P9-AFC-040

DATE DUE

DEMCO 38-296

CHRONOLOGY OF EUROPEAN HISTORY

R

CHRONOLOGY OF EUROPEAN HISTORY
15,000 B.C. to 1997

Volume 1
15,000 B.C. – 1469

Edited by
JOHN POWELL

Editor, Great Events from History
FRANK N. MAGILL

Associate Editors

E. G. WELTIN   JOSÉ M. SÁNCHEZ
THOMAS P. NEILL   EDWARD P. KELEHER

Project Editor
WENDY SACKET

Salem Press, Inc.
Pasadena, California   Englewood Cliffs, N.J.

Riverside Community College
Library
'98
APR   4800 Magnolia Avenue
Riverside, California 92506

D 11 .C57 1997 v.1

Chronology of European
history, 15,000 B.C. to

Editor in Chief: Dawn P. Dawson
Project Editor: Wendy Sacket
Acquisitions Editor: Mark Rehn
Research Supervisor: Jeffry Jensen
Photograph Editor: Karrie Hyatt
Production Editor: Joyce I. Buchea
Map Design and Layout: James Hutson

Copyright © 1972, 1973, 1980, 1997, by SALEM PRESS, INC.

All rights in this book are reserved. No part of this work may be used or reproduced in any manner whatsoever or transmitted in any form or by any means, electronic or mechanical, including photocopy, recording, or any information storage and retrieval system, without written permission from the copyright owner except in the case of brief quotations embodied in critical articles and reviews. For information address the publisher, Salem Press, Inc., P.O. Box 50062, Pasadena, California 91115.

This edition includes: materials from *Great Events from History: Ancient and Medieval*, Frank N. Magill, editor, E. G. Weltin, associate editor, 1972; *Great Events from History: Modern European*, Frank N. Magill, editor, Thomas P. Neill and José M. Sánchez, associate editors, 1973; *Great Events from History: Worldwide Twentieth Century*, Frank N. Magill, editor, Edward P. Keleher, associate editor, 1980; and material new to this edition.

∞ The paper used in these volumes conforms to the American National Standard for Permanence of Paper for Printed Library Materials, Z39.48-1984.

Library of Congress Cataloging-in-Publication Data

Chronology of European history, 15,000 B.C. to 1997 / edited by John Powell ; editor, Great events from history, Frank Magill ; associate editors, E. G. Weltin . . . [et al.] ; project editor, Wendy Sacket.

    p.   cm.

  "Combines updated entries from Magill's Great events from history : ancient and medieval series (1972) and Great events from history : modern European series (1973) with selected entries from Great events from history : worldwide twentieth century series (1980) and 266 completely new entries"—Vol. 1, Publisher's note.

  Includes bibliographical references and index.

  ISBN 0-89356-418-4 (set : alk. paper). — ISBN 0-89356-419-2 (v. 1)

  1. Europe—History—Chronology. I. Powell, John, 1954-   . II. Magill, Frank Northen, 1907-1997. III. Sacket, Wendy, 1962-   . IV. Great events from history. Ancient and medieval series. V. Great events from history. Modern European series. VI. Great events from history—worldwide twentieth century series.
D11.C57   1997
940'.02'02—dc21

97-33219
CIP

First Printing

PRINTED IN THE UNITED STATES OF AMERICA

CONTENTS

LIST OF MAPS

Volume I

Volume II

Volume III

PUBLISHER'S NOTE

For many years, the study of European history was equated with the rise of the West—the emergence of Western society and culture. With the end of the Cold War and the collapse of communism in the Soviet Union and Eastern Europe, however, historians have begun to reexamine the notion of history as an evolutionary process marked by cycles of growth and decline. Events of the 1990's, including the prolonged civil war among the former member-states of Yugoslavia and the signing of the Maastricht Treaty, are not easily charted as manifest evidence of a particular pattern or cycle. Thus, in compiling the three volumes of *Chronology of European History: 15,000 B.C. to 1997*, the editors have sought to include events that span the full spectrum of European experience, from prehistory to the present, examining these events from various perspectives in an effort to understand the social, political, economic, and intellectual currents behind them.

In outlining the events that constitute the shared historical experiences of the peoples of Europe, the articles endeavor to avoid a narrow, Eurocentric attitude by recognizing the diversity of cultures that have shaped enduring European traditions and ideas. A vast canvas of history is presented, giving attention to stateless nationalities and minority populations as well as great powers and nation-states. Events that reflect broad, familiar themes in European history—the Renaissance, the Reformation, the Scientific Revolution, and the Enlightenment—are found alongside events that reflect modern interest in environmental concerns, gender studies, peace movements, terrorism, and social reform. While including numerous events from ancient history, the set is focused more heavily on the medieval and modern periods of history to trace the evolution of a recognizably European community. At the same time, the set's geographical coverage seeks to give balanced treatment of all parts of the European landscape while including information on those areas which came into the European sphere of influence through conquest and colonization.

Chronology of European History: 15,000 B.C. to 1997 combines updated entries from Magill's *Great Events from History: Ancient and Medieval Series* (1972) and *Great Events from History: Modern European Series* (1973) with selected entries from *Great Events from History: Worldwide Twentieth Century Series* (1980) and 266 completely new entries. The new edition thus broadens the original publications' focus on European history through 1973 to cover historic events through 1997. Supplementing the text are more than 350 photographs and maps illustrating many of the key events. The result is this substantially updated and expanded edition, consisting of numerous illustrations and 614 articles on significant occurrences in European history.

The contents of this edition include nearly half of the articles in the *Ancient and Medieval Series* (163 out of 336 events) and almost three-quarters of the *Modern European Series* (237 out of 336 topics) are here, along with 13 topics germane to European history from the *Worldwide Twentieth Century Series*. Of these 413 articles, 348 were substantially updated and 65 were replaced with new essays. All information—dates, personages, categorization of events—was scrutinized, updated, and where necessary corrected by historians and other experts to ensure accuracy and currency. Each article's "Pertinent Literature" and "Additional Recommended Readings" sections were replaced by a more current annotated bibliography, entitled "Additional Reading," in which readers will find the best of both classic and recent publications for in-depth study.

In addition to the 413 articles updated or replaced from the original publications, 201 new articles have been commissioned to provide coverage of key events in the history of the ethnically diverse European peoples, including those from Eastern Europe, the Balkan Peninsula, and the Russian territories of central Asia; and important social, political, and economic milestones omitted from the original editions. Finally, two decades of history since the original publication dictated addition of many important political, legal, economic, and scientific developments since 1973, from German reunification, the dissolution of the former Soviet Union, and the proposed expansion of the North Atlantic Treaty Organization to the Chernobyl nuclear disaster and the opening of the Channel Tunnel.

Revision and updating extended to the articles' format as well as to the table of contents. Each article retains the same basic ready-reference listings, including event, date, locale, and principal personages ("Key Figures"). In the *Chronology of European History*, the editors have preceded each event's title with the year, in boldface, for ease in locating events that fall within a specified chronological period. Following the title, the editors have added a capsule summary identifying the significance of the event in the context of European history. A more precise "Date" line for each event was researched in order to add the exact month and day, as well as the year, of the event wherever appropriate. Finally, the top matter adds a list of Categories, replacing the old "Type of Event" with a listing of *all* categories to which the event is pertinent, from "Business and labor" through "Terrorism and political assassination" to "Wars, uprisings, and civil unrest."

As in the original publication, the text consists of a "Summary of Event" which rehearses the event itself and presents its impact. Depending on the event, this body of the article ranges from 1,000 to 1,500 words in length. In the case of the 348 updated entries, academicians in the fields of history, economics, and political science have reviewed the summaries' accuracy, have added material to correct or update the facts presented, and have reconsidered each event's impact in the light of new research during the years since 1973. The 266 new entries have likewise undergone editorial review for factual accuracy. Finally, the text of all articles has undergone a review for objectivity: Although history can never be impervious to viewpoint and interpretation, bias in both content and language has been strictly monitored in favor of reportorial presentation of the event and its impact, rather than interpretation. To the extent that interpretations do appear, it is the editors' hope that the broad range of academicians who have revised, updated, and newly written these articles—as well as the broad range of topics—will, in the aggregate, provide the emphasis on fact befitting a reference publication.

Each article's text ends with the signature of its author—or, in the case of updated entries, authors. Aesthetics dictated this positioning of the byline; the contributing authors were also responsible for compiling the bibliographies that appear at the ends of the articles.

The articles' end matter consists of two elements: the annotated bibliography of "Additional Readings," consisting of approximately five sources for further study with brief notes regarding their usefulness; and a listing of cross-references headed "See also." These "See also" cross-references list related events covered in the *Chronology of European History*. The cross-reference format begins with the event's year, followed by its title, to enable the reader to flip quickly to the event, whose heading includes the same information, boldfaced and in the same order.

Additional aids to accessing the information in these volumes exist in the form of two lists appearing at the end of each volume: a permuted index, the alphabetical Key Word Index, which lists titles by every key word appearing in them; and a Category List, listing each article in each of the twenty-three different categories to which it is pertinent. A count of entries in these categories reveals the following distribution: Business and Labor is a major focus of 9 entries; Communications, 6; Cultural and Intellectual History, 80; Diplomacy and International Relations, 63; Economics, 34; Education, 11; Environment, 10; Expansion and Land Acquisition, 67; Exploration and Discovery, 15; Government and Politics, 264; Health and Medicine, 11; Immigration, 4; Laws, Acts, and Legal History, 54; Organizations and Institutions, 16; Prehistory and Ancient Cultures, 6; Race and Ethnicity, 14; Religion, 100; Science and Technology, 47; Social Reform, 47; Terrorism and Political Assassination, 8; Transportation, 9; Wars, Uprisings, and Civil Unrest, 190; and Women's Issues, 6. Clearly the emphasis here is on social, political, and economic history; the significant number of intellectual, artistic, and scientific events covered reflects the extension of their impact beyond their immediate disciplines to the sociopolitical development of Europe.

Four more reference tools will be found at the end of volume 3: a Time Line, showing all events covered in the set; the Personages Index, listing all key figures and other personages who are listed in the articles' top matter *or* who receive significant discussion in the text; a Geographical List, providing a key to the empires, countries, and geopolitical regions in which these events occurred; and the Subject Index, which lists all events, movements, acts, terms, works, battles, treaties, locales, and concepts that receive significant textual discussion or that appear in contexts that cast further light on them.

The editors wish to thank the 175 contributors—historians, political scientists, economists, sociologists, and scientists—who prepared the material that appears in this publication. These academicians have provided not only their expertise but also their judgment in extracting the most important issues and facts for inclusion, as well as in updating their predecessors' work responsibly and seamlessly. A list of contributors to both the original editions and the *Chronology of European History* can be found in the opening pages of volume 1.

W. S.

INTRODUCTION TO GREAT EVENTS FROM HISTORY:
ANCIENT AND MEDIEVAL SERIES

The term "great" by necessity involves one in all sorts of value judgments bound to be colored by one's peculiar philosophy of history. While an event may be considered "great" in its own splendid isolation, such an evaluation rests ultimately on such a highly subjective individualistic commitment that it is not likely to be of much value to general readers. More safely, and more usefully, an event may be termed "great" if the general consensus of later history tends to view it as influential or important in an extended context. Whether history makes itself or whether historians make history is a question, however, best left to philosophers at this point. Considering the purpose of these volumes and their intended audiences, the term "great" is taken to mean important in the development of Western values, their preservation and propagation.

Any attempt to extract some three hundred fifty events as "great" and representative from the wide fields of ancient and medieval history is a task inviting controversy. In a case such as this, one is asked to evaluate all kinds of facts: political, technological, theological, sociological, philosophical, and economic, all of which are woven inextricably into the complicated pattern of unconscionably long eras. Under the circumstances, many readers are bound to decry the omission or inclusion of certain historical happenings about which they entertain definite views. For this reason, it seems judicious to state at the outset that events of "Oriental" ancient history which have no clear or heavy bearing on Western history are purposely omitted.

One of the unique difficulties involved in choosing significant events from ancient history, and to a large extent from medieval, stems from the fact that often, it appears, the ancient historian, more than his colleagues dealing with later periods, is impelled toward a pursuit of intellectual history. Apart from archaeological remains, ideas constitute the greatest part of the legacy from ancient times, ideas which are expressed in still extant writings from that period. Consequently there appears by necessity in these volumes what might seem to historians of later periods to be an excessive amount of literary compositions. Incidents usually termed "great" in relation to the founding of viable institutions are, for example, relatively scarce in ancient history in comparison to the medieval age, which was more prolific in the establishment of permanent institutions basic to the Western world. Most of the direct, concrete, institutional modern links with the ancient world, it appears, are found in the Jewish and Christian orbit.

In part, the choice of events has been dictated by the conviction that the ancient historian generally has been too prone to emphasize his period as an isolated era that comes to some mysterious ideological close with Constantine or to some sudden political end with the mythical "fall of Rome" in 476. These indefensible positions, arising from overspecialization or overdedication, slight an appreciation of the Christian contribution which, historically, probably should be viewed as the most significant legacy of Hellenistic and Roman history. It is hoped that the inclusion in these volumes of a generous amount of religious events, both Jewish and Christian, will help make this series more than usual an accurate and useful reflection of the composite Western tradition which rests so squarely on both a Greco-Roman and a Judeo-Christian foundation. If this view is correct, the development of Papal decretals is more important than the enunciation of Pericles' Funeral Oration, however cherished conventional periodization of history has made that masterpiece.

Assuming that Western history is a continuity from ancient times through the catalyst of Christianity with its Jewish background, the Middle Ages, far from being disparaged, must be considered an imposing period of inventive history when the West constructed its basic institutions to enshrine its newly distilled soul. Just as medieval banking presumes a far more sophisticated knowledge and creativity than the primitive economic exchange of the ancient world so, too, the Gothic cathedral is a daring architectural experiment compared to the static post-and-lintel structure of Greek temples, however magnificent the Parthenon may be in conception and execution.

The arrangement of the events has been made purposely chronological rather than alphabetical so that these volumes will serve as something more than an encyclopedic reference. The chronological juxtaposition of events quite often proves surprisingly enlightening as one discovers on proximate pages that isolated happenings are associated in time. In this way, a religious affair may be thrown, for example, in relief against a contemporary scientific development, or an event in Greek history set in chronological contrast with a Jewish episode.

Some defense should be made for what must appear to many as totally arbitrary dates assigned to the events. "Events" in ancient history are often more "topics" than isolated happenings: They tend to be developments often extending over hundreds or even thousands of years. To establish some workable chronology, a certain stage or distinct facet of a development often had to be chosen as a point around which the major "event" itself could be fixed and described. Arbitrariness is inevitable. Finally, it appears useful to remind ourselves that dates in ancient history are often quite controversial and in a state of flux perpetuated by the positions of different scholarly authorities.

It is axiomatic throughout that the nature and arrangement of these volumes imposes, by design, an artificial, disjunctive, isolated character on the course of history, making it impossible to deal in a sustained developmental way with any event, to relate it ideologically to any large extent with associated events, or to assess the importance of any happening in relation to others.

The matter of the interpretations appended to each event deserves some comment. In order to throw an event into high relief, efforts were made to obtain different, and preferably contrasting, interpretations to be found in the scholarly literature built up around the happening under consideration. Unfortunately, many matters in ancient history probably do not stand in as sharp a contrast as do those of "modern times," where relevancy supposedly is more readily apparent and biases definitely more virulent. One might say that only much of what was "best" or most useful in ancient times has been preserved over the years and is, therefore, not likely to be viewed in extremes. Moreover, the format of these volumes, limiting the interpretations to those available in English, has considerably curtailed the scope of interpretative material, much of which, in the fields of ancient and medieval history, is available only in foreign languages, generally German or French. The short bibliographies at the conclusion of each contribution also have been restricted to literature in English.

The editor wishes to thank the contributors to these volumes, writers all too few, especially in the field of ancient history, both secular and religious. Appreciation should also be expressed to Mr. James Turner, a graduate student of Washington University's history department, whose time and suggestions proved valuable in the preparation of these volumes.

E. G. WELTIN
Professor of History
Washington University

INTRODUCTION TO GREAT EVENTS FROM HISTORY: MODERN EUROPEAN SERIES

"History," great Dutch historian Pieter Geyl has observed, "is argument without end." Certainly, the course of Modern European history points out this basic truth. The period from 1500 to the present—the approximate limits of this series of volumes—can be viewed as the most dynamic and revolutionary upheaval in all human history. No other historical epoch concentrated in such a relatively short chronological period and in such a small geographical area has had such widespread influence upon the thought and action of the rest of the world. To select the three hundred and thirty-six most important events of this exciting period can boggle the imagination and lead to the "argument without end"; yet it must be done, for the historian's job is to select, organize, and interpret—in short, to put meaning into history. If the selections create controversy, then part of the historian's task if fulfilled; controversy excites the imagination and stimulates the mind, and in the process enables man to find his own place in history.

Modern Europe is above all the age of revolution. We are accustomed to thinking of revolution in a specifically political sense: The English, French, and Russian revolutions come to mind as exemplars of the revolutions that occurred in the United States two centuries ago, in Latin America at the beginning of the nineteenth century, and in Asia and Africa in recent times. However, these are only one aspect of the revolutionary upheaval, and in some ways the least important. Other revolutions have not only created the preconditions of the political eruptions but have been vastly more influential in their impact upon the modern world. When Martin Luther posted his ninety-five theses on the church door at Wittenberg in 1517, he lit the spark of a religious revolution that broke the unity of Western Christendom. When René Descartes meditated upon the processes of the mind in his cold room in Holland in November, 1620, he began an intellectual revolution that culminated in the Enlightenment and a shattering of the traditional mode of reasoning that had characterized Western thought for a millennium and more. And, when James Watt developed his minuscule steam engine in Glasgow in 1770, he unleashed the power of an industrial revolution that transformed the world's economy and reached into every human life. So also with Bach's development of polyphonic contrapuntal harmony that made modern music possible; and so also with the countless technological inventions that have shaped our own lives. These events rival and sometimes exceed the importance of political events. They have been included in this series.

Two problems in particular stand out as unique to modern history and to this series. One is the problem of perspective: The process of historical change has been so rapid in this century that it is difficult to select the more important events of recent times. In other words, will the selections stand the test of time? This is a problem that every modern historian has to face. In one sense, the problem of perspective in Modern European history is lessened by the rather clear delineation of 1945 as the end of the European era. After World War II, Europe was replaced as the world's impetal force by the power and influence of the United States, and the most cataclysmic events occurred chiefly in the Third World. But, the selection of recent events, like the selection of chronological time periods, is arbitrary, and creates even more controversy. It is a factor of which we must be aware. Who knows what a modern-day Luther, Descartes, Watt, or Bach may have done in the last few years that will shape the world of the future?

The other problem is one which this series was specifically designed to cope with: the problem of conflicting interpretation. Given the almost revolutionary impact of events in modern history it is not difficult to find opposing points of view and contrasting interpretations of the meaning of most important events. To take the most obvious example, Napoleon is interpreted by some historians as a positive progressive force in France and modern Europe; other historians see him as an unrelieved tyrant of despotic influence. These interpretations of people and events vary as do the events surrounding the historians' own biases, thus creating that fascinating branch of history known as historiography—the history of historical interpretation. In most instances in this series, the events are sufficiently controversial to have generated these conflicting interpretations, thereby giving meaning to the fact that history is indeed "argument without end."

Two final notes of caution seem necessary. First, because the shaping of this series has involved the coordination of the research and writing of over three dozen scholars in a number of different institutions, it has taken some years to complete the project. As a result, it has not been possible in all cases to incorporate all of the most recent historical works on a particular event in the bibliographical sections. Historical research, like other facets of what has been called "the knowledge explosion," has increased in almost startling proportions over the last decade: Even between the time that this series goes to press and its publication date, over a hundred historical monographs will appear in publication. Some works, published decades ago, will, of course, never be superseded, and we hope that these, having stood the test of time, will prove valuable to the reader.

Second, we have limited the historical literature to works in English on the assumption that the reader will find these most valuable and available for further consultation in his own library. In a series dealing with a continent only part of which is English-speaking, this has necessarily caused some omissions. Happily, the most important books have been translated and used in the series, but the reader should be aware of this limitation.

These volumes were begun under the editorial direction of Thomas P. Neill, professor of history at Saint Louis University. His untimely death in 1970 when the series was but three-fourths completed was a cause of sadness to everyone who knew him. As his former student and later colleague, I have attempted to complete them in the spirit of scholarship which he first taught me. If the reader finds these volumes useful, intriguing, and controversial, they will stand as a monument to his wisdom, dedication, and industry.

JOSÉ M. SÁNCHEZ
Professor and Chairman
Department of History
Saint Louis University

CONTRIBUTORS TO THE FIRST EDITIONS

(Affiliations are current as of publication of first editions.)

Paul Ashin
Stanford University

Martin J. Baron
Columbia University

Frederick B. Chary
Indiana University Northwest

Carl W. Conrad
Washington University

M. Joseph Costelloe
Creighton University

Martin L. Dolan
Northern Michigan University

Samuel K. Eddy
Syracuse University

Robert F. Erickson
Southern Illinois University

Miletus L. Flaningam
Purdue University

Charles J. Fleener
Saint Louis University

James H. Forse
Bowling Green State University

John G. Gallaher
Southern Illinois University

Jack H. Greising
Northern Michigan University

Manfred Grote
Purdue University

James M. Haas
Southern Illinois University

William Harrigan
Canisius College

John J. Healy
Saint Joseph Seminary

Hans Heilbronner
University of New Hampshire

Kevin Herbert
Washington University

James F. Hitchcock
Saint Louis University

Charles S. Inman
Royal Academy of Music, London

Mary Evelyn Jegen
University of Dayton

Christopher J. Kauffman
Marillac College

Edward P. Keleher
Purdue University at Calumet

Dorothy Kinsella
College of Saint Francis

Barry L. Knight
Northern Michigan University

Saul Lerner
Purdue University

Frances R. Lipp
Washington University

Elizabeth J. Lipscomb
*Virginia Highlands Community
   College*

John F. McGovern
*University of Wisconsin at
   Milwaukee*

Roderick E. McGrew
Temple University

Roger B. McShane
Trinity University

Russell M. Magnaghi
Northern Michigan University

Lynewood F. Martin
Lindenwood College

Paul T. Mason
Duquesne University

George R. Mitchell
Purdue University

Zola M. Packman
Washington University

Samuel C. Pearson
Southern Illinois University

George M. Pepe
Washington University

James W. Pringle
Purdue University

George F. Putnam
University of Missouri, Saint Louis

Thomas D. Riethmann
Saint Louis University

Carl F. Rohne
Southern Methodist University

Joseph J. Romano
Cabrini College

Joseph R. Rosenbloom
Washington University

José M. Sánchez
Saint Louis University

Wayne D. Santoni
Southern Illinois University

Raymond H. Schmandt
Saint Joseph College

Harold A. Schofield
Colorado Women's College

David Charles Smith
Bates College

Michael S. Smith
University of South Carolina

Norris K. Smith
Washington University

Harold L. Stansell
Regis College

James H. Steinel
*Saint John's University,
   New York*

Carl A. Volz
Concordia Seminary

Harry E. Wade
East Texas State University

J. A. Wahl
Saint Jerome's College

Paul A. Whelan
Air War College, Maxwell AFB

Richard J. Wurtz
Southern Illinois University

Edward A. Zivich
Calumet College

Lowell H. Zuck
Eden Seminary

Contributors

Amy Ackerberg-Hastings
Iowa State University

Richard Adler
University of Michigan—Dearborn

James A. Arieti
Hampden-Sydney College

Gerasimos Augustinos
University of South Carolina, Columbia

James A. Baer
Northern Virginia Community College

James T. Baker
Western Kentucky University

Ann Stewart Balakier
University of South Dakota

Art Barbeau
West Liberty State College

Xavier Baron
University of Wisconsin—Milwaukee

Paul Barton-Kriese
Indiana University—East

Douglas Clark Baxter
Ohio University

Milton Berman
University of Rochester

Jon L. Berquist
Westminster John Knox Press

Cynthia A. Bily
Adrian College

Nicholas Birns
The New School for Social Research

Arnold Blumberg
Towson State University

Steve D. Boilard
Western Kentucky University

John A. Britton
Francis Marion University

William S. Brockington, Jr.
University of South Carolina at Aiken

Kendall W. Brown
Brigham Young University

Anthony Brundage
California State Polytechnic University, Pomona

Jeffrey L. Buller
Georgia Southern University

Edmund J. Campion
University of Tennessee

Jack Carter
University of New Orleans

Donald E. Cellini
Adrian College

James T. Chambers
Texas Christian University

Paul J. Chara, Jr.
Loras College

Mark W. Chavalas
University of Wisconsin—La Crosse

Lawrence I. Clark
Independent Scholar

Bernard A. Cook
Loyola University of New Orleans

James J. Cooke
University of Mississippi

Arlene R. Courtney
Western Oregon State College

Daniel A. Crews
Central Missouri State University

Norma Crews
Independent Scholar

Jeff Cupp
Independent Scholar

Jennifer Davis
Independent Scholar

Frank Day
Clemson University

Thomas E. DeWolfe
Hampden-Sydney College

M. Casey Diana
University of Illinois

Stephen B. Dobrow
Fairleigh Dickinson University

Marjorie Donovan
Pittsburg State University

Daniel J. Doyle
Pennsylvania State University College of Technology

Jennifer Eastman
Clark University

H. J. Eisenman
University of Missouri, Rolla

Barbara M. Fahy
Albright College

James J. Farsolas
Coastal Carolina University

Stephanie Annette Finley-Croswhite
Old Dominion University

Alan M. Fisher
California State University, Dominguez Hills

David G. Fisher
Lycoming College

George J. Flynn
State University of New York College at Plattsburgh

James Flynn
Western Kentucky University

Michael J. Fontenot
Southern University—Baton Rouge

Robert J. Frail
Centenary College

Donald R. Franceschetti
University of Memphis

C. George Fry
Lutheran College

Gloria Fulton
Humboldt State University

Michael J. Galgano
James Madison University

Mitchel Gerber
Southeast Missouri State University

K. Fred Gillum
Colby College

Nancy M. Gordon
Independent Scholar

Margaret Bozenna Goscilo
Independent Scholar

Karen Gould
Independent Scholar

Lewis L. Gould
University of Texas at Austin

Daniel G. Graetzer
University of Montana

Johnpeter Horst Grill
Mississippi State University

Christopher E. Guthrie
Tarleton State University

David B. Haley
University of Minnesota

Irwin Halfond
McKendree College

Susan E. Hamilton
Independent Scholar

C. James Haug
Mississippi State University

Peter B. Heller
Manhattan College

Diane Lise Hendrix
New Mexico State University

Diane Andrews Henningfeld
Adrian College

Mark C. Herman
Edison Community College

John McDonnell Hintermaier
Purdue University

Hal Holladay
Simon's Rock of Bard College

Marian T. Horvat
University of Kansas

Raymond Pierre Hylton
Virginia Union University

John Quinn Imholte
University of Minnesota—Morris

John Jacob
Northwestern University

Duncan R. Jamieson
Ashland University

Albert C. Jensen
Central Florida Community College

K. Sue Jewell
Ohio State University

Raymond J. Jirran
Thomas Nelson Community College

Bruce E. Johansen
University of Nebraska at Omaha

Philip Dwight Jones
Bradley University

Charles L. Kammer III
The College of Wooster

Richard D. King
Ursinus College

Grove Koger
Boise Public Library

Michael Kugler
Northwestern College

Ralph L. Langenheim, Jr.
University of Illinois

Lawrence N. Langer
University of Connecticut

LaRae Larkin
Weber State University

Eugene Larson
Los Angeles Pierce College

Ernest H. Latham, Jr.
American Romanian Academy

Donald L. Layton
Indiana State University

Thomas T. Lewis
Mount Senario College

Victor Lindsey
East Central University

Herbert Luft
Pepperdine University

David C. Lukowitz
Hamline University

James Edward McGoldrick
Cedarville College

Douglas J. McMillan
East Carolina University

Paul Madden
Hardin-Simmons University

Robert Franklin Maddox
Marshall University

Bill T. Manikas
Gaston College

Nancy Farm Mannikko
Independent Scholar

Katherine S. Mansour
Jacksonville University

Chogollah Maroufi
California State University, Los Angeles

Ralph W. Mathisen
University of South Carolina, Columbia

Diane P. Michelfelder
California State Polytechnic University

Liesel Ashley Miller
Mississippi State University

Gordon R. Mork
Purdue University

Joseph L. Nogee
Independent Scholar

Norma Corigliano Noonan
Augsburg College

Thomas S. Noonan
University of Minnesota

Charles H. O'Brien
Western Illinois University

Gary A. Olson
San Bernardino Valley College

Patrick P. O'Neill
University of North Carolina, Chapel Hill

Maria A. Pacino
Azusa Pacific University

Connie Pedoto
Miles College

William A. Pelz
Institute of Working Class History

Marilyn Elizabeth Perry
Independent Scholar

James Persoon
Grand Valley State University

Marguerite R. Plummer
Louisiana State University in Shreveport

Clifton W. Potter, Jr.
Lynchburg College

Dorothy T. Potter
Lynchburg College

Edmund Dickenson Potter
Auburn University

Steven J. Ramold
Independent Scholar

John Ranlett
*State University of New York
College at Potsdam*

Betty Richardson
*Southern Illinois University at
Edwardsville*

Douglas W. Richmond
University of Texas at Arlington

Edward J. Rielly
Saint Joseph's College, Maine

Carl Rollyson
*Baruch College of the City University
of New York*

John Alan Ross
Eastern Washington University

Wendy Sacket
Independent Scholar

John Santore
Pratt Institute

Daniel C. Scavone
University of Southern Indiana

William C. Schrader
Tennessee Technological University

Larry Schweikart
University of Dayton

Elizabeth L. Scully
University of Texas at Arlington

Rose Secrest
Independent Scholar

Alfred Erich Senn
University of Wisconsin, Madison

Talaat E. Shehata
Miami University

Narasingha P. Sil
Western Oregon State College

John Edward Skillen
Gordon College

Gary Scott Smith
Grove City College

Roger Smith
Independent Scholar

John A. Sondey
South Dakota State University

Joseph L. Spradley
Wheaton College

Barbara C. Stanley
Independent Scholar

David L. Sterling
University of Cincinnati

Joan C. Stevenson
Western Washington University

Paul Stewart
Southern Connecticut State University

Leslie Stricker
Park College

Taylor Stults
Muskingum College

Glenn L. Swygart
Tennessee Temple University

Robert D. Talbott
University of Northern Iowa

Susan M. Taylor
Indiana University—South Bend

J. W. Thacker
Western Kentucky University

Nicholas C. Thomas
Auburn University at Montgomery

Leslie V. Tischauser
Prairie State College

William L. Urban
Monmouth College, Illinois

Fred R. van Hartesveldt
Fort Valley State College

Kevin B. Vichcales
Western Michigan University

Peter L. Viscusi
Central Missouri State University

Sharon B. Watkins
Western Illinois University

Thomas H. Watkins
Western Illinois University

Richard D. Weigel
Western Kentucky University

Henry G. Weisser
Colorado State University

Winifred Whelan
St. Bonaventure University

Richard Whitworth
Ball State University

Thomas Willard
University of Arizona

John F. Wilson
University of Hawaii at Manoa

John D. Windhausen
Saint Anselm College

Michael Witkoski
Independent Scholar

CHRONOLOGY OF EUROPEAN HISTORY

15,000 B.C.
CAVE PAINTINGS PROVIDE EVIDENCE OF MAGDALENIAN CULTURE

Paintings in the Lascaux Cave provide evidence of Magdalenian culture and demonstrate the behavioral sophistication of the first anatomically modern peoples in Europe.

DATE: 15,000 B.C.
LOCALE: Lascaux, Montignac (Dordogne), France
CATEGORY: Prehistory and ancient cultures
KEY FIGURES:
André Breton (1896-1966), French literary Surrealist
Abbé Henri-Édouard-Prosper Breuil (1877-1961), French archaeologist and historian of paleolithic art

SUMMARY OF EVENT. The first cultural remains of anatomically and behaviorally modern people in Europe are described by archaeologists as the Upper Paleolithic and are dated to the later part of the last glaciation of the very Late Pleistocene (40,000-35,000 to 12,000-10,000 years ago). A unique contribution of these Upper Paleolithic peoples is their "art" which was essentially absent in Europe prior to the appearance of anatomically modern peoples. One of the most dramatic examples of this art is Lascaux Cave discovered on September 12, 1940, by four teenage Montignac boys: Marcel Ravidat, Jacques Marsal, Simon Coencas, and Georges Agnel. At least six hundred paintings and nearly fifteen hundred engravings are found in this cave system. Charcoal discovered on the floor of the cave was dated to circa 15,000 B.C. indicating the paintings are at least that old.

It was Ravidat's idea to explore the cave. An elderly woman had buried a dead mule there and claimed that the hole extended to a medieval passage underground. She believed that it ended at a chateau at the base of a hill near Lascaux. The boys decided to test her assertion and had brought a lamp to light their way. They noticed the paintings and were quite excited. Soon many knew of their find, and their schoolteacher notified the priest, Abbé Breuil, who arrived on September 21, 1940, and was the first to describe and analyze the paintings.

The first Upper Paleolithic cave paintings were discovered by the landowner, Marcelino Sanz de Sautuola, in Altamira Cave in northern Spain in 1879, but many doubted their authenticity. Further examples were discovered in southwestern France by the early 1900's and this additional evidence reassured most doubters. The controversy resurfaced in 1952, when André Breton visited Pech-Merle and touched one of the apparently wet paintings. He was convinced it was a forgery. Breuil pointed out that the dampness of the caves prevented the paint from drying and that in many cases the pigments were overlain by whitish calcite deposits supporting their antiquity.

The Upper Paleolithic peoples were culturally very different from the peoples whom they followed. The tools and artifacts left by the preceding Neanderthals were remarkably uniform and differed only in the relative proportions of the same artifact types. Tools changed very slowly over thousands of years. That pace was altered dramatically with the appearance of Upper Paleolithic peoples who from thirty-four thousand to eleven thousand years ago left a series of tool industries known to archaeologists from older to younger as the Aurignacian, Gravettian (Perigordian), Solutrean, and Magdalenian. Each industry was distinguished by specific artifact types either rare or absent in other traditions. The Magdalenian culture with which Lascaux cave is identified is dated between 16,500 and 11,000 years ago and is found in France, northern Spain, Switzerland, Germany, Belgium and southern Britain. Its most diagnostic implements are composed of bone and antler which were fashioned into points, harpoons, and other tools.

Upper Paleolithic peoples lived by hunting and gathering wild animal and plant resources. Game was abundant at this time including woolly mammoth, reindeer, bison, horse, and saiga antelope. They were apparently more successful than the Neanderthals, because Upper Paleolithic sites are more numerous and populated more densely. Bird and fish bones in particular are more common than for older sites. There was also more contact and exchange among groups because archaeologists have found amber, finer flint, and seashells sometimes hundreds of kilometers from their source.

The social organization of these groups probably varied tremendously with small family groups in the harsher environments and likely complex, stratified societies, perhaps hereditary chiefdoms, in the richer environments. One of these resource rich areas was the Franco-Cantabrian region (southwestern France and northern Spain) inhabited 15,000-11,000 years ago by Magdalenian peoples. More than 150 caves with late Pleistocene paintings and engravings have been located in this area. Most of them cannot be dated precisely, but representations of extinct animals such as mammoth and bison suggest Pleistocene age and most are stylistically the same as the carved bone and antler animal figurines dated to the Magdalenian period.

Upper Paleolithic imagery has been arbitrarily subdivided into two kinds: wall (or parietal) art including paintings and the more numerous engravings on rock surfaces, and "portable" or home art (*art mobilier*), composed of movable artifacts such as engraved bone or antler. Paleolithic "art" has been used to describe materials that span 25,000 years in time and which are found from the Iberian Peninsula to Russia. The famous, mostly stylized, "Venus figurines" with exaggerated buttocks and breasts, are dated to the Gravettian period. Preserved images, numerous during the Upper Paleolithic, are new to the archaeological record, but what it means in terms of human existence is in dispute. That it is "art" in the contemporary sense of the term cannot be assumed.

The archaeologist, Margaret Conkey, has reviewed the two main ways by which this cultural expression has been interpreted as either sympathetic hunting magic or as a sort of language or type of communication about their worldview. She calls the former, originally promoted by Breuil, the "foundation interpretation," in that the animals and signs were devised in order to guarantee present and future hunting success. By the 1960's, André Leroi-Gourhan and others were criticizing this work and providing alternative explanations. One difficulty with the hunting hypothesis was that the animals represented in the art were not necessarily the most common animals in their refuse.

Leroi-Gourhan's work is described as the "mythogram interpretation," because analyses of where and how the images were made were explained as representing mythological structures and symbolic systems. Certain species of animals, particularly horse and bison, were more common than others and were thus assumed to have symbolic meaning. Conkey argues that this shift to describing the imagery as a sophisticated communication system is a profound statement about how Upper Paleolithic peoples were essentially mentally the same as contemporary peoples. In addition, this change to the production of wall and portable art has been observed all over the world. Thus, Conkey suggests that investigators should avoid the cultural preconceptions associated with the term "art" and try to understand the works in terms of local cultural adaptations. Unlike Western art, images are often superimposed and are usually not set off from each other or provided with a clear orienting context. Many images likely represent different times and peoples. For example, Lascaux Cave exhibits a heterogeneity in style.

Conkey is interested in where, when, and why these particular materials are found in these specific forms. For

This rendering of a bison pierced by an arrow found in the Niaux Caves in France is similar to the Paleolithic images found in the Lascaux Caves. (Archive Photos)

example, the use of pigments was sophisticated and varied. Studies at Lascaux show that pigments were ground and mixed with cave water and powered bone ash. Some pigments were applied directly and used to outline an image, and others were applied as a slurry and used to fill in the outlines in varying shades. Pigments were sometimes reapplied and not always in the same colors. Some were applied after some of the dissolved cave matrix had recrystallized indicating time gaps between applications. Lascaux's polychrome, mixed pigment imagery (not the only imagery) differs dramatically from the black outlines found at the French cave of Pech Merle. The drawings at Pech Merle may have been made quickly, whereas at Lascaux there is evidence for scaffolding.

New dating methods such as accelerator-dating may permit reevaluation of the relative dating strategies suggested by Breuil (two cycles of imagery) and Leroi-Gourhan (four style periods). Breuil assumed that superimposed images were made over an extended period of time over many generations as part of ritual to ensure hunting success. Pigment analysis has already demonstrated that some of the images were made with the same pigment recipes and probably represent shorter spans of time. Leroi-Gourhan's different styles will be dated and his sequence confirmed or the new dates used to generate alternative interpretations. —*Joan C. Stevenson*

ADDITIONAL READING:

Bahn, Paul G., and Jean Vertut. *Images of the Ice Age*. London: Woodward, 1988. Bahn and Vertut describe where and when these images were found around the world and their many interpretations.

Bataille, Georges. *Lascaux: Or, The Birth of Art*. Translated by Austryn Wainhouse. Lausanne: Skira, 1955. The interpretation of the cave paintings is dated, but this book is the next best thing to actually visiting the site.

Conkey, Margaret W. "Humans as Materialists and Symbolists: Image Making in the Upper Paleolithic." In *The Origin and Evolution of Humans and Humanness*. Boston: Jones and Bartlett, 1993. Conkey describes the latest critique of the interpretations and new advances in the studies of Upper Paleolithic imagery.

Klein, Richard G. *The Human Career*. Chicago: University of Chicago Press, 1989. One of the best descriptions of human biological and cultural evolution and places the Upper Paleolithic peoples and their associated artifacts into historical context.

Leroi-Gourhan, André *The Dawn of European Art*. Translated by Sara Champion. New York: Cambridge University Press, 1982. Leroi-Gourhan's interpretive framework is explained clearly, and there is much description

including a map and pictures of Lascaux Cave.

White, Randall. *Dark Caves, Bright Visions: Life in Ice Age Europe*. New York: W. W. Norton, 1986. White places the imagery into human development and the social context of their survival strategies.

SEE ALSO: 3100-1550 B.C., Building of Stonehenge; 1100-500 B.C., Hallstatt Civilization Ushers in Iron Age in Europe; 109-102 B.C., Celtic Hill Forts Appear; 60-61, Boadicea Leads Revolt Against Roman Rule.

3100-1550 B.C.
BUILDING OF STONEHENGE

The building of Stonehenge reveals that the late Stone Age and early Bronze Age cultures of Britain are as sophisticated as any of the contemporary civilizations of the Near East.

DATE: c. 3100-1550 B.C.
LOCALE: Southern England
CATEGORIES: Prehistory and ancient cultures; Religion; Science and technology
SUMMARY OF EVENT. Stonehenge is the most important prehistoric monument in Europe, a circular stone structure built on Salisbury Plain in southern England. Although it is only one of thousands of "megalithic," or large stone, structures erected in western Europe, its unique features have made it the most famous, generating centuries of speculation about who built it.

In his *History of the Kings of Britain* (A.D. 1136), Geoffrey of Monmouth attributed it to Merlin the Magician, claiming that it held the tombs of Aurelius, Constantine, and Uther Pendragon, father of King Arthur. Royal architect Inigo Jones, commissioned by King James I in 1620 to study the matter, concluded that it was Roman. According to antiquarians John Aubrey (1666) and William Stukeley (1740), Druid priests were its source, an idea still cherished by latter-day Druid cultists. In the late twentieth century, theorists have suggested that colonists from the lost continent of Atlantis or possibly extraterrestrial beings were responsible for constructing Stonehenge.

Until the 1970's, most archaeologists preferred to see Stonehenge as the result of Near Eastern influence. It was believed that civilization first arose in the Near East, later spreading advanced knowledge and skills outward to less capable peoples in a ripple effect. In a 1965 comment, Stonehenge authority R. J. C. Atkinson attributed the monument to Mycenaean Greeks, dismissing the local Britons of the period as "howling barbarians."

This diffusion theory was undermined by recalibrated radiocarbon dates, which showed that some European megalithic constructions existed as early as 4500 B.C.

The beveled curves and smooth joints found on the sandstone blocks at Stonehenge reveal a level of workmanship that sets it apart from other megalithic structures found in Europe. (R. Kent Rasmussen)

These dates helped classify such structures as the earliest stone architecture in the world. Rather than considering the megaliths to be imports, scholars turned their attention to understanding the *in situ* cultural evolution of late Stone Age farming peoples.

Farming was introduced to Britain in the Neolithic period, with wheat being grown in Wessex by 4000 B.C. Villages were small, organized socially as egalitarian tribes. This social organization is reflected in their burial practices, in which bones of people of all ages and sexes were placed in stone chambers, some with stone passageways. Excavated dirt from a surrounding ditch was placed over these megalithic structures, thus producing the long barrow.

Groups of barrows are associated with a larger British structure, the Causewayed Camp. These barrow enclosures were created by digging ditches with adjacent banks to the interior. Natural breaks, or "causeways," in the perimeter of ditches probably served as entrances. The use

of these ditches included excarnation, exposing bodies to remove flesh before interring the bones in the barrows. These structures required considerable labor to build and are believed to have served the living as well as the dead. Robin Hood's Ball, located three miles from the later site of Stonehenge, enclosed two and a half acres of land. It probably symbolized tribal identity and possession of the land and might have served as a community center.

A new feature appeared around 3200 B.C.—the henge. Similar to causewayed camps, the bank (or built structure) typically was constructed outside the ditch, with one or two entrances. Thirteen such structures include standing stones—the earliest British stone circles.

Scholars believe that after 3100 B.C., work began on Stonehenge by enclosing a circle 320 feet in diameter with a six-foot bank. Stonehenge is an unusual henge it that its ditch lies outside its bank, echoing the older causewayed camp. Flanked by two stones, Stonehenge's entrance is oriented to the northeast, the direction of the summer solstice sunrise. This axis is also marked by a sixteen-foot-high, thirty-five-ton Heel Stone, located ninety-six feet beyond (past) the entrance. Just inside the bank lies a circle 284 feet in diameter of fifty-six Aubrey Holes. Named for antiquarian John Aubrey, these holes are evenly spaced some sixteen feet apart, are from two to four feet deep, and were filled with chalk soon after being dug. Excavations revealed that some holes contained human cremations from a later date. In this form, Stonehenge was used for several centuries and then abandoned.

There is evidence that tribal societies were evolving into status-conscious chiefdoms around 2700 B.C. Communal long barrow graves were replaced by round barrows that covered a single rich grave. Copper daggers and gold earrings have been recovered from such sites, along with fine Beaker pottery, characterized by a distinctive drinking cup without handles.

Once believed to have reflected an actual invasion of "Beaker Peoples," such barrows and grave goods now seem to reflect an emerging leadership elite who were engaging in a wider trade in flint, copper, tin, and prestige items while continuing their rich Neolithic farming traditions. New henges began to appear, three of which are located within two miles of Stonehenge itself. At Avebury to the north, ninety-eight stones are enclosed by a ditch one mile in circumference. The prodigious labor required to construct these sites reflects the growing wealth and power of a royal elite entering the Bronze Age.

New work began at Stonehenge itself around 2100 B.C. By building two parallel chalk banks with exterior ditches more than one-third of a mile long, the new builders created an avenue leading up to the northeast entrance. Eighty bluestones, each measuring six feet in height and imported from the Preseli Mountains in Wales, were set up in two incomplete concentric circles. Researchers believe that this may have been the time when four "Station Stones" were set up on the Aubrey Circle, imposing on it a rough rectangle. In 1978, a Beaker burial was discovered in the ditch, continuing the association of enclosures with death and ritual.

It is in the period from 2000 to 1550 B.C. that Stonehenge became truly unique. The bluestones were removed, and large sarsen ("foreign") sandstone blocks were brought from Marlborough Downs some twenty miles to the north. Thirty upright blocks, weighing twenty-five tons each, were arranged three and a half feet apart to form a circle one hundred feet in diameter. These blocks were then topped by lintels, in essence creating a flat circular sidewalk elevated sixteen feet above the ground. Inside this sarsen circle is a horseshoe-shaped arrangement of five structures, known as trilithons, with the open

end of the horseshoe oriented on the northeast axis. Each trilithon was made of two upright blocks topped by a lintel; these structures include the largest stones in the monument. Bluestones were again added to the design. Sixty individual bluestones were positioned to form a circle seventy-five feet in diameter just within the sarsen circle. Nineteen bluestones placed within the trilithons formed a bluestone horseshoe.

The workmanship of these structures sets Stonehenge apart from other megalithic structures. The interior sides of all the sarsens reveal that workmen pounded them smooth with stone hammers. Each lintel had two depressions on the bottom that allowed them to fit over projections on the adjacent uprights. Tongue-in-groove joints were used between the lintels that met each other over the uprights in the sarsen circle. Beveling, curvature, and the use of perspective are evident, providing a glimpse of the skills of master craftsmen who seem to have adapted the art of fine woodworking on a massive scale to shape stone. Evidence of such attention to detail, along with the innovative design of the sarsen circle, occurs in no other megalithic monument on the earth.

Later alterations of Stonehenge have been attributed to the Wessex Culture of southern Britain's early Bronze Age. Dozens of their round barrows dot the surrounding ridges. In 1808, Sir Richard Colt Hoare excavated one such barrow in the Normanton group located just south of Stonehenge. Called Bush Barrow, it contained the skeleton of a tall male; with him were two bronze daggers and a bronze axe. A stone mace and a beautifully incised golden pectoral (breast ornament) found near him may have been the symbols of authority of one of the actual builders and lords of Stonehenge, a monument central to his reign.

In 1965, Harvard astronomer Gerald Hawkins claimed that Stonehenge served these people as a giant astronomical observatory. He explained that numerous stone alignments marked key positions of both the sun and the moon. Noting that the cycle of lunar eclipses occurs in a pattern of fifty-six years (nineteen plus nineteen plus eighteen), he believed that this pattern explained the purpose of the Aubrey holes, which were used as a lunar eclipse predictor.

Archaeologists have been skeptical of these claims, questioning the precision of the alignments and the builders' possession of the required knowledge to construct such an observatory. Missing and displaced stones at the site, as well as alterations in the ground plan over the centuries, combine to make an analysis of such precision difficult. Harvard researcher Alexander Marshack has made the claim that 25,000-year-old bones found in European sites have been engraved with precise day-to-day markings of the exact positions and phase of the moon. If Marshack is correct, ancient knowledge of astronomy that could validate Hawkins' claims for Stonehenge may have been available in Europe for a very long time. Within the vast scope of human history, the science of astronomy has only recently been divorced from astrology; control over cosmology and an ability to predict eclipses would have been of great value in reinforcing the power and prestige of the lords of Wessex.   —*Gary A. Olson*

ADDITIONAL READING:

Atkinson, R. J. C. *Stonehenge*. London: Hamish Hamilton, 1956. A standard reference on Stonehenge archaeology.

Chippindale, Christopher. *Stonehenge Complete*. Ithaca, N.Y.: Cornell University Press, 1983. A comprehensive overview of all facets of the topic.

Krupp, E. C. "The Stonehenge Chronicles." In *In Search of Ancient Astronomies*. New York: McGraw-Hill, 1979. A critical review of the astronomical controversies surrounding Stonehenge.

Renfrew, Colin. *Before Civilization*. New York: Pelican Books, 1976. Renfrew considers Wessex from a social rather than a diffusion perspective.

Zimmerman, Linda. *Set in Stone*. Berkeley: University of California Center for Media and Independent Learning, 1995. This twenty-four-minute film studies the challenge of balancing conservation needs and environmental concerns with the demands of Stonehenge's annual influx of ten thousand visitors and tourists.

SEE ALSO: 1620-1120 B.C., Rise of Mycenaean Civilization; 1100-500 B.C., Hallstatt Civilization Ushers in Iron Age in Europe; 109-102 B.C., Celtic Hill Forts Appear; 449, Saxon Settlement of Britain.

1620-1120 B.C.
RISE OF MYCENAEAN CIVILIZATION

The rise of Mycenaean civilization heralds the emergence of one of the most important cultural and political centers during the Heroic Age in Greece.

DATE: 1620-1120 B.C.
LOCALE: Greece
CATEGORY: Prehistory and ancient cultures
KEY FIGURES:
Aeschylus (525-456 B.C.), Greek dramatist who commemorated the legends of the House of Atreus of Mycenae in the trilogy of plays called the *Oresteia*
Agamemnon, powerful Mycenaean king believed to have led the Greeks against the Trojans in the Trojan War
Perseus, legendary founder of the city of Mycenae

Heinrich Schliemann (1822-1890), first archaeologist to excavate the site at Mycenae in 1876 and reveal its wealth
Michael Ventris (1922-1956), first linguist who claimed to have deciphered the Linear B tablets found in and around Mycenae in 1939

SUMMARY OF EVENT. In his epics the *Iliad* and the *Odyssey*, Homer recounted that Mycenae was a city rich in gold. When excavations of the city began in 1876, it became clear that this city contained more gold than any other Greek sites. The excavations further corroborated Homer's assertions that Mycenae was a powerful city as well as part of the most dominant civilization throughout Greece from 1620 until 1120 B.C.

Legends said that the city itself, located in the northeastern corner of the plain of Argos between two mountains, Mount Prophet Elias to the north and Zara to the south, was founded by Perseus in 1400 B.C. Perseus was the alleged son of Zeus and Danaë and the presumed destroyer of the Gorgon Medusa. His descendants ruled in Mycenae for three generations until Atreus, son of Pelops, was elected to rule around 1250 B.C. Atreus' brother, Thyestes, was consumed by jealousy and entered into a love affair with Atreus' wife. In revenge, Atreus prepared a banquet for Thyestes, consisting of Thyestes' two children. After Thyestes had eaten the meal and then learned of its contents, he shouted a curse which was to fall upon Atreus, his children, and his children's children. Indeed, according to legend as recorded in the *Oresteia* by the playwright, Aeschylus, the curse was borne out. When Agamemnon, the son of Atreus, returned from the Trojan War, his wife, Clytemnestra murdered him. Eight years later, Orestes, the son of Agamemnon, avenged his father's murder by killing Clytemnestra and her lover Aegisthus. According to Aeschylus, Orestes was then pursued by the Furies, avenging the mother's death, until after a trial in Athens, Athena declared that Orestes was not blameworthy for his deeds. He returned to Mycenae, which was already in decline. During his son's reign, the Dorians captured and virtually destroyed the citadel in 1120 B.C. From this date, the city and all of Greece entered into a period of obscurity.

Over the centuries, however, Mycenae has left visible signs of the power and attainments of its inhabitants. The oldest of these monuments are the Cyclopean Walls that surround the citadel of Mycenae. It was long alleged that Perseus built these walls with the help of the Cyclops, one-eyed giants mentioned in Homer, because the raising of such monumental walls (6.7 meters thick) seemed beyond the power of any human being to build. In actuality, these walls were probably constructed later in 1340 B.C. by humans who used ramps to push and pull the blocks of stone into place.

The entrance to the citadel, the Lion Gate, is one of the oldest pieces of monumental sculpture in the Western world. Its noteworthy features are the corbel vaulting with the sculpted lions. The corbel vaulting consists of blocks of wood carefully placed so that each projects a little beyond the one below it. This creates an empty triangular space over the lintel which relieves the lintel of the weight of the heavy walls above it. Sculpted figures of two lions (now headless) were placed inside the triangular space with their front paws on an altar, guarding the citadel. Interpretations vary as to the meaning of the Lion Gate. Some say that the lions were a secular emblem of Mycenae, the royal coat of arms; others believe that the lions were a religious symbol. It is believed that the gate was built during the reign of Atreus in 1250 B.C.

Once inside the Lion Gate, on the right is the Grave Circle A, a royal cemetery, excavated by Heinrich Schliemann in 1876. Schliemann discovered five shaft graves. After he left, another grave was unearthed. The six graves contained nineteen skeletons—eight men, nine women, and two children—presumably all of royal lineage. In addition to the skeletons, bronze swords and daggers, gold and silver cups, five masks of gold, discs of gold leaf, rhytons of gold and silver, and rings and necklaces were found. Among these artifacts was the noted mask of Agamemnon, so named by Schliemann. It was discovered later that this attribution was impossible because these graves dated from an earlier time—the sixteenth century B.C.

On the east side of Grave Circle A is a great ramp leading up to the palace on the summit. The most important room in the palace was the *megaron*, a long and narrow roofed structure. One entered the *domos*, or main room of the *megaron*, through a vestibule or *prodomos*. The *prodomos* and the *domos* contained fragments of frescoes which were later preserved in the National Archaeological Museum of Athens. The *domos* contained the throne of the king. It was in this room that banquets were held. Additional features of the palace were the grand stairway, domestic and guest quarters, the artist quarters, and the "House of Columns," storage rooms for the possessions of the royal family.

In the lower parts of the citadel, remains were discovered which indicate houses for the lesser royalty, state dignitaries and warriors defending the citadel. Just outside the citadel lived the citizens of Mycenae, their dwellings surrounded by the graves, known as Chamber Tombs, of their ancestors. These consisted of a passage, known as the *dromos*, open to the sky and a chamber hollowed out inside a hill.

Graves of the burial of royalty were more elaborate than the Chamber Tombs and were known as Tholos or Beehive Tombs. These were underground and reached by a open air passage, a dromos. Nine tholos tombs have been discovered at Mycenae to date. Among the best preserved of these tombs is the Treasury of Atreus. It is believed that this tomb was built at the same time as the Lion Gate. The proportions of the tomb are monumental: the width of the *dromos* leading up to the entrance is six meters, and its length is thirty-six meters. Above the lintel in the doorway is the characteristic relieving triangle. The ease with which the large stones were fitted into the round structure of the underground tomb make it one of the most impressive architectural achievements of the Mycenaean Age. Grave robbers had emptied all of the known tombs of their contents by the time they were discovered.

Most of modern knowledge of the Mycenaean world comes from artifacts such as frescoes, pottery fragments, metal work, and jewelry. In 1939, the excavation of another Mycenaean site, Pylos, produced tablets which contained a form of writing, known as Linear B. Only seventy of these tablets were discovered at Mycenae. In the

In 1876, German archaeologist Heinrich Schliemann conducted excavations in Mycenae, recovering artifacts that were eventually dated to the sixteenth century B.C. (National Library of Medicine)

1950's, linguist Michael Ventris was able to decipher the script. He discovered that the writing dated from just after 1400 B.C. and was an archaic form of Greek. The tablets consisted mostly of inventories of stores, livestock, agricultural products, and catalogs of the citizenry and their occupations. However limited in scope, the tablets have broadened modern perceptions of the Mycenaean civilization.

Pottery shards remain the chief index of how extensive the civilization was. At its peak, the Mycenaean civilization extended west to Italy and Great Britain and north to central Europe. In the east, by the end of the fifteenth century, the Mycenaeans dominated Crete. By the end of the Trojan War and the fatal return of Agamemnon to mainland Greece, the civilization was already in decline. Although later subject to domination by the Dorians at the end of the twelfth century and by the Argives in 468 B.C., Mycenaean civilization's richness and power at its height endured and provided the roots from which classical Greece arose.

—*Jennifer Eastman*

ADDITIONAL READING:

Aeschylus. *Oresteia*. Chicago: University of Chicago Press, 1953. An account of the legend of the sons of Atreus as reformulated in three plays by a classical Greek dramatist.

Bennett, Emmett L., Jr., ed. *Mycenaean Studies*. Madison: University of Wisconsin Press, 1964. A collection of essays with the primary focus on the deciphering of Linear B.

Mylonas, George E. *Mycenae: A Guide to Its Ruins and Its History*. Athens: Ekdotike Athenon, 1981. An accessible monograph detailing the remains at the site of Mycenae.

Schliemann, Henry. *Mycenae: A Narrative of Researches and Discoveries at Mycenae and Tiryns*. Reprint. Salem, N.H.: Ayer, 1989. First published in 1880, this work provides a firsthand account of Schliemann's excavations and an attempt to fit the findings within the Homeric tradition.

Taylour, Lord William. *The Mycenaeans*. New York: Thames & Hudson, 1983. The most detailed, scholarly, and up-to-date account of Mycenaean civilization.

Tsountas, Chrestos, and J. Irving Manatt. *The Mycenaean Age*. Boston: Houghton Mifflin, 1897. A classic, though dated, study giving detail of the daily lives such as clothing, weapons, and art of the Mycenaeans by an archaeologist who spent twenty years excavating the site.

SEE ALSO: 1600-1500 B.C., Flowering of Minoan Civilization; 1000 B.C., Greek Alphabet Is Developed; 800 b.c., Homer's Composition of the *Iliad*; 450-425 B.C., History Develops as Scholarly Discipline.

1600-1500 B.C.
FLOWERING OF MINOAN CIVILIZATION

The flowering of the Minoan civilization establishes the foundations of Mediterranean mythologies, religious practices, and social organization that influence classical Greek societies.

DATE: 1600-1500 B.C.

LOCALE: Crete

CATEGORY: Prehistory and ancient cultures

KEY FIGURES:

Sir Arthur Evans (1851-1941), British archaeologist

Minos (c. 1450 B.C.), legendary Cretan sea-king

SUMMARY OF EVENT. The ancient Greeks of the fourth and fifth centuries B.C. inherited legendary accounts of a wealthy, powerful Minoan civilization located on the Mediterranean island of Crete. Minos was supposedly the ruler of a thalassocracy (sea-empire) that controlled much of Aegean and mainland Greece in prehistoric times. According to Greek mythology, Minos was semidivine: He was the son of Zeus, ruler of the gods, and Europa, a Phoenician princess. Minos was remarkable for his justice as well as his power.

The Minos legend suggested deep historical roots to classical Greek civilization; but Minoan civilization remained mythic until 1900. Inspired by the discoveries of Heinrich Schliemann at Troy and Mycenae, Sir Arthur Evans began to excavate at Knossos. His findings were astonishing and revolutionary. They initiated an ongoing process of revision and reevaluation of Classical, Western, and finally world history.

Evans was deeply impressed by the Minos legend. An important part of that legend said, in brief, that there was a vast labyrinth at Knossos, built by Minos to imprison the fabulous Minotaur (a creature which was half-man, half-bull). As Evans excavated, the legend seemed to be confirmed. He unearthed the remains of a multi-story building which, on the ground floor, covered roughly five acres. The plan of the building was labyrinthine, with intricate corridors and hundreds of rooms arranged around a central court which seemed perfect for containing the Minotaur. Stone building blocks and various artifacts were found marked with the *labrys*, the double-ax, thus making the labyrinth the "house of the double-ax." A vivid fresco depicting male and female acrobats leaping over a powerful, noble bull seemed to refer to Athenian youths and maidens sacrificed as tribute to Minos the Overlord.

As Evans uncovered the ruins and their contents, he believed that he had found the "Palace of Minos"—that is, the political and administrative headquarters of a powerful monarch who ruled over all or most of Crete, many of the

MINOAN PALACES ON CRETE

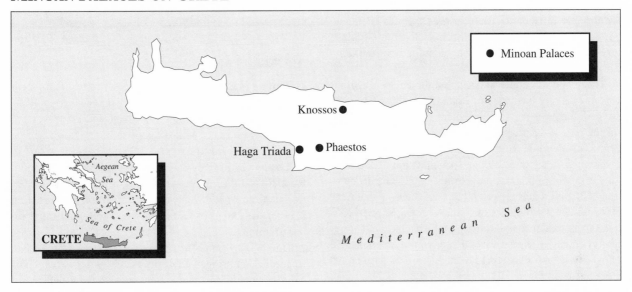

neighboring islands, and portions of the Greek mainland. He interpreted and named sections and rooms accordingly: the Royal Road, the North-West Treasure House, the Royal Magazines, the Corridor of the Procession, the Throne Room, the Central Court, the Hall of the Double-Axes, and the Queen's Toilet. Since virtually all major findings were in ruins or incomplete, Evans and his assistants reconstructed them as they imagined parts of a great palace might have looked.

As the work continued, two facts became evident. The first is the great length of prehistoric human habitation at Knossos. Evans uncovered about forty feet of human debris, roughly one-half of it from the Minoan period (c. 3000-1150 B.C.), one-half from the Neolithic period (6100-3000 B.C.). The Palace of Minos was built on the ruins of a prior, probably somewhat smaller, palace, itself built on the ruins of many layers of earlier Minoan and Neolithic buildings. To the extent to which the roots of classical Greek (and thus Western) civilization are Minoan, they are deep in the Cretan soil.

The second fact implied a similar conclusion about deep roots—now religious—in the earth. Classical Greek religion, like classical Greek society, was masculine, competitive, and oriented toward war. Characteristically, Zeus is depicted wielding his mighty thunderbolt: The Olympian gods are perpetually fighting, either among themselves or in human affairs. Minos as sea emperor fit easily into this scheme of male conquest and domination. Yet the hundreds and then thousands of artifacts—wall and vase paintings, cups, signet rings, cylinder seals and seal stones, jewelry items, rhytons (ritual vessels), and votive

offerings—found by Evans and later investigators did not fit this male-warrior picture. They suggested a Minoan religion and civilization of nearly opposite character.

A fundamental insight on religion is offered by the palace itself (and other, smaller palaces subsequently excavated at Phaistos, Mallia, and Zakros on Crete). Unlike mainland palaces, those on Crete had no defensive walls. The obvious implication is a peaceful society: The less obvious one is a society open to nature. Detailed archaeological evidence supports this view. The Minoans appear to have loved all aspects of nature—birds, animals, dolphins, fish, bees, flowers, trees and, interestingly, snakes. Aside from the labyrinth itself, the single most famous symbol of Minoan civilization is the figurine of a bare-breasted goddess holding snakes in each hand.

Evans himself was fully aware of the sacred character of many of his findings. Yet his view that the palace was the residence of priest-kings has been substantially amended. Archaeological evidence, combined with some documentary evidence from the Linear B tablets (inscribed with an early form of Greek), indicate that the Minoans worshiped and sacrificed to a Goddess. The Goddess may have taken a number of forms and been attended by one or more younger gods. Yet at the center of Minoan religion was Potnia (or the Lady). She was the prehistorical Cretan version of the Great Earth/Mother Goddess of Old Europe (7000-3500 B.C.). This powerful female deity was understood to be the source of all life, and the force behind the annual regeneration of nature.

The place of women in Cretan society paralleled the importance of the Goddess. They appear, from graphic representations, to have been at least equal to men. They figured prominently in palace life at Knossos, probably not directly as rulers but as priestesses. It has been suggested that a high priestess impersonated the Goddess, who was thus physically present as the lady of the labyrinth.

These considerations suggest that the Palace of Minos was more likely the abode of Potnia. Scholars of Minoan civilization have suggested a number of redesignations for the palace—perhaps it was a temple-palace, or a cult-center, or a temple. Even these names, however, may be misleading, since they imply a specialization of activities into religious, political, administrative, and so forth. Western civilization has inherited this orientation from the classical Greeks. What seems unique about Minoan civilization is that it was leisured, sophisticated, and (relatively) equalitarian, yet viewed life from the perspective of the wholeness of nature. Like the Labyrinth, it remained close to the earth.

It is no small irony, then, that the civilization of the earth-worshiping Minoans was very probably ended by the earth. Crete lies in a geologically unstable area and is subject to frequent and severe earthquakes. The Old Palace at Knossos was probably destroyed by an earthquake around 1700 B.C. It was rebuilt as the New Palace—excavated by Evans—along the same lines but on a somewhat grander scale. It was in and around this structure, be it termed palace or temple, that Minoan civilization reached its fullest development.

Very much remains uncertain about this "flowering." It is traditionally dated 1700-1450 B.C., with the "bloom" of the flowering being 1600-1500. The period 1500-1450 had been thought to date the Thera disaster, when an island seventy-five miles north of Knossos was blown literally to pieces by volcanic eruption. The resulting shock waves, tsunamis, and volcanic fallout, probably combined with local earthquakes, severely damaged Knossos. Yet considerable scientific evidence indicates a date of 1628 B.C. for the Thera eruption, thus raising the "flowering" by roughly a century.

It is clear that, at its height, Minoan civilization was a fruitful blending of cultures. Mainland peoples—certainly Mycenaeans, perhaps Luwians from Anatolia and Hyksos from Egypt—mingled with the Cretans, who themselves traveled throughout the eastern Mediterranean. The character of this intercourse is less clear. Did the Minoans colonize and dominate? Were they invaded and conquered? Did both patterns occur, giving rise to ambiguous legends of a "Minos" both powerful and just? Or, was the blending not only peaceful but divine, presided over by a great Goddess of Nature who nurtured the infant Zeus?

Did belief in that Earth Goddess dissipate as the earth repeatedly quaked and destroyed? There are no final answers; Minoan civilization continues to intrigue.

—John F. Wilson

ADDITIONAL READING:

Bernal, Martin. *Black Athena: The Afroasiatic Roots of Classical Civilization.* Vol II. New Brunswick, N.J.: Rutgers University Press, 1991. Brilliant and controversial, Bernal's work traces Minoan civilization to North Africa. He emphasizes the 1628 date for Thera eruption.

Castleden, Rodney. *The Knossos Labyrinth.* London: Routledge, 1990. An engaging and often persuasive reinterpretation of the labyrinth as "temple." Castleden stresses the extent of Evans' physical and conceptual reconstruction.

Chadwick, John. *The Mycenaean World.* Cambridge, England: Cambridge University Press, 1976. A nontechnical overview by the decipherer (with Michael Ventris) of Linear B, Chadwick's work grounds his analysis of Minoan civilization on the documentary evidence.

Gimbutas, Marija. *The Language of the Goddess.* San Francisco: HarperCollins, 1989. In her lavishly illustrated masterwork, the leading student of "O!d Europe" assimilates the Cretan artifacts to the symbol system of the Mother Goddess.

Marinatos, Nanno. *Minoan Religion: Ritual, Image, and Symbol.* Columbia: University of South Carolina Press, 1993. The author reconstructs Minoan religious ritual from archaeological evidence, concluding that Knossos was a "cult center."

Willetts, R. F. *The Civilization of Ancient Crete.* Berkeley: University of California Press, 1977. Perhaps the best single introduction to Minoan civilization, Willetts' work is especially sensitive to problems of interpretation and the resultant controversies.

SEE ALSO: 1620-1120 B.C., Rise of Mycenaean Civilization; 1000 B.C., Greek Alphabet Is Developed; 1000-900 B.C., Ionian Confederacy; 775 B.C., Oracle at Delphi.

1100-500 B.C.
HALLSTATT CIVILIZATION USHERS IN IRON AGE IN EUROPE

The Hallstatt civilization ushers in the Iron Age in Europe, setting the pattern of urban civilization in northern Europe for the next two thousand years.

DATE: c. 1100-500 B.C.
LOCALE: Northern Europe
CATEGORIES: Prehistory and ancient cultures

SUMMARY OF EVENT. In the early 1800's, a revolution in thinking about the past was occurring in Europe. Discoveries of the bones of extinct animals along with stone tools led people to consider a world that was vastly older than the few thousand years previously allotted to it, a world in which metals were not always available. This view was formalized in 1836 by Christian Jurgensen Thomsen, whose guidebook to the Danish National Museum in Copenhagen divided the past into a succession of a Stone Age, a Bronze Age, and then an Iron Age. This three-age system has continued to serve as a fundamental framework for prehistoric studies, and research since Thomsen's work was published has attempted to understand when and where these transitions took place and what impact they had on people's lives.

In 1824, K. P. Pollhammer uncovered an ancient tomb outside the small Austrian town of Hallstatt. Located by a lake in a picturesque Alpine valley some thirty miles southeast of the city of Salzburg, the community had been important for centuries as a source of salt. The tomb itself came from above the valley on the slope of a mountain named Salzberg, literally "salt mountain."

George Ramsauer, the manager of the local salt mines in 1846, followed up on Pollhammer's discovery and attempted to learn more about the area's early miners. On the same slope, Ramsauer located a vast cemetery that covered nearly one hundred thousand square feet. He conducted excavations there until 1863, uncovering nearly one thousand graves. Ramsauer's meticulous drawings recorded nearly twenty thousand items, including pottery, bronze vessels of Greek and local origins, jewelry of gold and Baltic amber, and many weapons of an unexpected material—iron.

More than one thousand additional graves have been discovered near Hallstatt since 1863. These graves have been shown to fall into two major periods: Hallstatt A and B, covering the time of the Late Bronze Age Urnfield Culture (1300-800 B.C.), and Hallstatt C and D, covering the early Iron Age (800-500 B.C.). It is to this latter phase that Hallstatt gives its name—the First Iron Age of northern Europe.

The Urnfield peoples helped to spread bronze working throughout Europe; they were named for their custom of cremating bodies and placing the ashes in urns for burial. Ramsauer excavated many such burials at Hallstatt, and it seems clear that the Hallstatt Culture evolved from Urnfield roots.

There were changes, however, which produced a culture now believed to be that of the early Celts. The advent of iron working was accompanied by the custom of inhumation instead of cremation—burial of the entire body instead of ashes. Groups of people began building and using large hill-forts, and chiefs were buried with costly grave goods, including four-wheeled carts, indicating that strong social differentiation was emerging, based on an energetic trade.

Mountain ranges, such as the Cévennes of France and the Maritime Alps between southern France and Italy, created a formidable barrier between temperate Europe and the Mediterranean world. The classic Hallstatt heartland developed where passes and rivers made access to trade routes possible. From the area of the Black Forest, headwaters of the Rhine River flow all the way to the North Sea, those of the Danube reach the Black Sea, and the Rhône joins the Saône on its way to the Mediterranean. Alpine passes, such as the Brenner Pass, connect Austria with Italy. Mediterranean wine, oil, bronzes, jewelry, and iron-working skills moved north, paid for with tin, copper, hides, textiles, amber, salt, and salt-cured fish and pork. Salt was so important that Rome later paid its legionnaires with it, a *salarium argentum* or "money for salt," the origin of the modern word "salary."

From Spain to Hungary, hill forts and settlements arose along these trade routes, evolving into industrial and commercial centers, In eastern France, the Hallstatt D hill fort on Mont Lassois dominated the headwaters of the Seine River. In an associated barrow located in the nearby village of Vix in 1953, René Joffroy discovered the spectacular tomb of a Celtic princess. Beneath the mound, she had been buried in a wooden chamber on a dismantled wagon, its wheels lined along one wall. She bore a golden crown, its ends terminating in winged horses. Her grave goods included jewelry of bronze and amber, a Greek Black Figure pot, and silver and bronze vessels. Dominating the chamber was a huge bronze jar, or krater, with a broad body, a wide neck, and two handles. A magnificent specimen of Greek manufacture, the jar stood five feet tall, measured thirteen feet in circumference, and weighed 460 pounds. The jar's decorated rim features a frieze showing a Greek charioteer, four horses, and hoplite infantrymen.

Iron continued to be relatively rare during the Hallstatt period, but its impact was evident in materials excavated from the Hohmichelle barrow, located near the Heuenburg hill fortress overlooking the Danube River in southern Germany. Forty feet in height, the barrow contained thirteen burials. Two were wagon burials—one containing a man and a woman, the other containing a solitary woman. Although the chambers had been looted by grave-robbers, intriguing traces of their richness remained, including the earliest known appearance of silk cloth in Europe. Iron arrowheads were found along with an archer's bow measuring six feet in length. Scholars were particularly interested in the planks used to construct the main chamber.

Twenty feet long, these planks apparently were sawn from logs with a two-man iron saw. Saws, adzes, and other tools of iron were transforming woodworking and other industrial activities.

Excavation of another wagon burial in 1978 at Hochdorf, Germany, uncovered other uses of the metal. The wagon itself was plated with sheets of iron. The grave's burial offerings included an iron drinking horn measuring more than three feet in length.

Early Celtic art of the Hallstatt period shows a concern with nature. Human beings are also portrayed, but they are rather rigid or patterned almost abstractly using triangles and circles. Fine pottery shows bold geometric incising of lozenges and circles. Animals, especially birds, are shown more realistically. One common design is the "Hallstatt duck" motif, usually associated with concentric circles. A classic example comes from the Hallstatt cemetery itself, a bronze bowl supported by six legs. Four small sculptured waterfowl seem to be swimming up each of the bowl's legs. Two horizontal friezes of waterfowl interspersed with spoke-wheeled forms decorate the bowl itself. These designs are thought to be mythic in nature and have their roots in bird and solar disc motifs found in the art of Urnfield and other Bronze Age cultures.

HALLSTATT AND LA TÈNE SITES

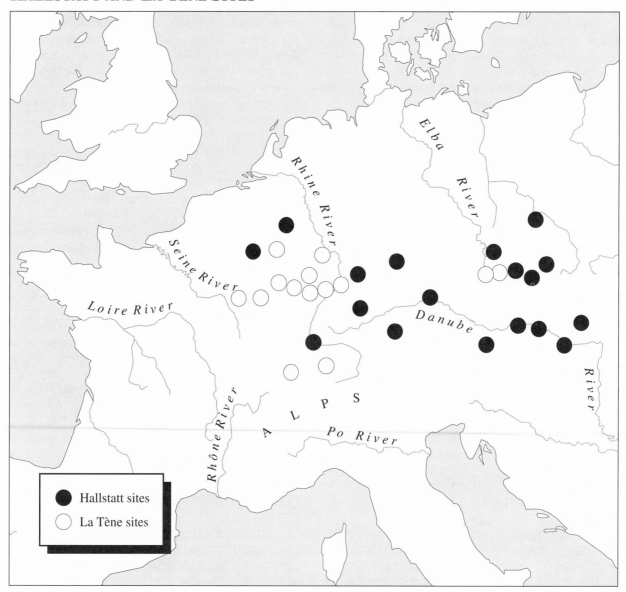

Materials dating from around 500 B.C. reveal a shift in art styles introducing a true Celtic art and culture. Some examples of this style were found in the later burials at Hallstatt, but the style was first recognized at the site of La Tène ("the shallows") on Lake Neuchâtel in Switzerland. During the severe winter of 1853-1854, the lake level dropped to reveal ancient wood pilings on the lake's margins. F. Keller dredged the area and turned up utensils and weapons. Work at the site during the 1880's and early 1900's produced more than twenty-five hundred items, decorated with a distinctive curvilinear art style. The site gave the name La Tène to the Second Iron Age in Europe, from 500 B.C. through Roman times.

La Tène culture clearly evolved out of Hallstatt culture. Conical helmets and oval shields found at sites from both periods were identical. "Hallstatt duck" and "solar" symbols continued. Wagon burials of chieftains also continued, although in two-wheeled chariots at La Tène sites. High status for women continued to be reflected in the richness of many of their burials. At places such as Manching in southern Germany, the hill forts evolved into true urban centers where there were industries in copper, iron, glass, amber, pottery, and textiles. Even coins were minted there.

Although they did not constitute a single united empire, the various Celtic peoples are jointly credited with an industrial revolution that produced horseshoes, iron-rimmed wheels, standardized tools, soap, the rotary flour mill, a harvester on wheels, and an iron plow that could open the heavier and more fertile soils for cultivation. They established courts, created a common market, and accorded rights to women. Even the dimension of the standard railroad track of the twentieth century descended from the measurements of the Celtic cart. The First and Second Iron Ages of Hallstatt and La Tène laid the social and economic foundation of northern European civilization.
—*Gary A. Olson*

ADDITIONAL READING:

Cunliffe, Barry. "Iron Age Societies in Western Europe and Beyond, 800-140 B.C." In *The Oxford Illustrated Prehistory of Europe*. New York: Oxford University Press, 1994. A comprehensive overview focusing on the relationship between Iron Age society and the environment.

Knauth, Percy. *The Metalsmiths*. New York: Time-Life Books, 1974. Knauth provides a global survey of metallurgy, including copper, bronze, iron, and gold.

Pleiner, R. "Early Iron Metallurgy in Europe." In *The Coming of the Age of Iron*. New Haven, Conn.: Yale University Press, 1980. Provides more technical aspects of iron metallurgy from early Europe.

Raymond, Robert. *Out of the Fiery Furnace: The Impact of Metals on the History of Mankind*. University Park: Pennsylvania State University Press, 1986. An ambitious survey of the history of metallurgy from the earliest copper artifacts up through aluminum.

Severy, Merle. "The Celts: Europe's Founders." *National Geographic* 151 (May, 1977): 582-633. Traces the rise of European civilization from the Bronze Age up to modern times.

SEE ALSO: 109-102 B.C., Celtic Hill Forts Appear; 58-51 B.C., Caesar's Conquest of Gaul; 635-800, Founding of Lindisfarne and Creation of the *Book of Kells*.

1000 B.C.
GREEK ALPHABET IS DEVELOPED

The Greek alphabet is developed, becoming the ancestor of all modern European alphabets, including English.

DATE: c. 1000 B.C.

LOCALE: Greece

CATEGORIES: Communications; Cultural and intellectual history

SUMMARY OF EVENT. An alphabet is a system of writing consisting of generally less than thirty symbols that represent all of the spoken sounds of a language. The Greeks were the first to assign a single sound to a single letter; hence, they were the first to develop a completely phonetic alphabet.

Every system of writing in existence ultimately derived from pictures used to represent words. Such pictographic writing emerged independently in many places around the world. In Mesopotamia around 3000 B.C., Sumerians had form of picture writing, followed by cuneiform in 2500 B.C. This was also the time of the earliest Egyptian hieroglyphs. China in 1500 B.C. developed a system in which each symbol designated a word. The Canaanites along the western shore of the Mediterranean had a pictographic writing system also, but they developed a syllabic alphabet around 1700 B.C. Syllables consisting of vowels and consonants were depicted as symbols, and peoples of the area, including a North Semitic group the Greeks came to call the Phoenicians, gradually devised alphabets consisting solely of consonants. All of the several hundred alphabets that came into existence can be traced back to this area of the Middle East.

The Mycenaean peoples inhabiting the area on and around the Greek mainland also had a writing system circa 1500-1100 B.C. Designated by twentieth century translators as Linear B, it derived from Crete, an island south of Greece, where Minoans devised a system designated

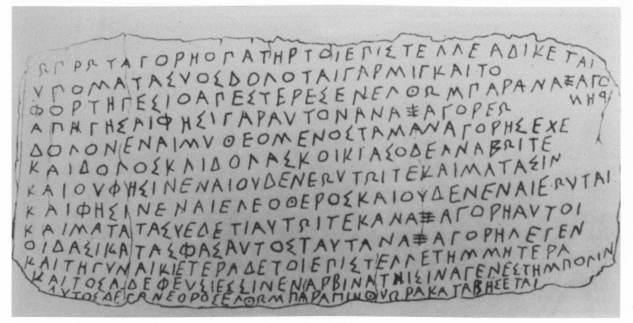

The distinctive shape of the characters of the Greek alphabet are clearly evident in this letter, originally inscribed on a thin sheet of lead, thus preserving text that might have disintegrated if written on paper. (Archive Photos)

Linear A to record items of commerce and official records. Linear B had at least eighty-eight signs with a few vowels, but it was a clumsy syllabic method of writing used only by the elite. During the twelfth century B.C., Doric-speaking invaders from the northwest or possibly Doric-speaking Greeks who were part of the Mycenaean culture overthrew the nobility. Greece was then illiterate for about four centuries around the time of Homer.

The twelfth century B.C. also saw the Phoenicians of the Canaanite region venture out to establish trade and colonies in the Mediterranean. They settled such places as Kition, Cyprus, Malta, Sicily, Sardinia, Spain, and possibly Carthage and Utica. Their alphabet was a series of consonants that is the distant ancestor of modern Hebrew. The Phoenicians might have provided the alphabet to the Greeks as they traveled around the Mediterranean trading with various peoples, yet it is not unlikely that Greeks and Phoenicians lived together in a bilingual settlement where the Greeks could learn the script at their leisure. Around 1000 B.C., the Greeks adapted the alphabet to fit the needs of their own speech.

The twenty-two-character Phoenician alphabet from aleph (Greek alpha) to taw (Greek tau) was accepted by the Greeks with few deletions. The Greeks were forced to add letters, however, for sounds that were present in their language but not used by the Phoenicians. The Greeks added psi for "ps," chi for "kh," and phi for "ph" around 800 B.C. Yet the most radical change that the Greeks

accomplished was to create vowels as letters that stood alone for the first time in history. Phoenician sounds at the beginning of some of the letter names were hard for the Greeks to pronounce, so they emphasized a vowel sound of their own speech which became the new sound of the letter. Alpha (a), epsilon (short e), eta (long e), iota (i), omicron (short o), upsilon (u), and omega (long o) formed the seven vowels in the twenty-four-character eastern Greek dialect of Ionian. The alphabet varied from region to region in the city-states of Greece. Some dialects, for example, adopted the Semitic qoph (an ancestor of the modern "Q") and digamma (an ancestor of the modern "F"). The Ionian dialect, however, was declared the official alphabet of Greece in a decree of Athens in 403 B.C., and it became the classical Greek alphabet.

Another important development attributed to the Greeks is the direction the letters eventually took. Every European language that is derived from the Greek alphabet writes from left to right. Phoenician, like modern Hebrew and Arabic, ran right to left, but early Greek inscriptions were not consistent. Some have been found running right to left, left to right, vertically either top to bottom or bottom to top, and even in a hairpin fashion that flipped some letters in reverse. Also common was the Greek practice of boustrophedon, or "as the ox plows." The letters in boustrophedon ran left to right, then right to left, so that they appear backward, then back to left to right, taking curves as they went. It must not have bothered readers of the time to read letters backward or upside-down. The practice is not as odd as it seems, for the readers would not have to automatically jerk their eyes back to the left margin in an unnatural fashion (yet one that is acceptable to readers of European alphabets). The Greeks standardized the left to right method around 600-500 B.C.

The orientation of symbols in the Phoenician language was important, because they were supposed to, in an abstract way, represent objects. The Greeks, however, were not constrained, for example, to leave aleph (Phoenician for "ox") as an upside-down "A," a representation of an ox face, because the word alpha to them only meant the name of the first letter of their alphabet. With all the different directions the Greeks gave their scripts originally, letters flipped back and forth (for example, a backward "B" flipped over to become a "B") before settling down to become the familiar ones of most modern European languages. Another possible reason the Greeks had to adjust the letters was to make them all taller than they were wide for uniform inscriptions into stone.

The versatility of a totally phonetic alphabet led to a widespread acceptance of the Greek alphabet. The alphabet was simpler to memorize than systems of writing based on thousands of picture symbols, so more people were able to master reading and writing. The concept of an alphabet worked its way to Egypt, where the Coptic alphabet replaced hieroglyphs. The phonetic system has even been applied in the transliteration of Far East symbols so that they can be read by speakers of European languages. The Greek alphabet was sent east around the ninth century A.D. at the hands of the Greek missionary Saint Cyril, making it the direct ancestor of the Cyrillic alphabet used in Slavic countries.

The most significant Greek influence came from the speakers of the Chalcidian dialect of eastern Greece. Unlike the Ionian dialect, it was not established as Greece's official alphabet. Nevertheless, the Chalcidian dialect traveled west from Kyme, Boeotia, and Euboia on the eastern shores of Greece to colonies on the island of Pithecusa around 775 B.C., as well as near the city of Cumae on Italy itself. The peoples of the area were called the Etruscans, and they accepted this Greek alphabet that had an "F" and a "Q" for use in writing their language. Etruscan symbols are the direct ancestor of the Roman alphabet, and, from there, all European alphabets.

—*Rose Secrest*

ADDITIONAL READING:

Claiborne, Robert. "The Gift of the Alphabet." In *The Birth of Writing*. New York: Time-Life Books, 1974. Easy-to-read summary of the transition from pictographs to the Greek alphabet, with inserts concerning other scripts such as the Mayan language.

Drucker, Johanna. "The Alphabet in Context," "Origins and Historians," and "The Alphabet in Classical History, Philosophy, and Divination." In *The Alphabetic Labyrinth: The Letters in History and Imagination*. New York: Thames & Hudson, 1995. For advanced students, this is a detailed but succinct summary of speculations concerning the origin of the Greek alphabet.

Havelock, Eric A. *The Literate Revolution in Greece and Its Cultural Consequences*. Princeton, N.J.: Princeton University Press, 1982. Discussion of how the alphabet was invented, absorbed, and promoted by the Greeks, whose greatest impact was to make the world literate.

Jeffery, L. H. "The Origin and Transmission of the Greek Alphabet" and "Writing in Ancient Greece." In *The Local Scripts of Archaic Greece: A Study of the Origin of the Greek Alphabet and Its Development from the Eighth to the Fifth Centuries B.C.* London: Oxford University Press, 1961. Despite its age, still the definitive study of the Greek writing system. While scholarly, the first two chapters yield a clear analysis of scripts.

McCarter, P. Kyle, Jr. *The Antiquity of the Greek Alphabet and the Early Phoenician Scripts*. Missoula, Mont.: Scholars Press, 1975. Technical and full of detail, yet a fascinating look at where, how, and when the Greek alphabet originated.

Moleas, Wendy. "Prehistoric and Ancient Greek." In *The Development of the Greek Language*. New Rochelle, N.Y.: Aristide D. Caratzas, 1989. Useful appendices show early Mycenaean and Greek signs, while the first chapter is an easily accessible introduction to the Greek alphabet.

Robinson, Andrew. *The Story of Writing: Alphabets, Hieroglyphs and Pictographs*. New York: Thames & Hudson, 1995. A colorful book with plenty of illustrations, it traverses the history of writing from cuneiform and hieroglyphics to the 1990's.

SEE ALSO: 1620-1120 B.C., Rise of Mycenaean Civilization; 1600-1500 B.C., Flowering of Minoan Civilization; 800 B.C., Homer's Composition of the *Iliad*; 850, Building of the Slavic Alphabet.

1000-900 B.C.
IONIAN CONFEDERACY

The Ionian confederacy brings together large settlements of Ionian Greeks who are responsible for the birth of Greek epic poetry, history writing, and natural philosophy.

DATE: c. 1000-900 B.C.

LOCALE: The western coast of Anatolia (modern Turkey)

CATEGORIES: Expansion and land acquisition; Government and politics

KEY FIGURES:

Androcles, son of King Codrus of Athens and founder of Ephesus

Neleus, son of King Codrus and founder of Miletus

SUMMARY OF EVENT. The central portion of the west coast of Anatolia (modern Turkey) has had a long and varied history. In the first half of the second millennium B.C., Minoan merchants from Crete established trading posts throughout the Aegean and eastern Mediterranean. Archaeologists have found Minoan type pottery on the west central coast of Anatolia in an area that would later be called Ionia. Moreover, Minoan settlements have also been found at Miletus. The pre-Classical mainland Greeks, known as Mycenaeans, also colonized the west coast of Anatolia, as evidenced by the beehive-shaped *tholos* tombs (dated from the fourteenth to the twelfth centuries B.C.) found at Colophon along the central coast. Hittite cuneiform records found in central Anatolia and dating to about 1300 B.C. mention a city named Milawata, probably the later Ionian city of Miletus. The records imply that Milawata was under the control of a polity known as Ahhiyawa, possibly the Hittite name for the Achaeans of mainland Greece during the Mycenaean period. It is not clear, however, who composed the indigenous population of the area during the second millennium B.C., although later tradition claims that they were a local Anatolian people called the Carians. By the twelfth century B.C., the Mycenaean and Hittite kingdoms were either destroyed or had become decentralized. Archaeological research has shown that the Mycenaean levels of Miletus were destroyed at this time, and Greek tradition claims that this period coincided with the sack of Troy.

At about this time, the Greek mainland was overrun by the Dorians, a group that had originated north of Greece. Greek historical tradition holds that migrations of Greeks from the mainland to Ionia began in response to the destruction of their cities at the end of the Bronze Age around 1200 B.C. Aeolian Greeks sailed to some of the Aegean islands, including Lesbos, and to the northwest Anatolian coast. Some Dorians evidently settled in the southern regions, while Greeks known as Ionians settled in the central coast. Their presence is evidenced by archaeological finds at Miletus, where the Mycenaean civilization settlement was succeeded by a group using pottery akin to that found in Attica on the mainland of Greece. This pottery type, called Protogeometric, has been found throughout Ionia.

The material remains concerning the Ionian migration can be complemented by a series of fragmented literary accounts in Greek. The memory of Ionians living in the mainland of Greece is recounted in Homer's *Iliad* (eighth century B.C.), which mentions them once in association with the Boeotians. A fragment from Solon, who flourished during the sixth century B.C., implies that the Ionians had come from Attica. The Greek historian Herodotus noted in his *Histories* that there had been Ionians in Boeotia, Attica, and in the Peloponnesus. The earliest extant account of the Ionian migration was written by the Athenian historian Pherecydes (c. 500 B.C.) and was paraphrased by the Roman geographer Strabo as well as by Pausanias (with slight variations). These accounts tell that the sons of Codrus, the Ionian king of Athens, and others migrated from there sometime around 1100 B.C. Miletus was founded by Neleus, a son of Codrus. The Ionians led by him killed the local male inhabitants and married the local women. Androcles, another son of Codrus, was the founder of the city of Ephesus. According to these accounts, Androclus drove out the Lydians but, unlike Neleus, was friendly with the local inhabitants. Tradition holds that others founded the remaining Ionian cities on the islands of Chios, Samos, and Mycale, as well as the mainland sites of Colophon, Priene, Lebedos, Phocaea, and Teos, among others.

The Ionian city-states forged a defensive confederacy that fostered a sense of community among them. The Greek writers state, however, that the Ionians fought between themselves and against the Carians, the local Anatolian inhabitants. In the eighth century B.C., the Ionians were successful in sending out colonies in the Aegean, the western Mediterranean (notably Sicily and southern Italy), inland Anatolia, and even the Egyptian delta region. By the early seventh century, the Ionians were attacked by the Lydian king Gyges, who threatened their existence. Even more dangerous was the threat posed by the Cimmerians and the Scythians later in the century who, according to Herodotus, plundered Ionia but did not destroy the cities. The Ionian confederacy was later forced to pay tribute to Lydia, and soon thereafter was conquered by Persia late in the sixth century B.C. In the beginning of the fifth century, with the support of Athens and other mainland Greek cities, Ionia staged an unsuccessful revolt against Persian rule. According to Herodotus, this revolt sparked the beginning of the great Persian Wars of the period.

Notwithstanding their importance to eastern Mediterranean political history, the Ionians were at the forefront of Greek civilization in the first half of the first millennium B.C. The great epic poetry of Greece, exemplified by Homer's *Iliad* and *Odyssey*, originated on the Asiatic Greek coast during the eighth century B.C. Moreover, the

Ionians appear to have been the first to promote a rational view of the world, thus founding the study of natural philosophy. Many of the greatest thinkers of the ancient world came from Ionia, including Thales, Anaximander, Heraclitus, and Anaximenes, all from Miletus, and Pythagoras of Samos. Furthermore, critical history writing originated from the Ionian coast with Hecataeus of Miletus, a forerunner of Herodotus. Finally, the Ionians made great innovations in art and architecture, creating a distinct style of sculpture known as Ionia. Thus, the Ionian impact on European poetry, philosophy, historiography, and sculpture is incalculable.   —*Mark W. Chavalas*

ADDITIONAL READING:

Bouzek, J. *The Aegean, Anatolia and Europe: Cultural Interaction in the Second Millennium B.C.* Göteburg, Sweden: Paul Astroms, 1985. This work surveys the cultural and artistic interconnections in the Aegean world during the Late Bronze and Early Iron ages, the periods of the Ionian migration to Anatolia.

Cook, J. M. *The Greeks in Ionia and the East.* New York: Frederick A. Praeger, 1963. Cook emphasizes the historical and material evidence for Ionian civilization and discusses Ionian art and architecture, including the Ionic sculpture style.

Drews, R. *The End of the Bronze Age: Changes in Warfare and the Catastrophe ca. 1200 B.C.* Princeton, N.J.: Princeton University Press, 1993. Drews provides the background for understanding the major cultural and political changes that occurred in the eastern Mediterranean from the Bronze to Iron ages, leading to the Ionian settlement of the Anatolian coast.

Dunbabin, T. J. *The Greeks and Their Eastern Neighbors.* Reprint. Chicago: Ares, 1979. First published in 1957, this volume emphasizes Greek relationships in the eastern Mediterranean, focusing on coastal Anatolia, the Aegean, Egypt, and Syro-Palestine.

Emlyn-Jones, C. J. *The Ionians and Hellenism: A Study of the Cultural Achievement of the Early Greek Inhabitants of Asia Minor.* London: Routledge & Kegan Paul, 1980. Surveys the cultural attributes of Ionia in the first half of the first millennium B.C. and the interaction of the Ionians with the local Anatolian populations.

Huxley, G. L. *The Early Ionians.* New York: Barnes & Noble, 1972. A general survey of Ionia from the beginning of the first millennium B.C. to the revolt against Persia five centuries later. Huxley studies both the literary traditions concerning early Ionia and the existing material remains.

Roebuck, C. *Ionian Trade and Colonisation.* New York: Archaeological Institute of America, 1959. Roebuck explores the economic aspects of Ionian civilization and colonization as found in primary literary sources and material remains.

SEE ALSO: 800 B.C., Homer's Composition of the *Iliad*; 776 B.C., Olympic Games; 600-500 B.C., Greek Philosophers Formulate Theories of the Cosmos; 530 B.C., Founding of the Pythagorean Brotherhood; 450-425 B.C., History Develops as Scholarly Discipline.

800 B.C.
HOMER'S COMPOSITION OF THE ILIAD

Homer's composition of the Iliad *produces a premier example of the Greek tradition of epic poetry.*

DATE: c. 800 B.C.
LOCALE: Ionia, on the coast of Asia Minor
CATEGORY: Cultural and intellectual history
KEY FIGURE:
Homer (fl. early to late ninth century B.C.), a Greek poet and author of the *Iliad* and the *Odyssey*

SUMMARY OF EVENT. The composition of the *Iliad* can be seen as both the beginning of Western literature and the culmination of a long tradition of oral epic poetry that probably dates from the height of Mycenaean civilization in the thirteenth and twelfth centuries B.C. Although few facts can be verified about the identity of Homer himself and the time and place of the composition of his epic poem, the *Iliad* itself provides evidence that can support some educated guesses as to its authorship and provenance. References to Homer's material in later Greek writings suggest that the epic must have been widely circulated by 700 B.C., and descriptions of sculpture and certain types of shields that can be closely dated by archaeologists indicate that the final version of the *Iliad* is unlikely to have been composed much before 725 B.C.

Elements of the Aeolic and Ionic dialects used in the poem have encouraged scholars to believe that its author lived in one of the Greek colonies on the coast of Asia Minor, where Hellenes, who had been powerful in Mycenaean days, had taken refuge from Dorian invaders during the eleventh century B.C. Somehow, in the nearly five hundred years between the legendary fall of Troy and the writing of the *Iliad*, the Ionian courts preserved the names of the Mycenaean heroes and cities powerful in the Aegean culture of the Bronze Age, as well as stories of events related to some conflict between Greeks and Trojans.

The preservation of these elements of a dead civilization has been attributed to the existence of a strong oral tradition. In books VII and XXII, the *Odyssey* describes court poets who entertained visitors with recitations of the deeds of heroes, and the characters of Demodocus and Phemius probably reflect Homer's own role in Ionian

As shown in this engraving, Homer is believed to have given oral recitations of his poetry as sagas that combined historical facts with folk tales and legends about heroic adventures. (Archive Photos)

society. Scholars have postulated the existence of poetic guilds that preserved and passed on, with their own embellishments, bodies of historical and legendary materials. Modern research into oral transmission of folk epics in Yugoslavia and Finland has proved what extraordinary amounts of material the human memory, properly trained, can retain.

These Ionian bards, like later ones who preserved and transmitted the Germanic sagas, developed sophisticated techniques to assist them in their composition. At some point in the growth of the oral epic, dactylic hexameter became the accepted metrical form. It is a complex meter, hardly more natural to the Greek language than it is to the English language. The bards therefore developed formulas or groups of words that fit metrically into various positions in the line and could be combined to form whole lines. Frequent use of the same epithets, such as "fleet-footed Achilles" or "Agamemnon, king of men," illustrates the technique; Hera is called "white-armed" or "Hera of the golden throne" according to whether she is mentioned at the beginning or end of a line, not because of the context in which she is mentioned.

Learning hundreds of these formulas must have been part of the training of Ionian court poets, for the same phrases seem to have been handed down for generations. Once a satisfactory pattern had been established, it appears to have been preserved, even though its words might have vanished from ordinary speech. The use of formulas probably explains why, for example, there are contradictory descriptions of weapons in the *Iliad*. The swords and shields of Ajax, Agamemnon, and Hector sometimes re-

sembled those which archaeologists have found among Mycenaean relics, and other times those of eighth century Ionia.

In addition, entire passages, such as the catalog of ships in book 2 of the *Iliad*, seem to have been handed down almost intact. Many of the cities mentioned were centers of commerce during Mycenaean times, but were obliterated long before Homer lived. It is interesting to note that Homer considered the list of heroes important enough to preserve in his poem, even though many of the leaders mentioned play little or no part in the epic itself.

Little is actually known about Homer's audience. Nevertheless, the nature of the *Iliad* makes it clear that the events surrounding the Trojan War were familiar to the poet's audience, for he begins in the middle of the action, declaring his intention to sing of the wrath of Achilles. There is no need to discuss the causes of the war or its conclusion, and the characters evidently need no introduction. The greatness of the poet was not his originality as a creator of plot, but rather his ability to bring a unified whole out of the masses of material at his disposal.

Perhaps even less is known about Homer as an individual. When the Greeks became interested in biography, nothing had been recorded about the man to whom they ascribed their greatest literary treasures. It is simply a romantic story that claims that Homer was a blind minstrel.

Homer used traditional materials and forms to create a work that embodied a radical and consistent interpretation of the world and of the position of man. As far as possible, he cleared away everything that could distract attention from his main theme: the terrible contrast of life and death.

The hero of Homer's epics represents the summit of human greatness, and his struggle to face death is fascinating enough to attract the gaze of the immortal gods, thus exalting human life to a level at which it achieves significance and becomes a fit subject for the song that celebrates its fragility and its greatness.

The *Iliad* does not tell readers that the world was made for human beings, or that the natural human state in this world is one of happiness. The epic does say that this state can be comprehended in human terms and that human life can be more than an insignificant or ignoble struggle in the dark. The human soul can rise to the height of the challenges and the suffering which are the lot of all humankind. That spirit, chastened but not despairing, which sees the world without illusion and confronts it without self-pity or evasion, was the gift of Greece to the world, and it is the deepest element in the thought of Homer.

Controversy has raged for years over the authorship of the *Iliad*. Some scholars see the epic as the work of one person, whereas others see it as the work of several individuals. The modern consensus seems to be that one controlling artistic imagination must have shaped the whole, regardless of the origin of its components. The consistent characterizations, the epic similes with their sympathetic glimpses into the life of the common people of Homer's day, and, above all, the unifying theme of the tragedy of Achilles can hardly have resulted from the work of a number of poets working separately.

It is equally clear, however, that the epic does contain inconsistencies. Some of these inconsistencies are related to the use of formulas and, probably, pieces of earlier epics. Others doubtless are the result of additions made by post-Homeric scribes and editors. It must also be remembered that since the *Iliad* was composed for recitation over a period of days and not for reading, both poet and audience might reasonably be expected to forget or confuse certain details.

It is nearly impossible to assess the enormous impact of the composition of the *Iliad* on Western civilization. Its story has been part of the education of every cultivated human for nearly three thousand years, testifying to the significance of the Homeric understanding of the nature of human beings and their place in the world. In addition, the Homeric epic has inspired many of the great works of European literature, including Vergil's *Aeneid* and Dante's *The Divine Comedy*.

—*Elizabeth J. Lipscomb, updated by Susan M. Taylor*

ADDITIONAL READING:

Bowra, C. M. *Tradition and Design in the "Iliad."* Oxford: Clarendon Press, 1950. Bowra presents a discussion of the historical background of the *Iliad*, Homer's use of traditional materials, and an analysis of Homer himself.

Crotty, Kevin. *The Poetics of Supplication: Homer's "Iliad" and "Odyssey."* Ithaca, N.Y.: Cornell University Press, 1994. This work discusses the criticisms of the *Iliad* as well as Homer's interpretation of heroes.

Edwards, Mark W. *Homer, Poet of the "Iliad."* Baltimore: The Johns Hopkins University Press, 1987. The author speaks to the rites and ceremonies in literature, concentrating on Homer's epic.

Frazer, Richard M. *A Reading of the "Iliad."* Lanham, Md.: University Press of America, 1993. Frazer discusses the history and literary criticism surrounding epic poetry, using the *Iliad* as an example.

Hadas, Moses. *A History of Greek Literature.* New York: Columbia University Press, 1950. This work provides a guide to Homer's place in the whole range of Greek literature.

Morrison, James V. *Homeric Misdirection: False Predictions of the "Iliad."* Ann Arbor: University of Michigan Press, 1992. Morrison provides a detailed discussion of Homeric technique and explores truths and falsehoods in literature.

Van Duzer, Chet A. *Duality and Structure in the "Iliad" and the "Odyssey."* New York: Peter Lang, 1996. Homer's technique is discussed at length, as well as the use of logic and polarity in literature.

SEE ALSO: 1620-1120 B.C., Rise of Mycenaean Civilization; 600-500 B.C., Greek Philosophers Formulate Theories of the Cosmos; 450-425 B.C., History Develops as Scholarly Discipline.

776 B.C.
OLYMPIC GAMES
The Olympic Games are established as one of four Panhellenic ("All-Greek") games in antiquity and help provide unity in a country otherwise isolated into competing city-states.

DATE: 776 B.C.
LOCALE: Olympia, Greece
CATEGORIES: Cultural and intellectual history; Diplomacy and international relations; Government and politics
KEY FIGURES:
Phidias (c. 490-430 B.C.), sculptor who created a massive statue of Zeus at Olympia
Pindar (518-438 B.C.), lyric poet whose works frequently celebrate Olympic victories
Theodosius the Great (A.D. 346-395), Roman emperor of the East, 379-395, and of the West, 394-395

Theodosius II (A.D. 401-450), Roman emperor in the East, 408-450, and grandson of Theodosius the Great

SUMMARY OF EVENT. It is unknown whether the date 776 B.C. represents the first Olympic Games or the first *recorded* celebration of the Olympic Festival. If the former, the Olympic Games arose at the end of the Greek Dark Ages, a period of roughly four hundred years extending from the fall of Mycenae (c. 1100 B.C.) until the dawn of the Archaic period. If the latter is true, however, the year 776 B.C. represents when writing returned to the Greek mainland, allowing people to begin preserving records of a celebration that began centuries earlier. Whichever of these is true (and evidence seems to support the second alternative), winners of each Olympic Festival were recorded from 776 B.C. until A.D. 217 in a list appearing in the writings of the chronographer Eusebius (c. A.D. 260-340). Winners of the earliest recorded events were thus roughly contemporary with the founding of Rome (April 21, 753 B.C.) and the earliest settlements on the Palatine Hill (c. 750 B.C.).

Olympia is located in the region of Elis, roughly ten miles inland from the Ionian Sea in the west-central Peloponnese. The festival celebrated there was, along with a common language and shared religion, one of the few aspects of Greek life promoting unity among the highly disparate city-states. Divided by local traditions, variant dialects, and diverse forms of government, the Greek *poleis* (singular: *polis*) or city-states were often rivals. At the Olympic Games, however, a truce was declared for the duration of the festival and political disputes were not allowed to interfere with the celebration. The Greeks believed, probably without foundation, that the Olympic Festival had been proposed by the Delphic Oracle as a means of promoting peace.

The Olympic Games were one of four Panhellenic Festivals or "All-Greek" athletic competitions held periodically in Greece. At the Pythian Games honoring Apollo at Delphi, the prize awarded to victors was a wreath of bay leaves gathered in the Vale of Tempe. The Nemean Games were held in honor of Zeus at Nemea, with winners receiving a wreath of wild parsley. At the Isthmian Games dedicated to Poseidon at Corinth, victors received a wreath of wild celery. Of these four festivals, the Olympic Games were by far the most prestigious. Held once every four years in honor of Zeus at Olympia, the prize awarded to victors was a wreath made of wild olive leaves. The four-year period between Olympic Festivals was known as an Olympiad and could be used as a means of calculating dates. The games began at Olympia at the first full moon after the summer solstice.

Like the other Panhellenic Festivals, the Olympic Games had a religious, as well as athletic and political, importance. The perfection of the human body was seen as an act of worship by which human beings tried to imitate the perfection of the eternal gods. In the odes of the poet Pindar, this physical achievement is often placed in a religious or mythological context. To aristocrats such as Pindar, the competition and the prize that the victor received were important, not because they were useful, but because they were useless. Time spent in activities having no practical utility must be the result of sheer love of the activity itself, not the pursuit of material gain. Honors and prizes conferred upon the victors by their native cities were, however, usually so large that they became rich for the rest of their lives.

Certain restrictions applied to those who were eligible for competition. Free men (and, after 632 B.C., boys) whose native language was Greek were allowed to participate in the Games. Those whose native language was not Greek were permitted to watch the Games but could not compete in them. (In the Roman period, this restriction was waived for the Romans themselves.) Slaves and all women, except for the local priestess of Demeter, were forbidden from entering the sacred area while the Games were in progress. Those violating this prohibition were hurled to their deaths from the Typaeon Rock.

The stadium that was built for the Olympic Festival was the earliest ever built by the Greeks, and it influenced the design of all that succeeded it. In Greece, a stadium was always used for footraces; it was never used, like Roman circuses, as an arena for chariot races. (A longer track, called a "hippodrome," was built for horse racing.) The term "stadium" is derived from the Greek word *stade* or *stadion*, a unit of measurement corresponding to six hundred Greek feet, each foot measuring slightly more than thirteen inches. A stade was thus 606.75 English feet in length. This became a standard unit of measurement in Greek racetracks of all periods. Because of the fierce independence of Greek city-states, however, some regional differences did occur.

The earliest events at Olympia appear to have been footraces, wrestling, and throwing events. As early as the seventh century B.C., races for chariots and individual horses occurred. In races, it was always the owner of the horse, not its rider, who was awarded the victory. From 472 B.C. onward, events at the Olympic Games were expanded to include horse races, the discus throw, the javelin throw, boxing, the pentathlon ("five contests": jumping, wrestling, the javelin, the discus, and running), and the *pancration* (a type of "no-holds-barred" wrestling). Contestants in the Games had to be in training for a minimum of ten months before their competition. For the last thirty days prior to the festival, athletes trained in a special gymnasium at Olympia itself, where they ran and threw the javelin or discus. This final month of training was supervised by the Hellenodicae, a board of ten men who also served as referees during the Games themselves.

As an important religious center, Olympia was also the location of the ancient world's most famous statue of Zeus, considered one of the Seven Wonders of the Ancient World. The statue was a forty foot high representation of the god in gold and ivory by the artist Pheidias that stood within the Temple of Zeus. Though approximately the same size as Phidias' statue of Athena in the Athenian Parthenon, this statue of Zeus was said to seem taller because it was a seated statue. The geographer Strabo (353 B.C.) thus noted that if "Zeus" would have risen from his chair, he would easily have lifted off the roof from the temple. The rhetorician Quintilian (*Institutio Oratoria*

12.10.9) claimed that this statue "could be said to have added something to traditional religion." The Roman statesman Cicero (*Orator* 2.8) noted that the statue was based, not upon any living model, but upon an idealized view of beauty, rather like that to which the athletes themselves aspired. Zeus was depicted as a bearded man, crowned with an olive wreath, and holding a life-size Winged Victory in his right hand.

In A.D. 393, the Roman emperor Theodosius, a Christian, ended all pagan athletic games in Greece. In 426, his successor Theodosius II ordered the destruction of the temples at Olympia. Then, in 1880-1881, the starting blocks and lines used for footraces in the ancient stadium were rediscovered. The modern Olympic Games began in the spring of 1896, largely through the efforts of the French educator Baron Pierre de Coubertin. In 1924, the Winter Olympics were added to this existing competition

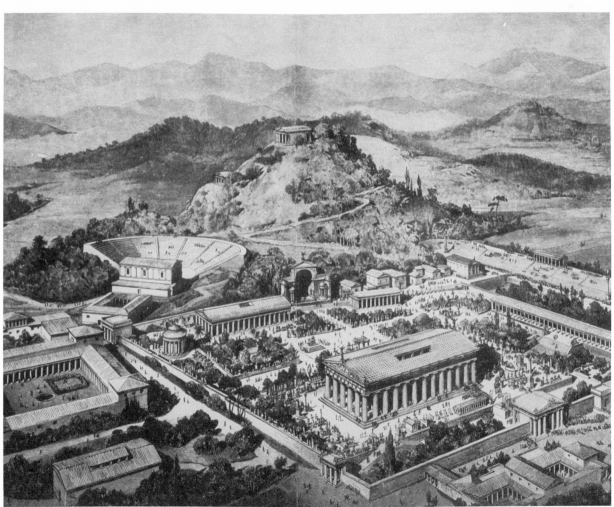

In this artist's rendering of the reconstruction of Olympia, the stadium used for footraces at the Olympic Games is visible on the left. (Archive Photos)

(now often called the "Summer Olympics"). For seventy years, both festivals were held in the same year. Beginning in 1994, however, winter and summer festivals began to alternate in even-numbered years. Like the ancient Olympic Festival, the modern Games are viewed as a means of promoting peace among peoples of different cultures.

—Jeffrey L. Buller

ADDITIONAL READING:

Ashmole, Bernard. *Olympia*. London: Phaidon, 1967. An archaeological and artistic examination of the major structures at Olympia, with major attention given to the sculptural decoration of the Temple of Zeus and its significance.

Drees, Ludwig. *Olympia: Gods, Artists, and Athletes*. New York: Praeger, 1968. An excellent place to begin; a broad account of the ancient Olympic Games and their importance in Greek society.

Gardiner, E. Norman. *Olympia: Its History and Remains*. Washington, D.C.: McGrath, 1973. Dated but still useful discussion of the physical evidence at Olympia and the role of the site throughout antiquity.

Harris, Harold Arthur. *Greek Athletes and Athletics*. Bloomington: Indiana University Press, 1966. A thorough examination of Greek athletic practice, relating the Olympic Games to other panhellenic festivals.

Schobel, Heinz. *The Ancient Olympic Games*. Translated by Joan Becker. Princeton, N.J.: Van Nostrand, 1966. A concise introduction for the general reader.

SEE ALSO: 775 B.C., Oracle at Delphi; 650 B.C., Greek City-States Use Coins as Means of Exchange.

775 B.C.
ORACLE AT DELPHI

The Oracle at Delphi provides a common meeting ground for early Greek city-states and a religious ratification for individual cities' decisions.

DATE: 775 B.C.

LOCALE: Central Greece

CATEGORIES: Government and politics; Religion

KEY FIGURES:

Lycurgus (fl. seventh century B.C.), traditional Spartan lawgiver

Phemonoe (c. 775 B.C.), traditional first priestess of Apollo

Solon (c. 639-c. 559 B.C.) Athenian lawgiver

SUMMARY OF EVENT. The ancient Greek cities, as they entered recorded history about 800 B.C., were disunited. Except for temporary, often strained alliances against foreign enemies, they developed no common political insti-

tutions. They were permanently in competition with one another, and often at war. Decisions had to be made, mostly about internal matters, but also about war, colonization, and occasional joint enterprises. These decisions were fundamentally matters of individual sovereignty. Yet there was enough sense of being "Hellenes"—Greeks—to permit the Oracle of Apollo at Delphi to emerge as somewhat of a common center. To understand this development, it is necessary to glance at prior religious and political arrangements.

From roughly 2000 until 1250 B.C., the brilliant, powerful "palace societies" of Crete and Mycenae dominated the area. The political-administrative form of these societies appears to have been bureaucratic aristocracy. Palace societies were originally worshipers of the Great (Earth) Goddess, but with increasing male military influence Poseidon, the earth-shaking lord of the sea, and then Zeus, the weather/sky god, emerged as major deities.

The period from 1200 through 800 B.C. is termed "The Dark Ages." The rich archaeological and even documentary evidence of a half millennium earlier does not exist. From what is known, Dark Age Greece was rudimentary and disorganized. The classical philosopher Aristotle (384-322 B.C.), in his *Politics*, held that the early Greeks lived "scattered about." Each clan was a little kingdom, ruled absolutely by an elder male who was father, master, and king. Aristotle may be overstating the extent of patriarchy, which he sees as analogous to Zeus's ascendancy as father and king of the Olympian gods. It was, however, precisely during this period that Zeus became dominant. His cult was established at Olympia in the early tenth century.

Zeus was a deity appropriate to a period dominated by small-scale, quasi-feudal monarchy. Slowly, however, and no doubt due in part to the relative order provided by authoritarian patriarchy-monarchy, the small Greek communities began to recover and grow. The classical Greek form of political organization, the *polis*, or "city-state," emerged. These early political communities were not yet the powerful, populous, often democratic cities of several centuries later; but neither were they scattered rural citadels of warrior chieftains. They represented the partial reemergence in Greece of civilized urban life, and as such required a revised religious orientation.

The god most related to this development was Apollo. The terms "Apollo" and "Apollonian" convey an image of beauty and harmony. Apollo is *the* god of Greek classicism, especially as "Phoibos Apollo," the Radiant Apollo. He is the god of healing, of purification, of music. Yet the Greeks could never forget the connotations of his name. With his characteristic bow and arrow, Apollo the "far-darter" seemed to be "The Destroyer." Even the adjective *phoibos* was frighteningly close to the noun *phobos*, "fear" or "terror."

This moral ambiguity is present in the tales of Apollo's arrival at Delphi. Apollo was the son of Zeus, begotten on the nymph Leto. Enraged, Zeus's sister-wife Hera sent the dragon-serpent Python to pursue Leto. Apollo was born on the Aegean island of Delos; met Python on Mount Parnassus and wounded him; pursued Python to Delphi, and killed him. Thus Apollo was established at Delphi.

At issue in the establishment is the question of precedence. Scholars debate whether the cult of Apollo took over an earlier oracle of the Earth goddess Ge, or Gaia. Complicating things is the question of whether Ge, Gaia, and Hera are all later personifications of the original Great (Earth) Goddess. Mythic traditions, combined with some archaeological and linguistic evidence, tend to affirm both prior occupation and theological identity. The moral implication is that both Zeus and Apollo acted unjustly, and that redress was required. Zeus appears to have suffered only through the growing influence of Apollo's cult. Yet Apollo is purified (on Crete, the Great Goddess' center); he shares the shrine with the Pythia, his priestess and oracle; and he further honors the memory of the slain Python with the Pythian Games, begun in 586.

There seems, then, to be an inner logic to the concomitant emergence of the Oracle of Apollo at Delphi and the *polis*. Apollo is the new, young god. He represents a fresh beginning, a break with both the obvious patriarchal order but also with the dimly remembered maternal religion lying behind it. Nevertheless, there is an evident compromise and implicit alliance of Son and Mother against Father. Apollo is the personification of beauty and harmony, but with an undercurrent of violence and injustice in his nature.

Given these characteristics, Apollo is the appropriate god for the classical Greek cities. They too represent a new principle, that of politics. Politics is the free intercourse of equal citizens, who conduct their affairs by speaking. Its authority is not that of the ancestral, but of individual, often youthful excellence. Politics is also a spirited, often violent, sometimes terrible competition. It is a kind of order deeply in need of a neutral ground, and of moderation.

Delphi provided that ground and attempted to provide the moderation. Supposedly carved over the entrance of one of the several successive temples of Apollo were the sayings "Nothing in Excess" and "Know thyself." These famous pieces of advice capture much of the permanent spirit of the oracle—a spirit communicated to cities and individuals with decreasing effectiveness as time passed.

Yet they are not themselves utterances of Apollo's Pythian priestess. To imagine the priestess "prophesying," that is, foretelling the future, or uttering pithy, cryptic sayings is to misunderstand, according to modern scholarship, normal Delphic procedure. (In this sense, Phemonoe, "prophetic mind," seems misnamed.) The oracle functioned approximately as a divine court of appeals. The "judges" were Apollo and, behind Apollo, at the omphalos stone marking the navel of the world, Earth Herself.

Representatives of cities or, less frequently, private individuals initiated an inquiry. They did not, however, do so at their own convenience. The Pythia gave responses nine times each year, on the seventh of each nonwinter month. She did so seated on a tripod in the innermost sanctuary of Apollo's temple. There is scholarly agreement that the most usual form of the response was "yes" or "no" to a policy question previously deliberated by a city; and, moreover, that the reply was almost always to

Delphic oracles were consulted for guidance in making important political decisions, as in this imagined encounter between Alexander the Great of Macedonia and a Pythian priestess. (Library of Congress)

affirm the policy. This simple, nearly automatic sort of "oracle" renders irrelevant the interesting question of the Pythia's state of mind when pronouncing. The traditional view, that she spoke under the influence of vapors emitted from a chasm in the earth, has been discarded. Those who admit as genuine some of the longer, more substantive responses reported speculate that the Pythia inhaled narcotic fumes, or induced self-hypnosis.

Given that the oracle's usual response was an affirmation of policy proposals, it is understandable that Delphi's greatest influence occurred in the first few centuries of its existence. The characteristic early political problems were the devising of law codes and the establishment of colonies. These proposals were both relatively easy to affirm and conducive to good reputation, since they provided both internal stability and widening Greek influence. The most famous examples of legislation, Lycurgus' at Sparta and Solon's at Athens, were noted for their balance and moderation, and closely associated with Delphi.

Delphi's broad political program, then, appears to have been twofold—acquiescence in particular *polis* decisions while encouraging development of moderate institutions. This program implicitly acknowledged Delphi's own limitations. At best, it might provide an opportunity for policy reconsideration in a setting suggestive of both a common Greekness and a superhuman perspective. Delphic moderation tended toward passivity, and was successful insofar as its member cities tended in the same direction. Early, most did; later, some, especially Athens, did not, and Delphi declined accordingly.   —*John F. Wilson*

ADDITIONAL READING:

Burkert, Walter. *Greek Religion*. Translated by John Raffan. Cambridge, Mass.: Harvard University Press, 1985. Widely recognized as the standard source, this book includes clear and balanced accounts of the Minoan-Mycenaean Great Goddess, sanctuaries and oracles, and Apollo.

Clay, Jenny Strauss. *The Politics of Olympus: Form and Meaning in the Major Homeric Hymns*. Princeton, N.J.: Princeton University Press, 1989. This interesting work emphasizes the gender aspects of divine politics, including the Gaia-Python-Apollo relationship.

Dempsey, Reverend T. *The Delphic Oracle: Its Early History Influence and Fall*. New York: Benjamin Blom, 1972. Superseded in scholarly terms, this short book is a useful, widely available introduction to the subject.

Fontenrose, Joseph. *The Delphic Oracle: Its Responses and Operations*. Berkeley: University of California Press, 1978. An important scholarly effort, this work consists largely of an exhaustive, sometimes controversial evaluation of the historicity of the Oracle's responses.

Morgan, Catherine. *Athletics and Oracles: The Transformation of Olympia and Delphi in the Eighth Century B.C.* New York: Cambridge University Press, 1990. This work effectively links the rise of the Delphic Oracle to early Greek city-state development.

Parke, H. W., and D. E. W. Wormell. *The Delphic Oracle: Volume 1—The History*. Oxford: Basil Blackwell, 1956. The classic source, this well-balanced account takes a middle position on the historicity of responses.

SEE ALSO: 1600-1500 B.C., Flowering of Minoan Civilization; 736-716 B.C., Spartan Conquest of Messenia; 600-500 B.C., Greek Philosophers Formulate Theories of the Cosmos; 594-580 B.C., Legislation of Solon.

736-716 B.C.
SPARTAN CONQUEST OF MESSENIA

The Spartan conquest of Messenia reduces the Messenian population to servitude and helps Sparta become the dominant military state in Greece.

DATE: c. 736-716 B.C.

LOCALE: The southwestern Peloponnesus, Greece

CATEGORIES: Expansion and land acquisition; Wars, uprisings, and civil unrest

KEY FIGURES:

Theopompus, Spartan king and commander in the First Messenian War

Tyrtaeus (fl. mid-seventh century B.C.), Spartan poet at the time of the Second Messenian War

SUMMARY OF EVENT. In the fifth and fourth centuries B.C., the institutions of the Peloponnesian city-state of Sparta, although not precisely imitated by other states, were universally judged to be unique. These institutions were admired by many, including the Athenian philosopher Plato. In a Greek environment increasingly dominated by economic commerce, Sparta remained almost exclusively agrarian. In a world in which other states had developed social diversity and rich cultural expression, Sparta retained a strict and simple social structure and a spiritual character rich in strength but seemingly wanting in creative artistic expression. Scholarly studies of the late twentieth century have shown the existence of some Spartan artistic creativity. Since archaeological and literary evidence indicates that Sparta was in the mainstream of Greek cultural development until the beginning of the seventh century B.C., the reason for Sparta's later uniqueness must be sought in a development of the seventh century. The most likely explanation is to be found in the deliberate crystallization of permanent military institutions made necessary by Sparta's conquest of Messenia as a response to the problem of overpopulation in the eighth century.

The Dorian invaders of Laconia, who settled in the valley of the Eurotas River during the twelfth century B.C., remained ethnically distinct from the residual non-Dorian inhabitants whom they had conquered and over whom they exercised administrative jurisdiction. The distinction seems to have been preserved especially by maintenance of a social code from the period of conquest that featured strict separation of the sexes, early military training for boys in kinship groups, and common daily gatherings of adult males within kinship groups.

During the eighth century B.C., most communities in the Greek world faced the problem of overpopulation and responded to the challenge by establishing overseas colonies throughout the Mediterranean world. Sparta stood aloof from the general movement of colonization, founding only a few colonies and solving its problem of overpopulation by conquering the neighboring province of Messenia. Located to the southwest, Messenia was one of the richest agricultural districts in a region known for its generally rocky, mountainous, and infertile terrain. The war between Sparta and Messenia extended over a twenty-year period from approximately 736 to 716 B.C. According to tradition, the Spartan army was led by Theopompus, one of its hereditary kings. There are abundant legends about the war, but little more can be firmly established beyond the bare facts recounted above and the Spartan organization of the land and its people following the conquest. Since the war had been fought in response to the challenge of overpopulation, Messenian land was divided into estates that were distributed among the victorious Spartan soldiers. The Messenians themselves continued to work the land as serfs and were obliged to pay one-half of their produce to the new Spartan landowners. The conquered Messenians were called *helots*, a term which probably had the original meaning of "prisoners of war."

Encouraged by Sparta's involvement in local wars against Argos, Arcadia, and Elis in the mid-seventh century, the Messenians attempted to throw off Spartan domination after several generations of servitude. The ensuing struggle was bitterly fought and apparently engendered a constitutional crisis from which Sparta emerged as a permanently militarist society with a rigid social and political structure. Primary sources describing events of this period include the poems of Tyrtaeus, exhortations of Spartan soldiers to resolution in the war with Messenia, a paraphrase of an oracle of Delphi sanctioning the constitution (apparently adopted or amended at this time), and the text of a document called the *Great Rhetra* (quoted by Plutarch in the *Life of Lycurgus*) containing information about the provisions of this constitution.

A major factor in this political crisis involved a shift in military tactics from fighting based on spear carriers and aristocratic cavalry to reliance on the close-knit phalanx of heavily armed foot soldiers known as hoplites. In Sparta and throughout the Greek world, the shifting of the burden of community defense to the shoulders of the hoplite infantry was accompanied by a demand by these soldiers for greater political authority. The imperative economic necessity of the reconquest of Messenia forced aristocratic leaders to grant concessions that were formalized by the *Great Rhetra*. In addition, the Spartan assembly (*Apella*) of nine thousand warriors adopted the framework of a military organization based on local considerations rather than one based solely on claims of kinship. According to the *Great Rhetra*, this assembly was to be sovereign in the state and would hold final authority over the *Gerousia*, an aristocratic council of thirty elders. Some adjustment of land distribution was evidently involved as well, for the nine thousand were henceforth called "equals" and were so content with their new lot that they did not resist the formulation of an amendment to the *Great Rhetra* granting veto power to the *Gerousia* over decisions made by the *Apella*.

Although they successfully suppressed the Messenian revolt, the Spartans were fully conscious that their economic security depended upon the continued subjection of a large population of serfs under the control of a relatively small Spartan army. The Spartan commitment to a life of relentless military preparedness was maintained at the cost of cultural stagnation—a price which the Spartans were willing to pay.

—*Carl W. Conrad, updated by Mark W. Chavalas*

ADDITIONAL READING:

Bowra, C. M. *Greek Lyric Poetry from Alcman to Simonides*. 2d ed. Oxford: Clarendon Press, 1961. This general survey of Greek lyric poets includes fragments of the work of Tyrtaeus, the Spartan poet whose work serves as a primary source for understanding the Messenian wars.

Fitzhardinge, L. F. *The Spartans*. London: Thames & Hudson, 1980. Fitzhardinge provides an overview of the material remains of the Spartans, placing the Messenian wars in an appropriate archaeological context and arguing that modern archaeological research has confirmed that Sparta was not as distinct from the other Greek city-states as was previously supposed.

Hooker, J. T. *The Ancient Spartans*. London: J. M. Dent & Sons, 1980. A good summary of Spartan culture and history that attempts to incorporate both literary traditions and archaeological research.

Jeffrey, L. H. *Archaic Greece: The City-States c. 700-500 B.C.* London: Methuen, 1976. Jeffrey's work focuses on a comparative analysis of the formative period of the Greek city-states. Useful for placing Sparta in its historical and archaeological context.

Lazenby, J. F. *The Spartan Army*. Warminster, England: Aris & Phillips, 1985. The best comprehensive survey of Spartan military techniques during the Archaic and Classical periods.

Powell, A., ed. *Classical Sparta: Techniques Behind Her Success*. Norman: University of Oklahoma Press, 1989. Contains a series of articles on Spartan culture and warfare that provide general information for understanding the Spartan victories in Messenia.

Snodgrass, A. *Archaic Greece: The Age of Experiment*. Berkeley: University of California Press, 1980. In his survey of the various cultural factors conditioning the growth of ancient Greece, Snodgrass includes occasional reference to Spartan affairs. Although far from exhaustive, this volume does provide an excellent context in which to study Spartan history.

SEE ALSO: 1000 B.C., Greek Alphabet Is Developed; 733 B.C., Founding of Syracuse; 650 B.C., Greek City-States Use Coins as Means of Exchange; 478-448 B.C., Athenian Empire Is Created.

733 B.C.
FOUNDING OF SYRACUSE

The founding of Syracuse by the Greek city-state of Corinth on the island of Sicily establishes one of the major political and cultural centers of the Greek world in the western Mediterranean.

DATE: c. 733 B.C.
LOCALE: The southeastern coast of Sicily
CATEGORIES: Expansion and land acquisition; Exploration and discovery; Government and politics
KEY FIGURE:
Archias, Corinthian nobleman and founder of Syracuse
SUMMARY OF EVENT. Since ancient times, Greece has been a country with sparse natural resources. Its deposits of minerals are not extensive, and the soil itself is thin and stony. Much of the terrain is covered by mountains, limiting its arable land to only one-quarter of its surface. At the dawn of Greek history, Homer wrote that Hellas (Greece) was married to poverty. As time passed and the population of Greece grew, many city-states found themselves unable to support their citizens. The acute need for more land could be satisfied only by emigration overseas. As a result, Greek city-states began a program of colonization around 750 B.C. that continued for nearly five centuries.

One of the first states to establish overseas colonies was Corinth, even though it possessed notable wealth by Greek standards. Corinth's position on the isthmus placed it at an important crossroads, where the land route between the Peloponnesus and central Greece intersected the short overland connection between the Gulf of Corinth and the Saronic Gulf. The city-state charged tolls on both routes, but the revenue received was insufficient to pay for much-needed imported food. As a result, Corinth decided to dispatch two expeditions overseas sometime around 733 B.C. Archias, a member of the noble family of the Bacchiadae, was selected to be the founder of the colony that settled on the east coast of the fertile island of Sicily. It is possible that the Corinthians consulted the god Apollo at Delphi to receive his sanction for the venture and to seek useful advice.

Unfortunately, virtually nothing is known of the story of the voyage to Sicily or of the early years of the new colony. Scholars believe that the risks faced by the Corinthians were similar to those encountered by European settlers who colonized North and South America in the seventeenth century. Although the Atlantic Ocean was more dangerous than the Mediterranean Sea, such dangers were mitigated by the larger and stronger ships used by seventeenth century colonists, as well as the compasses they used and improved knowledge of celestial navigation they possessed. These later colonists also had firearms and armor to defend themselves in encounters with the original inhabitants of the lands they claimed, whereas the Greeks had essentially the same weapons as the people they dispossessed. Archias and his Corinthian force succeeded in establishing their colony, and within a generation or two, Syracuse became a large and flourishing state. As a colony, Syracuse was not governed by Corinth, but was fully autonomous. Corinth and Syracuse enjoyed the typically friendly relationship that developed between most Greek city-states and their offshoots, since war between a colony and its mother city was considered to be a particularly shameful occurrence. There were exceptions, however, as in the case of Corcyra, another colony founded by Corinth around 733 B.C. Historians are aware of two wars fought between Corcyra and Corinth before the end of the fifth century B.C., and there are indications that there were other conflicts as well.

Syracuse became so powerful and populous that it was forced to establish its own colonies in other parts of Sicily; these daughter states also came to play an important role in the life and history of Sicily. Under the rule of the tyrant Dionysius at the beginning of the fourth century B.C., Syracuse temporarily imposed its hegemony on all of Sicily and much of southern Italy. The city became a brilliant center of Greek learning and culture and served as a conduit for transmitting elements of Hellenic culture from the Greek mainland and from Hellenized Alexandria to later Roman civilization.

After 650 B.C., a second motive for colonization supplemented the drive for agricultural expansion: Many colonies were founded for commercial gain. For example, the colony of Naucratis was established in Egypt shortly before 600 B.C. by Miletus, Aegina, Samus, and some smaller city-states as a depot for exporting much-needed grain from Egypt to Greece. In the west, Massilia (modern Marseilles) founded the city of Emporium, whose name may be translated from the Greek as "trading station," thus indicating the intention of its founders. Massilia also propagated Greek civilization up the valley of the Rhône River into southern Gaul.

Corinth was not the only city to colonize extensively. Other important colonizers included Eretria, located on the island of Euboea, which settled many colonies on the northern coast of the Aegean Sea, and Miletus, an Ionian city with numerous colonies along the coast of the Black Sea. This colonizing activity was of great significance, since the Black Sea, virtually all of Sicily, and the coastal regions of southern Italy were Hellenized by descendants of the original settlers of the western Mediterranean.

—*Samuel K. Eddy, updated by Mark W. Chavalas*

ADDITIONAL READING:

Berger, S. *Revolution and Society in Greek Sicily and Southern Italy*. Stuttgart, Germany: Steiner, 1992. A survey of the social and political institutions of Magna Grecia, or western Greece (Sicily and southern Italy), before and after the Roman conquest. Berger places special emphasis on the study of Syracuse and the impact of Greek tyranny.

Bernabo Brea, L. *Sicily Before the Greeks*. Translated by C. M. Preston and L. Guido. London: Thames & Hudson, 1957. This work is an important summary of Sicilian material culture that existed before Greek colonization. Readers should read this work in conjunction with the numerous excavations reports concerning prehistoric Sicily.

Boardman, J. *The Greeks Overseas*. 2d ed. London: Thames & Hudson, 1980. One of the more concise works on Greek colonization, with pertinent information concerning Sicily and southern Italy as well as areas in other parts of the Mediterranean and near the Black Sea.

Dunbabin, T. J. *The Western Greeks*. 2d ed. Chicago: Ares, 1979. Dunbabin's work is the fundamental study of Magna Grecia, surveying political history, natural philosophy, art, architecture, and other important subjects.

Finley, M. I. *Ancient Sicily to the Arab Conquest*. New York: Viking Press, 1968. A comprehensive historical survey of Sicily until Byzantine times that contains valuable information concerning Sicily. This volume is part of a three-volume series surveying the entire history of Sicily to modern times and its incorporation into the nation-state of Italy.

Hopper, R. J. *The Early Greeks*. New York: Barnes & Noble, 1977. Hopper gives a comprehensive account of early Greek civilization from prehistoric times to the beginning of Classical civilization in the sixth century B.C. Interested readers may use this source to place the history of Greek Sicily in its proper historical and archaeological context.

Malkin, I. *Religion and Colonization in Ancient Greece*. Leiden, the Netherlands: E. J. Brill, 1987. This volume surveys the religious aspects of Greek colonization in the Mediterranean and near the Black Sea. It also focuses on syncretism between Greek religious customs and those of the local inhabitants.

SEE ALSO: 736-716 B.C., Spartan Conquest of Messenia; 650 B.C., Greek City-States Use Coins as Means of Exchange; 625-509 B.C., Rise of Etruscan Civilization in Rome; 478-448 B.C., Athenian Empire Is Created; 415-413 B.C., Athenian Invasion of Sicily.

700-330 B.C.
PHALANX IS DEVELOPED AS A MILITARY UNIT

The phalanx is developed as a military unit, creating the first truly cohesive unit in Western warfare and making heavy infantry supreme on the battlefield.

DATE: 700-330 B.C.

LOCALE: Greece and Macedonia

CATEGORIES: Science and technology; Wars, uprisings, and civil unrest

KEY FIGURES:

Alexander the Great (356-323 B.C.), king of Macedonia, who combined the phalanx with light infantry and cavalry to conquer the Persian Empire

Epaminondas (c. 418-362 B.C.), Theban general who brought new flexibility to the phalanx

Miltiades (c. 540-c. 488 B.C.), Athenian general who defeated the Persians at Marathon

SUMMARY OF EVENT. While many factors help determine the characteristic military tactics of a time and place, culture and geography are certainly key among them. These were undoubtedly the two most important elements leading to the rise of the phalanx as the essential military unit among the ancient Greeks.

Quite early in their development, the inhabitants of Greece coalesced around a surprisingly large number of city-states, each of which controlled a limited portion of the Hellenic countryside. Arable lands on the slopes and hillsides were used to raise vines and olive trees for wine and oil; the relatively small amounts of flat lands were reserved for the growing of the cereal crops which formed the basis of the Greek diet. During the frequent wars between the city-states, it was the practice of the invader to attempt to seize the level farmland and destroy the crops, thus bringing eventual starvation and surrender to their opponent. The natural defensive strategy was therefore to meet the invader as quickly and as close to the border as possible, defeating him in one climactic battle. Thus was born the need for a quick decision in ancient Greek warfare.

Since Greece is a highly uneven land, often mountainous and with few expanses of level land—and those often narrow and hemmed in by hills and other rough terrain—even moderately sized forces could be deployed in relatively few areas. This meant that the focus on quick, decisive battle limited the type of warfare and the range of tactics which were available. Essentially it came down to the clash of two forces confined to a limited space; out of this necessity the phalanx was developed as a military unit.

The word "phalanx" itself comes from a Greek term which means, essentially, "a roller," and that is precisely what the unit was intended to do: roll over the enemy's battle line through sheer weight of mass and momentum. Throughout most of its career, the essence of phalanx warfare was to push forward until the opposing line broke; once that happened, defeat for the enemy was almost always inevitable.

The phalanx developed, apparently simultaneously throughout Greece, sometime during the eighth century B.C. It seems to have grown out of informal, small infantry units of citizen-soldiers armed with spears and shields. In order to increase their cohesiveness and impact, these units generally ranked shoulder to shoulder in a compact mass. The Greeks seemed to have found that eight ranks was the optimum depth for the spear. This length allowed at least three lines of spearpoints to project beyond the front rank, confronting the enemy with an imposing threat.

By the end of the eighth century, these troops were uniformly equipped. As citizens and landowners, however, each man was expected to purchase his own arms and armor. The primary arm was the spear, typically six to eight feet long and approximately one inch in diameter. It was usually made of ash or cornel wood with an iron

spearhead and a bronze butt spike, and generally seems to have weighed only two to four pounds. The spear was invariably held in the right hand, while the shield was grasped in the left.

Armor consisted of a helmet, breastplate, greaves (shin guards) and a round, bowl-shaped shield, which seems to have been about three feet in diameter and which may have weighed around sixteen pounds. It was clearly unwieldy and difficult to hold, for there are numerous references to those facts by ancient writers. Still, it seems to have offered considerable physical protection, and even greater psychological comfort, during the initial clash of lines in a phalanx battle. This shield was known in Greek as the *hoplon*, thus giving birth to the term for such a Greek soldier, a hoplite; the phalanx is hoplite warfare par excellence.

From ancient sources such as Thucydides and more recent archaeological evidence, hoplite warfare seems to have been highly ritualistic. Battles were often agreed to beforehand by the combatants and followed a prescribed course. This agreement was, for all practical purposes, necessary, since the phalanx was maneuverable only on fairly level ground; an army which had no wish to fight could simply withdraw into more rugged terrain. Such a shameful act, however, would have been unthinkable to the ancient Greeks. Prior to battle, each army offered sacrifices, followed by a ceremonial communal breakfast. Once ranged into position, the hoplites heard rousing speeches by their commanders. Then, shouting their battle cry, or *paean*, they charged.

Throughout most of phalanx warfare, this straightforward charge was the essence of the battle. As the two front lines collided, those in the front sought to find some opening through which to push their spear points; failing that, they resorted to a simple push of their *hoplon* against their opponent's, seeking to knock him off balance or at least force him backward.

As this struggle went on at the front, the men behind them pushed forward, adding their weight and impetus to the struggle. Eventually, one front line was pushed back until it began to break up in disorder, allowing its opponents to exploit the gap by striking into the heart of the phalanx. That was generally the point when the defeated phalanx collapsed and its men fled, many of them to be slaughtered from behind as they sought to escape. If there were any light troops or cavalry with the victorious army, this would be the time when they might be most useful in pursuing a beaten enemy. Even so, such pursuit seems to have been relatively limited, for generally speaking, the purpose of a phalanx battle was to repulse the enemy, not annihilate him.

The works of the Greek dramatist Sophocles reveal the military traditions and ceremonies connected with phalanx and hoplite warfare. (Library of Congress)

After the battle, the ritualistic aspects of Greek warfare would continue, for there would be a truce which allowed for the exchange of the bodies of the dead, followed by their ceremonial burial on the field, often with memorials to honor them. As Homer's *Iliad* and Sophocles' *Antigone* clearly show, refusal to permit proper burial was a shocking and indeed sacrilegious action.

The power of the traditional phalanx was convincingly demonstrated at the battle of Marathon (490 B.C.) in which Miltiades, the Athenian commander, completely defeated a Persian force overwhelmingly superior in numbers. Ancient writers remark on how shocked the Persians were by the ferocity and power of the attack of the Greek phalanx.

The brilliant Theban general Epaminondas made further refinements to the phalanx by increasing its flexibility. The ancient historian, Thucydides, among others, had noticed that in battle a phalanx tended to shift to the right, as each soldier unconsciously moved toward the protection of his neighbor's shield. Others had sought to make use of this fact, but Epaminondas and the Thebans achieved the greatest flexibility and, therefore, the greatest

results. At the battles of Leuctra (371 B.C.) and Mantinea (362 B.C.), Epaminondas defeated the Spartans by skillfully swinging a select force against their exposed and drifting flank.

The ultimate development of phalanx warfare came under the Macedonians, especially in the conquering army of Alexander the Great. The Macedonians, northern neighbors of the Greeks, doubled the length of the spear; their *sarissa* was held in both hands. The first five rows of *sarissas* projected beyond the front rank; the other rows held their *sarissas* at increasing angles of elevation, giving the formation a "hedgehog" effect. The Macedonians also further improved the flexibility of the phalanx, and trained it to act as a unit.

Even under Alexander the Great, however, the phalanx remained essentially the same: a compact body of heavily armed spearmen, willing to form up and charge equally courageous and well-armed opponents, until the issue was decided.

—*Michael Witkoski*

ADDITIONAL READING:

Devine, Albert. "Alexander the Great." In *Warfare in the Ancient World*, edited by General Sir John Hackett. New York: Facts On File, 1989. A brief but informative explanation of the weaponry and organization of the Macedonian phalanx.

Hanson, Victor Davis. *The Western Way of War: Infantry Battle in Classical Greece*. New York: Alfred A. Knopf, 1989. An outstanding work that presents the full range of phalanx warfare, including its psychological and sociological aspects.

Jones, Archer. *The Art of War in the Western World*. Urbana: University of Illinois Press, 1987. An eminent scholar clearly and concisely presents the tactical nature of battle between opposing phalanxes, and explains how victories such as Leuctra came about.

Keegan, John. *A History of Warfare*. New York: Alfred A. Knopf, 1993. Within this general survey of human conflict this work presents an outstanding section on phalanx and hoplite warfare, written in Keegan's unmistakable and entirely admirable style.

Pritchett, W. K. *The Greek State at War*. 4 vols. Berkeley: University of California Press, 1965-1985. A classic, multivolume set which provides extensive detail about all aspects of ancient Greek warfare.

SEE ALSO: 550 B.C., Construction of Trireme Changes Naval Warfare; 483 B.C., Naval Law of Themistocles; 480-479 B.C., Persian Invasion of Greece; 431-404 B.C., Peloponnesian War.

650 B.C.
GREEK CITY-STATES USE COINS AS MEANS OF EXCHANGE

The Greek city-states use coins as means of exchange as they expand their area of settlement and become economically sophisticated in their trade relations.

DATE: 650 B.C.

LOCALE: Greece

CATEGORIES: Business and labor; Economics

KEY FIGURE:

Xenophanes (fl. 525 B.C.), the principal ancient source for the origin of Greek coinage

SUMMARY OF EVENT. The earliest Greek trade occurred during the Neolithic era of Greece and was opportunistic in nature. In answer to a particular need or an unusual situation, Greeks ventured on the sea and engaged in rudimentary barter to secure what they needed or to gain an economic advantage. The leaders of the earliest Greek communities were eager to import luxury goods such as jewelry, decorative pottery, and ornamented weapons that they ultimately used as grave goods. The Greeks usually obtained their luxury goods from Levantine or Minoan traders who called upon the Greeks of the mainland at infrequent intervals.

When the Greeks needed additional food supplies or raw materials such as wood or metals, they sought to trade their locally grown produce or locally manufactured goods for that which they needed from various traders who happened into the area. In terms of competition, however, the earliest Greek traders were at a decided disadvantage because Greece offered little in the way of natural resources to use as beginning trading capital. To compensate for this deficiency, the Greeks participated in a combination of commerce and piracy, trading or attacking passing ships as the occasion allowed.

Greek merchant adventurers traded with the people who inhabited the Aegean islands and the various people who lived along the coasts of the Black, Ionian, and Mediterranean seas. With increased experience at sea and a growing familiarity with overseas territories and peoples, the Greeks began the process of overseas colonization. Over an extended period of time, from the Late Bronze Age through the Iron Age, mainland Greeks colonized the islands of the Aegean and the coastal areas of Asia Minor. The greatest period of colonization, however, occurred from about 750 to 550 B.C., when the Greeks succeeded in founding more than three hundred Greek communities along the Mediterranean coasts of Africa, Spain, France, southern Italy, and the northern shore of the Black Sea. With the notable exception of the Greek communities of the Black Sea region, all of these Greek colonies developed into independent city-states.

For the most part, the newer areas of colonization had similar climates to that of mainland Greece. This factor not only enabled the Greeks overseas to practice their usual forms of agriculture without change but it helped them to adapt to their new surroundings quickly. In addition, the colonial areas commonly offered the Greeks more economic opportunities than they ever had before. The Greeks in colonial areas wanted to have the foods and products they were used to having in their former homelands. There developed a significant and steady trade between the mother cities of mainland Greece and the daughter cities overseas in foodstuffs (olives, olive oil, wine, grain, and fish), raw materials (timber, marble, and

Early Greek city-states established the practice of using mint marks to distinguish their coins; these later coins bear the image of Philip of Macedonia, who ruled from 359 to 336 B.C. (Library of Congress)

metal ores), and manufactured goods (such as pottery).

Through their trade and colonization efforts, the Greeks came into contact with a number of people (particularly in Asia Minor and the Levant) who were more economically advanced than they were and who had developed more sophisticated political organizations than they had. Some of these people had writing and numerical systems through which they could record tax collections and maintain inventory lists of produce and weapons. The traders from these more advanced economies were able to conduct more complex economic transactions than just barter. To participate in these more complicated and many times more lucrative economic transactions, the Greeks had to adjust to these new realities. In addition to adapting the Phoenician alphabet to the Greek language, the Greeks adopted and improved upon a new economic development—coinage.

Both archaeology and Greek tradition attribute the beginnings of coinage to the Lydians of the interior of Asia Minor. The Greeks, having colonized the coastal areas of Asia Minor, would have come into economic contact with the Lydians at a very early date and would have been one of the first people introduced to the concept of coinage. Coinage is simply a method of designating value on a specific amount of precious metal. When a state struck or marked a coin with its mint mark, it certified the purity and weight of the precious metal in the coin and guaranteed its value. Coinage enabled an individual or state to store value or wealth in the form of a coin of precious metal that could be used again at some time in the future. The earliest coins, however, represented relatively high values and were probably issued to facilitate large payments between and among the various independent states of Asia Minor. Whether used as tribute payment or for payment for goods and services, the advent of coinage marked a great advance. Now when a state or an individual had to pay an obligation, the obligation did not have to be paid in bullion that would have to be weighed and assayed each time it was used in a transaction.

The Lydians appear to have struck their first coins sometime around 640 B.C., and the Greeks soon followed suit. The earliest Lydian coins were of electrum, an alloy of gold and silver, while the Greeks usually struck their coins in silver. Although both the Lydians and the Greeks had access to gold, they rarely coined it because it represented such a high value in relationship to silver. It was the Greeks who developed, refined, and expanded the use of coinage. The island of Aegina off the Greek mainland was the first Greek city-state to issue a large number of silver coins and struck them with the image of a sea turtle. Soon, the Greeks recognized the Aeginetan "turtles" as a practi-

cal coin standard and used them as a medium of exchange throughout their trading area. Aegina came to dominate the seaborne trade within Greece and the Greek trade with Egypt and the other countries of the eastern Mediterranean. With the expansion of trade, other Greek city-states struck coins and used mint marks unique to their cities as their guarantee of value. Gradually by the fifth century B.C., Greek city-states began to mint smaller denomination coinage to facilitate the economic transactions of the average person.

Although there was no international regulation of coinage, the Greeks realized early that there would be economic chaos if every Greek city-state issued coins according to its own arbitrary standard of weights and measures. Although Aegina was the earliest Greek city-state of the mainland to strike coins, its standard did not end up the sole standard for Greece. Greek city-states roughly adhered to, with local variations, one of two standards of coin weights and measures—the Aeginetan standard and the Euboic standard. Of the two weight systems, the Aeginetan system possessed the heavier weights, since it contained more silver in its coins. During the history of ancient Greece, the Euboic system gradually replaced the Aeginetan standard as the most common coin standard.

—*Peter L. Viscusi*

ADDITIONAL READING:

Carradice, Ian. *Greek Coins.* Austin: University of Texas Press, 1995. An up-to-date and thorough publication written by one of the leading authorities on Greek and Roman coinage.

Glotz, Gustave. *Ancient Greece at Work.* Translated by M. R. Dobie. New York: W. W. Norton, 1927. Although not specifically on Greek trade and commerce, this book is an excellent summary of what Greeks did to make a living.

Graham, A. J.. *Colony and Mother City in Ancient Greece.* Manchester, England: Manchester University Press, 1964. Widely recognized as the best introduction to the subject, this work gives a detailed historical analysis of the process of establishing a Greek colony.

Hasebroek, Johannes. *Trade and Politics in Ancient Greece.* Translated by L. M. Fraser and D. C. Macgregor. New York: Biblo and Tannen, 1965. Originally published in German in 1928, this book has been recognized by the world's leading authorities as a classic work for a topical overview of the subject.

Lowry, S. Todd. *The Archaeology of Economic Ideas: The Classical Greek Tradition.* Durham, N.C.: Duke University Press, 1987. An unusual economic history that examines archaeological finds in the light of their economic significance and their relationship to the overall evolution of classical Greece.

Seltman, Charles T. *Greek Coins*. 2d ed. London: Methuen, 1955. The author, a noted British scholar, takes a detailed and chronological approach to Greek coinage in general before examining the coinage of individual city-states.

Starr, Chester G. *The Economic and Social Growth of Early Greece, 800-500 B.C.* New York: Oxford University Press, 1977. This economic history provides a clear and concise account of the factors that led to the great cultural achievements of the classical period of Greece.

SEE ALSO: 483 B.C., Naval Law of Themistocles; 431-404 B.C., Peloponnesian War.

625-509 B.C.
RISE OF ETRUSCAN CIVILIZATION IN ROME

The rise of the Etruscan civilization in Rome transforms scattered agricultural villages into an advanced city-state with the capacity to grow into a major world empire.

DATE: 625-509 B.C.

LOCALE: Rome, Italy

CATEGORIES: Cultural and intellectual history; Prehistory and ancient cultures

KEY FIGURES:

Lucius Brutus, leader of the revolution to expel the Etruscans in 509 B.C.

Lucretia, legendary figure whose rape and subsequent suicide set the overthrow of the Etruscan monarchy in motion

Servius Tullius, second Etruscan king, 569-525 B.C.

Tarquinius Priscus, first Etruscan king, 607-569 B.C.

Tarquinius Superbus, third and last Etruscan king of Rome, 525-509 B.C.

SUMMARY OF EVENT. Modern scholars continue to disagree about the origins of the Etruscans. The non-Indo-European language of these remarkable civilizers of Italy still has not yet been satisfactorily translated. Between 800 and 600 B.C., the Etruscans expanded into west central Italy, establishing Etruria (in later Tuscany) as a home base. The Etruscans became neighbors of the Latins in Rome, who had established villages there as early as 1000 B.C.

The Etruscans grew wealthy on the copper, tin, zinc, lead, and iron deposits in Etruria. Fertile soil and favorable climate led to abundant crops of wheat, olives, and grapes. The Etruscans traded widely with the ancient world. They

were trading partners and periodic hostile adversaries of two other maritime powers, the Greek city-states and the Phoenicians.

The Etruscans built a loose confederation of twelve independent city-states such as Veii, Caere, Tarquinia, Vuki, and a number of large towns. Judging from paintings depicting scenes from everyday life, the realistic figures of the dead placed on top of sarcophagi or funerary urns, and artifacts uncovered from tombs, the Etruscans were a luxury and pleasure loving people with much leisure time and were voracious consumers. Splendor was enjoyed even in death, for the Etruscans built large cities of the dead (necropolis), laid out in grid fashion. Etruscan women enjoyed the luxury of fine jewelry, elegant clothing, diverse cosmetics, and appear to have been granted a high degree of equality in Etruscan life.

Militarily, the Etruscans developed an excellent navy and a formidable army which was based on heavy body armor and the use of bronze chariots. Cities were built on defensible hilltops, protected by heavy walls and gates, as well as ravines to provide security. Their military power was projected south into the Bay of Naples, and toward the Latin villages of Rome, which the Etruscans easily dominated as an aristocratic military ruling elite from 616 to 509 B.C. The seven hills of Rome, situated in the middle of a coastal plain, and the potential of the area as the hub of major trade routes, was not lost on the Etruscans.

In the course of a century, Etruscan Rome rapidly developed from a collection of villages into a major city. For Rome, the Etruscan cultural and technological legacy was immense. In building the city, the arch and vault, which could support considerable weight, was first used by the Etruscans. Later, the arch would be used with great proficiency by the Romans. The practice of placing temples on a high platform (podium) at the far end of a sacred enclosure, so as to elevate both the structure and the gods, making the individual feel relatively insignificant, would later become a standard Roman practice. The Romans also adopted the science of boundaries (*limitatio*), which divided land into rectangular grids. Also the marking of formal city boundaries in a circle (*pomerium*), to define a holy and protected space, became a basic Roman preoccupation. To expand land for cultivation and to eliminate unhealthy marshlands, the Etruscans employed the tunnel method of draining river bottoms (*cuniculus*), a method which the Romans would continue. The general use of drainage and irrigation systems, the construction of excellent hydraulics works, the building of roads, bridges, and sewers, were all aspects of Etruscan technology which the Romans would borrow and continue.

In relation to religious beliefs, the Etruscans also had a

IMPORTANT ETRUSCAN CITIES, 530-520 B.C.

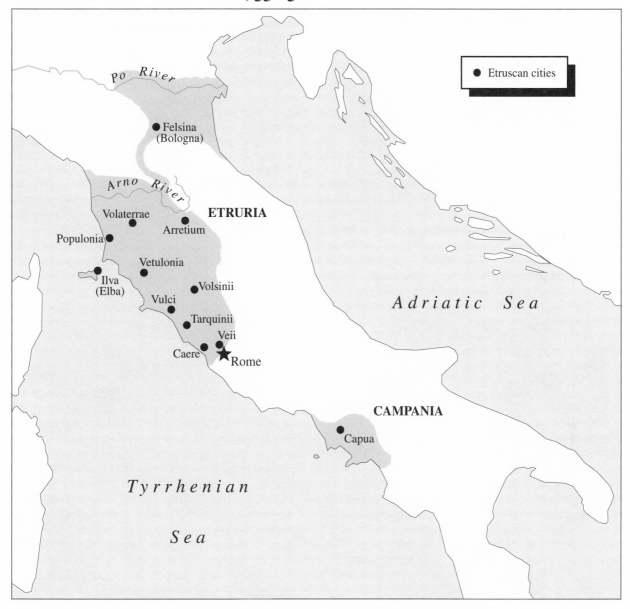

major impact. Their preoccupation with foretelling the future (divination) also became a Roman preoccupation, though one which was usually relegated only to times of emergency. Examination of animal entrails, most commonly the liver, became a pseudo-science designed to uncover the will of the gods. Similarly, the interpretation of lightning and thunder was used by the Etruscans to decipher the will of the gods, a practice the Romans would continue. In fact the Romans would insist on discovering signs (*auspices*) before making any major decision.

Like the Greeks, the Etruscans pictured their gods to have human form. The three major Etruscan gods—Tinia, Uni, and Menrva—were adapted by the Romans. Having much leisure time, the Etruscans celebrated many official holidays in honor of their gods. The Romans would also mark the year with many religious festivals.

For recreation on religious festivals, the Etruscans staged gladiator duels. While these Etruscan duels may seem to be basic martial contests when compared to the later Roman gladiatorial extravaganzas, still the Romans appear to have first developed their love of gladiator shows from the Etruscan experience. Tomb paintings also indicate that chariot racing was a favorite Etruscan recreation. This entertainment also became popular in Rome, with the Circus Maximus later outdoing anything the Etruscans could have fantasized. Undoubtedly, the major event in Etruscan Rome was the elaborate, semireligious procession following victorious campaigns, containing victors, captive prisoners, displays of seized treasures, musicians, and dancers. This ritual of the triumphant victory processional would continue throughout the Roman Republican and Imperial eras. The Etruscan propinquity toward rampant consumerism, fine foods, and elaborate banquets provided a hedonistic model which the Romans would first reject during the early centuries of the Republic, and eventually succumb to an extent that would have made the Etruscans envious.

Politically, the Romans were ruled by Etruscan kings. The king's power was called *imperium* and was conferred by a popular assembly. Imperium was symbolized by an eagle headed scepter and an ax bound in a bundle of rods (*fasces*). After the Etruscans, both these symbols continued as Roman symbols, as did the concept of imperium.

The first Etruscan king, Tarquinius Priscus according to tradition, consolidated Roman villages and began the building of the city. His successor, Servius Tullius, extended the city boundaries and continued building projects, including fortified city walls. He also implemented social reform, dividing the population, according to wealth, into six classes. He introduced the system of centuries into the Roman citizen army, grouped in phalanx formation into legions. According to Livy, he also cemented bonds with the Latin nobles (patricians) who formed an advisory council to the king. The patricians were grouped into clans and were known by both personal name and clan name. The common people (plebeians) were divided into thirty wards, which constituted a committee, and could only discuss matters set by the king on the agenda. In embryonic form, Rome's second king set up the senate and assembly of tribes.

The third and last Etruscan king, Tarquinius Superbus, reversed the Servian Reforms, established absolute rule, and succeeded in antagonizing both plebeians and patricians. Arrogant, tyrannical, and a lavish spender, Tarquinius built a temple to Jupiter larger than the Parthenon. He is also credited with building Rome's great sewer, the Cloaca Maxima. According to legend, Tarquinius' son raped Lucretia, the wife of a friend. To regain her honor, Lucretia stabbed herself, inspiring a friend, Junius Brutus to lead a revolt against Tarquinius' tyranny. In 509 B.C., the revolt was successful. In reaction to monarchical tyranny, the Romans turned legislative power over to the senate. Preventing overbearing executive power, Rome estab-

lished a system of two consuls, elected only for a single one year term, each with the power to veto the other. Junius Brutus was the first consul of the newly established Republic of Rome.

Following its defeat in Rome, Etruscan power received a serious setback. In 474 B.C., the Etruscan navy was defeated by the Greeks off of Cumae. Rome and its Latin allies gradually expanded toward the Etruscan cities. In 396 B.C., Veii fell after a long siege. By 250 B.C., what was left of Etruscan autonomy was integrated into the Roman system. Yet what had been integrated long before was the Etruscan concept of civilization, and technological knowhow to make advanced civilization possible.

—Irwin Halfond

ADDITIONAL READING:

Grant, Michael. *The Etruscans*. New York: Charles Scribner's Sons, 1980. Explores the Etruscan relationship with the Near East, the expansion of Etruscan influence, and the Etruscan role in seven city-states in Italy.

Hus, Alain. *The Etruscans*. New York: Grove Press, 1963. A highly readable yet detailed treatment of Etruscan culture and its influence.

Keller, Werner. *The Etruscans*. New York: Alfred A. Knopf, 1974. An analysis of the advent of the Etruscans, the creation of empire, the decline and legacy of the Etruscans.

Pallottino, Massimo. *A History of Earliest Italy*. Translated by M. Ryle and K. Soper. Ann Arbor: University of Michigan Press, 1991. A scholarly and well-illustrated treatment of the development of early Italy and the Etruscan role in that development.

Scullard, H. H. *A History of the Roman World 753 to 146 B.C.* New York: Routledge, 1991. A comprehensive and clearly written study of Rome's development, and a good starting point to obtain background material.

Spivey, Nigel J., and S. Stoddart. *Etruscan Italy*. London: Batsford, 1990. An excellent portrayal of Etruscan settlement, their technology, social and political organization, economic activity, methods of warfare, and religious beliefs.

SEE ALSO: 525 B.C., The Sibylline Books; 494 or 493 B.C., Institution of the Plebeian Tribunate; 312-264 B.C., Building of the Appian Way; 312 B.C., First Roman Aqueduct Is Built.

621 or 620 B.C.
DRACO'S CODE

Draco's code represents the beginning of Athenian legal and constitutional history and formulates, for the first time in Europe, a distinction between intentional and unintentional homicide.

DATE: 621 or 620 B.C.

LOCALE: Athens, Greece

CATEGORIES: Government and politics; Laws, acts, and legal history

KEY FIGURES:

Draco (fl. 621/620 B.C.), semimythical lawgiver

Xenophanes (or Athenophanes, fl. 409/408 B.C.), who had Draco's homicide law written on a *stele* in front of the Royal Portico

SUMMARY OF EVENT. According to ancient traditions, Draco was a Greek statesman who drew up the first code of law for the Athenians during the archonship of Aristaechmus in 621/620 B.C. Although Draco and his laws are mentioned more than fifty times in various sources, the evidence is so conflicting that it is difficult to determine the nature and extent of his legislation. It has even been denied by some noted scholars that there ever was a human lawgiver with this name, the Greek *drakon* referring instead to a "serpent god" that the Athenians credited with drawing up their first legal code. Yet, Draco was also a common personal name. Prodicus was aware of the difficulty surrounding the word *drakon*, and his famous pun reported in Aristotle's *Rhetoric* scarcely makes sense if the Athenians believed that their lawgiver was a snake: "They are not the laws of a man but of a 'snake,' so severe are they."

Other scholars have maintained that much of the evidence regarding Draco's legislation is the product of fourth century research and merely proves, if anything, that he drew up some laws regarding homicide. Such narrow interpretation of his activities, however, does not agree with all the evidence. Aristotle obviously attributed laws other than those on homicide to Draco. He states in his *Constitution of Athens*, for instance, that after Solon had drawn up a constitution and enacted new laws, "the ordinances of Draco ceased to be used, with the exception of those pertaining to murder [i.e. homicide]." Writers as early as Xenophone (c. 428-354 B.C.) and Lysias (c. 459-380 B.C.) refer to Draconian laws which were no longer in force. In 403 B.C., Tisamenus enacted a decree providing for the enforcement of the laws of Solon and of Draco as in earlier times. Various sources indicate that the legislation of Draco appeared to cover, in addition to homicide, such crimes as theft, vagrancy, adultery, the corruption of youth, neglect of the gods, and violation of the oath taken by jurors. Like other early lawgivers, Draco probably did not so much initiate new legislation as reduce customary law to an orderly and usable form in writing. He may also have drawn upon the decisions of earlier magistrates as

recorded by the thesmothetes, or judges. According to Aristotle's *Politics*, there was nothing unusual enough to mention about Draco's laws "except the greatness and severity of their penalties." Indeed, the severity of these laws had become legendary; Plutarch in his life of Solon reports that Draco's laws, except those relating to homicide, were repealed by Solon because they prescribed punishments regarded as too severe. Idleness or stealing a cabbage or an apple were capital offenses as serious as sacrilege or murder, and it was held that his laws were written not in ink but in blood. When Draco was asked why he assigned the death penalty for most offenses, he is reputed to have replied: "Small ones deserve that, and I have no higher for the greater crimes."

Such severity should not cause surprise. Most early codes of law were harsh in assigning severe penalties for petty crimes, as attested by early Hebrew law, Zaleucus' code, and the Twelve Tables of Rome. Not until the time of the Enlightenment was there concern to make the punishment fit the crime, and in England some severe and unreasonable penalties prescribed in Elizabethan times remained in force throughout the nineteenth century. Consequently, Draco's harshness, considering the times, can be exaggerated. Death was not the only penalty inflicted on violators; lesser infringements drew fines, disfranchisement, or exile. In the case of homicide, his legislation appears enlightened in that it drew careful distinction between willful murder and accidental or justifiable manslaughter. Evidence for such a view comes not only from the legal procedures which were established in his day but also from a copy of his homicide law which was erected in front of the Royal Portico in 409/408 B.C. by a decree of the Council and People initiated by Xenophanes.

Moreover, Draco's laws marked definite advances. By designating crimes, fixing penalties, and establishing rules of procedure, he made it easier for the poor and the weak to obtain justice. His laws on homicide so effectively put an end to the blood feuds which had plagued Athens that other primitive communities adopted Athenian laws generally.

The ancient city developed out of a gradual federation of groups, and it never was an "assembly of individuals." Draco's code represents the time when the coalescing city was forced to curtail the sovereignty of the tribe and family and to interfere first of all, for the sake of peace, in its prerogative of the blood feud. In the case of intentional homicide, old tribal rights were still honored; in the case of self-defense, however, the new city saw a reasonable place to begin its encroachments on tribal rights. In the case of involuntary homicide, probably often occurring between persons of different groups and unknown to each other, the city again saw wisdom in restricting old tribal blood feuds. Consequently, Draco's code is interesting not only for a history of Athenian jurisprudence but also as an index of the growing jurisdiction of the city of Athens itself. That the "state" did not concern itself with murder in Homer's day is quite likely inasmuch as the "city" in that era had not developed out of tribal associations but still represented the concerns of a noble family.

—M. Joseph Costelloe, updated by Jeffrey L. Buller

ADDITIONAL READING:

Gagarin, Michael. *Drakon and Early Athenian Homicide Law.* New Haven, Conn.: Yale University Press, 1981. The most complete academic analysis of Draco's law code, with attention to its historicity and impact, by a distinguished scholar of early Greek law.

Jones, J. Walter. *The Law and Legal Theory of the Greeks.* Oxford: Clarendon Press, 1956. Questions the historicity of the Draconian law code; useful in placing the code in the context of the Greek legal tradition.

Sealey, Raphael. *A History of the Greek City States, 700-338 B.C.* Berkeley: University of California Press, 1976. Discusses the figure of Draco and his legal tradition in the light of other semimythical lawgivers, including Lycurgus of Sparta and Charondas of Sicily.

Stroud, Ronald S. *The Axones and Kyrbeis of Drakon and Solon.* Berkeley: University of California Press, 1979. A brief but scholarly examination of the legal codes of Draco and Solon. (*Axones* and *kyrbeis* are technical terms for legal codes, derived from the tablets on which laws were inscribed.)

_____. *Drakon's Law on Homicide.* Berkeley: University of California Press, 1968. Contains the complete text of Draco's law code, with an English translation and commentary, using the text appearing on a marble inscription of 409/408 B.C. now in the Epigraphical Museum in Athens.

SEE ALSO: 594-580 B.C., Legislation of Solon; 483 B.C., Naval Law of Themistocles; 451-449 B.C., The "Twelve Tables" of Roman Law; 335-323 B.C., Aristotle Writes the *Politics.*

600-500 B.C.
GREEK PHILOSOPHERS FORMULATE THEORIES OF THE COSMOS

Greek philosophers formulate theories of the cosmos, setting aside previous mythopoeic explanations and launching an empirical and scientific intellectual revolution.

DATE: 600-500 B.C.
LOCALE: Greece
CATEGORIES: Cultural and intellectual history; Education; Science and technology
KEY FIGURES:
Anaximander of Miletus (610-545 B.C.), Greek philosopher often called the founder of astronomy
Anaximenes of Miletus (fl. 545 B.C.), Greek philosopher and scientist
Heraclitus of Ephesus (fl. 505-500 B.C.), Greek philosopher known for his book *On Nature*
Hesiod (fl. c. 700 B.C.), Greek epic poet
Parmenides of Elea (c. 515-c. 436 B.C.), Greek philosopher associated with study of metaphysics
Pythagoras of Samos and Crotona (c. 580-504 B.C.), Greek philosopher, astronomer, and mathematician
Thales of Miletus (c. 624-c. 548 B.C.), Greek philosopher and scientist
Xenophanes of Colophon and Elea (562-470 B.C.), Greek philosopher and poet

SUMMARY OF EVENT. Before the sixth century B.C., human beings everywhere explained the world in mythological terms. These myths depicted humankind dependent on the wills of inscrutable gods who created the world and acted on their all-too-human personal whims. Nonliving and powerful natural forces were "animated," given living souls by the pre-logical mentality of early people, otherwise quite sophisticated in building pyramids or irrigation canals. No other explanation was available to them, no scientific foundation on which to build a real understanding of the world and nature.

Similarly, most Greeks honored the epic poets Homer (c. 750 B.C.) and Hesiod as their teachers. Hesiod's *Theogony* ("Generations of Gods") is the earliest Greek version of the origins of the cosmos. The Greek term *kosmos* means the organized world order.

In Hesiod's account, the origin of all things was *chaos*, formless space or yawning watery deep, the opposite of *kosmos*. In time there emerged, either independently or by sexual union, Gaia (Earth), Tartaros (Hades), Eros (Love), Night, Day and Aither (upper air), Sea and Ouranos (Sky), and boundless Okeanos (Ocean). A generation of powerful Titans was engendered, and finally the Olympian gods descended from Ouranos and Gaia.

About 600 B.C., in Ionia (western Turkey), a new way of perceiving the world was beginning. Confronted by the confusing mythologies of ancient Near Eastern peoples, their own no better, a handful of Greeks over three generations attempted to explain the origins and components of the seen world without mythology. Their great discovery was that to one seeking knowledge—the philosopher—

the world manifests internal order and discernible regularity. Nature can be understood. The world is a *kosmos*.

From allusions in Homer and Hesiod came hints. The sky was thought to be a metallic hemispheric bowl covering the disk of earth. The lower space immediately above the disk was *aër*, breathable air; the upper part of the bowl-space was *ouranos* or *aither*. Below its surface, the earth's deep roots reached down to *Tartaros*, the deepest part of Hades (the underworld realm of the dead), as far below earth as sky is above it. *Okeanos*, infinitely wide, encircled the disk of earth and was the source of all fresh and salt waters. Such a mixture of the empirical and the imaginative was common to most mythopoeic cosmologies.

Thales of Miletus was the first to rationalize the myths. He conceived the earth-disk as floating upon the ocean and held the single substance of the world to be water. His reasoning, according to Aristotle, was that water can be gaseous, liquid, and solid; life requires water; Homer had surrounded the earth by *Okeanos*. As a unified source of all things, Thales' choice of water was a good guess, but it begged for alternatives. More important, in reducing multiple things to water, Thales had taken a first step in establishing inductive reasoning (from particular examples to general principles) as a scientific methodology.

Anaximander, companion of Thales, was a polymath: astronomer, geographer, evolutionist, philosopher-cosmologist. It is nearly impossible to do justice to his intellectual achievement. He was the first Greek to write in prose. He said animal life began in the sea and humans evolved from other animals. He made the first world map, a circle showing Europe and Asia plus Africa equal in size all surrounded by ocean. Anaximander's cosmos was a sphere with a drum-earth floating in space at its center. The sun, stars, and moon revolved around the earth, seen through openings in the metallic dome of the sky.

In place of Thales' water, Anaximander offered *apeiron*, an eternal, undefined, and inexhaustible basic stuff from which everything came to be and to which everything returns. It is a sophisticated Chaos. Convinced by his own logic, Anaximander imputed an ethical necessity to this process. Things coming to be and claiming their share of *apeiron* thus deprive others of existence. So, in his words, "they must render atonement each to the other according to the ordinances of Time." This eternal process operates throughout the cosmos. Using terms such as *kosmos* (order), *diké* (justice), and *tisis* (retribution), Anaximander enunciated the exalted idea that Nature itself is subject to universal moral laws.

The contributions of Anaximenes pale before those of Anaximander. What best defines Anaximenes is his empirical approach. He posited air as the primal stuff that gives rise to all things. Observing air condensing into water, he conceived a maximum condensation of air into stone. Similarly, by rarefaction, air becomes fire or soul. The earth and other heavenly bodies, being flat, ride upon air in its constant motion.

Xenophanes represents a new generation of thinkers. An Ionian, he had moved to Italy. The new natural explanations of the universe had challenged the older Hesiodic mythopoeic construct. Xenophanes interpreted this as the abandonment of the old, often immoral, anthropomorphic gods, who dressed in clothes and spoke Greek. He held a single spiritual creator god who controls the universe without effort, by pure thought. In this monotheism he was alone among the Greeks.

Insightfully, Xenophanes said human knowledge about the universe is limited and the whole truth may never be known. He taught that natural events have natural, not divine, causes. The rainbow is only a colored cloud. The sea is the source of all waters, winds, and clouds. From sea fossils found in rocks, his cosmogony deduced a time when land was under water. Civilization is the work of men, not gods. Xenophanes was a skeptic who trusted only his own observations about the world. Pythagoras, an Ionian mathematician in southern Italy, had noticed that the sounds of lyre strings varied according to their length and that harmonies were mathematically related. He saw that proportion can be visually perceived in geometrical figures. From these notions he and his followers described a cosmos structured on a mathematical model. Instead of adopting Anaximander's "justice" or Heraclitus' *Logos* as the dominant organizing principle, the Pythagoreans preferred numerical harmony.

Pythagoras thus added a dimension to the ancient concepts of due proportion and the golden mean that pervaded Greek thought. These concepts are seen in Greek sculpture and architecture and as moral principles in lyric and dramatic poetry and historical interpretations, where *hybris* (excess) and *sophrosyné* (moderation) were fundamental principles of human behavior.

Inevitably, Greek physical philosophy began to investigate the process of knowing. Number is unchanging; ten is always ten. In a world of apparently infinite diversity and flux, numbers can be known more perfectly than other objects of experience. Though the Pythagoreans went too far in trying to explain everything by numbers, they taught that a Nature based on mathematical harmony and proportion was knowable.

Heraclitus argued that change, though sometimes imperceptible, is the common element in all things. All change, he said, takes place along continuums of opposite qualities, such as the hot-cold line or dry-moist line. His contribution, however, was his idea of *Logos* as the hidden organizing principle of the cosmos. *Logos* maintains a protective balance (the golden mean again) among all the oppositional tensions in the world.

Although Parmenides and Democritus fall outside the chronological scope of the sixth century B.C., their contributions of logic to the Greek discovery of the cosmos merit some attention. In the mid-fifth century, Democritus of Abdera reasoned to a world built of the smallest thinkable indivisible particles, atoms.

Parmenides—struck by the constant flux of the physical world and seeking, as Pythagoras, an unchanging object of knowledge that mind can grasp—saw existence, or Being, as the common element of things in the cosmos. He proposed the logic that while things change, Being itself cannot change, for nothing and no place exists outside of the sphere of Being, so nothing could enter or leave. He is thus the most metaphysical of the philosophers, initiating ideas that would only be completed by Plato and Aristotle, the greatest of the philosophers.

The significance of the Ionian philosophers is that, within little more than a century after breaking with the mythopoeic interpretations of the world, they asserted its atomic makeup, conceived human evolution, discovered induction and logic, and practiced a curiosity about all natural phenomena. This was one of history's great intellectual revolutions, the origins of scientific speculation.

—*Daniel C. Scavone*

ADDITIONAL READING:

Jaeger, Werner. *Paideia: The Ideals of Greek Culture.* 3 vols. New York: Oxford University Press, 1939. Indispensable chapters on all aspects of the Greek intellectual achievement and the individuals involved.

Kirk, G. S., and J. E. Raven. *The Presocratic Philosophers.* Cambridge, England: Cambridge University Press, 1957. Best collection of Greek texts and English translations, with commentary based upon the words of individual philosophers.

Lesky, Albin. *A History of Greek Literature.* New York: Thomas Y. Crowell, 1966. A great German scholar has written the most detailed and scholarly study of Greek literature in one volume.

Sagan, Carl. *Cosmos.* New York: Random House, 1980. Current and authoritative, the noted scientist places the Greek contribution in the larger context of astronomy.

Sarton, George. *A History of Science: Ancient Science Through the Golden Age of Greece.* 2 vols. Cambridge, Mass.: Harvard University Press, 1952. A classic in its field, this volume treats the scientific value of the ideas of the Presocratics.

SEE ALSO: 530 B.C., Founding of the Pythagorean Brotherhood; 500-400 B.C., Greek Physicians Develop Scientific Practice of Medicine; 450-425 B.C., History Develops as Scholarly Discipline; 440 B.C., Teachings of the Sophists; 399 B.C., Death of Socrates; 380 B.C., Plato Develops His Theory of Ideas; 335-323 B.C., Aristotle Writes the *Politics*.

594-580 B.C.
LEGISLATION OF SOLON

The legislation of Solon allows Athens temporarily to avoid revolution in the sixth century B.C. and gives greater rights and authority to the non-noble citizens of Athens.

DATE: c. 594-580 B.C.

LOCALE: Athens, Greece

CATEGORY: Laws, acts, and legal history

KEY FIGURE:

Solon (c. 638-c. 559 B.C.), Athenian aristocrat

SUMMARY OF EVENT. At the beginning of the sixth century B.C., Athens was threatened with disaster. The aristocratic families fought among themselves for supremacy, and their struggles sometimes verged on civil war. The nobles also used their power against farmers of middle and low income in order to expand their own estates. Some poor farmers became serfs or were enslaved through debt. The resultant tendency was to diminish the class of men upon which the military strength and safety of Athens depended.

Other states solved similar problems by resorting to tyranny, a kind of one-man benevolent despotism which tended to favor the nonaristocrats, including the poor. The great magnates of Athens, fearful lest such a tyrant might arise and dispossess them, agreed to have limits set upon their power. Solon, himself a member of the aristocracy, was chosen archon about 594 B.C. In that year, and probably later as well, as special "conciliator" he brought about social and political relief by revising the laws of Athens.

Solon's social reforms were important; he himself referred to them as the "lifting of burdens." He abolished serfdom and slavery for debt, ridding Athens of those curses once and for all. New laws on debt were enacted, though details have been lost, and in this way the number of men eligible for military service was maintained.

Solon also appears to have considered building up Athens' commerce, possibly to provide employment for skilled foreigners such as potters and shipbuilders who were allowed to settle in Athens with the protected status of *metic* or "resident alien." How far Solon went along

In his life of Solon, the Greek biographer Plutarch chronicled the social and legal reforms enacted by Solon in Athens. (Library of Congress)

these lines is disputed. The tyrant Pisistratus undoubtedly did more later, so that by the end of the sixth century Athens was successfully competing with important trading states such as Aegina and Corinth.

To protect his social gains, Solon sought to strengthen political institutions through which the middle income group could voice its desires. The citizens were divided into four census classes based on wealth: The richest men were the *pentacosiomedimni* with an income of five hundred measures of olive oil, wine, or grain, a measure being 11.5 gallons wet or 1.85 bushels dry; next came the *hippeis* or cavalry whose farms produced three hundred measures and enabled them to keep a warhorse; then there were the *zeugitae* who plowed their land with a yoke of oxen, had an income of two hundred measures, could afford armor, and served as infantrymen; and last were the remaining citizens who belonged to the lowest class of the *thetes*, the laborers or hired men.

The top three classes had certain duties and privileges in the public affairs of the city and served in the first-line field army. Only members of the two richest classes, however, could hold the office of archon, or ruler. Three archons were selected annually, each having jurisdiction

over a specific sphere of public business. The *archon eponymus* had charge of internal affairs and presided over the Assembly. The *archon basileus* was responsible for the conduct of the state religion. The *archon polemarchos* commanded the army. These three officials and the other six archons called *thesmothetes* were also magistrates of the courts. Solon probably believed that only the nobility, by reason of birth and training, had sufficient knowledge and experience to carry out these important duties. The archons were, however, selected by lot by the people sitting as the *Ecclesia* or assembly. It is disputed whether the *thetes* were members of this body. The same people differently organized were the *heliaea*, or court. All citizens now had the right of appeal to this court from a judgment handed down by one of the archons, an advantage for the poor. This right, and the right of the assembly to examine the acceptability of candidates for archonship and to scrutinize the conduct of the magistrates in office, were safeguards of the few rights enjoyed by non-noble Athenians. There is no reason to believe that the assembly did more than elect the archons once a year and assent to declarations of war. There is no sure evidence that it passed laws, although it may have done so from time to time. How the laws of Solon were enacted is not known.

Solon is also said to have created an annual Council of Four Hundred whose function was to act as a steering committee for the whole assembly. Considerable doubt has recently been cast on the existence of this body. There was certainly another council at this time, the *areopagus*, made up of former archons serving for life, and it was also important. While scholars are unsure of its exact duties, it had some sort of power to safeguard the laws. It was also claimed in antiquity that Solon handed down a mass of detailed legislation amounting to a whole written code. It is extremely unlikely that he did, in fact, do so.

Solon's work was of great significance for Athens. He found the state dominated by a hereditary aristocracy, and he left it an aristocratic republic. The nobles had accepted limitation of their power, which gave the downtrodden peasantry a chance to develop.

—Samuel K. Eddy, updated by Jeffrey L. Buller

ADDITIONAL READING:

Anhalt, Emily Katz. *Solon the Singer*. Lanham, Md.: Rowman & Littlefield, 1993. A broad analysis of Solon and his influence, exploring not only his political contributions but also his poetry.

Fitt, Mary. *The Work and Life of Solon*. New York: Arno Press, 1976. A somewhat dated biographical treatment of Solon, of primary importance because it contains Kathleen Freeman's translation of Solon's poems.

Linforth, Ivan. *Solon the Athenian*. Berkeley: University of California Press, 1949. Dated but still useful examination of Solon and his contributions to Athenian legal history. An excellent place to begin.

Rexine, John E. *Solon and His Political Theory*. New York: William-Frederick Press, 1958. The classic study of Solon with special attention paid to the lawgiver's influence upon later legal history.

Sealey, Raphael. *A History of the Greek City States, 700-338 B.C.* Berkeley: University of California Press, 1976. A clear analysis of the distinction between the historical and mythical elements in the tradition of Solon.

Stroud, Ronald S. *The Axones and Kyrbeis of Drakon and Solon*. Berkeley: University of California Press, 1979. A brief but scholarly examination of the legal codes of Draco and Solon. (*Axones* and *kyrbeis* are technical terms for legal codes and are derived from the tablets on which laws were inscribed.)

Woodhouse, William John. *Solon the Liberator*. New York: Octagon Books, 1965. An examination of Solon's role in helping to avert Athens' agrarian problem in the seventh century B.C.; valuable analysis of the social and economic issues involved in Solon's reforms.

SEE ALSO: 508-507 B.C., Reforms of Cleisthenes; 478-448 B.C., Athenian Empire Is Created; 335-323 B.C., Aristotle Writes the *Politics*; 300 B.C., Stoic Conception of Natural Law.

550 B.C.
CONSTRUCTION OF TRIREME CHANGES NAVAL WARFARE

The construction of the trireme changes naval warfare, making possible the sophisticated ramming tactics that dominated Mediterranean naval warfare during the fifth and fourth centuries B.C.

DATE: 550 B.C.

LOCALE: Greece

CATEGORIES: Science and technology; Transportation; Wars, uprisings, and civil unrest

KEY FIGURES:

Ameinocles, early Corinthian shipwright

Phormion (died c. 428 B.C.), expert Athenian naval commander during Peloponnesian War

Themistocles (c. 524-c. 460 B.C., Athenian general at time of Persian Wars

SUMMARY OF EVENT. Although warships with rams appeared early in the Mediterranean region, sophisticated ramming tactics had to await the evolution of specialized warships designed specifically for optimum use of the ram. As early as the eighth century B.C., Greek vase paintings depict warships with rams and a single file of rowers on each side. Like most ancient warships, these vessels could cruise under sail but relied on oar power in battle. Later literary sources refer to larger and smaller versions of this type of ship: a *triakontor* (thirty-oared ship) with fifteen rowers per file, and a *pentekontor* (fifty-oared ship) with twenty-five rowers per file. With only two files of rowers at one level, these ships had roomy holds and considerable capacity for passengers and cargo in addition to their rowing crews. This roominess suited a style of warfare that involved the transport of sizable numbers of soldiers for coastal raids and boarding attacks on other ships. In naval battles between fleets, the *pentekontors* primarily functioned as fighting platforms from which armored soldiers, javelin throwers, and archers fought for control of immobilized adjacent vessels. Rams were no doubt used when the opportunity to hole an enemy ship presented itself, but the *pentekontor*'s limited rowing power restricted its effectiveness as a ram.

Since the *pentekontor*'s length approached the ancient design limit of 25-30 rowers, in order to substantially augment rowing power, it was necessary to increase the number of files. The bireme accomplished this by putting two additional files of oar men in the hold area, so that there were now two banks of rowers on each side of the ship. The trireme, with three banks of rowers per side, simply took this concept one step further to produce a vessel with more than three times the oar power of a *pentekontor*. For centuries, historians have argued over the exact design and rowing configuration of the trireme, but the recent construction of a functioning full-scale replica appears to settle most questions. In particular, it demonstrates that with outriggers, rowers at three different levels can operate efficiently using oars of the same length. With 170 rowers in three banks packed within its narrow, lightly built hull, the trireme sacrificed strength, stability, and cargo capacity for speed and maneuverability. An improved bronze ram at the bow's waterline completed the transformation of the *pentekontor*. The result was a virtual guided missile perfectly matched to the hit-and-run ramming tactics that would rule naval warfare in the two centuries following the trireme's widespread adoption.

While the overall evolution from *pentekontor* to bireme to trireme seems clear enough, the question of the date and place of trireme's invention is still debated. The earliest explicit report of triremes used in war refers to ships built in Egypt by the pharaoh Necho (610-595 B.C.). Because of Egypt's proximity to Phoenicia and the later fame of Phoenician triremes, some historians attribute the innovation to the Phoenicians. Other scholars note Necho's close relations with the Greeks and prefer to credit them with the breakthrough. According to the Greek historian Thucydides, the earliest naval battle took place when the Corcyraeans fought the Corinthians, who were the first among the Greeks to build triremes. Thucydides also names a noted Corinthian shipwright, Ameinocles, who built four triremes for the island city-state of Samos. If these events are correctly dated to the middle and late seventh century, then Necho may well have learned about triremes from Corinth. Regardless of who is given credit for the invention, in later times both the Phoenicians and the Greeks were acknowledged as masters of trireme construction and use.

Despite its early invention and its superiority as a ramming weapon, the expense of building and operating the trireme slowed its adoption. The construction of first class triremes required not only skilled shipwrights but also costly materials such as pitch and wax for waterproofing and fir, which gave lightweight strength to hull and oars. In addition, because each ship required a skilled crew of two hundred, the operational cost of a fleet of triremes exceeded the means of all but the wealthiest states. Thus,

in addition to Necho in Egypt, early trireme users included commercially prominent city-states, such as Corinth in Greece and Sidon in Phoenicia, and the powerful Greek tyrant, Polycrates of Samos, who replaced his fleet of one hundred *pentekontors* with one of triremes. In the late sixth century, the adoption of the trireme by the superpower of the day, Persia, guaranteed its predominance and made it the warship of choice for those Greek states that wished to resist the expansion of the Persian Empire into the Aegean region. Drawing upon his Phoenician, Egyptian, and eastern Greek subjects, Xerxes put together a gigantic fleet of twelve hundred triremes for his invasion of Greece in 480 B.C., an assault that may well have succeeded except for the Greeks' historic naval victory at Salamis. Greek triremes were the key to this victory, above all the two hundred ships that Themistocles had convinced the Athenians to build using the proceeds of a fortunate silver strike. Following the defeat of Xerxes, triremes and the tactics associated with them dominated Greek naval warfare for more than a century.

Although it was used sometimes in what Thucydides called the "old-fashioned manner," with marines in boarding attacks, the trireme excelled when the ship itself was

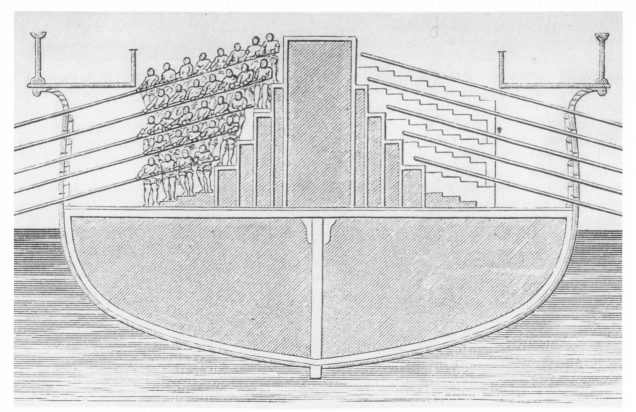

This cross-section of a Greek warship shows how the trireme later evolved into a quinquereme with a five-tiered arrangement of oarsmen. (Archive Photos)

used as a ramming weapon. Rival fleets of triremes typically faced each other in line abreast, and the defender attempted to avoid presenting vulnerable sides and sterns to the rams of the enemy. A drastically inferior force might form a defensive circle with bows facing outward. The attacking force sought to achieve *diekplous*, a breakthrough by a squadron of ships in line, or *periplous*, a flanking maneuver, either of which permitted ramming the enemy broadside. Once a ship had been holed, the attacker quickly disengaged to avoid a counterattack and resumed the offensive. Given these tactics, the advantage normally went to the swifter and more agile ships, a status determined partly by their design but also by how long the ships had been in the water and the expertness of their crews. In the victory at Salamis, for example, the normally slower Greek triremes probably had the advantage of speed, because their ships were drier and their crews more rested than those of the Persian force. The Athenians were renowned for the speed of their triremes, and their mastery of hit-and-run ramming tactics regularly let them defeat larger, less-skilled forces. In a famous encounter early in the Peloponnesian War, for example, a twenty-ship Athenian squadron commanded by the expert Phormio twice defeated larger Peloponnesian fleets.

As long as ramming tactics prevailed and skilled oarsmen were available, the trireme dominated ancient naval warfare. Beginning in the fourth century, however, a shortage of skilled crewmen encouraged the development of new rowing configurations that made use of less-skilled personnel. By manning each oar with a pair of rowers, only one of which needed real expertise, it was possible to produce a two-banked "four," which required one third fewer expert rowers but maintained the sleekness and speed of the trireme. The first "four" is attributed to the Phoenicians at Carthage. By 323 B.C., the Athenians planned a new fleet based primarily on "fours" rather than triremes. The use of rowers in teams of three or more produced ships of broader beam, which were slower and less agile than the trireme, but by the end of the fourth century new tactics were beginning to favor larger, more stable ships. By using various combinations of rowers in gangs of three, four, or more per oar, Hellenistic navies introduced much larger warships, from "fives" up to huge "sixteens," that provided stable firing platforms for catapults and excellent protection to their large crews of rowers and marines. Aptly suited to naval combat in the "old-fashioned manner," these vessels marked a return to tactics completely alien to the trireme and relegated it to an ancillary role in Hellenistic warfare.

—*James T. Chambers*

ADDITIONAL READING:

Casson, Lionel. *Ships and Seamanship in the Ancient World*. Princeton, N.J.: Princeton University Press, 1971. This study offers a general overview of ancient seafaring and includes a chapter on the trireme.

Morrison, John S., and J. F. Coates. *The Athenian Trireme: The History and Reconstruction of an Ancient Greek Warship*. New York: Cambridge University Press, 1986. The most important volume on this subject, this study analyzes all aspects of the trireme's history and incorporates knowledge gained from the modern replica.

Morrison, John S., and R. T. Williams. *Greek Oared Ships, 900-322 B.C.* Cambridge, England: Cambridge University Press, 1968. This volume provides a comprehensive collection of the written and visual evidence with commentary and interpretation.

Shaw, Timothy, ed. *The Trireme Project: Operational Experience 1987-90, Lessons Learnt*. Oxbow Monograph 31. Oxford: Oxbow Books, 1993. This anthology contains essays, some quite technical, on many aspects of the construction and operation of the full-scale replica.

SEE ALSO: 483 B.C., Naval Law of Themistocles; 480-479 B.C., Persian Invasion of Greece; 478-448 B.C., Athenian Empire Is Created; 431-404 B.C., Peloponnesian War.

530 B.C.

FOUNDING OF THE PYTHAGOREAN BROTHERHOOD

The founding of the Pythagorean brotherhood develops ideas about knowledge that influence classical Greek philosophers and last more than one thousand years.

DATE: c. 530 B.C.

LOCALE: Croton, in southern Italy

CATEGORIES: Cultural and intellectual history; Education

KEY FIGURES:

Alcmaeon of Croton (fl. sixth century B.C.), Pythagorean philosopher of medical interests

Archytas of Tarentum (fl. first half of fourth century B.C.), Pythagorean philosopher and mathematician

Philolaus of Croton (fl. second half of fifth century B.C.), Pythagorean philosopher

Pythagoras of Samos (572-c. 500 B.C.), Ionian polymath and philosopher

SUMMARY OF EVENT. The doctrines espoused by the Pythagorean brotherhood were repeated by a number of thinkers. For example, the final conversations of Socrates with his friends as described in the *Phaedo* reveal Plato's immense debt to Pythagoras and his school. In addition,

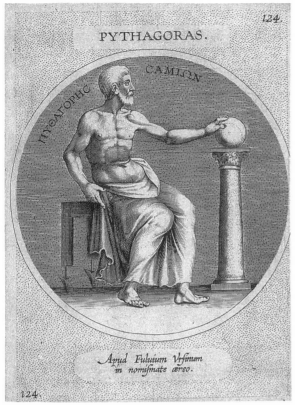

Known for his breadth of knowledge in the fields of astronomy, mathematics, and philosophy, Pythagoras organized a secret society in the Greek colonial settlement of Croton that became the basis of the Pythagorean brotherhood. (Archive Photos)

the Pythagoreans stand out in the history of science as precursors of understanding the structure of the universe in terms of mathematics. Even Nicolaus Copernicus and Johannes Kepler incorporated the mystical importance of "number" in their heliocentric theories of the sixteenth and seventeenth centuries A.D. It is unfortunate, then, that the facts about Pythagoras and his brotherhood are shrouded in legends that began in his own lifetime and grew more colorful during the millennium after his death. Adding to the confusion is the fact that the followers of Pythagoras usually signed his name to their own writings, which did not necessarily contain orthodox Pythagorean philosophy.

Although reliable information is scant, it can be stated that Pythagoras was born about 572 B.C. and lived until maturity on the Ionian island of Samos when it was economically and culturally prominent. He had already acquired fame as a sage well-versed in the learning of his age and also as an exponent of doctrine about the immortality of the soul when he left Samos about 540 B.C. According

to tradition, he left Samos because he was opposed to the tyranny of Polycrates. He then settled in Croton, one of the Greek cities in southern Italy and Sicily which made up the region known as Magna Graecia. In Croton, he organized a secret society of mixed religious, philosophic, and political interests which had become dominant by 510, and he played a leading role in the war between Croton and Sybaris which established the hegemony of Croton over the other cities of Magna Graecia. In 509 B.C., a democratic rebellion expelled the Pythagorean party from power in Croton, and Pythagoras moved to Metapontum, where he died about 500 B.C.

His followers founded a number of Pythagorean societies of an oligarchic nature. These groups played a leading role in several cities of Magna Graecia until about the middle of the fifth century B.C., when they were expelled in a violent upheaval. Afterward, several survivors migrated to the Greek mainland and established communities in Thebes and in Phlius. The foremost of these Pythagoreans was Philolaus. He is referred to in the *Phaedo* even though he wrote only one genuine book. In this work, he argued that "unlimited" and "limiting" substances were bound together through harmony to form the natural world. After the beginning of the fourth century, Pythagorean influence in southern Italy was reestablished with its center at Tarentum under the leadership of Archytas. This philosopher is noted for his collection of a variety of evidence in an attempt to prove that there is a relationship between the pitch of a musical note and its "speed," or measure.

It is a matter of debate which doctrines may reasonably be attributed to Pythagoras and the society that he founded. The most prevalent view is that the society's activities were based upon a curious fusion of religious belief and speculative cosmology dominated by mathematics. The religious doctrine shared an affinity with so-called Orphic conceptions of the transmigration of souls. The soul, according to this doctrine, is distinct in origin from the body in which it is imprisoned during a person's life span. Originally akin to the fires of heaven, it has entered at birth into a body from which it is released at death, only to enter anew into another body in a continuing cycle of successive reincarnations. The soul cannot free itself permanently from the cycle of reincarnation until it has successfully purified itself of the corruption to which its bodily imprisonment has subjected it. The distinctive element of the Pythagorean concept of purification is that, although one must engage in ascetic practices of bodily denial, the primary purifying activity is the intellectual endeavor to understand the nature of the heavenly bodies and their harmony.

This endeavor was based on the assumption that understanding the essence of the astral harmony enables the soul to "recollect" its primal astral purity and actualize at last its divine nature. The Pythagoreans believed that the essence of the heavenly bodies and their interrelationships was number: One came to understand the heavens by understanding the geometrical and arithmetical ratios involved in the constitution of the cosmos. They noted that harmonious sounds were in whole number ratios, and they believed that these ratios could be extended to describe all natural objects. The resulting cosmos was a single and nonmaterial system of reality which included a correspondence between inanimate and living objects. The Pythagoreans claimed, however, that only the elite could achieve this mystical process of knowing. Aristotle did report on their view of the ultimate reality in the *Metaphysics*, although he on occasion purposely misunderstood them in his works in order to minimize their philosophical influence.

Plato, on the other hand, had visited the Pythagoreans and incorporated the concept of number as the essence of

reality into his theory of matter. His sharp distinction between the sense-experience mediated by organs of the body and the intellectual awareness of pure concepts is essentially Pythagorean, as is the notion that mathematical relationships are eternal objects of knowledge. Once Plato had taken the step of identifying the eternally valid moral concepts which Socrates sought to define as of the same nature with the Pythagorean eternal mathematical objects of knowledge, the ground was laid for the doctrine of Ideas. It was probably also through the mediation of the Pythagorean tradition that Plato came to appropriate the notions of the soul's eternal nature, of its transmigration, and of learning as a process of "recollection" of truths once known by the soul when free from the corrupting influences of the bodily prison. All these notions find expression in the *Phaedo* of Plato, a dialogue deliberately fashioned so as to present Socrates as a Pythagorean sage and a paradigm of the disciplined philosophic life of progressive actualization of one's innate potential divinity through the acquisition of wisdom.

—*Carl W. Conrad, updated by Amy Ackerberg-Hastings*

ADDITIONAL READING:

Barnes, Jonathan. *The Presocratic Philosophers.* 2 vols. London: Routledge & Kegan Paul, 1979. Single-volume revised reprint, 1982. Pythagorean scholars of the 1980's and 1990's, among others, have drawn upon this book for background information and issues to be discussed.

Furley, David. *The Greek Cosmologists. Volume 1: The Formation of the Atomic Theory and Its Earliest Critics.* New York: Cambridge University Press, 1987. Furley keeps a general audience in mind while discussing the Pythagoreans in terms of the early Greek theories of the universe.

Huffman, Carl A. *Philolaus of Croton: Pythagorean and Presocratic.* New York: Cambridge University Press, 1993. Huffman's book includes scholarly commentary on the fragments attributed to Philolaus as well as essays on his life and philosophy.

Kirk, G. S., J. E. Raven, and M. Schofield. *The Presocratic Philosophers.* 2d ed. New York: Cambridge University Press, 1983. The landmark work that has been stimulating discussion since the 1960's and 1970's.

Lloyd, G. E. R. *Early Greek Science: Thales to Aristotle.* New York: W. W. Norton, 1970. The classic textbook for the beginning scholar, providing assistance with placing the Pythagoreans in context in the history of science and with explaining their mathematics.

Navia, Luis E. *Pythagoras: An Annotated Bibliography.* New York: Garland, 1990. A reference which con-

Although scholars are uncertain about his identification as a disciple of Pythagoras, Alcmaeon of Croton published writings on medicine, astronomy, and physics that were influenced by the Pythagoreans and their cosmological theories. (Library of Congress)

tains detailed information on more than eleven hundred journal articles, books, and dissertations on a variety of topics related to Pythagoras.

SEE ALSO: 440 B.C., Teachings of the Sophists; 399 B.C., Death of Socrates; 380 B.C., Plato Develops His Theory of Ideas; 335-323 B.C., Aristotle Writes the *Politics*; 300 B.C., Stoic Conception of Natural Law.

525 B.C.
THE SIBYLLINE BOOKS

The Sibylline Books are developed early in Roman history as a means of state divination and as a senatorial mechanism for effecting collective religious responses to critical situations.

DATE: c. 525 B.C.

LOCALE: Rome

CATEGORIES: Cultural and intellectual history; Religion

KEY FIGURE:

Tarquinius Superbus, king of Rome, traditionally believed to have ruled 534-510 B.C.

SUMMARY OF EVENT. The Sibylline Books were a collection of oracles written in Greek hexameters that were carefully guarded in ancient Rome and were consulted in times of great distress as a result of war, famine, pestilence, or other public calamity.

The Sibyls, from whom the adjective "Sibylline" is derived, were women oracles who gave responses to questions posed to them. The etymology of "Sibyl" is unknown, although numerous attempts have been made in ancient and modern times to explain it. The Sibyls originated in Asia Minor during the seventh century B.C. and spread from there to various sites throughout the Mediterranean world. The philosopher Heraclitus of Ephesus (c. 560-500 B.C.) was the first writer to refer to women of this type, but he only knew of one Sybil. Heraclides Ponticus (c. 390-310 B.C.), a philosopher and writer, was aware of two Sibyls, and later authors mention three, four, eight, ten, and twelve of them, or leave the number indefinite. The most famous listing of these seers is that given by Marcus Terentius Varro in his *Res Divinae*, where he names all sorts of Sibyls: Persian, Libyan, Delphic, Cimmerian, Erythraean, Samian, Cumaean, Hellespontic, Phrygian, and Tiburtine.

The Sibyls could be consulted on a private or public basis, and collections of their responses were compiled and circulated. One of these collections reached Rome toward the end of the sixth century B.C. There, it received official approval and came to be known as the *Libri Sibillini*, or "Sibylline Books."

The famous story connected with the advent of these books is an obvious legend devised to increase their pres-

tige. The story is related by both Greek and Latin authors with some minor alterations in detail. The fullest account is that found in Dionysius of Halicarnassus (30-8 B.C.), who taught history and rhetoric in Rome. According to him, Rome, through the favor of some divinity, was the recipient of wonderfully good fortune during the reign of Tarquinius Superbus (also known as Tarquin the Proud). A foreign woman tried to sell the king nine books of Sibylline oracles. When he refused to buy them, she burned three of the nine books and then offered him the remaining six at the original price. Rebuffed again, she burned three more of the books. When she finally offered the remaining three for the same price as the original nine, the baffled king asked the advice of his augurs, or official diviners. These augurs decided by certain signs that he had rejected a divine blessing in not buying all the books and urged him to purchase at least those that remained. Tarquinius appointed two prominent men to guard the books and gave them two public slaves to assist them in their task. Dionysius states that these books were kept in a stone chest beneath the temple of Jupiter on the Capitoline hill until the time of the Social War in 91-88 B.C., and that they perished in the fire that destroyed the temple in 83 B.C. The books were replaced with oracles gathered from other Italian cities, from Eythrae in Asia Minor, and other places. According to Dionysius, these oracles were the most guarded possession of the Romans, whether sacred or profane, so that the senate decreed that they could be consulted only during times of strife and misfortune in war, or when some baffling prodigy or apparition appeared.

Some attempts have been made to derive the Sibylline Books from Etruria because of their resemblance to the *Libri fatales*, or "Books of Fate," which are assumed to be of Etruscan origin. This title, however, is a generic term used for both Etruscan and Greek rituals. It seem more probable that the oracles were brought to Rome from Cumae, whence they had originally come from Erythrae. Unlike the Greeks, who freely allowed private persons as well as public officials to consult their oracles and even permitted private copies of the responses to be made, the Romans surrounded the books with great secrecy and restricted their use to state officials. Not even the priests in charge could consult them without a special order of the senate.

Scholars have traditionally credited the Sibylline Books with the progressive introduction of Greek and Eastern deities and modes of worship into Rome. Among the gods introduced in this manner were Demeter, Dionysius, and Kore under the Latin names Ceres, Liber, and Libera, and most famous of all, Cybele. Among the rites introduced were the *lectisternium*, or public offering of food to the gods as they were displayed on pillows or couches; the *supplicatio*, a general thanksgiving in honor of the gods, and the *ver sacrum* (sacred spring), a sacrifice of all fruits and animals produced in a particular spring. In a paper presented to the American Philosophical Association's annual meeting in 1994, Eric Orlin showed that the introduction of some of the so-called Greek cults and practices represented the senate's attempt to strengthen ties with south Italy and Sicily and that the Sibylline Books were thus used to sanction senatorial diplomatic policy rather than to serve as a mechanism for importing foreign religious customs.

The original priesthood in charge of the books, the *Duoviri sacris faciundis*, was increased from two to ten individuals, known as the *Decemviri*, and then to fifteen, the *Quindecimviri*. This priesthood formed one of the four major priestly colleges. As part of his religious reform, Augustus ordered a revision to be made of the oracles and had them transferred to the temple of Apollo on the Palatine hill, but by then their days of influence had largely passed. Although interest in them revived under the emperors Aurelian and Julian the Apostate, the Sibylline Books were reportedly burned during the reign of Honorius by order of his general Stilicho.

—*M. Joseph Costelloe, updated by Richard D. Weigel*

ADDITIONAL READING:

Beard, Mary, and John North. *Pagan Priests.* Ithaca, N.Y.: Cornell University Press, 1990. A collection of essays that focus not only on Roman divination and priesthoods but also on the activities of other pagan societies.

Boyce, Aline. "The Development of the *Decemviri Sacris Faciundis.*" *Transactions of the American Philological Association* 69 (1938): 161-187. Provides an overview of the rituals prescribed by the priesthood charged with consulting the Sibylline Books.

Coulter, Cornelia. "The Transfiguration of the Sibyl." *Classical Journal* 46 (1950-1951): 65-71, 78, 121-126. The author surveys the changing role of the books over time.

Momigliano, Arnaldo. "Sibylline Oracles." In *The Encyclopedia of Religion*, vol. 13. New York: Macmillan, 1987. An account of Sibylline Oracles in different religious traditions.

North, John. "Religion in Republican Rome." In *The Rise of Rome to 220 B.C.* Vol. 7, part 2 in *The Cambridge Ancient History*, edited by F. W. Walbank et al. New York: Cambridge University Press, 1989. North provides an overview of the development of Roman cults, games, and traditions during the course of the Republic.

Ogilvie, R. M. *The Romans and Their Gods in the Age of Augustus.* New York: W. W. Norton, 1969. The author

discusses Roman religious life during the late Republic and early Empire.

Parke, H. W. *Sibyls and Sibylline Prophecy in Classical Antiquity.* London: Oxford University Press, 1988. A study of sibyls and their prophecies in religion, poetry, and politics of the ancient world.

SEE ALSO: 775 B.C., Oracle at Delphi; 625-509 B.C., Rise of Etruscan Civilization in Rome; 494 or 493 B.C., Institution of the Plebeian Tribunate; 451-449 B.C., The "Twelve Tables" of Roman Law; 445 B.C., The Canuleian Law; 287 B.C., The *Lex Hortensia.*

508-507 B.C.
REFORMS OF CLEISTHENES

The reforms of Cleisthenes decrease the authority of the noble factions in Athens and establish the foundations of Athenian direct democracy.

DATE: 508-507 B.C.

LOCALE: Athens, Greece

CATEGORIES: Government and politics

KEY FIGURES:

Cleisthenes (c. 560-505 B.C.), Athenian aristocrat of the Alcmaeonid family

Cleomenes (died c. 490 B.C.), king of Sparta, c. 521-490 B.C.

Isagoras, Athenian aristocrat who opposed Cleisthenes

SUMMARY OF EVENT. After the passage of Solon's legislation early in the sixth century B.C., Athens continued to experience political turmoil. Pisistratus established a tyranny which after his death in 527 B.C. passed to his two sons, one of whom was assassinated in 514 and the other expelled with the assistance of King Cleomenes of Sparta in 510. The tyranny was followed by government by the nobility, apparently a narrow oligarchy whose leader was the aristocrat Isagoras. Cleisthenes, of the noble family of the Alcmaeonidae, incited the common people against the oligarchs. In 508-507 B.C., he besieged the conservatives and their Spartan supporters on the Acropolis. The Spartans acknowledged defeat and were permitted to withdraw, whereupon the aristocratic faction surrendered.

Cleisthenes, with the support of most Athenians, then drew up a fresh series of laws which superseded the established constitution by Solon. The reform was essentially political in nature, although it inevitably had repercussions on Attic society as a whole.

Social change was made mainly through abolishing the four traditional tribes of citizens and creating new ones which were not territorial, though they were made up of members of the old *demes*, the villages of Attica. There were then about 170 *demes* of varying sizes. Groups of ten *demes* called *trittyes* were formed by assigning *demes* by lot from the three geographical regions of Attica: the city itself and the countryside immediately around it; the coastal district; and the interior. The *demes* were not necessarily contiguous, especially as Cleisthenes intended to break up regional interest groups of the nobility which had hitherto caused civil unrest, but they were approximately equal in population. New cults were created for the tribes with the approval of the Delphic Apollo in order to bind new loyalties.

The organization of Solon's assembly was also changed, and there is reason to suppose that Cleisthenes assigned to it a more active and important role. It continued to supervise the annual election of magistrates and to be consulted on the issue of war or peace, but it now passed new laws from time to time. With thirty thousand male citizens including the *thetes* (lower-class citizens) eligible to attend, though not to vote, the assembly was unwieldy. An important constitutional innovation of Cleisthenes was creation of the *Boule* or Council, an executive committee of the Assembly made up of five hundred councilors, fifty from each tribe. Each *deme* elected councilors in proportion to its population. It is a matter of controversy whether the *Boule* was a new institution or merely replaced the Council of Four Hundred said to have been constituted by Solon.

Though the precise functions of the *Boule* in the time of Cleisthenes are not clear, it began somewhat later to draw up formal bills for consideration by the assembly, receive foreign embassies, discharge certain judicial functions, and look after the construction of warships, fortifications, and other public works.

Each tribal group of fifty men, a *Prytany*, lived continuously at public expense in the city of Athens for a tenth of the year, an arrangement which was the closest Cleisthenes came to giving payment for holding public office. These groups were ready in emergency to call either the full *Boule* or the assembly into session. One man of the *Prytany* was chosen each day to be the *Prytanis* or "President" of Athens for twenty-four hours. He was responsible for the safekeeping of keys to the temples and treasuries, and he presided over any sessions of the council or assembly which might take place on his day in office. The *Boule* familiarized the people of Athens with the organization, finances, and resources of the state. It also prepared the generation which followed Cleisthenes for the more democratic 460's and 450's under Pericles.

The nine archons (rulers) continued to function as heretofore, but Cleisthenes has also been credited by some authorities with creating the new office of "General" or *Strategos*, which was a more democratic office than ar-

chon because generals were elected without regard to census rating. As the office actually dates from 501/500 B.C., it was probably the creation of some other man because Cleisthenes drops out of Athenian history abruptly after 507 B.C. Some ancient writers also ascribed to him the honorable form of legalized exile known as "ostracism," but since it was not used until 487 B.C., it, too, was in all probability the creation of someone else.

—*Samuel K. Eddy, updated by Jeffrey L. Buller*

ADDITIONAL READING:

Bicknell, P. J. *Studies in Athenian Politics and Genealogy.* Wiesbaden, West Germany: F. Steiner, 1972. An important analysis of partisan politics in ancient Athens with extensive treatment of the reforms of Cleisthenes.

Eliot, C. W. J. *Coastal Demes of Attika.* Toronto: University of Toronto Press, 1962. A scholarly study of the policy of Cleisthenes in reorganizing the political structure of the Athenian *demes*. Contains a valuable bibliography.

Fornara, Charles W., and Loren J. Samons. *Athens from Cleisthenes to Pericles.* Berkeley: University of California Press, 1991. A legal and constitutional history of Athens that treats Cleisthenes as a pivotal figure in the development of the Athenian constitution.

Hignett, C. *A History of the Athenian Constitution to the End of the Fifth Century B.C.* Oxford: Clarendon Press, 1952. A readable summary of the Athenian constitution from Draco and Solon, through the reforms of Cleisthenes, to the time of the Peloponnesian War.

Jones, A. H. M. *Athenian Democracy.* Oxford: Basil Blackwell, 1957. Describes the day-to-day functioning of the Athenian government, providing an excellent picture of the political bodies developed or reformed by Cleisthenes.

Sealey, Raphael. *A History of the Greek City States, 700-338 B.C.* Berkeley: University of California Press, 1976. Provides a concise yet reliable summary of the reforms by Cleisthenes and details his political conflicts with Isagoras.

SEE ALSO: 594-580 B.C., Legislation of Solon; 483 B.C., Naval Law of Themistocles; 478-448 B.C., Athenian Empire Is Created; 431-404 B.C., Peloponnesian War.

500-400 B.C.
GREEK PHYSICIANS DEVELOP SCIENTIFIC PRACTICE OF MEDICINE
Greek physicians develop the scientific practice of medicine, allowing reason to triumph over superstition in their search for knowledge about disease and its treatment.

DATE: c. 500-400 B.C.

LOCALE: Greece

CATEGORIES: Health and medicine; Science and technology

KEY FIGURE:

Hippocrates (c. 460-360 B.C.), Greek physician associated with a medical school on Cos and a body of early medical writings

SUMMARY OF EVENT. One of the great accomplishments of the ancient Greek world, and of all antiquity, was the development in the late fifth century of the *scientific* practice of medicine. Doctoring is as old as civilization itself, but only when the Greeks developed a purely rational way of looking at the world did medicine become a science.

Early Greek thought resembles that of other peoples: Illness, like all other facets of human life, is in the hands of the gods. Two of the brilliant masterpieces of Greek literature, Homer's *Iliad* and Sophocles' *Oedipus Rex*, begin with plagues sent by an angered Apollo. The idea that God is responsible for causing and for curing illness is also found in biblical writings, especially in the New Testament, where among the principal activities of Jesus are the casting out of demons and the healing of the sick. Curative powers were attributed to the pagan gods, and among the most common archaeological finds are votive offerings (many of which are models of the affected parts needing cure) and amulets. As attested by the *Oneirocritica* of Artemidorus (second century A.D.), Greeks believed also in the curative power of dreams. These nonscientific medical views were never abandoned by the ancient world (nor, indeed, have they been abandoned by the modern world either, as the continued use of amulets, lighting of candles, and faith-healing all attest), but existed side by side with scientific medicine.

The fifty years following the Persian Wars saw spectacular intellectual development in the Greek world. Philosophy, which started with Thales in the preceding century, came into its own. The natural philosophers of Ionia (what is now the western part of Turkey) sought an explanation of nature that did not rely on supernatural causation. They sought, instead, to show that all nature operated by the same set of physical laws. They offered different solutions to the questions of what the world was made out of and how it functioned, and their theories were developed from arbitrary assumptions. Anaximenes asserted air to be the basic element; Anaxagoras, a substance of indeterminate nature; Heraclitus, fire; Empedocles, the four elements air, earth, fire, and water.

Because of the tremendous success of Greek mathematics, and of geometry in particular with its system of deductive reasoning based on very few axioms, there was a tendency among natural philosophers to seek systems of the physical universe that were deductive. Deductive reasoning produces the highest degree of certainty, and Aristotle is typical of the Greeks in affording the prize for scientific knowledge to sciences such as geometry and logic, sciences whose conclusions are reached through deductive reasoning from axioms and definitions. The results of the natural philosophers, however, were not satisfying: the material world does not yield to deductive reasoning. Medical writers of the fifth century and later very much wanted to separate themselves from the arbitrary axioms of the natural philosophers, and Celsus (A.D. 14-37) claims that Hippocrates was the first actually to do so. Thus the author of *On the Nature of Man* criticizes those physicians who claim that because humans are

Despite the difficulty in determining his actual writings, Hippocrates of Cos is credited as the founder of an enduring body of medical ideas and practices that are summarized in the Hippocratic oath. (Library of Congress)

a unity, they are composed of only one of the four elements. He says that their proofs amount to nothing and that victory in their debates goes to the one with the glibbest tongue. Yet the same author, though attacking others for their lack of evidence, accepts as axiomatic that humans are made of four humours—blood, yellow bile, black bile, and phlegm, each derived from one of the four elements.

A key feature of Greek medical science is its rejection of gods and magic in the interpretation of disease. In popular Greek language, epilepsy was called the "sacred disease." The Hippocratic author who wrote the treatise "On the Sacred Disease" claims that this disease is no more sacred than any other:

> I do not believe that the "Sacred Disease" is any more divine or sacred than any other disease, but, on the contrary, has specific characteristics and a definite cause. Nevertheless, because it is completely different from other diseases, it has been regarded as a divine visitation by those who, being only human, view it with ignorance and astonishment.

He continues by attacking as charlatans and quacks those who try to cure the disease by means of charms. He himself explains the disease as resulting from a discharge in the brain, and he supports this theory with the dissection of a goat that has suffered from the same disease. In addition to the physiological explanation, what is remarkable is that the author sees the same laws of nature operative in both humans and goats.

The man most identified with the development of Greek medicine is Hippocrates of Cos, who is said to have established a medical school on his native island. Virtually nothing is known of Hippocrates himself, though he is treated respectfully by writers of his era. Plato refers to him as a typical doctor, and Aristotle calls him the perfect example of a physician. Plato attributes to Hippocrates the revolutionary idea that in order to understand the body it is necessary to understand it as an organic whole, that is, as a unity whose parts function together. This organic view, however, is not explicitly stated in any of the extant Hippocratic books. The consensus of scholarly opinion is that there was no single author "Hippocrates." None of the fifty to seventy surviving books of the so-called Hippocratic corpus agree with the views attributed in antiquity to Hippocrates and, moreover, the contents of these books are often at odds with one another. Nevertheless, even if his actual works are not known, he appears to have been a real person and to have had—if Plato may be credited—a scientific outlook.

One of the important features of Greek medicine is the

The Roman writer Aulus Cornelius Celsus compiled a medical encyclopedia known as De medicina *(c. A.D. 30), which was largely based on the teachings and works of Hippocrates.* (Library of Congress)

inquiry into the causes of disease. As in the case of natural philosophy, where a variety of views explained the universe, so in medicine there are various theoretical formulations, ranging from a single unitary cause for all disease to specific causes for each. The author of the Hippocratic work *On Breaths*, for example, thinks that because some breathing irregularity accompanies illness, breath is at the root of every disease. On the other hand, the author of *Peri archaies ietrikes* (fifth or fourth century B.C., *Ancient Medicine*), criticizes physicians who do not distinguish between symptoms and causes. He also criticizes those who think that if a disease follows a certain action, the action was the cause of disease—a mistake known in philosophy as the *post hoc propter hoc* fallacy. An example would be eating a certain food, and, when illness followed shortly after, assuming the food to be the cause of the illness.

Another feature of Hippocratic medicine, as detailed in the work *Prognostics*, was the careful study of the progress of diseases. Once a physician had diagnosed a particular illness, he could tell the patient what to expect in the future as the disease ran its course. The ability to predict was certainly essential in establishing medicine's status as a science.

Diagnosis and prognostication both incorporate the fundamental principle of Hippocratic medicine that disease is a part of nature and acts in accordance with natural laws. As humans share a common nature and as diseases share a nature that is regular and hence predictable, a science of medicine is possible. For a disease to be treatable, what works for one patient must work for another. Thus, medicine must carefully analyze nature, catalog the types of diseases, and define the appropriate treatment for each. The underlying assumption of ancient medicine, as of modern medicine, is that the body functions best when its nature is maintained. Hence the physician's job is twofold: First, he should not interfere with the body's nature but should maintain it by means of preventive medicine, the principle forms of which are diet and exercise; second, when the patient is already ill, the physician, using therapeutic medicine, should restore the body to its nature.

From its birth in fifth century B.C. Greece, the scientific practice of medicine has been continually alive in the West. The centuries following Hippocrates saw advances in anatomy, as *post mortem* dissections became common. Specialized work in gynecology, orthopedics, and other branches of medicine continued and flourished. Later, in the Roman period, there followed major advances in public health, and the Romans bequeathed to posterity insights about hygiene, sanitation, water supplies, and public health.

—*James A. Arieti*

ADDITIONAL READING:

Edelstein, Ludwig. *Ancient Medicine*, edited by O. Temkin and C. L. Temkin. Baltimore: The Johns Hopkins University Press, 1967. Although an older work, this collection provides a useful context for understanding the origins of Greek medical practice.

Magner, Lois. *A History of Medicine*. New York: Marcel Dekker, 1992. Magner's work offers a fine introduction to Greek contributions to the study of medicine.

Majno, G. *The Healing Hand: Man and Wound in the Ancient World*. Cambridge, Mass.: Harvard University Press, 1975. A wide-ranging scholarly study that is accessible for the general reader.

Sargent, Frederick. *Hippocratic Heritage: A History of Ideas About Weather and Human Health*. New York: Pergamon Press, 1982. Sargent focuses on the legacy of Hippocrates and his impact on modern medical science.

Smith, Wesley. *The Hippocratic Tradition*. Ithaca, N.Y.: Cornell University Press, 1979. A particularly useful overview of the contributions of Hippocrates.

SEE ALSO: 325-323 B.C., Aristotle Isolates Science as a Discipline; 157-201, Galen Synthesizes Ancient Medical Knowledge; 1010-1015, Avicenna Writes His *Canon of Medicine*; 1150, Moors Transmit Classical Philosophy and Medicine to Europe.

494/493 B.C.
INSTITUTION OF THE PLEBEIAN TRIBUNATE

The institution of the plebeian tribunate by the Roman senate recognizes the rights of the lower orders of Roman society.

DATE: 494/493 B.C.
LOCALE: Rome
CATEGORIES: Government and politics; Social reform
KEY FIGURES:
Menenius Agrippa, ambassador of the Roman senate to the dissident plebeians
Gaius Licinius and *Lucius Albinus*, first tribunes to be chosen by the plebeians
Sicinius, leader of the plebeian revolt
Manius Valerius, Roman dictator in 494 B.C.

SUMMARY OF EVENT. Because of the lack of contemporary sources and because evidence was at times deliberately suppressed and falsified for purposes of family aggrandizement or moral and artistic edification, much early Roman history lies shrouded in obscurity and myth. Despite conflicting details, however, there seems to be a core of fact relating to the institution of the plebeian tribunate as described by Dionysius of Halicarnassus and Livy. A secession of the plebs, prompted by their abuse at the hands of the patricians, was followed by the election of officers to represent plebeians and defend their rights. Ultimately, an oath was sworn by the plebeians to regard as inviolable the persons of their new tribunes. Conflicting accounts exist about the place of secession, whether on the Aventine hill or the Sacred Mount; about the number of tribunes elected, whether two, four, or five; about the manner of their election; and about the oath taken making them sacrosanct.

According to Livy, trouble broke out during the consulship of Appius Claudius and Publius Servilius in 495 B.C. The plebeians complained that while they were fighting in the army to preserve Roman independence, they were being enslaved at home by patrician creditors. They were particularly exasperated by the pitiful sight of a former soldier who, having lost his home and his crops to the enemy, had to borrow money in order to pay his taxes. To induce plebeians to take up arms against a Volscian army, Servilius was forced to order that no Roman citizen should be held in chains or in prison to prevent him from enlisting, that no one should seize or sell a soldier's property while he was in service, and that no one should harass his children or grandchildren.

Continued pressure on debtors, however, caused the plebs to become violent. They began to assemble at night on the Aventine and Esquiline, and they refused to fight against the invading Sabines. An edict by the dictator Manius Valerius giving greater protection to plebeians from their creditors made it possible to muster an army. In the absence of permanent adjustments, however, the plebs took the advice of a certain Sicinius and withdrew to the Sacred Mount three miles from the city across the Anio River. This secession caused panic in the city among the patricians, who were afraid of hostile foreign invaders and those plebeians who remained behind. According to Livy, the senate compromised with a constitutional innovation.

This new agreement, a milestone in the struggle between the orders, created an exclusive plebeian office to protect "the people" from the aristocratic consuls. The "tribunes of the people" at first had only a negative function because they could do no more than "forbid" an overt act inimical to a plebeian at the instant of its perpetration. Moreover, aid had to be initiated by a complaining plebeian, so a tribune could not absent himself from the city for a whole night or shut his doors at any time. The person of the tribune was declared sacrosanct by a *lex sacrata*; anyone who interfered with a tribune doing his duty became an outlaw, liable to be killed by plebeians.

At first, there were two tribunes—or possibly four or five, according to some sources. That number, however, eventually grew to ten. This strange negative office, creating a set of parallel officials working at cross-purposes with the old magistrates of the state, was intended partly to satisfy plebeian unrest and partly to keep plebeians from becoming regular magistrates, thus usurping the prerogative of the nobility. In 471 B.C., a law transferred the election of tribunes from the assembly of the *curiae* to the *comitia tributa*, an event and date that Eduard Meyer and some other scholars have associated with the actual creation of the plebeian tribunate itself. Eventually, the veto of a plebeian tribune permitted him to negate the passage of any legislation prejudicial to plebeian concerns. Thus, it was only natural that tribunes began to sit in the senate to make known their objections to laws before they were actually passed, or to suggest legislation and even to call together the senate. The tribunes were also able to veto acts of the consuls and other magistrates, with the exception of dictators. In 287 B.C., plebiscites of their *comitia tributa* were given the same force as laws passed by the senate or the *comitia centuriata*.

Because of its invaluable power of veto, the office of plebeian tribune came to be sought avidly. Even patricians had themselves adopted by plebeians in order to become eligible. It is ironic that this weak, makeshift office became so powerful that the Emperor Augustus used the authority of the plebeian tribunate to rule Rome in preference to consular *imperium* because of the unique right of the former to initiate or veto legislation.

—*M. Joseph Costelloe, updated by Jeffrey L. Buller*

ADDITIONAL READING:

Alfoldi, Andreas. *Early Rome and the Latins*. Ann Arbor: University of Michigan Press, 1965. An exhaustive history of the early Roman republic by the foremost scholar in the field. Based upon Alfoldi's Jerome Lectures.

Ferenczy, Endre. *From the Patrician State to the Patricio-Plebeian State*. Translated by G. Dedinsky. Amsterdam: A. M. Hakkert, 1976. An excellent survey of the major reforms in the Roman government expanding the legal rights of non-nobles.

McDonald, Alexander Hugh. *Republican Rome*. New York: Frederick A. Praeger, 1966. For the general reader, the best survey of early Roman history currently available. A good place to begin.

Pinsent, John. *Military Tribunes and Plebeian Consuls*. Wiesbaden, West Germany: Steiner, 1975. Not a historical survey per se, but a listing of the early *Fasti Triumphales* (records of official triumphs) and *Fasti Consulares* (catalogs of Roman magistrates). Invaluable for those seeking primary source material on the effects of such developments as the institution of the plebeian tribunate.

Robinson, Cyril Edward. *A History of the Roman Republic*. New York: Barnes & Noble, 1932. Though now somewhat superseded by more recent research, this volume still contains a great deal of invaluable material on the earliest periods of Roman history.

Scullard, Howard Hayes. *A History of the Roman World: 753-146 B.C.* 4th ed. New York: Methuen, 1980. Lavishly detailed and comprehensive in scope, this book interweaves early Roman economic, military, and social history.

SEE ALSO: 451-449 B.C., The "Twelve Tables" of Roman Law; 445 B.C., The Canuleian Law; 340-338 B.C., Origin of *Municipia*; 287 B.C., The *Lex Hortensia*; 180 B.C., Establishment of the *Cursus Honorum*.

483 B.C.
NAVAL LAW OF THEMISTOCLES

The naval law of Themistocles is intended as a limited defensive measure but becomes essential to the defense of Greece against Persia and provides the foundation for the Athenian empire.

DATE: 483 B.C.

LOCALE: Athens, Greece

CATEGORIES: Government and politics; Laws, acts, and legal history

KEY FIGURES:

Pericles (c. 495-429 B.C.), Athenian statesman and general

Themistocles (c. 524-460 B.C.), Athenian archon and general

SUMMARY OF EVENT. In 483 B.C., Themistocles, one of several political leaders in the recently established Athenian democracy, made a proposal to the assembly that had far-reaching implications for Athens and the whole of Greece. For many years, the Athenians had obtained silver from their state-owned mines at Laurium and frequently distributed the modest annual output as a bonus to citizens. In 483 B.C., however, spectacularly rich veins of silver were exposed, and a debate ensued as to the disposal of this bonanza. Many argued for the customary (if unusually large) distribution to citizens, but Themistocles proposed that the windfall be used to build two hundred warships of the advanced trireme type. His proposal carried the day, and by 480 B.C. Athens had a fleet that made it a major naval power in Greece. To understand how Themistocles achieved acceptance of his proposal and his rationale, one must consider the democratic constitution of Athens, its previous troubled encounters with Persia and Aegina, and changes in naval technology.

Before this buildup, Athens had a small fleet of old-fashioned *pentekontors* (fifty-oared ships), which served well for coastal raids and boarding attacks on other ships but had limited effectiveness in the ramming tactics that were emerging with the spread of a newer style of warship, the trireme. With three banks of rowers per side, providing more than three times the oar power of a *pentekontor*, the trireme had great speed and ramming power. Despite its early invention and its superiority as a ramming weapon, however, the expense of building and operating the trireme slowed its adoption. Because each ship required a skilled crew of two hundred men, the operational cost of a fleet of triremes exceeded the means of all but the wealthiest states, such as Persia, Sidon, and a few of the richest Greek city-states. The silver strike at Laurium gave Athens the opportunity to join this elite group.

In advancing his naval policy, Themistocles operated within the democratic constitution, which had been instituted by Cleisthenes in 509 B.C. This reform placed primary power in the hands of an Assembly composed of all adult male citizens and a Council of Five Hundred selected annually by lot, while retaining limited aristocratic features. For example, only wealthier citizens could hold the office of archon and serve on the Council of the Areopagus. Pay was not provided for service on the councils or for jury duty. The new arrangement was also prone to factionalism, as rival aristocratic leaders competed for

popular support. Fortunately, the system included the peculiar procedure of ostracism, whereby the Athenians might annually vote to exile one individual for ten years. Designed to preempt a revival of tyranny, it emerged in the 480's B.C. as a political weapon that allowed a leader such as Themistocles to eliminate rivals and forge a consensus for a policy such as the naval law.

In proposing this costly program, Themistocles had in mind two potential threats: Aegina and Persia. Situated less than fifteen miles from the Athenian harbor, the island city-state of Aegina had achieved commercial and naval power well ahead of Athens. Rivalry between the two city-states went back many years, and since at least 506 B.C., an undeclared state of war had existed between them, with Aegina getting the better of the conflict. A naval expedition to avenge an Aeginetan raid on the Athenian harbor district had failed miserably and demonstrated Athenian naval inferiority. By building the new fleet, Themistocles hoped to put Athens in a position to retaliate for earlier aggressions and make the harbors of Attica safe from future Aeginetan predations. Punishment of Aegina had to wait, however, because the Persians presented a greater and more immediate threat.

In 545 B.C., the Persian king Cyrus had conquered Asia Minor and incorporated the Greek city-states of Ionia into the Persian Empire. His successor Darius asserted power across the Bosporus into European Thrace. When the Ionian city-states rebelled against Persian rule in 499 B.C., the Athenians alone of the mainland Greeks sent military support, an act that greatly incensed Darius. After suppressing the revolt by 494 B.C., he resolved to punish the Athenians for their interference. In 490 B.C., Darius sent an expeditionary force by sea, which landed at Marathon and suffered a humiliating defeat at the hands of the Athenians. Outraged at this outcome, Darius began preparations for a full-scale invasion of Greece, but his death in 486 B.C. forestalled this attack. His successor Xerxes took up Darius' plan for invading Greece, and, by 483 B.C. (the year of the silver strike at Laurium), Persian advance forces were already in Thrace and cutting the famous canal across the Athos peninsula that would facilitate passage of their fleet.

In proposing his naval law, Themistocles surely had this threat in mind as well as the continuing Aeginetan nuisance. Themistocles possessed the strategic insight to see the weakness of the immense Persian army: Its very size made it dependent upon seaborne supplies, which were protected by the Persian navy of more than one thousand triremes. Thanks to Themistocles, when the Persian onslaught came, the Greeks had an effective naval strategy and a substantial fleet to implement it. In the decisive naval battle at Salamis in 480 B.C., Athenian triremes made up more than half the combined Greek fleet that defeated the larger Persian force and broke the back of Xerxes' invasion. Ironically, the Aeginetans, who had temporarily suspended hostilities with Athens in the face of the Persian threat, were awarded the prize for valor at Salamis.

Once Xerxes' invasion had been repulsed, the Athenians eagerly assumed leadership of a continuing offensive against the Persians. In 478 B.C., they organized the Delian League, a voluntary alliance of Aegean city-states in which members contributed either triremes or money to support the league's common navy. In that same year, Themistocles employed a clever diplomatic ruse to secure the rebuilding of the city walls of Athens over the objections of other city-states, and he oversaw the fortification of the Athenian harbor at Piraeus. His antagonistic attitude toward Sparta led to his own ostracism in 473 B.C., but by this time the Athenians were committed to maintaining the navy program and pursuing the war against the Persians. During the next two decades under Athenian command, the forces of the Delian League expelled the Persians from Greek waters and liberated the city-states of Ionia. At the same time, however, the Athenians used the fleet to coerce Greek states to join or remain in the league, which rapidly became the Athenian empire. Aegina, the original target of Themistocles' naval buildup, succumbed in 458 B.C. and became a tribute-paying member of the Delian League. That same year also saw construction on the final part of the defensive system begun by Themistocles—the famous long walls that linked the city of Athens with its harbor. Secure within these walls and with its commerce and imperial tribute protected by its navy, Athens now entered its greatest period of power and prosperity.

The naval empire provided great material benefits to Athenians of all classes in the form of jobs, grants of land confiscated from subject city-states, and magnificent public buildings, most famously the Parthenon. It also greatly enhanced the influence of the poorest class of citizens and engendered constitutional changes that resulted in the "radical democracy" so hated by conservative critics. The security of Athens now depended less on the wealthier citizens who made up the infantry and cavalry forces than on the poorer citizens, called *thetes*, who rowed the triremes. Recognition of the increased importance of the lower classes led statesmen such as Pericles to introduce reforms that further democratized the political system. Thus, the wealth qualification for the office of archon was lowered; the powers of the Council of the Areopagus were drastically limited; and pay was now extended to members of the Council of Five Hundred and to jurors. Since the

aristocrats and conservative theorists who attacked these constitutional changes clearly associated them with the rise of the navy, it is not surprising that they singled out Themistocles for special condemnation.

—*James T. Chambers*

ADDITIONAL READING:

Jordan, Borimir. *The Athenian Navy in the Classical Period.* Berkeley: University of California Press, 1975. A detailed study of the navy created by Themistocles.

Meiggs, Russell. *The Athenian Empire.* Oxford: Oxford University Press, 1972. This book analyzes the empire's origins, course, and effects on Athens and the Greek world as a whole.

Morrison, John S., and J. F. Coates. *The Athenian Trireme: The History and Reconstruction of an Ancient Greek Warship.* New York: Cambridge University Press, 1986. The most important volume on this subject, this study analyzes all aspects of the trireme's history.

Plutarch. *The Rise and Fall of Athens.* Translated by Ian Scott-Kilvert. New York: Penguin Books, 1960. This excellent translation of nine of Plutarch's biographies has the lives of nine Athenian statesmen, including Themistocles.

Starr, Chester G. *The Influence of Sea Power on Ancient History.* New York: Oxford University Press, 1989. Chapter 3, "Athens on the Sea," provides an excellent overview of the rise and decline of Athens as a naval power.

SEE ALSO: 480-479 B.C., Persian Invasion of Greece; 478-448 B.C., Athenian Empire Is Created; 431-404 B.C., Peloponnesian War; 401-400 B.C., March of the "Ten Thousand."

480-479 B.C.
PERSIAN INVASION OF GREECE

The Persian invasion of Greece is repulsed by Greek city-states, who join together to defeat Persia, halting future invasions.

DATE: 480-479 B.C.

LOCALE: Greece, the Aegean Sea, and western Asia Minor

CATEGORIES: Expansion and land acquisition; Wars, uprisings, and civil unrest

KEY FIGURES:

Adimantus, Corinthian general, 480 B.C.

Eurybiades, Spartan admiral, commander in chief of the Greek fleet, 481-480 B.C.

Leonidas (died 480 B.C.), king of Sparta, 487-480 B.C.

Pausanias (died c. 470 B.C.), nephew of Leonidas and regent of Sparta 480-c. 470 B.C.

Themistocles, (c. 524-460 B.C.), Athenian general

Xerxes (c. 519-465 B.C.), king of the kings of the Persian Empire, 486-465 B.C.

SUMMARY OF EVENT. Cyrus the Great, founder of the Persian Empire, subjected the Greek states of western Asia Minor, or Ionia, to Persia. The Ionians resented the loss of their sovereignty, and in 499 B.C., they rebelled against Cyrus' successor, Darius I. Their action was supported by two states in Old Hellas, Eretria and Athens. At first the Ionian revolt went well, but Darius soon gathered overwhelming forces and reimposed Persian authority by 493 B.C. He then determined to invade Old Greece, to punish the states which had assisted the Ionian cities, and to end a vexatious frontier problem. Persia had been reasserting its strength along its western boundaries, but a campaign against Greece required different strategies, including a much greater reliance on naval battle than Persia had experienced before.

Darius' first attack in 492 B.C. miscarried when much of the Persian fleet was wrecked in a storm, and his second attempt in 490 B.C. failed when his army was driven into the sea at Marathon in Attica. He therefore planned a third invasion on a lavish scale. Darius, however, died in 486 B.C., and it fell to his son Xerxes to complete the preparation of his empire's forces.

The great invasion finally began in the spring of 480 B.C. An enormous host of more than one hundred thousand soldiers was supported by a fleet of six hundred warships. Part of the Persian military strategy in this campaign and others for fifty years prior was to let the opponents know that the Persian army was coming. They counted on terror and the effects of psychological warfare, rather than the element of military surprise. The Greeks could not fail to learn about the assembling of such masses, and in the winter of 481-480 B.C. representatives of the larger states met at Corinth to discuss resistance. The Delphic Oracle had to be persuaded to modify its initial prophecy of doom to one of doubtful outcome, and it was with some trepidation that a decision was taken to fight under Spartan leadership. Appeals to other Greek states to join the patriotic cities were rejected by some of the more important ones, notably anti-Spartan Argos. Ultimately, only thirty-one states fought on the Greek side. There were actually more Greek states on the side of Xerxes, although these served under compulsion.

The Greeks decided to delay the Persians' advance by holding the narrow pass at Thermopylae with eight thousand men and the adjacent strait between Thermopylae and the island of Euboea with their fleet. It was not until August that the Persians came up against these fortified positions. Three days passed as Xerxes vainly sent his best

troops against the well-armored Peloponnesian infantry fighting under King Leonidas of Sparta. Simultaneously, a series of inconclusive but costly naval engagements were fought off Cape Artemisium on Euboea; the Persians had earlier lost about two hundred warships in a storm. Xerxes, however, turned the position at Thermopylae by marching around it through the mountains. Most of the Greeks escaped encirclement in time, but Leonidas with his bodyguard of three hundred Spartans and the seven-hundred-man army of Tespiae were cut off and could only die resisting bravely to the end.

With the position on land lost, the Greek fleet retreated and took station on the island of Salamis off the western coast of Attica. The population of Athens had already been evacuated to the Peloponnesus. There was more wavering among the Greeks at Salamis, some even considering defection, but at last honor prevailed, and led by Eurybiades of Sparta, Themistocles of Athens, and Adimantus of Corinth, the Greek sailors prepared to fight. The Persians, fearing that the Greek fleet might escape westward decided upon an immediate attack, and late in September the Battle of Salamis was fought in the narrow strait between the island and the mainland. The Persians had about 350 ships, the Greeks probably 310, of which the majority were Athenian. The conflict lasted most of the day, and by sunset the Greeks were victorious. With the campaigning season nearly over Xerxes withdrew from devastated Attica and left half his army to winter in Boeotia. The rest of the army and the shattered fleet retired with the king to Asia.

The war was resumed the following spring. After a second Persian devastation of Attica, a hard-fought land battle took place at Plataea, a small state between Athens and Boeotia. Under the command of the Spartan regent Pausanias, the Greeks gained the victory, and the Spartan infantry showed once more their undoubted excellence. The Persian army was forced into rapid retreat.

While this campaign was being fought in Greece, the Hellenic fleet had crossed the Aegean to seek out the remnants of Xerxes' navy. Off the island of Mycale, the Greeks completed its destruction. Thus, the great force which Xerxes had led against the Hellenes was either destroyed or forced back into Asia, and, as the poet Simonides wrote, "Hellas put on the crown of freedom."

These victories did not end the war with Persia, but they did end Persian efforts to invade Greece. The liberation of Ionia now became the goal of the Greek states, and by 477 B.C. most of it had been freed. As a result of these campaigns Athens became one of the most important military powers of Greece.

After these wars, the Persian Empire never again seri-

MAJOR BATTLES AGAINST DARIUS AND XERXES

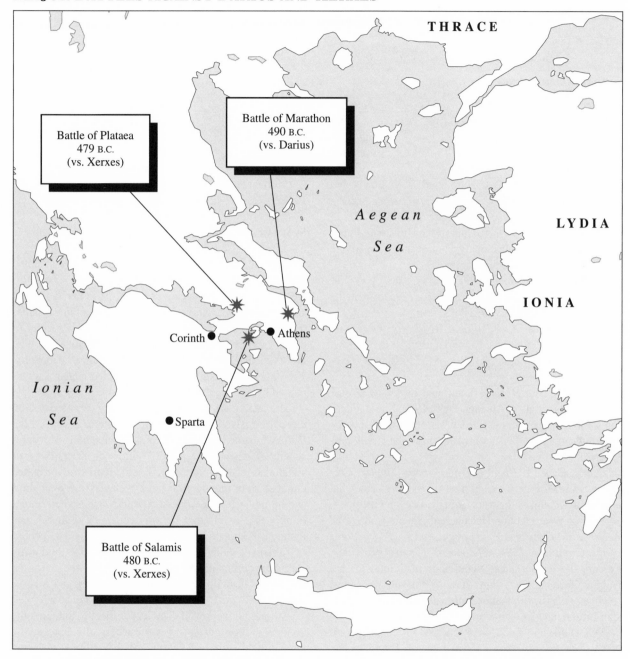

ously threatened the Greek city-states. Greece became the major power in the Mediterranean Sea, and this allowed the city-states to prosper through trade and to increase their political power. Athens' role in leading the fight against Persia continued in time of peace, as Athens was the most influential of the Greek city-states and the center of Hellenic cooperation. In contrast, the Persian Empire began its slow shrinking that set the stage for Alexander's

conquest, nearly one hundred fifty years later.

In the centuries after the Persian wars, Greek culture blossomed, expanding into the greatest variety of its classical period. The cultural vibrancy came to expression in literature such as the drama of Aeschylus of Athens and the poetry of Pindar of Thebes, as well as in the philosophy, mathematics, and athletics that flourished in this period. Greek hegemony over the eastern Mediterranean allowed its wealth to grow and its Hellenistic culture to begin its spread throughout the region, preparing the way for the later military conquests of what became Alexander the Great's empire.

—*Samuel K. Eddy, updated by Jon L. Berquist*

ADDITIONAL READING:

Bengston, Hermann, ed. *The Greeks and the Persians from the Sixth to the Fourth Centuries.* New York: Delacorte Press, 1968. A collection of essays dealing with different aspects of Persian-Greek relations surrounding the invasion.

Boardman, John, N. G. L. Hammond, D. M. Lewis, and M. Ostwald, eds. *The Cambridge Ancient History. Volume 4: Persia, Greece and the Western Mediterranean, c. 525 to 479 B.C.* 2d ed. New York: Cambridge University Press, 1988. The most complete analysis of events from before the invasion through Persia's defeat.

Burn, A. R. *Persia and the Greeks.* New York: St. Martin's Press, 1962. A narrative covering events from the sixth century to Xerxes' defeats in 479 B.C.

Dandamaev, M. A. *A Political History of the Achaemenid Empire.* Leiden, the Netherlands: E. J. Brill, 1989. A remarkably thorough treatment of the Persian involvement in the war.

Herodotus. *The History.* Translated by David Grene. Chicago: University of Chicago Press, 1987. The standard translation of the famous Greek historian who records (and interprets) the Persian invasion from the Greek perspective.

Olmstead, A. T. *History of the Persian Empire.* Chicago: University of Chicago Press, 1948. A somewhat uncritical account of the wars from the Persian viewpoint.

Sancisi-Weerdenburg, Heleen, and Amélie Kuhrt, eds. *Achaemenid History II: The Greek Sources. Proceedings of the Groningen 1984 Achaemenid History Workshop.* Leiden, the Netherlands: Nederlands Instituut voor het Nabije Oosten, 1987. Part of an eight-volume series, *Achaemenid History*, that examines all aspects of the Persian Empire and its interaction with its neighbors.

SEE ALSO: 550 B.C., Construction of Trireme Changes Naval Warfare; 483 B.C., Naval Law of Themistocles; 478-448 B.C., Athenian Empire Is Created; 431-404 B.C., Peloponnesian War; 401-400 B.C., March of the "Ten Thousand."

478-448 B.C.
ATHENIAN EMPIRE IS CREATED

The Athenian Empire is created, transforming a defensive alliance against Persia into a political empire that prevents the peaceful unification of Greece and leads to the Peloponnesian War.

DATE: 478-448 B.C.
LOCALE: Athens, Ionia, and other Greek city-states
CATEGORIES: Expansion and land acquisition; Government and politics
KEY FIGURES:
Aristides (c. 525-c. 468 B.C.), Athenian statesman and leading organizer of Delian League
Cimon (c. 512-450 B.C.), Athenian general and conservative political leader
Ephialtes (c. 505-461 B.C.), Athenian democratic political leader and reformer
Pericles (c. 495-429 B.C.), Athenian general and democratic political leader

SUMMARY OF EVENT. After the Persian invasion of Greece had been repulsed in the spring of 477 B.C., delegates from the liberated Greek cities of Ionia and Athens assembled and agreed to combine forces in a league whose stated aims were to protect the Aegean area from fresh Persian offensives and to ravage Xerxes' territory. The Spartan Pausanias (c. 515-c. 471 B.C.) had been the commander in chief of the allied Greeks. His behavior was so arrogant and brutal, however, that the allies rejected all Spartan leadership. The Athenian Aristides became the allied leader, accompanied by his younger colleague Cimon.

The headquarters of this confederacy was located on the sacred island of Delos, and it came to be called the Delian League. In the beginning an assembly of representatives determined policy, with each state, large or small, exercising one vote. Each member contributed either ships or money; the respective assessments of ships and money were the work of Aristides, whose determinations were so fair that he was called "The Just." The money was kept on Delos under the supervision of a board of Athenians called Hellenic Treasurers. Fleet and army were both commanded by Athenians since Athens was the largest and most powerful of the allied states, and Athenians had won great prestige in both war and peace.

At first, all went well. The league fleet maintained the security of the Aegean and even successfully attacked the Persian-held island of Cyprus. Such victories led some members of the confederacy to regard the Persian menace as broken, and about 470 B.C. Naxos, tired of onerous naval service, seceded. The Athenians, supported by a majority of the allies, felt that the withdrawal of Naxos might portend the dissolution of the league to Persia's advantage. Naxos was therefore besieged and reduced to obedience. This act set an important precedent. Moreover, the league's assessment of the situation was confirmed the next year, when the reconstituted Persian navy sailed toward the Aegean but was defeated in the Battle of Eurymedon by the league fleet ably commanded by Athens' Cimon.

Because providing ships year after year was a hardship for some members, Athens, upon the suggestion of Cimon, introduced the policy of allowing any state to convert its obligation to one of paying money. The exact date of this change is unknown; it probably occurred in the mid-460's, at the height of Cimon's power and prestige. Gradually most confederates made payments until, by 445 B.C., only seven states of a regular membership of some 150 still contributed triremes. At the time the change must have seemed statesmanlike, but it actually cloaked a great danger to the league. As time went on, only the Athenians and the few other states with fleets were capable of serious naval action; the ships of the money-paying cities decayed and their crews lacked practice. The Athenians, meanwhile, not only increased the size of their navy but also introduced improved models of triremes and new naval tactics, so that their navy was a virtually invincible force by the 440's.

In another unintended way Cimon furthered Athenian imperialism. League member Thasos seceded in 465 B.C., was defeated at sea and then besieged by the Athenians, and finally appealed to Sparta for help. Athens and Sparta remained formally allied, but Sparta, fearing Athens' growing power, agreed to aid Thasos. Before they could act, a severe earthquake struck Sparta, causing much destruction and many deaths. Seizing this opportunity, Sparta's subject-peoples revolted, and eventually were besieged at Ithome. Meanwhile, the Thasians, lacking Spartan aid, surrendered.

Sparta, recognizing Athenian prowess in siege operations, appealed to Athens for help. Cimon, relatively conservative and pro-Spartan, argued in favor; his more democratic, anti-Spartan opponent Ephialtes, against. Cimon prevailed, and was chosen to lead the assisting army. Yet the Spartans, probably fearing both the presence of an Athenian army in their territory and the effects of Athenian liberalism on current and would-be rebels, changed their minds. Delivering a "slap in the face," they asked the Athenians to leave but retained their other allies. As a result, Cimon's pro-Spartan policy was repudiated, and he was ostracized in 461. His conservative institutional ally, the Aeropagetic Council, was stripped of most of its powers by Ephialtes. Athens became more democratic, more anti-Spartan and, almost immediately, more imperial.

In 460 B.C., the Delian confederates attacked the Per-

To protect the financial resources of the Delian League from Persian attack, the Athenian government stored the league's treasury at the Acropolis. (Archive Photos)

sians in Egypt, but the offensive ended with the annihilation of a league fleet in 454 B.C. For a time, it seemed that Persian naval forces might again invade the Aegean. To meet the immediate danger posed to the league's treasure on the unfortified island of Delos, it was agreed to move the fund to the heavily guarded Acropolis at Athens. When peace was made with Persia in 448 B.C., however, the money was not moved back. The leaders of Athens assumed sole control of this enormous sum of five thousand talents, and insisted that the annual sums thereafter be paid to Athens. During the following decades, this money was used to maintain the Athenian navy, to erect the remarkable series of buildings on the Acropolis, and to finance future wars. Meetings of the league's assembly stopped; the league had become an Athenian empire.

Some members of the league strongly objected to this new regime and rebelled against it, but their naval weakness made them easy to suppress. Rebellious states were compelled to accept democratic, pro-Athenian governments; other states had their legal and commercial relations with Athens subjected to regulation. A few were forced to accept Athenian garrisons, or to cede territory for Athenian settlers. Pericles was mainly responsible for this program. He envisioned an idealized Athens, both as a supreme military power and as a model of political organization and advanced culture. "Our state," he said, "is the education of Hellas."

Pericles' more extreme acts of imperialism were condemned by conservatives such as the statesman Thucydides (c. 485-c. 425 B.C.), but by the 440's some thousands of Athenians received wages for various services from the annual payments of the allies. As a result the majority backed Pericles, and Thucydides was ostracized. "It may have been wrong to acquire the empire," said Pericles, "but it would certainly be dangerous to let it go." Thus, while defense had dictated the punishment of Naxos, imperial power compelled the Athenians to keep their grip on their former allies. Athens, in its own eyes "the educator of Hellas," was the tyrant-city to other Greeks. When the Peloponnesian War broke out in 431 B.C., most Greeks supported Sparta in the hope of seeing Athenian power destroyed.

Athenian imperialism was regrettable because it was, in most respects, the most advanced state in Greece. Athens was democratic. It tolerated free speech to a remarkable degree. Athens provided work for its poor and treated its slaves with relative humanity. From all parts of the Hellenic world artists, poets, and scholars streamed in, so that Athens became the cultural and philosophical center of Greece, a first "world city." Yet the Athenians' passion for empire turned much of the world against them, and

perhaps prevented the Delian League from becoming a vehicle for the gradual and voluntary unification of the numerous small, quarrelsome Greek states.

The possibility of this transformation highlights the relationship between internal politics and foreign policy. The early Delian League was nonimperial largely because Athens was balanced internally—in leadership, between an Ephialtes and a Cimon; institutionally, between an Aeropagetic Council and a popular Assembly. The events about 462 B.C. permanently upset these balances, opening the way for imperial policies. In time, Pericles became as dominant internally as Athens did externally. Each had ceased to be a first among equals, the condition necessary for a peaceful transformation.

—Samuel K. Eddy, updated by John F. Wilson

ADDITIONAL READING:

Fornara, Charles W., and Loren J. Samons II. *Athens from Cleisthenes to Pericles*. Berkeley: University of California Press, 1991. Comprehensive in historical scope and interestingly detailed, this work emphasizes the interplay of Athenian democracy and the acquisition of empire.

Kagan, Donald. *Pericles of Athens and the Birth of Democracy*. New York: Free Press, 1991. Part history, part biography, this semipopular work presents Pericles as commanding Athenian figure and model for contemporary democratic leadership.

McGregor, Malcolm F. *The Athenians and Their Empire*. Vancouver: University of British Columbia Press, 1987. Thorough, readable, and relatively succinct, McGregor's work concludes that the Persian threat justified Athenian actions.

Plutarch. *The Lives of the Noble Grecians and Romans*. New York: Modern Library, n.d. The indispensable primary source for the lives of "Aristides," "Cimon," and "Pericles."

Rhodes, P. J. "The Delian League to 449 B.C." and "The Athenian Revolution." In *The Cambridge Ancient History*, by D. M. Lewis et al. 2d ed. Vol 5. New York: Cambridge University Press, 1992. Scholarly, critical, yet accessible, these and related essays in this newly revised standard source provide a sound overview.

Stockton, David. *The Classical Athenian Democracy*. New York: Oxford University Press, 1990. The early chapters of Stockton's work discuss the reforms which led to "Periclean democracy."

SEE ALSO: 483 B.C., Naval Law of Themistocles; 480-479 B.C., Persian Invasion of Greece 447-438 B.C., The Parthenon Is Built; 431-404 B.C., Peloponnesian War; 415-413 B.C., Athenian Invasion of Sicily; 401-400 B.C., March of the "Ten Thousand."

451-449 B.C.

THE "TWELVE TABLES" OF ROMAN LAW

The "Twelve Tables" of Roman law establishes a code of laws to check the power of the patricians against the lower orders of Roman society.

DATE: 451-449 B.C.

LOCALE: Rome

CATEGORY: Laws, acts, and legal history

KEY FIGURES:

Appius Claudius,
Publius Curiatius,
Titus Genucius,
Gaius Julius,
Aulus Manlius,
Spurius Postumius,
Titus Romilius,
Publius Sestius,
Publius Sulpicius, and
Lucius Veturius, decemvirs in 451 B.C.
Appius Claudius,
Spurius Oppius Cornicen,
Caeso Duillius,
Marcus Cornelius Maluginensis,
Titus Antonius Merenda,
Lucius Minucius,
Quintus Poetelius,
Manius Rabuleus,
Marcus Sergius, and
Quintus Fabius Vibulanus, decemvirs in 450 B.C.

SUMMARY OF EVENT. The formulation of the Twelve Tables of Roman Law, as recorded by Livy and Dionysius of Halicarnassus, was one of the most significant events in the "struggle of the orders" between patricians and plebeians in Rome during the fifth century B.C. In 462 B.C., according to the tradition date, Gaius Terentilius Harsa, a tribune of the plebs, made a spirited attack on the authority of the consuls, charging that their unregulated and unlimited power brought down all the terrors and penalties of the law upon the plebs. Harsa suggested that five men should be appointed to compose a code of laws that would put a check upon the patricians, who, as judges, were interpreters of the unwritten customary law and, as priests, determined the validity of the complex legal procedures. His proposal was rejected, as was another in 454 when the tribunes suggested that a commission composed of both patricians and plebeians should draw up the code.

In 452 B.C., the tribunes insisted that the work of codification should begin. To expedite the task, it was decided that the ordinary magistracies should be suspended and

that, instead, *decemviri legibus scribundis* (ten men for writing the laws) should be chosen to rule the state the following year without being subject to appeal. After some debate, the plebeians agreed to surrender their demand to be represented on the board along with the patricians, but they did so with the understanding that their sacral laws would not be abrogated.

The ten elected decemvirs set about framing the laws and set them up on ten tables in the Forum. After amending them according to suggestions received, they presented their work to the *comitia centuriata* for formal ratification. It soon became apparent that two more tables would have to be added to make the corpus complete, and so the decemvirs were again elected by the *comitia centuriata* after considerable canvassing. Appius Claudius, who had been chairman of the first decemvirate, was reelected with nine new colleagues.

The second decemvirate is traditionally pictured as drafting the two additional tables amid a reign of terror. For some unknown reason, they began to act like tyrants by oppressing the plebeians, and only a secession of the plebs forced them out of office at the expiration of their commission. Legendary though much of this account of the formulation of the Twelve Tables may be, there is little doubt about the antiquity of the ancient code, which Livy, with some exaggeration, describes as "the source of all public and private law" for Rome.

While the original text of the Twelve Tables is said to have been lost in the sack of Rome by the Gauls around 390 B.C., copies remained so that Cicero reported in his *De legibus* that boys still had to memorize them in his day. Provisions of the code were never repealed, although many lapsed through neglect and irrelevancy. Some 140 fragments or paraphrases show that the code was genuinely Roman in content and largely a codification of already existing custom. The code had only two constitutional provisions: one forbidding *privilegia*, and the other forbidding trial of a citizen on a capital charge by any assembly except the *comitia centuriata*. Dealing with private, public, and sacral law, the code concerned itself, among other matters, with the guardianship and status of women and property, the guardianship of lunatics and prodigals, division of inheritances, and rights concerning land. Assembly at night was forbidden. The laws were absolute imperatives and protected property above life; an insolvent debtor, for example, could be fettered for sixty days and then executed or put up for sale. Many believed that the code allowed dismemberment of a debtor's body to satisfy several creditors. A person was permitted to kill a thief only if the thief came at night or actually used a weapon. Deformed children were to be killed. Blood revenge was recognized if satisfaction was denied in other ways. As absolute head of the family, the father could, with certain safeguards, sell his sons into slavery. Although marriage rites were simple, intermarriage between plebeian and patrician was forbidden. Penalties were harsh, and death was meted out in five different ways, including burning at the stake and casting from the Tarpeian rock. Bribery, libel, sorcery, cutting other people's crops, and even theft were capital offenses. Besides the death penalty, other forms of punishments that were recognized included being fined, fettered, or flogged; retaliation in kind; civil disgrace; banishment, and slavery. Fines for injuring persons were graduated according to the value traditionally ascribed to individuals. Plebeians gained benefits through a law allowing a thirty-day interval to discharge a debt before the infliction of penalty. Interest was fixed, probably at eight and one-third percent, and "not according to the free choice of the wealthy."

Apart from obvious legal significance, the Twelve Tables are of great interest to philologists because of the archaic language used and to historians because the ordinances provide the best information available on the economic and social conditions of Rome during the fifth century B.C.

—*M. Joseph Costelloe, updated by Jeffrey L. Buller*

ADDITIONAL READING:

Coleman-Norton, P. R. *The Twelve Tables Prefaced, Arranged, Translated, Annotated*. Princeton, N.J.: Princeton University Press, 1952. The best place to begin for readers interested in examining the primary source material on the Twelve Tables.

Diosdi, Gyorgy. *Contract in Roman Law: From the Twelve Tables to the Glossators*. Translated by J. Szabo. Budapest: Akademiai Kiado, 1981. Limited to only one aspect of the legal code, this work traces the development of Roman contract law from its origins in the Twelve Tables.

Gardner, Jane F. *Being a Roman Citizen*. New York: Routledge, 1993. A good introduction for the general reader on the impact of Roman law upon private life. Written in a popular style but well researched.

Lobingier, Charles Sumner. *The Evolution of the Roman Law*. Littleton, Colo.: F. B. Rothman, 1987. Although now somewhat dated (it was originally released in 1923), this work is still an excellent survey of Roman law from the period before the Twelve Tables to the major legal codes of the late Empire.

Scott, S. P. *The Civil Law*. Cincinnati: Central Trust Company, 1973. First issued in 1932, this work provides a translation of the Twelve Tables, along with other legal

codes later influenced by it, including the Institutes of Gaius, the Rules of Ulpian, the Opinions of Paulus, the Enactments of Justinian, and the Constitutions of Leo.

Watson, Alan. *The Evolution of Law*. Baltimore: The Johns Hopkins University Press, 1985. A good general introduction on the history and development of Roman law.

SEE ALSO: 445 B.C., The Canuleian Law; 340-338 B.C., Origin of *Municipia*; 300 B.C., Stoic Conception of Natural Law; 287 B.C., The *Lex Hortensia*; 90 B.C., Julian Law.

450-425 B.C.
HISTORY DEVELOPS AS SCHOLARLY DISCIPLINE

History develops as scholarly discipline, establishing historiography as a literary and scientific genre.

DATE: c. 450-425 B.C.

LOCALE: Samos, Athens, and the Greek colony of Thurii in Italy

CATEGORIES: Cultural and intellectual history; Education

KEY FIGURES:

Hecataeus of Miletus (fl. c. 575 B.C.), early geographer and genealogist

Herodotus (484-c. 425 B.C.), Greek historian

Thucydides (c. 460-c. 400 B.C.), Greek historian

SUMMARY OF EVENT. Herodotus' monumental history of the Persian wars, written during the second half of the fifth century B.C., established its author as, in Cicero's words, "the father of history." It is an extraordinary work, combining history in the modern sense with geography, anthropology, and comparative religion.

Part of the unprecedented intellectual movement that began in the fifth century B.C., Herodotus was in the midst of a philosophical revolution initiated by Socrates, perfected by Plato, and culminating with Aristotle. In an analogous fashion, Herodotus initiated the new style of historiography, Hecataeus of Miletus solidified the notion of scientific historical and geographical evidence, and Thucydides crowned their efforts.

Like most genres, history did not achieve maturity in its first form. Herodotus, while groping for the historical perspective mastered by Thucydides a generation later, retained many characteristics of his diverse predecessors. Homer influenced him significantly; critics have pointed out that epic poetry, for centuries the repository of records of the Greek past, probably hindered the development of history as a discipline through its emphasis on the biographical, rather than the institutional, its theistic-humanistic philosophy, and its appeal to romance and excitement.

Herodotus clearly derived much from the poets: the art of holding interest by intermingling digressions with narrative, the significance put on characterization of leaders, and, most important, a view of history as controlled to a great degree by the gods. Like his contemporaries, the great dramatists Sophocles and Aeschylus, Herodotus followed Homer in viewing human affairs as divinely ordained; man is a creature of fate, often a suffering victim. Like the heroes of classical tragedy, Herodotus' kings and princes become arrogant in their wealth and power and bring catastrophe upon themselves. Once Xerxes chastises the sea, the reader knows his great host crossing the Hellespont is headed toward destruction.

Although Herodotus worked objectively, sometimes resembling a modern-day anthropologist or ethnographer, he imbued his work with divine plans and predestinations in the Homeric tradition. The use of history to defend the existence of a divine power is common in ancient and modern historiography. The eighteenth century historian Edward Gibbon believed in divine cycles in history, each of which was initiated by a divine figure such as Moses, Jesus, or Mohammed. Thucydides, in contrast to Herodotus, treated history in a more dispassionate manner. He was interested in the simple formula of "Who, what, where, and when?" His *History of the Peloponnesian War* is a masterpiece of historiography. He advised historians not to be "masked by exaggerated fancies of the poets" or the stories of chroniclers who "seek to please the ear rather than to speak the truth."

While epic was the most popular record of the past in the Greek world of the seventh and sixth centuries B.C., Ionian writers were gradually developing prose accounts of the geography and customs of the areas they visited as they sailed on trading expeditions around the Mediterranean. The exposure to a variety of cultures seems to have developed in them a rational, often skeptical spirit, and they began to cast the eye of reason upon the myths that passed for history among their people. Only fragments have survived to indicate the nature of these semihistorical works. The remains of two treatises by Hecataeus of Miletus, who wrote during the latter part of the sixth century B.C., are probably representative of the new school of thought. In his *Genealogies*, he attempted to give rational explanations for familiar tales of the gods and heroes who were purportedly the ancestors of the Greeks of his own day. More significant for Herodotus was Hecataeus' *Periezesis*, his account of his observations on his journeys into Egypt, Persia, mainland Greece, and the countries near the Black Sea.

Thus, Herodotus began his work with a foundation in the epic concept of the relationship of god and man, and an Ionian-inspired curiosity about man and society, along with a rationalistic and skeptical approach to mythical history. To these perspectives must be added his strong pro-Athenian bias. Born in the Dorian city of Halicarnassus on the coast of Asia Minor, Herodotus lived in Athens for much of the period between 454 and 443, when he helped to colonize Thurii in Italy. He was thus a part of the flowering of Periclean Athens during the years between the end of the Persian wars in 479 and the beginning of the Peloponnesian conflict in 431. It was during these years that he probably derived his strong faith in the free state and its ability to triumph over tyranny, a belief that becomes a significant theme in the histories.

To assess the *Persian Wars* as history, it is perhaps useful to note that the Greek word *histor* means "observer," or "recorder," rather than "analyst of facts," and Herodotus is a historian in this sense more than in the modern one. Especially in the first six books he refers over and over again to what he has seen or what he has been told. He does not uncritically accept everything he hears, but neither does he attempt to sort out every conflicting account.

Like Thucydides, Herodotus was committed to objective reporting. In Book VII of his *Persian Wars* he writes, "My duty is to report all that is said, but I am not obliged to believe it all alike." For the most part he was fair and impartial. For example, despite his fervent Greek patriotism, he gave a meticulous and largely accurate account of the enemy's history and cultural practices.

Herodotus' work begins with a discussion of the earliest conflicts between the near-eastern and western Mediterranean cultures and an account of the growth of the Persian Empire. As he recounts each new conquest, he digresses to describe the customs of the soon-to-be-invaded nation: Lydia, ruled by the legendary Croesus, Assyria, Egypt, Ethiopia, Scythia, India, and Arabia. He traces the careers of successive Persian monarchs, Cyrus, Cambyses, and Darius, setting the stage for the massive expedition of Xerxes against the Greeks. Initially more digression than narrative, Herodotus' work sharpens its focus as it moves toward the climax, the account of the battles that culminated in the Persian defeat at Salamis.

Herodotus was criticized by ancient and modern historians on various charges. Plutarch dubbed him "the flatterer of Athens." He was considered by various historians a mere industrious compiler of gossip, a moralizer, inept in military tactics and statistics. For example, he reported the size of the Persian army as five million—too inflated by any ancient or modern estimation. He was also accused of plagiarism, dishonestly using Ionian chronicles as eyewitness reports and even doing that uncritically. Some downplayed his *Persian Wars* as inconsistent, lacking unity of purpose or direction.

Some of these accusations have been proven false or exaggerated. Herodotus worked within the limitations of his time. He had little evidence to verify the accounts of his eyewitnesses. He was careful in crediting what he heard, distinguishing between things he saw and things he only heard. He revisited battlefields and alleged army routes. He often used inscriptions on monuments and quoted extensively from temple records at Delphi. As a tourist-historian at Egyptian pyramids, he gave a meticulous, although at times speculative, account of what he saw. Only in the last two centuries have geographers, archaeologists, and anthropologists confirmed many of his observations.

Herodotus was an intelligent and observant historian with good faith and tolerance for diverse cultures. The unity of his work comes from his deep religious convictions and notion of history as divine epic. Many historians consider him the father of history without whose work modern readers would have been deprived of invaluable insights into the ancient world.

—*Elizabeth J. Lipscomb, updated by Chogollah Maroufi*

ADDITIONAL READING:

Bury, J. B. *The Ancient Greek Historians*. New York: Dover Publications, 1958. The classic account of Greek historiography.

Brunt, P. A. *Studies in Greek History and Thought*. New York: Oxford University Press, 1993. Meticulous accounts of early Greek ideas on historiography and historical analysis.

Gentili, Bruno, and Cerri Giovanni. *History and Biography in Ancient Thought*. Amsterdam: J. C. Gieben, 1988. An analysis of the notions of truth, observation, and divine causality in ancient historiography.

Hornblower, Simon, ed. *Greek Historiography*. Oxford: Clarendon Press, 1994. This is a challenging and rich book. It has a thorough and extensive introduction (seventy-two pages) and an extensive bibliography.

Myers, John. *Herodotus: Father of History*. Oxford: Oxford University Press, 1953. A general and thorough account of Herodotus' life and accomplishments.

SEE ALSO: 480-479 B.C., Persian Invasion of Greece; 440 B.C., Teachings of the Sophists; 431-404 B.C., Peloponnesian War; 380 B.C., Plato Develops His Theory of Ideas; 335-323 B.C., Aristotle Writes the *Politics*; 325-323 B.C., Aristotle Isolates Science as a Discipline.

447-438 B.C.
THE PARTHENON IS BUILT

The Parthenon is built, using a revolutionary combination of Doric and Ionic orders to create a higher standard of architectural excellence while giving rise to still newer forms in Greek art.

DATE: 447-438 B.C.
LOCALE: Athens, Greece
CATEGORY: Cultural and intellectual history
KEY FIGURES:
Ictinius and *Callicrates* (fl. 440 B.C.), architects in charge of design and construction of the Parthenon
Pericles (c. 495-429 B.C.), political leader of Athens, 461-429 B.C.
Phidias (490-430 B.C.), master sculptor and overseer of art work for the Parthenon

SUMMARY OF EVENT. The Parthenon, dedicated to Athena the Maiden, is the most famous of Greek temples, the crowning monument of the Athenian Acropolis. It was built on the remains of an older temple begun in 490 B.C. to celebrate the Athenian victory over the Persians in the Battle of Marathon. This temple was destroyed when the Persians returned and invaded Athens in 480 B.C. With the help of Sparta, Athens was able to defeat the Persians in 479 B.C. near Plataea. There, on the battlefield, the Greeks took an oath not to rebuild the ruined temples as a reminder of the devastation caused by the Persian invasion. By 449 B.C., Athens had made peace with Persia and this oath was no longer binding. Thus, in 447 B.C., Athens began to build a new Parthenon. Of the Doric order but with Ionic architectural features such as the continuous frieze, the new Parthenon was built under Pericles in 447-438 B.C. by the architects Ictinius and Callicrates. The sculptor Phidias was responsible for the design and composition of its decorative reliefs and statuary, which continued to be added to the structure through 432 B.C. Constructed entirely of Pentelic marble upon a limestone foundation, it is peripteral octastyle in plan, being encompassed by a single row of columns, with eight at each end and in this instance seventeen on each side. At the top step of the stylobate or substructure, the building measures 228 feet by 101 feet, so that it is exceptionally wide in proportion to its length. Within the peristyle of columns stood the enclosed cella, or main room, and a back chamber, each fronted by a porch with six columns. At both ends, metal grilles between these columns completely enclosed the two chambers. The cella, with its door facing east, had interior columns in two levels at the sides and rear. Within this main gallery, visitors could view the colossal cult statue, the gold and ivory Athena of Phidias, set at the far

Although the Parthenon was partially restored during the twentieth century, many of the friezes and other decorative elements remain in the collections of foreign museums, including the Elgin Marbles housed at the British Museum. (Library of Congress)

end of the room. The foundation of the pedestal, all that remains of this great work, measures twenty-six by thirteen feet. The back chamber or *opistodomos*, with its door opening to the west and with four interior columns, may have served as a treasury for gifts dedicated to the goddess. It was this chamber, officially known as the Parthenon or Chamber of the Virgin, which gave rise to the name of the building as a whole. The chamber of the virgins, or the Parthenon, was that room set aside in Athenian homes for the use of the virgin daughter before her marriage.

Chief among the sculptural decorations of the Parthenon were the metopes in high relief on the entablature, the continuous frieze in low relief above the wall of the two chambers, and the fully sculptured groups in the pediments at each end of the temple. The themes of this art glorify the goddess and the city of which she was patron; the metopes depicted notable combats—Lapiths against Centaurs, Olympians against giants, and Greeks against Amazons—to symbolize the victory of civilization over barbarism which was how the Athenians viewed their vic-

tory over the Persians. The frieze was remarkable in that it showed the Athenian citizenry involved in the contemporary event of the great Panathenaic procession in honor of the goddess. This procession took place every four years. Until this time, Greeks had been ambivalent about depicting current historical events. Now they did so and though the procession was in honor of Athena, the goddess, many of the human beings themselves portrayed godlike qualities.

The western pediment portrayed the contest between Athena and Poseidon for dominion over the city, while the eastern one depicted the birth of Athena. Here, the gods portrayed humanlike qualities. Of the purely architectural features, the columns stand thirty-four and a half feet high, the equal of about five and a half lower diameters of the columns. From the stylobate to the peak of the gabled roof, the structure stood more than sixty-one feet in height. Rectangular coffered blocks of marble supported by a sequence of pillars, beams, and walls, made up the ceiling, above which was a network of timbers to sustain the low-pitched roof. Yet even the roof tiles were cut from marble.

Although the earliest Greek temples were constructed of sun-dried brick and wood, hard limestone, conglomerate, and marble became the chief materials after the seventh century B.C. Athens was well endowed with marble from Mount Pentelicus to the northeast of the city. After being roughly cut in the quarries there, the blocks were brought to the Acropolis in wagons. Hoisting was accomplished by means of pulleys and tongs, the lewis or iron tenon fitting into a dove-tailed mortise in the stone. To bond the stones set vertically, such as the individual drums of the columns, iron or bronze dowels set in molten lead connected the top of one drum to the bottom of the one above it. Horizontal bonding of stone beams was achieved by the double-T or H type of clamp. The Greeks never used mortar or nails in this kind of construction, and great care was taken to assure perfect contacts along the surface joins of the marble. Even in the twentieth century, many of these joins were so tight that a razor blade could not be inserted between the blocks.

Many elements in the Hellenic temple came from other Mediterranean cultures—the floor plan from Crete, the columnar structure from Egypt, and the capitals from Assyria—but the genius of the evolving Doric form was typically Greek in its simplicity, its balance of proportions and its complementary use of Ionic sculpture and decoration. As the perfection of this type, the Parthenon also includes a number of unique refinements which make it a dynamic creation and a moving visual experience. Among these are the drooping or horizontal curvature of the stylobate toward all four corners, so that, for example, on the long sides the rise from the ends to the center of the structure is about four inches. The columns have both diminution or tapering of the shaft from the bottom up and also entasis or a slight convex swelling in the shaft. Furthermore, all the outside columns incline slightly toward the cella walls; the four angle columns are thicker than the others and by virtue of their position have a double inclination. Last, the chief vertical surfaces such as the cella wall have a backward slope, but the entablature above the columns has a slightly forward tilt. These and other refinements were probably incorporated to correct optical illusions which would otherwise make the stylobate appear to sag, the entablature to recede, and the angle columns to appear thin against the sky. Whatever the reasons, the refinements combine with other features of the Parthenon, such as the Ionic frieze and the tendency of the overall sculpture in the building to deify the humans and to humanize the Gods, to make it a nearly perfect building at the same time as it revolutionized conceptions of what was human and divine and brought into question what would

be the future basis of architectural forms in Greek society.

The Parthenon survived in fairly whole condition until 1687, when it was badly damaged by an explosion during a war between the Turks and the Venetians. More than a century later, Lord Elgin brought most of the surviving sculptures to London in order to save them from piecemeal destruction. Consequently, a full appreciation of the Parthenon requires a visit to the British Museum in London, where the so-called Elgin Marbles are on display, and to Athens, to view the partially restored temple.

—Kevin Herbert, updated by Jennifer Eastman

ADDITIONAL READING:

Bruno, Vincent J., ed. *The Parthenon*. New York: W. W. Norton, 1974. Collection of essays and illustrations on the history and construction of the Parthenon. Includes an essay by Dinsmoor.

Dinsmoor, W. B. *The Architecture of Ancient Greece*. 3d ed. London: Batsford, 1950. A comprehensive and reliable handbook with many illustrations.

Jenkins, Ian. *The Parthenon Frieze*. Austin: University of Texas Press, 1994. Concise history of the Parthenon with varying interpretations about the meaning of the frieze.

Rhodes, Robin Francis. *Architecture and Meaning on the Athenian Acropolis*. New York: Cambridge University Press, 1995. Rhodes stresses the importance of the combination of the Doric and Ionic orders and the tendency to deify the human and humanize the divine in the building of the Parthenon.

Woodford, Susan. *The Parthenon*. Cambridge, England: Cambridge University Press, 1981. Concise and accessible overview of the entire history of the Parthenon from 490 B.C. through the late twentieth century.

SEE ALSO: 775 B.C., Oracle at Delphi; 480-479 B.C., Persian Invasion of Greece; 312 B.C., First Roman Aqueduct Is Built; 240 B.C., Exploitation of the Arch.

445 B.C.
THE CANULEIAN LAW

The Canuleian Law continues a process of Roman political reform through the issuance of social legislation.
DATE: 445 B.C.
LOCALE: Rome
CATEGORIES: Laws, acts, and legal history; Social reform
KEY FIGURE:
Gaius Canuleius, plebeian tribune of Rome in 445 B.C.
SUMMARY OF EVENT. During the last decade of the sixth century B.C., the political community already established in Rome took its first steps toward the Republican consti-

tution of the first century B.C. The traditional system of kingship was overthrown and replaced by two magistrates equipped with broad executive powers who were elected annually. Legislative initiative and political power were vested in the senate, a self-sustaining body of elder counselors. Although both these organs of government appeared to be republican in character, they were unable to forestall civil strife at Rome and reflected the basic discrepancy in Roman society behind that strife. This dichotomy was the so-called struggle of the orders, a class conflict that was contested on almost all levels of communal life.

The two classes engaged in the struggle were known as patricians and plebeians. After 509 B.C., the traditional date for the beginning of the Roman Republic, the plebeians held an inferior position within the Roman state. They were excluded from political office and the senate, since such honors were reserved for the patricians. Furthermore, the plebeians were barred from the official religious bodies of the state and, by one of the laws in the Twelve Tables, from intermarriage with the patricians. The cause and significance of these prohibitions can be found in the underlying social structure of Rome.

The predominant social unit was the *gens* or clan, which was composed of a group of families linked by a common name and the veneration of a common male ancestor. The origin of the *gens* structure has been keenly disputed, but there is general agreement among scholars that it was an outgrowth of the economic progress within the early agrarian society of Rome. Increased wealth caused a split into upper and lower classes that hardened into richer and poorer families. Members of the richer and more powerful clans called themselves patricians from their exclusive hold on the senate, whose original members were termed *patres*, or fathers. This nobility of wealth eventually became a nobility of blood that claimed for itself full citizenship and total dominance in all aspects of political life. For the fifth century B.C., scholars have found evidence of the existence of fifty such patrician clans, entrenched in power and maintained by privilege.

Opposed to the patricians were the plebeians. Scholars have debated their origin, but plebeians were probably not racially distinct from the patricians. In general, plebeians were the poorer elements of Roman society who had not shared in the economic advances of the early years of Roman history. This original core was augmented by the workers and peasants who had either been attracted to Rome by its commercial growth or engulfed by the spread of Roman conquest. Together, these various strands formed the *plebs*, or multitude. The plebeians were not a servile class; they always possessed a number of political and civil rights. Furthermore, the plebeians also had a *gens*

structure within which individual plebeian clans gradually increased in size and wealth. They gradually became discontented with their second-class status; throughout the first half of the fifth century, they repeatedly demanded, and obtained, greater equity within the state. The plebeians acquired their own officials, the tribunes of the *plebs*, to act as their protectors and leaders. In 449 B.C., a special commission completed the first written codification of law at Rome, the famous Twelve Tables, which made knowledge of the law accessible to everyone. These gains were not obtained without patrician resistance, however, as evidenced by the inclusion in the Twelve Tables of the ban on intermarriage—a blatant reminder that the plebeians did not enjoy total equality.

It is misleading to say that marriage between the two groups was completely forbidden. Roman law recognized various forms of marriage, the simplest being the mere cohabitation of a man and a woman. If such an arrangement persisted without interruption for one year, the two parties were considered legally married, except in the case of patricians and plebeians. A plebeian woman could share the house of a patrician man for the required period without becoming patrician, and the children of such a union were not considered patrician. The decisive factor in this arrangement was a religious one. The only valid marriage ceremony for patricians was the solemn religious ritual called *confarreatio*. For a valid marriage between the two groups, therefore, the plebeians would have to be permitted entrance into the tenaciously guarded domain of patrician religion.

This impasse was circumvented in 445 B.C. by Gaius Canuleius, a tribune of the people, who proposed a law rescinding the ban on intermarriage. The law did not eliminate the exclusion of plebeians from the ceremony of *confarreatio*; instead, it recognized cohabitation and another secular form of marriage as legally binding so that a wife and her children gained patrician status. It seems probable that the patricians at first rejected even this compromise, which left their religion intact. The plebeians countered with their most effective weapon, a mass withdrawal from the communal life of the city. This drastic measure compelled the patricians to accept the law. With its enactment, the plebeians shed another vestige of their inferior status. Civil strife between the two classes persisted, but for the plebeians, the Canuleian Law came to stand as one of their more gratifying victories.

—George M. Pepe, updated by Jeffrey L. Buller

ADDITIONAL READING:

Buckland, William Warwick. A Manual of Roman Private Law. 2d ed. Cambridge, England: Cambridge University Press, 1953. Still the best source available for a detailed analysis of the major laws affecting Roman citizenship and private life.

Crook, John Anthony. *Law and Life of Rome*. Ithaca, N.Y.: Cornell University Press, 1967. Discusses the evolution of ancient Roman law within the context of social conditions.

Gardner, Jane F. *Being a Roman Citizen*. New York: Routledge, 1993. A good introduction for the general reader on the impact of Roman law upon private life. Written in a popular style but well researched.

Kunkel, Wolfgang. *An Introduction to Roman Legal and Constitutional History*. Translated by J. M. Kelly. Oxford: Clarendon Press, 1973. Presents, in a manageable format, a survey of the major developments in the Roman legal code.

Last, Hugh. "The Servian Reforms." *Journal of Roman Studies* 35 (1945): 30-48. A major revisionist interpretation of Roman law, arguing that intermarriage of the classes had actually occurred before the formal passage of the Canuleian Law.

Watson, Alan. *The Evolution of Law*. Baltimore: The Johns Hopkins University Press, 1985. A good general introduction on the history and development of Roman law.

SEE ALSO: 340-338 B.C., Origin of *Municipia*; 300 B.C., Stoic Conception of Natural Law; 287 B.C., The *Lex Hortensia*; 180 B.C., Establishment of the *Cursus Honorum*.

440 B.C.
TEACHINGS OF THE SOPHISTS

The teachings of the Sophists mark the emergence of an educational movement.

DATE: c. 440 B.C.

LOCALE: Greek-speaking communities throughout the Mediterranean world

CATEGORIES: Cultural and intellectual history; Education

KEY FIGURES:

Antiphon the Sophist (c. 480-410 B.C.), Athenian Sophist and rhetorician associated with distinguishing between *nomos* and *physis*

Gorgias of Leontini (c. 483-376 B.C.), Greek Sophist important in the development of rhetorical theory

Hippias of Elis (c. 475-400 B.C.), prominent Greek Sophist

Prodicus of Ceos (c. 470-400 B.C.), Greek Sophist noted for his concern with precise language; influenced Socrates

Protagoras of Abdera (c. 481-411 B.C.), Greek Sophist prominent for doctrines of epistemological relativism and agnosticism

Thrasymachus of Chalcedon (fl. c. 459 B.C.), Greek Sophist known for his belief that justice is a matter of human convention

SUMMARY OF EVENT. The Sophists, literally "wise ones," arose in the second half of the fifth century B.C. in response to a recognized need in the more advanced Greek states for training in the skills needed for active participation in political life. Traditional education consisted of appropriation of aristocratic ideals embodied in the poetic tradition and in military education, but this training was felt to be inadequate to impart the skills of political leadership in states where success depended upon the ability to sway votes in the courts and the popular assembly, and upon awareness of the principles of community organization. To meet this need, the Sophists emerged as itinerant educators making the rounds of Greek cities and offering courses of instruction to anyone willing to pay. Although their name suggests they were organized into a school, the Sophists had no direct affiliation with one another. They did, however, all claim to teach *politite arete*, the civic virtues considered necessary for a life of public service. One of the better known Sophists, Protagoras, claimed that any man who went through his course of instruction would learn "to order his own house in the best manner and be able to speak and act for the best in the affairs of the state."

While the Sophists offered courses of instruction in a variety of subjects, including history, mathematics, and literature, the ability to sway votes in courtroom or assembly was a fundamental political skill, so the Sophists placed special emphasis on the teaching of rhetoric and were the first to organize it into an art. Credited with being the first to suggest that there were two sides to every controversial question, Protagoras defined the nature and function of the orator as the ability to speak with equal persuasiveness to them both and to fortify a weaker argument so as to make it the most convincing. Gorgias simply defined rhetoric as "the art of persuasion."

The methods of rhetorical training employed by the Sophists were the debate and the set speech. The debate was an imitation of the courtroom situation, wherein speakers had to present, as convincingly as possible, the arguments for both the prosecution and the defense. The set speech might exemplify the presentation of a policy before the popular assembly or present a persuasive reinterpretation of some conventional myth, offering a convincing reversal of value judgments on characters in the myth. Thus, the *Encomium of Helen*, a set speech by Gorgias, argued the view that Helen, far from being guilty of criminal adultery, was the innocent victim of forces beyond her control. Gorgias' *Encomium of Helen* neatly exemplifies some of the assumptions of Sophistic rhetorical theory: that human psychology may be understood in terms of physico-chemical causation, that speech bears no necessary relationship to objective reality but plays upon men's hopes and fears to dislodge firmly held convictions and moral principles and to implant new perspectives with the same inevitable efficacy that drugs have when administered to the body.

The impact of Sophistic rhetorical training on Athenian life is clearly evident in the literature of the later years of the fifth century B.C., especially in the history of Thucydides and the plays of Euripides and Aristophanes. A critical disposition of mind toward traditional values was fostered; eloquence of speech came to be admired and often to be practiced with a cynical awareness that an argument need not be valid to be persuasive; and there were growing doubts of the efficacy of traditional values to govern human conduct, which was increasingly viewed as governed by nonpredictable compulsions.

Unlike their most immediate intellectual predecessors, the Greek natural philosophers, the Sophists were more interested in exploring the relation of human beings to

The Wasps *and other works by the Athenian dramatist Aristophanes reflect the influence of the Sophists, who emphasized the importance of eloquent speech and rhetoric.* (Library of Congress)

each other than to the cosmos. Sophistic anthropology and political science were consciously founded on humanistic assumptions rather than on traditionally recognized divinely sanctioned principles. Protagoras made the first widely publicized open declaration of agnosticism concerning the nature and activities of the gods, and he also propounded the doctrine of the relativity of human knowledge: "Of all things the measure is [each single] man, of things that are, that they are, and of things that are not, that they are not." With the logical priority of the individual over the group thus assumed, it is only reasonable to argue that the Sophists saw the values of any particular human community as artificial conventions, distinct from the conventions of other communities and imposing arbitrary limitations upon an individual human being, whose natural inclination could be empirically recognized as essentially self-interested and aggressive. That *nomos*, the conventional values and laws of a particular community, were artificial limitations imposed upon the universally self-assertive nature, or *physics*, of the individual man thus became a widely accepted view in the later years of the fifth century, a view finding varied expression in literature as well as in formulations of public policy.

As a consequence of this view of the nature of individual man and of human communities, the principle of justice came to be defined by some Sophists, most notably by Thrasymachus, as the "advantage of the stronger party" in any community. Traditionally, justice had been held to be a divinely sanctioned principle of distribution of rights and privileges in the human community, but it was now held by the Sophists to be a reflection of the power structure of any state. For example, in an oligarchy, a minority, by virtue of its control of army and police, enforces a distribution of wealth and privileges which benefits itself; in a democracy, the majority has seized and maintains power to assure an equality of distribution of rights and privileges. In Plato's *Republic*, Socrates sharply criticizes Thrasymachus' view of justice and argues that not only justice but all moral virtues are objectively real and good in themselves. In other dialogues, Socrates opposes additional Sophistic teachings, including the idea that virtue is teachable. While Socrates is arguably the most famous Athenian opposed to the views and practices of the Sophists, their oligarchical associations, their skepticism about traditional beliefs concerning the gods, and their educational emphasis on the credibility of an argument rather than its truth made them the objects of criticism of many Athenian citizens.

The impact of this analysis of human society in terms divorced from traditional moral sanctions was to undermine public confidence in, and voluntary submission to, constituted authority. Encouraged by the new perspective on man and society, groups of young noblemen, who were naturally most directly influenced because they were best able to afford Sophistic instruction, carefully studied the means of gaining power without scruples, and the later years of the Peloponnesian War were marked by violent social upheavals in many Greek states, upheavals made the more violent by the undermining of traditional moral scruples.

—*Carl W. Conrad, updated by Diane P. Michelfelder*

ADDITIONAL READING:

Barrett, Harold. *The Sophists: Rhetoric, Democracy and Plato's Idea of Sophistry.* Novato, Calif.: Chandler and Sharp, 1987. A brief, balanced guide to the thinking of Protagoras, Gorgias, and several other Sophists, as well as a discussion of Plato's antagonism toward their views.

Guthrie, W. K. C. *A History of Greek Philosophy, Vol. 3: The Fifth-Century Enlightenment.* Cambridge, England: Cambridge University Press, 1969. A classic study by a famous scholar of Greek philosophy, with an emphasis on the relation between their moral and political views and their metaphysical ones.

Irvin, Terence, ed. *Classical Philosophy, Vol. 2: Socrates and His Contemporaries.* New York: Garland, 1995. Contains recent and classical essays concerning the moral and political views of the Sophists, as well as their relation to Socrates and Plato.

Rankin, H. D. *Sophists, Socrates, and Cynics.* Totowa, N.J.: Barnes & Noble, 1983. A thorough look at the ideas of both well-known and lesser-known Sophists, as well as an examination of their influence on the writings of Thucydides.

Reale, Giovanni. *From the Origins to Socrates: A History of Ancient Philosophy.* Edited and translated by John Cahn. Albany: State University of New York Press, 1987. This accessible, scholarly investigation considers the problems addressed by the Sophists in light of modern philosophical concerns.

SEE ALSO: 399 B.C., Death of Socrates; 380 B.C., Plato Develops His Theory of Ideas; 332 B.C., Founding of Alexandria.

431-404 B.C.
PELOPONNESIAN WAR

The Peloponnesian War, a military conflict between the two greatest powers of ancient Greece, Athens and Sparta, is also the final stage of a long-standing struggle between conflicting political, economic, and social systems.

DATE: May, 431-September, 404 B.C.
LOCALE: Greece
CATEGORIES: Expansion and land acquisition; Wars, uprisings, and civil unrest
KEY FIGURES:
Alcibiades (c. 450-404 B.C.), the unscrupulous Athenian general who betrayed his city to the Spartans for several years in the late 410's
Brasidas (c. 460-422 B.C.), the greatest Spartan general of the late fifth century
Cleon (c. 465-422 B.C.), Athenian demagogue and political leader
Demosthenes (c. 450-413 B.C.), Athenian general
Lysander (c. 440-395 B.C.), Spartan statesman and general who finally defeated Athens
Nicias (c. 470-413 B.C.), a vacillating and superstitious general who was the leader of the peace party in Athens
Pericles (c. 495-429 B.C.), the greatest Athenian statesman and general of the mid-fifth century

SUMMARY OF EVENT. In the late spring of 431 B.C., the tensions that had existed between Athens and Sparta since the end of the Persian Wars suddenly erupted into open conflict. The resulting war became known as the Peloponnesian War because Sparta's area of greatest influence was the Peloponnese ("the Island of Pelops"), the peninsula on which it was located. The causes of the war were longstanding. Yet tensions between Athens and Sparta finally erupted into war when Athens defended the island of Corcyra against Corinth and excluded the city of Megara from commerce with any city in the Athenian empire. Both Corinth and Megara were Spartan allies and the Athenians' actions were taken as open acts of aggression, provoking a war between the two cities that had long vied for domination in Greece.

The military leader Pericles developed a strategy intended to win an easy victory for Athens. Pericles avoided direct conflicts with the much larger Spartan land army and took his forces to the sea, where Athens had an advantage. The entire population of Attica, the region in which Athens was located, withdrew behind the Long Walls, a defensive structure that connected the city to its port. Safe behind these defenses, the Athenians allowed the Spartans to invade Attica. The loss of Attic grain caused by this invasion was not a significant problem. The protection of the Long Walls permitted the Athenians to import substantially all the food they needed by sea.

Nevertheless, the crowding that resulted in Athens because of Pericles' strategy had one effect that the general had not foreseen: the spread of disease. After the first year of the war, a plague erupted in Athens, killing as much as one-quarter of the population. Pericles was fined and not selected as general for the following year. In the intervening period, Pericles himself became ill and died of the plague in the autumn of 429 B.C. Without the guidance of Pericles, the Athenians began to take increasingly brutal measures against their adversaries.

In 428 B.C., Mitylene, a city on the island of Lesbos, attempted to free itself from the Athenian empire. The Athenians resisted this action and starved the city into submission by May of 427 B.C. Back in Athens, the assembly decreed that all Mitylenaean men were to be killed, with the women and children sold into slavery. After a ship had already been dispatched to carry out this decree, the assembly reconvened to examine the severity of its sentence. Cleon, a politician popular with the masses, argued that the punishment of Mitylene had to be carried out as planned. He described the Athenian empire as a tyranny, saying that the state was now compelled to act like a despot and use terror and cruelty in order to keep its subjects in check. In the end, Cleon's arguments failed. The Athenians voted to "lighten" Mitylene's penalty by executing "only" about one thousand of the rebels, seizing the island's fleet, and destroying its defensive walls. Within six years, however, the harsh penalties proposed by Cleon would be used against rebel cities as a matter of ordinary policy, without any further opposition from the assembly.

By 425 B.C., the Athenians appeared to be winning the Peloponnesian War. Demosthenes (not the famous orator, but an earlier general of the same name) established a stronghold at Pylos on the southwest coast of the Peloponnesian peninsula. When the Athenians could not be dislodged from this base, the Spartans sued for peace. Nicias—who was often accused of being pro-Spartan—wanted the Athenian assembly to accept this proposal, but he was resisted by Cleon, who argued that Athens should hold out for better terms. As a result of this argument, Cleon was placed in command of the Athenian force on the Peloponnese and arrived in Pylos to discover that the army there was already planning a massive attack against the Spartans. When this attack occurred, the Spartans endured a loss of nearly a third of their troops and then surrendered, providing the Athenians with a group of hostages that included 120 full Spartan citizens. As Cleon had hoped, the Spartans then offered peace without concessions, proposing that Athens be allowed to keep its empire and all of its possessions.

Cleon sought an even greater victory. He suggested an aggressive campaign against the Spartans that would compel them to yield territory. In 424 B.C., the Spartan general Brasidas captured an Athenian ally (Amphipolis) in north-

ern Greece through a combination of negotiation and strategy. In 422 B.C., in a second battle over Amphipolis, both Cleon and Brasidas were killed. With the death of the leading Athenian opponent to peace, Sparta and Athens signed a treaty in March of 421 B.C. This treaty, known as the Peace of Nicias after its leading negotiator, held until the summer of 416 B.C., when the Athenians attacked the island of Melos, forcing it to join the empire. When Melos was captured, all men of military age were executed and all other citizens were enslaved.

In the following year, the Athenians also began a campaign to extend their empire westward into Sicily. The plan proved to be a disaster. Alcibiades, the former ward of Pericles and one of the Athenian generals sent to Sicily, was recalled just before the battle began on suspicion of having profaned the religious rites of Demeter. On his way back to Athens, Alcibiades slipped his guard and fled to Sparta. Partly because of Alcibiades' betrayal and partly because of the arrival of the Spartan commander Gylippus, a major portion of the Athenian fleet was destroyed in the campaign. Of a total force of forty thousand, only seven thousand soldiers survived the battle and a subsequent retreat inland. Nicias and Demosthenes were killed. The rest of the troops were imprisoned in a quarry, where the harsh conditions killed many.

Although its economy was nearly ruined, Athens used its limited resources to build additional ships and recruit soldiers. The Spartans also chose a new commander, Lysander, an incorruptible politician who had distinguished himself both as a diplomat and as an admiral. In 405 B.C., Lysander captured the Athenian fleet at Aegospotomi ("Goat's Creek") along the Hellespont. Some 170 ships were seized and 4,000 Athenian soldiers were executed after the battle. Lysander then swept the coast of Asia Minor, forcing all Athenians and Athenian supporters to return to Athens. Filled with this excess population and with no means of importing food, Athens was starved out, finally offering unconditional surrender to Sparta in 404 B.C.

The terms imposed by the Spartans were relatively mild: Athens had to adopt Sparta's foreign policy, allow its exiles to return, reduce its fleet to a defensive force of twelve ships, and breach the Long Walls. The defeat of Athens prevented what might otherwise have been a spread of direct democracy throughout much of Greece (and possibly elsewhere in Europe as well). The Peloponnesian War also came to symbolize for many people the conflict between democracy and military oligarchy, freedom and totalitarianism, passion and control.

—Jeffrey L. Buller

ADDITIONAL READING:

Forrest, William George Grieve. *A History of Sparta, 950-192 B.C.* New York: W. W. Norton, 1969. The standard history of Sparta for the general reader; Forrest condenses the Peloponnesian War to a concise account of fewer than twenty pages.

Hooker, J. T. *The Ancient Spartans.* London: J. M. Dent, 1980. A useful history of the Spartans including significant background material on the Peloponnesian War.

Jones, A. H. M. *Sparta.* Oxford: Blackwell and Mott, 1967. A scholarly account of ancient Sparta providing detailed information on its culture, economy, and military structure. Includes both a bibliography and a valuable genealogical table.

Kagan, Donald. *The Fall of the Athenian Empire.* Ithaca, N.Y.: Cornell University Press, 1987. An extensive history of the Peloponnesian War. Extremely readable but with sufficient detail for advanced study.

Lazenby, J. F. *The Spartan Army.* Warminster, England: Aris and Phillips, 1985. A thorough examination of the Spartan military structure and its strategy. Invaluable for an understanding of Spartan campaigns against Athens.

McGregor, Malcolm Francis. *The Athenians and Their Empire.* Vancouver: University of British Columbia Press, 1987. Focuses on the period of Athenian supremacy from the end of the Persian Wars through the fall of Athens in the closing days of the Peloponnesian War.

Meiggs, Russell. *The Athenian Empire.* Oxford: Clarendon Press, 1972. A classic work on Athens in the fifth century B.C. by the twentieth century's foremost scholar of ancient Greek history.

Powell, Anton. *Athens and Sparta.* New York: Routledge, 1991. An excellent study of the political and social relationship between Athens and Sparta from 478 B.C. onward, with special attention given to the period of the Peloponnesian War.

SEE ALSO: 550 B.C., Construction of Trireme Changes Naval Warfare; 478-448 B.C., Athenian Empire Is Created; 415-413 B.C., Athenian Invasion of Sicily.

415-413 B.C.
ATHENIAN INVASION OF SICILY

The Athenian invasion of Sicily fails when the invasion force sent by Athens to Sicily is totally destroyed, setting Athens on its course to inevitable defeat in the Peloponnesian War.

DATE: June, 415-September, 413 B.C.
LOCALE: Syracuse and its environs, island of Sicily

CATEGORIES: Expansion and land acquisition; Wars, uprisings, and civil unrest

KEY FIGURES:
Alcibiades (c. 450-404 B.C.), radical Athenian politician and general
Demosthenes (died 413 B.C.), Athenian general
Gylippus (c. 450-400 B.C.), Spartan general
Hermocrates (c. 455-407 B.C.), Syracusan politician and general
Nicias (c. 470-413 B.C.), conservative Athenian politician and general

SUMMARY OF EVENT. Following the successful conclusion of the series of wars with Persia during the sixth century B.C., the Greek city-states gradually settled into a system of conflicting alliances headed by Athens on the one hand and Sparta on the other, or perched in dangerous neutrality between these two great powers. In 477 B.C., Athens became head of the Delian League, supposedly a purely defensive association of some 150 Greek city-states. Within fifty years, the Delian League had grown to encompass more than 250 city-states and was, for all practical purposes, the Athenian empire, with all league riches flowing into Athens and with Athens setting league foreign policy.

Sparta, Athens' major Greek rival, watched its northern neighbor grow steadily more powerful, especially on sea, where the Spartans were weakest. According to Thucydides, whose history of the great conflict is one of the earliest and greatest of histories, it was this fear of Athenian expansion that led to the outbreak of the Peloponnesian War in 431 B.C. It would last, with several interruptions for uneasy truces that pretended to be peace, until the final and apparently utter defeat of Athens in 404 B.C. One of the factors that led directly to the downfall of Athens was the disaster which overtook its expedition against the city of Syracuse, on the island of Sicily, in 415-413 B.C.

The first phase of the war, known as the Archidamian War for the name of the Spartan king who began it, ended inconclusively in 421 B.C. The years from 421 through 415 B.C. were known as the Peace of Nicias, for the Athenian leader who negotiated a treaty with the Spartans. In Athens, the young and brilliant but unscrupulous Alcibiades, a ward of the great Athenian leader Pericles, urged a renewal of the conflict and an invasion of Sicily, which, Alcibiades claimed, would cut off Sparta's vital supply of Sicilian wheat. It is also speculated that Alcibiades may have dreamed of further conquests of southern Italy or Carthage.

Although the invasion plan was vigorously resisted by Nicias and other conservative leaders, it was enormously popular and, in June, 415 B.C., the Athenians launched

After laying siege to the walled city of Syracuse, the Athenian invasion force was unable to maintain its naval blockade—a failure that led to the defeat of the Athenian army, the execution of its generals, and the imprisonment and enslavement of its soldiers. (Archive Photos)

what was then an enormous fleet of at least 134 warships carrying between 5,000 and 6,500 heavy infantry ("hoplites") and light armed troops. In joint command of the expedition were Alcibiades, Nicias, and Lamachus, the last more a professional solider than a politician.

Just before the armada sailed (some sources say the very night before), a number of religious statues throughout Athens were mutilated. Since these Herms, as they were known, were sacred to Hermes, the god of travel, the act could be seen either as a bad omen or as a deliberate sacrilege; in either event, considerable suspicion fell upon Alcibiades, largely because of his scandalous past, which included participation in mocking celebrations of some of the Greeks' most solemn religious mysteries. Alcibiades was recalled after the fleet had sailed; fearing for his life, he fled to Sparta and urged a strong defense of Syracuse and a prompt attack on Athens.

In the absence of Alcibiades, the Athenian expedition sailed on and landed in Sicily. Lamachus urged an immediate attack on Syracuse, which might well have carried the city, but Nicias preferred caution. When Lamachus was killed in an early skirmish, Nicias procrastinated and

the campaigning season of 415 B.C. ended with Syracuse scarcely damaged. The Athenians were forced to withdraw into winter quarters, while the Syracusans appealed for and received help from their mother city of Corinth and its ally Sparta. The Spartans sent one contingent under Gylippus and the Corinthians another under Gongylus.

In 414 B.C., Athenian reinforcements arrived in Sicily, and Nicias pressed the siege of Syracuse, a strong, walled city built on a peninsula which separates a large bay, the Grand Harbor, from the sea. The Athenians seized part of the Grand Harbor, fortified it, and blockaded the city by the sea, hoping by building a wall across the landward end of the peninsula to invest Syracuse completely and force its surrender through lack of food. Lacking a siege train of battering rams, catapults, and other, similar weapons, the Athenians had no choice but to attempt the long and arduous process of starving out their opponents—or to have the city betrayed by a faction within its walls. Starvation or betrayal were, in fact, the typical fashion in which sieges were conducted during classical times, since a walled city such as Syracuse was, for all practical purposes, invulnerable to assault. After months of inaction, and at the moment when the Athenian strategy seemed about to force the city's surrender, Gongylus slipped inside the city to report Gylippus' approach with relief forces. Gylippus' strategy was to extend a counterwall from Syracuse at right angles to Nicias' wall and head off its completion. During the summer, fierce combats ranged around the ends of the two walls. By a narrow margin, Gylippus carried his fortifications past those of Nicias and thus frustrated the Athenian offensive. In the autumn, operations stalled and Nicias asked for reinforcements.

During the winter of 414-413 B.C., although under Spartan attack on the Greek mainland, the Athenians dispatched seventy-three additional triremes and five thousand hoplites under the command of Demosthenes. Their arrival barely restored the balance in favor of the Athenians. Fresh naval forces had reached Syracuse from the Peloponnesus and parts of Sicily. The Syracusans had made a bid for victory and in June and July, 413 B.C., they had won a series of naval actions in the Grand Harbor. It was at this point that Demosthenes had arrived, reestablished Athenian naval supremacy, and dashed Syracusan hopes.

Demosthenes and Nicias next decided to capture Gylippus' counterwall in order to retrieve gains made in the campaign of the year before. The Athenian army went forward by night and came extremely close to success, but in the darkness it lost cohesion and was repulsed. Demosthenes promptly advised Nicias to begin immediate withdrawal by sea, but once more Nicias delayed, believing an eclipse of the moon an omen against evacuation. The Syracusans then resumed their naval offensive, and in September defeated the Athenian fleet in a great battle in the Grand Harbor, compelling Nicias to resort to the forlorn hope of escaping by land. Complete disaster followed. The Syracusan cavalry and light troops harried their enemy and wore them down under a hail of missiles until Nicias surrendered. The Syracusans executed both him and Demosthenes, and imprisoned their men in stone quarries for months. Those who did not die under these conditions were sold into slavery.

This military defeat of Athens marked the beginning of the end for the city's struggle in the Peloponnesian War, primarily because it struck at Athens' political solidarity. At first enthusiastically united behind Alcibiades' scheme, the city was devastated first by his defection to the Spartans and then by the complete disaster which overtook the bulk of its relatively limited armed forces. Athens experienced a crisis of confidence from which it never fully recovered.

Although the Sicilian disaster encouraged some revolts within the Athenian empire, and lured Persia into an alliance with Sparta, its main effect—and Alcibiades' enduring legacy—was to sow distrust and dissension within Athens. It was this internal disarray, which brought distrust to its citizens and timidity to its military commanders, that led to its eventual collapse and final surrender in 404 B.C. —*Samuel K. Eddy, updated by Michael Witkoski*

ADDITIONAL READING:

Ellis, Walter M. *Alcibiades*. New York: Routledge, 1989. A brief but penetrating study of the Athenian who, almost single-handedly, convinced his native city to embark upon its most dangerous and ultimately disastrous adventure during the long war with Sparta.

Kagan, Donald. *The Peace of Nicias and the Sicilian Expedition*. Ithaca, N.Y.: Cornell University Press, 1981. The best, most extensive and most scholarly modern treatment of the subject, exhaustive in its scope but exhilarating in its narrative. Kagan places the events into their wider historical perspective while maintaining the vividness of an almost first-hand account.

Strauss, Barry S., and Josiah Ober. *The Anatomy of Error: Ancient Military Disasters and Their Lessons for Modern Strategists*. New York: St. Martin's Press, 1990. In addition to providing a brief but clear explanation of what happened, Strauss and Ober explain in more detail why the Athenian expedition met such a disastrous fate—and indeed, why the entire war resulted in an Athenian defeat.

Thucydides. *The Peloponnesian War*. Translated by Rex Warner. London: Harmondsworth, 1972.

_____. *The Peloponnesian War*. Translated by Thomas Hobbes, with notes and introduction by David Grene. Chicago: University of Chicago Press, 1989. The definitive source for the Sicilian expedition are books 6 and 7 of Thucydides' history of the war. It is interesting and informative to contrast the translation by the seventeenth century English philosopher Thomas Hobbes with that of the modern English poet, Rex Warner. Despite the changes in linguistic usage, the underlying and eternal meaning remains fairly constant.

SEE ALSO: 478-448 B.C., Athenian Empire Is Created; 450-425 B.C., History Develops as Scholarly Discipline; 431-404 B.C., Peloponnesian War.

401-400 B.C.
MARCH OF THE "TEN THOUSAND"

The March of the "Ten Thousand" is a failed military expedition against Persia, but it confirms the superiority of Greek hoplites over Asian infantry and reveals the growing importance of mercenaries in Greek warfare.

Date: 401-400 B.C.

Locale: The Persian Empire

Categories: Expansion and land acquisition; Wars, uprisings, and civil unrest

Key figures:

Artaxerxes II (died c. 359 B.C.), king of Persia, 404-359 B.C.

Clearchus (fl. c. 400 B.C.), Spartan exile, chief commander of the Greek mercenaries

Cyrus the Younger (c. 424-401 B.C.), Persian satrap in Asia Minor, brother of Artaxerxes

Tissaphernes (fl. c. 400 B.C.), Persian satrap in Asia Minor, general at the battle of Cunaxa

Xenophon (c. 428-c.355 B.C.), Athenian officer, chronicler of the march

Summary of event. The March of the "Ten Thousand" refers to the fifteen-hundred-mile journey of a Greek mercenary army into the heart of the Persian Empire, its valorous but vain combat near Babylon, and its arduous trek back to Greek territory more than a year later. The story is vividly recounted in the Anabasis, or "March Up Country," by Xenophon, an Athenian officer who participated in the expedition. Because Xenophon's straightforward style makes his account an ideal primer for learners of classical Greek, generations of modern students are familiar with the saga of the "Ten Thousand," which reveals much about Greek military practice and the non-Greek peoples encountered by the army. This adventure made a huge impression on contemporary Greeks, who took it as an indication of the vulnerability of the Persian Empire, and the campaign greatly influenced relations between Persia and Sparta. Nevertheless, the expedition arose out of Persian dynastic strife and is best understood in that context.

The ambitious Persian prince, Cyrus the Younger, organized this expedition in order to depose his older brother, Artaxerxes II, who had recently assumed the Persian throne on the death of their father, Darius II, in 404 B.C. Under Darius, Persia had played a key role in the later phase of the Peloponnesian War between Athens and Sparta (431-404 B.C.), when it intervened on the side of the Spartans by subsidizing the fleet that brought about the defeat of Athens. In return for this Persian support, the Spartans agreed to allow the Persians to reassert their control of the Ionian Greek cities, which had been part of the Athenian Empire. Sent out to Asia Minor in 407 B.C. to implement this pro-Spartan policy and given an extraordinary command at the age of sixteen, Cyrus quickly displayed his regal ambitions. Among those he offended were the Ionian satrap, Tissaphernes, whose authority and poli-

Following the death of Cyrus the Younger of Persia at the Battle of Cunaxa in 401 B.C., the Athenian soldier Xenophon was elected to lead his fellow Greek mercenaries back to their homeland. (Archive Photos)

cies Cyrus largely displaced, and two of Cyrus' royal cousins, whom he had executed for refusing to go along with his kingly ceremonial pretensions. When Artaxerxes assumed the throne in 404 B.C., Cyrus immediately plotted to dethrone him but was denounced by Tissaphernes and placed under arrest at the imperial capital. He escaped execution thanks to the intercession of his mother and was allowed to return to Ionia, although with drastically reduced authority. There, he immediately began preparations for a military challenge to Artaxerxes. To augment his sizable force of Asian troops Cyrus recruited approximately thirteen thousand mercenary soldiers from many areas of Greece. Most were heavily armored infantry, or hoplites, whose superiority to Asian infantry had been demonstrated in earlier conflicts. By sending a company of soldiers under a Spartan general and providing naval support, the Spartans became the only Greeks to participate as a city-state.

Cyrus attempted to disguise his treasonous objective by saying that the army would be used against rebellious tribes in Asia Minor, but he did not fool Tissaphernes, who dashed to alert Artaxerxes as soon as Cyrus' army left Sardis in the spring of 401 B.C. As the march progressed, the Greeks became suspicious of their destination and mutinied twice. Only the exhortations of the Spartan general, Clearchus, and promises of huge increases in pay induced the mercenaries to continue the march and cross the Euphrates into Mesopotamia. By turning south toward Babylon instead of proceeding east against the northern capital city of Ecbatana, Cyrus may have surprised Artaxerxes, who had to defend Babylon without his full army. In the battle at Cunaxa during September, 401 B.C., the Greeks acquitted themselves well, routing the more numerous Asian troops opposite them and beating off a counterattack organized by Tissaphernes. Not until the next day did they learn that Cyrus' Asian troops had been defeated and that Cyrus himself had died leading a cavalry charge against the king.

Demoralized by the death of Cyrus and aware of their precarious position, the Greeks nevertheless refused to surrender their weapons and acknowledged Clearchus as their leader. Clearchus entered into an uneasy truce with Tissaphernes, who promised the Greeks safe conduct on their return home and began to escort them out of Mesopotamia by way of the Tigris valley. Either out of pure treacherous impulse, as Xenophon would have it, or be-

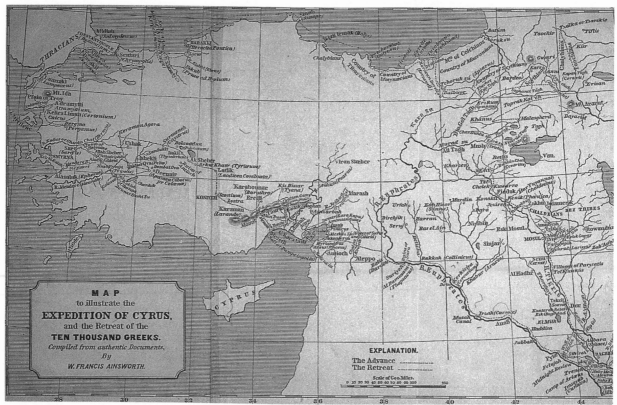

This map shows the overland route taken by the Greek mercenaries to support Cyrus against his brother, King Artaxerxes II, and the mercenaries' difficult return via the Black Sea to the straits of Bosporus. (Archive Photos)

cause he had learned that Clearchus was plotting to kill him, Tissaphernes surprised the Greeks by calling a parley at which he arrested their generals and executed the officers attending them. Clearchus and the other generals were put on display in Babylon before being put to death.

The leaderless army showed its resilience by electing new leaders, including Xenophon, and continued its march up the Tigris. Leaving Mesopotamia and Persian harassment behind, the mercenaries faced many hardships during the winter of 401-400 B.C., as they made their way through the mountains of Kurdistan and Armenia. In the spring of 400 B.C., they arrived at Trapezus on the Black Sea coast, where they rejoiced at the sight of the sea and recuperated before continuing their journey west by land and ship. At one point Xenophon suggested that they settle and found a new city, but this idea was not well received by his fellow soldiers, who were determined to return to Greece. When they finally reached the Bosporus in the autumn of 400, their number had shrunk to approximately six thousand. After their return, most of the "Cyreans," as they were called, did not go back to their home city-states but reentered mercenary service. They first served the Thracian king, Seuthes, and then crossed back to Asia Minor in 399 B.C. to fight for the Spartans, who had decided to go to war with the Persians in Ionia.

Contemporary Greeks may have exaggerated the significance of the army's successful retreat out of Asia as a sign of Persian weakness, for Artaxerxes certainly could have isolated and destroyed them, if he had wished to do so. His primary concern, however, was to get them out the rich province of Mesopotamia with a minimum of damage. Still, the encounter at Cunaxa confirmed the superiority of the Greek infantry phalanx over Asian troops and would inspire future invaders of the Persian Empire. The ease with which Cyrus recruited these soldiers, the first large mercenary Greek army, demonstrated the wide appeal of mercenary service among impoverished Greeks with no better means of earning a living. In coming years such mercenaries would play an important role in Greek warfare.

The expedition also brought about a change in Spartan-Persian relations that had enormous importance for the future of Sparta. Spartan support of Cyrus' failed attack on Artaxerxes soured relations between the empire and its former allies and led to Sparta's decision to fight the Persians in Asia. This Asian war weakened Sparta and prompted Artaxerxes to organize a coalition of Greek city-states to fight the bitter "Corinthian War" (395-386 B.C.) against Sparta. In order to face this conflict at home, Sparta abandoned the contest in Asia and acknowledged Persian overlordship of the Ionian Greeks. Sparta eventually won the war in Greece, but emerged with its manpower drained and its prestige among the Greeks badly damaged.   —*James T. Chambers*

ADDITIONAL READING:

Anderson, John K. *Military Theory and Practice in the Age of Xenophon*. Berkeley: University of California Press, 1970. This volume details Greek military practices as revealed in the writings of Xenophon.

Hackett, John, ed. *Warfare in the Ancient World*. New York: Facts On File, 1989. This excellently illustrated volume contrasts Greek and Persian styles of warfare in two chapters, "Hoplite Warfare" and "The Persians."

Hanson, Victor Davis. *The Western Way of War: Infantry Battle in Classical Greece*. New York: Alfred A. Knopf, 1989. The best study of Greek hoplite warfare, the book vividly recounts the soldier's experience of war.

Nussbaum, G. B. *The Ten Thousand: A Study in Social Organization and Action in Xenophon's Anabasis*. Leiden, the Netherlands: Brill, 1967. This study analyzes the decision-making process of the Greeks during their retreat and argues that the army functioned as a mobile city-state.

Parke, H. W. *Greek Mercenary Soldiers: From the Earliest Times to the Battle of Ipsus*. Oxford: Oxford University Press, 1933. This classic piece of scholarship is still the best study of the larger phenomenon represented by Cyrus' mercenary army, which is treated in chapter 5.

Roy, J. "The Mercenaries of Cyrus." *Historia* 16 (1967): 287-323. This detailed examination analyzes the origins, motivations, and fate of the Greeks who fought for Cyrus.

Xenophon. *The Persian Expedition*. Translated by Rex Warner. New York: Penguin, 1972. This translation of the Anabasis provides an entertaining firsthand record of the expedition. The extended introduction by George Cawkwell alerts the reader to the shortcomings of Xenophon's account and discusses some of the larger strategic and tactical problems associated with the march.

SEE ALSO: 700-330 B.C., Phalanx Is Developed as a Military Unit; 480-479 B.C., Persian Invasion of Greece; 450-425 B.C., History Develops as Scholarly Discipline.

399 B.C.
DEATH OF SOCRATES

The death of Socrates is decreed after he is tried, found guilty, and sentenced to die by an Athenian jury for crimes against the state, but his final days offer a lasting model of moral integrity and composure in the face of death.

DATE: 399 B.C.

LOCALE: Athens, Greece

CATEGORIES: Cultural and intellectual history; Government and politics

KEY FIGURES:

Alcibiades (c. 450-404 B.C.), talented Athenian citizen and military commander who defected to Sparta during the Peloponnesian War; later assassinated

Aristophanes (c. 448-c. 385 B.C.), Athenian comic dramatist

Critias (c. 480-403 B.C.), Athenian oligarchic leader of the Thirty Tyrants in 404 B.C.

Crito (fl. 490 B.C.), wealthy Athenian disciple of Socrates who first sought acquittal and then a means of escape for the condemned Socrates

Meletus and *Anytus*, Athenian citizens who brought the indictment against Socrates

Plato (427-347 B.C.), Athenian disciple of Socrates who wrote the most vivid account of the trial, imprisonment, and death of Socrates in his *Apology*, *Crito*, and *Phaedo*

Socrates (c. 470-399 B.C.), Athenian citizen and informal teacher

Xanthippe, wife of Socrates

SUMMARY OF EVENT. The conclusion and aftermath of the Peloponnesian War left Athenian democrats bitter and resentful. By the time this war ended in 404 B.C., the empire had crumbled and the fleet and walls of Athens had been dismantled. Democracy had finally been restored in 403 B.C. following two periods of oligarchic rule, one beginning in 411 B.C. under a group of aristocrats known as "The Four Hundred," the other under "The Thirty" in 404 B.C. In the person of Socrates there seemed to stand the symbol, if not the principal cause, of all the factors of intellectual and moral enervation which had destroyed from within the power of Athenian democracy to prosecute the war successfully and to sustain the integrity of its own governmental institutions. An indictment was therefore brought against Socrates in 399 B.C. by a religious fanatic, Meletus, supported by the politician Anytus and by the orator Lycon, on the charge of impiety. Socrates was officially charged with failing to worship the gods of the state, introducing new gods of his own, and corrupting the youth of Athens. Although his accusers demanded the death penalty, their intention seems to have been to drive Socrates into self-imposed exile, a sentence which they believed he himself would propose if found guilty.

Plato's *Apology* makes it clear that Socrates was identified in his accusers' minds with the natural philosophers and Sophists, whose teaching had indeed contributed to the deterioration of the traditional Athenian religious and political values. The natural philosophers had promulgated doctrines of a world sustained by impersonal laws rather than by personal deities, and the Sophists had encouraged their young noble pupils to be skeptical of all forms of institutional authority. Most damaging of all in their teaching was the doctrine of political power based on the assumptions that every individual's natural inclination was toward self-aggrandizement, and that the law of the state was an artificial restriction upon the individual's self-realization.

It was the Sophists, rather than Socrates, who were responsible for these demoralizing ideas. Socrates himself scrupulously lived by the laws of Athens and fully participated in the formal religion of the states. He did, however, openly criticize the tendency of the democracy to entrust tasks of professional competence to amateurs chosen by popularity or, worse still, by lot. Moreover, he freely associated with the young aristocrats who were then the most conspicuous pupils of the Sophists. To the Athenian who did not know him intimately, Socrates must have appeared to be a typical Sophist, and it was as such that he was caricatured in the *Clouds* of Aristophanes in 423 B.C., a play which must have left an indelible impression on many Athenian minds. After the double humiliation of defeat and revolution in 404 B.C., people remembered Alcibiades, who had deserted to the enemy during the war and severely damaged the Athenian war effort by helping to bring about a major Athenian naval defeat at the battle of Syracuse, and Critias, who was despised by Athenian democrats for his role as leader of "The Thirty." They also recalled that these two men had been pupils of Socrates in their youth, and so Socrates seemed an ideal scapegoat for the frustrated resentment of many Athenians.

Despite these considerations, the vote to convict Socrates was fairly close. Out of a total of 500 jurors, 280 voted to find him guilty; a switch of only 30 jurors would have acquitted him. As Plato shows in his *Apology*, Socrates spoke forcefully in his own defense, denying all the charges brought against him. The *Apology* of Plato presents a portrait of Socrates as an earnest moralist who, though no Sophist, was indeed a real threat to whatever aspects of the Athenian traditional could not be rationally grounded. Far from the atheist his accusers would have proved him, Socrates believed in objective moral values and a transcendent deity of truth. Athenians who were personally confronted by him were faced with a relentless challenge to their pretense of certain knowledge in matters of religion and morals. Although he himself professed ignorance in these areas, he claimed a wisdom unique among men by virtue of his awareness of ignorance.

Socrates stood on common ground with the Sophists in

Accused of failing to observe religious customs and corrupting the young, the Athenian philosopher Socrates refused to seek exile and was sentenced to be executed by drinking poisonous hemlock. (Archive Photos)

refusing to acknowledge any self-evident authority in traditional Greek theological and moral ideals. Yet he differed from them in that his skepticism was methodological rather than radical; he believed that valid moral ideals could ultimately be grounded rationally, although the effort might be long and arduous. To this end, he committed himself to a life of intellectual inquiry through conversation with any who would join him, and he honestly believed that his informal intercourse with the Athenian man-in-the-street was a divine commission of vital concern to Athens. The only life worth living, he insisted, was the life based on values formulated through rigorous, honest, personal self-examination. Through such individual self-examination alone might come about eventual moral regeneration in the state.

Once found guilty on the counts brought against him, Socrates refused the traditional option of voluntary exile and obstinately insisted, goading the jury, that only death would make him cease from his customary activities in Athens, whereupon the jury felt compelled to sentence him, this time by a larger margin, to execution by poison. During the interval between his trial and death, Socrates

conversed freely with his disciples, who sought to persuade him to go into exile. Plato's *Crito* gives Socrates' reason for resisting these entreaties: the command of the state, which he had heeded throughout his life, must be heeded now even though the condemnation was unjust.

The death of Socrates is dramatically portrayed in the *Phaedo* of Plato. On the day of his execution, Socrates appeared calm and relaxed. After a final reunion with Xanthippe, distraught over the idea that her husband would no longer be able to have philosophical conversations with his disciples, Socrates dismissively ordered Crito to take her home. Before drinking, without any protest, the cup of hemlock that would bring about his death, Socrates had one last philosophical conversation with his disciples, in which he argued for the immortality of the soul and the nature of human existence as a constant struggle between the body and the mind. The lasting value of this conversation, however, goes beyond the substance of Socrates' arguments, as Plato's *Phaedo* exalts the pattern of philosophic life consummated in Socrates' death to a transcendent ideal for all people.

—*Carl W. Conrad, updated by Diane P. Michelfelder*

ADDITIONAL READING:

Brickhouse, Thomas C., and Nicholas D. Smith. "The Formal Charges Against Socrates." In *Essays on the Philosophy of Socrates*, edited by Hugh H. Benson. New York: Oxford University Press, 1992. An analysis of Socrates' response to the three charges brought against him, in the light of the authors' interesting suggestion that Socrates takes these charges more seriously than most commentators previously suggested.

Irwin, Terence. *Classical Thought*. New York: Oxford University Press, 1989. A clear discussion of the philosophical method and moral views of Socrates are included in this book for the nonspecialist, written by a leading scholar of ancient philosophy.

Levin, Richard, ed. *The Question of Socrates*. New York: Harcourt, Brace & World, 1961. An introduction to the life and thinking of Socrates through selections from Aristophanes, Plato, Xenophon, Aristotle, Diogenes Laertius, and others.

Stone, I. F. *The Trial of Socrates*. New York: Doubleday, 1989. This best-selling book by a famous independent journalist is a lively investigation of the democratic values of ancient Athens and Socrates' relation to them.

Zeller, Eduard. *Socrates and the Socratic Schools*. New York: Russell & Russell, 1962. Part of a larger classic study of the philosophy of the Greeks, this book addresses the figure of Socrates in light of the culture of his times and assesses the reasons behind the decision to bring him to trial.

SEE ALSO: 478-448 B.C., Athenian Empire Is Created; 431-404 B.C., Peloponnesian War; 440 B.C., Teachings of the Sophists; 380 B.C., Plato Develops His Theory of Ideas.

380 B.C.
PLATO DEVELOPS HIS THEORY OF IDEAS

Plato develops his theory of ideas, providing a philosophical formulation of the concept of the ultimate reality.

DATE: c. 380 B.C.

LOCALE: Athens, southern Italy, and Sicily

CATEGORY: Cultural and intellectual history

KEY FIGURES:

Plato (427-347 B.C.), Athenian philosopher, disciple of Socrates and founder of the Academy

Socrates (c. 470-399 B.C.), Athenian citizen and informal teacher

SUMMARY OF EVENT. Plato's concept of "eidos," meaning "vision" in Greek, has influenced thinkers from Aristotle, to medieval scholastics and theologians, to modern philosophers such as René Descartes, Baruch Spinoza, Gottfried Wilhelm Leibniz, and even Gottlob Frege—the twentieth century German mathematician.

The Forms or Ideas are the penultimate reality of things. The Platonic realm of ideas contains the pure Forms of mathematical entities, such as numbers and geometrical shapes, and moral and aesthetic ideas, such as "the just," "the beautiful," and "the good." These Forms are immutable and timeless, unlike the phenomena in the actual world, which are shadowy, unreliable reflections of their Forms. Although humans can never fully articulate or define the Forms using limited conceptual terms, they can grasp them intuitively. The purer the mirror of the mind, the clearer the reflection received from the realm of Ideas.

In one sense, the emergence of this theory is the consummate logical expression of the classical Greek way of viewing human experience of the world, but in another it is possible to trace the emergence of Plato's theory in the context of pre-Socratic and Socratic thought.

For example, from Parmenides and the Sophists, Plato borrowed language for describing the nature of the Forms and their relationship to things in the actual world; from Heraclitus, he derived the idea of self-sufficiency and completeness of the Forms; from the Pythagoreans, he abstracted the idea of transcendence of the Forms and how the human soul has access to that heavenly realm from the lower realm of phenomena.

Plato's master and spiritual father, Socrates, had sought in the later years of the fifth century B.C. to discover a science of life, an objective system of knowledge of life's goals, and the means by which such goals might be achieved. While questioning his young aristocratic friends, Socrates found that no man had made this discovery, and that all men held no more than mere opinions about these ends and means of life. Yet Socrates was convinced that the technique of life was a matter of the mind's knowing objective principles and, once they were known, communicating them rationally; at the divine level he was convinced that they were grasped by a deity essentially good and truthful. The individual mind, or psyche, had intuitive access to these divinely known principles; moreover, Socrates believed that the psyche was obligated to bring them to explicit rational formulation in dialogue with other men. The earlier Socratic dialogues, notably the *Euthyphro, Charmides,* and *Laches* of Plato, which are generally held to be reasonably accurate descriptions of the characteristic aims and procedures of Socrates, portray him as engaged in the effort to define inductively the precise nature of the traditional Greek moral virtues of piety, temperance, and courage. Thus, implicit in the philosophical activity of Socrates is a dualism of common opinion and transcendental moral truth to which the psyche has intuitive access.

In Plato's account of the Forms, however, there is no dualism, because the only things that genuinely exist are the Forms. Everything else, such as rocks, plants, and animals, are mere shadows of the Forms. Thus, Plato's abhorrence of poetry and the arts. If the actual world is mere shadows of the Forms, then art and poetry are shadows of shadows. Ironically, Plato himself used a poetic and fictional literary style to narrate his philosophy.

Plato, however, preferred the speculative and analytic mode of thought over imaginative ones. He argued that in order to speculate about the Forms, humans must avoid the realm of opinion (*doxa*) and embrace the science of knowledge (*epitome*) or the pure intellect which uses logical inferences to abstract the truth of the Forms. Thus,

Plato separated the knowing subject from the knowledge of the realm of Ideas.

The Ionian philosophical tradition had already distinguished two types of experience: that of the senses on the one hand, revealing a multiplicity of distinct impressions; and that of the mind on the other, comprehending a rational pattern having the character of unity, order, and permanence. It was characteristic of the Greek mind, moreover, to value more highly, and attribute greater reality to, the static pattern of order—visualized by the mind and recognized as a recurrent feature of experience—than the continually shifting flux of concrete phenomena. Greek art and literature, especially the richly exploited store of mythical paradigms, amply exemplify this Greek preoccupation with the eternal and recurrent pattern. It is consis-

Shown here with his pupils in the garden of the Academy, Plato developed a theory of ideas that combined many of the concepts advanced by the Pythagoreans and by Socrates. (Archive Photos)

tent with this intellectual perspective that the Pythagorean community of southern Italy discovered that meaningful patterns of sense-experience are based on mathematical relations grasped not by the senses but by the psyche alone in inner vision. It was thus the Pythagoreans who distinguished the universal (the triangle, the square, the circle), seen by the mind alone, from the particular mode of the universal seen by the eye and found meaningful only by virtue of the psyche's grasp of the universal.

Plato, who spent some time following the death of Socrates in 399 B.C. in southern Italy and Sicily in company with Pythagoreans, appears to have brought together the Pythagorean idea of the universal and the Socratic idea of the objective and eternally valid moral concept. All meaningful patterns of human experience, Plato felt, must be founded on an eternal Form or Idea known by the psyche through intuitive experience and recognized by the senses as immanent in or imitated by concrete particular objects or phenomena. In the *Meno*, a transitional dialogue between his early and middle period, Plato gave the first clear formulation of this doctrine in terms of Orphic-Pythagorean dualistic mysticism. The doctrine is given ample expression in several dialogues of the middle period of Plato, notably in the *Phaedo* and the *Republic*. The destiny of the individual psyche is a function of its participation in successive life-periods, in two distinct realms of experience: a transcendental realm in which the psyche, free from the bodily limitations of sense-experience, apprehends the eternal forms in their purity; and a physical realm of generation and corruption in which the psyche, through the bodily medium of the senses, apprehends imperfect and perishable concrete exemplifications of eternal forms. The function of the philosopher is to purify his vision of the eternal forms in their ideal transcendental order so that in the physical realm he may creatively order his own life and, if permitted, the life of his human community, in accordance with this vision.

Plato was keenly aware of the difficulties and paradoxes involved in his notion of Forms. There are allusions to these difficulties throughout his work, especially in *Parmenides* and *Meno*, where learning and teaching become paradoxical because humans are supposed to have access to knowledge of the Forms prior to their experience with the world.

The impact of this doctrine upon the history of philosophy, however, is immeasurable. Some believe that philosophy started with Plato's famous dialogues. With certain modifications, Aristotle made it the basis of the first great systematic understanding of all human experience. The ontological status of Forms, be they mathematical concepts or moral ideals, has been a major subject of controversy between opposing philosophical schools throughout

the Western tradition, and empiricists' logical objections to the Doctrine of Ideas have never fully succeeded in dismissing its cogency and appeal as a necessary foundation for a secure epistemology.

—*Carl W. Conrad, updated by Chogollah Maroufi*

ADDITIONAL READING:

Fine, Gail. *On Ideas: Aristotle's Criticism of Plato's Theory of Forms*. Oxford: Clarendon Press, 1993. A rigorous and insightful account of how Aristotle incorporated his teacher's conception of the Forms.

Hare, R. M. *Plato*. New York: Oxford University Press, 1989. Written by an eminent philosopher, this book lucidly and briefly describes Plato's major theories. Especially see chapter 6, "Definition, Dialectic and the Good," pages 38-47.

Reynold, Noel. *Interpreting Plato's Euthyphro and Meno*. Provo, Utah: Brigham Young University Press, 1988. A comparative look at different notions of the Forms in *Euthyphro*, *Meno*, *Timous*, and other dialogues.

Ross, David. *Plato's Theory of Ideas*. Oxford: Clarendon Press, 1976. An account of the development and ramifications of Plato's theory.

Vlastos, Gregory, ed. *Plato: A Collection of Critical Essays*. Notre Dame, Ind.: University of Notre Dame Press, 1978. See chapters 2 through 3 for various critiques of the theory.

SEE ALSO: 600-500 B.C., Greek Philosophers Formulate Theories of the Cosmos; 440 B.C., Teachings of the Sophists; 335-323 B.C., Aristotle Writes the *Politics*.

340-338 B.C.
ORIGIN OF MUNICIPIA

The origin of Municipia *represents an advance in the development of diplomatic relations between Rome and its neighbors.*

DATE: 340-338 B.C.

LOCALE: Rome, Latium, and Campania, soon spreading throughout Italy

CATEGORY: Diplomacy and international relations

KEY FIGURE:

Titus Manlius Torquatus, military tribune, dictator, and consul, later general in 340 against the Latin League

SUMMARY OF EVENT. Vital to the expansion of Roman dominance in Italy was the discovery of a way to cement close relationships with other small neighboring states. Although the bonds gradually forged with Italian towns and tribal groups since the mid-500's were diverse in character, Roman diplomacy exhibited unprecedented sophistication in the terms imposed in the settlement in 338 B.C.

Some thirty to forty smaller communities in Latium south of Rome had long been united for mutual defense and common religious rites before Rome itself entered into agreement with them, possibly as early as 493 B.C. Surviving records reflect a Roman bias, according to which Rome dominated League decisions; in the 400's, all members cooperated in rough equality against the Aequi and Volsci in the hills east of Latium. By the 300's, the chief enemies were farther afield: Gauls in northern Italy, who had sacked Rome in 390, and Samnite tribes in the southern Apennine mountains, whom overpopulation and poor soil compelled to attack the Latins of the rich coastal plain. Latin League members exchanged some citizenship privileges such as intermarriage and recognition of commercial contracts; individuals could also abandon their home and acquire a new citizenship by establishing residence in another league town. The league occasionally founded colonies at strategic sites to serve as garrisons against its enemies; the *coloniae* became new members. From the 380's, Rome achieved a supremacy which its partners resented. About 358 B.C., several league towns supported an attack on Rome, and in 340 B.C. almost the entire league and a number of places in Campania took up arms against Roman hegemony.

Led by Titus Manlius Torquatus, hero of a famous duel against a giant Gaul, the Romans defeated their opponents by 338 B.C. The terms imposed at the restoration of peace are a milestone in Italian history, for the Roman senators established the principle of flexible treatment of beaten enemies. Rome retained and adapted the essential features of this settlement for centuries. Two points preface the ensuing discussion. First, as in civil law, Romans distinguished categories of people (free-slave, citizen-foreigner, *in patria potestate-sui juris,* and so forth), so in diplomacy they distinguished types of community; consequently, some technical terms are essential. Second, at the time citizenship was membership in one's home community, not some larger unit. Two hundred and fifty years later, the Romans devised a national citizenship: the Julian Law of 90 B.C. built on the principles formulated in 338 B.C. and applied over the next century, as it extended Roman citizenship to all free inhabitants of Italy.

In 338 B.C., Rome disbanded the old Latin League and replaced it with a new system. With the addition of other peoples, it became the Roman alliance system. (This is a modern term of convenience; it was not a federation, which implies an approximate equality among members.) The victor ended the independence of five nearby towns by incorporating their inhabitants as citizens of Rome. These places, at least as old as Rome, became the first *municipia* (*municipium* in the singular) and their residents

Roman *municipes* (*municeps* in the singular), so called because they undertook (*ceperunt*) the obligations (*munera*) of citizenship. *Coloniae* were new foundations, whether on a new site or replacing a destroyed town. Fresh treaties with the other Latin cities, chiefly League colonies, defined them as allies (*socii*) of Rome. These peoples retained their old rights, but henceforward only with Rome.

Further south there were a number of populous communities that controlled the fertile lowland plain called Campania, situated between the Samnites to the east and south and the Romans to the north. Capua, the largest city in Campania, appealed in 343 B.C. for Roman aid against Samnite aggression and received help. During the Latin War of 340-338 B.C., citizens of Capua and a few other Campanian communities assisted the Latins against Rome, but the upper-class Campanian cavalry remained loyal to Rome. Rome consequently rewarded the nobles of Capua and several smaller towns in Campania with what the historian Livy calls *civitas romana*, that is, Roman citizenship. Also described as *civitas sine suffragio*, or "citizenship without suffrage," this qualified citizenship specifically excluded the right to vote in Roman elections or to hold offices in Rome, but it did include the obligation to serve with the Roman legions when called upon to do so. These towns were also designated as *municipia*. *Cives sine suffragio* were similar to Latin *socii*: already citizens of Rome, they had the rights of marriage and commerce with Romans; neither group could vote or hold office at Rome. This partial Roman citizenship subordinated the *municipia* to the military and diplomatic dominance of Rome, but it also allowed Italian cities to retain almost complete freedom in local self-government. This autonomy was a practical necessity, as Rome lacked the machinery to govern its enlarged territory. Itinerant prefects (*praefecti*) sent out from Rome kept a watch on the *municipia*. Inscriptions reveal a considerable variety in the titles of municipal magistrates for years; for instance, Capua continued to be governed by its own traditional magistrates.

The *municipium* with *civitas sine suffragio* was one of two highly effective political weapons in Rome's steady expansion after 338 B.C.: Nineteen were established in 303-270 B.C., the first few among the Volsci but most in central Italy outside Latium. The other was the Latin colony, of which eighteen were founded in 338-268 B.C. The *municipia sine suffragio* and *coloniae Latinae* showed remarkable loyalty during the Samnite Wars between 327 and 290 B.C.; slowly they confined the Samnites to their mountain homelands and cut them off from potential allies such as the Etruscans. Though Rome probably intended *civitas sine suffragio* to be a permanent condition, it gradually elevated these *municipia* to full citizenship (*civitas optimo iure*). Some Sabine communities moved up in 268 B.C., the first block grant of full citizenship to non-Latin people; the rest followed in 241 B.C.; the people of Arpinum (including the families of Marius and Cicero) and Formiae received *civitas optimo iure* in 188 B.C., a consequence of loyalty during Hannibal's invasion of Italy. *Civitas sine suffragio* disappeared over the second century. The Latins, however, did not acquire *civitas Romana,* though like the *cives sine suffragio* they shared some of the fruits of Roman military victories and preserved their own self-government. Of less importance was the Roman citizen colony: few in number (eight by 264 B.C.), small in size (three hundred families), their inhabitants remained full citizens of Rome with little autonomy. Diplomacy was as important as battlefield superiority in the spread of Roman political power. Some fifty-five communities below a line from Cosa on the west to Ariminum on the east combined with the growing mass of Roman citizens to extend Roman culture and Latin language throughout peninsular Italy.

Incorporation of the remaining people of Italy as allies (*socii*) completed the Roman alliance system. These groups lacked the relatively privileged status of the Latins and *cives sine suffragio,* for though allowed a measure of autonomy they could not intermarry or conduct business with Romans and had no hope of full citizenship. This inferior treatment explains why the revolt of 90 B.C. was almost entirely confined to the Italian allies.

As Rome's domination extended in later centuries beyond Italy, terms such as *municipia* changed in meaning. The Julian Law of 90 B.C. extended citizenship to all people south of the Po River. Existing towns easily converted into *municipia,* and the less urbanized people formed *municipia* by amalgamating their villages and hamlets (*fora, conciliabula,* and so forth). Over the next century, these towns gradually adopted annual *quattuorviri* (two *duoviri iure dicundo,* judicial officials modeled on Rome's consuls, and two *aediles*). From then on, all Italian towns were either *coloniae* or *municipia.*

In the Roman Empire, the institution of the *municipium* spread widely. Grants of municipal status in the form of charters conferring increased rights to manage local affairs with Roman-style government emanated from the capital. Town elites became Roman citizens by holding local office, a practice appearing in the 120's B.C., in Italy. The process is best known in Spain, where Vespasian, recognizing their Romanization, elevated all the native (noncolonial) communities to Latin municipalities in A.D. 70-79.

—*Roger B. McShane, updated by Thomas H. Watkins*

ADDITIONAL READING:

Galsterer, H. "*Municipium Flavium Irnitanum*: A Latin Town in Spain." *The Journal of Roman Studies* 78 (1988): 78-90.

González, J. "The *Lex Irnitana*: A New Copy of the Flavian Municipal Law." *The Journal of Roman Studies* 76 (1986): 147-243. Galsterer and González discuss improved knowledge of municipal charters resulting from bronze tablets found at Irni.

Salmon, E. T. *The Making of Roman Italy.* Ithaca, N.Y.: Cornell University Press, 1982.

_____. *Roman Colonization Under the Republic.* Ithaca, N.Y.: Cornell University Press, 1969.

_____. *Samnium and the Samnites.* Cambridge, England: Cambridge University Press, 1967. These three works are probably the best introduction to the role and historical context of *coloniae* and *municipia*; consequences of enfranchisement from 90 B.C. forward.

Sherwin-White, A. N. *The Roman Citizenship.* 2d ed. Oxford: Clarendon Press, 1972. An authoritative and technical source.

Taylor, L. R. *The Voting Districts of the Roman Republic.* Vol. 19. Rome: Papers of the American Academy at Rome, 1960. The role and location of the tribes in Republican times; incorporation of the *municipia.*

SEE ALSO: 445 B.C., The Canuleian Law; 287 B.C., The *Lex Hortensia*; 90 B.C., Julian Law.

338 B.C.
BATTLE OF CHAERONEA

The Battle of Chaeronea results in a Macedonian victory that heralds the dawn of the Hellenistic Age.

DATE: August 2, 338 B.C.

LOCALE: Chaeronea, in Boeotia northwest of Thebes

CATEGORY: Wars, uprisings, and civil unrest

KEY FIGURES:

Alexander the Great (356-323 B.C.), son of Philip and his successor as king, 336-323 B.C.

Demosthenes (384-322 B.C.), Atheneian statesman and orator

Isocrates (436-338 B.C.), Athenian publicist and rhetorician

Philip II (382-336 B.C.), king of Macedonia, 359-336 B.C.

SUMMARY OF EVENT. The Peloponnesian War ended Athens' hegemony in Greece and marked the beginning of Spartan dominance. The result was the outbreak of new destructive wars aimed at the overthrow of Sparta. At the Battle of Leuctra in 371 B.C., the Thebans, allies of Athens, inflicted a decisive defeat on the Spartans, and Greece passed to the hegemony of Thebes. This hegemony proved to be exceedingly short-lived. Athens changed sides and, in concert with Sparta and other states, overcame Thebes in the closely fought Battle of Mantinea in 362 B.C. Meanwhile, Athens had revived the Delian confederacy, but most of its allies successfully revolted against Athens in the Social War of 357-355, and Athenian power was badly shaken.

Men who participated in these unsuccessful wars for the hegemony of Greece called out for relief from conflict. As the vital necessity for escaping continual competition and bloodshed, the Athenian Isocrates advocated the unification of Greece under the leadership of a strong state with a strong ruler. Demosthenes of Athens dreamed of an Athens revitalized culturally and militarily and preeminent in Greece. The philosopher Plato hoped for government by philosophers.

A more likely savior than one of Plato's scholars appeared in Philip of Macedonia, who began his reign in 359 B.C. He set about to Hellenize and modernize Macedonia with ingenuity and energy. He brought the factious nobility of his country to heel and taught them to serve him with heavy cavalry. He also created a phalanx better drilled and more effective than that of the Greeks. His army was of professional quality, far superior to the citizen militias or hired mercenaries that made up the bulk of the armies of the Hellenic cities. The Macedonian army was, moreover, supported by efficient financial institutions. Philip intended to establish his own hegemony over Greece, although he wished it to be merciful and enlightened. In the 340's, he began to penetrate southward through Thessaly. The principal Greek states of Athens, Sparta, and Thebes, distracted by their own perpetual feuds and weakened by their precarious fiscal circumstances, only halfheartedly resisted Philip.

In 340 B.C., the decisive war broke out between Macedonia and the Greeks. In August of 338, the Macedonian army of two thousand cavalry and thirty thousand infantry came face to face with the united Greek armies of weak cavalry and thirty-five thousand infantry near the small town of Chaeronea in northwestern Boeotia. The Greeks deployed with their right flank near a small stream; it was held by twelve thousand Thebans and Boeotians. The center was composed of various allies from central Greece and the Peloponnesus, and the left was made up of ten thousand Athenians. The Greek phalanx was to make its usual straightforward attack, hoping to crush the enemy by the weight of its charge. On the other side, Philip was a master of more subtle tactics, combining the use of cavalry and infantry. His own left, opposite the Thebans, was headed by his cavalry, which was to thrust itself into a gap

to be made in the Greek line. The gap would be opened by luring the Athenians into charging Philip's own right as it purposefully drew back in pretended retreat.

The battle was probably fought on August 2, 338, and everything went according to Philip's plan. The Athenians rushed forward, shouting "On to Pella!" (the capital of Macedonia), and when the Greek center and the Theban left moved obliquely to keep in close ranks, a hole opened in the Theban line. Led by the eighteen-year-old crown prince Alexander, the Macedonian heavy cavalry charged into this gap in wedge formation. They were followed by crack formations of infantry, which attacked the flanks on either side of the gap. The Thebans, after heroic resistance, were beaten; the Greek center and left, panic-stricken, broke and ran. The result was a decisive victory for Philip.

During the next few weeks, the Greek states surrendered one after the other. In 337 B.C., Philip organized them into a Hellenic League with its seat at Corinth. He served as president of the league, and members were forced to follow his foreign policy. Wars among them were forbidden, as was internal constitutional change except by constitutional methods. Philip's intentions were to secure a tranquil and contented Greece as the necessary first step in his new plan to liberate the Greeks of Asia Minor from the Persian Empire.

The Battle of Chaeronea was the great event that destroyed the sovereignty of the Greek states. There was a revolt against Macedonia in 323-321 B.C. called the "Lamian War," and several more occurred in the third century B.C., bringing temporary freedom. Nevertheless, the old, unbridled parochialism and imperialism of Athens, Sparta, and Thebes was extinguished.

—Samuel K. Eddy, updated by Jeffrey L. Buller

ADDITIONAL READING:

Bradford, Alfred S., ed. and trans. *Philip II of Macedon.* Westport, Conn.: Praeger, 1992. A lavishly illustrated biography of Philip with its texts drawn from ancient sources. Also includes a good set of maps.

Cawkwell, George. *Philip of Macedon.* Boston: Faber & Faber, 1978. A good biographical introduction to Philip II and the events leading up to the battle of Chaeronea; intended for the general reader.

Hammond, Nicholas Geoffrey Lempriere. *Philip of Macedon.* Baltimore: The Johns Hopkins University Press, 1994. The most complete scholarly discussion of Philip II currently available. Includes extensive information on the Battle of Chaeronea and valuable bibliographic references.

Hatzopoulos, Miltiades B., and Louisa D. Loukopulos, eds. *Philip of Macedon.* Athens, Greece: Ekdotike Athenon, 1980. An overview of the historical, cultural, and military aspects of Philip II's reign. Includes maps that are particularly useful in illustrating the background to the battle of Chaeronea.

Montgomery, Hugo. *The Way to Chaeronea.* New York: Columbia University Press, 1983. Primarily focusing on Demosthenes' role before the Battle of Chaeronea, this work provides a thorough analysis of Athenian foreign policy in the period before Philip's conquest.

SEE ALSO: 478-448 B.C., Athenian Empire Is Created; 431-404 B.C., Peloponnesian War; 401-400 B.C., March of the "Ten Thousand."

335-323 B.C.
ARISTOTLE WRITES THE POLITICS

Aristotle writes the Politics, *establishing a classic body of political concepts capable of being applied by later generations of Western political analysts.*

DATE: c. 335-323 B.C.

LOCALE: Athens, Greece

CATEGORIES: Cultural and intellectual history; Government and politics

KEY FIGURE:

Aristotle of Stagira (384-322 B.C.), a major Greek philosopher and founder of the Lyceum

SUMMARY OF EVENT. Aristotle's *Politics* is but one of a number of treatises compiled in the Lyceum from school discussions of the philosopher on every conceivable realm of phenomena that was of interest to the Greek mind. In his discussion of politics, Aristotle did not seek, as Plato had done, to lay foundations for a moral reconstruction of human community existence; instead, he sought to understand the distinctive form of Greek community life, the *polis.* The result of his work was the establishment of a classic body of normative political concepts capable of being applied by later generations of Western political analysts.

Characteristic of Aristotle's organismic perspective on the whole spectrum of phenomena is his concept of the city-state as a natural entity developing in response to inherent needs and drives in man. Man has a natural place in a hierarchy of life in which each genus and species of creature has its own distinctive inherent possibilities of development and modes of formal self-realization. At their own level in this hierarchy, human beings not only enjoy and participate in the plant and animal forms of development and realization but, as creatures uniquely endowed with reason, humans build upon the foundation of these lower life-activities a distinctively human mode of development and formal perfection.

Because they have the power of reason, humans are able not only to experience pain and pleasure like the lower animals but also to discriminate between good and evil, justice and injustice, and to share with others of their kind a community of values. For this reason human beings, more than any other animal, fulfill themselves naturally in forms of shared existence. The forms of community are themselves derived from a natural complementarity of the differing natures of human beings participating in a community. At the most primitive level, the household reaps the advantages of the association of man and woman for procreation and of ruler and ruled for mutual security. In those suited by nature for rule, the power of reason is sufficiently developed to discern what is advantageous for the common welfare, while in those who are by nature servile resides the physical power to effect such policy and sufficient reason to recognize the advantage of obedience to their wiser master.

Beyond the primitive community of the household is the village, a community of households established in order to secure, on a more permanent basis, the advantages of shared existence. Beyond the village-community stands the natural form of fully realized community life—the association of villages, or *polis.* While the *polis* comes into existence, according to Aristotle, in order to sustain human life in a fully self-sufficient form, it continues to exist in order to achieve the optimal perfection of human existence.

It should be noted that in designating the *polis* as the natural form of fully realized human community, Aristotle was thinking not of the large nation-state or of the industrial state or other historical times and places, but specifically of the relatively small Greek city-states, whose members could be reasonably familiar with one another. Once these circumstances are understood, the meaning of Aristotle's dictum, "Man is by nature a *polis*-animal," can be appreciated in its uniquely Greek and Aristotelian context.

Polis-communities may differ widely from one another, but the factor determining the distinctive form of each is its *politeia,* or constitution, which defines who are the citizens of the *polis* and in what category of citizens the primary authority for judicial and policy decisions resides. According to Aristotle, the citizen is that individual who participates in dispensing justice and determining policy. While a constitution may confer supreme authority upon one man, upon a few, or upon all freeborn members of the *polis,* Aristotle viewed as a legitimate constitution one in which the authoritative body in the *polis* dispenses justice and formulates policy with a view to the well-being of all freeborn citizens, and not the well-being of the authoritative body itself alone. In the latter case, the constitution would not be a legitimate form but a perversion. On this basis, Aristotle distinguished between three legiti-

In his treatise Politics, *Aristotle described the essential features of the Greek* polis-*community, explaining how aristocrats, soldiers, farmers, and laborers fulfilled important functions that sustained the community's collective well-being.* (Library of Congress)

mate forms, which he terms monarchy, aristocracy, and *politeia* (in a distinctive sense that could be translated as "republic" or "constitutional democracy"), and three corresponding perversions, which he called tyranny, oligarchy, and *demokratia* (which might perhaps be translated as "rule of the proletariat").

A survey of the functions necessary to a fully self-sufficient *polis* that maximizes the potentials of human well-being and of Aristotle's distribution of status among those who perform these functions makes fully clear to the modern mind that Aristotle's political theory was not so much a universally applicable conceptual scheme as it was a distillation of distinctively Greek aristocratic notions of what constituted optimal human well-being in a *polis*-community. These necessary functions included food production, provision of essential goods and services, maintenance of order within and defense against enemies, accumulation of surplus wealth to sustain private expenditures and security forces, cultic functions of *polis* religion, and policy making and dispensation of justice. In Aristotle's view, the farmers and laborers who performed the first two of these functions, while essential to the self-sufficiency and well-being of the *polis*, could not be citizens. Lacking the higher uses of reason necessary to participate in judicial and policy-making decisions, farmers and laborers were servants sustaining the plant and animal

functions of a corporate body, of which only the true citizens could achieve full realization of the well-being possible to humans. The last three of the necessary functions were performed by the true citizens at the ages at which they were best suited by nature to discharge them, and surplus wealth would also be in the possession of the citizens proper.

Several ideas emerge from a reading of Aristotle's *Politics*. First, the state has a natural history, and part of its meaning must be sought in its development. Second, the state has a natural basis in economics, family structure, and in ethics, Third, there are basic state forms into which political activity falls, and the art of politics lies in the choice among those forms and their combinations. Fourth, the art of government is the art of finding a proper equilibrium for the forces in the state. Aristotle was interested in the rise and fall of political systems, but he did not make the mistake of tracing that rise and fall to autonomous factors within politics. Like Plato, he believed that much in politics depended on the image which was stamped on the young by birth, education, nature, and habit. Above all, Aristotle was interested in what constituted the strength and weakness of the political community. He saw that the strength of the state depends not so much upon the machinery of government as upon the moral sense of the community.

Aristotle said "man is by nature a political animal" and "he who by nature and not by mere accident is without a state, is either above humanity or below it." By this, he meant that in their origin and impulses, in terms of the end toward which their development tends, human beings must be part of a whole that is greater than the sum of its parts. Except as he is a member of a collectivity, a man ceases to be a man and becomes either something greater or something less. The most important element of strength in a community is the sense of greatness that it can generate. The most important political emotion in human beings is the thirst for greatness, which, under pressure, stretches them beyond their everyday selves so that they reach the full outline of their human personality.

—Carl W. Conrad, updated by Susan M. Taylor

ADDITIONAL READING:

Davis, Michael. *The Politics of Philosophy: A Commentary on Aristotle's "Politics."* Lanham, Md.: Rowman & Littlefield, 1996. This work provides a sound discussion of Aristotle's contributions to political science.

Johnson, Curtis N. *Aristotle's Theory of the State*. New York: St. Martin's Press, 1990. Johnson discusses Aristotle's conception of the *polis* as a natural entity fulfilling a human impulse toward perfection.

Loizou, Andros, and Harry Lesser. *Polis and Politics: Essays in Greek Moral and Political Philosophy*. Brookfield, Vt.: Avebury Press, 1990. A series of papers that concentrate on Greek political thought.

Miller, Fred Dycus. *Nature, Justice, and Rights in Aristotle's "Politics."* Oxford: Clarendon Press, 1995. Focusing on Aristotle's concept of natural law and justice, Miller provides a good analysis of Aristotle's contributions not only to law but also to political science.

Mulgan, R. G. *Aristotle's Political Theory: An Introduction for Students of Political Theory*. Oxford: Clarendon Press, 1977. Mulgan presents a discussion of Aristotle's view of politics as well as the thoughts of other political theorists through 1800.

Nicholas, Mary P. *Citizens and Statesmen: A Study of Aristotle's "Politics."* Lanham, Md.: Rowman & Littlefield, 1992. Contains useful insights into Aristotle's view of the *polis* and how he has contributed to modern ideas of political science.

Voegelin, Eric. *Plato and Aristotle*. Vol. 3 in *Order and History*. Baton Rouge: Louisiana State University Press, 1957. This older study presents both the positive achievements and the shortcomings of Aristotle's investigation of political order.

SEE ALSO: 600-500 B.C., Greek Philosophers Formulate Theories of the Cosmos; 380 B.C., Plato Develops His Theory of Ideas; 325-323 B.C., Aristotle Isolates Science as a Discipline.

332 B.C.

FOUNDING OF ALEXANDRIA

The founding of Alexandria creates a new city that becomes a center of Hellenistic culture and learning.

DATE: 332 B.C.

LOCALE: The Nile Delta in Egypt

CATEGORIES: Cultural and intellectual history; Expansion and land acquisition

KEY FIGURES:

Alexander the Great (356-323 B.C.), king of Macedonia, 336-323 B.C.

Dinocrates of Macedonia, architect who planned Alexandria

Ptolemy Philadelphus (308-246 B.C.), king of Egypt, c. 282-246 B.C.

Ptolemy Soter (c. 367-c. 282 B.C.), king of Egypt, 306-c. 282 B.C.

Sostratus of Cnidus, architect of the lighthouse at Alexandria

SUMMARY OF EVENT. When Alexander the Great took Egypt from the Persians in 332 B.C., he had no intention of

restoring the country as an independent kingdom. He meant to make it a province of his own, and he believed that a new Hellenic city would make a more suitable capital than one of the old Egyptian towns. This capital was to be named Alexandria in honor of himself as its founder. The site chosen was on the coast, on the western edge of the Nile Delta, where the city would have easy communications with the interior by river and with the outside world by sea. Labor was conscripted from adjacent villages of Egyptian peasants and fishermen, and the work began in 331 B.C. with impressive religious ceremonies. Greek seers prophesied that the city would become "large and prosperous, a source of nourishment to many lands." Construction of the metropolis took years to complete and was still proceeding in the time of Alexander's successors, Ptolemy I and Ptolemy II.

The original plan of the city was prepared by the architect Dinocrates, who had it laid out on the grid pattern developed in the fifth century. It was divided into four large quarters by two broad avenues. Canopus Street, a processional boulevard one hundred feet wide, ran east and west along the long axis; a lesser street running north and south bisected it. At this intersection was the civic center containing the Court of Justice; the Gymnasium, a handsome, colonnaded building two hundred yards along its front; a series of sacred groves; and, most remarkable of all, an artificial hill dedicated to the god Pan. Its summit could easily be reached by a spiral path, and, from this point, visitors—of whom there were many—could survey the entire metropolis.

The most striking characteristic of Alexandria was its size. By the third century B.C., its population had already reached perhaps half a million. By the beginning of the Christian era, it stood at nearly one million, rivaling even the capital of the Roman Empire. One quarter of the city was inhabited mostly by Egyptians and half-caste Greeks, who had no civic rights and performed the menial labor of the city. Another quarter was the residence of the Jews, who came to Egypt in considerable numbers during the reign of Ptolemy I. They enjoyed a certain autonomy under their own ethnarch and council and constituted one of the most important Jewish settlements in all the ancient world.

The Greco-Macedonian quarter seems to have been near the sea breezes of the waterfront. It is probable that the Europeans were organized into *demes* and tribes, with an autonomous council and assembly. From east to west along the waterfront stretched warehouses and harbors that received merchant ships from upriver, from Mediterranean ports, and even, via a canal connecting the Nile River with the Red Sea, from the Far East. By the second century B.C., there was contact with India, and Buddhist missionaries visited the port. Here, too, were the efficient dockyards of the Ptolemaic navy.

The Royal Quarter was the most imposing of all. It was ornamented with the palaces of the Ptolemies and the nearby monumental tomb of Alexander. Here also was the great Serapeum, a magnificent temple dedicated to the dynasty's new god. The palace complex contained the famous library and museum, where the first two Ptolemies gathered the most distinguished minds of the third century for science and scholarship.

Dominating the skyline and even overshadowing the palace itself rose the great stone lighthouse designed by Sostratus of Cnidus. It stood on the island of Pharos, which was connected to the mainland by a manmade mole nearly three-quarters of a mile long, pierced by two bridged channels for ships. The tower was more than four hundred feet high and was provided with a windlass so that firewood could be drawn to the top. Here, fires blazed by night in front of a reflector of polished bronze, warning ships of dangers and guiding them into the harbor.

In the third century, the culture of Alexandria eclipsed even that of Athens. The scholarship of Aristophanes of Byzantium, the astronomy of Aristarchus, the poetry of Callimachus, and the medical studies of Erasistratus all were the products of Alexandria. The city was also an important bridge between the cultures of the Greeks and the Jews. The Septuagint, the Greek translation of the Old Testament, was begun in Alexandria in the third century, and the scholar Philo later worked there.

Alexandria contained both the positive and negative qualities of Hellenistic culture. While the city was the birthplace of much that was good, it was also infected with urban ills. Mobs of the poor sometimes rioted against the government and staged massacres. The city's pleasure domes housed the most sophisticated debauchery; its slums, the most sordid depravity. There was conflict between ethnic groups, with Egyptians swelling the ranks of the proletariat while most Greek immigrants enjoyed lives of privilege. Because intermarriage between Egyptians and Greeks was prohibited by law, few Egyptians found themselves sharing fully in the benefits of Greek civic culture. —*Samuel K. Eddy, updated by Jeffrey L. Buller*

ADDITIONAL READING:

Fraser, Peter Marshall. *Ptolemaic Alexandria.* Oxford: Clarendon Press, 1972. A scholarly three-volume study, not only of the origins of Alexandria but also its continued history and development in the period after Alexander the Great.

Hammond, Nicholas Geoffrey Lempriere. *Alexander the Great.* Park Ridge, N.J.: Noyes Press, 1980. Detailed biography of Alexander by one of the twentieth century's foremost scholars of the Hellenistic Age.

Jouguet, Pierre. *Alexander the Great and the Hellenistic World.* Translated by M. R. Dobie. Chicago: Ares, 1985. Originally published in 1928, this volume still provides an excellent overview of Alexander's Hellenization of the east, including Africa.

Lane Fox, Robin. *The Search for Alexander.* Boston: Little, Brown, 1980. Intended for the general reader, this work provides an excellent combination of current research, photographs, and readable narration. Contains useful information about the founding of Alexandria.

Warry, John. *Alexander, 334-323 B.C.: Conquest of the Persian Empire.* London: Osprey, 1991. A concise biography that places the founding of Alexandria within the context of Alexander's eastern campaign. Also contains useful maps.

SEE ALSO: 338 B.C., Battle of Chaeronea; 275 B.C., Advances in Hellenistic Astronomy; 250 B.C., Discoveries of Archimedes.

331 B.C.
BATTLE OF GAUGAMELA

The Battle of Gaugamela pits Alexander the Great's Macedonian forces against the Persians in a decisive battle for supremacy in Asia Minor.

DATE: October 1, 331 B.C.

LOCALE: Mesopotamia

CATEGORIES: Expansion and land acquisition; Wars, uprisings, and civil unrest

KEY FIGURES:

Alexander the Great (356-323 B.C.), king of Macedonia, 336-323 B.C.

Bessus (died c. 329 B.C.), Persian satrap of Bactria, who ruled as Artaxerxes IV after Darius' death in 330 B.C.

Darius III (died 330 B.C.), king of the kings of the Persian Empire, 336-330 B.C.

Parmenio (c. 400-330 B.C.), Macedonian general who served as Alexander's second in command in conquest of Persia

SUMMARY OF EVENT. After King Philip II of Macedonia had defeated the Greek states in the Battle of Chaeronea, he made plans to invade the Persian Empire. His assassination in 336 B.C., however, forestalled this scheme until his son Alexander made his succession to the throne secure. In 334 B.C., Alexander invaded Asia Minor and quickly defeated the Persians on the Granicus River. Alexander advanced eastward and, at the town of Issus in northern Syria, defeated King Darius II himself in 333. Next, Alexander took the wealthy province of Egypt in 332.

ALEXANDER'S EARLY CAMPAIGN AGAINST THE PERSIAN EMPIRE, 334-331 B.C.

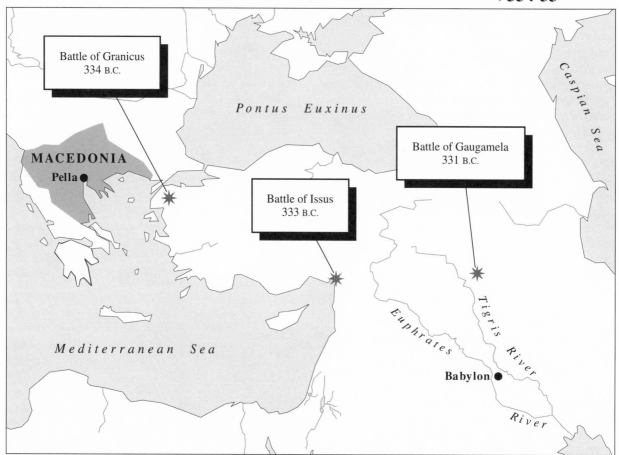

By 331 B.C., Alexander was ready for a second and decisive battle with Darius for the supremacy of Asia. The Persian king had been collecting a large army, and he came westward as far as the plains near the village of Gaugamela (Tel Gomel in modern Iraq), where he waited to be attacked. Darius' army consisted mainly of cavalry posted in long lines on level ground. The left wing was made up of his good Iranian horsemen, the Persians, some heavily mailed Saca, and the Bactrians, all commanded by Bessus, the satrap of Bactria. Syrian, Mesopotamian, and Median cavalry took stations on the right. Behind the cavalry was the infantry, mostly troops of little fighting value who had been conscripted recently. Behind the center of the two fighting lines was Darius, with his personal bodyguard and fifteen elephants. The Persian forces numbered more than fifty thousand men.

In the autumn, Alexander arrived in Gaugamela, and, on October 1, he led his army out of camp. Alexander had forty thousand infantry and seven thousand horsemen, both Greek and Macedonian. His army was also in long lines, with the infantry placed in the center and half the cavalry on either flank. Parmenion commanded the left, while Alexander himself took charge of the right with his best squadrons of Macedonian heavy cavalry. Alexander's chief virtues as a general were his understanding of how to use cavalry and infantry together and his gift for inspiring his men, either in battle or in the relentless, disciplined pursuit of a disorganized and fleeing foe. He now slowly advanced to his right while studying the enemy's array until the Hypaspists, a brigade of crack Macedonian infantry, were facing scythed chariots in front of the Persian center. Alexander turned to confront the enemy. Bessus sent the Saca charging at the extreme right of Alexander's cavalry. Alexander countered by bringing forward squadrons deployed behind them. There was a sharp fight with losses on both sides until Bessus' cavalry drew off to regroup. Meanwhile, the scythed chariots bounded forward against the Macedonian center, but here Alexander had posted troops armed with arrows and javelins who were able to shoot down most of the chariot horses before they reached the phalanx. The chariots, which did little damage to the Macedonians, were routed.

The cavalry action on Alexander's front had opened a gap between Bessus and the center of the long line of Persian horsemen. As soon as Alexander had his own horsemen under control, he charged into this gap, with the infantry phalanx following him on the run. This blow was irresistible, and the Persian lines began to crumple and stream toward the rear. For the second time, Darius turned to flee. His personal guard of two thousand Greek mercenaries stood their ground and lost five hundred men, sacrificed to win time for Darius to escape. As Alexander was reforming his troops to pursue Darius, he received distress messages from Parmenion that the Persian right was pressing him hard. Alexander rushed across the field with his own cavalry, and his timely arrival sent the Persian right reeling back. As the battle became a general rout, Alexander drove his horseman rapidly after the remnants of the Persian army, dispersing large numbers of fugitives until

he reached the city of Arbela after nightfall. Despite these efforts, Alexander did not succeed in catching up with Darius.

The Battle of Arbela (Gaugamela) was decisive. The Persian forces were so scattered that they could not be reorganized. The Persian nobles believed that Darius was responsible for the debacle, and they accordingly deposed and killed him. Bessus, whose troops were the only ones to withdraw in fairly good order, became king as Artaxerxes IV. He was unable, however, to collect enough men to oppose Alexander's swift and inexorable advance. The Persians quickly lost their wealthiest provinces, and the rich plains of Babylonia surrendered without resistance. Persis, the heartland of the Persian Empire, fell, and the religious capital of Persepolis was also taken, along with some fourteen years' worth of accumulated tribute. Alexander eventually caught Artaxerxes and had him executed, alleging the murder of Darius as an excuse. Alexander also burned the magnificent royal buildings at Persepolis. This

As seen in this engraving, elephants, horses, and scythed chariots played roles in the clash between the Persian and Macedonian armies at the Battle of Gaugamela. (Archive Photos)

act signaled the fall of the Persian Empire, the beginning of Alexander's own empire, and the subjugation of the East to Macedonian imperialism.

—*Samuel K. Eddy, updated by Jeffrey L. Buller*

ADDITIONAL READING:

Adcock, F. E. *The Greek and Macedonian Art of War.* Berkeley: University of California, 1957. A reprint of Adcock's Sather lectures delivered at the University of California, this slim volume provides insight into Alexander's military strategy. Adcock regards Gaugamela as the Persian army's only serious attempt to win a battle by using chariots; this was a strategy that failed utterly.

Fuller, J. F. C. *The Generalship of Alexander the Great.* New Brunswick, N.J.: Rutgers University Press, 1960. Still the most thorough analysis of Alexander's military strategy. Written by a British major general who was himself renowned as a strategist.

Hammond, Nicholas Geoffrey Lempriere. *Alexander the Great.* Park Ridge, N.J.: Noyes Press, 1980. Detailed biography of Alexander by one of the twentieth century's foremost scholars of the Hellenistic Age.

Lane Fox, Robin. *The Search for Alexander.* Boston: Little, Brown, 1980. Intended for the general reader, this work provides an excellent mix of current research, photographs, and readable narration. Contains an extensive discussion of the Battle of Gaugamela.

Marsden, Eric William. *The Campaign of Gaugamela.* Liverpool, England: Liverpool University Press, 1964. A brief but comprehensive account of nearly every aspect of the battle. Also contains a useful map and a list of helpful sources for further study.

Wepman, Dennis. *Alexander the Great.* New York: Chelsea House, 1986. Concise though reliable biography of Alexander the Great. Also noted for an introductory essay on leadership written by Arthur M. Schlesinger, Jr.

SEE ALSO: 700-330 B.C., Phalanx Is Developed as a Military Unit; 480-479 B.C., Persian Invasion of Greece; 338 B.C., Battle of Chaeronea.

325-323 B.C.
ARISTOTLE ISOLATES SCIENCE AS A DISCIPLINE

Aristotle isolates science as a discipline, becoming the first philosopher to approach the study of nature in a systematic way and providing a starting place for natural philosophers into the Middle Ages.

DATE: 325-323 B.C.
LOCALE: Athens, Greece

CATEGORIES: Cultural and intellectual history; Education; Science and technology
KEY FIGURE:
Aristotle of Stagira (384-322 B.C.), founder and head of the Lyceum

SUMMARY OF EVENT. Born in Stagira in northern Greece and the son of the physician to Amyntas II of Macedonia, Aristotle came to Athens when he was seventeen years old and studied at Plato's Academy for twenty years. When Plato died in 347 B.C., Aristotle left the Academy and traveled for twelve years, visiting various centers of learning in Asia Minor and Macedonia. During this period of travel, he developed his interest in the natural sciences, to which he applied his method of inquiry. He returned to Athens in 335 B.C. after a brief period of tutoring Alexander the Great, Amyntas' grandson, and established the Lyceum, a school which became a center of learning. He taught there until a year before his death.

The range of topics discussed and developed by Aristotle at the Lyceum is overwhelming: natural philosophy with its considerations of space, time, and motion; the heavenly bodies; life and psychic activities; ethical and political problems; animals and biological matters; and rhetoric and poetics. Further, he is sometimes credited with creating new fields of research, such as terrestrial dynamics and optics. He also taxonomized plants and animals and organized earlier Greeks' ideas about planetary astronomy in *On the Heavens.*

Perhaps the most significant aspect of Aristotle's work is his development of a "scientific" approach to these studies. This "scientific" approach recognizes the existence of independent disciplines, each employing its own principles and hypotheses. Such an approach also works out a methodology or procedure for each field of study, aiming at true and certain knowledge.

The Greek term that Aristotle uses for "scientific knowledge" is *episteme* which can best be translated as "true knowledge" or the "most certain knowledge." This knowledge includes the awareness of an object, of its causes, and that it can be no other way. Medieval scholars translated the Greek *episteme* as the Latin *scientia* which came into English as "science."

In recognizing independent fields of study, Aristotle showed a significant departure from Plato's philosophy. Plato had envisioned one single science. For him, true knowledge was the contemplation of the Forms: Virtue, Justice, Beauty, and Goodness. All other disciplines were subordinate to knowledge of the Forms. Aristotle, on the other hand, did not advocate a hierarchical structure of knowledge. Each study locates its own particular subject matter and defines its principles from which conclusions are to be drawn. Almost all his treatises begin with the same format: "Our task here concerns demonstrative science," that is, logic; or "Human conduct belongs to political science."

Aristotle's insistence upon the division of sciences, each using special principles, is indicative of his rejection of any absolute master plan of knowledge. He does, however, recognize "common principles," or principles shared by more than one science. For example, the "equals from equals" principle of mathematics can be used in geometry to deduce a conclusion about a line. Aristotle warns the geometrician, however, that this can be done "if he assumes the truth not universally, but only of magnitudes." Aristotle never intends the same common principles to be universally applied in exactly the same way throughout all the sciences. If this were the case, there would not be "sciences," but rather "Science."

The second important feature of Aristotle's scientific approach concerns methodology. In the *Posterior Analytics*, he develops the general technique which the particular disciplines are to employ in order to achieve scientific knowledge. First, an investigation must always begin with what is "better known" to humans. They must begin with observable data and facts, and not construct wild hypotheses. Second, human beings must proceed to a knowledge of the cause of the facts; mere observation is not enough. Observing something only indicates that something is the case; it does not explain why it is the case. Learning the cause tells people why, and this involves a logical demonstration. Third, the cause or reason of the fact must be of "that fact and no other." This criterion is the basis for a scientific law, since it demands a universal connection between the subject and its attributes.

The second and third criteria listed above require a deductive system of demonstration which is expressed in the universal positive form of the syllogism that Aristotle developed in the *Prior Analytics*. There is also what might be called an "inductive" approach to his method of science. Aristotle raises the question of how humans know the universal principles from which demonstration is to proceed. He answers that human knowledge of such principles begins with many sense perceptions of similar events. Human memory unifies these perceptions into a single experience. The human intellect or mind then understands the universal import of the experience. From many similar experiences, humans recognize a universal pattern.

Aristotle's method of science combines the theoretical and the practical. The theoretical aspect includes logical demonstrations and universal principles. The practical includes the necessary role of sense perception as it relates to particular objects. In the *Metaphysics* he warns that

In recognizing independent fields of study within the broad realm of the sciences, Aristotle helped pave the way for the botanical studies of Theophrastus, depicted here to the left of the title of this seventeenth century work on plants and herbal remedies. (Library of Congress)

physicians do not cure men-in-general in a universal sense; rather they cure Socrates or Callias, a particular man. He adds that one who knows medical theory dealing with universals without experience with particulars will fail to effect a cure. Instead, he advises the use of procedures grounded in common sense that have proven their validity in practice.

One application of this method is in Aristotle's writings on biology. He makes theoretical interpretations based on his dissection of marine animals and empirical observations, although he does also rely on other writers' descriptions of some animals. Based on these researches, he arranges a "ladder of nature." Because he can see changes in the realm of plants and animals, he affirms the reality of nature and the value of its study. He is optimistic that he could use natural history to find causal explanations of physiology.

For Aristotle, therefore, scientific knowledge includes the observation of concrete data, the formulation of universal principles, and the construction of logical proofs. Greek "science" prior to Aristotle, largely a melange of philosophical and quasi-mythological assumptions, blossomed after his investigations into the specialized work of Theophrastus in botany, Hierophilus in medicine, and Aristarchus in astronomy.   —*Joseph J. Romano,*
updated by Amy Ackerberg-Hastings

Additional Reading:

Barnes, Jonathan. *Aristotle*. Oxford: Oxford University Press, 1982. A straightforward, readable review of Aristotle's literature and the context in which it arose.

Bolton, Robert, and Robin Smith, eds. *Logic, Dialectic, and Science in Aristotle*. Special issue of *Ancient Philosophy* 14 (1994). Seven scholars of ancient Greek philosophy try to resolve puzzling sections in Aristotle's works on these subjects.

Ferejohn, Michael. *The Origins of Aristotelian Science*. New Haven: Yale University Press, 1991. An in-depth discussion of the theoretical structure of Aristotle's scientific method.

Golthelf, Allan, and James G. Lennox, eds. *Philosophical Issues in Aristotle's Biology*. Cambridge: Cambridge University Press, 1987. Noted Aristotelian scholars focus on the relationship between Aristotle's biological researches and writings and the methods he proposed in works such as the *Analytics*.

Lindberg, David C. *The Beginnings of Western Science*. Chicago: University of Chicago Press, 1992. An introductory-level, award-winning book which aims clear and thorough explanations of ancient and medieval scientific ideas to a diverse audience.

Lloyd, G. E. R. *Aristotle: The Growth and Structure of His Thought*. Cambridge: Cambridge University Press, 1968. Lloyd deals with Aristotle's intellectual development, as well as the fundamentals of his ideas with respect to logic, physics, ethics, and the like, and further introduces the reader to the views of other scholars in this work.

McKeon, Richard. *Introduction to Aristotle*. 2d ed. Chicago: University of Chicago Press, 1973. A general introduction to Aristotle which mainly includes selections from a number of his works, with some discussion of his scientific method.

See also: 335-323 B.C., Aristotle Writes the *Politics*; 275 B.C., Advances in Hellenistic Astronomy; 250 B.C., Discoveries of Archimedes.

312-264 B.C.
Building of the Appian Way

The building of the Appian Way improves transportation within the Roman Empire through the construction of a major highway.

Date: 312-264 B.C.
Locale: Latium and Campania, south of Rome
Categories: Science and technology; Transportation
Key figures:
Appius Claudius Crassus (surnamed Caecus "the Blind"), Roman consul, censor in 312 B.C.
Trajan (Marcus Ulpius Traianus Augustus; A.D. 53-117), Roman emperor, A.D. 98-117

Summary of event. During the first centuries of the Roman conquest of Italy, there were no major roads to connect the growing city on the Tiber River with other areas on the peninsula. Whereas the Persians had created a partially paved road system through their wide domain, Italian travel was limited before 300 B.C. In the early fourth century, short gravel or dirt trackways reached out from Rome to Alba Longa twelve miles to the south, and east to the salt beds in the mountains. Among his many duties, the Roman magistrate known as the *censor* was charged with maintaining such roads.

The earliest paved highway of any length in Italy was begun in the year 312 B.C., when the censor Appius Claudius Crassus took the initiative in projecting a military highway south from Rome. Appius was a vigorous patrician and two-time consul who was also credited with constructing Rome's first aqueduct and with enrolling plebeians in the senate. His chief monument, however, was the road he began, which was named the Via Appia.

Surveyors laid out the first fifty miles of the road on a straight southwest line paralleling the seacoast, about a dozen miles inland. Rapid military access to the coast may have been one purpose for the highway. Its chief original objective, however, was the key city of Capua, in the heart of the fertile Campanian plain. Capua had recently been captured by Roman armies, and Roman military colonies had been founded in strategic sites near Capua.

Less than twelve miles of the new road was paved immediately. Here, laborers dug a trench fifteen feet wide and three feet deep. Lining this with layers of loose gravel and small rock, they carefully fitted large slabs of polygonal stone into place as a surface. This segment of the road climbed to a ridge, from which it provided panoramic views of flat lands toward the sea as well as the Alban Hills to the east. An old village, Bovillae, was the first post-station at the end of the original paved area in 292 B.C.

Climbing and descending more steeply, travelers

reached the village of Ariccia, where many travelers, including the poet Horace, spent the first night out of Rome. At such points, the road was intersected by a crossroad, used by farmers to bring produce to a village market. Beyond Ariccia were the broad Pomptine Marshes, where it was necessary to drive in wooden pilings to raise a causeway six feet above the swamp land. At a trade center called Forum Appii, the road ended temporarily. Travelers could take boats twenty miles to Terracina or choose a long detour inland.

South of Terracina were mountains, forcing a zigzag route until a sea-level road was cut into the cliffs during imperial times. A four-arch brick bridge crossed the Liri River, and at Sinuessa the road turned sharply eastward along the Volturno River until it crossed on another massive bridge into Capua, 132 miles from the Roman Forum.

Too blind to see the finished project, Appius was said to have walked barefoot on the road to feel that the stones were well placed. Later, the highway was stretched out to Venusia, a colony settled by twenty thousand inhabitants. By 264 B.C., the road reached the sea at the ports of Tarentum and Brundisium, a total of 366 miles from Rome.

Other highways later shared the traffic, but the Via Appia remained the chief route south of Rome well into imperial times. About 250 B.C., milestones were placed at intervals measuring five thousand Roman feet. Trees planted by the roadside shaded travelers. In ancient times and later during the medieval period, rich Italians built tombs alongside the road, which eventually became lined with markets, towns, temples, monasteries, and other landmarks. One famous location was the Quo Vadis Church, where, according to legend, Saint Peter was said to have met his Lord and turned back during his flight from Rome.

Finally paved to Brundisium by the Emperor Trajan in A.D. 114, the Appian Way was called the "Queen of Roads" by the poet Statius. By that time, a complex web of roadways, built to the same pattern, crisscrossed the Roman Empire. Built to last and constructed on deep-set roadbeds resistant to flood or frost, these roads bound together Rome's conquests. Although originally used as military passageways, these roads served many other purposes. Roman civilians, such as Cicero, and provincials, such as the Apostle Paul, traveled on these roads.

In paving their fifty-three thousand miles of roads, the Romans used many local stones. The most common type of stone found in Italy was the hard green-black volcanic basalt used along much of the Appian Way. While floods or cultivation have obliterated the old road in many places, long stretches are still usable, paralleling more modern highways.

—*Roger B. McShane, updated by Jeffrey L. Buller*

ADDITIONAL READING:

Hamblin, Dora Jane. *The Appian Way, a Journey*. New York: Random House, 1974. Part travelogue, part history, this work provides a highly readable introduction to the Appian Way. Short but useful bibliography.

MacKendrick, Paul. *The Mute Stones Speak*. 2d ed. New York: W. W. Norton, 1983. Expertly combining archaeological information with historical and social insight, this work contains a valuable short survey of Roman road construction, including the Via Appia.

Paget, Robert F. *Central Italy: An Archaeological Guide*. Park Ridge, N.J.: Noyes Press, 1973. In addition to providing a wealth of archaeological information about Italian prehistory and Villanovan, Etruscan, Samnite, Italic, and early Roman remains, this work also discusses the ancient Roman road system.

Scullard, Howard Hayes. *A History of the Roman World: 753-146 B.C.* 4th ed. New York: Methuen, 1980. Lavishly detailed and comprehensive in scope, this book places the construction of the Via Appia in its context of Roman economic, military, and social history.

Wiseman, T. P. "Roman Republican Road-Building." *Papers of the British School at Rome* 38 (1970): 122-152. A scholarly discussion of early construction techniques used to plot and construct Roman roads.

SEE ALSO: 447-438 B.C., The Parthenon Is Built; 312 B.C., First Roman Aqueduct Is Built; 240 B.C., Exploitation of the Arch.

312 B.C.
FIRST ROMAN AQUEDUCT IS BUILT

The first Roman aqueduct is built to transport water into cities to supply community baths, inaugurating an advance in hydraulic engineering and architecture that continues to operate in Europe for many centuries.

DATE: 312 B.C.

LOCALE: Rome and numerous cities under its dominion

CATEGORIES: Science and technology; Transportation

KEY FIGURES:

Appius Claudius Crassus (surnamed Caecus "the Blind"), Roman consul, censor in 312 B.C. and builder of the first Roman aqueduct

Sextus Julius Frontinus, appointed water commissioner by Nerva in A.D. 97, author of the *De Aquis Urbis Romae*

Quintus Marcius Rex, builder of the first high-level aqueduct between 144 and 140 B.C.

SUMMARY OF EVENT. The engineering of aqueduct construction was complicated and based on a piecemeal evolution of techniques over five hundred years. The water, tapped from springs, streams, or reservoirs, was allowed to descend down a gently sloping channel until it reached a point of distribution. The main conduit was generally rather tall and narrow, approximately five by two feet. Because of the gravitational flow of the water, aqueducts had to be laid out carefully. If their slope was too slight the water became sluggish; if it was too steep pressures would build up to cause overflowing and ruptures. Vitruvius, the celebrated architect of Augustus' time, recommended a fall of one in two hundred, an excellent gradient which could not, however, always be maintained. Because the velocity of the water needed to be controlled, and hills and valleys had to be circumvented, an aqueduct was usually much longer than the straight distance between inlet and outlet. The aqueducts operated on the principle of constant offtake, so the outlets within the city were always open. Once an aqueduct was finished, it required constant maintenance to clean out deposits left by the hard Roman water.

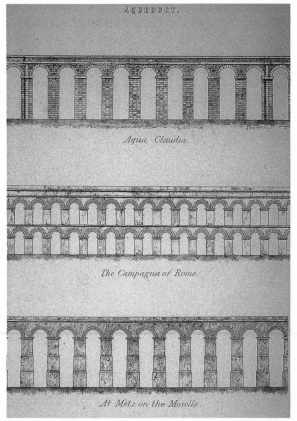

This engraving depicts the varied architectural designs of Roman aqueducts: the Aqua Claudia, *which brought water to the hilltops of Rome; the double-tiered* Campagna, *which fed into the* Aqua Claudia; *and the aqueduct at Metz on the Moselle River in northeastern France.* (Archive Photos)

An aqueduct could be constructed in three different ways. It could be led through a tunnel cut into the ground, laid in a ditch and covered over, or raised above the surface of the ground on a wall or series of arches. This last procedure generally recommended itself because its building materials were cheap while lead pipe for laying underground was expensive. Still, a long aqueduct often made use of all three methods. The first Roman aqueduct, the *Aqua Appia* of 312 B.C., ran its ten-mile course mostly underground, as did the *Anio Vetus* of 272 B.C. The third Roman aqueduct, however, the *Aqua Marcia*, built in 144-140 B.C., drew its waters from the Anio behind Tivoli only sixteen miles northeast of Rome and traveled fifty-eight miles before it reached the city. It was a high-level type aqueduct that crossed the Roman campagna on a series of arches nearly six miles long and entered the city at a level of 195 feet above the Tiber, high enough to supply the Capitoline, Caelian, and Aventine hills. When the *Aqua Tepula* of 125 B.C. and the *Aqua Julia* of 40 B.C. were built, their channels were superimposed upon those of the Marcian aqueduct near its approach to the city, making *Tepula and Julia* high-level types as well. The *Aqua Virgo* of 19 B.C. terminating in the Campus Martius, and the *Aqua Alsietina* of 2 B.C. supplying the Trastevere, were again underground. The famous *Aqua Claudia* was a very lofty structure reaching the highest hills of the city including the Palatine. The *Aqua Traiana* of A.D. 109, with its outlet on the Janiculum, had underground conduits, while the *Aqua Alexandrina* of A.D. 226 was carried on arches for most of its course.

The same methods of construction were used in the provinces. Occasionally refinements were made, as in the aqueducts of Lyons where siphons were used to carry water down and then up the other side of a valley or ravine. Siphons were probably used more often than most scholars have yet recognized. Bridges of arches were only utilized by Roman engineers in valleys that were up to fifty meters deep. Deeper valleys were crossed by means of siphons, and the number of siphons also depended on the number of valleys traversed by the aqueduct. Among the more famous remains of provincial aqueducts is the magnificent Pont du Gard, the bridge of the aqueduct for the city of Nîmes in southern France. This aqueduct, thirty-one miles long, crossed the Gard on a triple row of arches nine hundred feet long and 162 feet above the river. Built during the reign of Augustus, it remains one of the finest extant examples of Roman engineering. Hardly less spectacular is the gray granite bridge of the aqueduct of Segovia in Spain. Still in use, it crosses the valley next to the city on a series of arches 2,530 feet in length and 94 feet at their greatest height. In this category belongs

The ancient geographer Strabo admired the engineering skills displayed in Roman aqueducts, including his observations in his magnum opus, Geography. *(Library of Congress)*

drawing water from a spring near Tivoli to enter Rome by the now-famous *Porta Maggiore,* the eastern entrance into the city. Of its far-reaching line of arches, one section of 154 still stands intact together with many smaller groups of arches, one of which preserves the highest point of the aqueduct at more than eighty-eight feet. The enormous size of the undressed stones, laid dry, makes the work remarkable. Together with its associated aqueduct, the *Anio Novus*, it cost the Roman government fifty-five million sesterces.

Beyond Frontinus, primary accounts of the aqueducts are limited. Strabo praised the skills of the engineers in his geographical works, while Vitruvius included one chapter on aqueducts in his famous ten books of architecture. Frontinus himself appears to have been an administrative manager with no hydraulic experience, composing *De Aquis* to show that he had mastered knowledge of the aqueducts. Yet, enough has been learned of the aqueducts to know that Romans perceived them as the mark of civilized living, well worth the constant maintenance and expense they required. Successfully supplying millions of gallons of water to Rome's major cities, aqueducts were made to look beautiful to display them as the focus of civic pride that they were.
                                        —*M. Joseph Costelloe,*
                                updated by Amy Ackerberg-Hastings

ADDITIONAL READING:

Ashby, Thomas. *The Aqueducts of Ancient Rome.* Edited by I. A. Richmond. London: Oxford University Press, 1935. Reprint. Washington, D.C.: McGrath, 1973. A reprint of a classic standard which provides a meticulous description of the eleven aqueducts in Rome.

Barton, I. M., ed. *Roman Public Buildings.* Exeter, England: University of Exeter, 1989. The article on aqueducts in this undergraduate textbook on Roman architecture is by A. Trevor Hodge and breaks their construction down into understandable parts.

Evans, Harry B. *Water Distribution in Ancient Rome: The Evidence of Frontinus.* Ann Arbor: University of Michigan Press, 1994. Evans, a historian of ancient engineering, includes a translation of *De Aquis* and analysis of Frontinus' descriptions of Roman aqueducts.

Hodge, A. Trevor. "Siphons in Roman Aqueducts." *Scientific American* 252 (June, 1985): 114-119. An author of several books and articles on aqueducts here gives a well-explained account of the technology involved.

O'Connor, Colin. *Roman Bridges.* Cambridge, England: Cambridge University Press, 1993. O'Connor's explanation of Roman engineering in this area treats the aqueduct as a special bridge.

Owens, E. J. "The Kremna Aqueduct and Water Supply

also the magnificent span of the Roman aqueduct at Cherchel in Algeria which served ancient Caesarea. One of the most impressive sights in north Africa is the ruins of the aqueduct built by Hadrian to bring water from inland mountains to Carthage. It was eighty-two miles in length and some of its arches, 341 of which are still standing, reached a height of 130 feet.

Although it is impossible to say when Roman aqueduct construction reached its apogee, one might well hold that the building of the famous *Claudia* best represents that point in history. When this aqueduct was dedicated on August 1, 52, the birthday of the emperor whose name it bears, the famous Frontinus was already seventeen. Frontinus was the man who, as *curator aquarum* from A.D. 97 until some time before 103, was to be the authority on Roman aqueducts through his celebrated work *De Aquis Urbis Romae*.

The *Claudia*, begun in 38 under Caligula, is often regarded as the highest sustained achievement in Roman aqueduct construction. As the last and in many ways the most impressive stone aqueduct, Frontinus considered it especially magnificent. Conceived on a greater scale than any before it, it stretched virtually across the Campagna, in Roman Cities." *Greece and Rome* 38 (1991): 41-58. In a journal published for the Classical Association by Oxford University Press, a specific aqueduct is used to illustrate some general features of aqueducts.

SEE ALSO: 312-264 B.C., Building of the Appian Way; 240 B.C., Exploitation of the Arch.

300 B.C.
STOIC CONCEPTION OF NATURAL LAW

By positing a universal moral law independent of cultures and religions, the Stoics establish the foundations of modern conceptions of human rights and law based upon human reason.

DATE: c. 300 B.C.

LOCALE: Athens, Greece

CATEGORIES: Cultural and intellectual history; Laws, acts, and legal history

KEY FIGURES:

Marcus Aurelius (A.D. 121-180), a Roman emperor and important Stoic philosopher

Chrysippus of Soloi (280-207 B.C.), third scholarch of the Stoa who was chiefly responsible for the systematic formulation of the doctrines of the Old Stoa

Cicero (106-43 B.C.), a Roman philosopher and politician who focused on the issue of law

Cleanthes of Assos (331-232 B.C.), successor of Zeno as Scholarch of Stoa

Epictetus (A.D. 55-135), born a slave, he became the founder of a Stoic school at Nicopolis

Seneca (4 B.C.-A.D. 65), a Roman philosopher who was a tutor to Nero and also a playwright

Zeno of Citium (325-263 B.C.), founder of the Stoic school of philosophy

SUMMARY OF EVENT. The formulation of the Stoic concept of natural law was the logical culmination of trends in cosmological thought and political development in the Greek world after the time of Hesiod. Implicit in Hesiod's *Theogony* is an understanding of the world order as political in nature and of physical nature as obedient to the orderly processes of thought in the human mind. Early Ionian philosophy, especially that of Anaximander, had given explicit formulation to these implications of Hesiod's poem in the concepts of a cosmic justice governing all natural phenomena; the logos of Heraclitus expressed an active rational principle permeating all nature and directing its phenomena. Nevertheless, although these cosmological ideas were themselves derived from the political framework of the *polis* (city-state), there seems to have been no reapplication of them to the political and moral relationships of persons within different political and eth-

nic communities of the world until the mid-fifth century B.C. At that time, the Sophists called attention to the relativity of current moral and political standards, or *nomos*, in different communities and then pointed to a common human nature, or *physis*, with laws of its own which might well conflict with laws of human communities. As the institutions of the Greek *polis* were losing their power to command the loyalties of individuals, the Athenian Socrates postulated an objective and rational standard of moral human behavior based on the nature of the individual man as a rational and social being. Plato further developed this conception of a rational human nature and a rational moral law in the *Republic* and the *Laws*. Philosophy of the fourth century B.C. failed to realize the universalist implications of these ideas, probably because the *polis* remained the only obviously self-validating type of human community; but the conquests of Alexander demolished such claims for the *polis* and created in fact a universal human cultural community throughout the civilized areas of the eastern Mediterranean world. *Koine* Greek became a common language of international commerce and culture, and through this medium the cultural heritages of Greeks and "barbarians" cross-fertilized each other.

The earliest explicit recognition of the community of humankind seems to have been more a negative statement of the individual's rejection of ties to the local community than a positive affirmation of human brotherhood. The Cynic Diogenes of Sinope (413-327 B.C.) is said to have been the first to call himself a "citizen of the world" by way of denying any personal obligation to the *polis*. Far from being a political idealist, Diogenes held that all humans and beasts are related inasmuch as humans are beasts. All culture is artificial; a person keenly aware of what nature requires will find contentment without heeding the conventions of the community in which the person happens to reside.

The Stoic school of philosophy was established by Zeno of Citium about 300 B.C. and received its name from Zeno's practice of teaching from the porch (*stoa*) at the Athenian market. It was more fully developed and disseminated by Zeno's successors, Cleanthes of Assos and Chrysippus of Soloi. Stoicism was the dominant philosophy of educated persons in the Hellenic world for five hundred years until it was replaced by Christian thought which incorporated many of its tenets, especially that of natural law. Stoicism has three main periods referred to as Old Stoicism, Middle Stoicism, and Roman Stoicism. It is the first and last periods which are important to the conception of natural law.

The basis for natural law theory is developed in Old Stoicism and is given its practical application in the form of Roman law and governance during the period of Roman Stoicism. Stoicism developed out of Cynicism and evolved more systematically the Cynic school's conception of "the life according to nature." While the Cynics, however, had set a low estimate on a person's rational capacity, the Stoic conception of persons and their place in nature laid a supreme value on this rational capacity. Taking the cosmology of Heraclitus as a physical foundation for his system, Zeno postulated a cosmic monism of a pantheistic nature in which *logos*, or "active reason," pervades all nature and determines all events and also provides a moral law. God is present in all nature, yet God, or *logos*, has consciousness only in the souls of persons and in the totality of the universe. Since God and persons as conscious participants in the events of nature and of history are thus distinguished from plants, animals, and inorganic nature, God and all persons are bound together in a natural community of all rational beings.

The Stoic ethic comprises two complementary levels of the rational life according to nature. One is the inner level of assent by the *logos* within to the pattern of events determined by the universal *logos*, a recognition of the necessity and rationality of all which does in fact occur, contentment with fate, or in Stoic diction *apatheia*, imperturbability. Yet on the external level of practical moral response to critical choices confronting the individual, reason guides choice to fulfillment of duty. Duty is that portion of the responsibility for fulfilling the rational operation of nature and history which confronts the individual moral agent. Duty is not limited by geographic, ethnic, political, or even social boundaries. It is laid upon the individual not by the state or ancestral mores but by the rational principle which governs the universe, and therefore it extends to all human beings who, since they are endowed with reason, are members of the world community, the *cosmopolis*.

Although the early Stoic concepts of *cosmopolis* and natural law defining the duties of all rational beings are stated in positive form, in the period of the Old Stoa these ideals are essentially nonpolitical; they do not lead to any positive vision of the political unity of humankind. Citizenship is not a person's highest obligation, and while it is asserted that the laws of a state ought to reflect the natural laws and ought to be disobeyed if they contradict them, Stoic idealism in the early period could not envision a universal state over which a single code of law reigned supreme. With the emergence of the Roman Empire, however, Roman rulers were confronted with the very practical problem of finding a universal law and morality which was to govern persons of diverse cultural and religious backgrounds. It was during this period that Roman philosophers, especially Cicero, Seneca, Epictetus, and Mar-

cus Aurelius, more fully developed the practical aspects of natural law theory to provide a foundation for political, civil law based on universal moral principles. These universal principles were understood to be accessible to all persons by virtue of their participation in universal reason (the *logos*). Stoicism was so influential that Seneca served as the tutor of the emperor Nero, and Marcus Aurelius was himself emperor of Rome. The concepts of *cosmopolis* and natural law were thus ultimately influential in the formulation of the Roman imperial *ius gentium* (universal applied law). Stoic moral thought, especially the concept of natural law, was also very influential in the systematic formulation of the moral philosophy of the Christian Church, and received formal development in the work of the medieval theologian Thomas Aquinas. The entire conception of natural law became a basis for modern theories of the equality of all persons since all participate in universal reason. It also provides the primary source for modern conceptions of human rights and international law.

—*Carl W. Conrad, updated by Charles L. Kammer III*

ADDITIONAL READING:

Inwood, Brad. *Ethics and Human Action in Early Stoicism*. Oxford: Clarendon Press, 1987. A discussion of the philosophical origins of Stoicism with a focus on ethics.

Long, A. A. *Hellenistic Philosophy: Stoics, Epicureans, Sceptics*. New York: Charles Scribner's Sons, 1974. Locates Stoicism in the context of Hellenistic philosophy and the cross influences of the various traditions.

Schofield, Malcolm. *The Stoic Idea of the City*. New York: Cambridge University Press, 1991. A discussion of the Stoic ideas of political order.

Verbeke, Gerard. *The Presence of Stoicism in Medieval Thought*. Washington, D.C.: Catholic University of America Press, 1983. A discussion of Stoicism's influence on Christian thought and its role in shaping Western conceptions of ethics and natural law.

Weinreb, Lloyd. *Natural Law and Justice*. Cambridge, Mass.: Harvard University Press, 1987. A general discussion of natural law.

SEE ALSO: 445 B.C., The Canuleian Law; 380 B.C., Plato Develops His Theory of Ideas; 51 B.C., Cicero Writes His *De Republica*; 1265-1273, Thomas Aquinas Compiles the *Summa Theologiae*.

287 B.C.
THE LEX HORTENSIA

The Lex Hortensia *brings about constitutional reform by making plebiscites equal to laws and enforceable on the entire community.*

DATE: 287 B.C.

LOCALE: Rome

CATEGORY: Laws, acts, and legal history

KEY FIGURE:

Quintus Hortensius (died 287 B.C.), plebeian dictator in 287 B.C.

SUMMARY OF EVENT. Throughout the fifth and fourth centuries B.C., persistent class conflict raged between the privileged patrician class and the plebeians over the distribution of political rights and powers. Eventually, the plebeians managed to win increasing degrees of equality with the patricians. By means of various laws, they had gained recognition of intermarriage with patricians and the right of election to all major political offices. The patricians had also recognized the plebeians as a distinct political body within the state by granting to them the power of electing their own officials, the tribunes of the people. Most of these gains (essentially tactical concessions to the new economic and military power of the plebeians) were won only grudgingly from the patricians, who retained ultimate control over the state by dominating the legislative process.

In the early Roman constitution, a measure became law after it had been proposed to and ratified by a validly convened assembly, or *comitia*, of the community. Such assemblies had to be convoked by a consul or a praetor, could meet only on specified days after the performance of stipulated religious rituals, and could only vote "yes" or "no" to properly submitted proposals. Even after a proposal had been affirmed, it still required ratification by the patrician senators before it became valid. To ensure further patrician control over the legislative process, the main assembly in the early period was the *comitia centuriata*, in which the voting groups were unequal and a minority of wealthy patrician citizens could influence the final ballot. Once a proposal had navigated this complex process, it became law and was binding on all members of the community regardless of class affiliation; but the restrictions on the autonomy of the legislative body allowed the predominantly patrician senate (which did not itself have the power to enact laws) to subordinate legislation to senatorial interests and programs.

From the earliest days of the Republic, the plebeians had formed their own assembly (the *Concilium Plebis*), which contained only plebeian members and attended to their interests alone. Although convened by its own legitimate authority, one of the tribunes, it was not considered to be a *comitia* since it was limited to the enactment of proposals which were binding only on the plebeians themselves. Such enactments were termed plebiscites and were rigidly distinguished from laws, which obligated everyone.

The first attempt to change this situation was contained in one of the provisions of the Valerio-Horatian laws of 449 B.C., which stipulated that validly enacted plebiscites were to enjoy the same standing as laws and bind the entire citizen populace. The ineffectiveness of this law required a similar enactment by Publilius Philo in 339 B.C., which again attempted to convert plebiscites into laws. Some historians have seen both these laws as fictitious anticipations of the later Hortensian Law of 287 B.C., while others have argued that both laws were real enough but contained some qualifying condition, such as the necessity of senatorial ratification, before plebiscites became legally binding on everyone. It is likely, however, that both laws were passed without any qualification but were simply disregarded by the patricians as invalid since they had been passed without their approval.

This situation developed into a crisis in 287 B.C., when the plebeians, who had contributed greatly to the recent victory over the Samnites, imposed a general strike by withdrawing as a group from the city to force the patricians to meet their demands. In this emergency, the extreme measure was taken of appointing as dictator the plebeian and otherwise undistinguished Quintus Hortensius. Hortensius put through a law, called the *Lex Hortensia*, again making plebiscites equal to laws and enforceable on the entire community. The plebeians returned to the city after the acceptance of this constitutional reform by the patricians, and thereafter there was no further opposition to this particular issue by the patricians. Roman legal theorists treat subsequent plebiscites and laws as equivalent legislative enactments differing only in their point of origin. Armed with the power of making laws, the plebeians became an influential part of Roman political life; the tribunate, as the initiator of plebiscites grew into a more powerful office; and the democratic aspects of the Roman constitution became more evident and effective.

—George M. Pepe, updated by Jeffrey L. Buller

ADDITIONAL READING:

Buckland, William Warwick. *A Manual of Roman Private Law*. 2d ed. Cambridge, England: Cambridge University Press, 1953. Still the best source available for an analysis of the laws affecting Roman citizenship and private life.

Bush, Archie C. *Studies in Roman Social Structure.* Washington, D.C.: University Press of America, 1982. A general treatment of issues affecting Roman class and society, including marriage, the family, and kinship. The discussion of the conflicts inherent in Rome's social structure will help clarify the issues leading to the passage of the *Lex Hortensia*.

Crook, John Anthony. *Law and Life of Rome*. Ithaca,

N.Y.: Cornell University Press, 1967. Discusses the evolution of Roman law within the context of social conditions.

Mitchell, Richard E. *Patricians and Plebeians: The Origin of the Roman State*. Ithaca, N.Y.: Cornell University Press, 1990. An excellent discussion of class as an issue in Roman society and its impact upon the development of Roman legal and constitutional history.

Watson, Alan. *The Evolution of Law*. Baltimore: The Johns Hopkins University Press, 1985. A good general introduction on the history and development of Roman law.

Yavetz, Zvi. *Plebs and Princeps*. Oxford: Clarendon Press, 1969. The classic study of the Roman class system. Though focusing primarily upon the imperial period, this work provides important background on social conflicts that extended early into republican society.

SEE ALSO: 445 B.C., The Canuleian Law; 180 B.C., Establishment of the *Cursus Honorum*; 90 B.C., Julian Law.

275 B.C.
ADVANCES IN HELLENISTIC ASTRONOMY

Advances in Hellenistic astronomy are made when the ancient Greeks consider theories of an earth-centered and a sun-centered universe; the geocentric epicycle-on-deferent system proves to explain the most observations.

DATE: c. 275 B.C.

LOCALE: Alexandria, Egypt

CATEGORIES: Cultural and intellectual history; Science and technology

KEY FIGURES:

Apollonius of Perga (c. 262-c. 190 B.C.), Alexandrian astronomer and mathematician

Aristarchus of Samos (c. 310-230 B.C.), Alexandrian astronomer and mathematician

Eratosthenes of Cyrene (c. 275-195 B.C.), Alexandrian astronomer, geographer, and mathematician

Heraclides of Pontus (c. 388-310 B.C.), Greek astronomer and head of Plato's Academy

Hipparchus of Nicaea (c. 190-c. 120 B.C.), Greek astronomer and mathematician

Claudius Ptolemy (A.D. 100-178), Alexandrian mathematical astronomer

SUMMARY OF EVENT. That the earth was spherical was known to learned Greeks of the fourth century B.C. by the shape of its shadow on the moon during a lunar eclipse. The accepted view of the universe, however, was that the earth remained unmoving at its center while around it in concentric spheres moved the seven planets of the ancient

world: the Moon, Mercury, Venus, the Sun, Mars, Jupiter, and Saturn. About 340 B.C. at Athens, Heraclides of Pontus postulated that the earth rotated daily on its axis and that the sun and the other planets revolved around the earth. His book *On Things in the Heavens* is lost, so modern scholars do not know how he arrived at these conclusions.

This theory was the most advanced position taken by Greek astronomers by the time of Alexander's conquest of Persia, which opened up a new world to scientists. At Babylon, Uruk, and Sippar, in Mesopotamia, fairly accurate observations of the movements of the heavenly bodies had been recorded and kept for centuries. Part of this mass of new knowledge became known to Greek scientists in the third century B.C. The Greeks also had their own means of acquiring data, for among the wonders of the new museum established in Alexandria as a sort of university was an observatory, a simple tower whose only instrument was a device without lenses for measuring the azimuth and angle of height of a star or planet.

Although somewhat fanciful in its detail, this engraving depicts the simple instrument used by scientific observers at the astronomical observatory in Alexandria. (Archive Photos)

APOLLONII PERGÆI
CONICORUM
LIBRI OCTO,
ET
SERENI ANTISSENSIS
DE SECTIONE
CYLINDRI & CONI
LIBRI DUO.

OXONIÆ,
E THEATRO SHELDONIANO, An. Dom. MDCCX.

Known for his mathematical treatise on Conics, *Apollonius of Perga was also an Alexandrian astronomer who proposed a theory explaining the retrograde, or backward, motion of the planets.* (Library of Congress)

From these small beginnings Greek astronomers reached astonishing conclusions. Aristarchus of Samos, invited to Alexandria, showed by the use of observations and of plane geometry that the sun was some three hundred times larger than the earth. This estimate was a considerable improvement over the fifth-century estimate that the sun was about the size of the Peloponnesus. Aristarchus demonstrated his findings through geometrical proofs in his extant treatise *On the Sizes and Distances of the Sun and the Moon.* Having established this fact to his own satisfaction, Aristarchus went on to deduce that the Sun, apparently because it was so much larger than Earth, must itself be the unmoving center of the cosmos, with Earth and the other planets revolving about it in circles, the Moon about Earth, and Earth rotating on its axis. The unmoving fixed stars were at an infinite distance.

The book in which he explained his reasons for holding these bold hypotheses is lost; and, because his system violated ancient authority and common sense and predicted a shift in the position of the stars that was actually too small to be observed at that time, his ideas were not widely accepted.

Apollonius of Perga, on the other hand, made adjustments to the earth-centered system that Greeks found to be more reasonable. He proposed the theory that the planets moved in epicycles around imaginary points on spheres called deferents. The points were also supposed to move in spherical orbits around the earth, but their centers were not the earth itself. The complex scheme accounted for variations observed in the speeds of the planets and their distances from the earth. It also explained why a planet sometimes seemed to be moving backward and why that "retrograde" motion coincided with the planet's brightest appearance.

Meanwhile, at Alexandria and Syene, Eratosthenes of Cyrene conducted an imaginative experiment during which he measured the circumference of the earth to within perhaps less than two percent. He noticed that at Syene on the Nile River (modern Aswan) at noon on the summer solstice the Sun was exactly overhead. His proof began with the observation that then a vertical pole cast no shadow and the bottom of a deep well with vertical sides was completely illuminated. He arranged for an assistant at Alexandria to measure the angle cast by a vertical pole there at the same time on the same day. This angle measured one-fiftieth of a complete turn ($7°12'$), so he concluded that the distance between Syene and Alexandria was about one-fiftieth of the circumference of the earth. Determining this land distance, Eratosthenes then calculated the circumference of the earth as 250,000 stadia. This is an error of only about 250 miles according to some scholars' estimates of the length of a stade. He later changed his estimate to 252,000 stadia, although it is not known on what basis.

Eratosthenes actually made two mistakes: He wrongly assumed that Alexandria and Syene were on the same great circle, and his measurement of the distance between the two cities was inaccurate. Fortunately the two errors tended to cancel each other out, and his method was otherwise sound. Because he also knew that the distance from Gibraltar to India was only some sixty-nine thousand stadia, he made the remarkable prediction that another continental system would be found at the Antipodes by sailing west into the Atlantic Ocean or east into the Indian Ocean, an opinion held later by Christopher Columbus.

Like most of these astronomers, Hipparchus of Nicaea said that he acted "to save the phenomena." Theoretically, he accepted the geocentric system, but he is most noted for numerous observational contributions. He measured the length of the solar year to within six minutes, fourteen and three-tenths seconds, discovered the precession of the equinoxes, and cataloged more than 850 fixed stars together with their magnitudes into an accurate star map. He estimated the mass of the Sun as 1,800 times that of Earth and its distance as 1,245 earth diameters, improvements on those of Aristarchus, whose system had otherwise faded away.

The theories of the Hellenistic astronomers reached their culmination in Ptolemy. He added circular orbits and the concept of an equant point to the epicycle-on-deferent model of Apollonius, in part to resolve difficulties raised by the observations of Hipparchus. The equant point was as far from the true center of the universe as was the earth. A planet in orbit swept out equal areas of its circle around the earth in equal times with respect to the equant point. This system, which admittedly involved some complicated mathematics, remained influential into the Renaissance.

—*Samuel K. Eddy, updated by Amy Ackerberg-Hastings*

ADDITIONAL READING:

Gingerich, Owen. *The Eye of Heaven: Ptolemy, Copernicus, Kepler.* New York: American Institute of Physics, 1993. Gingerich places the Hellenistic astronomers in relation to these three; he also introduces the reader to notable themes and scholars in the history of science.

Grasshoff, Gerd. *The History of Ptolemy's Star Catalogue.* New York: Springer-Verlag, 1990. This work contains a sizable bibliography and in part considers the extent to which Ptolemy's catalog came from the observations of Hipparchus.

Heath, Sir Thomas. *Aristarchus of Samos: The Ancient Copernicus.* Oxford: Clarendon Press, 1913. Highly favorable treatment of the ancient heliocentrist by an extremely influential translator and scholar.

Lloyd, G. E. R. *Greek Science After Aristotle.* London: Chatto & Windus, 1973. A classic general work on Hellenistic science, including chapters on social context, astronomy, and Ptolemy.

Neugebauer, Otto. *Astronomy and History: Selected Essays.* New York: Springer-Verlag, 1983. Collection of republished articles that provides a good introduction to Neugebauer's more detailed and very technical full-length works, which are standards in the history of ancient mathematical astronomy.

Van Helden, Albert. *Measuring the Universe: Cosmic Dimensions from Aristarchus to Halley.* Chicago: University of Chicago Press, 1985. History of attempts to compute and expectations of astronomical sizes and distances, with a chapter on Aristarchus, Hipparchus, and their contemporaries.

SEE ALSO: 600-500 B.C., Greek Philosophers Formulate Theories of the Cosmos; 332 B.C., Founding of Alexandria; 325-323 B.C., Aristotle Isolates Science as a Discipline; 1543, Copernicus Publishes *Revolutions of the Heavenly Bodies*; 1610, Galileo Confirms Heliocentric Model of the Solar System.

264-225 B.C.
FIRST PUNIC WAR

The First Punic War pits Roman military forces against Carthage in an effort to expand Roman authority in the Mediterranean.

DATE: 264-225 B.C.

LOCALE: Italy, Sicily, and Africa

CATEGORIES: Expansion and land acquisition; Wars, uprisings, and civil unrest

KEY FIGURES:

Gaius Lutatius Catulus, Roman consul in 242 B.C. and

Quintus Lutatius Catulus, Roman consul in 241 B.C., brothers who were in command at the war's end

Appius Claudius Caudex, Roman consul in 264 B.C. who led the initial campaign

Gaius Duilius, Roman consul in 260 B.C. who won a great naval victory

Hiero II (c. 309-216 B.C.), king of Syracuse, 270-216 B.C.

Hamilcar Barca, Carthaginian commander in Sicily from 247 B.C. on; father of Hannibal

Marcus Atilius Regulus, Roman consul in 267 B.C. and 256 B.C. who commanded an invasion of Africa

SUMMARY OF EVENT. The First Punic War was a milestone in Roman history. Modern scholarship rejects the old interpretation that entry into this conflict committed Rome to a policy of expansion on an altogether new scale. The Roman victory in 241 B.C. marked the emergence of Rome as the dominant power in the western Mediterranean. The policies Rome adopted in Sicily and elsewhere at the conclusion of the war had permanent repercussions both at home and in foreign affairs.

The Mediterranean world in the early third century B.C. consisted in the east of large territorial empires in areas conquered by Alexander the Great. In the west were three major states and numerous tribal peoples. Carthage, a merchant oligarchy, dominated the coast of Africa from modern Tunisia westward to Morocco, Spain, the western corner of Sicily, Sardinia and Corsica. Rome, the second state, controlled the southern two-thirds of Italy. The portion inhabited by Roman citizens was the *ager Romanus*;

the rest belonged to nominally independent allies (*socii*), of whom the Latins were relatively privileged while the majority were subordinate to Rome. As of yet, Rome had no possessions and scant interest beyond the peninsula. The small kingdom of Syracuse in the southeast corner of Sicily, the leading Greek power in the west, was the third state. Sicily was an anachronism, certain to attract efforts on the part of the Hellenistic monarchies to attach it to one or another of the eastern Empires. Carthage and Rome were equally certain to resist the establishment of Hellenistic powers in the western Mediterranean. When Pyrrhus, king of Epirus, led his armies into Italy and Sicily, he first met the resistance of Rome, then of Carthage. The failure of his Italian and Sicilian campaign between 280 and 275 B.C. left a power vacuum little different from that which existed before, and it was only a matter of time before Rome and Carthage could be expected to come into conflict there.

The occasion of Roman involvement in Sicily, and the beginning of the First Punic War, may have seemed of relatively slight importance. The Mamertines, once mercenary soldiers of Syracuse who had seized the city of Messana and used it as a base of operations in northeast Sicily, found themselves threatened by the growing power of Hiero, king of Syracuse. They called on the Carthaginians for aid, but then fearing domination by these traditional rivals, requested aid from Rome in order to expel the Carthaginian garrison. Rome was a land power with no navy. The Roman senate, fearing overseas campaigns against a naval power, refused to accept the Mamertines' overtures. Rome had been almost continually at war for several generations (three Samnite wars in 343-290 B.C., then the struggle against Pyrrhus). Further, Rome had no desire to get involved in Sicily, from which the Roman government occasionally purchased grain, and had long had good relations with Carthage, highlighted by treaties of friendship and trade (507, 348, and 306 B.C.) and a defensive pact against Pyrrhus in 279 B.C. Yet Rome did not want Carthage to control Sicily. The Roman assemblies, perhaps beguiled by thoughts of the prosperity to be gained from involvement in the rich territories of Sicily, perhaps merely failing to foresee the extent of the military operations they were initiating, voted to aid the Mamertines. Claudius, a leader in the prowar faction, was elected consul for the year 264 B.C. and led an expedition to Sicily.

In the first phase of the war, the Roman forces aided Messana, while Carthage supported Syracuse. Yet this phase, and with it the original pretext for the war, was soon over. Hiero of Syracuse had no interest in matching his power against Rome's, nor in being dominated by his erstwhile allies. In 263 B.C., Hiero made peace with Rome

on terms that left him extensive territories as well as his independence. Syracuse and Messana gained treaties (*foedera*) by which they became allied to Rome. Yet Carthage and Rome were now in a struggle that neither cared to give up.

Between 262 and 256 B.C., Rome pressed hard, driving the Carthaginians into a limited number of military strongholds, and mounting the first Roman fleet, which under Duilius met with surprising success against the experienced Carthaginian navy. In 256, under Regulus, Rome transported an army into North Africa; it had initial successes, but the Carthaginians, directed by the Greek mercenary Xanthippus, succeeded the next year in destroying the forces of Rome. Regulus and his Carthaginian captors passed into legend as models of Roman adherence to their sworn word (*fides*) and Punic perfidy. Back in Sicily, the fortunes of war took many turns. Rome won most of the island but Carthage kept its naval bases in the west. At sea, the Roman navy was often victorious even though the loss of one fleet in battle and of others in storms weakened its position. By 247 B.C., both powers were fatigued. Peace negotiations stalled, but military efforts were at a minimum for some years.

In 244 B.C., the Roman government, too exhausted to build a new fleet, allowed a number of private individuals to mount one with the understanding that they should be repaid if the war were brought to a successful conclusion. In 242, this fleet arrived in Sicily. When a convoy of transports bringing supplies to Carthage's troops was captured, Carthage came to terms. The Carthaginians agreed to evacuate Sicily and pay an enormous indemnity over a long period of time.

Rome now confronted the consequences of victory. Skeptical of the volatile Sicilians' military capacities, Rome deemed it unwise either to include them among the Italian allies or to leave them free to stir up troubles among the Greeks of southern Italy, who resented their recent subordination to Rome. Nor would Rome permit Syracusan expansion throughout all Sicily. The easiest course of action was to rule Sicily directly, which Rome did by decreeing that taxes previously paid to Carthage or the Greek cities would henceforth go to Rome. Three years later, Rome evicted Carthage from Sardinia and Corsica and adopted the same policy. In 227 B.C., Rome increased the number of praetors from two to four, making the new ones governors of Rome's first possessions beyond Italy, Sicily and Sardinia-Corsica. A governor's "assignment" was his *provincia*; gradually this term became a geographical concept, corresponding to the modern word "province." Early in the Second Punic War, Hiero II's grandson and successor, Hieronymus, switched sides and supported Carthage. Turmoil followed. Rome captured the city of Syracuse (the mathematician Archimedes was killed in the fighting) and incorporated it into the province in 211 B.C. All Sicily was a Roman province except for treaty-bound Messana and several other cities made "free and immune" (autonomous and exempt from the Roman taxes) as rewards for joining Rome.

Rome's annexation of these islands as subject, tribute-paying territory, marked the start of the Roman Empire. By annexing a Hellenistic territory, Rome became, in a sense, a Hellenistic state, a fact that had a profound effect upon Roman cultural life as well as upon foreign relations. Rome's development of naval capacity made possible commercial and military involvement with all the Mediterranean world. Its need to govern conquered territory caused it to modify city-state institutions and begin constitutional developments that in the end undermined the republican form of government in Rome.

—Zola M. Packman, updated by Thomas H. Watkins

ADDITIONAL READING:

Badian, E. *Foreign Clientelae, 264-70 B.C.* Oxford: Clarendon Press, 1957. Chapters 1 and 2 analyze Roman control of Italy before 264 B.C. and of Sicily during and after the First Punic War.

Charles-Picard, Gilbert, and Colette Picard. *The Life and Death of Carthage.* Translated by Dominique Collon. New York: Taplinger, 1968. Valuable presentation of the Carthaginian perspective.

Cornell, T. J. *The Beginnings of Rome: Italy and Rome from the Bronze Age to the Punic Wars (c. 1000-264 B.C.)* London: Routledge, 1995. This detailed history of early Rome analyzes expansion in Italy and relations with Carthage before the war.

Dorey, T. A., and D. R. Dudley. *Rome Against Carthage.* Garden City, N.Y.: Doubleday, 1972. Good discussion, especially for beginners, of all three Punic Wars.

Eckstein, A. M. *Senate and General: Individual Decision Making and Roman Foreign Relations, 264-194 B.C.* Berkeley: University of California Press, 1987. Chapters 3 and 4 and four appendices analyze the outbreak of the First Punic War.

Errington, R. M. *The Dawn of Empire: Rome's Rise to World Power.* Ithaca, N.Y.: Cornell University Press, 1972. Chapters 1-3 cover the period from 264 to 220 B.C. Generally follows Badian's analysis but less technical.

Harris, W. V. *War and Imperialism in Republican Rome, 327-70 B.C.* 2d ed. Oxford: Clarendon Press, 1985. The thrust of Harris' work is Rome's almost constant aggression and readiness to annex.

Warmington, B. H. *Carthage.* New York: Praeger, 1960. Traditional, but (like Charles-Picard's study) dated because of recent archaeological work on Carthage.

SEE ALSO: 733 B.C., Founding of Syracuse; 218 B.C., Second Punic War; 439, Vandals Seize Carthage.

250 B.C.
DISCOVERIES OF ARCHIMEDES

The discoveries of Archimedes lead to innovations in mathematical theory as well as technological inventions.

DATE: c. 250 B.C.

LOCALE: Syracuse, Sicily

CATEGORIES: Cultural and intellectual history; Science and technology

KEY FIGURES:

Apollonius of Perga (c. 262-c. 190 B.C.), scientist and younger contemporary of Archimedes

Archimedes (c. 287-212 B.C.), Syracusan mathematician and inventor

Conon of Samos (died c. 235 B.C.), astronomer and friend of Archimedes at Alexandria

Euclid (fl. 323-285 B.C.), Greek mathematician and pioneer geometrician

Hiero II (c. 309-216 B.C.), king of Syracuse, 270-216 B.C., for whom Archimedes provided inventions and discoveries

Marcus Claudius Marcellus (c. 265-208 B.C.), Roman general who led the successful siege of Syracuse from 213 to 211 B.C.

SUMMARY OF EVENT. By far the best-known scientist of the third century B.C. was Archimedes of Syracuse, a man revered in his own age for his skill as an inventor and since recognized as one of the greatest Greek mathematicians, ranking with Pythagoras and Euclid.

Although tradition holds that Archimedes was born in Syracuse, virtually nothing is known of the scientist's early life. No one thought of writing a biography of Archimedes during his era, and posterity has had to depend on legend, Roman historical accounts, and the inventor's own works to piece together his life story. He may well have been of aristocratic descent, for the young Archimedes spent several years in study at Alexandria in Egypt, where he was introduced to the best mathematical and mechanical researchers. While there, he seems to have become such a close associate and admirer of the astronomers Conon of Samos and Erastosthenes that in later years he deferred to their judgment on the publication of his own mathematical treatises. Following his stay in Egypt, Archimedes spent most of his remaining life in Syracuse, where he enjoyed the patronage of King Hiero II. It is around this monarch that many of the legendary episodes of Archimedes' life cluster, especially his development of a system of pulley for drawing newly constructed ships into the water, his construction of military machinery, and his discovery of the fraudulent alloy in Hiero's crown.

Contemporaries and later generations of ancient writers praised Archimedes more for his colorful technical ingenuity than for his significant mathematical formulations. His discovery of the "law" of hydrostatics, or water displacement, and his application of this theory to determine the actual gold content of Hiero's crown may be true, but the exact methodology, if indeed he pursued any, is not at all clear in the ancient accounts. Similar vagueness surrounds the development of the *cochlias*, or Archimedian screw, a device by which water could be raised from a lower level to a higher level by means of a screw rotating inside a tube. Supposedly, Archimedes developed this invention in Egypt, but he may well have taken an existing mechanism and improved it. Other pieces of apparatus he

This portrait of Archimedes reflects his mathematical interests in geometry, showing him holding a compass in his right hand and drawings of geometrical figures in his left. (Library of Congress)

either invented or constructed include a water organ and a model planetarium, the latter being the sole item of booty that the conqueror of Syracuse, Marcus Claudius Marcellus, took back to Rome.

The great historians of the Roman Republican period, such as Polybius, Livy, and Plutarch, give accounts of Archimedes' genius in inventing military weapons. In his *Life of Marcellus*, Plutarch emphasized Archimedes' dramatic role in the defense of Syracuse. In constructing military weapons, Archimedes seems to have put to use all the laws of physics at his disposal. His knowledge of levers and pulleys was applied to the construction of ballistic weapons, cranes, grappling hooks, and other devices, so that the Roman siege of Syracuse was stalemated for two years, from 213 to 211 B.C. Even the improbable use of large mirrors for directing sharply focused rays of sunlight in order to ignite the Roman fleet is credited to Archimedes. Doubtless, he was the mind behind the defense of Syracuse, and the Romans respected his ability. Although Marcellus wished to capture Archimedes alive, the scientist was killed by a Roman legionnaire when the city of Syracuse fell.

Archimedes preferred to be remembered for his theoretical achievements rather than his discoveries in mechanics. In the third century B.C., Greek mathematical thought had advanced as far as it could in terms of geometric models of reasoning without algebraic notation, and the mathematical work of Archimedes appears as the culmination of Hellenistic mathematics. His work on plane curves represented an extension of Euclid's geometry, and it predicted integral calculus. Archimedes' studies included conic sections, the ratio of the volume of a cylinder to its inscribed square, and some understanding of pure numbers as opposed to the then prevalent notion of infinity. Through his sand-reckoner, Archimedes supposedly could express any integer up to 8×10^{16}. In his own lifetime, Archimedes' works were forwarded to Alexandria, where they were studied and dispersed. Two major Greek collections of Archimedes' works made by the mathematical schools of Constantinople were later passed on to Sicily and Italy, and then to northern Europe, where they were translated into Latin and widely published after the sixth century A.D. Since none of the Greek collections is complete, Arabic collections and associated commentaries have been used to tabulate the works attributed to Archimedes. Through these legacies, modern scholars have been able to study Archimedes' work, and some modern scholars consider him to be the greatest mathematician of antiquity.

—Richard J. Wurtz, updated by Jeffrey L. Buller

ADDITIONAL READING:

Bendick, Jeanne. *Archimedes and the Door of Science.* New York: Franklin Watts, 1962. A biography of Archimedes with an explanation of his contributions to physics, astronomy, and mathematics. Illustrated.

Clagett, Marshall, ed. *Archimedes in the Middle Ages.* Madison: University of Wisconsin Press, 1964. A series of texts in Latin, with English translation, that illustrate the continuing influence (and reinterpretation) of Archimedes in the Christian and Islamic worlds during the medieval period.

Dijksterhuis, Eduard Jan. *Archimedes.* Translated by C. Dikshoorn, with a new bibliographic essay by Wilbur R. Knorr. Princeton, N.J.: Princeton University Press, 1987. The most thorough treatment of Archimedes available. Also provides an extensive look at the development of Greek mathematics.

Ginzburg, Benjamin. *The Adventure of Science.* New York: Tudor, 1932. A popularizing history of science that discusses the influence of Archimedes and Ptolemy during the Alexandrian Period. Places Archimedes in the context of earlier figures such as Pythagoras and Aristotle, as well as such later scholars as Copernicus and Galileo.

Hoffman, Paul. *Archimedes' Revenge: The Joys and Perils of Mathematics.* New York: W. W. Norton, 1988. Uses the figure of Archimedes as a springboard for a general discussion of mathematics.

SEE ALSO: 530 B.C., Founding of the Pythagorean Brotherhood; 332 B.C., Founding of Alexandria; 264-225 B.C., First Punic War.

240 B.C.
EXPLOITATION OF THE ARCH

The exploitation of the arch as both a structural and decorative device revolutionizes architecture.

DATE: From 240 B.C.

LOCALE: Western Europe

CATEGORIES: Cultural and intellectual history; Science and technology

SUMMARY OF EVENT. Although the structural benefits of the arch were known as early as 3500 B.C., both the Egyptians and later the Greeks chose a simpler form of construction. As they adapted the Greek orders, so too the Romans took the structural form of the arch and exploited it throughout the Roman Empire. Through numerous barbaric invasions the arch remained a symbol of civilization long after the power of Rome disappeared.

The earliest architects used post and lintel construction to create the first shelters. In this type of structure, weight

Despite deterioration from exposure to the elements, the remains of the Colosseum in Rome clearly reveal the importance of the arch in engineering and strengthening the design of large public structures. (Robert McClenaghan)

is not distributed on the posts but is placed directly on the lentil, thus limiting a structure's height, weight of materials, and number stories. Large structures required massive pieces of stone and an equally massive labor force. In 3500 B.C., Egyptian architects began experimenting with vaults at both Dendera and Abydos. Constructed of wedge-shaped voussoirs with the joints between radiating from the center, the arch permits the dispersement of weight directly on to the posts. Though this support system proved successful, a rigid artistic tradition relegated the arch to underground storage areas.

As in Egypt, the Greeks chose to perfect post and lintel construction. Using weight, iron rods, and exact measurement, architects created what appeared to be seamless monumental structures. The Greek "order" featured a simple post and lintel construction of column and entablature, which produced a structure of beams, horizontal and upright, made of stone, and featuring the colonnade designed to suppress the wall. The Greeks disliked the arch because it gave distinctive form to a hole. It was characteristic of Greek thought to conceive of form or shape as that which determines the reality of what truly exists and to think of space or emptiness as the prime symbol of nonbeing.

The first architects to accord the arcuated aperture an important role in their construction were the Etruscans. These residents of Latium first used the arch in vaulted drains dating from the fourth century. By 240 B.C., architects employed this technology for bridges on the Via Amerina and city gates such as the Porta Augusta in Perugia. As the Romans began to gain an upper hand in the struggle for the control of the Italian peninsula, they freely adopted cultural traits from the peoples they conquered.

Unlike either the Egyptians or Greeks, the Romans made the brick their major medium of construction. While such a small building block hampers post and lentil construction, it is ideal for the arch. The genius of the Roman architect was combining the arch and the Greek orders by building a wall pierced with arches and then placing the Greek colonnade against it so as to show an arch between two columns which appeared to carry the entablature above. To fully ally the two elements, the impost molding was put around the pier to receive the arch while the base moldings and the band about the arch echoed the architrave. Finally, a keystone was used as an inventive aesthetic detail to bind the arch and the Greek order at its most critical point. This architectural innovation first appeared at the beginning of the first century B.C. in structures such as the Tabularium and the Temple of Hercules Victor at Tivoli.

As their engineering skills increased, the Romans employed the arch in a variety of ways, ranging from the strictly utilitarian Cloaca Maxima and the Pont du Gard to the purely commemorative or monumental arches of triumph. As Rome expanded outside of the Italian peninsula communication became vital. It was as "Pontifex Maximus" or "bridge builder" that the ruler could best visibly assert his authority by binding the Empire together with roads and bridges. The scale of public works such as the aqueduct at Segovia, from the first century A.D., dwarfed earlier Etruscan examples.

The Etruscan first employed the arch in a city gate, but it was the Romans who isolated the gateway as a symbol of power. Augustus ordered the construction of the first triumphal arch at Rimini in 27 B.C. to celebrate the restoration of the highway system in northern Italy. The arch thus became a metaphor of the state's control over the passageway and its ability to regulate and control the citizen's movements. This idea is enforced by the use of the triumphal arch on imperial coinage beginning during the reigns of the Julio Claudians.

The pinnacle of Rome's exploitation of the arch was, however, not visible to the average person, but it did make the grandeur of the imperial city possible. In works such as the Pantheon, built by Hadrian in the early second century A.D., a series of arches are used as internal buttress which support the domed rotunda. Hidden by the interior design of the building, these arches are then supported by a series of vaulted galleries. The development of the vault forced the column eventually to stand alone below this device, since with this form of arch there is no place for an entablature. The first time arches were set directly on capitals of columns with no architrave was in the palace of Diocletian at Spalatum in 300.

Following the shift of imperial power from the West to the East after the founding of Constantinople in 330, the arch played an important role in attempting to reverse the technical decline of European architecture. In 547, under Justinian's plan to reunify the Roman Empire, the Church of S. Vitale was constructed in Ravenna. Centrally planned, its eight piers rely on two sets of arches to support the gallery and the roof.

This engraving of the interior of the ancient baths of Caracalla in Rome shows the interrelationship between arches, columns, and vaulted galleries. (Archive Photos)

Although Justinian's successors found it unprofitable to maintain the reconquered provinces in the West, S. Vitale and its combination of the column and arch became an architectural model in Europe for another five hundred years. When Charlemagne began a cultural revival in 800, he used the architecture of his palace at Aachen to express his ties to Rome. His Palatine Chapel, consecrated in 805, follows the plan of S. Vitale with a simplified elevation since a thorough knowledge of Rome's engineering practices had been lost among western builders. Charlemagne was not alone in his desire to employ Roman forms, because they are clearly apparent in such structures as the abbey gatehouse of Lorsch, which is meant to be a triumphal arch.

By 1140, the Roman arch and many of the vaulting forms developed during the imperial period once more appeared in many of the religious structures of Western Europe. Abbot Suger's revolutionary use of the flying buttress and pointed arches at Saint-Denis made the first intellectual break with Christianity's architectural past. For the next four hundred years, the arch's structural and aesthetic uses were combined to create edifices of greater height with multiple window openings which were dedicated to the glory of God.

In 1421, Filippo Brunelleschi's design for the Foundling Hospital in Florence not only ushered in the Renaissance but also restored the rounded Roman arch to its place as a symbol of civilization. Expanding from Italy, both Imperial and Republican architecture were used by successive generations to express their place on the international political stage.

Although the arch has played a role as a decorative motif in the twentieth century, its last development as a structural form took place in the nineteenth. With the harnessing of steam and industrialization, architects and engineers faced new design problems. For many, Joseph Paxton's prominent use of the arch in the iron supports of the Crystal Palace demonstrated how a "noble" Roman form could be adapted for modern needs. With the advent of reinforced concrete and steel, however, the arch no longer fulfilled a structural need.

—*Norris K. Smith, updated by Edmund Dickenson Potter*

ADDITIONAL READING:

Boëthius, Axel, and J. B. Ward-Perkins. *Etruscan and Roman Architecture*. Baltimore: Penguin Books, 1970. A detailed work explaining the importance Etruscan culture had on Rome.

Hitchcock, Henry-Russell. *Architecture: Nineteenth and Twentieth Centuries*. New York: Penguin Books, 1978. Hitchcock shows how the arch played an important

role as architects explored new structural materials.

MacDonald, William L. *The Architecture of the Roman Empire*. New Haven, Conn.: Yale University Press, 1982. MacDonald focuses on a limited number of structures, for which original source materials survive, in order to provide an accurate picture of Roman innovation.

Pevsner, Nikolaus. *An Outline of European Architecture*. New York: Viking, 1963. One of the great architectural historians, Pevsner provides an excellent overview of architecture since the rise of Christianity.

Sear, Frank. *Roman Architecture*. London: Batsford, 1989. A fundamental, illustrated account integrating the arch into the development of Roman architecture.

Smith, E. Baldwin. *Architectural Symbolism of Imperial Rome and the Middle Ages*. Princeton, N.J.: Princeton University Press, 1956. Smith conveys the important intellectual connection that links Rome with the Christian kingdoms that followed.

Thorpe, Martin. *Roman Architecture*. London: Bristol Classical Press, 1995. Thorpe illustrates the vast subject of Roman architecture by focusing on several important examples.

SEE ALSO: 625-509 B.C., Rise of Etruscan Civilization in Rome; 447-438 B.C., The Parthenon Is Built; 312-264 B.C., Building of the Appian Way; 312 B.C., First Roman Aqueduct Is Built; 1150-1200, Development of Gothic Architecture; 1410-1440, Florentine School of Art Emerges.

218 B.C.
SECOND PUNIC WAR

The Second Punic War allows Rome to incorporate the Iberian Peninsula into the Roman Empire and paves the way for Roman domination of the western Mediterranean.

DATE: 218 B.C.

LOCALE: The Iberian Peninsula

CATEGORIES: Expansion and land acquisition; Wars, uprisings, and civil unrest

KEY FIGURES:

Hamilcar Barca (270-228 B.C.), Carthaginian general, father of Hannibal and Hasdrubal Barca

Hannibal (247-182 B.C.), Carthaginian general

Hasdrubal Barca (died 207 B.C.), Carthaginian general

Hasdrubal (died 221 B.C.), Carthaginian general, son-in-law of Hamilcar Barca

Gnaeus Servilius Scipio (died 211 B.C.), Roman consul and general, brother of Publius Cornelius Scipio

Publius Cornelius Scipio (died 211 B.C.), Roman consul and general

Publius Cornelius Scipio Africanus (236-183 B.C),
  Roman proconsul and general, son of Publius
  Cornelius Scipio

SUMMARY OF EVENT. By 275 B.C., Rome controlled the Italian Peninsula. The Romans then began to acquire an empire around the Mediterranean. Their expansion south brought them within three miles of Sicily, where Carthage, a major power situated on the Bay of Tunis on the north coast of Africa, was contending with Greek colonists for control. Its strategic location at the narrowest part of the Mediterranean helped Carthage develop into a great commercial state.

To protect and expand its commercial interest, Carthage built one of the largest navies of the time and expanded to include North Africa from Bengazi to Gibraltar, Spain, Portugal, Corsica, Balearic Islands, and parts of Sicily. With the capture of Malta, the people of Carthage were able to exclude the Greeks, their greatest commercial and colonial rivals, from the Western Mediterranean.

Carthage forced the captured peoples to become tribute-paying subjects and failed to win friends and allies as Rome had done in Italy. This unwise policy caused Carthage enormous difficulties and helps explain its defeat. During the wars with Rome, revolts broke out among Carthage's subject peoples in North Africa and Spain. Even the wealth and commercial domination of Carthage were not enough to fight both internal uprisings and Rome.

Other problems contributing to the Carthaginian defeat resulted from its political and military institutions. Carthage was an oligarchic republic dominated by a small group of wealthy men who were greedy and corrupt. The Carthaginian army was composed of conscripted soldiers from the empire. Their loyalty was questionable. Additionally, Carthaginian generals who won too many battles were considered dangerous and punished, but generals who lost battles were sometimes nailed to the cross. Only the navy, manned by Carthaginians and commanded by experts, was excellent.

During the First Punic War, 264-241 B.C., Rome had defeated Carthage, forcing it to surrender Sicily and to pay an indemnity. Carthage's sea power and its control of the western Mediterranean were lost. Rome became a major sea power and involved in the western Mediterranean.

Following the war, Rome distrusted Carthage and continued its own imperial expansion. Carthage resented its defeat at the hands of Rome and wanted to regain its former position. To achieve this goal, Carthage turned to Spain as a source of money, men, and supplies. Under the leadership of Hamilcar Barca, general of the Carthaginian army during the First Punic War, and his son-in-law Hasdrubal, Carthage extended its control over most of the

Iberian Peninsula south of the Ebro River. Hannibal, eldest son of Hamilcar Barca, took command in Spain after Hasdrubal was assassinated in 221 B.C. He continued the Iberian campaign until only the city of Saguntum (Sargunto), a trading partner of Rome's ally Massilia (Marseille), remained. In 219 B.C., Hannibal captured Saguntum, and the Second Punic War (218-201 B.C.) began.

Hannibal had one large, loyal, and well-trained army but had no navy. Roman naval superiority prevented Carthage from transporting large amounts of supplies and men to the Iberian Peninsula and enabled Rome to establish beachheads when and where it wanted. Because Hannibal had only one army and only Spain as a supply base, he chose to create a single front, preferably in Italy. As long as the city of Rome was in danger, the Romans would be forced to concentrate most of their power in Italy. Hannibal also believed that an invasion of Italy would break up the Roman Confederation, and the Roman allies in central and southern Italy would join him against their Roman overlords. Sometime around May 1, 218 B.C., Hannibal left New Carthage (Cartagena) with about forty thousand infantry, six thousand cavalry, and sixty elephants to invade Italy. He had crossed the Ebro River, the Pyrenees, and the Rhone River by the middle of August.

Rome planned an offensive war using its naval power. Rome sent an army to Sicily to invade Africa and landed another army under Consul Publius Cornelius Scipio at Massilia, where the Roman army could either invade Spain or intercept Hannibal in France. The Roman occupation of Massilia, however, was too late to stop Hannibal. When Scipio discovered that he had missed Hannibal, he ordered his brother Gnaeus Servilius Scipio to lead the army to Spain. He returned to Italy to lead the two legions in Cisalpine Gaul against Hannibal as he crossed the Alps.

It is not known what pass Hannibal used to cross the Alps. None of the passes would have been easy, and he lost approximately one-third of his forces to dangerous terrain, deep snow, and the attacks of mountain tribes. When he reached the plain of northern Italy, Hannibal had about twenty-six thousand infantry, four thousand cavalry, and twenty elephants. Nevertheless, the Carthaginians fought well. Between 216 and 212 B.C., the Romans suffered a series of defeats that forced them to give up temporarily the idea of invading Africa. In 217 B.C., Rome gained control of the coastal waters off Spain and prevented the Carthaginians from using Spain as a supply base or from sending reinforcements to Hannibal in Italy. Hannibal could not win new allies in Italy nor protect those cities that had gone over to him, but he continued to fight in Italy until he was recalled to Carthage to stop the invasion Rome began in 204 B.C.

Spain was one of the major areas of the war both on land and sea. In 215 B.C., the Scipio brothers defeated Hasdrubal Barca near Iberia. Two years later, the recall of Hasdrubal to Africa to put down a Numidian revolt gave Rome an even greater opportunity to strengthen its position. Many Spaniards went over to Rome. When Hasdrubal returned shortly after Rome captured Saguntum in 211 B.C., the Spaniards deserted Rome, and the Carthaginians defeated the Roman army. Publius Cornelius and Gnaeus Scipio were killed in separate battles.

In 210 B.C., Scipio Africanus was appointed proconsul and given command of the Roman forces in Spain. He reformed battle tactics and adopted the better weapons of Spain—the short sword and probably the javelin. After extensive training, his army became a more efficient battle force. In 209 B.C., New Carthage was captured, giving Rome a strategically located stronghold, money, ships, supplies, weapons, and the ten thousand Spanish hostages held by the Carthaginians. Scipio Africanus earned substantial good will by allowing these hostages to return home with part of the loot. Hasdrubal was defeated in 208 B.C., but managed to escape with his army. He joined his brother Hannibal in Italy. Scipio defeated the remaining Carthaginian generals, who were quarreling with each other. By 207 B.C., Carthaginian power in Spain was gone, and Rome decided to retain the peninsula to prevent any nation from using the area as a base to invade Italy. Rome also wanted Iberian wealth to help pay for the war.

Rome had difficulty subduing Spain. There were no large kingdoms or states that could be held responsible for collecting taxes or maintaining order. The interior had not been effectively controlled by Carthage or even explored. The tribes in the interior had long raided the richer and more civilized areas controlled by Carthage and now by Rome. Rome had to conquer the peninsula to actually control it or to benefit from its wealth.

Spain was divided by mountains into many small communities and separated clans. Communications and access were difficult. Rome could not conquer the tribes in a few battles. Even though the Second Punic War ended in 201 B.C., the Spaniards continued to fight the Romans until 133 B.C., and even then Spain was not fully subdued.

—*Robert D. Talbott*

ADDITIONAL READING:

Bradford, Ernle. *Hannibal.* New York: McGraw-Hill, 1981. A highly readable and interesting account of Hannibal's contributions to the Second Punic War. Includes information about the other Carthaginian generals.

Charles-Picard, Gilbert, and Colette Picard. *The Life and Death of Carthage: A Survey of Punic History and*

Culture from its Birth to the Final Tragedy. Translated by Dominique Collon. New York: Taplinger, 1969. A detailed description of the rise and fall of Carthage and of Hannibal.

Crawford, Michael. *The Roman Republic.* 2d ed. Cambridge, Mass.: Harvard University Press, 1993. Places the conquest of Spain in the context of the Roman expansion into the eastern and western Mediterranean. Includes a list of important dates.

Heichelheim, Fritz, Cedric A. Yeo, and Allen M. Ward. *A History of the Roman People.* Englewood Cliffs, N.J.: Prentice-Hall, 1984. Includes explanation of the developments in Rome and Carthage before, during, and after the three Punic Wars and a complete discussion of the wars.

Sutherland, C. H. V. *The Romans in Spain, 217 B.C.-A.D. 117.* New York: Barnes & Noble, 1971. Describes the expulsion of the Carthaginians and more extensively the establishment of Roman administration.

SEE ALSO: 264-225 B.C., First Punic War; 202 B.C., Battle of Zama; 439, Vandals Seize Carthage.

202 B.C.
BATTLE OF ZAMA

The Battle of Zama marks a pivotal engagement between Roman and Carthaginian armies.

DATE: 202 B.C.

LOCALE: About sixty miles southwest of Carthage in North Africa (modern Tunisia)

CATEGORIES: Expansion and land acquisition; Wars, uprisings, and civil unrest

KEY FIGURES:

Hannibal (248-182 B.C.), Carthaginian general

Hasdrubal Barca (died 207 B.C.), younger brother of Hannibal

Gaius Laelius, consul in 190 B.C. and Roman commander under Scipio

Massinissa (c. 240-148 B.C.), king of eastern Numidia and an ally of Rome

Publius Cornelius Scipio Africanus (236-184 B.C.), Roman consul and general

SUMMARY OF EVENT. After Hannibal had finally been trapped in southern Italy by the "Fabian tactics" of Rome, the tide of the Second Punic War turned against him. Scipio's victories in Spain from 208 to 206 B.C. and the frustration of the efforts of Hasdrubal Barca, Hannibal's younger brother, to reinforce Hannibal in 207 B.C., prepared the way for an invasion of Africa by Scipio in 204 B.C. It was then Rome's turn to ravish the enemy's countryside as Hannibal had done for fifteen years in Italy. With a large and well-disciplined army composed mostly of volunteers, Scipio outwitted two defense forces col-

BATTLES OF THE SECOND PUNIC WAR, 218-202 B.C.

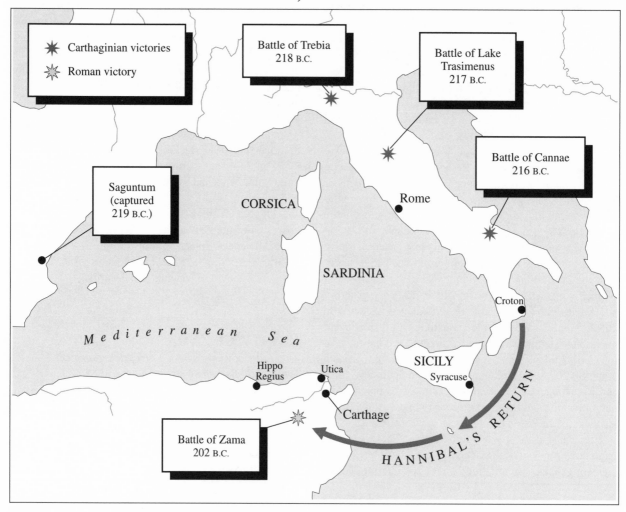

✴ Carthaginian victories

✴ Roman victory

Battle of Trebia
218 B.C.

Battle of Lake
Trasimenus
217 B.C.

Battle of Cannae
216 B.C.

Saguntum
(captured
219 B.C.)

CORSICA

Rome

SARDINIA

Croton

Mediterranean Sea

Hippo
Regius

Utica

SICILY

Syracuse

Carthage

HANNIBAL'S RETURN

Battle of Zama
202 B.C.

lected by Carthage, captured the rural areas around the city, and damaged its economy. The Carthaginians offered a truce to gain time in order to effect Hannibal's return from Italy; he succeeded in getting away with a force of more than ten thousand veterans.

Hannibal spent the winter of 203-202 B.C. collecting and training an army for the decisive meeting with Scipio. Since both Roman and Carthaginian cavalry were limited, the rival generals each sent out appeals for aid to various North African chieftains. Scipio turned to an old companion in arms, the wily desert sheik Massinissa, who had fought with the Romans in Spain. In 204-203 B.C., Scipio had helped Massinissa defeat a rival for control of a kingdom in Numidia, west of Carthage. In 202 B.C., however, Massinissa was slower to respond to Scipio than were other local princes who brought cavalry and elephants to aid Hannibal. As a result, Scipio moved his army

inland and westward to avoid a major battle until he had secured more cavalry.

Hannibal marched his army in pursuit of the Romans, hoping to force a confrontation before Scipio was ready. When the Carthaginian army came near the village of Zama, about five days' march southwest of Carthage, Hannibal sent scouts to search out Scipio's position. These spies were captured, but after being shown through the Roman camp, they were released. By this device, Scipio hoped that their reports would discourage an immediate Carthaginian attack. The Greek historian Polybius, who lived in the first half of the first century B.C., reported that the two generals actually had a dramatic face-to-face meeting before the battle, alone on a plain between two opposing hills where their armies were encamped. Nevertheless, Hannibal's peace proposals were rejected by Scipio, who had recently been encouraged by the arrival of Massinissa with four thousand cavalrymen and other reinforcements.

On the following day, the two armies were drawn up for battle. They were probably roughly equal in size, although some scholars estimate that Hannibal's force was as large as fifty thousand men while Scipio's was as small as twenty-three thousand. Certainly the Roman cavalry was stronger. Hannibal placed his eighty elephants in front of his first-line troops, who were experienced mercenaries from Europe and Africa. Scipio's front line was divided into separate fighting units with gaps between them to allow the elephants to pass through without disturbing the line.

When the battle began, bugles caused the Carthaginian line of elephants to stampede and then turn sideways onto Hannibal's own cavalry stationed on the wings. The Roman cavalry under Laelius and Massinissa took advantage of the confusion to drive the Carthaginian cavalry off the battlefield.

During the infantry battle that ensued, the disciplined front rank of Roman legionnaires, closely supported by their second-rank comrades, managed to penetrate Hannibal's line. The second-line troops of Carthage, apparently not as well coordinated, allowed both Punic lines to be driven back with heavy casualties. Hannibal had kept in reserve a strong third line of veterans, intending to attack with this fresh force when the Romans were exhausted, but he allowed a fatal pause during which Scipio regrouped his detachments. The final stage of the battle raged indecisively until the cavalry of Laelius and Massinissa returned to the field to attack the Carthaginians in the rear and destroy most of those encircled by this maneuver. Polybius reported that the Carthaginians suffered twenty thousand casualties, compared to only fifteen hundred Romans killed.

Hannibal escaped, but Carthage was exhausted and surrendered without a siege, accepting peace terms that took away all Carthaginian possessions outside Africa, imposed a heavy indemnity, and guaranteed the autonomy of Massinissa's kingdom. Scipio returned in triumph to Rome, where he was awarded the title "Africanus." Remarkably undaunted by defeat, Hannibal led Carthage to economic recovery within a few years; later, he fled eastward to aid adversaries of Rome in further wars.

By their victory at Zama, the Romans gained supremacy in the western Mediterranean and launched an imperialistic program that eventually made them dominant throughout most of Europe and the Near East, repressing eastern leadership until the rise of Muslim power.

—*Updated by Jeffrey L. Buller*

ADDITIONAL READING:

Bath, Tony. *Hannibal's Campaigns*. Cambridge, England: P. Stephens, 1981. A brief biography of Hannibal, focusing upon his development as a strategist.

Lazenby, John Francis. *Hannibal's War: A Military History of the Second Punic War*. Warminster, England: Aris and Phillips, 1978. Thorough analysis of the Second Punic War by one of the twentieth century's recognized experts in Roman military history.

Russell, Francis H. "The Battlefield of Zama." *Archaeology* 23 (April, 1970): 120-129. An illustrated study of the Battle of Zama, with emphasis upon the role that topography played in that conflict.

Scullard, H. H. *Scipio Africanus: Soldier and Politician*. Ithaca, N.Y.: Cornell University Press. Still the definitive biography of Scipio by one of the twentieth century's foremost Roman historians.

Smith, Philip J. *Scipio Africanus and Rome's Invasion of Africa*. Amsterdam: Gieben, 1993. Part of McGill University's series of monographs in classical archaeology and history, this historical commentary on Book 29 of Livy's history contains a wealth of information on Scipio, Hannibal, and the site of Zama.

SEE ALSO: 264-225 B.C., First Punic War; 218 B.C., Second Punic War; 439, Vandals Seize Carthage.

180 B.C.
ESTABLISHMENT OF THE CURSUS HONORUM

The establishment of the cursus honorum *restructures Roman government through new regulations governing officeholders.*

DATE: 180 B.C.

LOCALE: Rome

CATEGORIES: Government and politics; Laws, acts, and legal history

KEY FIGURES:

Marcus Porcius Cato, a *novus homo* who achieved the consulship in 195 B.C. and the censorship in 184 B.C.

Publius Cornelius Scipio Africanus (236-183 B.C.), consul in 205 B.C.

Lucius Villius, plebeian tribune in 180 B.C.

SUMMARY OF EVENT. The growth of Rome from an insignificant river city to the administrative center of a far-flung empire brought with it numerous changes in the machinery of its government. Many of these changes were made gradually but some were concessions forced by new political situations. A significant stage in this process was marked by the law passed in 180 B.C., the *Lex Villius*

Annalis. Understanding of its full significance, however, requires a historical description of the Roman magisterial offices.

Before the establishment of the Roman Republic, all final political power in Rome resided in the person of the king, while the executive officers of the state acted solely as his personal representatives. With the overthrow of the monarchy, these officials, called magistrates by the Romans, became effective representatives of the entire community; their powers, duties, and privileges were thought to be derived from the senate and people conjointly, even though in the early period the people were limited solely to ratifying the election of patrician candidates. At that time the most powerful officials were the two consuls, elected for terms of one year. Only patricians were eligible for this office until the Licinian laws of 367 B.C. threw it open to the plebeians. So strong was the aristocratic domination of Roman political life, however, that only in 172 B.C. were both consuls plebeians. The duties of the consuls were diverse; they were charged with conducting the affairs of the senate, maintaining public order throughout Italy, and leading the army in time of war.

The second most powerful office was the praetorship. It seems probable that the first praetor was elected in 360 B.C., although there are some indications that the office may have formed part of the original constitution of the republic. Plebeians first became eligible for it in 337 B.C. The praetor was above all the supreme civil judge. In 242 B.C., the number of annually elected praetors was increased to two, so that one could be placed in charge of lawsuits between Roman citizens and aliens. As Rome's overseas dominions increased, the number of praetors was raised to four in 227 B.C., allowing two praetors to serve as governors of the newly formed provinces of Sicily and Sardinia. In 197 B.C., the number was raised to six, the additional two officers being assigned to administer the two provinces of Spain.

An office not constitutionally essential for election to higher offices, but extremely influential in itself, was the aedileship. At the beginning of the Roman Republic, two aediles were appointed to supervise the temples and religious practices of the plebeians. Ultimately, they were given control over public buildings, street maintenance, the distribution of the corn supply, and, above all, production of the public games. This capacity enabled ambitious politicians to stage lavish and spectacular games in an attempt to gain popularity with the urban electorate.

The lowest political office was the quaestorship. The office was probably created at the beginning of the republic, with the number of annually elected quaestors raised to four in 421 B.C. At the same time, plebeians were also made eligible for the office. Ultimately the number of quaestors was fixed at twenty. Two of the quaestors had charge of the state treasury and official archives. The others were attached as aides either to generals on campaign or to provincial governors. Their duties were diverse: financial, judicial, and military.

These four offices formed the so-called *cursus honorum*, the order in which political offices had to be held, although the aedileship was not necessarily a prerequisite for election to any other office. The *cursus honorum* did not exist before 180 B.C., since until that time there were no age qualifications assigned to any of these offices, nor was the holding of any one office a necessary condition for election to another higher office. Thus Scipio Africanus, the conqueror of Hannibal, was elected consul for 205 B.C. at the age of thirty-one, and Flaminius, the victor at Cynoscephalae in 197 B.C., was elected consul in 198 B.C. at a similarly early age. This situation was drastically altered by a law carried in 180 B.C. by the tribune Lucius Villius that set fixed age qualifications for the various offices. The probable age limits established were forty for the praetor and forty-three for the consul. Although no minimum age was placed on the quaestors, it was generally understood that candidates who stood for this office would have already completed their ten-year military obligation and thus be approximately twenty-eight years old. Through these strictures, a regular and restrained order was placed over the advancement of all political careers.

—George M. Pepe, updated by Jeffrey L. Buller

Additional reading:

Adcock, F. E. *Roman Political Ideas and Practice.* Ann Arbor: University of Michigan Press, 1959. A discussion of how theory and practice intersected in ancient Roman politics. An excellent place for the general reader to begin.

Bush, Archie C. *Studies in Roman Social Structure.* Washington, D.C.: University Press of America, 1982. A general discussion of class and society in ancient Rome, including such issues as marriage, the family, and kinship. The work provides useful background information for an understanding of the role the *cursus honorum* played in the lives of Roman aristocrats.

Gardner, Jane F. *Being a Roman Citizen.* London: Routledge, 1993. A good introduction to the duties and responsibilities of Roman citizenship, including the political offices of the *cursus honorum.* Written in a popular style but well researched.

Scullard, Howard Hayes. *A History of the Roman World: 753-146 B.C.* 4th ed. New York: Methuen, 1980. Lavishly detailed and comprehensive in scope, this book sets a discussion of Roman politics against the background of early economic, military, and social history.

_____. *Roman Politics, 220-150 B.C.* 2d ed. Oxford: Clarendon Press, 1973. A thorough discussion of Roman politics, focusing upon the very period when the *cursus honorum* was established in Roman society. Explores the Roman government from a prosopographical perspective, examining how family connections affected politics. Also contains valuable genealogical tables and bibliographical references.

SEE ALSO: 494 or 493 B.C., Institution of the Plebeian Tribunate; 287 B.C., The *Lex Hortensia*; 90 B.C., Julian Law; 51 B.C., Cicero Writes His *De Republica*.

146 B.C.
SACK OF CORINTH

The sack of Corinth marks the end of Greek political autonomy and displays the harsh tactics of mature Roman imperialism.

DATE: 146 B.C.

LOCALE: Greece

CATEGORY: Wars, uprisings, and civil unrest

KEY FIGURES:

Callicrates, pro-Roman Achaean statesman

Critolaus, Achaean general

Diaeus, Achaean general

Titus Quinctius Flamininus (c. 227-174 B.C.), Roman general

Quintus Caecilius Metellus (died 115 B.C.), Roman general

Lucius Mummius, Roman general who sacked Corinth in 146 B.C.

Lucius Aurelius Orestes, Roman senator and diplomat

Philopoemen, Achaean statesman

SUMMARY OF EVENT. Corinth's fall in the summer of 146 B.C. came as the final event of what the Romans called the *bellum Achaicum*, or Achaean War, the fifth Roman military intervention into the eastern Mediterranean region since 200 B.C. Unlike earlier invasions, which had targeted the powerful kings of Macedonia and Syria, in this conflict the Romans went to war against a Greek state—the Achaean League, one of several confederacies of city-states that had come to prominence during the late classical and Hellenistic periods. Since joining the league in 243 B.C., Corinth had emerged as an influential member and frequently served as a site for Achaean League congresses and meetings with foreign ambassadors. As a result, Corinth was a logical target for punitive action following the Roman victory over the league. The fame of its wealth and artistic treasures made it an even more

appealing victim, and its international prominence as overseer of the panhellenic Isthmian Games heightened the lesson of its destruction.

The motives behind Rome's halting assertion of control over Greece are too complex to discuss here, but two things must be understood: the Romans did not set out to conquer Greece, and initially the Greeks did not find the Roman presence unwelcome. For example, the Romans undertook the Second Macedonian War (200-196 B.C.) against Philip V at the behest of several Greek states that had suffered Philip's depredations, and they fought the war with the support of most Greek states, including the Achaean League. Following Philip's defeat, the victorious commander Titus Quinctius Flamininus held a grand panhellenic ceremony at Corinth at which he declared the Greek states to be free and then evacuated all Roman forces from the region. The Achaeans also supported Rome in its war against King Antiochus of Syria (192-188 B.C.), but friction soon arose as the aggressively independent Achaean general Philopoemen ignored Roman appeals for restraint and forcibly incorporated the city-state of Sparta into the league. His death in 182 B.C. allowed a pro-Roman Achaean leader, Callicrates, to adopt a more cooperative relationship with Rome, but this stance invited charges of collaboration. Stung by these attacks, Callicrates urged the Roman senate to support their Greek friends and show displeasure with their enemies—something the Romans would do with a vengeance during their next military intervention.

The Third Macedonian War (172-168 B.C.) revealed a hardening of Roman attitudes, not only toward defeated opponents but also toward Greek states that had displayed lukewarm support for the Roman war effort. Thus, Illyrians and Macedonians saw their monarchies abolished and their countries divided. In Epirus, the Romans sacked seventy Greek towns that had sided with Macedonia and enslaved 150,000 people. In Boeotia, the fate of Haliartos exactly presaged the doom that would later befall Corinth: slaughter, enslavement, and destruction. With the aid of a Roman garrison, the pro-Roman faction of the Aetolian League executed 550 citizens suspected of antipathy to Rome. Some one thousand leading Achaean citizens named by Callicrates were deported to Italy, where they remained for seventeen years. The absence of these opposition leaders at first strengthened the hand of the pro-Roman faction in Achaea, but the continued holding of the hostages engendered growing resentment.

The release of the surviving Achaean captives in 150 B.C., along with the death of Callicrates in the following year, stiffened the Achaean League's sense of independence at a crucial time, for Sparta had chosen this moment to reassert its autonomy and appealed to Rome. Diaeus, a rival of Callicrates, defended the Achaean position before the Roman senate, which promised to send a ten-man commission to settle the dispute. Perhaps because of the senate's preoccupation with Rome's Third Punic War (149-146 B.C.) against Carthage, the commission was not sent for more than a year, during which the dispute intensified. At this moment, the appearance of a pretender to the Macedonian throne brought forth the army that would soon threaten Achaea. In 148 B.C., Quintus Caecilius Metellus defeated the pretender and stayed on with his army to complete the pacification of Macedonia. Again the Achaeans had supported the Roman campaign, but they did not respond positively to Metellus' initial request that they show restraint in their conflict with Sparta. A second embassy from Metellus finally convinced the league to call a truce and await the promised Roman commission.

Headed by Lucius Aurelius Orestes, the commission arrived at Corinth in the summer of 147 B.C. and delivered a stunning decision: It not only endorsed Sparta's secession from the league but also decreed that Corinth, Argos, Heracleia, and Orchomenos were to be detached as well. News of this ultimatum provoked a furious response throughout the city. The Roman commissioners tried in vain to save Spartans who had taken refuge with them and at one point were themselves pelted with filth. An outraged Orestes returned to Rome, where he claimed that the lives of the Roman commissioners had been in danger and demanded retaliation. Another Roman embassy accomplished little, and formal contacts between the league and the senate ceased at this point. The Achaean general Critolaus spent the winter of 147-146 B.C. preparing for war, and the senate authorized Lucius Mummius to raise an army and proceed against Achaea.

When Critolaus led the Achaean League army north in 146 to lay siege to the rebellious town of Heracleia, he was probably unaware of Mummius' preparations. On the one hand, perhaps recalling Philopoemen's successful acts of defiance, he may not have expected the Romans to back up their threats with force. Alternatively, he may have anticipated an eventual attack by Metellus but thought he had time to take up a position at Thermopylae, where he might reasonably attempt to confront Roman forces coming down from Macedonia. In any case, he was unprepared for Metellus' ferocious onslaught, which routed the Achaean army. Critolaus himself disappeared in the confusion, a victim of the battle or a suicide. Metellus then took control of the Isthmus of Corinth and tried to upstage Mummius by offering a negotiated settlement, but the Achaean leadership refused and resolved to resist with a

hastily assembled force made up primarily of freed slaves. At this juncture Mummius arrived, dismissed Metellus back to Macedonia, and with a fresh army overcame Diaeus and the Achaeans in battle at the Isthmus. Diaeus fled to his home city of Megalopolis, where he killed his wife and himself to avoid capture.

The destruction of Corinth followed shortly in two phases. Two days after the battle at the Isthmus, Mummius subjected the city to a brutal sack. Most of the men were killed, the women and children enslaved, and the city systematically looted. Scores of artistic treasures were shipped back to Italy, where they adorned temples and public buildings. Some weeks after this initial sack, a ten-man commission arrived from Rome to impose a final settlement. The commissioners dismembered the Achaean League and placed Greece under the oversight of the military governor in Macedonia, which was now organized as a Roman province. As for Corinth, part of its territory was declared Roman public land and reserved for exploitation by Romans; the rest was ceded to the neighboring city-state of Sicyon, which also received control of the Isthmian Games. Finally, citing as justification the insolent treatment of Orestes' commission, the commissioners ordered that the city be razed and burned. For a century, the site remained a wasteland inhabited by a few squatters and tomb robbers, who raided the cemeteries for valuables. Thus, Corinth ceased to exist, until Julius Caesar refounded the city in 44 B.C. as a colony for his veterans and others. Ironically, in this reincarnation the city would later flourish as the capital of the entire Greek region, now called the Roman Province of Achaea.

—*James T. Chambers*

ADDITIONAL READING:

Derow, P. S. "Rome, the Fall of Macedon and the Sack of Corinth." *Cambridge Ancient History*. Vol 8. 2d ed. New York: Cambridge University Press, 1989. Chapter 9 provides an excellent study of the background to the sack.

Fuks, Alexander. "The *Bellum Achaicum* and Its Social Aspect." *Journal of Hellenic Studies* 90 (1970): 78-89. This analysis argues that Achaean resistance to Rome arose from a sense of national solidarity in the face of unacceptable Roman demands.

Gruen, Eric S. *The Hellenistic World and the Coming of Rome*. 2 vols. Berkeley: University of California Press, 1984. A comprehensive study of Rome's entry into the east that stresses Rome's lack of design.

_____. "The Origins of the Achaean War." *Journal of Hellenic Studies* 96 (1976): 46-69. This detailed investigation attributes the war to the inconstancy of Roman policy and Greek misunderstanding of Roman intentions.

Harris, William V. *War and Imperialism in Republican Rome 327-70 B.C.* Oxford: Oxford University Press, 1979. Harris provides a realistic look at Roman imperialism that attributes Roman expansion to a habit of war and a keen sense of war's economic rewards.

SEE ALSO: 431-404 B.C., Peloponnesian War; 340-338 B.C., Origin of *Municipia*; 133 B.C., Pergamum Is Transferred to Rome.

133 B.C.
PERGAMUM IS TRANSFERRED TO ROME

The Pergamum is transferred to Rome, allowing for the expansion of Roman imperialism.

DATE: 133 B.C.

LOCALE: Pergamum, northwestern Asia Minor (modern Bergama, Turkey)

CATEGORY: Diplomacy and international relations

KEY FIGURES:

Manius Aquillius, succeeded Perperna as consul in 129 B.C. and proconsul 128-126 B.C.; head of the senatorial commission that established the *provincia* of Asia

Aristonicus, illegitimate claimant to the throne of Pergamum

Attalus III, last king of Pergamum, 138-134/133 B.C.

Publius Licinius Crassus Dives Mucianus (died 130 B.C.), consul in 131 B.C., Scipio's successor as pontifex maximus, and later proconsul in Asia (where he died)

Eumenes II (died c. 160 B.C.), king of Pergamum, 197-c. 160 B.C.

Tiberius Sempronius Gracchus, plebeian tribune in 133 B.C.

Marcus Perperna (died 129 B.C.), consul in 130 B.C. who replaced Crassus and died while proconsul

Publius Cornelius Scipio Nasica Serapio (died 132 B.C.), Gracchus' cousin who served as pontifex maximus from 141 B.C., as consul in 138 B.C., and as legate to Pergamum to supervise annexation in 132 B.C.

SUMMARY OF EVENT. The kingdom of Pergamum was originally part of the Seleucid state carved out of Alexander's empire. When Philetaerus, a satrap (governor, a title taken over from the Persians) in the Seleucid Empire, detached the area, he founded what came to be known as the Attalid dynasty; the name comes from the first king, Attalus I (241-197 B.C.). In any study of the politics of the area, it must be remembered that Pergamum, along with all successor states in the East, was ruled by a Greek minority that dominated the native-born population.

In time, Pergamum came to adopt a pro-Roman policy since it became increasingly clear that Rome could be counted upon to favor Greek culture and its supporters over that of the native Easterners. Attalid involvement with Rome became active during the reign of Attalus I, who early discovered that it was advantageous to favor Roman fortunes in the involved Macedonian-Seleucid conflicts of the period. It was mainly under Eumenes II, however, that the fortunes of Pergamum were cast. He first fomented a war between Rome and the Seleucid Antiochus III, and then supported the former. At the peace of Apamea, which concluded this Syrian war in 187 B.C., Rome gave him much of Anatolia west of Galatia and north of the Maeander River. Roman policy for fifty years sought to maintain a stable balance of power without direct involvement. Accordingly, Rome weakened and confined the major powers, Antigonid Macedonia and Seleucid Syria, and strengthened various lesser states, notably Pergamum but also Rhodes, Bithynia, and even Pontus. It seems to have crossed Eumenes' mind that Roman legions could be used again to advantage in suppressing any unrest fomented against the dominant Greek aristocracy by the native population, a threat which became increasingly more realistic after 200 B.C.

By this time, the city of Pergamum was a desirable prize. Adorned with majestic architecture and sculpture, it became more and more the home of artists and scholars. Its library rivaled that of Alexandria, and the famous Altar of Zeus further attests its artistic greatness. From Pessinus and with the help of Attalus, in 204 B.C. Rome obtained the fabled black stone of the Mother of the Gods, Cybele, thought to bring help in the final stages of the war against Hannibal. Rich in industry and agriculture, Pergamum became the trade outlet for much of the economic transactions in northern Asia Minor. Moreover, on it centered much of the balance of power in the East.

Eumenes II pursued a policy that apparently was an attempt to create a solidarity of the Greeks against the Orientals. He did at times panic, however, and employed a tortuous diplomacy which eventually cost him Roman favor, especially when he changed his mind and belatedly helped Perseus of Macedonia, son of Rome's old enemy Philip V, in the Third Macedonian War, 171-167 B.C. The temporary defection cost Pergamum the loss of Galatia. Attalus II, his brother, restored friendship with Rome, and, in 146 B.C., the Pergamene navy supported Lucius Mummius, Rome's commander in the Fourth Macedonian War at Corinth. Scipio Aemilianus Africanus Minor made a state visit to Pergamum in 140 B.C., but as was true of the senate as a whole, he had little interest in or knowledge of affairs east of Macedonia. Rome's attempt at remote management by occasional diplomacy was ineffective, and the states did not regard themselves as Roman clients.

Little is known about the last Attalid king, Attalus III, who died at age thirty-six and bequeathed his kingdom to Rome. Why he did so is uncertain. Rome had shown no interest in annexation. Without substantiation, Strabo charges that Attalus III was insane. Although childless, he could have adopted a successor. The only living Attalid claimant to the throne was his half-brother Aristonicus, an illegitimate son of Eumenes II and a slave. Perhaps Attalus only designated Rome his heir to deter both Aristonicus (possibly already in revolt) and ambitious neighbors (the kings of Bithynia and Pontus) from attacking, but then died unexpectedly before making other arrangements. Less probably, he envisioned Greek and Roman cooperation in maintaining Greek culture in the Orient and was interested in providing a peaceful future for his people. Aristonicus evidently appointed himself leader of the submerged Oriental elements. Recruiting his followers from natives, he called them "Citizens of the Sun-city" (Heliopolis), an appeal to Mithraic sentiments if not a utopian dream, in an effort to unite and inspire the local population, said to have detested Attalus. His war was under way before Roman authorities arrived.

Attalus' gift was unexpected at Rome, which had acquired all previous provinces through its own decisions at the conclusion of major wars. Consequences of the bequest follow two paths over several centuries: increasing Roman involvement in Asia Minor, culminating in direct rule over the region west of the upper Euphrates valley; polarization of Roman domestic politics, accelerating the failure of the traditional state and leading to the Augustan Principate. The will arrived at Rome in mid-133 B.C., some six months after the king's death. Reacting slowly, the senate dispatched Scipio Nasica Serapio and four others in 132 B.C. to oversee annexation. Alternatively, the envoys' task was to determine whether Rome would accept the legacy. The mission conveniently removed Scipio from Rome, where he had incurred widespread hatred for leading the violent suppression of the reforming tribune Tiberius Gracchus. Scipio soon died and his successor Crassus, commander of the first legions in Asia Minor since 187 B.C., was killed in battle in 131 or 130 B.C. Perperna captured Aristonicus at Stratonicea but then died at Pergamum. Aquillius ended the war and, assisted by a senatorial commission, organized the area as the province of Asia. Rome minimized its obligations: It gave outlying portions of the former kingdom to the rulers of Pontus, Bithynia, and Cappadocia, and did not keep a garrison in the province.

Unfortunately, the great age of Pergamum had already passed. Its wealth became fair game for ambitious Roman speculators, as well as idealistic reformers. For example, Tiberius Gracchus, probably with good intentions and before the senate had formally accepted the will, proposed that the Attalid treasury be used to stock new farms for the Roman poor of Italy. The bill was controversial, as it implied tribunician and legislative control over areas the senate had long regarded as its prerogative, foreign policy and finance. When Gracchus stood for reelection, his opponents labeled him a revolutionary. A mob of senators led by Scipio clubbed him and some followers to death. Gracchus' tribunate has long been seen as opening the Late Republic.

Rome would have remained disinterested in the region indefinitely had the regional kings kept the peace. Instead, the weakness of Nicomedes of Bithynia and the Ariarathrid rulers of Cappadocia tempted the territorial ambitions of Mithradates VI of Pontus. Gracchus' brother Gaius in 123-122 B.C. opened the door for financial exploitation. Tax farming companies sometimes combined with corrupt governors soon caused widespread hatred of the Roman regime. In 89 B.C., Mithradates swept through Asia as a liberator and Rome was slow to regain control. Nicomedes IV of Bithynia bequeathed his kingdom to Rome at his death in 74 B.C.; by 63 B.C., Pompey eliminated Mithradates, annexed Pontus as a province and reduced the other states to client kingdoms. To the south, he annexed Syria and converted Palestine to client status. Addition of the latter had incalculable results on Judaism and Christianity, and indeed on the entire intellectual history of the West.

—*Richard J. Wurtz, updated by Thomas H. Watkins*

ADDITIONAL READING:

Badian, E. *Foreign Clientelae, 264-70 B.C.* Oxford: Clarendon Press, 1958. Rome was reluctant to annex and preferred to extend the domestic patron-client institution into foreign affairs.

Boren, H. C. *The Gracchi.* New York: Twayne, 1968. Emphasizes the annexation of Pergamum in the context of the Gracchan reform program.

Broughton, T. R. S. *Roman Asia.* Vol. 5 in *An Economic Survey of Ancient Rome*, edited by Tenney Frank. Baltimore: The Johns Hopkins University Press, 1938. Reprint. Paterson, N.J.: Pageant Books, 1959. The economic focus of this work remains valuable.

Gruen, Eric S. *The Hellenistic World and the Coming of Rome.* 2 vols. Berkeley: University of California Press, 1984. Sometimes controversial analysis; excellent bibliography and notes.

Hansen, Esther V. *The Attalids of Pergamum*. 2d ed. Ithaca, N.Y.: Cornell University Press, 1971. Originally published in 1947 as part of the Cornell Studies in Classical Philology series, Hansen's work explores the history of Pergamon and its Attalid rulers.

Jones, A. H. M. *Cities of the Eastern Roman Provinces*. 2d ed. Oxford: Clarendon Press, 1971. Traces the fortunes of the cities under Roman rule.

Magie, D. *Roman Rule in Asia Minor*. 2 vols. Princeton, N.J.: Princeton University Press, 1950. Magie's work is dated but still of immense value.

Sherwin-White, A. N. *Roman Foreign Policy in the East, 168 B.C. to A.D. 1*. London: Duckworth, 1984. A cautious and reliable source that stresses Roman reluctance to act.

SEE ALSO: 340-338 B.C., Origin of *Municipia*; 146 B.C., Sack of Corinth; 27-23 B.C., Completion of the Augustan Settlement.

133 B.C.
TRIBUNATE OF TIBERIUS SEMPRONIUS GRACCHUS

The tribunate of Tiberius Sempronius Gracchus attempts to reform Roman society, but Gracchus' murder inaugurates an era of political violence that eventually destroys the Roman Republic.

DATE: 133 B.C.

LOCALE: Rome

CATEGORIES: Government and politics; Social reform

KEY FIGURES:

Tiberius Sempronius Gracchus (163-133 B.C.), Roman tribune

Marcus Octavius, Roman tribune, 133 B.C., opponent of Tiberius

Appius Claudius Pulcher (died 130 B.C.), *princeps senatus* and father-in-law of Tiberius

Scipio Aemilianus, uncle of Tiberius and the leader of senate opposition to his reforms, consul in 147 and 134 B.C.

Scipio Nasica, Roman senator, chief opponent and murderer of Tiberius, and consul in 138 B.C.

SUMMARY OF EVENT. By the 130's B.C., conditions in Roman Italy were deteriorating. The acquisition of empire made the posting of garrisons in distant provinces necessary and provoked a long-drawn-out war of pacification in Spain. Soldiers were conscripted for these duties from the small farmers of the Italian peninsula, and the long periods of time some of them had to spend overseas made it very difficult for them to keep their farms going at home. Many of the farms of these soldiers were ultimately sold to their wealthy creditors, who then added this land to their large rural plantations (*latifundia*), worked by non-Italian slaves taken in vast numbers during the provincial wars. For these reasons, the danger of mutiny grew in many foreign-based Roman legions. Moreover, landless citizens swelled the growing numbers of the demoralized urban proletariat, who, without property, were no longer subject to military service with the Roman field armies. This progressive pauperization of small farmers, who made up the bulk of recruits into the Roman army, threatened the long-term stability and survival of the state. A few attempts had been made to repair this situation, but they all had been blocked by the conservative Roman senate.

In December, 134 B.C., Tiberius Gracchus took office as one of the ten plebeian tribunes. Shortly thereafter, he proposed passage of the Sempronian Agrarian Law, a measure intended to reform the use of "public" land (land owned by the state). This land was occupied, but not owned, by farmers and ranchers, many of whom were wealthy latifundia proprietors. The Agrarian bill stipulated that the amount of public land being used by any single individual should not exceed three hundred acres. A man would be allowed to work an additional one hundred and fifty acres for each of his first two sons. The state would repossess areas above the stipulated three hundred acres, paying compensation for improvements made by the occupier, and divide this excess into eighteen acre parcels which the state would then rent to landless citizens. This measure was designed to reduce the number of landless citizens in Rome and simultaneously increase the number of men eligible for military service overseas.

Tiberius presented this plan to the Assembly of the People, the *Consilium Plebis*, which voted it into law. At this point, however, Marcus Octavius, one of the other tribunes who was said to have enormous tracts of public land, exercised his legal veto and nullified the assembly's act.

Tiberius counterattacked with a legal innovation that provoked a constitutional crisis of the first order. He argued that a tribune should not hold office if he acted against the interests of the people. Whether he did act against them should be decided by the people themselves through the *Consilium Plebis*. Conservatives, led by Tiberius' own uncle Scipio Aemilianus, strongly opposed this proposal, arguing that tribunes were inviolable and therefore not subject to recall. Moreover, they argued that there was no precedent for the deposition of a tribune. Tiberius, however, ignored these constitutional objections and presented his proposal to the *Consilium Plebis*, which voted overwhelmingly to recall Octavius. The assembly then immediately voted the Agrarian Bill into law and

CELTIC HILL FORTS APPEAR

Chronology of

appointed a commission, which included Tiberius, his brother Gaius, and another relative, to survey the public land and proceed with its redistribution.

This commission required money to function and the conservative-dominated senate, which traditionally controlled state finances, refused to grant it sufficient funds to operate. It was at this point that the news arrived that the Hellenistic state of Pergamum had been bequeathed to Rome by its recently deceased king, Attalus III. Tiberius, apparently with the approval of the *Consilium Plebis*, appropriated part of the financial reserve of Pergamum and used it to finance the commission's work. This action, while necessary to implement the Agrarian Law, nevertheless outraged conservative Romans, who viewed it as a serious breach of constitutional practice and a threat to the traditional authority of the senate. The senate therefore made up its collective mind to resist Tiberius.

As the time for the election of magistrates for the year 132 approached, Tiberius feared that his opponents would make an effort to elect men in sympathy with their own views and attempt to then repeal the Agrarian Law. To head off this possibility, he presented himself for reelection as tribune, another unprecedented action since tribunes had traditionally only served a single-year term. Conservatives charged that Tiberius was implementing a nefarious strategy designed to increase his personal power every year until he was in a position to proclaim himself king.

On election day, a crowd of senators and their clients gathered in the Roman Forum. When it became clear that Tiberius was going to be returned to office, this mob, led by Scipio Nasica, stormed the crowded voting areas armed with staves and knives. They seized Tiberius, beat him to death, and then murdered more than three hundred of his supporters. Their bodies were unceremoniously flung into the Tiber River.

Tiberius, in attempting to reform Roman society, had had to resort to extraconstitutional measures, which turned the senate, which included many of his relatives and former friends, sharply against him. Instead of attempting some sort of legal redress to deal with the renegade tribune, the senate resorted to the drastic expedient of murder. This act inaugurated an era of violence which gradually swelled into a full-scale civil war that would ultimately destroy the Roman Republic.

—*Samuel K. Eddy, updated by Christopher E. Guthrie*

ADDITIONAL READING:

Astin, A. E. *Scipio Aemilianus*. Oxford: Clarendon Press, 1967. A biography of the life of Tiberius Gracchus' famous uncle and his role in the crisis of 133 B.C.

Brunt, P. A. "The Fall of the Roman Republic." In *The Fall of the Roman Republic and Related Essays*. Oxford: Clarendon Press, 1988. A highly original and thought provoking essay which places Tiberius Gracchus within the larger framework of the breakdown of the republican system of government in Rome.

Scullard, Howard Hayes. *From the Gracchi to Nero: A History of Rome, 133 B.C. to A.D. 68*. London: Routledge, 1989. A classic study which places Tiberius Gracchus at the beginning of a process which led to the installation of the Julio-Claudian dynasty.

Shotter, David. *The Fall of the Roman Republic*. London: Routledge, 1994. A concise and easy-to-read analysis which argues that Tiberius Gracchus was essentially an opportunist who adopted the position of social reformer to further the interests of his senatorial faction.

Smith, R. E. *The Failure of the Roman Republic*. Cambridge, England: Cambridge University Press, 1955. A largely interpretative book on the collapse of the Roman Republic and the rise of an imperial monarchy which places the actions of Tiberius Gracchus as a major turning point.

SEE ALSO: 494 or 493 B.C., Institution of the Plebeian Tribunate; 287 B.C., The *Lex Hortensia*; 133 B.C., Pergamum Is Transferred to Rome; 90 B.C., Julian Law.

109-102 B.C.
CELTIC HILL FORTS APPEAR

Celtic hill forts and fortified towns begin to spread and are used by Iron Age tribes as defense points against invading Roman armies.

DATE: 109-102 B.C.

LOCALE: Western and central Europe

CATEGORIES: Prehistory and ancient cultures; Science and technology

KEY FIGURES:

Julius Caesar (c. 100-44 B.C.), the Roman general, statesman, and dictator who conquered the Celts in Gaul in 58 B.C.

Vercingetorix (died 46 B.C.), the Celtic leader who united the Celts against Julius Caesar in Gaul in 52 B.C.

SUMMARY OF EVENT. By the beginning of the second century B.C., the Celtic expansion, which encompassed lands from Asia Minor to the British Isles, was waning. In Austria, southern Germany, and western Hungary, the fierce and warlike Celts, who spoke Indo-European dialects later classified as Celtic languages, were beginning to feel the force of mighty Rome. By the middle of the first century B.C., when the Roman legions marched into western Europe, many of the old Celtic hill forts had been replaced by newly established fortified towns. These towns, referred to by the invading Romans as *oppida*, had grown into large commercial centers as a result of lucrative trading. The Celts, referred to by Greek scholars as the *Keltoi*, traditionally built fortified hilltop settlements that were defended by multiple earthwork ramparts, wooden palisades, and ditches. Prehistoric people used antlers to dig the soil and willow baskets to remove it. Two hundred people could dig a ditch and erect a thirteen-foot-high bank topped with one thousand stakes in a matter of one hundred days. By the time of Rome's advancement, scores of Celtic hill forts were scattered throughout western Europe and were used as defenses against the Roman armies. In his annals of the Gallic Wars, Julius Caesar listed *oppida* belonging to twenty-nine different Gallic tribes and regarded each *oppidum* as a commercial center.

Some hill forts were permanently inhabited during the Iron Age and others were occupied only during times of crisis. The oldest date from 1500 B.C. Originally constructed as refuges, storage sites, or as domiciles for kings,

many of these forts could be entered only through a series of mazes. They enclosed villages or towns of circular huts and could house permanently up to one thousand people and large numbers of refugees during times of crisis. According to Julius Caesar, the *oppidum* of Avaricum, sheltered forty thousand individuals during one Roman siege. The fully enclosed weatherproofed huts measured about thirty-six feet in diameter, were roofed with thatch made of reeds, and walled with vertical wooden planks. Many large grain storage pits as deep as ten feet were also dug within the forts ensuring survival during long Roman sieges. A 1955 excavation in Bavaria, Germany, revealed that the *oppidum* of Manching housed between one thousand and two thousand people. In southern Germany, another site known as Heuneburg Towers, which was excavated in 1876, revealed a Celtic stronghold dating back to 1500 B.C. By examining the layers of debris left by successive generations, scientists were able to determine that the particular hill fort had been demolished and rebuilt

This picturesque castle on the Rhine River occupies a strategic defensive location; many of these medieval fortresses were built on sites where earlier Celtic hill forts were located. (Robert McClenaghan)

more than twenty times. The central building of each enclosure served as a religious shrine.

By 600 B.C., an era referred to by archaeologists as the Hallstatt period and named after the Austrian village where it still remains, the use of iron-working technology had advanced to the point that the Celts had spread their culture and Celtic hill forts across a geographic area that covered Italy to Ireland and Spain to the Ukraine. By the fifth century B.C., partly as a result of trade disruptions, many of the early Hallstatt hill forts were abandoned, and the wealth of the early Celts began to fade. By 450 B.C., however, the second Iron Age period of Celtic culture, known as the La Tène period, emerged and the earlier hill fort sites were refurbished and restored. From the third century B.C., the expansive world of the La Tène Celts increasingly shrank until the early first century B.C., when Rome began to penetrate Celtic lands in Gaul (modern France). Julius Caesar first began to tame the Celts in Gaul in 58 B.C. without too much resistance until he finally met an army of united Celts under Vercingetorix at Alesia in 52 B.C. Victory for Caesar here meant the collapse of Celtic dominance of Gaul. Independent Celtic kingdoms were maintained in southern Britain until their conquest by Claudius in A.D. 43, and in Ireland and parts of Scotland up into the Middle Ages. Gaul was finally subjugated by Julius Caesar in the Gallic Wars of 51 B.C., and the Romans went on to conquer Britain in the first century A.D.

Named after a key archeological site on the east side of Lake Neuchatel in Switzerland, archaeologists called the second major Celtic era the La Tène period. Numerous artifacts were found in the shallow waters of the lake, including iron swords and household utensils decorated with distinctive curvilinear patterns that express the vigorous and exuberant Celtic art style. The La Tène period lasted from the mid-fifth century B.C. until the Roman conquest and spread across France, Germany, Austria, Switzerland, Britain, Ireland, Bohemia, parts of Iberia, and Italy.

The Celtic hill forts had used natural topographic features such as cliffs for defense prior to 400 B.C. After that time, the La Tène Celts constructed contour forts, in which an entire hilltop, encircled by banks and ditches, made enemy assault almost impossible. The best-known British hill forts from this period, built by a Celtic tribe known as the Western Belgae, are Hod Hill (later turned into a military establishment by the Romans), Hambledon, and the large Maiden Castle.

Maiden Castle, in Dorset, England, remains one of the best-known extant hill forts. In its many archeological layers, it clearly demonstrates how one culture built upon another on the prehistoric hill forts. Excavated by Sir Mortimer Wheeler between 1934 and 1937, the Iron Age hill fort was initially developed from a single-rampart, fifteen-acre enclosure in about the fourth century B.C. By the Roman conquest in the first century A.D., however, it had grown to an immense fortress made up of four concentric ramparts that enclosed nearly forty-five acres. Maiden Castle is believed to have surrendered to the Second Roman Legion under Vespasian shortly before A.D. 45. Yet the mighty Maiden Castle was occupied in an earlier form long before this. Neolithic constructions at the site include a prehistoric camp, enclosed by concentric ditches and an immense earthen mound 1,805 feet in length. In addition, the remains of a Roman-Celtic temple attest to the mighty hill fort's later occupation by Roman-Britons in the fourth century A.D.

The Roman Empire's occupation of western Europe instituted a strong central government and accelerated the development of unfortified *oppida* resulting in the decline of independent hill forts such as the one in Dorset, England. The Celtic hill forts in unoccupied Ireland, however, remained in use for about another five hundred years. When the Romans were ousted from Britain in the fifth century A.D., some forts were again occupied by the native Britons as a defense against the invading Saxons. As Roman power declined, invading Germanic tribes—the Saxons, the Angles, and the Jutes—renewed their drive westward into the former Celtic lands. Only along the Atlantic fringe of Europe did Celtic culture survive in distinct form. The modern populations of Ireland, Scotland, Wales, Cornwall, and Brittany retain strong Celtic elements and the sites of thousands of Celtic hill fort settlements are still scattered throughout Europe.

—*M. Casey Diana*

ADDITIONAL READING:

Audouze, Françoise, and Oliver Büchenschütz. *Towns, Villages and Countryside of Celtic Europe*. Translated by Henry Cleere. Bloomington: Indiana University Press, 1992. A scholarly but approachable work detailing many aspects of Celtic life and history.

Cunliffe, Barry. *English Heritage Book of Danebury*. London: B. T. Batsford, 1993. Exposition of the popular Celtic archeological site discovered under Heathrow airport. Covers the structures erected consecutively over five hundred years.

Eluére, Christine. *The Celtic Conquerors of Ancient Europe*. New York: Harry N. Abrams, 1993. Although this work primarily covers the earlier advance of Celtic culture throughout western Europe, it provides good coverage of Celtic hill forts.

King, Anthony. *Roman Gaul and Germany*. Berkeley:

University of California Press, 1990. An in-depth, scholarly study of the spread of the Roman Empire throughout France and Germany.

Sharples, Niall M. *English Heritage Book of Maiden Castle*. London: B. T. Batsford, 1991. Traces the history of the largest known Celtic Iron Age hill fort: Maiden Castle, in Dorset, England. Sharples also discusses the Celts' abandonment of the fort after the Roman invasion.

Wiseman, Anne, and Peter Wiseman. *Julius Caesar: The Battle of Gaul*. Boston: David R. Godine, 1980. Discusses Caesar's invasion of Celtic France and his siegecraft involving hill forts.

SEE ALSO: 1100-500 B.C., Hallstatt Civilization Ushers in Iron Age in Europe; 58-51 B.C., Caesar's Conquest of Gaul; 43-130, Roman Conquest of Britain; 449, Saxon Settlement of Britain Begins.

107-101 B.C.
MARIUS CREATES A PRIVATE ARMY

Marius creates a private army, changing recruitment procedures and revolutionizing the organization of the Roman army.

DATE: 107-101 B.C.

LOCALE: Rome, North Africa, and north Italy

CATEGORIES: Government and politics; Wars, uprisings, and civil unrest

KEY FIGURES:

Jugurtha (died 104 B.C.), one of three princes who inherited the kingdom of Numidia in 118 B.C.

Gaius Marius (157-86 B.C.), commoner who gained high civilian status through military achievements

SUMMARY OF EVENT. Marius' reforms of the Roman army were the culmination of developments arising out of Rome's emergence as an imperial power. These reforms marked the beginning of developments that led to the civil wars of the late first century and the end of the Roman Republic.

From the earliest period, the Roman army was recruited on an ad hoc basis for specific campaigns. Levies were held in each year in which military operations were proposed; recruits were conscripted from free-born citizens whose properties enabled them to provide their own arms. Although the property qualifications for military service were often loosely observed, and although the extended campaigns required from the First Punic War onward brought about the institution of military pay for soldiers, the armies of Rome were still thought of, and in large part were still treated as, a citizen militia rather than a professional force. Possession of property, regarded as a pledge of good faith and a commitment to the nation, remained a requirement for eligibility to serve.

During the third and second centuries B.C., the traditional system of recruitment was subjected to increasing strain. The requirements of empire created a need for larger numbers of troops recruited for longer periods of time. Small landholders, who made up the bulk of the army, found it increasingly difficult to maintain their farms while fulfilling their military responsibilities. The importation of cheap grain from conquered territories created additional hardships for small farmers, whose small holdings fell more and more into the hand of large landowners. These prosperous landowners operated their tracts with the help of slaves and tenants who were disqualified, by lack of property, from army service. In short, the need for troops was increasing while the class of citizens who supplied that need was diminishing.

The reforms of Tiberius and Gaius Gracchus, designed to reestablish the small farmer class, failed to achieve their purpose while creating a climate of mutual suspicion and hostility between the ruling senatorial order and the rest of the Roman population. When Gaius Marius, an experienced soldier unconnected with the senatorial order, offered to remove the conduct of the Jugurthine War from the hands of the senate-appointed generals, he was elected to office by a large popular majority. Furthermore, over the objections of the senate, Marius was entrusted with the African campaign. Seeing the difficulties of raising an army in the traditional way, and less bound by tradition than generals of higher birth, Marius refused to order a conscription. Instead, he called for volunteers, accepting all who appeared to be physically fit, with no consideration of property qualifications.

Marius' action, superb in its simplicity, solved once and for all the problems of recruiting military forces. While the Roman countryside had been depleted of small farmers, the propertyless masses of the city had grown large. From these urban residents and from the large rural population of tenant farmers, Marius forged an army of volunteers who regarded military service not as a civic obligation but as a means of earning a living.

The change from a citizen militia to a professional army, however, created difficulties of a new kind. Thereafter, the Roman army was not a force raised by the state, but one that had attached itself to a particular commander. Soldiers fought not to protect their possessions, but to earn a living. Their advantage lay not in a quick resolution of a specific campaign, but in the continuation of military action. The commander of these forces had to guarantee their pay and booty; he also had to ensure them some form of pension, usually a small landholding, at the end of their service. To offer such guarantees, he had to maintain a high degree of control over Roman policies, both foreign and domestic. So Rome came under the twin threats of civil war and military dictatorship, a situation that was not resolved until the collapse of the Roman Republic, when military and civil government were combined under the emperors.

With the creation of a truly professional army came extensive reorganizations in tactics and equipment. The Roman legion, regarded as a standing force, was given an identity symbolized by a permanent name and a legionary standard. Armor and pack were improved and standardized; training and discipline received greater attention. The maniple, a tactical unit of approximately 120 men of proven maneuverability against the larger and tighter Greek phalanx, was replaced by the cohort. This tactical unit of six hundred men proved itself more effective against the non-Greek forces that had become more common as Rome's opponents. Whatever its unfortunate effects upon the republican form of government, the professional army created by Marius served the Roman Empire well for centuries of conquest, occupation, and defense.   —*Zola M. Packman, updated by Jeffrey L. Buller*

ADDITIONAL READING:

Adcock, Frank Ezra. *The Roman Art of War Under the Republic.* Cambridge, Mass.: W. Heffer and Sons, 1970. A publication of Adcock's Martin Classical Lectures at Harvard University, this volume concisely explores the development of the Roman military and navy.

Carter, John Marshall. *War and Military Reform in the Roman Republic, 578-89 B.C.* Manhattan, Kans.: MA/AH Publishing, 1980. A brief survey of the changes in the Roman military from the origins of Rome until the time of Marius. Includes a useful bibliography.

De Blois, Lukas. *The Roman Army and Politics in the First Century Before Christ.* Amsterdam: J. C. Gieben, 1987. Explores the political dimension to developments in the Roman military. An excellent source on the reforms of Marius.

Keppie, L. J. F. *The Making of the Roman Army: From Republic to Empire.* London: B. T. Batsford, 1984. A survey of the historical development of the Roman army, tracing changes in strategy and organization as a result of political as well as military factors.

Peddie, John. *The Roman War Machine.* Stroud, Gloucestershire, England: A. Sutton, 1994. A good general introduction to the evolution of the Roman army and navy.

SEE ALSO: 700-330 B.C., Phalanx Is Developed as a Military Unit; 550 B.C., Construction of Trireme Changes Naval Warfare; 264-225 B.C., First Punic War; 133 B.C., Tribunate of Tiberius Sempronius Gracchus; 58-51 B.C., Caesar's Conquest of Gaul.

90 B.C.
JULIAN LAW

Julian Law extends Roman citizenship to the southern two-thirds of Italy, transforming the concept of citizenship and creating the first nation in history.

DATE: 90 B.C.

LOCALE: Rome and all Italy

CATEGORIES: Government and politics; Laws, acts, and legal history; Social reform

KEY FIGURES:

Lucius Julius Caesar (died 87 B.C.), Roman consul, 90 B.C.

Marcus Livius Drusus (died 91 B.C.), Roman tribune

Gaius Marius (died 86 B.C.), Roman consul in 107, 104-100, and 86 B.C.

Silo Pompaedius, leader of the Italic allies

Publius Sulpicius Rufus (died 88 B.C.), Roman tribune

Gnaeus Pompeius Strabo (died 87 B.C.), Roman commander who became a consul in 89 B.C.

SUMMARY OF EVENT. For centuries the Romans, as did all the peoples of ancient Italy, thought of their community in ethnic rather than geographical terms: The state was a people, the *Res Publica Populi Romani.* Its members (citizens, *cives*) possessed distinct duties, privileges, and rights. The foremost duties were the payment of various taxes and compulsory service in the military; the chief privilege was eligibility for elective public office. The rights of citizenship (*civitas*) were more comprehensive and ultimately, for most people, more valuable: *conubium,* the right to contract a valid marriage; *commercium,* the right to own private property and to enter into contracts that were enforceable in court; the right of appeal in the face of cruel and arbitrary punishment by a public official; and the right to vote on proposed legislation and on candidates for elective office.

Two and a half centuries of constant warfare gave Rome domination of Italy by the end of the First Punic War in 241 B.C. In the course of the fighting, Rome devised a flexible three-tiered system to control its defeated rivals. Roman citizens were the first category. Nearly all Romans were citizens from birth. On rare occasions individuals received citizenship through government grant, and the children of freed slaves became citizens.

The Latins received preferential treatment; they were geographically and culturally close to Rome and prior to 338 B.C. were Rome's full partners. These "allies of the Latin name" (*socii nominis Latini*), the second tier, were given *commercium* and *conubium* together with limited voting rights in Rome. For a time, Latins could migrate to Rome and obtain Roman citizenship, though this right (*ius migrandi*) ceased in the 170's B.C. Within another fifty years, Latins who held local political office thereby won Roman citizenship. This ingenious and not altogether disinterested provision ensured each city a small ruling class, primarily loyal to Rome. All "Latins-become-Romans" had to abandon their original citizenship, for one could not be a citizen of two communities simultaneously. The Latins were numerically the smallest of the three categories. A few peoples received citizenship without the vote (*civitas sine suffragio*), a category which was close to *Latinitas;* by the end of the second century they had acquired full *civitas.*

The remaining communities of Italy were treated as allies, *socii,* bound to Rome by formal treaties that specified their obligations and rights. These peoples varied widely, from urbanized Greeks and Etruscans to the numerous tribal *populi* lacking central governments, notably the Samnites and Marsi. The common feature of this third tier was its members' cultural difference from Rome. They retained their local autonomy except in matters of foreign policy, where they had to follow the will of Rome. Although they were exempt from the payment of tribute and taxes, they had to provide troops at Rome's request even for wars which did not affect their own security directly. Furthermore they were under the vague and general obligation to respect Rome's dignity and to preserve its power.

This threefold alliance system with its fine gradations functioned smoothly in the beginning. Hannibal's efforts at fomenting insurrection among Rome's allies in the Second Punic War had insignificant results. In the course of the second century, however, the situation gradually worsened. Enormous changes swept over the peninsula. Rome established control over north Italy, called Cisalpine Gaul, whose largely Celtic population joined the number of *socii.* By this time, Rome was acquiring lands outside Italy, called provinces, and Rome compelled the Latins and Italians to provide a disproportionate share of the incessant and heavy military demands—and discriminated against them when sharing out the spoils of war. Further, Roman citizenship had become far more valuable than earlier and Roman officials are known to have violated the allies' treaty rights. By the 140's, the allies were demanding the protection of full citizenship, but the conservative senate and jealous Roman assemblies rejected their appeals. In 125 B.C., Rome destroyed the Latin colony of Fregellae when it revolted in frustration, and then the voters rejected the proposals of Fulvius Flaccus and Gaius Gracchus to extend the citizenship. The terms of the bills are uncertain (perhaps full *civitas* to the Latins and Latin rights to the Italians), and in any case failed to pass.

In 91 B.C., the reform program of the tribune Drusus included a proposal to extend citizenship to the allies. Passions ran high on both sides. The bill failed, he was murdered, and fighting broke out. The war goes by various names: Social (from *socius*), Marsic (Marsi were among the leaders), or Italian (from the belligerents). Under the command of the Marsian Silo Pompaedius, the allies revolted and established their own confederation of Italia, with its seat at Corfinium. They began issuing their own coinage and put a huge army in the field. For a time Rome was close to disaster but slowly gained the upper hand. Several factors combined to bring about a Roman victory. With one exception, Venusia, the Latins remained loyal and Rome used their towns as strongholds. Few Etruscans, Gauls, other northern peoples, or Greeks defected. The Samnites and Marsi were the most resolute enemies, as they had been among Rome's bitterest enemies in the fourth century B.C. The rebels had no tradition of union and failed to coordinate effectively. Most important, Rome undercut the rebellion by judicious concessions.

In 90 B.C., the consul Lucius Julius Caesar, second cousin once removed of the more famous Gaius Julius Caesar, carried the *Lex Julia: De Civitate Latinis et Sociis Danda* (Julian Law on giving citizenship to the Latins and [Italian] allies), which granted full citizenship to all communities south of Cisalpine Gaul—and the four Latin colonies in it (Piacenza, Cremona, Bologna, and Aquileia)—which had not joined in the revolt or promptly abandoned it. This was the major act of enfranchisement and it decisively changed the nature of Italy. Urbanization proceeded rapidly, and with it relative administrative uniformity, as *populi* were upgraded to *municipia* and joined the older *coloniae.* Roman citizenship was now well on the way to becoming a national institution, and Italy was distinct from the provinces.

Subsequent laws supplemented the Lex Julia. In 89 B.C., Pompeius Strabo's Lex Pompeia evidently made Cisalpine Gaul a province (its southern border set at the Arno and Rubicon rivers), granted Latin status to the mostly Celtic peoples north of the Po River, and attached them to the former Latin colonies which were now Roman *municipia.* This extension of *Latinitas* manifests Roman flexibility: Latinity was coming to be seen as a condition halfway to full citizenship and independent of its homeland in Latium. The Gallic Latins became citizens in 49 B.C., and Cisalpine Gaul was incorporated into Italy in 42 B.C. Rome was henceforward the common *patria* of all free Italians, including women. In later centuries both Latin status and full citizenship spread throughout the Roman Empire.

Registration of the masses of new citizens was controversial. Fearing the loss of their ability to control political life, conservatives wanted to pack them in a few of the older tribes. In 88 B.C., the tribune Sulpicius Rufus proposed that they be distributed evenly through all thirty-five tribes. He turned to the military hero Marius for help. The sixty-eight-year-old Marius favored equitable treatment for the Italians and through marriage had become an in-law of the Caesars. Rufus transferred to him the eastern command which the senate had assigned to Sulla, one of the consuls elected in 88 B.C. In the ensuing civil war, Sulla marched on Rome and killed Rufus. Marius fled, returned, proscribed his enemies (including the Caesar who passed the law of 90 B.C.), and died in January, 86 B.C., two weeks into his seventh consulship. A few years later, Sulla became dictator, but accepted the distribution of the new citizens in all thirty-five tribes.

—*George M. Pepe, updated by Thomas H. Watkins*

ADDITIONAL READING:

Brunt, P. *Italian Manpower, 225 B.C.-A.D. 14.* Oxford: Clarendon Press, 1971. Places the question of citizenship in the context of population trends, including emigration.

McCullough, Colleen. *The Grass Crown.* New York: Avon, 1992. Part of a series of novels based on Roman history, this work demonstrates author Colleen McCullough's thorough research and captures the spirit and personalities of the era.

Salmon, E. T. *The Making of Roman Italy.* Ithaca, N.Y.: Cornell University Press, 1982. Salmon's valuable work adopts a broad Italian rather than narrowly Roman focus in exploring the country's ancient history.

_____. *Samnium and the Samnites.* Cambridge, England: Cambridge University Press, 1967. Detailed history of the most persistent of Rome's Italian foes.

Sherwin-White, A. N. *The Roman Citizenship.* 2d ed. Oxford: Clarendon Press, 1973. This work remains the definitive treatment of the subject. The revised edition contains a new chapter on the political goals of the rebels of 91-87 B.C.

Taylor, L. R. *The Voting Districts of the Roman Republic.* Rome: Papers of the American Academy at Rome, 1960. A technical study of the distribution of the voting tribes.

Toynbee, A. J. *Hannibal's Legacy.* New York: Oxford University Press, 1965. A detailed social history of Italy from 200 B.C. to the end of the Roman Republic.

SEE ALSO: 340-338 B.C., Origin of *Municipia*; 287 B.C., The *Lex Hortensia*; 133 B.C., Tribunate of Tiberius Sempronius Gracchus; 58-51 B.C., Caesar's Conquest of Gaul.

58-51 B.C.
CAESAR'S CONQUEST OF GAUL

Caesar's conquest of Gaul reshapes Gallic culture, alters the nature of the Roman Empire, and propels Caesar toward domination of Rome.

DATE: 58-51 B.C.

LOCALE: Modern France, Belgium, the German Rhineland, Switzerland, and Britain

CATEGORIES: Expansion and land acquisition; Wars, uprisings, and civil unrest

KEY FIGURES:

Ambiorix (fl. mid-first century B.C.), Gallic chieftain whose troops slaughtered a Roman legion and who was never captured by the Romans

Julius Caesar (100-44 B.C.), Roman politician and general; proconsul of Gaul, 58-50 B.C.

Indutiomarus (fl. mid-first century B.C.), chieftain of the Gallic Treveri

Publius Vatinius (died after 42 B.C.), tribune in 59 B.C. and a political ally of Caesar

Vercingetorix (died 46 B.C.), Gallic chieftain chosen in 52 B.C. to lead the Gauls

SUMMARY OF EVENT. Julius Caesar's conquest of Gaul is among the most significant campaigns in Roman and Western European history. In the Roman context, Caesar's campaigns fit into the pattern of Roman imperialism. For centuries, commanders ambitious to enhance their political careers by military glory had initiated wars of aggression. (Caesar's *Gallic War Commentaries*, released in annual books, were self-promotional press releases.) The annexation of Gaul, the largest single acquisition, shifted Rome's interest from Mediterranean possessions to involvement in northwest Europe and led to campaigns across the Danube and Rhine rivers (abandoned in A.D. 9) and then to the conquest of Britain from A.D. 43.

For Caesar personally, his brilliance as a commander won him glory, immense (and very useful) wealth, the devotion of his soldiers, widespread popularity, and the enmity of those senators who began to fear his ultimate intentions. Having gained a strong military, financial, and political base through the wars, Caesar challenged the Roman establishment in civil war when he marched troops across the Rubicon River in January, 49 B.C. When the fighting ceased, Caesar had unprecedented powers as master of Rome—which led directly to his assassination. His career was fundamental in the transition from the failing "Republic" to the "Empire."

Viewed from a different perspective, Caesar's warfare in the 50's also altered the culture of the Celtic tribes. Greeks had been settled in southern Gaul and spreading their culture northward since the sixth century B.C. Answering an appeal for help from the leading Greek city, Marseilles, Rome conquered the coastal strip in the late 120's and made it the province of Narbonese Gaul, named for the colony of Narbo founded in 118 B.C. The recent discovery of quantities of Italian wine am-

FINAL CAMPAIGN AGAINST GALLIC TRIBES, 52 B.C.

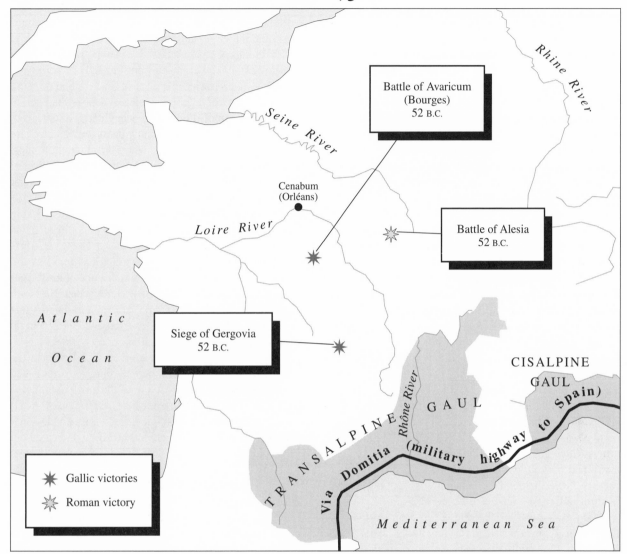

phoras prove that Roman merchants were soon operating beyond the provincial boundaries. Commercial activities thus preceded Caesar's wars by fifty years and may have influenced his policies. Rome applied various labels to this extensive territory: Gallia Transalpina ("Gaul beyond the Alps," contrasted with north Italy, Cisalpina), Ultima ("Farthest"), Comata ("long-haired"), and Bracata ("trousered").

In 59 B.C., the tribune Vatinius sponsored a law which gave Caesar the proconsular governorship of Cisalpine Gaul and Illyricum with three legions for five years. The opportune death of the governor of Narbonensis allowed him to tack on an amendment adding this province and another legion. North of "the Province," as Narbonensis

was often known, lay most of Gaul, a diverse but fertile area between the River Rhine and the Pyrenees and inhabited mostly by Celts. Divided into more than one hundred tribes, the Gauls were unstable politically, with a feuding nobility and rival factions even within tribes.

In the spring of 58 B.C. the Helvetii, a group of tribes in western Switzerland, were migrating in search of richer lands and requested the right to pass through the Roman province. Perceiving an opportunity use his newly formed legions and gain military renown Caesar rushed from Rome to Geneva to block the Helvetii at the Rhone River. Those he did not annihilate he forced to return to their Alpine homes. Later that year, under the pretext of defending Gallic allies, Caesar boldly marched northward to drive back across the Rhine a Germanic chieftain whose aggressions were threatening central Gaul as well as Roman political and presumably economic interests.

Recruiting additional legions in the winter and gaining more Gallic allies, Caesar in 57 B.C. ravaged Belgic territory in northern Gaul, overwhelming one tribe after another. When one town resisted a siege, he sold more than fifty thousand of the Belgae into slavery. The following year, building a fleet, Caesar crushed the Veneti who lived along the Atlantic coast. Thus by the end of 56 B.C., he had ruthlessly asserted Roman dominance in most of Gaul.

Back at Rome, Caesar's political enemies charged that he had far exceeded his authority. In 56 B.C., however, his political allies obtained the extension of Caesar's proconsulship for another five years, which encouraged him to press on toward permanent occupation of northern Gaul.

In 55 B.C., two German tribes crossed the Rhine seeking land. When their leaders came to Caesar to negotiate, he detained them and by a surprise attack massacred the Germans, his cavalry hunting down even their women and children. Caesar's enemy Cato demanded in the senate at Rome that Caesar be handed over to the Germans to atone for his butchery. Bridging the Rhine, Caesar's forces briefly invaded Germany, to forestall further Germanic inroads. That same summer he led two legions in a reconnaissance of Britain, and in the following year, 54 B.C., he led a large-scale invasion army across the English Channel, receiving the nominal submission of a British king north of the Thames River. Although Caesar claimed victories, Rome gained no lasting control in Britain or Germany and paid little attention to the island for almost a century. Nevertheless, these expeditions were impressive features in Caesar's reports to Rome.

Many Gallic tribes refused to accept Roman rule, and Caesar faced several dangerous rebellions in the years 54-52 B.C.. One crafty chieftain, Ambiorix of the Belgic Eburones, wiped out a Roman legion; Roman merchants as well as Roman supply trains were butchered by the Gauls. Simultaneously, Indutiomarus of the nearby Treveri threatened Rome's control in the Moselle valley and along the left bank of the Rhine. Enlarging his army to ten legions or about fifty thousand men, Caesar vowed vengeance. Yet a new leader, Vercingetorix, unified a Gallic coalition. His "scorched-earth" policy forced the Romans to besiege Gallic hill forts. Frustrated, Caesar's men massacred the inhabitants of several towns. His siege of a stronghold at Gergovia, however, failed miserably, encouraging further desertions by Gauls who had once supported Rome. Only by employing German mercenary cavalry and by dogged discipline and shrewd strategy did Caesar finally outmaneuver and corner Vercingetorix. Af-

ter a bitter and bloody siege the Gallic hero surrendered. Caesar had him executed after his triumph in 46 B.C.

For Caesar, this eight-year campaign brought prominence and increased ambition. His reports to Rome cleverly justified his actions, and his veteran army, intensely loyal to him, enabled him to return to Italy to seize sole power after a civil war. Caesar never had time to do more than begin recovery. Gaul was devastated, perhaps more than half its men of military age slaughtered or enslaved, and its agriculture and towns badly damaged. Scholars are uncertain as to what his plans were. By playing on inter- and intratribal enmities, he had won the allegiance of some Gauls. Many Gauls were soon named Julii; they or their ancestors won Roman citizenship through Caesar's grants. (Most others obtained it from Augustus.) Using demobilized veterans as settlers, Caesar reinforced the colony at Narbo and founded new ones at Baeterrae (Beziers), Arelate (Arles), and probably Noviodunum (Nyon). Evidently following Caesar's intentions, one of his former officers founded colonies at Raurica (Augst near Basel) on the Rhine and Lugdunum (Lyon) at the confluence of the Rhone and Saone. Because of renewed civil wars, general recuperation only began after 30 B.C.

Caesar's great-nephew and adopted son Octavian, better known as Rome's first emperor, Augustus, established the basic administrative structure of the newly conquered lands. Three provinces lay north of Narbonensis: Aquitania, Lugdunensis, and Belgica. Each was divided into administrative units called *civitates* (cantons), created out of the old tribes. Two military zones, Upper and Lower Germany, ran along the west bank of the Rhine; they became provinces in the early 90's A.D. Augustus founded several more colonies in Narbonensis, notably Forum Julii (Fréjus) and Arausio (Orange). A network of roads, linked to Narbonensis, radiated from Lugdunum, the chief city of the north. Roman rule soon brought relative peace and order, economic prosperity, and the development of this extensive, agriculturally rich, and prosperous land.

—Roger B. McShane, updated by Thomas H. Watkins

ADDITIONAL READING:

Cunliffe, Barry. *The Celtic World*. New York: McGraw-Hill, 1979. Well-illustrated overview of Celtic culture and the changes caused by contact with the Greeks and Romans.

Drinkwater, J. *Roman Gaul*. London: Duckworth, 1983. Basic narrative and administrative history; clear on importance of Caesar and Augustus.

Gelzer, M. *Julius Caesar*. Translated by Peter Needham. New York: Blackwell, 1968. Political biography of Caesar; cursory on Gallic War.

Gruen, Eric S. *The Last Generation of the Roman Republic*. Berkeley: University of California Press, 1974. Political life and maneuvering in Rome from 78 to 49 B.C.

Harris, W. V. *War and Imperialism in Republican Rome, 327-70 B.C.* New York: Oxford University Press, 1985. An examination of the role of the quest for military glory in Roman politics in the pre-Caesarian period.

Rivet, A. L. F. *Gallia Narbonensis: Southern France in Roman Times*. London: Batsford, 1988. History of the region with a focus on administration.

Wightman, E. M. *Gallia Belgica*. London: Batsford, 1985. A history of northeast Gaul.

SEE ALSO: 107-101 B.C., Marius Creates a Private Army; 15 B.C.-A.D. 15, Rhine-Danube Frontier Is Established; 43-130, Roman Conquest of Britain.

51 B.C.
CICERO WRITES HIS DE REPUBLICA

Cicero writes his De republica, *arguing that the mixed constitution of the Roman state (*res publica*) is the perfect government because it evolved naturally and was not the creation of a single lawgiver.*

DATE: 51 B.C.

LOCALE: Rome

CATEGORIES: Cultural and intellectual history; Government and politics

KEY FIGURE:

Marcus Tullius Cicero (106-43 B.C.), Roman orator and statesman, consul in 63 B.C.

SUMMARY OF EVENT. For centuries, the only known substantial portion of *De republica* (51 B.C.; *On the State*, 1817) was the "Dream of Scipio" (*Somnium Scipionis*). Scattered quotations, many in St. Augustine's *City of God*, provided hints of the main text. In 1820, a manuscript of much of the rest was found in the Vatican Library. Although scholars still do not possess the full text of *On the State*, it is sufficiently intact to reveal its main argumentation and to justify an assessment of its contribution to political theory. (*On the Commonwealth* is a more accurate rendering of Cicero's title; the Roman state was not a republic in the modern sense of the word.)

It is fairly certain that Cicero had completed the writing of the *De republica* before his term as the governor of the province of Cilicia in Asia Minor in 51 B.C. This date is decisive for proper appraisal of the work. Cicero's political career had peaked when he suppressed the Catilinarian conspiracy as consul in 63 B.C. Politics were turbulent. Cicero had a powerful enemy in Publius Clodius. In 59 B.C., Julius Caesar was consul and formed the first triumvirate with Gnaeus Pompeius Magnus and Marcus

Licinius Crassus. Cicero opposed this coalition and Caesar's readiness to use violence to gain passage of measures he supported. The next year, Clodius was tribune and exiled Cicero, ostensibly because he had summarily executed some of the Catilinarians without a trial (although with the moral support of the senate) at the end of 63 B.C. Although Cicero was recalled to Rome the next year, his political initiative was henceforth curtailed severely. The triumvirs forced him into submission in 56 B.C. and compelled him to speak on behalf of some of their allies, although Caesar always sought to keep Cicero a friendly neutral. By 54 B.C., Cicero had essentially dropped out of politics. During this period, as he himself records, he turned to philosophy, especially to Plato, for consolation. The result was *De republica*, to which was added later a companion piece on the nature of law, the *De legibus* (which was never completed).

Cicero's efforts are not to be seen as translations of Plato. Both works have a Roman setting and famous Romans as the interlocutors of the dialogues. In *De republica*, the chief speaker is Publius Cornelius Scipio Aemilianus Africanus Minor, the most distinguished Roman of his generation (consul in 147 and 134 B.C., censor in 142 B.C., and *princeps senatus*) and one of Cicero's heroes; he is best known as the conqueror of Carthage in 146 B.C. The remaining eight participants are his political allies and clients. *De republica* is set in 129 B.C., shortly before Scipio's death. Cicero himself leads the discussion in *De legibus*, so his role corresponds to that of Scipio; his brother Quintus and friend Titus Pomponius Atticus are the other participants in the discussion.

The two works are not merely Roman replicas of Greek originals. In both works, Cicero is more dependent on Platonic format (the dialogue form and concluding dream) than content. He draws upon the teaching of many other philosophical schools, especially Stoic philosophy, and on the Greek historian Polybius (a friend of Scipio Aemilianus), to form his own conception of the ideal state and of the nature of law. Above all, Cicero utilizes his own experiences as Roman patriot, statesman, and theoretician. Cicero, for all his wisdom and patriotism, is fundamentally romantic. Politics in Scipio's time were much more complex than Cicero presents them. As history the work is flawed, but as theory it was intended to be practical, not utopian.

Cicero's *De republica* is composed of six books. Unlike Plato's *Republic*, its theme is not the nature of justice reflected in the workings of the perfect state, but the state itself reflected in its constitution and government. In book 1, Scipio examines the three types of government: monarchy, aristocracy, and democracy. He shows that the

Known for his brilliant oratorical skills, Cicero also incorporated his firsthand political experience as a Roman statesman to write his De republica. *(Library of Congress)*

best state is formed from a mixture of elements drawn from the three separate types. In book 2, he shows how the Roman state, itself a mixed form of government, achieved in the course of history this composite form. Book 3 discusses the nature of justice and its relation to the state. Book 4 treats education, while books 5 and 6 portray the ideal statesman (variously styled *princeps*, *moderator*, or *rector*), who guides the state by the force of personal integrity and reputation (*auctoritas*). The work ends with an almost mystic vision of the rewards to be enjoyed in the afterlife by those who have administered the state properly.

This last section had a life separate from the rest of the dialogue as the *Somnium Scipionis*. In it, Scipio has a dream in which he discourses with two distinguished Roman senators, his adoptive grandfather (Scipio Africanus Major [the Elder]) and his real father (Lucius Aemilius Paulus), and learns of the eternal fame and deifica-

tion of the true statesman. Cicero's propensity to simplify complexities, to idealize those he regarded as good and vilify those he thought bad, proved fatal, for in 44-43 B.C., seeing himself as *rector*, his vitriolic attacks on Marc Antony led to the civil war many sought to prevent and to his own death.

Two aspects of *De republica* have been especially influential among later thinkers: the theory of the mixed constitution, and the relation of justice to the state. Cicero was not the originator of either idea, but he is primarily responsible for transmitting them to later ages. A third aspect is controversial. Cicero's theory may have influenced Augustus and his advisers in the early 20's B.C. to model Augustus' role as *princeps* on the Ciceronian *princeps* or *rector*, who guides by *auctoritas* (prestige) instead of ruling through *potestas* or *imperium* (power).

The virtue of the mixed constitution is that it is immune to the defects inherent in the three types of government. In ancient political theory there was an inevitable cycle in which monarchy degenerated into tyranny, aristocracy into oligarchy, and democracy into anarchic mob rule. Yet if the three types are combined into a single system of government, their differences interact upon one another and form a series of checks and balances to prevent the dominance and subsequent degeneration of any one type. The influence of this theory is readily apparent in the structure of the U.S. Constitution.

Cicero's treatment of the role of justice within the state is equally relevant. The initial argument is that justice is inimical to the efficient operation of the state since it is opposed to self-interest. Since each state has diverse laws and customs, there is no universal concept of justice which all states can follow. Among states as among men the accepted principle is that the stronger dominate and exploit the weaker to ensure their own security and self-interest. If a state attempts to observe justice, it will only expose itself to mediocrity and external control. Against this view it is argued that justice forms the very fabric of the state, without which the state cannot even exist since by definition the state is the union of persons who are joined by a common agreement about law and rights and by a desire to share mutual advantages. Yet justice is concerned precisely with the due observance of law and rights. Without justice the members of the state can have nothing to share in and can only become a band of mutual exploiters. Cicero thus placed as the bedrock of his republic the inextricable bond of justice and law, and he transmitted to the West the concept that the very existence of the state depends on its being just; indeed, the unjust state has no right to continue.

Plato's *Republic* has appealed to political thinkers more

as an allegory than as a practical treatise for real politicians. Cicero's *De republica* and his *De officiis*, however, typified a Roman practicality tempered by moderate idealism urging upon men a role of action as statesmen. To the philosophers, Cicero remained the ideal of the active man, a thinker in action, in spite of the faulty policy that led to his death in the proscription on December 7, 43 B.C.

—*George M. Pepe, updated by Thomas H. Watkins*

ADDITIONAL READING:

Astin, A. E. *Scipio Aemilianus.* Oxford: Clarendon Press, 1967. Authoritative study of the real—not Cicero's idealized—Scipio.

Gruen, Eric S. *The Last Generation of the Roman Republic.* Berkeley: University of California Press, 1974. Detailed study of political life that places Cicero's career in context.

Habicht, C. *Cicero the Politician.* Baltimore: The Johns Hopkins University Press, 1990. Brief but detailed account that accepts Cicero's possible influence on Augustan principate.

Rawson, E. D. *Cicero: A Portrait.* Ithaca, N.Y.: Cornell University Press, 1975. Reliable overview of the life and work of Cicero.

_____. *Intellectual Life in the Late Roman Republic.* Baltimore: The Johns Hopkins University Press, 1985. In this work, Rawson's focus is on individuals other than Cicero.

Sabine, G. H., and S. B. Smith, eds. *"On the Commonwealth" of Marcus Tullius Cicero.* Columbus: Ohio State University Press, 1929. An old but excellent commentary on Cicero's work.

Stockton, D. *Cicero: A Political Biography.* Oxford: Oxford University Press, 1971. Minimizes possible influence of the *De republica.*

Wood, N. *Cicero's Social and Political Thought.* Berkeley: University of California Press, 1988. Although somewhat beyond the grasp of laypersons Wood's study provides a reliable scholarly exploration of the topic.

SEE ALSO: 380 B.C., Plato Develops His Theory of Ideas; 300 B.C., Stoic Conception of Natural Law; 90 B.C., Julian Law; 43-42 B.C., Proscriptions of the Second Triumvirate; 27-23 B.C., Completion of the Augustan Settlement.

43-42 B.C.
PROSCRIPTIONS OF THE SECOND TRIUMVIRATE

Proscriptions of the Second Triumvirate remove many political opponents in Rome, raise funds to help pay the triumviral armies, and set a standard for ruthless bloodshed that will be a negative model for Western civilization.

DATE: 43-42 B.C.

LOCALE: Rome

CATEGORY: Government and politics

KEY FIGURES:

Marc Antony (Marcus Antonius; c. 82-30 B.C.), colleague and later rival of Octavian

Marcus Tullius Cicero (106-43 B.C.), statesman, orator, and philosopher who was a victim of the proscriptions

Marcus Aemilius Lepidus (c. 89-12 B.C.), member of the Second Triumvirate who was ultimately deposed

Octavian (Gaius Julius Caesar Octavianus; 63 B.C.-A.D. 14), heir of Julius Caesar, first Roman emperor, 27 B.C.-A.D. 14, later called Augustus

SUMMARY OF EVENT. The Roman Republic was increasingly troubled after 135 B.C. The inadequacy of its city-state constitution to meet the needs of a growing empire, the stranglehold of great families on its offices, the rise of the equites and the consequent class struggle, and the twisting of its constitution initiated already by the Gracchi between 133 and 120 B.C. and by Marius and Sulla between 105 and 80 B.C., all contributed to the Republic's travail. Especially significant were the great rivals born in the decade between 110 and 100 B.C., men such as Pompey, Crassus, Julius Caesar, Catiline, and Sertorius, who were ready to fulfill their ambitions between 70 and 60 B.C. Most of these men proved to be too big for the constitution to contain. The rise of private armies, extraordinary commands, absentee governorships, extended tenures of office, bribery, demagoguery, political manipulation, and outright violence became more and more commonplace. Marius and Sulla even dared to liquidate each other's adherents by outright purges, a precedent set for the leaders who were to emerge as the Second Triumvirate. By decimating the old patrician stock and silencing Republican sentiments, the proscriptions of the Second Triumvirate brought an end to the civil wars by enabling Octavian to become the first emperor of Rome.

The formation of the Second Triumvirate by Octavian, Marc Antony, and Marcus Aemilius Lepidus in 43 B.C. was a pragmatic arrangement of three leaders who were united by their personal connections to Julius Caesar and because of their common enemies: a faction under the leadership of Brutus and Cassius and another under the leadership of Sextus Pompey, the son of Pompey the Great. Unlike the First Triumvirate, this three-man dictatorship was given legal sanction. The three leaders met on a small island in a river near Bologna, and formulated a joint policy. Although in effect they established a three-man dictatorship, of necessity they avoided the term, since Antony, when consul, had abolished the office of dictator for all time. They formed themselves into an executive committee which was to hold absolute power for five years in order to rebuild the Roman state. The triumvirs planned to unite their armies for a war against the Republican forces in the East. The West, already under their control, was divided among themselves: Lepidus keeping his provinces of Hither Spain and Narbonese Gaul and picking up Farther Spain as well, Antony taking the newly conquered parts of Gaul together with the Cisalpine province, and Octavian (as junior member) being assigned North Africa, Sardinia, Corsica, and Sicily, territories largely held by Pompeian adherents. Italy itself was to be under these three men's combined rule.

At the same meeting, the triumvirs determined to ensure the success of their rule by declaring a proscription against their Republican enemies. In this purge, hundreds of senators and about two thousand wealthy equites were marked for destruction. The historian Livy records that 130 senators were proscribed, Appian indicates that 300 were proscribed, and Plutarch records that 200 to 300 were proscribed. The names of almost one hundred of the proscribed have been recorded. Not all of these individuals were killed; a few obtained pardon and many successfully escaped from Italy. In most cases, the victims suffered only the confiscation of their properties.

In the official proclamation of the proscription, the triumvirs emphasized the injustices suffered at the hands of the enemies of the state and pointed out the necessity of removing a threat to peace at home while they were away fighting against the Republican armies. To justify their position and gain for it some semblance of respectability, they pointed out that when Julius Caesar had adopted a policy of clemency toward his enemies, he had paid for that policy by forfeiting his life.

While personal vengeance and political pragmatism played a part in the proscriptions, economic necessity also played a role. Octavian, Antony, and Lepidus had bought the support of their troops with lavish promises, and it was imperative that they pay them with more than words. Altogether, the triumvirs commanded forty-three legions, and they needed their support in the impending campaign against Brutus and Cassius. F. Hinard, in his book *Les Proscriptions de la Rome Républicaine* (1985), however, revises downward the numbers actually proscribed and supports the argument of political motivation to avenge Caesar and terrorize their opponents over that of economic demands for paying the soldiers.

In drawing up the lists, each of the three triumvirs had to give up some of his friends or relatives to satisfy the vengeance of one or the other of his colleagues and to make a public demonstration of their collective "toughness." So it was that the most famous of the victims, Cicero, was found on the list of the condemned. Octavian might have spared the famous orator, but Antony insisted on his death. While many of the proscribed acted quickly and escaped, Cicero dallied, uncertain of the best course to take, and died as a result. Livy, as quoted by Seneca, has given a full account of Cicero's death. The bloodshed of the proscriptions, highlighted by the execution of Cicero, tainted the historical reputations of the triumvirs, and especially those of Antony and Lepidus. During the religious wars of the sixteenth century, the French painter Antoine Caron (1521-1599) produced a series of massacre paintings showing the triumvirs watching or joining in the slaughter of unarmed citizens.

—Mary Evelyn Jegen, updated by Richard D. Weigel

ADDITIONAL READING:

Gowing, Alain. "Lepidus, the Proscriptions and the Laudatio Turiae." *Historia* 41 (1992), 283-296. An account of the funerary inscription that tells of the devotion of a wife to her proscribed husband and slanders Lepidus at the same time.

_____. *The Triumviral Narratives of Appian and Cassius Dio*. Ann Arbor: University of Michigan Press, 1992. The author compares the accounts that Appian and Cassius Dio present of the principal personages of the triumviral period.

Huzar, Eleanor G. *Mark Antony: A Biography*. Minneapolis: University of Minnesota Press, 1978. Huzar surveys the slanted sources on Antony and sees him in a moderate light, while admitting that the proscriptions revealed him at his worst.

Mitchell, Thomas. *Cicero: The Senior Statesman*. New Haven, Conn.: Yale University Press, 1991. A biography of the orator and defender of the Republic from his consulship in 63 B.C. until his honorable death in the proscriptions.

Syme, Ronald. *The Roman Revolution*. Oxford: Oxford University Press, 1939. The classic study of the transition from Republic to Empire that credits the proscriptions with a chilling, yet major, role in this process.

Weigel, Richard. *Lepidus: The Tarnished Triumvir*. London: Routledge, 1992. A biography of the "third triumvir" that attempts to reassess the biased sources and create a relatively objective account of his career.

SEE ALSO: 107-101 B.C., Marius Creates a Private Army; 51 B.C., Cicero Writes His *De Republica*; 31 B.C., Battle of Actium; 27-23 B.C., Completion of the Augustan Settlement.

31 B.C.
BATTLE OF ACTIUM

The Battle of Actium establishes the Roman Empire by ending the lengthy Roman civil wars with the victory of Octavian over Marc Antony and Cleopatra.

DATE: September 2, 31 B.C.

LOCALE: The Ambracian Gulf, on the west coast of northern Greece

CATEGORY: Wars, uprisings, and civil unrest

KEY FIGURES:

Marcus Vipsanius Agrippa (63 B.C.-A.D. 12), general and admiral serving Octavian

Marc Antony (Marcus Antonius; c. 83-30 B.C.), Roman general, member of the Second Triumvirate

Cleopatra VII (69-30 B.C.), queen of Egypt, consort of Marc Antony

Octavian (Gaius Julius Caesar Octavianus; 63 B.C.-A.D. 14), grandnephew of Julius Caesar, later called Augustus

SUMMARY OF EVENT. In the decade following the assassination of Julius Caesar in 44 B.C., a political struggle developed between Marc Antony and Octavian. Alternately rivals for power and reluctant allies, they became bitter enemies after Antony in 34 B.C. openly attached himself to Cleopatra, thus repudiating his legal wife who was Octavian's sister. In Italy, Octavian's supporters excoriated Antony for his liaison with Cleopatra and published a purported will of Antony deposited with the Vestal Virgins by which Antony donated eastern territories to Cleopatra and her children. In 32 B.C., the two consuls and three hundred senators went east to join Antony, thus terminating negotiations between him and Octavian.

Antony had recruited a heterogeneous army, variously estimated from forty thousand to a hundred thousand men, while Octavian raised an Italian force almost as large. Battle strategy eventually depended on navies, with Octavian's admiral Agrippa the most experienced commander at sea. Antony's fleet, perhaps at first slightly greater in size, was composed of larger, slower ships, some of his "sea castles" having eight or ten banks of oars.

In the mid-winter of 31 B.C., Marcus Agrippa sailed from Italy across the Ionian Sea and, after establishing Epirus as his base, began seizing important strong points along the Greek coast. At about the same time, Antony had moved his forces forward to block Agrippa's eastward advance. The Antonine fleet was stationed in the Gulf of Ambracia (Arta) with the army occupying a fortified camp on the nearby sandy promontory of Actium, one of the two peninsulas that pointed toward each other across the mouth of the gulf. Octavian, arriving with the remainder

Although shown with Cleopatra in this artistic rendering of the Battle of Actium, Antony commanded his own naval fleet before being forced to escape in the wake of Cleopatra's reserve squadron of ships. (Archive Photos)

of his forces, seized Corinth and other strategic inland positions, then occupied the northern peninsula of the gulf. Through skillful use of his cavalry he severed Antony's communications with the interior, and when the fleet under Agrippa sealed the Ambracian Gulf, Antony's forces were effectively blockaded. Soon, they began to suffer from hunger and disease. Significant desertions and lowered morale now impelled Antony to act.

In a council held in Antony's camp on September 1, 31 B.C., his officers were divided over strategy. A Roman faction advocated retreat by land; Cleopatra with some supporters favored a naval attack or an escape to Egypt. While Antony's enigmatic aims and actions are variously reported by later historians, it seems less likely that Antony wanted a showdown by naval action than that he hoped to break out of the blockade in order to fight later in a more favorable situation. Any ships he may have burned were probably unusable. All records agree that he left some of his troops ashore to retreat by an inland route, and that he kept aboard his ships the masts and sails, which were ordinarily jettisoned before action, in order to allow his fleet either to escape if the battle went against it or else pursue its defeated enemy.

The following day's battle was a chaotic imbroglio, shrouded from modern view in conflicting accounts. Antony's ships advanced through the narrow exit from the gulf, aligned so as to take advantage of an expected shift in the wind at midday. The Caesarian fleet blocked their passage. One squadron of sixty ships under Cleopatra was placed in the rear, carrying the treasure chest which undoubtedly belonged to her more than to Antony. After several hours of tense inactivity one wing of Antony's fleet was drawn into conflict, forcing Antony to commit the remainder of his forces. His soldiers aboard the large ships hurled missiles and shot arrows into Octavian's smaller vessels, which attempted to ram or surround and capture their clumsy opponents. Except for the use of oars, the battle vaguely resembled the one fought later between the sixteenth century Spanish Armada and the small English ships of Francis Drake.

Suddenly, at the height of the conflict, when a breeze rose from the northwest, Cleopatra's reserve squadron hoisted purple sails and moved through the battle line, in evident flight southward. Although Antony's flagship was entrapped, he transferred to a smaller ship and with a small portion of his fleet followed Cleopatra. Plutarch vividly portrays the gloom of defeat on the escaping ships.

Abandoned by their leader, the remnants of Antony's fleet backed into the gulf. More than five thousand men had been killed or drowned. Octavian and Agrippa made little attempt to pursue Antony; instead, they kept their ships at sea to bottle up the enemy and thus prevented further escape. Within about a week the ships and soldiers left behind by Antony surrendered. Octavian claimed to have captured three hundred vessels.

The battle of Actium remains one which is difficult to reconstruct and even more difficult to understand. The conflicting accounts of the battle can be interpreted as evidence either of Antony's determination to fight a serious, climactic naval battle with Octavian, or as an attempt to break Octavian's blockade in order to return to Egypt. Once there, Antony and Cleopatra could have reinforced their army, resupplied their navy, and either seized the initiative or waited for Octavian to attack them at their strongest point.

Scholars who favor the decisive battle theory generally suggest that Antony attempted to turn one flank of Octavian's fleet, but that Agrippa, a solider with a first-class military mind, skillfully countered the thrust with his smaller, more maneuverable ships. As the battle unfolded, Antony's fleet began to retire in some disorder, while a gap opened in Octavian's line. Seeing the battle was going against Antony, Cleopatra fled through this gap with her ships and Antony followed.

Those who support the breakout hypothesis read the same evidence, generally the accounts of the ancient historians Plutarch and Dio Cassius, in their favor. According to this view, Antony realized that his outnumbered and blockaded fleet had no real chance of defeating Octavian and Agrippa. Therefore, he feigned an attack at one point of the line in order to open the gap through which his key units— including the ships carrying his war chest—could escape.

Whichever theory is accepted, the battle of Actium was a decisive engagement, with profound and lasting impact on Roman and world history. Antony and Cleopatra returned to Egypt, where some final desperate expedients were contemplated but not effectively carried out. The next year Octavian came to Egypt, where he met little resistance and precipitated the romanticized suicides of both Antony and Cleopatra. The civil wars and the Republic were at an end, for Octavian was now the undisputed ruler of the Mediterranean world.

—Roger B. McShane, updated by Michael Witkoski

ADDITIONAL READING:

Brunson, Matthew. *Encyclopedia of the Roman Empire*. New York: Facts On File, 1994. A good introductory volume which provides the essential facts and information both about the battle itself and the larger civil war of which it was a part.

Green, Peter. *Alexander to Actium: The Historical Evolution of the Hellenistic Age*. Berkeley: University of California Press, 1990. The political, social and cultural undercurrents which pitted the Latin west against the Greek east during the final phases of the Roman Civil War are admirably expounded, clearly revealing the divergence of the Roman and Alexandrian worldviews.

Murray, William M., and Photios M. Petsas. *Octavian's Campsite Memorial for the Actian War*. Philadelphia: American Philosophical Society, 1989. Although this volume has archaeology as its main focus, it does provide an interesting and insightful review of the battle itself and its consequences.

Richardson, G. W. "Actium." *The Journal of Roman Studies* 27 (1937): 153-164. Accepts the traditional historical version of the battle which holds that Antony was attempting an escape, rather than a pitched battle, at Actium.

Rodgers, William. *Greek and Roman Naval Warfare: A Study of Strategy, Tactics and Ship Design from Salamis to Actium.* Annapolis, Md.: U.S. Naval Institute, 1964. The volume as a whole places the battle within the general context of ancient naval warfare, while the specific sections on Actium are detailed and informative.

Tarn, W. W. "The Battle of Actium." *The Journal of Roman Studies* 21 (1931): 173-199. Takes the view that Antony planned to fight a decisive battle at Actium but was betrayed by disloyal or disheartened elements within his own forces. Tarn explains Cleopatra's "flight" as a valiant but failed attempt to bolster the Antonine battle line.

SEE ALSO: 43-42 B.C., Proscriptions of the Second Triumvirate; 27-23 B.C., Completion of the Augustan Settlement.

27-23 B.C.
COMPLETION OF THE AUGUSTAN SETTLEMENT

The completion of the Augustan settlement marks a transition from the traditional res publica *to a new form of government, the Principate.*

DATE: 27-23 B.C.

LOCALE: Rome

CATEGORY: Government and politics

KEY FIGURE:

Octavian (63 B.C.-A.D. 14), great-nephew of Julius Caesar and his son by testamentary adoption in 44 B.C. (legally becoming Gaius Julius Caesar Octavianus); usually called Octavian until 27 B.C., and Augustus *princeps* thereafter

SUMMARY OF EVENT. For years, Julius Caesar outmaneuvered and outfought his enemies in war and politics but was never able to achieve permanent supremacy. Each victory on the battlefield and each new political office and honor produced more enemies. On March 15, 44 B.C., Julius Caesar was struck down in the name of liberty by a conspiracy led by men whom he had pardoned, trusted, and promoted. Caesar's plans are unknown. In 44 B.C., he was consul for the fifth time, *dictator perpetuo* ("for life"), and *pontifex maximus* (head of the state religion). Caesar had also received a number of honors deriving from Rome's kings in the sixth century. Whether he wanted to be king is uncertain and irrelevant: Although he had publicly rejected a crown, his whole position was regal and incompatible with Roman political opinion. To the conspirators, led by Gaius Cassius Longinus and Marcus Junius Brutus, it was patriotism, not murder, to kill the tyrant.

Julius Caesar's assassins restored neither *libertas* nor the *res publica*. For months, senators who dreaded the renewal of civil war sought to work out a compromise. Antony abolished the offensive dictatorship, but Cicero assailed him as a tyrannical threat to freedom and drove Rome to war. In November, 43 B.C., Caesarians came together in the Second Triumvirate: Antony, Lepidus, and young Gaius Octavius, who had just been made consul and insisted on being called Caesar. Everyone misjudged Octavian. Cicero dismissed him as "the boy," and Antony once remarked that he owed everything to his name (Caesar). The triumvirs eliminated their domestic enemies, most conspicuously Cicero, through massive proscriptions. In 42 B.C., they deified Julius Caesar (permitting Octavian to style himself *divi filius*, son of the god), and then destroyed the conspirators' army at Philippi. The triumvirate gradually failed, in good part because of the ruthless Octavian. He removed Lepidus from power in 36 B.C., but allowed him to live because Lepidus was *pontifex maximus*. Octavian turned public opinion against Antony, claiming that in 32 B.C. "all Italy" and the western provinces took an oath of loyalty to him as leader (*dux*, not a magistracy). As consul in 31 B.C., he destroyed Antony's forces at Actium and drove Antony and his consort, Cleopatra, to suicide the next year. The young Caesar had won supremacy. He had more power than the elder Caesar had ever had, but had yet to win acceptance.

Octavian wisely did not revive the dictatorship and kept clear of kingship. Yet it was not enough to avoid Caesar's errors. He had to devise a new position in the state and a new image for himself. The triumvir who had risen to power as *divi filius* moved away from his bloody Caesarian past. For a time after 31 B.C., he relied on consecutive consulships. Octavian returned to Rome in 29 B.C., celebrated a huge triumph, proclaimed the return of peace, and spent the following year in Rome to symbolize the end of the civil wars.

Years later, he wrote that in 28-27 B.C. he restored the *res publica* from his control to the judgment of the senate and Roman people. Outwardly he did. On January 13, 27 B.C., Octavian went before the senate and renounced all extraordinary powers given him during the period of the triumvirate. The senate promptly asked him to stay on as consul and undertake the governorship of Spain, Gaul, and Syria for ten years, together with his dominion over Egypt as a kind of private possession. Octavian allowed himself to be persuaded to accede to the senate's wishes. He was a model of Roman duty: He did not grasp unprecedented powers or titles, but rather, having saved the state from its enemies he offered to resign and then accepted a specific assignment which the senate asked him to undertake. It was a carefully scripted maneuver which he had worked out with a group of advisers. The lands given him contained about two-thirds of Rome's army and came to be designated the imperial (or armed) provinces. He governed them through legates. (A *legatus* was someone holding *imperium*, the right to command troops, delegated to him by a superior.) The senate governed all other provinces.

Three days later, the senate conferred upon him a number of singular honors. The most important of them was a new name, "Augustus," chosen after rejection of an alternative, Romulus, the founder of the city. Romulus cannot have been seriously considered: a king who had supposedly been murdered by the senators and then declared a god was uncomfortably like Caesar, whose statue had stood in the Temple of Quirinus (the deified Romulus). The month Sextilis was changed to August because Augustus' greatest achievements had occurred in that month.

From then on, Augustus was widely known as *princeps*, a word long used in Roman politics but raised to a new level of meaning. Leading senators were loosely designated *principes*, the "first men" in the state; and the most distinguished member of that body was formally designated *princeps senatus*, an honor that allowed him to speak first in debate. Augustus, however, was the *princeps*, "First Man" in a way that no one had ever been. Although scholars have debated this point, the title *princeps* may have been emphasized to recall the *princeps* of Cicero's essay *De republica*. The Ciceronian *princeps* was a distinguished and patriotic senator who guided the state by wisdom, not love of power, and on death won deification at the acclamation of his grateful citizens. This "settlement of 27" is generally taken as the opening of the imperial period in Roman history.

Following a long absence from Rome, suppression of a conspiracy, and recovery from a serious illness, Augustus adjusted his position on July 1, 23 B.C., when he resigned the consulship. This act was good propaganda: He had been consul consecutively since 31 B.C., which both made him appear monarchical and monopolized the office. In practical politics, however, it left Augustus without the power to control the government. The senate gave him twofold compensation: proconsular *imperium* and *tribunicia potestas*. Proconsular power enabled him to intervene and correct abuses in all provinces, for it was specified as *maius*, "greater" than of any provincial governor. Tribunician power (granted for ten years and periodically renewed) conferred the all-important right to initiate or veto measures (which he had done as consul), and made him a protector and champion of the ordinary people. Largely because of its *popularis* traditions, the tribunician power was renewed annually. Augustus emphasized this purely civilian power and downplayed his *imperium*.

Subsequent modifications in his position are minor, but two are noteworthy. After the death of Lepidus, Augustus was elected *pontifex maximus* in 12 B.C. In 2 B.C., he was hailed as *pater patriae*, "Father of his Country." The fundamental imperial powers thereafter were those he held, because Augustus was the first emperor: *imperium proconsulare maius*, *tribunicia potestas*, and *pontifex maximus*. (*Pater patriae* was standard but not essential.) From the late first century A.D., emperors also held the powers of the old censors, which Augustus had avoided.

Scholars debate whether Augustus actually hoped to "restore the Republic." In reality there is no question. To Romans, the *res publica* was not "Republic" in the modern sense but "the traditional state"—lawful government with the familiar magistracies and senatorial preeminence. *Res publica* was incompatible with kingship, dictatorship, or any obvious domination by a single individual. The conservative Italian upper classes and the senatorial aristocracy were emotionally attached to the ancient institutions. Julius Caesar had scorned them as outmoded and had moved to establish some type of personal rule. His failure to appreciate the widespread devotion to the old ways and how grievously his lifelong dictatorship and quasi-royal trappings had offended the political classes put him on the wrong end of numerous daggers on the Ides of March. Octavian's genius was his ability to retain the control of the state he had won in civil war by devising a new position which was based on tradition. Every element of his ultimate status had "republican" antecedents, but cumulatively they were new. His position was no charade. It was the Principate, and he was *princeps*. His wiser successors modeled themselves on him.

—*M. Joseph Costelloe, updated by Thomas H. Watkins*

ADDITIONAL READING:

Lacey, W. K. "Octavian in the Senate, January 27 B.C." *Journal of Roman Studies* 64 (1974): 176-184. Octavian carefully followed traditional procedure in returning the government to normal operations.

Millar, F., and E. Segal. *Caesar Augustus: Seven Aspects*. New York: Oxford University Press, 1984. A collection of scholarly essays by experts on Augustus.

Raaflaub, K. A., and M. Toher. *Between Republic and Empire: Interpretations of Augustus and His Principate*. Berkeley: University of California Press, 1990. Essays by experts interpret the political strength and legacy of Augustus.

Salmon, E. T. "The Evolution of Augustus' Principate." *Historia* 5 (1956): 456-476. Salmon explores the successive modifications in Augustus' position.

Syme, Ronald. *The Roman Revolution*. Oxford: Clarendon Press, 1939. A magisterial study, but one hostile to Octavian. Syme interprets Roman history against a twentieth century backdrop: the rise of Fascism and Nazism.

Zanker, Paul. *The Power of Images in the Age of Augustus*. Translated by Alan Shapiro. Ann Arbor: University of Michigan Press, 1988. Explores the intriguing thesis that conservatism in Roman art during the Augustan period matched that in politics.

SEE ALSO: 51 B.C., Cicero Writes His *De Republica*; 43-42 B.C., Proscriptions of the Second Triumvirate; 31 B.C., Battle of Actium; 50, Creation of the Imperial Bureaucracy.

15 B.C.-A.D. 15
RHINE-DANUBE FRONTIER IS ESTABLISHED

The Rhine-Danube frontier is established, fixing boundaries between the Roman Empire and European tribes to the north.

DATE: Primarily between 15 B.C. and A.D. 15

LOCALE: The Rhine and Danube Rivers and the Balkan peninsula south of Danube valley

CATEGORIES: Expansion and land acquisition; Government and politics

KEY FIGURES:

Arminius (c. 17 B.C.-A.D. 19), chieftain of the Germanic Cherusci

Augustus (Gaius Julius Caesar Octavianus; 63 B.C.-A.D. 14), first emperor of Rome, 27 B.C.-A.D. 14

Julius Caesar (100-44 B.C.), proconsul in Gaul, 58-50 B.C., and dictator of Rome, 49-44 B.C.

Nero Claudius Drusus (38-9 B.C.), brother of Tiberius and equally prominent

Nero Claudius Drusus Germanicus (15 B.C.-A.D. 19), Roman general who was the son of Drusus and Augustus' niece Antonia Minor; husband of Augustus' granddaughter Agrippina Major; father of the emperor Caligula; brother of the emperor Claudius

Maroboduus (c. 18 B.C.-A.D. 41), king of the Marcomanni in Bohemia

Tiberius Claudius Nero (42 B.C.-A.D. 37), prominent general under his stepfather Augustus, whom he succeeded as emperor in A.D. 14

Publius Quintilius Varus (died A.D. 9), served as legate on the lower Rhine, where he directed campaigns to annex the land between the Rhine and the Elbe

SUMMARY OF EVENT. The Rhine-Danube frontier was mostly established between 15 B.C. and A.D. 15 through the

determination of Emperor Augustus to limit the boundaries of the immense empire of which he was the first emperor (*princeps*).

Julius Caesar had conquered Gaul between 58 and 50 B.C., thereby extending Roman rule to the Rhine. In the course of his campaigns against the Celts and the Germans who had come into eastern Gaul, Caesar came to realize the value of the Rhine as a frontier. To coerce the Germans into similar respect for this natural boundary, Caesar built a temporary wooden bridge, crossed the river in 55 B.C., conducted extensive raids in German lands for two weeks, and then returned to Roman territory. His intimidating campaign had the effect of keeping the Germans away from Gaul for thirty years, though there was no true frontier.

Gaul (with the Rhine valley) was one of the "imperial" provinces assigned to Augustus from the start of the Roman Empire in 27 B.C. His enormous powers allowed him to create Rome's first unified frontier policy. Equally advantageous, all newly created provinces were automatically designated "imperial." Governors of imperial provinces were styled "propraetorian legates of the emperor" (*legati propraetore Augusti*); the emperor was commander in chief, possessed proconsular *imperium*, and delegated *imperium* to his appointees.

At the opening of Augustus' reign, Rome had extensive possessions in the west and the east but lacked control of the Alps and the Balkan peninsula. Northern Italy, Illyricum, and Macedonia could not be defended against serious attack by barbarian tribes. Augustus determined to expand Roman holdings up to the Danube and perhaps beyond. There were three theaters of campaigns. In the first theater, Augustus sent legions under the command of his capable stepsons Tiberius Claudius and Nero Claudius Drusus through the Alps to the upper Danube region in 16 B.C., while he himself took charge in Gaul. Within two years, Tiberius and Drusus were largely done. A legion soon occupied Vindonissa (Windisch, on the Aare near Brugg). Modern Switzerland, southern Bavaria, and western Austria became the province of Raetia. Rome annexed Noricum (central Austria) and administered it through prefects (*praefecti*) headquartered at the natives' mountaintop commercial center, the Magdalensberg. Later, in A.D. 40-49, Claudius converted Noricum into a procuratorial province, so called because the governor was an equestrian *procurator* (not a senator), and moved the capital to Virunum (Waisenberg, near Klagenfurt).

Campaigns in the second theater, south of the middle Danube, proved difficult. Augustus' son-in-law Marcus Agrippa was to have directed operations but died in 12 B.C. Tiberius took over and had apparently completed the war by 9 B.C. Other generals extended Roman control over the lower Danube (modern Bulgaria) to create the province of Moesia and to reduce Thrace to a client state. The Pannonians, however, rose in an extensive revolt in A.D. 6, and Tiberius, assisted by several senior commanders, took three years to crush the uprising. Illyricum was divided into two imperial provinces: Pannonia, centering on the Drava and Sava River valleys to their confluence with the Danube, and Dalmatia, in the Balkan peninsula north of Macedonia. These conquests brought Roman rule to the western coast of the Black Sea. Fortifications were established along the Danube and probably in the tributaries to its south. The location of many legionary fortresses in the early Roman Empire remains uncertain, although bases at Emona (Ljubljana) and Poetovio (Ptuj) are probable. Dalmatia had two legions: one at Burnum on the Krka and the other at Tilurium (Gardun) on the Cetina.

Meanwhile, Drusus had marched northward from Raetia along the Rhine to establish the third theater of the campaign. Because the German tribes had renewed attacks on Gaul, it was decided to invade Germany again and push back the German frontier to the Elbe (less probably as far as the Vistula). The plan was to shorten Rome's northern frontier by some three hundred miles and also to put Gaul beyond the reach of German attacks. Drusus entered the German heartland in 12 B.C., planting Roman eagles on the Elbe after fortifying the lower Rhine. He was accidentally killed in 9 B.C., and his brother Tiberius replaced him.

Rome overran but never really organized the lands east of the Rhine. The Germans revolted, and under Arminius, a young chieftain who had served with the Romans as an auxiliary commander and won Roman citizenship, they annihilated some twenty thousand Romans belonging to three legions under the command of Publius Quintilius Varus in the famous Battle of the Teutoburger Forest in A.D. 9. The site of the battle has recently been located, in the Lippe valley. The elderly Augustus was severely shaken when news of the disaster reached him, and though Drusus' son Germanicus undertook some punitive action and restored Roman prestige in A.D. 14-17, Rome made no further effort to encompass or restrain the Germanic tribes. They remained outside the mainstream of Roman civilization.

In the early Roman Empire, the Rhine commands were among the most important in the empire and senators of consular rank held them. Two military districts, called Upper and Lower Germany (*Germania Superior* and *Inferior*), stretched along the Rhine; they became provinces only in A.D. 90 with capitals at Moguntiacum (modern Mainz) for Superior and Colonia Agrippinensis (modern Cologne or Köln) for Inferior. Each legate commanded four legions plus auxiliary troops. By the early second century, the garrison was reduced to just four. Other legionary fortresses along the Rhine are also the origins of modern cities: Argentorate (Strasbourg), Bonna (Bonn), Novaesium (Neuss), and Castra Vetera (Xanten). Another base was converted into a civilian colony in A.D. 49, as Colonia Claudia Ara Agrippinsium. In the 70's and early 80's, Rome occupied the Black Forest area between the Upper Rhine and Upper Danube, a noticeable shortening of the frontier. By the early second century, these garrisons had been reduced to two legions each, plus auxiliaries, as the Danube became the military center of the empire.

The Danube area had been pacified after the fall of Maroboduus as king of the Marcomanni in A.D. 19, but slowly it came to have the Empire's largest concentration of forces. The bases in the Balkans were closed and their legions transferred to the Danube from Dalmatia, from the Rhine army, and even from Britain. Augusta Regina (Regensburg), Vindobona (Vienna), Aquincum (Budapest), and Singidunum (Belgrade) are legionary fortresses which have become modern cities. Trajan conquered Dacia (roughly Romania) in 101-106; his famous column in Rome commemorates the war. Ironically, it was the Marcomanni who (with the Quadi) in the reign of Marcus Aurelius (A.D. 161-180) first seriously challenged the frontier after two centuries of the *Pax Romana*. Rome's ultimate establishment of the Rhine-Danube line as its northern frontier, the subsequent Dacian conquest notwithstanding, was not a matter of choice but of necessity. Rome's inability to conquer further was dictated by spreading internal weaknesses and revolts, the generally troublesome Parthian frontier, and the strength of Rome's German adversaries. The establishment of the northern frontier entailed much more than the mere definition of a border; it represented both the height and the eclipse of Roman imperialism in Europe and therefore the spread of *Romanitas* as well.

—*Edward P. Keleher, updated by Thomas H. Watkins*

ADDITIONAL READING:

Alföldy, Geza. *Noricum*. Translated by Anthony Birley. London: Routledge & Kegan Paul, 1974. Part of Routledge's *History of the Provinces of the Roman Empire* series, this work is detailed and archaeological, and its scholarship is superb.

Drinkwater, J. *Roman Gaul*. London: Croom Helm, 1983. Provides an overview of activities on the Rhine frontier.

King, Anthony. *Roman Gaul and Germany*. Berkeley: University of California Press, 1990. King also treats the

Rhine frontier. When compared to the work of Drinkwater, cited above, King's volume is more accessible for beginners.

Luttwak, E. *The Grand Strategy of the Roman Empire.* Baltimore: The Johns Hopkins University Press, 1976. An analyst for the Department of Defense rather than an ancient historian, Luttwak has stimulated considerable debate; many doubt Rome had a "grand strategy."

Mocsy, A. *Pannonia and Upper Moesia.* London: Routledge & Kegan Paul, 1974. Like the work by Alföldy, cited above, this well-written volume is part of Routledge's *History of the Provinces of the Roman Empire.*

Syme, Ronald. "The Northern Frontier Under Augustus." In *Cambridge Ancient History*, Vol. X, edited by S. A. Cook et al. Cambridge, England: Cambridge University Press, 1934. Syme's study remains irreplaceable; archaeological work has provided some new information.

Wilkes, J. *Dalmatia.* London: Routledge & Kegan Paul, 1969. Yet another superb entry in Routledge's *History of the Provinces of the Roman Empire* series.

SEE ALSO: 58-51 B.C., Caesar's Conquest of Gaul; 9, Defeat in the Teutoburger Forest.

9
DEFEAT IN THE TEUTOBURGER FOREST

Its defeat in the Teutoburger forest causes the Roman Empire to shift to a defensive stance after three Roman legions are ambushed on the German frontier.

DATE: A.D. 9

LOCALE: Northwest Germany

CATEGORIES: Government and politics; Wars, uprisings, and civil unrest

KEY FIGURES:

Arminius (c. 17 B.C.-A.D. 19), chieftain of the Cherusci, a small Germanic tribe

Asprenas (died c. A.D. 30), consul in A.D. 6, Varus' nephew and legate who led two legions to Mainz to halt the German advance

Octavian Augustus, Roman emperor, 27 B.C.-A.D. 14

Tiberius, future Roman emperor (A.D. 14-37) and successor to Augustus who led his troops to the Rhineland to help recover Varus' losses

Publius Quintilius Varus (died A.D. 9), consul in 13 B.C., Roman general assigned to the Roman province between the Rhine and Elbe Rivers in A.D. 7

SUMMARY OF EVENT. After the Battle of Actium in 31 B.C. and the subsequent Roman conquest of Egypt, which secured his hold upon the Roman world, Emperor Augus-

tus (as Octavian was hailed by the senate in 27 B.C.) reduced the Roman army to almost half its former strength, leaving only twenty-eight legions in service. This was the period of the famous Pax Romana, which some historians see as a period of national fatigue and inertia, the inevitable result of more than a century of incessant civil war, rather than as a time of good will.

Because it was difficult to maintain equilibrium on the northern frontier, Augustus' policy called for an expansion into Germanic territory. By A.D. 6, the region north of the Main River between the Rhine and the Elbe was a Roman province administered by Publius Quintilius Varus, a general chosen by Augustus and married to the emperor's grandniece. Varus appears to have been more an administrator than a soldier, a view hinted at by the Latin historian Velleius Paterculus and one that may have been shared by Arminius, who saw an opportunity to overthrow Roman imperial rule before it was firmly established in German territory. Certainly, Varus did not understand the German temperament nor sufficiently appreciate its warlike nature.

After being routed in battle by Germanic forces led by Arminius, the Roman general Publius Quintilius Varus committed suicide by falling upon his sword. (Archive Photos)

In A.D. 9, three legions under Varus were defeated in the Teutoburger forest by Arminius, a chieftain of the Cherusci, a small Germanic tribe, in a battle that marked a watershed in the history of the Roman Empire. From that time onward, the open secret of Roman policy in the territory beyond the Rhine was to divide, not conquer. Rome had changed from an offensive to a defensive position vis à vis the Germanic peoples.

The frontier problem was related to one of the major defects in the Roman imperial system, namely the nature of the imperial succession. Since the principle of succession by heredity was not firmly established during the early years of the Roman Empire, the ambiguity of the succession process played into the hands of strong leaders in the army, men who had little reason to be loyal to a Roman tradition which, in many cases, they did not even know. While it was many years before a barbarian general ascended the imperial throne, the victory of Arminius signaled the growing political function of the Roman barbarized army.

Arminius himself was a Roman-trained soldier and, at the time of his victory over Varus, the leader of only a faction of the Cherusci. Varus' appointment as governor was an unfortunate choice. He tactlessly treated the high-spirited Germans as inferior and tried to Romanize them against their will. This policy roused resentment in the Cherusci and led to Varus' disastrous defeat. Enticed by the report of an uprising, Varus led the seventeenth, eighteenth, and nineteenth legions out of summer quarters into the Teutoburger forest, probably located somewhere between the modern towns of Osnabrück and Detmold. There, the army was ambushed and massacred, and Varus himself committed suicide. The episode can hardly be classified as a battle, for the Germans had the odds in their favor as they fell on the Roman columns encumbered by their baggage train in wooded country. The Roman cavalry attempted to escape but did not succeed.

Velleius Paterculus, in a translation by F. W. Shipley, describes the result. Hemmed in by forests and marshes and ambuscades, the column was exterminated almost to a man by the very enemy whom it had always slaughtered like cattle, whose life or death had depended solely upon the wrath or the pity of the Romans. The general had more courage to die than to fight, for, following the example of his father and grandfather, Varus ran himself through with his sword.

After the rout of Varus, the Germans swept on to capture Roman forts east of the Rhine. Asprenas, Varus' legate, led two legions to Mainz, but the enemy did not attempt to cross there. Having just succeeded in quelling a major revolt in Pannonia after three years of difficult fighting, the Roman general (and future emperor) Tiberius was forced to postpone a triumphal celebration in Rome in order to hurry to the Rhine, where the garrison was raised to eight legions. To bring the forces to this level, two Roman legions were withdrawn from the province of Raetia (modern Austria) and four were taken from Spain and Illyricum (the eastern Adriatic coast).

While the Rhine defenses were thus strengthened, the three lost legions were not replaced in the Roman army, so that its total strength was reduced to twenty-five legions. Any thought of further expansion beyond the Elbe was abandoned. Even before the disaster in the Teutoburger forest, slaves were being pressed into military service, a practice that revealed a serious shortage of Roman manpower.

Augustus, who was seventy-two years old at the time, was shocked by Varus' defeat. According to the Roman biographer and historian Suetonius, for several months Augustus cut neither his beard nor his hair, the traditional Roman sign of mourning, and sometimes would bash his head against a door, crying: "Quinctilius Varus, give me back my legions."

The major impact of the defeat, however, was to shift Roman policy to a defensive posture on the German frontier, which became fixed under Augustus' successor, Tiberius. In this sense, the defeat in Teutoburger forest was a pivotal point in European history, allowing the Germanic tribes to remain outside Roman influence.

—Mary Evelyn Jegen, updated by Michael Witkoski

ADDITIONAL READING:

Drummond, Stephen K., and Lynn Nelson. *The Western Frontiers of Imperial Rome*. Armonk, N.Y.: M. E. Sharpe, 1994. An expansive description of the ebb and flow of Rome's borders which illustrates the long-range impact of the event in the Teutoburger forest.

Grant, Michael. *The Twelve Caesars*. New York: Charles Scribner's Sons, 1975. Written by an outstanding historian of Rome, this work contains a section on Augustus that provides a concise summary of the event and its impact.

May, Elmer C., Gerald Stadler, and John F. Votaw. *Ancient and Medieval Warfare*. Wayne, N.J.: Avery Publishing Group, 1984. Prepared for the Department of History of the United States Military Academy at West Point, this volume helps the student understand the nature of warfare on the Roman frontier.

Newark, Tim. *The Barbarians*. Poole, Dorset, England: Blandford Press, 1985. An illustrated study that discusses Germanic tactics and weapons during their contests with the imperial legions.

Scarre, Christopher. *Chronicle of the Roman Emperors.*

New York: Thames & Hudson, 1995. This account of imperial Roman history provides a brief but excellent survey of the disastrous battle and its impact on Roman frontier policy.

Suetonius, Gaius. *The Twelve Caesars.* Translated by Robert Graves. Revised, with an introduction by Michael Grant. London: Allen Lane, 1979. The section on "Augustus" in this illustrated version of Graves's translation memorably describes the emperor's reaction to the destruction of the frontier legions.

SEE ALSO: 58-51 B.C., Caesar's Conquest of Gaul; 31 B.C., Battle of Actium; 15 B.C.-A.D. 15, Rhine-Danube Frontier Is Established.

43-130
ROMAN CONQUEST OF BRITAIN

The Roman conquest of Britain creates a new province through the subjugation of the island's Celtic tribes.

DATE: 43-130

LOCALE: Britain south of Hadrian's Wall

CATEGORIES: Expansion and land acquisition; Wars, uprisings, and civil unrest

KEY FIGURES:

Agricola, Roman governor (imperial legate) of Britain, A.D. 77/78-83/84

Julius Caesar (100-44 B.C.), first Roman to campaign in Britain, in 55 and 54 B.C.

Claudius, Roman emperor, A.D. 41-54; ordered conquest in A.D. 43

Hadrian, Roman emperor, A.D. 117-138

SUMMARY OF EVENT. At the beginning of the Christian era, Britannia—the Roman name for England, Wales, and southern Scotland—had an Iron Age culture. Before the sixth century B.C., waves of Celts had crossed the English Channel from the Continent and, by the time of Julius Caesar, had imposed their culture throughout the island. Little is known of their history because the Celts were preliterate, and Greek and Roman writers were not much interested in them. Archaeology allows an estimate of their development. Tribal kingdoms dominated by warrior aristocracies fought incessantly. Possessing rich farmland, engaging in frequent trade with their Celtic kin of Gaul and the Rhineland, and sharing their La Tène culture, the tribes of the southeast were developing rapidly; their villages approximated true towns and their kings struck coins, proof of emerging royal power. The tribes of the north and west were isolated, poorer, and still relied on hill forts for defense.

Caesar's campaign against the Nervii in northern Gaul led him in 55 B.C. to make an expedition across the Chan-

SITES IN ROMAN BRITAIN

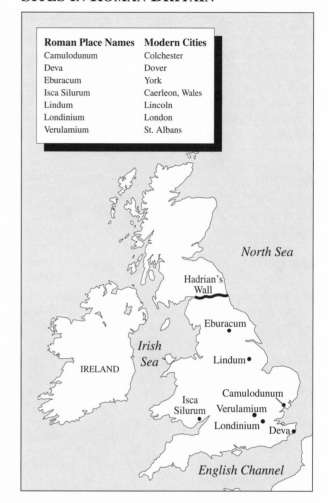

Roman Place Names	Modern Cities
Camulodunum	Colchester
Deva	Dover
Eburacum	York
Isca Silurum	Caerleon, Wales
Lindum	Lincoln
Londinium	London
Verulamium	St. Albans

nel against their British allies. With a small force, he landed on the Kentish coast, but storm damage to his fleet and British resistance forced his withdrawal that fall. He was more successful the following year, as he defeated Cassivellaunus of the Catuvellauni (near St. Albans), took hostages, required payment of tribute, claimed to have conquered Britain, and left, never to return. Civil wars from 49 to 30 and then the organization of Gaul and the establishment of the Rhine frontier kept Rome out of Britain for almost a century. Diplomacy sought to maintain a rough equality among the tribes by supporting kings or factions, and to prevent British assistance to revolts inside Roman Gaul. Finds of Roman coins and wine amphoras indicate sporadic luxury trade. Anti-Roman Catuvellaunian expansion in Essex and across the south necessitated a change in Roman policies.

Claudius decided to conquer Britain. He dispatched Aulus Plautius at the head of an army of four legions

(5,500 men each) plus an equal number of auxiliary troops in 43. The force landed in Kent, crossed the Thames, and captured Camulodunum (Colchester), recently become the Catuvellaunian capital. Leaving Legio XX Valeria at Camulodunum, three army corps fanned out to overrun the lowlands. Legio II Augusta pacified the southern region under the command of Vespasian (who ruled as emperor from 69 to 79). Legio XIV Gemina—joined by XX Valeria in 49—thrust into the Midlands, and IX Hispana marched through East Anglia. By the year 47, the new province embraced lands south and east of the Humber and Severn Rivers. A military road, the Fosse Way, ran from Exeter (a base of Legio II) northeast to Lincoln (a base of Legio IX) and marked the limit of Roman control. The decommissioned fortress at Camulodunum became a *colonia* and the provincial capital; Verulamium (near St. Albans) and Londinium (London) were flourishing symbols of Roman rule. Two tribal kings surrendered in time to preserve independence as client rulers: Cogidubnus in Surrey-Hampshire and Prasutagus in Norfolk. Subsequent advance was much more difficult because of highland terrain and stiffening resistance. The Silures in east Wales, the Ordovices in north Wales, and the Brigantes in Yorkshire proved to be intractable. The harsh annexation of Prasutagus' kingdom after his death sparked a revolt led by his widow Boudica in 60-61. Her army sacked Camulodunum, Londinium, and Verulamium but the disciplined army of the governor Suetonius Paullinus destroyed it; the XIVth and XXth became known as Victrix for their valor.

Under the Flavian dynasty (69-96), Rome expanded the province and improved the quality of her rule. The laudatory biography of Agricola by his son-in-law Tacitus has made that governor's activities famous. His predecessors Cerealis and Frontinus subjugated the Brigantes and the tribes of Wales, freeing Agricola to push against the Caledonians (Scotland) and begin construction of a fortress for Legio XX at Inchtuthil on the Tay. It was abandoned unfinished, as troubles on the Danube compelled the withdrawal from the Highlands and the reduction of the British garrison to three legions. Legion IX occupied Eburacum (York), while Legions II and XX moved to Isca (Caerleon) and Deva (Chester); all three proved to be permanent. The cities destroyed by Boudica were rebuilt and Londinium, the hub of the road network and with an excellent harbor, soon became the capital; archaeology has uncovered the governor's palace, forum, some streets and wharves. Two former legionary fortresses became *coloniae*: Lindum colonia (Lincoln) and Glevum *castra* ("fort") (Gloucester). To promote Romanization and easier provincial administration, the governors fostered Roman-style towns as *civitas*-capitals ("canton-capitals"); each

controlled the surrounding countryside. Early examples are Canterbury and Chelmsford; more appeared under the Flavians—Chichester, Silchester, and Winchester (on the annexation of Cogidubnus' kingdom), Dorchester, Exeter, Cirencester, Caistor-by-Norwich, Leicester, and Wroxeter. Nearly all these places continued to flourish as cities through the late twentieth century, so knowledge of them has increased piecemeal through urban archaeology. Wroxeter and Silchester are uninhabited, and studies of them have provided the most complete information of Romano-British towns.

Literary sources necessary for narrative history practically cease at the recall of Agricola in 83/84. Legio IX was transferred out of Britain about 110 (the old view that it was destroyed in a rebellion around the year 117 is wrong). Hadrian came to Britain in 121, bringing a new governor (Platorius Nepos), a new legion (VI Victrix, which occupied York), and new ideas. The last *civitas*-capitals appeared in these years. He initiated the building of the famous wall, the best-known example among a number of linear barriers around the Roman Empire and stretching some eighty Roman miles from coast to coast from the mouth of the River Tyne to Solway Firth. Auxiliary troops (infantry and part-mounted cohorts) garrisoned

Archaeological excavations at the site of Hadrian's Wall in Scotland have uncovered artifacts associated with the Roman military occupation of Britain. (Robert McClenaghan)

forts at five- or six-mile intervals. Between each pair of forts were "milecastles" housing small contingents sent out from the forts, and watchtowers rose at one-third mile intervals, thus within sight of one another. Command headquarters and the largest single unit (a "milliary" cavalry wing, *ala*) were at Stanwix near Carlisle. There were also several cavalry forts to the north of the wall, from which mounted patrols increased Roman surveillance. Hadrian's Wall marked the northern boundary of Britannia and the Roman Empire, stood guard against the tribes of the far north and prevented them from joining restless peoples within the province. The wall allowed the Romans to collect customs. While the wall made raids difficult (and returning home laden with booty more so), it was not intended to withstand large attacks. Invaders who overran it would have to contend with the legions moving up from York and Chester and reinforced auxiliary units closing in from behind.

The reign of Hadrian marks the end of the Roman conquest of Britain. In later years there were only occasional campaigns beyond the wall. Antoninus Pius' effort to hold a line between Edinburgh and Glasgow was soon abandoned. Septimius Severus fought up into the Highlands and died at York; his son Caracalla pulled back to the wall.   —*Kevin Herbert, updated by Thomas H. Watkins*

ADDITIONAL READING:

Birley, A. *The Fasti of Roman Britain*. Oxford: Clarendon Press, 1981. Reference work, discussing all known Roman officials.

Britannia. This scholarly journal provides specialized articles, reviews of books, and annual updates of work in progress.

Cunliffe, B. *The Iron Age Communities of Britain*. 2d ed. Oxford: Clarendon Press, 1978. Best study of the topic.

Frere, S. *Britannia*. 3d ed. London: Routledge & Kegan Paul, 1987. Detailed history, heavily military and archaeological.

Hanson, W. S. *Agricola*. Totowa, N.J.: Barnes & Noble, 1987. One of the few up-to-date studies of Agricola available in English.

Jones, B., and D. Mattingly. *An Atlas of Roman Britain*. Oxford: Blackwell, 1990. Good maps, discussion, and bibliography.

Webster, G. *Boudica: The British Revolt Against Rome, A.D. 60*. Totowa, N.J.: Rowman & Littlefield, 1978. A useful biographical study of the revolt of the native Britons against Roman rule.

_____. *Fortress into City: The Consolidation of Roman Britain*. Totowa, N.J.: Barnes & Noble, 1988. Archaeological study of the major military-turned-civilian sites.

SEE ALSO: 1100-500 B.C., Hallstatt Civilization Ushers in Iron Age in Europe; 109-102 B.C., Celtic Hill Forts Appear; 58-51 B.C., Caesar's Conquest of Gaul; 60-61, Boadicea Leads Revolt Against Roman Rule.

50
CREATION OF THE IMPERIAL BUREAUCRACY

The creation of the imperial bureaucracy establishes civil service reform within the political machinery of the Roman Empire.

DATE: c. 50
LOCALE: Rome and the Roman Empire
CATEGORIES: Government and politics; Organizations and institutions
KEY FIGURES:
Augustus (Gaius Julius Caesar Octavianus; 63 B.C.-A.D. 14), Roman emperor, 27 B.C.-A.D. 14
Caligula (Gaius Caesar; A.D. 12-41), Roman emperor, A.D. 37-41
Claudius (Tiberius Claudius Drusus Nero Germanicus; 10 B.C.-A.D. 54), Roman emperor, A.D. 41-54
Hadrian, Roman emperor, A.D. 117-138
Pallas,
Narcissus, and
Callistus, freedmen heads of bureaus under Claudius, and regarded by Roman tradition as archetypes of the all-powerful bureaucrat
Tiberius (Tiberius Claudius Nero; 42 B.C.-A.D. 37), Roman emperor, A.D. 14-37

SUMMARY OF EVENT. The imperial bureaucracy was the creation of the early Roman emperors, especially of the first, Augustus, and the fourth, Claudius. Augustus' reorganization of Roman government provided the framework for the development of such a bureaucracy; Claudius' deliberate elaboration of the bureaucracy that had developed during preceding reigns brought this branch of government service to the peak of its power.

The imperial bureaucracy was comparable to, and at first existed alongside, an older and less elaborate bureaucracy of the Republican period. The Republican magistrates had drawn their supporting staffs from two sources. One was the pool of permanent employees attached to the central government treasury. The other was each magistrate's personal staff. The Roman magistrate was invariably a man of property, and it was customary for such a person to use his personal staff, composed in large part of his own slaves and freedmen, to conduct public as well as private business.

Under the political settlement effected by Augustus, the government of Italy and of about half the provinces continued to be conducted according to Republican custom, by annually elected magistrates whose supporting staff was drawn from personal employees and from employees of the treasury, which remained under the control of the senate. In the remaining provinces, government was the personal responsibility of the emperor, who governed through representatives whom he appointed. The emperor's representatives, once again men of property and political standing, may have been assisted by their personal staffs but they were not provided with personnel from the central treasury. Instead, the supporting staff for administration of the emperor's provinces was drawn from the emperor's own household, and was composed, for the most part, of the emperor's slaves and freedmen.

Information about the development of the imperial bureaucracy under Augustus and under his successors Tiberius and Caligula, is limited. One may assume that as an emperor gathered ever greater powers into his own hands, the bureaus that assisted him grew in number, complexity, and power. With Tiberius' retirement from Rome in his later years and with Caligula's erratic preoccupations, much of the business of the Roman Empire must have been left to the chiefs of bureaus. It is a tribute to the capabilities of the bureaucracy and of the bureaucrats that civilian government did not collapse, even under the burden of unrest and resentment that led to Caligula's assassination.

The importance of a capable imperial bureaucracy did not escape the notice of Claudius, and it is during his rule that scholars have found much evidence of the consolidation and expansion of this organization. Claudius' personal agents collected certain taxes even in provinces governed, in theory, by elected magistrates. These financial agents were granted political powers, particularly the right to preside over certain kinds of litigation, that had formerly been reserved for elected officials. The emperor's staff in Rome was organized into distinct bureaus whose chiefs, the emperor's freedmen, were granted extraordinary dignity and authority. Five chief bureaus are known: *a rationibus* dealing with finance, *ab epistulis* with state correspondence, *a libellis* with petitions, *a cognitionibus* with justice, and *a studiis* with culture.

In his elaboration of the imperial bureaucracy, Claudius was no doubt motivated by the desire to achieve efficient central administration, and there is evidence that the Roman Empire in general, and particularly the outlying regions, benefited from his reforms. Yet the population of Rome, jealous of its ancient privileges, resented the assumption of power by foreign-born former slaves.

Claudius may have actually granted his ministers enough power to govern even him. Narcissus, chief of the bureau *ab epistulis*, is said to have disposed of Claudius' wife Messalina more or less without his consent. Pallas, chief of *a rationibus*, was believed to have cooperated with Claudius' next wife, Agrippina, in bringing about the emperor's death by poisoning, and in establishing as next emperor, not Claudius' son and heir-elect, Britannicus, but Agrippina's son, the infamous Nero who reigned from A.D. 41 to 68.

As Nero devoted himself increasingly to his own amusement, the imperial bureaucracy continued to wield nearly unsupervised power, and there is little doubt that the abuses of the emperor's freedmen contributed to the alienation that led to open revolt and warfare in A.D. 68-69. Succeeding emperors attempted to restrain their agents without enacting any major reform of the bureaucracy, which continued to function in the form given it by Claudius until the reign of Hadrian. By that time, the principle of one-man rule was well accepted, and the service of the emperor was recognized as the service of the state. Hadrian reorganized the imperial bureaucracy accordingly, relying less on the services of his personal dependents and opening the more important positions to free-born Roman citizens. The rift between bureaucracy and citizenry was repaired without diminishing the usefulness of the bureaucracy itself.

—*Zola M. Packman, updated by Jeffrey L. Buller*

ADDITIONAL READING:

Braund, David C., ed. *The Administration of the Roman Empire, 241 B.C.-A.D. 193*. Exeter, England: University of Exeter, 1988. A concise series of essays exploring the development of the Roman imperial bureaucracy.

Carney, Thomas F. *Bureaucracy in Traditional Society*. Lawrence, Kans.: Coronado Press, 1971. Although focusing primarily on the late Roman Empire and the Byzantine Period, this work provides excellent background on the operation of the Roman bureaucratic mechanism. Includes useful maps and diagrams.

Dise, Robert L. *Cultural Change and Imperial Administration*. New York: Peter Lang, 1991. Using the middle Danube provinces as an example, explores the operation of the Roman bureaucracy in outlying regions of the empire. Covers the period from the beginning of the empire to the third century A.D. and provides excellent insight into the day-to-day administration of the Roman government.

Lydus, Ioannes. *On Powers or the Magistracies of the Roman State*. Translated by Anastasius C. Bandy. Philadelphia: American Philosophical Society, 1983. Contains both the Greek text and a good translation (in parallel columns) of an informative sixth century work on the operation of the Roman imperial bureaucracy. Also includes an introduction, critical text, and commentary.

Matthews, John. *Political Life and Culture in Late Roman Society*. London: Variorum Reprints, 1985. Covering the period from 30 B.C. until the late fifth century A.D., this work explores the gradual development of the Roman imperial bureaucracy. Also contains illustrations and maps.

Mattingly, Harold B. *The Imperial Civil Service of Rome*. Cambridge, England: Cambridge University Press, 1910. Although somewhat dated, this work still provides the best general introduction to the development of the Roman imperial government.

SEE ALSO: 340-338 B.C., Origin of *Municipia*; 51 B.C., Cicero Writes His *De Republica*; 27-23 B.C., Completion of the Augustan Settlement

60-61
BOADICEA LEADS REVOLT AGAINST ROMAN RULE

Boadicea leads a revolt against Roman rule, uniting southern tribes in the province of Britain in a failed attempt to resist the forces of imperial Rome.

DATE: 60-61

LOCALE: England

CATEGORY: Wars, uprisings, and civil unrest

KEY FIGURES:

Boadicea, queen of the Iceni

Caratacus, son of Cunobelinus, king of the Catuvellauni

Claudius (Tiberius Claudius Drusus Nero Germanicus; 10 B.C.-A.D. 54), Roman emperor, A.D. 41-54

Catus Decianus, Roman procurator of Britain

Nero (Nero Claudius Caesar Drusus Germanicus; A.D. 37-68), Roman emperor, A.D. 54-68

Prasutagus, king of the Iceni

Publius Ostorius Scapula, Roman governor of Britain, A.D. 50-52

Caius Paulinus Seutonius, Roman governor of Britain, A.D. 58-61

SUMMARY OF EVENT. Queen Boadicea of the Iceni, one of the larger tribes in Britain, led a revolt against Roman rule in A.D. 60. There is greater agreement regarding the meaning of this warrior queen's name than regarding its spelling. The word for victory in Gaelic is *bouda*; and in modern Welsh, *buddug*. Many linguists translate Boadicea as meaning "Victory" or "the Victorious." There is little consensus regarding its proper spelling. Variations include

Boudicca, Boudica, Bodicca, Boudicea, Bonducca, Bunduica, and Boadicea. Many modern writers have adopted the spelling "Boudicea," which occurs frequently in various manuscripts of the Roman historian Tacitus, with the substitution of an "a" for "u."

Prasutagus, king of the Iceni, died in A.D. 60 at a time when Caius Paulinus Seutonius, the Roman governor of Britain, was subduing lands in the west later known as Wales. The chief tax collector or procurator of Britain, Catus Decianus, acted swiftly to ensure that Prasutagus' entire estate reverted to Rome. Decianus also declared that loans previously made by Emperor Claudius had to be repaid immediately, with interest. Accompanied by his staff, Decianus enforced his orders. In the process, members of his staff stripped and lashed Queen Boadicea and raped her two virgin daughters, whose names were never listed in the historical record. Impelled by these outrages, Boadicea and the Iceni took up arms. They were joined by the Trinovantes, a neighboring tribe, and by others.

Boadicea's army of 120,000 people attacked and destroyed the *colonia* of Camulodunum (Colchester), a settlement of retired Roman army veterans, along with its entire population, estimated at some two thousand people. The Iceni and their allies then sacked and burned Londinium (London), the largest city in the province, killing its population estimated at some twenty thousand. According to Greek historian Cassius Dio, the women had their breasts cut off and stuffed into their mouths, and then they were impaled on long, sharp skewers run through their bodies lengthwise. The rebels likewise killed the entire population of Verulamium (St. Albans), the third-largest city in the province and burned the town to the ground. They also decimated a large part of the IX Legion. The revolt finally was defeated by the XIV and XX Legions under the command of Seutonius.

Tacitus describes the location of the final confrontation between the forces of Boadicea and Seutonius. Boadicea's army, estimated at this point to have numbered anywhere from 100,000 to 230,000, advanced into a front of diminishing width. Her army faced eleven thousand to thirteen thousand Roman soldiers, consisting of the XIV Legion, detachments of the II and XX at the center, and cavalry and auxiliaries on the wings. Behind the Romans lay a thick forest on rising ground that gave protection to Seutonius' rear. Ahead the ground was open, affording no cover to the advancing Britons.

Seutonius defeated Boadicea's forces and gained a massive victory. Tacitus indicates that eighty thousand Britons were killed in the battle, while Roman losses were four hundred dead and slightly more than that number wounded. Boadicea went away and poisoned herself.

As leader of the Iceni, Boadicea gathered support from other local tribes in staging a rebellion against Roman rule in Britain. (Archive Photos)

Prior to the invasion of Britain in 54 B.C. by Julius Caesar and later in A.D. 43 by General Aulus Platius, many tribes lived in southern England. These tribes were polytheistic, believing in many deities. The deities of one tribe were not necessarily those of another. One tribe could not hope for assistance from another on the basis that they worshiped the same gods or goddesses. Druid priests, recruited from the landowning nobility immediately below the ruling tribal families, became chief priests to all these differing religions. They could travel unharmed from one tribe to another, protected by their religious status. In this respect, they were more powerful than any tribal queen or king. They were the one social element potentially capable of uniting the disparate tribes.

In A.D. 43, Emperor Tiberius Claudius Drusus Nero Germanicus sent Platius with four legions to conquer Britain. Many tribes, including the Iceni, welcomed the Romans or surrendered without a fight. Other tribes were

defeated. Still others, including the Catuvellauni, resisted Roman rule. Resistance coalesced around Caratacus, son of the Catuvellauni king, Cunobelinus. When it became impossible to continue fighting in southeast Britain, Caratacus and his followers fled to the west, into lands now known as Wales.

Rome rewarded those who had helped them during the invasion. Emperor Claudius loaned various chiefs the sum of forty million *sesterces*. One recipient was Prasutagus of the Iceni. Prasutagus was given a client kingdom to rule with some degree of independence, an arrangement common on the borders of the Roman Empire, where pro-Roman sympathies were harnessed to create buffer zones to protect Roman territory from outside attack. For the Roman Empire, a client relationship was a tool of short-term political expedience, the achievement of rapid conquest in an area and the consolidation of Roman power therein. When the individual died with whom a client relationship had been established, the client relationship ended. The fortune and estates of a client king or queen reverted in full to Rome.

Publius Ostorius Scapula was governor of Britain from A.D. 50 until his death in A.D. 52. Scapula unsuccessfully tried to eradicate the forces of Caratacus in Wales. Scapula dared not count on the tribes remaining loyal to Rome while he waged battle in Wales, so preparatory to that campaign, he collected all weapons from the tribes. This search and seizure angered some of the tribes, including the Iceni. Camulodunum, the former capital city of the Trinovantes, became the capital of the new province. A large temple was built there to honor the spirit of Claudius. The Romans also created a *colonia* at Camulodunum. Rome appropriated needed lands from the tribes. Rome similarly appropriated lands from the Catuvellauni to build the city of Varulamium (St. Albans).

After the assassination of Claudius in A.D. 54, his stepson Nero became emperor. The government under Nero seriously considered giving up Britain altogether. A decision was reached by A.D. 57 to retain Britain and to conquer and hold the whole area later known as Wales. The soldier chosen to subdue these western areas was Seutonius. He realized that discontent and hostility toward Rome were centered in the sacred groves of the Druids in the west, where those Britons had gathered who followed the lead of Caratacus in refusing to submit to Rome.

Seutonius, victorious in the west, was informed of Boadicea's revolt. He proceeded to the south, assessed the situation, marshaled his forces, selected a battle site, and defeated the hosts of Boadicea. Afterward, some seven thousand reinforcements were sent from Germany, and Seutonius led a systematic campaign of retaliation, from which it took ten years for the province to recover.

A living history museum in the English town of West Stow has re-created the structures and environment of a typical Iceni village. (Robin W. Diel)

Boadicea's revolt profoundly affected Britons and Roman imperial policy toward Britain. There was a genuine attempt by Rome to recognize the tribes as civilized peoples rather than as non-Romans. Temples were raised to Celtic gods in the guise of their Roman equivalents. All hopes vanished of Roman defeat or withdrawal. Not until the gradual breakup of the Roman Empire some five hundred years later did the Britons reassert themselves.

—*Marjorie Donovan*

ADDITIONAL READING:

Andrews, Ian. *Boudicca's Revolt*. Cambridge, England: Cambridge University Press, 1978. This work provides a sense of what life was like in the different levels of society in the areas of England where the revolt occurred. Illustrated with drawings by Graham Humphreys and Trevor Stubley.

Dio, Cassius. *History of Rome*. Translated by Ernest Carey. London: Loeb Classics, 1925. At the end of the second century, the Greek historian used corroborated and uncorroborated sources to write one of two classical histories of the revolt.

Dudley, Donald R., and Graham Webster. *The Rebellion of Boudicca*. New York: Barnes & Noble, 1962. This work explores the treatment of Boadicea in British history and tradition and illumines the relationships among the Iceni, their neighbors, and the European continent.

Matthews, John. *Boadicea: Warrior Queen of the Celts*. Poole, Dorset, England: Firebird Books, 1988. An entry in Firebird's Heroes and Warriors Series for young readers, this book provides a concise history of the social, cultural, and political events leading to the revolt. Enhanced by many color and black-and-white drawings and pictures.

Spence, Lewis. *Boadicea: Warrior Queen of the Britons*. London: Robert Hale, 1937. This work draws on the histories of Tacitus, Dio, and others to provide a balanced account of the revolt. Illustrated.

Tacitus. *The Annals*. 4 vols. Books XIII-XVI. Translated by John Jackson. Cambridge, Mass.: Harvard University Press, 1956. Tacitus, a Roman senator and consul, wrote his *Annals* just fifty years after the revolt. The noted Roman historian had access to imperial archives.

Webster, Graham. *Boudica: The British Revolt Against Rome in A.D. 60*. Totowa, N.J.: Rowman & Littlefield, 1978. Archaeological knowledge and aerial reconnaissance join with classical sources in this indispensable narrative of the political, social, economic, and demographic factors surrounding the revolt.

SEE ALSO: 109-102 B.C., Celtic Hill Forts Appear; 43-130, Roman Conquest of Britain; 50, Creation of the Imperial Bureaucracy.

64-67
NERO PERSECUTES THE CHRISTIANS

Nero persecutes the Christians, marking the beginning of the Roman Empire's prolonged harassment of a religious group for political purposes.

DATE: 64-67

LOCALE: Rome, Italy

CATEGORIES: Government and politics; Religion

KEY FIGURES:

Nero (A.D. 37-68), Roman emperor, A.D. 54-68

Saint Paul (Saul of Tarsus; died c. 64), Christian apostle

Saint Peter (Simon; died c. 64), Christian apostle

SUMMARY OF EVENT. Nero, fifth emperor of Rome and the last of the Julio-Claudian line, ruled the Roman Empire from A.D. 54 to 68 and is generally considered one of the cruelest men in history. Born on December 15, A.D. 37, in Antium, Italy, to consul Gnaeus Domitius Ahenobarbus and Agrippina the Younger, daughter of Germanicus Caesar and great-granddaughter of Emperor Augustus, Nero was originally named Lucius Domitius Ahenobarbus. After the death of his father in approximately 40, Nero's scheming mother married her uncle, Emperor Claudius I, in A.D. 49, and persuaded him to adopt her son, whose name was then changed to Nero Claudius Caesar Drusus Germanicus. Nero then married Claudius' daughter Octavia, an act which marked him out as Rome's next emperor, thus bypassing Claudius' biological son Britannicus. Agrippina then poisoned Claudius in 54 and the Praetorian Guard and the senate united in declaring Nero emperor at the age of seventeen. Nero had blotchy skin, a fat belly, spindly legs, and a thick neck, a feature which is recorded in his coinage.

Guided by the Praetorian prefect Burrus and the Stoic philosopher-tutor Seneca, Nero began the first five years of his reign as a man of moderation, known for his clemency. He also made several popular changes within Roman government, including his proposal to abolish some forms of taxation. Although many of Nero's subjects initially received him with great enthusiasm, Burrus and Seneca were unable to hold the boy emperor's cruelty in check for long. Nero soon began to rule unrestrained, violently plotting against people he perceived as threats to his power. Britannicus, his stepbrother and rightful heir to the throne, was poisoned in A.D. 55 and Agrippina, whose plotting gained Nero the throne in the first place, was murdered in 59 after criticizing Nero's mistress, Poppaea Sabina. He later divorced and murdered his wife Octavia and married Poppaea. Nero later kicked Poppaea to death while she was pregnant. His third marriage was to Statilia Messalina, whose husband he had ordered to be executed.

The Stoic philosopher Seneca served as tutor and adviser to the young Nero, who became emperor of Rome at the age of seventeen. (Library of Congress)

A great fire swept through Rome in the hot July weather of 64. Flames raged for about ten days, burning nearly two-thirds of the city. Three of the fourteen Augustan municipal districts were completely gutted, and seven others were badly damaged. Rumors quickly circulated that Nero himself had started the fire to make room for his new palace, but most historians believe there is no factual evidence to support this theory. Some historians have suggested that Nero was away at Antium while legend says that Nero viewed the blaze from the Tower of Maecenas, amusing himself by playing his lyre and reciting his own epic poem "The Sack of Troy" on his private stage while thousands died and Rome was reduced to ashes. This story led to the popular expression "fiddling while Rome burns," a label often bestowed on public officials who fail in their civil duty during an emergency. According to some accounts, Nero sought to avert rumors accusing him of irresponsibility by accusing Rome's Christian inhabitants of starting the fire, thereafter making Christians the victims of vicious and cruel tortures. Up to this time, Rome had been tolerant of nonnational monotheistic religions such as Judaism and Christianity but was always watchful. Jews generally were treated relatively well by

Pompey, Caesar, and Augustus, in part as a result of support by Herod the Great and Herod Agrippa, and were envied by other religious groups. The Christian apostle and preacher Paul enjoyed Roman protection and "appealed to Caesar" when persecuted by followers of his own Jewish heritage.

The year 64, however, marked a dramatic change in Rome's attitude toward Christians for the next 250 years. Christians were charged with incendiarism, were torn by lions and dogs, crucified, and burned alive as torches to light nocturnal games during which Nero paraded around the Palatine Gardens and Vatican Circus dressed as a charioteer. Tacitus recorded that public reaction to Nero's atrocities generally tended to pity the Christians as victims of Nero's brutality, with few observers believing they were perpetrators of actual crimes. Suetonius, the other classical authority, mentions that Christians began to be driven out of Rome but does not associate them with the accusation of starting the great fire. Christian executions increased in 65, when an assassination plot by a group of aristocrats, senators, and equestrians was uncovered and Nero revived the wide-ranging law of treason, under which many were executed on spurious charges or forced to commit suicide. Questions as to the legal basis behind the attacks on the Christians and the specific charges filed against them will undoubtedly never be answered.

The number and names of the early Christian martyrs under Nero and those persecuted by Roman authorities after his death were not reliably documented. Tradition beginning with Clement of Rome in approximately A.D. 95 lists Peter and Paul, as martyrs under Nero in Rome, whereas later tradition holds that their deaths occurred several years later and may not have even happened in Rome. Biblical references in the New Testament book of 1 Peter indicate that Nero's Christian persecutions reached far beyond the city of Rome into Asia Minor, Pontus, Galicia, and Bithynia. The trials conducted under Nero established that crimes such as secret assembly were punishable by death, with numerous Christians regularly convicted of such acts. Rome set a precedent for all its governors in that no formal law was necessary for prosecution, and proof of a definite crime was not required. Persecution of people called by the name "Christian" was begun during Nero's reign, possibly to divert attention away from the arson, and was continued with Christians being generally condemned as a sect dangerous to public safety and permanent enemies of civilization. Orosius later popularized the idea of ten persecutions against the Christian church, which were often lackadaisically carried out by half-hearted Roman officials. Arguably the worst period of Christian persecution occurred in 303 under

Diocletian and continued under Galerius and Maximinus until 313, when the Edict of Milan gave official recognition to the Christian religion. The total number of Christians tortured and executed between A.D. 64 and 313 remains controversial but is commonly estimated to be between ten thousand and one hundred thousand.

Nero proceeded to rebuild Rome with fire precautions and shelters for the homeless on a much more extravagant scale than before, including the construction of a magnificent palace called the Golden House (Domus Aurea) in the center of Rome where he held lavish parties. Nero's building projects were financed by heavy taxation on his subjects, with buried ruins of the Golden House stretching back into a hillside overlooking the Coliseum. Promoting himself as an artist, singer, musician, chariot driver, and religious visionary, Nero appeared publicly in dramas, the Olympic Games, and other events, with the Greeks awarding him first prize in contests when he would visit. Only the Greeks, he said, really appreciated him as he returned home with 1,808 first prizes. After fourteen years of Neronian rule, the loss of many costly battles against Parthia, and a successful revolt by Nero's own Gaelic and Spanish armies, the Roman senate proclaimed Nero a public enemy and crowned Galba as emperor. When the Praetorians also deserted him, Nero attempted to flee but was overtaken not far from Rome. At age thirty on June 9, 68, Nero committed suicide by stabbing himself. His last words allegedly were, "What an artist dies in me!" Nero was so hated for his cruelty and ruthlessness after his deeds were exposed that his name was erased from records and monuments, his palace was torn down, and his statues were broken. Nero, the last male relative of Augustus, was buried by two of his nurses and his longtime concubine, Acte, in the mausoleum of his father's family.

—*Daniel G. Graetzer*

ADDITIONAL READING:

Freud, W. H. C. *Martyrdom and Persecution in the Early Church.* Garden City, N.Y.: Doubleday, 1967. This well-written text documents numerous theories as to the underlying causes and legal basis for the sudden onset of Christian persecution in 64.

Guterman, S. L. *Religious Toleration and Persecution in Ancient Rome.* London: Aiglon Press, 1951. A well-

This engraving captures Nero's brutal disregard for Christians, who were crucified and burned alive as torches as part of the emperor's entertainments. (Archive Photos)

documented analysis of several possible reasons for the treatment of religion in the Roman Empire.

Hardy, E. R. *Christianity and the Roman Government*. London: Allen & Unwin, 1925. An excellent text on Roman-Christian relations with details on Nero's persecutions.

Massie, Allan. *The Caesars*. New York: Franklin Watts, 1984. This text details the relationships between Rome's first twelve emperors and the Roman Empire, including Nero's manipulative control over those by whom he felt threatened.

Ramsay, William. *The Church in the Roman Empire*. London: Hodder & Stoughton, 1907. This often-cited text attempts to assess the meaning of the Neronian persecution and often cites writings by Tacitus and Suetonius, considered the only two reliable witnesses.

Workman, H. B. *Persecution of the Early Church*. London: Epworth Press, 1923. A history of the Christian persecution under Nero.

SEE ALSO: 110, Trajan's Religious Policy; 200, Christian Apologists Develop Concept of Theology; 284, Inauguration of the Dominate.

79

DESTRUCTION OF POMPEII

The destruction of Pompeii through the eruption of Mount Vesuvius annihilates thousands of Pompeians, but preserves the remains of this former great Roman colony for discovery in later archaeological excavations.

DATE: August 24, A.D. 79

LOCALE: Pompeii, in the Roman province of Campania in southern Italy

CATEGORIES: Cultural and intellectual history; Environment

KEY FIGURES:

Giuseppe Fiorelli (1823-1896), Italian archaeologist who directed the systematic excavation of Pompeii later in the nineteenth century and who invented a plaster procedure to recapture human bodies and animals frozen in time

Joachim Murat (1767-1815), king of Naples and Sicily, 1808-1815, during whose reign archaeologists excavated houses and streets in Pompeii

Pliny the Elder (A.D. 23-79), uncle of Pliny the Younger and commander of a Roman fleet, who lost his life during the eruption

Pliny the Younger (A.D. 62-113), who witnessed the eruption of Mount Vesuvius and the ensuing destruction of Pompeii and who wrote two factual letters to the historian Tacitus about his observations

SUMMARY OF EVENT. The destruction of Pompeii and two other cities as a result of the eruption of Mount Vesuvius in A.D. 79 has provided a rich archaeological treasure for excavators of the past two centuries. Pompeii was originally part of a large coastal area founded by the Greeks (c. 650 B.C.) called Neapolis (Naples) or "the New City," and it became a prosperous harbor town along the Sarnus (Sarno) River. The Samnites controlled the city after 420 B.C. until it fell to Rome in 290 B.C. Pompeii became a more independent colony after 91 B.C. and a thriving center of oil and wine production, as well as a strong exporter of fish sauce, fruit, and volcanic stone or tufa. Yet the city's significance should not be overestimated, for it had a population of only twenty thousand and an importance which was solely regional. Its pleasant climate and proximity to the sea, however, made it a fashionable resort for wealthy Romans, some of whom, including the orator Cicero, maintained homes there.

During the reign of Emperor Nero on February 5, A.D. 62, a severe earthquake rocked and badly damaged towns circling Mount Vesuvius, especially Pompeii and its Forum area and temples. In fact, the great reservoir near Porta Vesuvius gave way, unleashing flood waters throughout the city, and huge chasms opened in the fields with reports of people and flocks of sheep being swallowed.

Along with the neighboring cities of Herculaneum and Stabiae, the city came to an abrupt end on August 24 in the year 79, when the volcano Vesuvius erupted in full fury. Located some twelve miles north of Pompeii across the southern end of the Bay of Naples, the volcano aided by strong winds rained down tons of fiery ashes and pumice upon the three helpless cities. First, a mass of lava pebbles (*lapilli*) and boulders shot thousands of feet into the sky and crashed to the surface adding about eight to nine feet of debris on the ground. Then, a cloud of pumice covered the terrain of the city up to six to eight feet in height. A new wave of earthquakes, caused by the collapse of the sides of the volcanic cone, contributed to an explosion of gaseous pumice, dust, ash, and cinders. This material eventually turned downward, adding another seven feet to the ash-covered city—not to mention the addition of various lethal gases as well.

Pliny the Younger, an eyewitness, describes the event graphically. About 7:00 A.M., Pliny relates, a dark cloud shaped like a pine tree appeared over the summit of Mount Vesuvius. The volcano emitted "flashes of fire as vivid as lightening" and produced "darkness more profound than night." A thick vapor enveloped the entire area. Although all three cities were destroyed, Herculaneum appears to have received the full force of the eruption, being engulfed in a flood of volcanic waste which solidified into a level

The Roman naval commander Pliny the Elder was one of the victims who died from asphyxiation near Herculaneum in the wake of the eruption of Mount Vesuvius. (National Library of Medicine)

mass between fifty and seventy feet thick. Fortunately, the Roman fleet from Misenum commanded by Pliny the Elder, uncle of Pliny the Younger, was able to evacuate some of the inhabitants of the city. Nevertheless, the loss of life was great; by the 1990's, archaeologists had removed some two thousand bodies. Tragically, later sea escape attempts were thwarted because of fiery stones, winds, and waves that made embarkation impossible; the burning, flowing mud and ashes also prevented ships of rescue from making any landings. Unfortunately, Pliny the Elder himself was overcome by the deadly fumes and died at a point near Herculaneum (west of the volcano). Indeed, the main cause of death was not incineration but asphyxiation caused by carbon monoxide or sulfur dioxide. The submerged cities were not rebuilt. A small village did for a time occupy the site of Pompeii but it was deserted after another eruption of Mount Vesuvius in A.D. 472. Subsequent eruptions of the volcano so changed the coastline that by the time exploration of the region was undertaken in the mid-eighteenth century, the exact site of Pompeii and the other two cities was uncertain.

Excavation actually began in 1748, when a peasant digging a well made some interesting finds which he reported to the authorities. King Charles IV of Naples became interested in the work, and, in 1755, the amphitheater and other public buildings were uncovered. During the following fifty years, little systematic excavation took place, although miscellaneous rare objects were found

from time to time. Under Joachim Murat, appointed king of Naples by Napoleon, archaeologists excavated some houses and streets, but only later in the nineteenth century under Giuseppe Fiorelli, professor of archaeology at the University of Naples, were extensive excavations undertaken. He wanted to maintain the historical authenticity of the site by preserving objects found on location. His great contribution to Western civilization was his invention of a way to recapture the forms, or appearances, of people and animals caught in the horror of the destruction of Pompeii. Since ashes preserved the exteriors of dead bodies after decomposition, by inserting a tube into hollow areas where bones no longer existed he would inject a special liquid plaster which, when hardened, would assume the shape of the original body. Details of Pompeian clothes, hair texture, feet imprints, and facial expressions are amazingly preserved.

The city was shaped like an irregular oval, the length being on an east-west axis. The mile-and-a-half wall that surrounded the town had eight gates at which sentry boxes were located. Magnificently preserved streets and homes have been unearthed, the latter containing numerous utensils, jewelry, doctors' and tradesmen's tools, lamps, and mirrors in addition to beautifully painted walls displaying frescoes which reflect various themes of Roman life. Some of the larger Pompeian homes or villas date from the second century, while the style of wall paintings in others indicate that they were built during the Augustan period. The most pretentious villas were located two miles outside Pompeii at Boscoreale. In one villa there, besides artifacts of the traditional type, numerous wine storage jars were found which could accommodate an annual production of twenty thousand gallons. The income from the sale of so much wine is clearly reflected in the luxurious appointments of the estate.

Excavations at Pompeii, besides broadening knowledge about the daily life and routine of all ranks of Roman people, has had other unexpected repercussions. In the eighteenth century, they reinforced the neoclassical traditions popular during the Enlightenment. In France, the discoveries influenced the so-called Imperial style of Louis XV, while in England they gave birth to the so-called Adam Period of architecture and decorative art during the second half of the eighteenth century.

—Edward P. Keleher, updated by Connie Pedoto

ADDITIONAL READING:

Brilliant, Richard. *Pompeii A.D. 79: The Treasure of Rediscovery.* New York: Clarkson N. Potter, 1979. A remarkable literary-narrative approach to the story of Pompeii with 295 pages filled with excavation photos, restora-

Volcanic ash preserved the exterior shape of the victims at Pompeii, allowing archaeologists to make plaster casts for scientific study. (Library of Congress)

tion drawings, color paintings, and poetry—a true album of Pompeii.

Brion, Marcel. *Pompeii and Herculaneum: The Glory and the Grief.* New York: Crown Publishers, 1961. A text with 132 beautiful illustrations of the cultural artifacts of Pompeii with 50 works in full color.

Grant, Michael. *The Art and Life of Pompeii and Herculaneum.* Milan: Arnoldo Mondadori Editore, 1979. A great historical text with about one hundred excellent photos, mostly in color, of the Pompeii ruins and artistic treasures and accompanied by an index of illustrations.

Maiuri, Amedeo. *Pompeii.* Novara, Italy: Istituto Geografico De Agostini, 1957. A source with an index of tombs, villas, and portas of Pompeii and with a street-to-street and wall-by-wall detailed tour of Pompeii, including maps.

Ward-Perkins, John, and Amanda Claridge. *Pompeii A.D. 79.* New York: Alfred A. Knopf, 1978. A large 250-page text with 450 plates (50 in color) with striking photos of sculpture and artifacts in well-divided sections of government, politics, and daily life.

SEE ALSO: 15,000 B.C., Cave Paintings Provide Evidence of Magdalenian Culture; 3100-1550 B.C., Building

of Stonehenge; 1620-1120 B.C., Rise of Mycenaean Civilization; 1600-1500 B.C., Flowering of Minoan Civilization; 1100-500 B.C., Hallstatt Civilization Ushers in Iron Age in Europe; 109-102 B.C., Celtic Hill Forts Appear.

110
TRAJAN'S RELIGIOUS POLICY
Trajan's religious policy establishes an imperial precedent for the suppression and persecution of Christians.

DATE: c. A.D. 110

LOCALE: The Roman province of Bithynia-Pontus in northern Asia Minor (Turkey)

CATEGORIES: Government and politics; Religion

KEY FIGURES:

Pliny the Younger (Caius Plinius Caecilius Secundus), Roman governor of Bithynia-Pontus, c. 109-111, with the title *legatus Augusti propraetore consulari potestate* ("propraetorian legate of the emperor with consular power")

Trajan (Marcus Ulpius Traianus), Roman emperor, 98-117

SUMMARY OF EVENT. The province lies along the south coast of the Black Sea. King Nicomedes IV bequeathed Bithynia to Rome in 74 B.C. Rome governed through a dozen Hellenized cities, each of which controlled the surrounding countryside. Pompey annexed Pontus at the conclusion of the war against king Mithradates VI in 63 B.C. This region was less urbanized: three Greek cities along the coast (Sinope, Amisus, Amastris) and a few half-Hellenized places in the interior, notably Amaseia. To facilitate provincial governance, he founded a number of cities, naming some after himself (Pompeiopolis, Magnopolis). Augustus re-created the kingdom for the client ruler Polemo, but it fell under Roman rule again in A.D. 64 and was joined to Bithynia. The senate assumed supervision of this peaceful province and annually dispatched senators of praetorian rank (termed proconsuls) to govern it. Each year the governor made a circuit of his province, holding court in the major towns, inquiring into a wide range of matters and rendering punishments. In these *cognitiones* the proconsuls had enormous power over ordinary provincials; they had to proceed more carefully when dealing with Roman citizens and sometimes chose to transmit their cases to Rome.

Bitter rivalries within and between cities, combined with lax senatorial supervision and corrupt governors, put urban finances in critical condition, and, in about A.D. 108, Trajan intervened. Using his greater proconsular *imperium*, he removed Bithynia-Pontus from the senate, placed it under temporary imperial control, and dispatched the former consul and treasury expert Pliny as special legate. Trajan provided a broad set of instructions (*mandata*). The Tenth Book of Pliny's "Letters" contains correspondence with the emperor; letters 15-121 are a mixture of his inquiries and Trajan's answers (*responsa*), which thus constitute imperial policy. (It is incorrect to label Pliny a *curator* or *corrector*; these officials supervised one or several cities, whereas he was in charge of the entire province. Pliny is customarily designated "the Younger" to distinguish him from his maternal uncle, the polymath and naval officer Pliny "the Elder," who was killed in the eruption of Mount Vesuvius in A.D. 79. Pliny evidently died in his third year in office.

Pliny encountered Christians, a novel annoyance interrupting his more important concerns, while on circuit in Pontus. The location is unknown; Amastris is likely (cf. letter 98), though Amisus (numbers 92 and 110) or Sinope (number 90) are possible. Lacking personal familiarity with Christianity and possessing no guidance in his *mandata*, he relied on his *imperium* and *coercitio* (power of a legitimate authority to compel obedience and punish refusal) and then checked with the emperor whether he was correct: letters 96-97. These letters are the earliest Roman

account of "the Christian problem"; a few years later Tacitus described the Neronian persecution of 64 (*Annals* 15.44). The Christian community was small and generally kept a low profile, though the New Testament is clear that it had been spreading through Asia Minor for years. Acts 2:9-10, Acts 18:2, and 1 Peter 1:1 mention Christians from Bithynia, Cappadocia, Galatia, Pamphylia, Phrygia, and Pontus; Paul and Barnabas had journeyed through Pisidia, Galatia, and Asia; there are letters to Colossae, Ephesus, Galatia, and Laodicea. The notorious heretic Marcion was from Sinope (Eusebius, *Hist. Eccl.* 4.23).

Pliny's report raised three questions. First, should a distinction be made in age or sex, or "should the weakest offenders be treated exactly like the stronger?" Second, should pardon be given to those who recant, or must they be punished nevertheless for having been Christians? Third, does punishment attach to the mere name of Christian apart from the secret crimes allegedly committed by the new sect, or are Christians to be punished only for the actual crimes they may commit? In other words, was simply being a Christian a (capital) crime or did one have to have done something more?

Pliny continued by reviewing the actions he has already taken against the Christians. Whenever accusations were made against them, he brought them to trial. Some denied that they had ever been Christians, and then offered proof by worshiping with incense and wine before a statue of the emperor; after they had reviled Christ, they were released. A second group admitting having been Christian but asserted that they had ceased to be such; these also were released after making offerings to the emperor and reviling Christ. The third group, those who confessed to being Christians, were told of the consequences of their acts and allowed three opportunities to recant. Employment of *coercitio* emerges when Pliny said that those who refused were executed: "whatever the nature of their admission, I am convinced that their stubbornness and unshakable obstinacy ought not to go unpunished." Roman citizens constituted an exception: They were remanded to Rome for sentencing.

Pliny also reported that his investigation of the Christians indicated they were a relatively harmless cult whose only guilt consisted in the habit of meeting "on a certain fixed day before it was light, when they sang in alternate verses a hymn to Christ, as to a god, and bound themselves by a solemn oath not to do any wicked deeds." The torture of two female slaves styled deaconesses revealed to the governor that the new religion was merely "a perverse and extravagant superstition." The letter concludes with the observation that because of these stringent measures against the Christians, "the almost deserted temples begin to be resorted to, long disused ceremonies or religion are restored, fodder for victims finds a market, whereas buyers until now were very few." As far as Pliny could see, Christians did not constitute a threat to public order. Yet as an unsanctioned group, a *religio illicita*, they deserved punishment. Rome tolerated far stranger beliefs and practices than Christianity. It did, however, have a longstanding suspicion that unauthorized groups might be subversive of morality. Refusal to obey, *contumacia*, implied conspiratorial subversion. Trajan refused to permit a fire department because this seemingly commendable cause might serve to cover covert political action (letter 33). Rome's hostility toward the Bacchanalian cult in the 180's B.C., though tinged with hysteria because it was in Italy, is similar to her attitude toward the Christians.

Trajan's reply, embodying his statement of religious policy, is here cited in full. "You have adopted the proper course, my dear Secundus, in your examination of the cases of those who were accused to you as Christians, for indeed nothing can be laid down as a general rule involving something like a set form of procedure. They are not to be sought out; but if they are accused and convicted, they must be punished—yet on this condition, that whoever denies himself to be a Christian and makes the fact plain by his action, that is by worshiping our gods, shall obtain pardon for his repentance, however suspicious his past conduct may be. Papers, however, which are presented unsigned ought not to be admitted in any charge, for they are a very bad example and unworthy of our time."

This *responsum* constituted imperial precedent; although it was directed to Pliny in Bithynia-Pontus, it could be extended throughout the Roman Empire. Soon imperial *responsa* became law. Christians were not to be actively sought out. The government had more important concerns; Trajan essentially instructed Pliny not to bother unless provoked. The movement remained illegal. If Christians caused trouble and accusers brought charges in open court (not anonymously), the authorities should suppress them. The open profession of Christianity continued to be a capital offense, apparently because it implied disloyalty in its refusal to worship the Roman gods. Punishment of Christians was local, sporadic, and, on occasion, nasty for years; the persecution of Gallic Christians at Lyon in 177 illustrates what could happen, even under the "good" Marcus Aurelius. The first empire-wide persecutions began in the crisis of the 250's.

—*Carl A. Volz, updated by Thomas H. Watkins*

ADDITIONAL READING:

Jones, A. H. M. *The Cities of the Eastern Roman Provinces*. 2d ed. Oxford: Clarendon Press, 1971. A wealth of information on the cities of Bithynia and Pontus.

Jones, C. P. *The Roman World of Dio Chrysostom*. Cambridge, Mass.: Harvard University Press, 1978. From Prusa in Bithynia and known to Pliny; his orations give much information about conditions in the cities.

Lane Fox, Robin. *Pagans and Christians*. New York: Alfred A. Knopf, 1987. Lively account of the vitality of paganism and the challenge of the new religion.

Liebeschuetz, J. H. W. G. *Continuity and Change in Roman Religion*. Oxford: Clarendon Press, 1979. Puts Christianity in the history of Roman religion and religious policy.

Magie, D. *Roman Rule in Asia Minor*. Princeton, N.J.: Princeton University Press, 1950. Detailed history of the region.

Millar, F. *The Emperor in the Roman World*. London: Duckworth, 1977. Analysis of how the emperors governed and limitations on their authority; good on *mandata, responsa, edicta*, and so forth.

Sherwin-White, A. N. *The Letters of Pliny: A Historical and Social Commentary*. Oxford: Clarendon Press, 1966. Massive volume; two hundred pages and two appendices on book 10. Convenient translation of the letters is by B. Radice in the Penguin Classics.

SEE ALSO: 64-67, Nero Persecutes the Christians; 200, Christian Apologists Develop Concept of Theology; 312, Conversion of Constantine; 313-395, Inception of the Church-State Problem.

157-201
GALEN SYNTHESIZES ANCIENT MEDICAL KNOWLEDGE

Galen synthesizes ancient medical knowledge, combining preexisting medical knowledge with his own ideas in writings that dominate European medical thinking for some fifteen hundred years after his death.

DATE: c. 157-201

LOCALE: Rome

CATEGORIES: Cultural and intellectual history; Health and medicine; Science and technology

KEY FIGURES:

Saint Thomas Aquinas (1225-1274), advanced psychological thinking and reconciled faith and Aristotelian reason

Sir Francis Bacon (1561-1626), "father" of modern science

René Descartes (1596-1650), "father" of modern philosophy

Galen (Claudius Galenus; 129-c. 199), Roman physician and medical author

Hippocrates (c. 460-c. 377 B.C.), considered the Greek "father of medicine"

Ivan Pavlov (1849-1936), Nobel Prize-winning Russian physiologist and psychologist

SUMMARY OF EVENT. Galen, a Greek subject of the Roman Empire, was born about A.D. 131 in Pergamon, a city in Asia Minor considered to be second only to Alexandria as the greatest center of learning in the Roman Empire. After studying philosophy in Pergamon and serving as a surgeon to gladiators, he moved to Alexandria to study anatomy. In 169, Galen took a position as the personal physician of the Roman emperor Marcus Aurelius Antonius, and his eminence as a medical teacher was widely recognized. At Rome, he had access to the imperial library's vast collection of medical writings from the farthest reaches of the empire. Combining his own observations and research with this great store of medical knowledge, Galen's writings, more than any other source, influenced Western medical thinking for approximately fifteen hundred years after his death.

Galen wrote down for posterity the accomplishments of the great early figures of medicine. Hippocrates, "the father of medicine," is largely known to the modern world through the writings of Galen. The Hippocratics, followers of Hippocrates, built upon the scientific foundation laid by Hippocrates. Their collections of observations and research were also kept alive by Galen for subsequent generations. If not for Galen, most of the Hippocratic literature would have perished and the modern world would know nothing about the work of the great Alexandrian anatomists of the fourth and third centuries B.C. such as Herophilus and Erasistratus who pioneered work on the nervous and circulatory systems. Galen's seventeen-volume medical treatise *On the Usefulness of the Parts of the Body* (written between A.D. 165 and 175) summarized the medical knowledge of his day and preserved the medical knowledge of his predecessors.

Galen, in his book *On the Natural Faculties*, expanded upon Hippocrates' theory of the four "humors," or bodily "wet substances": black bile, yellow bile, blood, and phlegm. According to Galen, in addition to the physiological abnormalities caused by imbalances of these humors, psychological differences would also result. Furthermore, overabundances of different humors were linked with distinct temperaments (personality predispositions). Thus, excess black bile could result in sadness (melancholic temperament); too much yellow bile in excitability and being easily angered (choleric temperament); excess phlegm in sluggishness and introversion (phlegmatic temperament); and too much blood in a cheerfulness and extroversion (sanguine temperament). The influence of

this theory is still seen in the contemporary use of words such as sanguine and phlegmatic and in expressions such as, "Are you in a good humor today?" Even the red-striped barber's pole was originally the sign of an individual who would drain blood to improve the health of others.

Although he was not a Christian, Galen was strongly opposed to atheistic, materialistic explanations of nature and the human body. He believed that nature reflects a divine design and so does the body. God breathes life into nature and, according to Galen, the divine life-giving principle in humans is called *pneuma* (from the Greek "breeze"). Three adaptations of pneuma give the following attributes of living creatures: the "natural" spirit produces growth; the "vital" spirit causes locomotion; and the "animal" (from the Latin term *anima*, meaning soul) spirit is what makes intellectual functioning possible. Galen's studies of anatomy and physiology were often conducted to determine the flow of these spirits throughout the human body. Pneuma theory dominated Western medical thinking until well into the eighteenth century.

Galen not only wrote on the impact of physiological factors on mental activities, but also concluded that thinking could affect physiology. This is illustrated in an incident in which Galen was treating a female patient. Galen noticed that when the name of Pylades, a male dancer, was mentioned, the patient's heart rate became irregular. When

In addition to summarizing the medical knowledge of his predecessors, Galen conducted detailed studies of the anatomy and physiology of the human body. (Archive Photos)

the names of other male dancers were mentioned, there were no effects on her pulse. Galen concluded from this that the patient was "in love" with the dancer and that thinking can lead to physiological consequences. Thus, the first clear description of a psychosomatic (mind-body) relationship can be said to originate with Galen.

Dealing with psychological problems was also a concern of Galen. He wrote of the importance of counsel and education in treating psychological problems. Therapy, according to Galen, should involve a mature, unbiased older person, confronting clients whose passions, such as anger and jealousy, were thought to be primarily responsible for their psychological problems. Such advice by Galen illustrates an ancient idea of psychotherapy. Other advice by Galen on psychological matters is contained in his book *On the Diagnosis and Cure of the Soul's Passions*.

Galen's ideas dominated Western medical thinking from his era until the Renaissance. His strongly theistic attitudes were embraced by the Christian thinkers who began to prevail over the affairs of the later Roman Empire. Early Christian writers from the second to the fourth centuries A.D., such as Tertullian, Lactantius, Nemesius, and Gregory of Nyssa, integrated Galen's ideas into many of their works. Unfortunately, Galen's numerous medical treatises (more than four hundred) were often summarized and distorted by other, inferior, writers and the Galenism that dominated Western medical thinking from the Dark Ages through medieval times was often far removed from Galen's original writings. Nevertheless, Galen's influence was so profound that even many Renaissance texts began with an acknowledgment to the great contributions of Galen, particularly his emphasis on observation and experimentation.

The profound impact of Galen on subsequent Western thinking is demonstrated most clearly in examining the influence of his theories of *pneuma* and *humors*. The three adaptations of pneuma can be seen to be influential in the writings of the great theologian St. Thomas Aquinas in his description of the faculties (or powers) of the soul. René Descartes' philosophy is often considered to mark the beginning of the modern period of philosophy. He has also been called the "father of physiology" for his descriptions of the workings of the human body. These descriptions contained something new, the demonstration of the circulation of the blood by William Harvey (1578-1657), and something old, the animal spirits from Galen's writings.

The old theory of humors, expanded upon by Galen, resurfaced in the twentieth century in the work of two noted psychologists. Ivan Pavlov, whose work on classical conditioning is one of the greatest contributions to the history of psychology, accepted Galen's classification of temperaments and even extended the theory to dogs, the primary subjects of his research. The distinguished British psychologist Hans Eysenck presented a personality theory in 1964 that incorporated some of Galen's ideas. Indeed, modern research on introversion and extraversion can be seen to have its philosophical antecedents in Galen's theory of humors.

The work of Galen united philosophy with science, rationalism (major source of knowledge is reason) with empiricism (major source of knowledge is experience). His writings are a connection to ancient thinkers and yet, his influence on twentieth century theories can be seen. Galen was a practical man dedicated toward discovering the facts of medicine, and his influence will continue to be found in future medical practices.   *—Paul J. Chara, Jr.*

ADDITIONAL READING:

Eysenck, Hans J. "Principles and Methods of Personality Description, Classification, and Diagnosis." *British Journal of Psychology* 55 (1964): 284-294. A description of twentieth century personality theory in consideration of Galen's theory of humors.

Galen. *On the Natural Faculties*. Translated by Arthur John Brock. New York: Putnam, 1916. Considered Galen's most important psychological work.

_____. *On the Usefulness of the Parts of the Body*. Translated by M. T. May. Ithaca, N.Y.: Cornell University Press, 1968. A seventeen-volume work containing Galen's most extensive description of the ancient anatomical literature.

Jackson, S. W. "Galen: On Mental Disorders." *Journal of the History of the Behavioral Sciences* 5 (1969): 365-384. Galen's thoughts on psychosomatic relationships and psychotherapy are examined.

Murray, David J. *A History of Western Psychology*. 2d ed. Englewood Cliffs, N.J.: Prentice Hall, 1988. One of the most extensive treatments of Galen's subsequent influence is presented.

Robinson, Daniel N. *An Intellectual History of Psychology*. 3d ed. Madison: University of Wisconsin Press, 1995. A brief description of Galen is presented, emphasizing his scientific thinking.

Viney, Wayne. *A History of Psychology: Ideas and Context*. Boston: Allyn & Bacon, 1993. Contains a summarization of Galen's life with unique (such as his influence on Pavlov) emphasis on his contributions to psychology.

SEE ALSO: 500-400 B.C., Greek Physicians Develop Scientific Practice of Medicine; 1010-1015, Avicenna Writes His *Canon of Medicine*; 1150, Moors Transmit Classical Philosophy and Medicine to Europe.

165

GAIUS' EDITION OF THE INSTITUTES OF ROMAN LAW

Gaius' edition of the Institutes *of Roman Law codifies classical Roman law in textbook form and survives as the only authentic work of classical legal scholarship still extant and unaltered by the ministers of Justinian.*

DATE: c. 165

LOCALE: Rome

CATEGORIES: Cultural and intellectual history; Laws, acts, and legal history

KEY FIGURES:

Gaius (fl. A.D. 160), Roman jurist and author

Justinian (483-565), Byzantine emperor, 527-565, who imitated Gaius in his work

SUMMARY OF EVENT. When Justinian published *Corpus Juris Civilis* (body of civil law), his monumental codification of Roman law, in the sixth century, he proscribed the use of any other legal texts. As a result, the older collections lay unused and forgotten, falling prey during the course of centuries to the ravages of time. Since Justinian also ordered that all excerpts included in his *Code* should be altered if necessary to make them consistent with contemporary legal practice, it seemed impossible for modern scholars to ascertain the ancient texts. It was therefore of some importance to legal historians when B. C. Niebuhr, a German scholar of the early nineteenth century, discovered a fifth century text of the *Institutes* of Gaius, which up to that time was known only from fragments in the *Digest* (part of Justinian's *Code*) and barbaric codes of the sixth century A.D.

Gaius, the author of this textbook of Roman law, is a shadowy figure. Although his *Institutes* was prescribed as a basic text in the law schools of the Western Empire and citations from eighteen of his works appear in Justinian's *Code*, he does not seem to have been cited by other jurists. From the text, it would appear that the *Institutes* was compiled shortly after A.D. 162. Other than this dating, and the conjecture that he may have studied and taught in Rome, little else is known about Gaius. Even his complete name remains unknown.

Since it was meant to be used as a textbook, the *Institutes* is devoid of penetrating analyses of law or profound solutions to complex legal problems. Nevertheless, it is important to legal historians and students for several reasons. It remains the only authentic work of classical legal scholarship still extant and unaltered by the ministers of Justinian. Beyond that, however, it provides insights into classical Roman law that would not otherwise be available. It is from the *Institutes* of Gaius, for example, that

scholars have obtained knowledge of the *legis actiones* ("actions of law") of ancient Roman law. Apparently in early Roman law, a plaintiff could initiate an action or claim at law only by using one of the five distinct ritual modes, or *actiones*, recognized as legal. As might be expected, these ritual formulas did not cover all possible situations. Even when the situation was covered by an appropriate action, the plaintiff had to take care to state his claim in words acceptable to the formula pertinent to his situation.

Gaius gives a clear example of this anomaly in the *Institutes* 4:11, when he states that "the actions of the practice of older times were called *legis actiones* either because they were the creation of statutes . . . or because they were framed in the very words of statutes and were consequently treated as no less immutable than statutes." He cites the case of a man who, when suing for the cutting down of his vines, would lose his claim if he referred to trees, since "the law of the Twelve Tables, on which his action for the cutting down of his vines lay, spoke of cutting down trees in general."

These actions were probably a form of verbal combat, the vestigial remains of a time when Roman society had emerged from a primitive state and was making its first attempts to regulate self-help. Although the *legis actiones* had become obsolete by Gaius' time, his discussion of this ancient form of legislation has provided valuable knowledge of ancient Roman law and has contributed to an understanding of the concepts that shaped development of the Roman legal system and determined its form.

Even a cursory reading of Gaius' *Institutes* indicates that it is the model followed by Justinian in his own *Institutes*, published as an introduction to his *Corpus Juris Civilis*. Following Gaius, Justinian divided Roman law into three main categories: the law of persons, the law of things, and the law of obligations. Although there is some overlap among these categories, the first section contains those laws referring to people, the second refers to the rights and duties of persons, and the third contains laws relating to remedies, or the way in which rights and duties are to be enforced or protected. This last section involves legal concepts that fall under the modern category of procedural law. As a result of Justinian's borrowings from Gaius, nearly all modern legal systems are generally divided into these three categories. Although Gaius was not clear about these divisions, he nevertheless bequeathed a method of studying and teaching law that has endured, clarifying and making legal concepts more concise and manageable.

Gaius' *Institutes* offers modern readers more than an opportunity to read an authentic document of ancient classical law; it also allows them to understand more about Roman law in general and about contemporary approaches to modern law and legal philosophy.

—*J. A. Wahl, updated by Jeffrey L. Buller*

ADDITIONAL READING:

Gordon, W. M., and O. F. Robinson. *The Institutes of Gaius*. Ithaca, N.Y.: Cornell University Press, 1988. Contains a complete translation, as well as the original Latin text, of Gaius' *Institutes*. The excellent introduction provides invaluable background and is the best place for the serious reader to begin.

Kunkel, Wolfgang. *An Introduction to Roman Legal and Constitutional History*. Translated by J. M. Kelly. Oxford: Clarendon Press, 1973. Presents, in a manageable format, a survey of the major developments in the Roman legal code.

Prichard, Alan Martin. *Leage's Roman Private Law*. 3d ed. New York: St. Martin's Press, 1961. Using the *Institutes* of Gaius and the legal code of Justinian as a basis, this work provides an extensive introduction and discussion of Roman private law and its impact upon modern legal systems.

Scott, S. P. *The Civil Law*. Cincinnati: Central Trust Company, 1973. Reprinting an edition first issued in 1932, this work provides a translation of Gaius' *Institutes*, along with other legal codes, such as the Twelve Tables, the Rules of Ulpian, the Opinions of Paulus, the Enactments of Justinian, and the Constitutions of Leo.

Watson, Alan. *The Evolution of Law*. Baltimore: The Johns Hopkins University Press, 1985. A good general introduction on the history and development of Roman law.

Wolff, Hans Julius. *Roman Law: An Historical Introduction*. Norman: University of Oklahoma Press, 1951. A survey of Roman law, emphasizing the importance of Gaius' *Institutes* to a complete understanding of Roman jurisprudence.

SEE ALSO: 451-449 B.C., The "Twelve Tables" of Roman Law; 90 B.C., Julian Law; 529-534, Justinian's *Code*

200
CHRISTIAN APOLOGISTS DEVELOP CONCEPT OF THEOLOGY

Christian apologists develop a concept of theology, providing the young Christian Church with a solid core of durable beliefs about man and his relationship to God.

DATE: 200
LOCALE: Rome and the eastern Mediterranean region
CATEGORIES: Cultural and intellectual history; Religion

KEY FIGURES:

Marcion (fl. 120-150), Greek Christian who came to Rome, helped establish the New Testament canon, and quarreled with Tertullian

Montanus (fl. late second century A.D.), charismatic teacher whose appeal to many women followers resulted in women being banned from the ministry

Origen (c. 185-c. 254), powerful Christian thinker born in Alexandria and founder of the science of biblical theology

Saint Paul (Saul of Tarsus; died c. A.D. 64), Christian convert who created the early Church by his tireless teaching efforts and powerful personality

Tertullian (c. 160-c. 230), eloquent Carthaginian polemicist and believer in the importance of faith as a force in the lives of the elect

SUMMARY OF EVENT. Christian theology begins with Paul's trip around A.D. 49 from Antioch to Jerusalem to meet with Jesus' surviving followers. According to the Acts of the Apostles, this conference, or Council of Jerusalem, came about because of the insistence of James, Jesus' brother, and others of the Jerusalem church that circumcision was demanded by the law. Disputing this, Paul went from Antioch with Barnabas to settle the issue, and left with a compromise dispensing with circumcision, while agreeing to Jewish laws governing sex and diet. Yet in chapter 2 of his epistle to the Galatians, Paul mentions no compromise on the law, stating only that his congregation would go to the heathens (Gentiles) while the Jerusalem church went to the circumcised, or the Jews.

For Paul, the Apostolic Conference raked over no mere legal dispute among sects but forced a momentous showdown over the importance of Jesus' life. He insists in Galatians 2, verse 16 that "man is not justified by the works of the law, but by the faith of Jesus Christ," adding later (chapter 3, verse 13) that "Christ hath redeemed us from the curse of the law." In Paul's theology, Jesus of Nazareth was descended from David and born of a woman, but through his resurrection he proved himself the Son of God. He was crucified for man's sins and was raised to the throne at God's right hand. He was Jesus Christ, or the Messiah, whose death redeems all humanity. This world will fade away and Christ will return from heaven as the Son of Man. Much of this new salvationist theology is outlined in Paul's epistle to the Romans.

The success of Paul's revolutionary vision was guaranteed by the political unrest in Jerusalem and its subsequent destruction by Titus in A.D. 70 after four years of civil war. In 135, Hadrian put down another revolt and built a new Roman colony on the site of the old city. These events destroyed the Jewish-Christian congregation, leaving

Rome to become the center for the propagation of Paul's teachings. Certain fringe sects soon condemned Paul as a heretic, and although these charges introduced the notion of heresy into the new Church, just what constituted heresy was not at all clear.

The emerging Church was threatened by dangerous external foes. Greek philosophy, for instance, would have rationalized the Gospels, Hellenizing them in a dangerous way. Another Greek element that persists to this day among many Christians is a sharp conflict between matter and spirit, with a concomitant conviction that salvation demands the spirit's escape from the bondage of the human flesh.

Further competition came from Gnosticism, a combination of beliefs from many Mediterranean and Eastern sources. The Greek word *gnosis*, or "knowledge," denotes a direct apprehension of spiritual truth, and the Gnostics received their name from their belief in a secret knowledge that can be passed on to initiates. They also stressed the dualism of flesh and spirit, teaching that the emancipation of the spirit could be accomplished only by initiation into the Gnostic mysteries.

One powerful thinker influenced by Gnosticism was Marcion. Marcion was wealthy, and he gave generously to the church in Rome when he gravitated there from the Black Sea region around 140. Marcion's preaching attracted enough followers that he could begin his own church. Although he believed in the dualism of the Gnostics, he supplanted Gnostic insistence on initiation with a radical faith in the Gospel. Marcion preached a God of love who revealed himself in Christ, who, in Marcion's Gnostic-influenced theology, only seemed to have a physical body (an argument called "docetism").

Marcion's emphasis on salvation through faith made him a natural follower of Paul, and he collected Paul's letters and edited the Gospel of Luke to his own primitive Gospel taste. This work made Marcion one of the earliest collectors of Christian documents. Although Marcion was also an effective organizer who brought his followers together into churches, his insistence on absolute celibacy and the separation of husbands and wives spelled eventual doom for his teachings.

Another group that flourished in the late second century were the Montanists, named after their leader, Montanus. They were also known as Phrygians after the region of Asia Minor from which they came. They were chiliasts, or believers in the imminent second coming of Christ. Montanus spoke in tongues, declaring that the Paraclete, the Holy Spirit, spoke through him. Montanus had two women disciples who also claimed to speak for the Holy Spirit, but ironically it was opposition to Montanus' women followers that helped bar women from the ministry.

Montanism had a wide following in Asia Minor and North Africa as late as the fifth century, including among its converts the wealthy Carthaginian-born Tertullian. Well educated in philosophy and history, Tertullian practiced law in Rome until he converted to Christianity in middle age and returned to Carthage to spend his remaining years writing on questions of theology. Tertullian wrote beautiful prose, which he used to condemn heretics and to attack Marcion and his teaching that love is sufficient to guide rational man through life. Tertullian's innate pessimism reflected his conviction of human corruptibility and his contempt for Greek philosophy and rational inquiry in general. Like Paul, Tertullian valued most highly the faith of the elect and proclaimed the absolute necessity of the individual spirit in direct, unmediated communion with God.

The need to harmonize the clamor of competing voices within the church led to the shaping of an apostolic succession that created an episcopate, to the stabilization of a New Testament canon, and to the formulation of the Apostles' Creed.

The first of these demands was met partly by Ireneaus, a native of Smyrna and an outstanding theologian who became bishop of Lyons. He stressed the reliability of the apostles' accounts and the validity of the line of bishops descended from them. Ireneaus exerted a vital influence in establishing a secure episcopacy. The episcopal system was strengthened by the insistence of Cyprian, bishop of Carthage, that the impossibility of salvation through direct communion with God necessitated the mediation of bishops.

The need for a New Testament canon was partly met by Marcion's work with Paul's letters and the Gospel of Luke, and it was furthered by Irenaeus' firm insistence on a total of four Gospels. By 200, the final canon of twenty-seven works was fairly well settled as a companion to the Jewish scriptures.

Although the declaration known as the Apostles' Creed was not fixed in its present form before the sixth century, an early version, the "Roman Symbol," was known in part by Tertullian and Irenaeus. The Roman Symbol may have evolved from the primitive baptismal statement, altered in response to Marcion's idiosyncratic view on God's role in the creation of the universe.

Among the early shapers of Christian theology, none was more intellectually gifted and creative than the Alexandrian scholar Origen. He identified three levels of meaning in the scriptures: a surface meaning accessible to any common reader; a didactic sense offering moral edification; and a hidden, allegorical meaning available only to the spiritually pure. Origen was a prodigious scholar whose thinking was shaped by Greek thought as well as Hebrew, and his fluent writings did much to give the young Christian Church a coherent vision of God and man by the time he died around 254. —*Frank Day*

ADDITIONAL READING:

Chadwick, Henry. "The Early Christian Community." In *The Oxford Illustrated History of Christianity*. New York: Oxford University Press, 1990. A beautiful book throughout.

Durant, Will. *Caesar and Christ*. Vol. 3 of *The Story of Civilization*. New York: Simon & Schuster, 1944. Durant is a secular historian whose chapter 28, "The Growth of the Church: A.D. 96-305," tells its story straightforwardly.

Johnson, Paul. *A History of Christianity*. New York: Atheneum, 1976. Part 1, "The Rise and Rescue of the Jesus Sect (50 B.C.-A.D. 250)," is an excellent source, especially good on the genius of Paul.

Latourette, Kenneth Scott. *A History of Christianity*. Vol. 1: *Beginnings to 1500*. Rev. ed. New York: Harper & Row, 1975. Chapter 6, "Christianity Takes Shape in Organization and Doctrine," is richly detailed.

Meeks, Wayne. *The Origins of Christian Morality: The First Two Centuries*. New Haven, Conn.: Yale University Press, 1993. Excellent philosophical discussions—for those who have read one of the above accounts.

SEE ALSO: 312, Conversion of Constantine; 313-395, Inception of the Church-State Problem; 325, The Nicene Creed.

220
ULPIAN'S DICTUM

Ulpian's dictum constitutes an early statement on theories of government, clothing an absolutist reality with a veneer of constitutionalism.

DATE: c. 220
LOCALE: Rome
CATEGORIES: Government and politics; Laws, acts, and legal history
KEY FIGURES:
Accursius (1182-1260), glossator and professor of Roman law at Bologna
Baldus de Ubaldis (c. 1320-1400), Roman lawyer and canonist
Bartolus of Sassoferrato (1314-1357), Roman lawyer
Henry de Bracton (c. 1210-1268), English jurist
Hostiensis (Henry de Segusio, c. 1200-1271), canonist
Ulpian (Domitius Ulpianus, c. 170-228), classical jurist who was Praetorian Prefect in 222

SUMMARY OF EVENT. One of the most famous phrases in the *Digest* of Justinian's *Corpus Juris Civilis*, or body of civil law, is Ulpian's statement concerning the origin of the emperor's authority: "What pleases the prince has the force of law since by the *lex regia* which was passed concerning his authority, the people transfers to him and upon him the whole of its own authority and power."

Early Roman law asserted that law was an enactment of the whole people in assembly. In time, however, decrees of the senate were accepted as replacements for laws because of the impracticality of calling together and consulting the entire populace. By the first century A.D., however, the power of the *princeps* had so overshadowed the authority not only of the people but also of the senate that it could no longer be ignored. While it was an established fact of political life that imperial decrees were also laws, Ulpian attempted to protect the ancient popular rights by assuming that this authority rested on a grant of power by the people through a so-called *lex regia*. There is no evidence of such a law except possibly an extant "*lex de imperio Vespasiani*" (A.D. 69-70), whereby Emperor Vespasian was granted sovereignty and in which is mentioned the rights held by his predecessors. It is doubtful that any such formal grant was made later than that. In this fiction of the *lex regia*, Ulpian clothed an absolutist reality with a veneer of constitutionalism.

Thus, two apparently contradictory concepts are contained in this one statement: unlimited imperial authority and the ultimate sovereign rights and power of the people. This opinion of Ulpian caused the Roman people no difficulty since the power of the emperor was a fact, while the sovereignty of the people was a theory accepted by all, even the emperors.

In the course of the Middle Ages, however, two divergent traditions developed from Ulpian's statement: the absolutist and the constitutional concepts of monarchy. Ulpian's dictum did not create these terms of reference, but supporters on either side of the issue made use of his authority after the rediscovery of Roman law in the eleventh century.

In the twelfth century, a doctrine of sovereignty arose which ascribed to the ruler an absolute plenitude of power; all inferior authority came by way of delegation. The adherents of this doctrine pointed to the first part of Ulpian's statement that the prince's will has the force of law. Not only was he unfettered by any statute but he could also apply or break them as he believed the circumstances warranted.

One such proponent was Henry de Bracton, a jurist of King Henry II of England and a writer on English law, who concluded from the "quod principi" dictum that the king as supreme lawgiver could not be legally bound by any earthly authority or the law even though he was morally bound to obey the law. Legally, the ruler was an absolute ruler; morally, he was a constitutional monarch.

Opposition to this exalted view of the monarchical office took the form of an emphasis on popular sovereignty. The proponents of this view also relied upon Ulpian's dictum, laying their stress on the second part. According to them, the king's power rested on a grant of authority by the people. Should the people be convinced that he was not acting in their interests, they could legally depose him and choose a new ruler.

Since both camps appealed with equal vehemence to Ulpian in support of their arguments, the discussion quickly began to revolve around the question of the nature of the cession of authority to the king by the people. The proponents of the absolutist view, while conceding that a grant of authority had been made, insisted that it was irrevocable and complete. The people not only were powerless to rescind the grant they had made but also no longer possessed any legislative power. Among the advocates of this view was Accursius, who wrote what became the standard gloss, or commentary, on Justinian's *Code*, and Hostiensis, one of the foremost canonists of the thirteenth century.

Hostiensis, who studied at Bologna and lectured in Paris, was particularly influential. He served King Henry III of England and Pope Innocent IV, and became cardinal bishop of Ostia. His two commentaries on the Decretals, written between 1250 and 1271, assured his fame. Bartolus of Sassoferrato and Baldus de Ubaldis, two of the greatest Roman lawyers of the fourteenth century, also supported the absolutist powers of the prince.

The Enlightenment did much to settle the question by advocating the doctrine that the will of the people was the ultimate authority in government. Modern democratic countries have determined that, in the final analysis, Ulpian was correct when he proposed that the ruler's authority was founded ultimately on the will of the people.

—*J. A. Wahl, updated by Jeffrey L. Buller*

ADDITIONAL READING:

Giercke, Otto. *Political Theories of the Middle Ages.* Translated by Frederic William Maitland. Boston: Beacon Press, 1958. Among the many issues discussed in this wide-ranging text, there is a full discussion of the impact of Ulpian's dictum upon later legal and constitutional theory.

Honore, Tony. *Ulpian.* Oxford: Clarendon Press, 1982. The most complete scholarly resource available on the contributions of Ulpian to the Roman legal system. Going far beyond the importance of Ulpian's dictum, this work

summarizes all that is known about the early third century jurist.

McIlwain, Charles Howard. *Constitutionalism: Ancient and Modern.* Ithaca, N.Y.: Cornell University Press, 1947. Traces the impact of Ulpian's dictum on the development of constitutionalism in the West.

Scott, S. P. *The Civil Law.* Cincinnati: Central Trust Company, 1973. Reprinting an edition first issued in 1932, this work provides a translation of the Rules of Ulpian along with other legal codes, including the Twelve Tables, the Institutes of Gaius, the Opinions of Paulus, the Enactments of Justinian, and the Constitutions of Leo.

Ullmann, Walter. *Principles of Government and Politics in the Middle Ages.* New York: Barnes & Noble, 1961. An excellent presentation of medieval political theory, including the influence that various doctrines of the Roman Empire had upon it.

SEE ALSO: 335-323 B.C., Aristotle Writes the *Politics*; 51 B.C., Cicero Writes His *De Republica*; 529-534, Justinian's *Code*.

284
INAUGURATION OF THE DOMINATE

The inauguration of the Dominate places the rule of the Roman Empire on a formally and explicitly authoritarian basis in order to provide stability in a troubled political climate.

DATE: 284
LOCALE: The Roman Empire
CATEGORY: Government and politics
KEY FIGURES:
Constantius I (Flavius Valerius Constantius Chlorus; died 306), Roman emperor, 293-306
Diocletian (Gaius Aurelius Valerius Diocletianus; c. 245-316), Roman emperor, 284-305
Galerius (Gaius Galerius Valerius Maximianus; died 311), Roman emperor, 293-311
Maximian (Marcus Aurelius Valerius Maximianus; died 310), co-emperor with Diocletian, 285-305, and sole emperor, 306-308

SUMMARY OF EVENT. The era of the Roman Empire has been traditionally divided into these two great periods: the Principate as founded by Augustus, and the Dominate as reconstituted by Diocletian. The difference in tone between the two periods is well indicated by their separate names: Principate, derived from *princeps*, or "first man," indicates that the emperor was, at least in theory, a constitutional magistrate. Dominate, on the other hand, taken from *dominus*, meaning lord or master, acknowledges the fact that the emperor was an absolute ruler.

From the assassination of Alexander Severus in A.D. 235 to the accession of the Dalmatian peasant Diocletian, a successful general, in 284, the Roman Empire had been in a state of almost continuous anarchy. Thanks to assassinations and wars, only one of the more than twenty emperors who ruled during this period had died a natural death. Ruinous taxes, a plague that lasted from 253 to 268, wars with the Persians, and barbarian threats further afflicted the empire.

In the face of these difficulties, Diocletian effected a series of controversial reforms. Changes to make the army more mobile, arrangement for planned retirement of emperors after twenty years and for peaceful successions by trained caesars, and division of the state into four major districts with courts and capitals in Nicomedia, Milan, Trier, and Sirmium were ways in which Diocletian further divided the empire for administrative purposes into twelve dioceses. Each diocese was under a vicar subject to the praetorian prefect of his respective Augustus or Caesar, and Diocletian enlarged the number of provinces to one hundred. In the new provincial arrangement, military authority was separated from the civil, the former under *duces* or "dukes," the latter under *comites* or "counts." The old haphazard land tax was replaced with a new system based upon a division of land into *juga* of uniform value in each diocese and a similar division of men and animals into units known as *capita*. At stipulated periods, praetorian prefects had to estimate the budget in terms of goods and make an assessment, or *indictio*, according to *juga* and *capita*.

These reforms, however wise or necessary, were not made without cost. Already during the Severi, the emperorship and the state had been brutalized by falling under military domination. Liturgies had to be resorted to in order to bolster the flagging collection of taxes. Rich men and members of *collegia* were forced to provide free services and supplies in order to balance the budget. During the Severi, moreover, Roman jurisprudence divorced both criminal and civil jurisdiction from vestiges of Republican institutions such as the senate of Rome, which under Diocletian became a provincial city. Ulpian's dictum well presaged the absolutism of Diocletian in asserting that the "will of the prince has the force of law." It was becoming more and more obvious that citizens were existing for the benefit of the state rather than the other way around.

Diocletian's reign can readily be seen as representative of this trend toward totalitarian control. The cost of supporting four elaborate courts and the enlarged army added to the burden of the already impoverished economy. Inadequate issuance of new gold and silver coins and overdevaluation of others encouraged rapid inflation. Consequently in 301, Diocletian attempted to control the economy by issuing his famous Edict of Prices fixing the maximum that could be paid for all kinds of goods and services. Despite severe penalties, the law proved to be unworkable and eventually had to be permitted to lapse. To prevent people from avoiding the more thorough collection of taxes, farmers became bound to their land and workmen to their trades. Moreover, sons had to take up the same labors as their fathers, thereby creating a kind of serfdom in the country and a caste system in the cities.

Historians have often tended to overemphasize the rigidity of Diocletian's regime. Whether because of a misleading comparison with twentieth century socialism or a dislike of Diocletian's persecution of the Christians, historians have underestimated the significance of Diocletian's constitutional reforms. These reforms proceeded from a genuine vision of how the Roman Empire could be reconstituted and once again be made a formidable and cohesive force. Particularly important was the mechanism Diocletian devised for the imperial succession. Typically, the reigning emperor had been suspicious of any particularly strong man among those who served him; this suspicion led either to the elimination of the rivals or their preemptive overthrow of the emperor. By granting ambitious, energetic men a junior share in government and promising them eventual leadership, Diocletian defused the air of suspicion and intrigue that had plagued Roman statesmanship for several decades. Although his system ultimately collapsed, it still provided the Roman Empire with twenty years of good government, and the imperial succession would never again be so unstable as it had been in the third century. Also notable (and rare in Roman imperial history) was Diocletian's willingness to abdicate the throne after serving his twenty years. This action, which hearkened back to the old Roman virtues of rectitude and patriotic self-sacrifice and was only reluctantly emulated by Maximian, indicates that Diocletian adhered to his own standards of conduct and was not merely an opportunistic dictator. Diocletian's authoritarianism, unlike so many others, possessed a rationale and a logic.

Indicative of the new atmosphere, Diocletian introduced an elaborate ceremonial protocol into his court borrowed from Persian and earlier Hellenistic rulers. On formal occasions, he wore a robe of purple silk and shoes adorned with jewels and was seated on a throne. He insisted upon being styled *dominus*, or lord, and those admitted to his presence had to perform the *proskynesis*, or prostration, to kiss the hem of his robe. Many historians profess to see in the declining art of the period the trend toward domination by the emperor.

Finally, although not as an innovator, Diocletian took control over the consciences of his subjects. Diocletian believed in using the prestige of the classical gods to buttress his own power; thus he allowed himself to be described as "Jove" and Maximian as "Hercules." A conservative polytheist convinced that the prosperity of the state depended upon the favor of the gods, Diocletian issued decrees against Manichaeans in 297 and instituted the great persecution against the Christians in 303-304. This dragnet, which required all to display a certificate of sacrifice to the gods, came to a permanent end only with the Edict of Milan in 313 and the so-called Peace of the Church.

—*M. Joseph Costelloe, updated by Nicholas Birns*

ADDITIONAL READING:

Barnes, Timothy. *The New Empire of Diocletian and Constantine.* Cambridge, Mass.: Harvard University Press, 1982. A compendium of laws and records make this source useful for research on Diocletian.

Cameron, Averil. *The Later Roman Empire A.D. 284-430.* London: Fontana, 1993. Cameron provides a crisply written and cogent analysis of the period.

Corcoran, Simon. *The Empire of the Tetrarchs: Imperial Pronouncements and Government, A.D. 284-324.* Oxford: Clarendon Press, 1996. Explores the legal and political basis of the Dominate.

Jones, A. H. M. *The Later Roman Empire, 284-602.* Baltimore: The Johns Hopkins University Press, 1986. Describes Diocletian's impact on the entire period of late antiquity.

Victor, Sextus Aurelius. *Liber de Caesaribus of Sextus Aurelius Victor.* Translated with an introduction and commentary by H. W. Bird. Liverpool, England: Liverpool University Press, 1994. Bird has provided a fine translation of the main primary source for Diocletian, accompanied by an excellent, modern-day commentary.

Williams, Stephen. *Diocletian and the Roman Recovery.* London: B. T. Batsford, 1985. This source is particularly recommended as the most thorough analysis of Diocletian and his time available.

SEE ALSO: 133 B.C., Tribunate of Tiberius Sempronius Gracchus; 27-23 B.C., Completion of the Augustan Settlement; 220, Ulpian's Dictum.

312
CONVERSION OF CONSTANTINE

The conversion of Constantine marks the emergence of Christianity as the dominant religion of the slowly disintegrating Roman Empire, a development that leads to the creation of a common European culture.

DATE: October 28, 312
LOCALE: The Milvian Bridge, a few miles north of Rome
CATEGORIES: Government and politics; Religion
KEY FIGURES:
Constantine the Great (c. 272-337), emperor in the West, 312-324, and sole Roman emperor, 324-337
Valerius Licinianus Licinius (c. 250-325), co-emperor with Constantine, 313-324, who ruled the eastern part of the Roman Empire
Marcus Aurelius Valerius Maxentius (c. 265-312), son of Maximian, former co-emperor with Diocletian, and self-proclaimed Roman emperor, 306-312

SUMMARY OF EVENT. By the end of third century A.D., the Roman Empire was politically and religiously divided and in decline. Diocletian, one of the claimants to the title of Roman emperor, in an attempt to create religious and cultural unity, issued a series of decrees beginning in 303 against Christianity. The decrees included instructions to burn churches, destroy copies of the Scripture, and eventually to murder Christians themselves. After the abdication of Diocletian in A.D. 305, at least eight rivals emerged to claim the imperial title. By 312, only four remained: Maxentius and Maximinus Daia were aligned against Constantine and Licinius and continued the policy of encouraging religious unity by persecuting Christians. When Constantine defeated Maxentius at the Battle of the Milvian Bridge and Lucinius conquered Maximinus Daia, the two victors divided the Roman Empire between them. The division lasted for ten years until Constantine defeated Licinius in 324 and became sole ruler.

At noon on the day before the battle against Maxentius at the Milvian Bridge, Constantine, according to Eusebius' *Life of Constantine*, saw a sign appearing in the sky as a fiery cross with the legend: "Conquer by this." The same night, the Christian God allegedly appeared to him in a dream and instructed him to place the Christian emblem on the imperial standards if he wished to be victorious. Eusebius claims that he heard the story from the lips of Constantine, but he wrote after the emperor's death and he does not tell the same tale in his *Ecclesiastical History*. At the head of his legions, Constantine placed the *labarum* displaying the famous *chi rho*, combining to form a cross the first two letters of the word "Christ" in Greek. Subsequent victory against Maxentius convinced Constantine that the Christian God was more powerful than the classical deities worshiped by his rivals. Clearly Constantine was taking a risk, since only about one-tenth of the Roman Empire was Christian at the time. Nevertheless, Constantine seems to have understood Christianity's long-term potential for providing religious unity to the Roman Empire.

According to his biographer Eusebius, Constantine's vision of a cross lighting up the noonday sky on the day before an important battle led to his conversion to Christianity. (Archive Photos)

Whether the emperor's conversion was contrived or genuine is still a matter of debate, but there can be no doubt that his rule was beneficial for Christianity. In 313, Licinius agreed upon the terms of the so-called Edict of Milan, which granted toleration to Christianity, reimbursed Christians for losses suffered in recent persecutions, and exempted the clergy from certain compulsory civil obligations. While the edict simply affirmed religious toleration and continued to provide support for the continuance of traditional forms of Roman religion, subsequent legislation certainly provided Christianity with a favored status. In 315, Constantine enacted legislation which prohibited retributions against Jewish converts to Christianity, and in 318, the emperor ordained, in a precedent-making decree, that a civil suit might, with the consent of both litigants, be removed to the jurisdic-

tion of a bishop, whose verdict would be final. By 321, the Church could inherit property and bishops could manumit slaves. Sunday was declared a holiday for imperial employees. By convening church councils at Arles and Nicaea, Constantine set up ecclesiastical machinery for the adjudication of problems caused by dissenting groups such as Donatists and Arians. At the first ecumenical council, the emperor himself put his prestige behind the famous *homoousian* formula, which has remained Christian dogma ever since. Associating his Christian piety with the welfare of the state, Constantine built basilicas, composed prayers, and paid for translations of the Christian Scriptures. Finally, he was baptized on his deathbed by Eusebius, bishop of Nicomedia.

Christianity's sudden change in fortune from a persecuted, outlawed sect to a tolerated and favored religion posed special problems. Christianity's strong commitment to pacifism and its status as a religion of the lower classes were both significantly modified. The attitude of the Church toward the Roman Empire also underwent a drastic change. The seventeenth chapter of Revelation, probably written at the end of the first century, is generally supposed to refer to Rome when it speaks of the woman "drunk with the blood of saints," but Eusebius now saw the emperor as the viceregent of God. Nevertheless, the dilemma had to be faced concerning where jurisdictional lines should be drawn between the Church and the state. Since Christians enjoyed political preferment in the imperial government after the conversion of Constantine, the Church in the fourth century was inundated with large numbers of half-convinced pagans. This mixed blessing led to early reform movements in the Church and the institution of monasticism.

The favored position of Christianity in the Roman Empire also led to a different interpretation of history. Whereas Christians during the persecutions had looked for the immediate return of Christ and the establishment of the new Jerusalem to replace the vicious rule of Rome, it now appeared that the golden age had dawned. Eusebius saw in Constantine the fulfillment of God's promises to his chosen people through Abraham. Such a sanguine view of the state remained typically eastern; in the West, a dualist attitude that held the Church and the state in tension was destined to become dominant.

Clearly the conversion of Constantine was a turning point in imperial and Christian history which ultimately affected the entire Western world. Historians have variously interpreted the sincerity of Constantine's change of heart. One view holds that his conversion was motivated by political expediency so that he might use the Church for purposes of state. The opposite position maintains that

Constantine's acts can be explained only in the light of a genuine change of heart and full conversion. A mediating position attempts to postulate a gradual change in the emperor from that of a deistic humanitarian trying to integrate Christianity with the current paganism, to one of nominal conversion by the time of his death. It should be noted that Constantine was noted for placing great significance on dreams and visions, and one legend reports an earlier experience in which Constantine adopted Apollo as his god because of a promise that he would prosper in Apollo's name. It is noteworthy that Apollo was linked to the Sun-god, a form of monotheistic faith which Constantine seems to have adopted, perhaps preparing the ground for his conversion to Christianity, also a monotheistic religion.

—*Carl A. Volz, updated by Charles L. Kammer III*

ADDITIONAL READING:

Barnes, Timothy D. *Constantine and Eusebius*. Cambridge, Mass.: Harvard University Press, 1981. An extensive treatment of Constantine and Eusebius in the context of the political situation in the Roman Empire at the end of the third and beginning of the fourth centuries.

Burckhardt, Jacob. *The Age of Constantine the Great*. Translated by Moses Hadas. New York: Doubleday, 1956. First published in 1852, this is still an influential work in understanding the conversion of Constantine and its significance.

Cochrane, Charles Norris. *Christianity and Classical Culture: A Study of Thought and Action from Augustus to Augustine*. New York: Oxford University Press, 1957. The most significant treatment of the emergence of Christianity as a source of cultural unity.

Grant, Michael. *Constantine the Great: The Man and His Times*. New York: Charles Scribner's Sons, 1993. A recent study that focuses especially on the complex religious policies and personal development of Constantine.

Jones, A. H. M. *Constantine and the Conversion of Europe*. 6th ed. London: The English Universities Press, 1964. A discussion of the conversion of Constantine and the religious practices he implemented as emperor.

Nicene and Post-Nicene Fathers of the Christian Church. 2d ser. Grand Rapids, Mich.: Wm. B. Eerdmans, 1952. Includes the text of Eusebius' *The Life of Constantine*, as well as text of a speech attributed to Constantine and an additional speech by Eusebius, "In Praise of Constantine."

SEE ALSO: 110, Trajan's Religious Policy; 313-395, Inception of the Church-State Problem; 325, The Nicene Creed.

313-395
INCEPTION OF CHURCH-STATE PROBLEM

The inception of the church-state problem develops from conflicting interpretations of the relationship between the organized church and civil government concerning the extent of their powers within each other's sphere of activity.

DATE: 313-395
LOCALE: The Roman Empire
CATEGORIES: Government and politics; Religion
KEY FIGURES:
Ambrose (c. 339-397), bishop of Milan, 374-397
Athanasius (c. 293-373), bishop of Alexandria, 328-373
Saint Augustine (354-430), bishop of Hippo, 396-430, and author of the *City of God*
Constans I (c. 323-350), son of Constantine and emperor in the West, 337-350
Constantine the Great (c. 272-337), sole emperor of the Roman Empire, 324-337
Constantine II (317-340), son of Constantine and emperor in the West, 337-340
Constantius II (317-361), son of Constantine, emperor in the East, 337-350, sole ruler, 350-361
Gratian (359-383), emperor in the West, 375-383
Theodosius the Great (346-395), emperor in the East, 379-393, sole ruler, 393-395

SUMMARY OF EVENT. The phrase "Church and state" represents a framework for understanding how religion and politics are related when both institutions are allowed to make formal jurisdictional claims within the same society. Historians have recognized that church and state have managed to coexist in three basic ways: as totally detached entities, as distinguished but not necessarily separated from each other, and joined together as one. Since the time of the Roman Empire, Christian theology has swung back and forth between viewing the Church as supreme, with the state merely a vassal of the Church, to viewing the state as supreme, with the Church purely a spiritual power. Most societies exist with a mutually dependent church and state, as in the United States, where church-state issues have centered on the U.S. Constitution and its First Amendment "freedom of religion" clause, interpreted by a large body of constitutional law.

The inception of church-state problems occurred with the organization of the early Christian Church within the Roman Empire and its recognition of the existence and legality of the state by praying for the good of the state and its magistrates. The empire, however, did not begin to acknowledge the legality or authority of the Church until the Edict of Milan in A.D. 313, which gave official recognition to the Christian religion. Before the edict, there was essentially no common ground of acknowledgment on which conflicts of jurisdiction could be settled or even discussed. Thus, the persecuted Church enjoyed considerable early freedom in its doctrinal formulations and other functions mainly because Rome denied its legal existence. The coming "age of toleration" made it evident that both Church and state would soon find it necessary to define the limits of their respective boundaries. During the fourth century A.D., some church fathers adopted the stance that the two institutions should remain fundamentally separate, particularly in matters of faith. Others developed the opinion that the Church should be subject to the state, assuming that the major state religion was Christianity.

One controversial issue that emerged as organized Christianity developed within the Roman Empire involved the emperor's title and influence as *pontifex maximus*. Beginning in 12 B.C., Roman emperors claimed this position with authority over all religious activities within the Roman Empire. When Christianity was recognized as the official state religion under Theodosius, controversy developed whether Christianity should and could be governed by the same public laws as the earlier pagan cults. Prior to Christianity, Roman emperors and other secular rulers held religious and civil authority either in a priestly role as intermediaries between people and gods, or as actual gods themselves.

The inception of church-state problems was furthered by the teaching of the Church and state as dual authorities, known as the "two swords" doctrine, and the activities of Constantine, the first public leader to convert to Christianity. Tradition relates that Constantine became converted after a battle when he saw a vision of a cross in the sky on which were written the words "By this sign, thou shalt conquer." The dualistic view advanced by Constantine actually began much earlier with the Jewish nation, which was forced to submit to conquerors from Egypt, Assyria, Babylon, Medeo-Persia, and Greece, but managed to retain an independent religious identity and thus a separation between spiritual and worldly matters.

Growing out of Judaism, Christianity preserved this distinction in the words of Jesus Christ recorded in the book of Saint Matthew, "Render to Caesar the things that are Caesar's, and to God the things that are God's." Constantine not only assisted the new state religion by convening councils and actively supporting its propaganda but also threatened heretics and implemented social restrictions against them. Constantine did not aspire to act as head of the Church, and he disclaimed any rights of defining dogma or judging bishops in matters of the Christian

faith. Under Constantine's leadership, Church and state first recognized each other as legal and independent institutions, clearly setting the stage for later jurisdictional conflicts. After Constantine's death, the Roman Empire was divided among his three sons, Constantine, Constantius, and Constans, which served to create three weak governments out of one relatively strong one.

Strife between Church and state became inevitable when Constantius II sought to assume numerous controversial ecclesiastical prerogatives which his father, Constantine, never attempted to claim. One notable example is that Constantius II sought to impose an Arian creed upon all bishops, quickly bringing the protest of several Western clerics. The basis for Constantius' attempts at controlling Christianity was derived from the same constitutional rules that previously had placed paganism under imperial control. The Arian incident resulted in conclusions from Athanasius, Hilary, and Ambrose that only a true and complete separation of Church and state would avert further conflict. Problems initiated by church-state issues became more volatile with a trend toward Church leaders resisting the emperor's authority in the spiritual domain, while allowing him more extensive jurisdiction in civil matters. The duties of defending and propagating the Christian faith and of taking disciplinary action against paganism were included under imperial authority and later began to be expected by the Church.

After Gratian became the first Roman emperor to refuse the title of *pontifex maximus*, future Christian emperors claimed their right to authority over the Church by saying that their office was conferred directly by God for the welfare of the Church. With decrees by Gratian and Theodosius making the empire legally Christian, the relationship between Church and state became more confrontational, with intense disagreements between Bishop Ambrose and Emperor Theodosius. The theology of fourth century fathers, such as Athanasius, Hilary, and Ambrose, rejected the attempt to unite Church and Roman Empire within one institution but sought independent juristic existence, as long as the empire continued to guarantee the Church's integrity.

The principle of separation between Church and state became well established in the West by the end of the fourth century, but the Christian Church in the East still looked to the emperor for guidance and approval in Church matters. The Western tradition of separation between the two powers was bequeathed to the medieval Church largely through St. Augustine's *City of God*. Augustine considered all earthly governments, regardless of their form, as representative of the fallen and imperfect "city of man." Under his theology, the state was necessary to provide the "sword" to discipline fallen man through law and education. Augustine's church represented the perfect and eternal "city of God" set up to preserve the divine values of peace, hope, and charity. Church and state were separate in that they occupied different realms and held different values, but remained very much related. Gelasius, pope in the late fifth century, laid down many of Augustine's principles for separate spiritual and temporal jurisdiction.

With the fall of the Roman Empire in A.D. 476, the Church gained enormous political and administrative power as it had become the main source of educated leaders. Charlemagne, Frankish emperor from 800 to 814 who greatly influenced Western civilization during the early Middle Ages, sought to subordinate ecclesiastical power and advance an independent secular state by personally appointing bishops and requiring political allegiance from them. Pope Gregory VII attempted to reverse Charlemagne's trend and excommunicated Emperor Henry IV for his resistance. The Protestant Reformation, begun by Martin Luther in 1520, replaced the medieval doctrine of two swords with the doctrine of the sovereign state, under which the Church was clearly subordinated to secular authority in worldly matters.

—*Daniel G. Graetzer*

ADDITIONAL READING:

Greenslade, S. L. *Church and State from Constantine to Theodosius*. London: Student Christian Movement Press, 1954. Greenslade outlines and analyzes the attitudes of Constantine, Constantius II, Constans, and others.

Loetscher, Frederick W. "St. Augustine's Conception of the State." *Church History* 4 (March, 1935): 16-41. An excellent treatise on Augustine's "dualistic" approach to Church and state separation.

Morrison, Karl Fredrick. *Rome and the City of God*. Vol. 54 of the Transactions of the American Philosophical Society. Philadelphia: American Philosophical Society, 1964. Part 1 assesses legal principles and part 2 analyzes the theologies of Athanasius, Hilary, and Ambrose as they relate to Church and state.

Setton, K. M. *Christian Attitude Toward the Emperor in the Fourth Century*. New York: Columbia University Press, 1941. An excellent text which meets the scope of its title in a very readable way.

Williams, G. H. "Christology and Church-State Relations in the Fourth Century." *Church History* 10 (September, 1951): 3-33, and 10 (December, 1951): 3-26. An interesting treatise focusing on the divine and human roles of Christ, the emperors, and others.

SEE ALSO: 200, Christian Apologists Develop Concept of Theology; 312, Conversion of Constantine; 325, The Nicene Creed; 413-426, Augustine Writes the *City of God*.

325
THE NICENE CREED

The Nicene Creed attempts to standardize Christian doctrine and restore Christian unity, becoming the only creed accepted by all major bodies of the Christian church—Catholic, Orthodox, and Protestant.

DATE: 325
LOCALE: Nicaea in Asia Minor
CATEGORY: Religion
KEY FIGURES:
Alexander (died 328), bishop of Alexandria, 313-328
Arius (c. 250-336), presbyter of Alexandria, 313-325
Athanasius (c. 295-373), deacon of Alexandria, 319-328; bishop, 328-373
Constantine the Great (c. 272-337), sole Roman emperor, 324-337
Eusebius of Caesarea (c. 260-c. 340), Eastern bishop and supporter of Arius
Eusebius of Nicomedia (died c. 342), bishop and supporter of Arius; bishop of Constantinople, 339-c. 342
Hosius of Cordova (c. 257-357), bishop and ecclesiastical adviser to Constantine, 312-326

SUMMARY OF EVENT. At the beginning of the fourth century A.D., faith in the divinity of Christ was firmly established in Christian worship but it was not precisely defined theologically, especially in relation to the divinity of God the Father. Arius, a presbyter in the Baucalis district of Alexandria, hoped to clarify these matters and, in line with a strong trend in Hellenistic philosophy, was anxious to assert the unity and immutability of God. For Arius, God must of necessity be one, alone, eternal. The world, the realm of change so completely foreign to the nature of God, must be created by an intermediary being, the Son, or Word. Arius was willing to countenance the worship traditionally given the Son because as Son he was a perfect creature standing in such a special relation to God that he might well be called "only begotten God." Yet he remained a creature whose "substance," or nature, was separate and related to the eternal Father. Unlike God the Father, the Son had a beginning, and, in the words of a popular Arian slogan concerning the Son, "There was when he was not."

Alexander, the bishop of Alexandria, totally rejected Arius' denial of the full divinity of Christ. When Arius made an appeal for popular support by composing theological songs based on his teachings, such as *Thalia* or

Spiritual Banquet, Alexander denounced him, took steps to depose him, and forced him into exile in Syria where he had powerful friends in Bishops Eusebius of Caesarea, Theodotus of Laodicea, and Eusebius of Nicomedia.

The dispute, which by now had assumed serious proportions, came to the attention of Emperor Constantine. While Constantine seems to have had little understanding of the complex issues which were being debated, he was anxious to secure theological agreement within the Church as a bulwark of political stability. Since both sides in the dispute could find both Scriptural support and support from earlier theological writers for their positions, there was no immediate way to resolve the dispute. When imperial letters and the efforts of his ecclesiastical adviser Bishop Hosius of Cordova failed to end the contention, Constantine decided, with little or no precedent, to call together a council of all Christian bishops. In taking such action, he established the precedent of calling Church councils to resolve theological disputes as a means of preserving ecclesiastical unity. To facilitate matters, he extended to the bishops the courtesy of the imperial coach service. On May 20, 325, the council opened in Nicaea near Constantinople with about three hundred bishops in attendance. Except for seven bishops from the Western Empire and a few from beyond the Eastern frontier, all were from the East. For the most part, they were not learned theologians. The absent Arius had his mouthpieces in Eusebius of Caesarea and Eusebius of Nicomedia; Alexander had at his elbow his deacon and successor Athanasius, who was later to play the leading part in the post-Nicene disputes with the Arians.

The council, which opened with great splendor with Constantine's greetings and admonitions, was presided over by Hosius of Cordova. The actual course by which the council drafted a creed is obscure. It appears that a radical Arian creed was almost unanimously rejected early in the course of debate, but the formulation of the orthodox belief proved to be more difficult.

To help combat heretical teachings, bishops of the Christian Church met at the Council of Nicaea and devised a uniform theological doctrine known as the Nicene Creed. (Archive Photos)

As a number of anti-Arian phrases attest, the creed represents a complete condemnation of the teachings of Arius. The term "begotten, that is, from the substance of the Father," directly rejected the Arian position that the Son was created out of nothing. The Nicene Creed further asserts that the Son was "Very God of very God," denying the Arian stand that God the Father was unique and that the Son was God in some secondary sense, not "true God." The phrase "begotten not made" again states the belief that the Son was one in nature with the Father and related to him in a way that the Creation was not. In response to the Arian objection that the begetting of the Son required a Father who was prior, the Nicene defenders referred to Origen's teaching of the eternal generation of the Son by the Father. The wording "of one substance with the Father" asserted the full deity of the Son in a way which admitted no Arianizing interpretation. Yet, the word *homoousios*, "of the same substance," presented certain difficulties. It was not a biblical term and moreover had been condemned in another context by an earlier synod. To some, it suggested a materialistic concept of God and courted the danger of the Sabellian heresy, which completely identified the persons of the Father and the Son. Later, in the 350's, the word *homoousios* became the keynote in a three-way struggle between the radical Arians, who said that the Son was not of the same substance as the Father; the conservatives, who believed that the Son was of "like" substance with the Father; and the defenders of the Nicene formula. Finally, the creed explicitly condemned a number of Arian teachings. When the supporters of Arius at the council were given the choice of signing the creed or going into exile, all but two signed. Arius himself was banished and his writings burned by imperial order. The Church also anathematized all those who claimed there was a time when the Son did not exist.

Prior to Nicaea, Christian symbols had been primarily local and liturgical creeds, used for the instruction of catechumens. The Nicene formula was a theological creed intended for universal subscription, not as a replacement for the older creeds but as a theological test for Church leaders.

The Council, however, did not finally end the dispute. Arius' followers were able to exert pressure on the emperor and the Church, and Arius was readmitted in 327. At the Council of Tyre in 335, Athanasius was banned from the Church. The dispute continued until a further council was called at Constantinople in 381, the Second Ecumenical Council. It was there that the more fully developed Nicene Creed was formally adopted. It included the provisions of the Creed adopted by the Council of Nicaea and enlarged the section on the Holy Spirit.

The creed formulated by the two Councils of Nicaea and Constantinople is the "Nicene" or "Niceno-Constantinopolitan Creed" found in the liturgy of most Christian churches, including Roman Catholic, Greek Orthodox, and Protestant faiths.

—*David Charles Smith, updated by Charles L. Kammer III*

ADDITIONAL READING:

Barnes, Timothy D. *Constantine and Eusebius.* Cambridge, Mass.: Harvard University Press, 1981. Contains a discussion of the Council of Nicaea as part of Constantine's attempt to create a unified Roman Empire.

Flint, Thomas P., ed. *Christian Philosophy.* Notre Dame, Ind.: University of Notre Dame Press, 1990. Contains a discussion of the contemporary significance of the Nicene Creed.

Grant, Michael. *Constantine the Great: The Man and His Times.* New York: Charles Scribner's Sons, 1993. Discusses the Council of Nicaea in terms of Constantine's concern for a unified faith.

Harnack, Adolph. *History of Dogma.* 3d ed. New York: Dover Publications, 1961. A central work in the study of the development of Christian doctrine which discusses the creed in the context of the Arian controversy.

Kelly, J. N. D. *Early Christian Creeds.* London: Longmans, Green, 1950. Presents a careful analysis of the theological claims of the creed in the context of the Arian controversy.

SEE ALSO: 200, Christian Apologists Develop Concept of Theology; 312, Conversion of Constantine; 313-395, Inception of the Church-State Problem.

326-330
CONSTANTINOPLE IS FOUNDED
Constantinople is founded, making the city instrumental in the survival of the Byzantine Empire and the extinction of the Western Roman Empire.
DATE: November 24, 326-May 11, 330
LOCALE: Constantinople (modern Istanbul), Turkey
CATEGORIES: Cultural and intellectual history; Government and politics
KEY FIGURE:
Constantine the Great (c. 272-337), emperor of Rome, 306-337
SUMMARY OF EVENT. During the third century A.D., the Roman Empire faced a crisis. Beginning in the year 235, armies around the empire acclaimed their generals as emperors, leading to constant civil wars as each new emperor attempted to gain control of Rome, the capital, for only the emperor who controlled Rome was the legiti-

mate emperor. Furthermore, with the armies engaged in civil wars, the borders were left unguarded, and the empire was attacked on all sides, by Franks and Alamans on the Rhine, Goths on the Danube, and Persians in the east. During the 250's, with the empire at its lowest ebb, the emperor Valerian turned the western part over to his son and took the east for himself. This marked the beginning of a trend toward multiple emperors and an administrative splitting of the empire, although officially there was only one empire and only one capital city, Rome.

Beginning in the year 284, the emperor Diocletian was able to reestablish control of the entire empire, defeat all the invaders, and put an end to the interminable warfare. At the same time, he instituted a number of reforms that were so overwhelming that his reign has been called the beginning of the "Late Roman Empire." Diocletian formalized the practices of having two emperors (Augustuses), each with a junior emperor (Caesar), in charge of the eastern and western parts of the empire. As senior emperor, Diocletian took control of the more populous and prosperous eastern part of the empire and established his court at Nicomedia in Asia Minor. Rome, however, remained the official capital of the entire empire.

After Diocletian retired in 305, civil war broke out again. The victor this time was Constantine, the son of one of Diocletian's junior emperors. In 324, Constantine defeated Licinius, his last rival, and he continued, and even expanded upon, Diocletian's reforms. Like Diocletian, Constantine recognized that the eastern section of the empire—the Balkans, Asia Minor, Syria-Palestine, and Egypt—was strategically, politically, and economically more important than the west. In recognition of this reality—not because of dislike of the Romans of Rome, as some later commentators thought—Constantine decided to establish not merely another court-city, but an actual second capital city of the empire, located in the east. This step was a sharp blow to the status and prestige of Rome. By this time, however, Rome was living on its past glories, a backwater area where nothing of significance happened any longer.

The selection of a site was accompanied by a good bit of soul-searching. After deciding against places such as Serdica (modern Sofia) near the Danube, Thessalonica in northern Greece, and Chalcedon in northern Asia Minor, Constantine initially decided to found his city on the site of ancient Troy. This was the home of Aeneas, the legendary ancestor of the ancient Romans, and would have been a worthy site for a second Rome. Constantine even went so far as to lay out the city and build the city gates. It was later said, however, that God came to him in a vision and told him to abandon this pagan site and select another.

Another legend said that eagles carried the measuring tapes from the proposed site at Chalcedon north to the old Greek city of Byzantium.

Byzantium was strategically located on the north side of the Bosporus, the strait that linked the Aegean and Black Seas and separated Europe from Asia. It was surrounded on three sides by water: the Golden Horn on the north, the Bosporus on the east, and the Sea of Marmora on the south. This was the place where the land route from Europe to Asia crossed the sea route from the Aegean to the Black Sea. Whoever controlled the site controlled both commercial and military traffic going east and west, north and south. As long as the crossing could be held, Rome's eastern, and richest, domains were protected from invasion from the north.

The new capital was officially "founded" on November 4, 326, at an astrologically auspicious time with the sun in Sagittarius and Cancer ruling the hour. At this time, only the western wall was laid out. Constantine himself, spear in hand, marked out the remaining extent of the city. According to a later legend, his courtiers thought he was incorporating too much ground and asked, "How much further, my Lord?" Constantine replied, "Until he who walks before me stops walking." Work then proceeded apace—some said too quickly, for Constantine subsequently was accused of wasting public funds and shoddy construction. The latter charge, at least, has some substance, for some of the buildings had to be propped up, and others soon had to be reconstructed.

The new city was encompassed by a wall that extended north to south and quadrupled the previous size of the city. In many regards, it was an imitation of Rome. Like Rome, it was built, allegedly, on seven hills, and it had fourteen districts and a forum. In the forum stood a porphyry column of Constantine, nearly one hundred feet tall, which had on top a gold encrusted statue of Constantine with a nail from the true cross embedded in its diadem and a piece of the cross in the orb which he held. In order to emphasize the city's role as the "New Rome," Constantine placed beneath the column the *palladium*, an ancient wooden statue of Athena said to have been brought from Troy to Rome by Aeneas himself, the legendary ancestor of the Romans.

Toward the eastern end of the peninsula, the imperial palace and the 440-yard-long hippodrome (racing course for chariots) adjoined each other, just as the imperial palace and Circus Maximus adjoined in Rome. The city was decorated with monuments removed from other famous sites. In the hippodrome stood the famous serpent column, which had been dedicated at Delphi after the Greek victory over the Persians at Plataea in 479 B.C. Also

LANDMARKS OF CONSTANTINOPLE

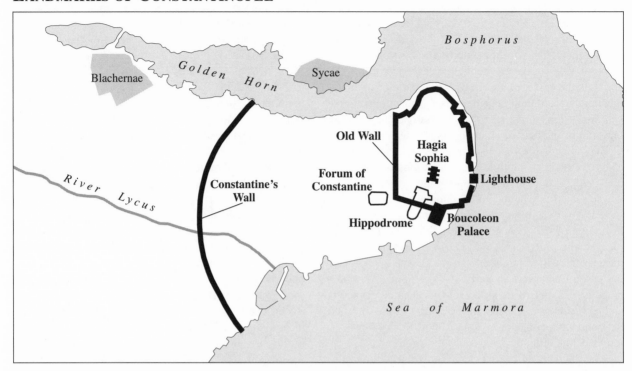

there was the *milarion*, the milestone from which the distances of all roads in the east were measured. Many statues of pagan gods, including the Pythian Apollo, the Samian Hera, and the Olympian Zeus, were removed from their temples and brought to the city, where they could be appreciated for their material beauty rather than their divine power. Indeed, St. Jerome noted in his chronicle under the year 330, "Constantinople is dedicated, while almost all other cities are stripped."

Unlike old Rome, however, Constantinople was a Christian city from the very beginning. Constantine built three churches in honor of Dynamis (power), Irene (peace), and Sophia (wisdom), the last of these with 427 pagan statues aligned in front. At a later time, the last two were combined into a much larger church of St. Sophia (Hagia Sophia). The only pagan temples in the city were those of Castor and Pollux in the hippodrome, and of Tyche, the patron goddess of the city—and even she had a cross incised in her forehead.

Although it was yet incomplete, the new city was officially dedicated on May 11, 330, and endowed with the name "Constantinople," that is, "The City of Constantine." The celebrations lasted forty days, and the pagan writer Zosimus later reported that they included further astrological ceremonies and that the Neoplatonist philosopher Sopatros took part. On the Christian side, processions

left the forum singing *Kyrie eleison*. There were chariot races in the Hippodrome, the Baths of Zeuxippus were officially opened, and commemorative coins were issued—one for the old capital of Rome, showing the wolf and twins, the other for Constantinople, with a depiction of the goddess Victoria.

As for the name of his foundation, Constantine himself stated that he "bestowed upon it an eternal name by the commandment of God." What this name was is uncertain. It was not "Constantinople," although it may have been "New Rome" or "Second Rome," names the city also went under. Yet the "eternal name" may have been *Flora, Anthusa* in Greek, which means "flourishing," and which also had been the sacred, occult name of Rome itself.

For Constantinople to be a true city, moreover, a population was necessary. Settlement by influential individuals was encouraged by promises of land grants and tax remissions. A later legend recounted, "Wishing to populate his city, and in particular to draw Romans to Byzantium, the great Constantine secretly took their signet rings from senators, one from each, and sent them [to fight] against the king of the Persians, who was called Sarbarus." Meanwhile, he moved the families of these men to Constantinople and built houses for them, and on their return from the east they decided to remain there as well. In spite of such efforts, it was not until about ten years later that the city received its own senate. Even this senate had the image, but not the substance, of the Roman one. The new senators gained social rank and prestige, but no political power.

Another thing Constantinople had in common with Rome was an increasingly large population of urban poor who were fed and entertained at imperial expense. The foodstuffs came largely from Egypt, and the entertainment was provided primarily by the chariot races in the hippodrome. The four teams (blues, greens, reds, and whites) each gained large cheering sections. The "blues" and "greens," as the fans of these teams were known, were the most numerous and most vociferous, and given to expressing opinions on matters not merely athletic, but political as well.

In later years, Constantinople justified Constantine's choice of a site. The population expanded rapidly, approaching one million. In the early fifth century, there were 20 public bakeries, 120 private bakeries, 9 public baths, 153 private baths, and 4,388 houses (not including apartment buildings). Constantine's walls were demolished in the year 413, and the famous "land walls" were built, doubling the size of the city. During the barbarian invasions of the late fourth and the fifth century A.D., Constantinople protected the rich provinces of the East, with the end result that the western part of the empire fell, but the eastern section—later known as the Byzantine Empire—survived. Another reason for the fall of the West was that the establishment of a second capital effectively split the empire in two, and left each to fend for itself. Thus, it was no surprise that the more populous, more "civilized," and more financially sound portion survived.

During the same period, Constantinople also appropriated status from old Rome in another way, for the bishops of Constantinople laid claim to first rank among Christian bishops. The result was a festering quarrel with Rome that ultimately led, in 1054, to the "Great Schism," and the development of separate Greek Orthodox churches in the East and Roman Catholic in the West.

In 1204, Constantinople was captured for the first time in its history, by treacherous western crusaders with no stomach for fighting the Muslims. When it was retaken by the Byzantines in 1261 it was but a shadow of its former self. The shrunken Byzantine Empire, now under constant attack by the Turks, held out until 1453, when the city finally fell. The last emperor, appropriately named Constantine XI, died defending the walls and was recognized in death only by his red shoes.

Despite its conquest, the city's importance did not end. Under the name Istanbul, Constantinople became the capital of the Ottoman Empire, and as such continued to be one of the most important cities in the world. It has been said that the building of Constantinople alone would place Constantine among the great figures of history. Given the significance of the city through subsequent ages, few would deny this claim.   —*Ralph W. Mathisen*

ADDITIONAL READING:

Barnes, Timothy D. *Constantine and Eusebius*. Cambridge, Mass.: Harvard University Press, 1981. This biography concentrates particularly on religious issues, incorporating the perspective of Constantine's contemporary biographer, Eusebius of Caesarea, to comment on the various issues that affected Constantine's commitment to creating a Christian empire.

Doerries, H. *Constantine the Great*. Translated by R. H. Bainton. New York: Harper & Row, 1972. Pages 69-76 of this biography provide a useful background for understanding the founding of Constantinople.

Kazhdan, A. "'Constantine Imaginaire': Byzantine Legends of the Ninth Century About Constantine the Great." *Byzantion* 57 (1987): 196-250. This scholarly article presents and evaluates the legends that have become associated with Constantine and the founding of Constantinople.

MacMullen, Ramsay. *Constantine*. New York: Dial Press, 1969. This well-written biography of Constantine by a serious scholar is accessible to the general reader. MacMullen provides an excellent summary of the various aspects of Constantine's life, including the founding of Constantinople.

Ostrogorsky, George. *History of the Byzantine State*. Translated by Joan Hursey. New Brunswick, N.J.: Rutgers University Press, 1957. The author, a leading German authority on the institutional life of the Byzantine Empire, includes a useful, though somewhat dated, bibliography.

SEE ALSO: 332 B.C., Founding of Alexandria; 312, Conversion of Constantine; 532-537, Building of Hagia Sophia.

361-363
FAILURE OF JULIAN'S PAGAN REVIVAL

The failure of Julian's pagan revival represents an attempt to replace Christianity with a government-sponsored pagan renaissance.

DATE: 361-363
LOCALE: The Eastern Roman Empire
CATEGORIES: Government and politics; Religion
KEY FIGURES:
Athanasius (c. 295-373), bishop of Alexandria, 328-373, who was exiled in Julian's reign

Cyril (c. 375-444), bishop of Alexandria, 412-444, who wrote a refutation of Julian's treatise *Against the Galileans*

Iamblichus (c. 250-c. 330), Neoplatonist philosopher who influenced Julian

Julian the Apostate (Flavius Claudius Julianus; 333-363), Roman emperor, 361-363

Maximus (died 370), theurgist who interested Julian in eastern mystery religions

SUMMARY OF EVENT. Julian, known as "the Apostate" for his renunciation of Christianity, was a descendent of Constantine the Great, the emperor who first adopted the faith as the state religion. Educated in the classical traditions of rhetoric and philosophy, Julian found Christianity intellectually and morally lacking; once he became emperor in A.D. 361, he pursued two goals: the rejection of Christianity in favor of classical paganism and the renewal of the empire through a vigorous campaign against the Persians in the east. He failed at both endeavors.

His attempts, however, began well. In 355, Constantius II, Julian's cousin and the ruling emperor, summoned Julian from his studies in Milan to serve as caesar, or junior emperor. At the same time, Julian was married to Constantius' daughter Helena and sent to Gaul. There, Julian defeated an invading force of the Alemanni, then conducted two years of vigorous and successful campaigning against the Germans. In 360, the troops of Julian declared him emperor against Constantius. The two rivals were marching toward one another when Constantius died suddenly, naming Julian as his successor.

Julian, once dutiful in his outward obedience to Christianity, now revealed his allegiance to paganism. Tutored in Neoplatonic philosophy by the noted scholars Iamblichus and Maximus, Julian had developed an advanced, mystical paganism. A monotheist, he regarded paganism as a unified system of worship which needed its moral dimension expanded and strengthened to combat the Christian faith. Julian believed in one, abstract deity of whom the individual gods and goddesses represented various aspects or qualities. The combined influence of Iamblichus' Neoplatonism and Maximus' eastern mystery religions are clearly seen in Julian's own thoughts and writings.

When he became emperor, Julian was able openly to champion paganism against Christianity, which he sincerely regarded as a corrupting influence in society. While carefully avoiding the persecution of Christians, he used legal and political measures to destroy the Church. He removed the privileges extended to the Christian institution by Constantine, granting toleration for all in the late Roman Empire—Jews, Christians, and heretics alike. The clergy were no longer exempt from such civil duties as the

office of *curiale*, or member of a municipal council, a position which was often incompatible with their pastoral responsibilities. Pagan temples were reopened, temple lands were restored, and public cults of the gods were reestablished.

The step that caused the greatest reaction was Julian's edict forbidding Christians to teach literature in the schools. By this measure, the emperor planned, astutely enough, to cut off Christians from a chief source of influence and ultimately to destroy their social position. The rationale behind his edict assumed that those who did not subscribe to the pagan system of values as expressed in classical letters had no right to teach literature because they could not do so with integrity. Julian maintained that Christians who insisted on their own form of worship in their own churches should likewise maintain their own schools. He knew that upper-class Christians would not sacrifice their children's chances for an education that would prepare them for high positions in society by exposing them to makeshift training. It is impossible to know how Julian's strategy would have worked, since he died within two years and his plans never materialized. Attempts of two Christian professors to translate the Scrip-

Some scholars have theorized that a disgruntled Christian sympathizer may have caused the death of Roman emperor Julian the Apostate during a Persian military campaign. (Archive Photos)

tures into classical verse forms and Platonic dialogues proved a waste of time in the face of standard pagan educational fare.

Julian brought other pressure to bear against the Christians. Pagans were preferred in the emperor's service, and cities that cooperated with the restoration of pagan worship were favored. Although Julian never implemented a vicious imperial policy of open persecution, there were petty attacks in some provinces. A punitive action was taken on at least one loyally Christian city, and private acts of vindictiveness were perpetrated by both Christians and pagans.

At the same time, paganism was actively promoted in many ways. Pagan rites were made part of civic celebrations and military ceremonies. Official sacrifices celebrated for the army included lavish and attractive feasts of sacrificial meat. Julian also attempted to provide the pagan revival with a trained elite corps of pagan clergy. He appointed a priest for each city and a high priest of each province; he wrote personally to several of his high ecclesiastics, outlining for them the courses they were to follow. Several of these extant letters show the high ideal and the elevated ethical code that Julian proposed for his revival. His instructions were remarkably parallel to the teachings of Christian morality in that he encouraged his pagan bishops to lead holy and austere lives, to avoid the theater and races, and to organize works of social welfare for the poor and unfortunate. The social welfare program was supplemented by state grants. On one occasion, Julian instructed his pagan high priest of Galatia to spend at least a fifth of a government subsidy on the poor who served the priests and to distribute the rest to strangers and beggars. "For it is a disgrace," wrote Julian, "that no Jew is a beggar, and the impious Galileans feed our people in addition to their own, whereas ours manifestly lack assistance from us." The emperor insisted that pagans must be taught to subscribe to such services and benefits to humanity.

Julian was deeply interested in classical learning and literature. His own writings include orations, letters, satires, and pagan hymns. His most famous piece, the satire "Against the Galileans," has not survived, but is known from the refutation written by Cyril, bishop of Alexandria.

It is possible that Julian's campaign against Persia was motivated partly by his desire to find a location outside the Christian Roman orbit where his pagan renaissance might have a better chance of success. At any rate, when Julian met his death on his Persian campaign in 363, his pagan revival ended with him. It is possible that Julian may have been mortally wounded by one of his own soldiers, for many of them deeply resented his paganism. While sincere, Julian apparently did not understand the hold of

Christianity on the popular mind and imagination. His own religion was largely negative, a revulsion against what he saw as a barbarism and the loss of classical values; his pagan revival was chiefly an attempt to retain the Hellenistic cultural heritage. His efforts were further hampered by the fact that his personal religion was esoteric and appeared bizarre to his contemporaries. If Julian's attempt proved anything, it showed that the day of paganism as a formative cultural influence was past, although pockets of paganism remained in both the East and West for centuries.

—*Mary Evelyn Jegen, updated by Michael Witkoski*

ADDITIONAL READING:

Athanassiadi-Fowden, Polymnia. *Julian and Hellenism: An Intellectual Biography*. Oxford: Clarendon Press, 1981. An examination of Julian's thought as it was influenced by the Greek experience and how he wished to extend that heritage throughout the empire.

Head, Constance. *The Emperor Julian*. Boston: Twayne, 1976. A good, basic introduction to the man and his times.

Ricciotti, Guiseppe. *Julian the Apostate*. Translated by M. Joseph Costelloe. Milwaukee: Bruce Publishing Company, 1959. Using contemporary sources, this study provides a good examination of how Julian was perceived during his own times and the impact, or lack of, of his pagan revival.

Smith, Roland. *Julian's Gods: Religion and Philosophy in the Thought and Action of Julian the Apostate*. New York: Routledge, 1995. An ambitious review of Julian's career in terms of his religious and philosophical influences.

Vidal, Gore. *Julian*. New York: Ballantine, 1986. First published in 1964, this novel remains the finest re-creation of Julian and his times. Deeply and at times passionately informed on the religious and philosophical debates of the age.

SEE ALSO: 312, Conversion of Constantine; 313-395, Inception of the Church-State Problem; 380-392, Theodosius' Edicts Promote Christian Orthodoxy.

378
BATTLE OF ADRIANOPLE

The Battle of Adrianople marks the first time that tribal invaders from outside Rome's borders manage to inflict a full-fledged defeat on the Roman army and gain permission to enter the Roman Empire as refugees.
DATE: August 9, 378
LOCALE: Adrianople

CATEGORY: Wars, uprisings, and civil unrest
KEY FIGURES:
Fritigern, leader of the Visigoths
Gratian (359-383), Roman emperor in the West, 367-383
Lupicinus, Roman official of the province of Moesia
Sebastian, commander of the Roman infantry
Valens (c. 328-378), Roman emperor in the East, 364-378
SUMMARY OF EVENT. The group that historians eventually termed the Visigoths (their own name for themselves was "the Tervingi") first came into contact with the Roman Empire because the Huns, a group of powerful Asian nomads, were pushing them westward. The Goths were less an ethnically homogeneous nation than an armed group comprising various people, largely Germanic in origin but containing people from other backgrounds as well. At first, the Goths had contracted to serve in the imperial armies, but had accumulated many grievances against the Romans and had begun to rebel.

For almost two years, rebellious Visigoths had spread death and destruction throughout the Roman provinces that made up the area of modern Bulgaria. The emperor Valens was in residence at Antioch pursuing his campaign against the Persians, and it was there in A.D. 376 that he learned of the disastrous breakdown of his agreement with the Visigoths. Without undue haste, he arranged a truce with Persia so that he might deal with the Germanic threat; it was not until April, 378, that he departed for Constantinople. Dissatisfied with the efforts of his commander Trajan against the Visigoths, he replaced him with a capable officer recently arrived from the West, Sebastian by name, who had a distinguished military record. To him, Valens entrusted a selected infantry force which Sebastian quickly whipped into shape and then led off toward the troubled provinces. Sebastian experienced no difficulty in clearing the countryside of the roving bands of marauders, but he was not prepared for a major engagement. With additional troops, Valens himself left his headquarters near Constantinople at the end of June and advanced toward Adrianople to join his general in preparation for a decisive blow.

Fritigern, the Visigothic leader, became alarmed. He realized that his scattered countrymen, impeded by the presence of their wives, children, and possessions, were highly vulnerable. They were more like a group of refugees on the move than an army. Fritigern therefore ordered his people to concentrate near Cabyle, and at the same time, he sent out agents to enlist auxiliaries for the impending clash with the Romans. Bands of Huns and Alans from beyond the Danube River joined him, and a wandering contingent of Ostrogothic cavalry under the ethnic Alans Alatheus and Saphrax promised to do the same. Fritigern had already recruited runaway slaves and a variety of discontented Roman subjects, and while these additions to his fighting force swelled his numerical strength, the diversity of their interests and their undisciplined nature placed heavy demands on his leadership. Food supplies were uncertain since the Germans were living off the countryside, and time worked against them.

Unfortunately for the Romans, Emperor Valens threw away his advantages. Reinforcements from the West led by his nephew, the co-emperor Gratian, were marching eastward; a small advance unit reached Adrianople about August 7, while Valens and his officers were discussing strategy. Some urged caution and delay until the Western army arrived. Sebastian and others, however, favored an immediate attack, and their advice confirmed Valens' own inclination. He had been incorrectly informed that the Visigoths numbered only ten thousand men. No figures are available about the numerical strength of either side, but the Roman army probably totaled at least twenty thousand. At the same time, unknown to Valens, the Goths actually outnumbered the Romans.

Possibly Valens was also motivated in his decision by jealousy. Gratian had shortly before achieved a notable victory over the Germans in the West, a feat which Valens seems to have desired to emulate. Gratian was vastly preferred by the majority of the Roman people because he was an orthodox, Catholic Christian whereas Valens was an Arian heretic. Ironically, the Goths were also Arian Christians, having been converted a generation before by the heroic Gothic missionary Ulfilas, so Valens was in religious communion with the very barbarians who opposed him in battle. His religious differences with Gratian made Valens less inclined to cooperate. To wait for the Gallic reinforcements would mean sharing the glory of victory rather than enjoying it alone. Whatever the reason, Valens decided on an immediate offensive.

While these councils were being held, Fritigern sent an Arian Christian priest as an envoy to negotiate with Valens. The envoy promised peace in return for a guarantee of land in Thrace for the Visigoths to settle upon as their own, together with an adequate food supply. In effect, this had been Valens' original agreement with the Goths two years earlier, so that Fritigern asked little more than what had been previously conceded. Yet Valens rejected any talk of a truce or treaty. Perhaps he was convinced that the rebellious depredations of the Germans could not be left unpunished. Perhaps, too, he doubted Fritigern's sincerity, for the Visigothic leader was awaiting the arrival of the Gothic cavalry of Alatheus and may have been stalling for time.

Early on the morning of August 9, 378, the Romans broke camp and advanced eight miles out from Adrianople to within sight of the Visigoths. Fritigern had drawn up his forces in a defensive position with his wagon train forming a circle enclosing his noncombatants and supplies. Tired from their morning's march, the Roman soldiers also suffered from the summer heat as well as from the smoke and heat of the fires that the Visigoths set in the surrounding fields to confuse and discomfit them. A second offer of negotiations from Fritigern induced Valens to dispatch one of his officers toward the Visigothic camp for a consultation. Before the officer could reach the camp, some of the Roman troops impetuously opened the attack.

The details of the battle cannot be reconstructed accurately. The Gothic army, largely cavalry, overwhelmed the Roman infantry, who evidently broke under the shock and the superior numbers of the Visigoths. By nightfall, scarcely one-third of the Romans survived. Among the slain were Valens and Sebastian. The emperor's body was never recovered. Two stories circulated about his death: one that he had been killed by an arrow while fleeing in a band of common soldiers, the other that he had been carried wounded into a farmhouse that the Visigoths destroyed by fire. not knowing the identity of the Romans within who refused to surrender.

Fritigern's victory at Adrianople did not solve his problem. Even with numerical superiority, the Visigoths could not follow up their success properly because they lacked the equipment and knowledge needed to conduct siege operations. As a result, they could not strike at the towns where Roman wealth and power were concentrated. Two days after the battle, they tried to take Adrianople itself, but had to abandon this vain effort. They soon made their way southward and reached the outskirts of Constantinople before retiring.

Essentially, the Visigoths desired land on which to settle and make new homes for themselves, but they could attain their objective only by coming to terms with the Roman authorities. Shrewdly understanding this aim, Theodosius, the new emperor of the East, combined diplomacy with military pressure and subdued the barbarians with a treaty in 382. They received what they desired and also the right to rule themselves. They agreed to pay an annual tribute in return for peace and guaranteed they would serve in the Roman army whenever called upon to do so.

Valens' Arianism made him hated by Catholic historians; thus the calamitous nature of his loss at Adrianople has perhaps been exaggerated in the historical record. Yet it cannot be denied that there were two significant results of the Battle of Adrianople. First, the Visigoths became the first Germanic tribe to win territory within the Roman Empire and a degree of autonomy that placed them generally beyond the government's control. This situation portended the future dismemberment of the Roman Empire.

Second, the destruction of a Roman army on its own soil demonstrated the deterioration of the once-powerful legions, thereby encouraging the Visigoths themselves and later other Germanic tribes to risk further campaigns against Rome. The period of the peaceful penetration of the Roman Empire by the Germans thus came to an end, and the age of invasions by conquest and force began on the battlefield of Adrianople.

—Raymond H. Schmandt, updated by Nicholas Birns

ADDITIONAL READING:

Ammianus Marcellinus. *The Later Roman Empire*. Selected and translated by Walter Hamilton. New York: Penguin, 1986. The major primary source of knowledge about the battle of Adrianople. Of necessity, it emphasizes the Roman perspective and is not sympathetic to Valens.

Gibbon, Edward. *History of the Decline and Fall of the Roman Empire*. Reprint. New York: AMS Press, 1974. This work by the great eighteenth century British historian places Adrianople within a general account of the Roman Empire's collapse. Gibbon's account is weak on Gothic history, for which readers should consult works by P. J. Heather and Herwig Wolfram below.

Grant, Michael. *The Fall of the Roman Empire*. London: Weidenfeld & Nicolson, 1990. Grant reevaluates whether Adrianople constituted a crucial loss for the Roman Empire.

Heather, P. J. *Goths and Romans, 332-489*. New York: Oxford University Press, 1991. Provides a close examination of Gothic history during the migration period.

Williams, Stephen, and Gerard Friell. *Theodosius: The Empire at Bay*. London: Batsford, 1994. A provocative and detailed account of the battle of Adrianople and its aftermath.

Wolfram, Herwig. *History of the Goths*. Berkeley: University of California Press, 1988. Contains several detailed pages on Adrianople and provides a good explanation of the battle within the context of Gothic history.

SEE ALSO: 410, Gothic Armies Sack Rome; 445-453, Invasions of Attila the Hun; 476, "Fall" of Rome; 533-553, Justinian's Wars Against the Vandals, Ostrogoths, and Visigoths.

380-392
THEODOSIUS' EDICTS PROMOTE CHRISTIAN ORTHODOXY

Theodosius' edicts promote Christian orthodoxy, establishing Nicene Christianity as the state religion of the Roman Empire.

DATE: 380-392

LOCALE: The Roman Empire

CATEGORIES: Government and politics; Religion

KEY FIGURES:

Ambrose (c. 339-397), bishop of Milan, 374-397

Damasus I (c. 304-384), bishop of Rome, 366-384

Gratian (359-383), Roman emperor in the West, 375-383

Theodosius the Great (346-395), Roman emperor in the East, 379-395, sole ruler, 392-395

SUMMARY OF EVENT. In the late fourth century A.D., government policies made one form of Christianity a mainstay of a troubled Roman Empire. The reign of Theodosius brought to a close the turbulent controversy over the nature of the Trinity. Basically the question revolved around the issue of relationships within the Godhead. Arius had said that the Son and the Holy Ghost, because not fully spirit and eternal, were inferior to the Father, whereas the bishops assembled in the first ecumenical council at Nicaea in 325 had affirmed the equality of Son and Father. In succeeding years, many of these bishops also agreed that the Holy Ghost shared essential deity with the Father and the Son. Argument raged throughout the empire for years, aggravated by religious splits among the successors of Constantine. After the death of Jovian in A.D. 364, the Roman Empire was again divided politically, this time between Valentinian (364-375) in the West and his brother Valens (364-378) in the East. The Western emperor was little inclined toward interfering in Church affairs, but in the East, Valens adopted a modified form of Arianism and harassed Christians who adhered to the Nicene formula. Gratian, succeeding his father Valentinian, refused to become *pontifex maximus*, an imperial title since 12 B.C., and in 382 ordered the statue of Victory removed from the Senate House in Rome, the citadel of conservatism and paganism. In general he supported the Nicene faith and began to place both heretics and pagans under civil penalties. In 382 and 384, delegations of senators pleaded for the traditional freedom to allow all persons to seek "the Divine Mystery" (in the words of Symmachus) in their own way. Damasus and Ambrose opposed the petitions and the government remained firm.

When Valens was killed by the invading Goths at Adrianople in 378, Gratian appointed Theodosius to succeed him. Theodosius, of Iberian family origin and whose father (*comes*, or "Count," Theodosius) had been a distinguished general, was a devout adherent of the Nicene views espoused by most Western bishops. At the same time a Nicene group was emerging in the East, and Theodosius evidently felt the time was ripe for his own vigorous participation in the controversy among the Christians.

He issued his edict of February 27, 380, from Thessa-lonica (Saloniki), one month after baptism at the hands of the Nicene bishop of the city and recovery from illness. It has come to be known as *Cunctos Populos* from its opening words. The text of the edict is translated as follows: "It is our pleasure that all the nations which are governed by our clemency and moderation should steadfastly adhere to the religion which was taught by St. Peter to the Romans; which faithful tradition has preserved; and which is now professed by the pontiff Damasus and by Peter, Bishop of Alexandria, a man of apostolic holiness." In accordance with the teaching of the Gospel and of the early apostles, he enjoined belief in the sole deity of the Father, the Son, and the Holy Ghost, "under an equal majesty and a pious Trinity." Only followers of this doctrine could assume the title of "Catholic Christians"; all other were judged extravagant madmen, and were branded with the "infamous title of heretics." Their conventicles should no longer be called churches and they could expect to suffer the penalties which the emperor, under divine guidance, would deem justifiable (Theodosian Code 16.1.2). By imperial edict, orthodox ("correct") Christianity was established, and deviationists were threatened with penalties. In 381, the government convened the second ecumenical council at Constantinople. It reissued the Nicene Creed and the emperor gave the force of civil law to the conciliar canons.

Arianism faded away inside the empire, but missionaries spread it among the Germans. After A.D. 400, Visigoths settled in southern Gaul and Spain, Ostrogoths in Italy, and Vandals in North Africa. Religious hostility exacerbated the tensions between the heretical invaders and the mostly Nicene natives.

Although Theodosius took a rigid attitude toward Christian heretics, he allowed considerable latitude to non-Christians during the first twelve years of his reign. In 391, however, two edicts were issued against the pagans, and the following year a more comprehensive law was promulgated. In this decree, which came to be known as *Nullus Omnino*, he ordered that no one was to kill innocent victims in the worship of idols, nor was anyone henceforth permitted to venerate *lares*, *genii*, or *penates*. The reading of entrails was likewise forbidden, and he encouraged informers to reveal infractions of the law. Idol worship was ridiculed as a violation of true religion. Houses where pagan rites were conducted were to be confiscated, and a fine of twenty-five pounds in gold was to be imposed on all who sacrificed to idols or circumvented the law. The edict concluded with threats against officials who might be lax in enforcing this law (Theodosian Code 16.10.12).

Theodosius' solicitude for Christianity was not confined to the promulgation of these two edicts. By *Nullus Haereticis* in 381, he ordered that there be "no place left to the heretics for celebrating the mysteries of their faith," and he went on to assign the name Catholic only to those who believed in the Trinity. Heretics were forbidden to conduct assemblies within the limits of towns. During the next two years, the emperor set aside wills of apostate Christians, and he denied them the rights of inheritance. Likewise his attitude toward pagans resulted in the laws of 391, which prohibited sacrifices and the visiting of shrines. Possibly as a result of these laws the great temple to Serapis in Alexandria was destroyed about 391.

The pretender Magnus Maximus eliminated Gratian in 383, but Theodosius took revenge. While in Italy from 388 to 391, he had several disputes with Ambrose, the West's most prominent bishop. In 390, Ambrose refused to allow the emperor to receive communion until he accepted responsibility and did penance for the massacre of civilians at Thessalonica by imperial troops. Theodosius also ended the pagan Olympic Games (considered immoral because participants competed naked); those held in 392 were the last to be staged until the modern Olympic Games were revived in 1896. Valentinian II, brother of Gratian, was murdered or committed suicide in 392, but Theodosius eliminated the pretender Eugenius and the Frankish general Arbogast. He was the last emperor to rule the entire Roman Empire.

Theodosius' policies went beyond those of Constantine, who had been content to legalize Christianity and endow the Church with wealth, buildings, and legal privileges. Damasus and Ambrose convinced Gratian and Theodosius that diversity in belief was wrong now that the truth was known. Theodosius ended Rome's traditional religious toleration when he decreed the Nicene-Catholic form of Christianity to be the official religion of the state and made liable to the harsh penalties of the law all who did not accept it. This established two enduring principles: religious persecution and the state church. Temples of the old gods were reconsecrated to the Christian God or fell into disrepair; Christian mobs destroyed others in riots their bishops encouraged and the government permitted. Imperial religious processions, occasions of display to the people, were henceforth only to Christian basilicas. For centuries, Europe regarded diversity as synonymous with disunity. Accepting the proposition that political and social unity required religious uniformity, governments enforced such uniformity through a state church. The policy began to break down with the Edict of Nantes in France in 1598, but the constitutional separation of church and state established in the United States two centuries later constituted the clearest rejection of the Theodosian policy.

—Carl A. Volz, updated by Thomas H. Watkins

ADDITIONAL READING:

Barnes, T. D. "Religion and Society in the Age of Theodosius." In *Grace, Politics and Desire: Essays on Augustine*, edited by H. A. Maynell. Calgary: University of Calgary Press, 1990. Judicious, traditional scholarship.

Brown, P. *Power and Persuasion in Late Antiquity: Toward a Christian Empire*. Madison: University of Wisconsin Press, 1992. Bishops, some with access to the emperors, became the elite of society as Christianity superseded paganism.

Cochrane, C. N. *Christianity and Classical Culture*. Rev. ed. Oxford: Oxford University Press, 1944. An older study that contains a masterful summary of the topic. Chapters 5-9 argue that Theodosius completed the revolution begun by Constantine.

Jones, A. H. M. *The Later Roman Empire, 284-602*. Oxford: Blackwell, 1964. Church affairs are analyzed in the broad context of an administrative history.

King, N. Q. *The Emperor Theodosius and the Establishment of Christianity*. Philadelphia: Westminster Press, 1960. Traditional interpretation of Theodosius' role in advancing the Christian faith.

Liebeschuetz, J. H. W. G. *Continuity and Change in Roman Religion*. Oxford: Clarendon Press, 1979. Although ending with Constantine, this study puts Christianity in the context of twelve centuries of Roman religion and religious policies.

McLynn, N. B. *Ambrose of Milan: Church and Court in a Christian Capital*. Berkeley: University of California Press, 1994. Chapters 3 and 7 analyze the Altar of Victory controversy, the relationship between Ambrose (as Nathan) and Theodosius (as David) and reinterpret the events of 390-391.

Markus, R. *The End of Ancient Christianity*. Cambridge: Cambridge University Press, 1990. Excellent study of the revolutionary redefinition of society and individuals in the period 380-430, although it contains little on Theodosius and church-state relations.

SEE ALSO: 313-395, Inception of the Church-State Problem; 325, The Nicene Creed; 361-363, Failure of Julian's Pagan Revival; 378, Battle of Adrianople; 428-431, The Nestorian Controversy.

410
GOTHIC ARMIES SACK ROME

Gothic armies sack Rome and reveal the crisis afflicting the Roman Empire in the West, shattering the myth of Rome's invincibility and security.

DATE: August 24-26, 410
LOCALE: Rome
CATEGORY: Wars, uprisings, and civil unrest
KEY FIGURES:
Alaric (c. 370-410), leader of the Visigoths, 395-410
Ataulf (Atawulf; died 415), brother-in-law of Alaric and his successor as Gothic leader
Saint Augustine (354-430), bishop of Hippo, 395-430, and author of the *City of God*, in which he refuted charges that Christianity was responsible for the decline of Rome
Honorius (384-423), Roman emperor in the West, 395-423
Jerome (c. 340-420), scriptural scholar who popularized the idea that the sack of Rome meant the destruction of civilization
Flavius Stilicho (c. 360-408), Vandal general in control of Rome as regent for Honorius, 395-408

SUMMARY OF EVENT. When Emperor Theodosius died in A.D. 395, the breakup of the Roman Empire into eastern and western halves was inevitable. From that time onward, the civil rulers in the West were under the power of barbarian leaders. The sack of Rome by the Visigoths under Alaric in 410 should be seen as one episode in the final stages of the disintegration of the united Empire.

Theodosius' successors were his sons: eighteen-year-old Arcadius, who was designated Augustus in the East; and Honorius, a mentally impaired child of eleven who was designated Augustus in the West. Actual rule in the West was in the hands of the army under the leadership of a Vandal, Flavius Stilicho, chosen by Theodosius as regent for Honorius.

Alaric, a member of the Balth dynasty of Gothic kings and a leader of the Visigothic allies of the Romans, took advantage of the death of Theodosius to make a bid for power in the Balkans and southern Greece. Stilicho tried to stop Alaric in the North, but was deflected by an order from Arcadius to lead his army back to Constantinople. Later, Stilicho managed to come to terms with Alaric in Greece. Alaric and his Goths settled in Epirus, and Alaric had the satisfaction of receiving the title *Magister Militum*, or "Master of the Soldiers," from the Eastern court. This title was tantamount to official recognition as a military dictator.

The Visigoths have often been pictured in popular lore and culture as an aggressive, war-hungry group of barbarian invaders. Modern historians, however, have stressed the one-sidedness of this view. Far more than invaders, the Goths were refugees fleeing the turmoil in their homelands, which were being invaded by waves of nomads from the east. The Goths were not an ethnically homogeneous group; they were a collection of warriors and their dependents who were largely Germanic but included Alan and Sarmatian elements as well. By the time Alaric became Visigothic leader, the Goths had lived within Roman borders for a generation. They were no longer fully "barbarians"; they were far more interested in gaining a piece of Roman prosperity than in destroying the empire by warfare and looting. The Visigoths were Christians, although they adhered to the Arian heresy. Despite their acculturation into Roman ways, however, the Goths still constituted a large group on the move, hungry and skilled at fighting. Their management presented a formidable challenge to Stilicho and the other Roman authorities.

In 401, Alaric first invaded Italy but was forced to withdraw by Stilicho. Stilicho checked a similar attempt in 403. For a time, Alaric joined forces with Stilicho to help him in taking Illyricum, which Stilicho was attempting to restore to Honorius. News of an uprising in Gaul, however, caused Alaric to sense an opportunity for advancing his own cause. He hurried north, demanded employment for his troops, and succeeded in obtaining four thousand pounds of gold from the senate. Alaric's adviser in this negotiation was Stilicho, who soon after, in 408, was killed by enemies in court who thought he was plotting to make his own grandchild emperor. Stilicho's murder was an imprudent action accompanied by an antibarbarian purge in which soldiers, along with their wives and children, were brutally murdered. The result was that barbarian troops defected to Alaric.

With Stilicho out of the way, Italy was defenseless, and Alaric had his opportunity to strike at the heart of the Western Empire. He demanded lands and supplies for his men. Honorius refused and barricaded himself at Ravenna, northeast of Rome. In 408, Alaric and his Goths marched on Rome, but were bought off. They marched on Rome again in 409, and Alaric set up a rival emperor, Priscus Attalus. Having secured supporting troops from the Eastern Empire, however, Honorius refused to capitulate. Indeed, Honorius sought to counter Alaric by setting up Sarus, a Gothic bandit, as a rival candidate for chieftain of the Goths, and internal dissension between Alaric and his puppet Attalus led to the latter's deposition.

Finally, on August 24, 410, Alaric and some forty thousand Goths seized Rome and plundered it for three days. The actual physical destruction was relatively slight, but the impression on contemporaries was shattering. The event marked the first time in more than eight hundred years that Rome had been taken by an enemy. It appeared that an era or even a civilization had come to an end. When the news reached Bethlehem in Palestine, the scriptural scholar Jerome wrote that all humanity was included in the ruins of Rome. Augustine was moved by the event to write his great masterpiece of political and historical theory, the *City of God*, in which he answered those who charged that Christianity was the cause of Rome's decline.

After his attack on Rome, in which he took Honorius' sister Galla Placidia as one of his own prizes, Alaric attempted to invade Africa, the granary of Italy. This invasion failed when his ships were wrecked in a storm. Alaric died soon after and was buried in the Busento River, near modern Cosenza, by followers who were killed thereafter to prevent anyone from knowing the exact location of the body and desecrating the remains.

If Alaric had any consistent policy, it seems to have been the acquisition of lands in the Roman Empire, preferably in Italy, where his people might settle. In this attempt, he failed. According to Jordanes, historian of the Goths, another aim of Alaric was the union of the Goths and the Romans as a single people. In this, Alaric had unrealistic expectations in terms of his own time, although later generations saw the assimilation of the two peoples in Spain and southern Gaul. Alaric's successor, his brother-in-law Ataulf, married Honorius' sister, Galla Placidia, and thus cemented the terms of peaceful coexistence between Goths and Romans. Ataulf led the Goths into Gaul and from there into Spain, where he died in 415. The next Visigoth leader, Wallia, negotiated with the Romans and was given lands in southern Aquitania, in Gaul, in 418. Spasmodic struggles between Goths and Romans continued for another sixty years, but after 477, with the total collapse of Roman authority in the West, the Goths' sovereignty in southern Gaul and Spain—the so-called kingdom of Toulouse—was assured.

—*Mary Evelyn Jegen, updated by Nicholas Birns*

ADDITIONAL READING:

Grant, Michael. *The Fall of the Roman Empire*. London: Weidenfeld, 1990. Good discussion of Honorius' relationships with Flavius Stilicho and Alaric.

Heather, P. J. *Goths and Romans, 332-489*. New York: Oxford University Press, 1991. In contrast to Wolfram below, Heather seeks to diminish the emphasis on Alaric's belonging to the Balth dynasty of Gothic rulers.

Herrin, Judith. *The Formation of Christendom*. Princeton, N.J.: Princeton University Press, 1987. Emphasizes Alaric as a historical participant in fifth century Roman politics.

O'Flynn, John M. *Generalissimos of the Western Roman Empire*. Edmonton: University of Alberta Press, 1983. The definitive source on Stilicho.

Paulus Orosius. *The Seven Books of History Against the Pagans*. Translated by Roy J. Deferrari. Washington, D.C.: Catholic University of America Press, 1964. This fifth century historian established the theme of Alaric's sack as the calamitous end of Roman greatness.

Wolfram, Herwig. *History of the Goths*. Berkeley: University of California Press, 1988. A detailed and well-researched account of the Gothic migrations.

SEE ALSO: 378, Battle of Adrianople; 445-453, Invasions of Attila the Hun; 476, "Fall" of Rome; 533-553, Justinian's Wars Against the Vandals, Ostrogoths, and Visigoths.

413-426
AUGUSTINE WRITES THE CITY OF GOD

Augustine writes the City of God, *a key work that embodies the transformation from the humanistic, world-centered viewpoint of classical thought to the God-centered concept of eternity that characterizes the Christian Middle Ages.*

DATE: 413-426

LOCALE: Hippo Regius in North Africa

CATEGORIES: Cultural and intellectual history; Religion

KEY FIGURES:

Alaric (c. 370-410), leader of the Visigoths, 395-410

Saint Augustine (354-430), bishop of Hippo, 395-430

Honorius (384-423), Roman emperor in the West, 395-423

Marcellinus, a friend of Augustine who suggested writing the book

SUMMARY OF EVENT. Under their chieftain Alaric, the barbarian Visigoths captured the city of Rome in August, A.D. 410. For almost eight hundred years, Rome had escaped the ravages of invaders, but at last the Germans succeeded where even Hannibal's military genius had failed. The event was not totally unexpected. For two years, the Visigoths had been tramping practically at will through central Italy. In Ravenna, then the capital of the western half of the Roman Empire, the timorous Emperor Honorius cowered in fright, having himself ordered the murder of Stilicho, the general who might have delivered Italy from the barbarian menace. When Innocent I, the bishop of Rome, came to beg military assistance for his flock, Ravenna had nothing to offer.

The physical damage was relatively light, but the psychological shock was great. If the Eternal City was no longer safe, doom seemed to threaten civilization itself. Jerome, far off in his murky cave in Bethlehem, reacted typically: he poured out his heart in lamentation to one of his correspondents, prophesying the imminent end of the world. For Rome was the ideological heart of all that was mighty and worthwhile in secular life and culture.

How could the disaster be explained? One interpretation that quickly made itself heard traced Rome's misfortune to the displeasure of the ancient deities who had stood guard over the city during its long history before being displaced by the Christian God. Scarcely a generation had passed since Emperor Theodosius I had proscribed the ancient cults and declared Christianity to be the Roman Empire's official faith. Mars, Jupiter, and the old pantheon had been discarded; and now they were having their revenge. It was not the first time that Christianity had been blamed for calamities of one sort or another. The writings of Tertullian, Cyprian of Carthage, and Arnobius of Sicca testify to similar accusations during the preceding centuries, and the Church Fathers had striven to counter the charges.

One of the last significant groups of Romans still holding fast to the old paganism, privately, was an educated cultured elite, men of good lives and sound learning who grasped the true grandeur of the empire and its civilization, and who formed an influential body of conservative public opinion that continually looked back nostalgically to "the good old days." These men felt the fall of Rome acutely, and the last gasp of dying paganism was their protest against the new religion which they held responsible for the decay that was everywhere evident. Christianity to these conservative minds seemed completely incompatible with the best interests of the state and its culture. The events of 410, to them, unmistakably confirmed their diagnosis.

This sentiment was voiced forcefully among the refugees from Rome who had fled to the security of North Africa when the Visigoths approached. Volusianus, the imperial proconsul in the province, shared their views. When his friend Marcellinus tried to convert him to Christianity, Volusianus let it be known that his reluctance stemmed not from doctrine but from cultural and historical reasons. This Marcellinus, another imperial official but a fervent Christian, had been sent to North Africa by Emperor Honorius for the purpose of mediating between orthodox Christians and Donatist heretics. He had become a close friend of the bishop of Hippo Regius, Augustine, and he turned to him for help in answering Volusianus' objections. As a result, Augustine was alerted to the larger issue of the relations between Christianity and Rome within the newest context of the barbarian menace. With Marcellinus urging him on, he decided to defend his faith in the volume entitle the *City of God*, which he began in 413 and finished in twenty-two books thirteen years later. When Marcellinus approached him, Augustine already enjoyed a reputation as one of the most penetrating of Christian thinkers. More than half his numerous books, many sermons, and hundreds of letters had already been written. Most of this material sprang from an immedi-

ate challenge. Always an unsystematic, intuitive thinker, Augustine wrote best when responding to an immediate problem. Proof of his greatness is the fact that his responses generally had much more than a circumstantial value or application; ephemeral circumstances elicited from him immortal replies. This was certainly true of the *City of God*.

Augustine started with the intention of answering the current charge against Christianity, but he soon gave up such a limited plan and turned that project over to the Spanish priest Orosius who stopped by for a visit and an exchange of ideas in 414. Augustine delegated to him the purely historical task. As Orosius related in his *Seven Books Against the Pagans*, Augustine had directed him to "discover from all the available data of histories and annals whatever instances past ages have afforded of the burdens of war, the ravages of disease, the horrors of famine, of terrible earthquakes, extraordinary floods, dreadful eruptions of fire, thunderbolts and hailstorms, and also instances of the cruel miseries caused by parricides and disgusting crimes." This sort of information would demonstrate how miserable the world had actually been under the tutelage of the old gods. With Orosius composing this

Although influenced in childhood by his pious mother, Saint Augustine did not turn to Christianity and theological endeavors until he was in his thirties. (Archive Photos)

sort of book, Augustine felt justified in devoting his energies to a more philosophical approach to the subject.

For himself, Augustine decided to take up the vaster burden of interpreting the whole of human history in the light of the principles of Christian theology. He would write not history, but a philosophy or a theology of history. He desired to show that everything had its place in the divine plan. Himself one of the greatest of Romans, he labored to reconcile Roman culture with Christianity, not to drive them apart. His vehicle was an analogy that he apparently found in the writings of another African, the Donatist intellectual Tyconius: the scheme of the organization of all people and human events into two vast groups, the City of God and the Worldly City, the society of those who lived in conformity with divine law, and the society of those who did not.

It is difficult to re-create the precise stages of composition and evolution of Augustine's thought during the thirteen years that he wrote the *City of God.* As a bishop in an unsettled time for the Christian church, he had many preoccupations and duties that kept him from devoting full attention to this particular work. The completed treatise, which consists of twenty-two books, has two major compositional parts. The first, comprising books 1-10, primarily defends Christianity and counters pagan accusations, especially relating to the recent attack on Rome. The second part, books 11-22, presents Augustine's new view of history in Christian terms. He sees history as a progressive course leading from Creation to the ultimate end in the city of God.

Using all the secular learning at his disposal, Augustine wrote a theological tract of universal value, creating an ideology which became a satisfactory substitute for the classical *polis.* Still regarded as one of the greatest books of Western civilization, it has taken a remarkable share in the shaping of Christendom.

—*Raymond H. Schmandt, updated by Karen Gould*

ADDITIONAL READING:

Brown, Peter. *Augustine of Hippo.* Berkeley: University of California Press, 1967. The most complete biography of Augustine by a scholar with a thorough knowledge of Christianity in late antique culture. The *City of God* is discussed in several chapters within the context of Augustine's life.

Figgis, John Neville. *The Political Aspects of St. Augustine's "City of God."* Gloucester, Mass.: Peter Smith, 1963. A short book that examines the political ideas in the *City of God.* Figgis also traces the influences of Augustine's statements on politics in Western culture to the present.

Markus, R. A. *Saeculum: History and Society in the*

Theology of St. Augustine. Cambridge, England: Cambridge University Press, 1970. A study that primarily analyzes Augustine's concept of history, but also looks at Augustine's views on politics and society within the framework of his historical schema.

Van der Meer, F. *Augustine the Bishop.* London: Sheed and Ward, 1961. Since Augustine composed the *City of God* while he was bishop of Hippo, this book is valuable in showing the activities in which he was engaged while he was writing this important work.

Van Oort, Johannes. *Jerusalem and Babylon: A Study into Augustine's "City of God" and the Sources of His Doctrine of the Two Cities.* Leiden, the Netherlands: E. J. Brill, 1991. A complete study of the *City of God* from multiple standpoints: compositional structure, the meaning of the two cities, its character as an apologetic and theological work, and the sources of Augustine's ideas.

Versfeld, Marthinus. *A Guide to "The City of God."* London: Sheed and Ward, 1958. A study of the second part of Augustine's *City of God* (books 11-22), which the author analyzes from the perspective of moral philosophy.

SEE ALSO: 450-425 B.C., History Develops as Scholarly Discipline; 200, Christian Apologists Develop Concept of Theology; 313-395, Inception of the Church-State Problem; 410, Gothic Armies Sack Rome.

428-431
THE NESTORIAN CONTROVERSY

The Nestorian controversy heralds the beginning of a long series of political and theological controversies concerning the divine and human natures of Christ.
DATE: 428-431
LOCALE: Antioch, Syria, and Alexandria, Egypt
CATEGORIES: Government and politics; Religion
KEY FIGURES:
Celestine I (died 432), Roman Catholic pope, 422-432
Cyril (c. 375-444), bishop of Alexandria, 412-444
Nestorius (died c. 451), bishop of Constantinople,
    428-431
Theodosius II (401-450), Roman emperor in the East,
    408-450
SUMMARY OF EVENT. In the early 400's, there were two rival theological schools of thought concerning Jesus Christ. The theologians in Alexandria in Egypt, led by Cyril of Alexandria, held that Jesus was the eternal Word of God, living under the conditions of humanity. The other school, based in Antioch, in Syria, believed that Jesus was the result of a union between the divine Son of God and the man Jesus. In Alexandria, more emphasis was placed on the divinity of Christ, whereas Antioch feared

that too much emphasis on divinity would obscure Jesus' humanity.

In A.D. 428, Nestorius, a Syrian, became bishop of Constantinople, the eastern capital of the Roman Empire, a position that ranked second only to Rome itself in ecclesiastical prestige. Following the school of Antioch, he preached that Jesus had two distinct natures, human and divine. He also preferred the term "christotokos" (mother of Christ), for Jesus' mother, rather than the more popular "theotokos" (mother of God), because, he said, "theotokos" implies that Mary gave birth to God. To Cyril, denial of the concept of "theotokos" meant that Mary was not the mother of God, and hence that God had not become human in Jesus. Nestorius seemed to be teaching that there were two persons in Christ, the man Jesus and the divine Son of God.

Nestorius was quickly challenged by Cyril of Alexandria, who considered it his duty to strike down heresy wherever it might appear. Nestorius retaliated by encouraging renegade Egyptians living in Constantinople to file charges of misconduct against Cyril. Cyril complained to Emperor Theodosius II, who had appointed Nestorius. During the Easter season in 430, Cyril convoked a synod of all the bishops under his jurisdiction, and after a formal investigation, they condemned Nestorius as a heretic.

Early in his term of office, Nestorius had written to the pope about various matters and had incidentally mentioned something of his novel opinions. Concerned about these opinions, Pope Celestine kept Constantinople under observation. The pope took no action until Cyril of Alexandria sent him a dossier of the documents that had been used at his synod, along with information of that body's verdict. Celestine then brought together the Italian bishops during August of 430, studied the matter, and concurred in the Egyptian decision. In a letter to Nestorius, Celestine informed the bishop of Constantinople of his verdict and gave Nestorius ten days after receiving the letter to repudiate the erroneous doctrine or suffer excommunication. To see to it that Nestorius obeyed, Celestine commissioned Cyril to enforce his decision. Meanwhile, however, Theodosius II intervened; on November 19, he summoned a general council to meet in Ephesus early in 431 to investigate the controversy. The pope tacitly agreed to suspend his sentence in the interval.

On June 7, 431, the date set by Theodosius for the opening of the council, Nestorius and Cyril were in Ephesus. Each had a coterie of supporters, but the pope's legates were absent, as were the delegates in the jurisdiction of John, bishop of Antioch. Although this last group did not support Nestorius, they also did not care for Cyril's theology. During his anti-Nestorian campaign, Cyril had drawn up a list of theses, known as the Twelve Anathemas, in an effort to pinpoint the errors of Nestorius. The language of these propositions, however, was equivocal and suspicious to the Antiochene theologians.

After waiting two weeks for the tardy bishops, and against the protests of the emperor's civil supervisor, Cyril opened the council on June 22. Summoned officially to account for his ideas and defend himself, Nestorius refused to attend, so his views were studied in his written documents. The assembled theologians found him guilty of advocating heretical ideas, excommunicated him, and declared him deposed.

During the course of the remaining sessions of the council, all the latecomers finally arrived, and immediately the Antiochenes quarreled with Cyril and those who accepted his leadership. They declared him excommunicated and proclaimed themselves a rival council. In the end, the emperor ordered the arrest of both Cyril and John of Antioch. Irritated and somewhat puzzled, he wanted time to conduct a personal investigation. Cyril lavishly distributed money and gifts to the important people at Theodosius' court, but whether or not this activity influenced the emperor himself cannot be determined. With the advice of the pope's legate and of others whom he consulted, Theodosius ratified the condemnation of Nestorius and exonerated the other two bishops. Not until 433 did Antioch and Alexandria reach an agreement that removed all suspicion from Cyril.

As a result of these controversies, a reaction set in against Nestorianism called monophysitism, a Greek term meaning "a single nature." Whereas Nestorians believed that Jesus had two separate natures, Monophysites stressed his predominately divine nature. In 451, the Council of Chalcedon finally declared Jesus to be both fully human and fully divine, and that he was one person who was divine.

Nestorian supporters thought that their views were vindicated by this council. Nevertheless, Nestorius was exiled by the emperor's order, at first back to his home near Antioch and then to a distant oasis in Upper Egypt. Some twenty years later, he died in obscurity. His ideas, however, did not die. They fell on fertile ground outside the Roman Empire in Armenia and Persia; from there, Nestorianism penetrated eastward as far as China. Europeans visiting Peking in the time of Marco Polo found Nestorian Christians there. Of even greater significance for Christianity was the legacy of ill will created by the Nestorian affair. The virulent theological hostilities that it engendered released a current of controversy that swept over the Roman world during the following century.

—*Raymond H. Schmandt, updated by Winifred Whelan*

ADDITIONAL READING:

Constas, Nicholas. "Weaving the Body of God: Proclus of Constantinople, the Theotokos, and the Loom of the Flesh." *Journal of Early Christian Studies* 3 (Summer, 1995): 169-194. Constas describes the conflict between Nestorius, who did not believe in honoring Mary as Mother of God, and Proclus, his successor, who defended the Theotokos title.

Kee, Howard Clark, et al. *Christianity: A Social and Cultural History.* New York: Macmillan, 1991. This book includes a short section telling the story of the Nestorian controversy. It describes the role of the emperor's sister Pucheria in the event, and the blustery personality of Nestorius.

LaPorte, Jean. "Christology in Early Christianity." In *Christology: The Center and the Periphery*, edited by Frank K. Flinn. New York: Paragon House, 1988. LaPorte describes the bitter conflict between Cyril and Nestorius. The Council of Chalcedon in 451 actually agreed with Nestorius that there are two natures in Christ, but said that the two natures are united in a "hypostasis" or person.

Marthaler, Berard. *The Creed.* Mystic, Conn: Twenty-Third Publications. Chapter 6, "Christology: Two Approaches," describes two opposite tendencies in Christian theology. On the one hand, Jesus is human and bound to the earth as other humans. The other approach dwells more on ideas such as, "He came down from heaven."

Morris, Thomas V. *The Logic of God Incarnate.* Ithaca, N.Y.: Cornell University Press, 1986. This work constitutes a useful reference for a more complete discussion of the arguments on both sides of the God-human debate.

Sellers, R. V. *The Council of Chalcedon.* London: Society for Promoting Christian Knowledge, 1961. A more lengthy and thorough explanation of the Nestorian controversy, which was a catalyst for a series of political and theological debates. These debates resulted in the official clarification of the Church's doctrine of the single person of Christ.

SEE ALSO: 200, Christian Apologists Develop Concept of Theology; 325, The Nicene Creed; 1271-1291, Travels of Marco Polo.

439

VANDALS SEIZE CARTHAGE

Vandal forces seize Carthage, seriously expediting the erosion of Roman authority in the West.

DATE: 439

LOCALE: Carthage, on the northwest coast of Africa

CATEGORIES: Expansion and land acquisition; Wars, uprisings, and civil unrest

KEY FIGURES:

Flavius Aetius (died 454), master-general and chief minister to Valentinian III

Bonifacius (died 432), Roman governor in Africa, 425-431, alleged to have sought the Vandals as allies in rebellion against Rome

Gaiseric (Genseric; died 477), king of the Vandals, 428-477, and leader of the attack on Carthage

Galla Placidia (c. 390-450), regent for Emperor Valentinian III, 425-c. 440

Wallia, Visigoth leader, 415-418, who was authorized by Rome to attack the Vandals in Spain

SUMMARY OF EVENT. The Vandals appear to have entered the stage of European history suddenly and with little prior attestation, aside from various legends that point to a sometime residence in the area that later became modern Poland. In the mid-fourth century, the Vandals split into two groups, the Asding and the Siling. It is the Asding Vandals who participated in the events of the fifth century A.D. Driven west by the swiftly moving Huns, the Vandals crossed the Rhine River near Mainz in 406. For several years, the Vandals ravaged Gaul and at one point seemed poised to cross the English Channel and invade Britain. Instead, they crossed the Pyrenees and settled in Spain in 409. In 411, the Vandals became *foederati* or official allies of the Romans. The Vandals remained in Spain for twenty years, but the Roman-Vandal peace was an uneasy one. It was broken in 416, when Rome authorized the Visigoths, under Wallia, to attack the Vandals in the name of the emperor. The Vandals suffered severely under this treatment, but recovered their strength within a decade.

Under the leadership of their king, Gaiseric, the Vandals crossed to North Africa in 429, lured by the prospect of controlling the rich grain lands there. Conditions in Africa made an invasion an attractive prospect to the enterprising Vandals, because the local ruler, Count Boniface, had rebelled against Galla Placidia, regent for the child emperor Valentinian III. It cannot be proved that Count Boniface actually invited the Vandals as allies; nevertheless, an estimated eighty thousand Vandals arrived, of whom twenty thousand were fighting men. The Vandals found further advantages in the restlessness of the native Berbers and in the turmoil fomented by the religious discord of the Donatists, a group of schismatic Christians.

Although Gaiseric did not capture any of the chief cities of North Africa then, he did ravage the country and defeat Boniface's troops in battle in 431. Gaiseric also laid siege to Hippo for fourteen months, during which time the city's great bishop and writer, Augustine, died. Finally in 435, terms of peace were concluded by which the Vandals were permitted to settle in Numidia.

In 439, Gaiseric threw off the Roman yoke and seized Carthage, the leading city and key to the control of North Africa and the Mediterranean. Next, a fleet was organized to operate off the Sicilian coast. In 442, despite the vigorous efforts of Aetius, the generalissimo and chief minister to Valentinian III, Rome was forced to acknowledge the independence of the Vandal kingdom.

For the next century, under Gaiseric and four of his successors, the Vandals ruled independently in North Africa, holding Sicily, Corsica, and Sardinia as well, thus controlling the Mediterranean. In 455, when Valentinian III was assassinated, Gaiseric descended upon Rome. The Vandals spared the buildings and monuments but otherwise plundered the city's art treasures.

Shortly after becoming emperor of the East in 457, Leo I sent a fleet to try to reconquer Carthage; his troops suffered a humiliating defeat, and Gaiseric was left in total control of the province of Africa. The Vandals continued to administer the rich, grain-producing North African territory in much the same manner as had the Romans, even using the same administrative personnel. The significant differences were to be seen in the confiscation of large landed estates (which became properties of the Vandals), in the independent stance toward the Roman emperor in Constantinople, and in the religion of the people. The Vandals were Arian Christians, and Gaiseric and several of his successors waged bitter persecution against the non-Arian Christians; they were largely successful in destroying orthodox Christianity and replacing it with Arianism. This attitude was different from the policies of other barbarian kingdoms, such as the Visigoths and Ostrogoths, who, although adherents of Arianism themselves, were tolerant of the religions of their Catholic subjects. The Vandals' hollow victory over Catholicism proved to be the seed of their own undoing.

Vandal control of Africa came to an end when the emperor Justinian decided to reincorporate the western portion of the old Roman Empire and to enforce orthodoxy throughout his dominions. Belisarius, Justinian's general, defeated the Vandals at Ad Decimam and soon after captured Gelimer, the Vandal king, thus bringing Vandal rule in Africa to a close. The Vandals who survived became slaves of the Romans and disappeared as a people from history.

Although the Vandals held North Africa for more than a century, their influence was more negative than positive. They made little or no lasting cultural contribution to North Africa and left almost no records. The coming of the Vandals marked the denouement of Roman culture in North Africa, which had been among its most advanced areas. The career and writings of Augustine of Hippo serve as a reminder of the achievements and potential of North African civilization, had the Roman-Christian synthesis there survived the barbarian onslaught. There were exceptions, such as the work of the poet Luxorius and the allegorist Fulgentius, that showed the spirit of Roman culture could still flourish in Vandal-occupied Africa, but a full-scale cultural revival was impossible. Justinian's recovery of North Africa in 534 proved ephemeral, for the area soon succumbed to another shock of invasion when the Muslims took over the region in the seventh century, permanently destroying the unity of the Mediterranean area economically, religiously, and politically.

—*Mary Evelyn Jegen, updated by Nicholas Birns*

ADDITIONAL READING:

Clover, Frank. *The Vandals and the Late Roman West*. Aldershot, England: Variorum, 1993. A collection of essays, ranging from general to more specialized topics, written by the late twentieth century's leading historian of the Vandals.

Grant, Michael. *The Fall of the Roman Empire*. London: Weidenfeld, 1990. Grant analyzes the Vandal invasion in light of the dissolution of Roman rule in the West.

Isidore of Seville. *History of the Goths, Vandals, and Suevi*. Translated by Guido Donini and Gordon B. Ford. Leiden, the Netherlands: E. J. Brill, 1970. A leading primary source on the Vandals.

O'Flynn, John M. *Generalissimos of the Western Roman Empire*. Edmonton: University of Alberta Press, 1983. Good coverage of the relationship between Gaiseric and Aetius.

Vasiliev, A. A. *History of the Byzantine Empire: Volume One*. Madison: University of Wisconsin Press, 1952. This older source provides a fine description of the cultural and social life of the Vandals in relation to Justinian's reconquest.

SEE ALSO: 445-453, Invasions of Attila the Hun; 476, "Fall" of Rome; 533-553, Justinian's Wars Against the Vandals, Ostrogoths, and Visigoths.

445-453
INVASIONS OF ATTILA THE HUN

Invasions of Attila the Hun highlight Roman weakness, push some German tribes into new regions, and dislocate much of the population of Italy.

DATE: 445-453

LOCALE: The Eastern and Western Roman Empires

CATEGORIES: Expansion and land acquisition; Wars, uprisings, and civil unrest

KEY FIGURES:

Flavius Aetius (died 454), master-general of the joint
　　Roman-Visigothic army at Châlons

Attila (c. 406-453), king of the Huns, 434-453

Honoria, sister of Valentinian III

Leo I, the Great (c. 400-461), Roman Catholic pope,
　　440-461

Theodoric I (died 451), king of the Visigoths, 419-451

Valentinian III (Flavius Valentinianus; 419-455),
　　Western Roman emperor, 423-455

SUMMARY OF EVENT. Although the issue is still disputed
by some, the Huns are generally identified with the Hsiung-
Nu, a nomadic tribe from the Gobi Desert who first attracted the attention of the civilized world when they
attacked Han China in the second and first centuries B.C.
According to Edward Gibbon, the Hsiung-Nu were ultimately defeated by the Han emperor Vouti, precipitating
the permanent division of the tribe. One group remained
in the Gobi Desert where they were soon conquered by
another Mongol tribe called the Sienpi. Another group
settled in southwestern China on land allotted to them by
the emperor. A third group, however, headed west and split
into a northern and a southern branch as they left central
Asia. The southern branch eventually settled around the
Caspian Sea while the northern branch, the "Huns" which
so disrupted the Late Roman Empire, headed for Europe.

The Huns advanced very rapidly across the Ukraine,
central Europe, and as far south as the junction of the
Rhine and Danube Rivers. They organized the territory
they conquered into a loose confederation of subservient
tribes. The Alans, Scythians, Ostrogoths, and many other
lesser tribes were subjected to Hunnish rule in this manner.
Other tribes, such as the Visigoths, fled their homelands to
avoid a similar fate and thereby contributed to increasing
German pressure on Roman territory. The Visigoths fled
en masse to the banks of the Danube and begged the
Roman emperor Valens to allow them to enter the relative
safety of the empire. He agreed and thereby introduced a
dangerous and unstable element into the Western Empire
which many Roman leaders would later regret.

When Attila assumed leadership of the Hunnish empire, it was at its greatest extent, with all German tribes,
except the Frisians and Salian Franks, bound to the Huns
in one way or another and the Eastern Roman Empire
reduced to paying annual bribes to keep them at bay (a
policy introduced by the emperor Theodosius). Attila
originally assumed kingship of the Huns jointly with his
brother, Bleda, in A.D. 434. The two men ruled together
until 444, when Attila murdered his brother and seized
exclusive control of the tribe and its extensive possessions.

Attila became involved shortly thereafter in the internal
politics of the family of the Western Roman emperor,
Valentinian III. The emperor's sister, Honoria, had dis-
graced herself by having an affair with one of her servants
and had been excluded from her inheritance and former
position within the royal family. She appealed to Attila for
aid and seems to have promised him her hand in marriage
and a tremendous amount of money if he would help her
regain her lost prominence and prestige. This offer seems
to have flattered Attila, and he began to demand that
Valentinian hand Honoria over to him so that he could
formalize her marriage offer. He also began to claim that
half of the Western Roman Empire was his by right of the
fact that he was Honoria's fiancé. Valentinian, naturally,
rejected these demands and the uneasy truce that had
existed between the Huns and the Western Roman Empire
steadily deteriorated.

This deterioration culminated in Attila's invasion of
Gaul in 451. The king of the Franks had just died and a
dispute over his throne had erupted among several of his
sons. Attila hoped to take advantage of this confusion to
add this valuable piece of the Western Roman Empire to
his possessions. At the same time he once again repeated
his demand that Valentinian surrender Honoria to him and
give him half of the Western Empire. The ensuing campaign has been described as one of the decisive events in
European history. Attila was more than simply a danger to
Roman political control of the West. He also represented
a serious threat to Latin civilization and to the Christian
religion. Even though most of the Germanic tribes who
had settled in Gaul were independent in a political sense,
most of them had adopted Christianity and were at least to
a degree appreciative of the merits of Roman civilization.
Attila possessed no such appreciation and had no use at all
for Christianity.

In the end, it was this realization of the terrible ramifications of a Hunnish conquest of Gaul that caused all the
Germanic tribes in the region—the Salian Franks, Burgundians, and Visigoths—to join together with Roman
forces to stop Attila. This combined force was commanded by the Roman master-general Aetius and the king
of the Visigoths, Theodoric I. This army met Attila's force
near Châlons in a bloody battle which cost, according to
contemporary sources, between 162,000 and 320,000
lives. Theodoric himself was mortally wounded during the
battle, but the joint German-Roman army did manage to
halt Attila's advance in Gaul and force him to retreat back
beyond the Rhine River. It did not, however, have the
strength left to follow Attila and finish him off.

Attila's defeat at Châlons did nothing to weaken his
powerful ambitions. The very next year, 452, he invaded
Italy and laid siege to the large and prosperous city of

Hun cavalry forces conducted raids against neighboring Germanic tribes before targeting the Roman province of Gaul for conquest. (Archive Photos)

Aquileia, on the northern Adriatic coast. After a three-month siege, the city fell to the Huns and was so thoroughly destroyed by them that it never rose again. Attila then headed south toward Rome, destroying any other city in his path which did not immediately surrender to him. His original intention was to capture and sack the city but he began to waver in this goal after some of his advisers warned him that every other invader who had sacked Rome (most notably, Alaric, former king of the Visigoths) had died shortly thereafter. It was just at this point that an embassy, led by Pope Leo the Great, met Attila north of Rome and offered him a substantial bribe if he would spare the city. This bribe, combined with the fact that a famine was ravaging Italy and making it difficult for the Huns to support themselves, convinced Attila to alter his plans, and he withdrew from the peninsula shortly thereafter. One long-term consequence of Attila's invasion of Italy was that a large number of refugees settled on the low islands on the northern Adriatic coast. They became the nucleus of what would become the future republic of Venice.

After his withdrawal from Italy, Attila made another attempt to invade Gaul, only to be stopped by the forces of the new Visigothic king, Thorismund. He then began to make threats of invading the Eastern Roman Empire. Before he could carry this threat out, however, he died suddenly of a hemorrhage after excessive drinking during one of his frequent wedding celebrations. Attila's empire quickly disintegrated after his death in 453, with many of the survivors drifting back into central Asia, and the Huns ceased to be a force in world history.

—*Christopher E. Guthrie*

ADDITIONAL READING:

Gibbon, Edward. *The Decline and Fall of the Roman Empire*. Reprint. New York: Penguin Books, 1980. Classic account of the collapse of the Roman Empire which contains several interesting and valuable sections on the impact of Attila and the Huns on this event.

Goffart, Walter. *Rome's Fall and After*. London: The Hambledon Press, 1989. An excellent collection of essays which place the invasions of the Huns within the larger context of Rome's problems during the third and fourth centuries A.D.

Gordon, C. D. *The Age of Attila: Fifth Century Byzantium and the Barbarians*. Ann Arbor: University of Michigan Press, 1961. Despite its title, this book contains only one chapter which specifically deals with Attila and the Huns. It does, however, contain long quotations from contemporary observers of the period and is thus quite valuable in obtaining a feel for the times.

Jones, A. H. M. *The Later Roman Empire, 284-610 A.D.* Norman: University of Oklahoma Press, 1964. Excellent survey of the last centuries of the Roman Empire and the role that Attila and his Huns played in its ultimate collapse.

Thompson, E. A. *The Huns*. London: Blackwell, 1996. A reissue of the author's 1948 classic, *A History of Attila and the Huns*, this revised edition remains the best single source in English on the history of both the Huns as a people and Attila as a leader.

SEE ALSO: 410, Gothic Armies Sack Rome; 451, Battle of the Catalaunian Plains; 476, "Fall" of Rome.

449
SAXON SETTLEMENT OF BRITAIN BEGINS

The Saxon settlement of Britain begins, bringing an end to Roman occupation and establishing the origins of English language and culture.

DATE: 449

LOCALE: England

CATEGORIES: Expansion and land acquisition; Wars, uprisings, and civil unrest

KEY FIGURES:

Ambrosius Aurelianus, surviving member of the Roman ruling class, organized the Britons against the Saxon invaders

Artorius, Roman British leader and successor of Ambrosius Aurelianus, said to be the prototype of the medieval King Arthur

Bede (673-735), historian and scholar who composed the famous *Ecclesiastical History of the English Nation* in 731, putting in written form the legends of England that reached as far back as the Roman occupation

Hengist, a Jutish leader responsible for establishing the first Saxon settlement in Britain in 450 in the vicinity of modern Kent

Vortigern, a British warlord indirectly responsible for the establishment of the first Saxon settlement in Britain in 450

SUMMARY OF EVENT. Three separate tribes make up what is now referred to as the Anglo-Saxons. Beginning in about A.D. 250, three disparate but racially and culturally similar groups—the Angles, the Saxons, and the Jutes— invaded and settled in different parts of Britain. The Angles (whose name serves as the origin for the word English) settled in the north of Britain. A similar tribe known as the Saxons settled in the southern part of the island, and the Jutes, whom some scholars believe originated in Jutland (Denmark), settled in the middle. Although these were the major invading groups, there were also a small percentage of Frisians from the northern part of what is now the Netherlands, Swabians from the innermost parts of Germany, and very likely some smaller tribes that had originally inhabited Sweden. The causes behind this geographical migra-

tion (like that of the Vikings later) were overcrowding, poor farmland, and the constant battles with nature in their homeland in Northern Europe. At this point in history, the land held by these groups was literally shrinking as sections of the northern German coasts sank into the sea.

The first Anglo-Saxon raids began around 259 with small raiding parties that also invaded the opposite coasts of Gaul. These raiders surprised the native Britons and carried off plunder and captives. Although its hold was weakening, the Roman Empire, which dominated Britain at this time, was still strong enough to fight back. The real invasions, however, started about 449 and lasted for more than one hundred years. First called Saxons, the German invaders were later referred to as Angles. By 601, the pope referred to the leader of southern Britain, Aethelbert of Kent, as *rex Anglorum* ("king of the Angles").

Arriving without warning in their long-boats, the Saxons first landed on the southern and eastern coasts of Britain and then moved to the island's interior. Some of the boats these Saxons used to invade Britain have been preserved in peat bogs. The Nydam boat, named for its place of discovery, was seventy-seven feet long and up to eleven feet wide. It used oars for propulsion, and resembled a long rowboat. These invaders carried thrusting spears, bows, swords, and Roman-made armor. Their shields were round and made of wooden planks with a large metal spike in the center.

In the year 400, Britain was still a Roman province, with Roman style towns, villas, roads, and armies. Unlike the Romans, who had earlier invaded Britain with strong and highly trained armies, the Saxons carried out their invasion of Britain more slowly with wave after wave of invaders. Also, unlike the Romans, who desired to overthrow the native Celtic Britons, and absorb them into the vast Roman Empire, the Saxons wanted to stay, cultivate the earth, and prosper in a new land. When the Saxon warrior-adventurers first arrived, they were repelled by the Roman army. By the early fifth century, however, Roman Britain had reached the point of collapse. By 410, the British people found themselves without Roman protection on an isolated and vulnerable island at the edge of the known world. Emperor Honorius, who was under attack himself from the Goths, was unable to send Roman military forces. Slowly, the Saxons made their way up the British rivers, plundering and taking captives all the way, but always returning to their native country. The first permanent Saxon settlement was not established until about 450, when the British warlord, Vortigern, presented a tract of land to a group of Saxons in return for protection from other native warlords. Although the Jutish leader, known as Hengist, provided protection for awhile, he soon turned against Vortigern and quickly conquered Kent for himself. Soon after, the next wave of Saxon invaders were made up of farmers and their families intent on seizing rich farmland, instead of warrior-adventurers and plunderers. By the second half of the fifth century, the Saxons had gained settlements along the rivers and coasts without much opposition from the native British people. They wanted peace, and were intent on gaining land and farming it well. They were prepared to fight only if necessary. While the native Britons traditionally farmed on the lighter soil found on hill slopes, the newcomers preferred the clay soil, similar to that found in their native land. In many parts of England, the two peoples were able to coexist peacefully for a time.

At the end of the fifth century, however, the Britons rallied around a leader, a survivor of the Roman ruling class named Ambrosius Aurelianus. Some scholars believe Aurelianus held the Anglo-Saxons at bay for forty years. His successor, Artorius (thought to be the model for the mythical King Arthur), is said to have replaced Aurelianus as leader of the Britons. Riding into battle in Roman-style chain-mail armor, Artorius defeated the Saxons at Mount Badon. To the Anglo-Saxons, who fought only on foot, the Britons, who sometimes fought in Roman-style cavalry units, must have seemed quite formidable. It is said that Artorius halted the Saxon invasion for fifty years. Unfortunately, the British people, who were broken up into at least five separate kingdoms, could not unite under a single leader. By the middle of the sixth century, the temporary British revival had ended. The fair-haired Anglo-Saxons eventually claimed victory, and rapidly moved inland, erecting their timber huts many times among Roman ruins. They lived side by side and intermarried with the darker-haired Celtic-speaking British peasantry. Although the Celtic language was eventually replaced by the language of the Angles, Saxons, and Jutes, it continued to survive in various forms in Ireland, Wales, and Scotland. By the seventh century, there were seven Saxon kingdoms in Britain: Kent, Essex, Sussex, Wessex, Mercia, East Anglia, and Northumberland.

Early Anglo-Saxon society was built on families and clans, or tribes, and centered on the warrior and a method of reciprocity that was to lead to the medieval feudal system known as the *comitatus*. The lord (earl) expected the service and loyalty of his thanes (similar to the later feudal knights), who expected the reciprocal protection from the lord. The West Germanic language of the invaders has been always referred to as English, whether spoken by Angles, Saxons, or Jutes, but it was not until about 890 that the name "Engla lande" (the land of the Angles) became popular.

The Saxon culture maintained a strong oral tradition rich in poetic form. The Venerable Bede, who completed his famous *Ecclesiastical History of the English People* in Latin in 731, is chiefly responsible for preserving in written form the legends of England reaching as far back as the Roman occupation. In addition, the *Anglo-Saxon Chronicle* (900), written in Old English, has provided scholars with many incidents of Anglo-Saxon life and history. Although the famous epic *Beowulf* is set in Scandinavia, it is written in English and gives modern readers a glimpse of Anglo-Saxon life.

The decline and fall of the Roman Empire ensured the success of the Anglo-Saxon invasion of Britain. The geographical movement of the Anglo-Saxons from what later became Germany, Denmark, and the Netherlands to the British Isles was only part of the general upheaval that affected Europe for generations. With the introduction of Christianity in 597, the Anglo-Saxons began using the Latin alphabet. By the end of the seventh century, the Saxon pagans had been converted to Christianity by Saint Augustine of Canterbury and other missionaries from the European continent.   —*M. Casey Diana*

ADDITIONAL READING:

Hamilton, John, and Alan Sorrell. *Saxon England.* Chester Springs, Pa.: Dufour, 1968. Complete, concise, and approachable account of the Anglo-Saxon invasion of and absorption into Britain.

Jones, Michael E. *The End of Roman Britain.* Ithaca, N.Y.: Cornell University Press, 1996. A comprehensive account of the Germanic invasions with a focused account of movements between the third and sixth centuries. Contains a forty-page bibliography and is illustrated with maps.

Nye, Robert. *Beowulf.* New York: Dell, 1982. Also found in many English literature anthologies, this classic three-thousand-line poem is the first major English-language epic and provides insights into Anglo-Saxon life.

Spellman, R. R. *The Anglo-Saxons.* New York: Roy Publishers, 1959. Although barely sixty-six pages, this work provides a comprehensive, well-illustrated account of the Saxon invasion of Britain along with social and cultural accounts of Saxon life. Contains detailed maps.

Woods, J. Douglas. *The Anglo-Saxons: Synthesis and Achievement.* Waterloo, Ontario: Laurien University Press, 1986. A scholarly but approachable work highlighting Saxon civilization to 1066. Includes a comprehensive bibliography.

SEE ALSO: 43-130, Roman Conquest of Britain; 60-61, Boadicea Leads Revolt Against Roman Rule; 878, King Alfred Defeats the Danes at Edington; 1016, Danish Invaders Led by Canute Conquer England; 1066, Battle of Hastings.

450
CONVERSION OF IRELAND

The conversion of Ireland precipitates a form of monasticism that ensures the preservation of the records and literature of Western civilization after the fall of Rome.

DATE: c. 450
LOCALE: Ireland and the Celtic parts of the British Isles
CATEGORIES: Cultural and intellectual history; Religion
KEY FIGURES:

Saint Brendan (484-577), traveled widely before founding a monastery at Clonfert in Galway
Saint Briget (453-523), founder of several monasteries in Ireland, also held in reverence in Scotland
Celestine I (died 432), Roman Catholic pope, 422-432, and first Roman bishop to interest himself in the Irish
Saint Colman (c. 605-676), principal spokesperson for the Celtic position at the Synod of Whitby (664)
Saint Columba (c. 521-597), founder of several monasteries in Ireland
Saint Columban (543-615), founder of Luxeuil in France (590) and Bobbio in Italy (612)
Saint Finnian (c. 470-c. 552), founder of the monastery of Clonard in Ireland
Saint Patrick (c. 389-c. 461), semilegendary missionary bishop traditionally associated with the conversion of Ireland
Pelagius (c. 355-425), British monk whose heretical beliefs (Pelagianism) upheld the essential goodness of human nature

SUMMARY OF EVENT. The Irish of history have their roots in the Celtic La Tène civilization, which was probably established in Ireland by the end of the third century B.C. The Celtic cultural base remained predominant through the first millennium A.D., virtually the only modification being the introduction of Christianity.

Christianity certainly existed in Ireland before the fifth century A.D., although it was probably limited to the southern part of the island where it had presumably been carried by inhabitants of Britain and Gaul who had fled to Hibernia from the Vandals and Huns. Augustine of Hippo, (a city in Roman Africa) believed that his rival, the archheretic Pelagius was from Hibernia, and Gallic bishops such as Victricius of Rouen, Lupus of Troyes, and Germanus of Auxerre journeyed to the British Isles in the late fourth and early fifth centuries to counter Pelagianism, which taught that salvation could be achieved by the exercise of human powers. Pope Celestine I commissioned Palladius, a Roman deacon, to convert Ireland in A.D. 431. Little is known about this missionary bishop other than that he was either the original Saint Patrick or,

Credited with converting the Celtic residents of Ireland to Christianity in the fifth century A.D., Saint Patrick has traditionally been associated with ridding Ireland of snakes. (Library of Congress)

more likely, a predecessor. On the death of Palladius, Patrick was ordained a bishop and set out for Ireland.

Research on Patrick trying to establish a chronology for his life and work has yielded few positive results. His own writings, his *Confessions*, a reply to his detractors, *Letters to the Soldiers of Croticus*, and several letters, date from the fifth century, but the earliest extant biographies come from the seventh. Patrick was born in Roman Britain where, at the age of sixteen, he was captured and sold into slavery in Ireland. During his captivity, he turned to religion. After six years of labor as a shepherd, he returned to Britain determined eventually to convert the Irish to Christianity. Although the record of his actual missionary activity among the Irish is not clear, Patrick is credited with securing toleration for Christians, developing a native clergy, fostering the growth of monasticism, and establishing dioceses. Patrick's doctrine is considered orthodox and has been interpreted as anti-Pelagian. There is no account of his immediate successors nor any knowledge of ecclesiastical establishments attributable to him.

The ecclesiastical polity introduced by Palladus and Patrick was probably episcopal, but their establishment of monasticism was to influence Irish Christianity profoundly. By the sixth century, the Irish church became a monastic church under the control of powerful abbots within a system closely akin in tone to the Eastern anchoritic traditions which had filtered into Ireland by way of Wales, Aquitaine, a region in present day southwestern France, and Galicia in Spain. The monasteries were organizational centers for the *paruchiae*, or parishes, areas often corresponding to the boundaries of the tribe from which the founder had sprung, or that tribe which patronized the establishment. Powerful personages of the tribes became abbots.

The monasteries were centers of learning, with the Irish monks transmuting into a rich literary style with Christian implications, the law and poetry of their pagan predecessors: the *brehon*, whose ancient Irish customary Brehon laws were used to arbitrate claims, and the *filidh*, which was made up of bardic poets, physicians, and druids. Latin learning in Ireland in the fifth and sixth centuries laid solid foundations in grammar and rhetoric, as well as knowledge of the scriptures, church fathers, and lives of saints.

As noteworthy as their zest for learning was the Irish monks' penchant for poverty, asceticism, contemplation, and solitude. This form of monasticism, reminiscent of earlier *brehon* and *filidh* spartan characteristics, reflects the Celtic spirit of individualism. During the sixth century, this ascetic spirit of the Irish was manifest in the activities of Finnian at Clonard, Cieran at Clonmacnoise, and Comgall at Bangor. Of particular note were Briget of Kildare, a miracle-working transmutation of the Celtic goddess Ceridwen, who founded four monasteries, and Brendan at Clonfert, the subject of the Irish epic *Navigatio Brendani* (voyage of Brendan), who is rumored to have traveled to North America. For the sake of solitude more than for proselytizing, Irish outposts were founded on pagan frontiers. Thus in the British Isles, monasteries were founded by Columba in 563 on Iona, an island off the coast of western Scotland, and by Aidan in 634 at Lindisfarne, an island off the northeast coast of England. These centers were responsible for the spread of the Christian faith into Scotland and Northumbria. On the Continent, the works of Columban at Luxeuil and Bobbio, Gall in Switzerland, and Kilian at Wurzburg were similar in method and intent. Each of these foreign missions provided a great stimulus for the maintenance of Latin learning and Christian ascetic piety in Western Europe in the early Middle Ages.

In the realm of spiritual discipline, Irish innovations made a lasting impression. The Irish monks first replaced public penance with private penance, consisting of prayers and works of mortification directed by the confessor for the penitent.

By the mid-seventh century, certain practices of Irish and the whole of Celtic Christendom were considered irregular in the eyes of the Roman Church, which was then episcopally governed and Benedictine in its monasticism. Differences between Irish and Roman practices included peculiarities of liturgy and rituals in the Mass, single immersion in baptism, extensive rites for ordinations, procedures in episcopal consecration, and especially differences in the celebration of Easter, the Irish tonsure, and the use of leavened bread in the communion. England was the scene of the clash between the Roman and the Celtic (Irish) traditions in the fifty years following Augustine's mission and the death of Columba at Iona (597). The Synod of Whitby in 664, witnessed the debate between the Roman Wilfrid and the Celtic Colman, but the resolution resulted in King Oswald of Northumbria's preference for Roman practices. By the beginning of the eighth century, the Irish had conformed to Roman practices as they understood them, and Armagh, a district of Northern Ireland said to be the site of Patrick's first mission settlement, emerged as the chief episcopal center. The harsh rules of innovators such as Columban made the more moderate papal-sponsored Benedictine form of monasticism seem attractive by comparison. Complete alignment with continental practices was impeded, however, by Viking invasions beginning in A.D. 795.

What was for most of Europe the Dark Ages was for Ireland the golden age. During this era, religious art, such as the Ardagh Chalice and the *Book of Kells* and other illuminated manuscripts, flourished. As the invading Germanic tribes burned the books of the Roman cities, the Irish monk scribes, perched on remote islands, copied all the Western literature they could obtain, thereby preserving Western civilization.

—*Richard J. Wurtz, updated by M. Casey Diana*

ADDITIONAL READING:

Bury, J. B. *The Life of St. Patrick and His Place in History*. London: Macmillan, 1905. Influential biography of Saint Patrick that illustrates the fifth century Irish Church.

Cahill, Thomas. *How the Irish Saved Civilization: The Untold Story of Ireland's Heroic Role from the Fall of Rome to the Rise of Medieval Europe*. New York: Doubleday, 1995. Scholarly yet approachable work that argues that although Ireland knew neither Renaissance nor Enlightement, its monks refounded Western civilization by preserving Western literature. Contains a pronunciation guide to Irish words, illustrations, a bibliography for each chapter, and a chronology from approximately 3000 B.C. to 1923.

Hanson, R. P. C. *St. Patrick: A British Missionary Bishop*. Nottingham, England: Hawthorne's, 1965. Analyzes Saint Patrick's own works and early Church biographies and references.

Hughes, Kathleen. *The Church in Early Irish Society*. Ithaca, N.Y.: Cornell University Press, 1966. Examines the Irish Church from the fifth to the twelfth centuries by blending the work of earlier major scholars. Effectively demonstrates the Irish Church's accommodation of earlier Celtic tribal practices.

Thompson, E. A. *Who Was Saint Patrick?* New York: St. Martin's Press, 1986. Uses both primary and secondary sources to account for Saint Patrick's life, including his own written works. Reconstructs the conversion of Ireland.

SEE ALSO: 635-800, Founding of Lindisfarne and Creation of the *Book of Kells*; 793, Northmen Raid Lindisfarne.

451

BATTLE OF THE CATALAUNIAN PLAINS

The Battle of the Catalaunian Plains stops the advance of the Huns into Europe and is the last effective act of the Roman Empire in the West.

DATE: July, 451

LOCALE: The Mauriac Plain, northwest of Troyes, France

CATEGORY: Wars, uprisings, and civil unrest

KEY FIGURES:

Flavius Aetius (died 454), Roman general

Attila (c. 406-453), king of the Huns, 434-453

Honoria, Roman princess

Sangibanus, king of the Alans

Theodoric I (died 451), king of the Visigoths, 419-451

Theodosius II (401-450), Eastern Roman emperor, 408-450

Thorismund (died 453), king of the Visigoths, 451-453

Valentinian III (Flavius Valentinianus; 419-455), Western Roman emperor, 425-455

SUMMARY OF EVENT. The Huns appear to have been related to the Hsiung-Nu, a Turkish-Mongolian people who appear in Chinese records of the early centuries A.D. They eventually made their way across central Asia and acquired a fearsome reputation as savage warriors who lived out their lives on horseback. They defeated and absorbed one barbarian group after another, and in the process they created a nomad horde. Pressure from the Huns forced other barbarian groups into the Roman Empire, and even has been blamed for the so-called barbarian invasions.

In the 370's, the Huns halted their advance north of the

Danube River. For a time, their relations with the Romans were like those of other barbarians, and they often served as auxiliaries in the Roman army. In the fifth century A.D., however, they once again grew restive. In the early 420's, the Hun king Rua had to be bought off by the Romans with a subsidy of 350 pounds of gold per year. This created an unfortunate precedent, for the barbarian taste for gold obtained in this manner could never be satiated.

In the late 430's, the brothers Attila and Bleda, sons of Rua, succeeded to the throne. Sometime around 445, Attila murdered his brother and became sole king. He imposed increasingly severe terms upon the Eastern Roman emperor Theodosius II, raising the yearly subsidy first to seven hundred pounds of gold, and then to twenty-one hundred pounds. In 447, the Romans even agreed to evacuate a strip south of the Danube five-days' march wide.

Subsequently, Attila's interests seem to have turned toward the west and to the Princess Justa Grata Honoria, elder sister of Emperor Valentinian III. Around 449, she had been apprehended in an illicit love affair and exiled to Constantinople. She then sent her ring to Attila and appealed to him for help. At this, Theodosius II, who already had enough problems with the Huns, immediately dispatched her back to Italy—with the recommendation that Valentinian turn her over to Attila.

Valentinian refused, and what happened next is described by the historian Priscus, who had visited Attila's camp in 448. Attila, he says,

> sent men to the ruler of the western Romans to argue that Honoria, whom he had pledged to himself in marriage, should in no way be harmed. . . . He sent also to the eastern Romans concerning the appointed tribute, but his ambassadors returned from both missions with nothing accomplished. . . . Attila was of two minds and at a loss which he should attack first, but finally it seemed better to him to enter on the greater war and to march against the west, since his fight there would be not only against the Italians but also against the Goths and Franks.

Priscus continues, "He sent certain men of his court to Italy that the Romans might surrender Honoria. . . . He also said that Valentinian should withdraw from half of the empire. . . . When the western Romans held their former opinion, he devoted himself eagerly to preparation for war."

Meanwhile, in the western part of the empire, things were not going well. Britain, Africa, and much of Gaul (modern France) had been lost to the barbarians. By mid-century, only a shadow of the Western Roman Empire was held together by the "Patrician and Master of Soldiers" (field marshal) Flavius Aetius, a hostage of Attila in his youth, who for twenty-five years had skillfully played one barbarian group off against another.

When Attila led the Huns and their subject peoples across the Rhine into Gaul in 451, the situation looked bleak for the Romans. The Roman army, so-called, now consisted of little more than barbarian mercenaries in the personal service of Aetius. The other powers in western Europe, the Visigoths in Aquitania and the Franks in the Rhineland, could be expected only to use to their own advantage a further weakening of the Romans. As things turned out, however, the western barbarians decided they had more to fear from the Huns than the Romans, and Aetius became the leader of an unlikely coalition of what remained of the Roman army, Visigoths, and Franks.

Scholars have pieced together the progress of the invasion from several sources. The Gallic chronicler Prosper, writing only a few years later, noted, "Once the Rhine had been crossed, many Gallic cities experienced Attila's most savage attacks." The Spaniard Hydatius, writing in the 460's, reported, "Having broken the peace, the nation of the Huns ravaged the provinces of Gaul; many cities were destroyed"; he names Metz in particular. In the next cen-

tury, Gregory of Tours related that after destroying Metz, the Huns "ravaged a great number of other cities" before finally attacking Orléans. Other reports from about the same time tell of an attack on Rheims, and an approach toward Paris. It would seem, therefore, that the Huns crossed the Rhine near Strasbourg, traveled west by way of Metz and Rheims, but then turned south before reaching Paris, and so came to Orléans.

At that time, Orléans was under the protection of a group of barbarian Alans in Roman service. The mid-sixth century historian Jordanes, a Goth himself, reports, "Sangibanus, the king of the Alans, terrified by fear of the future, promised to surrender himself to Attila and to betray into his power the Gallic city of Orléans, where he then was stationed." In the meantime, however, Anianus, bishop of Orléans, had gone south to seek the aid of Aetius, and the imperial coalition arrived in the nick of time, apparently after a breach had already been made in the walls.

Unable to take the now strongly defended city and not having expected to be resisted in force, Attila began a strategic retreat northward. In July, it seems, between Troyes and Châlons-sur-Marne (ancient Catalauni), Attila

Attila's attacks against wealthy Roman residents of Gaul prompted Roman armies under general Flavius Aetius to join forces with Visigothic troops led by King Theodoric to defeat the Huns in battle near Châlons. (Archive Photos)

was brought to battle. The actual location of the battle, which traditionally has been referred to as the Battle of Châlons, is in some doubt. Jordanes says, "They came together in the Catalaunian Plain, which also is called Mauriac. It is one hundred leagues in length and seventy in breadth." This is a large area, about 150 by 105 miles, which demonstrates even Jordanes' uncertainty about the location of the battle. Among other sources, the Spaniard Hydatius says the battle took place "in the Catalaunian fields," but the Gallic sources all agree that it occurred "at Troyes in the place called Mauriac." Modern scholars have favored the French view that the battle took place on the "Mauriac Plain" (modern Mery-sur-Seine), about twenty miles northwest of Troyes, thirty-five miles south of Châlons, and next to the "Catalaunian fields."

The only detailed account of the ensuing "battle of the nations" comes, again, from Jordanes. He reports that on the night before the general engagement, the Franks, perhaps under king Merovech, and Gepids fell upon each other, and that fifteen thousand were slain. On the next day, the Roman battle line consisted of the Visigoths under their king, Theodoric, on the right wing and the Romans under Aetius on the left, with the unreliable Alans under Sangibanus in the center. The location of the Franks is unspecified, suggesting that they may have received the worst of the fighting the night before. Perhaps they were stationed behind the Alans. On the other side, the Huns took the center, with the wings occupied by the Ostrogoths, under Valamer, on the left, and the remaining Gepids, under Ardaric, on the right. The rest of the "crowd of kings," says Jordanes, "attended to Attila's whims like lackeys."

The battle proper began rather late, at the "ninth hour" (that is, at about 5:00 P.M.), with a skirmish for the possession of a strategic ridge of high ground. The Romans, led by the Visigothic prince Thorismund, reached the summit first, and were able to repel the Huns as they came up the slope. Stung by this initial reverse, Attila gave his soldiers a brief pep talk, concluding, "I shall hurl the first spear against the enemy, and if any man thinks to take his leisure while Attila fights, he is a dead man."

Next, there ensued "a battle ghastly, confused, ferocious, and unrelenting, the like of which history has never recounted." The streams, it was said, ran red with blood. Initially, the motley Roman forces retained their line. The Visigoths were able to drive back the Ostrogoths, although in the course of this fighting the aged Visigothic king Theodoric was thrown from his horse and trampled to death by his own men. The Visigoths then separated from the Alans on their left and fell upon the left flank of the Huns themselves. In the ensuing melee, Attila was nearly slain, and the Huns then retreated to their camp, which

had been fortified by their encircled wagons. As darkness fell, the Visigoths made an attack on the Hun camp but were repulsed. On the Roman right, meanwhile, Aetius and his forces seem to have broken through the weakened Gepids; Aetius himself became separated from his men and only after wandering through enemy lines did he return safely to camp.

The next day, neither side felt strong enough to resume the battle—it was later said that 165,000 men had been slain. While the members of the Roman coalition debated what to do next, Attila himself, it was said, stood atop a funeral pyre threatening to immolate himself rather than be taken captive. According to Jordanes, Aetius, fearful that if the Huns were destroyed totally the Visigoths would be left with a free hand in Gaul, advised Thorismund, the new Visigothic king, to return home to consolidate his own place on the throne. Gregory of Tours reports that Aetius also persuaded the Franks to leave—so that he could claim all the booty. Perhaps a more realistic reconstruction is that both the Visigoths and Franks, weakened themselves, departed because they believed that their job was complete. Attila had been weakened to the point where he no longer posed them a threat, and to continue to fight would only be to serve Roman interests.

However that may be, neither Attila nor Aetius was in any condition to carry on the fight. Attila withdrew back across the Rhine to fight another day. Indeed, in the next year he returned, and passed through the inexplicably undefended Alps into Italy. Aquileia was destroyed and Milan was captured. Then, according to a pious legend, the Huns were induced to withdraw by an embassy of pope Leo, who was assisted in his efforts by apparitions of Saints Peter and Paul. Disease, starvation, and the rumored arrival of reinforcements from the east also would have influenced the decision. In 453, Attila died on his wedding night, and in the next year the subject peoples of the Huns revolted, inflicting a disastrous defeat upon their erstwhile masters at the Battle of the Nedao River. The Huns never again posed a serious threat to the empire.

As for the Battle of the Mauriac Plains, it subsequently assumed a prodigious place in the popular imagination. A fifteenth century writer, for example, listed Rheims, Cambrai, Trier, Tetz, Arras, Tongres, Tournai, Therouanne, Cologne, Amiens, Beauvais, and Paris, not to mention Worms, Strasbourg, and Langres, as having been destroyed by Attila. Attila himself subsequently obtained a reputation as a barbarian par excellence. Christian moralists referred to him as the "scourge of God" for his perceived role in punishing sinful Christians. In modern times, it has been suggested that a victory by the Huns would have caused irreparable damage to the future of

Western civilization. The battle has been portrayed as a victory of civilization over barbarism, and a major turning point in history. —*Ralph W. Mathisen*

ADDITIONAL READING:

Gordon, C. D. *The Age of Attila: Fifth-Century Byzantium and the Barbarians.* Ann Arbor: University of Michigan Press, 1966. Provides the commentary of Priscus.

Gregory of Tours. *The History of the Franks.* Translated by L. Thorpe. London: Penguin, 1974. A modern translation of the history of the battle as written by Gregory of Tours.

Jordanes. *The Origin and Deeds of the Goths.* Translated by C. C. Mierow. Princeton, N.J.: Princeton University Press, 1915. A translation of Jordanes' account of the battle.

Maencheh-Helfen, Otto. *The World of the Huns.* Berkeley: University of California Press, 1973. Provides an overview of barbarian tribal culture and the Huns' interactions with the Roman Empire.

Thompson, Edward A. *Attila and the Huns.* Oxford: Oxford University Press, 1948. An older study that is still useful for understanding Attila and his impact.

SEE ALSO: 410, Gothic Armies Sack Rome; 445-453, Invasions of Attila the Hun; 476, "Fall" of Rome; 533-553, Justinian's Wars Against the Vandals, Ostrogoths, and Visigoths.

476
"FALL" OF ROME

The "fall" of Rome occurs as the result of internal strife and external attacks, resulting in a transfer of imperial power to Constantinople.

DATE: September 4, 476

LOCALE: Ravenna, Italy

CATEGORY: Wars, uprisings, and civil unrest

KEY FIGURES:

Julius Nepos (died 480), Roman emperor in the West, 474-480

Odovacar (434-493), son of Edica, a Scirian warlord, and barbarian ruler of Italy, 476-493

Romulus Augustulus, son of Orestes, usurper of the position of Roman emperor in the West, 475-476

Zeno, (died 491) Roman emperor in the East, 474-491

SUMMARY OF EVENT. The decline and eventual fall of the powerful Roman Empire can be traced back to severe problems beginning with the reign of Marcus Aurelius, a brutal persecutor of the Christians. His violent reign (161-180) experienced increased interior rebellions in addition to attacks on the empire's borders. The subsequent reign of his brutal and incompetent son Lucius Aelius Aurelius Commodus from 180 to 192 (when he was strangled) is regarded by many historians as the beginning of Rome's long decline.

The third century A.D. saw increased tension between the opulent city-dwellers and the barely civilized peasants. Caracalla reigned from 211 to 217 and granted Roman citizenship to all freemen living in the Roman Empire, with the intent of imposing additional taxes on them. Alexander Severus (208-235) ruled with "wisdom and justice" from 222 to 235, with his death beginning a period of great confusion throughout all Italy. Of his twelve successors who ruled in the next thirty-three years, all but one died a violent death, usually at the hands of the soldiers who had established them. The internal strife that began under Aurelius continued, and the increased taxation necessary to finance the military resulted in economy-crippling inflation. The defenses of the empire on the Rhine and Danube collapsed under the attack of Germanic and other tribes, and the Eastern provinces were invaded by the Persians.

A very temporary restoration of peace and prosperity was achieved by the Illyrian emperors Claudius (surnamed Gothicus), who drove back the Goths, and by Aurelian, who was victorious over the Goths, Germans, and Zenobia, queen of Palmyra, who had occupied Egypt and Asia Minor. This brief restoration lasted until the accession of Diocletian, who ruled from 284 to 305. Diocletian introduced many social, economic, and political reforms, including removal of many political and economic privileges that Rome and Italy had enjoyed at the expense of the provinces. He sought to regulate rampant inflation by controlling prices on many necessary goods and on the maximum wages of workers. Diocletian controlled Thrace, Egypt, and Asia. He assigned control of Italy and Africa to Maximian, control of Gaul, Spain, and Britain to Constantius, and control of Danubian provinces to Galerius. This system created a strong administration but greatly increased the size of the already monstrous governmental bureaucracy, thus creating a tremendous financial burden on the empire's resources. The abdication in 305 of Diocletian and Maximian, who both had taken the title of Augustus, resulted in the outbreak of several civil wars which did not end until the accession of Constantine the Great in 312. Constantine I, who had previously become Caesar of the army in Britain, overcame all rivals and reunited the Western Roman Empire under his rule. The defeat of Eastern emperor Licinius in 314 made Constantine the sole ruler of the Roman world.

Christianity had recovered from Diocletian's attempts to destroy it by persecution, and the politically minded

LANDMARKS OF ROME

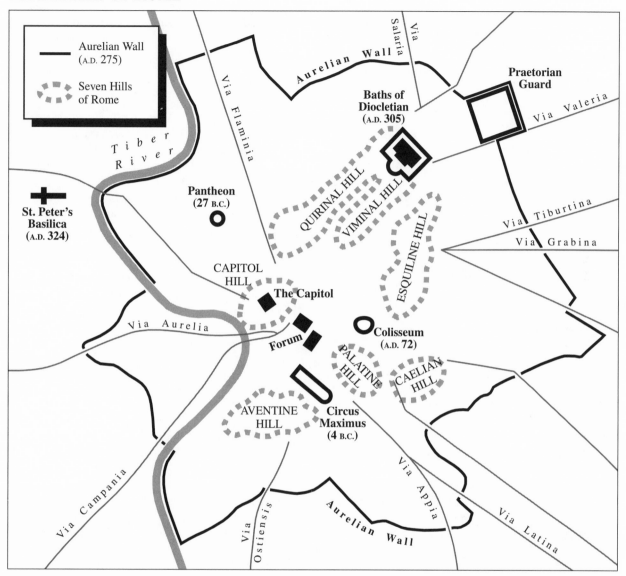

Constantine adopted Christianity, claiming a personal conversion and proclaiming it the official religion of the Roman Empire. The other event of far-reaching significance during Constantine's reign was his establishment of a new governmental seat in Byzantium, which eventually was named in his honor as Constantinople (later called Istanbul). Constantine reigned from 306 to 337 and is often regarded as the second founder of the empire. He successfully fought off numerous opponents, reorganized local government into prefectures, dioceses, and provinces, legalized Christianity after his self-proclaimed conversion, and enlisted the church in service to the state. The death of Constantine in 337 began more civil wars be-

tween the rival Caesars, which continued until Constantine's only surviving son, Constantius II, was successful in briefly uniting the empire. Constantius II was followed by Julian, who ruled from 361 to 363 and was known as the Apostate because of his renunciation of Christianity. The reforms begun under Constantine, however, proved to be far from successful enough to halt the fall of the empire.

Upon the death of Theodosius in 395, the empire was permanently divided into the Latin Western and the Greek Eastern Byzantine empires. The Eastern Empire, with its capital at Constantinople, lived on until 1435, when it was conquered by the Turks. The Western Empire was overrun and gradually dismembered by Germanic tribes with various Roman leaders initially conciliating a victorious invader with military commands and administrative offices. The conquest of Africa by the Vandals under Gaiseric and the seizure of Gaul and Italy by the Huns soon followed. Led by their famous leader Attila, the Huns ruled central and northern Europe and confronted the emperors of East and West alike as an independent power. The city of Rome was plundered by the Visigoths in 410 and by the Vandals in 455, after which Julius Nepos and Leo I briefly held the Western and Eastern thrones, respectively. The death of Leo I passed the Eastern throne to his seven-year-old grandson, Leo II, whose father, Zeno, became the Eastern emperor when Leo II died in 474. Nepos' insecure rule in Rome was highlighted by his appointment of Orestes, a former lieutenant of Attila the Hun.

It quickly became evident that Orestes desired the imperial throne for his son Romulus and when Nepos fled Rome, Orestes crowned his young son in late 475. The crowning of Romulus was without any legal authority, but historians from the sixth century on have accepted that the boy was the last emperor of the West. Orestes was soon at odds with his Germanic army and was slain in 476. A leader of this rebellious army was the mercenary Herulian leader Odovacar (sometimes called Odoacer) who is credited with overthrowing the child Romulus Augustulus on September 4, 476, thus finalizing the fall of ancient Rome.

Historians have been analyzing the "world-changing" decline and fall of ancient Rome ever since the founding of the science of history in the eighteenth and nineteenth centuries. The result of their work probably will never result in a single definitive answer to the complex question of what caused the decline of the mighty Roman Empire. Any answer to this question must take into account the fact that the Eastern Empire in Constantinople did not decline simultaneously with the West but endured almost another thousand years. Some scholars have stressed that the well-documented sharp decline in population in the Western regions severely limited agricultural and industrial growth, and defense against invasion. Economic explanations were initially accepted as adequate but nearly all have since been refuted or seriously weakened. Some scholars have looked for evidence that the soil of the Western provinces was of poorer quality than the East, while others have tried to show that patterns of rising and ebbing rainfall made Italy fluctuate in prosperity. Furthermore, most barbarians invaded Europe from the West along the flatter regions as compared to mountain ranges of southeastern Europe. Geographically speaking, it is obvious why invaders appeared in Germany along the Danube River and in Italy itself, while Byzantium lay protected by the Balkan Mountain ranges. One scholar

points to data that suggest that a contributing factor to Rome's fall was widespread lead poisoning among the Roman upper class. The richer citizens consumed a Greek diet, with their food cooked in lead containers or lead-glazed pottery and drinking water that flowed through lead pipes. As they ingested diluted lead, they may have sterilized themselves and thus prevented the survival of the more talented men and women.

Regardless of how historical theories are evaluated, what is well documented in history are the numerous ideas of Rome that survived its decline and fall. Many scholars contend that the mighty Roman Empire did not "fall" but was merely transformed as a result of the merging of the papacy, Holy Roman Empire, Papal States, Italy, and various German elements into the nation-states of medieval Europe.   —*Daniel G. Graetzer*

Additional reading:

Chambers, Mortimer, ed. *The Fall of Rome: Can It Be Explained?* 2d ed. New York: Holt, Rinehart and Winston, 1970. This often-referenced text details the numerous interpretations of modern historians as to why Rome fell.

Gibbon, Edward. *The History of the Decline and Fall of the Roman Empire.* New York: Penguin Books, 1985. Acclaimed as a masterpiece by other historians and literary critics, Gibbon's work was first published in seven volumes.

Massie, Allan. *The Caesars.* New York: Franklin Watts, 1984. This text details the relationships between Rome's first twelve emperors and the Roman empire.

Ramsay, William. *The Church in the Roman Empire.* London: Hodder & Stoughton, 1907. This often-cited text attempts to assess the meaning of the Christian persecution and its relationship to the fall of the empire.

Vogt, Joseph. *The Decline of Rome.* London: Weidenfeld & Nicolson, 1967. An English translation of a broad study by a well-known German scholar of the fall of Rome.

See also: 410, Gothic Armies Sack Rome; 439, Vandals Seize Carthage; 445-453, Invasions of Attila the Hun; 451, Battle of the Catalaunian Plains; 533-553, Justinian's Wars Against the Vandals, Ostrogoths, and Visigoths.

496
Baptism of Clovis
The baptism of Clovis facilitates the conversion of the Franks, spreading Catholicism into France and Germany.
Date: 496
Locale: France
Categories: Government and politics; Religion

KEY FIGURES:

Clovis I (c. 466-511), king of the Franks, 482-511

Saint Gregory of Tours (c. 539-c. 594), bishop of Tours, 573-c. 594

SUMMARY OF EVENT. The conversion of Clovis to Christianity was one of the major events of the early Middle Ages and established a pivotal political and religious relationship between the Germanic tribe of the Franks and the papacy. The Franks are central to much of early medieval history, because they were the basis of the political and religious institutions and of the social and economic organization that distinguished the medieval world of Gaul, which became the geographic center of Charlemagne's empire, and of the subsequent rise of the principalities and kingdoms of France and Germany.

The significance of Clovis' baptism was that he converted to the Nicene faith—the belief of Roman Catholicism and eastern Byzantine Orthodoxy. Most other Germanic tribes occupying the Western Roman Empire were followers of Arian Christianity. Arianism had been condemned as a heresy at the first ecumenical council in 325, because it denied the full humanity of Jesus. The Nicene faith proclaimed the Holy Trinity (Father, Son, and Holy Ghost) and declared Jesus to be both God and man. Germanic Arians included the Goths (both the Ostrogoths in Italy and the Visigoths in Spain), who were converted to Arianism by the missionary Ulfilas in the mid-fourth century, the Vandals in North Africa, Lombards in Italy, and the Burgundians in southern Gaul. Clovis was the first important Germanic ruler to become Catholic. Others followed later: The Visigoths under Recared became Catholic in 589; the Burgundians converted under Sigismund (516-523); and the Lombards had a Catholic ruler, Liutprand (712-744); but these lacked the political significance of the Franks.

In the fifth century, the Franks were probably a client state of the Romans. Frankish aid was critical in the Roman victory over the Huns in 451 near Orléans. Clovis' father, Childeric, was a protector of the Gallo-Roman population and the Catholic Church. Clovis (Chlodovic) succeeded his father in 482 and, although a pagan, continued his father's policies. This meant he sought to preserve friendly relations with and to seek the advice of the Church. During the 480's, Clovis extended his power into the kingdom of Soissons, defeating and killing Syagrius, the last Roman commander in Gaul. Until his death in 511, Clovis waged constant wars against the Armorican Celts in Brittany, the Thuringi in the lower Rhine, the Alamanni north of Trier, and the Burgundians.

The fundamental source for the conversion of Clovis is the *History of the Franks*, written by Gregory of Tours a century after the event. According to Gregory, Clovis was a pagan and a plunderer of churches. Like any Germanic warrior Clovis could be ruthless and violent. Gregory describes Clovis as personally capable of splitting the head of an enemy or of anyone who demeaned his honor. Clovis worshiped Roman deities, such as Saturn, Jupiter, Mars, and Mercury. He also venerated various statutes made of stone, wood, or metal, and he may have adhered to certain Celtic and Scandinavian deities as well as a sea god that was part man, beast, and bull. Since the powerful Burgundians, Ostrogoths, and Visigoths were all Arian, it is possible that Clovis may have considered converting to Arianism. His Burgundian wife, Clotild, was Catholic, however, and had urged him to accept the Nicene faith. To his wife's entreaties, Clovis responded that Jesus was a god who could do nothing; perhaps Jesus was not even a god at all.

Clotild had their infant son baptized, but he died while still in his baptismal robes. Angry, Clovis blamed the Christian god for his son's death. To his surprise, Clotild accepted it and tried to assure Clovis that the boy was now in heaven. It was a difficult concept for Clovis to understand. A second son, Chlodomer, was born and baptized and also

As king of the Franks, Clovis was the first important Germanic ruler to convert to the Catholic faith and accept the Nicene Creed. (Archive Photos)

became ill. This only further convinced Clovis of the ineffectiveness of the Christian god, but the child recovered because, according to Gregory, of Clotild's prayers.

Clovis' war with the Alamanni had decimated both armies. In desperation Clovis now turned to Christ, calling upon him to aid the Franks in battle. Only with victory, as a sign and proof of the existence and favor of Christ, would Clovis accept baptism. The Franks won the battle of Tolbac, and Clovis informed Clotild he would be baptized. With the urging of his wife Clovis received secret religious instruction from the Bishop Remigius of Rheims. Secrecy was important because Clovis was not sure of the support of his troops for such a change. Gregory glosses over the difficulty by having the Frankish leaders already willing to accept their own and the king's baptism. On Christmas Day in 496 (though 498 or even 506 are possible), Clovis was baptized in Rheims by Bishop Remigius. Gregory portrays Remigius as a learned and holy man, who performed miracles and even raised a man from the dead, thereby underscoring the centrality of the Resurrection to Christianity. Three thousand Frankish warriors followed the example of their king and were baptized. Clovis affirmed the Nicene creed by accepting the Holy Trinity and by marking the holy chrism (oil) with the sign of the cross. A sister, Albofled, was also baptized. Although she died soon after, Clovis' faith held. A second sister later converted from Arianism.

For Gregory, Clovis was another Constantine the Great, a pagan warrior who converted to the true faith and brought that faith to his people. As a Catholic, Clovis could also justify new wars against the heretical Arian Burgundians and Goths in Gaul. Although Gregory chronicles the bloody events and brutality of Clovis, which included the elimination of family rivals and even his expressed regret that he no longer had living relatives to kill, he still describes Clovis as one who did what was pleasing to God, because Catholicism had become the official faith of the Franks.

Gregory does imply that Clovis' faith rested on the belief that Jesus was a powerful god, who could aid the Franks in battle. It is not even certain whether Clovis became a strict monotheist. The consequences of the conversion, however, were immense. Unlike other Arian Germanic tribes who stood apart from the indigenous Catholic populace, there was no religious separation between the Franks and the Gallo-Romans. This allowed for a greater assimilation between the two peoples. Clovis' wars could also marshal the support of the Gallo-Roman aristocracy, particularly of those who remained under Arian domination. The conversion had therefore an important political dimension in that it was part of Clovis' political challenge

against the Visigoths at Toulouse and the Burgundians. It also helped Clovis obtain the support of the Byzantine emperor Anastasius, whose fleets prevented the Ostrogoths from aiding the Visigoths in their conflict with the Franks. Anastasius also bestowed on Clovis the honorific title of consul. Clovis probably hoped for an imperial title, because he is described as having appeared at the Cathedral of St. Martin of Tours dressed in purple and wearing a crown. The conversion permitted a closer political and working relationship with the Merovingian bishops, many of whom were of noble birth and whose families controlled such bishoprics such as Paris, Tours, and Sens.

Clovis' conversion also made the cult of St. Martin of Tours a central part of the religious faith of the Franks. Born around the year 316 in Hungary (Pannonia), Martin was a Roman soldier, who gave half of his cloak to a beggar. His remaining half became a sacred relic of Frankish kings. Martin was in the tradition of ascetic hermits, a holy man, who attracted followers and preached in central and western Gaul. In 371, he was made bishop of Tours, and though he continued to live in a solitary cell, he did travel, even as far as Rome, to defend orthodoxy. At first the cult and monasticism of Martin did not extend much beyond the Loire River, yet Clovis was attracted to this soldier who had become an ascetic, a defender of the Nicene faith, and an administrator of a bishopric. Because of Clovis, the cult of Martin spread to Paris, Chartres, Rouen and other cities throughout the Frankish lands. In Gregory's *History of the Franks*, Martin and Clovis are the two pivotal figures defining Christianity in Frankish Gaul—the homeland of later France and Germany. Clovis founded the Church of the Apostles in Paris, later called Sainte-Genviève. —*Lawrence N. Langer*

ADDITIONAL READING:

Brown, Peter. "Relics and Social Status in the Age of Gregory of Tours." In *Society and the Holy in Late Antiquity*. Berkeley: University of California Press, 1982. An important analysis of religious attitudes among the Franks.

Geary, Patrick. *Before France and Germany*. Oxford: Oxford University Press, 1988. A study of society in Merovingian Gaul.

Gregory of Tours. *The History of the Franks*. Translated by L. Thorpe. New York: Penguin Books, 1974. The fundamental source for the reign of Clovis.

Wallace-Hadrill, J. M. *The Frankish Church*. Oxford: Oxford University Press, 1983. An important study of the Frankish church.

_____. *The Long-Haired Kings*. New York: Barnes & Noble, 1962. The standard study of early Frankish history.

SEE ALSO: 312, Conversion of Constantine; 325, The Nicene Creed; 450, Conversion of Ireland; 735, Christianity Is Introduced into Germany; 754, Coronation of Pepin.

506
BREVIARIUM OF ALARIC IS DRAFTED

The Breviarium *of Alaric is drafted, codifying a transmitted body of Roman statutes and jurisprudence in a form accepted by a European barbarian ruler.*

DATE: February 2, 506

LOCALE: Toulouse, France

CATEGORIES: Government and politics; Laws, acts, and legal history

KEY FIGURES:

Alaric II (died 507), king of the Visigoths, 484-507

Clovis (c. 466-511), king of the Franks, c. 481-511

Euric (died 484), king of the Visigoths, 466-484

Theodosius II (401-450), Eastern Roman emperor, 408-450

SUMMARY OF EVENT. In A.D. 418, the Roman Master of Soldiers Constantius concluded a treaty with the barbarian Visigoths that settled them in Aquitania, the name given then and now to southwestern Gaul (modern-day France). This marked the beginning of the so-called kingdom of Toulouse, the first of what were to become several barbarian kingdoms carved out of the western Roman Empire. In 477, the Visigoths, under their king Euric (466-484), occupied the last Roman territory of southern Gaul, and, in Gaul at least, the Roman Empire was at an end.

The Visigoths, however, were but a drop in a Roman sea, and in many ways ruled only by the sufferance of the Roman majority. By this time, Gallo-Roman bishops had become the de facto rulers of the Roman population, and powerful Gallo-Roman senators were a force to be reckoned with. Barbarian rulers offended influential Romans at their peril.

One of the most significant areas of incompatibility between Visigoths and Romans was religious: both peoples were Christian, but the Romans were Nicene (Catholic) and the Visigoths Arian, resulting in an insurmountable obstacle to any meaningful integration of the two societies, for each considered the other to be heretics. The ambitious Euric, in attempts to consolidate his authority, forbade the ordination of Catholic bishops as sees became vacant, and as a result seriously antagonized the Roman aristocracy. Bishops of newly acquired Roman cities were often exiled or imprisoned.

At the same time, Euric attempted to regularize the legal affairs of his kingdom by issuing a law code known as the *Codex Euricianus* ("Code of Euric"). He did so not only to impose his control more firmly upon his Visigothic subjects, but also to assert Visigothic independence of any vestige of Roman authority. It has been suggested in the past that the Code was based on Visigothic custom and intended only for the Visigoths, but it would appear that many of the pronouncements were in fact based on Roman provincial law and applied to Visigoths and Romans equally. The surviving entries in his code, about 60 of an original 350, touch on matters of property, buying and selling, loans, and gifts. When Euric died in 484, his son Alaric II inherited a very tense social and political situation. Even though Alaric subsequently allowed vacant sees to be filled, Visigothic relations with the Gallo-Roman aristocracy continued to be strained.

In the north, meanwhile, another ambitious barbarian chieftain, Clovis, became the ruler of one of the many fragmented bands of Franks in 481-482. In 486, he doubled the size of his kingdom by defeating Syagrius of Soissons, the last independent Roman ruler in Gaul. Subsequently, perhaps in the mid-490's, Clovis adopted Nicene Christianity, and immediately became the darling of the Gallo-Roman establishment. In the Visigothic kingdom, a number of Roman bishops were exiled or imprisoned for supposedly favoring the Franks.

By the early sixth century, Clovis had incorporated most of the other Frankish groups into his own kingdom, and it was clear that he had his eyes on the kingdom of Toulouse. Faced with this northern threat, Alaric attempted to shore up his sagging Gallo-Roman support. In 506, he permitted the Catholic bishops to summon, in the small coastal town of Agde, the first church council to be held in Aquitania since the arrival of the Visigoths.

On February 2 of the same year, Alaric sanctioned the issuance at Toulouse of yet another law code, this one strictly Roman in nature. Although described in the text simply as a *Corpus* ("collection"), it later became known as the *Breviarium Alarici* ("Breviary of Alaric"), or the *Lex romana Visigothorum* ("Roman law of the Visigoths"). Its publication was overseen by the *vir inlustis* (illustrious gentleman) Count Goiaricus, and it was edited by the *vir spectabilis* (respectable gentleman) Anianus and distributed by the *vir spectabilis* Count Timotheus. Its heading noted, "In this body (*corpus*) are contained the laws (*leges*) and the image of justice (*ius*), selected from the Theodosian and other books and, as it was commanded, interpreted." Its prologue proclaimed that it had been issued "So that all the obscurity of Roman laws (*leges*) and ancient jurisprudence (*ius*), led into the light of a better intelligence with the assistance of bishops and the nobility, might be made clear and so that nothing might remain in doubt," and it asserted that "the assent of the venerable bishops and chosen provincials has strengthened" it.

The *Breviarium* is a typical product of Roman provincial jurisprudence. It complemented, but did not replace, the Code of Euric by giving Visigothic sanction to selected elements of Roman law. In doing so, it reinforced the notion that the Visigothic kings were the direct successors of the Roman emperors. It was excerpted from the two primary sources of Roman law: the statutes (*leges*) issued by Roman emperors and the opinions (*ius*) put forth by eminent Roman jurists. In the former category were entries from the *Codex Gregorianus* ("Code of Gregorius") and *Codex Hermogenianus* ("Code of Hermogenianus"), both originally issued in the 290's under the emperor Diocletian (284-305) (and both known primarily only from their entries in the *Breviarium*); 398 constitutions (less than one-eighth of the total) from the *Codex Theodosianus* ("Theodosian Code"), issued by the eastern emperor Theodosius II (402-450) in 438; and the *Novellae* ("New Laws"), which were issued between 438 and 471. The only jurists cited were Gaius, Paul, and Papinian.

Yet this is not to say that the *Breviarium* merely copied, or even summarized, the *Codex Theodosianus*. Far from it. A clear selection process was at work. For example, some Roman legislation, such as that on *hospitium* (the billeting of troops), *agri deserti* (deserted lands), and heretics, was omitted. Other laws were revised: the *Breviarium* repeated the prohibition of intermarriage between Romans and barbarians dating from the 370's, but substituted the words *Romani* (Romans) and *barbari* (barbarians) for *provinciales* (provincials) and *gentiles* (foreigners)—a curious instance of the Visigoths self-identifying as barbarians. Furthermore, the *Breviarium* also included, at the express request of Alaric, extensive legal *interpretationes* (interpretations) of the Theodosian provisions, which give an indication of the enormous scope of legal activities in late and post-Roman Gaul. Although it has been generally assumed that Alaric's Gallo-Roman legal advisers completed the task of assembling and issuing the code within the remarkably short space of a few months, it would seem more likely that the work had been going on for a very long time in private Gallic legal circles, and that the politically astute Gauls merely used Alaric's dire straits to their own advantage in securing his approval for work which was already essentially complete.

It is impossible to say where Alaric's initiatives might have led. In the following year, 507, the armies of Alaric and Clovis met at Vouillé, and the result was the destruction of the Visigothic army and the death of Alaric. During the next year, Clovis occupied nearly all of the kingdom of Toulouse. All that remained to the Visigoths, now firmly entrenched in Spain, was Septimania, a coastal strip focused on Narbonne. The Gothic kingdom of Toulouse was at an end, and the history of post-Roman Gaul was to be written not by the Visigoths but by the Franks.

The *Breviarium*, however, refused to die, and went on to enjoy a distinguished and influential afterlife. Although other more complete sections of various parts of the Theodosian Code survived elsewhere, the *Breviarium* is the only extant document that preserves the organizational structure of the entire code.

Furthermore, Alaric's initiative gave a barbarian *imprimatur* to Roman law that was seconded in other barbarian kingdoms which also introduced in the sixth century and later law codes heavily influenced by Roman law in general and by the *Breviarium* in particular. These include the *Lex romana Burgundionum* ("Roman Law of the Burgundians") of the Burgundian kingdom (which included a mere forty-seven clauses), and even the *Pactus legis salicae* ("Record of Salic Law") of the Franks.

The publication of the *Breviarium* also was one reason why subsequent Western barbarian law was based on the Theodosian Code rather than the updated and expanded *Codex Justinianus* ("Code of Justinian"), issued by the Romans at Constantinople in the early 530's. Other forms of the Theodosian Code, perhaps based in part on the *Breviarium*, also were used in post-Roman western Europe and attest to the code's continued vitality. These include the *Lex romana curiensis* ("Roman law of Chur") dating from the period A.D. 800. In general, the *Breviarium* demonstrates in a microcosm the ways in which Roman law and custom had a decisive role in barbarian Europe that continued to have an effect even in the twentieth century.

—*Ralph W. Mathisen*

ADDITIONAL READING:

Drew, Katherine Fischer. "The Barbarian Kings as Lawgivers and Judges." In *Life and Thought in the Early Middle Ages*, edited by Robert S. Hoyt. Minneapolis: University of Minnesota Press, 1967. Drew's study assesses the influence of the *Breviarium*, especially in southwestern Gaul and the Rhone valley, even after it was superseded by the seventh code known as *Liber*, or *Forum Judicum*.

Harries, J., and Ian Wood, eds. *The Theodosian Code*. Ithaca, N.Y.: Cornell University Press, 1993. Provides a background for understanding the Roman legal precedents on which the *Breviarium* was based.

Mathisen, Ralph. *Roman Aristocrats in Barbarian Gaul: Strategies for Survival in an Age of Transition*. Austin: University of Texas Press, 1993. A useful study of the period.

Wood, Ian. "Disputes in Late Fifth and Sixth-Century Gaul: Some Problems." In *The Settlement of Disputes in Early Medieval Europe*, edited by Wendy Davies and Paul Fouracre. New York: Cambridge University Press, 1986. This scholarly article places the *Breviarium* in a helpful legal and historical context.

Ziegler, Aloysius K. "The Visigothic Code of Civil Law." In *Church and State in Visigothic Spain*. Washington, D.C.: Catholic University of America, 1930. Although this dissertation is an older study, it offers important insights.

SEE ALSO: 165, Gaius' Edition of the *Institutes* of Roman Law; 529-534, Justinian's *Code*; 533-553, Justinian's Wars Against the Vandals, Ostrogoths, and Visigoths

524
IMPRISONMENT AND DEATH OF BOETHIUS

The imprisonment and death of Boethius results in the composition of one of the Western world's most influential books—The Consolation of Philosophy.

DATE: 524

LOCALE: Pavia (Ticinum), Italy (twenty miles south of Milan)

CATEGORIES: Cultural and intellectual history; Government and politics

KEY FIGURES:

Anicius Manlius Severinus Boethius (c. 480-524), philosopher, theologian, Roman senator and consul

Quintus Aurelius Memmius Symmachus (died 524 or 525), adoptive father, father-in-law, and friend of Boethius, Roman senator and consul

Theodoric (c. 454-526), king of the Ostrogoths, Roman governor of Italy, and an Arian Christian, 474-526

SUMMARY OF EVENT. The philosopher, theologian, poet, and statesman Boethius was unjustly accused of treason by Theodoric, king of the Ostrogoths and governor of Italy, imprisoned at Pavia (Ticinum), tortured, and executed in the year 524. While imprisoned, he composed what many consider to be the single most influential book for the medieval, Renaissance, and early modern Western world: *The Consolation of Philosophy*.

Boethius belonged to an ancient, noble Roman family. He was a Roman senator, Roman consul in 510, and *magister officiorum* ("master of the palace") in 522. He had had a very successful career as a statesman under Theodoric, he was actually a friend of Theodoric, and yet he was accused of treason, banished from Rome, imprisoned, tortured, and executed at Pavia under orders of this

same person. Theodoric, king of the Ostrogoths (the East Goths), had migrated with his whole tribe from the eastern end of the Roman Empire to Italy itself. In addition to being king of the Ostrogoths, Theodoric became, as a result of conquest, governor of Italy with the approbation of the Roman emperor in Constantinople.

The situation in brief is part of the so-called fall of Rome, that is the change from ancient classical Rome with its emperors and senators to early medieval Rome with its so-called barbarian overlords. Boethius was part of the old order; Theodoric was a leader of the new order. The situation would be complicated enough if it were political alone; however, there was the further complication of religion. Boethius is believed to have been a Catholic Christian; Theodoric was an Arian Christian. What this means at core is that Boethius' Christian faith was orthodox according to the Roman episcopal teaching about Christ as true God and true man, whereas Theodoric's Christian faith was considered heretical, holding that Christ was neither truly God nor truly man but a being having a human body with divine essence. The accusation of treason against Boethius may very likely have been as much a religious charge as a political charge and may have been thought to involve an attempt to reunite the eastern and western parts of the Roman Empire both politically and doctrinally. (The emperor in Constantinople at that time was a Catholic Christian.) The accusation also seems to involve Pope John I, who was the current pope. The charge was treason, but what was behind the charge is not clear. Nevertheless, there seems to be universal agreement that Boethius was not guilty of the offenses of which he was accused. This innocence makes his torture, which was most unusual for a Roman senator anyway, even more heinous. It is said that a strap was tied around his eyes and temples and then tightened to inflict great pain. The mode of execution itself is also clearly out of keeping with the dignity of a Roman senator; he was clubbed to death. Boethius' adoptive father and father-in-law, Symmachus, also a Roman senator and consul, was executed under similar vague charges of treason with Boethius or within a year later.

Before the imprisonment, Boethius was not only a trusted and influential statesman but also a prominent philosopher and theologian. He learned Greek early in his training and had set a goal for himself to translate into Latin, and to comment on, all the works of both Plato and Aristotle. His further goal was to reconcile the two philosophies based on his understanding of their essential agreement with one another. Because of his political duties and particularly because of his untimely death he did not get very far with his major project of reconciling Plato and Aristotle. He did make some important beginnings particularly with the writings of Aristotle including the *Categories* and the *Organon*. In addition he composed original books on logic, arithmetic, geometry, music, and astronomy. Further, he is thought to be the author of several Christian theological books including the following: *The Trinity Is One God Not Three Gods, Whether Father, Son, and Holy Spirit Are Substantially Predicated of the Divinity*, and *On the Catholic Faith*. Although much of his work is unfinished, he left a legacy both of syntheses of ancient writings and of his own original writings. Much of what he accomplished and published became standard and basic textbook material for medieval, Renaissance, and early modern schools and universities. This alone would have made him memorable and worthy of admiration and study.

What he composed while imprisoned is truly amazing and even more worthy of attention. Under the shadow of torture and anticipated execution, he composed *The Consolation of Philosophy*. This work is in five books each consisting of alternating prose and poetical sections. The prose sections may be said to represent the philosopher Boethius; the poetical sections may be said to represent the poet Boethius. He is a master in both. Also he is very Platonic and neo-Platonic in both with a focus on real reality as otherworldly. Interesting questions here are where is the theologian Boethius? Why a consolation of philosophy rather than theology? There is not a really good answer for these questions assuming Boethius was the Christian scholars think he was and particularly in light of a man facing death turning to philosophy, logic, and reason rather than to religion, revelation, and the Bible. Be that as it may, this work is a consolation of philosophy not of religion nor even of literature. An allegorical figure called Lady Philosophy helps the imprisoned Boethius through his doubts and troubles to a reasoned acceptance of the way things are. The comings and goings of this earthly life are not as important as one might think. Lady Fortune also plays a role in this allegorical instruction. Lady Philosophy not only teaches about Fortune's fickle role in human destiny but also takes up more important questions such as the concept of true happiness, the supreme good, evil, providence, free will, and the simplicity and perfection of divine knowledge. From this short list of important questions alone, however, it can be seen that barely under the philosophical layer there is a theological layer of inquiry. Succeeding generations found this philosophical and poetical approach to theological questions most intriguing, most convincing, and truly consoling. The result is that the book quickly became the favorite and comforting reading of thousands and thousands of persons. As with the biblical Job, Boethius and Lady Philosophy teach readers how little humans really understand about themselves and about God. It is interesting to consider the stature of some of the early translators into English of this book: King Alfred the Great into Old English, Geoffrey Chaucer into Middle English, and Queen Elizabeth I into early modern English. Students who come to appreciate the lessons of *The Consolation of Philosophy* will also come close to understanding the core of medieval, Renaissance, and early modern thinking. They are indeed that closely linked. To know Boethius is to know the beginnings of medieval culture. As much as one regrets Boethius' imprisonment, torture, and execution, these conditions produced a major work of prison literature.   —*Douglas J. McMillan*

ADDITIONAL READING:

Astell, Ann W. *Job, Boethius, and Epic Truth*. Ithaca, N.Y.: Cornell University Press, 1994. An exploration of Boethius' role in the history of the genres of allegory and epic.

Barrett, Helen M. *Boethius: Some Aspects of His Times and Work*. Reprint. New York: Russell & Russell, 1965. First published in 1940, this is a standard account of the life, times, and thought of Boethius.

Boethius. *The Consolation of Philosophy*. Translated and edited by Richard Green. The Library of Liberal Arts. Indianapolis: Bobbs-Merrill, 1962. In addition to a standard translation, this edition includes good basic information on Boethius and his major work plus an invaluable summary of *The Consolation of Philosophy*.

Gibson, Margaret, ed. *Boethius: His Life, Thought and Influence*. Oxford: Basil Blackwell, 1981. A collection of fourteen major scholarly essays to celebrate the fifteen hundredth anniversary of Boethius' birth: 480-1980.

Lewis, C. S. "Boethius." In *The Discarded Image: An Introduction to Medieval and Renaissance Literature*. Cambridge, England: Cambridge University Press, 1964. A brilliant definition of the central role of Boethius in medieval and Renaissance culture.

Patch, Howard Rollin. *The Tradition of Boethius: A Study of His Importance in Medieval Culture*. Reprint. New York: Russell & Russell, 1970. First published in 1935, this is a standard literary account of Boethius' importance.

Varvis, Stephen. *The "Consolation" of Boethius: An Analytical Inquiry into His Intellectual Processes and Goals*. San Francisco: Mellen Research University Press, 1991. A standard historical and philosophical account of Boethius' importance.

SEE ALSO: 325, The Nicene Creed; 428-431, The Nestorian Controversy; 476, "Fall" of Rome.

529-534
JUSTINIAN'S CODE

Justinian's Code *creates a comprehensive, authoritative compilation of Roman law that serves as the foundation of European law.*

DATE: 529-534

LOCALE: Constantinople

CATEGORIES: Government and politics; Laws, acts, and legal history

KEY FIGURES:

John the Cappadocian (fl. 525-550), praetorian prefect of the East, c. 531-January, 532; 532-541

Justin I (c. 450-527), Byzantine emperor, 518-527

Justinian I (c. 497-565), Byzantine emperor, 527-565

Theodora (c. 500-548), Byzantine empress, 527-548

Theodosius II (401-450), Byzantine emperor, 408-450

Tribonian (died 545), quaestor of the Sacred Palace, 529-532, 534-545

Valentinian III (Flavius Valentinianus; 419-455), Western Roman emperor, 425-455

SUMMARY OF EVENT. When Justinian directed its reform, Roman law was the accumulated product of Rome's history from republican times. For centuries, emperors had repeatedly issued new laws and decrees (referred to as "constitutions"). They also issued rescripts (official statements) regarding specific questions. Although these did not necessarily agree with the general principles of the law, they had the force of law. In addition, laws were not systematically published and the archives did not always keep copies of new legislation. This accumulation of conflicting legislation made it difficult for lawyers and judges to cite the law accurately on specific legal points. Also jurisconsultants issued many opinions during the second and third centuries. These opinions, however, were sometimes contradictory, and many were difficult to find.

Toward the end of the third century, two different collections of laws were compiled and updating was attempted during following years. These publications, however, gradually lost their usefulness as time passed. In 426, Valentinian III, the Western Roman emperor, ordered that the opinions of only five past commentators could be cited before the courts. Opinions of earlier commentators cited by them also could be considered, but only if they were confirmed by comparison of manuscripts. If the commentators differed, the majority ruled. If they were equally divided, the authority of the group which included an opinion of Papinian, a prestigious second century jurist, was to be accepted. Theodosius II, after setting up commissions in 427 and 434 in order to prepare a collection of laws issued after 312, promulgated the Theodosian Code

in 438. His code, however, proved inadequate. In short, by the time of Justinian, the legal system badly needed streamlining.

Prior to succeeding the emperor Justin, who was his uncle, Justinian had long served in the emperor's administration. According to the historian Procopius, Justin appointed his nephew, Justinian, Count of the Domestics, and invested him with patrician rank immediately after beginning his reign in 518. In 529, Justin, having earlier adopted him, made Justinian co-emperor. Thus, Justinian became well aware of defects in the legal system, and, doubtless, began formulating plans for reform.

Justinian's long-term mistress, whom he married after the death of Justin's wife, was most influential in Justinian's rule. He considered her co-equal in many respects, and portions of his code, especially those relating to women's issues, apparently were heavily influenced by her opinions. She appears not, however, to have been officially recognized as sharing the throne.

On February 13, 528, in the first year of his reign, Justinian appointed a commission of ten experts to produce a new code of imperial law. The chairman of the commission was John the Cappadocian, praetorian prefect of the East, the highest administrative official of the eastern empire. The commission was charged with updating the laws recorded in the existing Gregorian, Hermogenian, and Theodosian Codes. In addition, the constitutions, as well as "novels" or supplementary laws, issued since promulgation of the Theodosian Code, were to be included. This accumulated mass of law was systematized and simplified in the *Codex Justinianus* and published April 7, 529. An updated edition later was published November 16, 534.

On December 15, 530, a second commission, under the direction of Tribonian, quaestor of the Sacred Palace (chief legal officer of the empire) and a highly qualified lawyer, set out to codify the works of Roman jurists. These works, written by Roman lawyers during the first through fourth centuries, comprised 1,528 "books." Each manuscript was the length of a papyrus roll. The entire text is estimated to comprise three million lines. Tribonian, who probably was a graduate of the school at Beirut, chose the other commissioners: Constantinus, the *register libellorum*, the official whose function was to prepare cases for the supreme court; Dorotheus, dean of the Beirut law school; Anatolius, a Beirut law school professor whose father had served on the first commission; Theophilus, a professor at the Constantinople law school; and Cratinus, another Constantinople professor. In addition, eleven barristers assisted the commission. All of these were *illustres*, belonging to the highest and least numerous class of senators who were permitted to deliberate in the senate. By December 16, 533, the commission published the Panadects, or Digest, consisting of 9,123 separate texts contained in fifty books totaling 150,000 lines.

During their work, the commissioners found many outmoded or unjust arguments and opinions. Many of these were simply abolished, but some questions required reform, so during the first three years of his reign, Justinian issued many new laws. These, then were compiled by the commission and published in late 530 or early 531 as *Fifty Decisions*, the text of which has been lost. This contained only decisions promulgated before work began on the *Digest*. Tribonian's commission quickly recognized that a new edition of the Code of 529 would be required, so Tribonian, Dorotheus, and three other lawyers immediately began work. The revised code, *Codex Justinianus repetitae praelectionis* or "Justinian's Code of Resumed Reading," published in 534, replaced the *Codex Vetus* of 529.

In addition, a committee consisting of Tribonian and the leading academic lawyers of Constantinople and Beirut also prepared, as a short textbook, the *Institutes* to be used by students of law. This was published November 21, 533, and was heavily indebted to Gaius, an earlier lawyer of the second century.

Justinian intended the entire work, *Codex*, *Digest*, and *Institutes* or *Corpus Iuris Civilis*, as it has been known since the sixteenth century, as a unified, consistent, literal, and straightforward body of law. Commentaries on the *Digest* were prohibited, although indices and supply headings were provided. In contrast to the *Codex*, literal translations of the *Digest* into Greek also were allowed.

The *Corpus* seems to have little affected the mass of the empire. In any event, civil courts were hardly used away from Constantinople. The fact that the *Code* and *Digest* were published in Latin, a language not understood in most of the eastern empire, limited use of the *Corpus*. Local laws and institutions continued to operate in many localities even though they contradicted imperial legislation, and arbitration and mediation were favored in the provinces, generally with bishops or local holy men as arbiters. Although slightly used in the Eastern Empire after the sixth century, the *Corpus* remained a most important philosophical contribution. In the eleventh century, rediscovery of the *Digest* led to the founding of the University of Bologna in 1088 and the revival of Roman law. Inerius' publication of the *Vulgate Digest* as a textbook for students at Bologna is, by some, considered the initial spark of the European Renaissance. In any event, Justinian's code of civil law became the *de facto* law in many parts of Western Europe. Furthermore, appropriate parts of Roman law were incorporated in new codes and func-

tioned as parts of them. In this way, the influence of Roman law persists through all subsequent European history.
                                    —*Ralph L. Langenheim, Jr.*

ADDITIONAL READING:

Browning, Robert. *Justinian and Theodora.* 2d ed. London: Thames & Hudson, 1987. Discusses Empress Theodora's contributory role in Justinian's administration.

Bury, J. B. *History of the Later Roman Empire: From the Death of Theodosius I to the Death of Justinian.* London: St. Martin's Press, 1923. Reprint. New York: Dover Publications, 1958. Comprehensive scholarly history with a full chapter on Justinian's legislative works. Bury's work on Byzantium is the definitive account by an English-speaking scholar.

Evans, James Allen Stewart. *The Age of Justinian.* New York: Routledge, 1996. An updated political and social history of Justinian's era, including many facets of the legal system.

Gerostergios, Asterios. *Justinian the Great: The Emperor and Saint.* Belmont, Mass.: Institute for Byzantium and Modern Greek Studies, 1982. Detailed account by a Greek historian of Justinian's religious policies, including the role of the *Codex*.

Moorhead, John. *Justinian.* New York: Longman, 1994. A concise biography that includes a succinct account of Justinian's legal reforms.

Thomas, J. A. C. *Textbook of Roman Law.* Amsterdam: North Holland, 1976. Account of the Justinian Code and its far-reaching consequences.

Vasiliev, A. A. *History of the Byzantine Empire, 324-1453.* Madison: University of Wisconsin Press, 1952. Written from the point of view of czarist Russian scholarship, this comprehensive account illuminates Justinian's legal reforms, their causes and effects.

SEE ALSO: 165, Gaius' Edition of the *Institutes* of Roman Law; 506, *Breviarium* of Alaric II Is Drafted; 533-553, Justinian's Wars Against the Vandals, Ostrogoths, and Visigoths.

532-537
BUILDING OF HAGIA SOPHIA

The building of Hagia Sophia marks the pinnacle of Byzantine architecture and engineering, creating a cathedral whose design influences future building in both the Muslim and Christian worlds.

DATE: 532-537

LOCALE: Constantinople

CATEGORIES: Cultural and intellectual history; Religion; Science and technology

KEY FIGURES:

Anthemios of Tralles, architect and designer of the building

Mustafa Kemal Atatürk (1881-1938), president of Turkey, 1923-1938

Isidore of Miletus, architect and assistant to Anthemius

Isidore the Younger, engineer who redesigned the dome

Justinian I (482-565), Byzantine emperor, 527-565

SUMMARY OF EVENT. When Justinian commissioned the construction of the Cathedral of Hagia Sophia in Constantinople in 532, he envisioned the structure to be a symbol of both Christianity and his ability to civilize and rule much of the known world. The first church to occupy the site was built and dedicated by Constantine II on February 15, 360. It followed a basilica plan similar to Old Saint Peter's in Rome. During the riots that followed the banishment of John Chrysostom, the structure burned on June 20, 404. Hagia Sophia was rebuilt by Theodosius the Younger and consecrated in 415. This second church was one of many architectural victims of the riots in January, 532, begun by the uniting of Hippodrome factions against the state. Through its failure, the Nika insurrection provided Justinian the opportunity to rebuild the imperial capital and usher in a new "golden age."

As architects for the cathedral of Hagia Sophia, or "Holy Wisdom," Justinian chose two scholars and master builders: Anthemius of Tralles, and Isidorus of Miletus. Anthemius, the principal designer, authored works on conic sections and reflectors. Isidorus, who taught physics and stereometry at the Universities of Alexandria and Constantinople, had collected and published the works of Archimedes of Syracuse, and had written commentary on the Kamarika of Heron of Alexandria concerning the construction of vaults.

Early Christian structures were built using two essentially different forms: the central plan and the rectangular basilica, with its focal point at one end. The inspiration for the first type of structure came from such buildings as the Pantheon in Rome and the mausoleums of Diocletian in Split and resulted in centralized churches such as San Stefano Rotundo in Rome (468-483) and San Lorenzo in Milan (founded circa 350, and rebuilt in the fifth century). The rectangular church form dominated in the West, where attention focused upon the altar and presbyterium. Its secular predecessors were the basilica facing the forum in Pompeii and the Basilica Julia in Rome. The Cathedral of Hagia Sophia represented a fusion of these forms employing a daring and complexity that had never before been attempted.

One of the major feats of construction was the erection of a dome on a square base. This dome rested upon a crown formed by the conjuncture of the tops of four arches and four pendentives rising from four massive piers. The thrust of the dome to the east and west was taken up by two semidomes abutting the arches, and these in turn discharged it upon vaults and piers still farther to the east and west. The lateral pressure to the north and south, on the other hand, was absorbed by the piers. This technical skill and balance of thrusts would be copied, but not equaled for centuries. The construction began on February 23, 532, with two teams of workers with a combined force of ten thousand men. Following traditional Roman practice, Hagia Sophia was built of brick and mortar except for the eight main piers, which were made of large blocks of stone. The use of standardized materials in conjunction with a sense of competitiveness between the work crews enabled the structure to be completed on schedule for its dedication on December 27, 537. The rebuilt cathedral's magnificent scale pleased Justinian to such a degree that he stated: "Glory to God who has deemed me worthy to complete such a work. O Solomon, I have surpassed thee."

Worshipers enter the sanctuary by first passing through a forecourt and two vestibules, each two hundred feet wide which fulfill the function of a narthex. Beyond is the large oval area 225 feet in length and 107 feet in width. Over the center of this open space, the architects placed a relatively shallow dome the same width as the nave, rising to a height of 160 feet. Light for the church came through many apertures including forty windows that puncture the great dome. The combination of a gold ceiling, multicol-

Elevation and Plan of the Cathedral of Sᵃ Sophia at Constantinople.

This cutaway view shows the interior vaulting that allowed for the construction of the central dome of the Cathedral of Hagia Sophia in Constantinople. (Archive Photos)

ored marble columns, walls, and pavement and large areas decorated with mosaics gave the church's interior a luminous effect.

The exaggerated thrust of the shallow dome, the haste with which it was constructed, and severe earthquakes in 553 and again in 557 contributed to a split in the arch to the east, so that on May 7, 558, part of the central dome collapsed. As both Anthemius and Isidorus had died, the task of restoration was given to Isidorus the Younger, who strengthened the arches to the north and south and filled in their spandrels with windowed walls. To diminish the lateral thrust of the central dome, he raised its center some twenty feet. Isidorus' work was necessary and remarkably successful, but he was more an engineer than an artist. The resulting inner shell of the dome is no longer as brilliantly illuminated, as the walls beneath the north and south arches, even though pierced with windows, cut off the light that once filled the nave.

Following the completion of Isidorus the Younger's work, Hagia Sophia changed little even as the power of the Byzantine Empire waned. In 1453, Constantinople fell to the Ottoman Turks and the Christian Orthodox cathedral became both a royal mosque and an architectural model for Muslim religious structures throughout the Ottoman Empire. Beginning in the second half of the fifteenth century, a dramatic shift took place in the architecture of the Islamic world as designers strove to create mosques equal to the empire their masters ruled.

Throughout its existence, Hagia Sophia has required repeated restorations to combat the effects of regional earthquakes. The work of repairing the structure in the years after the fall of Constantinople gave Muslim architects the opportunity to study the cathedral's vaulting system. As early as 1463, the combination of a dome flanked by a semidome was used at the mosque of Mehmed II in Istanbul. By 1505, two semidomes were used in the construction of the city's second imperial mosque of Bayezit II. It was the late sixteenth century architect Sinan, however, who sought to create works which directly competed with Justinian's masterpiece in the mosques of Süleyman and Kilic Ali Pasha.

In the West, St. Mark's Cathedral in Venice, the repository of much of the wealth of Constantinople stolen in the Fourth Crusade, bears the most direct relationship to Hagia Sophia. After Hagia Sophia was converted to a mosque, access to the building became restricted for non-believers. Only in the twentieth century were Westerners allowed to study Hagia Sophia's mosaics, which had long been covered for religious reasons. After the fall of the Ottoman Empire, following World War I, funding for the structures preservation diminished. On February 1, 1935,

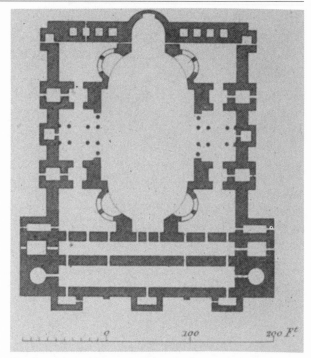

The floor plan of Hagia Sophia reveals the central oval space above which the architects placed the cathedral's distinctive dome and semidome. (Archive Photos)

Mustafa Kemal Atatürk, president of Turkey, had Hagia Sophia converted into a museum in order to permit a restoration of both its interior and exterior to take place. Although much of the ornament of Justinian's cathedral is lost, what remains provides testament to both the artist and architectural skills of the Byzantine Empire.

—*M. Joseph Costelloe,*
updated by Edmund Dickenson Potter

ADDITIONAL READING:

Kahler, Heinz. *Hagia Sophia's*. New York: Frederick A. Praeger, 1967. Kahler provides a concise history of the cathedral and detailed illustrations of its structure.

Kinross, Lord. *Hagia Sophia*. New York: Newsweek, 1972. As a supplement to his work, Kinross provides a large collection of commentaries made by visitors to Hagia Sophia in the many centuries since its consecration.

Krautheimer, Richard. *Early Christian and Byzantine Architecture*. Baltimore: Penguin Books, 1965. Krautheimer demonstrates Hagia Sophia's importance in the history of architecture through this survey, which illustrates church development in the first five hundred years of Christianity.

Mainstone, Rowland J. *Hagia Sophia*. New York: Thames & Hudson, 1988. Using archaeological evidence,

Rowland seeks to separate Justinian's cathedral from later restoration and demonstrate how it was used in religious ceremonies.

Mango, Cyril. *The Mosaics of St. Sophia at Istanbul.* Washington, D.C.: Dumbarton Oaks Research Library, 1962. Mango is regularly sighted as an expert of Hagia Sophia's mosaics, which were an integral part of the building's design.

Mark, Robert, and Ahmet S. Cakmak. *Hagia Sophia: From the Age of Justinian to the Present.* New York: Cambridge University Press, 1992. Examines the cathedral's structure, design, and material through a series of essays by leading scholars. The work addresses Hagia Sophia's influence on Muslim architects and how restoration and stabilization of the building has changed its design since the fall of Constantinople.

Procopius. *Buildings.* Translated by H. B. Dewing with the collaboration of Glanville Downey. Cambridge, Mass.: Harvard University Press, 1940. As the first historian to document Justinian's reign, Procopius provides the only surviving account of Hagia Sophia's construction. This work is volume 7 in the collected works of Procopius published as part of the Loeb Classical Library.

SEE ALSO: 447-438 B.C., The Parthenon Is Built; 312 B.C., First Roman Aqueduct Is Built; 1150-1200, Development of Gothic Architecture; 1410-1440, Florentine School of Art Emerges.

533-553
JUSTINIAN'S WARS AGAINST THE VANDALS, OSTROGOTHS, AND VISIGOTHS

Justinian's wars against the Vandals, Ostrogoths, and Visigoths mark the last major attempt to revive the Roman Empire as a great Mediterranean power.

DATE: 533-553

LOCALE: Spain, North Africa, and Italy

CATEGORIES: Expansion and land acquisition; Wars, uprisings, and civil unrest

KEY FIGURES:

Belisarius (c. 505-565), commander of the Byzantine army

Justinian I (483-565), Byzantine emperor, 527-565

Narses (c. 480-574), commander of the Byzantine army and grand chamberlain

Totila (Baduila; died 552), king of the Ostrogoths, 541-552

SUMMARY OF EVENT. One of the central and unifying policies of the reign of Justinian was the reconquest of western Roman lands lost to the Germanic tribes in the fifth and early sixth centuries A.D. By the reign of Justinian, the Visigoths occupied Spain, the Franks and Burgundians held Gaul, the Vandals ruled in North Africa from Carthage, and the Ostrogoths controlled much of Italy from their capital in Ravenna. Despite the harsh reality of Germanic rule in the West, Byzantine emperors never relinquished the idea of a single Roman empire, encompassing the West, with the rightful emperor sitting in Constantinople. Furthermore, as the defender of "true Christianity," Justinian felt compelled to uphold orthodox Christian belief. The Ostrogoths, Visigoths, and Vandals were all adherents of Christian Arianism—a doctrine stating that Christ the Son has a separate substance and nature from that of God the Father, making Christ less than fully divine. This doctrine had been condemned as heretical by the church council at Nicaea in 325. Thus, the reconquest of the West involved the subjugation of heresy as well as the liberation of the Roman population from Germanic rule.

Justinian's armies were small, perhaps no more than twenty thousand at any one time, and they often consisted of mercenaries whose payment demands drained the treasury. Wars against Persia further depleted manpower and treasure, and the Nika rebellion in 532 almost toppled Justinian and Empress Theodora from power. Nevertheless, the emperor was determined to take back lost Roman lands in the Mediterranean; to that end, he had two brilliant generals in Belisarius and Narses.

The war against the Visigoths (or West Goths) in Spain was generally inconsequential. The Visigoths first carved out a kingdom centered at Toulouse in Gaul but later moved south of the Pyrenees under pressure from the Franks. Justinian was principally concerned with Italy and North Africa; he saw an opportunity, however, to intervene in Spain in 500, when the Visigoths became divided between two rival claimants, Agila and Athanagild. Justinian supported Athanagild's request for aid, and a small Byzantine army took the southern coast along the Straits of Spain, including Cadiz. Once Athanagild secured his throne in 554, Byzantine expansion was halted.

The Vandals under Gaiseric sacked Rome in 455 and conquered North Africa, but Vandal power declined after Gaiseric's death in 477. In 523, his grandson, Hilderic, who was proud of his Roman lineage (his mother was Eudocia, daughter of Valentinian III, the Western Roman emperor), succeeded to the throne, converted to orthodox Christianity, and became an ally of Byzantium. Hilderic's cousin, Gelimar, seized power in 530, leading an anti-Roman and anti-Orthodox Christian faction. This event was the immediate impetus for Justinian's decision to intervene in North Africa.

Shown here presenting captives before Emperor Justinian I, Belisarius defeated the Vandals at Carthage, bringing North Africa under Byzantine control. (Archive Photos)

The Vandal war lasted from 533 to 548. Using Sicily as a staging area for his assault, Belisarius landed near Hadrumentum in 533, with a force numbering only sixteen thousand. Gelimar had Hilderic executed and then engaged the Byzantine army ten miles from Carthage (Ad Decimum—"the tenth milestone") on September 13, 533. Belisarius won the battle and entered Carthage two days later. Gelimar regrouped his forces but was again defeated in December, 533, at Tricamaron. He fled to Numidia, taking refuge in the mountains. Unable to continue resistance, he surrendered in March, 534, and was brought to Constantinople in a triumphal procession accorded to Belisarius in the hippodrome. Gelimar was allowed to live out his days peacefully near Constantinople, and the Vandal kingdom ceased to exist.

It was a striking victory and no doubt encouraged Justinian to extend his military adventures into Italy. The Ostrogoth war of 535-553 presented a far more formidable power. Under Theodoric (493-526), as the viceroy of the

Byzantine emperor Zeno, the Ostrogoths ruled Italy. As Arians, however, they were perceived as a foreign occupying force by the Roman populace. At first tolerant, Theodoric attempted to assimilate Roman cultural and administrative traditions. In his later years, however, he became more suspicious and ruthless. He executed the philosopher Boethius and Boethius' father-in-law Symmachus, the leader of the senate. Theodoric's death left the throne in the hands of his widow, Amalasuntha (Almalaswintha), who acted as regent for her son Athalaric. Her reign was torn by pro- and anti-Byzantine factions. The death of her son in 534 and later her own murder by her new husband, Theodahad, gave Justinian the justification to intervene militarily in Italy as a defender of a fallen ally.

Justinian had hoped for a surprise landing. One army sailed under Belisarius, but the second, commanded by Mundus, failed in its land march through Dalmatia. Belisarius' first objective was to take Ostrogoth territory in Sicily. With little resistance, he occupied Syracuse in December, 535. After a short campaign to end a revolt in Carthage, he landed in Italy and marched against Naples. A difficult siege followed, but the city was taken and pillaged. The humiliated king Theodahad was deposed and executed by the Ostrogoths, who elected Wittigis as their new leader.

Belisarius advanced on Rome and the population opened the gates to his army on December 9, 536. Wittigis raised an army of fifteen thousand—three times the number of Byzantine troops—and besieged Rome for more than a year. Repeated assaults were repulsed, and disease racked both armies. Eventually, reinforcements and the Byzantine fleet forced Wittigis to withdraw in March, 538, with heavy losses.

The arrival of the eunuch Narses with new troops enabled Belisarius to break the Gothic siege of Ariminum, but the two generals became bitter rivals, and their conflict made it difficult to save Milan—the Goths were said to have massacred three hundred thousand.

Narses was recalled by Justinian, and Belisarius turned toward Ravenna, the Gothic capital. Frankish attacks into north Italy further weakened the Gothic position. Justinian, concerned about impending conflict with Persia, sought negotiations that would have left the Goths in control of territory north of the Po River. Some Gothic leaders were ready to submit to Belisarius as the new emperor of the West and surrendered Ravenna in May, 540. Once in Ravenna, Belisarius renounced any plan to make him emperor and arrested Wittigis. With Wittigis as captive, Belisarius returned to Constantinople to command the Persian front.

In 541, a new stage of the war began when the Goths

selected Totila as king. In Totila, they found a commander equal to Belisarius. By 543, the Goths occupied Naples. Belisarius was removed from the Persian front and sent back to Italy, but Totila continued to take Byzantine outposts and then besieged Rome in late 545. The rivalry between Belisarius and the general John destroyed Byzantine efforts to relieve the city. Rome fell on December 17, 546, and the Goths massacred the population. Totila's abandonment of Rome allowed Belisarius to enter and rebuild the Roman fortress sufficiently to withstand a counterattack by Totila. Rome notwithstanding, Belisarius' authority was largely confined to the coast, where he had access to the fleet. When his political supporter, the empress Theodora, died in 549, Justinian was persuaded to recall Belasarius.

Rome fell again to the Goths on January 16, 550. Gothic success was checked by another Frankish invasion in the north and the return of Narses, who quickly destroyed the Gothic navy. At the battle of Busta Gallorum in Umbria, Narses routed the Goths, and Totila was killed in the retreat. Rome again was Byzantine. The Goths made a stand near Mount Vesuvius (Mons Lactarius) but were badly defeated. The battles of Busta Gallorum and Mons Lactarius marked the end of the Gothic kingdom.

Justinian had won, but Italy was devastated. Resources poured into North Africa and Italy left Byzantium unable to defend the Balkans and the eastern frontier adequately against Persia. Soon after Justinian's death, the Avars and Slavs began to penetrate the Balkans. In 568, only three years after Justinian's death, the Lombards invaded Italy. In North Africa, attacks by the Moors were a constant problem, and Byzantium lost its territory in Spain by 624. The restoration of the old Roman Empire was beyond Byzantine resources. In the end, the wars weakened more than they strengthened the empire, leaving Byzantium susceptible to later Persian and Arab conquests in the next century.
                                                                  —*Lawrence N. Langer*

ADDITIONAL READING:

Barker, John W. *Justinian and the Later Roman Empire*. Madison: University of Wisconsin Press, 1966. A concise history of Justinian's reign and an excellent survey of his wars and foreign policy.

Burns, Thomas. *A History of the Ostrogoths*. Bloomington: Indiana University Press, 1984. An important study of the Gothic kingdom in Italy.

Bury, J. B. *A History of the Later Roman Empire from the Death of Theodosius I to the Death of Justinian (A.D. 395-565)*. 2 vols. London: Macmillan, 1923. Reprint. New York: Dover, 1958. The second volume of this classic work contains a fine study of Justinian.

Clover, Frank. *The Late Roman West and the Vandals*. Brookfield, Vt.: Variorum, 1993. Collected specialized studies on the Vandals.

Musset, Lucien. *The Germanic Invasions: The Making of Europe, A.D. 400-600*. Translated by Edward and Columba James. University Park: Pennsylvania State University Press, 1975. General survey of the Germanic invasions in the era of the fall of the Western Roman Empire.

Procopius. *History of the Wars; Anékdota (Secret History); On the Buildings*. Translated by H. B. Dewing. 7 vols. London: Loeb Classical Library, 1914-1940. The fundamental source on Justinian's wars written by the secretary to Belisarius.

SEE ALSO: 410, Gothic Armies Sack Rome; 439, Vandals Seize Carthage; 445-453, Invasions of Attila the Hun; 451, Battle of the Catalaunian Plains; 476, "Fall" of Rome; 568-571, Lombard Conquest of Italy.

568-571
LOMBARD CONQUEST OF ITALY
The Lombard conquest of Italy makes the Byzantine reconquest ephemeral and underlines the permanent political separation of the eastern and western halves of what had once been the Roman Empire.

DATE: 568-571

LOCALE: Italy

CATEGORIES: Expansion and land acquisition; Wars, uprisings, and civil unrest

KEY FIGURES:

Alboin (died 572), king of the Lombards who led the invasion of Italy

Cunimund (died 567), king of the Gepids defeated by Alboin in a fierce struggle

Justin II (565-578), Byzantine emperor during whose reign Italy was lost to the Lombards

Longinus, Byzantine governor of Italy dispatched by Justin II

Narses (478-573), Byzantine general who had conquered Italy from the Ostrogoths

Rosamund, daughter of Cunimund; forced to marry Alboin

Sophia, wife of Justin II

SUMMARY OF EVENT. From 535 to 552, Italy had been ravaged by the war between the Byzantine (East Roman) army, which was trying to reconquer the Italy lost by the Roman Empire in 476, and the Ostrogothic tribal leadership, which had dominated Italy for the previous sixty years. The Byzantine army, commanded by the aged Armenian eunuch Narses, had been ultimately victorious. Both the army and the finances of the Byzantine Empire itself, however, were exhausted, leaving Italy easy prey for future invaders.

The Lombards were one of numerous German tribes of obscure origin and even more obscure subsequent migrations that played an unexpected political role in Europe in the wake of the dissolution of the Roman Empire. The Lombards called themselves the Longobards or "long-beards"; they are called the Lombards by modern-day historians because they settled in a part of Italy later known as Lombardy. In Italian, their name is "I Lango-bardi." Although the Lombards were among the last to make their historical mark, they had lived for centuries on the northeastern borders of the empire, most lately in the area of Pannonia (modern Hungary). By the mid-sixth century, they were serving as Byzantine allies against the Ostrogoths. Most of their military energies, though, were devoted to a bitter and protracted struggle against their fellow Germanic tribesmen and eastern neighbors, the Gepids. This struggle, taking place in a wooded region that later passed into Germanic legend as "Mirkwood," culminated when Alboin, the Lombard chieftain, slew his hated rival, the Gepid leader Cunimund, in 567. Alboin forced Rosamund, the daughter of Cunimund, to marry him; it is reported that he fashioned a drinking cup out of the skull of Cunimund and then made Rosamund drink from it on the day of their wedding.

This anecdote, and many others relating to the Lombard invasion, may or may not be historically reliable: The problem here is that the only real written source for Lombard history is the work of Paul the Deacon, which was written more than two hundred years after the events in question. Archaeological evidence, though, has proven much of Paul's account to be reasonably accurate. It is known from other sources that the Lombards were not able to rest easy in Pannonia after the defeat of the Gepids, as the area was shortly invaded by the powerful Asiatic tribe, the Avars. The Lombards had previously allied with the Avars to assure the defeat of the Gepids, but they now found themselves confronted by the far stronger Avaric power. From their longtime status as allies of Byzantium, Alboin knew that, despite the recent imperial successes in Italy, the Byzantine army was far weaker than it appeared. The combination of Lombard self-confidence, the Avar threat, and Byzantine vulnerability made the Lombards decide to invade Italy in 568.

The situation in Byzantine-occupied Italy was unstable because of the recent retirement of Narses, the eighty-five-year-old eunuch who had proved an improbably brilliant general, conquering much of Italy from the fierce Ostrogoths. Several historical accounts (of unsure reliability) report that this was because Narses was disliked by So-

phia, the wife of Justin II, the new Byzantine emperor. Justin, who had succeeded his uncle, Justinian I, on the throne in Constantinople in 565, was an incompetent ruler, and Sophia made many of the decisions during his regime. It is related that Sophia had said that Narses, as a eunuch, was not entitled to be a general; instead, she believed he should have been stationed in the women's quarters of the palace at Constantinople. Behind this perhaps-apocryphal story lies the very real suspicion that the new emperor and his wife had of Narses' power and prestige; there also exists evidence that they thought he had taken too many of the revenues of the Italian province for himself. Narses is then supposed to have invited the Lombards to invade Italy as a final form of retaliation against Constantinople.

Whatever the reasons, Narses was recalled (though he never left Italy, dying there in retirement five years later), and a man named Longinus appointed to take his place. Before Longinus even reached the Italian administrative capital of Ravenna, though, the Lombards had marched into Italy. Alboin and his men had begun the march two days after Easter. The Lombard retinue included not only the Lombards themselves but also the recently defeated Gepids, a few Alamanni, and a group of thousands of Saxons whom Alboin had invited along to share the booty. The Lombards were not a tightly organized army, but an unsystematic group of warriors; yet they were militarily effective. The Lombards encountered little opposition as they entered Italy, because the province was exhausted from the Gothic war as well as from a severe plague that had occurred in 565. The Lombards quickly occupied such key northern Italian cities as Milan, Modena, and, after a lengthy siege, Pavia. The only cities that stood successfully against the Lombards were the imperial capital of Ravenna, which was practically impregnable, and the city of Rome itself, protected by the authority of the pope.

The Lombards received a mixed welcome from their new subjects. The Italians were unenthusiastic about Byzantine overlordship and welcomed a strong government that would offer them a respite from constant war. Yet the Italians were overwhelmingly Catholic Christians (except for a few residual Ostrogoths) and the Lombard conquerors were predominantly Arian heretics, although there were Catholic and even pagan factions within Alboin's people. The Lombards were eventually to convert to Catholicism a century and a half later under the leadership of King Liutprand (712-744), but until then religion was a constant source of tension between them and their subjects.

The new Byzantine governor, Longinus, arrived soon enough to protect Ravenna and the area around it that bordered the Adriatic Sea and was called the Pentapolis. Rome also remained loosely associated with the Byzantine dominions, and the Byzantines also preserved Naples and some areas near the extreme south of Italy that indeed were to remain under Byzantine rule until the eleventh century. The Lombards, though, ended up occupying the majority of the peninsula, and the Byzantines could do nothing to dislodge them, though they tried by intrigue, armed assaults (one of them led by Justin's son-in-law), and attempted cooperation with the Frankish rulers of Gaul in order to catch the Lombards in a kind of pincer movement. The Lombard invasion had permanently punctured the dream of restoring the Roman Empire in the West; from this point on, Byzantium was to be only a weak and limited force in Italy. The Lombards established a strong realm in the north with its capital at Pavia. They also ruled two separate duchies to the south of the thin Byzantine corridor stretching between Ravenna and Rome. These duchies, centered at Spoleto in Umbria and Benevento in the southeast respectively, were subject to the Lombard king in Pavia but not under his total control. This arrangement lasted for more than two centuries.

Alboin, though, was not to enjoy the fruits of his victory. He was assassinated at Verona in 572 in a conspiracy launched by Rosamund, still intent on avenging Alboin's cruelty to her and his murder of Cunimund. Rosamund was aided by a henchman, Helmechis, and was also subsidized by the Byzantine governor, Longinus, who hoped to marry Rosamund. Rosamund herself was murdered shortly after, however, and Lombard rule was consolidated under the leadership of the kings Authari and Agilulf.

—*Nicholas Birns*

ADDITIONAL READING:

Christie, Neil. *The Lombards: The Ancient Langobards*. Oxford: Blackwell, 1995. An accessible survey of the history of the Lombard peoples, both before and after their settlement in Italy.

Fauber, Lawrence. *Narses: Hammer of the Goths*. New York: St. Martin's Press, 1990. This entertaining biography of the aged Byzantine general gives needed background.

Goffart, Walter. *The Narrators of Barbarian History: A.D. 550-800*. Princeton, N.J.: Princeton University Press, 1988. In discussing Paul the Deacon's account of Lombard history, Goffart also discusses that history itself.

Paul the Deacon. *History of the Langobards*. Translated by William Dudley Foulke. Philadelphia: University of Pennsylvania Press, 1974. Valuable primary source.

Tabacco, Giovanni. *The Struggle for Power in Medieval Italy*. Cambridge, England: Cambridge University Press, 1989. Places the invasion in the context of the sweep of medieval Italian history.

Wickham, Chris. *Early Medieval Italy: Central Power* *and Local Society, 400-1000*. Ann Arbor: University of Michigan Press, 1989. Good for social background.

SEE ALSO: 410, Gothic Armies Sack Rome; 476, "Fall" of Rome; 533-553, Justinian's Wars Against the Vandals, Ostrogoths, and Visigoths.

590-604
REFORMS OF POPE GREGORY THE GREAT

The reforms of Pope Gregory the Great establish papal primacy and provide for a reorganization of Church practices and activities.

DATE: 590-604
LOCALE: Italy and the Roman Empire
CATEGORIES: Religion
KEY FIGURES:

Augustine of Canterbury (died 604), prior of the monastery of St. Andrew and sent by Gregory as missionary to England

Benedict I (575-578), Roman Catholic pope who made Gregory a deacon to administer charity in Rome

Gregory the Great (c. 540-604), an Italian aristocrat who became a monk and scholar of theology before being elected as Roman Catholic pope, 590-604

Pelagius II (died 590),Roman Catholic pope, 579-590, who sent Gregory to serve as a papal legate to Constantinople

Peter the Deacon (died c. 605), friend and fellow monk who appears in one of Gregory's works as Gregory's faithful companion

SUMMARY OF EVENT. In the early Christian centuries, disputes about theology agitated the Church and threatened to divide it irreparably. Influential bishops took the lead in resolving such controversies, and the bishops of Rome thereby acquired a reputation as defenders of orthodoxy and authoritative teachers of doctrine. Among such powerful personalities was Gregory I, who became bishop at a time when the primacy of authority within the church was much debated and church-state relations were still undefined. The capital of the Roman Empire had moved to Constantinople, and Italy was in danger from barbarian attacks.

Gregory came from an aristocratic Roman family, and among his ancestors were popes Felix III (483-492) and Agapetus (535-536). Gregory obtained a fine education, especially in the law. In 570, he became prefect of Rome, a position in which he led the senate and supervised matters of defense, finances, and internal security. Civil service did not satisfy him, however, so Gregory abandoned it around 575 and became a monk. His family's estate became a renowned monastery, known as a site of learning and rigorous asceticism. Gregory intended to spend his life there pursuing monastic virtues.

Soon, however, Pope Benedict I made Gregory a deacon to administer charity in Rome; the next pontiff, Pelagius II, dispatched Gregory to Constantinople for seven years to be his legate at the imperial court. In 585, Gregory returned to his Roman monastery, hoping to enjoy its seclusion. Devastating floods and an epidemic of plague propelled him into public life again. When Pelagius died in the midst of the crisis, public acclaim demanded that Gregory succeed him as bishop of Rome.

In addition to the miseries that resulted from disease, Italy suffered from barbarian attacks, and Rome received numerous refugees. Gregory used crops from Church lands to feed hungry people, and he purchased more grain from Egypt. He was a skillful economic and political leader, and his deep sense of charity led him to ransom prisoners taken by the Lombards and to pay tribute in order to discourage further attacks.

Gregory I did more than any previous Roman bishop to advance papal primacy. As a theologian, Gregory had a profound influence because he was the first to present a well-formulated doctrine of Purgatory, which became a major theme in medieval belief. Gregory was rather naïve, however, in spiritual matters, accepting reports of miracles without substantiation. As one who believed in the imminent approach of the Apocalypse, which would mark the destruction of the world, he sometimes discouraged study of secular learning despite his own knowledge of classical literature.

Although Catholic rulers had sometimes compelled pagans to accept Christianity, Gregory decried the practice of forced conversion. He contended that compulsion produced hypocrites, not converts. Among his most significant achievements was the extension of papal jurisdiction through missions to evangelize pagans and establish the authority of Rome in parts of Christendom where it did not prevail, particularly in Britain. In his desire to subject churches to the rule of bishops obedient to his authority, Gregory dispatched Augustine, a monk from the monastery of St. Andrew in Rome, to England in 597 to seek the salvation of the Anglo-Saxons and to bring the British church to accept pontifical rule. Gregory rewarded Augustine's success by making him first archbishop of Canterbury. In a similar way, Gregory improved his position in Gaul and Spain, and he insisted that Italian bishops confer with him and submit to his supervision. He was highly successful in establishing the authority of the Vatican over broad areas of Christendom.

Gregory I reigned at a time when relations between the papacy and the patriarchs of the Eastern churches were undefined and sometimes hostile. Gregory recognized the right of the patriarchs of Constantinople, Antioch, Alexandria, and Jerusalem to govern their own jurisdictions, but he asserted his own primacy and at times entertained appeals from clergy within those patriarchates. He disapproved of the Archbishop of Constantinople's use of the title "Ecumenical Patriarch," and he declared unequivocally the universal extent of papal authority, asserting that the Church of Rome was "the head of all churches."

In addition to his success in cementing papal rule, Gregory I exerted broad influence through his theological writings, some of which were composed before he became pope. *Liber regulae pastoralis* (*Pastoral Care*, 1950), *The Four Books of Dialogues on the Lives of the Italian Fathers and on the Immortality of Souls* (594), and a collection of his letters were all produced while he was pope.

In *Pastoral Care*, the pontiff explained his conception of a bishop's duties with regard to the spiritual well-being of his people, among which he emphasized the ministry of preaching as incumbent upon all bishops, for only through that medium could they fulfill their responsibilities as successors to the apostles, the preeminent preachers of the New Testament. Gregory opposed the belief that a clergy member's main duties were ceremonial. *Pastoral Care* enjoyed wide circulation during the Middle Ages and appeared in Greek and Old English. As the Rule of St. Benedict was the guide for monks, Gregory's work became the manual for bishops.

The Four Books of Dialogues on the Lives of the Italian Fathers and on the Immortality of Souls was addressed to general readers as well as to clerics. Gregory composed this work in the form of a conversation with Peter the Deacon, and therein he extolled the pious lives of saints from the sixth century (to whom he was quick to attribute miracles). The second dialogue deals with Benedict of Nursia (480-546), founder of the Benedictine order, and is the main source of information about the most influential figure in Western monasticism. Gregory believed that the intercession of Benedict was responsible for numerous miracles, but he hastened to add that some of the finest saints had no miracles to their credit, their holy lives being the attestation to their sanctity.

In thus acclaiming the saints, Gregory encouraged the practice of invoking their intercession with God, a practice that became customary in medieval devotion. In the same way, Gregory promoted the veneration of relics and images of the saints. In letters to various bishops, the pontiff reprimanded clerics who denigrated the use of images in Catholic worship, even when ignorant people worshiped them in violation of the divine law against idolatry. Gregory held that the duty of the clergy was to teach against superstition while not contending that the use of images per se was sinful.

Gregory's formulation of the doctrine of Purgatory is an especially significant feature of his *Dialogues*. He taught that judgment comes right after death and that a purgation by fire awaited believers as a means to purify them of offenses that did not merit damnation. The prayers of living Christians could benefit souls in Purgatory because the good deeds of people on the earth could be reckoned to those in torment. The fourth dialogue includes graphic depictions of Hell as well as Purgatory, and it portrays Heaven as the realm of eternal bliss. Gregory's teaching about life after death promised immediate entry into Heaven for those souls who were worthy. According to him, these worthy souls would not have to wait until judgment day, as previous theologians had affirmed.

Gregory's pontificate occurred during Europe's transi-

In The Four Books of Dialogues, *Pope Gregory the Great recounts the activities of Saint Benedict of Nursia, founder of the Benedictine order, shown here with Saint Scholastica.* (Archive Photos)

tion from classical to medieval times. His influence helped carry that movement forward in church organization, missions, moral and doctrinal theology, as well as in mystical and ascetical practices of devotion. Eventually, the church arranged masses on thirty consecutive days and assigned a special indulgence for all who participated. The series became known as the "Gregorian Masses," named after a story that appeared in Gregory's *Dialogues* in which a monk obtained release from Purgatory after people on earth had transferred the benefits to his soul. Medieval authors cited Gregory as the author of chants that became popular in that era. His exact role in that development is not clear, but the influence of Gregorian chants upon church music is undeniable. In 1298, Pope Boniface VIII declared Gregory a doctor of the Church, thus laying the foundation for the custom of referring to him as Gregory the Great.   *—James Edward McGoldrick*

ADDITIONAL READING:

Duckett, Eleanor Shipley. *The Gateway to the Middle Ages: Monasticism.* Reprint. Ann Arbor: University of Michigan Press, 1961. This reprint of Duckett's 1938 edition contains a lengthy essay about Gregory written in splendid style by a first-class medievalist.

Dudden, F. Holmes. *Gregory the Great.* 2 vols. New York: Russell & Russell, 1969. The classic biography of Gregory, Dudden's work established a benchmark to which all subsequent scholarship has responded.

Evans, G. R. *The Thought of Gregory the Great.* New York: Cambridge University Press, 1986. A thorough analysis of Gregory's beliefs with an appraisal of his influence.

Payne, Robert. *Fathers of the Western Church.* New York: Viking Press, 1951. This highly readable work contains a chapter about Gregory. A skillful professional writer, Payne has produced a work that serves as a fine introduction for laypersons.

Richards, Jeffrey. *Consul of God: The Life and Times of Gregory the Great.* London: Routledge & Kegan Paul, 1980. Richards endeavors to provide a balanced interpretation of Gregory and his times. Contains an extensive bibliography of primary and secondary sources, as well as a fine index.

Straw, Carole. *Gregory the Great, Perfection in Imperfection.* Berkeley: University of California Press, 1988. Marked by its erudite scholarship, Straw's work constitutes the best analysis of Gregory available.

SEE ALSO: 380-392, Theodosius' Edicts Promote Christian Orthodoxy; 428-431, The Nestorian Controversy; 568-571, Lombard Conquest of Italy; 596-597, See of Canterbury Is Established.

596-597

SEE OF CANTERBURY IS ESTABLISHED

The See of Canterbury is established, assisting in the conversion of the Kentish kingdom by bringing England back into the Catholic Church and firmly reestablishing English ties to the Continent.

DATE: 596-597

LOCALE: Kent, England

CATEGORIES: Organizations and institutions; Religion

KEY FIGURES:

Augustine of Canterbury (died 604), head of Gregory's missionary party and first archbishop of Canterbury

Bertha, Frankish Christian wife of Ethelbert, possibly the source of Christian influence on Ethelbert's court prior to the arrival of Augustine

Ethelbert, king of Kent, 560-616, and chief English ruler south of the Humber River, converted by Augustine

Gregory the Great (c. 540-604), Roman Catholic pope, 590-604, who sent out a missionary party to Kent in 596

Paulinus (died 644), Roman priest and head of a mission from Canterbury to Northumbria in 625

SUMMARY OF EVENT. Although the Church in England was sufficiently well established by the fourth century to be represented by bishops at church councils on the Continent, it survived the Anglo-Saxon invasion only in remote areas in the west and north and, like other aspects of English culture, failed to influence the heathen Germanic settlers to any significant extent. Nearly a century and a half after the first settlements, the conversion of the English was undertaken by Pope Gregory the Great. The Venerable Bede recorded that Gregory's interest in the English was aroused by the sight of English youths sent to Rome to be sold as slaves. Gregory, then an abbot, was impressed by their fair complexions and was moved to inquire about their origin, expressing a desire that their people be saved from the darkness of heathenism. As a consequence of this encounter, Gregory is said to have sought permission to undertake the mission himself. The pope granted permission, but popular demand forced Gregory to abandon the project and remain in Rome.

In 595, five years after he himself became pope, Gregory wrote to a priest to arrange for the education of Anglo-Saxon boys in monasteries in Gaul, perhaps so that they could later contribute to missionary work in their native land. In the following year, he dispatched a missionary party from Rome to preach to the English in Kent, the chief kingdom south of the Humber River. Augustine, prior of St. Andrew's, a monastery which Gregory had founded and where he had served as abbot, was put in charge of a party of about forty monks. In southern Gaul, the mission lost heart and sent their leader back to ask Gregory to give up his plan. The pope ordered the group to continue and gave Augustine absolute authority by making him abbot over the monks. Gregory also provided commendatory letters to influential secular and ecclesiastical officials in Gaul in order that the dangers of the journey might be lessened.

In 597, Augustine and his party arrived in Kent and met King Ethelbert on the Isle of Thanet. Ethelbert was acquainted with Christianity, for he had married a Christian Frankish princess, Bertha, some nine years before. Bertha had brought with her a priest, Luithard, and had continued to practice her religion in her new country, using a church that had survived from Roman times. Moreover, Kentish merchants engaged frequently in trade with their Frankish neighbors and must have brought back information about Christianity. Whatever the influence of these political and economic ties may have been, Ethelbert received Augustine with hospitality and granted the missionaries permission to preach, endowing the group with land for churches.

Some scholars speculate that Ethelbert welcomed the mission from Rome so quickly because it provided him with a means of showing his independence from the growing power of the Franks, giving allegiance to Gregory in Rome instead. Scholars disagree about the date of Ethelbert's conversion; some place it in 597, soon after Augustine's arrival; others believe that it was postponed until as late as 601. The date of Augustine's consecration as Archbishop of Canterbury is also in dispute. Most scholars agree that it took place at Autun late in 597, when the success of the mission seemed assured, but a few maintain that Augustine was consecrated before he arrived in Kent.

The work in Kent apparently went well, for in one of his letters written in 598, Gregory mentioned that ten thousand Anglo-Saxons had been baptized. This information he doubtless received from messengers whom Augustine sent to Rome that year to report on the progress of the mission and to request additional help and answers to questions about the new Church. Gregory's response to Augustine was delayed until 601, when he sent competent men to join the mission, a pallium for Augustine, letters to Ethelbert and Bertha urging their support of the Church, answers to Augustine's questions, and instructions for the episcopal organization of all England. In answering Augustine's questions, the pope instructed his archbishop to bring the native Church in England under the authority of Rome because, during its long isolation from Rome, it had developed practices that differed from those of the

Built on the site of the monastery founded in 602, Canterbury Cathedral reflected the importance of the See of Canterbury as the center of Roman Catholicism in England. (R. Kent Rasmussen)

Western Church as a whole and which distinguished Celtic from Roman Christianity. Gregory's desire for a Christian England, unified in its acceptance of Roman Catholic doctrine and having a well-defined and efficient episcopal structure was not realized for many years. In addition, the archbishopric he established at Canterbury did not play a major role in the Catholic Church in England until more than seventy years after Augustine's landing. Augustine and his successor, Lawrence, attempted to extend the Christian faith outside Kent into the neighboring kingdoms of Essex and East Anglia, but the results proved to be superficial and short-lived.

A later mission to Northumbria under Paulinus was dramatically successful for a brief period, but was brought to an end by a resurgence of heathenism. The manner of Paulinus' conversion of the Northumbrians, however, remained significant in the development of Christianity in England. In his instructions to Paulinus regarding the best way to proceed in his mission, Gregory counseled him not to destroy the pagan temples or their customs and observances, but rather to transform what he found, baptizing or Christianizing the old observances to make them new. The

story is told memorably by Bede. A Northumbrian counselor, listening to Paulinus preach, counsels his king that this life on earth is like warriors feasting in a hall when, at one door, a sparrow flies in from the dark and cold, circles the warmth and light for a few minutes, and then is gone out the other door into darkness again. Christianity, the counselor argues, unlike their paganism, offers an answer to what lies beyond the two doors. The Chief Priest then rides into the temple and pulls down the idols worshiped there, but the temple remains and is consecrated to Christian worship.

Most of the work of conversion outside Kent fell to others, primarily to the Irish, who, like the Britons, were adherents of Celtic Christianity. Augustine's effort to enlist the support of the Celtic Church merely aggravated hostility in southern England between the two churches. Here, too, the lead was eventually taken by others.

Augustine's success, then, was limited to the establishment of the See of Canterbury. With its establishment and survival, written learning and written law, Latin architecture, liturgy, and civilization were established in England. Despite a strong revival of heathenism under Eadbald, Ethelbert's successor, the see remained occupied and the succession of archbishops was uninterrupted until 664. Christianity in Kent was soon well established. Although it did not play a major role for many years, the see was the traditional center for Roman Christianity in England and provided a model to others in its organization and in its school for bishops. When, in 669, Theodore arrived from Rome to fill the vacancy at Canterbury, he made use of the foundations that had already been laid for the organization of the Church under the leadership of Canterbury and for the establishment of centers of learning which were to make England the intellectual leader of the Western world in the eighth century. Canterbury's emergence from its struggle for primacy with the rival See of York in the later Middle Ages and its close association with the English monarch as spiritual father, adviser, and consecrator elevated its power further in English national life until the advent of the Reformation, when the monarch emerged not only as protector of the Church but as its head as well. In succeeding centuries, the See of Canterbury continued to be inseparably linked with king and country in national life.   —*Frances R. Lipp, updated by James Persoon*

ADDITIONAL READING:

Bede. *A History of the English Church and People.* Translated by Leo Sherley-Price. Baltimore: Penguin, 1955. Originally written in Latin in the eighth century, this work constitutes the chief source of written information about the early English Church.

Deanesly, Margaret. *Augustine of Canterbury*. London: Thomas Nelson and Sons, 1964. Written by a distinguished scholar and accessible to the general reader, this biography includes details of the Roman environment Augustine came from, the people to whom he ministered, and the impact of his mission on the English people and nation.

Edwards, David L. *Christian England: Its Story to the Reformation*. New York: Oxford University Press, 1980. A readable narrative giving a longer-range view of the English Church, from the Romans through the Reformation.

Gallyon, Margaret. *The Early Church in Eastern England*. Lavenham, Suffolk, England: Terence Dalton, 1973. Gallyon provides a scholarly but readable account of the earliest missions in Kent, Sussex, Essex, and East Anglia, including those of Augustine and St. Wilfrid. Illustrated.

Godfrey, John. *The Church in Anglo-Saxon England*. Cambridge, England: Cambridge University Press, 1962. A general and fairly comprehensive account of the early English Church.

Sims-Williams, Patrick. *Religion and Literature in Western England, 600-800*. New York: Cambridge University Press, 1990. Although it does not specifically cover the founding of the See of Canterbury, this work demonstrates how a concentrated examination on the regional level of all the evidence can reconstruct a fuller picture.

Yorke, Barbara. *Kings and Kingdoms of Early Anglo-Saxon England*. London: Seaby, 1990. Yorke provides a detailed discussion of the origins of the Anglo-Saxon kingdoms and the relations between king and church.

SEE ALSO: 449, Saxon Settlement of Britain Begins; 450, Conversion of Ireland; 590-604, Reforms of Pope Gregory the Great; 635-800, Founding of Lindisfarne and Creation of the *Book of Kells*; 731, Bede Concludes His *Ecclesiastical History of the English People*.

635-800

FOUNDING OF LINDISFARNE AND CREATION OF THE BOOK OF KELLS

The founding of Lindisfarne and the creation of the Book of Kells *establishes a monastic community that in turn becomes the inspirational source for much of the religious, educational, and cultural renewal of "Dark Age" Europe.*

DATE: 635-800
LOCALE: Northern Britain and Ireland
CATEGORIES: Cultural and intellectual history; Religion
KEY FIGURES:
Saint Aidan (died 651), first bishop of Lindisfarne, 635-651

Saint Colman (c. 605-676), third abbot of Lindisfarne, 661-664, who represented the Irish position at the Synod of Whitby
Saint Columba (c. 521-597), missionary monk who founded the monastery at Iona
Saint Cuthbert (c. 635-687), abbot, hermit, and bishop of Lindisfarne who was its most illustrious saint
Hilda (614-680), Northumbrian noblewoman and influential first abbess of Whitby
Oswald (c. 605-641), Northumbrian king, 635-641, who sponsored the founding of Lindisfarne

SUMMARY OF EVENT. Since its settlement before the seventh century, the small island of Lindisfarne, located a mile off the northeast coast of England, has been accessible from the mainland only by a causeway exposed at low tide. The monastic community first established on "Holy Island" in 635 was one of the key sites of the encounter between two different Christian missions to pagan Saxon England during the 600's.

The establishment of Lindesfarne's monastery can best be understood within the historical context of the Roman settlement of Britain. The withdrawal of Roman troops from Celtic Britain in the early fifth century allowed the successful colonization of Britain by invading Germanic peoples from the northern European mainland, isolating the indigenous Celts in the "fringes" of Wales, Ireland, and Scotland. Those Celts who had been Christianized were largely cut off from regular intercourse with the continental Church under the authority of Rome. Nevertheless, the vibrancy of the Irish church during the 500's is evidenced by its fame for scholarship, by the evangelizing missions back to the continent by people such as Columbanus, and by the number of admired founders of monastic communities. One of these was Columba, born of Irish nobility, who journeyed across the Irish Sea in the 560's to establish a monastic community on the tiny island of Iona off the western coast of Scotland.

The several tribal kingdoms of the Anglo-Saxon invaders engaged in their own jockeying for power. In the rivalry between two northern kingdoms, for instance, Aethelfrith of Bernicia forced Edwin of Deira into exile in the early 600's and became sole overlord over a combined Northumbria. After Aethelfrith's death in battle in 616, Edwin regained power and forced Aethelfrith's two sons Oswald and Oswy into exile among the Irish and Scottish peoples to the northwest.

Into the context of this tribal rivalry, a new evangelistic mission arrived in southeastern England in 597, sent by Pope Gregory the Great and led by an Italian monk named Augustine. After converting the Kentish king Aethelbert and establishing a bishopric at Canterbury, Augustine and his successors sent missions northward during the early seventh century to other of the Saxon kingdoms. Paulinus' mission to Edwin's Northumbria in 625 is described in considerable detail by the monk and scholar, Bede, on whose work *An Ecclesiastical History of the English People* (completed in 731) every account of the period depends.

When the now-converted Edwin was defeated in 633 by Caedwalla, king of the Welsh Britons, Aethelfrith's exiled sons Oswald and Oswy returned to reestablish their family's overlordship in Northumbria. Yet Oswald and Oswy had themselves been converted by the Irish Christians among whom they had lived in exile, in all likelihood under the influence of the Irish mission on Iona, whose founder Columba had died in the year of Augustine's arrival at Canterbury. Soon after establishing his authority in Northumbria, Oswald invited the Ionan church to send a mission to oversee the evangelization of his kingdom. From Iona came Aidan, to whom Oswald gave the island of Lindisfarne as a base of operations.

The half-century following the founding of Lindisfarne in fact saw a complex web of Christian enterprise moving in all directions throughout Britain, and involving people from Augustine's Roman mission, from Ireland or the indigenous Welsh church directly, and from the Irish mission based at Lindisfarne. Nevertheless, historians commonly identify Lindisfarne as the most influential center of ecclesiastical influence through the 660's, even as the church throughout Britain became increasingly aware of the importance of bringing itself into conformity with the Church of Rome.

In 664, a church counsel was called at Whitby to address the main points of conflict between the Irish and Roman "camps." Underlying issues involved the differences between the Irish monastic system of church government and the Roman diocesan system. Yet one of the critical sticking points concerned different means of calculating the date of Easter. The resolution of these matters in favor of Roman custom represented a watershed moment of reorientation toward Catholic unity with the continental Church. Nevertheless, respect for the virtues and piety of the Irish tradition remained strong.

To be sure, there occurred among Irish diehards a reorientation back toward Ireland. Colman, the abbot of Lindisfarne and leading spokesman for the defeated Irish position, resigned his abbacy and led a group of monks (some of whom were certainly English) to Ireland to establish a new community at Mayo. Ireland remained a pilgrimage direction for many who found Irish scholarship preeminent. Thus the Irish church was invested with significant new vibrancy during the 700's in large part through the intercourse sought by Saxon converts. The threads of mutual influence become so difficult to separate as to warrant the modern term "Hiberno-Saxon." For example, the Celtic elements in the products of the Lindisfarne scriptorium clearly demonstrate Irish influence, yet the brilliant synthesis of Celtic, Germanic, Mediterranean, and even Coptic elements found in the Lindisfarne Gospels also influenced the design of later Irish manuscripts.

Lindisfarne became the northern Irish pole of an axis reaching southward to the developing family of monasteries under Roman influence, including those established in 674 and 682 by Benedict Biscop only thirty miles down the coast at Wearmouth and Jarrow. Clearly the monasteries collaborated collegially with one another. Bede, who spent his entire life at Jarrow, was invited by the Lindisfarne community to compose the biography of its most illustrious saint, Cuthbert. The elaborately illuminated

The illuminated pages of the Book of Kells *reflect distinctive elements of Celtic art, including the extensive use of the Celtic knot design and the fanciful animal heads, tails, and feet adorning the letter "T."* (Archive Photos)

On this page reproduced from the Book of Kells, *the abstract and sinuous decorative elements on the page appear to overshadow the actual text of the manuscript.* (Archive Photos)

gospel books, of which the Lindisfarne Gospels is the most splendid survivor, clearly represent a synthesis—both textual and artistic—of sources from Irish tradition and from the continental scholarship imported by Benedict Biscop and other leading seventh century churchmen such as Wilfrid and Archbishop Theodore. In turn, Lindisfarne influenced the production of such manuscripts as the Codex Amiatinus, a complete Bible sent to Italy in 718 as a gift to the pope from Wearmouth and Jarrow, and for centuries supposed to be of Italian, not Northumbrian, origin.

Yet Lindisfarne also continued as the eastern pole of an axis oriented westward toward Iona and the family of monastic communities throughout Ireland. This axis accounts for Lindisfarne's connection with the problematic second subject of this entry: the *Book of Kells*, the most famous of the surviving Hiberno-Saxon gospelbooks

whose unfathomable intricacy of ornamentation marks it as one of Ireland's national treasures.

Although datable to somewhere around 800, the *Book of Kells* remains a mystery text. Where was it made, and by whom? The longest surviving tradition associates the book with St. Columba and Iona, although it is clearly of later provenance than the sixth century. Most scholars accept the likely relevance of the fact that Iona was attacked by Viking raiders in the late 700's (as were the Northumbrian monasteries), and that a band of Ionan monks seeking refuge established a daughter house at Kells in County Meath. By the eleventh century, the gospelbook that became known as the *Book of Kells* was associated with this monastery. Many questions remain. It is possible that it was created by the monks there, or it may have been created at the scriptorium at Iona and then brought with the monks escaping the Vikings. Another theory claims that it was begun at Iona and completed at Kells. One of the most controversial yet respected arguments suggests that it was produced at Lindisfarne or at one of the northern English monasteries but was at some point brought back to Kells, which an Irish faction might have considered to be its proper keeping-place.

—*John Edward Skillen*

ADDITIONAL READING:

Backhouse, Janet. *The Lindisfarne Gospels*. London: Phaidon Press, 1981. Oriented toward the general reader, this study provides a good introduction to the early illuminated gospelbooks.

Blair, Peter Hunter. *The World of Bede*. 2d ed. New York: St. Martin's Press, 1990. While focusing on Bede, this eminent historian of Saxon England provides the layperson with an overview of the entire Hiberno-Saxon world.

De Hamel, Christopher. *A History of Illuminated Manuscripts*. London: Phaidon Press, 1994. The chapter on "Books for Missionaries" emphasizes the intended uses of the splendid illuminated gospelbooks such as *Kells*.

Mayr-Harting, Henry. *The Coming of Christianity to Anglo-Saxon England*. London: B. T. Batsford, 1972. Oriented toward the general reader, this study includes the Irish and Mediterranean influences on early English Christianity.

Meehan, Bernard. *The "Book of Kells": An Illustrated Introduction to the Manuscript*. London: Thames and Hudson, 1994. This richly illustrated popular guide is written by one of the foremost contemporary Kells scholars.

SEE ALSO: 450, Conversion of Ireland; 731, Bede Concludes His *Ecclesiastical History of the English People*; 793, Northmen Raid Lindisfarne.

700-1000
USE OF HEAVY PLOW INCREASES AGRICULTURAL YIELDS

The use of the heavy plow increases agricultural yields, eliminating the need for cross plowing and allowing for the exploitation of rich, damp soils in northern Europe.

DATE: 700-1000

LOCALE: Northern Europe

CATEGORIES: Business and labor; Economics; Science and technology

SUMMARY OF EVENT. Throughout the Middle Ages, farming remained the most important economic activity in Europe. It absorbed the daily labor of nearly all inhabitants and determined social customs and practices. Development and widespread use of the heavy plow, which began gradually in Europe between the eighth and eleventh centuries, was the principal transformation in rural life during this period. The new wheeled plow, fitted with a coulter or heavy knife fixed to the pole to cut vertically into the soil, a flat, asymmetrical plowshare set at right angle to the coulter to cut the earth horizontally at the root level, and a moldboard to turn the sliced turf to the left or right and create furrows, did not immediately supplant the earlier scratch plow which was fitted with a symmetrically shaped share that merely broke the ground and threw the earth to either side depending on where the "ears" were attached. The advantages of the scratch plow were its lightness, ease of assembly and handling, and low cost. A single plowman could fit together its wooden pieces which were sometimes reinforced with metal strips. The scratch plow could be pulled by a team of oxen and operated by a lone plowman. This plow remains in use in the Mediterranean areas of Europe where the soils are thinner and the climate more arid. In these regions, the heavier wheeled plow brings too much precious moisture to the surface and thereby reduces fertility. Although it was easier to manipulate and cheaper to operate, the scratch plow required intense manual labor and could not be used efficiently on the heavier soils of northern Europe. Also, because it left a wedge between furrows, cross plowing was necessary. Thus, each field had to be plowed twice. In addition, the fields had to be dug with spades as often as every four years.

The wheeled plow overcame these disadvantages and proved suitable to the heavier turf and damper climate of the north. Its origins can actually be traced to imperial Roman times. Pliny refers to its presence in the lands south of the upper Danube and archaeological evidence indicates its use in the areas inhabited by Slavs, Bulgarians, and Byzantine peoples on the lower Danube, as well as along the North Sea. A hoard of tools uncovered at Osterburken, dating from the fifth century, includes a smaller, similar version, possibly a precursor to the heavy plow. Comparable in shape, the Osterburken plowshare differs only in the worn symmetry of its coulter. Plowshares dating from Carolingian and Anglo-Saxon times were worn on one side indicating use of a moldboard that forced the plow to cut at an incline and create a furrow.

Changes in the rural environment occasioned by the end of the Roman Empire in the west led to the temporary abandonment of the heavier wheeled plow. The Roman *latifundia* ceased to exist and villages were more scattered. As monarchical states formed and monastic foundations settled wastelands, the rural population first stabilized then grew, larger fields were once again cultivated, and the heavier wheeled plow became desirable. The Benedictines were particularly important in promoting settled agriculture. Saint Benedict emphasized the virtues of manual labor and many of his followers wore a pruning hook in their girdles symbolic of their agrarian labor. According to Benedictine tradition, Theodulf, from a monastery near Rheims, operated a plow daily for twenty-two years. After his death, his fellow monks venerated his plow at the church of Saint-Thierry. Archaeological discoveries of plows from Poland, Bohemia, the Rhineland, and Savoy place the redevelopment of the heavy plow between the eighth and tenth centuries. While there is scattered earlier evidence from Cornwall and Wales, the heavy plow was not widely used across England and Wales until the eleventh century. Fossilized furrows from other parts of Europe support the idea of a gradual transformation in plow technology.

The heavy wheeled plowshare reduced manual labor by eliminating the need to cross plow and spade fields by hand. Its weight, coupled with the nature of the soil, demanded greater reliance upon animal power. The single team of oxen gave way to teams of eight or more and ultimately to teams of horses once the fixed wooden head collar was developed. Horses could work a field more rapidly than oxen, though they were more expensive to maintain. The Bayeux Tapestry shows a horse-drawn harrow, and its presence there may help explain the reluctance of English farmers to abandon the oxen for the horse. While manual labor was saved, it hardly disappeared. An Anglo-Saxon plowman described his daily routine: "O my lord, I work very hard: I go out at dawn, driving the cattle to the field, and I yoke them to the plow. Nor is the weather so bad in winter that I dare to stay at home, for fear of my lord: but when the oxen are yoked, and the plowshare and coulter attached to the plow, I must plow one whole field a day, or more." The plowman's fear was well-founded. He had to remain in the field as his tax was tied to the plowing he was expected to perform during the year. The English plowland or hide came to be the unit of assessment and eventually the day's plowing was standardized at an acre.

The new wheeled plow also improved drainage and increased crop yields. The moldboard turned the furrow to one side only, piling the soil to the center of the field and creating shallow trenches between plowlands. These trenches improved drainage. The better drained fields ensured greater yields in wet and dry years. In wet years, crops flourished on the drier crest of each ridge while in dry ones, crops grew in the furrows. Deeper plowing brought richer soil to the surface, also enhancing soil productivity. At a minimum, fields in France produced four times what had been customary in Charlemagne's time. Slowly, knowledge of marling and manuring became more widespread, and eventually farmers devised the three-field rotation with one field lying fallow every third year. As a result of these changes, all tied to the widespread adoption of the heavier wheeled plow, crops of wheat, rye, spelt, barley, and oats—staples of the European bread diet—rose dramatically across the continent.

Finally, the heavier wheeled plow altered field shape and necessitated agrarian cooperation. Cross plowing resulted in square Roman field types; furrow plowing, especially with large teams of animals, was more suited to longer fields. As farms were divided into the lands of the lord and those of the tenant, field shape adapted to the new technology. The expense of a plow team forced most peasants to either share teams or borrow them from wealthier neighbors in exchange for labor. Thus, even tenurial relationships were revised by the plow as fewer tenants could maintain a purely independent status. Cooperation enhanced and stabilized community.

The end result of the heavy wheeled plow was economic growth, a rise in population, the expansion of trade, and the growth of towns and cities. In a very real sense, the heavy wheeled plow nourished the feudal and religious establishments of medieval Europe.

—*Michael J. Galgano*

ADDITIONAL READING:

Astill, Grenville, and Annie Grant, eds. *The Countryside of Medieval England*. Oxford: Basil Blackwell, 1988. Essays blend multidisiplinary and traditional scholarship to examine how the countryside was exploited in medieval England.

Duby, Georges. *Rural Economy and Country Life in the Medieval West*. Translated by Cynthia Postan. Columbia: University of South Carolina Press, 1968. Though somewhat dated, this work is still a valuable introduction to the European rural economy from the Carolingian period to the fourteenth century by a leading French *Annales* historian.

Fossier, Robert. *Peasant Life in the Medieval West*. Translated by Juliet Vale. Oxford: Basil Blackwell, 1988. Synthesis of recent scholarship by a modern French scholar to defend the controversial argument that lasting agricultural improvements began only after the tenth century.

Rösener, Werner. *Peasants in the Middle Ages*. Translated by Alexander Stützer. Urbana: University of Illinois Press, 1992. Most comprehensive modern synthesis of the difficult and challenging world of European peasants by a leading German scholar.

Slicher Van Bath, B. H. *The Agrarian History of Western Europe, A.D. 500-1850*. Translated by Olive Ordish. London: Edward Arnold, 1963. Surveys agrarian history from the fall of Rome to industrialization. Good treatment of agricultural productivity based upon statistical evidence.

Sweeney, Del, ed. *Agriculture in the Middle Ages: Technology, Practice, and Representation*. Philadelphia: University of Pennsylvania Press, 1995. Collection of essays place changes in agriculture and economics in a cultural context and examine how societal changes shaped views of the peasants and their labor.

White, Lynn, Jr. *Medieval Technology and Social Change*. Oxford: Oxford University Press, 1980. Sound introduction to the relationship between technology and social change. Arguments that the wheeled plow led to agricultural expansion and that the stirrup caused feudalism are no longer accepted.

SEE ALSO: 1086, The Domesday Survey; 1150-1200, Rise of the Hansa; 1200, Fairs of Champagne.

711
TARIK'S CROSSING INTO SPAIN

Tarik's crossing into Spain begins the Muslim political conquest that allows Muslim influences to pervade all aspects of Spanish life.

DATE: April or May, 711

LOCALE: Western North Africa and Iberian peninsula

CATEGORIES: Expansion and land acquisition; Wars, uprisings, and civil unrest

KEY FIGURES:

Count Julian (fl. c. 710), ruler of the Christian city of Ceuta

Mūsa ibn Nusair (c. 660-714), Arab governor of North Africa and commander of Arab troops

Roderick (died 711), last king of Visigothic Spain, 710-711

Tarik ibn Ziyad (died c. 720), Berber lieutenant of Mūsa

Witiza, king of Visigothic Spain, 697-710

SUMMARY OF EVENT. The entire question of the Muslim conquest of Spain is shrouded in mystery and romance. Some historians think it was religious zeal on the part of newly converted Arabs; others maintain that the invasion of Spain was part of a grand strategy planned by the Islamic caliphs and aimed at the subjugation of Europe. The latter school points to the Muslim siege of Constantinople in 717 and to the entry into Spain in 711 as opposing eastern and western pincer movements. Still others see an economic motive only.

Recent scholarship shows that the caliph of Damascus actually had little control over Mūsa ibn Nusair, his governor in North Africa, and that the latter's push from Egypt was the result of his personal ambition and only incidentally led to independent raiding parties bent on plundering Spain.

The first of these expeditions across the Strait of Gibraltar did little more than report the ease with which booty could be obtained. Mūsa accordingly outfitted a larger raiding party led by his lieutenant, Tarik ibn Ziyad, a Berber and a former slave. With about seven thousand Berber warriors, none from Mūsa's army, Tarik landed in April or May, 711, on the great rock which has since borne his name, the Jebel Tarik or Gibraltar. King Roderick, a usurper of the Visigothic throne from the sons of his predecessor Witiza, marched south with between forty and one hundred thousand men to intercept Tarik.

At the seven-day Battle of La Janda fought between the Barbate River and the Sierra de Retin, treachery by members of the disposed Visigothic line assured Tarik of victory. King Roderick became a figure in Spanish legend. Although his horse and sandals were found on the river bank, the body of Roderick was not with them. He undoubtedly was killed and his body washed out to sea. In Spanish legends, King Roderick would return in triumph to lead the Christians against the Moors.

Fearful and jealous of his lieutenant, Mūsa led another army across the strait to complete the subjugation of the peninsula. He degraded Tarik publicly and moved north, taking city after city, and finally driving the Visigothic nobles under Christian leaders such as Pelayo into the mountainous region of Asturias in the northwest. These Christian pockets were destined to hold in isolated fortresses for more than three hundred years. They ultimately coalesced into the Christian kingdoms of Leon, Castile, and Navarre and began to reconquer the peninsula from Muslim control.

Most historians regard much of the Visigothic version of the conquest as legend. King Roderick, largely unknown, appears to have reigned for only one year. Evidence that the sons of Witiza played some part in Tarik's success is only partly credible. The identities of Count Julian, the governor of Cueta, and his daughter Florinda are either vague or fanciful.

Tarik's crossing marked the beginning of Muslim influence in Spain, often symbolized by the majestic beauty of the Alhambra in Granada. (Robert McClenaghan)

According to Spanish legend, Count Julian sent his beautiful daughter to the court of King Roderick at Toledo to be educated. Instead of protecting her as he was honor bound to do, Roderick seduced her. Because Julian's wife, the daughter of deposed King Witiza, was of royal blood, the disgrace was even greater. Count Julian revenged himself by aiding Tarik. Although the legend may not be true, it is known that Julian supplied the four ships used by Tarik to cross to Gibraltar and those used by Mūsa in the second invasion. Another explanation for Julian's action is his desire to retain his position of governor in Ceuta after the inevitable Muslim conquest of the city.

Instead of such colorful and romanticized accounts, historians prefer to cite the disorganized internal situation in Visigothic Spain to explain its sudden collapse. The kingdom had been weak since the fifth century, when the Visigoths seized the area from the Romans. The Visigoths remained a minority because they would not be assimilated into the hostile local population, whom they cruelly exploited. The serfs were legally tied to the land and without rights or recourse. The middle class was burdened with crushing taxes, and slaves, who had no hope of betterment or freedom, labored on the large estates owned by a small group of nobles.

The Visigoths were Arian Christians when they conquered Spain, and most of their subjects were staunch orthodox Christians. Furthermore, the Visigoths sporadically persecuted a large Jewish element who had made their homes in the peninsula. Finally, in the sixth century, the Visigothic king and most of his followers converted to orthodox Christianity, but the monarchy fell under the domination of Spanish bishops. By the time of Roderick, the kingship was almost powerless, insecure, and still regarded as an alien influence by most of the population.

When Tarik arrived, the kingdom was incapable of united action in any form. The native population did not seem to care one way or the other. The Jews threw in their lot with the Arabs and actually held the city of Toledo for the invaders. The nobles were jealous and disorganized, and the high-ranking clergy, including the archbishop of Toledo, were interested only in saving their treasures and themselves. The result was that Christian Spain disintegrated and collapsed.

The Spanish people found scant consolation in the fact that Mūsa ibn Nusair fell into disfavor. Summoned to Damascus by the caliph, he was stripped of his rank and possessions and forced to retire to Medina, where he died penniless. Tarik ibn Ziyad journeyed to Damascus with his master, but he returned to live out his days on the riches he had gained from his unexpected and phenomenal conquest.

The Iberian peninsula was dominated by Muslims for the next four hundred years, with the Muslim presence continuing until the fall of Granada in 1492. During this period, Arabic learning flourished at Muslim courts, and Spain became one of the primary sources from which western Europeans in the twelfth century drew much of their knowledge of mathematics, medicine, astronomy, and particularly Aristotelian philosophy. Muslim culture has been one of the continuing influences in many aspects of Spanish life. In the face of Islamic penetration, Spain developed an aggressive devotion to orthodox Christianity, a characteristic which has been typical of Spain through the Reformation until the late twentieth century.

—James H. Forse, updated by Robert D. Talbott

ADDITIONAL READING:

Chejne, Anwar G. *Muslim Spain: Its History and Culture*. Minneapolis: University of Minnesota Press, 1974. The author attempts to give a panoramic view of the whole field of Hispano-Arabic culture and covers all aspects.

Hitti, Philip K. *History of the Arabs*. New York: Macmillan, 1951. Views the Arabs as carrying the torch of culture to Spain and to Europe and includes a complete description of Arab culture in Spain.

Lowe, Alfonso. *The Spanish: The Intrepid Nation*. London: Gordon Cremonisi, 1975. The author, a Spaniard, attempts to give the "feel" of the nation through thumbnail sketches of historical figures.

Marías, Julián. *Understanding Spain*. Translated by Frances M. López-Morillas. Ann Arbor: University of Michigan Press, 1990. The author, a Spaniard, tries to describe the reality of Spain from the inside, an account based upon historical reason.

Thompson, E. A. *The Goths in Spain*. Oxford: Clarendon Press, 1969. The author wrote a history of the Goths not of Gothic Spain that includes all aspects of Gothic Spain.

Trend, J. B. "Spain and Portugal." In *The Legacy of Islam*, edited by Thomas Arnold and A. Guillaune. New York: Oxford University Press, 1952. A summary of the views of leading Spanish historians of the importance of the Moorish invasion.

SEE ALSO: 950, Flourishing of the Court of Córdoba; 1031, Fall of the Caliphate of Córdoba; 1092-1094, El Cid Conquers Valencia and Becomes Its Ruler; 1150, Moors Transmit Classical Philosophy and Medicine to Europe.

726-843
ICONOCLASTIC CONTROVERSY

The Iconoclastic Controversy, a major religious crisis, divides Byzantium and causes a split between the Christian centers of Constantinople and Rome.

DATE: 726-843
LOCALE: Constantinople and the Byzantine Empire
CATEGORY: Religion
KEY FIGURES:
Charlemagne (742-814), king of the Franks, 768-814
Constantine V (718-755), Byzantine emperor, 741-775
Saint Gregory II (669-731), Roman Catholic pope, 715-731
Irene (c. 752-803), wife of Leo IV and ruler of the Byzantine Empire, 797-802
Saint John of Damascus (c. 675-749), Eastern monk and theologian
Leo III, the Isaurian (c. 680-741), Byzantine emperor, 717-741
Leo IV, the Khazar (749-780), Byzantine emperor, 775-780
Leo V, the Armenian (died 820), Byzantine emperor, 813-820

SUMMARY OF EVENT. The Iconoclastic Controversy (726-787, and 815-843) constituted a profound religious and political crisis within Christendom. It divided the religious worlds of the Western Roman Catholic Church from Eastern Orthodoxy, and it shook the religious, political, and military foundations of Byzantium.

First, the controversy concerned the use and religious significance of icons. They became very popular in the sixth century A.D., when imperial images were replaced by those of Jesus. Icons were perceived as more than simply paintings. They were holy objects, capable of working miracles to heal the sick or to offer divine protection against foreign invasion. They represented the Christian belief in intercession, offering a way by which human fears and aspirations, suffering and pain, joy and faith, and common superstition could reach God. Icons stood at the intersection of the human and divine worlds. The difficulty, however, was that icons might appear as objects of idolatry, thereby violating one of the sacred Ten Commandments.

The problem of idolatry was compounded by the rise of Islam in the seventh and early eighth centuries. Islam adhered to a strict monotheism and rejected the concept of intercession and the use of images in worship. The Arabs conquered vast Byzantine territories stretching from Syria, Palestine, Egypt, and through North Africa. Many Byzantines believed the explanation for their defeats was God's punishment for idolatry. Although political and military issues became intertwined with Iconoclasm, the central question remained religious.

Emperor Leo III was an Iconoclast who, like Jews and Muslims, considered icons to be idol worship. Leo broke the great Arab siege of Constantinople in 717 and promul-gated an important law code (*Ecloga*). Because of his hostility to icons, he was called "Saracen-minded." In 726, Leo III ordered the removal of the image of Jesus to the entrance of the imperial palace and banned the worship of icons. Despite opposition from the patriarch, elements of the army, and even the populace in Constantinople, he reaffirmed his decision to ban icons in 730 in a kind of council (*Silentium*). Pope Gregory II and his successor Gregory III refused to recognize Leo's imperial authority in such religious matters. Gregory III condemned Iconoclasm in 731. The emperor responded by removing Dalmatia from the ecclesiastical jurisdiction of Rome to that of Constantinople—an action that would later bring many Balkan Slavs under the Eastern Orthodox Church.

Leo was succeeded by his son Constantine V Copronymus ("called from dung"). For his first two years, Constantine fought a civil war with his father-in-law Artavasdus, who supported icons. Constantine triumphed with loyal troops from Anatolia. At times, though not always, the eastern provincial armies (themes) were more sympathetic to Iconoclasm than European troops.

Although it was not attended by any eastern patriarch or papal legate, Constantine called a council in 754 to condemn icons as the work of the Devil and to place offending believers under imperial laws. This change allowed the administration to begin a widespread persecution of monks, some of whom were forced to wear secular dress, marry, or to march through the hippodrome holding the hands of women. Torture and executions of icon worshipers—Saint Stephen of Mount Auxentius being the best-known victim—were not uncommon. Monastic lands were confiscated and monasteries turned into military barracks; thousands of monks were said to have fled the empire, particularly to Cyprus, southern Italy, and Sicily. It is probable that Constantine wished to destroy the entire Byzantine monastic order.

Not all monks opposed Constantine, especially those who had a formal religious education and resided in urban monasteries, or who came from aristocratic families. The most fervent opponents of Constantine were usually popular holy men, often poor and uneducated, who were the focal point of popular unrest. These holy men were largely responsible for bringing icons into the church liturgy.

The concept of the incarnation of Jesus (Jesus as both God and man) was at the heart of the theological dispute over icons. Constantine may have been a dualist (perhaps even a Manichean), one who believed that matter (the wood of icons) was created in sin by a lesser deity, or he may have been a Monophysite, one who believed Jesus to be only divine. (Monophysite doctrine was declared heretical and denounced in the Fourth Ecumenical Council held at Chalcedon in 451.) Constantine argued that icons could never depict what was divine in Jesus because divinity cannot be limited in paint and wood. On the other hand, if icons portray only what is human in Jesus, then they divided what could not be separated. For Constantine, only the miracle of the Mass transformed matter into spirit.

The theological defense of icons was given by John of Damascus. Jesus as God, having taken on flesh, had sanctified the flesh as holy. Therefore, icons could not be condemned simply because they were made of matter. Icons were an imitation (*mimesis*) and not of the same substance or essence (*ousia*) of the divine. By themselves, icons had no independent significance but through imitation they partook of the divine.

Constantine's successor, Leo IV "the Khazar," halted the assault on monasticism, and his wife Irene was an advocate of icons. After Leo's death, Irene ruled as regent for her ten-year-old son Constantine. In 787, the Seventh Ecumenical Council met in Nicaea and sanctioned icons, excommunicated those who declared icons to be idols, condemned seizure of monasteries, and declared that Christians could give reverence (*proskynesis*) to icons but could not literally worship (*latreia*) them.

In August of 797, Irene deposed her son and had his eyes put out; he died shortly thereafter. Her reign coincided with that of Charlemagne in the West. At the Frankfurt Council in 794, Charlemagne attacked the council of 787 and the Byzantines as too iconodule and as idolatrous. Icons were useful only for didactic purposes. From the point of view of Charlemagne and Pope Leo III (795-816), the fact that a woman reigned in Constantinople meant that the Byzantine throne was effectively empty. Pope Leo III hoped to unite East and West under Charlemagne by crowning him emperor on December 25, 800. To solidify his claim as emperor of Rome, Charlemagne proposed marriage to Irene, but her fall from power in 802 ended any possibility of such a union. In 812, Byzantine emperor Michael I recognized Charlemagne as emperor but not of the Romans, a title which belonged only to the Byzantine East.

As with the Arab conquests, icons may have been once more associated with apostasy and foreign victory. Emperor Nicephorus I was killed by the Bulgars in 811, and had his head turned into a victorious drinking cup. In the council of 815, Leo V "the Armenian" condemned icons and ushered in the second Iconoclastic era. He was opposed by the abbot Theodore of the Studion monastery. Theodore became a leader of the Iconodules and struggled for church independence from imperial power. He had the support of Pope Paschel I (817-824), who offered asylum to Greek monks and sent legates in an unsuccessful attempt to end Iconoclasm.

Iconoclasm continued to divide Byzantium. A terrible revolt by Thomas the Slav (821-823) sought to restore icons. The Arab conquest of Crete in 826, the appearance of Arab forces in Sicily in 827, and the Arab sack of Amorian in Anatolia in 838 argued against the idea that Christ favored Iconoclasm. After the death of the emperor Theophilus, Empress Theodora restored icons on March 11, 843—the date marks the Byzantine Feast of Orthodoxy, celebrated to this day on the first Sunday of Lent. Icons were to remain an integral part of the faith of the Eastern Orthodox Church, but they had created a schism between the churches of the East and West. The Roman Church could not accept the right of an emperor to interfere and define religious doctrine.

—Lawrence N. Langer

ADDITIONAL READING:

Alexander, P. J. *The Patriarch Nicephorus of Constantinople: Ecclesiastical Policy and Image Worship in the Byzantine Empire.* Oxford: Oxford University Press, 1958. An important study on Byzantine church policy.

Brown, Peter. "A Dark Age Crisis: Aspects of the Iconoclastic Controversy." In *Society and the Holy.* Berkeley: University of California Press, 1989. An interpretation of the controversy as an issue on the nature of the holy in the Dark Ages.

Kaegi, Walter. "The Byzantine Armies and Iconoclasm." *Byzantinoslavica* 27 (1966): 48-70. A study of the role of the armies in Iconoclasm.

Magoulias, Harry J. *Byzantine Christianity: Empress, Church and the West.* Chicago: Rand McNally, 1970. A good introduction to the beliefs of the Eastern Orthodox Church.

Martin, E. J. *A History of the Iconoclastic Controversy.* London: S.P.C.K., 1930. An older work but still an excellent overview of Iconoclasm.

SEE ALSO: 864, Boris Converts to Christianity; 1054, Beginning of the Rome-Constantinople Schism; 1204, Knights of the Fourth Crusade Capture Constantinople.

731
BEDE CONCLUDES HIS ECCLESIASTICAL HISTORY OF THE ENGLISH PEOPLE

Bede completes his Ecclesiastical History of the English People, *creating a contemporary history of Anglo-Saxon England that popularizes the system of dating events from the birth of Christ rather than by the years of a ruler's reign.*

DATE: 731

LOCALE: Jarrow, Northumbria, England

CATEGORIES: Cultural and intellectual history; Religion

KEY FIGURES:

Albinus (c. 672-732), abbot of the monastery of St. Peter and St. Paul, Canterbury

Bede, the Venerable (672-735), scholar-priest of Jarrow and father of English history

Benedict Biscop (627-689), founding abbot of Jarrow

Ceolfrith (642-716), second abbot of Jarrow

Ceolwulf, king of Northumbria, 729-737, to whom Bede's *History* is dedicated

Eanflaed (626-685), Northumbrian princess and second abbess of Whitby

Hilda (614-680), founding abbess of Whitby

Paulinus (died 644), Roman priest who baptized Edwin of Northumbria in 627

SUMMARY OF EVENT. Elevated after his death by the Church to the status of "the Venerable" and honored by the secular world as "the Father of English History," Bede was born into unlikely circumstance for such honors. Northumbria, in the psychological geography of the times, was a remote part of a remote island on the very edge of a fallen Roman Empire. The Anglo-Saxon king Edwin, who had first received Christianity at the hands of Paulinus some forty-five years before Bede's birth in 672, was killed soon after by a pagan claimant to the throne. Politically and religiously, Northumbria was an unsettled place.

Into this peripheral and unsettled time and place, Bede was born, most likely to a noble family. Nothing further is known about his origins, for he was given at the age of seven to the abbot Benedict Biscop to be educated. Benedict Biscop was a former Northumbrian thegn who had left secular life around the age of twenty-five to go on a pilgrimage to Rome. Returning with books, religious relics, and skilled stonemasons from France, Biscop was granted land first at Wearmouth and later at Jarrow to found monasteries. He recruited Ceolfrith, another Northumbrian nobleman turned monk, to help; it was Ceolfrith who, more than anyone, became Bede's spiritual father.

Benedict Biscop made six visits to Rome during his life, each time returning to England with copied books, vestments, and even pictures. As a result, the twin monasteries of Wearmouth and Jarrow grew as centers of learning, with Bede as their greatest jewel. Under Ceolfrith, a revised and edited version of the Bible was produced based on the best available manuscripts. This work to produce a good text of the Bible made Bede's writings on biblical interpretation and meaning possible. In his lifetime, Bede wrote prolifically: biblical commentaries, histories of the saints, books of homilies, of hymns, of epi-

grams, or martyrology, books on time, on poetry, on orthography, and in five books, the church history of his island and people.

This latter work, completed when Bede was fifty-nine years old, is considered his masterpiece. One reason for this is his system of dating events. Bede created a cumulative dating system beginning with *annus domini*, the year of Christ's birth, rather than with *annus mundi*, the year of the Creation, used by Eusebius, Jerome, and Isidore in their histories. This change required a massive effort of calculation, taking into account previous chronicles with different starting points, imperial Roman regnal years in the East and the West, the regnal years of six or more Anglo-Saxon kings ruling at the same time. It also required a knowledge of the multitude of starting points for various systems of calculating a year, such as the calendar year, which might begin on January 1, in September, or at Christmas; or the Indiction beginning dates of September 1, September 25, or January 25; or the date in a particular kingdom when a king took up his reign. With so much variation possible, complete accuracy could never be achieved by anyone, resulting in uncertainties that neither Bede nor those who followed him could resolve. Bede's own birth date, for example, is uncertain—either 672 or 673. Given these small variations in accuracy, however, Bede produced a trustworthy chronology, a monumental achievement.

Bede's careful method in seeking out sources for past events, as well as the near-contemporaneity of many of the events he writes about, are a second reason his history is so remarkable. It has an importance as a historical document unmatched by anything else of the time. The history begins with a prefatory letter to the Northumbrian king Ceolwulf, telling readers that the king already had a draft copy of the work and wanted to have this revised version for copying. Albinus of Canterbury, whom Bede names as his source for information on the Kentish church, also had a copy for review. Scholars know that when Bede wrote a *Life* of Cuthbert, he sent it on to the monastery at Lindisfarne, where Cuthbert had been abbot, so that those still alive who knew Cuthbert could comment on it. Bede relied on interviews he conducted and on those conducted for him by others. A priest of London visited Rome to search the archives there and copy out for Bede the letters of Pope Gregory the Great concerning the mission of Augustine and Paulinus to convert the English. Eanflaed, daughter of Edwin, the first king of Northumbria to receive Christianity, was still alive during Bede's lifetime and served as the abbess of Whitby. As an infant, Eanflaed had actually been the first person to be baptized by Paulinus. Some of the most interesting stories, for example, how the pagan *Bretwalda* (overlord) of East Anglia kept both a pagan altar and a Christian one side by side, most likely came to Bede from royal family history, in this case through King Ceolwulf or through Hilda, founding abbess of Whitby. Thus Bede was dealing in his history with events whose witnesses were still alive.

The *Historia ecclesiastica gentis Anglorum* (*Ecclesiastical History of the English People*) is first and foremost an ecclesiastical history. It seeks to tell the details of Britain and its peoples only insofar as those details help tell the story of God's providence. Thus Bede focuses on the mission from Rome and the conversion of the English to Christianity, with the subsequent history of church establishments, abbots, and bishops, but also includes political history, pagan and Christian, to illustrate the workings of divine providence. Hagiography, or the lives of saints and holy men, as well as the recording of miracles, are also a necessary part of his history, fitting his larger purpose. Bede's particular genius is weaving all of these disparate elements into a cohesive story.

The history is divided into five books. The first book begins with a description of Britain as a rich, almost paradisiacal land, in the tradition of the garden before the Fall in the book of Genesis. It then moves to the Roman history of Britain, its despoiling by the Anglo-Saxon invaders of the fifth century, and the mission of Augustine to re-Christianize Britain. The second book concentrates on Paulinus' mission to Northumbria, down to the death of King Edwin and the failure of the mission. Book 3 deals with the second planting of Christianity in Northumbria from Ireland and its spread to Mercia and East Anglia, with the Easter controversy and the Synod of Whitby in 664, which resolved the controversy in favor of the Roman way over the Irish. Book 4 treats the life of Cuthbert, who began his life's work as an Irish monk but moved firmly into the Roman camp, and of Hilda, who founded Whitby and made it a center of learning.

In its recounting of the successions of various abbots and bishops, book 5 moves the story up to 731, but it is given over much more to miraculous visions and healing than the first four books were. Book 5 includes stories of the afterlife: One man returns from the dead to tell of the dreadful and desirable things he saw, and another is given a preview by devils of the fate awaiting him for his sins. Thus one can see in Bede's history the general movement of the Bible from the book of Genesis to the book of Revelation and of the Christian soul from baptism to the afterlife. Although it is a competent history, Bede's most famous work is finally a spiritual document. The large number of surviving manuscript copies attests its widespread popularity in its own day.   —*James Persoon*

ADDITIONAL READING:

Bede. *A History of the English Church and People.* Translated by Leo Sherley-Price. Baltimore: Penguin, 1955. A readily available English translation of Bede's most famous work.

Blair, Peter Hunter. *The World of Bede.* New York: St. Martin's Press, 1970. A thorough evocation of Bede's times by an eminent historian of Anglo-Saxon England.

Chance, Jane. *Woman as Hero in Old English Literature.* Syracuse, N.Y.: Syracuse University Press, 1986. A discussion of the treatment of women in Old English literature, including in Bede's *Historia ecclesiastica.*

Mayr-Harting, Henry. "Bede's *Ecclesiastical History.*" In *The Coming of Christianity to England.* New York: Schocken Books, 1972. Chapter 2 gives a readable and succinct judgment of Bede's place in the larger context of church history.

Sims-Williams, Patrick. *Britain and Early Christian Europe.* Great Yarmouth, England: Galliard, 1995. A collection of scholarly articles on Bede and his contemporaries.

Thompson, A. Hamilton. *Bede: His Life, Times, and Writings.* New York: Russell & Russell, 1966. A collection of articles on such topics as Bede's library, his manuscripts, and his accomplishments as a historian.

Wallace-Hadrill, J. M. *Bede's "Ecclesiastical History of the English People": A Historical Commentary.* Oxford: Oxford University Press, 1993. Extended scholarly notes and a bibliography accompany this serious study of Bede's *Historia ecclesiastica.*

SEE ALSO: 450, Conversion of Ireland; 596-597, See of Canterbury Is Established; 635-800, Founding of Lindisfarne and Creation of the *Book of Kells*; 793, Northmen Raid Lindisfarne.

732
BATTLE OF TOURS

The Battle of Tours discourages further Muslim incursions beyond the Pyrenees after they are defeated by Christian Frankish forces.

DATE: October 11, 732

LOCALE: Near Poitiers, France

CATEGORIES: Religion; Wars, uprisings, and civil unrest

KEY FIGURES:

'Abd al-Rahman (died 732), governor of Spain

Charles Martel (c. 688-741), Frankish mayor of the palace, c. 719-741

Eudo (665-735), duke of Aquitaine, c. 714-735

SUMMARY OF EVENT. The first thing to know about the Battle of Tours is that it was really the Battle of Poitiers, because it was fought closer to Poitiers than Tours; but it is convenient to use the traditional name to distinguish this battle from ones fought near Poitiers in 507 and 1356. The second thing to know about the battle is that little is known about it, other than that a Christian army under the Frankish ruler Charles, later nicknamed *Martel* ("Hammer"), defeated a Muslim army under the Arab governor ʿAbd al-Rahman, probably in October, 732. Contemporary accounts are so sketchy, and sometimes unbelievable, that accounts by modern historians vary in details, and the following summary is a presentation as much of what likely happened as of what undeniably happened.

By the end of 725, the Islamic empire spread from central Asia through North Africa into Spain and even across the Pyrenees into Septimania, in southern Gaul. Meanwhile, in that part of Gaul still under Christian rule, such central military and political power as there was lay not with the Frankish king, a figurehead, but with Charles, his mayor of the palace. Among the noblemen more or less under Charles's rule was Eudo, the duke of Aquitaine, who had defeated the Muslims at Toulouse in 721, but gave his daughter as a bride in 730 to the Muslim ruler of Septimania to form an alliance to secure Eudo's own position against both Charles and the Spanish Muslims. In 731, Eudo declared himself independent of Charles, but Eudo's son-in-law died that year in a revolt against ʿAbd al-Rahman, the Muslim governor of Spain, who gave the young widow to his own master, the caliph in Damascus.

Then Eudo learned that ʿAbd al-Rahman had crossed the western Pyrenees and was heading into Aquitaine. Trying to divert Christian forces by sending a small army east toward Arles, ʿAbd al-Rahman himself led a bigger force north. Arriving too late to keep the Muslims from pillaging and burning Bordeaux, Eudo's soldiers then lost in battle to ʿAbd al-Rahman's at the Dordogne. Humbling himself, Eudo appealed to Charles for help as perhaps seventy thousand Muslims went toward the rich abbey at Tours. When Charles's probably smaller army of Franks and their German allies eventually crossed the Loire River near Tours, ʿAbd al-Rahman led his men back toward Poitiers, near which the battle occurred at a site now unknown.

The two armies that faced each other were different in more than religion. The Franks and their allies were mainly an infantry force relying on shields, chain mail, and helmets for armor, and on axes, javelins, daggers, and swords for weapons. Charles's personal troops were experienced and probably better armed and armored than the militias raised by his vassals; even so, the discipline and organization of the army as a whole was poor by the standards of most modern nations. ʿAbd al-Rahman's army, which had more Berbers than actual Arabs, was similar in armor and weaponry to the Arab armies that had

won so many victories in the century since Muhammad's death. Most of the men rode horses and carried little armor, forgoing shields and preferring turbans to helmets. Their typical weapons were lances and swords.

The different armies faced each other six days with little fighting. On the seventh day, the Muslims, primarily an offensive force, attacked the Christians, who had taken a defensive position. Although at first the Muslim cavalry could not penetrate the massed Christian infantry, eventually the horsemen broke through in a few places. After a while, however, many Muslims heard a rumor that Christians were stealing the goods the Muslims themselves had earlier stolen in the invasion, and a number of Muslim squadrons rode off to protect their camp. Then, thinking their comrades were fleeing, many other Muslims started riding away from the battle, to the dismay of ʿAbd al-Rahman, who, in his attempt to stop the chaotic retreat, died at his enemies' hands. On the eighth day, when no Muslims came to fight, Charles sent scouts to the enemy camp. They reported that the Muslims had fled and taken some of their loot with them. Aware of the enemy tactic of feigned retreats, the severity of his own losses, his soldiers' fatigue, and the ease with which horsemen could outdistance infantrymen, Charles decided not to pursue.

The significance of the battle is debatable. For Edward Gibbon and many other historians who have followed his lead, the battle changed world history, because, had Charles not led his Christian army to victory, Muslim conquerors might have reached Poland and Scotland and Islamic theology been taught in Gibbon's own day to an entirely Muslim student body at Oxford.

Such events *might* indeed have happened had the Christians lost the Battle of Tours, but evidence suggests that, while important to the men who fought there, especially those who died, the battle did not have by itself all the importance Gibbon claims for it. In reality, the spread of Islam through war had not been one fast victory after another. In 642, only ten years after Muhammad's death, Muslims had conquered Egypt, but not until 709 did they conquer the rest of North Africa. Before the Battle of Tours, two Muslim sieges of Constantinople had failed; the Christian victory under Leo III in the second siege, which ended in 718, was probably more important than the victory under Charles fourteen years later in the West. Furthermore, by 732 Muslim soldiers often lacked the zeal that had led their predecessors to fight and risk death for God and were generally more concerned with pillaging than with winning Europe for Islam. That loss of belligerent fervor, combined with civil strife in Muslim Spain and a revolt of the Berbers in North Africa, worked against an extension of Muslim territory in western Europe. A final indication of the relative unimportance of the Battle of Tours is that the Muslims later were militarily successful in Charles's territory and held Arles and Avignon awhile. Only by 759, eighteen years after Charles's death, did the Franks end the Muslim occupation of Gaul.

Yet the Christian triumph in the Battle of Tours discouraged Muslim raids deep into Gaul and let Muslim generals know that conquering the Franks would be harder than conquering the Visigoths in Spain, and Charles's success at the Battle of Tours and elsewhere against Muslims strengthened the position of his son Pepin the Short, who actually became king, and led to the celebrated rule of Pepin's son Charlemagne. —*James H. Forse, updated by Victor Lindsey*

ADDITIONAL READING:

Fuller, J. F. C. *A Military History of the Western World: From the Earliest Times to the Battle of Lepanto.* Vol. 1 of *A Military History of the Western World.* 3 vols. New York: Funk & Wagnalls, 1954-1956. Fuller calls Charles's victory significant as an "epilogue" to Leo's.

Gibbon, Edward. *The History of the Decline and Fall of the Roman Empire.* 6 vols. 1776-1788. With notes by Dean Milman, M. Guizot, and Dr. William Smith. DeLuxe ed. Vol. 5. Philadelphia: John D. Morris, n.d. Even if Gibbon overstates the significance of the battle, his description of the consequences of a Christian defeat is classic.

Lewis, Archibald R. *Naval Power and Trade in the Mediterranean, A.D. 500-1100.* Vol. 5 of the Princeton Studies in History. Princeton, N.J.: Princeton University Press, 1951. Lewis sees the battle as the thwarting of only a raiding party.

Mitchell, Lt. Col. Joseph B., and Sir Edward S. Creasy. *Twenty Decisive Battles of the World.* New York: Macmillan, 1964. Giving the battle the significance Gibbon gives it, Mitchell and Creasy describe the action in as much detail as they can find.

Oman, Charles. *The Dark Ages, 476-918.* 6th ed. Vol. 1 of the Periods of European History series. London: Rivingtons, 1919. Oman argues against Gibbon's interpretation of the battle.

SEE ALSO: 711, Tarik's Crossing into Spain; 754, Coronation of Pepin; 781, Alcuin Becomes Adviser to Charlemagne; 950, Flourishing of the Court of Córdoba.

735
CHRISTIANITY IS INTRODUCED INTO GERMANY

Christianity is introduced into Germany, expanding the borders of Christendom beyond the boundaries of the Roman Empire.

DATE: 735
LOCALE: Frisia, Hesse, Thuringia, and Bavaria
CATEGORY: Religion
KEY FIGURES:
Saint Boniface, (672-754), apostle of Germany, archbishop of Mainz, 747-754
Pope Gregory II (669-731), head of the Roman Catholic Church, 715-731, and patron of Saint Boniface
Willibrord (658-739), apostle of Frisia, bishop of Utrecht
SUMMARY OF EVENT. From A.D. 500 to 700, Irish and later English missionary monks under religious conviction attempted to create a new Europe out of its wreckage from previous wars. Anglo-Saxon monks and the papacy were hard at work in the mission field during the eighth century in a dual attempt to transform the Frankish church and to convert the pagan continental Germanic tribes. An early evangelical pioneer was Willibrord, a Northumbrian monk, who began a minimally successful forty-year effort to convert the Frisians in approximately 690 in the area around the town of Utrecht (located in modern Belgium). Willibrord was later joined in Frisia by one of his missionary associates, Wynfrith, a celebrated English nobleman and Benedictine monk. Wynfrith would later be renamed "Saint Boniface" and be given the title "Apostle of Germany" from his patron, Pope Gregory II, who called him in 718 to preach in Germany. Wynfrith's personal call by the papacy, however, did not come immediately as Gregory II was initially disturbed to see a member of the Roman Church trying to organize a band of pilgrims instead of permanently settling in a monastery. Only after Wynfrith produced an episcopal letter of recommendation and explained his intentions did Gregory II authorize him to go into the German mission field and represent the Roman Church.

Wynfrith, born in a noble Anglo-Saxon family in Kirton, Devonshire, and christened as Winfrid, labored at making converts for three years before the pope made him bishop for all of Germany east of the Rhine River in 723 and gave him the name "Saint Boniface." In approximately 743, Saint Boniface founded the Abbey of Fulda, which later became one of the most famous monasteries in Germany, and served as archbishop of Mainz from 747 to 754. Visiting the Frankish ruler Charles Martel on his way to minister in the rebellious heathen province of Hesse, Saint Boniface was granted protection by Frankish officials. This civil protection greatly assisted his ability to further institute and strengthen papal authority in France and allowed his missions to succeed where others had previously failed. Ten years of missionary work in the areas of Hesse and Thuringia followed, during which tradition relates that Saint Boniface felled a famous oak tree sacred to the pagan gods at Geismar to reinforce one of his teachings and then used the timber to build a church in honor of Saint Peter. Saint Boniface's work among the heathen was later opposed by Frankish bishops and Irish monks who accused him of working in regions under their jurisdiction. News of this resistance to his work brought numerous English volunteers to his aid, which served to advance the young German church but at some cost to the Church of England. When Gregory III became pope in 732, Saint Boniface was granted metropolitan rank with power to consecrate other bishops, although he remained without an episcopal see until he secured the chair of Mainz. With great organizing skill and loyalty to the Holy See, Saint Boniface founded missionary works for Bavaria in Salzburg, Regensburg, Freising, and Passau. By 742, he had established episcopal seats for Hesse and Thuringia at Wurtzburg, Buraburg, and Erfurt.

Saint Boniface visited Rome in 738 for the third time when the structure and organization of the German church was completed. Even though Saint Boniface enjoyed the numerous advantages of papal support during his missionary projects, his work among the heathen Saxons resulted in very limited success. He had apparently underestimated the difficulties of converting the Saxons, his continental blood brothers, and met such fierce resistance that military efforts by Charlemagne a half-century later were necessary to make them permanent converts. Although Christianity is founded on the teachings of Jesus Christ who sought to prepare his disciples to convert followers for the coming kingdom of God, Saint Boniface found through his studies and struggles that the Bible includes very few organizational instructions how to accomplish this. After his failure with the Saxon tribes, Pope Gregory III instructed Saint Boniface to continue the organization of the church in southern Germany on a diocesan basis, which he accomplished with tremendous skill and dedication.

History will remember Saint Boniface being clearly more successful as a missionary than other notable missionaries during the Middle Ages such as Saint Augustine, apostle to the English nation and first archbishop of Canterbury. One contributing factor may have been that Saint Boniface had considerably more military protection and financial support from Charles Martel and Pepin the Short than Saint Augustine did from King Ethelbert of Kent. Saint Boniface also had the advantage of working among people less different from himself than missionaries either before or after him. Additionally, the previous attempts by Irish monks to convert the Saxons and other Germanic tribes in the area had undoubtedly helped prepare the way for Saint Boniface and his talent for attracting helpers and financial support.

Saint Boniface left his mark on German religion and culture by starting the Benedictine-dominated German church of the early Middle Ages and to some extent, the Carolingian monarchy of the eighth and ninth centuries. Saint Boniface's love for and devotion to the papacy also contributed to the final emancipation of the papacy from the Roman Empire in the East, to the penetration of the idea of the theocratic monarchy into western Europe, and to the legal founding of the papal states. Willibrord, Wilfred, and Saint Boniface are credited by most historians as "heroes whose labor established the Roman Church as the ultimate standard in the heart of Europe." The festival of Saint Boniface is celebrated in both the Catholic and Anglican churches on June 5, the anniversary of his death in 754 at the hands of an angry pagan mob.

The Roman Catholic form of Christianity continued to prosper in all German lands until the advent of the Protestant Reformation. A majority of the Protestants of the sixteenth century followed the teachings of Martin Luther, which were based on the scripture "the just shall live by faith" and thus became known as Lutherans. Other German Protestants followed the teachings of the French Protestant reformer John Calvin and thus organized Reformed and Evangelical churches. Many of the Polish-speaking people of eastern Prussia remained in the Roman Catholic faith, as did many peoples of Austria, Bavaria, and some of the Rheinland cities of western Prussia. Most of Prussia, Saxony, and northern and central Germany increasingly turned away from the Roman Catholic form of Christianity to the Protestant church after the Great Reformation.   —*Daniel G. Graetzer*

ADDITIONAL READING:

Deanesly, Margaret. *The Pre-Conquest Church in England.* New York: Oxford University Press, 1961. This volume contains excellent and well-organized chapters on Boniface and other English missionaries to Germany in the eighth century.

Duckett, Eleanor Shipley. *Anglo-Saxon Saints and Scholars.* New York: Macmillan, 1947. A biographical account of numerous Anglo-Saxon saints and scholars who shaped the religious development of Europe during their time.

Godfrey, John. *The Church in Anglo-Saxon England.* Cambridge, England: Cambridge University Press, 1962. Godfrey eulogizes Boniface as a creator of Europe, a founder of German Christianity, a reformer of the Frankish church, and a chief architect of the monumental alliance between the papacy and the Carolingian family.

Greenaway, George W. *St. Boniface.* New York: Humanities Press, 1955. A brief account of the life, struggles, and dedication of Saint Boniface.

Levison, Wilhelm. *England and the Continent in the Eighth Century*. Oxford: Oxford University Press, 1946. A text that contains a full, standard, and learned account of the work of English missionaries in the time of Saint Boniface.

Schnurer, Gustav. *Church and Culture in the Middle Ages: Volume I, 350-814*. Paterson, N.J.: Saint Anthony Guild Press, 1956. Schnurer emphasizes the numerous difficulties which Boniface had to overcome and calls him "probably the most able missionary ever produced by a north European country."

Talbot, C. H., ed. *The Anglo-Saxon Missionaries in Germany: Being the Lives of SS. Willibrord, Boniface, Sturm, Leoba, and Lebuin, Together with the Hodoeporicon of St. Willibald and a Selection from the Correspondence of St. Boniface*. New York: Sheed and Ward, 1954. An excellent write-up on the "Life of St. Boniface" is included in this well-edited text, with all sources translated into English.

SEE ALSO: 596-597, See of Canterbury Is Established; 754, Coronation of Pepin; 781, Alcuin Becomes Adviser to Charlemagne; 843, Treaty of Verdun.

754
CORONATION OF PEPIN

The coronation of Pepin marks the first time that a European dynasty is given formal religious sanction.

DATE: 754

LOCALE: Ponthion, France

CATEGORIES: Government and politics; Religion

KEY FIGURES:

Childeric III (died 754), last Merovingian king, 741-751, deposed by Pepin

Pepin the Short (c. 714-768), son of Charles Martel, mayor of the palace under the Merovingians from 741, and father of Charlemagne

Stephen II (died 757), Roman Catholic pope, 752-757

Zacharias (died 752), Roman Catholic pope, 741-752

SUMMARY OF EVENT. The Franks conquered much of France under the leadership of Clovis, who founded the dynasty of kings known as the Merovingians. They continued to rule during the seventh and eighth centuries, assisted by officials called mayors of the palace. Because of periods of minorities, dwindling royal resources, and the physical deterioration of the dynasty, the mayors of the palace eventually became the actual power behind the throne, although they were careful to cloak their actions behind the formal prerogative of the Merovingian kings, who were held in quasi-sacred respect by the Frankish people. In time, the mayoral power became concentrated

As mayor of the palace under Childeric, the last Merovingian king, Pepin the Short cemented an alliance with Rome, leading to his consecration as king of the Franks by Pope Stephen II. (Archive Photos)

in the Arnulfing family. In 750, Pepin the Short, mayor of the palace and son of Charles Martel, sent two messengers to Pope Zacharias to inquire whether it was right that a ruler with no power should continue to be called "king." The pope replied that it was better for the man who actually possessed power to be the legal ruler, and he authorized Pepin to assume the title. Historians have debated whether this was a spontaneous interchange or the enactment of a carefully choreographed script. The Merovingians were so established a dynasty that nothing less than the pope's explicit approval could have sanctioned their removal. As a result, Childeric III and his son, the last remaining Merovingians, were sent to a monastery in November, 751, and Childeric was ritually shorn of his long hair, long a symbol of kingship in Frankish eyes. Pepin thus became king of the Franks. This new dynasty of Arnulfing rulers later became known as the Carolingians, after the most illustrious representative of the line: Charlemagne, son of Pepin.

Meanwhile, the Lombards under King Aistulf had conquered Ravenna, expelled the emperor's viceroy, and directed their armies toward Rome. Pope Stephen II dispatched messengers to Pepin requesting an escort for the pope to visit the Frankish kingdom in person. Pepin agreed to cooperate. The emperor in Constantinople likewise dispatched an envoy to the pope, insisting that he negotiate with Aistulf the Lombard. Stephen did stop briefly in Pavia to confer with Aistulf, but he proceeded to the meeting with Pepin at Ponthion on January 6, 754. The pope's biographer later reported that Pepin prostrated himself on the ground and then held the bridle of the papal horse. He vowed to reconquer papal territories that had been taken by the Lombards. At the monastery of Saint-Denis, the pope anointed Pepin and his wife and sons, and bestowed on him the title "Patrician of the Romans." Stephen also prohibited, under pain of excommunication, the choice of a king other than from the line of Pepin. With the papal-Frankish alliance firmly concluded, Pepin entered Italy, defeated Aistulf, and, in 756, gave to the pope all the territories of the exarchate around Ravenna, which had formerly been the possession of the emperor. This bequest has come to be known as the "Donation of Pepin."

Traditionally, the pope had regarded the emperor in Constantinople as his secular counterpart and protector. This was true even after the Lombard invasion disturbed the imperial hold over much of Italy. During the eighth century, however, the Iconoclastic Controversy in Byzantium alienated the papacy and made the popes conscious of the distinctly Western foundation of the spiritual culture over which they presided. Therefore, the popes began to look across the mountains toward the Frankish kingdom for their secular sponsors.

Controversy over the significance of Pepin's coronation continued for centuries. Papal theorists contended that by appealing to Zacharias for an opinion, Pepin was actually acknowledging papal superiority over kingship; by accepting the unction from Stephen, Pepin recognized the right of the pontiff to create kings. By accepting the Donation of Pepin, the pope was merely receiving back his own land from a loyal son of the Church. Supporters of the emperor in Constantinople challenged the right of the pope to create kings or bestow titles, since this was solely the prerogative of the emperor. Furthermore, they maintained that the Donation of Pepin was illegal because the exarchate around Ravenna had belonged to the emperor. Pepin's successors, on the other hand, pointed out that the pope came to France as a suppliant seeking aid against the Lombards, and that Pepin was in no way dependent on the pope. They said that by defeating Aistulf and bestowing land, Pepin was actually patronizing the pope. He never used the title of patrician conferred by the pope, nor did he return to Rome after 756.

No matter how the event is interpreted, Pepin's coronation resulted in an intimate relationship between kings and popes. The ambiguities implicit in this relationship were the cause of papal-imperial tensions for the remainder of the medieval period. In a concrete way, the episode raised the question of ultimate sovereignty, creating a precedent for the coronations of Charlemagne and of Otto the Great.

—*Carl A. Volz, updated by Nicholas Birns*

ADDITIONAL READING:

Barraclough, Geoffrey. *The Medieval Papacy*. London: Thames & Hudson, 1968. Barraclough views the coronation of Pepin as an incident in the centuries-old East-West tension. The Donation of Pepin established the papacy as a temporal power.

Ganshof, François Louis. *The Carolingians and the Frankish Monarchy*. Translated by Janet Sondheimer. London: Longman, 1971. Somewhat old-fashioned and underestimates the importance of religious issues, but still a helpful basic source.

Herrin, Judith. *The Formation of Christendom*. Princeton, N.J.: Princeton University Press, 1987. Describes the evolution of a distinctively Western idea of a Christian commonwealth which underlay the coronations of both Pepin and Charlemagne.

McKitterick, Rosamond. *The Frankish Kings and Culture in the Early Middle Ages*. Aldershot, England: Variorum, 1995. Essays on the period by the leading late twentieth century historian of the Carolingians.

Nelson, Janet. "Kingship and Empire in the Carolingian World." In *Carolingian Culture: Education and Innovation*, edited by Rosamond McKitterick. Cambridge, England: Cambridge University Press, 1994. Scholarly look at the significance of coronation rituals and the royal prerogatives that emanated from them.

Riché, Pierre. *The Carolingians*. Philadelphia: University of Pennsylvania Press, 1993. Very detailed, reliable, and reflective account of the origins of the Carolingian dynasty; compares the political skill of Pepin in displacing the Merovingians to his less accomplished ancestors.

Scherman, Katherine. *The Birth of France: Warriors, Bishops, and Long-Haired Kings*. New York: Random House, 1987. Written for the general reader; good on the nature of the Merovingian dynasty and its decline and fall.

SEE ALSO: 781, Alcuin Becomes Adviser to Charlemagne; 843, Treaty of Verdun.

781

ALCUIN BECOMES ADVISER TO CHARLEMAGNE

Alcuin becomes adviser to Charlemagne, initiating a flowering of intellectual and cultural achievement that is known as the Carolingian Renaissance.

DATE: 781

LOCALE: Parma, Italy

CATEGORIES: Cultural and intellectual history; Education; Government and politics

KEY FIGURES:

Alcuin (c. 735-804), head of Charlemagne's palace school and abbot of Saint-Martin at Tours

Charlemagne (742-814), king of the Franks and Carolingian emperor, 768-814

Einhard (c. 770-840), historian and biographer of Charlemagne

Paul the Deacon (c. 720-800), historian

Paulinus (726-802), patriarch of Aquileia

Peter of Pisa (died c. 800), grammarian

Theodulf (c. 760-821), abbot of Saint-Benôit-sur-Loire, Saint Aignan, and bishop of Orléans

SUMMARY OF EVENT. Alcuin was a scholar and teacher. He was educated at the cathedral school at York where he remained first as a scholar in residence and later as head of the school and its library.

In 780-781, the Northumbrian king Elfwald sent Alcuin on a mission to Rome to ask for papal confirmation of Eanbald as the new archbishop of York. Around Easter, 781, as Alcuin was returning from Rome to York, he met Charlemagne in northern Italy at Parma. Because Charlemagne was eager to foster a program of education for clergy and laypersons throughout his kingdom, he urged Alcuin, who was famous for his educational endeavors at York, to join his court. Although Alcuin hated to leave his native York, Charlemagne persuaded him. Alcuin arrived at the Frankish court of Charlemagne in 782. With the exception of several visits to England, Alcuin remained in the Frankish kingdom, first connected with the court and, from 796 until his death in 804, as abbot of the great Carolingian monastery of Saint-Martin at Tours.

With the fall of the Roman Empire in A.D. 476, classical culture, including Latin literature, education, literacy, and the arts, declined. In the various Germanic kingdoms that succeeded the Roman Empire in Europe, monasteries became the primary centers of literate culture. In some areas, for example Northumbria in England, monks and scholars such as the Venerable Bede (c. 672-735) continued to study classical literature and write works of theology and history. Alcuin was trained in this tradition.

When Charlemagne became king of the Franks in 768, the levels of education and literacy were low. During the first decade of his reign, Charlemagne was primarily occupied with securing his rule through military conquest which eventually made him ruler of most of Europe, including lands in France, Germany, and Italy. Around 780, his concerns turned toward governing his extensive territories. As a Christian ruler, he assumed responsibility for the spiritual welfare of the Church and the people throughout his empire, a concept which drew on the imperial heritage of the later Roman emperors. Charlemagne's encouragement of a widespread program of education and cultural development in literature and the arts had both practical and idealistic components. Because it looked to Classical Greco-Roman culture for many of its models, modern historians have called this movement the "Carolingian Renaissance."

When Charlemagne recruited Alcuin to join his court in 781, he had already embarked on various initiatives to improve education and to promote cultural literacy. Several scholars and intellectuals were in residence at Charlemagne's court. Peter of Pisa focused particularly on grammar. Paul the Deacon was a Lombard who spent four years at the court. He wrote on grammar, but his interests also included history, poetry, and mathematics. Another Italian, Paulinus, also taught grammar at the court for a time until he became patriarch (bishop) of Aquileia in 787. Theodulf, a Visigoth from Spain, joined the court in the late eighth century. He became involved with several theological debates, particularly concerning the Iconoclastic Controversy. These scholars formed a core of the various intellectuals and students who maintained an ongoing and changing group of *literati* who enlivened and edified the court and spread the educational program and cultural ideals of the Carolingian Renaissance to many parts of Charlemagne's empire.

While Alcuin was only one among many intellectuals who constituted a "palace school," he became Charlemagne's chief adviser on matters relating to education and culture. Alcuin's career during his years in the Frankish kingdom exemplifies many of the key facets of the Carolingian Renaissance under Charlemagne's leadership.

Above all, Alcuin was a teacher. He instructed members of Charlemagne's family, especially his children. Other young people, usually from noble families, also received an education at the court of Charlemagne. Einhard presents an example of someone who benefited from this educational opportunity. After Charlemagne's death, Einhard wrote a life of Charlemagne modeled on the biographical writing of the Roman historian Suetonius, which became one of the best-known literary works of the Carolingian Renaissance.

Alcuin's influence on education was not confined to his personal instruction at the palace school. He also wrote a number of pedagogical treatises that became popular books of instruction for schools in the Carolingian period. Alcuin was also responsible for organizing the educational curriculum of the seven liberal arts into three basic disciplines, the trivium, consisting of grammar, dialectics, and rhetoric, and four advanced subjects, the quadrivium, composed of arithmetic, geometry, astronomy, and music.

Although educational training utilized classical foundations of the seven liberal arts, the ultimate goal of learning and literacy was in the service of the Christian religion. Through several treatises and many letters, Alcuin articulated the emperor's position on several important theological debates. He argued against adoptionism (the belief that Jesus was God's adopted son) and iconoclasm (the prohibition against images). His theological position on the Trinity in the *filioque* controversy supported the view that the Holy Spirit proceeded from both God the Father and Christ the Son. Alcuin's most important and long-ranging contribution to religious practice in the Carolingian empire was his revision and standardization of liturgy in developing the lectionary of biblical readings for church services and bringing the sacramentary used by the priest in performing the sacrament of the Mass in accord with usage of the Church in Rome.

In 796, Alcuin became abbot of the monastery of Saint-Martin at Tours. Although he remained in close contact with Charlemagne's court, he directed his primary attention toward the text of the Bible, chiefly clarifying passages that had become corrupted through scribal transmission of the text. The monastery at Tours became a center for copying manuscripts of the Bible with a corrected text that were disseminated throughout the Carolingian empire. These manuscripts were written in a script known as Caroline minuscule. Although Alcuin did not personally develop the script, the clarity of the letters and the spacing between words and lines was a visual embodiment of the goals of the Carolingian Renaissance in the improvement of literacy.

Alcuin and the circle of court scholars were primarily concerned with literature and education, but the Carolingian Renaissance also encompassed the visual arts and music. Architecture, especially of churches and monasteries, revived Roman plans of basilicas and baptisteries, as well as the structure and aesthetics of arches and columns. Wall-paintings and mosaics decorated these buildings. Although few of these edifices have survived, one example is the small church with apse mosaic at Germigny-des-Prés whose construction and iconographical program was probably guided by Alcuin's colleague, Theodulf of Or-

léans. Manuscripts of Bibles, liturgical texts, and secular books preserve miniatures whose figure style and decorative patterns recall Roman paintings. Sumptuous ivory and jeweled bindings on many of these books also revive the style and magnificence of late antique ivory carving and metalwork. Music supported the liturgy with Roman practice of Gregorian chant.

In political terms, Charlemagne's empire did not survive the division among his heirs, but the Carolingian Renaissance that Alcuin and his contemporaries promoted was passed down through several generations of scholars who continued these literary traditions even while the political fabric of the Carolingian empire disintegrated. Indeed, the Carolingian Renaissance has had a long-lasting influence. It preserved and transmitted much of the classical Roman literature that has survived. It established standards for an education in the liberal arts. Its texts were copied in a clear, legible script that remains the foundation of typographical letters to the present. The text of the Bible owes much to the work of Alcuin and the Carolingian dissemination of biblical manuscripts. The collaboration of Alcuin and Charlemagne along with other intellectuals and artists thus had a major impact on the cultural heritage of Western civilization. —*Karen Gould*

ADDITIONAL READING:

Bolgar, R. R. *The Classical Heritage and Its Beneficiaries.* Cambridge, England: Cambridge University Press, 1954. As the most complete study that traces the fate of classical literature from late antiquity through the Renaissance, it places the Carolingian Renaissance in historical context.

Boussard, Jacques. *The Civilization of Charlemagne.* London: Weidenfeld & Nicolson, 1968. This history of Charlemagne's rule focuses on Carolingian culture within its political and social context.

Duckett, Eleanor Shipley. *Alcuin, Friend of Charlemagne.* New York: Macmillan, 1951. Written by an important medieval historian, this study remains the only complete biography of Alcuin.

Hubert, Jean, Jean Porcher, and W. F. Volbach. *The Carolingian Renaissance.* New York: George Braziller, 1970. A beautifully illustrated book that discusses all aspects of the visual arts during the Carolingian Renaissance.

McKitterick, Rosamond, ed. *Carolingian Culture: Emulation and Innovation.* New York: Cambridge University Press, 1994. This book contains eleven essays by leading scholars that discuss the literary and artistic contributions of the Carolingian Renaissance.

_____. *The Carolingians and the Written Word.* New York: Cambridge University Press, 1989. This study examines the extent and uses of literacy and education in the Carolingian period.

SEE ALSO: 731, Bede Concludes His *Ecclesiastical History of the English People*; 754, Coronation of Pepin; 843, Treaty of Verdun.

793

NORTHMEN RAID LINDISFARNE

Northmen raid Lindisfarne and foreshadow the large-scale Scandinavian migrations that permanently alter the culture and politics of the British Isles.

DATE: June 7, 793

LOCALE: The northeast coast of Northumbria, northern England

CATEGORIES: Religion; Wars, uprisings, and civil unrest

KEY FIGURES:

Aethelred (died 796), king of Northumbria

Alcuin (735-804), Northumbrian-born monk and an official in Charlemagne's court

Charlemagne (742-814), king of the Franks, 768-814

Higbald (died 802), bishop of Lindisfarne

Offa (died 796), king of Mercia, 757-796

SUMMARY OF EVENT. On June 7, 793, three ships beached on the small island of Lindisfarne, a few hundred meters off the east coast of northern Northumbria, just south of modern England's border with Scotland. A band of warriors, about one hundred strong, disembarked and attacked the monastery at the southern tip of the island. They looted the church and surrounding buildings, killed the old monks who had not fled, and captured the young for slavery. Packing the booty and captives into their ships, they sailed back in the direction whence they had come, the north.

Nothing else definite is known about the Lindisfarne raid from the fragmentary records that survived this turbulent period in Anglo-Saxon England. Its immediate effects, however, are well attested. Contemporaries, especially churchmen, reacted with shock and outrage at the sacrilege to the Lindisfarne monastery, one of England's wealthiest and most distinguished religious institutions, where St. Cuthbert, a patron saint of the Anglo-Saxons, lay buried. They blamed "heathen northmen" who were taking advantage of the moral and political degeneration of the northern English kingdom of Northumbria and worried that more such piratical bands might follow. The worries were well founded. Although probably not the first appearance of northern marauders, the Lindisfarne incident traditionally begins a period of escalating raiding and then large-scale invasion of the British Isles and western France. Scholars called this period the Scandinavian

Migration Age, the Viking Age, or, as Anglo-Saxons thought of it, the Viking terror.

Based on archaeological evidence and histories written late in the Anglo-Saxon period (450-1066), scholars have conjectured further details about the Lindisfarne raid. Originally from southern Norway, the raiders operated out of a base in the Orkney Islands, north of Scotland. They called themselves *v'kingar*, an Old Norse word of obscure origin. To the English they were "northmen" or "shipmen," names that immediately became synonymous with pirates. These pirates were probably berserkers, members of a pagan warrior cult known for their battle frenzy. In fact, although they might fight like madmen, they were raiders who planned their attacks carefully based upon information gathered from traveling merchants: a Viking band typically sought a wealthy monastery easily accessible from the sea; they preferred to hunt in areas where the local rulers were weak or fighting among one another; and they tried to maximize their profits by plundering during church festivals when people thronged together and were not on their guard. The Vikings carried away anything that could be resold, but gold, silver, and slaves were their chief goals.

The monks of the Lindisfarne monastery were far from helpless. A mixture of Anglo-Saxons, Irish, and British Celts, they frequently came from the warrior class themselves, performed hard physical labor farming the monastery's holdings, and were almost certainly capable of mounting a spirited defense. Yet, even though outnumbering the Vikings, they stood little chance. The northmen wielded swords, axes, and pikes with devastating skill as they charged, all the while shouting a blood-chilling berserker battle cry that was famous for unnerving opponents. Moreover, the monks were almost certainly caught by surprise, thanks to the Viking longship. The finest vessel in northern waters during the early Middle Ages, the longship could be rowed or sailed swiftly, and because it had a shallow draft and a strong keel, its crew could run the vessel aground close to shore to discharge warriors and horses for a quick assault into the hinterland.

According to local tradition, the Vikings landed on the north side of the island and charged across farm fields, routing the monks as they went, to the monastery grounds. There, they found two churches, a guest house, and a dormitory, all surrounded by an earthen wall. The monastery's considerable wealth consisted primarily of adornments for the main church. The Vikings took chalices, candelabra, crucifixes, and other ritual objects, made of silver and often having inlaid gold and amber, and stripped the golden ornamentation from the altar and holy books. Yet the destruction, while great, was not complete. The

Lindisfarne Gospels, an ornately decorated vellum manuscript similar to the *Book of Kells*, survived, as did the remains of Saint Cuthbert, the single most valuable possession to the monastery. Most significantly, the monastery remained in operation.

The names of the Vikings are lost to history, and there is no indication that Anglo-Saxons tried to identify them. What mattered, especially to ecclesiastical leaders, was that the raiders were pagans. That pagans could succeed in robbing and killing servants of God was horrifying and ominous. The most outspoken about the danger was Alcuin, an adviser to Charlemagne, king of the Franks. Alcuin had been born in Northumbria and trained in monasteries there. He viewed the attack on his homeland as a sign of moral and political corruption. In a series of letters, he suggests to Higbald, the bishop in charge of Lindisfarne, that monastic discipline had slipped and darkly hints that some monks must have secretly sinned and brought on God's displeasure. The Vikings performed His punishment. Alcuin also upbraids the Northumbrian king, Aethelred, accusing him of self-indulgent habits and lack of valor. To Alcuin's great disgust, the raid went entirely unpunished. The anonymous writers of the *Anglo-Saxon Chronicle* entries for 793 also saw the raid as a moral portent, along with famine, strange flashes of lightning, and fiery dragons reportedly seen the same year.

Whatever the moral conditions of Northumbria, Alcuin was right that the kingdom was weak. Once the strongest kingdom of England, it had degenerated during the previous one hundred years because of infighting among claimants to the throne. The feuding had left the coasts undefended, as the Vikings surely knew. Alcuin vaguely promised bishop Higbald military help from Charlemagne, but the Frankish king soon had Viking troubles of his own. Viking attacks on trading ports in Frisia and France prompted Charlemagne to build a coastal fleet and harbor defenses. In Northumbria, Aethelred seemed to have taken no such measures. Yet in Mercia, the kingdom to the south, King Offa was already preparing coastal defenses in 792.

Small bands of Northmen, or Viking sea raiders, began conducting daring attacks against Lindisfarne and other wealthy monasteries long before establishing permanent settlements in the British Isles. (R. Hyatt Archive)

In any case, the Vikings soon shifted their hunting grounds. After 800, raids on England declined, and those on the west coast of Scotland and on Ireland dramatically increased, as the Norse sea raiders took advantage of the incessant feuds that obsessed Celtic kings. Vikings repeatedly plundered the monastery founded by the Irish saint Columcille at Iona, an island establishment as prestigious as Lindisfarne. Soon the northmen were raiding far inland, and in 841 they established a permanent town, Dublin, to support their trade in slaves and stolen goods. When northmen returned to England they did so in army-sized invasions. Following 865 they began to settle the areas that they had conquered and eventually controlled most of northern England, permanently affecting the political balance, social structure, legal system, language, and arts of England.

Historians have cited a variety of social and political causes for the sudden outburst of Scandinavian raiders in the late eighth century. Population pressure and political instability in parts of Norway probably supplied the main impetus for warrior bands to seek their fortune in the rich Christian islands to the south, and improvements in weaponry and the longship gave the Vikings considerable tactical advantage. Overall, however, the Scandinavian Migration Age should not be seen in isolation. It was the last in a series of Germanic migrations, including that of the Angles and Saxons to Britain in the fifth century, that spread tribes throughout Europe after the dissolution of the Roman Empire.   —*Roger Smith*

ADDITIONAL READING:

Farrell, R. T., ed. *The Vikings*. London: Phillimore, 1982. A collection of articles by scholars considering the causes of the Viking Age, the Viking image, Vikings in the British Isles, and northern art, history, and literature.

Jones, Gwyn. *A History of the Vikings*. Rev. ed. New York: Oxford University Press, 1984. The most comprehensive and readable treatment available, describing Scandinavian history and culture from prehistoric times to 1066. The Lindisfarne raid receives brief attention.

Logan, Donald F. *The Vikings in History*. Rev. ed. New York: Routledge, Chapman, and Hall, 1991. A general history of the Vikings, with one chapter devoted to the raids on the British Isles. Helpful illustrations and maps.

Loyn, H. R. *The Vikings in Britain*. Cambridge, Mass.: Blackwell, 1995. Loyn devotes three chapters to the early raids and subsequent large-scale invasions of England by Scandinavians. A highly regarded history of the Viking Age.

Marsden, John. *The Fury of the Northmen: Saints, Shrines and Sea-Raiders in the Viking Age*. New York: St. Martin's Press, 1995. Marsden details Viking depreda-tions on monasteries, particularly Lindisfarne, quoting medieval sources extensively. He views the Vikings as barbarian pirates and the monasteries as repositories of civilization.

SEE ALSO: 450, Conversion of Ireland; 635-800, Founding of Lindisfarne and Creation of the *Book of Kells*; 878, King Alfred Defeats the Danes at Edington; 1016, Danish Invaders Led by Canute Conquer England.

843
TREATY OF VERDUN

The Treaty of Verdun provides broad lines of territorial demarcation within Charlemagne's empire and establishes a temporary measure of stability for nascent France and Germany.

DATE: 843

LOCALE: Northern France

CATEGORIES: Diplomacy and international relations; Expansion and land acquisition

KEY FIGURES:

Charles the Bald (823-877), Holy Roman Emperor, 875-877, son of Louis the Pious by his second wife Judith

Gregory IV, Roman Catholic pope, 827-844, and supporter of Lothair

Lothair I (795-855), son of Louis the Pious and coemperor, 817-855

Louis the Pious (778-840), emperor of the Franks, 814-840, and successor of Charlemagne

Louis II, the German (c. 804-876), youngest son of Louis the Pious and heir to the eastern part of the Frankish empire, 843-875

Pépin I (c. 803-838), second son of Louis the Pious and king of Aquitaine, 817-838

SUMMARY OF EVENT. More than almost any event of early European history, the Treaty of Verdun of 843 is intriguing because it not only established the broad line of modern France and Germany but also gave political and legal recognition to an area which became a matter of tension and dispute between the two nations ever after.

The Treaty of Verdun, however, did not provide for the resolution of national rivalries. In 843, neither France nor Germany, as such, existed. What happened at Verdun was, rather, a temporary settlement of a family feud of some twenty-six years' standing, in which each of the major parties was supported by a sizable following with vested interests in the land.

Louis the Pious, Charlemagne's sole surviving son, succeeded him as king of the Franks and Italy, and as emperor of the West. Father of three legitimate sons when

DIVISION OF CHARLEMAGNE'S EMPIRE

he took over the throne in 814, Louis made immediate provision for two of them. Although neither of the boys was old enough to rule the territory granted him, Lothair was named king of Bavaria and Pepin was named king of Aquitaine. Louis, the youngest son, known later as Louis the German, was not assigned a portion of the empire at this first division.

Three years later, Louis the Pious modified this arrangement. By the *Division Imperii* of 817, Lothair was made coemperor with his father. Louis the German received Bavaria, which had been Lothair's, and Pepin added Gascony, Toulouse, and some Burgundian counties to Aquitaine, his original holding. On the death of Louis the Pious, the rest of the empire was to go to Lothair. Although each of the sons was sovereign in his own domain and was recipient of its revenues, the emperor's supremacy was ensured by the requirements that they consult him on all occasions of importance, that they obtain his consent before waging war or making treaties, and that they seek his approval for their marriages. A further provision required the brothers to attend the emperor's court every year to confer with him on public affairs. Finally, disputes among the brothers were to be settled by a general assembly of the empire.

The first test of the 817 arrangement came not from one of the sons but from the emperor's nephew Bernard, king of Italy. Seeing his own position threatened, Bernard crossed the Alps and staged an abortive revolt against Louis. After the revolt was crushed, Louis retaliated by having his nephew blinded. Bernard died a few days later. Louis' remorse led him to make a public confession and penance at Attigny in 833. The public humiliation that followed put Louis under the power of the ecclesiastics who supported Bernard and whose loyalties changed with the conflicting ambitions of Louis' sons. Meanwhile, Louis' wife died, and he married Judith, the daughter of a Swabian magnate. In 823, Judith bore Louis a son, Charles the Bald, a key player in the power struggle which was temporarily resolved by the Treaty of Verdun.

In 829, after an assembly at Worms, Louis issued an edict giving Charles a portion of the empire which had belonged to Lothair. Lothair was sent to Italy, and charters ceased referring to him as coemperor. What followed was a struggle between Louis' three sons by his first wife and the party of Judith's son Charles.

In this phase of the struggle, the emperor succeeded in wooing Louis the German and Pepin away from Lothair by promising them additional territories. Soon, however, the emperor had to face Louis and Pepin in separate battles. Aquitaine was wrested from Pepin for Charles, but the Aquitanians refused to accept the new arrangement and drove the emperor's forces out in 833. In his next bid, Lothair found an ally in Pope Gregory IV, who crossed the Alps on Lothair's behalf but returned disillusioned by the opportunism he witnessed on all sides of the struggle. Louis the Pious' fortunes reached a low ebb in 833, when he was again subjected to public penance and for all practical purposes was deposed, only to be restored to power in 835.

In 838, Pepin died and Aquitaine went to Charles, but again partisans of Pepin resisted in favor of Pepin's son, Pepin II. When Louis the Pious himself died in 840, he could have had small consolation in knowing that he had succeeded in having Lothair proclaimed emperor once more.

It was after the death of his father that Lothair attempted to press vigorously the provisions of the *Divisio Imperii* of 817. He was supported by ecclesiastics but not by a large enough number of lay magnates and therefore was doomed to lose. With all these personal feuds, it is impossible to interpret the complicated struggle as a nationalistic one, although Louis the German's followers were predominantly residents of what was to become Germany, and Charles's followers were from what was to become France. Both Louis the German and Charles found themselves opposed to the imperial claims of Lothair.

When Lothair failed to appear at Attigny in 841 for peace negotiations, his cause was for all practical purposes finished. Although there was a major battle at Fontenoy which proved indecisive, it was fatigue rather than military action that brought a willingness to talk peace late in 842. The division was concluded in 843, after consideration by 120 representatives selected to arrange the partition. Lothair was able to hold out for the middle portion of the old empire, a territory including northern Italy and a narrow corridor, about 150 miles wide, running to the North Sea. Louis the German received the territories east of the Rhine River and the dioceses of Spires, Worms, and Mainz on the west side. Charles received all else as far as Spain. The brothers swore to secure one another's shares, a promise that was to be honored only when convenient.

With the exception of Lothair's "middle kingdom," which was geographically and culturally unnatural, the divisions established at Verdun have essentially lasted throughout the course of European history. It is significant that in the later phase of their struggle and in the presence of their followers, Louis the German and Charles swore oaths in each other's languages. These are the famous Strasbourg Oaths, which provide one of the earliest examples of the emerging German and French languages. In this incident there is a reminder that what can be seen primarily as a war ending in the temporary settlement by Verdun was a struggle colored by cultural differences so deep as to be reflected in diverging languages.

—*Mary Evelyn Jegen, updated by John Quinn Imholte*

ADDITIONAL READING:

Cantor, Norman F. *Medieval History: The Life and Death of a Civilization.* New York: Macmillan, 1963. The author's section on Europe in the eighth and ninth centuries places the Treaty of Verdun in perspective.

Deanesly, Margaret. *A History of Medieval Europe: 476-911.* New York: Barnes & Noble, 1962. Deanesly argues that only Charlemagne could command a united Frankish effort. Neither Louis the Pious nor Lothair could prevent the internal disintegration of the empire.

Ganshof, F. L. *The Carolingians and the Frankish Monarchy: Studies in Carolingian History.* Ithaca, N.Y.: Cornell University Press, 1971. This scholarly and readable account presents some brief observations on Charlemagne's failure, Louis the Pious' intellectual strengths, and the origin and importance of the Treaty of Verdun.

Previte-Orton, Charles W. *The Shorter Cambridge Medieval History*. Volume 1: *The Late Roman Empire in the Twelfth Century*. Cambridge, England: Cambridge University Press, 1952. The author argues that the Carolingian Empire weakened because it was too large, its agrarian economy was unable to produce the necessary leadership, and its "Frankish custom" of dividing an estate among all of the sons amounted to self-destruction.

SEE ALSO: 754, Coronation of Pepin; 781, Alcuin Becomes Adviser to Charlemagne.

850

BUILDING OF THE SLAVIC ALPHABET

The building of the Slavic alphabet helps to promote the cultural identity of the Slavic peoples and the spread of Christianity.

DATE: c. 850

LOCALE: Moravia and southeastern Europe

CATEGORIES: Communications; Cultural and intellectual history

KEY FIGURES:

Saint Cyril (Constantine, c. 827-869), alleged creator of the Slavic alphabet

Saint Methodius (c. 825-884), brother and associate of Cyril

Peter the Great (1682-1725), czar of Russia

Rotislav (c. 846-869), prince of Great Moravia

Vladimir I (c. 956-1015), grand prince of Kiev, 980-1015

SUMMARY OF EVENT. One of the most important linguistic developments in medieval Europe was the building of the Slavic alphabet. This alphabet, uniquely adaptable to the richness of the spoken Slavic tongues, has been paramount in promoting the cultural identity of the Bulgarians, Serbs, Ruthenians, Ukrainians, and Russians. It was also forcibly adopted by non-Slavic peoples under Russian and Soviet domination in the nineteenth and twentieth centuries until the breakup of the Soviet Union's republics into separate countries in the late 1980's and early 1990's.

Little is known of the Slavs prior to their adoption of a written language, although they did have a notch and stick system of communication. The earliest evidence of their settlements is in and about the region between the Oder and Vistula Rivers. Their expansion in all directions from this area was noted by Greek and Latin writers. Their southern and western movement was eventually restricted in the late eighth century by the nascent Germanic *Drang nach Osten* of Charlemagne and the Magyar incursion in

the next century. This resistance to Slavic expansion explains the division of the southern Slavs of the Balkan peninsula and the western Slavs of east central Europe, who managed on their own to expand slowly eastward, a process not completed until the Russian settlement on the Bering Sea in the late nineteenth century.

The development of writing among the Slavs had its origin in their conversion to Christianity beginning in the later ninth century. Traditionally the brothers Constantine, better known as Cyril, and Methodius, two Greek priests from Salonika in upper Macedonia, have been recognized as the apostles of the Slavs. Both were well prepared for their mission, coming as they did from that part of the Eastern Empire with the greatest exposure to Slavic peoples and culture. Cyril had studied and taught philosophy at Constantinople, and both brothers had served in court in a mission to the Khazars beyond the Black Sea in 860-861. Soon after their return, they came to Great Moravia at the request of Prince Rotislav. This mission had religious as well as political overtones, because Rotislav wished to curb the influence among his people of Roman-rite German missionaries from Salzburg and Passau led by Bishop Wiching, a symptom of the stress developing between Rome and Constantinople in the battle for souls in Slavic territories. Moreover, because of the long-term economic relationship between the Slavs and Constantinople and the security that Constantinople provided from a Frankish invasion, Rotislav was politically motivated to request missionaries from Constantinople. Cyril and Methodius were to spread the Christian message among the pagan Slavs by preaching in the vernacular, training a native clergy, and providing a written Slavic language for the transmission of the Scriptures and liturgical texts. In the process, their efforts would underscore the need for a Slavic alphabet. Unfortunately, the immediate success of the Byzantine mission was limited because of the ecclesiastical debate between Rome and Constantinople. Cyril and Methodius' efforts were, however, ultimately recognized by Rome; the former died in 869 while on a mission to Rome, and the latter was created Archbishop of Sirmium and papal legate. Even so, Methodius' work was thwarted at nearly every turn in Moravia by the efforts of Bishop Wiching and the German party. Following Methodius' death in 884, his disciples were persecuted and driven from Moravia. The brothers' influence proved more effective among the Slavic people of the Balkans, where their orthodox form of Christianity prevailed as well as their Slavic alphabet.

The spread of the Slavic alphabet was limited because of ethnic, regional, and political differences. With the acceptance of Christianity as the state religion by the

Kievan prince Vladimir in 988 or 989, however, the use of the Slavic alphabet grew. Although almost exclusively limited to religious sermons, tracts, and church service books, these documents formed the backbone of the Russian literary language until the seventeenth century.

The appearance of two alphabets presents a problem in early Slavic literature: the Cyrillic, with its forty-three letters; and the Glagolitic, with its thirty-eight or forty characters, depending how diphthongs were counted. While differing widely in the form of their letters and their eventual development, both alphabets were admirably suited for representing the many Slavic sounds and subtle nuances of pronunciation. Scholarship is much divided over which was the creation of Cyril, although it seems likely that the more primitive Glagolitic was created by Cyril, while the Glagolitic alphabet was modified by the followers of Cyril and Methodius, probably in Bulgaria, into the Cyrillic alphabet, named in honor of Saint Cyril. The shapes of the Glagolitic letters are unlike any known variety of Greek, and the general impression of its nonligatured quadrangles, squares, and appended circles is that they have an Ethiopian, Samaritan, Armenian, or even Hebrew base. This appearance may have been a deliberate attempt on Cyril's part to create a unique and original alphabet to document the Slavic culture, while yet maintaining a similarity to the alphabets of other civilized nations of his time. Nevertheless, the Glagolitic characters had a numerical and phonetic value nearly identical to the Cyrillic letters, and in the early stages of Slavic writing Glagolitic was an important rival of the Cyrillic. This Bulgarian Glagolitsa, as it is called, was used widely in northern and eastern Balkan areas until the thirteenth century, when it was superseded by the Cyrillic alphabet. There did remain, however, some localized use of Glagolitsa in Dalmatia and Montenegro until early modern times.

The basis for the Cyrillic is clearly the Greek script found in Salonika in the ninth century. Adaptations of this script to correspond to the sounds of the Slavic language of the day were so effective that it has been considered one of the most complete systems of writing in the family of languages. This Cyrillic alphabet became the vehicle for the religious literature, devotional and scriptural, of those Slavic peoples who received their Christianity from Constantinople. Although the script was modified in the early eighteenth century by Peter the Great, and again by the Bolshevik Revolution of 1917, the Cyrillic alphabet itself remained the basic tool used to express the literary aspirations of the Russians, Ukrainians, Bulgarians, and White Russians, as well as those countries which fell under Soviet domination after the Russian Revolution. The Slavic peoples of central and southeastern Europe who accepted their Christianity from Rome, adapted their language to the Roman alphabet. The alphabetic break with their Slavic brethren to the east is not complete, however, for the Glagolitic characteristic of diacritical marks is found in several of the western Slavic languages.

—*Richard J. Wurtz, updated by Elizabeth L. Scully*

ADDITIONAL READING:

Diringer, David. *The Alphabet: A Key to the History of Mankind.* 2 vols. London: Hutchinson, 1968. This two-volume work provides a brief treatment of the Slavic alphabet.

Duichev, Ivan, ed. *Kiril and Methodius: Founders of Slavonic Writing: A Collection of Sources and Critical Studies.* Translated by Spass Nikolov. Boulder, Colo.: East European Monographs, 1985. Series of monographs covering various aspects of Slavic alphabet development.

Dvornik, Francis. *Byzantine Missions Among the Slavs: Saints Constantine-Cyril and Methodius.* New Brunswick, N.J.: Rutgers University Press, 1970. Views development of the Slavic alphabet as an outgrowth of religious missions.

Entwistle, W. J., and W. A. Morrison. *Russian and the Slavonic Languages.* 2d ed. London: Faber & Faber, 1974. First published in 1964, this work provides a detailed examination of the historical and cultural development of all Slavonic languages. The introductory chapters are of import for the layperson.

MacKenzie, David, and Michael W. Curran. "Kievan Rus: Economic Life, Society, Culture, and Religion." In *A History of Russia, the Soviet Union, and Beyond.* 4th ed. Belmont, Calif.: Wadsworth Publishing, 1993. A brief overview of the bonds between religion, politics, economics, and the development of the Slavic alphabet.

SEE ALSO: 1000 B.C., Greek Alphabet Is Developed; 850-900, Vikings Settle in Kiev; 893, Beginning of Bulgaria's Golden Age; 988, Vladimir, Prince of Kiev, Is Baptized

850-900
VIKINGS SETTLE IN KIEV

Vikings settle in Kiev, making it the capital of the first Russian, or Rus', state.

DATE: c. 850-900

LOCALE: Kiev, Ukraine

CATEGORY: Expansion and land acquisition

KEY FIGURE:

Oleg (died c. 912), the Viking leader from northern Russia who conquered Kiev and initiated its transformation into the center of a Rus' state

SUMMARY OF EVENT. Starting around A.D. 750, Vikings coming mainly from Sweden began to settle in northern Russia and develop trade ties with the Near East via the Khazar khaganate. One group of these Vikings was said to have been led by a certain Riurik who apparently established himself in northwestern Russia shortly after 850. By the second half of the ninth century, some of the Vikings from northern Russia began to settle in Kiev which is located along the middle course of the Dnieper River. One report states, for example, that two Vikings from Riurik's band, Askold and Dir, had moved to Kiev already in the 860's. Around 882, Oleg, who succeeded Riurik as the head of Vikings in northwestern Russia, left some of his men in the north and led the rest south where they seized Kiev and killed Askold and Dir. Under Oleg, Kiev began to emerge as the center of the first Russian or Rus' state.

Vikings such as Oleg were attracted to Kiev because it was ideally located for developing a profitable trade with the Khazar khaganate and the Near East as well as with Constantinople, which was the greatest city in all Europe at the time. Kiev was far enough south to control the trade of the upper and middle Dnieper with the Black Sea. This stranglehold over the Dnieper's commerce enabled Oleg's band in Kiev to subordinate the other Viking groups in Rus', and it provided the wealth that allowed them to recruit the forces needed to conquer the indigenous peoples and compel them to pay tribute. At the same time, Kiev was far enough north to give it reasonable protection from the raids of steppe nomads such as the Pechenegs. Rus' towns further south were constantly threatened by such raids. The Vikings led by Oleg thus exploited Kiev's location to make it the center of a huge tributary state that was engaged in an active commerce with the Khazars, the Near East, and Byzantium.

Before the Vikings arrived in Kiev, the middle Dnieper region had been ruled by the Khazars who collected tribute from the East Slavic tribes of the area, including the Polianians who dwelt around Kiev. The movement of Vikings into this region posed a serious challenge to Khazar rule. Although the written sources say nothing about Viking-Khazar conflicts in the middle Dnieper, such conflicts are quite probable. The Khazars would not willingly give up their control of this area while the Vikings were determined to establish themselves here. It is possible that the first Vikings to settle in Kiev (Askold and Dir) acknowledged some type of Khazar overlordship while later Vikings such as Oleg refused to do so and expelled both the Khazars and their Viking allies from the area. In any event, Khazar rule over the middle Dnieper and Kiev disappeared after the Vikings of Oleg's band established themselves here around 882.

Under Oleg, the Vikings of Kiev pursued two main objectives. The first was to replace the Khazars as collectors of tribute from the East Slavic tribes of the middle Dnieper. This task was accomplished in a series of campaigns. The Derevlians northwest of Kiev, the Severians east of Kiev, and the Radimichians northeast of Kiev were all compelled to pay tribute to Oleg. At the same time, Oleg specified the amount of the tribute which the inhabitants of northwestern Russia had to pay him while his lieutenants in the north continued to expand his tributary domain there. Under Oleg, Kiev thus emerged as the center of a growing state which collected large quantities of furs, wax, honey, and slaves from the peoples under its domination.

The second objective of Oleg's band was to find markets for the goods obtained from their tributaries. Discoveries of Islamic coins from Kiev indicate that the city's commerce with Khazaria, the Near East, and central Asia grew rapidly starting in the early tenth century. Developing Kiev's trade with Constantinople proved difficult, since the Byzantine government supervised foreign commerce very carefully. In addition, Viking raids had made Byzantium highly suspicious of any Vikings, even those who appeared outside Constantinople claiming to be merchants. Oleg's band therefore had to pressure the Byzantines into concluding a satisfactory trade treaty (c. 907-912) by launching a raid against Constantinople. The guidelines were now established under which merchants from Kiev and other Rus' towns conducted their trade in the Byzantine capital.

There is disagreement about the origins of Kiev. Some scholars date the earliest East Slavic-Polianian remains from Kiev to the sixth century and claim that there was a continuity of settlement from that time forward. Other scholars find little or no evidence of permanent early medieval settlement here prior to the 880's and believe that Kiev's emergence as a town dates to the time when Oleg's band is said to have arrived here. In any event, early Kiev consisted of two main sections. The upper city appeared on the high west bank of the Dnieper some ninety meters above the river. This plateau (approximately fifteen kilometers long and three to four kilometers wide) was broken up into smaller neighborhoods by a number of ravines. Prior to Oleg's time, several small agrarian settlements had appeared on these easily defended hills. By the late ninth through early tenth century, the so-called Old Kiev Hill (*Starokievskaia Gora*) was emerging as the most important neighborhood. Protected by an earthen rampart and moat, Oleg's residence, perhaps a large log building, was most likely located here. The princes, their followers, and, later, the church hierarchy all resided in the upper city which thus became the political, military, and religious center of the city.

The lower part of the town along the Dnieper was called the *Podol* or *Podil*. It was first settled in the 880's and soon was divided into a number of rectangular plots ranging between 300 and 800 square meters. Each plot was surrounded by a fence and contained a log cabin as well as several storage and service buildings. With its adjoining harbor and wharfs, the *Podol* became an ideal location for the markets, warehouses, merchant quarters, and craft workshops that supplied Kiev's population and serviced the commercial traffic along the Dnieper.

Following Oleg's conquest, the separate settlements on the plateau as well as the newly established settlement in the Podol began to coalesce into a single urban center. The majority of the population, which grew from approximately a few hundred in the late ninth century to a few thousand in the early tenth century, were local East Slavs. Nevertheless, among Kiev's residents were a Viking military-political elite, some Khazars, and Islamic as well as Byzantine merchants and artisans. The increasingly complex society included the prince (Oleg) and his family, the prince's important followers and agents, merchants and artisans, the low-ranking servitors of the prince, and various servants and slaves. The process by which these peoples of diverse ethnic and social backgrounds first began to think of themselves as Rus' inhabitants of Kiev can be dated to Oleg's time. It was Vikings such as Oleg who transformed Kiev from a few scattered hamlets into the prosperous capital of the first Russian state.

—Thomas S. Noonan

ADDITIONAL READING:

Callmer, Johan. "The Archaeology of Kiev ca. A.D. 500-1000: A Survey." *Figura* 19 (1981): 29-52. This is probably the best introduction to the early history of Kiev.

_____. "The Archaeology of Kiev to the End of the Earliest Urban Phase." *Harvard Ukrainian Studies* 11 (1987): 323-353. An updated version of the author's earlier study on the origins and development of Kiev to the early eleventh century.

Cross, S. H., and O. P. Sherbowitz-Wetzor, eds. and trans. *The Russian Primary Chronicle: Laurentian Text.* Cambridge, Mass.: The Medieval Academy of America, 1953. In this most important primary source on early Rus' history, the anonymous chroniclers provide the standard account of Oleg's seizure of Kiev and the city's subsequent development.

Ioannisyan, Oleg M. "Archaeological Evidence for the Development and Urbanization of Kiev from the Eighth to the Fourteenth Centuries." In *From the Baltic to the*

Black Sea: Studies in Medieval Archaeology, edited by D. Austin and L. Alcock. London: Unwin Hyman, 1990. A Soviet perspective on Kiev's origins and growth.

Mezentsev, Volodymyr I. "The Emergence of the Podil and the Genesis of the City of Kiev: Problems of Dating." *Harvard Ukrainian Studies* 10 (1986): 48-70. An examination of what Soviet archaeological excavations revealed about the origins of the commercial-craft section of Kiev.

Pritsak, Omeljan. "The Time of the Conquest of Kiev by the Rus'." In *Khazarian Hebrew Documents of the Tenth Century*, edited by Norman Golb and Omeljan Pritsak. Ithaca, N.Y.: Cornell University Press, 1982. While difficult for nonspecialists, this chapter provides a detailed examination of the written sources and offers a different interpretation from the one given above.

SEE ALSO: 976-1025, Reign of Basil II; 988, Vladimir, Prince of Kiev, Is Baptized; 1240, Mongols Take Kiev.

864
BORIS CONVERTS TO CHRISTIANITY

Boris converts to Christianity, firmly anchoring Bulgaria into civilized, Christian Europe in a way that determines its national destiny.

DATE: 864
LOCALE: Bulgaria
CATEGORIES: Government and politics; Religion
KEY FIGURES:
Boris (c. 830-907), khan of the Bulgarians
Saint Cyril (Constantine; c. 827-869), Byzantine missionary to the Slavs and Bulgars
Saint Methodius (c. 825-884), Byzantine missionary to the Slavs and Bulgars
Michael III (838-867), Byzantine emperor, 842-867
Nicholas I (c. 819-867), Roman Catholic pope, 858-867, who sought to convert Bulgarians
Photios (820-893), patriarch of Constantinople and the intellectual architect of Bulgarian conversion

SUMMARY OF EVENT. The Bulgarians were originally a Turkic people residing to the northeast of the Sea of Azov and ruled, according to legend, by the house of Dulo. Under a semilegendary figure, Kubrat, they enter history in the seventh century as a powerful tribal confederation. Kubrat's grandson, Asperukh, led a portion of the people south across the Danube River in 681, deemed the founding date of Bulgarian nationhood. Asperukh and his heirs soon found themselves in conflict with the mighty Byzantine Empire, which yearned to reoccupy its former possessions in the Thracian territories the Bulgarians now held. The ferocious Bulgarian leader, or "khan," Krum so annihilated a Byzantine army in 811 that Byzantium became convinced it did not have the strength to conquer Bulgaria. Krum's son and successor, Omortag, was more conciliatory to the Byzantines. By 852, with the accession of Khan Boris, Byzantine-Bulgar relations were more amicable. In particular, whereas the ferocious Krum had been an unrelenting pagan, rejoicing in drinking blood out of the skulls of his enemies, Boris began to understand the air of sanctity and authority which Christianity provided to the Byzantine ruler. Christianity also appealed to Boris for more local political reasons. The Turkic-descended Bulgars ruled over a majority of Slavs who were beginning to acquire increasing political power in the kingdom. Boris was interested in appealing to these Slavs as he wished to weaken the power of the Bulgar nobles or "boyars." The Slavs and Bulgars were beginning to become one people. Yet the Slavs would never subscribe to the traditional Bulgar religion, and therefore the supra-ethnic nature of Christianity became a decided boon in Boris' eyes.

Though desirous of converting to Christianity, Boris was also conscious that he had more than one version of Christianity from which to choose. Although Bulgaria was geographically closer to the Eastern church at Constantinople, that very proximity made the Western church centered at Rome a potentially less controlling alternative. Yet it was the Eastern church that had begun to realize the importance of missionary activity among the Slavic peoples. In the late 850's, the Byzantine emperor, Michael III, had approved the sending of the missionaries Cyril and Methodius to preach Christianity in the kingdom of Great Moravia, a kingdom to the northwest of Bulgaria whose exact location is still disputed by historians. Seeing Moravian power as a threat, especially if exercised in concert with Byzantium, Boris sought an alliance with the German emperor as a counterweight, a potential alliance which entailed, as well, acceptance of the Western form of Christianity. This frightened the Byzantines into action, and a frantic rivalry began between East and West as to which would be the one to convert the Bulgars.

Both the Eastern and Western churches were blessed with excellent leadership in this period. The eastern patriarch at this time was Photios, one of the greatest intellects of Byzantine history and possibly the most gifted individual ever to occupy his position. The Roman Catholic pope was the capable and energetic Nicholas I, who was the most assertive pope the West was to have in the period covering the ninth and tenth centuries. Both Photios and Nicholas fully realized the importance of Bulgaria to the power of their churches. Photios, though, had the immediate advantage of the Byzantine army being ready to assist his cause. Michael sent his troops into Bulgaria, and welcomed Boris' rapid surrender in order to impose terms consisting of Boris' adoption of eastern Christianity for his nation. In a diplomatic turnabout, Boris was not only baptized, but accepted the sponsorship of the emperor and received thereby the symbolic name "Michael."

Yet all was not harmonious in the newly Christian Bulgaria. The boyars sensed that Boris' enthusiasm for Christianity stemmed partially from his eagerness to centralize power in the monarchy, and thus revolted bloodily, a revolt which Boris quelled only with much effort. Boris also was vexed by the rigor of the Eastern rite, with its seemingly minute and arcane modes of observation. Especially, he was annoyed by the sudden irruption of Greek-speaking clergy into his kingdom, since he realized that the priests would have no loyalty to him but only to the emperor, and would limit the effectiveness of the Bulgarian church as a national organ. Thus the continuing entreaties of Pope Nicholas took on a renewed appeal to Boris. In a letter to the pope, Boris enquired as to the necessity of the various practices of Eastern Christianity, as well as the extent to which he had to reform pagan practices, such as polygamy, that still flourished among his people. Nicholas' response was firm in its insistence on the basic truths of Christianity but pleasingly flexible on certain details. Since Nicholas and Photios were simultaneously quarreling on a massive scale over the theological issue of whether or not the Holy Spirit proceeded from both the Father and the Son, an issue that would lead to schism between the Eastern and Western churches centuries later, their duel over Bulgaria took on an added urgency. Nicholas sent in a detachment of bishops and priests, and the Greek supremacy in the Bulgarian church was overturned. Although Boris was pleased by the fact that the new clergy owed allegiance only to the pope and therefore were unlikely to provide support for a rival sovereign, he still was uneasy about the amount of local control Rome would permit. Nicholas made some vague promises of a future autonomous Bulgarian church, but, upon further pressure from Boris, retrenched and made clear that the only permissible model for the papacy was a centralized church hierarchy completely controlled by Rome. Boris decided that he preferred Eastern Christianity because of its tendency to leave political matters to the monarch and concentrate on spiritual questions alone.

The Byzantines, meanwhile, had decided to change their tactics. A new and more energetic emperor, Basil I, succeeded Michael and decided to fire Photios as patriarch in order to repair relations with the Western church. The new patriarch smoothed over matters with Rome sufficiently to obtain grudging consent to Bulgaria being within the Eastern sphere. The Byzantines had made a huge concession: They sanctioned the liturgy being preached not in Greek, but in Bulgarian, a language which by now had a heavy admixture of Slavic syntax and structure. This would ensure that the priests would themselves be Bulgarian and thus owe allegiance to the Bulgarian king. After 870, Boris enthusiastically promulgated the new order and, as a symbol for the evolution of his people, prepared to move the seat of government from the old capital, Pliska, with its pagan associations, to the new city of Preslav. Although his conversion was motivated by political expediency, Boris became personally pious and ended his days as a monk.

The new Bulgarian liturgy flourished, as did the Cyrillic alphabet especially developed for the Slavic languages by the missionaries Cyril and Methodius and propagated by their disciples, such as St. Clement of Ohrid. This liturgical language eventually came to be called "old Church Slavonic" and was the basis for the church language used in later Slavic countries, such as Russia, which followed Bulgaria in converting to Eastern Christianity. Perhaps the most far-reaching effect of Boris' conversion was to sanction the use of vernacular languages in Orthodox Christianity, which had previously permitted worship in only the three "sacred" languages of Hebrew, Greek, and Latin.

The Bulgarians, like their contemporaries the Anglo-Saxons in England, had managed to keep their own language and culture while fully participating in the classical and Christian heritage. It is for this that Bulgarians are often termed "the Englishmen of the Balkans." After Boris' conversion, Bulgaria was to hold a permanent place in the framework of European civilization.

—*Nicholas Birns*

ADDITIONAL READING:

Bowlus, Charles R. *Franks, Moravians, and Magyars: The Struggle for the Middle Danube, 788-907.* Philadelphia: University of Pennsylvania Press, 1995. Radical revisioning of early Central European history which highlights relations between Bulgaria and the West.

Browning, Robert. *Byzantium and Bulgaria.* Berkeley: University of California Press, 1975. Accessible account of Bulgarian-Byzantine relations.

Fine, John. *The Early Medieval Balkans.* Ann Arbor: University of Michigan Press, 1983. Learned and comprehensive work aimed at the advanced student.

Lang, David Marshall. *The Bulgarians.* Boulder, Colo.: Westview Press, 1976. A convenient overview of early Bulgarian history.

Obolensky, Dimitri. *The Byzantine Commonwealth.* Crestwood, Ill.: St. Vladimir's Seminary Press, 1971. This epochal book describes how Byzantine Christianity was

spread to the emerging nations of Eastern Europe. Particularly recommended.

Runciman, Steven. *The First Bulgarian Empire.* London: Bell, 1930. Although somewhat dated, this work is still the best narrative account of the period in English.

Tsvetkov, Plamen. *A History of the Balkans.* San Francisco: Mellen Press, 1993. A densely written account that situates Bulgarian history in a regional context.

SEE ALSO: 850, Building of the Slavic Alphabet; 893, Beginning of Bulgaria's Golden Age; 1014, Basil II Conquers the Bulgars.

878

KING ALFRED DEFEATS THE DANES AT EDINGTON

King Alfred defeats the Danes at Edington, encouraging further Anglo-Saxon resistance against Viking invasion and establishing the foundation for his transition from king of Wessex to king of the English.

DATE: 878

LOCALE: Wiltshire, Wessex

CATEGORIES: Expansion and land acquisition; Wars, uprisings, and civil unrest

KEY FIGURES:

Aethelred I (died 971), king of Wessex, 866-971, and elder brother of Alfred the Great

Alfred the Great (849-899), king of Wessex, 871-899

Asser (died c. 909), a monk from St. Davids (Wales) and later bishop of Sherborne (Somerset), Alfred's biographer

Guthrum (Godrum; died 890), Danish king of East Anglia, 880-890

Halfdan, son of the Viking chief Ragnar Lothbrok, conqueror of York

Ivar the Boneless, Halfdan's brother and conqueror of East Anglia

Ragnar Lothbrok, Viking leader

SUMMARY OF EVENT. The Vikings (general designation of the invaders from Denmark, Norway, and Sweden) first visited England in 789, raiding Dorchester, Wessex, then under Mercian control. The raiders did not commit any plunder but exhibited their superior strength. When the royal reeve from Dorchester commanded them to meet the king (Brihtric), he was killed on the spot. In 793, the Vikings sacked the monastery of Lindisfarne off the coast of Northumbria. The following year, they hit the monastery of Jarrow at the mouth of the Don. Nearly half a century later, in 835, a Danish raiding party devastated the Isle of Sheppey in the Thames estuary. In 836, thirty-five

Viking ships landed at Carhampton (Somerset) but King Egbert put up a stiff resistance. Two years later, a Viking fleet joined forces with the Britons of Cornwall, but the allies were defeated by Egbert's West Saxon army at Hingston Down.

A more serious phase of Viking operations in England began when they took to wintering on island bases in the river mouths, conveniently situated for quick resumption of campaigning at the onset of spring. In 851, after wintering on the Isle of Thanet, an army of 350 ships stormed Canterbury and London. It routed the army of King Berhtwulf of Mercia but was defeated by Aethelwulf, king of Wessex, and his son Aethelbald at *Aclea* ("oak field") in Surrey.

The *Anglo-Saxon Chronicle* for 865 records how the people of Kent promised the Viking army at Thanet protection money, or *Danegeld*, and how the "heathens" broke their promise. In 866, a "Great Army" of Danes commanded by two brothers, Halfdan and Ivar, took up winter quarters in East Anglia and the East Angles paid them money to buy their peace. For fifteen years, this army terrorized England. According to Scandinavian folklore, the two young Danes wished to avenge the horrible murder of their father Ragnar Lothbrok, "Hairy Breeches," the most notorious Viking of his time. Evidently some years earlier, Ragnar's ships had been wrecked by a great storm off the Northumbrian coast. He was captured by the Northumbrian king, Aelle, and flung into a pit of adders where the violent Viking met a horrible death.

The Great Army conquered York in 866, East Anglia in 868, and by 870, seized Reading at the junction of the Thames and Kennet. In January, 871, they were checked by Alfred the Atheling, brother of King Aethelred of Wessex, who, as Asser writes, charged the enemy "acting courageously, like a wild boar," cutting them down at Ashdown. Although the Vikings were vanquished, they yet held their own and fought nine more battles through that year. In April, 871, Alfred became king of Wessex upon his brother's death and decided to make peace by paying protection money to the Danish host. The Danes then turned to Mercia, forced King Burhred to abdicate in 874, and in his place appointed one of the royal thegns, Ceolwulf II, "a foolish king's thegn," in the contemptuous phraseology of the *Chronicle*.

The peace that Alfred bought from the Danes gave his kingdom a respite for reorganizing its defense, though it must be recognized that the West Saxon army, the *fyrd*, was nothing more than an emergency, though quite effective, expedient. Neither ealdorman nor king could keep it in the field indefinitely nor lead it far beyond the borders of the shire of its origin. The inability to keep a battle-worthy army constantly at hand resulted in the near-destruction of

Wessex when the second Viking invasion began toward the end of 875. This was the southern division of the army, commanded by the three kings: Oscetel, Anwend, and Guthrum, who was the foremost and most forceful. Under Guthrum's leadership, the Danes quickly settled themselves at Wareham on the Dorset coast in 876 before the West Saxons could intercept them in the open country.

Unable to dislodge them by force, Alfred soon came to terms with the Danes, who promised to leave the West Saxon kingdom. In actuality, however, they merely transferred their camp further west and took up winter quarters for 876-877 at Exeter. Again, Alfred offered terms; this time, the Danes actually honored the agreement. In August, 877, they crossed the border into Mercia and established camp at Gloucester. Here they proceeded to share out some of the land and to give some to King Ceolwulf of Mercia, their protégé. The Viking settlement covered an extensive region of central and eastern Mercia comprising the Five Boroughs—Lincoln, Stamford, Nottingham, Leicester, and Derby—as well as the land further south and southeast, around Northampton, Bedford, and London. Ceolwulf's share lay in the southwesterly part of the kingdom including the towns of Gloucester, Worcester, and Warwick.

The settlement of parts of Mercia in the autumn of 877 must have diverted Viking manpower, but still they had enough fighting men to undertake a third invasion of Wessex. The English had, on the other hand, mistakenly believed that their invaders followed a single method of attack: campaigning in summer and holding up in a fortified lair in winter. After departing from Exeter in August, 877, Guthrum's army tarried for five months and then "in midwinter" 878, descended on Chippenham. Guthrum chose a surprise attack when the land of the West Saxons had hibernated for the winter and its army long dispersed. Chippenham was the royal residence and most probably the invaders attempted to kill Alfred and his body of councilors at one stroke. Although the attempt failed and Alfred decamped, this winter-descent of the Danes surprised, confused, and appalled the West Saxons, who thought their king to be dead and thus lay at the mercy of the intruders.

Alfred actually fled southeast into the heart of Somerset, where he set up a guerrilla base on the Isle of Athelney and began mounting periodic incursions against the Vikings. His preparations were severe and precarious. He could not raise the full muster of Wessex but had to make do with the *fyrds* of Somerset, Wiltshire, and western Hampshire. In any case, in the late spring of 878, he rode to Egbert's Stone east of Selwood, took command of the host, and led his men toward the northern fringe of the Salisbury Plain, where Guthrum's men paused on their march through Wessex. At Ethundune (Edington), as the

Chronicle records, Alfred drove the entire Danish army away from the battlefield, and they promised to quit Wessex and have their king Guthrum baptized. Accordingly, "three weeks later King Guthrum with thirty of the men . . . came [to] Athelney, and the king [Alfred] stood sponsor to him at his baptism there." Guthrum may have faced growing unrest among his battle-weary host, who compared their uncertain and unstable condition on the field to the peaceful and settled life of Halfdan's men in Northumbria and thus looked for a peace with the Christians of the south so that they would be free to pursue a normal settled life in East Anglia and southern Mercia.

Alfred's flight to Athelney and triumphant return to Egbert's Stone, "where men were fain of him," as well as his victory at Edington followed by Guthrum's conversion to Christianity have become part of the folk history of England. These episodes showed Alfred in his magnificent best and glorified Christianity as a civilizing force for the pagan and nomadic Vikings who were to be Christianized and civilized. The immediate threat to Wessex was eliminated. Edington led to the eventual creation of a united Christian, Anglo-Scandinavian kingdom. To cite the concluding remarks of a distinguished historian, "whatever Alfred's shortcomings as a military commander in the future might prove to be, Edington was truly his finest hour." —*Narasingha P. Sil*

ADDITIONAL READING:

Graham-Campbell, James. *The Viking World.* New Haven, Conn.: Ticknor & Fields, 1980. A succinct account with a brief but helpful bibliography.

Keynes, Simon, and Michael Lapidge, eds. *Alfred the Great: Asser's Life of King Alfred and Other Contemporary Sources.* Harmondsworth, Middlesex, England: Penguin Books, 1983. Meticulous, scholarly account of Alfred's life. Indispensable reading.

Loyn, H. R. *The Vikings in Britain.* New York: St. Martin's Press, 1977. A concise history by a renowned medievalist.

Smyth, Alfred P. *King Alfred the Great.* New York: Oxford University Press, 1995. Erudite critical study of Alfred. Chapter 3 is especially pertinent to an understanding of the Battle of Edington.

Sturdy, David. *Alfred the Great.* London: Constable, 1995. In an effort to counterbalance prevailing accounts, Sturdy's biography is extremely critical of Alfredian myths and legends.

Whitelock, Dorothy. "The Importance of the Battle of Edington." In *From Bede to Alfred.* London: Variorum Reprints, 1980. This lecture to the Society of Friends of the Priory Church of Edington has some interesting concluding comments on the long-term significance of the Battle of Edington.

Whitelock, Dorothy, David C. Douglas, and Susie I. Tucker, eds. *The Anglo-Saxon Chronicle: A Revised Translation.* New Brunswick, N.J.: Rutgers University Press, 1961. An authoritative annotated translation of an important primary source from the period.

SEE ALSO: 793, Northmen Raid Lindisfarne; 930, Vikings Establish the Althing in Iceland; 1014, Battle of Clontarf; 1016, Danish Invaders Led by Canute Conquer England

Legend has it that King Alfred was able to defeat the Danes by disguising himself as a harper and spying in their camp. (Archive Photos)

893

BEGINNING OF BULGARIA'S GOLDEN AGE

The beginning of Bulgaria's Golden Age, from the ascension of Symeon to the end of his reign in 927, witnesses Bulgaria's territorial expansion and its aspirations to capture the imperial city of Constantinople.

DATE: 893

LOCALE: Preslav, Bulgaria

CATEGORIES: Cultural and intellectual history; Government and politics

KEY FIGURES:

Alexander (870-913), Byzantine emperor, 912-913

Boris I (died 907), Bulgarian khan, 852-889

Constantine VII Porphyrogennetos (905-959), Byzantine emperor, 945-959

Leo VI (866-912), Byzantine emperor, 886-912

Nicholas I Mystikos (852-925), patriarch of Constantinople, 901-907 and 912-925

Romanus I Lecapenus (870-948), Byzantine emperor, 920-944

Symeon (863-927), czar of Bulgaria, 893-927

Zoe Karbonopsina (died c. 920), Byzantine empress, 914-919

SUMMARY OF EVENT. Bulgaria's Golden Age began with the reign of Symeon (893-927), following a church council convened in Preslav in 893. Boris, the Bulgarian ruler who had first accepted Christianity in 864, left his kingdom to his eldest son Vladimir in 889 in order to retire to a monastery. Vladimir, however, consorted with the aristocratic Bulgar boyars to overturn the Christian religion that Boris had introduced. Clergy were persecuted, the alliance with Byzantium was dropped in favor of one with King Arnulf of Germany, and a revival of paganism seemed imminent. After four years of this retrograde regime, Boris reappeared in Pliska, the capital, recovered the crown, and deposed and blinded his son. Boris then called a church council in 893, which recognized Vladimir's deposition and proclaimed Symeon the new ruler, and Christianity the state religion, with Slavonic the state language instead of Greek. The new capital was to be Preslav instead of the former capital Pliska.

Symeon, the younger son of Boris, was trained for a religious vocation, having spent almost ten years as a novice at a Byzantine monastery in Constantinople. While there, he had also received a secular education, and was well versed in the philosophical and literary culture of his day. He had returned to Bulgaria in 888 to pursue Greek studies and to oversee the translation of Greek religious and historical texts into Bulgarian. In 893, he became czar of Bulgaria.

Under Symeon's leadership, the new Bulgarian capital Preslav became a monastic, cultural, and crafts center. Under him, the Bulgarian Orthodox Church first became independent of Greek clergy. Symeon fully supported the adaptation of Greek liturgical texts to the Slavic vernacular, as well as the translation of numerous secular literary texts. Bulgaria at this time was experiencing a flourishing

of the literary arts, not only continuing and expanding on the mission of the disciples Cyril and Methodius, but even carrying this work to other Slavic nations within the Byzantine sphere of influence. The new capital, Preslav, rivaled Constantinople in the splendor of its royal palace, which the new czar constructed by importing builders and artists from the imperial capital.

By this time also, the Slavicization of the Turkic Bulgars, the conquerors of the indigenous Slavic population, was practically complete, the more numerous Slavs having assimilated the Bulgars both linguistically and culturally. This assimilation had come about through intermarriage, trade, Christianization, and the numerical superiority of the Slavs.

Soon after his accession, Symeon came into conflict with Byzantium over the expulsion from Constantinople of Bulgarian merchants trading there. He invaded the imperial domains in Thrace and let his troops lay waste to the countryside. When the Byzantine emperor retaliated, his troops were defeated by those of Symeon. The emperor then mobilized a larger force, including the Magyars, which caused Symeon to sue for peace. Symeon's secret negotiations with the Pechenegs, a central Asian nomadic people, however, served to divert the Magyars from the Bulgarian flank and enabled him to continue his quarrel with Leo VI, the Byzantine emperor. Symeon demanded the return of all Bulgarian captives and, unsatisfied, engaged the imperial army at Bulgarophygon in Thrace and triumphed.

The Bulgarians and Byzantines signed a treaty in 897, whereby the Byzantines agreed to pay the Bulgarians tribute, commercial rights of Bulgarian traders were restored in Constantinople, and Symeon was given some territory along the frontier.

From 902 to 904, the Arabs were depredating the Aegean area, especially the coast of Thessaly and the Peloponnesus. In 904, they captured Thessaloniki but later withdrew with prisoners and booty. Symeon used this opportunity to garner further territory from the Byzantine Empire in return for refraining from attacking the devastated city. He acquired parts of Thrace and obtained Byzantine recognition for Bulgarian dominion over most of Macedonia. This allowed Bulgaria to claim sovereignty over Slavic tribes west of the original Bulgarian state.

With Emperor Leo VI's death in 912 and the ascension of his brother Alexander, a number of new political figures came into power, among them the former patriarch Nicholas I Mystikos. Nicholas had been deposed by Leo for refusing to acknowledge his fourth marriage, from which the future emperor, Constantine VII Porphyrogennetos, had sprung.

FIRST BULGARIAN EMPIRE UNDER CZAR SYMEON

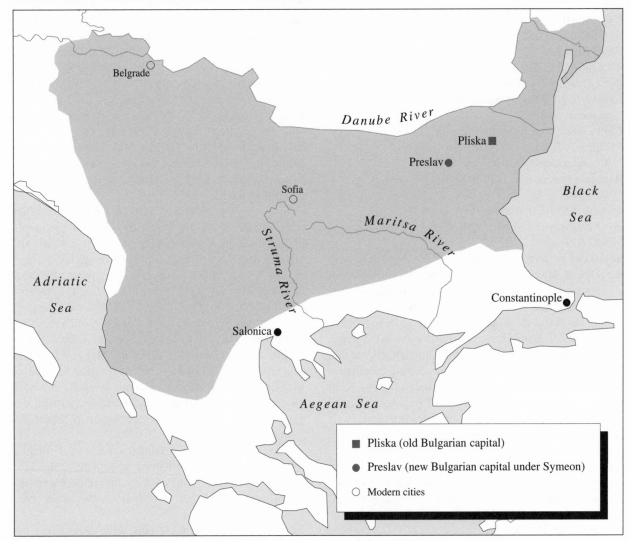

Alexander alienated Symeon by refusing to pay tribute to his envoys under the terms of the 897 treaty. This refusal gave Symeon the pretext he needed for launching an attack on Byzantium, which he did by spring of 913. Shortly thereafter, the degenerate Byzantine emperor Alexander died, leaving the seven-year-old Constantine Porphyrogennetos under the regency of Nicholas I Mystikos, with Constantine's mother Zoe exiled to a monastery.

In August of 913, Symeon led his army to the massive walls surrounding Constantinople, claiming the emperor's crown for himself. Symeon, educated in Constantinople, sometimes called "the half-Greek," and filled with imperial ambition, wished to be recognized as the sole "Roman" emperor of a combined Greek-Bulgarian state. Like so many of his precursors, however, Symeon was unable to break through the thick walls surrounding the city.

The patriarch and regent Nicholas Mysticos agreed to meet and confer with Symeon, and, in so doing, placed a crown on Symeon's head. Nicholas also agreed to a marriage between the young Constantine Porphyrogennetos and Symeon's daughter. Whether this coronation was genuine or a sham is disputed by scholars, as is the nature of the crown with which Symeon was honored. At any rate, Symeon believed that he, as future father-in-law of the future Byzantine emperor, had come closer to the throne of Byzantium, his ultimate goal.

Shortly after this "coronation" early in 1914, Constantine's mother Zoe returned to the capital, led a palace coup, replaced Nicholas as regent, and reversed Symeon's marriage plans for her son. The infuriated Symeon, frustrated in his hopes, retaliated by resuming his war against the empire, which he continued for the next decade.

For the next five years, Symeon's campaign in the Balkans was largely successful as he moved from one conquest to another. Symeon and the Byzantine army clashed at Anchialos on the Black Sea on August 20, 917. The Byzantines were routed. Then Symeon invaded Serbia, which had earlier been consorting with the Byzantines, and placed his own candidate, Pavel, on the Serbian throne. He then proceeded to attack Greece.

Then, in 919, the regent Zoe was deposed in Byzantium by the admiral Romanus Lecapenus, who married his own daughter to the hapless Constantine. He then had himself crowned coemperor with Constantine VII in December, 920.

Disappointed in his own imperial ambitions, Symeon overran Thrace. Now the Serbian crown went to Zaharije, the Bulgarian's candidate. Zaharije, however, proved to be unreliable and turned against his kingmaker, defeating Symeon's troops and beheading his officers.

Symeon then attempted to create a navy by proposing an alliance with the Fatimid dynasty in North Africa. When the Byzantines subverted this plan he finally agreed to meet with Romanus.

His imperial designs foiled, Symeon turned a large army against Serbia in 924 and annexed it, greatly increasing his state, and reoccupied several cities in Thrace. In 926, he launched an invasion against his new neighbor to the west, Croatia, then at the height of its fortunes under its king, Tomislav. This attack was repelled, and Symeon made peace with Tomislav.

In 927, Symeon set out once again against Byzantium, but died on the road, never having achieved his ultimate goal of becoming emperor of the Romans.

—*Gloria Fulton*

ADDITIONAL READING:

Browning, Robert. *Byzantium and Bulgaria: A Comparative Study Across the Early Medieval Frontier.* Berkeley: University of California Press, 1975. Focuses on the ninth and tenth centuries and the relationship between Byzantium and Bulgaria.

Fine, John. *The Early Medieval Balkans: A Critical Survey from the Sixth to the Late Twelfth Century.* Ann Arbor: University of Michigan Press, 1983. A scholarly work stressing the many uncertainties about the historical sources for the earliest Bulgarian period. Chapter 5 treats the reign of Symeon.

Obolensky, Dimitri. *The Byzantine Commonwealth: Eastern Europe, 500-1453.* New York: Praeger Publishers, 1971. Historical and geographical study of the nations of Eastern Europe, particularly the Slavs, during the Byzantine Empire.

Runciman, Steven. *A History of the First Bulgarian Empire.* London: Bell, 1930. A classic history of the First Bulgarian Empire, focusing on religious and political developments from the earliest times to 1014.

Tzvetkov, Plamen. *A History of the Balkans: A Regional Overview from a Bulgarian Perspective.* 2 vols. San Francisco: Edwin Mellen Press, 1993. Volume 1 covers the early period, giving the Bulgarian version of the historical events.

SEE ALSO: 850, Building of the Slavic Alphabet; 864, Boris Converts to Christianity; 1014, Basil II Conquers the Bulgars.

896

MAGYAR INVASIONS OF ITALY, SAXONY, AND BAVARIA

The Magyar invasions of Italy, Saxony, and Bavaria introduce a new ethnic element into the European population.

DATE: 896

LOCALE: Central Europe

CATEGORIES: Expansion and land acquisition; Wars, uprisings, and civil unrest

KEY FIGURES:

Árpád (died 907), leader of the Magyars, c. 890-907
Arnulf (c. 850-899), king of Germany, 887-899
Lambert (c. 875-898), claimant to the throne of Italy
Zwentibald (c. 840-894), king of Great Moravia

SUMMARY OF EVENT. The origin of the Magyars is obscure and half-legendary. Yet historians have surmised that the Magyars were originally a Finno-Ugric people, related to the Finns, the Estonians, and the Mordvinians. These peoples tended to be sedentary forest-dwellers. Sometime in the earlier centuries of the first millennium, the Magyars abandoned their sedentary way of life and adopted the nomadic habits of the Turks and other Altaic peoples of the steppes. It was at this time that they were given the name "On-Ogur" or "ten tribes," which later was corrupted by Europeans into "Hungarian" even though they always called themselves "Magyars" and continued to do so.

In this era, the steppes were in constant turmoil, and nomads constantly invaded westward toward Europe in search of food and territory. The most famous of these incursions was by the Huns in the mid-fifth century. Although Hungarian tradition sees the Huns as ancestors of the Hungarians, and although the famous Hunnish name "Attila" is a popular Hungarian given name, there is no evidence but that the Huns were anything more than collateral relatives of the Magyars.

After the Huns, steppe people such as the Avars and Bulgars continued to pour into central Europe. Whereas the Bulgars occupied a corner of southeastern Europe and settled down there permanently, the Avars, although amassing a large realm that included modern Hungary and which posed a threat to the Byzantine Empire in the seventh century, never jelled into a sovereign nation-state. The Avar realm soon collapsed and was replaced by the state of Great Moravia, the first major Slav-dominated political entity. Traditionally, historians assumed that great Moravia was in the area of modern Moravia (in what is now the Czech Republic). Lately, though, some scholars have claimed that Great Moravia actually lay in portions of Serbia stretching toward the Hungarian border, and that only that location explains why Great Moravia had as much to do with Byzantium as with the Latin West. This is important because the location of Great Moravia explains where exactly the lands were that the Magyars initially conquered.

At the time of the height of Great Moravia's power, the Magyars were still living on the steppes, as vassals of the ethnically Turkish (and Jewish by religion) Khazar empire. Despite their Turkish lifestyle, the Magyars had retained their Finnish-related tongue, which enabled them to preserve their tribal identity. Because the Magyars had no written language and did not keep their own records, historical sources for the early Magyars are sparse, relying on Arabic, Greek, and Latin accounts far removed from the action. Nonetheless, a bare narrative of events can be pieced together. The Magyars left the Khazar confederation about 830 and moved westward to Ukraine. They were just about to put down roots in this fertile breadbasket when pressed from the east by a ferocious Turkic tribe, the Pechenegs. The Pechenegs, who were later to establish an impermanent state on the shores of Romania and Moldova, also expelled some Khazar tribes who became attached to the Magyars in a grand federation. Recognizing the need to defend themselves against their opponents and secure a permanent home for all the tribes, the federation established a more stable leadership structure than was customary among the steppe peoples. The person chosen to lead this federation was a man named Árpád, a senior chief of the most powerful Magyar tribe.

The opportunities for the Magyars to attack central Europe had increased because of the decline of the Carolingian Empire, which had conquered the region under Charlemagne. By the 890's, the empire had been divided and subdivided into several states. The eastern, German portion was ruled by Arnulf, who had only a peripheral

connection to Carolingian ancestry and whose legitimacy was thus questioned. Arnulf lay claim to the symbolic center of the empire in Rome, but his authority was strongly challenged by Lambert, the young son of the late Italian count Guido of Spoleto, who was not a Carolingian at all but who nevertheless manifested a claim to the throne of, at least, Italy. The Magyars probably could have taken advantage of this dissension to invade, but there was no need for this. In a manner so often repeated throughout history, Arnulf willingly risked barbarians on his own soil in order to gain a temporary advantage over his opponent by asking the aid of the Magyars against Lambert. The Magyars swept into the central European plain in 892 and completely conquered Great Moravia, which had been attacking Arnulf on his east just as he was trying to subjugate Lambert on his south. Zwentibald and much of the Moravian aristocracy were killed. Árpád and the other Magyar leaders were impressed by the space and fertility of the flatlands to the west of the Carpathian range and, given the presence of the Pechenegs on the Black Sea coast, decided to move the entire Magyar people there in 895 now that there was a vacuum after the end of the Moravian state. Arnulf was too busy with his other problems to prevent this. The Magyars did not become vassals of Germany; they did not convert to Christianity or adopt Latin institutions. All this was to come later. Indeed, for several decades thereafter the Magyars lived and behaved like traditional steppe warriors, launching swift and massive invasions of Italy, Germany, France, and Serbia (often, as in the case of Arnulf, at the behest of embattled rulers of these countries who required aid) during which they captured booty and then quickly withdrew. A German attempt to conquer the Magyars was handily rebuffed at a battle near Bratislava in 907.

For Western Europeans, the Magyars represented as much of a problem as the ubiquitous Viking raids taking place at the same time, as is evidenced by the apparent derivation of the word "ogre" from "On-Ogur." A new wave of terrible barbarian invasions seemed set to undermine Carolingian culture much as late Roman culture had been disjointed by the Germanic tribes centuries before. Yet what happened to the Magyars turned out to be different. Whereas the Huns, for instance, had amassed a large territory during the lifetime of Attila only to see it totally collapse with his death, the Magyars settled a more compact, easily cultivated territory in which they established a permanent stake and identity. Instead of merely subjugating the Slavic populace that remained from Great Moravia, the Magyars integrated the Slavs into their tribal structure and, to some extent, assimilated them. This was symbolized by Árpád's son Zolta marrying a Moravian princess in 904. A stabilizing secondary element in the ethnic mix were the Szekelers, a people related to the Avars who occupied a small but defined role in the Magyar realm. Historians are unsure whether the Szekelers had been part of the original Avar state or traveled in with the Magyars from the steppes. By the time of Árpád's great-grandson Geza eighty years after the Magyar conquest, there was a firmly established central Asian ethnic presence in the heart of Europe, a presence which changed the ethnic mix of the European continent and has affected it up through the twentieth century and beyond.

—*Nicholas Birns*

ADDITIONAL READING:

Barraclough, Geoffrey. *The Crucible of Europe: The Ninth and Tenth Centuries in European History*. Berkeley: University of California Press, 1976. A general history of the period which places some stress on the Magyar invasion.

Bobula, Ida Miriam. *Origin of the Hungarian Nation*. Gainesville, Fla.: Danubian Research and Information Center, 1966. Speculative, not always responsible account heavily influenced by Hungarian nationalism, but has useful background information.

Bowlus, Charles R. *Franks, Moravians, and Magyars: The Struggle for the Middle Danube, 788-907*. Philadelphia: University of Pennsylvania Press, 1995. Controversial in its contention that Great Moravia was actually located in modern Serbia; a lightning-rod for renewed debate about early Magyar history.

McCartney, C. A. *The Magyars in the Ninth Century*. London: Cambridge University Press, 1968. Exhaustively detailed, scholarly account that is quite reliable and informative.

Riché, Pierre. *The Carolingians*. Philadelphia: University of Pennsylvania Press, 1993. Useful on the roles of Arnulf and Lambert in the events of 896.

Sugar, Peter F., ed. *A History of Hungary*. Bloomington: Indiana University Press, 1990. Readable, reliable, and up-to-date account; the best for an elementary overview.

SEE ALSO: 445-453, Invasions of Attila the Hun; 843, Treaty of Verdun; 955, Otto I Defeats the Magyars.

930
VIKINGS ESTABLISH THE ALTHING IN ICELAND

The Vikings establish the Althing in Iceland, a legislative assembly that is generally considered to be the oldest in Europe.

DATE: 930
LOCALE: Thingvellir, Iceland
CATEGORY: Government and politics
KEY FIGURES:

Ulfljot (fl. early tenth century), formulated a legal code, Ulfljot's Law, derived from Norwegian law

Thirty-six godar, or chiefs, who agreed to Ulfljot's Law at the first Althing in 930

SUMMARY OF EVENT. The events preceding the establishment of the Althing are of great interest in themselves. The story begins in 864, when the blood brothers Ingolf Arnarson and Leif Hrodmarsson, later called Hjörleif, or Leif the Sword, left Norway with families, warriors, and Irish slaves to settle in Iceland. Their ships got separated in the mist along Iceland's southern coast, and Hjörleif came to anchor that autumn seventy-two miles west of Ingolf. When spring came and Hjörleif ordered his Irish thralls to pull the plow to save his sole ox, the slaves rebelled and murdered Hjörleif and his followers, only to be slain themselves by Ingolf and his men when they happened upon the bodies. Ingolf soon after discovered a beautiful bay, with steam rising from the meadows, and he settled there and called the place Reykjavik, Bay of Smoke.

In the next half-century, as many as twenty thousand immigrants had settled all around the coast and taken up all the arable land for growing barley and raising sheep and cattle. When a Norse chief settled in Iceland, he built a temple for his own dependents and any others of the region who had resources of their own. The chief became the *hof godi* (*godi* is a cognate of the word "God"), or temple priest, but he was almost exclusively a secular chieftain rather than a religious personage. The *godi* would hold assemblies, or Things, of the freemen at the temple to dispose of matters demanding action. (The English cognate "hustings" means literally "house thing.") The members of a chieftain's Thing looked to his patronage and protection and he expected their support, but all the Thingmen (yeomen, in effect, who could afford to pay a temple tax) were free and allowed to join another Thing at their wish.

Although the Thingmen were required to pay a toll to meet temple expenses, the tolls were not large enough to enhance the chieftain's powers. Moreover, the Thing had no land specific to it, and this lack of a territorial identification thus distinguished the system of Things from feudalism. The chieftain's office, his *godard*, was transferable in the way of any private property and could even be held by several individuals jointly. Finally, the same *godi* might buy or inherit a number of *godards*.

The strongest bonds among Thingmen were based on kinship, and since the individuals loyal to one *godi*, or chieftain, were not all blood-related, family feuds were not necessarily between Things. If the family of a murdered man did not get satisfaction in either blood or money, it could sue through the Thing; but since the Thing had no enforcement powers, the plaintiffs, even when found in the right, were themselves responsible for exacting punishment of the guilty party.

Given the violent, aggressive nature of the Vikings, every kind of grievance was rife both within individual Things and between rival Things, and since there was no Icelandic state to which all Things belonged, this semi-anarchy made life difficult for all. At about 927, an elder chief, Ulfljot, proposed one general Thing for the whole young country. (The word "Thing" is believed to be a short form of *almannathing*, a "Thing for all people." There were also local spring and autumn Things. The term is many-faceted, referring to the law of the whole nation, to a specific geographical site, and to a special time of year. After pressing his case to many of the most powerful chiefs, Ulfljot even sailed to Norway to learn how its laws worked. While he was away, his foster-brother Grim Geitskor (goat's shoe), famous for his agility in the rocky terrain, went in search of a proper site for the great assembly. He finally discovered a beautiful spot northeast of Reykjavik that has since been known as Thingvellir, or "The Plains of the Thing."

Thus in 930, upon Ulfljot's return from Norway, the first Althing, or general assembly, was held, and these Althings were continued every year until 1800. They were always held the last two weeks of June when the summer solstice assured the most hours of daylight and the weather was at its best. Each chief had a sort of booth, and the political and legal business was leavened heavily with social rejoicing. The atmosphere must have suggested a mix of New England town meeting, grand jury proceeding, and county fair, all conducted in a carnival mood conducive to marriage arrangements and other social contracts.

The constitution shaped at the first Althing called for a total of thirty-six Things, each with its chieftain. This number grew later into thirty-nine when in 965 the island was divided into quarters and each quarter got nine Things, except the north quarter, which enjoyed twelve. Each of the quarters then lumped its Things together into groups of three to create thirteen so-called Thing-districts. The rules demanded that the lawspeaker, the chiefs, and certain Thingmen be present.

The Althing was unusual in that it had legislative and judicial branches but no executive arm. Legislative power was exercised by the assembled chiefs, and they elected the "lawspeaker," who presided over the body constituted by the chiefs. The lawspeaker served a three-year term, over the course of which he was required to recite the whole body of law. (The laws were not written down until 1117.) A special ledge, the "law rock," was the lawspeaker's podium, from which he was also instructed to announce any new laws. He was responsible for answering questions about the law but not for passing judgment in particular lawsuits. The lawspeaker held the highest appointment in the country, a position recognized by his being the only officeholder to be paid.

Judicial power was vested in a court established at the Althing. Originally the court comprised thirty-six Thingmen, one appointed by each of the chiefs, but when the island was quartered in 965 each quarter got its own court. Eventually, in 1004, a fifth court was established much like a supreme court. The whole system was enormously complicated by the other two Things, the one in the spring and the one in autumn.

The spring Thing had two parts: a "law-suit Thing" and a "payment Thing." If the thirty-six judges could not all agree, a case could be referred to the Althing or even to the fifth court. The autumn Thing, coming as it did after the Althing, served mainly to convey to everyone the decisions of the grand assembly at Thingvellir.

The system that evolved gave the chiefs control over the Things without themselves being overseen by any legislative body, and yet the freedom of the Thingmen to switch allegiances among chiefs ensured a form of representative democracy. All in all, the judicial system rooted in the Althing was intricate and fluid, but the main features endured to guarantee that all Icelanders, except the slaves, had their place in the hierarchy and were subject to the rule of the Althing.

—Frank Day

Additional reading:

Bryce, James. *Studies in History and Jurisprudence*. New York: Oxford University Press, 1967. A long essay on "Primitive Iceland" on pages 263-300 puts into perspective the whole story of the rise and fall of the Icelandic republic.

Graham-Campbell, James, et al., eds. *Cultural Atlas of the Viking World*. New York: Facts On File, 1994. The four pages on Thingvellir offer beautiful illustrations and a brief summary of the Althing and its history.

Hastrup, Kirsten. *Culture and History in Medieval Iceland: An Anthropological Analysis of Structure and Change*. Oxford: Clarendon Press, 1985. A very scholarly—but completely readable—study that describes the institution of the Thing in detail, with a diagram of the political-administrative structure of the Althing (pages 118-130). Includes a rich bibliography.

Jones, Gwyn. *A History of the Vikings*. New York: Oxford University Press, 1968. Includes several pages on the origins of the Althing, many diagrams, maps, and photos, a bibliography, and a valuable detailed index.

_____. *The Norse Atlantic Saga: Being the Norse Voyages of Discovery and Settlement to Iceland, Greenland, America.* London: Oxford University Press, 1964. The second half of this book reprints many sources, including several pages about the Althing excerpted from Ari Thorgilsson the Learned's *The Book of the Icelanders* (c. 1122-1125).

Scherman, Katharine. *Daughter of Fire: A Portrait of Iceland.* Boston: Little, Brown, 1976. This popular history of Iceland gives a succinct account of the provisions of the Althing and is a good place to begin studying the history of the country.

SEE ALSO: 793, Northmen Raid Lindisfarne; 850-900, Vikings Settle in Kiev; 878, King Alfred Defeats the Danes at Edington; 1014, Battle of Clontarf; 1016, Danish Invaders Led by Canute Conquer England.

950
FLOURISHING OF THE COURT OF CÓRDOBA

The flourishing of the court of Córdoba produces cultural and intellectual accomplishments in al-Andalus that have a profound significance for western Europe.

DATE: c. 950

LOCALE: Córdoba, Spain

CATEGORIES: Cultural and intellectual history; Education; Government and politics; Religion

KEY FIGURES:

'Abd al-Rahman I (731-788), founder of the Umayyad Dynasty at Córdoba and emir of Córdoba, 756-788

'Abd al-Rahman II (788-852), emir of Córdoba, 822-852

'Abd al-Rahmān III al-Nasir (891-961), emir of Córdoba, 912-928, and first caliph of Córdoba, 929-961

Al-Hakam I (770-822), emir of Córdoba, 796-822

Al-Hakam II (died 976), caliph of Córdoba, 961-976

Abu 'Āmir al-Mansūr (c. 938-1002), vizier of Hishām II, 976-1002

Hishām I (757-796), emir of Córdoba, 788-796

SUMMARY OF EVENT. The foundation of the court of Córdoba, which in the tenth century became one of the greatest centers of learning in Europe, reads like a story out of the *Arabian Nights' Entertainments*. In 750, a revolution by the Abbasid family against the Umayyad caliph broke out in Iraq and Syria. A young Umayyad prince, 'Abd al-Rahman, escaped the proscription and traveled to North Africa, where he gained the support of his Berber

relatives. He eventually went to Spain, where he established himself at Córdoba as an independent ruler.

After his death in 788, civil wars and revolts threatened the state he had created. In 912, a strong successor came to the throne: 'Abd al-Rahmān III, who firmly established control over Muslim Spain and carried on successful campaigns against small Christian outposts in the North. He and his successors al-Hakam II and Hishām II brought Muslim Spain to its greatest heights until the ambition of Hishām's vizier, al-Mansūr, caused dynastic difficulties which brought about the collapse of the caliphate of Córdoba by 1035. About the same time the long reconquest of Spain by the Christians began.

The Umayyads of Damascus had been notable patrons of art and learning, and their descendants at Córdoba continued the family tradition. Cultural and intellectual edification at the new court was so emphatic that its spiritual impact outlived its political life. While 'Abd al-Rahman I was still struggling to secure control of Spain, he found time to promote such artistic endeavors as initiation of the construction of the great mosque of Córdoba, which became the model for future Moorish mosques. He wrote poetry extolling the beauties of his Syrian homeland, imported fruit trees and vegetables from the eastern Islamic lands, and built the Rusafah Palace in the midst of gardens which were regarded as a wonder. Under his successors Hishām I and al-Hakam I, the great mosque was enlarged and extensive building campaigns were undertaken. 'Abd al-Rahman II, a poet himself, imported scholars and artisans from the East and carried on an extensive building program.

This early activity came to fruition during the reign of 'Abd al-Rahmān III, called "the Great," and his immediate successors. Once he had centralized his authority over Muslim Spain and coastal areas of North Africa, forcing the powerful Fatimid Dynasty to move eastward to Egypt, he determined that his court would surpass that of his Abbasid rivals in Baghdad, who were on the decline. Perhaps for political reasons, 'Abd al-Rahmān III was the first Andalusian Umayyad dynast to declare himself "caliph," establishing throughout his reign absolute authority and increased isolation from his subjects, circumscribed by complex court etiquette. He brought prosperity as well as political unity to al-Andalus; during his reign Córdoba was the most prosperous city in Europe and foreign delegates marveled at the splendors of his court. He introduced new agricultural techniques and carried on a massive building program in and around Córdoba, including the lavish all-inclusive government city, Madinat al-Zahra on the outskirts of Córdoba. He was a dedicated patron of the ever-increasing body of poets, historians, physicians, geographers, astronomers, mathematicians, musicians, and philosophers who gathered at his court. His son al-Hakam II continued such patronage, as did the powerful vizier of Hishām II, al-Mansūr. The Cordoban tradition of scholarship based on Greco-Arabic learning was so strong that even as late as the twelfth century, long after the fall of the caliphate, the old capital produced two celebrated medieval thinkers, the Islamic philosopher Averroës (Ibn Rushd) and the Jewish scholar Moses Maimonides.

The court of the Cordoban emirate and caliphate, and the al-Andalus which it ruled, was culturally heterogeneous. Although the rulers maintained the eastern Umayyad ideal of Arab supremacy, in reality the population consisted of large numbers of Berbers, Hispanic Jews and Christians, Slavs, and others, many of whom rose to positions of prominence. This unique blend of cultural and religious elements contributed to the ease with which Andalusian accomplishments were disseminated throughout the West.

As early as the tenth century A.D., certain concepts of Arabic mathematics and astronomy were apparently introduced into Western Europe through contacts with Córdoba and Islamic Spain. John, a monk from the abbey of Gorze, was sent as ambassador to Córdoba by Emperor Otto I of Germany and returned with books on mathematics that soon made Gorze and other Lotharingian monasteries centers of study in this field. Gerbert d'Aurillac, a young monk who later became Pope Sylvester II, owed much to Islamic learning when he became one of the greatest Western European scholars of the tenth century. When he visited Barcelona, he absorbed much mathematical and astronomical knowledge which had spread northward from Muslim centers. Many scholars believe that, as the most learned mathematician of his time, Pope Sylvester introduced the abacus and also Arabic numerals into Europe. Because he was familiar with superior Islamic learning, legends after his death pictured him as a wizard created by Saracen sorcery and magic.

The dissemination of Islamic learning in Spain had its greatest impact on Europe in the twelfth and thirteenth centuries, when Latin translations of Arabic texts and treatises on Aristotle began to appear in the North. Such translations spurred the development of Scholasticism, and the philosophical works of Averroës and his school at Córdoba played an influential role in the process.

The intellectual impact of Muslim scholarship was wide and varied. The works of Avicenna (Ibn Sina), the eleventh century Islamic medical theorist, became standard texts for Western physicians. The colorful stonework of the Romanesque churches of Auvergne bears striking resemblance to the variegated patterns of Moorish archi-tecture; development of the Gothic arch can possibly be traced to the colonnades and horseshoe arches of Islamic Spanish masterpieces such as the mosque of Córdoba and the Alhambra. Considering the close contacts between southern France and northern Spain, the similarity between the themes and descriptions of Arabic love poetry and the roots of medieval courtly love poetry and music may be found in Moorish prototypes. One Spanish scholar, Miguel Asin-Palacios, even maintains that Muslim legends about heaven and hell influenced that supreme poetic creation of medieval Western Europe, Dante's *La divina commedia* (c. 1320; *The Divine Comedy*, 1802).

—*James H. Forse, updated by Katherine S. Mansour*

ADDITIONAL READING:

Chejne, Anwar G. *Muslim Spain: Its History and Culture.* St. Paul: University of Minnesota Press, 1974. Written as a text for graduate students, this work provides a well-written and interesting overview of the history, culture, and intellectual life of al-Andalus.

Fletcher, Richard A. *Moorish Spain.* New York: Henry Holt, 1992. This work incorporates current scholarship on al-Andalus and offers a concise treatment of the Moors.

Hayes, John R., ed. *The Genius of Arab Civilization: Source of Renaissance.* 2d ed. Cambridge, Mass.: MIT Press, 1983. A lively collection of essays, suitable for the lay reader, discussing Arab intellectual and cultural accomplishments.

Reilly, Bernard F. *The Contest of Christian and Muslim Spain: 1031-1157.* Cambridge, Mass.: Blackwell, 1992. Enlightening use of recently published primary sources to provide insight into the political and cultural changes in Iberia during this critical period.

Sordo, Enrique. *Moorish Spain.* New York: Crown Publishers, 1963. A work that concentrates on the three greatest cultural centers of Islamic Spain: Córdoba, Seville, and Granada.

SEE ALSO: 711, Tarik's Crossing into Spain; 1010-1015, Avicenna Writes His *Canon of Medicine*; 1031, Fall of the Caliphate of Córdoba.

955
OTTO I DEFEATS THE MAGYARS

Otto I defeats the Magyars and halts their raids of central Europe, encouraging their peaceful settlement in the plains of Hungary as a civilized and Christianized nation.

DATE: August 10, 955
LOCALE: Lechfield, outside Augsburg, Germany
CATEGORY: Wars, uprisings, and civil unrest

KEY FIGURES:

Adelaide (931-999), widow of King Lothair of
Lombardy and second wife of Otto I (married in 951)

Berengar II (died 966), marquis of Ivrea

John XII (Octavian; c. 937-964), Roman Catholic pope,
955-964

Otto I, the Great (912-973), king of Germany, 937-973,
and Holy Roman Emperor, 962-973

SUMMARY OF EVENT. Otto I, whom contemporaries
named "the Great," has been called "the Charlemagne of
Germany proper." His reign marked the beginning of
Germany's First Reich, known for almost a thousand years
(until 1806) as the Holy Roman Empire of German Nations.

He inherited the kingship from his father Henry I, the
Fowler. Although exercising little royal power over the
strong and independent tribal dukes, Henry nevertheless
increased the prestige of the crown by his charismatic
personality. His successor, the twenty-four-year-old Otto,
took a different view of the German kingship than his
father. The great Frankish emperor Charlemagne was his
model. Consequently, he held his coronation at Charlemagne's favorite residence, Aix-la-Chapelle (Aachen).
The ceremony was attended by all the tribal dukes of
Germany who unanimously elected him king. The archbishop of Mainz anointed him king and invested him with
Charlemagne's gigantic crown, scepter, sword, and golden
mantle.

King Henry's death became a signal of revolt among
the Slavic and Hungarian peoples to the east of the kingdom. In 895, the Magyars, a restless nomadic people,
began taking possession of the ancient Roman province of
Pannonia, from which they raided central Europe for more
than half a century. In 937, they made their first incursion
into Germany during Otto's reign, raiding Saxony and
ransacking their way to the borders of France. They were
defeated by forces led by Otto himself at a place unknown.

In addition, the early part of Otto's reign was fraught
with insurrection and challenges to his crown by the
independent-minded dukes of Germany, aided by archbishops and his own brother, Henry, and half-brother,
Tankmar. Otto was able to defeat these rebellious nobles
and consolidate his power by giving their territories to
faithful relatives and other followers. In addition to these
internecine challenges, Otto had to fight incursions of the
Danes to the north, the Slavs and Wends to the east,
Bohemians and Hungarians to the southeast, and the duke
of Lorraine on the western frontier. Being the embodiment
of the Germanic warrior king at the head of his troops, he
succeeded in beating back these onslaughts. In many instances he was not only able to secure the borders but to

subjugate and Christianize these pagan peoples and bring
them into the orbit of the German realm. During his reign,
Germany extended its colonization of Slav territory from
the Elbe to the Oder River. These policies, in imitation of
Charlemagne, earned Otto the title "the Great."

His most decisive victory came over the marauding
Magyars, who had made repeated incursions into Germany in 937, 944, 948, and 950. In 955, they were invited
into Germany by some Bavarian nobles as part of their
civil strife against Otto. The Hungarian hordes, arrogant
of success on account of their sheer numerical strength
(contemporaries estimated one hundred thousand horsemen; the Hungarians boasted that their horses could drain
every river in Germany), laid siege to the city of Augsburg
which was heroically defended by its bishop. Badly outnumbered and with only dilapidated walls to protect it, the
city seemed incapable of withstanding the assault. When
Otto heard of the Magyar invasion, he hastily assembled
an army from all parts of Germany and hurried to
Augsburg. The decisive Battle of Lechfield took place on

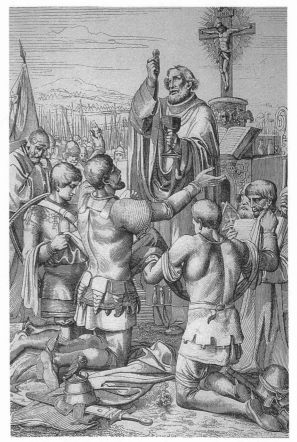

*Before the Battle of Lechfield took place, King Otto and his
German forces attended a mass performed by the bishop of
Augsburg.* (Archive Photos)

August 10, 955, outside of the city on the Lech River. Before the battle started, Otto and his armies consecrated themselves in a mass where they took the Holy Eucharist and the king vowed to found a bishopric at Merseburg if God granted him victory. The upcoming battle took on the characteristic of a crusade.

In the scorching heat of August, the Magyar troops were attacked by three waves of Bavarians, followed by a wave of Franks, a fifth wave of elite Saxon troops led by the king himself, followed by five lines of Swabians and a rear guard composed of Bohemians, under the banner of the archangel Michael. At first, the Magyars were able to avoid the direct attack, even causing havoc by falling into the rear of Otto's army. Nevertheless, valor saved the day. Sword in hand, Otto himself fought in the thick of battle. Conrad of Lorraine, the most valiant warrior of the day who led the Franks in combat, died from an arrow in his throat while lifting his helmet to wipe his face and catch some air. As the tide of battle turned, the Hungarians tried to escape across the Lech River, where many of them drowned. The rest of the Magyar invaders were routed and killed. If one can believe the statistics of the age, some one hundred thousand Hungarians died.

So decisive was the victory that, after the battle of Lechfield, the Magyars gave up their restless wandering, accepted Christianity, peacefully settled on the plains of Hungary, and eventually became allies of the Holy Roman Empire.

With his prestige enhanced by this victory, Otto tried to further consolidate the German monarchy by seeking to extend his influence to Italy and eventually to be crowned Holy Roman Emperor. Adelaide, widow of the Lombard king, had lost her northern Italian kingdom to the local pretender Berengar II. In 951, Otto, in response to a call for help, crossed the Alps and defeated Berengar. A widower himself at the time, Otto married Adelaide and reincorporated her lands into the empire. This began Germany's fateful involvement in the chaotic affairs of Italy. In an attempt to win an empire, the German emperors lost Germany, as later history was to witness.

While Otto's attention was absorbed with his rebellious and disloyal vassals in Germany and his defense against the Magyars, Berengar had reconquered the Lombard kingdom, seeking independent sovereignty in Italy. Consequently, in 961, Otto crossed the Alps again, expelled Berengar, continued on to Rome, where the reluctant Pope John XII on February 2, 962, crowned him Holy Roman Emperor. This union of Germany and Italy under the imperial crown created the Holy Roman Empire.

This coronation marked the apex of Otto's emulation of Charlemagne. Yet with it he also had set the agenda for the Holy Roman Empire for the remainder of the Middle Ages.

His successors would see the need to keep the reluctant northern Italians in the empire as the rationale to obtaining the Roman crown. Their dream of an empire would prevent the consolidation of the monarchy in Germany.

The eastward expansion of Germany into Slavic territory became a constant theme of German history, as did the colonization of eastern central Europe where the Poles, Bohemians, and Hungarians remained in the orbit of the Holy Roman Empire. The battle of Lechfield, however, not only ended Hungarian incursion into central Europe but also marks the beginning of the Magyars as a sedentary people and civilized nation.   —*Herbert Luft*

ADDITIONAL READING:

Falco, Georgio. *The Holy Roman Empire*. Westport, Conn.: Greenwood Press, 1980. This general history of the Holy Roman Empire profiles the Middle Ages in German history.

Fichtenau, Heinrich. *Living in the Tenth Century: Mentalities and Social Order*. Chicago: University of Chicago Press, 1991. This is a survey of Carolingian and post-Carolingian in *Annales* style.

Hill, Boyd H., Jr. *Medieval Monarchy in Action: The German Empire from Henry I to Henry IV*. New York: Barnes & Noble Books, 1972. A history of the reigns of German emperors with emphasis on their domestic and foreign policies.

Leyse, Karl J. *Rule and Conflict in Early Medieval Society: Ottonian Saxony*. Bloomington: Indiana University Press, 1979. This collection of studies includes a discussion of Otto I and his enemies.

Reuter, Timothy. *Germany in the Early Middle Ages*. London: Longman, 1991. This largely political history incorporates the latest scholarship.

SEE ALSO: 735, Christianity Is Introduced into Germany; 781, Alcuin Becomes Adviser to Charlemagne; 896, Magyar Invasions of Italy, Saxony, and Bavaria.

963
FOUNDATION OF MOUNT ATHOS MONASTERIES

The foundation of Mount Athos monasteries provides a cultural and intellectual center for the Eastern Orthodox religion, particularly during the prolonged period of Ottoman Turkish domination of the Balkan Peninsula.

DATE: 963

LOCALE: Mount Athos, on the Chalkidike Peninsula in northern Greece

CATEGORIES: Organizations and institutions; Religion
KEY FIGURES:
Athanasios of Athos (925-1001), saint and founder of
  Great Lavra monastery
Gregory of Sinai (c. 1255-c. 1337), Hesychast monk and
  writer
John I Tzimiskes (925-976), Byzantine emperor, 969-976
Leo VI (866-912), Byzantine emperor, 886-912
Nicephorus II Phocas (912-969), Byzantine emperor,
  963-969

SUMMARY OF EVENT. Although the legend of Mount
Athos as a Christian religious sanctuary goes back to a
purported visit to the Holy Mount by the Virgin Mary in
A.D. 49, this area has a religious tradition that predates
Christianity. Named after Athos, son of Poseidon, accord-
ing to tradition it was the home of the Greek gods before
Olympus.

Throughout the early Middle Ages, Athos held a reputation as a holy place. In the ninth century, it was the home
of Saint Peter the Athonite, a semilegendary hermit who
lived there in a cave for thirty-five years. By the end of the
ninth century, there were several small *lavras* (monasteries) there. A *chrysobul* (imperial document) from the Byzantine emperor Leo VI was issued around A.D. 900, confirming the possession of the entire peninsula to certain
hermits already there.

Around 961, the Byzantine general Nicephorus Phocas
and his adviser, the monk Athanasios, decided to build a
great monastery on Athos to which they might retire from
public life. Instead, Nicephorus became the emperor, leaving Athanasios to complete the monastery. This monastic
establishment, the Great Lavra, still stands as the oldest
and largest monastery on Athos, although Athanasios himself was killed supervising its construction.

The hermits living on Athos at that time were not
pleased by the rise of the Great Lavra, and they complained to Nicephorus' successor John Tzimiskes about its
size and worldliness. The latter reconfirmed the monastery, however, and increased the number of monks allowed
to live there. He established a common council of hermit-
monks who would meet regularly in Karyes, a small town
in the center of the peninsula.

By the end of the tenth century, several more monasteries, including Iveron, Vatopedi, Chilandar, Esphigmenou,
Pantaleimon, Xenophontos, and Zographou, had been
built. At about this time monks from other nations, including Georgia, Italy, and Armenia, began to come to Athos,
while the following two centuries saw the addition of
Slavic monks from Serbia, Bulgaria, and Russia. New
monasteries were founded during the next hundred years
with a steadily increasing population of monks and her-

mits. This continued until the fall of Constantinople, in
1453, caused the building impetus to slow.

Many of these larger monasteries became wealthy
from royal subsidies, as well as the sale of agricultural
products produced by the monks and trees from the forests.

The later Middle Ages represent the most active era in
the establishment of the monasteries of Mount Athos. All
of the Ruling Monasteries had been established by 1540,
less than a century after the fall of Constantinople to the
Turks. The largest monasteries had extensive libraries and
treasure houses, as well as archives relating to the founding of each of the monastic houses. The purpose of the
monastic establishments was to provide a place for prayer
and contemplation away from the tribulations of everyday
life. These monasteries were usually supported by gifts
from various rulers or by donations solicited from the
faithful. The monks themselves took responsibility for the
daily tasks involved in the upkeep of their own monastic
communities.

Among issues of importance to the monasteries on
Athos was the question as to whether the Byzantine emperor or the Orthodox patriarch had supreme authority
over the Mount. Another matter of importance was the
proscription of eunuchs, beardless youths, women, and in
fact all female creatures, from the area. Although traditionally at the behest of the Virgin herself, this proscription
was instituted in 1045 under the constitution approved by
Constantine Monomachus, the Byzantine emperor.

In 1204, when Byzantium was invaded and pillaged by
the legions of the Fourth Crusade, there was great danger
that the treasures on Mount Athos, which included a great
jeweled Bible, a reliquary of the True Cross, and many
priceless manuscripts, might be seized by the crusaders.
Pope Innocent III, however, guaranteed the autonomy of
the Mount, which prevented this disaster from occurring.
After the restoration of the Byzantine emperors to the
throne, however, and the consequent attempt to end the
schism between the Eastern and Western Catholic Church
by recognizing the supremacy of the pope of Rome, many
of the monks on Athos were executed by inquisitors.

Another disaster which befell the inhabitants of Mount
Athos occurred in 1307, when the Grand Company of
Catalans, mercenaries who had been hired by Andro-
nikos II Palaiologos to defend the Byzantine Empire
against the Turks, turned to devastation against their host
and pillaged the monasteries on Athos, despoiling their
treasures and slaughtering many of the monks.

Up to that point, the monastic organization of Mount
Athos had been cenobitic, with all of the monks living in
a communal environment. After the Catalans departed, for

the first time arose the alternative idiorrhythmic style of monasticism. Based on the Christian ideal of brotherly love, the cenobitic example of monastic living, as developed by Saints Pachomius and Basil in the fourth century, stressed the desirability of living together in a rule of poverty, chastity, and obedience, with all meals, worship, and living space in common. The idiorrhythmic principle, on the other hand, allowed the possession of personal property, the solitary taking of food, and worship in private if desired. It also allowed for a much more rigorous eremetic existence, and thus appealed to those monks who wished to become more fervent practitioners of the monastic ideal.

Of the twenty Ruling Monasteries on Athos, nine eventually adopted the idiorrhythmic way of life. It was forbidden for any more monasteries to choose the idiorrhythmic organization, although the formerly idiorrhythmic monasteries were allowed to opt for the cenobitic style.

In monastic governance, the idiorrhythmic monasteries are governed by a committee of three elected representatives and a permanent council of elders, while the cenobitic houses are governed by an abbot, who is elected for life and may assume almost dictatorial power.

The Hesychast regimen, based on a movement introduced to Athos by Gregory of Sinai in the early fourteenth century, was adopted by some of the Athonite monks. Basically, the Hesychasts believed in perpetual prayer and self-illumination from within, and joy through meditation. This mystical approach to spiritual communion with God later became associated with social and political movements that led to a civil war within the Byzantine state. This issue was not resolved until John VI Cantacuzenus presided over a council which upheld the Hesychasts.

Of the twenty Ruling Monasteries on Athos, one is Serbian (Chilandar), one is Russian (Pantaleimon), one is Bulgarian (Zographou), and the remainder are Greek. They are each represented by one member at the Holy Synod at Karyes, the parliament of Athos. For those desiring it, however, there are other options besides the Ruling Monasteries. There are a dozen or so *sketes*, both cenobitic and idiorrhythmic, where a more austere lifestyle and an interest in trade or handicraft obtains. Smaller than the *sketes* are the *kellia*, usually occupied by two to four monks, and usually following agricultural pursuits. Then there are the true hermits. They are in the tradition of the earliest eremitic inhabitants of Athos, leading an ascetic existence in caves and single huts, spending their days in prayer, self-mortification, and solitude.

During the almost half-millennium of Turkish occupation of the Balkans, the cultural legacy of the past survived almost entirely because of the influence of the Orthodox Church. Athos because of its independence was a great center of Byzantine and Hellenistic thought, and because of its isolated location was as well a refuge for those seeking to escape from Ottoman disfavor. Because the Ottomans were tolerant of other religions, and because the monks did not politically display their lack of sympathy for the Turkish authorities, they were largely left alone to pursue their intellectual and religious endeavors.

The monasteries on Mount Athos continued to exist through the twentieth century, although the number of monks was much smaller than during its flourishing in the Middle Ages. —*Gloria Fulton*

ADDITIONAL READING:

Amand de Mendieta, Emmanuel. *Mount Athos: The Garden of the Panaghia*. Berlin: Akademie Verlag, 1972. Basic work covering geographic setting, administration, monastic life, art, and liturgy.

Fine, John V. A. *The Late Medieval Balkans: A Critical Survey from the Late Twelfth Century to the Ottoman Conquest*. Ann Arbor: University of Michigan Press, 1987. Discusses the later development of Mount Athos in the context of general developments in the Balkans.

Hasluck, F. W. *Athos and Its Monasteries*. New York: E. P. Dutton, 1924. An older work that still retains its usefulness.

Hussey, J. M. *The Orthodox Church in the Byzantine Empire*. Oxford: Clarendon Press, 1986. An exhaustive work on the history, principles, and organization of the Eastern Orthodox religion as it developed under the Byzantines.

Norwich, John Julian, and Reresby Sitwell. *Mount Athos*. New York: Harper & Row, 1966. An account of the monasteries and their history arising from visits to Mount Athos by Norwich and Sitwell.

Obolensky, Dimitri. *The Byzantine Commonwealth: Eastern Europe, 500-1453*. New York: Praeger, 1971. Chapter 10 discusses monasticism under the Byzantines, particularly as practiced by the Slavs at Athos and elsewhere.

SEE ALSO: 726-843, Iconoclastic Controversy; 850, Building of the Slavic Alphabet; 976-1025, Reign of Basil II.

976-1025
REIGN OF BASIL II

The reign of Basil II marks the apex of Byzantine power and produces remarkable achievements in the military, religious, and economic realms, despite controversies over Basil's successor.

DATE: 976-1025
LOCALE: The Byzantine Empire
CATEGORY: Government and politics
KEY FIGURES:

Bardas Phocas (died 989), nephew of Nicephorus II Phocas, member of a powerful aristocratic house and general who claimed the imperial office in 987

Bardas Scleros, powerful general who challenged Basil's succession in 976 and again in 987

Basil II (958-1025), Byzantine emperor, 976-1025

Basil the Eunuch (died 985), great-uncle of the Byzantine emperors Basil II and Constantine VIII

John I Tzimisces (925-976), Byzantine emperor, 969-976

John XVI (Giovanni Filagato; died c. 1013), antipope, 997-998, bishop of Calabria and Basil's candidate as Roman pontiff

Nicephorus II Phocas (912-969), Byzantine emperor, 963-969

Samuel of Bulgaria (died 1014), czar of Bulgaria, 987-1014

Theophano (died after 976), empress and wife of Romanus II, Nicephorus II Phocas, and John I Tzimisces; mother of Basil II and Constantine VIII

Vladimir I (c. 956-1015), grand prince of Kiev, 980-1015

SUMMARY OF EVENT. In spite of its bloody beginnings, the Macedonian dynasty of the Byzantine Empire, founded by the illiterate Armenian peasant Basil I who, as imperial chamberlain and then co-emperor, assassinated his rival to the throne, attained its zenith of power during the reign of Basil's great-great grandson Basil II, son of Emperor Romanus II and the beautiful Theophano, who may have murdered a series of emperor-husbands. Although crowned in 960 as a child, Basil II ascended to the throne in Constantinople in 976 after fifty years of court dissension and intrigue. Always able to control his brother and joint emperor, Constantine VIII, Basil moved to control the empire by himself only in 985, when he drove his able adviser-minister and great-uncle, Basil the Eunuch, into exile. In the same year, according to the chief contemporary source, Michael Psellus, Basil reached another turning point in his life. Whereas in his early years Basil had been given to the banquet table and pleasures of the flesh, he now became secretive, ascetic, and effectively autocratic. His sole concern was to forge a strong state, defending it from enemies within and without. By this time, his military skills had been sharpened in frustrated campaigns against Czar Samuel of Bulgaria in the Balkans, and his administrative and diplomatic aptitude had developed in the absence of Basil the Eunuch. In cultural and intellectual pursuits, however, the emperor showed little interest, and during his administration government patronage of learning and the arts declined.

His rule continued to be plagued with unrest until 989 through such contenders as the general Bardas Scleros, who was raised to the imperial purple by his troops in 976, and the pretender Bardas Phocas, who in 987 tried to usurp the throne with the support of army officers and the landed aristocracy of Asia Minor. Basil put down these rebellions in 987 by the expedient of inviting Prince Vladimir of Kiev and his Varangian troops to his aid, in return for which Vladimir was promised the hand of Basil's sister, the Byzantine princess Anna. Vladimir ensured the fulfillment of this promise by seizing the Byzantine colony of Cherson in the Crimea. After the marriage, and following his own research into the Byzantine ritual, Vladimir accepted the Orthodox rite of Christianity for himself and the Russian state in 988.

In 996, Basil attacked the powerful landed aristocracy by demanding that they restore property to those whom they had dispossessed. Although this action was motivated partly out of revenge against the Bardas family and their supporters, there were legitimate economic considerations involved. These programs revived the intentions of Basil's predecessor and great-grandfather, Romanus Lecapenus, insofar as agrarian reforms were promoted and the tax base was broadened. No longer was the aristocracy able to ignore imperial assessments or transfer property to monastic establishments, for Basil threw the weight of taxation on all the propertied classes including the Church.

As commander in chief, Basil II had no equal among the Byzantine emperors before or after him. Not always a victor in battles, he was inevitably successful in wars, following a policy of careful consolidation of his victories along each step of his military campaigns. The Caucasian provinces were in a state of constant unrest as a result of the independent spirit of the Georgian and Armenian aristocracy, but a show of strength by Basil in 998 ensured imperial control. The expansionist policy in Syria of an Egyptian Fatimid caliph was countered by successful campaigns in 994 and 999 by the emperor himself.

Basil's greatest military triumph was against the Bulgars of Czar Samuel. The Bulgarian war occupied Basil's attention intermittently for thirty years. John I Tzimisces, Basil's usurping predecessor, had fragmented Bulgarian power in the Balkans, but it became a threat again under Czar Samuel, who in 985 ravaged Thrace to the Corinthian Isthmus and overran the strategic territory around Thessalonica. Basil himself narrowly escaped with his life after a sound defeat at the hands of the Bulgars in the summer of 986. The revolts of Phocas and Bardas between 986 and 996 interrupted the emperor's Bulgarian campaign, and Samuel was able to make himself the arbiter of the Balkans, killing or capturing with impunity the Byzantine administrative officials who attempted to drive him from Thessalonica. In 996, however, the imperial general Nicephorus Uranus crushed Samuel's army at Spercheus River, and the Bulgarian czar directed his attention to the more accessible goals of Dalmatia, Bosnia, and Dioclea, petty kingdoms federated to Constantinople. So successful was Samuel's campaign in the western Balkans that he was able to arrange, about 1000, the marriage of his son and successor, Gabriel Radomir, to a daughter of Stephen of Hungary.

Basil pursued a relentless policy of encirclement, negotiating a treaty with the Venetians to cut off Bulgarian access to the Adriatic, and deploying his own forces in a pincer movement along the lower and middle Danube and into the central Balkans. Although Basil surprised the army of Samuel in the spring of 1003 near Skoplje, and nearly captured him, Bulgarian resistance dragged on until 1019 as a result of the tenacious spirit of the Bulgarians and the impregnable nature of their strongholds. The turning point was Basil's summer campaign of 1014 aimed at the Bulgarian capital of Ochrid, when the emperor captured a Bulgarian force of fourteen thousand men. The eyes of ninety-nine out of every hundred were put out; the hundredth man was left with only one eye so he could lead his fellows back to their hapless czar. Samuel was so struck by this tragic sight that he suffered a seizure and died on October 6, 1014. Basil, the "Bulgar-slayer," could as a result hold the Balkan Peninsula securely in the empire.

Basil's skill as a diplomat presents a record more mixed in its success. While he himself never married and seemingly had little liking for women, he used marriage freely to cement relationships with his allies. In addition to the alliance with the Kievan dynasty of Vladimir, another royal princess was promised in marriage to the Venetian John Urseolo in order to seal an alliance with that naval power against the Bulgarians in 998. The Crown Princess Zoe, eldest daughter of Constantine VIII, was given in marriage to the young Otto III, who died in 1002 before consummation was effected. In the latter case, there was a precedence for such a foreign marriage, since the mother of Otto III was a Byzantine princess.

In regard to the Church, Basil maintained a truly autocratic policy. He personally appointed three successive patriarchs in Constantinople and controlled the appointments at Antioch and Jerusalem. Probably unappreciative of the complexity of Western papal-imperial politics, he tried to promote a Calabrian bishop, John Philagathus, as a rival for the German papal candidate, Gregory V. The ambitious plan failed in 998 when Philagathus was cap-

tured, mutilated, and imprisoned by Ottonian supporters. It is noteworthy, however, that at his death in December, 1025, Basil was preparing an offensive against the Normans in southern Italy, the objective being to resurrect Byzantine power in the West.

—*Richard J. Wurtz, updated by Gloria Fulton*

ADDITIONAL READING:

Browning, Robert. *The Byzantine Empire*. Rev. ed. Washington, D.C.: Catholic University of America Press, 1992. A survey of the history of the Byzantine Empire. Chapter 3 discusses the golden age of Byzantium, which covers the reign of Basil II.

Fine, John V. A. *The Early Medieval Balkans: A Critical Survey from the Sixth to the Late Twelfth Century*. Ann Arbor: University of Michigan Press, 1983. A detailed historical survey of the entire Balkans, with good discussion of original sources and areas of scholarly dispute.

Jenkins, Romilly. *Byzantium: The Imperial Centuries, A.D. 610-1071*. London: Weidenfeld & Nicolson, 1966. A scholarly study of the apex of Byzantine power.

Kazhdan, A. P., and Ann Wharton Epstein. *Change in Byzantine Culture in the Eleventh and Twelfth Centuries*. Berkeley: University of California Press, 1985. A scholarly treatment of the cultural, social, and economic background to the reign of Basil II and his successors.

Norwich, John Julius. *Byzantium: The Apogee*. New York: Alfred A. Knopf, 1992. A very readable account of the fortunes of the Byzantine Empire, including considerable detail on the relationship with Bulgaria.

Runciman, Steven. *A History of the First Bulgarian Empire*. London: Bell, 1930. The classic history of the First Bulgarian Empire, focusing on religious and political developments from the earliest times to the end of the reign of Samuel.

SEE ALSO: 963, Foundation of Mount Athos Monasteries; 1014, Basil II Conquers the Bulgars.

987

HUGH CAPET IS ELECTED TO THE THRONE OF FRANCE

Hugh Capet is elected to the throne of France, founding a dynasty that will rule France continuously until 1328.

DATE: 987

LOCALE: France

CATEGORY: Government and politics

KEY FIGURES:

Adalbero of Rheims (fl. 960), archbishop of Rheims, supporter of Hugh Capet

Charles of Lorraine (953-991), duke of Lorraine, hereditary heir to the throne of the Franks and uncle of Louis V

Gerbert d'Aurillac (c. 940-1003) secretary to Adalbero, later became Pope Sylvester II in 990

Hugh Capet (941-996), duke of the Franks, 956-996, king of the Franks, 987-996

Lothair (941-986), Carolingian king of the Franks, 954-986

Louis V (c. 966-987), last Carolingian king of the Franks

Robert II, the Pious (c. 973-1031), son of Hugh Capet, king of the Franks, 996-1031

SUMMARY OF EVENT. Little is known about Hugh Capet. Although he was described by contemporary sources as a man of "nobility and vigor," neither his character nor his appearance emerge from the scanty source material dating from his reign. Nevertheless, he founded a dynasty which ruled without interruption for almost three hundred years and under whose rule emerged the beginnings of the nation of France.

The situation in the region known as Western Francia was not propitious in 987 for the beginning of the reign of Hugh Capet and his Capetian successors. During the ninth and tenth centuries, the descendants of Charlemagne who ruled the territory steadily lost power to the landed nobility, especially those entrenched in large feudal principalities such as the duchies of Normandy, Burgundy, and Aquitaine, and the counties of Champagne and Anjou. Clashes between the monarchs and these powerful barons were frequent, and at virtually every point the great nobles proved their determination to hamstring the authority of their king. Indeed, even before Hugh's election, the nobles had already deposed of two Carolingian monarchs and had elected three of Hugh's relatives as kings. The first, after the dethronement of Charles the Fat in 888, was Hugh's great-grandfather Odo; later, with the deposition of Charles the Simple in 922, Hugh's grandfather Robert and then Hugh's granduncle Raoul had been chosen as kings. In each case, however, the kingship had been returned to the Carolingians, but precedents for an elective monarchy had been set.

The powers of the king declined dramatically during the tenth century, as the ongoing deposition and election of monarchs by the nobles reveal. Further, the lands under royal authority continued to shrink until the royal principality included little else than the lands immediately surrounding Paris.

In 954, Lothair became king on the death of Louis IV. Because Lothair was only twelve, his uncles protected his rights. In so doing, they called upon Hugh Capet for succor and support of the young king, which Hugh Capet granted. Upon Lothair's death, his son Louis V was elected king; however he only survived his father by one year. Louis V's nearest blood relative was his uncle, Charles, the duke of Lorraine.

It has been suggested that Charles's claim was overlooked on the basis of his marriage to a woman of lower birth; others suggest that Charles's shifting allegiances cost him the throne. It is also possible that Hugh Capet's relationship through his mother to Otto II contributed to his appeal to the assembled nobles and church officials responsible for electing a king. In any event, at an assembly at Senlis in 987, Hugh Capet was considered to be the more attractive candidate, and he was elected king in spite of Charles's claim. Though Charles and his few supporters tried to appeal to the concept of legitimate succession by birth, his claims were countered and frustrated by the intrigues of two of Hugh's most active supporters: Adalbero, the archbishop of Rheims, and his secretary Gerbert d'Aurillac, one of the most respected scholars of the tenth century and later Pope Sylvester II.

According to the sources, Adalbero of Rheims flatly denied any principle of hereditary right, affirming instead that the crown was conferred only through election by the nobles of the kingdom. Ironically, Hugh himself quickly reestablished hereditary rights by installing his own son as heir shortly after his own ascension.

In 987, Hugh himself was far from being more powerful than the nobles. His county of Paris, the only realm he could call his own, was small, poor, and badly organized compared to great feudal lands such as Normandy and Champagne. Indeed, he could scarcely control the lesser nobles who were his vassals within the county of Paris, let alone the powerful dukes and counts throughout the realm. Hugh at his accession was perhaps the weakest of the great lords of France, and it had been made clear at the outset that he held his throne only at the sufferance of the nobility and the church.

The election of Hugh Capet was an event of prime importance in the history of France, in spite of the fact that the decentralization of political power and the decline in royal authority continued on for another century. In the first place, he successfully defended his throne against the intrigues and armed revolts launched against him by Charles of Lorraine, thereby preserving the throne for his Capetian descendants. He apparently also continually insisted upon recognition of the theoretical supremacy of the crown over the claims of nobles and upon the unique nature of the royal dignity. Furthermore, it would appear that he began the policy of gradual accumulation of power through the legal exercise of rights as feudal suzerain, directing his efforts primarily at trying to subdue the

nobles within his own territory. There is also evidence to suggest that Hugh resorted to diplomacy more frequently than to war to establish his claims. Some historians claim that this is because he knew he was likely to fail on the battlefield. Finally, in seeing to the preservation of his royal line, he encouraged the reestablishment of the principle of hereditary succession. With the election and consecration of his son Robert II as his successor in 987, Hugh Capet assured that the kingdom would pass on to his direct descendant. The facts that the Capetian kings enjoyed remarkably long reigns, the average being thirty years, and were generally able to pass the crown to mature males were, of course, caused more by chance than astuteness. The device of crowning the heir apparent during his father's lifetime was not abandoned until the reign of Philip II (1180-1223), and the practice of insistence upon royal prerogatives and gradual extension of monarchical authority through the exercise of feudal law was carried on by Hugh's successors. Hugh's greatest accomplishment was, quite simply, the founding of a dynasty. It was for his heirs to establish the centralized monarchical authority of the later Middle Ages.
—James H. Forse,
updated by Diane Andrews Henningfeld

ADDITIONAL READING:

Duby, Georges. *France in the Middle Ages, 987-1460: From Hugh Capet to Joan of Arc.* Translated by Juliet Vale. Oxford: Blackwell Publishers, 1991. A noted French historian traces the development of the French state during the Middle Ages, paying particular attention to the intellectual climate of the time.

Dunabin, Jean. *France in the Making, 843-1180.* Oxford: Oxford University Press, 1985. This book covers the end of the Carolingian Empire through the rise of the Capetian dynasty and the formation of the French state and includes a comprehensive bibliography.

Fawtier, Robert. *The Capetian Kings of France: Monarchy and Nation, 987-1328.* Translated by Lionel Butler and R. J. Adams. New York: St. Martin's Press, 1960. Long considered the standard text of the roles played by the Capetian kings in the creation of a French dynastic state, this book stresses Capetian continuity.

Hallam, Elizabeth M. *Capetian France, 987-1328.* New York: Longman, 1980. Hallam offers a useful and well-organized book containing narrations of political events as well as clear analyses of social and economic conditions.

James, Edward. *The Origins of France: From Clovis to the Capetians, 500-1000.* New York: St. Martin's Press, 1982. A thorough study of the Carolingian background of Capetian France with an extensive bibliography, James's

work offers a counterpoint to Duby's interpretation of the same period.

SEE ALSO: 754, Coronation of Pepin; 781, Alcuin Becomes Adviser to Charlemagne; 843, Treaty of Verdun; 1025, Scholars at Chartres Revive Interest in Classical Learning.

988
VLADIMIR, PRINCE OF KIEV, IS BAPTIZED

Vladimir, Prince of Kiev, is baptized, linking the cultural, economic, and political fortunes of the Rus' with the Byzantine world by his conversion to Orthodox Christianity.

DATE: 988

LOCALE: Kiev (later, the capital of Ukraine)

CATEGORIES: Government and politics; Religion

KEY FIGURES:

Anna, sister of Basil II and wife to Vladimir of Kiev
Basil II (958-1025), Byzantine emperor in Constantinople, 976-1025
Igor (c. 877-945), grand prince of Kievan Rus', 912-945
Olga (c. 899-969), grand princess of Kievan Rus' and regent, 945-964
Svyatoslav I (died 972), grand prince of Kievan Rus', 945-972
Vladimir I (c. 956-1015), grand prince of Kievan Rus', 980-1015

SUMMARY OF EVENT. In 1988, the Russian Orthodox Church celebrated the millennial anniversary of its founding. Early sources reveal that Vladimir, grand prince of Kievan Rus', was baptized an Eastern Christian in 988 and then compelled his subjects to be baptized in the Dnieper River. Christianity certainly penetrated Russian society much earlier. Russian churchmen insist that Saint Andrew visited Russia in the first century, an event used by chroniclers to show the apostolic origins of Russian Orthodoxy. In reality, he probably never got farther than the Crimea. The Christian Church of Saint Elias existed in Kiev during the rule of Igor, and members of his military retinue were Christians when the Rus' signed a treaty with Constantinople in 945. Igor's widow, Grand Princess Olga, grandmother to Vladimir, was even baptized a Christian in the Byzantine capital ten years later, although the pagan faith remained the religion of her Kievan state. A number of merchants in Kiev were known to be Christians as well, but Christianity gained official status only with Vladimir.

Born in Kiev sometime after 950, Vladimir Svyatoslavich was the son of Malusha (Malfried), a former

EXPANSION OF KIEVAN RUS', 900-1000

Initial Holdings in 912

Additions in 972

housekeeper of his grandmother, Grand Princess Olga, and Svyatoslav I, grand prince of Kievan Rus'. When the latter died in 972, civil wars erupted among the sons over the succession to the grand princely throne: Yaropolk, Oleg, and Vladimir. With Viking armies, Vladimir emerged, and as grand prince he forged a new union of Novgorod and Kiev. To maintain this empire required a common religious bond.

Early in his reign, Vladimir considered the adoption of a new pagan cult to unify the realm, binding ruled and ruler. He had already created a pagan pantheon of gods, using regional cults in conjunction with the state cult of Perun, the god of thunder and lightning. He came to realize that the pagan cult could have limited use in foreign affairs and that a modern religion would best facilitate territorial expansion. The Rus' were surrounded by adherents of the new religions: the Khazars adopted Judaism in the ninth century; the Volga Bulgars chose Islam in the early tenth century, and Latin Christianity was spreading among the Poles, Hungarians, and other Eastern Europeans.

Chroniclers relate the famous story of emissaries sent to investigate the various religions and the discussions which the grand prince had with each of them. There is undoubtedly some truth to the prince's aversion to the fasting from drink and to the practice of circumcision among the Jews and Muslims, as well as to his particular attraction for the beauty of the Byzantine liturgy over that

of the Roman and his dislike of Islamic mosques. Yet it seems that the decisive issue involved the establishment of close political and economic ties of Kiev with Constantinople, as well as strong apprehension concerning submission to the central authority of Rome.

There was yet another factor. In January of 988, Vladimir sent a bodyguard of six thousand Varangian warriors to aid Emperor Basil II to quell a rebellion in his empire. This force was the origin of the famed Varangian Guard in Constantinople. When Basil hesitated on his promise to send his sister to Vladimir in marriage, however, an angry grand prince attacked the Byzantine port of Chersonesus (Kherson) in the Crimea. The emperor relented and sent his sister, Anna, to marry Vladimir in Chersonesus on the condition that he become a Christian. The local bishop and the priestly retinue of Anna were responsible for Vladimir's formal conversion to the Christian religion that year in Chersonesus. Upon returning to his capital city, Vladimir ordered the statue of Perun to be dragged through the main avenue of Kiev and tossed over the falls in the Dnieper River. The populace was ordered to the river for their own baptism, and a similar command was sent to all the towns of the Kievan realm.

The decision of Vladimir for the Orthodox faith meant the adoption of an entire culture, replete with the artistic tradition of icon painting, Byzantine style architecture, monasticism, religious education, legal principles and other patterns of thought. It is worth noting that one feature was absent from the legacy of Byzantium— namely, the interest in theological speculation. Several modern authorities argue that Vladimir and the Kievan Rus' were so entranced by the beauty of Orthodoxy that tampering with doctrinal formulations was thought to be tampering with perfection. Another modern analysis holds that the Russians were not really converted to Christianity so much as they overlaid a shallow veneer of Christianity upon a pagan base.

How much Vladimir himself was changed by the religious conversion is disputed. Chroniclers make frequent mention of his weekly feasts, wherein he invited his retinue and others to dine at court, while servants would distribute food to the poor in the streets. Notice is also made of his newfound aversion to capital punishment and the cessation of his harem. He continued to exercise little restraint in warfare, allowing his soldiers to pillage at will, although it was the usual custom of the time.

Some Western elements are found in Vladimir's religious policies, such as his introduction of the tithe to support his plans for a cathedral. Vladimir gave the Church a broad charter of immunity from the civil law and allowed the Church's own jurisdiction to include not only moral and liturgical matters but also family disputes and inheritances. Such issues corresponded more to Western than Greek practices.

Russian churchmen adopted two central features of the Byzantine traditions: the sacramental and mystical element of Christianity, that was best expressed in the veneration of icons; and the Platonic ideal which stressed the Spirit as reality. This last was illustrated by the strength of monasticism in Russia. In both traditions, the liturgy assumed major importance with its icon screens, chants, and a general air of the unworldly. Like the Byzantine Caesar, Vladimir also assumed the role as a church leader in Kievan Russia.

Byzantine traditions sometimes blended with the Russian pagan traditions, which included the Cult of Mother Earth: the Paraskeva, when the crops, rivers, and forests were venerated, where one is lost in nature. These traditions included the Rusolki, or stories of female spirits, and the inclination to ancestor worship evident in the continued use of the patronymic. There was the residue also of other pagan customs such as beating with palms, decorating Easter eggs, and the cult of Grandfather Frost. Such a blend of Christian and pagan practices was the case in the early Roman Church as well.

Russians refute the accusation sometimes made in the West that they were not Christianized before Vladimir's time because they were too savage, barbaric, and illiterate. Yet evidence shows the existence of a written language in Smolensk from a much earlier period. Scholars have also made note of a complicated trade agreement between the Rus' and Byzantines in 907, which must have involved sophisticated language. Pre-Christian artistic traditions lasted even into the age of Andrei Rublev in the early fifteenth century. The voluminous secular graffiti and business discussions on the walls of the Saint Sophia in Kiev and in Novgorod in the early eleventh century indicate that the society was not unsophisticated in this genre. In short, Vladimir's decision to become a Christian did not begin Russian civilization.   —*John D. Windhausen*

ADDITIONAL READING:

Cross, Samuel Hazard, and Olgerd P. Sherbowitz-Wetzor, eds. and trans. *The Russian Primary Chronicle*. Cambridge, Mass.: The Medieval Academy of America, 1953. Contains the Laurentian Chronicle, the principal annals of Vladimir's era.

Fedotov, George P. *The Russian Religious Mind: Kievan Christianity*. Cambridge, Mass.: Harvard University Press, 1946. A classic exploration of the historical roots of Russian Orthodoxy and its relations with the state by a writer who combines scholarship with beautiful prose.

Fennell, John. *A History of the Russian Church to 1448*. New York: Longman, 1995. This last work by a respected medieval scholar stresses the extent of Christianity in Kievan Rus' as the context for Vladimir's conversion.

Grekov, B. A. "The Reign of Prince Vladimir Svyatoslavich." In *Kievan Rus*. Moscow: Foreign Languages Publishing House, 1959. The most noted work by a Soviet scholar on the Kievan era of Russian history. In it he argues that paganism yielded to Christianity because the former was a tribal religion whereas the latter was essentially class oriented.

Grunwald, Constantin De. "Saint Vladimir." In *Saints of Russia*. New York: Macmillan, 1960. A concise, intelligent account of his life, using many Nordic sources, that stresses Vladimir's Scandinavian ties. He argues that the conversion of the Kievan people took place in 990.

Lobachev, Valeri, and Vladimir Prevotorov. *A Millennium of Russian Christianity*. Moscow: Novosti Press, 1988. A concise view of the Soviet point of view on this question.

Vernadsky, George. *Kievan Russia*. New Haven, Conn.: Yale University Press, 1948. The standard account of Vladimir's conversion by a well-respected scholar whose discussion of the grand prince is still not challenged.

SEE ALSO: 850-900, Vikings Settle in Kiev; 976-1025, Reign of Basil II; 1240, Alexander Nevsky Defends Novgorod from Swedish Invaders; 1240, Mongols Take Kiev.

1009

THE CHURCH OF THE HOLY SEPULCHRE IS DESTROYED

The Church of the Holy Sepulchre is destroyed by the Fatimids, but is later rebuilt by Byzantine emperors and inspires the conquest of Jerusalem during the Crusades.

DATE: 1009

LOCALE: Jerusalem

CATEGORIES: Religion; Wars, uprisings, and civil unrest

KEY FIGURES:

Al-Ḥākim bi-Amrih Allāh (Abu ʿAli al-Mansūr al-Ḥākim; 985-1021), the sixth ruler of the Egyptian Shiite Fatimid dynasty, 996-1021

Constantine I (died 337), Roman emperor of the East, 306-377

SUMMARY OF EVENT. The Holy Sepulchre is the tomb in which the body of Jesus Christ was laid after his death. No mention of the place is found in history until the early 300's, but converts to Christianity very probably visited the Holy Sepulchre soon after the Resurrection, and taught their children to venerate it. Roman armies destroyed the city of Jerusalem in the year 70, and Christians who were in Jerusalem fled, but it was possible for them to go back again in the year 73. No doubt there were many who knew the location of the tomb. In 135, however, Emperor Hadrian built a sanctuary of Venus (Aphrodite) at the site where the sepulchre of Christ had stood. Alexander of Jerusalem (died 251) "visited the places for the investigation of the footsteps of Jesus and of His disciples," and by the beginning of the fourth century, the custom of visiting Jerusalem for the sake of information and devotion had become so frequent that Eusebius wrote that Christians "flocked together from all parts of the earth." By the early 400's, two hundred hostels and monasteries had been built to accommodate pilgrims in and around Jerusalem.

According to legend, Constantine sent his mother Helena to build a church on the spot. They looked for the cross of Christ but could not find it, so they decided to build on the place of the Passion and Resurrection. As they began to tear down the temple of Venus which had been built there, they found three crosses, a few nails, and Pilate's inscription. In 335, Constantine dedicated the new basilica, and it is on this site that the Church of the Holy Sepulchre now stands.

Within the basilica, the Holy Sepulchre was in the center of a rotunda sixty-five feet in diameter. It extended eastward from this to a distance of 250 feet. An atrium and vestibule gave a total length of 475 feet. Beyond this was a second open court where the rock of Calvary stood in the open air, rising some twelve feet above the ground. The tomb that had been the sepulchre of Christ was enclosed by a round domed building that became known as the *Anastasis* because it commemorated the place of the Resurrection.

After the church was built, many Christians began to visit the Holy City. Along with Jerome and Rufinus, ascetic women from Rome, such as Paula and Melania, traveled to Jerusalem and searched out as many biblical sites as possible. Melania settled on the Mount of Olives while Paula and Jerome, along with a group of women who traveled with them, went to Bethlehem. Both established monasteries for men and women, built with money the women had inherited.

The Constantinian buildings were destroyed by fire in 614 during the Persian invasion under Chosroes II; in 878, the Egyptian Ulunids annexed Palestine. In 935, a mosque was built on the site of the exterior atrium. This regime did not last long, however, because the Egyptians were conquered in 969 by Ubaydulla ("little slave of God" in Arabic) al-Mahdi, father of the Fatimid dynasty. This administration ruled all of the lands around the Mediterranean Sea, including Egypt.

Although the Fatimids were generally tolerant, it was a descendant of this dynasty, al-Hākim bi-Amrih Allāh (Arabic for "ruler by God's command"), the sixth ruler of the Egyptian Shiite Fatimid dynasty, who came to power in Jerusalem. From 1004 until 1014, he went on a fiery rampage against churches in Syria and Palestine, burning and looting some thirty thousand before he finished. He built mosques on the roofs of those churches he did not burn. He was known for his cruelty and persecution of Christians, Jews, and even Sunni Muslims. He went so far as to destroy all dogs because their barking annoyed him, and he banned various kinds of shellfish and vegetables. It is said that al-Hākim took offense at the Holy Fire ceremony performed in the church annually at Easter. During famines, however, he distributed food and tried to stabilize prices. He also founded mosques and patronized scholars and poets. In 1017, he began to encourage the teachings of some Ismaili missionaries who held that he was the incarnation of the divinity. Some authors note that the persecution only stopped when al-Hākim became convinced that he himself was divine. After this he changed completely and began to provide money for the rebuilding of churches and to allow those who had been forcibly converted to Islam to return to Christianity.

Al-Hākim is known for having initiated Druzism, which developed out of the Ismaili teachings, and which has thousands of devotees in southern Lebanon and the Syrian district of Hawran. This is a relatively small Middle Eastern religious sect with a very close-knit identity. They call themselves *muwahhidun* or monotheists. They permit no conversion, either away from or to their religion, and no intermarriage. Their religious system is kept secret from the outside world. Only an elite of initiates participate fully in their religious services and have access to the sacred teachings of the Druze religious doctrine. According to this doctrine, in times of persecution, a Druze is allowed to deny his faith outwardly if his life is in danger. Al-Hākim mysteriously vanished while taking a walk on the night of February 13, 1021, and it is believed by some Druze people that he will again return in triumph to inaugurate a golden age.

After the devastation in 1009, very little can have remained of Jesus' tomb. Al-Hākim's successors showed more tolerance. The Byzantine emperor Michael IV persuaded the Fatimid caliph in 1034 to allow the rebuilding of all the churches of the Holy Land. In 1048, Constantine IX Monomachus was able to reconstruct the cave in masonry, obliterating, however, the last trace of the natural state of the tomb.

In 1099, the crusaders found the basilica in ruins. They built a Romanesque church, which was consecrated on

July 15, 1149. A rotunda at the western end rose over the Holy Sepulchre. They established Jerusalem as their capital, and the city prospered during the 1100's. Again, extensive building was undertaken, but crusader occupation of Jerusalem meant persecution for local Muslims and Jews. The basilica built by the crusaders was partially destroyed by fire in 1808, when the rotunda fell in upon the Sepulchre. A new church was built at the expense of Greeks and Armenians and was dedicated in 1810.

The modern church consists of two main sections: the chapel of St. Helena with the cave of the Finding of the Holy Cross, and the church proper with its many adjacent chapels. The sections are divided up among the Latins, the Greeks, the Armenians, the Syrians, and the Copts, but there are sections that are common to all. There are arguments as to whether the present church is the actual site of the original tomb. According to the Gospel, it is outside the walls of the city, whereas the present church is inside. Yet the walls have been in different places in different historical eras; it seems there is no archaeological evidence to suggest that any other site might be more accurate.

—*Winifred Whelan*

ADDITIONAL READING:

Hawkins, Peter S. "Sacred Time Share: At the Church of the Holy Sepulchre." *The Christian Century* 113 (January 3, 1996): 4-5. The author describes how the Church of the Holy Sepulchre is again being restored under the joint direction of six churches.

Hitti, Philip K. *Makers of Arab History*. New York: St. Martin's Press, 1968. The chapter in part 1 of this book on ʿUbaydullah al-Mahdi describes the reign of the Fatimid dynasty under which the Church of the Holy Sepulchre was destroyed.

Idinopulos, Thomas A. *Jerusalem Blessed, Jerusalem Cursed: Jews, Christians, and Muslims in the Holy City from David's Time to Our Own*. Chicago: Ivan R. Dee, 1991. A history of the city of Jerusalem; the fifth chapter of this book, "God Wills It!" describes the particular era in which the Church of the Holy Sepulchre was destroyed by the Muslim rulers.

Kochav, Sarah. "The Search for a Protestant Holy Sepulchre: The Garden Tomb in Nineteenth Century Jerusalem." *Journal of Ecclesiastical History* 46 (April, 1995): 278-301. Protestants came too late to claim a stake in the Church of the Holy Sepulchre. In 1893, therefore, a committee of Englishmen bought an ancient tomb and called it the "Garden Tomb," the Protestant Holy Sepulchre.

Powell, James M. *Muslims Under Latin Rule, 1100-1300*. Princeton, N.J.: Princeton University Press, 1990. Shortly after the destruction of the Church of the Holy

Sepulchre, the crusaders entered Jerusalem and began to rebuild the city. The book dwells on Muslim minorities and how they fared under Christian rule.

SEE ALSO: 312, Conversion of Constantine; 1095, Pope Urban II Calls the First Crusade; 1120, Order of the Knights Templar Is Founded.

1010-1015
AVICENNA WRITES HIS CANON OF MEDICINE

Avicenna writes his Canon of Medicine, *a five-book medical encyclopedia that serves as the authoritative source in both the Islamic world and Europe for half a millennium.*

DATE: C. A.D. 1010-1015

LOCALE: Hamadan, Persia (west central Iran)

CATEGORIES: Cultural and intellectual history; Health and medicine

KEY FIGURES:

ʿAlaʾ al-Dawlah, ruler of Isfahan, 1008-1042, and the last prince served by Avicenna

Shams al-Dawlah (died 1022), Buyid prince of Hamadan whom Avicenna served as physician and vizier

Andrea Alpago (died 1522), scholar who produced a widely disseminated Latin translation of the *Canon of Medicine*

Avicenna (Abu ʿAli al-Husain ibn ʿAbdallah ibn Sina; 980-1037), author of the *Canon of Medicine* and one of the most influential Islamic philosopher-scientists

Gerald of Cremona (died 1187), scholar who first translated the *Canon of Medicine* into Latin, providing a standard translation until the sixteenth century

Nuh ibn Mansur (died 997), Samanid ruler at Bukhara who first brought Avicenna to court as a physician

SUMMARY OF EVENT. In 1015, at the age of thirty-five, Avicenna (ibn Sina) completed the first of five books that would make up his *Canon of Medicine*, a task undertaken because he believed that neither the Classical nor Islamic world had produced a book that could teach the practice of medicine as an integral whole. The end result of his efforts was a medical encyclopedia that would become the most influential single work in the history of medicine, remaining the authoritative text for both the Islamic and European worlds for five centuries.

Avicenna was one of the greatest philosophical and scientific minds produced by medieval Islam as well as a highly capable physician and political administrator. He was born in 980 near Bukhara, then the capital of the Persian Samanid dynasty, the son of a local governor who opened his house for learned men to meet and discuss theological and philosophical issues. Avicenna, who had a private tutor since early childhood, mastered the Koran and a substantial body of Arabic poetry by the age of ten and then was instructed in Aristotelian logic and metaphysics. He impressed his tutor, al-Natili, by his independent thought and then soon outgrew his teacher. In his early teens, while grappling with Aristotle's *Metaphysics*, Avicenna decided to turn to medicine, which he found easy to master by reading the numerous works of Galen translated into Arabic. He found Galen hard to reconcile with some of Aristotle's conclusions, and continued his intellectual struggles with *Metaphysics*.

At the age of sixteen, Avicenna began the practice of medicine, establishing a reputation for originating his own methods of treatment based on careful observation of symptoms and attention to detail. One year later, when the reigning Samanid prince (ibn Mansur) fell ill, Avicenna was invited to court, successfully treating him along with other doctors. He remained at court, receiving permission to use the vast royal library containing numerous Greek

A noted physician who served many Muslim princes, Avicenna worked to produce a comprehensive medical encyclopedia known as the Canon of Medicine. *(Library of Congress)*

works that Avicenna had never imagined to be in existence. His self-education grew by quantum leaps, along with his reputation as a skilled physician.

The fall of the Samanids to the Turkish-led Ghazavids forced Avicenna from court, sending him on a journey across central Persia to the courts of Buyid princes where he continued his role as a physician, before finally settling at the court of Shams al-Dawlah at Hamadan in central western Persia. Here he became court physician while also serving as the prince's vizier. Avicenna's nights were spent at Hamadan with a large retinue of students, composing and transcribing what would become the *Canon of Medicine*.

Also finalized was *The Book of Healing*, probably the largest philosophic and scientific treatise written by a single individual, an encyclopedic synthesis of Greco-Roman knowledge, both theoretical and practical, with Islamic beliefs.

Following the death of Shams al-Dawlah in 1022, Avicenna fled to Isfahan, where he was accepted as an esteemed member of the court of 'Ala' al-Dawlah and continued his prolific writing, turning in his later years toward mystical spiritualism. More than one hundred of Avicenna's major works and treatises would survive the ravages of time. He died in 1037, while accompanying his prince on a military campaign at Hamadan. About half a century later, with the first comprehensive Latin translation by Gerald of Cremona, Avicenna's *Canon of Medicine* would be born as a rapidly growing work of authority in Europe.

Avicenna's work comprised five books which, sharing an Aristotelian penchant for classification, were each subject to three subdivisions by Avicenna. Book 1 would rapidly be adopted on its own as a textbook on medical theory and as a standard setter for the major operating principles underlying the medical profession. Unlike Hippocrates, who viewed medicine as an art or craft, Avicenna showed it to be a science which used both philosophy and logical reasoning for practical ends. Book 1 was heavily based on Greek sources, particularly Aristotle and Galen. Avicenna pointed out the differences between the two (such as marked differences in defining the function of the heart and brain), and then proceeded to synthesize Galen, Aristotle, and Neo-Platonic thought. Basically, Avicenna took Aristotle's thought and updated it with Galen's superior anatomical knowledge and the practical observations of Islamic physicians such as himself. Hence, book 1 contained a lengthy general discussion of the anatomy of the body.

In book 1, Avicenna tried to clarify the causes for both health and sickness which he found, like his Greek predecessors, subject to the laws of nature, a proper balance of hot, wet, cold, and dry, and a balance of four primary humors (blood, phlegm, red bile, and black bile). For Avicenna, imbalances in urine and pulse were also important monitors of the state of health.

In book 2 on *meteria dedica*, Avicenna blended Aristotle and Galen, while opening medical methodology to Stoic logic. Here he expounded on rules for isolating causes of disease, treatments, and means of measuring recurrence.

Book 3 was an analysis of specific diseases which affected twenty-one separate organs or organ systems, along with descriptions about how to treat each, while book 4 analyzed diseases that affect whole systems. Central ideas put forth in book 4 were the concept of crisis in fevers and the effects of toxins and tumors. Also of significance was the recognition that disease could be spread not only by bad air, but by contaminated water and soil as well, the contagious nature of tuberculosis, and the system weakening effects of intestinal worms. Avicenna also stressed the importance of minor surgery to correct whole system maladies, thus considering surgery to be part of the practice of medicine, not separate from it. Similarly, pharmacology was considered an important part of the practice of medicine, not in a world of its own, and book 5 was devoted to this end.

In book 5 on pharmacology, 760 drugs and herbs were discussed, including directions on how to prepare and administer them. In this book, Avicenna made many original contributions to medicine, including discussion of the antiseptic qualities of alcohol, the curative effects of mineral waters, and even the significance of animal experimentation in testing new drugs, along with general rules for experimental use of drugs.

The first Latin translation of the *Canon of Medicine* was made by Gerald of Cremona at a time when universities were beginning to rise in Europe and Scholasticism was orienting students to the ancients. Book 1 of the *Canon*, with its heavy reliance on Greek sources, found its way into the universities at Padua and Salerno. By the late 1200's, using the *Canon* (although not the total encyclopedia) was a standard part of a university medical education. The *Canon* could even be found in both monastic and personal libraries. By the fourteenth century, major parts of the *Canon* were translated into a variety of vernacular languages. A major retranslation of the *Canon* was made by Andrea Alpago. More than sixty Latin editions would be printed in the sixteenth century, along with a tremendous amount of commentary to modernize the *Canon*.

The *Canon of Medicine* was weakest where Avicenna identified Aristotle and Galen to be weakest, namely

physiology. With the increasing use of dissection, and the scientific revolution of the second half of the seventeenth century, the *Canon*'s five-hundred-year authority would be undermined by the direct observation that Avicenna advocated. While Avicenna would be removed as a current influence in the Western world by 1700, he would remain as one of the most influential figures in the historical evolution of medicine.   —*Irwin Halfond*

ADDITIONAL READING:

Afnan, Soheil. *Avicenna: His Life and Works*. London: Allen & Unwin, 1958. A standard treatment of Avicenna for the general reader with a chapter devoted to his work in medicine and the natural sciences.

Goodman, Lenn E. *Avicenna*. London: Routledge, 1992. A thorough philosophical analysis of Avicenna's work viewed within the wider context of his times.

Huff, Toby E. *The Rise of Early Modern Science: Islam, China and the West*. Cambridge, England: Cambridge University Press, 1993. Provides a strong cross-cultural background for the rise of science and medicine in Avicenna's time.

Sirasi, Nancy G. *Avicenna in Renaissance Italy: The Canon and Medical Teaching in Italian Universities After 1500*. Princeton, N.J.: Princeton University Press, 1987. The best English analysis of Avicenna's work and its influence on Western medical education.

Wickens, G. M., ed. *Avicenna: Scientist and Philosopher*. London: Luzac, 1952. Contains relevant millennial symposium papers by leading experts on Avicenna.

SEE ALSO: 500-400 B.C., Greek Physicians Develop Scientific Practice of Medicine; 157-201, Galen Synthesizes Ancient Medical Knowledge; 1150, Moors Transmit Classical Philosophy and Medicine to Europe.

1014
BASIL II CONQUERS THE BULGARS

Basil II conquers the Bulgars, devastating the Bulgar troops and ending the First Bulgarian Empire with the death of Czar Samuel, thus ensuring the continued existence of the Byzantine state.

DATE: 1014

LOCALE: Kleidion, on the river Struma, near Salonika, Macedonia

CATEGORIES: Expansion and land acquisition; Wars, uprisings, and civil unrest

KEY FIGURES:

Basil II (958-1025), Byzantine emperor, 976-1025

Boris II (c. 930-c. 985), czar of Bulgaria, 969-971

John Vladislav (died 1018), ruler of Bulgaria, 1015-1018

John I Tzimiskes (925-976), Byzantine emperor, 969-976

Nicephorus II Phocas (912-969), Byzantine emperor, 963-969

Samuel of Bulgaria (died 1014), czar of Bulgaria, 987-1014

Svyatoslav I (died 972), prince of Kiev, 945-972

SUMMARY OF EVENT. Relations between the Bulgarians and the Byzantines, peaceful for forty years following the tumultuous reign of Symeon, again became problematic during the coregency of Nicephorus Phocas with his two stepsons, Basil and Constantine. In 965, when Bulgarian envoys appeared at his court demanding their accustomed tribute, Nicephorus claimed that no tribute was owed, had the envoys beaten and sent back to Bulgaria, and then attacked Bulgarian fortresses.

Deciding to destroy Bulgaria as a nation and incorporate it into the Byzantine Empire, Nicephorus then prompted the Russians, led by Prince Svyatoslav of Kiev, to attack and plunder the Bulgarians, which they did. Svyatoslav, however, decided that he would then use his access through Bulgaria to launch an attack on the Byzantine Empire itself. He proceeded to occupy some of Bulgaria's Danubian territory in 967, including the important trading city Perejaslavec, as his base of operations.

Peter, the ailing Bulgarian czar, abdicated in favor of his son Boris, and entered a monastery. Boris II entered Preslav and was proclaimed czar.

By this time, the Byzantines were concerned about the Russian presence on the lower Danube. Nicephorus signed an alliance with the Bulgarians against the Russians, the boy emperor Basil II was engaged to marry the daughter of the new Bulgarian czar, while his younger brother Constantine (VIII) was to wed Boris' other daughter in order to ensure harmonious relations between the two dynasties. Boris, in his turn, needed Byzantine aid to recover his lost territory.

The Bulgarians and Byzantines then enlisted the Pechenegs, a nomadic central Asian people, to help drive out the Russians. Svyatoslav defeated this coalition, captured the capital Preslav and the Bulgarian royal family, although Boris was given nominal authority as vassal under Russian hegemony, and considered moving his capital from Kiev to Perejaslavec. The city was then recaptured, but lost again before the Bulgarians finally conceded its loss.

In Constantinople in December of 969, Nicephorus Phocas was murdered by Empress Theophano's lover, the general John Tzimiskes, who then became regent and co-emperor with Basil and Constantine. He immediately exiled the dowager empress Theophano and opened negotiations with Svyatoslav. Svyatoslav, however, by this time had imperial ambitions himself.

This led Svyatoslav's Russia, together with its vassal ally Bulgaria, into a direct clash with Byzantium in 972. Although the fortunes of war favored first the Russians, then the Byzantines, finally, at Silistria, the Russians were defeated and a truce was declared. Svyatoslav signed a treaty in which he withdrew from his Danubian stronghold, trading rights were restored to the Bulgarians, Svyatoslav agreed to abandon his claims on Bulgaria and Kherson, a strategic city on the Black Sea, and the emperor promised to send food supplies to Svyatoslav's army. On his way back to Kiev, however, Svyatoslav was ambushed by the Pechenegs and his skull made into a drinking cup.

This connection between the Bulgarians and the Russians, inimical as it was to the interests of both sides, may have exerted an influence on the later conversion of the Russians, in 988, under Svyatoslav's son Vladimir.

For Bulgaria, the consequences of the war were even more ruinous. Bulgarian lands were now considered imperial territory and converted to a military theme, the Bulgarian royal treasures were surrendered to Byzantium, and Boris II was captured in Preslav by John Tzimiskes and forced to abdicate, ending any treaty obligations between Bulgaria and Byzantium. The Bulgarian national church was brought under the control of Constantinople, the Bulgarian patriarchate was abolished, and the Byzantine Empire once more extended to the Danube. Tzimiskes also transferred many of the Bulgarian boyars to locations in Constantinople or Anatolia, a frequent Byzantine policy in disposing of potentially dangerous enemies.

In spite of the changes in eastern Bulgaria, Macedonia, in the west, remained virtually independent. It was to this territory that Boris and his brother Romanus returned, where in fact Boris died. Romanus, castrated by the Byzantines, was not eligible for the Bulgarian throne. Bulgaria followed the same tradition as the Byzantines in demanding that the ruler be physically perfect, which caused potential candidates for the throne to be blinded or otherwise mutilated by adversaries.

There was, however, a native family of Bulgarian magnates, sons of Count Nicholas Cometopuli, who held power in Macedonia. One of the sons of this family was Samuel, who took the title of czar in 997. This western Bulgarian state was centered in Ohrid, where Samuel established a new patriarchate. By this time, as a result of conquests over both members of his own family and Byzantium, Samuel was in control of all Macedonia, Bulgaria, Thessaly, Epirus, Durazzo, and most of present-day Albania. John Tzimiskes was occupied with establishing Byzantine control in other newly conquered provinces, and unable to turn his attention to the new developing Bulgarian state before his death in 976.

The new emperor, Basil II, had been unable to oppose Samuel's conquest because of internal problems within the Byzantine Empire. By 990, however, he had decided that he must take measures to stem Samuel's growing power.

In the 990's, Basil entered into relations with the state of Duklja, which comprised the former Serbian state, along with present-day Montenegro and Herzegovina, and was ruled by John Vladimir. This caused Samuel to move against Duklja and capture John Vladimir, thus gaining control over both Raška (Serbia) and Duklja, which de facto controlled land stretching from the Black Sea to the Adriatic, and from the Danube to the Aegean. Samuel also concluded an alliance with Stephen I, king of Hungary, although that was short-lived.

Basil II himself led a campaign to recover Byzantine territory lost to Samuel beginning around 1000. He recaptured Sardika (Sofija), then occupied the region around Preslav. He then sent troops into Macedonia and Thessaly, restoring Byzantine rule there. Finally he directed his efforts against the Danube area, recapturing Vidin after a protracted siege. Basil's and Samuel's forces clashed in 1004 at Skopje, with Emperor Basil the victor. Then, in 1005, Basil recaptured Durazzo to the west.

After another decade of fighting, Basil surrounded the Bulgarian forces near the river Struma, although Samuel himself escaped. At the battle of Kleidion, he took fourteen thousand of Samuel's men as prisoners. All the men captured were blinded except that one eye was left for every hundredth man, who was thus able to lead his blinded army back to Samuel. Samuel, at the sight of his returning troops in Prilep, died within days. For this atrocity, Basil II is remembered as the "Bulgar killer."

After Samuel's death, his empire gradually disintegrated as Basil continued his methodical reconquest of the Balkans. Samuel's nephew John Vladislav, after dispatching Samuel's son Gabriel Radomir, renewed the conflict with Basil, murdering John Vladimir, ruler of Duklja, before being killed himself in an attempt to retake the western port of Durazzo in 1018. In that year as well Ohrid, Samuel's former capital, surrendered to Basil, where he received homage from Samuel's widow. Thus ended the First Bulgarian Empire, now a Byzantine province instead of a powerful autonomous state.

The legacy of the Bulgarian state was cultural rather than political. As opposed to the native Slavic populations of the Byzantine territories, who had become almost totally Hellenized by this time, the Slavic populations of Bulgaria retained their language and culture. This made possible the resurgence of Bulgaria as a new political entity during the Second Bulgarian Empire of the twelfth to the fourteenth centuries. —*Gloria Fulton*

ADDITIONAL READING:

Browning, Robert. *Byzantium and Bulgaria: A Comparative Study Across the Early Medieval Frontier.* Berkeley: University of California Press, 1975. A study of relations between Bulgaria and Byzantium. Chapter 3 discusses relations in the ninth and tenth centuries.

Fine, John V. A. *The Early Medieval Balkans: A Critical Survey from the Sixth to the Late Twelfth Century.* Ann Arbor: University of Michigan Press, 1983. A detailed historical survey of the entire Balkans, with good discussion of original sources and areas of scholarly dispute.

Norwich, John Julius. *Byzantium: The Apogee.* New York: Alfred A. Knopf, 1992. A very readable account of the fortunes of the Byzantine Empire, including considerable detail on the relationship with Bulgaria.

Runciman, Steven. *A History of the First Bulgarian Empire.* London: Bell, 1930. The classic history of the First Bulgarian Empire, focusing on religious and political developments from the earliest times to 1014.

Sedlar, Jean W. *East Central Europe in the Middle Ages, 1000-1500.* Seattle: University of Washington Press, 1994. Organized in large comprehensive topics, includes much information on early Bulgaria along with other countries treated in this work.

Tzvetkov, Plamen S. *A History of the Balkans: A Regional Overview from a Bulgarian Perspective.* Lewiston, N.Y.: Edwin Mellen Press, 1993. Volume 1 of this two-volume work covers the medieval and Ottoman periods, focusing on unique attributes of the Bulgarian people and their history.

SEE ALSO: 864, Boris Converts to Christianity; 893, Beginning of Bulgaria's Golden Age; 976-1025, Reign of Basil II; 1876, Bulgarian Massacres.

1014
BATTLE OF CLONTARF

The Battle of Clontarf pits the Irish forces of Leinster and their Norse allies against the Munster forces of Brian Boru, resulting in Boru's victory on Good Friday.

DATE: April 23, 1014
LOCALE: Clontarf, Ireland
CATEGORIES: Expansion and land acquisition; Wars, uprisings, and civil unrest
KEY FIGURES:
Brian Boru mac Cennétig (941-1014), leader of the Dál Cais tribe
Brodar and *Ospak*, two prominent Viking leaders who had a fleet on the Isle of Man
Murchad, son of Brian

Sitric, Viking ruler of Dublin

Sigurd, Viking earl of the Orkneys

SUMMARY OF EVENT. Few battles in Irish history command the fame that has been attached to Brian Boru's victory at Clontarf on Good Friday (April 23), 1014. Since medieval times, the Battle of Clontarf has been presented as a struggle between Irish forces and Norse invaders for the control of Ireland. Correspondingly, the Irish victory has been seen as breaking the power of the Norse in Ireland and as a defining moment in Ireland's progress toward national unity under a single king. Moreover, the fact that Brian, a Christian king, was killed by a pagan Norseman on Good Friday, the day of Christ's death, made for suitable hagiographical comparisons. Most of these claims belong to legend rather than history, however, and originated in a propagandistic Irish work, entitled *Cocad Gáedel re Gallaib* (the war of the Irish with the foreigners), that was designed to glorify Brian.

For a more objective and reliable account of what happened, the primary source is the *Annals of Ulster*, a year-by-year chronicle of Irish events, whose entry on the battle may be almost contemporaneous. Not only does it detail the military movements in the preceding months, but it also lists the main contestants and fatalities in the battle. Curiously, the *Annals of Inisfallen*, the chronicle that originated in Munster (the province from which Brian hailed) and might have been expected to provide the fullest and most detailed account, is disappointing on both counts. Next in importance to the annals as a source is the *Cocad*. This work, composed around the year 1100 during the reign of Brian Boru's great-grandson, was designed to glorify Brian. It is cast in the form of a native saga with heroes and villains, contains much dramatic incident, and is written in a suitably hyperbolic style. Obviously, its propagandistic intent, coupled with its adherence to the conventions of a literary genre, make it suspect as a historical source. At best, it can be described as a "tale with a historical background."

Even more unreliable are the various versions of the Middle Irish saga *Cath Cluana Tarbh* (the battle of Clontarf), which, among other marvels, has supernatural figures visiting the protagonists before the battle. Yet, if nothing else, these tales bear witness to the extraordinary importance later assumed by the battle among the literate classes in Ireland. A final source is *Njál's Saga*, the most famous of the Icelandic prose sagas, which was probably composed in the thirteenth century. While attesting that the reverberations of the Battle of Clontarf were also felt in the Scandinavian world, this source provides a unique Norse perspective on events. Although its account of the battle is jejune, it does provide details about the Norse combatants that may well be genuine.

Brian Boru mac Cennétig belonged to the Dál Cais, a minor tribe occupying an area of southwest Ireland roughly equal to eastern County Clare of the twentieth century. This strategic location guaranteed the tribe's control of the estuary and waterway of the Shannon, Ireland's main river, which provided access to the Midlands. When Brian was growing up early in the second half of the tenth century, this tribe began to emerge as a major player on the local political scene. Taking advantage of a power vacuum in the southern province of Munster, the Dál Cais formed alliances with various Munster parties, including the Norse city of Waterford. On the death of his brother Mathgamain in 976, Brian became the leader and prime mover of Dál Cais expansion. By the end of the tenth century, Brian Boru was well on his way to establishing himself as the foremost king in Ireland. His extraordinary success was partly the result of natural ability and of divisions among his rivals that he was able to exploit.

At the turn of the eleventh century, Ireland was a political conglomerate of numerous petty kingdoms, known as *tuatha*, loosely bound together in five major provinces: Leinster in the east, Munster in the south, Connaught in the west, Ulster in the north, and Meath in north-central Ireland. Each of these provinces had its own over-king. In the thirty years after he became king of the Dál Cais, Brian progressively extended his influence, first over Munster, over the southern part of Ireland by 997, later over Meath, and eventually over Ulster by 1005. His relations with Leinster, however, were more problematic. In order to assert his authority over the southern part of Ireland, Brian needed to control Leinster, including the independent Norse city of Dublin. Following earlier forays into Leinster in 984 and 991, Brian defeated the Leinstermen at Glenn Máma in late 999. Early in 1000, he plundered Dublin and compelled its ruler Sitric to submit. (Brian was well aware of the commercial and military advantages found in controlling Viking cities such as Dublin.) A few years later, Brian intervened politically in Leinster affairs by deposing Domhnall mac Donnchada as king of Leinster, replacing him with Máel Mórda mac Murchada, who hailed from a north Leinster tribe.

Nevertheless, Leinster's longstanding resentment against outsider control erupted again in 1013, possibly as a result of an insult suffered by Máel Mórda at the hands of Brian's son Murchad. Máel Mórda not only withdrew his submission to Brian but also encouraged other subject tribes to do the same. In addition, Máel Mórda entered an alliance with the Norse residents of Dublin.

In the meantime, Brian was also gathering his forces. Along with his own army of Munstermen, Brian recruited forces from the southern Connaught kingdoms of the Uí

Although the victory at Clontarf was attributed to Brian Boru, his son Murchad (shown here capturing an enemy flag) was responsible for leading Brian's army. (Archive Photos)

Fiachrach Aidne and the Uí Maine. He advanced eastward through the border territory of Ossory at the same time that Murchad proceeded northward through Leinster from the south. The two armies converged on the north side of Dublin, which Brian then besieged all through the autumn of 1013. After failing to take the city, Brian withdrew his forces by Christmas and returned home to Munster.

Realizing that Brian and his forces would return, the Norse of Dublin made preparations. Sitric visited his Norse allies in western Scotland and the Isle of Man. He won over Earl Sigurd of the Orkneys and two prominent Viking leaders, Brodar and Ospak, who had a fleet on the Isle of Man. These allies agreed to be in Dublin with their ships by Palm Sunday of 1014. They may have deliberately chosen this date as a time when their Christian enemies would be preoccupied with the observance of Holy Week.

This time, Brian returned with an even larger army, although the advantage of superior numbers was wiped out when his ally, Máelsechlainn II of Meath, withdrew his forces on the eve of the battle. Arriving near Dublin, Brian ravaged the Norse suburbs of Fingal and Howth.

The Norse and their Leinster allies marched out of the city to meet Brian. The battle was joined on the plains of Clontarf on the north side of Dublin, where the river Tolka runs into Dublin Bay. By this time an elderly man, Brian remained in his tent and left the conduct of the battle to his son Murchad.

The battle was fought all day, but by evening the Leinster and Norse armies gave way and fled toward the sea. The victory was marred by the slaughter of Brian in his tent by Brodar during his retreat inland from the battle. Other prominent casualties included Murchad and kings of the subject Munster tribes, as well as a grandson and nephew of Brian; casualties on the other side included Máel Mórda, Sigurd, and Brodar, as well as most of the prominent Leinster leaders. The victorious Munster army, led by Brian's surviving son, Donnchad, returned home, but not without harassment from another Leinster tribe, the Osraige.

In no real sense could this battle be described as a decisive conflict between two national armies. Brian's army consisted essentially of men from his own tribe and province; with the exception of Leinster, the rest of Ireland remained unengaged. Likewise, his enemies could not be characterized as Norse invaders, since the majority of them were residents of Leinster. The role played by the Norsemen of Dublin was relatively minor, and the majority of these men were residents of Ireland, not invaders. As for the portrayal of Brian as the first real high-king of Ireland, it also falls short of being accurate. Brian certainly gave new definition and potential to this notion, but he never achieved a national monarchy and did not establish the institutions and administration normally associated with such an office.

How then does one explain the enormous significance that later time attached to the Battle of Clontarf? The memory of a protracted and bitterly fought battle, the death of a man who had already carved out for himself a special place in Irish history, and the propaganda produced a few decades later by Brian's own people in the *Cocad* all ensured a permanent place for the battle in Irish literary and pseudo-historical tradition.   —*Patrick P. O'Neill*

ADDITIONAL READING:

Byrne, Francis John. *Irish Kings and High-Kings*. New York: St. Martin's Press, 1973. Information on the Irish tribes and the rivalries leading up to the Battle of Clontarf can be found on pages 267-268.

Moody, T. W., and F. X. Martin, eds. *The Course of Irish History*. Rev. ed. Niwot, Colo.: Roberts Rinehart, 1994. A scholarly collection of articles that provides a useful introduction to Irish history. Contains illustrations and a chronological table.

Ó Corráin, Donncha. *Ireland Before the Normans*. Vol. 2 in *The Gill History of Ireland*. Dublin: Gill, 1972. Pages 120-131 provide insights into events surrounding the Battle of Clontarf.

Otway-Ruthven, A. J. *A History of Medieval Ireland*. 2d ed. New York: Barnes & Noble, 1993. This well-written overview of medieval Irish history is a good starting point for understanding events during the period before 1496.

SEE ALSO: 793, Northmen Raid Lindisfarne; 1016, Danish Invaders Led by Canute Conquer England; 1169-1172, Norman Troops Invade Ireland.

1016
DANISH INVADERS LED BY CANUTE CONQUER ENGLAND
Danish invaders led by Canute conquer England, launching the nineteen-year reign of Canute, a period

of benign leadership, relative peace, and strengthening bonds between England and the Christian Church in Rome.

DATE: 1016
LOCALE: England
CATEGORIES: Expansion and land acquisition; Wars, uprisings, and civil unrest
KEY FIGURES:
Canute (also Cnut; c. 994-1035), Danish Viking and king of England, 1016-1035
Edmund Ironside (c. 993-1016), son of Ethelred and Saxon king of England who ruled jointly with Canute for seven months
Emma of Normandy (died 1052), wife of Ethelred the Unready who married Canute in 1017 after Ethelred's death in 1016
Ethelred II ("the Unready"; c. 968-1016), Saxon king of England, 978-1016
Sweyn Forkbeard (c. 985-1014), father of Canute and first Danish king of England, 1013-1014
William the Conqueror (1027-1087), led Norman conquest of England and served as first Norman king of England, 1066-1087

SUMMARY OF EVENT. For more than two hundred years, starting about 789, Viking warriors from Denmark and Norway harassed the peoples of the British Isles. Indeed, a familiar prayer uttered by the hapless Britons petitioned God, "From the fury of the Norsemen, good Lord deliver us!" Adding to the slaughter, warrior earls and would-be kings among the resident Saxons battled for the right to rule Britain. A nineteen-year interlude of peace transformed the country when Canute, a Danish Viking who had been baptized a Christian, became the ruler of all of England in 1016.

Historians are not in full agreement about the meaning of the word *viking*. As a verb, the term had been used in the original written sources to mean piracy or a pirate raid; as a noun, it was used to mean a pirate or raider. Whatever the term's exact meaning, the Vikings were bold, bloodthirsty plunderers. Roaming the seas in their well-crafted long boats or dragon ships, they primarily attacked the British Isles. In 793, a Viking raid on the monastery of Lindisfarne, located off the Northumbrian coast, horrified the Christian world. The invaders slaughtered some of the monks, took others to sell as slaves, and looted the monastery of gold and jeweled religious objects. After this raid, Viking attacks increased in fury and frequency.

The east coast of England took the brunt of the raids as the Vikings sailed their dragon ships up the rivers to harass the inland villagers. The invaders frequently found allies among the resident peoples, particularly the Celts, who joined the Danes in battles against the Saxon rulers of England. In 838, a large Danish force landed in Cornwall, where many of the residents joined the Vikings to fight their enemy, Wessex.

For the next century and a half, the battles between the Vikings and the various peoples of the British Isles see-sawed across England. In the end, the Vikings occupied large sections of the country and established their head-quarters in London. Local British resistance continued, however, and the Vikings, now well organized under a sound Danish government at home, launched their forces for the final conquest of England.

Sweyn Forkbeard, king of Denmark, led a major thrust against England in 994. He was supported in the field by forces from Norway. The battles raged on for nearly twenty years. In 1013, Sweyn's army defeated the disorganized and weary Britons, led by Ethelred the Unready. In a curious twist of fate, Sweyn died on February 3, 1014, just as he had secured this total victory. Command of the Danish troops was turned over to Sweyn's younger son, Canute, who was unable to prevail against a counterattack launched by the Britons and fled to Denmark.

Born in Denmark around 994, Canute was the younger son of Sweyn Forkbeard. Little is known of his early years before he accompanied his father on a raid to England in 1013, when he was about nineteen years old. Canute's older brother, Harold, may also have accompanied Sweyn on the raid. In the wake of his success, Sweyn was accepted as king over the Danelaw, the Danish-held part of eastern England, where he collected the Danegeld, an enforced contribution of money, precious metals, and jewels taken from resident Britons to support the needs of the Viking occupation forces. After Sweyn's death in 1014, his followers considered Canute to be heir to their English territory. Believed to be a Viking as able as his father, Canute assembled a fleet and set sail for England in 1015. The ruling structure of England was in shambles, and treachery and distrust prevented effective resistance to the Vikings. After landing his forces, Canute carried the battle to Nottingham and York in the north before moving south to London. After a prolonged siege of London, which ultimately ended in a stalemate, Canute and Edmund Ironside signed a peace settlement in 1016 giving Edmund continued control of Wessex while granting Canute control over the lands north of the Thames River. After Edmund's death later that year, Canute became sole ruler of England.

As king, Canute ushered in a period of peace for his new kingdom, the first the people had enjoyed for several decades. The Saxon English and the Danes managed to live in harmony, although Canute had appointed many Danish officials to govern the land. Saxons and Danes intermarried, and many adopted new names befitting these unions.

Many years of paying the Danegeld had seriously depleted the nation's finances. Canute imposed widespread taxation to replenish the treasury. As a warrior, Canute recognized that England's defenses had to be rebuilt to withstand future attacks, and most of the tax revenue was used to improve the system of walls, bulwarks, and ditches.

Canute also sought to strengthen his standing with the English by marrying into the Saxon royal line. In 1017, he married Emma of Normandy, widow of Ethelred the Unready. This shrewd stroke of policy pleased the English and appeared to assure a sound line of succession to the English throne. Canute's marital arrangements, however, suffered some complications. Canute acknowledged two sons, Sweyn and Harold Harefoot, whom he had fathered by his Anglo-Danish mistress, Aelgifu of Northampton. Of the children Canute later had with Emma, young Hardecanute was in the line of succession to the English throne. Both Harold Harefoot and Hardecanute were to serve briefly as English monarchs after Canute's death.

Canute's governing policy for England lay along two lines. First, he sought to continue a national government that followed that of King Edgar, Anglo-Saxon ruler from 359 to 375, who was considered one of the best of the preceding English monarchs. Second, Canute sought to strengthen relations with the Catholic Church in Rome. Although he had been born a pagan, Canute had been baptized a Christian sometime before he accompanied his father on the 1013 raid against England. Canute gave generous donations to the Catholic Church and traveled to Rome in 1027 to attend the coronation of Emperor Conrad II, whose son Henry had married Canute's daughter Gunhild.

In addition to maintaining peace in England, Canute became king of Denmark in 1018 (after the death of his brother Harold) and king of Norway in 1028. As a result, he brought England into a Scandinavian empire that facilitated healthy commerce among the nations.

Canute ruled wisely and was held in high regard by his English subjects, many of whom believed he was all-powerful and could command anything, including the tides of the sea. According to one story, which may well be apocryphal, Canute had his throne placed at the seashore to demonstrate that he was, after all, only a man. In this story, Canute commanded the sea to fall back. The tide continued to rise, however, dampening both Canute's shoes and the flattery of his courtiers. Their sincere admiration could not be dampened, however, and Canute was extolled as the first Viking king to be ranked as a civilized Christian ruler.

Canute died at Shaftesbury, England, on November 12, 1035. His son Harold Harefoot ruled as regent for his half brother Hardecanute from 1035 to 1037 and then took the kingship for himself and ruled from 1037 to 1040. Canute's legitimate son Hardecanute ruled England from 1040 to 1042. Because Canute's sons lacked their father's strength and popularity, the English soon restored a Saxon heir to the throne. Hardecanute was succeeded by his Anglo-Saxon half brother Edward the Confessor, the son of Ethelred the Unready and Emma of Normandy, who ruled from 1042 to 1066. Edward was succeeded by Harold II, who ruled briefly in 1066. The entire Danish-Saxon dynasty collapsed with the Norman invasion of 1066, led by William the Conqueror.   —*Albert C. Jensen*

ADDITIONAL READING:

Adams, Phoebe-Lou. "From York to Jorvik: The Viking Past Lives on in England." *Atlantic Monthly* 275 (March, 1995): 46-50. Describes the role of the Vikings not only as plunderers but also as traders who converted the Saxon town of Eoforwic into an international port they named Jorvik (modern York).

Brønsted, Johannes. *The Vikings*. Translated by Kalle Skov. London: Penguin Books, 1965. A valuable source for the general reader. In addition to providing an introduction to Viking history, this work is illustrated with many photographs.

Christiansen, Eric. "Canute and His World." *History Today* 36 (November, 1986): 34-39. A well-rounded view of Canute that presents him as a good Christian monarch who married into the English nobility despite his previous reputation as a murderous Viking outlaw.

Jones, Gwyn. *A History of the Vikings*. New York: Oxford University Press, 1968. Written by a professional historian, this work provides a detailed, informative history of the Vikings.

Lawson, M. K. *Cnut: The Danes in England in the Early Eleventh Century*. White Plains, N.Y.: Longman, 1983. A solid survey of Canute's career, with valuable insight into his relations with the Holy Roman Empire and Anglo-Danish government.

May, Robin. *Canute and the Vikings*. New York: Bookwright Press, 1985. Brief but authoritative account of the Viking king of England written for a young high school audience.

SEE ALSO: 793, Northmen Raid Lindisfarne; 878, King Alfred Defeats the Danes at Edington; 1066, Battle of Hastings.

1025
SCHOLARS AT CHARTRES REVIVE INTEREST IN CLASSICAL LEARNING

Scholars at Chartres revive interest in classical learning, providing the foundation for the twelfth century Renaissance through the use of the seven liberal arts, a program of learning reflected in sculpture and stained glass windows at Chartres Cathedral.

DATE: c. 1025

LOCALE: The cathedral of Chartres, France

CATEGORIES: Cultural and intellectual history; Education; Religion

KEY FIGURES:

Fulbert of Chartres (960-1020), bishop of Chartres who led the effort to rebuild the cathedral at Chartres

Gerbert d'Aurillac (c. 955-1003), French scholar in charge of the cathedral school at Rheims, later archibishop of Rheims and finally elected pope as Sylvester II, 999-1003

SUMMARY OF EVENT. By the eleventh century, the cathedral at Chartres was already known as an important pilgrimage center. The Carolingian cathedral held the *Sancta Camisia*, the garment that allegedly had been worn by Mary at the time of the Annunciation. As the cult of Mary grew during the High Middle Ages, so did the importance of Chartres Cathedral.

The year 1020 proved to be an ominous one for the cathedral. On September 7, 1020, a fire consumed the cathedral. Fulbert of Chartres, the local bishop, rallied financial support from King Robert of France, King Canute of England, and other sovereigns in a successful effort to rebuild the cathedral. Monetary magnanimity allowed Fulbert to commission the architect Beregar to construct the apse, the ambulatory, and the chapels for the eastern portion of the cathedral. Another fire in 1030 delayed consecration of the rebuilt cathedral until 1037. Fulbert's new cathedral was built in the Romanesque style and was the predecessor of the twelfth century Gothic structure now found at Chartres.

While Fulbert was the decided inspiration for the reconstruction of the cathedral and its restoration as a major pilgrimage site, he is equally important for his revitalization of the classics studied at the Chartres Cathedral school. The eleventh century witnessed the shift of learning from the sometimes remote monastic centers to the urban cathedral schools. Because of the general prosperity resulting from commercial trade in cities and towns, the urban cathedral schools were able to attract the best scholars and the most promising young students. Fulbert laid the cornerstone for the new learning and was the academic coordinator for the curriculum at Chartres. Educated at the cathedral school at Rheims under the tutelage of Gerbert d'Aurillac, the future Pope Sylvester II, Fulbert came to Chartres in the 980's and established the cathedral school there. Chartres was considered the foremost school in France until the University of Paris and other similar institutions forced the cathedral schools into oblivion during the thirteenth century.

The cathedral school at Chartres fostered the classical tradition through its curriculum. Martianus Capella's fifth-century treatise, the *Marriage of Mercury and Philology*, provided the pedagogical foundation for learning. Boethius (c. 480-524) later fine-tuned Capella's work and formally activated the trivium and quadrivium into divisional entities and outlined their specific functions within the ideal curriculum. The trivium consisted of grammar, rhetoric, and dialectic (or logic), while the quadrivium included arithmetic, geometry, music, and astronomy. The trivium allowed the educated person to speak, to communicate, and to persuade clearly and cogitantly. The quadrivium, on the other hand, provided a theoretical background necessary to understand the workings of the universe. According to the traditions of Plato and Pythagoras, much in evidence at Chartres, mathematics held the key to understanding order in the universe.

Grammar was the foundation for the trivium. The texts of Donatus and Priscian were available from the cathedral's vast library. The method of teaching grammar was incessant drilling conducted by underlings and probably not by the major scholars at Chartres. If the later sculpture of Grammar holding a switch, located on the portal of the Gothic cathedral at Chartres, is any indication, flogging assumed a part of the pedagogical methodology through which the student suffered (in addition to the drilling) as he proceeded along the path toward mastering the trivium.

Rhetoric and logic emerged triumphant in the eleventh century in response to the growing need to persuade an audience of readers or listeners toward goodness. This persuasion was part of a religious mission for the monks at Chartres. The work of Quintillian served as the basis of oratorical study, but rhetoric was subordinate to logic at this time. Having studied logic with Gerbert at Rheims, Fulbert strongly advocated the pursuit of logic. Porphyry's introduction to the *Categories* and Boethius' *Introduction to Categoric Syllogisms* were the starting points for the fledgling subject of logic at Chartres, since Aristotle and his rationalism were not to appear in France until the twelfth century. Yet the importance of syllogisms here points directly toward the advent of Scholasticism in the twelfth and thirteenth centuries.

Although the trivium was more in evidence than the quadrivium at Chartres, the cathedral school still managed to earn an outstanding reputation for mathematics. A rare book on geometry written by Albinus circulated throughout the cathedral school. Fulbert's talents in mathematics attracted Ragimbold of Cologne to come to Chartres and study with Fulbert. Ragimbold's experience, however, was not an entirely happy one. Ragimbold claimed that on one occasion Fulbert was able to demonstrate one geometric problem but not a second one. Ragimbold left Chartres in frustration. Since Ragimbold was to become a major mathematician of the eleventh century, perhaps Fulbert was overmatched by a brilliant student who not only was much better that the other students at Chartres but also may have surpassed Fulbert himself in the study of mathematics. Aside from this one criticism, most students had nothing but praise for the mathematical instruction they received at Chartres.

Medicine was taught and practiced at Chartres under the watchful eye of Heribrand. Richer, the monk of St. Remy and a former student of Gerbert d'Aurillac, described the process of a long and complicated journey to Chartres in 991. It seemed that the trip was beset by difficulties at every turn. With his perilous travels behind him, Richer recounts that he studied the *Harmony of Hippocrates, Galen and Suranus*, along with the *Aphorisms* of Hippocrates. From his studies with Heribrand and from his readings of the classical texts, Richer recounted that he was prepared to write theoretical analyses of medical problems and surgical procedures. Richer praised the generosity of his teacher and claimed that pharmacy, botany, and surgery were well within Heribrand's range of expertise. Although Richer and Heribrand were thoroughly acquainted with the ancients and the medical manuscripts in the Chartres library, other capable scholars, such as Fulbert, understood the rudiments of home remedies and their application toward healing even though they failed to grasp the more advanced theoretical treatises on medicine. It appears that divisional study and expertise were in evidence at the cathedral school.

From the quadrivium, astronomy was another popular subject at Chartres. Fulbert was responsible for introducing the astrolabe, a device long used by the Muslims to gauge celestial altitudes and to tell time. The Muslims were chiefly responsible for the transmission of ancient Greek astronomical texts. Tenth century contact with the Muslims introduced the astrolabe and astronomy to Christian Europe. Gerbert d'Aurillac had traveled to Muslim Spain, where he studied the ancient texts as seen through Muslim eyes. Gerbert himself used the astrolabe and wrote a book about the device. It is likely that Fulbert's knowledge of the astrolabe and astronomy came from his association with Gerbert. Fulbert's interest in astronomy is demonstrated by his writings, which are sprinkled with reference to zodiacal signs and the tabulations of constellations. Astronomical observation and subsequent computation provided a rational way to understand the motions of the planets and the process of time; this study subsequently allowed one to penetrate the very workings of God's wondrous universe.

An eleventh century Vatican inventory of books at Chartres reveals the breadth and the depth of classical sources in the cathedral school library. Martianus Capella accompanies Fortunatus, Juvenal, Ovid, Porphyry, Vergil, and Cicero. An eleventh century monk brought a list of books that he had read to St. Emneram's monastery in Regensburg. It is not exactly clear whether he had studied either at Chartres or Rheims, but the surviving list is instructive about the availability of books at both Rheims and Chartres. The student monk mentions works by Cicero, Quintillian, Pliny, and Livy, among others. If this student knew these sources, it is clear that Fulbert and his scholarly circle were thoroughly conversant with the same texts. These books would have formed the backbone of the most important classical Roman literature.

It is true that Fulbert, his colleagues, and his students admired the classical tradition and all that it had to offer them. Nevertheless, it must be remembered that the primary goal of the cathedral school was not to train students in the liberal arts for their use in the secular world, but rather to educated orthodox and moral clergymen who would temper the vicissitudes of daily life faced by their parishioners who lived in the secular world. The classics, then, were to support Christian principles and ideals.

The classics were an appropriate background for the study of theology. In the twelfth century, Bernard of Chartres understood the blending of the Christian and classical world. He saw no conflict between them when he said, unabashedly, that scholars of his own time were dwarfs standing on the shoulders of the giants from a more glorious past. The scholars of Chartres gave proper tribute to the value of the classical tradition.

—Barbara M. Fahy

ADDITIONAL READING:

Bolgar, R. R. *The Classical Heritage and Its Beneficiaries*. New York: Cambridge University Press, 1958. Although somewhat dated, this scholarly work continues to serve as the single most important text on classical learning in the Western world. Accessible to general readers.

MacKinney, Loren C. *Bishop Fulbert and Education at the School of Chartres*. Vol. 6. Notre Dame, Ind.: The Mediaeval Institute, 1957. MacKinney attempts to be balanced and comprehensive in this portrait of Fulbert and his role as teacher and mentor at the cathedral school. Recommended for advanced readers familiar with medieval history.

Sandys, John E. *A History of Classical Scholarship*. 3 vols. Harper & Row, 1964. A standard, comprehensive work on the classics. Essential reading for those who want to understand the evolution of classical scholarship throughout the ages.

Southern, R. W. *Medieval Humanism and Other Studies*. New York: Harper & Row, 1971. In this survey of medieval Humanism, Southern covers many topics on intellectual history and provides an original presentation of the material.

Wagner, David L. *The Seven Liberal Arts in the Middle Ages*. Bloomington: Indiana University Press, 1986. This collection of superb essays written by key scholars provides an excellent, in-depth guide to the study of the seven liberal arts throughout the Middle Ages.

SEE ALSO: 635-800, Founding of Lindisfarne and Creation of the *Book of Kells*; 781, Alcuin Becomes Adviser to Charlemagne; 1100-1300, Emergence of European Universities; 1150, Moors Transmit Classical Philosophy and Medicine to Europe.

Many classical sources were among the inventory of books at the cathedral school at Chartres, including works written by the Roman poet and scholar Vergil. (Library of Congress)

1031

FALL OF THE CALIPHATE OF CÓRDOBA

The fall of the caliphate of Córdoba marks the receding political power of Muslim Spain and its loss of cultural influence.

DATE: 1031

LOCALE: Córdoba, Spain

CATEGORIES: Government and politics; Religion; Wars, uprisings, and civil unrest

KEY FIGURES:

ʿAbd al-Rahmān III al-Nasir (891-961), emir who proclaimed himself caliph of Córdoba in 929

Al-Hakam II (died 976), son of ʿAbd al-Rahmān III and caliph of Córdoba, 961-976

Al-Mansur (Muhammad ibn Abu ʿĀmir al-Mansur, often Romanized to Almanzor; c. 938-1002), prime minister-chancellor of Córdoba, 976-1002

Al-Mushafi, first minister under al-Hakam II and Hishām II

Al-Muzaffar (ʿAbd al-Malik), son of al-Mansūr who served as chamberlain, 1002-1008

Ghalib, general and military head under al-Hakam II and Hishām II

Hishām II (965-1013), caliph of Córdoba, 976-1009 and 1010-1013

Subh, first a concubine then favored wife of al-Hakam and queen mother of Hishām II

SUMMARY OF EVENT. The tenth century was the golden age of Muslim Spain, and Córdoba was its political and intellectual center. Yet the roots of the downfall of the Umayyad caliphate in al-Andalus can be found in the caliphate's rapid rise to power.

On January 16, 929, ʿAbd al-Rahmān III proclaimed himself caliph, an act which separated Córdoba from the caliphate at Baghdad. Córdoba, a city with a population of one hundred thousand inhabitants, was noted for its extensive markets, the architecture of its mosques, its official residences, palace, industrial zones, baths, and gardens. Beginning in 936, ʿAbd al-Rahmān built a new palace and administrative headquarters, Medinat az-Zahra, approximately three miles from the city. Until 961, al-Andalus, or Muslim Spain, prospered during his reign. ʿAbd al-Rahmān quieted the Christian campaigns in the north as well as the Fatimid navy that threatened the Mediterranean from North Africa. To maintain this peace, he relied heavily on mercenary soldiers, and imported Slavs from Europe for his personal protection.

ʿAbd al-Rahmān was succeeded as caliph by his son al-Hakam II, who continued many of the policies of his father. Always the scholar, he accumulated a library of more than four hundred thousand books, an impressive collection in its time. Al-Hakam tended, however, to rely more strongly than his father on officials to conduct routine activities of the caliphate. Although he failed to prepare a successor to assume the caliphate upon his death, his concubine Subh gave birth to a son, Hishām, who succeeded his father.

Because Hishām was only eleven years old when his father died, there was some difficulty in determining who would assume the position of caliph while several groups, including the Slav bodyguards, attempted to place their own choices. Ibn Abu ʿĀmir, chancellor under al-Hakam, accepted the guardianship of Hishām until he came of age and was able to serve as caliph. Al-Mansur, as Ibn Abu ʿĀmir came to be known, with al-Mushafi, the first minister, and Ghalib, the head of the military, formed a triumvirate to carry out the responsibilities of the young caliph. Unfortunately, Hishām was isolated in the palace for the remainder of his life, however, and others ruled for him. Al-Mansur manipulated himself into a position of absolute power; he was aided in his acquiescence of power by Subh who, by that time, held great influence outside of Córdoba. His Medinat al-Zāhira equaled in splendor the palace of ʿAbd al-Rahmān III. With his administration relocated to the new center, Hishām was left a veritable prisoner within the palace. By 981, al-Mansur was named mayor of the palace and ruled until 1002. During his reign, he built extensively, cut taxes, and increased the size of the army by the use of Berbers from Africa. Despite his means of obtaining control of the caliphate, al-Andalus was stable and prosperous under his rule.

Al-Mansur not only centralized authority in his own hands but also nominated his son, ʿAbd al-Malik (al-Muzaffar) as chamberlain. After the death of al-Mansur, the change in authority was again challenged by several groups, particularly the Slavs. Al-Muzaffar and al-Mansur had both maintained the absolute power which was bequeathed to them by the caliph, who was left completely unfit to assume the responsibilities of the office. Since al-Muzaffar and al-Mansur had done nothing to harm the caliph nor diminish the respect for the office, the populace generally accepted their rule. When al-Muzaffar died after only six years of rule, his brother tried to succeed him and, ultimately, gain the title of caliph. These actions quickly led to his downfall and to the end of Āmirid dictatorship.

From 1008 until the dissolution of the caliphate in 1031, al-Andalus suffered an ongoing civil war. In the absence of the tight control that al-Mansur and his son had maintained, chaos suddenly erupted. Mercenaries who were no longer being paid soon resorted to lawlessness and violence. Various groups, particularly the Slavs and the Berbers as well as the people of Córdoba, again put forward leaders who tried to establish control, but none was successful. Some were in control for only a few months, others for as long as a few years. Medinat az-Zahra, the royal city built by ʿAbd al-Rahmān, and Medinat az-Zāhira, the administrative center built by al-Mansur, were both destroyed completely in the civil war. Hishām II retained the title of caliph through the early years of the civil war, but remained impotent and was eventually killed in 1013.

Following so many years of war and internal struggles, al-Andalus was eager for the peace and stability it had enjoyed previously. In 1031, the elders of Córdoba met under the leadership of Abū Hazm Ibn Jahwar and abolished the institution of the caliphate. In its place, a governing council was established, which was to rule the region of Córdoba. Shortly thereafter, towns established their own independent rulers, who became known as party kings.

In considering this period of al-Andalus, the historian is left with few primary sources of material. While some caliphs employed professional historians to record the events of the period, much of their writing was destroyed during the civil war. Historians also caution that these writers made no attempt to hide their allegiances in their efforts to explain the reasons for the downfall of the caliphate. Some Muslim writers of the time followed a religious line of thought which claimed that the events were a trial or test for Muslims from God. They were defeated, they believed, because of losing their way from the right path.

Other writers point to more political and social causes for the great downfall. Many, for example, point to ʿAbd al-Rahmān's reliance on mercenary soldiers and Slavs, which led to ethnic divisions within Muslim society. In the same way, al-Mansur increased the size of the military by importing Berber soldiers and, at the same time, eliminated tribal groupings. Society was unable to assimilate so many new groups, and a great deal of friction resulted. There was also concern that the caliphate did not have the resources to maintain such a large military force.

Another cause for concern was al-Hakam's relinquishment of his authority to various officials of the palace. This action may have enabled al-Mansur and others who followed to usurp the power of the caliph and then centralize that power outside of the office of caliph.

Despite such reasons, history clearly shows that with the abolishment of the caliphate in 1031, al-Andalus was divided into many independent kingdoms and the glory of the tenth century caliphate was not seen again. It also seems safe to assert that the loss of the Umayyad caliphate

marked a shift in the relations between Christian Spanish kings of the north and the Muslims of al-Andalus. The Christian kings' efforts to reconquer Spain from the Muslims gained greater strength and momentum after the fall of Córdoba.   —*Donald E. Cellini*

ADDITIONAL READING:

Chejne, Anwar G. *Muslim Spain: Its History and Culture*. Minneapolis: University of Minnesota Press, 1974. The second chapter of this work, "The Caliphate 929-1031," includes a discussion of both the rise and fall of the caliphate of Córdoba.

Fletcher, Richard. *Moorish Spain*. New York: Henry Holt, 1992. While this work deals with various aspects of the Spanish-Islamic state, chapter 4, entitled "The Caliphate of Córdoba," considers the glories of the caliphate as well as its collapse.

Reilly, Bernard F. *The Medieval Spains*. New York: Cambridge University Press, 1993. The caliphate and its decline is discussed within the general context of medieval Spain.

Scales, Peter C. *The Fall of the Caliphate of Córdoba: Berbers and Andalusis in Conflict*. Leiden, the Netherlands: E. J. Brill, 1994. In this scholarly work, Scales examines the primary sources available in his discussion of the fall of the caliphate.

Watt, W. Montgomery. *A History of Islamic Spain*. Edinburgh: Edinburgh University Press, 1965. In this detailed history of Islam in Spain, Watt provides extensive background on the events leading up to and following the collapse of the caliphate of Córdoba.

SEE ALSO: 711, Tarik's Crossing into Spain; 950, Flourishing of the Court of Córdoba; 1092-1094, El Cid Conquers Valencia and Becomes Its Ruler; 1150, Moors Transmit Classical Philosophy and Medicine to Europe; 1492, Fall of Granada.

1054

BEGINNING OF THE ROME-CONSTANTINOPLE SCHISM

The beginning of the Rome-Constantinople schism intensifies, reaching its culmination after the conquest of Constantinople by the soldiers of the Fourth Crusade in 1204 and later weakening Christianity against the influx of Islam during the Turkish conquests of the fourteenth and fifteenth centuries.

DATE: 1054
LOCALE: Constantinople, the Byzantine Empire
CATEGORIES: Government and politics; Religion

KEY FIGURES:

Alexius I Comnenus (1048-1118), emperor of Constantinople, 1081-1118

Argyros (died 1058), son of Melo of Bari and commander of Italy, Calabria, Sicily, and Paphlagonia, 1051-1058

Bohemond (c. 1052-1111), Norman adventurer, son of Robert Guiscard and commander of the Normans against Byzantium

Constantine IX Monomachos (c. 980-1055), Byzantine emperor, 1042-1055

Humbert of Mourmoutiers (c. 1000-1061), cardinal of Silva Candida and papal legate

Leo IX (Bruno of Egisheim; 1002-1054), Roman Catholic pope, 1048-1054

Michael I Cerularius (c. 1000-1059), patriarch of Constantinople, 1043-1058

Urban II (Odo of Lagery; c. 1042-1099), Roman Catholic pope, 1088-1099

SUMMARY OF EVENT. The gradual alienation between the Eastern and Western Christian churches may be traced as far back as the physical division of the Roman Empire in A.D. 395, when the Eastern Church, with its capital in Constantinople, was separated from the Western Roman Church by the Theodosian line, a geographic demarcation that traversed the Balkan peninsula. Founded in A.D. 330 by Emperor Constantine I the Great and heavily influenced by Hellenic Greek culture, the Eastern Church adopted the Greek language and became the center of an empire in which church and state were equally under the authority of the Byzantine emperor, the representative of God on earth. Doctrinal matters were decided by ecumenical councils called by the emperor, which were attended by the bishops of the five patriarchal cities: Rome, Constantinople, Antioch, Alexandria, and Jerusalem. Of these Rome was considered the most important, since it was the see founded by St. Peter. Constantinople, the residence of the emperor, was second in importance after Rome.

The weakening of the Latin-speaking Church based in Rome following the barbarian incursions of the fourth century meant that the Byzantines saw themselves as the legitimate heirs of the Roman Empire and the repository of the Christian tradition. As bishop of Rome, however, the pope maintained his primacy because of the apostolic foundation of his see.

Over time, disagreements between the two branches of Christianity developed, in part because of communication difficulties and also because of cultural differences between them. These differences touched on issues both of authority and doctrine. The concept of schism, a split within the Christian community, is distinguished from heresy, which is a division based on doctrinal differences.

Past schisms had developed between the churches, the most noteworthy being the Acacian schism of 483-518, in which Acacius, patriarch of Constantinople, was excommunicated for making concessions to the Monophysites, and that of 607, when Pope Gregory I objected to the title of ecumenical patriarch being applied to the patriarch of Constantinople. Further ill-will developed in Rome when the Byzantines instigated the iconoclastic movement under Emperor Leo III, which was later condemned at the seventh ecumenical council of Nicaea in 787. This estrangement was exacerbated by the papal crowning of Charlemagne as emperor of the Romans in 800 and subsequently, when attempts were made to substitute the primacy of the pope for that of the emperor.

A more serious doctrinal dispute was occasioned by the insertion of the *filioque* clause into the Nicene Creed, first proposed by the German popes elected after Emperor Otto I restored the Western Roman Empire. The *filioque* was inserted into the language approved at the Council of Nicaea concerning the procession of the Holy Spirit, which was believed to come from the Father. The addition of language indicating that it proceeded also from the Son, in Latin *filioque*, was considered heretical by the Eastern Church. A further area of disagreement touched upon celibacy of the clergy, an innovation in the Roman Church imposed by the western Franks, and Latin condemnation of the use of leavened bread in the celebration of the eucharist by the Greeks.

Some date the Eastern schism from 1009, when the pope sent a copy of the creed with the *filioque* included to the Patriarch Sergios of Constantinople. From that date, the Byzantines no longer included the pope's name in the diptychs of their Church. Nevertheless, practitioners of the Greek and Roman rites did not feel that the churches were in schism at that time.

The immediate cause of the controversy of 1054 was the refusal of Michael I Cerularius, the patriarch of Constantinople, to countenance the use of unleavened bread in the communion ceremony as practiced in Byzantine territory in southern Italy. To the Greeks, the leaven in the bread was symbolic of the life of Christ. So Cerularius closed down churches using the Latin rite in Constantinople in 1052. Leo, the Eastern Orthodox archbishop of Ochrida, dispatched a letter of protest against the use of unleavened bread. The archbishop's action outraged Pope Leo IX, who replied to the letter and demanded the submission of the patriarch to the primacy of Rome. After a further exchange of letters, the pope dispatched legates to Constantinople with a letter to Cerularius that was insulting in tone, as well as a more amicable one to the emperor.

Wishing to avoid controversy, Constantine IX Monomachos, the Byzantine emperor, cordially received the legates, headed by Cardinal Humbert of Silva Candida. Although Constantine proposed a compromise, it was unacceptable to Patriarch Michael Cerularius, who saw the views of the Romans as heretical. The papal legates composed a bull of excommunication, written in Latin, against the patriarch and all his supporters. After placing this document upon the altar of the cathedral of Hagia Sophia in Constantinople, the legates left the city. When it was translated back into Greek, this bull was mistranslated, extending the excommunication against the entire Eastern Church. Cerularius used this pretext to recall the legates to Constantinople and imprison the supporters of Argyros, his archenemy in Italy. Cerularius also had the translators beaten and convened a holy synod to excommunicate the legates and pronounce anathema. His precipitate action outfaced the emperor of Constantinople, who wished to adopt a conciliatory policy toward Rome.

In the meantime, Pope Leo IX had died in 1054, thus invalidating the bull of excommunication. Confusion as to the implications of the actions of Humbert and Cerularius made it unclear whether a state of schism actually existed between the churches of Rome and Constantinople.

While these events were taking place, the Turks of Anatolia were continuing to threaten Christendom. Urban II, who was elected pope in 1088, and Alexius I Comnenus, emperor of Constantinople, were in accord on the need to form a crusade to resist the Turks. Although the emperor was hesitant to throw open the doors of his empire to armed soldiers from the West, he and Pope Urban II decided to pursue a crusade. For his part, the pope saw a crusade as a way to repair the rupture between the Eastern and Western churches. The Byzantine emperor reached an understanding that any formerly Byzantine cities captured by the crusaders should revert to Byzantium. Unfortunately, this did not happen when Antioch, one of the five patriarch cities, was recovered by the crusaders. Bohemond, a Norman adventurer, kept the city in spite of his oath to Emperor Alexius I and nominated a Latin patriarch, exiling the Greek patriarch to Constantinople.

Nominally intended to recapture the Holy Land but more frequently causing pillage and destruction throughout the imperial realms of the Byzantines, subsequent crusades only served to deepen the distrust of the Byzantine Greeks toward the adherents of the Latin Church. The Greeks maintained their unwillingness to recognize the primacy of the pope of Rome. This mutual bitterness reached a bloody culmination in 1182, when the Greeks massacred the population of the Latin colony of Constantinople, and again in 1185, when the Greeks of Salonika were in their turn massacred by the Normans. Because they attempted to negotiate with the Turks, the Byzantine Greeks were accused of treachery by the Latins. Bohemond used this argument as a rationale for diverting the armies of the Fourth Crusade to attack Constantinople in 1204. The crusaders sacked and plundered the city, massacred many of the inhabitants, destroyed churches, works of art, and architectural monuments, appointed a Latin patriarch, and founded Constantinople as a Latin empire.

Although the Greek rule of Constantinople was restored during the following century, this destruction of their beautiful city by fellow Christians remained in the Greek memory as an unforgivable transgression, and doomed all subsequent attempts to reunify the Eastern and Western churches.

—*Gloria Fulton*

ADDITIONAL READING:

Angold, Michael. *The Byzantine Empire, 1025-1204: A Political History*. London: Longman, 1984. This study focuses on political events and discusses the schism within that context.

The Cambridge Medieval History. Vol. 4. New York: Macmillan, 1927. This standard work discusses the schism from the Roman point of view.

Norwich, John Julius. *Byzantium: The Apogee*. New York: Alfred A. Knopf, 1992. A popular, highly readable account of the Byzantine Empire from 800 to 1081.

_____. *Byzantium: The Decline and Fall*. New York: Alfred A. Knopf, 1996. Continuation of Norwich's earlier account, covering the period from the Crusades to the fall of Byzantium to the Turks in 1453.

Runciman, Steven. *The Eastern Schism: A Study of the Papacy and the Eastern Churches During the Eleventh and Twelfth Centuries*. Oxford: Clarendon Press, 1955. The classic work on events leading up to the schism, reasons for the positions of each side, and the aftermath, focusing on the devastating impact of the schism for the Byzantine Empire. This study represents the Greek point of view.

SEE ALSO: 726-843, Iconoclastic Controversy; 1204, Knights of the Fourth Crusade Capture Constantinople; 1215, The Fourth Lateran Council; 1414-1418, Council of Constance.

1066
BATTLE OF HASTINGS

The Battle of Hastings marks the defeat of Anglo-Saxon forces by the French-speaking Normans and the decline of the Anglo-Saxon language and culture.

DATE: October 14, 1066
LOCALE: England
CATEGORY: Wars, uprisings, and civil unrest
KEY FIGURES:
Edward the Confessor (1003-1066), Anglo-Saxon king
    of England, 1046-1066, who died without an heir
Harold Godwinson (c. 1022-1066), Anglo-Saxon king
    of England, 1066, elected by the Witan and crowned
    after Edward the Confessor's death
Harold Hardrada, (1015-1066), king of Norway,
    1045-1066, and claimant to the English throne
William I (1028-1087), duke of Normandy, 1035-1087,
    victor over Harold Godwinson at the Battle of
    Hastings and first Norman king of England,
    1066-1087
SUMMARY OF EVENT. In 1066, on the death of Edward the
Confessor, the childless Anglo-Saxon king, there were
three rivals for the throne: Harold Hardrada, king of Nor-
way, who based his claim on his relationship to Cnut (also
known as Canute) of Denmark, who had ruled England
from 1016 to 1035; Harold Godwinson, accepted as heir
to the throne by the dying Edward and by the Witan, the
Anglo-Saxon assembly of nobles; and William, duke of
Normandy, who based his claim on blood relationship as
well as on promises from both Edward the Confessor and
Harold Godwinson that the throne should be his.

William's claim to the throne was no surprise. Edward,
although English on his father's side, had been born of a
Norman mother and had spent his early years in Normandy.
He included many Normans in his court and received
frequent Norman visitors, William among them. William
maintained that Edward had promised him the English
throne when William had visited Edward in England. In
addition, William based his claim on a promise he had
exacted from Harold Godwinson himself when Harold
had been held captive in Normandy after a shipwreck.
William also had the support of the pope, who wanted to
bring the English Church into closer ties with Rome.

To enforce his claim, William assembled a feudal army
composed not only of Normans but also of knights from the
neighboring duchies of Main and Brittany and from Flanders, central France, Aquitaine, and the Norman colonies
in southern Italy. These mercenary troops were mostly
composed of landless men, looking to gain wealth and
land in England by fighting for William. Their strength lay
in their cavalry tactics and in the leadership of William,
who had proven himself an indomitable soldier in the
campaigns in Normandy and elsewhere in France. As they
waited in Normandy for good sailing weather, William's
troops numbered conservatively between five thousand and
six thousand men, a massive force by medieval standards.

Harold Godwinson's force had two parts: the standing
army, made up of *housecarles*, trained members of the
king's bodyguard, and *fyrdmen*, a part-time force made up
of men who owed service to the king. When Harold
received news of William's preparations, he marched his
army to the coast to wait for William's attack. When he
heard that his brother, Tostig, and the Norwegian Harold
Hardrada had attacked England, however, Harold Godwinson turned his army northward, engaging the invaders at
Stamford Bridge in Yorkshire and defeating them soundly.

Three days later, William landed at Pevensey on the
south coast of England on September 28. Still in the north,
Harold received word of William's landing after the decisive victory at Stamford Bridge. By a forced march of
some two hundred miles, Harold brought his weary army
to meet the fresh enemy. He reached London by October 5-6 with the vanguard of his army. He stayed in London for several days, resting his troops and waiting for the
rest of his army to arrive from Yorkshire. Ignoring the
advice from his brother Gyrth to wait longer, Harold left
London on October 11 with less than his full force to meet
William. Had he delayed, time would have proven his best
ally, because William needed to fight before his supplies
ran out and winter set in. Instead, on a field between
Hastings and Senlac in Sussex, the two armies met on
October 14, 1066. The famous Bayeux tapestry, a 231-foot
piece of linen needlework created to commemorate the
battle, provides a graphic representation of the fighting,
detailing the Normans and Anglo-Saxons in battle.

The battle started at about 9:00 A.M. and continued
throughout the day. For all their disadvantages, the English troops fought tenaciously and almost won the day.
They depended on a close phalanx formation, a long line
of men shoulder to shoulder with spears raised. This formation held during the early hours of the battle, and the
Saxons successfully repulsed William's Breton troops
who were in the lead. As the afternoon wore on, large
numbers of both Saxons and Normans were killed, including Leofwin and Gyrth, Harold's brothers. By late afternoon, the Normans began to force their way through the
Saxon line. Even then, according to the chronicler William
of Malmesbury, the English fought bravely and "by frequently making a stand, they slaughtered their pursuers by
heaps." King Harold was killed during the last stages of
the battle, and without leadership, the Saxon defense
crumbled. William had won the day and England.

During the Battle of Hastings, many of the Anglo-
Saxon nobility were killed; those who survived had their
lands confiscated. The defeat at Hastings led effectively to
the end of the Anglo-Saxon ruling class.

It took William another seven years to put down all the

The Norman victory at the Battle of Hastings was a watershed event in English history, since it effectively brought England into the European orbit. (Archive Photos)

resistance in the north and in the west. Meanwhile, he began successfully his great task of fusing Norman and Saxon institutions, so that England became, much earlier than France, a consolidated monarchy with an efficient central government. William introduced Norman feudal practices into England and made himself an effective sovereign over his nobles by insisting that they acknowledge him as liege lord. At the same time, he left the machinery of government on the local level much as he found it, keeping the Anglo-Saxon shires with their sheriffs responsible to the king. William also inaugurated a remarkable census when he ordered the Domesday survey, which recorded properties and their holders at the time of the Norman Conquest. It was this record which enabled the royal government to provide for itself an adequate and consistent income, since officials knew what revenues could be expected from any piece of land.

The Norman Conquest also meant that French, along with Latin, became the language of the upper class, the government, and power for the next three hundred years at the expense of Anglo-Saxon. Ecclesiastical life was greatly affected also, as William repaid the pope for his support by bringing the English Church into closer ties with Rome.

If Duke William had not won the Battle of Hastings, England might have developed an isolated culture or maintained an orientation toward Scandinavia. In the opinion of some historians, the battle constitutes the most important single event in English history. It not only marks the last time that the island was successfully invaded, but, more important, it is also the event that effectively brought England into the European orbit.   *—Mary Evelyn Jegen, updated by Diane Andrews Henningfeld*

ADDITIONAL READING:

Barber, Malcolm. "The Kingdom of England." In *The Two Cities: Medieval Europe, 1050-1320.* London: Routledge, 1992. Barber carefully traces the events leading to Hastings as well as the aftermath of the Norman Conquest, paying particular attention to medieval mentality.

Brown, R. A. "The Battle of Hastings." *The Proceedings of the Battle Conference on Anglo-Norman Studies* 3

(1981): 1-21. Brown's article explores military tactics and strategy of Hastings.

Furneaux, Rupert. *Invasion 1066*. Englewood Cliffs, N.J.: Prentice-Hall, 1966. Furneaux presents a vivid account, complete with maps, diagrams, and a reconstruction of the scene of battle.

Stenton, F. M. *Anglo-Saxon England*. 2d ed. Oxford: Clarendon Press, 1947. This is the second volume of the *Oxford History of England*, edited by Sir George Clark. Hastings is described near the end of the book in a section on the Norman Conquest.

Walker, David. *The Normans in Britain*. Oxford: Blackwell, 1995. Walker offers an overview of the Anglo-Norman period in England, Scotland, Ireland, and Wales, beginning with the Battle of Hastings.

Wright, Peter Poyntz. *The Battle of Hastings*. Salisbury, England: Michael Russell, 1986. In a short book filled with illustrations and maps and devoted entirely to the Battle of Hastings, Wright traces the events leading to the battle, tactics, strategies, and the immediate aftermath.

SEE ALSO: 1016, Danish Invaders Led by Canute Conquer England; 1086, The Domesday Survey; 1154-1204, Establishment of the Angevin Empire.

1071

BATTLE OF MANZIKERT

The Battle of Manzikert undermines Byzantine control of Asia Minor through a catastrophic military loss to the Turks.

DATE: August 26, 1071

LOCALE: Manzikert, in eastern Turkey

CATEGORY: Wars, uprisings, and civil unrest

KEY FIGURES:

Alp Arslan (c. 1030-1072), nephew of Toghrïl and victor at Manzikert

Romanus IV Diogenes (died 1071), Byzantine emperor, 1067-1071, who was captured at Manzikert

Seljuk, Turkish chieftain, c. 956-970

Toghrïl Beg (Tughril Beg; c. 990-1063), grandson of Seljuk and founder of the Turkish Seljuk dynasty

SUMMARY OF EVENT. Soon after the Arabs emerged from the Arabian peninsula in the seventh century to extend their conquests eastward and westward, they attempted to conquer the Byzantine Empire by capturing Constantinople. Their repeated failures, however, kept Asia Minor and eastern Europe closed to them. In the middle of the eleventh century, the Seljuk Turks, who were later converts to Islam, arose to restore the power and prestige of the debilitated Muslim caliphate. In turn, they inherited Arab ambitions against Byzantium.

The Seljuks took their name from the chieftain of a tribe of Turkish nomads who wandered from the Kirghiz steppes of Turkestan into the Transoxiana region, settling there about the middle of the tenth century. The true founder of the dynasty was Seljuk's grandson, Toghrïl, who fought his way slowly westward until he came to the gates of Baghdad in 1055. His nephew, Alp Arslan, followed him as sultan and succeeded in further extending his empire until it reached from modern-day Turkmenistan to the Mediterranean.

Expansion into Armenia caused the decisive Battle of Manzikert in 1071, when Byzantine Emperor Romanus IV Diogenes was taken prisoner and Asia Minor was laid open to complete occupation by the Turks. The outcome of the battle had been partially determined by the unexpected desertion of a portion of Romanus' troops who were ethnic Turks to the Turkish enemy. Whether this was done out of ethnic solidarity or because of Romanus' unpopularity is unknown, but the desertion fatally undermined the cohesiveness and confidence of the Byzantine army. Alp Arslan did not take Constantinople, although he did conquer up to the Sea of Marmora.

The conquest of Asia Minor may well have been facilitated by disaffection, especially in Armenian areas, because of high taxes. The Battle of Manzikert itself may have been intended by Alp Arslan merely as a strategic act to guarantee his right flank while he subdued Syria and Egypt and not as a step in the conquest of Asia Minor. Nevertheless, the occupation of the area had far-reaching result, less for the Seljuks than for the Byzantines. Prowess and booty invested Baghdad once again with some of the past glory it had enjoyed under the Abbasids. With the death of Sultan Malikshah and his vizier, Misam al-Mulk, by 1092, the unity of the Seljuks collapsed. Civil wars and dissidence in the provinces caused the empire to break up into petty states. One such Turkish band, which eventually carried on the further investment of Asia Minor by occupying and redistributing the land, established the independent sultanate of Rum, or Roman lands. Members of this band in turn lost their independence when they were conquered by Mongol invaders in 1243. It remained for the Ottomans, cousins of the Seljuks, to bring a stable political regime into the area once more.

The impact of the Battle of Manzikert was far more intense and disastrous to Byzantium. The complete conquest of Asia Minor included even the Asiatic shore of the Sea of Marmora directly across from Constantinople, which dominated commercial routes vital to the Greek capital. The further investment of the peninsula at the hands of Suleiman, one of Alp Arslan's distant cousins, was so thorough that Hellenization of Asia Minor, finally being completed by Byzantium, was wrecked forever. It seems significant and ironic that Suleiman chose Nicaea, a city in western Asia Minor noted for the first Christian ecumenical council, as his capital. Byzantium's loss of food supplies, raw materials, revenues, commerce, and trade routes was serious indeed, and it was never redeemed. Especially disastrous was the loss of Asia Minor as a source of manpower, for the best army recruits of the Byzantine state came from the interior of that peninsula.

It was not immediately clear that Asia Minor would be permanently lost. After all, Byzantine armies had lost considerable territory in the past and much of it had been reconquered. Under the capable Comnenus dynasty of the twelfth century, Byzantium, with Crusader assistance, reconquered much of Asia Minor. Yet, after Manzikert, the Turkish presence, in the form of either the Seljuks or their successors, was always there. When Emperor Manuel I suffered a devastating defeat to the Turks at Myriocephalon in 1176, it was clear that the majority of Asia Minor would be permanently Turkish. The Battle of Manzikert had an immediate repercussion of wide significance. When Byzantium called upon Western Christendom for aid, the Crusades were launched. As Italian merchants followed in the wake of the crusaders and the Latin states were founded, trade routes tended to shift from Byzantium in favor of Syria. The fall of Constantinople to Venetian merchants and soldiers in 1204 wrought such damage to Byzantium that, even though Michael Paleologus managed to overthrow the Latin domination in 1261, the Byzantine Empire never regained its full strength before its final defeat in 1453 at the hands of the Ottoman Turks.

—*Joseph R. Rosenbloom, updated by Nicholas Birns*

ADDITIONAL READING:

Angold, Michael. *The Byzantine Empire 1025-1204: A Political History.* London: Longman, 1984. Provides background on both Alp Arslan and Romanus IV Diogenes.

Bryer, Anthony, and Michael Ursinus, eds. *Manzikert to Lepanto: The Byzantine World and the Turks 1071-1571.* Amsterdam: A. M. Hakkert, 1991. A detailed source on Byzantine-Turkish relations in the wake of the Battle of Manzikert.

Friendly, Alfred. *The Dreadful Day: The Battle of Manzikert, 1071.* London: Hutchinson, 1981. Friendly provides a thorough and detailed account of the battle and its consequences.

Kafesoglu, Ibrahim. *A History of the Seljuks.* Translated and edited by Gary Leiser. Carbondale: Southern Illinois University Press, 1988. A fine translation of a contemporary Turkish treatment of Seljuk history.

Norwich, John Julius. *Byzantium: The Apogee.* New York: Alfred A. Knopf, 1992. Norwich offers a well-written narrative history that gives a vivid description of the Battle of Manzikert.

Psellus, Michael. *Fourteen Byzantine Rulers.* Translated by E. R. A. Sewter. Baltimore: Penguin, 1966. A contemporary translation of the best primary source on the battle.

SEE ALSO: 1054, Beginning of the Rome-Constantinople Schism; 1095, Pope Urban II Calls the First Crusade; 1204, Knights of the Fourth Crusade Capture Constantinople; 1453, Fall of Constantinople.

1086
THE DOMESDAY SURVEY

The Domesday Survey provides detailed information about the resources of individual landholders for purposes of identification, settling disputed titles and levying taxes while establishing feudal law and consolidating Norman rule.

DATE: 1086

LOCALE: England

CATEGORIES: Economics; Government and politics

KEY FIGURES:

Robert of Losinga, bishop of Hereford, 1079-1095

William I (1028-1087), first Norman king of England, 1066-1087

SUMMARY OF EVENT. During the Christmas court at Gloucester in 1085, William I, faced with the threat of armies from Denmark, Norway, and Flanders, met with his advisers in what the *Anglo-Saxon Chronicle* called "a deep discussion" about the state of the country. The outcome of their deliberations was William's decision to survey his kingdom in order to reveal the resources of the new feudal order he had established. At the same time, he probably announced an increase in the annual tax on land (*Danegeld* or geld) to what was perceived by his subjects as an exorbitant level. To carry out the proposed survey, William and his advisers divided the kingdom into seven circuits, each consisting of between three and six counties. The first circuit, for example, included Kent, Sussex, Surrey, Hampshire, and Berkshire. Yorkshire and Lincolnshire may actually have been surveyed separately from their designated circuits. He appointed a team of commissioners, prelates and barons, assisted by clerks and monks, to visit the circuits and record the responses to a series of questions about every manor and its wealth.

Robert of Losinga, bishop of Hereford, who was likely present at the Gloucester Council, provides the earliest contemporary reference to this event. According to his account, William "made a survey of all England; of the land in each of the counties; of the possessions of each of the magnates, their lands, their habitations, their men, both slaves and freemen, living in huts or with their own houses and lands; of plows, horses, and other animals; of the services and payments due from each and every estate." He also reports that the commissioners were to conduct a second survey in areas where they were not known to the inhabitants to verify the first and check for possible fraud. He corroborates that the survey coincided with a tax levy.

The commissioners began their task as early as January in some counties and probably finished it by August 1, 1086, when William held a court at Salisbury. He had summoned the substantial landowners there to swear oaths of loyalty and obedience shortly before he departed for Normandy. Afterward, he successfully taxed his vassals to support his military ventures and penalized those accused of wrongfully possessing their estates. He could only have accomplished these things if the survey was already complete.

Each commission relied upon the existing court structure to assemble their evidence. The sheriff of each county was responsible for collecting information and summoning those holding manors to appear. The king's tenants-in-chief were required to submit their responses in writing and there is good evidence that the barons and ecclesiastical tenants cooperated. Royal scribes used shorthand to write down the testimony given them in French or English, then, prepared drafts for delivery to Winchester, site of the Treasury and likely the central gathering place for all reports. At Winchester, the survey was translated into Latin, edited—possibly by one scribe—into 888 richly detailed leaves, and listed by county with individual manors highlighted in red. The leaves were subsequently bound into two books: Little Domesday, encompassing Essex, Norfolk, and Suffolk; and the larger Exchequer Domesday, covering the remainder of the kingdom. Both books were originally housed at Winchester in a large chest protected with lock and three keys. Later, they were moved to Westminster.

Although the survey is incomplete, omitting London, Winchester, and other places known to have existed in the eleventh century, it is still a magnificent testament to Norman administrative efficiency and a unique medieval document. While the Carolingian surveys of the late eighth century contain some parallels, none matches Domesday in breadth or thoroughness. It is quite literally a survey of the landed wealth of England. There is nothing comparable for the Middle Ages for any European country. It records the estates and manors before the Conquest (1066) and twenty years later (1086). In many cases, it also reports the value of an estate when it was acquired by its Norman landlord. Thus, the survey was both a land register and rent book for the upper levels of society.

While its sole purpose was not the collection of the land tax or geld, the survey illustrates William's obvious need to revise the tax lists in light of the altered pattern of ownership occasioned by the Conquest and consequent settlement. For example, Domesday includes nearly two hundred landowners who possessed estates yielding one hundred pounds yearly. By 1086, this aggregate included only two Englishmen. Among the lesser magnates, that number was one in fourteen and a single bishopric remained in English hands. There was less transfer of properties further down the social scale; however, the settlement transformed landholdings throughout the country and many who owned lands in 1066 found themselves leasing them twenty years later. Because of the immediate military threat from abroad, William had to know what resources he could draw upon to defend his territories. He also understood the advantages settling disputed land claims held for peace and stability in England. The survey allowed William to accomplish both goals.

The immediate significance of the Domesday survey was as an administrative document used to arbitrate disputes between central and local government. It is a precise record of the location and value of lands and, as such, was an essential reference to sheriffs and other royal officials charged with settling tenure disputes for nearly two hundred years. During William's reign, no estate, even those forfeit for rebellion, could be transferred without his approval. The value of the survey in this connection was it permitted him to know readily which of his vassals was acquiring too many estates and thereby becoming too powerful. Within a century of its completion its reputation was so profound that the survey had acquired the popular name "Domesday," according to Richard Fitz Nigel, author of *The Dialogue of the Exchequer* (c. 1179). The reference was to the Day of Judgment from which there was no appeal.

Although its principal purposes may have been feudal and fiscal, the Domesday Book's enduring importance is found in the comprehensive portrait it provides of English rural life in the eleventh century. It records more than thirteen thousand place names and permits a reasonably accurate population estimate for England of about two million in 1086. Of that total, there were more than one hundred thousand villeins, peasants tied to the land who owed labor service to the lord of the manor. They also held a share in the common field. This aggregate headed nearly one-third of the households in the country. The south and southwest especially, contained nearly thirty thousand slaves, more than twice the number of free men. The details of mills, ponds, plows, and livestock are similarly full.

The Domesday Book gave William precise knowledge of his kingdom. It facilitated collection of the geld, helped settle title disputes caused by the Conquest, and showed the general resources of England in a compact form useful to royal administrators at the time and ever since.

—*Michael J. Galgano*

ADDITIONAL READING:

Bates, David. *A Bibliography of Domesday Book*. Woodbridge, England: The Boydell Press (for the Royal Historical Society), 1986. Comprehensive survey of the literature since 1886. Less complete for pre-1886 period. Entries are grouped as general or local studies.

Darby, H. C. *Domesday England*. New York: Cambridge University Press, 1986. Summary volume to *Domesday Geography*, which was produced earlier in five volumes under Darby's direction. Compares contemporary lists with the Domesday Book, illustrates the feudal purpose of the survey, and includes full statistics.

Douglas, David C. *William the Conqueror: The Norman Impact upon England*. Berkeley: University of California Press, 1964. Standard biography of William. Examines William in Normandy, but focuses on the Conquest and the establishment of Norman rule and influence in England.

Galbraith, V. H. *The Making of Domesday Book*. Oxford: Clarendon Press, 1961. Galbraith stresses that the purpose of the Domesday was feudal, not fiscal. The finished book was part of the original plan, and it was completed before Wiiliam's death.

Holt, J. C., ed. *Domesday Studies: Papers Read at the Novocentenary Conference of the Royal Historical Society and the Institute of British Geographers, Winchester, 1986*. Woodbridge, England: The Boydell Press, 1987. Essays examine range of political, economic, administrative, and structural topics associated with the survey, the making of the Domesday Book, and the times.

Maitland, Frederic William. *Domesday Book and Beyond: Three Essays in the Early History of England*. New York: Cambridge University Press, 1987. First published in 1897, this work spurred the modern scholarly study of the Domesday. Concentrates on social structure, feudal tenure, and the hides. Maitland emphasizes the survey's fiscal purpose.

Sawyer, Peter, ed. *Domesday Book: A Reassessment*. London: Edward Arnold, 1985. Collection of articles that illustrate the range of recent scholarship on the survey, the survey's intent, the paleography of the manuscripts, and the problems executing the survey.

SEE ALSO: 1066, Battle of Hastings; 1154-1204, Establishment of the Angevin Empire; 1175, Common Law Tradition Emerges in England.

1092-1094
EL CID CONQUERS VALENCIA AND BECOMES ITS RULER

El Cid conquers Valencia and becomes its ruler, making use of excellent military strategies and tactics to defeat Muslims from northern Africa who invade Spain in the eleventh century.

DATE: November 1, 1092-June 15, 1094

LOCALE: Valencia, Spain

CATEGORIES: Government and politics; Wars, uprisings, and civil unrest

KEY FIGURES:

Alfonso VI (c. 1040-1109), younger son of Ferdinand, his successor as king of Léon, 1065-1109, and later king of Castile, 1072-1109

El Cid (Rodrigo Díaz de Vivar; c. 1043-1099), Spanish military leader who defeated the Almoravids at Valencia

Jimena Díaz, wife of the Cid

Ferdinand I (c. 1016-1065), king of Castile, 1035-1065, and king of León, 1037-1065

Sancho II (c. 1038-1072), eldest son of Ferdinand and his successor as king of Castile, 1065-1072

Urraca (c. 1080-1126), daughter of Ferdinand and queen of Castile and León, 1109-1126

Yūsuf ibn Tāshufīn (died 1106), emir of Almoravid Empire, 1061-1106

SUMMARY OF EVENT. Rodrigo Díaz de Vivar, best known as El Cid, is both a historical and a literary figure. Since his death in 1099, this hero's life has been celebrated in several works, particularly the thirteenth century epic poem *Poema del Cid*, also known as *El Cantar de Mío Cid*. History and legend have become so entangled that scholars still struggle to determine the exact events of his life.

In the year 711, thousands of Islamic Berbers from northern Africa crossed into Spain at Gibraltar, and Islam remained in Spain for nearly eight hundred years. Partially because the Christian kingdoms were divided among themselves, there was little resistance to this invasion. In 718, the leader Pelayo was the first to stop these Muslim troops as they attempted to cross the peninsula and invade the rest of Europe. Over the next several hundred years, until 1492 when the last Moorish leaders left Spain, Christians and Moors battled what was known as the "reconquest" of Spain.

The *reconquista* was not a period of continual warfare. Córdoba, Seville, and Granada became powerful political and cultural centers in the southern part of the peninsula under Muslim rule. Evidence of the glories of this culture can still be seen in the architecture which remains in these cities: The Great Mosque at Córdoba, the Alcázar in Seville, and the famous Alhambra in Granada. Boundaries between the Christian north and Muslim south were not fixed and one group or the other often initiated warfare in an attempt to control territory, while at other times there was relative harmony.

It is during the *reconquista* that the Cid emerges as a Christian military leader and later as legendary hero. Born in Vivar, near Burgos in 1043, Rodrigo Díaz de Vivar became known more widely as El Cid, a nickname derived from the Arabic *sayyid*, meaning lord.

At the age of seventeen, the Cid was knighted by Sancho II and later appointed commander of the royal army. Following the death of the king Fernando I, father of Sancho, a civil war erupted between Alfonso and his sister Urraca against their brother Sancho. When Sancho was murdered, Alfonso VI became king of Castile. For a time, the Cid seemed to have royal favor under this new king. In 1074, Alfonso arranged a marriage between the Cid and his niece, Jimena of the House of Aragón. His

Although shown in this engraving in the company of his wife, El Cid was often separated from his family during his long career as a soldier for hire who served under Christian and Muslim rulers in Spain. (Archive Photos)

status with Alfonso, however, quickly changed. In 1081, the Cid led a successful raid into the territory of Toledo without the king's approval. The Cid's enemies convinced Alfonso that the leader had taken the action for personal gain. His wife and children placed in a monastery for safety, the Cid was exiled from Castile and León. He took with him a small army of trained warriors and served as a mercenary for both Christian and Muslim kings. During this period, the Cid demonstrated his military genius through a series of successful campaigns.

During the time when the Cid was in exile in the eastern part of Spain, events in the southern part of the country were occupying Alfonso. He had taken the Moorish city of Toledo and extended his reign further in to Moorish territory. He controlled nearly all of Christian and Muslim Spain. Seeing the threat they were under, Muslim rulers eventually sought additional help from the Almoravid empire in northern Africa.

In June of 1086, Yūsuf ibn Tāshufīn crossed into Spain and was met by Muslim leaders of Seville, Granada, and Málaga. Alfonso VI ceased his attempt to gain control of Zaragoza and marched south with his troops to meet Yūsuf. The two met at Sagrajas, and Alfonso was humiliated in defeat. The military tactics of these North Africans was unlike that of the Spaniards; it was more compact and unified compared to the Spanish one-on-one style combat. Finally, Yūsuf returned to Africa and Alfonso called the Cid out of exile.

Alfonso gave the Cid free reign in large parts of eastern al-Andalus, that is Muslim-occupied Spain, and even promised the Cid and his heirs all the land that he freed from the Moors. The Cid gained control of several independent kingdoms and demanded tribute from them. He even succeeded in forcing Valencia to pay tribute owed to Alfonso.

In 1089, Yūsuf once again crossed into Spain and Alfonso demanded that the Cid join him in fighting against the Almoravids. Because of internal struggles between Yūsuf and other Muslim leaders, however, Yūsuf and his army had retreated before Alfonso reached Aledo. It is not clear exactly what occurred, but the Cid failed to meet up with Alfonso. Enraged, the king once again banished the Cid from his kingdom, confiscated his property, and imprisoned the Cid's wife and children, although the family was reunited later.

Exiled for a second time, the Cid again began to demand tribute from several of the independent kingdoms in the east and southeast of al-Andalus. He even persuaded al-Qadir, former ruler of Toledo, then ruler of Valencia to again pay tribute to ensure protection. The Cid remained a nuisance to both Yūsuf and to Alfonso, but became acceptable to many of the Moors. He practiced an authority which permitted tolerance rather than influence by power. Nevertheless, many Muslim resented the taxes which were imposed on them by Christian rulers.

When Yūsuf began his third campaign into Spain, many Muslim rulers decided they were safer without Yūsuf as an ally. They were prepared to ally themselves with Alfonso, instead.

This time, however, Yūsuf managed to reclaim several cities and Alfonso lost his control of al-Andalus. Only the Cid remained to exert pressure within the Moorish territory.

At the request of Alfonso's wife, Queen Constanza, the Cid joined the king near Granada. The reconciliation, however, was short lived. The Almoravids did not attack as anticipated, and eventually the royal troops were ordered back to Toledo. In a misunderstanding over protocol, the Cid pitched his tents close to the walls of the city. Alfonso was only too ready to misinterpret the Cid's actions and the Cid fled and returned safely to Valencia where both Muslim and Christian leaders sought his support against the Almoravids of northern Africa.

During this period, Alfonso was unable to regain control of the south, and Yūsuf reconquered several cities and kingdoms. While the Cid was in Zaragoza, Valencia's ruler al-Qadir was forced to flee the city and the populace planned to turn the city over to the Almoravids. Upon his return, the Cid began a siege of the city which took nearly nineteen months to complete. When the new ruler refused to honor the previous accord, the Cid cut off food supplies. News of another Almoravid invasion encouraged those in control of Valencia to hold out until the North African troops could arrive. The famine and death caused by the lack of supplies combined with further news that the Almoravids had eventually returned to Africa forced Valencia to negotiate a settlement. On June 15, 1094, the Cid took control of Valencia as its unofficial king.

Yūsuf, now aged and perhaps ill, sent his nephew to reconquer Valencia and bring back the Cid alive; his nephew was unsuccessful and Yūsuf never returned to Spain. In December of 1094, at the battle of Cuarte, the Cid again defeated the Almoravids

The Cid held the city of Valencia for another five years until he died suddenly on July 10, 1099. His widow Jimena held Valencia for only a few years before she was forced to withdraw from the city and Valencia once again fell to Muslim rule.   —*Donald E. Cellini*

ADDITIONAL READING:

DeChasca, Edmund. *The Poem of the Cid*. Boston: Twayne, 1976. Although the focus of this text is the epic poem about the Cid, the author provides extensive historical background as a basis for understanding the literary work.

Fletcher, Richard. *The Quest for El Cid*. New York: Alfred A. Knopf, 1990. This scholar provides a synthesis of research and refutes some earlier assumptions.

Fuentes, Carlos. "The Reconquest of Spain." In *The Buried Mirror: Reflection on Spain and the New World*. Boston: Houghton Mifflin, 1992. In this widely accessible work, Fuentes discusses the Cid within the context of the Spanish *reconquista* and describes its significance on the conquest of the Americas several hundred years later.

Matthews, John. *El Cid: Champion of Spain*. New York: Sterling Publishing, 1988. This publication provides an easy and concise introduction to the Cid and to Spain of the eleventh century, including maps, drawings, and photographs.

Menendez Pidal, Ramón. *The Cid and His Spain*. Translated by Harold Sunderland. Reprint. London: J. Murray, 1971. Menendez Pidal is the best-known scholar of the Cid. Six editions of this work were published before the author's death in 1969. This English translation first appeared in 1934.

SEE ALSO: 1031, Fall of the Caliphate of Córdoba; 1150, Moors Transmit Classical Philosophy and Medicine to Europe; 1230, Kingdoms of Castile and Léon Are Unified; 1469, Marriage of Ferdinand and Isabella; 1492, Fall of Granada.

1095

POPE URBAN II CALLS THE FIRST CRUSADE

Pope Urban II calls the First Crusade, initiating the first in a series of military expeditions from western Europe to the Middle East intent on recapturing the Holy Land from the Muslims.

DATE: November 27, 1095
LOCALE: Clermont, France
CATEGORIES: Religion; Wars, uprisings, and civil unrest
KEY FIGURES:
Adhemar de Monteil (Aimar de Le Puy, died 1098), papal legate with the First Crusade
Alexius I Comnenus (1048-1118), Byzantine emperor, 1081-1118
Bohemond (c. 1030-1111), son of Robert Guiscard of Italy and a leader of the First Crusade
Gautier Sans Avoir (Walter the Penniless; died 1097), French knight, a leader of the Peasants' Crusade
Godfrey de Bouillon (c. 1060-1100), duke of Lower

While presiding at the Council of Clermont, Pope Urban II delivered a speech calling upon Christians to support a military expedition to liberate the pilgrimage sites in the Holy Land from Muslim control. (Archive Photos)

Lorraine and protector of the Holy Sepulchre, 1099

Peter the Hermit (Peter of Amiens; c. 1050-1115), French ascetic and preacher of the Peasants' Crusade

Raymond of Saint Giles (1042-1105), count of Toulouse, a leader of the First Crusade

Robert of Flanders (1093-1111), Norman crusader and ruler of Jerusalem

Urban II (Odo of Ladery; c. 1035-1099), Roman Catholic pope, 1088-1099, who preached the First Crusade

SUMMARY OF EVENT. Fought between 1096 and 1464, the Crusades, or "Wars of the Cross," were a defining feature of the High Middle Ages in Europe. For almost four centuries, between nine and ten major military expeditions left the West for the Middle East in an effort to achieve two strategic goals. One was to prevent the conquest of the Byzantine Empire, a Christian stronghold, by the Muslim Turks. The other goal, which was more important to the Europeans, was to establish Christian control over the venerated pilgrimage sites in the Holy Land, especially Jerusalem. Ultimately, neither aim was permanently secured. The Turks conquered Constantinople in 1453, ending forever the Byzantine Empire. By 1515, all the East, including Palestine, fell under the control of the

Turks. The Crusades, however, represent the West's earliest effort to expand and create what has been rightly called "Europe's first adventure in colonialism."

On Tuesday, November 27, 1095, Pope Urban II preached the First Crusade before the Council of Clermont, an assembly of some two hundred bishops meeting in the south of France. Of French noble birth, Urban had been educated at Soissons and Rheims and had served as a prior in the reforming abbey of Cluny prior to becoming a papal legate and later pope on March 12, 1088, at Terracina. The agenda at Clermont included many items. The council adopted some thirty-two canons on a variety of topics. The main business, however, was the pope's call for a "Holy War" to liberate the East from the Turks. What language Urban used in his speech is not known, since there is not surviving transcript. The response to his speech was immediate and positive. From the congregation came the cry *"Deus volt"* ("God wills it"). The Crusades were launched.

The pope had two primary motives in calling the crusade. One was his hope for the reunification of the Christian world, which had been rent asunder by a schism between Rome and Constantinople in 1056. Another was his dream of a universal papacy, with the pope having hegemony over Christendom's three holiest cities—Rome, Constantinople, and Jerusalem. The crusade he called would facilitate both these visions.

The occasion for the pope's message was also two-fold. The Byzantine Empire was in danger of falling under the control of the Turks. In August of 1071, the Seljuk Turks had decisively defeated the Eastern Emperor at the Battle of Manzikert. In the wake of that victory, the Turks advanced across Anatolia, taking Antioch in 1085 and Nicaea in 1092. These reversals prompted the new Byzantine emperor, Alexius I Comnenus, to appeal to the West for help. A parallel problem involved the Turkish occupation of Palestine. The economic and religious revival of the West had resulted in an increased traffic of pilgrims journeying to the Holy Land. Tales of sacrilege, desecrations, and abuse were heard in Europe. Many individuals believed that only a Christian military presence in the East could guarantee the security and the integrity of Christian pilgrims and shrines from Turkish atrocities.

A variety of reasons account for the popularity of Pope Urban II's appeal among all classes—peasants, merchants, warriors, and clergy. Merchants and other residents of Italian towns were eager to secure commercial advantages in the Mediterranean from the Greeks and Arabs. Younger sons of the aristocracy could find fiefs of their own in *Outre Mer* ("the land beyond the sea"). Epidemic private warfare between Europe's nobility was expected to diminish as aggression was directed toward an external foe. A precedent for wars of reconquest had been established by Christian advances in Spain, Sardinia, and Sicily. Europe was in an expansive mood as new domains were added in Scandinavia, the Baltic, and the Balkans. An expanding population was seeking space all the way from Iceland to Cyprus. Military science had proved the potential for success of major international expeditions, as seen in the Norman Conquest of England in 1066. Peasants were eager for freedom and adventure in the exotic East. A major religious revival was evident, giving birth to the university, the cathedral, and now the Crusades, a kind of "spiritual journey." Very much a product of his times, Pope Urban II had touched the vibrant energies and the vivid imagination of a rejuvenated Europe.

Probably to the pope's surprise, the masses were the first to respond to the call. A French ascetic from Amiens known as Peter the Hermit and a French knight named Gautier Sans Avoir (Walter the Penniless) preached the Peasants' or People's Crusade. This popular movement attracted the innocent as well as the iniquitous, who in undisciplined fashion worked their way down the Balkans to Constantinople. Crossing the straits of Bosporus into Asia, participants in the Peasants' Crusade faced annihilation by the Turks at the Battle of Cibotus (Civetot) in August, 1096.

Meanwhile in Europe that same month, the expected response to the pope's sermon occurred among the nobility. Although no kings took up the cross, many European nobles did. The First Crusade, also known as the Barons' Crusade, set out for the East in four major contingents. One contingent was led by Godfrey de Bouillon, the duke of Lower Lorraine. A second group was headed by Bohemond, the middle-aged son of Robert Guiscard, a Norman noble with properties in Italy. Leading the third and largest forces was Raymond of Saint Giles, the count of Toulouse, who was the oldest and most experienced of the crusaders. Raymond was accompanied by Adhemar de Monteil, a warrior bishop who served as papal legate for the Crusade. A fourth group was directed by Robert of Flanders. Because the French predominated among the crusader forces, the soldiers of the First Crusade were known in the East as "the Franks" or "the Normans."

Passing through Constantinople, some four thousand mounted knights and twenty-five thousand infantry invaded Anatolia, taking Nicaea on June 19, 1097, and surrendering it to the Byzantine emperor. On June 3, 1098, the Syrian city of Antioch was taken and was retained by Bohemond as his own. Jerusalem itself was captured on

As seen in this engraving, crusader knights wearing chain mail and riding trained warhorses fought against lightly armored Turkish cavalry, who relied on bows as well as lances. (Archive Photos)

July 15, 1099, with much bloodshed. Within three years, the crusaders had obtained their goals of pushing the Turks back from Anatolia and securing western sovereignty in Palestine. Godfrey de Bouillon was appointed to remain as defender of the Holy Sepulchre in Jerusalem. Within a few years, a series of Latin feudal principalities were established along the Levantine coast. For Europe, the First Crusade appeared to be a resounding success.

Appearances were deceptive, however, since crusader victories occurred because of fragmentation of power in the Muslim East. Once the Turks and other Muslims recovered political control, the tide turned. Maintaining a Western military presence in the Middle East proved difficult, not only because of the proximity of enemies but also because of the distance of these military forces from the European base of power. Within a short time, it became necessary to wage the Second and Third Crusades, leading to a series of religious wars that would terminate in the eventual expulsion of European crusader forces from the Middle East.   —*C. George Fry*

ADDITIONAL READING:

Bridge, Anthony. *The Crusades*. New York: Franklin Watts, 1982. Written for a popular audience, this beautifully illustrated text provides a fine introduction to the history of the Crusades. Includes maps and a useful bibliography.

Duggan, Alfred. *The Story of the Crusades, 1097-1291*. New York: Pantheon Books, 1964. A popular account of the Crusades accompanied by a thorough index and line drawings by C. Walter Hodges.

Grousset, Rene. *The Epic of the Crusades*. Translated from the French by Noël Lindsay. New York: Orion Press, 1970. A premier French historian provides a readable and fast-paced survey, rich in anecdotal detail as well as interpretive analysis.

Hill, John Hugh. *Raymond IV, Count of Toulouse*. Syracuse, N.Y.: Syracuse University Press, 1961. This concise study provides a quick and readable introduction to the life of one of the great leaders of the First Crusade.

Riley-Smith, Jonathan. *The First Crusade and the Idea of Crusading*. Philadelphia: University of Pennsylvania Press, 1986. A scholarly overview of the initial Crusade and its motivations. Includes maps and an excellent bibliography.

Runciman, Steven. *A History of the Crusades*. 3 vols. Cambridge, England: Cambridge University Press, 1951-1954. Written by a celebrated British historian, this three-volume study is the classic work on the Crusades. The first volume provides a good overview of the First Crusade.

SEE ALSO: 1147-1149, The Second Crusade; 1189-1192, The Third Crusade; 1204, Knights of the Fourth Crusade Capture Constantinople; 1209-1229, The Albigensian Crusade; 1212, The Children's Crusade; 1217-1221, The Fifth Crusade; 1227-1230, Frederick II Leads the Sixth Crusade; 1248-1254, Failure of the Seventh Crusade.

1098
CISTERCIAN MONASTIC ORDER IS FOUNDED

The Cistercian monastic order is founded, adopting more austere practices than the Benedictines in following the Rule, returning to its original simplicity in Christian antiquity, and justifying this "new" way of life.

DATE: March 21, 1098
LOCALE: Burgundy, France
CATEGORIES: Organizations and institutions; Religion
KEY FIGURES:
Alberic, abbot of Cîteaux, 1099-1108
Benedict of Nursia (c. 480-c. 547), founder of Benedictine Order
Bernard of Clairvaux (1090-1153), abbot of Clairvaux, 1115-1153
Stephen Harding (c. 1060-1134), abbot of Cîteaux, 1108-1133
Hugh de Die, archbishop of Lyons and papal legate in France, late eleventh-early twelfth centuries
Robert of Molesme (c. 1027-1110), abbot of Cîteaux, 1098-1099

SUMMARY OF EVENT. The history of monasticism in the Roman Catholic Church has been said to be an account of a continuing series of internal reformations. The founding of the Order of Cistercians in 1098 is no exception. Reform was in the air during the eleventh century, and the reform of the Cistercians, or White Monks as they were called, changed monasticism during the twelfth century and the Roman Catholic Church was not the same thereafter.

This reform as well as other reforms of the eleventh and twelfth centuries were reactions to the changing times. The Carolingian reforms around 800 were by the eleventh century out of date. So, too, was the Cluniac reform begun in 909. In broad terms, what was needed at the time was institutional separation of church and state. More narrowly, within monasticism what was needed was a return to following strictly the excellent Rule of St. Benedict that had governed monastic life in western Europe since the sixth century. More specifically, a threefold reform was necessary: a return to poverty; an emphasis on the higher nature of eremetical (solitary) rather than conventional (communal) monastic life; and a desire to imitate the lives of Christ's first apostles as literally as possible, including providing for themselves through their labor while leading a life of poverty and simplicity. A return to the ideals and practices of the earliest hermits and monks also seemed desirable. The reformers wanted monks to leave the secular world as far behind as possible in order to lead a life of prayer, penance, and mortification. Specifically, the reform included living monastic life according to the literal interpretation of Benedict's Rule, having an abbot for each house rather than one for the whole order as with the Benedictine's and the Cluniacs, having a year-long novitiate probationary period, and setting a minimum age of fifteen for admission.

The Cistercian order began at Cîteaux, the place known in Latin as *Cistercium*. An important precursor to Cîteaux was the founding of the monastery of Molesme by Robert in 1075. The son of noble parents, Robert was born about 1027 in Champagne. Robert became a monk in his youth and rose rapidly to prior and abbot. Disillusioned with the practices of contemporary monastic life, he joined a group of hermit monks in the forest of Collan in 1074. The next year, he founded the reform monastery of Molesme. Many new men were called to monastic life because of Molesme, and gifts allowed for about forty daughter monasteries to be founded by 1100. These successes eventually made Molesme similar to the monasteries it had set out to reform. The need for reform and its success eventually begets the need for further reform.

In 1098, Robert and twenty-one other monks set out for another reformed "new monastery" in Burgundy that was to be Cîteaux, about twenty miles south of Dijon and about sixty miles north of Cluny. Archbishop Hugh de Die of Lyons, papal legate in France, gave permission for this establishment. Robert had told the archbishop that the observance of the Rule of St. Benedict at Molesme was "lukewarm and negligent." When Robert and his hermit monks arrived at Cîteaux they found a few peasant buildings and perhaps even the remains of an old chapel as the base for their monastery. For several years the name "Cîteaux" was not used; instead, it was called generically the New Monastery. The date officially given for the founding of the monastery of Cîteaux is March 21, 1098, Palm Sunday that year and appropriately the feast day of Saint Benedict. Exactly when the canonical erection of the abbey, the oath of obedience of Abbot Robert to the local bishop, or the stability vows of the monks to the New Monastery took place is not known. It is likely that it was during the same year, possibly during the summer.

Meanwhile the monastery of Molesme had fallen even

TIME LINE OF MONASTIC ORDERS

529 The abbey of Monte Cassino is founded by Saint Benedict of Nursia under the guidelines for communal living established by the Rule of St. Augustine.

910 The abbey of Cluny is founded in the region of Burgundy on land granted by Count William the Pious of Aquitaine.

1084 Carthusian order is founded by Saint Bruno at La Grande-Chartreuse near Grenoble, Switzerland.

1098 Robert de Molesmes founds a Cistercian monastery at Cîteaux. The Cistercian order founds four "daughter-houses" between 1113 and 1115.

1113 The order of the Hospital of St. John of Jerusalem (Hospitallers) is founded as a nursing order to serve pilgrims in the Holy Land. The order also founded houses in Spain, Italy and Germany.

1118 The order of Poor Fellow-soldiers of Christ and the Temple of Solomon (Knights Templar) is founded as a military order to defend pilgrimage sites in the Holy Land. Members originally established their headquarters near the Temple of Solomon. The order was granted official recognition by the Roman Catholic Church in 1128.

c. 1190 The Teutonic Knights is founded as a charitable order connected with a German crusader hospital in Jerusalem; it becomes a military order in 1198. Along with the Brothers of the Sword, founded in 1202, the Teutonic Knights bring Prussia and the Baltic region under Christian control.

1207-1212 Saint Dominic founds the Order of the Friars Preachers to stamp out Albigensian (Catharist) heresy in southern France.

1209 Saint Francis of Assisi founds the Order of the Friars Minor, requiring members of the order to accept strict levels of poverty. This restriction gives rise to other mendicant orders whose members traveled the countryside preaching rather than establishing monastic houses.

1243-1247 The order of the Hermits of St. Augustine is founded. Along with the Carmelite order, which encourages resettlement of the Holy Land, the Hermits of St. Augustine are linked to the Franciscan mendicant orders.

1534 Ignatius of Loyola founds the Society of Jesus, or Jesuit order, which assumes a prominent role in the defense and revival of Catholicism as part of the Counter-Reformation. The order is officially recognized by Pope Paul III in 1540. Jesuit priests occupy a central role in the establishment of missions in Asia, Africa, and the New World.

further from the ideals of Saint Benedict's Rule, and there was a call for Robert to return with the hope that he could bring about reforms. The nobles of the area around Molesme, the pope, the papal legate in France, and a number of bishops were involved in this attempt to get Robert to return. The papal legate Hugh called a synod probably during June, 1099; the current abbot of Molesme, Geoffrey, voluntarily resigned, and Robert was ordered by Hugh to return to Molesme. The monks of Cîteaux were given the option of remaining there or returning with Robert to Molesme. Several returned with him, leaving perhaps just eight monks at Cîteaux. Robert then served as Abbot of Molesme until his death in 1111. There was a struggle for survival of the New Monastery at Cîteaux that went on for twenty years. Recruits were hard to come by, and it looked as if this too would be a failed monastic experiment.

Shortly after Robert's departure, Alberic was elected abbot of Cîteaux. Alberic had been prior under Robert and seems to have been not only one of the founders of Cîteaux but also of Molesme earlier. Abbot Alberic with the material support of Odo, duke of Burgundy, and his son Hugh consolidated the founding of the monastery of Cîteaux and deserves along with Robert credit for the establishment of the Order of Cistercians. Independence from Molesme and other monasteries was obtained along with papal protection during the tenure of Alberic who died January 26, 1109.

The monastery's prior, Stephen Harding, an Englishman, was elected abbot. During Stephen's tenure, the new Cistercian Order was fully established. Stephen was born about 1060 of noble Anglo-Saxon parents. The Norman Conquest of England ruined his family and resulted in his moving to Scotland and then to France. After studying in Paris, and visiting Rome, he joined first the community at Molesme and then at Cîteaux. During his tenure, numerous additional woods and vineyards were added to the monastery holdings.

Also about April of 1112, a monk known later as Bernard of Clairvaux had entered Cîteaux. Bernard brought about thirty new monks along with him, many of them his relatives, and the reversal of the seemingly failing experiment was at hand. Bernard is given the credit for setting the New Monastery on a firm base and leading it to a time of impressive growth and influence. The number of monks had grown so that a second monastery was necessary at La Ferté by 1113. This expansion was followed quickly with new houses in 1114 at Pontigny, 1115 at Clairvaux and at Morimond, 1118 at Preuilly, and 1119 at La Cour Dieu, Bouras, Cadouin, and Fontenay. Abbot Stephen secured papal authorization from Pope Callis-

tus II in 1119 for a further independence of Cîteaux and its affiliated monasteries. The Order of Cistercians had indeed become a reality, and it soon spread to nearly every part of western Europe bringing a much needed renewed vitality to monasticism and, as a side effect of work with the land, major agricultural pioneering advances, most notably with sheep farming in England.

—*Douglas J. McMillan*

ADDITIONAL READING:

Bouchard, Constance Brittain. *Holy Entrepreneurs: Cistercians, Knights, and Economic Exchange in Twelfth-Century Burgundy*. Ithaca, N.Y.: Cornell University Press, 1991. Explores the Cistercian contributions to the economic development of Burgundy.

Brooke, Christopher. "The Cistercians." In *Monasteries of the World*. Ware, Hertfordshire, England: Omega Books, 1982. Presents the origin and history of the Cistercian order in words and pictures. Includes one map, ten diagrams, five color photographs, and thirty-seven black-and-white photographs.

King, Archdale A. *Cîteaux and Her Elder Daughters*. London: Burns & Oates, 1954. The major study of the first physical home of the Cistercians and of four daughter houses. Includes nine black-and-white photographs and one diagram.

Lawrence, C. H. "The Cistercian Model." In *Medieval Monasticism: Forms of Religious Life in Western Europe in the Middle Ages*. London: Longman, 1984. Explores the new form of monastic life developed by the Cistercians.

Lekai, Louis J. *The Cistercians: Ideals and Reality*. Kent, Ohio: Kent State University Press. 1977. The definitive study of the Cistercian order from its founding to Vatican II.

Lynch, Joseph H. "The Reformed Benedictines: Cistercians." In *The Medieval Church: A Brief History*. London: Longman, 1992. Lynch places the new order in its role as part of church history.

Southern, R. W. "The Cistercians." In *Western Society and the Church in the Middle Ages*. Vol. 2 of The Pelican History of the Church series. Grand Rapids, Mich.: Wm. B. Eerdmans, 1970. The story of the Cistercians told by a major church historian in the context of cultural and ecclesiastical history.

SEE ALSO: 590-604, Reforms of Pope Gregory the Great; 963, Foundation of Mount Athos Monasteries; 1025, Scholars at Chartres Revive Interest in Classical Learning; 1120, Order of the Knights Templar Is Founded; 1210, Founding of the Franciscans; 1534, Founding of the Jesuits.

1100-1300
EMERGENCE OF EUROPEAN UNIVERSITIES

The emergence of European universities provides a systematic organization for the transmission of learning and makes possible the exponential growth and transmission of knowledge across Western civilization.

DATE: 1100-1300

LOCALE: Europe

CATEGORIES: Cultural and intellectual history; Education

KEY FIGURES:

Peter Abelard (c. 1079-1142), French logician who taught at Notre Dame in Paris and was known as "the First Academic"

Saint Thomas Aquinas (Tommaso d'Aquino; c. 1224-1274), Italian-born scholastic philosopher, author of *Summa Theologica*

Irnerius (also Guarnerius; c. 1055-1125), Italian scholar known as "the Father of Scientific Jurisprudence"

SUMMARY OF EVENT. The rise of the universities from the abbey and cathedral schools is one of the great achievements of the Middle Ages, making possible the steady increase in education of large numbers of people and the explosion of knowledge upon which the modern world is based. The history of their rise is a complex subject covering the whole of Europe. Some of that history is unreliable, as the early universities attempted to establish a tradition for themselves by claiming to have been founded by famous individuals, such as King Arthur, Charlemagne, or the survivors of Troy. In actuality, the universities arose slowly over time, seldom established by but rather recognized by the pope or a ruler after having reached an established level of growth.

In the Middle Ages, the word *universitas*, or university, had no specific connection with the world of learning. It did not refer to the universe or universality of learning, but rather meant simply an association or group. The term could refer to a guild or group of barbers or carpenters or students, denoting only that its members were engaged in a common enterprise.

In the early Middle Ages, education was concerned chiefly with the preservation of minimal standards of clerical literacy. Education took place in schools organized in the parishes, abbeys, and cathedrals, and its subjects were the seven liberal arts. These seven were traditionally divided into two categories: the trivium, consisting of grammar, logic, and rhetoric, and the quadrivium, consisting of arithmetic, geometry, astronomy, and music. In the Greco-Roman world, sometimes

two other liberal arts are mentioned—medicine and architecture—but these two already appear to have started becoming professionalized. In the early Middle Ages, the trivium was emphasized, especially grammar, because the ability to read sacred texts and commentaries was the chief need. The only quadrivium subject to receive much attention was arithmetic, since it was needed in calculating the date of Easter. The Greek ideal, seconded by Cicero, of the importance of rhetoric and of the other quadrivium subjects to educate a person to become a capable citizen, able to engage fully in public life, received scant attention in a society that lacked the same public outlets for participation. Thus, education up until about 1100 was primarily concerned with ecclesiastical and administrative needs and chiefly centered on the transmission of the accumulated knowledge of the past.

The change that became known as the Twelfth Century Renaissance was led by logic, of all subjects, and its most famous early embodiment was Peter Abelard. A part of Aristotle's writings on logic, preserved by Boethius, had long been known, but Abelard put this "old logic" to work in a new way, testing Scripture and commentaries of the Church Fathers by reason rather than faith. Abelard is remembered for his bitter dispute with Bernard of Clairvaux over this point, and perhaps even more so for his amorous misadventure with Heloïse, but he was a brilliant teacher, flamboyant and arrogant, who attracted many students to the cathedral school at Paris. During the twelfth century, the cathedral school at Notre Dame had gathered a number of teaching masters, a large urban student population, and the support of the French monarchy. The school had a continent-wide reputation in the study of logic applied to theology and had developed the institutional framework of the cathedral school. These factors led to its establishment as a permanent center for learning. The development of the school at Notre Dame is an example of one pattern by which the university developed. The Paris model is one of organization by the scholars, or masters, who eventually received a charter from King Philip Augustus in 1200 and obtained recognition from Pope Innocent III in 1208 that gave the corporate body or university of masters certain rights of independence against the municipal authorities.

Another pattern of organization is exemplified by the school of law at Bologna, perhaps the earliest "university," which received formal recognition from Emperor Frederick Barbarossa in 1158. At Bologna, it was students who received the charter after they had organized into an association or university for economic protection against the town and eventually for power in choosing their instructors. As at Paris, however, it was a great teacher,

EUROPEAN UNIVERSITIES OF THE MEDIEVAL PERIOD

Founded before 1270

Bologna—1088

Cambridge—c. 1110/1209; St. Peter's College (the oldest at
      Cambridge) was founded in 1284 by Hugh Balsham,
      the bishop of Ely

Montpellier—1220

Naples—1224

Oxford—mid-twelfth century; Balliol College (the oldest at
      Oxford) is traditionally considered to date from 1263

Padua—1222

Palencia—1208

Paris—c. 1170

Salamanca—1218

Salerno—founded in eleventh century; chartered in 1224

Toulouse—1229

Founded after 1270

Angers—existed as an educational center as far back as 1080;
      chartered as a university with schools of law, medi-
      cine, and theology by King Charles V in 1364

Cahors—1322

Coimbra—1290

Florence—1321

Grenoble—1339

Heidelberg—1386

Orléans—1305

Perugia—established in 1200; chartered in 1307

Pisa—1343

Prague—1348 (Charles University)

Rome—1303

Valladolid—founded during the last quarter of the thirteenth
      century (prior to 1293)

Irnerius, who gave the school its initial reputation and impetus. Farther south at Salerno was an even older center of learning whose reputation in the study of medicine was equal to the reputations of Paris in theology and Bologna in law. Despite this reputation, the proto-university at Salerno remained only a center for medicine and never developed the institutional framework to capitalize on its expertise and reputation.

Salerno's early advantage was its location, which placed it in close contact with the Greek East. The great influx of new knowledge from the East served as the primary impetus for the rise of the new learning and of the university organizations that took advantage of this learning. Although much of this knowledge came to Europe from the Greek East by way of Italy, the most important works came chiefly from libraries in the Muslim world through the Arab scholars of Spain. Europe was awash in newly discovered works, chiefly those of Aristotle, with commentaries by Greek, Roman, Arabic, and Jewish scholars. Also included were works of Euclid, Ptolemy, Galen, and Hippocrates, with the new arithmetic expressed in Al-Khwarizmi's *Algebra*, which used Arab numerals (including the concept of zero) rather than clumsy Roman numerals. In addition, the *Corpus Juris Civilis* of Justinian helped lead the study of law.

During the thirteenth century, the university system expanded rapidly. In England, masters associations were formed at Oxford in 1214 and at Cambridge in the 1230's. At Montpellier in the south of France, a faculty of medicine assembled in 1220. Universities arose in France at Orléans and Toulouse that rivaled Paris in the study of law and the study of theology, respectively. For the universities

that arose after 1300, the archetypal universities of Paris and Bologna served as the organizing models. In general, the pattern of the student university (Bologna) was followed in southern Europe, and the masters university (Paris) prevailed in northern Europe, with the German universities strongly affected by both models.

Perhaps the greatest scholar of the period was Thomas Aquinas; his career reveals much about the new universities. Born near Naples in about 1224, he became a member of the Dominican Order in 1244 and was sent to Paris, where he studied under Albertus Magnus. Aquinas studied biblical exegesis and Peter Lombard's *Sentences*, and was given a teaching post in theology in 1257. He taught in Paris and Rome and began to write extensively, eventually producing the *Summa Theologica* as well as commentaries on all of Aristotle's works. In Aquinas' lifetime, the universities were transnational and attracted students by the fame of their teachers. Most were still connected with religious life and religious orders and emphasized a long program of study—usually four to eight years. Such programs led to a teaching apprenticeship, thus supplying much of the teaching labor force of a university, before one was licensed to enter the guild of masters. Upon entering this guild, a new master became entitled to the full privileges of his degree, which for practical purposes in theology—the highest of pursuits—meant the freedom to teach and write. Even in these early days, one of the disappointments expressed by faculty members was the preference of students for more lucrative and worldly degrees, such as law and medicine.

The apparatus that made the universities different from the cathedral schools and from earlier Greek and Roman education are familiar to the modern university—the power to grant degrees, a regulated curriculum, an organized faculty with a rector, the lecture, examinations, and commencements. It is this organizational achievement that constitutes the heart of the medieval invention of the university.   —*James Persoon*

ADDITIONAL READING:

Cobban, A. B. *The Medieval Universities: Their Development and Organization.* London: Methuen, 1975. Scholarly but readable account, with emphasis on developments at Salerno, Bologna, Paris, Oxford, and Cambridge.

Haskins, Charles Homer. *The Rise of Universities.* 2d ed. Ithaca, N.Y.: Cornell University Press, 1965. A short introduction for the general reader, covering the earliest universities, the medieval professor, and the medieval student.

Mundy, John H. *Europe in the High Middle Ages, 1150-1309.* London: Longman, 1973. A general history of the years in which the universities arose, placing that movement in larger political, economic, and social contexts.

Piltz, Anders. *The World of Medieval Learning.* London: Basil Blackwell, 1981. A survey for the general reader, with special attention to the life and academic career of Thomas Aquinas.

Rashdall, H. *The Universities of Europe in the Middle Ages.* 3 vols. 2d ed. Oxford: Oxford University Press, 1963. First published in 1895, this monumental three-volume work provides an excellent basis for further study of the medieval university.

SEE ALSO: 781, Alcuin Becomes Adviser to Charlemagne; 1025, Scholars at Chartres Revive Interest in Classical Learning; 1150, Moors Transmit Classical Philosophy and Medicine to Europe.

1120
ORDER OF THE KNIGHTS TEMPLAR IS FOUNDED

The Order of the Knights Templar is founded, enabling the Roman Catholic Church to gain political, military, and financial power.

DATE: c. 1120
LOCALE: Jerusalem
CATEGORIES: Organizations and institutions; Religion
KEY FIGURES:
Baldwin II (Baldwin du Bourg; died 1131), king of Jerusalem, 1118-1131
Bernard of Clairvaux (1090-1153), French saint and one of the most powerful men of his time, influential in establishing Knights Templar

Hugues des Payens (c. 1070-1136), French knight and cofounder, with Geoffroi de Saint-Omer, of Knights Templar
Philip IV, the Fair, (1268-1314), king of France responsible for destruction of Knights Templar

SUMMARY OF EVENT. During the Middle Ages, several orders of knighthood were founded while the Crusades against the Muslims were in progress. Among the first of twelve religious-military orders of knighthood were the Poor Knights of Christ and the Temple of Solomon, popularly known as the Knights Templars, founded around the year 1120. A religious-military order dedicated to the protection of the Holy Sepulchre in Jerusalem, since it was violently taken against the Turks during the First Crusade on July 15, 1099, the members conformed to both military and religious discipline. They were soldiers with the obligations and training of knighthood, but who also took the monastic vows of poverty, chastity, and obedience. The Knights Templars took their name from their headquarters located in the Temple of Solomon in Jerusalem. Described as "lions in war, lambs in the house, to the enemies of Christ implacable, but to Christians kind and gracious," the Knights built castles and hospitals in Palestine with ancillary branches in Europe.

The Knights Templar grew from a group of pious soldiers who gathered in Jerusalem during the second decade of the twelfth century when the crusaders controlled only a few strongholds in the Holy Land. An order that followed the rules of St. Augustine, in groups of eight or nine, they protected pilgrims from marauding Muslim bands on the roads between Jaffa, on the Palestine coast, and Jerusalem and other holy places. They also provided sustenance and medical treatment. The order was founded and led by a French nobleman, Hugues des Payens, who with nine or ten other knights, swore to offer protection to pilgrims. They were welcomed by and given quarters in Jerusalem in King Baldwin's palace which, it is said, stood upon the site of King Solomon's Temple. At the commencement of the Order, the Knights were laymen who promised to follow religious monastic rules. In 1127, Hugues de Payens traveling in Europe seeking funds, met Bernard, the abbot of Clairvaux (later St. Bernard), a spiritual leader with a large following. The idea of a military-religious order appealed to Bernard and at the Council of Troyes in 1128, the Poor Knights of the Temple were given official Church status, switching allegiance to Bernard's stricter Cistercian Order's regime of prayer, silence, plainness, simple diet, self-denial, and manual labor. The Knights were permitted to wear the white mantle of the Cistercians, to which Pope Eugene III had added the characteristic red cross. To overcome the discrepancy between the military purpose of the Knights Templar and the Church's idea of a peaceful man of God, sworn to nonviolence, St. Bernard argued that the Knights fought for Christ's purposes, protecting the Holy Land from unbelievers: "Not without cause does he bear the sword! He is the instrument of God for the punishment of the malefactors and for the defence of the just . . . he is accounted Christ's legal executioner against evildoers." Any land or property taken by the Knights became the property of the Church, and other Church orders tended to look down upon the Knights Templars and considered them inferior to the "true," monks who lived lives of peaceful contemplation within the walls of European abbeys. They were headed by a grand master, and each branch of the Order was headed by a commander who swore absolute obedience to the grand master.

Because of their defense of the Holy Land, the Knights Templars gained universal approval in Catholic Europe. Their reputation was constructed in part by the propagandistic writings of Bernard of Clairvaux. Immensely successful, they quickly increased their land and power, becoming influential in European political and religious circles. Because men of all classes were accepted into their Order, the feudal class came to identify with them and herein lay their primary strength. At their height, they numbered twenty thousand, and by the middle of the twelfth century, they owned estates and castles scattered throughout western Europe, the Mediterranean, and the Holy Land. While the Templar Knights proper had to be from the rank of knights, a lower bourgeoisie class rank of "sergeants," who were armed and wore brown, rather then white, were accepted. Other ranks of chaplain and servant were also decreed. They surrendered all their property, joining the Order for life, leaving only to join a stricter Order.

In Paris in 1147, just before the departure of the French king on the Second Crusade, 130 white-robed Templars offered homage to the king and pope. Thousands of estates in England, France, and Spain were given to the Templars, and millions throughout Europe contributed funds to the continuing cause of the Crusades. Templar houses and castles were the strongest and safest buildings. Their membership increased dramatically and their wealth and position grew, until they owned property throughout most of western Europe. At this point, they came to take on the role of international banker, oftentimes granting loans to European monarchs. They adopted absolute secrecy to cover all internal activities and because they were considered "defenders of the Church," they were free from tithes and taxes. With this diversification of roles, they became a vital element in the defense of the Holy Land, where they built numerous castles and garrisoned every town. While the Crusades went on in the East, men and materials were needed in the West and as long as the defense of the Holy Land was in question, political attacks on Templars were unsuccessful.

For more than one hundred years, the Templars maintained their power. Nevertheless, the fall of Jerusalem in 1187 led to the demise of the Order. After the Holy Land fell to the Muslims in 1291, the Templars transfigured themselves into an international mercenary force, available to any government that had the funds to pay them. With centers in London and Paris, they retained their international banking status, servicing nobles and commoners alike. Indeed, the king of France deposited the French royal treasury with them.

For at least forty years, rumors had circulated regarding the rites of initiation of the Templars. Because of the complete secrecy of all rituals, however, no proof was available. King Philip IV of France, known as Philip the Fair, was said to have manufactured accounts of these rumored sacrilegious and obscene rites, based on magical ritual, and sent them to Pope Clement V. On October 13, 1307, King Philip had the entire population of some two thousand members of the Knights Templar in France arrested. The king also confiscated all French property belonging to the Order. Accusing the Templars of heresy and immorality, Philip blamed them for the loss of the Holy Land. Although the reasons for Philip's actions are not entirely clear, many scholars believed that he coveted their financial resources. When Philip ascended the throne in 1285, the country was near bankruptcy but the Templars possessed land and money in great quantity.

Philip was not satisfied, however, with halting the activities of the Templars in France. In an effort to destroy the entire Order, Philip launched a propaganda campaign that painted the Templars as a rich, corrupt organization that used magic to accumulate power. In July, 1308, the pope approved an investigation of these charges, and Philip began an inquisition that coerced confessions under torture. Although a papal council voted against the abolition of the Templars in December, 1311, Philip ordered Jacques de Molay, the Templar Grand Master, and other high-ranking Templar officials burned at the stake in March, 1314. At this point, the Knights Templars were dissolved and their guilt remains a historical controversy.

—*M. Casey Diana*

ADDITIONAL READING:

Barber, Stephan. *The New Knighthood: A History of the Order of the Temple*. New York: Cambridge University Press, 1994. A well-known historian of the Knights Templar provides a fresh account of the Order.

_____. *The Trial of the Templars*. Cambridge, England: Cambridge University Press, 1978. Scholarly account of the latter years of the Templars with an emphasis on the politics surrounding the organization's demise.

Howarth, Stephan. *The Knights Templar*. New York: Atheneum, 1982. Covers in great detail the period from the First Crusade in 1095 to the collapse of the Knights Templar in 1308. Readable account that contains illustrations of significant sites and personages associated with the Order.

Partner, Peter. *The Murdered Magicians: The Templars and Their Myth*. New York: Oxford University Press, 1982. Although this book is directed more at the scholar of Masonic mysticism and can be challenging for the layperson, the introduction contains concise historical information on the Knights Templar.

Robinson, John. *Dungeon, Fire, and Sword*. New York: M. Evans, 1991. Provides a concise historical account of the Templars' religious-military mission in battling for control of the Holy Land. Contains illustrations and a comprehensive bibliography.

SEE ALSO: 1095, Pope Urban II Calls the First Crusade; 1098, Cistercian Monastic Order Is Founded; 1147-1149, The Second Crusade; 1291, Fall of Acre.

1125
CHARTER OF LORRIS

The Charter of Lorris serves as the model charter for more than eighty towns, defining the nature of urban liberties of townspeople in France.

DATE: 1125

LOCALE: France

CATEGORY: Laws, acts, and legal history

KEY FIGURES:

Louis VI, "the Fat" (1081-1137), king of France, 1108-1137

Louis VII (1120-1180), king of France, 1137-1180

SUMMARY OF EVENT. The Charter of Lorris was an early and significant charter guaranteeing urban liberties. It served as a model of urban privileges for French towns in the twelfth and thirteenth centuries. The granting of such urban charters represented a major transformation in medieval politics, society, and economy. Roman cities in the early Middle Ages had deteriorated into stagnant markets populated mostly by the administrative or military personnel of bishoprics or lay lords. Although markets never fully disappeared and local traders still plied their wares, towns no longer were the thriving centers of long-distance trade or handicraft production. Compared to cities of im-

perial Rome there were fewer governmental functions and cultural activities. The medieval population was overwhelmingly rural, and most peasants by the ninth century were serfs—they were not free and owed various forms of labor service and taxes to their lords. Serfs had to bake their bread in the lord's oven. Although legally not slaves, serfs had no access to public courts of law; they could not leave the estates and could not marry outside the estate without obtaining the lord's permission and paying a tax. Their dependency on their lords made them close to slaves.

Beginning in the tenth century, the medieval population began to grow and rural production of grain increased. The rise in population and food production, particularly in the eleventh and twelfth centuries, made possible the reemergence of urban life. Once again towns attracted long-distance traders in luxury commodities, such as spices and silk, and in sugar, salt, metals (iron, copper, tin), precious metals (gold and silver), furs, cloth, wine, foodstuffs (grain, salted fish), and so forth. Towns became centers of important manufacturing, especially in cloth. Merchants and craftsmen organized themselves into guilds and soon demanded privileges commensurate with their growing economic power. Towns sometimes staged violent revolts against their lay or ecclesiastical lords, or peacefully obtained charters securing a high degree of autonomy and, most important, freeing townspeople from many of the exactions owed by serfs.

In Mediterranean towns, as in Italy, the concept of citizen (*civis*) was retained, encompassing all the urban dwellers, whether aristocrats or commoners. Yet northern towns beyond the Alps, as in France and Germany, drew a distinction between those living in the central fortress (*bourg*) and the merchants and craftsmen living outside the bourg in a trading area called a port, *vicus*, or *Wik*. In the north, the term *burgher* was extended to mean townspeople, socially distinct from lay lords or knights, and personally free.

The town was an association (*universitas*)—a collective legal personality, where political power belonged to the town. Towns were theoretically autonomous in administrative, judicial, and fiscal matters; they were largely freed from monarchical government. This development was more fully realized in Italy, where towns became city-states. The principle of urban autonomy and independent councils with elected officers also spread to France, Flanders, and Germany. In France, the monarchy still retained administrative prerogatives. Monarchs and other great territorial princes found it to their economic benefit to support towns and to grant charters of liberties, because towns offered vast new sources of revenue through new taxes and payments for charters.

An important element in the development of urban liberties was the growing power of the church, which sought independence from lay control and lay investments of bishops. The church's policy of a *Pax Dei* (peace of God) sought to protect the clergy and others from war. This implied exemption from the policing power of the monarchy, and the idea of church privileges was applied to towns.

Towns, however, were not democracies. Government was generally in the hands of wealthy merchants, who formed the urban patriciate and dominated local politics through the merchant guild. Craft guilds were often represented in government but rarely exercised decisive government control, except through periodic rebellions and force. Yet the towns were also the vehicles of an economic revolution, bringing in new wealth in commerce and manufacture and offering new economic techniques and a new economic system in credit, banking and money exchange, investments and capital.

Towns became centers of intellectual life in the cathedral schools and universities. Their economies made possible the building of the great Gothic cathedrals. Towns attracted peasants seeking to escape serfdom. Peasants who could establish that they had lived a year and a day in a town could obtained their freedom. The rural nobility encouraged peasants to trade in towns in return for new taxes. Some rural villages were given "charters" to help promote the growth of markets. The nobility required money in order to obtain the goods traded and manufactured in towns. Peasant labor services and taxes in kind were commuted to money payments. Thus the rise of towns was instrumental in slowly changing and even ending serfdom in parts of western Europe.

The charter of Lorris was granted to a small town in north-central France, not far from Orléans. The original royal charter was given by King Louis VI, often called the "Father of Communes," but was later lost. The earliest extant document is a redaction written in 1155 and granted to the town and parish of Lorris by King Louis VII. Unlike Italian towns, Lorris retained an important presence of royal power in administrative and judicial matters in the office of provost. According the article 35, all provosts and sergeants were required to uphold the liberties or customs of the charter.

The charter's customs clearly differentiated townspeople from the peasantry. Townspeople were exempted from taxes common to peasants, such as the tallage (or *taille*—a tax levied upon people or land) described in article 9 and the inheritance tax (*mainmorte*). Through the provision in article 24, townspeople were freed from the peasant tax to bake bread in the lord's oven. Marriage fees were not imposed. The charter granted the right to sell one's home and to leave the town, unless one had committed a crime (article 17). Townspeople were exempt from labor service (*corvée*) typical of peasant life, except to cart the king's wine to Orléans twice a year (article 15). In article 18, the charter enshrined the concept that to live a year and a day within the town secured one's freedom.

The charter also provided important judicial privileges. These included autonomy from the abbot for those who had lands in the domain of the monastery of Saint Benedict. Townspeople had the right to be heard before the king's court within the town. They were not under the judicial authority of any provosts other than the royal provost in Lorris. These provisions effectively provided judicial freedom from neighboring powerful lay or ecclesiastical lords. The charter also preserved privileges in judicial procedures (the right to bail and the necessity of witnesses to crimes) and security over property. Judicial duels were regulated and various fines and provost fees were reduced.

Certain limited seignorial rights were preserved, however. A quitrent (*cens*), or fixed rent of six derniers for each house or acre of land in the parish, was levied; the king and his queen had the right to have provisions for a fortnight. Military duty could be imposed but townspeople were not required to go beyond one day's march. Taxes in rye for the provision of the sergeants were levied but restricted, and the king had the right to sell from the royal vineyards with public notice. According to article 2, however, no tax was imposed on food for one's own consumption or grain grown by one's own labor.

To encourage commerce, article 6 of the charter enacted the right of free movement of traders; commercial taxes were regulated; and no tolls were taken on the roads to Étampes, Orléans, or to Milly.

The charter became the standard custom of privileges for more than eighty towns, mostly small ones, located in the royal domain. Lorris was typical of French urban privileges in that it granted personal liberty, free movement, control over one's property, and limited autonomy. In the thirteenth century, royal power increased over many French towns, and the French bourgeoisie became politically and economically tied to the monarchy. This development would have extremely important consequences for the future political history of France.

—Lawrence N. Langer

ADDITIONAL READING:

Beatty, J., and O. Johnson. *Heritage of Western Civilization.* 8th ed. 2 vols. Englewood Cliffs, N.J.: Prentice Hall, 1995. Volume 2 contains a translation of the Charter of Lorris on pages 296-298.

Hilton, R. H. *English and French Towns in Feudal*

Society. New York: Cambridge University Press, 1992. A major comparative study of feudal urban life.

Petit-Dutailles, Charles. *The French Communes in the Middle Ages*. Translated by Joan Vickes. Amsterdam: North-Holland, 1978. Written in 1947, this work is a classic study of French towns.

Pirenne, Henri. *Medieval Cities*. Princeton, N.J.: Princeton University Press, 1925. The Pirenne thesis remains an important analysis of the rise of towns.

Reynolds, Susan. *Kingdoms and Communities in Western Europe, 900-1300*. Oxford: Clarendon Press, 1984. An examination on the nature of urban and rural communities in the Middle Ages.

SEE ALSO: 1100-1300, Emergence of European Universities; 1150-1200, Development of Gothic Architecture; 1150-1200, Rise of the Hansa; 1175, Common Law Tradition Emerges in England; 1200, Fairs of Champagne.

1127-1130
KINGDOM OF SICILY IS CREATED

The Kingdom of Sicily is created, establishing a realm that dominates the central Mediterranean.

DATE: 1127-1130
LOCALE: Sicily and southern Italy
CATEGORY: Government and politics
KEY FIGURES:

Robert Guiscard (Robert de Hauteville; c. 1015-1085), duke of Apulia, Calabria, and Sicily
Roger, the Great Count (1031-1101), conqueror of Sicily
Roger II (1095-1154), count of Sicily, 1105-1130, and later king of Sicily, 1130-1154

SUMMARY OF EVENT. In the early eleventh century, an increasing number of landless Norman knights found service as mercenaries in the confused struggles in southern Italy and on Sicily. This region was at the crossroads of three cultures—Byzantine, Latin, and Arabic. Apulia and Calabria remained under the power of the Byzantine Empire. The central provinces were governed by Lombard lords. Across the narrow straits of Messina the island of Sicily was under Muslim control.

Taking service with Lombard princes, the pope, or the Byzantines as circumstances prescribed, the Normans soon made a name for themselves in southern Italy, in 1030 acquiring their first territorial possession. As the family property proved unable to keep pace with the family fertility, increasing numbers of Norman warriors sought their fortunes in southern Italy, including nine of the twelve sons of Tancred d'Hauteville. By the end of 1042, William d'Hauteville was proclaimed count of Apulia and Calabria.

In 1046, the sixth son of old Tancred, Robert, called Guiscard (the foxy or the cunning), arrived and in 1057 effectively succeeding his brothers in Apulia and Calabria. At the synod of Melfi in 1059, Pope Nicholas II formally invested Robert Guiscard with Apulia, Calabria, and Sicily, even though at that time Robert had never set foot on the island and the only claim of the pope to sovereignty was the fictitious *Donation of Constantine*.

Before acting to enforce his claims to Sicily, Robert strengthened his position on the mainland, restricting the Byzantines to Bari in Apulia and eliminating them from Calabria. On Sicily, three Muslim emirs engaged in fratricidal conflict, while a large part of the population remained Christian, open to the blandishments of the Normans. A Byzantine attack on Apulia called Robert away from Sicily, so it was his youngest brother Roger who became the major force in the island's conquest.

In May, 1061, the Normans captured Messina, giving them an opening to the entire island. In alliance with Emir Ibn at-Timnah of Palermo, they soundly defeated Emir Ibn al-Hawas at Enna. Despite these early successes, limited resources and intermittent internecine quarrels meant that the Norman conquest would not be quick. The Norman victory at Misilmeri in 1068 broke the back of Saracen. Count Roger also built up his fleet, which appeared before Palermo. After a five-month siege, the city surrendered in 1071. Meanwhile, Duke Robert brought Byzantine power in southern Italy to an end with the capitulation of Bari, also in 1071. During the next fifteen years, he successfully fended off rebellions among his vassals, conflicts with other south Italian powers, and the enmity of Pope Gregory VII, expanding his holdings by the conquest of Amalfi and Salerno, and becoming the indispensable ally of the pope in his struggle with Emperor Henry IV. Duke Robert also turned his energies against his earliest opponents, the Byzantines, dying in 1085 on Cephalonia. He was succeeded by his son Roger Borsa, who was immediately challenged by a half brother, Bohemond.

Although Robert Guiscard remained the titular overlord of Sicily, he was busy with the defense and enlargement of his possessions on the mainland, and left control to his brother Roger, called "the Great Count." After the capitulation of Palermo, Roger began to incorporate elements of the native Muslim population into his administration and army. In 1075, he concluded a treaty of friendship with the Zirid sultan at Mahdia, thus depriving the Sicilian Muslims of any hope of aid from Africa. In 1085, Syracuse was captured, but it was not until 1091 that Noto, the last Muslim stronghold, surrendered.

Conquest was quickly followed by conciliation, creating a new, multilingual and multireligious society. Although Muslims and Jews had to pay a special tax, Latins, Greeks, Jews, and Saracens enjoyed the protection of their own laws. The Muslims were granted extensive religious toleration, continued possession of their lands, and inclusion in many military and administrative positions. The Greek Christians had to swallow the bitter pill of Roman primacy, but not only kept their own language and liturgy, but gained the rebuilding of their churches and the foundation of fourteen Basilian monasteries. The Latins obtained the Church hierarchy and the choicest fiefs. Court ceremonies were more Byzantine than feudal. Although allied with the papacy, Roger held firm control of the Sicilian Church, in 1098 receiving from Pope Urban II for himself and his successors the authority of a papal legate. By the time Count Roger died in 1101, he had established one of the most remarkable states of medieval Europe, a hybrid of three cultures at the focal point of the Mediterranean world.

The Great Count was succeeded by his son, Roger II, under the regency of his widow, Adelaide of Savona. Relying in large part on her Greek and Arab subjects, Adelaide weathered many difficulties, establishing her court at Palermo. By 1113, Roger II was ready to take up the government. The island realm was prosperous and well protected by the strong fleet founded by the Great Count. On the mainland, Roger Borsa and his son William showed none of the abilities of Robert Guiscard. In 1125, the childless Duke William recognized Count Roger II as his heir, and died two years later at the age of thirty. Roger rushed to Salerno, gained possession there, and, after ineffective resistance by the pope and disgruntled barons, in 1228 was invested by Honorius II as Duke of Apulia, Calabria, and Sicily. He then held a grand court at Melfi, where the feudal nobility of Apulia and Calabria were required to swear loyalty to himself and his sons, to forswear private warfare, and to surrender criminals to the ducal courts. Thus the foundations were laid for the extension to the mainland of the strong kingly power which his father has established on Sicily. Somewhat later in that same year the only remaining independent Norman lord in southern Italy, Robert of Capua, submitted to Roger's suzerainty. Taking advantage of a disputed papal election, Roger obtained a bull raising him to the royal dignity. After obtaining the agreement of his vassals at assemblies held at Salerno and Palermo, Roger was crowned the first king of Sicily in Palermo cathedral on Christmas Day, 1130.

King Roger ruled for another twenty-three years, continuing to strengthen his already impressive realm. He was succeeded in 1154 by William the Bad, and he in turn by his son, William the Good, who died in 1198. This period from the Great Count to William II was a golden age in

Sicilian history, when good government provided peace, some degree of protection against the greed and violence of feudal lords, and more toleration than anywhere else in the contemporary Mediterranean world.

With William II's death in 1198, the throne passed to the Hohenstauffen dynasty, which involved Sicily in the endless struggles between papacy and empire. This connection was especially strong under Emperor Frederick II (1212-1250), with the southern realm sharing in the glories and the downfall of this enigmatic sovereign, who died in battle against the forces allied with the papacy. Not long thereafter, Sicily passed under the control of Frederick's illegitimate son, Manfred. In his capacity as feudal suzerain, Pope Urban IV offered the crown to Charles of Anjou, brother of King Louis IX of France, who conquered Sicily in 1266. The harshness of Angevin rule encouraged dissatisfaction, and the island of Sicily rose in a rebellion known as the Sicilian Vespers in 1282. The crown of Sicily was offered to Peter III of Aragon, husband of Manfred's daughter Constance. The Angevins were never able to regain control, so there were two claimants to the Sicilian crown, on the island and on the mainland. In 1504, Ferdinand of Aragon conquered the mainland, after which the two Sicilies remained part of the Spanish monarchy until the extinction of the Spanish Habsburgs. In 1735, both Sicilies were joined under a Bourbon line which, with the exception of the Napoleonic period at Naples, ruled until 1860, when this monarchy, officially called the kingdom of the Two Sicilies only in the nineteenth century, was united to the new Italian national state.

—William C. Schrader

ADDITIONAL READING:

Brown, R. Allen. *The Normans*. 2d ed. Woodbridge, England: Boydell & Brewer, 1995. Emphasizes the capacity of the Normans for leadership and organization.

Haskins, Charles Homer. *The Normans in European History*. Reprint. New York: W. W. Norton, 1966. Originally published in 1915, this seminal work places the Sicilian events in a broader European context.

Kreutz, Barbara M. *Before the Normans: Southern Italy in the Ninth and Tenth Centuries*. Philadelphia: University of Pennsylvania Press, 1991. An account of the background into which the Normans came.

Mack Smith, Denis. *A History of Sicily*. Vol. 1: *Medieval Sicily*. New York: Dorset, 1968. Readable and concise account of the medieval period in Sicily, but with minor factual errors.

Norwich, John Julius. *The Other Conquest*. New York: Harper & Row, 1967. A detailed and readable work on the founding of the Norman realm.

Runciman, Steven. *The Sicilian Vespers*. Cambridge, England: Cambridge University Press, 1958. Primarily dealing with the breakup of the Sicilian kingdom, this work contains a fine summary of the earlier periods.

SEE ALSO: 415-413 B.C., Athenian Invasion of Sicily; 568-571, Lombard Conquest of Italy; 896, Magyar Invasions of Italy, Saxony, and Bavaria; 1147-1149, The Second Crusade; 1290-1306, Jews Are Expelled from England, France, and Southern Italy.

1147-1149
THE SECOND CRUSADE

The Second Crusade is launched by Pope Eugenius III, providing a model for the preaching of later expeditions and expanding the defintion of crusade to include holy wars against any enemy of the Church.

DATE: 1147-1149

LOCALE: Outremer (Jerusalem), Portugal, and lands east of the Elbe River

CATEGORIES: Religion; Wars, uprisings, and civil unrest

KEY FIGURES:

Bernard of Clairvaux (1090-1153), abbot of Clairvaux, 1115-1153

Conrad III (c. 1093-1152), king of Germany, 1138-1152

Eleanor of Aquitaine (c. 1122-1204), queen consort of Louis VII of France, 1137-1152, and Henry II of England, 1152-1204

Eugenius III (Bernardo Paganelli; died 1153), Roman Catholic pope, 1145-1153

Louis VII (1120-1180), king of France, 1137-1180

Manuel I Comnenus (c. 1122-1180), Byzantine emperor, 1143-1180

Raymond of Antioch (1099-1149), prince of Antioch, 1136-1149, and uncle of Eleanor of Aquitaine

Roger II (1095-1154), Norman king of Sicily, 1130-1154

SUMMARY OF EVENT. While crusades were preached in Europe after the First Crusade of 1096 and while Europeans continued to send reinforcements to the Latin settlements of the East (commonly known as Outremer), it was not until 1145 that a pope called for a large-scale crusade. The call was precipitated by the December 24, 1144, capture of Edessa by Prince Imad al-Din Zangi of the Seljuk Empire. Edessa had been in Christian hands since the First Crusade and its fall sent shock waves through Europe.

As a result, in 1145, Pope Eugenius III called for a new crusade to the East in his encyclical *Quantum Praedecessores*. This encyclical became the model for the formulation of later papal calls to crusade, including a summary of the threat, a call to take the cross, and a list of privileges granted to the crusaders.

Louis VII of France was the first to heed the call. Apparently Louis had long planned a pilgrimage to Jerusalem. He announced his plan to take up the cross in December, 1145, to an assembly of nobles gathered for the Christmas Court at Bourges; however, the response to Louis' call for a crusade was lukewarm.

It was not until Pope Eugenius appointed Bernard of Clairvaux to preach the crusade that Louis received widespread support. Indeed, contemporary chroniclers report that Bernard's preaching so moved the crowd at Vézelay on March 31, 1146, that Bernard ran out of the cloth crosses he had brought with him to give to those pledging themselves to the crusade.

Although crusade fever gripped France, the Germans were less enthusiastic. In spite of continued urging from the pope, Conrad III of Germany was reluctant to take up the cross himself or to commit his men to the crusade. It was not until Bernard himself traveled to Germany that Conrad acquiesced.

Pope Eugenius III appointed the Cistercian abbot Bernard of Clairvaux to preach in France and Germany to gain support for the Second Crusade. (Archive Photos)

During the Second Crusade, the Christian community at Antioch supported Louis VII's disastrous decision to attack Damascus; shown here is the facade of the oldest Christian church in Antioch. (Robin W. Diel)

During the two years of planning, the scale of the Second Crusade expanded to include three distinct arenas: Outremer; the Wendish lands beyond the Elbe River; and the Iberian Peninsula. Shortly before the departure of Conrad's German forces for Outremer, a group of Saxons asked to be allowed to crusade against the pagan Wends who lived beyond the Elbe River. The pope granted them permission, and so for the first time, the definition of crusade grew to include war against pagans or enemies of the Church.

The pope also included a call for the reconquest of the Iberian Peninsula, and crusaders who fought in this arena were accorded the same indulgences that crusaders headed for the East enjoyed. Consequently, when the Anglo-Flemish forces landed in Portugal on their way east in June of 1147, they were persuaded to participate in the siege of Lisbon. The subsequent crusader victory was the only real success of the entire Second Crusade.

The main thrust of the Second Crusade was the relief of Outremer. Conrad's forces left Germany in May, 1147, and Louis followed in June. They elected to travel overland, through the Byzantine Empire ruled by Manuel I Comnenus.

Although both armies had been offered sea passage to Outremer by Roger of Sicily, neither Conrad nor Louis fully trusted him. Conrad was on especially bad terms with Roger and preferred to negotiate with Manuel for safe conduct through the Byzantine Empire. Although the French were on better terms with Roger, they, too, elected the overland route. Significantly, Roger complicated the situation for the European crusaders by engaging in a war with the Byzantine Empire.

Initially, the Germans had little problem crossing Byzantine territory. Their refusal to bypass Constantinople, however, as well as crusader plundering led to problems. After leaving Nicaea, the German army not only ran out of supplies, it was ambushed by Turkish forces and routed. The survivors, including Conrad, fled to Nicaea to await aid from Louis.

Louis' departure from France was in grand style. Like the Germans, he had many noncombatant pilgrims with him. In addition, Eleanor of Aquitaine and her court traveled with Louis' forces. There are reports that Eleanor and her ladies frequently dressed like a troop of Amazons and rode alongside the troops headed to Outremer.

Louis was on less friendly terms with Manuel than Conrad and French troops had to pass through territory already plundered by the crusaders from Germany. Consequently, the French had little support from the Byzantines. Indeed, just as the French neared Constantinople, they received word that Manuel had been negotiating with the Turks.

When the French army reached Nicaea, they met with the remains of Conrad's army and continued eastward. Provisions grew low and by the time they reached Antalya, they were in serious trouble, both from starvation and from Turkish harassment. Although Manuel promised ships to take the crusaders on to Antioch, there were too few ships to transport all of Louis' forces, and so many crusaders were stranded in Byzantine territory to find their own way home or to Antioch.

Louis finally arrived in Antioch on March 19, 1148, where his troops remained as guests of Eleanor's uncle, Raymond of Antioch. In June, Louis, Conrad, and many Christians from the Latin settlements met and decided to attack Damascus. Contemporary writers alleged that Eleanor's impropriety with her uncle spurred Louis on to rashly starting out for Damascus; whatever the case, the combined forces meet with disaster when they attacked Damascus, thus ending the Second Crusade which had begun so grandly.

Many scholars have speculated on the causes leading to the failure of the Second Crusade. Some point to the large number of noncombatants who certainly drained critical resources. Others believe that the failure of the European forces to act in unity led to defeat; the strength of the European force in the East was diluted by the war against the Wends in Germany and against the Islamic holdings in the Iberian Peninsula. Still others suggest that the war between Roger of Sicily and Manuel led to fatal political maneuvering which cost the European forces important support in the East. Finally, some believe that Eleanor's alleged dalliance with her uncle, Raymond of Antioch, led to the disastrous decision to attack Damascus.

In all likelihood, all of these reasons contributed to the spectacular failure of the European forces in Outremer. The failure of the Second Crusade led to bitter recriminations among Europeans who variously blamed God's wrath with the Christian leadership or Byzantine betrayal for the failure. In any event, the morale of the Europeans in regard to Outremer was at an all-time low. No large-scale eastern crusade was planned for nearly forty years. Further, although the Second Crusade is remembered as the largest, and perhaps most dramatic, of any medieval crusade, Europeans met success only in the capture of Lisbon and the expansion of German territory into the land east of the Elbe. In the East, the Second Crusade only served to further inspire Muslim unity, ultimately leading to the collapse of Outremer in the following century.

—Diane Andrews Henningfeld

ADDITIONAL READING:

Hallam, Elizabeth, ed. "The Second Crusade." In *Chronicles of the Crusades*. New York: Weidenfeld & Nicolson, 1989. A collection of translated letters and documents from contemporary sources, this chapter provides the student with both well-written introductory material and primary sources.

Kelly, Amy. *Eleanor of Aquitaine and the Four Kings.* Cambridge, Mass.: Harvard University Press, 1950. A highly readable account of Eleanor of Aquitaine's participation in the Second Crusade.

Lloyd, Simon. "The Crusading Movement, 1096-1274." In *The Oxford Illustrated History of the Crusades*, edited by Jonathan Riley-Smith. New York: Oxford University Press, 1995. Simon places the Second Crusade within the context of the medieval crusading movement, arguing that "the crusading movement would emerge to become one of the most important components, and defining characteristics, of late medieval western culture."

Maalouf, Amin. *The Crusades Through Arab Eyes.* Translated by Jon Rothschild. New York: Schocken Books, 1984. Drawn from Arab chroniclers of the wars, this book provides an Arab version of the Crusades from 1096 to 1291.

Riley-Smith, Jonathan. *The Crusades: A Short History.* New Haven, Conn.: Yale University Press, 1987. This book traces the growth and decline of the crusading movement from 1096 through 1798 and includes discussions of the Crusades in Europe as well as in the East.

Runciman, Steven. *A History of the Crusades.* Vol. 2: *The Kingdom of Jerusalem and the Frankish East, 1100-1187.* Cambridge, England: Cambridge University Press,

1962. Runciman's series has long been considered the standard reference to the Crusades; however, he focuses almost exclusively on crusades to the East.

SEE ALSO: 1095, Pope Urban II Calls the First Crusade; 1127-1130, Kingdom of Sicily Is Created; 1189-1192, The Third Crusade; 1204, Knights of the Fourth Crusade Capture Constantinople; 1209-1229, The Albigensian Crusade; 1212, The Children's Crusade; 1217-1221, The Fifth Crusade; 1227-1230, Frederick II Leads the Sixth Crusade; 1248-1254, Failure of the Seventh Crusade.

1150
MOORS TRANSMIT CLASSICAL PHILOSOPHY AND MEDICINE TO EUROPE

The Moors transmit classical philosophy and medicine to Europe from their stronghold in Spain, sharing Muslim scholarship and classical philosophies with the Latin West and profoundly influencing medieval European intellectual development.

DATE: c. 1150
LOCALE: Spain
CATEGORIES: Communications; Cultural and intellectual history; Education; Health and medicine
KEY FIGURES:
Adelard of Bath (c. early twelfth century), English interpreter of Arabic works and scholastic philosopher
Saint Thomas Aquinas (Tommaso d'Aquino; c. 1224-1274, Italian theologian and leading scholastic philosopher
Avempace (Ibn Bajjah; 1095-1138), earliest known Moorish representative of Aristotelian-Neoplatonic tradition
Averroës (Ibn Rushd; 1126-1198) best-known Moorish philosopher and Aristotelian commentator
Avicenna (Abu ʿAli al-Husain ibn ʿAbdallah ibn Sina; 980-1037), Persian physician and most famous philosopher-scientist of Islam
Ibn Tufayl (1109-1185), Moorish philosopher and physician

SUMMARY OF EVENT. Contact between the Umayyad caliphs of Damascus (661-750) and Hellenic centers such as Antioch, Alexandria, and Edessa likely resulted in the first translations of Greek scientific and philosophical documents into Arabic. The succeeding Abbasid sultans moved the capital to Baghdad and undertook a systematic attempt to obtain and translate the major Greek philosophical works. Their dissemination throughout the Islamic world had a profound impact on Muslim theolo-

gians, philosophers, medical doctors, and scientists. In Moorish Spain, classical learning was interpreted and expanded upon by Muslim scholars before the blended Greco-Muslim philosophy and science were dispersed throughout Europe.

Interest in classical philosophy and medicine was initiated in Spain under its fifth Umayyad ruler, ʿAbd Al-Rahmān III (ruled 912-961). Early Andalusian scholarship benefited from the rivalry existing between its flourishing court and the waning Abbasid court of Baghdad in terms of the collecting of fine books and patronizing of Muslim intellectuals. Despite lengthy periods during which philosophy was viewed with disfavor by the successive Moorish courts, a number of Andalusian scholars visited the East and returned with books and ideas, thus preserving a level of intellectual unity throughout the Muslim world.

The first significant writer in Spain on philosophical issues, Avempace drew acclaim and disciples by his work with Aristotelian and Neoplatonic ideas. His work and that of Ibn Tufayl stimulated on a vast scale the interest of Andalusian scholars in classical learning. This interest came to fruition in the person of Averroës, acknowledged as the greatest Muslim commentator on Aristotle's works. Following his introduction to Caliph Abu Yaʿqub Yusuf (ruled 1163-1184) by Ibn Tufayl, Averroës was appointed as *qadi* (judge) of Seville and instructed to comment on the works of Aristotle, which the caliph found difficult to understand. During his remarkable career, he was promoted to the position of chief *qadi* at Córdoba and royal physician to the Córdoban court. Among his works, which attempted to harmonize philosophy and theological dogma, is his great philosophical rebuttal of the eastern Muslim philosopher al-Ghazali, *Tahafut at-Tahafut* (Incoherence of the Incoherence). His work was to become highly regarded throughout the West, as evidenced by his inclusion among the masters of Hellenic thought in Raphael's masterpiece *School of Athens*.

Averroës' championing of genuine Aristotelianism dichotomized philosophical pursuits in the western Muslim world from those in the East, which primarily endorsed the quasi-mystical illumination (*ishraq*) philosophy supported by Avicenna. Yet Avicenna advanced Western knowledge in his own right, primarily by the dissemination of his medical treatises into Europe via Andalusia.

During the eighth century, a time when medicine in the Latin West was based largely on superstition, Muslim medicine was based on scientific method as inherited from classical works such as those by Hippocrates and Galen. Muslim medical literature was later translated into Latin and used in some European universities as late as the seventeenth century. A number of scholars agree that Muslim philosophers did little to expand most branches of Greek medical knowledge, serving instead as the preservators of Greek medical heritage. Noted exceptions are the work of Ibn al-Jazzar (died 984) concerning the management and care of children and that of ʿArib bin Saʾid of Córdoba on gynecology, embryology, and pediatrics. Al-Razi (c. 865-925) wrote a discourse describing the causes and treatment of smallpox. Al-Zahrawi (c. 940-1013) compiled a medical encyclopedia devoted, among other things, to midwifery, implying the existence of a thriving profession of trained nurses and midwives in Moorish Spain.

Muslim contributions to the fields of pharmacology and medical botany, however, greatly surpassed the work of the classicists. Advancing well beyond Dioscorides' *Materia medica*, Muslims described identifications, modes of administration, and therapeutic qualities of more than one hundred plants known throughout the Muslim world. In addition, the increasing incidence of poisonings prompted an attempt by court physicians to expand their knowledge of toxicology. Galen's recipe for the theriac, the universal antidote, was translated and significantly modified before its introduction to the West in the thirteenth century.

While the Islamic world was translating and expanding classical works with great fervor, medieval Europe was for the most part ignorant of classical philosophy. Other than three dialogues of Plato, Aristotle's *Logic*, and several mistranslated versions of Aristotle, examples of Greek works were unavailable to scholars. Limited contact between the Latin West and the Byzantine Empire, which preserved Greek manuscripts but little understood them, and the dominant trend in medieval Europe to emphasize Christian theology over philosophy contributed to a general neglect of Greek knowledge north of Muslim Spain.

At the turn of the eleventh century, however, Greco-Muslim philosophy began its migration throughout the Latin West. Christian conquest of Muslim lands increased the level of interaction between European conquerors, merchants, pilgrims, and scholars and Muslim tributaries, spawning an effort to translate Arabic works into Latin in order to understand the past successes of Islam. Spain served as the major cultural and intellectual bridge between East and West and as the leading center for European scholars who wished to learn Arabic and engage in translation.

The first college of translators was established in Toledo by Don Raimundo, archbishop of that city from 1126 to 1151. Toledo was a natural center of translation and intellectual transmission because of the amicable coexistence there of Christians and Muslims and the existence of a large Jewish population, which was at home in

both worlds and fluent in both Arabic and in Latin or Romance. A number of Toledo's Jews, including Maimonides, were respected philosophers in their own right. Although many of Toledo's Christian translators used Jewish or Muslim intermediaries to translate into the vernacular before subsequent translation into Latin, others, such as Gerard of Cremona, learned Arabic in order to read the works and later render them directly into Latin. Gerard's translations eventually included virtually the entire field of science at that time.

Work in various disciplines, undertaken in Toledo under Church patronage by such scholars as Adelard of Bath and Peter the Venerable (c. 1091-1156), abbot of Cluny, revived classicism and increased acceptance of hitherto "heretical" disciplines in Western thought. As evidenced in the writings of Saint Thomas Aquinas, Dante (1265-1321), and Roger Bacon (c. 1220-1292), the religion of Islam continued to be regarded as anathema in the Christian West, although Muslim learning was held in high esteem. The development of Christian Scholasticism is indebted in large part to the philosophical works of Ibn Tufayl and Averroës.

As Toledo's eminence as a translation center waned toward the end of the thirteenth century, Christian elites

The Jewish philosopher Maimonides was part of the flourishing scholarly community of Toledo in Spain, known during the twelfth century as a center for the translation of Muslim and Classical learning. (The New York Academy of Medicine)

such as Alfonso X, ruler of Castile from 1252 to 1284, established new centers. In addition to translation, the Christian West made a concerted effort to obtain books, build libraries, and increase the number of Muslim and Jewish court scholars capable of elucidating classical learning. Throughout the Christian Reconquest, scholars of various religions and cultures maintained close collaboration. Ideas were transmitted with great speed, enabling a new work to make the journey from the Muslim East to Córdoba and on into Christian Europe in less than two years.

Classical and Greco-Muslim ideas, new to Christian Europe and in many cases contradictory to the teachings of the Church, were hotly debated. It was not until 1251 that Aristotle was recognized as an acceptable subject for study in the University of Paris. Yet the process of debate and consequent intense study of the works inherited from Muslim philosophers slowly released medieval Europe from narrow modes of thought and encouraged appreciation of classical ideas. Such appreciation ultimately resulted in the European Renaissance, built upon the foundation of classical achievements and a desire to emulate the all-embracing approach of classical thought.

—*Katherine S. Mansour*

ADDITIONAL READING:

Chejne, Anwar G. *Muslim Spain: Its History and Culture.* St. Paul: University of Minnesota Press, 1974. Written as a text for graduate students, this work provides a well-written overview of the history, culture, and intellectual life of al-Andalus.

_____. "The Role of al-Andalus in the Movement of Ideas Between Islam and the West." In *Islam and the Medieval West*, edited by Khalil I. Semaan. Albany: State University of New York Press, 1980. A defense of Muslim contributions to European culture and discussion of not easily documented contributions from Arabic literary genres.

Deitrich, Albert. "Islamic Sciences and the Medieval West: Pharmacology." In *Islam and the Medieval West*, edited by Khalil I. Semaan. Albany: State University of New York Press, 1980. A detailed and well-documented discussion of the expansion of Greek knowledge of pharmacology by medieval Muslims.

Fletcher, Richard A. *Moorish Spain.* New York: Henry Holt, 1992. This work incorporates current scholarship on al-Andalus and offers a concise treatment of the Moors.

Reilly, Bernard F. *The Contest of Christian and Muslim Spain: 1031-1157.* Cambridge, Mass.: Blackwell, 1992. Enlightening use of recently published primary sources to provide insight into the political and cultural changes in Iberia during this critical period.

SEE ALSO: 781, Alcuin Becomes Adviser to Charlemagne; 950, Flourishing of the Court of Córdoba; 1010-1015, Avicenna Writes His *Canon of Medicine*; 1025, Scholars at Chartres Revive Interest in Classical Learning; 1100-1300, Emergence of European Universities; 1350-1400, Petrarch and Boccaccio Recover Classical Texts.

1150
VENETIAN MERCHANTS DOMINATE TRADE WITH THE EAST

Venetian merchants dominate trade with the East, gaining commercial advantages as a result of the weakening and ultimate collapse of the Byzantine Empire.

DATE: 1150
LOCALE: Venice, Italy, and the Aegean Sea
CATEGORIES: Economics; Transportation
KEY FIGURES:
Alexius I Comnenus (1048-1118), Byzantine emperor, 1081-1118
Godfrey de Bouillon (c. 1060-1100), became leader of the First Crusade in 1099 and the ruler of Jerusalem under the title, Defender of the Holy Sepulchre
John II Comnenus (1088-1143), Byzantine emperor, 1118-1143
Manuel I Comnenus (c. 1122-1180), Byzantine emperor, 1143-1180
Pietro II Orseolo (991-1009), doge of Venice
Robert Guiscard (Robert de Hauteville; c. 1015-1085), Norman noble who conquered southern Italy and became duke of Apulia and Calabria
Urban II (Odo of Ladery; c. 1035-1099), Roman Catholic pope, 1088-1099

SUMMARY OF EVENT. Venice, a city founded on a group of small islands in a lagoon at the northern end of the Adriatic, eventually became known as the "Queen of the Adriatic" as a result of its commercial and military control of this important body of water. From its earliest beginnings, Venice seemed destined to become an important maritime power. Geographically, Venice was located on the edge of both the Byzantine and Holy Roman Empires and became the gateway for trade for both empires.

Faced with very limited natural resources, the early Venetians earned their living fishing and participating in the fish and salt trade with the people on the Italian mainland. On rare occasions, Greek or Syrian merchants traveling to or from the nearby Byzantine cities of Ravenna and Aquilia might visit Venice bringing with them trade goods from the East. When the Lombards, a Germanic tribe, took these cities in the eighth century, they quickly declined in importance. For a very brief time the city of Comacchio rose to become the economic focus for the region before the Venetians took the city in 886.

While being on the edge of the two greatest empires of the time had its advantages for Venice, it also had its perils. Pietro II Orseolo (doge, 991-1009) succeeded in balancing the Venetian interests with those of the Byzantine and Holy Roman Emperors without having Venice become subject to either power. The Venetians signed favorable trade treaties with both empires and was even able to sign commercial treaties with the Islamic states of north Africa. Building on their previous trade dominance in fish and salt with the mainland, the Venetians now became suppliers of incense, silks, spices, and other trade goods of the East.

Initially, Venetian trade with the Levant was in Slavic slaves and Italian lumber—two goods in ample supply. While the slave trade might rise and fall in importance to Venice, the significance of lumber remained a mainstay of Venetian commerce. The Mediterranean-based powers all had a need for lumber, particularly for shipbuilding, and Venice was no exception. Because they possessed access to lumber, pitch, iron, and hemp, the Venetians were able to develop a very profitable shipbuilding industry and a powerful navy.

The Venetian Republic made it its business to police the Adriatic Sea to maintain its vital trade routes. By fighting Slavic pirates operating from the Dalmatian coast, the Venetians earned the respect and favor of the Byzantine emperor. It did not take many years before the Dalmatian coastal cities came to recognize Venice as their nominal lord.

Each success in the Adriatic provided the Venetians with expanded opportunities in the eastern Mediterranean. By the late eleventh century, the Byzantines were losing control of their ports in southern Italy to the Normans of Robert Guiscard while simultaneously losing territories in the East to the Seljuk Turks. The Byzantine emperor, Alexius I Comnenus, appealed to Venice for naval aid against the Normans. It was in the Venetian self-interest to render the requested aid because the Normans wanted to control both shores of the lower Adriatic so they could plunder Venetian shipping. The Venetians quickly saw that they could both help themselves and earn some reward from the Byzantines. While the Venetians already had the right to trade in the Byzantine Empire as the result of a commercial treaty signed in 992, they now saw the possibility of trade with reduced tariffs. The Venetians were not only successful in defending Byzantine interests in the area, they were not disappointed in their expectations. The emperor Alexius

granted the Venetians expanded trading rights and exemption from tolls in the Golden Bull of 1082.

Having temporarily halted the Norman advance on Byzantine possessions in eastern Europe, Alexius called upon Pope Urban II in 1095 for military aid against the Seljuk Turks in the East. The pope preached the First Crusade to enlist Christian support for a holy war against the Islamic Seljuk Turks. Although Venice gained some trading rights and commercial concessions from Godfrey de Bouillon, leader of the kingdom of Jerusalem, most of the commercial activity in the area was in the hands of Venice's archrivals Genoa and Pisa. In the summer of 1123, Venice was able to deepen its relationship with the kingdom of Jerusalem when a Venetian fleet defeated a Muslim one at the Battle of Ascalon. This naval engagement ensured Christian control of the seacoast for the kingdom of Jerusalem for another generation.

Although the Byzantines regularly enlisted the aid of Venice against their enemies, they were never entirely happy about their relative relationship. Despite the successful Venetian efforts on behalf of the Byzantines against the Normans of southern Italy, the emperor Alexius began to show favor to Pisa in an effort to undermine Venice in the Adriatic and to play off one Italian maritime power against another. In 1118, Alexius died and the new emperor John II Comnenus refused to renew the charter granting Venice commercial concessions. Although they hoped to sow the seeds of war among the competing Italian maritime states, the Byzantines overestimated their own importance to the Italians. Pisa and Genoa were more concerned at that time with their respective territorial claims to Corsica (which was certainly geographically more important to them) than with any Byzantine commercial prize in the East. To force the Byzantines to recognize their rights, the Venetians sacked a number of Greek islands and cities of the Aegean. Grudgingly, the Byzantines renewed their commercial ties with Venice.

Despite the Byzantine efforts to disrupt Venetian trade, the primary Venetian goal throughout this period was to maintain official trade relations with the Byzantine Empire rather than to resort to opportunistic plundering. The Venetians were more interested in maintaining the Byzantine Empire as a state than in seeing its collapse. There were, however, problems ahead for both peoples. The Greeks were increasingly irritated and unhappy because of Italian trade privileges in general and the Venetian concessions in particular. The Venetians were increasingly contemptuous of the Greeks because of their obvious political and military weaknesses.

In 1171, the Byzantine emperor Manuel I Comnenus ordered the arrest of all Venetians in the Byzantine Empire and the confiscation of their possessions and properties. The Venetians sent a fleet to the Aegean to plunder the Greek possessions to force the Byzantines to release their compatriots and restore their property. In this instance, the Venetians were not only unsuccessful but they also returned to Venice carrying a plague which infected the city. When the Byzantines finally allowed the Venetians to renew their commercial concession, it was on a new, nonexclusive basis. The Venetians were now just one of a number of Italian states given trade rights in the Byzantine Empire. By the end of the twelfth century, piracy became the rule rather than the exception, and the Byzantine Empire was now preyed upon by the Genoese, Pisans, Muslims, Greeks, Saracens, Sicilian Normans, as well as the Venetians. From the Venetian perspective, the collapse of the Byzantine Empire was inevitable and imminent. Within this context, Venetian involvement in the Fourth Crusade (1202-1204) and the overthrow of the Byzantine government becomes understandable.   *—Peter L. Viscusi*

ADDITIONAL READING:

Cheetham, Nicolas. *Mediaeval Greece*. New Haven, Conn.: Yale University Press, 1981. This history of Greece during the Middle Ages reflects contemporary scholarship and provides a clear account of the political, military, cultural, and religious turmoil in medieval Greece.

Diehl, Charles. *Byzantium: Greatness and Decline*. Translated by Naomi Walford. New Brunswick, N.J.: Rutgers University Press, 1957. Despite its age, this survey is recognized as the best introduction to Byzantine civilization. It provides a balanced historical analysis of various aspects of Byzantium including its economic and trade policies.

Lane, Frederic C. *Venice: A Maritime Republic*. Baltimore: The Johns Hopkins University Press, 1973. Written by one of the world's leading authorities, this is the classic reference work for a quick topical overview of the subject.

Norwich, John Julius. *A History of Venice*. New York: Alfred A. Knopf, 1982. The author, a noted British scholar, takes a detailed and chronological approach to Venetian history that is both interesting and colorful.

Ostrogorsky, George. *History of the Byzantine State*. Translated by Joan Hussey. New Brunswick, N.J.: Rutgers University Press, 1957. Although providing more densely written and footnoted scholarly information than most general readers might need, this work is nevertheless a fascinating trove of historical detail.

Sapori, Armando. *The Italian Merchant in the Middle Ages*. Translated by Patricia Ann Kennen. New York: W. W. Norton, 1970. Although not specifically on Venetian commerce, this is an excellent summary of what Italian merchants did in their home cities and abroad.

SEE ALSO: 1095, Pope Urban II Calls the First Crusade; 1127-1130, Kingdom of Sicily Is Created; 1150-1200, Rise of the Hansa; 1204, Knights of the Fourth Crusade Capture Constantinople.

1150-1200
DEVELOPMENT OF GOTHIC ARCHITECTURE

The development of Gothic architecture introduces new structural techniques and creates an aesthetic style whose soaring, light-filled spaces typify late Medieval culture.

DATE: c. 1150-1200
LOCALE: The Île-de-France region of France
CATEGORY: Cultural and intellectual history
KEY FIGURES:
Jean d'Orbais, first architect of the Cathedral of
    Rheims, begun in 1211
Robert de Luzarches, first architect of the Cathedral of
    Amiens, begun in 1220
Suger (1081-1151), abbot of Saint-Denis, 1122-1151
SUMMARY OF EVENT. "Gothic," derived from "Goth," the generic name of the Teutons who invaded Europe in the fourth and fifth centuries, connotes cruelty and barbarity. It was in this opprobrious sense that "Gothic" was used by earlier art critics and architects such as Giorgio Vasari (1511-1574) and Sir Christopher Wren (1632-1723) to describe the dominant architecture of Europe from the twelfth century to the sixteenth. During the nineteenth century there was a change in sentiment toward the Middle Ages, and "Gothic" ecclesiastical buildings became objects of interest, admiration, and detailed studies.

It appears that this style had its origins in northeastern France, especially in the Île-de-France around Paris, and from there spread throughout the Continent and across the English Channel to England. It stems out of its immediate predecessor, the Romanesque basilica, which substituted stone vaulting for wooden ceilings and consequently required heavy walls and buttresses.

The Gothic church is distinguished by a masterful combination of ribbed vaults, pointed arches, and flying buttresses. Romanesque architects regularly employed "groined" vaults to span the aisles and naves of their churches. One of the first Romanesque churches to have the groined vault in the nave was Sant' Ambrogio at Milan. These vaults were constructed by arching over the space to be covered in two different directions, the "groin" being formed by the diagonal lines where the masonry met. Though vaults of this type concentrated their vertical

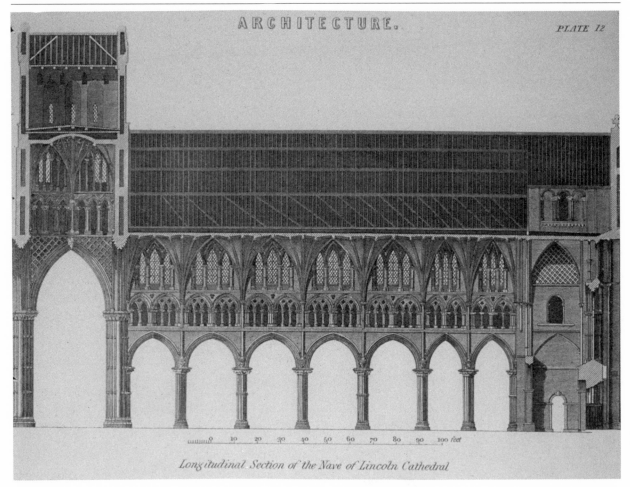

ARCHITECTURE.

PLATE 12

Longitudinal Section of the Nave of Lincoln Cathedral

This cutaway view of Lincoln Cathedral in England reveals the distinctive pointed arches and ribbed vaults associated with Gothic architecture. In the church nave, the ribbed vaults created a fan-like tracery leading to the ceiling—a feature associated with the Perpendicular Gothic style. (Archive Photos)

thrust upon columns and piers, and not along a continuous wall as in the case of "barrel" vaults, they were still heavy and difficult to construct. The introduction of "ogival," or "ribbed," vaulting in Romanesque buildings of the eleventh century in northern Italy was, therefore, a significant advance in technique. In vaults of this type the area was first outlined with diagonal, transverse, and longitudinal ribs of stone which were then filled in with webs of brick or stone. Since this type of vaulting was lighter and stronger, it became one of the distinctive features of Gothic architecture.

The Romans used only the classically proportioned round arch. Builders in Mesopotamia, on the other hand, had earlier employed the pointed arch as well. From there it passed to Persia, Armenia, Egypt, and Sicily. Probably the first use made of it on the European continent was in the nave arcades of the Romanesque abbey church of

Cluny (1089-1131). The pointed arch proved to have a number of distinct advantages over the round: It generated less of a lateral thrust; more important, the pointed arch was more flexible in that its height was not determined by its width. Consequently it could easily be adjusted so that the crowns of the transverse and longitudinal ribs of a vault were equal in height to the diagonal ribs, a matter of particular importance for cruciform churches. By pointing the diagonal ribs more sharply, any height commensurate with safety could be effected.

Vaulted construction required heavy buttressing by piers or relieving arches to carry the thrust to piers placed further out. Roman and Romanesque architects concealed these piers as far as possible behind the outer walls of their buildings. Gothic architects lightened appearances by exposing the framework, the piers, and the "flying" buttresses to open view.

In comparison to earlier architecture, Gothic was revolutionary. The earlier style of building was practically turned inside out. The new style anticipated modern skyscraper construction, but in a more sophisticated way than post and lintel usage, by erecting a skeleton so that the roof was not supported directly by the walls. Instead, the roof was held aloft by an elaborate framework of piers, arches, and buttresses which at the same time absorbed and carried most of the pressures generated by the vaulting of the nave so that the walls could be filled with stained glass windows to form an airy curtain.

The interior of a Gothic church proved to be even more impressive than its exterior. While length directed attention to the sanctuary at the east end of the nave, the ribbing of piers and vaults together with the great height pulled the beholder's eyes upward. In the Cathe-

dral of Amiens, the nave ceiling is 140 feet above the floor.

The new spirit dominating Gothic architecture was both philosophical and theological. From the Schoolmen, the medieval architects derived a feeling for order and a conviction that all temporal beauty was a reflection of divine beauty. At the same time a deeper mystical appreciation of the humanity of Christ and his role in salvation is reflected in the many carvings and stained-glass windows that adorned the new churches.

If one individual can be singled out in this new architectural movement, it is perhaps Abbot Suger, who largely rebuilt the west facade and choir of the abbey church of Saint-Denis on the outskirts of Paris between 1130 and 1144. With its ribbed vaults, interlinking spaces, and stained glass as well as the sculptural program of the facade this building campaign is generally conceded to be

The exterior of the famous Cathedral of Notre Dame in Paris shows the extensive use of flying buttresses, allowing the roof to be supported by an external skeleton so that the church walls can be filled with beautiful stained-glass windows. (R. Kent Rasmussen)

the first definitely Gothic structure. Suger fittingly commemorated the event in his *The Consecration of the Church of St.-Denis*, in which he recounted the reasons for the rebuilding and offered the theological basis of the architectural style which transformed the material into the immaterial.

Within a few years, notably at Chartres Cathedral and a number of churches located in the Île-de-France, the new style developed with increasingly greater sophistication. By the early decades of the thirteenth century, the structural principles of ribbed vaulting and flying buttresses had been refined to the point that mature statements of the Gothic style appeared in the churches of Rheims and Amiens begun by the architects Jean d'Orbais and Robert de Luzarches. These cathedrals represent the epitome of the verticality of space from floor to ribbed vault, the lightness of the stained glass, all supported by the exterior flying buttresses.

—*M. Joseph Costelloe, updated by Karen Gould*

ADDITIONAL READING:

Bony, Jean. *French Gothic Architecture of the Twelfth and Thirteenth Centuries*. Berkeley: University of California Press, 1983. A comprehensive survey of the origins and development of Gothic architecture in France.

Gerson, Paula Lieber, ed. *Abbot Suger and Saint-Denis*. New York: The Metropolitan Museum of Art, 1986. A collection of essays on all aspects of Saint-Denis, Abbot Suger, and the role of this structure in the origins of Gothic architecture.

Panofsky, Erwin. *Abbot Suger on the Abbey Church of St.-Denis and Its Art Treasures*. 2d ed. Princeton, N.J.: Princeton University Press, 1979. Panofsky includes the Latin text and English translation, together with extended notes, of two of the most important medieval documents on Gothic architecture.

_____. *Gothic Architecture and Scholasticism*. 2d ed. New York: Meridian Books, 1957. This essay makes connection between the aims of the Gothic architectural style and its contemporary philosophical system, Scholasticism.

Radding, Charles M., and William W. Clark. *Medieval Architecture, Medieval Learning: Builders and Masters in the Age of Romanesque and Gothic*. New Haven, Conn.: Yale University Press, 1992. Written by an intellectual historian and an architectural historian, this work juxtaposes relationships between ideas and architectural style in the transition from Romanesque to Gothic.

Simson, Otto von. *The Gothic Cathedral*. 3d ed. Princeton, N.J.: Princeton University Press, 1988. A study of the aesthetic impact of Gothic architecture as an expression of theological ideas.

SEE ALSO: 240 B.C., Exploitation of the Arch; 1025, Scholars at Chartres Revive Interest in Classical Learning; 1100-1300, Emergence of European Universities; 1410-1440, Florentine School of Art Emerges.

1150-1200
RISE OF THE HANSA

The Hansa, a loose union of merchants in northern Germany, evolves by 1350 into an association of cities that dominates the region's maritime trade for three hundred years.

DATE: c. 1150-1200
LOCALE: The Baltic region of northern Germany
CATEGORIES: Economics; Government and politics
KEY FIGURES:

Adolf II of Schauenburg, count of Holstein, founder of the new city of Lübeck in 1158-1559 after the destruction of the old city in 1138

Ethelred II ("the Unready"; c. 968-1016), king of England and early supporter of the rights of foreign merchants

Henry II (1133-1189), king of England and protector of Cologne wine merchants competing with French traders in England

Henry the Lion (1129-1195), duke of Saxony, 1142-1180, and duke of Bavaria, 1156-1180, whose enforced peace between Germany and Gotland encouraged trade in the Baltic

SUMMARY OF EVENT. "Hansa" is the Latin form of the German *Hense*, a very old word designating a group of warriors. In thirteenth century England, this term came to mean a tribute paid by merchants from abroad. At various times the word also referred to a tax on commerce as well as to an entrance fee imposed on members of the so-called Hanseatic League, a term that has been rejected by some scholars who prefer to refer to the confederation as the "Hanseatic Community." This confederation of merchants began roughly with the rebuilding of Lübeck in 1158-1159, and had evolved into a trade association of towns by the fourteenth century. The confederation expired in the seventeenth century. Although individual hansas were common in the Baltic region, the general use of the term "Hansa" for a specific association of merchants and towns was not adopted until 1370.

Merchants who traveled abroad faced many hazards during the Middle Ages. Many of the early traders in the Baltic and North Seas were hardly better than pirates seizing cargoes at will. The crews of wrecked ships could be enslaved, and the flotsam and jetsam of shipwrecks were fair loot for anyone on shore, often providing considerable wealth for some of the many monasteries. Besides these threats to the safety of their wares, traders were the frequent prey of noblemen greedy for exorbitant tolls. Given the hardships and the dangers they faced in foreign travel—and these early merchants were not deskbound, but quite the opposite—mutual protection on foreign shores was important right from the start in the rise of the Hansa.

As early as 978, under the reign of the young Ethelred II, English law granted equal protection to the merchants from across the North Sea. These rights were expanded under Henry II to allow traders from Cologne to sell wine under the same provisions accorded the French. Moreover, a grant made around the year 1157 provided protection for the Cologne merchants, who by this time had their own London Guildhall. King John contributed to England's importance in the early history of the Hansa by enforcing his predecessors' liberal policies during his own reign, and Hansa merchants were freed from their annual tribute of two shillings in 1194. The continued strength of the feudal system in England, however, prevented the development of rich cities served by a powerful middle class of English merchants.

During the reign of Frederick I ("Barbarossa"), German merchants fared much better. Seeking allies in his quarrels with the nobles, Frederick supported the middle class and then extracted money from it to finance his foreign interests. From one point of view, Frederick's support of this merchant middle class was shortsighted, since their independent power weakened Germany's political unity. Nevertheless, the freedom that merchants enjoyed fostered trade and encouraged the growth of the Hansa. Powerful, flourishing cities began to spring up in this period, and the Hansa emerged as a crucial factor in the decline of feudalism and the relative triumph of the middle classes over their crowns.

Once they received some support from sympathetic royalty, the merchant bourgeoisie effected many practical improvements in promoting maritime law, improving and charting the waterways, building lighthouses and digging canals, and introducing order and security into the mercantile traffic of northern Europe. The Baltic Sea had been for centuries the main trade route between eastern and western Europe. The traders from the West did not themselves sail the Baltic, however, but simply received goods from the Scandinavians and Slavs who came to Schleswig on the eastern shore of the narrow neck of the Danish peninsula. The overland journey from Schleswig to Hollingstedt on the Eider River leading to the North Sea was only fifteen kilometers. One prominent theory contends that the establishment of the city of Lübeck on the

Trave estuary south of Schleswig in 1158-1159 opened up the first stage of the growth of the Hansa by giving Western traders direct access to the Baltic in their new "cogs," slender ships better for commerce than the northerners' vessels. Whatever Lübeck's precise role, few scholars deny its central importance in the growth of the Hansa. The spread of German commerce north and east brought German language and culture along with it into the regions of Estonia and Prussia.

The Baltic island of Gotland, a customary stopover for merchants headed east, was at first oppressed by Henry the Lion, duke of Saxony. Later in 1161, he enforced a peace between Germany and Gotland and won German merchants the right to trade in Gotland. A community of visiting German merchants grew up in the Gottish town of Visby, and were often influential in founding churches. Of the six churches that can be traced to the late eleventh century, the German merchant church of Sancta Maria Teutonicorum became the warehouse and registry of the Gotland Company. The group created its own constitution featuring rule by four aldermen elected from the merchants of Visby, Lübeck, Soest, and Dortmund.

Parallel with the growth of Gotland's importance was the German entrance into the lucrative herring fishing industry thriving off Skania on the southern tip of Sweden. For Catholic Europe, salted fish was a sought-after commodity. Fishing provided great wealth, and the herring came in great numbers to the coasts of Skania and Pomerania during the twelfth through fifteenth centuries. The city of Kolberg became famous for its salt fish, and salted herrings were a common medium of exchange and an acceptable tax offering. For the Germans trading in herring, Visby became the center of their extensive commerce. Traders enjoyed the protection of the city, for the law held that it was bound to help any merchant devastated by robbery or shipwreck.

The Russians also had a presence in the Baltic, as evidenced by churches in Gotland and other cities. Merchants in Novgorod, an old trading port in northwestern Russia, carried on business in the Church of Holy Friday, built in 1156. Germans eventually arrived in the area from Gotland and by 1184 were competing successfully against the Russians from their trading post, the Peterhof, on the Volkhov River east of Novgorod.

At its peak of power, the Hansa reached from Bruges in the south, over the English Channel to the eastern cities of England, north to Bergen in Norway, around the coast of Sweden and north to southern Finland and Novgorod. The heaviest concentration of Hansa cities clustered around the big centers of Bremen, Cologne, Hamburg, Lübeck, and then north up the Baltic coast to Danzig and Riga. The

Hansa cities grew steadily in power until the middle of the fourteenth century, when the diverging interests of the Hansa merchants hurt their unity. From then on, the Hanseatic Community dwindled in importance, bleeding from its wars with the Dutch, the Danes, the English, and the Castilians, until the final Hanseatic diet was held at Lübeck in 1669.   —*Frank Day*

ADDITIONAL READING:

Dollinger, Phillipe. *The German Hansa*. Translated and edited by D. S. Ault and S. H. Steinberg. Stanford, Calif.: Stanford University Press, 1970. The standard work on the topic, stressing the evolution of the Hansa of Merchants into the Hansa of Towns.

Durant, Will. *The Age of Faith*. Volume 4 of *The Story of Civilization*. New York: Simon & Schuster, 1950. A brief account of the Hansa's importance is included in a chapter that places the development of the Hansa in a broad context.

Lloyd, T. H. *England and the German Hanse, 1157-1611: A Study of Their Trade and Commercial Diplomacy*. New York: Cambridge University Press, 1991. Authoritative on England's role in the history of the Hansa.

Schildhauer, Johannes. *The Hansa: History and Culture*. Translated by Kathleen Vanovitch. Leipzig: Edition Leipzig, 1985. Beautifully illustrated coffee-table book with detailed chapters on such topics as "The Hanseatic Townscape" and "Hanseatic Culture." It contains an excellent map, but its bibliography largely consists of German-language works.

Zimmern, Helen. *The Hansa Towns*. New York: G. P. Putnam's Sons, 1893. Zimmern's romantic narrative approach dates this study, which is nevertheless informative and extremely readable.

SEE ALSO: 1150, Venetian Merchants Dominate Trade with the East.

1152

FREDERICK BARBAROSSA IS ELECTED KING OF GERMANY

Frederick Barbarossa is elected king of Germany and his reign firmly establishes the ideal of a united German nation as opposed to a collection of small independent political entities.

DATE: 1152
LOCALE: The Holy Roman Empire
CATEGORY: Government and politics
KEY FIGURES:
Berthold IV of Zähringen (died 1186), duke of Zähringen

Conrad III Hohenstaufen (c. 1093-1152), duke of Swabia and king of Germany, 1138-1152
Frederick I Hohenstaufen (Frederick Barbarossa; c. 1123-1190), duke of Swabia as Frederick III, 1147-1190; king of Germany and Holy Roman Emperor, 1152-1190
Frederick of Rothenburg (1144-1167), duke of Swabia, 1152-1167
Henry II Jasomirgott (von Babenberg; c. 1114-1191), duke of Bavaria, 1143-1156, and later the first duke of Austria, 1156-1177
Henry the Lion (1129-1195), duke of Saxony, 1142-1180, and duke of Bavaria, 1156-1180
Count Welf VI (also known as Guelph; 1115-1191), margrave of Tuscany and duke of Spoleto, 1152

SUMMARY OF EVENT. By the time of Conrad III's coronation as king of Germany in 1138, the king-emperor's power and the stability of the realm had greatly eroded. The powers of a king-emperor, charged by God with the rule of Christendom and supreme lord of both the laity and clergy, had greatly diminished. The pope had taken the power of investing bishops from the emperor so the prince-bishops no longer were strictly subject to the king's control. In addition, the pope had become responsible for crowning the emperor, subordinating the emperor to the papacy. Also, the rise of strong feudal nobles had further circumscribed the king's powers so that the emperor was dominated by the powerful ducal families. As a consequence, Conrad III's election as king was strongly contested, and he never fully gained control of the kingdom. He also never was crowned emperor.

Conrad III died February 15, 1152, and designated Frederick II Hohenstaufen, duke of Swabia, as his successor. Frederick was elected king of Germany as Frederick I in 1152. The princes were almost unanimous in selecting Frederick, and the meeting apparently had been well planned to ensure a peaceful succession. According to one account, Conrad III designated Frederick his successor and guardian of Frederick of Rothenburg, his eight-year-old son, because Conrad realized his young son would, in all probability, be the target of inimical forces during his minority.

In any event, the election necessarily would be negotiated in the face of deep divisions among the German princes and bishops. Rivalry between the Hohenstaufen family of Conrad III and Frederick I Barbarossa, and the Welf family, led by Henry the Lion, plagued Conrad during his entire reign and easily could have disrupted the succession. Although Frederick was a Hohenstaufen, he also was the son of a Welf mother, Judith. Thus his election might be acceptable to both families. As duke of Swabia,

Frederick had consistently favored his mother's family, perhaps preparing for eventual promotion to kingship. During Conrad's final illness, Frederick, in concert with Conrad's closest advisers (Abbot Wibald and Bishop Eberhard of Bamberg), offered concessions to the Welfs. Henry the Lion was promised the duchies of Saxony and Bavaria. Count Welf VI was offered an autonomous position as margrave of Tuscany and duke of Spoleto. Henry the Lion's father-in-law, Berthold IV of Zähringen, was encouraged to carve out a sphere of influence in Burgundy. Henry II Jasomirgott, a Babenberg who feared loss of Bavaria, was prominent in a small opposition group led by Archbishop Henry of Mainz, a Hohenstaufen opponent.

After his election in Frankfort, Frederick received oaths of loyalty from the assembled princes. On March 6, he left for Aix-la-Chapelle and his coronation. There, he was met by a large crowd assembled to see the coronation. Seated on the throne of Charlemagne, Frederick was crowned king of Germany by Arnold, the archbishop of Cologne. Immediately thereafter, Frederick began preparing an expedition to Rome to be crowned emperor of the Holy Roman Empire and to assert control over his Italian vassals. First, as was customary for newly elected kings of Germany, Frederick Barbarossa immediately made a "grand tour" of the kingdom to receive fealty and to mediate conflicts within the kingdom. He also sent Bishop Eberhard of Bamberg to Rome to announce his election to Pope Eugene. Instead of begging papal confirmation of the election, Frederick merely informed the pope of the fact, reasserting imperial independence of papal authority.

Frederick quickly consolidated his position by confirming his Welf cousin, Henry the Lion, as duke of Saxony and granting him the dukedom of Bavaria as well. Henry, the most powerful of the German nobles, thus became Frederick's loyal ally for twenty years. In 1176, however, Henry demanded the imperial city of Goslar and its rich silver mines in return for supporting Frederick's campaign against the Lombard League. As a consequence, Frederick charged Henry with a breach of the king's peace in 1178, an event that ultimately led to Henry's eviction from his duchies in 1180. The powerful Babenberg family was compensated for its loss of Bavaria to Henry by separating the margraviate of Austria from Bavaria as a new dukedom. Frederick conferred the dukedom of Austria on Henry II Jasomirgott with rights of hereditary succession and immunity from many feudal obligations to the emperor. Thus, the Babenbergs were brought to accept Frederick's rule. Frederick also confirmed Berthold IV Zähringen's claims in Burgundy and Provence in return for Berthold's support during the coronation expedition.

Through these actions, Frederick established control in Germany and converted the powerful princes to be his sworn vassals.

In setting out to gain control of his Italian lands, Frederick mounted no less than five military campaigns. Although Frederick's protracted conflict with the Lombard communes and the pope failed to establish direct royal government, he was more successful in Tuscany and central Italy. After the Peace of Venice in 1177 and the Peace of Constance in 1183, Frederick was able to extend direct imperial administration throughout Tuscany. He thus obtained enough income to expand imperial properties and ensure his maintenance in Germany.

Although his control of the Holy Roman Empire was in large part indirect, Frederick reestablished its territorial integrity and inculcated a strong sense of German nationhood. Feudal centralization of the Holy Roman Empire began with Frederick; after Hohenstaufen rule decayed, however, the centralized German state quickly reverted to an assemblage of essentially independent states uncontrolled by the emperor. The sense of nationhood developed under Frederick, however, eventually inspiring reestablishment of a unified Germany in the nineteenth century.

Frederick's reign ended when he drowned in the Saleph River of northwestern Syria while leading the Third Crusade. The actual circumstances of his death are unknown. According to one story, he was swept away while fording the river. Another report suggests that he suffered a seizure while bathing in the cold river water. Yet another tale has him thrown from his horse while crossing the river.

Although Frederick Barbarossa's demise apparently was received calmly as a not unexpected event, he became the centerpiece of a national legend five hundred years later. According to the early nineteenth century myth, Frederick did not die, but was supposed to be living in a cave beneath Kyffhäuser Mountain in Thuringia, Germany. He was expected to return from that mountain and save the German nation in a future cataclysmic conflict. One mythic variation has Barbarossa returning when his red beard grows long enough to surround the giant round table at which he supposedly sits. These myths long antedate Barbarossa's identification as a German national hero and are steeped in contradictions. From 1250 until the sixteenth century, it was Barbarossa's grandson, Frederick II, who was believed to be in the cave. Even before Frederick II was incorporated into the legend, Kyffhäuser had been a mythic shrine from at least the time of the Celts. Many other heroes, including Julius Caesar and Wotan, had been associated with the magic mountain.

Although Frederick failed to establish lasting political order in the Holy Roman Empire, he is generally considered the most effective of medieval Holy Roman Emperors. He also has become the acknowledged German national hero who lives in the communal German mind, comparable only to El Cid in Spain, Joan of Arc in France, and King Arthur in England. —*Ralph L. Langenheim, Jr.*

ADDITIONAL READING:

Arnold, Benjamin. *Princes and Territories in Medieval Germany*. New York: Cambridge University Press, 1991. Concentrates on fundamental institutional changes in Germany during the twelfth and thirteenth centuries.

Barraclough, Geoffrey. *Factors in German History*. Reprint. Westport, Conn.: Greenwood Press, 1979. First published in 1946, this account has less detail than that found in his 1946 *The Origins of Modern Germany*. Instead, it provides a concise account of the major events in Barbarossa's career.

_____. *The Origins of Modern Germany*. 2d ed. Oxford: Basil Blackwell, 1947. Probably the most useful account of German history in the English language.

Fuhrmann, Horst. *Germany in the High Middle Ages, c. 1050-1200*. Translated by Timothy Reuter. New York: Cambridge University Press, 1986. Provides an overview of events before, during, and after Barbarossa's reign.

Haverkamp, Alfred. *Medieval Germany, 1056-1273*. Translated by Helga Braun and Richard Mortimer. New York: Oxford University Press, 1988. Haverkamp has written a political, social, and economic history of the period including Barbarossa's reign.

Kitchin, Martin. *The Cambridge Illustrated History of Germany*. New York: Cambridge University Press, 1996. Emphasizes cultural as well as political history. Recommended as an introduction for general readers.

Munz, Peter. *Frederick Barbarossa: A Study in Medieval Politics*. Ithaca, N.Y.: Cornell University Press, 1969. Scholarly biography of Barbarossa.

SEE ALSO: 1156, Emergence of Austria; 1189-1192, The Third Crusade; 1227-1230, Frederick II Leads the Sixth Crusade.

1154-1204
ESTABLISHMENT OF ANGEVIN EMPIRE
The establishment of the Angevin empire under the three Plantagenet kings expands English holdings to their widest extent, until Normandy is annexed in 1204 by the king of France.

DATE: 1154-1204
LOCALE: France and England
CATEGORY: Government and politics

KEY FIGURES:
Eleanor of Aquitaine (c. 1121-1204), queen of England through her marriage to Henry II
Geoffrey IV, "the Handsome" (Geoffrey Plantagenet; 1113-1151), count of Anjou, 1129-1149
Henry II (Henry Plantagenet; 1133-1189), successor to King Stephen as king of England, 1154-1189
Richard I ("the Lionheart"; 1157-1199), third son of Henry II and king of England, 1189-1199
John I ("Lackland"; 1166-1216), youngest son of Henry II and king of England, 1199-1216
Matilda (1102-1167), only daughter of Henry I, wife of Geoffrey Plantagenet, and mother of Henry II
Philip II (Philip Augustus; 1165-1223), son of Louis VII and king of France, 1180-1223

SUMMARY OF EVENT. Geographically, the Angevin empire of the twelfth century comprised England, Normandy, Anjou, and Aquitaine. The first two domains had been united by William the Conqueror and consolidated under his son, Henry I (1100-1135). Anjou was added by the marriage of Henry's daughter, Matilda, to Geoffrey Plantagenet, count of Anjou. Their son, Henry II, further enlarged the empire by his marriage to Eleanor of Aquitaine.

As summarized by historian John Gillingham, this four-part empire became, under Henry and his sons Richard and John, "the dominant polity in western Europe." Contemporaries did not speak of an "Angevin empire," however, nor does the term indicate a nation aware of its cultural identity. The Angevin kings did not create a political structure that might be perpetuated or conquered. Their achievement was to subordinate the feudal aristocracy, who, in spite of their diverse regions and dialects, all paid homage to their Angevin overlord.

The empire, therefore, was unified in the person of the king rather than by its subjects' loyalty to a common tradition or territory. Like his grandfather Henry and his great-grandfather the Conqueror, Henry II enjoyed the fealty of powerful lords. These barons and earls found it to their advantage to do homage to the king because only he could prevent their destructive quarrels and give them justice. Under feudalism in its crude form, the warrior caste, while protecting those who worked their manors, had constantly challenged one another's holdings. Under Norman feudalism, the warrior lords waived their rights of ownership and instead held their lands "in fee" (*feod*, related to the word for cattle) from the king, who was recognized as the sole legal owner (especially since William owned the England he had conquered). In return for these fiefs, the king's feudal tenants-in-chief, including bishops and abbots as well as barons, promised to pay certain taxes or dues, to attend the royal councils, and to support the king with a fixed number of armed and mounted knights.

Besides superseding the manorial courts of the feudal barons, the king's justice in England absorbed the old shire courts presided over by a sheriff ("shire reeve"). Henry II revived his grandfather's practice of sending out his royal officers on circuit to sit beside the sheriffs and enforce his rights to taxes. These officers gradually expanded their jurisdiction, giving judgment in trials for murder, rape, arson, robbery, forgery, and harboring criminals. In this way, the "king's peace" was extended to the whole nation, and the king was able to fulfill his coronation oath, which bound him to see justice done and to guarantee everyone's right of appeal to his courts. For a modest fee, any freeman forcibly dispossessed of his land could get a writ, or royal command, restoring immediate possession pending a full trial. To determine property disputes, William the Conqueror had ordered juries of twelve "free and lawful men" of the neighborhood to look into the facts of the case. Henry II extended this jury inquest to cover judicial processes of every kind.

Henry claimed not to be innovating, but merely to be restoring the good old laws. He was actually depriving the feudal aristocracy of their ancient right to decide all matters either by an oath or by appealing to force (trial by combat). Henry drove the barons and their manorial courts out of business, for most of his subjects wanted to have their cases tried in the king's courts. At the same time, Henry and his sons were developing a legal system. Their writs were recorded, and they became the first body of written law since late Roman times. Royal officials had to know this written law as well as local customs; hence was born, around 1200, the profession judge. Next came the lawyers—men trained in precedents and cases—who were hired as professional advocates by either side, recalling the professional fighters whom the parties had formerly retained for trials by combat. The fascinating evolution of English courts and law in the thirteenth century is compelling proof that the Norman/Angevin genius shaped the culture inherited by all modern English-speaking citizens.

Another innovation characteristic of the Norsemen enabled the Angevin kings to gain the upper hand over the feudal lords. This innovation was the institution of wardship, whereby the king asserted his right to take the heir of the greatest vassal into custody until the heir was of age. This right went back to the practice of Viking seafaring tribes, whose ethnic traditions were able to survive even after the ties of family had become weakened. In effect, the leader of a band of pirates held together primarily by their northern origin was transformed into the model of a feudal monarch. The model figures prominently in British

PLANTAGENET KINGDOM AND OVERSEAS POSSESSIONS, C. 1170

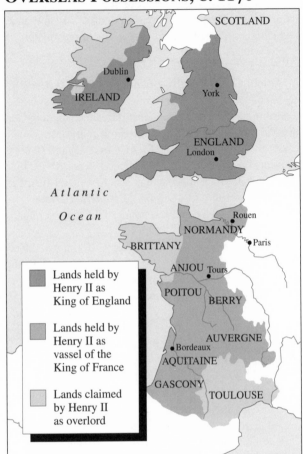

history. From the works of Geoffrey Chaucer and William Shakespeare to the eighteenth century novel, it can be observed in the custom of gentry who send their children away from home at a tender age to be reared in another, aristocratic household.

The Angevin kings could develop government in such a logical and systematic way because feudal relations were considered the material out of which the state had to be formed. Especially in England, these feudal materials were molded into an original polity, in contrast to conservative Normandy, where the lords' rights were strengthened at the expense of any state, and in equal contrast to France, where the king worked with the church to suppress feudalism in favor of an autocracy like that of Charlemagne and his Frankish forebears.

Having established the Angevin empire, Henry II was faced with the problem of bequeathing it whole to his successor. He wanted to provide for all of his sons while ensuring that the younger brothers paid homage for their provinces to the eldest. Henry's first son had died as a child and his second son (also named Henry) died in 1183, leaving Richard the Lionheart next in line. When Richard succeeded to the throne in 1189, he won great fame in Europe and the Holy Lands, and he was a reassuring presence to his Norman and Angevin vassals. Nevertheless, he spent a scant total of five months of his ten-year reign governing his inheritance in England. When Richard died unexpectedly in 1199, John, his youngest brother, took over the Crown. Although he was known to be Henry's favorite son, John was unable to command the fealty of the Norman and Angevin lords, who deserted him to pay their homage instead to the French king, Philip Augustus.

In the empire's final phase, which saw the loss of Normandy, the Catholic Church played a major role. First, the Norman bishops, not wanting the church to be torn apart by divided loyalty to two overlords, fell back on their original homage to the Frankish kings and their latest descendant, Philip Augustus. For ten years after losing Normandy and Anjou, John abused his rights over his English vassals. Stephen Langton, archbishop of Canterbury, acted to preserve the monarchy painstakingly built up by Henry I and Henry II. The nobility were threatening to get rid of John as a tyrant. Rather than allow them to throw off kingly rule and plunge England back into feudal chaos, Langton announced that he had found a charter of Henry I by means of which the nobles might regain their lost liberty. He urged them not to destroy the Crown but to demand that the king restore old customs. Although the Magna Carta that John's vassals forced upon him in 1215 insists upon their feudal rights as tenants-in-chief, fully thirty-two of the document's sixty-one clauses deal with the relations between the king and his *subjects*—that is, with the liberties of freemen and small property-owners that have become accepted by all those living under the common law.   —*David B. Haley*

ADDITIONAL READING:

Barber, Richard. *The Devil's Crown: A History of Henry II and His Sons*. London: British Broadcasting Corporation, 1978. This volume is based on a television series shown by the British Broadcasting Corporation. It is an extremely informative and popularly styled history of the Angevin period.

Bryant, Arthur. *The Medieval Foundation*. London: Collins, 1966. A very readable account of the growth of British legal and parliamentary systems.

Gillingham, John. *The Angevin Empire*. New York: Holmes & Meier, 1984. The most complete modern political account of the Angevin kings and their holdings.

_____. *Richard the Lionheart*. New York: Times Books, 1978. A sympathetic biography that portrays Richard as both a distinguished warrior and a capable ruler of the duchy of Aquitaine.

Kelly, Amy. *Eleanor of Aquitaine and the Four Kings*. Cambridge, Mass.: Harvard University Press, 1950. A celebrated biography of Henry II's wife, who had previously been married to King Louis VII of France and was queen mother of the Angevin empire.

Mortimer, Richard. *Angevin England, 1154-1258*. Cambridge, Mass.: Blackwell, 1994. An up-to-date account of social history and customs that flourished under the Angevins. Complements Gillingham's political history of the period cited above.

Painter, Sidney. *The Reign of King John*. Baltimore: The Johns Hopkins University Press, 1949. An enduring, respected study that still provides the best history of John's reign.

Powicke, F. M. *The Loss of Normandy, 1189-1204*. 2d ed. Manchester, England: Manchester University Press, 1961. First published in 1913, Powicke's work provides a fine history of the triumph and eventual supercession of Norman institutions.

SEE ALSO: 1066, Battle of Hastings; 1169-1172, Norman Troops Invade Ireland; 1175, Common Law Tradition Emerges in England; 1189-1192, The Third Crusade; 1215, Signing of the Magna Carta; 1453, English Are Driven from France.

1156
EMERGENCE OF AUSTRIA

The emergence of Austria heralds its status as a national entity after the East Mark is established as the duchy of Austria.

DATE: September 17, 1156
LOCALE: Regensburg, Bavaria
CATEGORY: Government and politics
KEY FIGURES:
Conrad III Hohenstaufen (c. 1093-1152), duke of
   Swabia and king of Germany, 1138-1152
Frederick I Hohenstaufen (Frederick Barbarossa;
   c. 1123-1190), duke of Swabia as Frederick III,
   1147-1190; king of Germany and Holy Roman
   Emperor, 1152-1190
Henry II Jasomirgott (von Babenberg; c. 1114-1191),
   duke of Bavaria, 1143-1156, and later the first duke
   of Austria, 1156-1177
Henry the Proud (c. 1108-1139), duke of Bavaria,
   1126-1139, and duke of Saxony, 1137-1139
Henry the Lion (1124-1194), duke of Saxony,
   1142-1180, and duke of Bavaria, 1156-1180

SUMMARY OF EVENT. Celtic and Roman civilization in Austria was crushed when Avars overran the region in the sixth century. After Charlemagne destroyed Avar power between 791 and 811, he organized the Austrian lands as the East Mark on Bavaria's eastern frontier. The East Mark then was colonized by German settlers, chiefly from Bavaria, but Hungarian invaders obliterated the East Mark's German settlements between 898 and 955. Little survived, but German colonization resumed after Otto the Great defeated the Hungarians at Lechfield in 955, confining them to the area that became known as Hungary.

The bishops of Passau and Regensburg and the monasteries of St. Polten, Kremsmunster, and St. Florian were instrumental in this colonizing, joining material considerations with zeal to convert pagan Slavs and Hungarians. In 973, Margrave Leopold of Babenberg assumed secular authority in the East Mark. Shortly thereafter, in 996, the name *osterrichi* (Austria) first appeared in an imperial document. Members of the Babenberg family governed the territory until the death of Frederick the Fighter in 1246. The margraves encouraged German immigration, slowly pushed the frontier eastward, and defended the territory against the Slavs and Hungarians.

The East Mark was a no-man's-land between German civilization and peripheral ethnic groups, with boundaries determined by the balance of power. By the mid-twelfth century, German settlement was halted by Hungarians who were deeply entrenched at the Leitha River. Led by Henry II Babenberg, known as Jasomirgott, the margraves began emphasizing consolidation and internal exploitation. By this time, Vienna had reappeared, most unoccupied land was converted to agriculture, and more refined cultural aspects were in evidence. Thus, the East Mark's colonial stage of development came to an end.

For a generation, Bavaria and the East Mark were disputed by the Welfs (Guelphs) and Hohenstaufens (Ghibelins), the two most powerful German families of the period. The controversy erupted in 1137, when Emperor Lothar II died without a male heir. His daughter Gertrude had married the Welf duke of Bavaria, Henry the Proud. Through Gertrude, Henry secured Saxony, the nucleus of Lothar's possessions. Joining Saxony to Bavaria, Henry the Proud became the most powerful German prince. As duke of Spoleto, Henry's authority also reached the gates of Rome.

Henry expected to become king of Germany in early 1138, but the princes disappointed him by electing Conrad III of Franconia, a member of the Hohenstaufen family who dominated the duchy of Swabia. Since the Hohenstaufens had often defied Lothar and had frequently fought with the duchy of Bavaria, Henry the Proud expressed his disappointment by preparing for war.

Conrad III deposed Henry, granting Saxony to Albert the Bear, the margrave of Brandenburg, and presenting Bavaria to Leopold of the East Mark. Yet Conrad could not enforce his decrees. Henry recovered most of Saxony and was poised to invade Bavaria when he died in October, 1139, leaving Henry the Lion, his ten-year-old son, as his heir. The boy's grandmother and an uncle managed to compel Conrad to return Saxony to young Henry in 1142. Conrad insisted, however, that Bavaria remain in the hands of Henry II Jasomirgott of the East Mark, brother and heir of the late Leopold of Babenberg. In consequence, young Henry the Lion renounced his claim on his Bavarian inheritance.

Henry II Jasomirgott's control over Bavaria was tenuous. Opponents within the duchy warred against him and the maturing Henry the Lion began to regret his renunciation of his claim to Bavaria. During the Second Crusade in 1147, Henry the Lion demonstrated military talent fighting against the pagan Wends. When Conrad III returned from the crusade, Henry the Lion pressed his claim to Bavaria. Fighting had already erupted when Conrad died in February.

In 1152, Conrad III's nephew, Frederick Barbarossa, was elected king of Germany. Barbarossa apparently recognized that Germany's constitutional structure had been forever altered by the investiture controversy and civil strife during the early twelfth century. The vast power of the princes had undermined the monarchy, and the newly crowned king needed to discover new methods of rule. Barbarossa based his plans on the inherent possibilities of feudalism, then well established in western Europe but existing only tangentially in Germany.

A strong feudal monarch required an extensive royal domain with its economic resources to create and maintain political power. Within Germany little remained of the old royal domain by 1152, so Barbarossa concentrated his initial efforts toward Italy. Here his perquisites as Holy Roman Emperor offered resources to regain his lost rights within Germany. Frederick Barbarossa therefore determined to subjugate Italy so he could eventually dominate Germany.

A second aspect of Barbarossa's policy consisted of strengthening the hierarchical structure of government within Germany with the monarch firmly entrenched at the summit, sustained by clear lines of authority and control. He needed the cooperation and support of the great dukes to construct a scheme of administration that would, with his outside resources, permit him to dominate these same dukes. He needed to grant concessions to placate powerful families, especially the Welfs, who would never rest content until they recovered their confiscated

Bavarian lands. To bring this about, Barbarossa also needed to grant concessions to the Babenbergs to buy their support. The backing of the Babenbergs would counterbalance the dangerous concentration of power in the Welf family.

Frederick Barbarossa was related to both Henry of Saxony and Henry II Jasomirgott of the East Mark. Apparently Barbarossa promised restoration of Bavaria to the Saxon duke before his election in order to ensure his support. For two years, however, Barbarossa could not persuade Henry II Jasomirgott to discuss the matter. Finally, Barbarossa and his court announced at the Diet of Goslar in 1154 that Henry the Lion's claim to Bavaria overrode that of the Babenbergs. Barbarossa invested Henry the Lion with the disputed territory. Jasomirgott stubbornly refused to accept this judgment for two more years, despite negotiations in which his son Otto, bishop of Freising, took part. Jasomirgott finally yielded in 1156, on condition that he be compensated. Barbarossa delivered his compensation through a charter that converted Henry's East Mark into the newly created duchy of Austria. He granted this duchy to Henry II Jasomirgott on September 17, 1156, at Regensburg.

According to this charter, known as the *privelegium minus*, the East Mark became the duchy of Austria and was legally equivalent to the other great German duchies. Furthermore, the emperor granted Duke Henry and his wife the right of inheritance in both the female and the male lines as an added guarantee of permanent succession in the Babenberg family. Moreover, no one was allowed any jurisdiction within Austria without the duke's consent, a provision that expanded the Austrian duke's sovereignty beyond that granted elsewhere. In apparent recognition of Austria's military obligations on the Holy Roman Empire's frontier, where the Babenbergs risked continuing warfare with bordering Magyars and the Slavs, Austria was exempted from all imperial military obligations except campaigns against lands on its own borders. None of the usual ducal services to the emperor were exacted from the duke of Austria, except attendance at diets held in Bavaria. In this way, Austria became essentially independent, a status immediately sought and eventually attained by the other duchies and political subdivisions of the Holy Roman Empire.

Finally, Barbarossa's constitutional reform reinforced the internal authority of the dukes. With this authority, they could end the endemic petty warfare among the lesser nobility that was destroying Germany's internal resources. As the monarchy dominated the dukes, the dukes were expected to dominate and control the lesser potentates beneath them. The Austrian charter of 1155 illustrates

Barbarossa's technique, bestowing full control of internal administration on the duke.

Of the German duchies that existed in 1156, only Austria persisted as an independent, sovereign state through the twentieth century. Many events intervened between the twelfth and twentieth centuries, but the year 1156 witnessed Austria's decisive break with its past. Its subsequent greatness flowed, indirectly, from the charter that Frederick Barbarossa bestowed on Henry Jasomirgott.

—*Raymond H. Schmandt,*
updated by Ralph L. Langenheim, Jr.

ADDITIONAL READING:

Arnold, Benjamin. *Princes and Territories in Medieval Germany*. Cambridge, England: Cambridge University Press, 1991. Details interrelationships between German rulers and the nature of their political status.

Barraclough, Geoffrey. *The Origins of Modern Germany*. Oxford: Basil Blackwell and Mott, 1957. Thorough discussion of medieval Germany, including the establishment of Austria.

Haverkamp, Alfred. *Medieval Germany, 1056-1273*. Translated by Helga Braun and Richard Mortimer. New York: Oxford University Press, 1988. Describes establishment of Babenberg Austria and its subsequent history.

Leeper, A. W. A. *A History of Medieval Austria*. Edited by R. W. Seton-Watson and C. A. Macartney. Oxford: Oxford University Press, 1941. This book is unrivaled for study of Austrian history through the end of the Babenberg dynasty in 1254.

Munz, Peter. *Frederick Barbarossa: A Study in Medieval Politics*. Ithaca, N.Y.: Cornell University Press, 1969. Definitive biography of Barbarossa, including an account of his role in establishing Austria.

SEE ALSO: 1147-1149, The Second Crusade; 1152, Frederick Barbarossa Is Elected King of Germany; 1189-1192, The Third Crusade.

1168

NEMANYID DYNASTY IS FOUNDED IN SERBIA

The Nemanyid dynasty is founded in Serbia and extends its power from the eastern Sava River to the south of Thessaly by the middle of the fourteenth century.

DATE: 1168

LOCALE: Serbia

CATEGORY: Government and politics

KEY FIGURES:

Stephen Nemanya (Nemanja; 1114-1200), ruler of

Serbia and founder of the Nemanyid dynasty,
c. 1067-1196

Stephen II Nemanya (Nemanja; died 1228), the
founder's son and successor as king of Serbia,
1196-1228

SUMMARY OF EVENT. As historian Ferdinand Schevill
observes, information about the Serb people in the early
medieval period is "fragmentary and unsatisfactory. Serbs
settled in the Balkan Peninsula in the sixth and seventh
centuries and were converted to Christianity in the ninth
century. Their petty principalities were nominally governed by a grand zhupan, who recognized Byzantine
authority.

By the eleventh century, Serbs were beginning to form
into large concentrations, opposed to both the Greeks and
the Magyars. Out of the rivalry of various Serb chieftains,
Stephen Nemanya (sometimes spelled Nemanja) triumphed, the Byzantine emperor acknowledging him as
grand *zhupan* (clan leader) in 1159. A man of extraordinary energy and audacity, Nemanya united the Serbs and
ruled for more than twenty-five years, resigning his throne
in 1196.

Not content with having forged a self-reliant nation,
Nemanya conducted several successful wars against the
Byzantine Empire, although he was never powerful
enough to conquer it, and at times he had to sue for peace.
Nor was he able to vanquish the Greeks, ending his career
as their vassal. Nevertheless, his record among the Serbs
was hallowed because he coupled his warrior's prowess
with a religious sensibility. At the end of his reign, he
entrusted power to his son Stephen and retired to a monastery on Mount Athos, preparing himself for death
through prayer and meditation.

The Nemanyid dynasty, then, was founded on this
legend of a ruler revered as a saint, who valued both this
world and the next. Indeed, Serbs believed that oil from
Stephen's grave performed miracles. One of Stephen's
sons became Saint Sava, a pilgrim and statesman, revered
by monks and treated by the Serbs as an embodiment of
both their religion and their national aspirations.

For two hundred years, the dynasty took Serbia to the
height of its power. The second Stephen Nemanya proved
to be as effective as his father, and more prudent in his
military exploits, preferring to gain the advantage by diplomacy rather than war. He also enhanced the prestige
and mystique of the dynasty by having himself crowned
twice—by a Roman papal legate in 1217 and by the
Orthodox Church in 1222. With the blessing of both the
western and eastern halves of the old Roman Empire, the
second Nemanya consolidated both his power and his
religious standing.

All the Nemanyas adopted the name of Stephen, emphasizing their direct descent from the hallowed founder
of their dynasty as well as invoking the protection of Saint
Stephen, whom the Serbs worshiped as a martyr to the
Christian faith and as their patron saint. Indeed, the Nemanya dynasty fused the idea of Christianity and Serb unity,
overriding the claims of village rulers and princelings.

By the third generation of Nemanyas, however, Serbia
ceased developing at the rapid pace set by the dynasty's
founders. The Nemanyas could not settle internal rivalries
that led to civil war; their disputes contributed to a serious
weakening of the nation, exploited by various Serb chieftains and the nobility. Nevertheless, as Schevill points out,
the nation did slowly progress, improving both its social
and economic organization. Even when the Serbs lost their
independence and were defeated by the Turks in 1389, the
Orthodox Church kept alive the memory of the Nemanyas,
of a free and Christian state—an idea that penetrated
deeply into all classes, including the peasants. The Serbs
who took part in the uprising against the Turks in 1804
sang songs evoking their Nemanyid heritage of a highly
developed civilization which they intended to create anew.
In October of 1915, when the Serbian army was faced with
extinction—confronting a combined Austro-Hungarian
and Bulgarian army of more than half a million men,
Serbian monks and soldiers carried the coffins of their
Nemanyid kings in bullock-carts, and when the roads no
longer were passable by vehicles, they hoisted the coffins
on their shoulders and kept going, so that their sacred
rulers would not be defiled by the enemy.

After the first two Stephens, the Nemanyid kings found
it difficult to protect the Serbs from the onslaught and
rivalry of various Slavic peoples. Only a rare combination
of shrewdness and boldness could have confirmed and
extended Serbian power. On the west, Serbia had to contend with Catholic Bosnia, allied with papal Rome in
efforts to attack the Orthodox Serbs. To the north, Hungary engaged in several attacks on the Serbs, and to the
south the Byzantine Empire represented a perennial threat
to Serb independence.

The Turkish conquest of Serbia served to embellish in
the Serbian imagination a dynasty that had withstood
pagan threats and remained loyal to Christianity. The
religious art of the Nemanya period, found in monasteries
and churches, is especially revered. The Turkish usurpa-
tion is viewed as only an interruption in Serbia's mission
to defend and spread Christianity.

The Nemanyid dynasty of old Serbia evokes images of
a heroic age—not merely of great kings but of a close-knit
people, fiercely independent and dynamic, creating beautiful works of art. It is an idealized image, of course, the

subject of countless romantic stories. Yet the Nemanyid period also reflects a people's aspiration, a vision of the past which is simultaneously a projection of their future. At its best, the Nemanyid period also conveys the quest for religious tolerance, for the most successful representatives of the dynasty were able to live beside both Catholic and Orthodox Slavs and even encourage peaceful coexistence between different religious communities. This history of tolerance, however, was marred by other Nemanyas, who confiscated Catholic monasteries and churches and turned them over to Orthodox priests.

In the early twentieth century, the idea of the unified Yugoslavia, with the Serbs in the vanguard of a coalition of southern Slavs (Catholic and Orthodox) owed much to the example of the Nemanyas. Not until after World War II, when Yugoslavia's Communist leader, Tito, took control, did the idea of a Serb-led union of southern Slavs dissipate. The dissolution of Yugoslavia awakened a yearning for a union of Serbs, but the resulting wars led to more division between the south Slavs, and the creation of new countries—Slovenia, Croatia, and Bosnia—establishing a fragmented region that the Nemanyid dynasty sought to integrate.   —*Carl Rollyson*

ADDITIONAL READING:

Halecki, Oscar. *Borderlands of Western Civilization: A History of East Central Europe.* New York: Ronald Press, 1952. See chapter 5 for a succinct account of the establishment and success of the Nemanyid dynasty in the context of the Fourth Crusade and the development of Bulgarian independence.

Kaplan, Robert D. *Balkan Ghosts: A Journey Through History.* New York: St. Martin's Press, 1993. Chapter 2, "Old Serbia and Albania: Balkan 'West Bank,'" offers insights into the legacy of the Nemanyid dynasty and describes the monasteries which perpetuate the dynasty's hold on the Serb imagination.

Laffan, R. G. D. *The Serbs: Guardians of the Gate.* New York: Dorset Press, 1989. A reprint of the 1917 edition. Chapter 1, "The Past," is still a good introduction to the geography and history of old Serbia, out of which the Nemanyid dynasty developed.

Palmer, Alan. *The Lands Between: A History of East-Central Europe Since the Congress of Vienna.* New York: Macmillan, 1970. Chapter 1 includes a brief discussion of the Nemanyid dynasty in terms of the eastern European tendency to glorify the past, especially episodes of valor that highlight a dedication to national mission and the quest for patriot-father figures.

Schevill, Ferdinand. *A History of the Balkans: From the Earliest Times to the Present Day.* New York: Dorset Press, 1991. Originally published in 1933, this volume still has one of the best straightforward accounts of the founding and perpetuation of the Nemanyid dynasty.

Stavrianos, L. S. *The Balkans Since 1453.* New York: Rinehart & Company, 1958. Chapter 2, "Historical Background," explains the origins of the Serbs, Stephen Nemanya's role in uniting them for the first time, and his son's consolidation of Nemanya power.

West, Rebecca. *Black Lamb and Grey Falcon: A Journey Through Yugoslavia.* New York: Viking Press, 1941. Still the most evocative and dramatic account of the Nemanyid dynasty, weaving its history and its impact on modern-day Serbia throughout this epic work of travel writing and history.

SEE ALSO: 850, Building of the Slavic Alphabet; 963, Foundation of Mount Athos Monasteries; 1389, Turkish Conquest of Serbia.

1169-1172
NORMAN TROOPS INVADE IRELAND
Norman troops invade Ireland in a series of small military expeditions, backed by Welsh and Flemish foot soldiers, establishing a foothold in southeastern Ireland that provides the basis for England's lengthy domination of Ireland and continuing involvement in Irish affairs.

DATE: 1169-1172
LOCALE: Ireland
CATEGORIES: Expansion and land acquisition; Wars, uprisings, and civil unrest
KEY FIGURES:
Adrian IV (Nicholas Brakespeare), Roman Catholic pope, 1154-1159
Richard FitzGilbert de Clare ("Strongbow"; died 1176), earl of Strigoil, earl of Pembroke, and titular leader of the Norman expeditionary forces in Ireland
Maurice Fitzgerald (died 1176) and *Robert Fitzstephen*, half brothers and Norman nobles who led the first wave of Normans into Ireland in 1169
Henry II (Henry Plantagenet; 1144-1189), king of England, 1154-1189
John of Salisbury (c. 1115-1180), English cleric and emissary from England to the papal court in Rome
Dermot (Diarmaid) MacMurrough (died 1171), deposed king of Leinster
Eva (Aoife) MacMurrough, daughter of Dermot MacMurrough and wife of "Strongbow"
Rory O'Connor, king of Connacht and high-king of Ireland, 1166-1198
Dervorgilla O'Rourke, wife of Tiernan O'Rourke

Tiernan O'Rourke, king of Breifne and archenemy of Dermot MacMurrough

Laurence O'Toole, archbishop of Dublin, 1162-1180, who later received sainthood

SUMMARY OF EVENT. There was no well-conceived design by England's Henry II to obtain control of Ireland. Henry, whose domains stretched from Scotland to the Pyrenees Mountains, was also duke of Normandy, count of Anjou, and ruler of Aquitaine through marriage to its duchess, Eleanor. As such, Henry was lukewarm to the idea of taking on additional responsibilities. At a royal council held at Winchester in 1155, the idea of invading Ireland had been discussed, but quickly put aside. It had been the English bishops, led by the archbishop of Canterbury, who had been the most enthusiastic in their support of such an invasion.

The two kingdoms were utterly different from each other. England was a centralized, medieval monarchy, with a well-developed system of bureaucracy and an efficient administration whose workings ultimately stemmed from the king himself. In the hands of an energetic, detail-oriented monarch such as Henry, it could be a highly effective instrument. The English Church followed the Roman model and acknowledged the pope's final authority. Ireland, however, maintained the centuries-old Celtic structure of its church. Government was decentralized, and territory was parceled into units controlled by tribal or clan groupings known as *tuath*. Tribal chieftains and clan leaders owed allegiance to different kings. Ultimately, all of the various kings theoretically pledged allegiance to an Irish high-king. The high-king, however, was considered a war leader or a "first among equals," rather than a governmental or administrative head; there was no set rule determining who would be high-king. Heredity was only one factor to consider, out of many. Order and authority were generally maintained by force of arms, and each separate kingdom often enjoyed abundant autonomy. At any given time, there might be as many as 150 Irish kingdoms. The Irish Church also operated on an independent basis, differing from the Roman Church in many of its ideas and practices. During the tenth and eleventh centuries, Danish Vikings set up independent colonies that developed into urban centers—notably Dublin, Limerick, Waterford, and Wexford—further complicating Ireland's fragmented political picture.

In 1152, Irish church leaders had angered Theobald, the influential archbishop of Canterbury, by ignoring his claims to authority over them. In response, the archbishop pressured Henry into dispatching his emissary, John of Salisbury, on a mission to Pope Adrian IV. Born Nicholas Brakespeare, Pope Adrian was the first and only English-man elevated to the papacy. In December of 1155, Adrian issued the papal bull *Laudabiliter*, which authorized Henry to take control of Ireland and to restore the Irish Church to Roman practices. At the time, the gesture was ineffectual; Henry did not follow up on it.

Ireland's internal politics, however, transformed the situation. Dermot MacMurrough, king of Leinster, had maintained a long-standing feud with Tiernan O'Rourke, king of Breifne. Animosity between the two kings reached such a level of intensity that MacMurrough once abducted O'Rourke's wife Dervorgilla and held her (not entirely against her will) for one year. O'Rourke never forgot this humiliation; when his powerful ally Rory O'Connor, king of Connacht, became high-king of Ireland in 1166, MacMurrough was dispossessed of his kingdom and forced into exile.

In an attempt to regain his crown, MacMurrough sought out Henry in Aquitaine and implored his assistance in its recovery. Although he expressed sympathy, Henry refused to commit himself. Nevertheless, he authorized his subjects to help in restoring MacMurrough if they so desired. MacMurrough chose to concentrate his efforts at recruitment in the border country of South Wales. There, many tough young Norman warriors had been tempering their battle skills in clashes with Welsh tribesmen.

MacMurrough found the Normans quite willing to embark on an adventure in Ireland—for a price. In return for the promise of lands, money, or both, bands of Norman knights, Flemish foot soldiers, and Welsh bowmen agreed to sail across the Irish Sea on MacMurrough's behalf. The most prominent of these mercenaries was Richard Fitz-Gilbert de Clare, earl of Strigoil and Pembroke, who was popularly known as Strongbow. What this powerful noble asked, and received, was the hand of MacMurrough's daughter Eva in marriage and the right of succession to the kingdom of Leinster. In 1167, MacMurrough led a small force of foreigners in his first attempt to reclaim his kingdom, and it proved to be an unqualified failure. In May, 1169, however, a more formidable contingent—thirty knights, sixty men-at-arms, and three hundred archers—under the command of half brothers Robert Fitzstephen and Maurice Fitzgerald landed in County Wexford. Other landings soon followed, with Strongbow himself disembarking at Passage in County Waterford in August, 1170.

The lightly clad Irish, relying on wild, headlong charges and antiquated weaponry, proved no match for the less numerous but effective and well-disciplined Norman forces, nor could the urban Danes stand up to the Norman invaders. After a spectacular Norman success at Baginbun and the taking of Wexford and Waterford cities, Strong-bow married Eva MacMurrough and marched on Dublin, which also fell into his grasp. Upon Dermot MacMurrough's death in May, 1171, Strongbow laid claim to his domains but had to defend his claims against various rivals. Murtough MacMurrough, Dermot's nephew, tried to wrest control of the kingdom of Leinster; Asculf, the exiled Danish ruler of Dublin, returned with Viking warriors from as far off as Norway. Cavalry charges scattered Asculf's forces, and he was beheaded after a brief trial. O'Connor and O'Rourke then besieged Dublin, but were beaten back after two months by a Norman surprise attack on the high-king's camp.

King Henry, who became alarmed at the possibility that Strongbow might establish himself as an independent ruler, took a belated interest in the invasion and landed at Waterford in October, 1171. In the negotiations that followed, Laurence O'Toole, archbishop of Dublin, played a key role. O'Toole was largely responsible for persuading a synod of Irish bishops meeting at Cashel to submit to Henry's rule and also negotiated Strongbow's submission to the English king. Henry entered Dublin in triumph and received the submission of one Irish king after another. Although he allowed Strongbow to retain his position as ruler (not king) of Leinster, Henry appointed Hugh de Lacy, a trusted Norman, to serve as justiciar of Ireland and gave him authority over the former kingdom of Meath in order to balance Strongbow's power.

Henry's ultimate victory in Ireland occurred when he successfully negotiated the Treaty of Windsor in October, 1175. Under the terms of the treaty, High-King Rory O'Connor acknowledged Henry as his suzerain. O'Connor proved to be Ireland's last high-king and was increasingly unable to assert his influence over the remaining lands of his realm. He died while on a religious pilgrimage to Cong in 1198.

Strongbow died at Dublin in 1176, leaving no male heir; he was buried in Christchurch Cathedral. The dominant position of the English government in Ireland, however, had been established on an enduring foundation.

—*Raymond Pierre Hylton*

ADDITIONAL READING:

Cambrensis, Giraldus. *Expugnation Hibernica: The Conquest of Ireland*. Edited and translated by A. B. Scott and F. X. Martin. Dublin: Royal Irish Academy, 1978. A primary source account of the period whose author, a Norman-Welsh cleric, expresses a distinct anti-Irish bias.

De Poer, Liam. *The Peoples of Ireland*. Notre Dame, Ind.: University of Notre Dame Press, 1986. An overview that covers the breadth of invasions, migrations, and influences entering Ireland from prehistory to the twentieth century.

Flanagan, Marie Therese. *Irish Society, Anglo-Norman Settlers, Angevin Kingship: Intervention and Interaction in Ireland in the Late Twelfth Century*. Oxford: Clarendon Press, 1989. Scholarly reevaluation of primary source material that is accessible to laypersons. Stresses the role of the English Church.

Foster, R. F. *The Oxford Illustrated History of Ireland*. New York: Oxford University Press, 1989. A good place to being reading on the subject. There is a greater amount of written content here than the title might indicate. Stresses the effects of Irish tribal politics.

Moody, T. W., and F. X. Martin. *The Course of Irish History*. Cork, Ireland: Mercier Press, 1984. One of the most complete scholarly accounts of the sequence of events culminating in the establishment of Norman political control.

SEE ALSO: 635-800, Founding of Lindisfarne and Creation of the *Book of Kells*; 793, Northmen Raid Lindisfarne; 1014, Battle of Clontarf; 1066, Battle of Hastings; 1154-1204, Establishment of the Angevin Empire.

1170
MURDER OF THOMAS À BECKET

The murder of Thomas à Becket and his subsequent canonization thwart the aristocracy's effort to bring the Catholic Church under secular control and has a considerable influence on the evolution and ecclesiastical law and royal custom in England.

DATE: December 29, 1170

LOCALE: Canterbury Cathedral, England

CATEGORIES: Government and politics; Religion; Terrorism and political assassination

KEY FIGURES:

Alexander III (Roland Bandinelli; c. 1105-1181), Roman Catholic pope, 1159-1181, who was torn between support of Becket and political expediency

Thomas à Becket (1118-1170), archbishop of Canterbury, 1162-1170

Gilbert Foliot, bishop of London, 1163-1188, and opponent of Becket

Henry II (Henry Plantagenet; 1144-1189), king of England, 1154-1189, a close personal friend and later an opponent of Becket

Louis VII (1120-1180), king of France, 1137-1180, supporter of Becket in exile

Roger of York (died 1181), archbishop of York and critic of Becket

Theobald (c. 1090-1161), archbishop of Canterbury, 1138-1161, and proponent of Becket as chancellor in 1155

SUMMARY OF EVENT. Thomas à Becket was born in London in 1118 to middle-class merchant parents. He was educated first at Merton Priory in Surrey and then at Paris. About 1141, he joined the household of Theobald, archbishop of Canterbury, who sent him to Bologna and Auxerre to study law. In 1154, Becket became archdeacon of Canterbury, and in the following year Henry II chose Becket as his chancellor. Loyal courtier, able diplomat, and trusted soldier, Becket became a close personal friend of the king and vigorously pursued the interests of the Crown.

Theobald's death in 1161 was followed by a long vacancy of the See of Canterbury. Henry was aware that the archbishop of Cologne was successfully serving as chancellor of the Holy Roman Empire, and he saw in his friend an ally in his lifelong effort to gain complete control of his kingdom. Henry passed over the worthy Gilbert Foliot and asked that Becket be invested as archbishop of the See of Canterbury. If Henry expected Becket to acquiesce in his efforts to limit the independence the church had won under Stephen, he was to be disappointed; Becket resigned the chancellorship in order to devote himself completely and wholeheartedly to the service of the Catholic Church.

A crucial dispute concerning jurisdiction over felonious clerics arose between Henry and Becket in 1163. By custom, clerics accused of a felony were tried and sentenced in church courts. Since these courts were not permitted to impose any penalty involving physical punishment, criminous clerics were usually expelled from office but were spared the capital punishment often meted out to laypersons in the king's courts. In 1163, Philip de Brois, a canon accused of murder, was acquitted by a church court. Public opinion insisted that he was guilty, and the sheriff brought him before the king's justice. On Becket's protest of the action, it was dropped, but the king was determined that felonious clerics should henceforth stand trial in the secular courts. At a council held at Westminster in October, 1163, Henry insisted that all bishops swear to observe the ancient customs of the realm, without specifying what they were. Although Becket and the other bishops were aware that the unwritten customs could seriously infringe on ecclesiastical liberties, they swore to uphold them.

In January of 1164, the king held a council at Clarendon that included bishops and the lay magnates of the kingdom. In sixteen decrees, Henry proposed the regulation which should henceforth govern the relations between the Church and the Crown. The most important clause concerned criminous clerics. Henry proposed that after a cleric had been found guilty in a church court he should be stripped of his orders so that, as a layman, he could be sent to the king's judge for sentencing and for confiscation of his chattels. Henry insisted that this was the ancient custom of the realm, observed by William the Conqueror and his sons. Becket and the bishops repeated their pledge to observe the ancient customs, but when the king put them in writing, they refused to agree to them. Since medieval custom was oral and flexible, any attempt to make custom absolute by writing was considered novel and dangerous.

The Constitutions of Clarendon not only dealt with felonious clerics but also stated that no appeal could be made from English courts to the pope, and that royal consent was required before a tenant-in-chief could be excommunicated, before a papal bull could be promulgated in the land, or before a cleric could leave England. Becket vacillated somewhat but ultimately took a position that was consistent with that of the Gregorian reformers on the Continent and of Alexander III, namely that the Church had the sole right to try and punish clerics in major orders. The question of criminous clerics and ancestral custom was actually a symptom of the deeper problem

Thomas à Becket's assassination within the transept of Canterbury Cathedral resulted in his canonization as a saint; later at the cathedral, Henry II made public penance to demonstrate his remorse over his role in the murder. (Archive Photos)

of two rival jurisdictions existing together in the same country.

When one of Becket's vassals claimed that he had been denied justice and appealed to the king, the archbishop was summoned before Henry at Northampton. Becket refused the first summons so that the assembled barons judged him guilty of contempt of court. Then the king added a demand that Becket account for the money he had handled when he was chancellor. Becket's request for time to get his accounts in order was refused. Seeing that Henry intended to ruin and imprison him or to force his resignation as archbishop, Becket fled to France, where Pope Alexander received him with honor.

During the negotiations between the pope and the French and English kings, Becket stayed at the Cistercian abbey of Pontigny in Burgundy. When Henry threatened to expel all Cistercians from England in 1166 in retaliation, Becket moved to a Benedictine abbey at Sens under the protection of King Louis VII. In 1169, Becket excommunicated two English bishops who had opposed him, and he threatened to place all England under interdict. In June of 1170, Henry had Roger, archbishop of York, crown young prince Henry, a ritual which was the prerogative of the archbishop of Canterbury. Becket, followed by the pope, excommunicated all responsible for the investiture; fearing an interdict for England, Henry was reconciled with Becket at Fréteval in Normandy in July, 1170. It was agreed that the endowments of Canterbury should be restored and the exiled followers of Becket forgiven, but nothing was said about the Constitutions of Clarendon, appeals to Rome, or any of the other matters in dispute.

Becket returned to England on November 30, 1170, and was received with enthusiasm. When Becket refused to lift the excommunication of Roger of York and Foliot, Henry was furious. In a fit of rage, he uttered the words, "What sluggards, what cowards have I brought up in my court, who care nothing for their allegiance to their lord. Not one will deliver me from this low-born priest!" This outburst was enough to inspire four knights to travel to Canterbury and assassinate Becket within the cathedral late in the afternoon of December 29, 1170.

The news of Becket's murder sent a shock of horror throughout Christendom. The pope refused to see any English citizens for several weeks, and Henry was afraid that his vassals would throw off their allegiance to him. The two articles of the Constitutions of Clarendon dealing with felonious clerics and appeals to Rome were dropped, but the remaining fourteen articles were observed, and Henry continued to control the English Church in the same manner as he had done before the struggle with Becket began.

Thomas à Becket was canonized by the Roman Catholic Church in 1173; he quickly became one of Europe's best-loved saints. Thousands of pilgrims visited his tomb, and churches were dedicated to him throughout Europe. Even in death, he was a champion of the principle of clerical supremacy.

—*Carl A. Volz, updated by Hal Holladay*

ADDITIONAL READING:

Barlow, Frank. *Thomas Becket.* Berkeley: University of California Press, 1990. A comprehensive biography by a distinguished scholar who writes astutely about the complex legal questions involved in the controversy.

Duggan, Alfred. *Thomas Becket of Canterbury.* London: Faber & Faber, 1967. A sprightly and critical account of Becket's life and death based on close familiarity with the sources.

Fitz Stephen, William. *The Life and Death of Thomas Becket.* Edited by George W. Greenway. London: Folio Society, 1961. A collection of data on Becket's life and death arranged chronologically and held together by the editor's explanatory comments.

Ide, Arthur Frederick. *Calendar of Death.* Irving, Tex.: Scholar Books, 1986. A brief study of the sociopolitical factors in Thomas à Becket's attitude toward his own death.

Knowles, David. *The Episcopal Colleagues of Archbishop Thomas Becket.* Cambridge, England: Cambridge University Press, 1951. Written by the author of several distinguished studies of Becket, this work contains the best account of the events of Northampton.

Pain, Nesta. *The King and Becket.* New York: Barnes & Noble, 1966. A compelling and well-documented study that takes a negative view of Becket.

Winston, Richard. *Thomas Becket.* New York: Alfred A. Knopf, 1968. A balanced, equitable, and readable study of Becket that is sensitive to the virtues as well as the flaws of both Becket and Henry.

SEE ALSO: 596-597, See of Canterbury Is Established; 1154-1204, Establishment of the Angevin Empire.

1175
APPEARANCE OF THE WALDENSIANS

The excommunication of the Waldensians from the medieval Catholic Church for preaching heretical beliefs is considered one of the marks of the beginning of the Protestant movement in Europe.

DATE: c. 1175

LOCALE: Lyons, France; Piedmont, Italy; and generally throughout Europe

CATEGORY: Religion

KEY FIGURES:

Alexander III (Roland Bandinelli; c. 1105-1181), Roman Catholic pope, 1159-1181, who tolerated the early Waldensian movement

Durand of Huesca, clerical organizer of the Catholic poor

Innocent III (Lothario of Segni; c. 1160-1216), Roman Catholic pope, 1198-1216, and author of coercive measure against the Waldensians

Peter II (Pedro II; 1174-1213), king of Aragon and Catalonia, 1196-1213, responsible for the death by burning edict of 1197

Peter Waldo (Pierre Valdès; died 1217), French religious leader who was banished from Lyons in 1184, advocate of ecclesiastical reforms

SUMMARY OF EVENT. The first Waldensians advocated a return to the simple type of Christianity reflected in the Gospels, unencumbered with ecclesiastical organization or hierarchical structure. They possibly named themselves after Peter Waldo, a rich merchant of Lyons who in 1176 decided to distribute his wealth to the poor and established a lay order known as "The Poor Men of Lyons." Other origins of the name Waldensians suggest Vaux, or valleys of Piedmont, where the sect flourished; or Peter of Vaux, a predecessor of Waldo.

According to early accounts, Peter Waldo, after hearing of the Gospels, asked two priests to translate them into everyday language for him. He immersed himself in these translations and resolved to follow the teachings of Christ he found there in a literal fashion. He sold his property, gave the proceeds to the poor, and began begging in the streets. Soon he was joined by many of the uneducated and unlettered poor of Lyons. From this group of followers, the lay order of The Poor Men of Lyons was established. The requirements for admission to the order were "conversion," accompanied by a turning away from worldly pursuits, divesting self of personal property and vocation, along with the dissolution of any existing marriage, and unquestioned submission to the superiors in the order. Training consisted of memorization of the entire New Testament and many of the writings of the Saints.

At first Peter Waldo's personal program consisted primarily of living a life of poverty, but as he became better acquainted with the Bible in the vernacular he began publicly to elucidate the Scriptures. In addition, his followers openly criticized the immorality of the clergy and their frequent indifference to Christian precepts. Although Waldo's activities, and those of his followers, were not heretical, it was contrary to the Canon Law of the Church and established practice for lay persons to preach. At the Third Lateran Council (1179), The Poor Men of Lyons sought and received authorization for their vow of poverty, and were given permission to preach provided they received authorization from local church authorities. When the Poor Men found it difficult to obtain such authorization, because they were found by the Council to be unacquainted with even the most basic teachings of the Church, they ignored the Council's restriction by expounding the Scriptures openly in the towns. At the Council of Verona in 1184, they were condemned along with the Albigensians and expelled from Lyons. They fled to Spain, Lombardy, the Rhineland, Bohemia, Hungary, and northern France; but as they went they came into contact with more radical heretical groups who influenced them into adopting more extreme unorthodox tenets.

As opposed to the Church, the Waldensians denied the existence of purgatory, and the efficacy of indulgences and prayers for the dead. They held that private prayer (praying in a closet) is preferable to praying in a church. From the beginning they especially stressed the need to make the Scriptures in the vernacular available to the laity—rather than to reserve them to the priesthood. Lying was considered an especially grievous sin, and they forbade the shedding of blood and the taking of oaths. In an age when society was bound together by a system of feudal oaths, this prohibition was considered deleterious to the social order. Furthermore, they condemned war and capital punishment. From preaching and expounding the Scriptures it was an easy transition to hearing confessions, absolving sins, and assigning penances. At the Council of Verona (1184), they were accused of refusing obedience to the clergy, usurping the right of preaching, and opposing the validity of masses for the dead. Although the Waldensians did not espouse any significant doctoral aberration, they opposed the entire sacerdotal system, declaring that the authority to exercise priestly functions was derived not from ordination but from individual merit and piety.

In Spain in 1194, an edict was issued allowing the confiscation of the property of all who gave food and shelter to the Waldensians. In 1197, Pedro II amended this edict to include the burning of Waldensians wherever they were found. This edict was the first public document in which death by burning was prescribed as the state punishment for heresy.

By the early 1300's, the Waldensians were in such conflict with the Church that they had become a secret organization. They divided themselves into two classes, the "Perfect" or *Perfecti*, and the "Believers" or *Credentes*. Only the male descendants of the original believers—women were no longer admitted to the order—were eligible to become members. The celibate *Perfecti*, having spent five or six years in study, were ordained as deacons and then required to spend as much as nine years more in theological study. They were bound by the vow of poverty, led an itinerant life of preaching and, being exempt from manual labor, they depended upon the *Credentes* for their support. The latter group continued to live in the world as others, even receiving the sacraments, except penance, administered by Waldensian bishops. The *Perfecti* were further classified as bishops, priests, and deacons. Bishops celebrated the Eucharist and administered penance and ordination; priests preached and heard confessions; deacons received alms and administered the temporal affairs of the church. Bishops were elected at joint meetings of priests and deacons. One bishop, the rector, seems to have enjoyed supervision over the others, but the supreme governing power was vested in a council of all the *Perfecti*.

After their condemnation by Pope Lucius III at Verona, the Waldensians scattered. Waldo led a group into upper Italy where the sect flourished in the Lombard climate of revolt and anticlericalism. As sporadic persecutions arose, however, they were gradually driven into the rugged valleys of the Piedmontese Alps. A dispute arose between the Italian and French factions in which the former, led by Waldo, rejected hierarchical organization, manual labor of the preachers, and moral requirements for one celebrating the Eucharist. The dispute reached such proportions that a majority of the sect repudiated Waldo's leadership and followed his chief opponent, Joannes de Roncho. It appears that Waldo and the French group favored a reconciliation with Rome, whereas the Italians supported the idea of a separate organization consciously opposed to Rome. Waldo left Piedmont and, according to tradition, traveled through Italy for some time and finally went to Bohemia where he died in 1217. The dispute was resolved at the Council of Bergamo, a city in Lombardy, in 1218, attended by delegates from several countries. During the thirteenth and fourteenth centuries, the center of Waldensianism shifted to Milan, where the chief bishop resided and a theological school was established. Each year during Lent, a council was held attended by delegates from every nation which had an organized Waldensian Church. Although harassed by numerous persecutions, the Waldensians persisted. In Bohemia, they paved the way for Jan Hus, in Switzerland for Calvin, and in France they eventually merged with the Calvinists in the seventeenth century. The Waldensian Church is considered by some to be the oldest Protestant church in existence. Some thirty thousand adherents continued to exist in Italy in the late twentieth century.

—*Carl A. Volz, updated by Barbara C. Stanley*

ADDITIONAL READING:

Clot, Alberto. "Waldenses." In *The New Schaff-Herzog Encyclopedia of Religious Knowledge*. Vol. 12. Grand Rapids, Mich.: Baker Book House, 1969. Detailed history of Waldensianism, describing its place in medieval church history and its spread to other countries in both hemispheres; contains an extensive annotated bibliography.

Coulton, G. G. *Inquisition and Liberty*. Boston: Beacon Press, 1959. Chapters 16 and 17 of this work detail the methodology and history of the Church's efforts to root out the heresy.

Dossat, Y. "Waldenses." In *New Catholic Encyclopedia*. Vol. 4. New York: McGraw-Hill, 1967. An article maintaining that contempt for the power of the Church was at the basis of the heresy.

Leff, Gordon. "Waldensians." In *The Encyclopedia of Religion*. Vol. 15. New York: Macmillan, 1987. An article setting out the historical chronology of the Waldensian movement, its belief system (biblical foundation and basic tenets), and its descent into heresy.

SEE ALSO: 1209-1229, The Albigensian Crusade; 1215, The Fourth Lateran Council; 1377-1378, John Wycliffe Is Condemned for Attacking Church Authority; 1415, Martyrdom of Jan Hus.

1175
COMMON LAW TRADITION EMERGES IN ENGLAND

The common law tradition emerges during the twelfth and thirteenth centuries in England, forming the foundation of the legal systems of Britain and most of its colonies.

DATE: c. 1175
LOCALE: England
CATEGORIES: Government and politics; Laws, acts, and legal history
KEY FIGURES:
Edward I (1239-1307), king of England, 1272-1307
Henry I (1068-1135), king of England, 1100-1135
Henry II (1133-1189), king of England, 1154-1189
SUMMARY OF EVENT. William the Conqueror, in an attempt to conciliate the recently subjugated Anglo-Saxons, promised that he would "restore the laws of their last king, Edward the Confessor." In doing so, he helped to ensure that England developed a distinctive set of procedures and rules which in time came to be known as the common law. This term is used in contradistinction to Roman, or civil law, which except to a limited degree, was never adopted in England. Civil law was a judicial system based on

written legal codes which were generally legislated by rulers. Common law, on the other hand, was never written down and developed on a case-by-case basis. Judges rendered decisions based on earlier cases, or precedents. Although legal theorists such as Ranulf de Glanville and Henry de Bracton wrote treatises on the common law, their books were not legally binding on judges. The treatises did, however, provide summaries of cases which were used as precedents by judges making decisions.

The term "common law" refers to that law which originated in the English royal court and gradually spread until it became common to much of the realm, dealing with all persons equally as subjects of the king regardless of class. Built up gradually by the king and his judges, the common law took effect in no single year. By about 1200 , however, the characteristic features of the common law were well established. William the Conqueror, in the years after the conquest of England, laid the foundations for the later emergence of the common law. A strong administrator, William introduced feudalism, grafting this system of government onto existing Anglo-Saxon legal customs. His work was mainly that of systemization and regularization. He both stated and enforced royal rights, out of which eventually grew the common law.

Although during the reign of William's son, Henry I, there was little that could accurately be called the common law, Henry I was responsible for a number of reforms and extensions of royal power. He commissioned judges to hear royal cases in the counties. Again, Henry's chief contribution to the emergence of the common law was his development of a well-run central administration which would provide the mechanism for the growth of the common law.

The most decisive period in the formation of the common law occurred during the reign of Henry II. Henry II extended the system of traveling judges. In addition, he issued the Assizes of Clarendon which provided instructions for his justices on how to try criminal cases. Under Henry II, royal courts could prosecute criminals. He ordered that twelve men from every hundred and four from each township testify if anyone in their district were suspected of committing crimes. He also encouraged the use of juries, systematized the grand jury, and developed a procedure for returning land to people from whom the land had been wrongfully seized.

The common law was called "the law of the land" in part because it constituted a body of rules about pieces of land; it was a body of real property law, a law of real estate. Such a development was natural in a community such as that of twelfth century England, where the most important form of wealth was land. Naturally, one of the most impor-

tant tasks of the legal system was to devise a body of rules to settle disputes concerning its ownership or possession.

Perhaps the most famous instrument of the common law was the writ. The number of writs grew from about thirty-nine in the late twelfth century to more than four hundred by the end of the thirteenth century, a clear indication of the growth of the common law. Writs were written orders in the king's name that required action by a defendant or court. Property rights were at the heart of much of the common law, and Henry II developed at least four writs to address the problem of seizure of property. Perhaps the most significant of these was the assize of novel disseisin, designed to quickly restore a property owner to his property. A dispossessed property owner would secure a writ, addressed to the sheriff, instructing him to assemble a jury of twelve men knowledgeable of the facts of the case. It was the task of this jury to decide before a judge whether or not the dispossession had occurred within a particular period of time. If it had, the sheriff was required to return the land to the original property owner. Since in the twelfth and thirteenth centuries the writs designed to settle the question of possession (possessory writs) were the ones most widely used, they were the ones characteristic of the common law in its formative stages. One such writ, the Assize of Mort d'Ancestor, was used to secure an inheritance of real estate, for example. One characteristic of common law which emerges from this is its emphasis upon the use of proper procedures; it does not begin with assertion of a right but designates a procedure to be used by the aggrieved party. It has been said that in the common law "substansive law, or right, is secreted within the interstices of procedure." Moreover, it is apparent that the common law, as exemplified by the assize of novel disseisin, demanded considerable citizen participation. The jury of inquiry was the heart of the whole procedure, the jury here serving the same function as witnesses in later courts by providing information.

Henry's order that no one be disturbed in the possession of his land without a king's writ gave the king's law wide jurisdiction over real property and caused royal justices to formulate more and more rules about the ownership of land. In addition, his itinerant justices extended the king's law under the guise of keeping the king's peace. The application of the "grand jury," men familiar enough with events in the vills and hundreds of the shire to report crimes, brought more and more cases under the competence of the royal justices. The establishment of new courts followed and the constant extension of the number of writs until the last quarter of the thirteenth century virtually ended the application of the old feudal baronial law.

By the time of Edward I, the system of royal courts,

then fairly well defined, consistently applied the common law as refined by more than a century of development. By regularly calling Parliament and systematically enforcing the common law, Edward moved England toward the realization of a "community of the realm."

—Martin J. Baron,
updated by Diane Andrews Henningfeld

ADDITIONAL READING:

Baker, J. H. *An Introduction to English Legal History.* 3d ed. London: Butterworths, 1990. Baker provides not only a standard history of English law, but also includes documents in Latin with accompanying English translations.

Hines, W. D. *English Legal History: A Bibliography and Guide to the Literature.* New York: Garland, 1990. A good starting place for research into English legal history, this volume provides an introduction for each facet of the law.

Hogue, Arthur R. *Origins of the Common Law.* Bloomington: Indiana University Press, 1966. Hogue emphasizes the interrelationships among the monarchy, the society, and the law, concluding with a chapter in which he examines the legacy of medieval common law.

Pollock, Sir Frederick, and Frederic William Maitland. *The History of English Law Before the Time of Edward I.* 2d ed. 2 vols. Cambridge, England: Cambridge University Press, 1968. Pollock and Maitland trace the history of English law through the maturation of the common law during the thirteenth century in this classic work.

Van Caenegem, R. C. *The Birth of the English Common Law.* 2d ed. Cambridge, England: Cambridge University Press, 1988. Van Caenegem outlines the development of the common law beginning with William the Conqueror. His discussion of royal writs and writ procedure illuminates a difficult topic.

SEE ALSO: 1086, The Domesday Survey; 1154-1204, Establishment of the Angevin Empire; 1215, Signing of the Magna Carta; 1258, The "Provisions of Oxford"; 1285, Statute of Winchester; 1628, Petition of Right.

1189-1192
THE THIRD CRUSADE

The Third Crusade fails to secure control of Jerusalem but strengthens the Western presence in the Middle East for generations through its acquisition of Acre and Cyprus.

DATE: 1189-1192
LOCALE: Anatolia, Cyprus, and Palestine
CATEGORIES: Government and politics; Religion; Wars, uprisings, and civil unrest

KEY FIGURES:
Berengaria (1165-1230), wife of Richard I, king of England
Frederick I Barbarossa (c. 1123-1190), Holy Roman Emperor, 1152-1190, and a leader of the Third Crusade
Gregory VIII (Alberto de Morra; died 1187), Roman Catholic pope, 1187, who preached the Third Crusade
Leopold V (1157-1194), duke of Austria, 1177-1192, and adversary of Richard I
Philip Augustus (1165-1223), king of France, 1179-1223, and a leader of the Third Crusade
Richard I ("the Lionheart"; 1157-1199), king of England, 1189-1199, and a leader of the Third Crusade
Saladin (Salah al-Din Yusuf ib Ayyub; c. 1137-1193), sultan of Egypt and Syria, and founder of the Ayyubid Dynasty

SUMMARY OF EVENT. Between 1096 and 1464, some nine or ten crusades went from the West to attempt to regain control of the Holy Land. There was a Peasants' Crusade (1096-1097), a Barons' Crusade (1096-1204), a Children's Crusade (1212), but one of the most colorful was the Crusade of the Three Kings (1189-1192), also known as the Third Crusade.

The Third Crusade was occasioned by the rise of the Muslim warrior Saladin. Born in Mesopotamia, Saladin became sultan in Egypt and Syria (after 1174), founding the famed Ayyubid Dynasty. Determined to expel the crusaders from the East, Saladin took Acre, Nazareth, and finally, on October 2, 1187, Jerusalem itself. Pope Gregory VIII, who was pontiff for only one year, called for a holy war to redeem Jerusalem. To his appeal, three famed kings responded.

The first of these kings was Frederick I, called Barbarossa, scion of the house of Hohenstaufen from Swabia, who was known for restoring peace and prosperity to his realm. As a youth, Frederick had served with the Second Crusade in 1147. Now, as a man nearing seventy, he desired once more to "take up the cross." In spite of his previous quarrels with the papacy, Frederick was reconciled to Rome and received favorably the papal legation asking him to march east. Well aware of the dangers he faced, Frederick gathered the largest crusading army yet assembled, a well-disciplined force that left Germany in May, 1189. The army peacefully crossed Hungary, but encountered hostility near Bulgaria.

Frederick promptly proposed to the pope that the crusade be redefined to target both Constantinople and Jerusalem. The Byzantine emperor quickly became more compliant. After wintering in Adrianople, Frederick avoided Constantinople, and in March, 1190, crossed the Helles-

The Third Crusade was notable for drawing the personal support of three European rulers: Frederick Barbarossa, the Holy Roman Emperor; Philip Augustus, king of France; and Richard I, king of England. (Archive Photos)

pont into Anatolia. By May, the Germans had defeated the Seljuk Turks in Iconium and the land route to Jerusalem was open. On June 10, 1190, while Frederick crossed the Calycadnus (Saleph) River in Cilicia (modern Turkey), he drowned. When his troops discovered Frederick's drowned body in full armor, they lost heart for the crusade. Many went home to Germany by sea. A much smaller force continued to Antioch under Frederick of Swabia and Duke Leopold V of Austria. Here, more discouragement occurred. Frederick's body was buried in Antioch, and not in Jerusalem, as has been planned. Without their emperor, the Germans suddenly ranked third, after the kings of England and France. A small remnant of the vast German army that had left Regensburg did prove useful in the siege of Acre in 1191. The German contribution to the Third Crusade was virtually ended.

The second of the three kings was the youthful Richard I of England, surnamed *Couer de Lion* ("the Lion-hearted"). Scion of the late Plantagenet king Henry II, Richard inherited his father's commitment to go crusading. The thirty-three-year-old "troubadour prince" was a colorful but unstable personality, dramatic but unpredictable. Often in disagreement with his family and engaged in rivalries with the king of France, Richard feared to leave his kingdom. Fortunately for the crusaders, he did and proved to be an excellent strategist.

The third of the three kings was Philip II, commonly known as Philip Augustus, of the French House of Capet. Although he was not fond of crusading, Philip had recently waged wars with England from 1187 to 1189 in an effort to enlarge his realm. A consummate politician, but an inadequate warrior, Philip agreed to meet Richard at Vezelay on July 4, 1190, to move eastward by sea.

While Philip crossed the Mediterranean and began the siege of Acre in April, 1191, Richard had landed on the island of Cyprus, where his sister, Joan, and his fiancée, Berengaria of Navarre, had been shipwrecked and were held by a local rebel prince. Richard simply conquered Cyprus. This was a fateful decision, probably the most significant outcome of the Third Crusade, since Cyprus became a permanent Western outpost in the Mediterranean. Meanwhile, Richard married Berengaria, had her crowned queen of England in the Church of Saint George at Limassol, and had his bride accompany him to Palestine.

Once in the Holy Land, Richard assisted in taking Acre, but he quarreled with Duke Leopold of Austria in the process. After Acre fell, Philip believed that he had fulfilled his crusader's vow and departed for France. Alone, Richard successfully took Jaffa in 1192, but decided to negotiate peace with Saladin. On September 2, 1192, a five-year peace treaty, recognizing Western control of the coast from Jaffa north, but acknowledging Muslim control of Jerusalem in exchange for guarantees of Christian access to the sacred sites. Regarding his mission as complete, Richard set out for Europe on October 9, only to be captured and held for ransom by Leopold of Austria until 1194. Upon his return to England, Richard went to war with his old rival, Philip of France. Richard died of mortal wounds near Limoges, France, in 1199.

If measured by its stated goal, the rescue of Jerusalem, the Third Crusade was a failure. Since access to the Holy Sepulchre was the intent of the mission, it could be maintained that this goal was attained by diplomacy, not war. Outremer (the land beyond the sea) was militarily strengthened by the possession of Acre and the Palestinian coast. The occupation of Cyprus was the most important result of the Third Crusade. Not only did it become a powerful kingdom in its own right, Cyprus was a crusader outpost in the East, a base for future campaigns, and a

Although unable to secure control of Jerusalem, the soldiers of the Third Crusade did occupy fortified outposts in Acre, on Cyprus, and along the Anatolian coast, as evidenced by the remains of this crusader castle. (Robin W. Diel)

Western foothold in the Mediterranean for almost three hundred years.   *—C. George Fry*

ADDITIONAL READING:

Erbstösser, Martin. *The Crusades.* Translated from the German by C. S. V. Salt. New York: Universe Books, 1979. In 214 pages, with maps and drawings, a noted German historian provides a nontechnical introduction to the Crusades "from the standpoint of the history of civilization."

Gibb, Christopher. *Richard the Lionhearted and the Crusades.* New York: Bookwright Press, 1986. This brief, introductory biography of the twelfth century English king treats the origins of the Crusades and their impact on Muslim-Christian relations.

Grousset, Rene. *The Epic of the Crusades.* Translated from the French by Noël Lindsay. New York: Orion Press, 1970. A celebrated French scholar offers a readable and reliable narrative of the Crusades that is rich in drama and detail.

Prawer, Joshua. *The Crusaders' Kingdom: European Colonialism in the Middle Ages.* New York: Praeger, 1972. A noted scholar at Hebrew University in Jerusalem, Prawer analyzes the impact of "a medieval society transplanted to the Eastern Mediterranean." Illustrated, with a complete bibliography.

Riley-Smith, Jonathan. *The Feudal Nobility and the Kingdom of Jerusalem, 1174-1277.* Hamden, Conn.: Archon Books, 1973. Riley-Smith examines the constitutional ideas embodied in the crusader kingdom of Jerusalem. Includes notes, appendices, and a bibliography.

Runciman, Steven. *A History of the Crusades.* 3 vols. Cambridge, England: Cambridge University Press, 1951-

1954. Prepared by a highly respected English historian, this work will long remain the definitive study of the Crusades. Volumes 2 and 3 are especially relevant to an understanding of the Third Crusade.

Smail, R. C. *The Crusaders in Syria and the Holy Land.* New York: Praeger, 1973. A fine introduction to the nature of crusader life in the Levant. Illustrated with seventy photographs, thirty-three line drawings, three maps, and two tables.

SEE ALSO: 1095, Pope Urban II Calls the First Crusade; 1147-1149, The Second Crusade; 1204, Knights of the Fourth Crusade Capture Constantinople; 1209-1229, The Albigensian Crusade; 1212, The Children's Crusade; 1217-1221, The Fifth Crusade; 1227-1230, Frederick II Leads the Sixth Crusade; 1248-1254, Failure of the Seventh Crusade.

1200
FAIRS OF CHAMPAGNE

The fairs of Champagne constitute the first major organized commercial venture in Europe and provide both the place and the means for trade between Mediterranean Europe and northern Europe.

DATE: c. 1200
LOCALE: Champagne, France
CATEGORY: Economics
KEY FIGURES:
The counts of Champagne, c. 1090-1300
SUMMARY OF EVENT. From about the middle of the eleventh century through most of the thirteenth century, the county of Champagne was the home of the fairs of Cham-

pagne, organized medieval trade fairs which encouraged and promoted interregional trade. Many factors contributed to the growth of the fairs. The location of Champagne, aristocratic patronage, technological developments, the growth of manufacturing, improved transportation, changes in business and banking practices, and the influence of the Crusades put the fairs of Champagne at the heart of the commercial revolution of the Middle Ages.

Trade fairs existed long before the Middle Ages. During the Roman period, trade fairs existed in coastal cities where people from throughout the Roman Empire met and exchanged goods. Gradually these trade fairs moved inland to locations along trade routes. In the twelfth century, virtually every trade route in Europe crossed Champagne. Champagne was well located east of Paris and between the upper Saone River and tributaries of the Rhine, Seine, and Loire. It was through these river valleys that the first traders from Flanders made their way south into Italy, and Italian traders with goods from the Mediterranean and the Arab world made their way north.

Other factors also contributed to the success of the Champagne fairs. Across Europe, improved farming techniques during the period led to growth in agriculture which in turn led to more goods available for exchange. At the same time, Europe saw an increase in the number of manufactured goods produced. Textiles and metal products took the place of furs and wood as primary exports from the northern countries. In addition, the discovery of the Frieburg silver mines led to an increase in currency. Shortages of negotiable coins had traditionally hampered trade in Europe. Furthermore, returning crusaders brought with them goods from the East, spurring the demand for luxury items. The conquest of cities in the Levant by European forces led to the import of spices, gems, and other goods from the Muslim world to Europe. The Italian cities of Genoa and Pisa grew rich through this increase in trade. By 1200, European merchants were importing goods from Africa, Asia, Constantinople, Syria, and Alexandria.

Perhaps most important, however, was the patronage given to the fairs of Champagne by the counts of Champagne, who understood the potential for profit from the growing trade moving across the Champagne borders. Consequently, the counts initiated and organized the fairs of Champagne in the towns of Troyes, Provins, Bar-sur-Aube, and Lagny.

Each fair lasted for forty-nine days and was held at the same time each year. The Lagny fair started the year in January, with the Bar-sur-Aube fair usually beginning in March during Lent. The next fair, at Provins, ran from May through June and was followed by the "warm" fair of Troyes, running from July through August. In Sep-

tember, Provins held the fair of Saint Ayoul, and in October and November, merchants returned to Troyes for the "cold" fair.

In addition to setting the time for each fair, the counts provided many necessary amenities: a place to hold the fair; booths for individual merchants; police supervision during the fair; money changers to provide standard currency and maintain accounts; and judges and courts to handle disputes. The counts appointed two keepers of the fair to oversee the daily details of administration. The counts also paid nobles who lived along the major trade routes an annual income in return for fealty and a promise to protect those merchants traveling to and from the fairs of Champagne. This arrangement was called a "money fief." The counts of Champagne thus provided a regular, safe meeting place for merchants from the Mediterranean and northern Europe, making possible regular, safe transport of goods from the south to the north and from the north to the south.

Clearly, the counts of Champagne invested much money in the enterprise. They profited greatly, however, from the success of the fairs. The counts received a sales tax on all goods sold at the fairs and also realized profit from booth rental. All of the fines levied against those who broke the rules of the fairs were given to the counts as well. As a result, the counts of Champagne became the richest lords in all of France.

During the first week of each fair, the merchants entered the city, registered with the Keepers, set up their booths, and displayed their wares. Each day of the fair was selected for a specific commodity. For example, the first ten days of the "warm" fair at Troyes were designated for the sale of cloth. The next days were devoted to the sale of goods which could be weighed, such as spices. One surviving medieval list names more than 288 different spices available at the fairs. Over the course of each fair, an impressive number of goods were bought and sold, including wool from England and Flanders; German iron, furs, and linens; Spanish leather and steel; Mediterranean spices and dyes; Scandinavian lumber and furs; Syrian sugar; and Egyptian alum. Both raw materials and handcrafted items were traded. For example, the Champagne fairs served as a source of ivory for ivory carvers as well as a place where intricate ivory carvings were sold. Luxury goods from the Arab world such as musk, diamonds, rubies, carpets, ambergris, and ebony also found their way into the fairs of Champagne.

Until the last week of the fair, no money changed hands; only accounts were kept. During the final days of the fair, accounts were settled. The money changers provided an essential service to the Champagne fairs and made business possible in a number of ways. First, the money changers converted all the currencies from around the world into the standard currency of the fairs, the Troyes pound. Second, the money changers maintained a credit system for the merchants; and because the money changers moved from fair to fair, the credit system worked among all the fairs. For example, a merchant could have an account follow him throughout the cycle of fairs and could settle at the end of the cycle before returning home. Also, the money changers offered loans and acted as pawnbrokers. These systems, as well as an accounting system independent of the money changers called the "letter of the fair," allowed business to be transacted by proxy. Thus, a businessman could send his agent to make trades throughout the cycle. About half of the money changers were Jews, not bound by the Christian rules concerning usury. The other half of the money changers were usually Italians. During the fairs, some of the Church usury laws were relaxed. In other cases, money changers and merchants were able to hide interest in currency exchange fees.

By the fourteenth century, the fairs of Champagne were on the wane. The kings of France controlled the fairs by this time, and they were notorious for overcharging for booths and levying taxes which were too high. Furthermore, sea transportation had become more reliable and alternate trade routes had opened up. Nevertheless, the fairs of Champagne were one of the most significant features of the medieval commercial revolution. They provided a conduit through which trade goods circulated throughout Europe and the Mediterranean. Further, because merchants from England, Scotland, Iceland, Scandinavia, Portugal, France, Germany, Switzerland, Spain, Italy, and Sicily all frequented the fairs, communication and languages spread throughout Europe. News of southern Europe reached northern Europe via the fairs. The fairs also began the process of standardization of weights, measures, and coinage necessary for trading in goods. The banking and accounting principles developed at the fairs as well as the mercantile law instituted by the counts allowed for the further expansion of commerce.

—*Diane Andrews Henningfeld*

ADDITIONAL READING:

Evergates, Theodore, trans. and ed. *Feudal Society in Medieval France: Documents from the County of Champagne.* Philadelphia: University of Pennsylvania Press, 1993. A translated and annotated collection of more than two hundred primary source documents from twelfth and thirteenth century Champagne, including documents describing the regulation of the fairs.

Gies, Frances, and Joseph Gies. *Life in a Medieval City.* New York: Harper & Row, 1969. A thoroughly accessible glimpse into life in Troyes, circa 1250, including a full chapter on the Champagne fair. Not academic in tone, the book offers the details of daily life at the fair.

Lopez, Robert S. *The Commercial Revolution of the Middle Ages, 950-1350.* Cambridge, England: Cambridge University Press, 1976. This work outlines the factors which made possible the rapid economic expansion of the tenth and eleventh centuries.

Lopez, Robert S., and Irving Raymond. *Medieval Trade in the Mediterranean World.* New York: Columbia University Press, 1955. Classic book on the development of trade between the Arab world and Europe.

Postan, M. M., and Edward Miller, eds. *Trade and Industry in the Middle Ages.* Vol 2. of *The Cambridge Economic History of Europe.* Cambridge, England: Cambridge University Press, 1987. *The Cambridge Economic History of Europe* has long been considered to offer the most comprehensive study of medieval economy; Postan and Miller's updated and revised volume is an important starting place for any study of trade.

SEE ALSO: 1150, Venetian Merchants Dominate Trade with the East; 1150-1200, Rise of the Hansa; 1271-1291, Travels of Marco Polo; 1602, Dutch East India Company Is Founded.

1204

KNIGHTS OF THE FOURTH CRUSADE CAPTURE CONSTANTINOPLE

The knights of the Fourth Crusade capture Constantinople, ushering in the triumph of militant Latin Catholicism and establishing Western political and economic power over the Byzantine Empire.

DATE: 1204

LOCALE: Constantinople

CATEGORIES: Religion; Wars, uprisings, and civil unrest

KEY FIGURES:

Alexius III Angelus (died 1211), Byzantine emperor, 1195-1203

Alexius IV Angelus (died 1204), Byzantine emperor, 1203-1204

Alexius V Mourtzouphlos (died 1204), Byzantine emperor, 1204

Baldwin I (1172-1205), count of Flanders as Baldwin IX and count of Hainault as Baldwin VI, 1195-1205; Byzantine emperor, 1204-1205

Enrico Dandolo (c. 1107-1205), doge of Venice, 1192-1205

Innocent III (Lothario of Segni; c. 1160-1216), Roman Catholic pope, 1198-1216

Isaac II Angelus (c. 1135-1204), Byzantine emperor, 1185-1195, 1203-1204

SUMMARY OF EVENT. The fall of Constantinople in 1204 was the culmination of a long historical process of Byzantine decline and the ascendancy of Western political, military, economic, and religious power in the eastern Mediterranean. Beginning with the First Crusade in 1096, Byzantium feared that the knights were as often interested in taking Byzantine territory as they were in conquering the Holy Land. Crusading armies, particularly when they passed through the Balkans, often pillaged Byzantine provinces. From the Byzantine perspective, the Norman conquest of southern Italy made them a constant military threat to the Balkans, especially at Dyrrakhion on the Adriatic coast.

In the twelfth century the Italian cities of Venice, Genoa, and Pisa obtained commercial privileges in Byz-

With the emblem of the lion of Saint Mark identifying its ships, the city of Venice agreed to assist the knights of the Fourth Crusade in reaching Constantinople in exchange for their assistance in restoring the Dalmatian city of Zara under Venetian control. (Archive Photos)

antium and established districts within Constantinople. Yet their economic power and presence within the capital were bitterly resented, and in 1182 the Latins in Constantinople were brutally massacred. Three years later, the Normans seized both Dyrrakhion and the important city of Thessalonica, which was ravaged in revenge for the Latin massacre of 1182. In the Third Crusade, the German emperor Frederick Barbarossa raided the Balkans, seized Adrianople, and sought to even take Constantinople before crossing into Anatolia where he died. In 1197, Barbarossa's son, Henry VI, gathered a huge fleet to attack Constantinople, but his death ended the expedition. The Crusades were a constant threat to Byzantium, but the empire had been militarily weak ever since the destruction of the Byzantine army by the Seljuk Turks at Myriokephalon in 1176. The Italians were needed to offset the Normans and Germans. The Venetians were permitted to return to Constantinople in 1189, and the Genoese and Pisans followed in 1198.

Tensions between Byzantium and the Western knights were further strained because Byzantium had entered into alliances with the Seljuks, as in the First Crusade, and with Egypt in the Third Crusade. Byzantium was accused of not sufficiently aiding the knights and was blamed for the failure of the Second Crusade. In addition, the Catholic and Orthodox churches were in excommunication since 1054. Doctrinal issues over the bread used in the Mass, the nature of the Holy Trinity of Jesus, and the claims of Rome as the head of the Christian world further divided east and west. In the Third Lateran Council of 1179, the pope claimed papal supremacy over the Orthodox church. Thus, the events of 1204 were the culmination of more than a century's hostility between Byzantium and the West.

In 1198, a new pope, Innocent III, ascended the papal throne and soon called for a new crusade. Most of the knights came from France, Flanders, England, Germany, and Sicily. They were led by Thibault of Champagne, who died just before the crusade began, Boniface of Montferrat, Baldwin of Flanders, and Louis of Blois.

In Venice, Enrico Dandolo became doge in 1192 at the age of eighty-five. Legend had it that he had been blinded some thirty years earlier in Constantinople as a hostage. Dandolo saw the crusade as a means for extending Venetian influence in the eastern Mediterranean. In addition to accusing Dandolo for turning the Crusade against Byzantium, scholars have variously accused Philip Hohenstaufen of Swabia, who succeeded his brother Henry VI as emperor of Germany and married the daughter of Byzantine Emperor Isaac II Angelus, and Boniface of Montferrat, who claimed Thessalonica. Such conspiracies are difficult to prove, but there was a general attitude of hostility toward Byzantium and a willingness to unify the two Christian churches.

The knights needed Venetian ships, and they agreed to pay eighty-five thousand silver marks for transport and supplies for forty-five hundred knights, nine thousand squires, and twenty thousand sergeants. Venice would also send fifty warships. A secret clause to the treaty stated that the crusade would in fact be directed against Egypt, the center of Ayubid power and the base from which the Muslims had retaken Jerusalem in 1187.

As the knights gathered at Venice in April, 1202, they were only able to muster ten thousand soldiers, but the Venetians refused to lower their fees. Unable to meet the Venetian fees, the knights agreed to the doge's demand to divert the crusaders toward Zara, a Venetian dependency on the Dalmatian coast that had been taken by the Hungarians in 1186. Zara fell to the crusaders, but the Cistercians in the army opposed the action and Innocent excommunicated the army. Innocent, however, did not want to lose all control of the Crusade; he later lifted the ban on the French and Germans but retained it for the Venetians. He did not forbid contact with the Venetians, however, and this allowed the army to remain together.

In Constantinople, Alexius III Angelus had taken power in 1195 by overthrowing and blinding his brother, Isaac II. Isaac's son, Alexius, escaped to the West in 1201 and sought help to restore his father to the throne. Alexius joined the Crusade; he offered two hundred thousand marks and declared his intention to unify the churches. It was an opportunity the Venetians could not refuse. Innocent, although reluctant to change the Crusade, did not condemn the turn toward Constantinople. On July 17, 1203, the crusaders attacked Constantinople by land and sea. Alexius III fled and the city was taken. The blind Isaac and his son were crowned as co-emperors. They managed to pay one hundred thousand marks to the Venetians and knights, but a popular tide of anti-Latin feeling swept the capital, and virtually all Latins were driven from the city to Galata where the knights were encamped. A new emperor took power as Alexius V Mourtzouphlos, and both co-emperors were murdered. The crusaders now decided to destroy Byzantine independence and to subjugate the Orthodox church to Rome. Alexius V was declared a usurper and murderer.

After agreeing among themselves on dividing Byzantium, the knights launched their attack on April 12, 1204. On April 13, they breached the walls. For three days, the crusaders ravaged the city. Alexius V was captured and executed by being thrown from a high column in the Hippodrome. Much of the plunder was dispersed to France and Venice, including the sixth century horses that adorn St. Mark's Cathedral. One knight, Robert of Clari, remarked that "that two thirds of the wealth of this world is in Constantinople."

An electoral council of six Venetians and six Frenchmen chose Baldwin, count of Flanders, as emperor of Romania—the Latin empire of Constantinople. He was crowned in the Cathedral of Hagia Sophia with the Latin rite. The Venetians had opposed the selection of Boniface of Montferrat but compensated him with Thessalonica. The Venetians and Baldwin divided Constantinople; Baldwin received five-eighths of the city and Dandolo three-eighths. Baldwin was also given southern Thrace, some area along the Bosphorus, and important islands such as Lesbos and Chios. Yet the Venetians obtained major acquisitions, including Dyrrakhion on the Adriatic, the Ionian islands, most of the islands of the Aegean, Crete, Gallipoli, and territory within Thrace. Dandolo took the Byzantine title of despot and was not required to pay homage to Baldwin. Venetian clergy were given control of Hagia Sophia, and a Venetian, Morosini, was made patriarch of the Catholic Church in Constantinople. The Venetians held the most important harbors of Byzantium and secured the seas between Venice and Constantinople. Byzantium had effectively become a colony of Venice. Innocent III at first welcomed the news of Constantinople's fall and its religious union with the West, but as he learned of the details of the sack and the dominance of Venice over the church in Constantinople, he expressed concern over the direction that the crusade had taken. In the end, however, he had to reconcile himself with the results.

Byzantine royalty and nobility formed three new kingdoms in exile: one was the empire of Nicaea just across the Sea of Marmora; a second was the despotat of Epirus in the Balkans; and the third was the empire of Trebizond on the Black Sea. The Latins occupied Constantinople but had great difficulty governing the rest of the empire. Finally, in 1261, a new Byzantine dynasty under Michael VIII Palaeologus was restored. Despite this development, Byzantium never fully recovered from the Fourth Crusade. It remained weak and dependent on the West until its final surrender to the Ottoman Turks in 1453. The sack of Constantinople also widened the breach between the Eastern and Western churches. —*Lawrence N. Langer*

ADDITIONAL READING:

Choniates, Nicetas. *O City of Byzantium*. Detroit: Wayne State Press, 1984. The major Byzantine source on the Fourth Crusade.

Clari, Robert de. *The Conquest of Constantinople*. New York: Columbia University Press, 1936. Translation of an account by an eyewitness to the sack of Constantinople.

Godfrey, John. *The Unholy Crusade*. Oxford: Oxford University Press, 1980. A good general survey of the Fourth Crusade.

Queller, Donald. *The Fourth Crusade*. Philadelphia: University of Pennsylvania Press, 1977. An excellent history of the crusade.

Villhardouin, Geoffroi de. *Memoirs of the Crusades by Villardouin and De Joinville*. New York: E. P. Dutton, 1965. A major French source on the Fourth Crusade.

SEE ALSO: 1095, Pope Urban II Calls the First Crusade; 1147-1149, The Second Crusade; 1189-1192, The Third Crusade; 1209-1229, The Albigensian Crusade; 1212, The Children's Crusade; 1217-1221, The Fifth Crusade; 1227-1230, Frederick II Leads the Sixth Crusade; 1248-1254, Failure of the Seventh Crusade.

1209-1229
ALBIGENSIAN CRUSADE

The Albigensian crusade represents an attempt by Roman Catholic authorities to control French unification in southern Europe, which had long been the crucible of exotic influences.

DATE: 1209-1229

LOCALE: Toulouse, southern France

CATEGORIES: Government and politics; Religion; Wars, uprisings, and civil unrest

KEY FIGURES:

Arnaud Amalric (c. 1160-1225), abbot-general of Cîteaux and papal legate to Toulouse, who preached the Albigensian crusade

Innocent III (Lothario of Segni; c. 1160-1216), Roman Catholic pope, 1198-1216, who instigated the Albigensian crusade

Louis VIII (1187-1226), king of France, 1223-1226

Simon de Montfort (c. 1165-1218), military leader of the Albigensian crusade

Peter II (Pedro II; 1174-1213), king of Aragon and Catalonia, 1196-1213

Philip II (Philip Augustus; 1165-1223), king of France, 1180-1223

Raymond VI (1156-1222), count of Toulouse, 1194-1222

Raymond VII (1197-1249), count of Toulouse, 1222-1247

SUMMARY OF EVENT. Adherents of Manichean or dualist ways of thinking emerged in Languedoc, or southern France, in the eleventh century. This part of Europe was outside the rigid control of the French Capetian dynasty and the Holy Roman Empire. Remnants of Jewish and Muslim cultures added to a divers population that absorbed Middle Eastern and North African heritages eas-

ily—especially during the era of the Crusades—and wedded such influences into a capricious, often secular spirit.

The Albigensians or Cathari (purists) apparently drew their numbers from disaffected migrants from Asia Minor (Paulicians) and Bulgaria (Bogomils) who had entered the Balkans and northern Italy. Because the clergy of southern France was notoriously inefficient and disorganized, the region tolerated heterogeneous thinkers whose ideas went beyond the neo-Platonist tendencies evident in other parts of Europe. Thus, the region around Toulouse became a stronghold for Cathari beliefs.

Since all Albigensian writings were destroyed, scholars have found it difficult to ascertain any clear, systematic principles associated with the Cathari. In general, adherents were divided into two groups: ascetics and believers. The priestly class and their adepts were generally considered to be models of stoic behavior. The believers, or "auditors," however, transformed sacred principles into abhorrent practices, running the gamut from deathbed suicides, infanticide, black masses, unbridled promiscuity, and other scandalous behaviors. As a result, in 1179, the papal authorities in Rome launched a full-scale attack against Albigensians during the Third Lateran Council. Some initiates of the Cathari sect became increasingly defiant of Roman Catholic authority, and rumors spread that the Albigensians were infidels who renounced marriage, the family, Christian sacraments, crosses, icons, saints, indulgences, relics, and almost any connection to the Old Testament—presumably the work of Satan, or the Demiurge. According to popular tradition, reinforced by the songs of troubadours, the Cathari held fourteen dioceses and acknowledged their own pope. Furthermore, the Cathari notion of *consolamentum* (an initiation ceremony) openly challenged the papal decree that crusaders were granted absolution if they died in the cause of Christian perseverance. The general mind-set of southern France, rooted in cultural autonomy, drifted further away from the centrality of Philip II, who was unwilling to challenge the feudal privileges accorded to Raymond VI of Toulouse.

Pope Innocent III tried to counteract unorthodox tendencies among the Albigensians (borrowed from primitive Christian societies) by sending legates to the local bishops. While leaving the church of St. Gilles du Gard in Toulouse, one of these legates, Peter of Castelnau, was killed by a knight in the service of Raymond VI. His death provided the pope with a pretext to call a Crusade against Languedoc. Arnaud Amalric preached this Albigensian crusade in the name of Saint Dominic, who (ironically) had tried to win over the Cathari by peaceful methods. A Christian army, nominally supported by Philip II of France, gathered at Lyon and laid siege to southern France. In 1209,

Béziers was assaulted, and as many as seven thousand people were indiscriminately killed. Many of the victims were unarmed citizens who had taken refuge in the church of the Madelaine. Arnaud Amalric apparently called out, "Kill them all. God will recognize his own!"

After this debacle, Simon de Montfort, a man known for his military acumen and fierce temperament, was appointed commander of the crusading army. Peter II, king of Aragon and Catalonia, sided with his brother-in-law, Raymond VI of Toulouse. Peter led a huge force into southern France and established headquarters at the castle of Muret. Despite being outnumbered, Simon de Montfort maneuvered around the Spanish forces and scored a resounding victory in 1213. Peter was killed and the followers of Raymond VI disbanded.

After learning about the bloodshed at Muret, Pope Innocent III suspended the crusade against the Cathari, who were renowned pacifists, and tried to find a diplomatic solution to what was essentially a political problem. Such diplomacy was conducted under the watchful eye of Philip II, who sent his son, Prince Louis, on a futile mission to force a settlement. Emboldened once again, Raymond VI fortified Toulouse. In 1218, Simon de Montfort died in an attempt to take the city.

After his father's death in 1222, Raymond VII of Toulouse continued to protect the city from invasion. Backed financially by Pope Honorius III, King Louis VIII of France crushed the Albigensian resistance in 1226 through the brutal massacre of the people of Marenaude and by securing the capitulation of Soignon and other cities in southern France. In 1229, a peace agreement was reached by which the management of Languedoc fell under the control of the French king. Caught up in this political dispute, the Albigensians went underground after Pope Gregory IV announced the Papal Inquisition of 1233 against their interest.

Scholars differ as to what contributed to the widespread appeal of the Cathari. Some note a strong attachment among merchants and soldiers (which partly explains the later accommodation of Calvinist ideology); others insist on the power of a recalcitrant nobility, with secret codes derived from Middle Eastern and North African influences, thus posing an obvious threat to northern European hegemony.   —*Robert J. Frail*

ADDITIONAL READING:

Gore, Terry L. *Neglected Heroes: Leadership and War in the Early Medieval Period*. Westport, Conn.: Praeger, 1995. A thrilling account of military techniques in an era of siege warfare.

Madaule, Jacques. *The Albigensian Crusade: An His-torical Essay*. Translated by Barbara Wall. New York: Fordham University Press, 1967. In this informative study, the author reinforces the cultural differences between northern and southern France and the role that the Albigensian crusade played in the formation of France as a national state.

Runciman, Steven. *A History of the Crusades*. New York: Cambridge University Press, 1988. Runciman places the Languedoc invasion within the context of the other crusades and notes that northern extremists moved beyond the authority of the popes.

Sayers, Jane E. *Innocent III: Leader of Europe, 1198-1216*. New York: Longman, 1994. Analyzes Innocent III's attempt to impose a theocratic dominance in Europe over and against secular tendencies such as those that surfaced in Albigensian France.

Strayer, Joseph Ree. *The Albigensian Crusades*. Ann Arbor: University of Michigan Press, 1992. Strayer provides a comprehensive study of the political conditions in Europe that contributed to the backlash against the Cathari.

Sumption, Jonathan. *The Albigensian Crusade*. Boston: Faber & Faber, 1978. A wide-ranging summary of the linguistic, religious, and political differences between southern and northern France that led to the clash of two cultures.

SEE ALSO: 1095, Pope Urban II Calls the First Crusade; 1147-1149, The Second Crusade; 1175, Appearance of the Waldensians; 1189-1192, The Third Crusade; 1204, Knights of the Fourth Crusade Capture Constantinople; 1212, The Children's Crusade; 1215, The Fourth Lateran Council; 1217-1221, The Fifth Crusade; 1227-1230, Frederick II Leads the Sixth Crusade; 1233, The Papal Inquisition; 1248-1254, Failure of the Seventh Crusade.

1209
FOUNDING OF THE FRANCISCANS

The founding of the Franciscans represents the first time in Catholic Church history in which religious brothers and sisters are allowed to live in strict poverty, owning nothing, and the first time that men of a religious order are allowed to go about preaching as opposed to living in a monastery.

DATE: April 16, 1209

LOCALE: Assisi, Italy

CATEGORIES: Organizations and institutions; Religion

KEY FIGURES:

Clare of Assisi (Clare Offreduccio; 1194-1253), a noblewoman who became the first female follower of Francis

Saint Francis of Assisi (Francesco di Pietro di
  Bernardone; c. 1181-1226), founder of the
  Franciscan Order

Innocent III (Lothario of Segni; c. 1160-1216), Roman
  Catholic pope, 1198-1216, who authorized the
  foundation of the order

SUMMARY OF EVENT. Francis Bernardone was born in
1181 or 1182, the son of a cloth merchant. He was an
ordinary young man, very popular with his friends, and he
dreamed of knighthood and marriage. When war broke out
between his home town and the neighboring Perugia, he
found himself in prison, captured by the enemy. Pietro, his
father, bailed him out, but Francis had contracted some
illness. When he recovered, Francis was changed. He still
went out with his friends, but he was more reflective and
thoughtful.

When the pope called for a crusade, Francis had the
chance to be a knight. His father dressed him in a new coat
of armor and gave him a new horse, and Francis rode off
to war. Within a short time, however, he again became ill
and returned home. He went to the little church of San
Damiano, which was falling down, and he heard the cru-
cifix telling him to "Rebuild my church." At first, Francis
thought that he should buy or beg for stones to rebuild San
Damiano. A turning point in his life occurred when he stole
money from his father's store to buy stones and his father
demanded the money back. Francis not only returned the
money but also took off all his clothes and gave them to
his father. As he handed over his clothing, Francis said that
from now on Pietro was no longer his father, but only God.

From this point forward, Francis was completely
changed. With a few followers, he wandered around fixing churches and preaching poverty. At this point a young
noblewoman, Clare Offreduccio, heard about Francis'
preaching. She was attracted to what Francis was saying about poverty, and wanted to follow his style of life
in a way that would be appropriate for women. Francis
established Clare, her sister, and several other women
from Clare's household at San Damiano. Other women
soon joined them, and the group became known as the
Damianites.

Lest he be thought heretical, Francis determined to
go to Rome to get permission for his group. At first,
Innocent III would not listen to what looked like a pack of
stragglers, but that night the pope had a dream that the
church was falling down, and a man dressed like Francis
was holding it up. The next day, Innocent III gave oral
permission for the new order.

From this time on, Francis and his brothers spent their
time preaching, rebuilding churches, and begging for
whatever they needed. Francis called his group "little

brothers," or friars minor. They refused money, and attempted to live literally like Jesus had, having no where to
sleep except for the ground, and no clothes except rags, a
rope around their waists, and no shoes. Clare and her
followers also lived according to this ideal. They did not
preach, but prayed and fasted, eating what people brought
to them or what the brothers begged for them. They spent
their time doing needlework, and raising some of their
own food. Clare insisted that the sisters be kind and loving
to one another, and Clare herself washed the feet of her
sisters and cleaned their mattresses.

Before Francis died in 1226, five thousand men were
accepted into the order. As human nature would have it,
controversies arose as to how the brothers should live.
Francis wanted no houses or property, but there were some
who could not see how the order would survive without
them. In countries where the weather was cold, the brothers needed shoes and warmer clothing. Since Francis'
talent was more charismatic than administrative, he
handed the running of the order to his trusted friend,
Brother Elias. Yet Brother Elias felt that the order should
own property. This disagreement caused dissention before
and after Francis died.

About a month before he died, Francis spent the night
at Mount Alverna. In the sky, there appeared a six-winged
angel who marked Francis' body with the wounds of Jesus
crucified. It seems that Francis' desire to live the way Jesus
did reached a climax with this incident, called the stig-
mata. Francis died on October 4, 1226, a date on which
Franciscans throughout the world celebrate his life and
death. On the way to the burial, his body was taken to
Clare and her sisters to view.

After Francis' death, the controversy over property and
spirituality continued. A group who called themselves the
Spirituals wanted to remain faithful to the primitive ideal
of Francis and Clare, living a life of poverty and prayer.
Before long, this movement disappeared, but in the
1300's, a group formed who called themselves Obser-
vants. They took what was best from the Spirituals and
committed themselves to living a more austere life. In
1517, the Franciscans divided into two groups: the Con-
ventuals and the Friars Minor of the Regular Observance.
Some broke away from this second group to form the
Capuchins, or "The Strict Observance." Pope Clement VII
recognized them in 1527 as the third independent branch
of the order. Also many others broke away and formed
new convents and monasteries. In 1897, Leo X joined all
families into one large order, the Order of Friars Minor.

Clare's community went through the same sort of
struggle. In 1227, at eighty-two years of age, Cardinal
Ugolino (1227-1241), one of the first followers of Francis,

was elected the new pope, Gregory IX. Clare asked to be allowed to live according to the poverty of Francis. The pope agreed, but he determined that he would restrict this privilege to the house of Poor Ladies at San Damiano because with no property, the Poor Ladies lacked the necessities of life. Pope Gregory pleaded with Clare to accept some possessions, but Clare refused. He offered to release Clare from her vows in order to stop their shortages of provisions and relieve their suffering, but Clare would not yield. "Never do I wish, Holy Father, to be released in any way from following Christ."

During Clare's lifetime, many houses of Damianites sprang up throughout Italy and in most of Europe. Some 147 houses were founded before Clare's death in 1253. At least forty-seven houses were founded in Spain during the thirteenth century. Under the influence of Agnes of Prague, houses of Clarisses were founded in Moravia between 1242 and 1248, and a house for sixty nuns was founded in Poland in 1254, but destroyed in 1259 by the invasion of the Tartars. Meanwhile, Saint Elizabeth of Hungary inspired many women, and a house of Poor Clares was established at Trnava in 1238. Isabelle of France, who was the only daughter of Louis VIII and Blanche of Castille, joined the Poor Ladies in 1252 and established a convent at Longchamps in 1261.

By living in poverty, the Franciscans stood in opposition to the wealth and often corrupt church of the Middle Ages. Men and women flocked to the brotherhood and sisterhood in order to live a spiritual and holy life.

—*Winifred Whelan*

ADDITIONAL READING:

Bodo, Murray. *The Way of St. Francis: The Challenge of Franciscan Spirituality for Everyone.* Garden City, N.Y.: Doubleday, 1984. A personal and rather intimate telling of the life of Saint Francis, and how Francis' spirit is continued in his contemporary followers.

Flood, David. *Francis of Assisi and the Franciscan Movement.* Quezon City, Philippines: FIA Contact Publications, The Franciscan Institute of Asia, 1989. This book relates the life of Francis and the brothers by concentrating on the rule of life which they wrote and by which they lived. It dwells on the history and context of the movement.

Leclerc, Eloi. *Francis of Assisi: Return to the Gospel.* Chicago: Franciscan Herald Press, 1983. This book concentrates on the human, economic, social, and political environment in which Francis' spiritual experience was rooted.

Peterson, Ingrid J. *Clare of Assisi: A Biographical Study.* Quincy, Ill.: Franciscan Press, 1993. Recent scholarship has begun to uncover the history of women of the

Middle Ages. For Clare, much of this work has been done in conjunction with the 800th anniversary of her birth.

Rotzetter, Anton, Willibrord-Christian Van Dijk, and Taddee Matura. *Gospel Living: Francis of Assisi Yesterday and Today.* St. Bonaventure, N.Y.: St. Bonaventure University, 1994. In three parts, this book tells the life of Saint Francis, the history of the order including the saints, writings and activities of the friars in many countries, and the present status of the order.

SEE ALSO: 635-800, Founding of Lindisfarne and Creation of the *Book of Kells*; 963, Foundation of Mount Athos Monasteries; 1098, Cistercian Monastic Order Is Founded; 1120, Order of the Knights Templar Is Founded; 1523, Franciscans Arrive in Mexico; 1534, Founding of the Jesuits.

1212
THE CHILDREN'S CRUSADE

The Children's Crusade inspires and shames adult Christians for centuries even though it achieves nothing in terms of conquest of land, because the children who participate are seen as fervent believers and martyrs.

DATE: 1212
LOCALE: France, Germany, and the Mediterranean coast
CATEGORY: Religion
KEY FIGURES:
Hugh Ferreus, a merchant seafarer of Marseilles
Innocent III (Lothario of Segni; c. 1160-1216), Roman Catholic pope, 1198-1216
Nicholas of Cologne, leader of the young German crusaders
Philip II (Philip Augustus; 1165-1223), king of France, 1180-1223
William Porcus, a merchant seafarer of Marseilles
Stephen of Cloyes, leader of the young French crusaders
SUMMARY OF EVENT. The Children's Crusade is probably one of the most familiar and least understood events of the Middle Ages. Most generally educated Western adults know the phrase "Children's Crusade," but have only vague notions about when and where it took place. The episode was not really a crusade—that is, it was not called for nor sanctioned by the pope, and those participating in it were not granted special blessings or indulgences.

Because of its spontaneous and humble beginnings, there are no official rolls of participants or contemporary records of the crusade. It was not until twenty and more years after the year of the Children's Crusade that written accounts began to appear; these chronicles are contradictory, and many are clearly fictionalized or contain fictional elements.

The traditionally accepted version of the events, pulled together from various chronicles, is as follows. The beginning of the thirteenth century was a troubling time for Christians. The Fourth Crusade (1202-1204) had failed to drive Muslims out of what the Christians considered their Holy Land, and in 1209 Pope Innocent III's crusading armies had massacred hundreds of Albigensians, non-Christians living in southern France. In the eyes of many Christians, the crusaders had revealed themselves to be greedy and corrupt, more interested in the spoils of war than in sacred duty and honor. The institution of the Church was found wanting, and many people looked to children as personifications of the innocence of true faith. In this climate, two boys came forward.

In France, in the small town of Cloyes near Vendôme, a shepherd boy named Stephen announced that Jesus had visited him dressed as a poor pilgrim, given Stephen a letter, and told him to present it to King Philip Augustus of France. The letter called for a new crusade, conducted by children who were pure of heart and who would be able to accomplish what their elders could not. Stephen, then about twelve or thirteen years old, set out toward Paris to see the king, accompanied by several of his fellow shepherds, who believed that Stephen had been called to some great duty. More and more groups of children joined Stephen and his band, fervently ignoring protests by their parents. These groups included both boys and girls, poor and rich, and eventually many adults as well; they carried banners and crosses, praying and chanting Christian messages of praise. By May, 1212, when the crusaders gathered in the city of St. Denys, just north of Paris, they numbered in the thousands.

Stephen called his followers to gather more friends and meet in Vendôme; from there they would go to the Holy Land, to free the tomb of Jesus from the Muslims who then controlled the region. The children carried no weapons, and had no intention of fighting. They believed that they had been called to liberate the Holy Land, and that if they showed their faith by marching in, the infidels would simply fall away.

As the army grew, both the king of France and the pope studiously avoided taking any notice of it. The pope did not take the movement seriously, and would not bless it. Philip Augustus, if he ever saw Stephen's letter, apparently did not believe it; he ordered the children to return home. The faith—or the hysteria—of Stephen's followers was too well established to be set aside by the orders of an earthly king, and they continued in their quest.

By late July or early August, 1212, the crusaders set off for the port city of Marseilles, more than three hundred miles away on the Mediterranean. They must have been quite a sight: a procession of several thousand (some accounts say thirty thousand), banners flying, crosses held high, singing hymns and chanting "To God!" No one knows how they intended to get to the Holy Land from Marseilles—whether they expected ships to be provided for them or, as some said, expected God to part the waters of the sea.

A month later, they arrived in Marseilles. Many of the young crusaders had turned back along the way, finding their enthusiasm for the cause weakening under the harsh conditions of travel. Others had been captured and sold into slavery, or fallen ill. Some new crusaders had joined the group as it passed by. When the army reached Marseilles, they asked permission to stay a short time, expecting to be on their way soon, and permission was granted. Somehow, transportation was arranged for five thousand crusaders on the ships of two merchants, Hugo Ferreus and William Porcus. With great ceremony, they sailed out of Marseilles in August, bound, they believed, for the Holy Land.

Meanwhile, in Germany, another army of singing, banner-waving children had gathered around Nicholas, an eleven- or twelve-year-old boy from Cologne. Doubtless each of the two groups had received word of the other, and of other spontaneous uprisings by children, feeding the frenzy. In June or July, 1212, Nicholas and nearly twenty thousand followers set out for the Holy Land, via Genoa. They traveled south along the Rhine and across the Alps. Records indicate that the tired, cold, and hungry children rested at a monastery in the Alps before continuing on. As with the French children, many of these German crusaders turned back, were waylaid by criminals, or died along the way. Fewer than seven thousand remained on August 25, 1212, when the group arrived at the gates of Genoa.

The army asked permission to stay only one night, expecting miraculous transportation across the sea to Palestine the next day. When it did not materialize, the group dispersed. Many returned home. Some went on to Pisa, still expecting to complete their journey. Two shiploads of children sailed from Pisa, but were never heard from again. One small band eventually reached Rome, and presented themselves before the pope to receive his further instructions. Innocent III coldly ordered them to return home, but reminded them that they had taken vows as crusaders, and would be called to fight when they reached adulthood.

The French children who had sailed from Marseilles never reached their destination, and for eighteen years their fate was a mystery. Then in 1230, an old priest came forward with a strange tale: He had sailed with the crusade out of Marseilles. Two days from port, a storm had sunk two of the ships, drowning all aboard. Those on the remaining five vessels were sold into slavery by the two merchants.

Although several contemporary chronicles tell of spontaneous gatherings of Christian children processing and praying to God, it is nearly twenty years after the events that the first chronicler describes them as crusaders, and claims that their destination was the Holy Land. Many scholars believe that the stories of the Children's Crusade are more legend than history. Whether factual or not, the stories of pure and innocent children setting off to do God's will, when the adults around them had failed to do so, have inspired Christians for centuries.

—*Cynthia A. Bily*

ADDITIONAL READING:

Armstrong, Karen. *Holy War: The Crusades and Their Impact on Today's World.* New York: Doubleday, 1988. An engaging history that delves into Christian, Jewish, and Muslim consciousnesses. A brief section explains the theory that a spontaneous uprising by bands of wandering poor was transformed by later chroniclers into the myth of the Children's Crusade.

Gray, George Zabriskie. *The Children's Crusade.* New York: William Morrow, 1972. Originally published in 1870, this volume pulls together six hundred years of lore about the Children's Crusade into a romanticized, and unabashedly pro-Christian, narrative.

Hallam, Elizabeth, ed. *Chronicles of the Crusades: Nine Crusades and Two Hundred Years of Bitter Conflict for the Holy Land Brought to Life Through the Words of Those Who Were Actually There.* New York: Weidenfeld & Nicholson, 1989. Lavishly illustrated and clearly annotated. Includes accounts of the Children's Crusade from the Annals of Marbach and the monk Aubrey of Trois-Fontaines, translated into lively English prose.

Raedts, Peter. "The Children's Crusade of 1212." *Journal of Medieval History* 3 (1977): 279-333. Based on an extensive study of primary and secondary sources, Raedts argues that it was not religious fervor so much as the peasants' dissatisfaction with the wealthier classes' failures to win the Holy Land that led to the Children's Crusade.

Riley-Smith, Jonathan, ed. *The Atlas of the Crusades.* New York: Facts On File, 1990. Especially helpful for tracing the paths of the three major groups of children Crusaders through regions whose geographical names have changed several times over many centuries. Includes bibliographical references.

Zacour, Norman P. "The Children's Crusade." In *A History of the Crusades.* Vol. 2. Edited by Kenneth M. Stetton. 6 vols. Madison: University of Wisconsin Press, 1969. A detailed account, clear at every point as to which evidence from medieval chronicles can be considered reliable, and which is only speculative, at best.

SEE ALSO: 1095, Pope Urban II Calls the First Crusade; 1147-1149, The Second Crusade; 1189-1192, The Third Crusade; 1204, Knights of the Fourth Crusade Capture Constantinople; 1217-1221, The Fifth Crusade; 1227-1230, Frederick II Leads the Sixth Crusade; 1248-1254, Failure of the Seventh Crusade.

1214
BATTLE OF BOUVINES

The Battle of Bouvines signals the advent of a new patriotism in France when a minor skirmish quickly takes on mythic proportions.

DATE: July 27, 1214
LOCALE: Near Tournai, Flanders (later, part of France)
CATEGORY: Wars, uprisings, and civil unrest
KEY FIGURES:
Ferrand (Ferdinand), count of Flanders and vassal of Philip II
John (1166-1216), youngest son of Henry II and king of England, 1199-1216
Otto IV (Otto of Brunswick; c. 1174-1218), Holy Roman Emperor, 1198-1215, and nephew of King John
Philip II (Philip Augustus; 1165-1223), son of Louis VII and king of France, 1180-1223
Renaud, count of Boulougne and vassal of Philip II

SUMMARY OF EVENT. Drawing upon four or five contemporary narratives of the brief encounter at Bouvines, poets and historians have formed the event into a legend. The essential facts reveal a much simpler story. On a hot Sunday in July of 1214, King Philip II of France was returning from Tournai, which he had devastated on the previous day to chastise Count Ferrand of Flanders, a rebellious vassal. Around midday, as the king and his knights were about to cross the bridge of Bouvines, they were unexpectedly set upon by a coalition of troops led by Ferrand, Renaud of Boulogne, and Otto IV of Bavaria. A three-hour battle ensued, involving perhaps four thousand mounted knights and twelve thousand infantry. Both of the rebellious counts were taken prisoner. King Philip himself, pulled to the ground by Otto's German foot soldiers, miraculously escaped death and remounted to pursue the "false" (the excommunicated) emperor, who managed to get away. Ferrand and Renaud were led in chains to Paris, and the king's triumph was made complete by news from Poitou that his son Louis (known as "the Lion") had defeated King John of England, the remaining party to the coalition against France.

Why, for historians, has this short and unprepared battle in the meadows of Bouvines seemed more decisive than most previous military encounters? The answer clearly lies in the importance of Philip's victory for the later development of the French monarchy. At the same time, it established the primacy of France as champion of the Catholic church and as the model of chivalry and knighthood. An examination of each of these aspects will shed light on the event.

The enemy coalition was financed by King John, who simultaneously attacked Poitou in an attempt to recover the inheritance of his Angevin predecessors. John had lost these lands ten years before, when Philip had taken Normandy and Anjou from him as a disloyal vassal. The year before Bouvines, Philip had been prepared to invade England when John forestalled him by securing an intercession from the pope. (In 1216, Philip's son Louis did invade England but was defeated by the barons under the command of William Marshal.) John had been joined by two other disloyal vassals, Ferrand and Renaud; by defeating all three, Philip and his host of knights proved that vassals to the French crown were more formidable than an illegitimate coalition of mercenaries. The French monarchy was a more cohesive force than feudalism. "After Bouvines," according to French historian Georges Duby, nothing could "stand in the way of the expansion of the royal domain."

The Catholic Church had managed to harness the forces of chivalry and feudal strife by launching the First Crusade, which had freed Jerusalem in 1099. The Third and Fourth Crusades (1191 and 1204), however, had been failures. Philip had taken part in the Third Crusade, but had fallen out with Pope Innocent III over his desire to be divorced from his second wife, Ingeborg of Denmark. Meanwhile, the pope had excommunicated and deposed Emperor Otto IV, and Philip had allied himself with the new emperor, Frederick II, in 1213. As a result, when Otto joined Philip's enemies in the surprise attack at Bouvines, Philip found himself in the heroic role of Christian champion pitted against the false emperor, or Antichrist. Coincidentally, Otto's emblem was a dragon (reminiscent of the evil dragon in the biblical Book of Revelation), which was displayed on the banner he dropped on fleeing from Bouvines. Opposing this symbol of the Antichrist, the French banner carried the Oriflamme, representing their patron, Saint Denis.

By forcing Philip to do battle on a Sunday, the enemy was violating the Lord's day. This situation invited historians to claim that God had made the king His instrument for punishing such sacrilege. The notion that the king was God's avenger powerfully supports the teaching that the Crown is the sovereign font of justice. This idea was far more potent than feudal conceptions, which held the king

to be merely the strongest of mortal overlords. As the legend of Bouvines developed, Philip was given prayers like those spoken by Moses and David, as if he had foreseen the battle and directly implored God's aid. Sacred meanings could be found in all of his gestures. For example, while watching his troops cross the bridge, Philip had rested under a tree and eaten pieces of bread that he dipped in his wine. The legends also endowed Philip with a golden goblet, so that the lunchtime snack of a practical and cautious monarch resembled the taking of Communion.

If the legend made Philip to be God's champion against unruly heretics and rebels who flouted the divinely ordained social order, the miraculous victory at Bouvines also confirmed France's national role in human destiny. The underlying idea here is not truly religious, but chivalric and superstitious. Bouvines was a trial by arms—a judicial combat in which God is seen as arbitrating between the two parties by awarding victory to the just cause. In this historical event, the French entered the lists—the *champel*, or closed field, in which duels took place—as combatants on the side of honor and "Romance" civilization. Their opponents were seen as evil "Teutonic" barbarians. God was believed to have rendered judgment at Bouvines by sending a definitive outcome. This divine judgment explains why Philip made no real effort to pursue and kill Otto. The flight of the Germans was the sign that judgment had been given; pressing the fight was to risk tempting God.

In what was probably the most important embellishment of the story, Bouvines was invoked, from the late thirteenth century onward, to reaffirm the belief that the king of France was "elected" by the voice of God speaking through the people. In the fullest contemporary account of the battle, Philip had completed his tour through Hainault and Flanders and had chastised his two rebel vassals by calculated destruction of their lands. He certainly did not plan on a pitched battle; indeed, when told of the coalition's approach, he tried to escape but could not get his army over the narrow bridge in time. Forced to make a stand, he took counsel with his knights, as was customary. He made a short speech, reminding them that although they were all sinners, they were not mercenaries like their foes and had not been excommunicated. He bade them to trust God, and, acting in his semisacred capacity, he raised his hand to bless them.

In the later legends, the king loses all trace of surprise or fear. On the contrary, Philip's self-possessed, almost theatrical speech has the effect of removing whatever perplexity and doubt the surprise attack must have raised among his followers. These legends claim that the king, obviously expecting the occasion, has brought his crown with him (even though the crown was always kept in Paris). Laying that national symbol before his men—in still later legends, his forces included commoners as well as knights—Philip tells them, "Without you, I cannot rule the kingdom anymore." In addition, he invites anyone who thinks himself more worthy to put on the crown and lead them. Naturally, the barons cry out that they will have no king but Philip. In this way, God speaks through the "people's voice" and renews His divine choice of the king of the Franks. It is a very old ceremony that still retains its effective power, despite the advent of modern democracy.

—*David B. Haley*

ADDITIONAL READING:

Denholm-Young, N. "The Tournament in the Thirteenth Century." In *Studies in Medieval History Presented to F. M. Powicke*, edited by R. W. Hunt, W. A. Pantin, and R. W. Southern. Oxford: Clarendon Press, 1948. Provides insight into the court's notion of warfare.

Duby, Georges. *The Legend of Bouvines: War, Religion, and Culture in the Middle Ages.* Translated by Catherine Tihanyi. Berkeley: University of California Press, 1990. A thorough and up-to-date account, written by a famous medievalist. Duby's work prints a translation of the chief chronicle of Bouvines by William the Breton, together with an appendix of other thirteenth century narratives and poems on Bouvines.

_____. *The Three Orders: Feudal Society Imagined.* Translated by Arthur Goldhammer. Chicago: University of Chicago Press, 1980. An authoritative study of the three estates that, under the crown, constituted the mature feudal system of France.

Hay, Denys. *The Medieval Centuries.* Rev. ed. New York: Harper & Row, 1964. Excellent source for understanding the development of the rivalry between the French and the Germans.

Painter, Sidney. *French Chivalry.* Ithaca, N.Y.: Cornell University Press, 1969. First published in 1940, this classic account of the period is one that is often reprinted and retains its fresh appeal.

SEE ALSO: 1154-1204, Establishment of the Angevin Empire; 1189-1192, The Third Crusade.

1215
SIGNING OF THE MAGNA CARTA

The signing of the Magna Carta is popularly remembered as the first great confrontation between the monarchy and the lower-ranking nobility in England and the root of many important judicial practices, although many of *its provisions become obsolete within a few centuries of its enactment.*

DATE: June 15, 1215
LOCALE: Runnymede, England
CATEGORY: Laws, acts, and legal history
KEY FIGURES:
Henry III (1207-1272), king of England, 1216-1272
John (1166-1216), king of England, 1199-1216

SUMMARY OF EVENT. Of the documents in which the constitutional tradition of the English-speaking peoples is enshrined, the Magna Carta is, if not the oldest, the first to have won for itself a place in the public memory. The sixty-three chapters of the Great Charter, wrung from King John by civil war, extend a grant of liberties to all the freemen of the kingdom including barons, churchmen, and townspeople.

At first sight the fame of the Magna Carta in later centuries seems puzzling. The doctrines which were to find a prominent place in the famous libertarian documents of later centuries are absent here. The Magna Carta does not advance against the king in the name of God, or the sovereignty of the people, or the inalienable rights of man. Yet its veneration is deserved.

The significance of the Magna Carta lies not in any one chapter or group of chapters, but rather in the fact that it established a degree of juridical equality between subjects and government, an indisputable prerequisite if the lowly subject was to claim successfully rights which the government must respect. The Magna Carta defined the legal relationship between king and subject in terms of the relationship that existed between a feudal lord and his vassal. The limitations that applied to the feudal lord, the Magna Carta held, were applicable in substantial measure to the king as well. In a sense a new juridical identity was created for the king; he was king no longer but feudal lord, and in this capacity his subjects could claim from him numerous rights.

Chapter 12, for instance, states in part that no aid, or demand for payment of money, "shall be imposed in our realm except with the common council of the realm" unless it be to ransom the person of the king, to knight his eldest son, or to marry his eldest daughter. Even in these cases "only a reasonable aid shall be levied." To obtain money beyond these three designated occasions, the king must have previously obtained the consent of his subjects. This common "counsel of the realm" is to be obtained, according to chapter 14, from the Great Council convened by specific letters of summons sent by the king to his tenants-in-chief.

The three designated occasions when the king need not obtain consent are at best infrequent and, as soon as the

King John signed the Magna Carta on the field of Runnymede to appease powerful English barons, but later appealed to Pope Innocent III to annul it. Despite the pope's action, the Great Charter became the cornerstone of an evolving definition of English civil liberties. (Archive Photos)

royal government had evolved beyond the most primitive stage, the sums supplied from these sources became more and more irrelevant and inadequate so that the king was bound to obtain consent for most exactions necessary to operate government. In effect, chapter 12 of the Magna Carta secures the property right of the subject: He need yield to the Crown only those sums to which he has consented. Looked at from another viewpoint, the property right of the subject constitutes a limitation on the power of the Crown; it forms an enclave into which the king may not, so to speak, intrude without permission. Moreover, the necessity of obtaining consent led easily in time to the institution of Parliament where eventually consent to taxation was given provisionally on the condition that the sums realized be spent for one purpose and not another.

The fact that the king needs the consent of his "tenants-in-chief" rather than of his "subjects" when he requires additional "aids," roots the Magna Carta's limitations in feudal law. The legal literature of England in the decades before the great Charter distinctly showed that the aids a feudal lord could ask of his knight or tenant-in-chief were specifically limited. For instance, the *Treatise on the Laws and Customs of the Realm of England*, a twelfth century summary of English law usually attributed to Ranulph de Glanville, similarly states that the aids a lord may demand from his knights must be moderate according to the size and wealth of their fiefs and that similar moderate demands may be made by the lord only when his son is knighted or his eldest daughter married. Already, the lord is limited in what he can ask of a knight. The notion of limitation, vague in the case of Glanville but precise in the Magna Carta, is common to both documents. Since in the Magna Carta the king's subjects are his tenants-in-chief and the king is considered a feudal lord, the limitations of a feudal lord are made to do duty in limiting the king. The kings of England since William the Conqueror had been feudal lords as well as kings. The Magna Carta exploited this fact.

The Magna Carta contains inklings of some modern political ideas, such as the "due process" clause of the U.S. Constitution. The following interpretation of the Magna Carta was handed down in the statutes of Edward III (1354): "No man of what estate or condition that he be, shall be put out of land or tenement, nor taken nor imprisoned, nor disinherited, nor put to death, without being brought in answer by due process of law."

While its precedents for modern law are well known, large parts of the Magna Carta have been largely forgotten to history. Sir Ivor Jennings, author of *Magna Carta and Its Influence in the World Today* (1965) asserts that "if the Magna Carta were redrafted in the form of an Act of Parliament, it would contain four parts." The first part, according to Jennings, would be "a single clause from Chapter 1, protecting the rights . . . of the English church . . . so general in its terms that it has never been very important." The second part would be drawn from the fourteen provisions relating to feudal land tenure, most of which have been repealed by later law. The third part would contain the fourteen provisions relating to the administration of justice. While chapters 8, 14, and 29 have had a seminal effect on later law, the other eleven provisions "were obsolete before the end of the thirteenth century," according to Jennings. Part 4 would contain the last nine provisions of the Magna Carta, of which five are still workable under present law.

The Great Charter also guaranteed that no freeman should be imprisoned or dispossessed except by legal judgment of his peers or by the law of the land. Furthermore, justice would not be denied, sold, or delayed. Chapter 61 allowed for machinery to provide means of enforcement. Although Pope Innocent III repudiated the charter for John after the king had declared himself a papal vassal, it was confirmed seven times during the reign of Henry III and reissued again in 1297 under Edward I.

—*Martin J. Baron, updated by Bruce E. Johansen*

ADDITIONAL READING:

Dickinson, J. C. *The Great Charter*. London: Historical Association Publications, 1955. This brief work outlines the principles and historical circumstances of the Magna Carta.

Holt, J. C. *Magna Carta*. New York: Cambridge University Press, 1992. First published in 1965, Holt's work examines the judicial roots of the Magna Carta, tracing the hostility toward the monarchy that developed in England after the Norman Conquest.

_____. *Magna Carta and Medieval Government*. London: Ronceverte, 1985. Studies presented to the International Commission for the History of Representative and Parliamentary Opinion.

Painter, Sidney. *The Reign of King John*. Baltimore: The Johns Hopkins University Press, 1966. First published in 1949, Painter's work traces the development of the Magna Carta against the background of King John's reign.

Swindler, W. F. *Magna Carta: Legend and Legacy*. Indianapolis: Bobbs-Merrill, 1965. Discusses the use of the Magna Carta by the later generations of English and American historians.

SEE ALSO: 1154-1204, Establishment of the Angevin Empire; 1175, Common Law Tradition Emerges in England; 1258, The "Provisions of Oxford"; 1285, Statute of Winchester; 1295, The Model Parliament.

1215
FOURTH LATERAN COUNCIL

The Fourth Lateran Council lays the cornerstone for medieval Christian devotion and reflects the authority of the papacy throughout Europe.

DATE: November 11-30, 1215
LOCALE: The Lateran Basilica in Rome
CATEGORY: Religion
KEY FIGURES:
Saint Dominic (Domingo de Guzmán; c. 1170-1221), founder of the Dominican Order of preaching friars
Saint Francis of Assisi (c. 1181-1226), founder of the Order of Friars Minor, also known as the Franciscans
Innocent III, Roman Catholic pope, 1198-1216
John (1166-1216), king of England, 1199-1216
Simon de Montfort (1160-1218), earl of Leicester, who was given the Albigensian county of Toulouse in southern France by the council

SUMMARY OF EVENT. Innocent III's reign is known as the "high noon of the papacy." He once likened the papacy to the sun and lessened the state to the satellite position of the moon. These concepts seemed to filter through the air at the Fourth Lateran Council, in which Innocent III made his expectations known despite opposition from laity and clergy alike.

Innocent III fit the mold of many twelfth and thirteenth century popes. He was more of a jurist and an administrator than a saintly individual. Educated at Bologna, he was elected pope at the rather early age of thirty-seven. Following in the tradition of the twelfth century popes Innocent II, who called the Second Lateran Council in 1139, and Alexander III, who called the Third Lateran Council in 1179, Innocent convoked a truly ecumenical council that rivaled even the earlier Eastern ecumenical councils. The number of participants (2,280) was imposing, in part because members of laity and clergy both were well represented. It was the first instance in which both estates were participants in a church council. Among the more than four hundred bishops were prelates from Bohemia, Poland, Hungary, Livonia, and Estonia, countries never before represented at a council. Innocent failed to persuade the Greeks to attend, but the Latin patriarchs of the East were present. Besides abbots, eight hundred legates of monastic chapters attended. Envoys on behalf of Frederick II of Sicily, the emperor of Constantinople, and the kings of France, Hungary, Jerusalem, Cyprus, and Aragon arrived. King John of England was not invited, since he was under the ban of excommunication, but he was represented by five proctors (three clerics and two laity).

Little is known about the council's organization. The only extant documents are Innocent's inaugural address, the record of one public session, the text of seventy approved canons, and the decree authorizing a new crusade. In addition, there are two eyewitness accounts. One describes the ceremonial splendors of the council's opening session. The council first met on November 11, following a papal mass celebrated at dawn. The ensuing papal address had such a vast audience that there were reports of several fatalities resulting from the crowded conditions, and the bishop of Amalfi was suffocated during the melee. There were two other public sessions held on November 20 and 30.

The first public session on November 11 addressed one of the major issues at hand. Innocent was anxious to call a crusade, perhaps to eradicate the memory of the devastation and damage committed during the Fourth Crusade (1201-1204), when the crusaders attacked Constantinople and succeeded in carrying off countless religious and secular treasures with reckless abandon. He ordered that all crusaders should be ready by June to embark at Brindisi for the recovery of the Holy Land. To attract participants, the property of potential crusaders was protected. Crusaders would pay no taxes nor would they need to address their debts during their absence. Indulgences were liberal. Despite all of the careful preparation, the crusade was doomed to failure. Frederick II was expected to participate, but did not fulfill this expectation. Because of the resulting lack of leadership and the death of Innocent III in the meantime, the Fifth Crusade (1217-1221) ended in disaster in Egypt.

In enacting internal Church reform, the Fourth Lateran Council was especially successful. It has been said that Innocent made more laws than fifty of his predecessors,

laws that were practical and workable and entitled him to be considered virtually a cofounder of the canon law of the Church, which had been begun by Gratian in his *Decretum* of the 1140's. These laws laid the groundwork for medieval canon law through the process of assimilation of Roman law and the introduction of new church laws.

Heresy was a major concern of the council. Innocent III continued his vehement opposition to the troublesome Albigensian heresy. The council's canon 1 carefully defined the Trinity and condemned Joachim of Fiore's views against the trinity. Canon 1 also made significant use of the Aristotelian word "transubstantiation," stating that bread and wine were "transubstantiated" into the body and blood of Christ. This statement was the most significant theological definition issued by the council. It was reiterated at the Council of Trent (1545-1563) and continued as a doctrine within the Roman Catholic Church. Another decree required the priest to elevate the Host with his back to the congregation. The laity subsequently became observers rather than participants in the Mass when this decree was put in place. (Following Vatican II in 1965, priests once again were able to face the congregation as they had prior to the Fourth Lateran Council.) Canon 21 commanded every Roman Catholic to make a yearly confession and to receive Communion at Easter. The Fourth Lateran Council established the number of sacraments at seven and stressed the necessity for believers to receive the sacraments in order to attain salvation. Canon 50 liberally restricted marriage to the fourth degree of consanguinity. Other regulations were aimed at clerical discipline. Clergy were not to hold secular offices and were not to act in an unbecoming or exhibitionist manner. Likewise, the clergy was to refrain from wearing decorous or inappropriate clothing.

Canon 2 elaborated on the pursuit of heretics. All who professed heresies contrary to the faith expressed in the first canon defining transubstantiation were condemned and left to be suitably punished by the state. In order to detect doctrinal deviations, bishops were ordered to visit suspected centers of heresy every year. Canon 8 marked the beginning of an episcopal Court of Inquisitions, although the Inquisition at this point in time was procedural and not fully developed until later in the thirteenth century. Innocent's intention at the council was to bring peace after seven years of bloody crusading against the Albigensians. The council developed these antiheresy measures into canon law, thus regularizing the legal process and making use of documentary evidence.

Canon 13 forbade the founding of new religious orders. There were new spiritual forces at work in the thirteenth century. No doubt there was fear about the radical nature of some of the new congregations compounded with a certain sense of rivalry from the older, established orders. The older orders—the Benedictines, the Augustines, the Cistercians—tried to prevail upon the pope not to recognize these new orders. Innocent seems to have countermanded the council. He had already permitted the radical Francis of Assisi to preach; according to some sources, Innocent recognized the Franciscans at the council. This acceptance does not find its way into the documents but it is assumed that Innocent interceded on behalf of the Franciscans. The Franciscan Rule would be recognized by Innocent III's successor, Honorius III, in 1223. The forty-five-year-old Dominic Guzmán from Spain, lacking previous recognition, was allowed by Innocent to establish his new order after initial hesitation and against the vote of the council. After Innocent's death, the Dominican order was sanctioned by Honorius III in 1216. With good diplomatic sense, Innocent was able to reconcile dissidents within the church while simultaneously accommodating the wave of new spiritual reform orders.

The council issued decrees against Muslims and Jews. Anti-Semitism had been on the rise since the period of the First Crusade, and the nature of the crusading movement itself directed hostility toward the Muslims. With the growing self-assurance of Christians about themselves, both Jews and Muslims became "outsiders" even though they had coexisted, sometimes quite peacefully, with Christians for centuries. Canon 68 stated that Jews and Muslims should wear distinctive clothing in Christian lands so that they would not be mistaken as Christians. In the three days before Easter, particularly on Good Friday, Jews and Muslims were not to be seen in public. Innocent III did not want Jews to suffer physical persecution, and he ordered crusaders not to harass Jews. Nevertheless, the requirement of distinctive dress paved an easier path toward the possibility of future persecution.

Other specific matters were then laid before the council for approval. These items included Innocent's choice of Frederick for German king; his suspension of Stephen Langton, the archbishop of Canterbury; his condemnation of the Magna Carta in favor of King John; and his advocacy of the claims of the Albigensian persecutor Simon de Montfort to the territory of Toulouse in southern France. Although violent opposition to the claims of de Montfort erupted among the delegates, Innocent was able to save a large part of the Toulouse inheritance for de Montfort's heir. Apart from his limited success in the Toulouse settlement, Innocent and his momentous Fourth Lateran Council failed only in launching vast crusading plans in the Holy Land.

—Lowell H. Zuck, updated by Barbara M. Fahy

ADDITIONAL READING:

Barraclough, Geoffrey. *Medieval Papacy*. New York: Harcourt Brace Jovanovich, 1968. A solid but readable book on the papacy by a noted medieval scholar.

Jedin, Hubert, *Ecumenical Councils of the Catholic Church: A Historical Survey*. New York: B. Herder, 1960. A well-balanced survey of all the ecumenical councils written by an able and judicious Catholic scholar.

Kuttner, S., and A. Garcia y Garcia. "A New Eyewitness Account of the Fourth Lateran Council." *Traditio* 20 (1964). Although challenging for the general reader, this scholarly look at primary source materials is worth the effort in getting a closer look at the inner workings of the council.

Powell, James M. *Innocent III: Vicar of Christ or Lord of the World?* Boston: D. C. Heath, 1963. A succinct collection of essays that outline the problems and interpretations of Innocent's reign.

Sayers, Jane. *Innocent III, Leader of Europe, 1198-1216*. New York: Longmans, 1994. A fresh and clear perspective of Innocent, his papacy, and the way in which his authority was viewed throughout Europe.

SEE ALSO: 1204, Knights of the Fourth Crusade Capture Constantinople; 1209-1229, The Albigensian Crusade; 1210, Founding of the Franciscans; 1217-1221, The Fifth Crusade; 1233, The Papal Inquisition; 1545-1563, Council of Trent.

1217-1221
THE FIFTH CRUSADE

The Fifth Crusade attempts to regain control of the Holy Land through military action against the Muslims living there, but ends as a dismal failure despite careful planning.

DATE: 1217-1221
LOCALE: Europe; Acre, Syria; Damietta, Egypt
CATEGORIES: Religion; Wars, uprisings, and civil unrest
KEY FIGURES:

Andrew II (1175-1235), king of Hungary, 1205-1235, who supported the cause of the Crusade

Honorius III (Cencio Savelli; died 1227), successor to Innocent III as Roman Catholic pope, 1216-1227, who carried out the preparations for the Fifth Crusade

Innocent III (Lothario of Segni; c. 1160-1216), Roman Catholic pope, 1198-1216, who promoted the Fourth and Fifth Crusades

John of Brienne (c. 1148-1237), king of Jerusalem, 1210-1225, who became the military leader of the crusaders *al-Kāmil* (al-Malik al-Kāmil; 1180-1238), sultan of Egypt, Palestine, and Syria, 1218-1238, who commanded the forces defending Damietta

Pelagius of Albano, papal legate under Honorius III who pressed the point that the pope's authority was superior to that of secular rulers

SUMMARY OF EVENT. One of several crusades that failed to drive Muslims out of what the Christians considered their Holy Land, the Fifth Crusade was nevertheless one of the most carefully planned. Pope Innocent III had been disappointed by the Fourth Crusade; although crusaders had seized Constantinople, victory had not led to conquest of the Holy Land. Seeing the popular religious fervor which had led to the Children's Crusade in 1212, Innocent began to prepare for another crusade in 1213. He believed that the prevailing enthusiasm for the cause would ensure a victory.

In 1213, Innocent sent a papal encyclical to Christian leaders, summoning them to a council to be held in November, 1215. The most important topic for discussion would be the formation of another crusade, and all bishops and clergymen should begin plans to send fighting troops, arms, and supplies when the time came. Innocent also ordered all Christian churches to commence public prayers for the restoration of the Holy Land; monthly processions and daily prayers were called for in an attempt to gather spiritual support from those who would not fight. Handbooks of sermons and prayers were distributed throughout Europe. Innocent's letters and subsequent sermons by local clergymen painted dramatic pictures of devout Christians suffering under Muslim oppression and of Jesus' own sepulchre defiled by disdainful Muslims. The common folk responded enthusiastically.

Inflaming his followers was one thing, but Innocent also needed the support of kings, princes, and barons. Innocent believed that because the spirit is superior to the flesh, the pope should have authority over earthly rulers. Not surprisingly, earthly rulers disagreed. The pope dispatched carefully chosen emissaries throughout Christendom to request—or demand—support.

At the Fourth Lateran Council, which opened on November 11, 1215, the final details were arranged. Those who had taken vows as crusaders in previous engagements would be compelled to fulfill them now. Spanish fighting against the Moors was demoted from crusade status, and Spanish soldiers would now join this crusade. The rules of conduct for crusaders were spelled out, and Innocent promised indulgences and redemption for those who faithfully fulfilled their vows. The crusaders would set off from Sicily on June 1, 1217, after the expiration of the truce between Jerusalem and the Mus-

lims, and Innocent himself would be there to bless them.

In spite of Innocent's strong organizational skills, his carefully laid plans were not followed. He won the full support of many common people, but men of power were less willing to submit to him. No previous pope had demanded taxes to pay for a crusade, or promised redemption as repayment, and these new programs were received with great skepticism. Without the leadership of the nobles, ordinary citizens could not be drawn together into an effective force. Before he could press his will on secular rulers who had their own, different, agendas, Innocent III died on July 16, 1216, almost a year before the Fifth Crusade was to begin.

Pope Honorius III tried to carry out Innocent's plans, believing God's destiny for him was that he should free the Holy Land, but the difficulties were beyond him. Although Hungary and the Netherlands could be counted on, French noblemen refused to join the Fifth Crusade. In Germany, Frederick II had taken up the cross, but his right to the throne was under challenge and he could not risk a long absence. The English nobility were locked in intense internal struggles, and the Spanish were unhappy at being taxed for this crusade after they had already funded the fighting against the Moors.

King Andrew II of Hungary took the first action. In July of 1217, he set out with a large army for Spalato, where they would meet a fleet of ships. As it turned out, the number of crusaders was larger than expected, and there were not enough ships to carry them all, resulting in a delay of several weeks. During the delay, many found their zeal weakening and returned home.

By the fall, more than one hundred thousand crusaders from Hungary, Austria, Merano, Cyprus, and Germany gathered in Acre, Syria. Unfortunately, Syria was experiencing a severe famine, and there was little food. Again, many crusaders deserted the group; others starved to death, or fell victim to crime and unrest. John of Brienne, the king of Jerusalem, decided to abandon his earlier plans for two massive campaigns, and called instead for a series of small attacks to buy time until more crusaders could arrive. Three times the crusaders attacked Muslim strongholds, and three times they were defeated.

Andrew II of Hungary returned home with his army, and replacements from Germany, Italy, and Frisia arrived. The new, larger force attacked Damietta, Egypt, on May 27, 1218. Over the next eighteen months, more crusaders gathered from Italy, France, Cyprus, and England. King John of Jerusalem was chosen as leader of the troops; he expected that once victory was theirs Egypt would fall under his rule. The papal legate Pelagius of Albano had also arrived, however, bringing the message that the pope intended Egypt to be his own, since his authority superseded the king's. Pelagius was the stronger—and more ruthless—personality, and he gradually gained ascendancy over John.

The crusaders camped outside Damietta. In August of 1218, they captured the Chain Tower in the middle of the Nile, and were able then to control the river. The Muslims sank several ships in the river, preventing Christian ships from passing, and the crusaders turned to an abandoned canal. Both sides were determined, and for months neither side seemed to be winning. In February of 1219, however, internal conflict and the deposition of the new sultan led to disorder in Egypt, and the Christians were able to move in.

The Egyptians decided to negotiate. Sultan al-Kāmil offered to surrender nearly all his territory in the kingdom of Jerusalem, and to hold to a thirty-year truce, if the crusaders would leave Egypt. King John and others favored accepting these terms, but Pelagius did not, and he had his way. By the time the crusaders finally conquered Damietta in November of 1219, Muslim forces outside the city were more determined than ever to resist the Christian intruders. The crusaders themselves were disorganized and disgruntled, torn apart by the arguments of their leaders. As for Damietta, it was by this time inhabited by only a small number of starving soldiers who put up no further defense.

With Damietta taken, the conflict between John and Pelagius intensified, further dividing the crusaders. The plan had been for Damietta to become a base from which to launch further attacks; instead, the crusaders remained inactive and disorganized. King John departed in disgust, leaving Pelagius as an unpopular and ineffective leader. As the Muslims' strength grew, Pelagius ordered attacks, but the crusaders were not willing to follow him. Finally, in July of 1221, ordered by the pope to rejoin the Fifth Crusade, John led the crusaders on a march down the Nile. By now, even John had lost the popular support of the men. Taking a route he advised against, the army was cut off and defeated by the Muslims. The crusaders had no choice but to surrender, agreeing on August 30, 1221, to retreat from Egypt. The crusade which had been so carefully planned, and which had at times seemed so near to success, had ended in complete failure.   —*Cynthia A. Bily*

ADDITIONAL READING:

Donovan, J. P. *Pelagius and the Fifth Crusade.* Reprint. Ann Arbor, Mich.: University Microfilms, 1971. First published in 1950, this is one of the most accessible of the book-length studies of the controversial papal legate and one of the most favorable to Pelagius. Donovan acknowl-edges Pelagius' blunders but argues against those who blame those errors for the Fifth Crusade's failure.

Powell, James M. *Anatomy of a Crusade, 1213-1221.* Philadelphia: University of Pennsylvania Press, 1986. Unlike most other studies, this book praises Innocent III's extensive preparations and attributes the Fifth Crusade's failure to implementation weaknesses on the part of secular leaders.

_____, ed. *Innocent III: Vicar of Christ or Lord of the World?* Washington, D.C.: Catholic University of America Press, 1994. A balanced biography, with insightful discussion of Innocent's theology and his extensive theological writings.

Riley-Smith, Jonathan. *The Crusades: A Short History.* New Haven, Conn.: Yale University Press, 1987. A readable history for the general reader, with helpful apparatus for the nonspecialist, including nine historical maps, a unique system of transliteration, and an extensive annotated bibliography.

Van Cleve, Thomas C. "The Fifth Crusade." In *The Later Crusades, 1189-1311*, edited by Robert Lee Wolff and Harry W. Hazard. Vol. 2 in *A History of the Crusades*, edited by Kenneth M. Setton. 2d ed. Madison: University of Wisconsin Press, 1969. An exceptionally clear and detailed accounting of the events of the Fifth Crusade, drawn from Western and Arabic sources. Includes a map of the Near East.

SEE ALSO: 1095, Pope Urban II Calls the First Crusade; 1147-1149, The Second Crusade; 1189-1192, The Third Crusade; 1204, Knights of the Fourth Crusade Capture Constantinople; 1209-1229, The Albigensian Crusade; 1212, The Children's Crusade; 1227-1230, Frederick II Leads the Sixth Crusade; 1228-1231, Teutonic Knights Bring Baltic Region Under Catholic Control; 1248-1254, Failure of the Seventh Crusade.

1227-1230
FREDERICK II LEADS THE SIXTH CRUSADE

Frederick II leads the Sixth Crusade under his imperial power, reestablishing Christian rule in the Holy Land in an almost bloodless victory and ironically earning papal condemnation and opposition of Christian feudal interests for his efforts.

DATE: 1227-1230

LOCALE: Southern Italy and the Holy Land

CATEGORIES: Religion; Wars, uprisings, and civil unrest

KEY FIGURES:

Richard Filangieri, Frederick's agent, representing imperial interests in the Holy Land, 1231-1243

Frederick II (1194-1250), Holy Roman Emperor, 1215-1250, and leader of the Sixth Crusade

Gregory IX (Ugo of Segni; c. 1170-1241), Roman Catholic pope, 1227-1241, who viewed Frederick, not Islam, as a primary concern

Honorius III (Cencio Savelli; died 1227), Roman Catholic pope, 1216-1227, who urged and helped plan the Sixth Crusade

Innocent III (Lothario of Segni; c. 1160-1216), Roman Catholic pope, 1198-1216, and Frederick's absentee guardian, whose major goal was the reconquest of the Holy Land

SUMMARY OF EVENT. In 1215, at the age of twenty-one, Frederick II took his vow as a crusader, apparently to the surprise of Pope Innocent III, who served as his absentee guardian after Frederick was orphaned at the age of four. Frederick's father, Henry VI, was heir to the Germanic empire of Frederick I (Barbarossa), while his mother, Constance of Sicily, was heiress to southern Italy. If he ever gained full control of his inheritance Frederick could be the most powerful Western ruler since Charlemagne.

Frederick spent much of his early life in Sicily, at the time a half Muslim kingdom also populated by a large number of Jews and Greeks. He had a succession of tutors and appears to have absorbed much on his own from the cultural diversity of Sicily, including an attitude of toleration. Arabic and Greek texts, Muslim mathematics and science fascinated him. By the time he reached adulthood, Frederick could speak nine languages (including Arabic) and could write in seven of them. He was not a typical medieval ruler, and when he finally departed on what was the Sixth Crusade, it was a most unusual crusade.

Also in 1215, Frederick was crowned German king at Aachen, having survived a bitter power struggle for the throne. The first five years of his reign was spent consolidating power in the north, largely by permitting considerable independent authority of the German princes. Clearly his Crusader's oath would have to await resolution of immediate political necessities. His "guardian," Pope Innocent III dreamed of a Fifth Crusade after the Fourth Crusade (1202-1204) was diverted by the Venetians into a rapacious sacking of the Christian cities of Zara and Constantinople, and the unofficial "Children's Crusade" (1212) turned into an incredibly embarrassing fiasco. Innocent's plans were put into effect by his successor, Honorius III. Yet this Fifth Crusade, an attack on Damietta in Egypt led by John of Brienne, the former king of Jerusalem, in March of 1218, ended in disaster three years later.

Frederick was too preoccupied to have anything to do with the Fifth Crusade. In November of 1220, he was crowned Holy Roman Emperor in Rome with Honorius

officiating. In return, he reaffirmed his vow to go on a crusade, affirmed church liberties, and promised to keep separate the crowns of southern Italy and Germany. Frederick then returned to Palermo, intent on exerting central control over what was at the time the wealthiest European kingdom because of its vast grain supplies and central position over Mediterranean trade routes.

In the wake of the failure of the Fifth Crusade, Frederick strategized with Honorius about launching a Sixth Crusade. At the suggestion of Hermann of Salza, Frederick's friend and master of the Teutonic Knights, Frederick decided to marry the fifteen-year-old daughter of John of Brienne, heiress to the crown of Jerusalem. Showing that this crusade would be in imperial and not papal control, Frederick had himself crowned king of Jerusalem. This was to be a well-planned military movement using the resources of southern Italy and the Teutonic Knights. At the Conference of San Germano held in 1225, Frederick pledged to the pope, under penalty of excommunication, that the Sixth Crusade would be launched by August 15, 1227.

Honorius did not live to see Frederick honor his vow as a crusader. For his successor, Gregory IX, the eighty-six-year-old nephew of Innocent III, gaining the upper hand in the pope-emperor relationship was a more important goal than was the crusade. Imperial control of northern and southern Italy produced serious encirclement anxieties for Gregory. Anxious to occupy the Holy Roman Emperor in dangerous adventures far away from Italy, Gregory sent Frederick a letter containing a stern warning to go on the Sixth Crusade as scheduled, or suffer the consequences.

Unbeknownst to Gregory, Frederick had already gone on the Crusade, using diplomats instead of soldiers. Taking advantage of a raging dispute between al-Kāmil, the sultan of Egypt, and his brother al-Mulazzam, the governor of Damascus, Frederick was able to communicate to al-Kāmil the advantages of his kingship over Jerusalem, and having troops at hand hostile to Syrian interests. While Gregory ordered Frederick to go east, the sultan of Egypt was inviting him to come.

Frederick and his army finally set sail from Brindisi on September 8, 1227. Disease had plagued the assembling army even before departure. Many were ill from either typhoid or cholera while on board ship. Among the sick was Frederick, who disembarked at Otranto to recover, while the rest of his fleet continued on its journey. Seizing the opportunity to catch Frederick on a technicality, Gregory excommunicated him, after denouncing the emperor in a long list of grievances. Gregory then began assembling an army to invade Sicily.

While Frederick recuperated, his wife died shortly after bearing him a son, thus clouding the issue of whether Frederick would be king or regent of Jerusalem. Meanwhile his forces, led by Duke Henry of Limburg, recaptured Sidon, and reenforced Caesarea. Hermann of Salza established the mighty fortress of Montfort as the main base of operations of the Teutonic Knights. During his recuperation, Frederick tried, to no avail, to come to terms with Gregory. Finally, while still under excommunication, Frederick set sail for Jerusalem in June of 1228, with forty additional ships. This act, which showed the sincerity of Frederick's intentions, was a major blow to Gregory's prestige.

On his way to the Holy Land, Frederick stopped off at Cyprus, using his army's force to gain recognition of his overlordship. From Cyprus, he ventured to Tyre and then on to Acre. By this time, al-Kāmil had little reason to negotiate further with Frederick, since his brother, the governor of Syria had suddenly died, leaving only a child to continue his claims. Yet pressure exerted by Frederick's original force (although much dwindled by the time of his arrival) and the new troops arriving with Frederick, convinced al-Kāmil to come to terms. By the Treaty of February 18, 1229, the sultan surrendered Bethlehem, Nazareth, and Jerusalem. He also provided Frederick with a land corridor to the coast for supplies.

In return, Frederick promised not to fortify Jerusalem, to respect Muslim control of holy places and mosques, and to protect the sultan's interests from all adversaries (including Christians) for the length of a ten year truce.

As a final act, Frederick went to the altar of the Holy Sepulchre and placed the crown of the kingdom of Jerusalem on his own head. Instead of celebration for the return of the Holy Land to Christian rule, Jerusalem was placed under interdict and Frederick was again excommunicated for entering the church while still under excommunication and collaborating with the infidel. That the Holy Land was returned to Christianity by Frederick, without bloodshed, using only eight hundred knights and ten thousand foot soldiers, was beside the point.

To protect his kingdom of Sicily from papal invasion, Frederick had to make a speedy exit from Jerusalem. He appointed two Syrian barons as regents and headed back to Sicily. Overlordship of Cyprus was sold to five other Syrian barons. To represent imperial interests in the Holy Land, Richard Filangieri was sent in 1231, and would remain for the next twelve years. By the end of 1230, the papal invading force had been defeated and Gregory was forced to make peace. Ten years later, the hundred-year-old pope died, still battling Frederick and facing the encirclement of Rome. His successor, Innocent IV, deposed

Frederick in 1245, and declared a Holy Crusade against the Holy Roman Emperor. The fact that Jerusalem had fallen the previous year, to a band of marauding Turks, was hardly noticed. It was not until many years later, during the aftermath of World War I, that the Holy Land was again, for a time, under European administration.

—Irwin Halfond

ADDITIONAL READING:

Abulafia, David. *Frederick II: A Medieval Emperor.* London: Penguin, 1988. An interpretive demythologizing biographical study of Frederick II, containing solid and detailed analysis of his crusading venture.

Billings, Malcolm. *The Cross and the Crescent: A History of the Crusades.* New York: Sterling, 1988. Good starting point for Frederick's role in the Crusades, and a very readable background for the Crusades as well.

Kantorowicz, Ernst. *Frederick the Second, 1194-1250.* Reprint. New York: Frederick Ungar, 1957. First published in 1931 and somewhat overdramatic in tone, this landmark biography of Frederick is still the most readable and comprehensive study of his reign.

Marshall, Christopher. *Warfare in the Latin East, 1192-1291.* New York: Cambridge University Press, 1992. An exhaustive military history of the strategies used in the later Crusades, including detailed analysis of conflicts between fellow Christians.

Riley-Smith, Jonathan. *The Feudal Nobility and the Kingdom of Jerusalem, 1174-1277.* London: Archon, 1973. In-depth study of the role of kings and nobles in the administration of the Latin kingdom, detailing the uncooperativeness of Frankish lords, with an excellent chapter on the Baillage created by Frederick II.

SEE ALSO: 1095, Pope Urban II Calls the First Crusade; 1147-1149, The Second Crusade; 1189-1192, The Third Crusade; 1204, Knights of the Fourth Crusade Capture Constantinople; 1209-1229, The Albigensian Crusade; 1212, The Children's Crusade; 1217-1221, The Fifth Crusade; 1228-1231, Teutonic Knights Bring Baltic Region Under Catholic Control; 1248-1254, Failure of the Seventh Crusade.

1228-1231
TEUTONIC KNIGHTS BRING BALTIC REGION UNDER CATHOLIC CONTROL

Teutonic knights bring the Baltic region under Catholic control, launching a series of military crusades against pagan peoples who have resisted peaceful conversion and assimilation.

DATE: 1228-1231

LOCALE: Prussia

CATEGORIES: Economics; Expansion and land acquisition; Religion

KEY FIGURES:

Hermann Balke, Prussian master, 1230-1239, and Livonian master, 1237-1239

Christian, bishop of Prussia, 1215-1245

Conrad of Masovia (1187-1247), Polish duke

Frederick II (1194-1250), Holy Roman Emperor, 1215-1250

Gregory IX (Ugo of Segni; c. 1170-1241), Roman Catholic pope, 1227-1241

Hermann von Salza, grandmaster of the Teutonic Order, 1209-1239

SUMMARY OF EVENT. East Prussia early in the late thirteenth century lay between Poland and the Baltic Sea, bounded on the west and south by the Vistula River, on the southeast and east by the wilderness of the Masurian Lake district, on the north by the Nemunas (Memel) River; it was inhabited by eleven tribes related by language, culture, and religion to the inhabitants of Lithuania and southern Livonia (modern Latvia). Pomerellia, or West Prussia, on the west bank of the Vistula, was inhabited by Slavs closely related to the Poles. Like Poland, Mecklenburg, and Pomerania, it was being rapidly settled by German immigrants who had been invited by the duke to settle in unpopulated areas. This aspect of the *Drang nach Osten* (push to the east) of the Germans was largely peaceful—in contrast to the crusading effort associated with the twelfth century Wendish Crusade and the later crusade led by the Teutonic Knights in Prussia and even later into Lithuania.

Efforts at a peaceful conversion of the Prussian pagans had failed. Earlier Slavic missionaries had become martyrs, while would-be Bishop Christian was discovering that the pagans had no desire to abandon bigamy, exposure of female infants, and occasional human sacrifice. Meanwhile in Livonia, German crusaders were exploiting their technological and organizational superiority and the ancient rivalries of the local peoples to establish themselves at Riga, and King Waldemar of Denmark was crushing Estonian resistance. The example of Bishop Albert of Riga (1198-1227) persuaded Bishop Christian and Duke Conrad that they could organize a similar crusade, with similar success. In 1217, the pope gave his blessing to the project. From initial victories in 1219, everything went wrong—Duke Conrad could not provide an occupation force for his conquests, then could not protect his own lands from the vengeful Prussians; the Polish kingdom was entering a period of disarray, so that help from the king and other dukes was seldom available; and Prussian paganism, which was based on a military ethos, inspired its worshipers with enthusiasm for their gods' ability to give them slaves and booty from among the worshipers of the Christian god. The pagan offensive reached even into Pomerellia.

Unable to obtain adequate help from relatives and neighbors to repel the pagan onslaught, Duke Conrad again emulated the German model from Livonia by first attempting to found a crusading order of his own (the Dobriners), then in 1225 calling upon established orders to come to his lands. Although a small number of Templars settled in Pomerellia, the only order to respond to the Masovian appeal was the Teutonic Order, and its commitment was small.

The Teutonic Order's formal name was the "Knights of the Hospital of St. Mary of the Germans at Jerusalem," which tells much about their own views of their origin and purpose. Actually founded as a hospital order at Acre in 1189, it was converted into a military order in 1197; as a result, in English it is often called the Teutonic Knights. *Der Deutsche Orden*, its most common German name, means only "the German Order." *Der Deutschritterorden* reflects a much later period when the grandmasters served the interests of the House of Habsburg. The gifted grandmaster Hermann von Salza oversaw the order's expansion in numbers, wealth, and influence until he found it difficult to deploy the warriors in the few castles available to him in the Holy Land. In 1211, von Salza established convent-castles in Hungary to protect that kingdom from steppe warriors, but King Bela, fearing that the newcomers were becoming too powerful, expelled them in 1225. As a result, Hermann von Salza was hesitant to give a greater response to Duke Conrad's invitation than to send a handful of knights to investigate the situation.

Frederick II issued the "Golden Bull" of Rimini in 1226, guaranteeing the order the protection of the Holy Roman Empire for its conquests. In 1228 and 1230, Duke Conrad signed agreements with the Teutonic Order granting the order ownership of any provinces they might conquer (apparently never anticipating that they would take more than a small area around Culm). Bishop Christian somewhat reluctantly made similar promises, but came to a formal agreement only in 1231, after which he was captured by Prussians and thus vanished from the political scene for critical years. Pope Gregory IX eventually issued a crusading bull. In 1230, the first sizable contingent of Teutonic Knights arrived in Prussia under the command of Hermann Balke.

The successes attained by the combined efforts of Polish, Pomerellian, and German crusaders allowed the Teutonic Order to crush all but the most westerly tribes

LANDS OCCUPIED BY THE TEUTONIC KNIGHTS DURING THEIR CRUSADES, 1198-1411

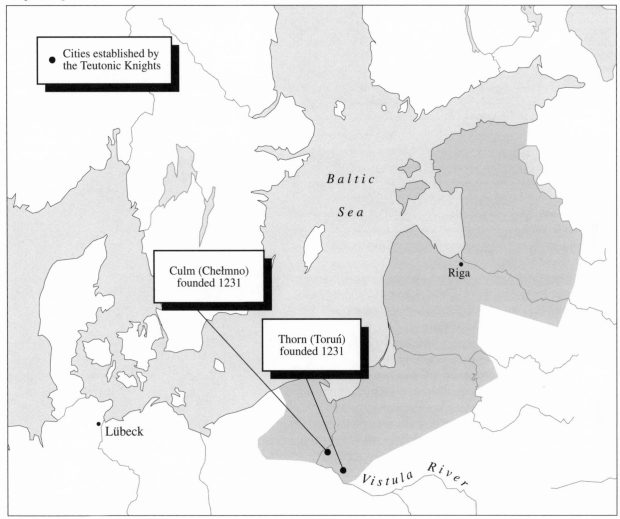

Cities established by the Teutonic Knights

Baltic Sea

Culm (Chełmno) founded 1231

Thorn (Toruń) founded 1231

Riga

Lübeck

Vistula River

quickly; and while civil wars and the Mongol invasion of 1241 occupied the Polish dukes fully, Hermann Balke and his successors resettled the pagans in areas where they could be watched and Christianized, then attracted immigrant farmers and burghers to settle on vacant lands. Within a few decades, the Teutonic Knights had made their Prussian conquests into an independent state. By the time Duke Conrad and his heirs could protest, it was too late.

The papal legate, William of Modena, who was active during these years in Prussia and Livonia, was a practical man. Though not approving of the actions of Hermann Balke, he was not about to dismantle the state in the middle of the continuing wars in Prussia and Livonia. The crusaders were far from attaining ultimate victory in either theater, and if the Teutonic Order were dismissed or dis-

solved, no competing bishop or duke had the resources to govern the areas already conquered, preach the crusade throughout a sufficiently wide area to raise a significant number of crusaders, and then garrison the castles after the armies of volunteers had returned home. The Teutonic Knights, with their resources in the Holy Roman Empire, could do all these things and even send replacements for fallen knights when the inevitable military disasters occurred. As a result, Masovian and Pomerellian complaints were not so much dismissed as ignored.

In 1237, Hermann von Salza sent Hermann Balke with a force of Teutonic Knights to Livonia to rescue the situation there after the local crusading order (the Swordbrothers) was largely destroyed in battle by pagan Lithuanians. In time that region came under the control of a semiautonomous branch of the Teutonic Knights called the Livonian Order. The principal distinguishing characteristic (other than the practicality of governing widely separated regions separately) was that the knights in Prussia generally spoke High German, those in Livonia Low German. To the end of the century, the grandmasters saw their order's principal duty as the defense of the Holy Land, and it was only after the loss of Acre that the order's resources in Italy, Germany, and Bohemia were used primarily to support its brethren in Prussia and Livonia.

—*William L. Urban*

ADDITIONAL READING:

Bartlett, Robert. *The Making of Europe: Conquest, Colonization, and Cultural Change, 950-1350.* Princeton, N.J.: Princeton University Press, 1993. Bartlett's work offers a comprehensive overview of the expansion of Europe during the period when the Teutonic Knights conducted their conquests.

Christiansen, Eric. *The Northern Crusades: The Baltic and Catholic Frontier, 1100-1525.* Minneapolis: University of Minnesota Press, 1980. Erudite and witty study of the period that is highly informative.

Henry of Livonia. *The Chronicle.* Translated by James A. Brundage. Madison: University of Wisconsin Press, 1961. One of the very best medieval chronicles. An eyewitness account of the missionary and crusader era, 1186-1227.

The Livonian Rhymed Chronicle. Translated by Jerry C. Smith and William L. Urban. Indiana University Publications, Uralic and Altaic Series, 128. Bloomington: Indiana University Press, 1977. A useful primary source for the history of the Teutonic Knights.

Urban, William. *The Baltic Crusade.* Rev. ed. Chicago: Lithuanian Research and Studies Center, 1994.

_____. *The Prussian Crusade.* Lanham, Md.: University Press of America, 1980. These two works provide complete narrative accounts of the activities of the Teutonic Order during this period.

SEE ALSO: 1204, Knights of the Fourth Crusade Capture Constantinople; 1217-1221, The Fifth Crusade; 1227-1230, Frederick II Leads the Sixth Crusade; 1240, Mongols Take Kiev; 1248-1254, Failure of the Seventh Crusade; 1291, Fall of Acre.

1230

KINGDOMS OF CASTILE AND LEÓN ARE UNIFIED

The kingdoms of Castile and León are unified, marking an early high point in the Christian reconquest of the Iberian Peninsula and the creation of the kingdom of Spain.

DATE: 1230

LOCALE: León and Castile, Spain

CATEGORIES: Government and politics; Religion

KEY FIGURES:

Alfonso IX (1171-1230), king of León, 1188-1230

Ferdinand I (c. 1016-1065), king of Castile, 1035-1065, and king of Léon, 1037-1065

Ferdinand III (c. 1201-1252), king of Castile, 1217-1252, and king of León, 1230-1252

SUMMARY OF EVENT. Spain was invaded by successive waves of German tribes. The Visigoths, the last of these invaders, obtained control of the Peninsula early in the fifth century and moved their capital from France to Toledo. The Visigoths were followers of the Arian heresy and maintained their own legal code. The Hispano-Romans were Catholic and continued to accept Roman law. Intermarriage between the two groups was forbidden. Conqueror and conquered remained separate.

Instability was characteristic of the Visigothic monarchy. The Visigothic nobles retained the elective kingship, which caused political intrigue and frequent deposition or assassination of the king. The disintegration of the Visigothic state was complete by the reign of Roderick (710-711), the last of the Visigothic kings.

Perhaps as a result of an invitation by the enemies of Roderick, Tarik ibn Mulluk, the Berber governor of Tangiers, crossed the Strait of Gibraltar and defeated Roderick. A second North African army led by Tarik's superior, Musa ben Nosair, conquered the area from Mérida to Salamanca. Only the Basque and the northwestern mountains were unoccupied.

Some Visigothic nobles and their retainers retreated before the Moors into the mountains of Asturias. They elected the Visigothic prince Pelayo (c. 718-737) as king of Asturias and began the Christian Reconquest. Future kings of Spain claimed descent from Pelayo.

Alfonso I of Asturias added Galacia by conquest to his kingdom and moved the capital to Olviedo at the end of the eighth century. The discovery of the tomb of Saint James the Greater at Compostela in Galacia around 830 made the Asturian king guardian of a shrine of European significance and made Compostela a symbol of national unity. Pilgrims from Christian Spain and from Europe brought foreign ideas, customs, money, and soldiers to assist in the Reconquest. Devotion to Saint James led to legends of his appearance to Christian armies on the eve of battle signifying victory.

Succeeding kings of Asturias added additional territory including, in the early part of the tenth century, the table-lands of León, south of the mountains. The capital was moved to the city of León, and the kingdom became known as León. Its territory included Galacia, Asturias, part of the Basque lands, Navarre, and Castile. Yet the local residents of Castile, Navarre, and the Basque lands refused to recognize the authority of the king of León. Disputes over the throne by members of the royal family weakened León and enabled the dissident areas to successfully resist the king.

Castile, located between León and Navarre, was created by the eastward expansion of León. The government of the area was given to the counts of Castile, who paid little attention the kings. Distance, difficulty of communications, and civil strife in León contributed to making Castile independent by the middle of the tenth century. Count Fernán González united the Castilian counties, enlarged his territory, and established his family as hereditary monarchs. In 1028, Sancho García the Great of Navarre captured Castile and annexed it. On his death the territories of Navarre were divided among his sons. To his son Ferdinand, Sancho granted Castile as an independent kingdom.

Ferdinand I of Castile was obsessed with the idea of the Reconquest and was successful in battle. In 1037, he defeated the King Vermundo III of León and united the two kingdoms. Taking advantage of the breakup of the caliphate of Córdoba and of the increase in population and wealth of his enlarged kingdom, Ferdinand expanded southward and westward to bring approximately a quarter of the Peninsula under his control. On his death in 1065, Ferdinand divided his lands among his three sons. Within the year Alfonso VI, who had been given Castile, conquered the territories of his brothers and reunited the three crowns. The fall of Toledo to Alfonso gave him a strategic city that provided protection for the lands to the north, adversely affected the morale of the Moors, and speeded up the Reconquest.

Queen Constance, the second wife of Alfonso VI, was French. Among the Frenchmen she brought to Spain was Bernard, a monk of the Order of Cluny. The king made Bernard archbishop of Toledo, and Pope Urban III made him primate of Spain. Religious toleration had existed until this time. Christians and Moorish rulers had cooperated when it served their purposes, and both Christian and Moorish rulers became vassals of rulers of the other faith. Archbishop Bernard introduced bigotry and the spirit of the Crusades into the Reconquest. He set out to reform the church in Spain and insisted upon strict adherence to orthodox Catholicism.

In 1109, Alfonso VI of Castile was succeeded by his daughter Queen Urraca, whose second husband was King Alfonso I of Aragon. The couple's marital problems caused conflict between Castile and Aragon. Alfonso seized all of Castile, Toledo, and most of León, leaving Queen Urraca Galacia and little else. Prince Alfonso, the queen's son by her first marriage to Raymond of Bur-

The royal families of Castile and Léon led early efforts to reconquer Spain from Moorish control; here, a castle stands next to windmills rising above the central plains of Castile. (Robert McClenaghan)

gundy, was crowned king of Galacia in 1111. He recovered Castile and León from his stepfather and became Alfonso VII of Castile and León. On the death of his stepfather, Alfonso VII became pretender to the throne of Aragon. He did not attempt to conquer the kingdom, which remained separate from the crown of Castile and León.

When Alfonso VII died in 1157, he divided his lands between his two sons, Sancho III, who received Castile, and Ferdinand II, who received León. Sancho ruled only one year and was succeeded by his three-year-old son, Alfonso VIII. Alfonso assumed power at age fourteen and became one of the most successful conquerors of Moorish territory. He advertised the campaigns as crusades, and the pope recognized them as such. Many foreigners joined the Spanish armies fighting the Moors. Alfonso also negotiated with Aragon the first of a series of treaties that determined the boundary between the two kingdoms.

In León, Ferdinand II and his son Alfonso IX greatly extended the Leónese borders southward, and Alfonso turned his attention to the conquest of Castile. The family conflict was settled in 1197 by the marriage of Alfonso IX of León to the daughter of Alfonso VIII of Castile. Their son was Ferdinand III, also known as Saint Ferdinand.

When Alfonso VIII of Castile died in 1214, he was succeeded by his son Enrique I, who died while still a minor. The crown passed to his sister, Doña Berenguela, who had been separated from her husband by the pope on grounds of consanguinity. Doña Berenguela ceded the crown to her son Ferdinand III. Alfonso IX of León opposed the cession even though he was Ferdinand's father and unsuccessfully invaded Castile to remove Ferdinand from the throne. Alfonso IX of León was so hostile to his son Ferdinand and to Castile that when he died in 1230, he bequeathed the throne of León to his two daughters by his first wife, the half sisters of Ferdinand III of Castile. Ferdinand was able to negotiate a settlement with his half sisters whereby he assumed the throne of León in return for rich dowries. The two kingdoms that were first separated in the tenth century and temporarily joined three times in the eleventh and twelfth centuries became permanently joined in 1230. Future kings did not divide their territories as earlier kings had done. The kingdom of León and Castile included Galacia, Asturias, León, Castile, and the territories south added by conquest. The family quarrels resulting from the division of their lands by the earlier kings ended.

—*Robert D. Talbott*

ADDITIONAL READING:

Altamira y Crevea, Rafael. *A History of Spain from the Beginning to the Present Day*. Translated by Muna Lee.

New York: D. Van Nostrand, 1949. Altamira is a world recognized jurist, historian, journalist, and art critic. His history combines all these areas, explaining "Why Spanish things are the way they are."

Descola, Jean. *A History of Spain*. Translated by Elaine P. Halperin. New York: Alfred A. Knopf, 1963. Descola has won worldwide recognition as a Hispanic scholar. This work illustrates his idea of history as an art that combines the writer's imagination and his knowledge.

Marías, Julían. *Understanding Spain*. Translated by Frances M. Lopez-Morillas. Ann Arbor: University of Michigan Press, 1990. The major emphasis of this work is to develop an understanding of the factors which created Spain, factors such as geography, the Reconqest, and Moorish influences.

Reilly, Bernard F. *The Conquest of Christian and Muslim Spain, 1031-1157*. Cambridge, Mass.: Blackwell, 1992. This work is a more complete coverage of the rise of León-Castile and Aragon and deals extensively with the military struggle and dynastic history.

_____. *The Kingdom of León-Castilla Under Queen Urraca, 1109-1126*. Princeton, N.J.: Princeton University Press, 1982. This work covers an important period of economic and cultural advance when the Reconquest achieved significant results, the final unification of León and Castile occurs, and Portugal achieved de facto independence.

SEE ALSO: 711, Tarik's Crossing into Spain; 1031, Fall of the Caliphate of Córdoba; 1092-1094, El Cid Conquers Valencia and Becomes Its Ruler; 1469, Marriage of Ferdinand and Isabella; 1478, Establishment of the Spanish Inquisition; 1492, Fall of Granada.

1233
THE PAPAL INQUISITION

The papal inquisition develops a legal mechanism for suppressing heresy and is instituted gradually during the course of a millennium, causing the suffering and death of thousands of people during the Middle Ages.

DATE: 1233

LOCALE: Primarily Italy, southern France, Spain, and Germany

CATEGORIES: Laws, acts, and legal history; Religion

KEY FIGURES:

Frederick II (1194-1250), Holy Roman Emperor, 1215-1250, who introduced capital punishment for heresy into secular law

Gregory IX (Ugo of Segni; c. 1170-1241), Roman Catholic pope, 1227-1241, and founder of the formal papal Inquisition

Innocent III (Lothario of Segni; c. 1160-1216), Roman
　　Catholic pope, 1198-1216, and instigator of the
　　crusade against the Albigensians
Innocent IV (Sinibaldo Fieschi; c. 1180-1254), Roman
　　Catholic pope, 1243-1254, and organizer of the
　　Inquisition

SUMMARY OF EVENT. When Christianity became the religion of the Roman Empire in 313, the sudden growth of
Christian believers created problems of authority for both
church and state. Maintenance of the social order required
the prohibition of antisocial behavior such as sorcery,
sacrilege, and treason. At first, coercion to ensure harmony
was avoided as being contrary to Gospel precepts. Under
the Christian emperors, notably Constantine's sons, physical force by the state was introduced to bring about unanimity of belief. Nonconformists were regarded as potential rebels and traitors whose activities undermined the
state. After Constantine, the unity of Christian belief was
considered a guarantee of the unity of the empire. The
church fathers were divided on the use of coercion, but
Augustine's views became dominant in the West. He
maintained that the state, like a benevolent father, was
required to encourage heretics to return to orthodoxy and
thus save their souls. Thus, church and state were united
in a common cause.

Shortly after the year 1000, a form of neo-Manichae-
ism, Catharism, or Albigensianism, spread over western
Europe. The popular revulsion against adherents of this
sect was especially strong in France, where thirteen
Cathari were burned at the stake in 1022 by order of
Robert II, and the three-year-old corpse of a heretic was
exhumed and taken out of Christian burial ground. Execution by fire was an innovation unheard of before that time,
but in 1028 heretics were burned by popular demand at
Milan. In 1051, some Cathari were hanged in the presence
of Emperor Henry III. These eleventh century outbursts
seem to have been prompted by the general populace
rather than by the Church. Toward the end of the twelfth
century, however, Catharism had spread to such an extent
in southern France that the very existence of the Church
seemed to be threatened.

Once attention was called to the danger, churchmen
became convinced that some machinery must be set in
motion to deal with it. The relatively casual approach by
many bishops to heresy was changed in 1184, when the
Council of Verona decreed that bishops were to make a
formal inquest in each diocese to root out heretics. This
was the beginning of the episcopal inquisition. The
Church prescribed imprisonment, excommunication, and
confiscation of property, but did not condone the burning
or death of the heretic. In 1199, Pope Innocent III equated

heresy with treason. The obstinate one was to be handed
over to the secular powers for unspecified punishment and
their lands were to be confiscated. In 1220, Frederick II
decreed that relapsed heretics were to be burned and that
lesser offenders were to lose their tongues.

The episcopal inquisition was not successful in stemming the tide of heretics. Pope Innocent III sent his own
legatine inquisitors to southern France, and it was the
murder of one emissary which touched off the crusade
against the Albigensians. With the Treaty of Meaux in
1229, the crusade came to an end, but heresy was still
prevalent. In 1233, Pope Gregory IX issued two papal
bulls establishing the papal Inquisition, which in theory
was to be implemented in cooperation with the bishops,
but in practice was often an instrument of papal control.
Dominicans and Franciscans were generally chosen as
papal inquisitors.

The inquisitor was a privileged person under the special favor of the papacy, who could be controlled by the
pope alone. He was surrounded by numerous assistants:
delegates who asked preliminary questions and heard witnesses, *socii* who accompanied the inquisitor, familiars
who acted as personal guards and agents, notaries, counselors, and servants. The careful preservation of records
promoted the success of the Inquisition, for it rendered
almost impossible the escape of any suspect. Some were
apprehended years later far from the scene of the original
trial on the basis of the trial records.

The inquisitor's task was formidable, as he was obliged
to determine the state of a person's innermost convictions.
The matter of interpretation of the nature of heresy gave
abundant scope for uncovering the smallest details of a
person's moral life. Inquisitors recognized a complex hierarchy of heretics, from those who were merely suspected
to those who obstinately adhered to error. In the latter case,
they were summarily handed over to the secular authorities to be executed, but even those who were merely
suspect received some type of penance, since it appeared
a wrong to God that anyone whose orthodoxy was in doubt
should escape penalty. The list of offenses included anticlericalism, association with heretics (including even
close relatives), moral offenses, sorcery, and witchcraft. It
was rare for an accused heretic to escape some form of
punishment despite protestations of innocence.

After arriving at a town within his province, the inquisitor let it be known that he would receive accusations and
confessions for a period of time. After that he proceeded
to summon suspects who had not voluntarily presented
themselves. The accused were not permitted to cross-
examine their accusers, but they were permitted to draw
up a list of any enemies who might gain from their convic-

Once they were found guilty by papal inquisitors, heretics could be sentenced to death by fire or subjected to extreme forms of punishment; here, a woman is tortured by having her arms and legs tied to ropes attached to four horses. (Archive Photos)

tion. Prejudiced evidence from such enemies was not to be admitted. The inquisitor was assisted by a council, and in theory he was to reach his verdict in consultation with the council and the bishop. In practice, the verdicts were often made by the inquisitor-judge alone. Torture, which had been permitted by Pope Innocent IV in his bull *Ad extirpanda* (1252), was abrogated by Pope Boniface VIII. The sentence was pronounced at the *sermo generalis* or *auto-da-fé* (act of faith), a public exhibition which all residents of the locality were urged to attend. Sentences varied from death by fire, carried out by the state, to imprisonments of varied duration, confiscation of goods, pilgrimages, and lesser penances.

In 1542, Pope Paul III established the Congregation of the Inquisition as the final court of appeals for heresy trials. (In 1908, this congregation became known as the Holy Office, and in 1965, it came to be called the Congregation for the Doctrine of the Faith.)

The Spanish Inquisition, which was not established until the end of the fifteenth century, bears a different character. It was established to discover heretics among converted Muslims (*Moriscos*) and Jews (*Marranos*), only later extending its activities to include Protestants. It was primarily an instrument of the state. In fact, many orthodox bishops and Jesuits were singled out for harassment and even death because of their criticism of the secular authorities.

—*Carl A. Volz,
updated by Winifred Whelan*

ADDITIONAL READING:

Kieckhefer, Richard. "The Office of Inquisition and Heresy: The Transition from Personal to Institutional Jurisdiction." In *Journal of Ecclesiastical History* 46 (January, 1995): 36-61. Kieckhefer indicates that there was no "Inquisition" as a systematic structured entity until 1542, a fact that is not recognized by many authors on the subject. At first, there were only individual local efforts, and only gradually did a systematic, centralized, curial inquisitional authority emerge.

Lea, Henry Charles. *The History of the Inquisition of the Middle Ages.* 3 vols. New York: Harper & Row, 1888. Lea's work is considered foundational for all significant study on the topic of the inquisition. The book outlines the gradual establishment of inquisitorial procedure and shows how after 1250 the papal legates served as an arm of central authority over the bishops as well as detectors of heresy, thus enhancing papal centralization.

Monter, E. William. *Frontiers of Heresy: The Spanish Inquisition from the Basque Lands to Sicily.* New York: Cambridge University Press, 1990. This book concentrates particularly on the Spanish Inquisition. It includes interesting tables and appendices showing the number of people who were put to death in various tribunals.

Peters, Edward. *Inquisition.* New York: Free Press, 1988. Peters contends that the inquisition began when the church employed clergy to preserve orthodox religious beliefs from the attacks of heretics. At the time of the Protestant Reformation, these localized inquisitions were transformed into the Inquisition, mainly because it served the purpose of various political regimes. The book also includes chapters on the inquisition in literature and art.

Shannon, Albert C. *The Medieval Inquisition.* Collegeville, Minn.: Liturgical Press, 1984. For its specific topic, this book singles out the period of the 1200's in Languedoc, southern France. It details how the beliefs of the Albigensians and the Waldensians resulted in the establishment of the Inquisition.

SEE ALSO: 1175, Appearance of the Waldensians; 1209-1229, The Albigensian Crusade; 1478, Establishment of the Spanish Inquisition.

1240

ALEXANDER NEVSKY DEFENDS NOVGOROD FROM SWEDISH INVADERS

Alexander Nevsky defends Novgorod from Swedish invaders, checking the Swedish advance into Russian territory and allowing Novgorod's merchants to have continued access to the Gulf of Finland via the Neva River.

DATE: July 15, 1240

LOCALE: Neva River and Gulf of Finland

CATEGORIES: Expansion and land acquisition; Wars, uprisings, and civil unrest

KEY FIGURES:

Alexander Yaroslavich Nevsky (c. 1220-1263), prince of Novgorod and later grand prince, 1252-1263

Andrei Yaroslavich, grand prince, 1249-1252

Batu (died 1255), Mongol leader who conquered Russia in the thirteenth century and established khanate of the Golden Horde in 1241

Birger Jarl (died 1266), regent of the Swedish crown, 1248-1252

Kirill (1246-1280), metropolitan of the Orthodox Church in Russia and author of Alexander's *Life*

Yaroslav Vsevolodovich, grand prince, 1238-1246

SUMMARY OF EVENT. Alexander's leadership in the defense of Novgorod and the other Russian lands from incursions of Swedes and Germans are well known. Metropolitan Kirill's *Life* of Alexander portrayed his hero as the savior of Orthodoxy. Twice Alexander was engaged in defense against Swedes, one of which took place along the Neva River on July 15, 1240, and explains the sobriquet "Nevsky." Alexander's mounted brigade surprised the encamped Swedes while infantry attacked Swedish ships in dock to prevent arrival of reinforcements. These battles (or skirmishes, as one authority avers) were part of the continuing struggle between Russians and Scandinavians for control of the Finnish and Karelian lands. Other sources, however, argue that such battles were designed by Grand Prince Yaroslav Vsevolodovich to stop the territorial and religious plans of Germans, Danes, and Swedes who hoped to absorb Novgorod at a time when it was weakened by Tatar rule. Yaroslav's action may have been designed to enhance Novgorod's military dependence upon the "downstream" princes of Vladimir upon whom it was already dependent for food.

Yaroslav, father of Alexander, sent him to become prince of Novgorod, a commercial city-state north of Vladimir. Unlike most Russian towns, Novgorod had a powerful assembly dominated by merchant lords and often divided in its allegiance to the grand principality of Vladimir to the south. Novgorod also maintained steady trade with the Hanseatic league of cities in northern Europe. Its furs, wax, walrus tusks, and woodwork were prized items at fairs. The so-called German quarter of Novgorod was the residence of many foreign merchants who came to the city by way of the Gulf of Finland, the Neva River, Lake Ladoga, and then south to Novgorod along the Volkhov River. When, in 1240, an army of Swedes, with Finns and Danes, arrived at the mouth of the Izhora River at the spot joining the Neva, Russians in Novgorod perceived this invasion as an effort to close their access to the sea. The merchants of Novgorod also regarded this incursion as a first step toward further acquisitions south toward the city-state, itself. Meanwhile, Yaroslav was concerned about the advances of Germans and Lithuanians from the west as well as the Swedes from the north.

According to most early and modern sources, when the Swedes arrived at the Neva in "very many ships," their leader, Birger, later regent to the young king of Sweden, sent news of their presence to Novgorod, challenging the entire province to take battle. The twenty-year-old prince, Alexander, summoned an army after spending many hours praying to the Blessed Virgin in the Saint Sophia Cathedral. He was impatient to wait for reinforcements from the outlying regions of the Novgorod territories as well as others from Russian territories downstream toward Vladimir. He probably doubted the ability to raise more troops given the recent Mongol destruction of Russian mounted retainers. Thus Alexander began his campaign against the Swedes with a much smaller force than his opponent.

Although the encounter on July 15, 1240, is sometimes described as a skirmish by some modern writers, the description of the battle indicates that it was more than that. A certain Pelgusius, a local chieftain of a Finno-Ugric tribe at Lake Ladoga offered to reconnoiter the Swedish encampment for Alexander. Although his tribe was pagan he was a Christian, and he told Alexander of a vision about the impending battle whereby the medieval Russian Saints Boris and Gleb appeared to him with news that they intended to aid the prince against the invaders.

Despite the Swedish notification to Alexander, the fact that his armies surprised the Swedish forces in the daylight indicates that Alexander's strategy of hasty advance without additional reinforcements may have been the correct strategy. In a plan to prevent enemy reinforcements from arriving, three Swedish vessels were sunk by Alexander's infantry, while two others escaped with fleeing soldiers. A Swedish general was killed, and one source mentions that the Earl Birger was even wounded by Alexander and that one of the Catholic bishops was killed. Russian horsemen killed a large number of enemy as well, although the hagiography of Alexander written by Metropolitan Kirill, told of an angel of death killing a multitude of Swedish soldiers who lay along the opposite banks of the Neva where Alexander's men had not crossed. At any rate the victory led to Alexander's new appellation as "Nevsky" in honor of this battle.

Among the men of Novgorod who distinguished themselves on the battlefield were six: Gavrilo Oleksich, who fought the general and son of Birger; Zbyslav Yakenovich, who fought daring encounters with his battle axe; Jacob of Polotsk, the huntsman of Prince Alexander, who charged the enemy with his sword; Mikhail, a foot soldier who led the infantry in the attack which destroyed three Swedish vessels; Savva, who stimulated his fellow soldiers to combat when he charged the big, golden-crowned tent of the enemy, cutting its central pole; and Ratmir, who died fighting when encircled by many foes. Alexander arrived back home with losses of but twenty of his men, including those well known to contemporaries such as Konstantin Lugotinits, Giuriata Pineshchinich, Nemest, and Drochilo, son of Nezdilo the tanner.

Although triumphant, the new popularity of Alexander was threatening to the merchant lords of Novgorod who dismissed him as their prince. Alexander, in anger, took his courtiers and family to his former home in Pereiaslavl. A few years later when the Germans invaded the satellite region of Pskov, Novgorod pleaded with Alexander to return. He did so and the famous battle on the ice took place on Lake Peipus as Alexander's forces routed the German Knights of Livonia (1242). The Swedes would return again in 1247, but Alexander was then en route to the capital of the Mongols to appease their demands for conscription and taxes. The policy of appeasement was considered essential to the survival of the Russian lands which could not have withstood both Mongols to the south and Catholics to the west at the same time. That very year of the battle on the Neva, the Russian town of Chernigov was overwhelmed by the Mongols, as was Kiev on the Dnieper River. One year later, the Germans invaded from the west. Metropolitan Kirill thought the Catholic threat was more to be feared, since the Mongols allowed the Orthodox Church to function in Russia so long as priests prayed for the khan. Did he overstate the importance of Alexander's military defenses against the West in order to deflect criticism of the prince's appeasement of the Tatars? In any case, in 1245 the Lithuanians attacked Russian lands from the West, seizing permanently many Russian communities. A formal treaty of peace between the Russians and the Swedes was not signed until 1326. As for Novgorod, its commercial prosperity and republican political organization continued for the duration of the "Tatar

Yoke" until the city-state was absorbed by the Muscovite state of Grand Prince Ivan III in the late fifteenth century.

—*John D. Windhausen*

ADDITIONAL READING:

Birnbaum, Henrik. *Lord Novgorod the Great: Essays in the History and Culture of a Medieval City-State*. Columbus, Ohio: Slavica, 1981. Birnbaum agrees with Soviet researchers who believe that the Swedish regent was not at the battle on the Neva, but at the later one in 1247.

The Chronicle of Novgorod. Translated by Robert Mitchell and Nevill Forbes. New York: AMS Press, 1970. An indispensable source for the study of Alexander's role in Novgorod, but written from the tendentious outlook of medieval churchmen.

Fennell, John. *The Crisis of Medieval Russia, 1200-1304*. London: Longman, 1983. A critical account of this medieval hero who doubts the importance of the Neva encounter.

Presniakov, A. E. *The Formation of the Great Russian State*. Translated by A. E. Moorhouse. Chicago: Quadrangle Books, 1970. First published in 1918, this work analyzes the disarray among the Russian leaders at the time of the Mongol and Western invasions. He stresses Alexander's family relationships and charismatic leadership.

Riasanovsky, Nicholas V. "Lord Novgorod the Great," *A History of Russia*. 5th ed. New York: Oxford, 1993. The author depicts the encounter as an ideological confrontation.

"Tale of the Life and Courage of the Pious and Great Prince Alexander." In *Medieval Russia's Epics, Chronicles, and Tales*, edited by Serge A. Zenkovsky. New York: E. P. Dutton, 1974. Although written forty years after the events, it remains the basic source for the era of Alexander and depicts him as the savior of the land from the Catholic West.

Vernadsky, George. *The Mongols and Russia*. New Haven, Conn.: Yale University Press, 1953. The classic account by the late dean of American scholars of medieval Russia. It should be read in conjunction with the revisionist version of Fennell.

SEE ALSO: 1228-1231, Teutonic Knights Bring Baltic Region Under Catholic Control; 1240, Mongols Take Kiev; 1391-1395, Timur Devastates Southern Russia; 1480-1502, Destruction of the Golden Horde; after 1480, Ivan III's Organization of the "Third Rome."

1240
MONGOLS TAKE KIEV

Mongols take Kiev, capturing the Rus' capital as part of the Mongol conquest of European Russia between 1236 and 1240.

DATE: December 6, 1240

LOCALE: Ukraine, Russia

CATEGORIES: Expansion and land acquisition; Wars, uprisings, and civil unrest

KEY FIGURES:

Batu (died 1255), grandson of Ghengis Khan and nominal leader of the Mongol forces that conquered European Russia

Dmitrii, the Rus' military commander of Kiev in late 1240

Guyuk (died 1248), grandson of Ghengis Khan and participant in the Mongol conquest of European Russia who later ruled as great khan, 1246-1248

Mongke (died 1259), grandson of Ghengis Khan and participant in the Mongol conquest of European Russia who later ruled as great khan, 1251-1259

SUMMARY OF EVENT. In 1234-1235, a Mongol *quriltai*, or council of clan leaders, approved ambitious plans for the conquest of the Sung empire in southern China, Korea, the Middle East, and Europe. Batu, son of Jochi and grandson of Ghengis Khan, was appointed the nominal head of the latter campaign. Kazakhstan and the yet un-conquered lands to the west had been earlier bequeathed to Jochi by his father, Ghengis Khan, as his inheritance and are thus sometimes referred to as Jochi's *ulus* or Jochi's share. Batu was thus setting out to conquer the lands which "belonged" to him by right of inheritance from his father Jochi, who had died in 1227. Since Batu did not have enough troops of his own for this western campaign, several other grandsons of Ghengis, including the future great khans Guyuk and Mongke, along with several very experienced generals such as Subedei, were designated by the Great Khan Ugedei to participate in the conquest of Europe. Batu also conscripted numerous Tur-kic steppe horsemen from his own *ulus* into the invasion force whose total number may have reached 150,000-250,000 (the estimates vary greatly).

The Mongols had long been interested in European Russia and the Caucasus. In 1222-1223, for example, a large Mongol scouting party led by Jebe and Subedei advanced along the southern coast of the Caspian Sea, crossed through the Caucasus easily crushing all local opposition, defeated the Alans and Polovtsians-Cumans of the northern Caucasus and south Russian steppe, invaded the Crimea, and then destroyed a joint Rus'-Polovtsian force at the Battle of the Kalka in 1223 before returning home to report to Ghengis on what they had learned about the "western lands." Between 1223 and 1236, additional intelligence-gathering campaigns had been conducted along the middle and lower Volga. Batu's army thus pos-sessed considerable information about the peoples of European Russia on the eve of its invasion. The Rus', by way of contrast, seem to have little or no knowledge about the Mongols. In any event, the various Mongol armies came together somewhere east of the Volga River in early 1236 and one part, led by Batu and Subedei, launched an attack against the Bulghars of the middle Volga River and neighboring peoples. A second Mongol force commanded by Mongke took the lower Volga region and moved into the northern Caucasus. By the fall of 1237, all the Finnic and Turkic peoples living to the east and southeast of the Rus' lands had been conquered.

In December of 1237, Batu's army invaded the north-eastern Rus' principalities of Riazan' and Vladimir which were quickly subdued. The local Rus' forces were deci-sively crushed by the Mongols at the Battle of the Sit' in early March, 1238. The Mongol armies then invaded the upper Volga lands and came within sixty-five miles or so of Novgorod, the greatest Rus' city in northwestern Rus-sia. At this point, the Mongols retreated to the steppes of southern Russia and Ukraine where they rested, re-grouped, and spent the period between the summer of 1238 and early 1239 suppressing revolts by the Polov-tsians of the steppe, the peoples of the northern Caucasus, the inhabitants of the Crimea, and the Finnic and Rus' natives of the middle and upper Volga. Having reaffirmed their domination over these areas, the Mongol forces were ready to invade the Pereiaslavl', Chernigov, and Kiev principalities of the middle Dnieper basin early in 1239.

By the spring of 1239, the city of Pereiaslavl' had been taken, and Chernigov fell to the Mongols in October of 1239. At this point, there was no doubt that Kiev would be the next Mongol objective. It was a large and well-fortified city, however, whose siege demanded careful preparations. The Mongols thus retreated into the steppe again and sent scouting parties to reconnoitre the areas around Kiev and gather information on the city's defenses. While heading one of these parties, Mongke sent several envoys to Kiev apparently demanding its surrender. Grand Prince Mikhail refused, allegedly had the envoys killed, and then fled to Hungary. Rostislav of Smolensk and Daniil of Galicia briefly served as grand prince of Kiev, but neither remained to face the impending siege. The latter, however, left Dmitrii, a *voevoda* or military com-mander, to take charge of Kiev's defense. When the Mon-gols again moved north during the late summer of 1240, the remaining inhabitants of Kiev were no doubt demoral-ized by the obvious fear of their princes and the tremen-dous success of the Mongols elsewhere in Rus' lands. To facilitate their attack, the Mongols conquered the nomadic auxiliaries of the Kievan princes who lived south of Kiev and then proceeded to the capital city.

The large Mongol army which besieged Kiev was commanded by Batu and included Guyuk and Mongke as well as Batu's brother Orda. The city was surrounded and catapults and battering rams were moved near the walls in the vicinity of the so-called Polish Gates. This site was chosen because the woods here provided cover for the attackers. The battering rams pounded against the walls day and night without interruption while the catapults fired missiles continuously. Many on both sides perished in this fighting. After this attack had gone on for some time, Batu offered to spare the lives of those inside Kiev if they would surrender. The people of Kiev refused and cursed Batu. The Mongols continued with the attack and finally broke through the walls and invaded the city. Fierce hand-to-hand fighting took place and there were numerous casualties. Slowly but surely the Mongols defeated the defenders and captured more and more of the city. The Rus' military commander, Dmitrii, was wounded and many of his best soldiers were dead. When night came, the remaining Rus' survivors fortified the Church of the Virgin Mary and prepared to make their last stand there. In the morning, fighting resumed and the Mongols broke through the Rus' defenses and entered the Church. The remaining Rus' fled to the church steeple where they were killed; the Church itself collapsed from the fighting. Kiev thus fell to the Mongols on December 6, 1240, the day of St. Nicholas. Extensive archaeological excavations in Kiev have confirmed the widespread destruction caused by the Mongol conquest. The wounded Rus' *voevoda*, Dmitrii, was brought before Batu who supposedly spared his life in recognition of his bravery. The first capital of the Rus' lands was now under Mongol rule.

Batu left a Mongol garrison in Kiev and then departed for Vladimir in Volynia and Galich in the western Rus' lands which he took before the Mongols launched their invasion of Hungary. By December of 1241, the Hungarian army had been routed, and Batu had crossed the Danube into Croatia pursuing the Hungarian king. Batu, however, withdrew from Hungary to the east in the spring of 1242 upon learning that the Great Khan Ugedei had died and the politicking to elect a new khan had begun. He established himself at Sarai along the lower Volga River, which soon developed into the capital of the Golden Horde, the name given to those Mongols who ruled European Russia from the time of Batu's conquest until the fifteenth century.   —*Thomas S. Noonan*

ADDITIONAL READING:

Chambers, James. *The Devil's Horsemen: The Mongol Invasion of Europe*. London: Weidenfeld & Nicolson, 1979. A good introduction to the European conquests.

Fennell, John. *The Crisis of Medieval Russia, 1200-1304*. London: Longman, 1983. The section on "The Great Invasion 1237-1240" (on pages 76-90) provides a useful account of the Mongol invasion of the Rus' lands and the conquest of Kiev.

Juvainī, ʿAlā-al Dīn ʿAtā-Malik. *The History of the World-Conqueror*. Translated by J. A. Boyle. 2 vols. Manchester, England: Manchester University Press, 1958.

Perfecky, George A., ed. and trans. *The Hypathian Codex Part II: The Galician-Volynian Chronicle*. Munich, Germany: Wilhelm Fink, 1973. In this annotated translation, the entries for 1236-1240 provide a southern Rus' perspective on the Mongol conquest which incorporates much firsthand information.

Rashīd al-Dīn. *The Successors of Genghis Khan*. Translated by J. A. Boyle. New York: Columbia University Press, 1971. The conquests of the Mongols, including European Russia, as seen from a Mongol perspective by Islamic authors.

Vernadsky, George. *The Mongols and Russia*. Vol. 3 in *A History of Russia*. New Haven, Conn.: Yale University Press, 1953. The most systematic attempt to integrate Rus' and Mongol history during the period when the Mongols conquered and ruled the Rus' lands.

Zenkovsky, Serge A., ed. *The Nikonian Chronicle, Volume Two: From the Year 1132-1240*. Translated by Serge A. Zenkovsky and Betty Jean Zenkovsky. Princeton, N.J.: Kingston Press, 1984. This annotated translation of a sixteenth century Muscovite chronicle combines information found in many earlier Rus' chronicles to provide, in the entries for 1236-1240, a detailed northern Rus' perspective on the Mongol conquest.

SEE ALSO: 1271-1291, Travels of Marco Polo; 1391-1395, Timur Devastates Southern Russia; 1480-1502, Destruction of the Golden Horde.

1248-1254
FAILURE OF THE SEVENTH CRUSADE

The failure of the Seventh Crusade contributes to the growing disillusionment and anti-Crusade sentiment characteristic of mid- to late thirteenth century Europe.

DATE: 1248-1254

LOCALE: Egypt

CATEGORIES: Religion; Wars, uprisings, and civil unrest

KEY FIGURES:

Alphonse of Poitiers (1220-1271), brother of Louis and a crusader

Blanche of Castile (1188-1252), mother of Louis, acted as regent of France in 1226-1234 and 1248-1252 in the king's absence

Charles of Anjou (1227-1285), brother of Louis and
   member of the Crusade army

Jean de Joinville (c. 1224-1317), baron who joined the
   Seventh Crusade and described it in his memoirs

Louis IX (1214-1270), king of France, 1226-1270, and
   leader of the Seventh Crusade

Margaret of Provence (1221-1295), wife of Louis who
   accompanied him on the Seventh Crusade

Robert of Artois, younger brother of King Louis IX who
   led the disastrous attack on Mansurah

William, earl of Salisbury (c. 1212-1250), leader of the
   English contingent

SUMMARY OF EVENT. A little more than one hundred and
fifty years after Pope Urban II called the First Crusade in
1095, King Louis IX of France embarked on what historians regard as the end of the crusading movement. Louis
can be seen as leader of two crusades, or of one crusade in
two phases. In either interpretation, it is the earlier effort
that is usually called the Seventh Crusade.

It is true that there were attempts to organize crusades
for several centuries after the failure of the campaigns of
Louis in 1248 and 1270, but none of them succeeded in
winning the kind of support that made possible the strong
offensives of the twelfth and thirteenth centuries. Indeed,
Louis' abortive crusade of 1270 marked the last full-scale
crusade mounted by a European king.

On the diplomatic scene there were compelling reasons
for a crusade in the 1240's. In the West, a succession of
popes had engaged in a long vendetta with the brilliant
Hohenstaufen emperor, Frederick II. In this struggle, crusading had been a factor in several ways. First, although
Frederick had promised to lead a crusade in 1215 and
1220, he did not leave until 1227. Pope Gregory, angered
by his stalling, finally excommunicated him, a ban which
was not lifted until Frederick's return from the Sixth Crusade. During the Sixth Crusade, Frederick won Jerusalem
in negotiations with al-Kāmil, the sultan of Egypt. The
Christian victory was not long-lived, however; Jerusalem
was subsequently retaken in 1244 by the Turks, who were
allies of the Egyptians. Second, Frederick once again
found himself the target of papal anger in 1245, when
Pope Innocent IV excommunicated him and called for a
crusade against Frederick himself at the Council of Lyons.

Although his loyalty to the church was unquestioned,
Louis did not support the pope in this venture. Rather,
during a serious illness, Louis made a vow that he would
take up the cross for the more traditional and popular
purpose of reconquering the Holy Land. Louis' mother,
Blanche of Castile, tried to dissuade him from his vow,
saying that a vow taken in illness was not binding. Louis'
response was to retake his vow upon his recovery.

Conditions in the East also indicated that the time was
ripe for a major thrust against the Muslims, because there
was internal rivalry between the Syrian and Egyptian
leaders. Another hopeful sign, though misinterpreted, was
an apparent chance of allying with the Mongols against
the Muslims. Several religious-diplomatic missions had
been sent to the Mongol khan, Hulagu, and though they
had produced no positive results, the possibilities of converting the Mongols and thus procuring a strong ally in the
East was a factor in the climate that supported Louis'
crusade.

Louis prepared for the Seventh Crusade in a number of
ways. First, he wanted to leave behind a stable France. He
had quelled two uprisings by barons in 1241 and 1243; as
he gathered his forces for the Seventh Crusade, he persuaded many of the dissident barons to accompany him.
He also sent emissaries around the country to investigate
any wrongdoings by his government or dissatisfaction of
his subjects. As a result of this investigation, he overhauled
his administration and left experienced, trustworthy officials in charge during his absence.

Second, Louis carefully planned for the material needs
of his expedition. The Seventh Crusade, which was more
carefully planned than any of the expeditions which had
preceded it, included the construction of a port of embarkation at Aigues-Mortes, not far from Marseilles, as well
as the shipping of a large number of supplies ahead to
Cyprus. Further, Louis embarked on negotiations with the
Genoese for transportation and the recruitment of an army
of at least ten thousand men. Apart from a small contingent from England under the earl of Salisbury, grandson
of Henry II, most of the force was French, and a large
proportion was supported directly by the king. Among the
leading barons were three of the French king's brothers:
Robert of Artois, Charles of Anjou, and Alphonse of Poitiers. Louis' wife, Margaret of Provence, also accompanied the expedition, a reminder that crusaders of knightly
rank were accustomed to bringing an entire household. In
this case, Margaret played a strategic role in the evacuation after Louis' defeat.

Louis received little help from the pope in organizing
his crusade. The pope's crusade against Frederick II as
well as his call for a crusade in Spain diluted the crusading
effort across Europe. Most of Louis' support came from
within France, with the Catholic Church contributing
funds that covered approximately two-thirds of his expenses. Louis also contributed a great deal of his own
money to support the expedition.

After three years of preparation, the expedition sailed
for Damietta after wintering at Cyprus. Louis reached the
Nile River near Damietta by June of 1249. The plan called

CRUSADE OF LOUIS IX TO EGYPT AND THE HOLY LAND

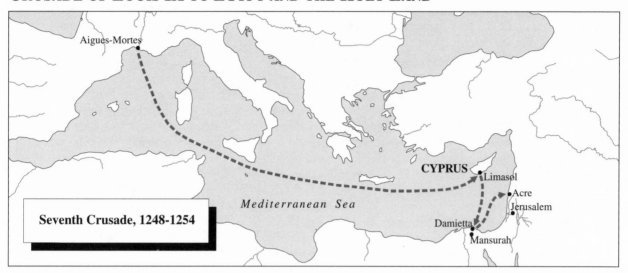

Seventh Crusade, 1248-1254

for conquering the Ayubite Muslims in Egypt, thus forcing them to make concessions in the Holy Places. Louis was following the strategy of the Fifth Crusade, when Damietta was offered in exchange for Jerusalem. In a rapid, excellently organized landing and attack, the crusaders routed an Egyptian force which had come to the coast to meet them. Pushing on to Damietta itself by June 6, the crusaders found the place deserted and were able to take it over with little or no loss, thus providing themselves with an ideal base of operations.

The crusaders did not begin their march into Egypt until November 20. They did not reach Mansurah, a fortified stronghold up the Nile, until February of 1250. Mansurah was an important military objective: Whoever held Mansurah could command Cairo, and thus bargain from a position of strength.

The attack on Mansurah was a complete disaster for Louis' forces. Robert of Artois, who led the vanguard, flagrantly disobeyed orders and stormed the city with the Knights Templars before the supporting troops had time to assemble. The vanguard was trapped in the narrow streets of Mansurah, and Robert was killed. Louis, who crossed the Nile with the main body of crusaders, fought all day and ended in possession of the battlefield outside of the city when the Muslims retreated to Mansurah. Over the next days, however, the crusaders were unable to take Mansurah and became increasingly isolated and without defense. By April, Louis and his remaining army recrossed the Nile and began their retreat to Damietta. The Muslims were easily able to capture the fleeing army. Captives worth a ransom, particularly the king, were spared. When news of the tragedy reached Damietta, the

Genoese responsible for transport planned to pull out and leave the remnant of the crusaders to their own devices. At this juncture Margaret, Louis' wife, bargained successfully with the Genoese and persuaded them to stay.

Louis was released on May 6, 1250, after partial payment of his ransom. He chose to remain in Acre about four years, however, as a protector of those who were waiting to be ransomed. When his mother, Blanche of Castile, who had acted as regent in his absence, died, Louis returned to France in 1254, believing that his failure had been a punishment for his sins.

Sixteen years later, Louis headed another expedition. This time, the response to the crusading call was disappointing and the army was considerably smaller than the earlier one. Some of Louis' closest associates, including Jean de Joinville, his biographer and loyal supporter on the earlier campaign, refused the second time. The army landed at Tunis, for reasons that continue to puzzle historians. It was the end for Louis, who died of a fever. It was reported that his last words were "Jerusalem, Jerusalem."

The failure of Louis' crusades cannot be alleged as the sole cause for the mood of disillusionment concerning the Holy War that was so pronounced a feature after Louis' time. Nevertheless, it was undoubtedly an important factor. Louis was revered even during his lifetime as an exemplar of Christian kingship; soon after his death, he became a legend. It was hard for the people of an age that looked to heaven for visible signs of approval to believe that a crusade could possibly be an expression of God's will, since the greatest of Christian kings that people knew had tried and failed. The old crusaders' cry, "God wills it," could never again have a convincing ring. Whether it was

Louis' failure or the political uses to which the Crusades were put during the last half of the thirteenth century which led to the end of the era is unclear. Nevertheless, although crusades continued to be mounted on a small scale for the next three hundred years, no crusade ever again achieved the scope or size of the Seventh Crusade.

—*Mary Evelyn Jegen,*
updated by Diane Andrews Henningfeld

ADDITIONAL READING:

Daniels, Norman. *The Arabs and Medieval Europe.* London: Longman, 1974. Daniels provides a good introduction to Islamic-Christian relations during the Middle Ages.

Hallam, Elizabeth, ed. *Chronicles of the Crusades.* New York: Weidenfeld & Nicolson, 1989. A large, lavishly illustrated volume of translated primary source documents and linking essays, the book includes Arabic as well as European texts.

Holt, P. M. *The Age of the Crusades: The Near East from the Eleventh Century to 1517.* London: Longmans, 1986. A short introduction to the subject of the eastern Crusades.

Riley-Smith, Jonathan. *The Crusades: A Short History.* New Haven, Conn.: Yale University Press, 1987. A comprehensive history of the Crusades including the crusades to the East as well as the political crusades in Europe.

Runciman, Steven. *The Kingdom of Acre and the Later Crusades.* Vol. 3 in *A History of the Crusades*. Cambridge, England: Cambridge University Press, 1954. Runciman devotes a chapter to King Louis, and shows the Crusades from an Eastern perspective.

SEE ALSO: 1095, Pope Urban II Calls the First Crusade; 1147-1149, The Second Crusade; 1189-1192, The Third Crusade; 1204, Knights of the Fourth Crusade Capture Constantinople; 1217-1221, The Fifth Crusade; 1227-1230, Frederick II Leads the Sixth Crusade; 1291, Fall of Acre.

1258
THE "PROVISIONS OF OXFORD"

The "Provisions of Oxford" transform the centralized despotism of the Angevin dynasty into a limited monarchy based on a written constitution.

DATE: 1258
LOCALE: Oxford, England
CATEGORY: Laws, acts, and legal history
KEY FIGURES:

Alexander IV (Rinaldo Conti; 1199-1261), Roman Catholic pope, 1254-1261, and nephew of Gregory IX
Hugh Bigod (died 1266), earl of Norfolk

Henry III (1207-1272), king of England, 1216-1272
Innocent IV (Sinibaldo Fieschi; c. 1180-1254), Roman Catholic pope, 1243-1254
Louis IX (1214-1270), king of France, 1226-1270
Simon de Montfort (c. 1208-1265), earl of Leicester and a favorite of Henry III
Edmund Rich (Edmund of Abingdon, also Saint Edmund; c. 1175-1240), archbishop of Canterbury, 1233-1240

SUMMARY OF EVENT. The origins of the baronial reform movement of 1258 can be traced to the early 1230's when Henry III, a minor at his accession who came of age in 1227, began his personal rule. He was a man of multiple faces—at once aesthetical and arrogant, devout and extravagant, regnant and yet incapable of leadership—and, to quote a distinguished historian of early medieval England, "obstinate, petulant, and mercurial . . . sharptongued, rather ungenerous." Shrewd but not subtle, the king exhibited a disarming childlike simplicity—impervious to failures and mistakes. His reign was a period of tug of war between the monarch bent on maintaining absolutism and his barons struggling to restrain him as well as his ministers and councilors.

The decade of Henry's minority—presided over by the regent William Marshal (earl of Pembroke, who died in 1219) and thereafter by Hubert de Bergh, the royal justiciar (1227-1232), followed by Peter des Roches and his nephew Peter des Rivaux (1232-1234) and their clerks—placed heavy strains upon the loyalty of the barons, whose traditional rights and privileges were repeatedly infringed upon in the interests of peace and order. They were, however, schooled in the art of politics. In the crisis of 1234, they showed their understanding of the rule of law and of the interests of the community and supported Archbishop Edmund Rich and the clergy in forcing the king to give up his absolutist style and conform to the traditional ways of "the joint enterprise." In 1236, a baronial demonstration against foreign participation in royal governance forced him to take refuge for a time in the Tower of London, but the incident did not affect the makeup of the royal council. At a great council meeting in 1237, the barons forced the king to purge his small council and recruit "natural counselors" on pain of denying his request for aid. He submitted, albeit momentarily, appointing twelve men acceptable to the barons. Once the great council disbanded, however, the king recalled his own men.

The barons expected their monarch to assume the direction of government himself after the purge of his court and council and they were even ready to put up with his mistakes and indiscretions in the conduct of business. Neither English nor even Norman, but French out and out,

Henry unmistakably but unwittingly betrayed his misgivings about the English (though French-speaking) barons and preferred instead the Savoyard relations of his queen and his own Poitevin half brothers, the infamous Lusignans (William and Aymer de Valence, Guy and Geoffrey, sons of Henry III's mother Isabella of Angoulême by her marriage to Hugh of Lusignan) and their cronies, men who remained despised foreigners until their expulsion from England in 1258.

Ignoring the counsel of his barons, the king heedlessly pursued his dream of recovering the lost French possessions—Normandy, Anjou, Touraine, Maine, and Poitou. He paid soldiers, bribed allies, and sponsored revolts against the French king, although to little effect. He also antagonized the marcher lords in Wales by his territorial claims and his intervention in Welsh affairs. His actions provoked a rebellion at Gwynedd in 1256 by Llywelyn ap Gruffudd, grandson of Llywelyn ap Iorwerth, lord of Snowdon.

Finally, against the best advice of his barons and prelates, the king played into the politics of Pope Innocent IV and agreed to his offer of the Sicilian crown to his second son Edmund. Until the death of Emperor Frederick II in 1250, Germany and Sicily had belonged to his Hohenstaufen family. The popes were determined to prevent the two kingdoms from being united and to destroy the influence of the Hohenstaufen dynasty. Henry's Sicilian venture in 1254 and the resulting papal ultimatum (from Pope Alexander IV, who succeeded Innocent in 1254) threatening him with excommunication unless he met the papal debts already incurred in the Sicilian war, forced the king to divert the clerical contributions (tenths of the revenues of the church) for the crusade (Henry had taken the cross in 1250) to Sicily—a venture that brought England nothing but the humiliating Treaty of Paris with France in 1259.

Yet Henry cannot be entirely faulted for all his actions and decisions. He patronized his half brothers because he wished to continue his influence in their homeland of Poitou and also because they could provide some security along the northern borders of Gascony, England's only substantial possession in France. Likewise, Henry's Sicilian scheme was not altogether misconceived. Sicily was wealthy and an English candidature would not only block a possible French one but was also likely to provide a springboard for English expansion in the eastern Mediterranean.

The financial straits arising out of the Sicilian venture and baronial determination to obtain effective measures of reform before they could help their desperate sovereign forms the background to the events of 1258. Henry summoned a parliament at Westminster on April 9, in which he conceded the baronial demand for reform. On May 2, an agreement was made in two instruments. According to the first, the king agreed to introduce reforms *a la* baronial demands and even submitted himself to the penalty of excommunication in event of noncompliance. The second instrument contained the royal promise to reform the gov-

Pressures from powerful English barons forced King Henry III to take refuge in the Tower of London, shown here across the Thames River. (R. Kent Rasmussen)

ernment by a body of twenty-four, made up of twelve of the king's council and twelve elected by the magnates who were to convene at Oxford on June 11. The king swore to observe the majority decision of this body.

Meanwhile, the king, had called upon his friends to come to the assembly at Oxford with their armed retainers. On May 25, a party of Burgundian knights and their followers were diverted from their Welsh engagement to Oxford. In self-defense, the reforming barons summoned their own armed retainers. Despite this tense atmosphere parliament met at Oxford on June 11, and the twenty-four set to work upon a scheme of reform. This scheme is enshrined in what is known as the Provisions of Oxford. These were never formally published, but took the form of a series of memoranda.

Central to that scheme was the formation of a new council of fifteen, chosen by a complicated electoral method, included seven of the baronial twelve and three of the king's twelve, with a twelve-year tenure. It was to oversee royal ministers, appoint the great officers (especially justiciar, chancellor, and treasurer), and advise the king constantly on all matters "affecting both the king and the realm." It was to cooperate with twelve representatives of parliament, which met three times a year (October, February, and June). The justiciarship, vacant since 1234, was revived with the appointment of Hugh Bigod. Among his specific responsibilities as justiciar, Bigod was to act as chief justice with an annual tenure rather than as a leading royal minister with undefined authority as was the case with traditional Angevin justiciars.

The Provisions of Oxford passed a large measure of initiative over to each county, where four knights were to collect complaints against officials for transmission to the justiciar as he toured the counties. The justiciar was to have jurisdiction well as royal officials. The sheriffs were to be local landowners, salaried and appointed for one year only. The provisions also promised future reform of the church, urban reforms including the city of London, the Jewry, the mint, and the royal household.

In these activities, the leading baron was Simon de Montfort, an aristocrat from northern France who was the king's brother-in-law and one-time favorite. Montfort was absent from the Oxford parliament on June 11, negotiating the Treat of Paris between England and France. He returned on June 14 and was present throughout the fortnight of the Oxford parliament. Together with the earls of Gloucester (Richard de Clare, d. 1262) and Norfolk, John fitz Geoffrey and Peter de Montfort (Simon's retainer but no relation), he was a member of the various committees concerned with reform. Although the reform movement was not solely Montfort's enterprise, his distinctive contri-

bution lay, to quote his most recent and influential biographer, "in the moral imperatives which were part of the driving force behind the movement."

—*Narasingha P. Sil*

ADDITIONAL READING:

Brooke, Christopher. *From Alfred to Henry III 871-1272*. Cardinal ed. London: Sphere Books, 1974. First published in 1961, this study provides a competent and compact critical history of the period.

Harding, Alan. *England in the Thirteenth Century*. New York: Cambridge University Press, 1993. A comprehensive account of politics, government, and society of thirteenth century England.

Maddicott, John R. *Simon de Montfort*. New York: Cambridge University Press, 1994. Arguably Montfort's best biography.

Prestwich, Michael. *English Politics in the Thirteenth Century*. Houndmills, England: Macmillan, 1990. Chapters 2 and 8 contain a succinct analytical account of English society and government in the thirteenth century.

Sayles, George O. *The King's Parliament of England*. New York: W. W. Norton, 1974. A sound analysis of the constitutional achievements of the Provisions of Oxford.

Treharne, Reginald F. *Simon de Montfort and Baronial Reform: Thirteenth-Century Essays*. Edited by E. B. Fryde. London: Hambledon Press, 1968. Although somewhat indulgent to Montfort, still a full account of his achievements as well as a competent analysis of the baronial reform movement.

Treharne, Reginald F., and I. J. Sanders, eds. *Documents of the Baronial Movement of Reform and Rebellion, 1258-1267*. Oxford: Clarendon Press, 1973. Superb selection and translation of primary materials.

SEE ALSO: 1154-1204, Establishment of the Angevin Empire; 1175, Common Law Tradition Emerges in England; 1215, Signing of the Magna Carta; 1285, Statute of Winchester; 1295, The Model Parliament.

1265-1273
THOMAS AQUINAS COMPILES THE SUMMA THEOLOGIAE

Thomas Aquinas compiles the Summa theologiae, *creating a theological treatise that attempts to combine secular and divine knowledge into one orderly rational system.*

DATE: c. 1265-1273
LOCALE: Paris, France, and Naples, Italy
CATEGORIES: Cultural and intellectual history; Religion

KEY FIGURES:

Albert the Great (1193-1280), Swabian count who taught Aquinas at Cologne

Saint Thomas Aquinas (1225-1274), Italian-born Dominican theologian

Raymond of Peñafort (c. 1180-1275), Spanish canonist

Reginald of Piperno (died 1290), confessor and companion of Thomas Aquinas

Étienne Tempier, bishop of Paris, 1268-1279, and chancellor of the University

William of Moerbeke (c. 1215-1286), archbishop of Corinth

SUMMARY OF EVENT. Thomas Aquinas was born near Monte Cassino, where his parents placed him in the famous Benedictine monastery at the age of five. He was of heavy German proportions with a large head, broad face, and blond hair. Although his friends called him "the great dumb ox of Sicily," history was to know him as Doctor Angelicus. His career throughout was a distinguished one. He studied art and philosophy at the University of Naples. At the age of twenty-five, he began what could be called graduate studies at the University of Paris. He was Master of Theology at Paris from 1256 to 1259 and again from 1269 to 1272, adviser to Pope Urban IV and Pope Clement IV as well as to Louis IX of France, active participant in the business of his Dominican order, founder of a study house in Rome, popular preacher and debater, reorganizer of the University of Naples, and archbishop-designate of Naples, an office which he declined. Death came while he was traveling to the Council of Lyons at the summons of Pope Gregory IX.

His *Summa theologiae* ("summation of theology"), an attempt to bring all knowledge, both secular and divine, into one orderly rational system, represents one of the most ambitious intellectual programs ever undertaken by a theologian. Aquinas deals with hundreds of theological problems, providing answers that were simultaneously consistent with Aristotelian and Platonic philosophies, medieval Christian theology, and theoretical and commonsense reasoning. "Summa" in the thirteenth century had a technical connotation: a teaching tool for a curriculum of study in a specific scientific field. A *summa* was concise and abridged, ready to be used by the teacher and the students. Aquinas' work, of course, was facilitated by earlier scholarship, since virtually all revelationary religions that came into contact with Hellenism realized that sooner or later they must harmonize, in a monumental way, their deposit of faith with the dictates of reason. Philo and Maimonides undertook the task for the Jewish tradition, Averroës for the Muslim. Within the Christian orbit, Aquinas was heir to a thousand years of scholarship which

had attempted to forge a synthesis between faith and reason, revelation and observation.

Summa theologiae was created in a milieu of scholastic upheaval and in the midst of rediscovery of Aristotle. The university debate about Aristotle's inclusion in Christian theology was at a peak. Aquinas, according to his own writings, was one of the leaders of these debates in the university and theological communities in Paris.

The teaching of Saint Augustine had dominated Western thought for more than eight hundred years, and Augustinian thought insisted that in his search for truth man must depend upon inner ideas rather than sensory experience. Aristotle had said the opposite, and it was Aristotle's insistence on empirical knowledge and the value of sense experience which caused the dichotomy between the two schools of thought. In Aquinas' time, the works of Aristotle were beginning to appear in translations accompanied by the commentaries of Arabian scholars, and French philosophers were asserting that philosophy was independent of revelation. The question was whether Aristotle could be adequately tamed to Christian theology in order to prevent weakening of the faith and even heresy.

In learning about such matters, Aquinas was greatly indebted to his famous teacher at Paris and Cologne, the eminent Albert the Great. The contents of books of "sentences" commenting on the Scriptures and the church fathers were so influential in calling attention to the need for theological scholarship that Aquinas himself responded by first writing a *Commentary on the Sentences* of Peter Lombard. The new Latin translations of Aristotle prepared by William of Moerbeke and the early thirteenth century translation of Averroës were influential in Aquinas' conception and execution of his great work.

When he was teaching in Italy, the noted Spanish Dominican canonist Raymond of Peñafort urged him to write a new kind of *summa* as a guide for Dominican missionaries in Spain. This *Summan contra Gentiles* was directed in great measure against the radical Christian Averroists and Muslim intellectuals. According to Aquinas' fellow student Bartholomew of Lucca, the plan of the great *Summa theologiae* was conceived at Rome in 1265. Ninety-three major questions had been answered when death came to Aquinas, and the work was completed by his confessor and companion Reginald of Piperno, who extracted material from Aquinas' earlier work on Lombard's *Sentences*, mainly from book four.

Recognizing in an enlightened way the desirability of harmonizing Aristotle and Arabic science with Christian revelation (instead of barring non-Christian scholarship as the Obscurantists insisted upon doing), the *Summa theologiae* sets out to establish once and for all a compatibility between divine and human knowledge, theology and philosophy, faith and reason, and in a sense, Plato and Aristotle. It is this kind of successful synthesis that made Aquinas indispensable to Christian theology. To cope with questions in which reason can make little progress, such as the nature of the Divine Being or Christ as the mediator of transcendency and love, Aquinas included a third epistemological category by which such knowledge was possible through a mix of reason and revelation.

He made his reputation where even Albert the Great had failed. Aquinas insisted that the truths of faith and those of sense experience are compatible and complementary; some truths, such as the mystery of the Incarnation, can be known only through revelation, while others, such as knowledge of the composition of earthly things, can be known only through sense experience. Moreover, Aquinas took a further step forward: Some truths require both revelation and sense experience for their perception, and among such truths he included man's awareness of God. Man becomes aware of God through knowledge of the material world around him, but in order to comprehend the highest truths about God he needs revelation as well. Aquinas' realism placed the universals firmly in the human mind, in contrast to the extreme realists who insisted that such universals existed independently of the human mind. The argument actually involved Platonism more than Aristotelianism. In this sense he was more like Augustine, but he used Platonic notions only when Aristotelian concepts failed; namely, he used Plato's ideas of emanation and return, and efficient and final cause.

Aquinas was concerned to show through dialectic that all revealed knowledge could be demonstrated as being not contrary to reason even if every item could not be logically proven. He relied heavily on three Aristotelian hypotheses: that since cognition starts with sense perception, then argumentation must begin with facts about the natural world; that a distinction must be made between substance and accident; and that a polarity exists between potency and action.

At first blush, *Summa theologiae* seems like a cut-and-paste project covering a collage of quasi-related topics. On closer scrutiny, however, one finds that the work is a meticulously unified and masterfully argued line of analogic reasoning, leading to a unified system of theological metaphysics. The work is in three parts, and thirty-eight sections supply answers to some 630 theological questions by quoting authorities, notably Augustine and Aristotle, and by applying impeccable logic. In the process, Aquinas answers some ten thousand objections to his own conclusions. The work remains today the greatest exposition of Christian ethics. It represents the apex of the

As a young scholar, Thomas Aquinas was indebted to the theological training he received from his eminent teacher, Albert the Great. (Library of Congress)

synthesis between classical and Christian learning which had been going on since the second century. By distinguishing between philosophy and theology, it facilitated the development of Western philosophy as a distinct discipline. There was opposition to his work from Franciscans and some Dominicans; and it was condemned in 1277 by Étienne Tempier, bishop of Paris and chancellor of the University. Despite such detraction, Thomas Aquinas was canonized in 1328 and declared a doctor of the Church in 1567. Pope Leo XIII made Thomism the basis for instruction in all Roman Catholic schools, and Pius XII affirmed in an encyclical that Thomist philosophy should be regarded as the surest guide to Catholic doctrine; all departure from it should be condemned. The Roman Catholic Church, at the urging of Belgian theologians, among others, has now tended to tone down the bold rationalism of Aquinas.

The monumental work of the *Summa theologiae* shook the thirteenth century scholastic and theological worlds, as Karl Marx's writings shook political and moral sensibilities and institutions in the nineteenth and twentieth centuries. The success of Aquinas' work is also attributed to his pedagogical skill rather than to his sainthood, mysticism, or complex philosophy. On closer scrutiny of his writing, we also find a man of unwavering faith, with a compassionate soul and fatherly warmth, always aware of his limitations and always in search of God.

—*Lowell H. Zuck, updated by Chogollah Maroufi*

ADDITIONAL READING:

Boyle, Leonard. *The Setting of the Summa Theologiae of Saint Thomas*. Toronto: Pontifical Institute of Mediaeval Studies, 1982. A brief and thorough intellectual history of the work.

Gilson, Etienne. *The History of Christian Philosophy in the Middle Ages*. New York: Random House, 1955. This survey of the whole of medieval Christian philosophy puts Thomism in its historical context.

Kenny, Anthony. *Aquinas*. Oxford: Oxford University Press, 1980. Kenny, an eminent Oxford philosopher, gives a lucid, brief, and accessible account of Aquinas' theological philosophy.

Knasas, John, ed. *Thomas Papers, Volume VI*. Houston, Tex.: Center of Thomist Studies, 1994. A challenging book, discussing the evolution of Aquinas' philosophy in various forms. See especially the section titled "Neo-Thomism, and Christian Philosophy."

Martin, Christopher, ed. *The Philosophy of Thomas Aquinas: Introductory Reading*. London: Routledge, 1988. It contains a representative sampling of all of Aquinas' important works, including an ample selection of his *Summa theologiae*, with excellent introductions of each selection.

SEE ALSO: 380 B.C., Plato Develops His Theory of Ideas; 335-323 B.C., Aristotle Writes the *Politics*; 413-426, Augustine Writes the *City of God*; 1150, Moors Transmit Classical Philosophy and Medicine to Europe; 1310-1350, William of Ockham Attacks Thomist Ideas.

1271-1291
TRAVELS OF MARCO POLO

The travels of Marco Polo in Asia stimulate Western interest in Eastern commerce and influence later explorers, such as Christopher Columbus.

DATE: 1271-1291

LOCALE: Venice, Italy; Peking and Canton, China; Persia

CATEGORIES: Economics; Exploration and discovery

KEY FIGURES:

Gregory X (Teobaldo Visconti; 1210-1276), Roman Catholic pope, 1271-1276

Kublai Khan (c. 1251-1294), ruler of China at Peking

Maffeo Polo, brother of Niccolò Polo and also a Venetian merchant

Marco Polo (c. 1254-1324), Venetian traveler and merchant

Niccolò Polo, Venetian merchant who traveled to the East in 1261, father of Marco Polo

SUMMARY OF EVENT. In 1254, the year of Marco Polo's birth, Italy was divided into warring city states, and Genoa and Venice vied for naval dominance. Although deep in the Middle Ages, thirteenth century Europe witnessed an amazing increasing geographical knowledge as well as an increase in contact between western Europe and the Far East. China, remote and exotic, held such a fascination for Europeans that tales of travel to that land were eagerly sought and circulated by the educated.

Before the Tartar conquest of Asia Minor and the consequent arrival of Tartar embassies in the West by the late thirteenth century, contact with the Far East had already been made by such men as John of Piano Carpini and William of Rubruck, the latter being sent by Louis IX of France. Trade routes and opportunities which had not existed since the time of Roman rule, were finally reopened. By 1260, Niccolò and Maffeo Polo, the father and uncle of Marco Polo, members of an adventurous Venetian family, left the young Marco behind and began their epic journey eastward to the court of the khan of the Pipchak Tartars at Serai. Their hardships were compensated for by trading so successful that the brothers lingered for more than a year while amassing considerable profit. When they decided to return to Venice, however, they found that their route was cut off by local wars and mutinies, and so they made a momentous decision to visit the court of the great khan of China. In Peking, they were received graciously by that powerful medieval monarch and, after concluding business there, they were urged to return home and bring back Christian missionaries from the West for the further edification of the royal court. To expedite their journey they were given the services of a trusted Tartar guide.

After an arduous journey overland to Venice they learned in 1268 that Pope Clement IV had already died and that no successor had yet been elected. By 1271, they managed to secure from the new pope, Gregory X, the services of two inept Dominicans who soon decided to desert the mission. The Polos, nevertheless, went back to Peking taking with them the teenage son of widower Niccolò Polo, the famous Ser Marco Polo, a lad destined to leave an immortal record of his wanderings in the company of his father and uncle. In Marco's famous account of his journeys, *Il milione* (literally, the million; usually translated into English as *The Travels of Marco Polo*), his uncle and father soon fade into the background, allowing the young and adventuresome author to become the dominant figure. His clear, colorful, and eminently readable travel account made a great and immediate impression on a credulous medieval Europe. Indeed, this account of Polo's travels in Asia was the primary source for the European image of the Far East until the late nineteenth century.

Ser Marco and his two relatives began their remarkable journey in 1271, going by sea to Acre. After arriving at the mouth of the Persian Gulf, they abandoned their plan of traveling by sea and turned north following the ancient caravan routes through Iraq and Persia traversing Persia and Turkmen until they reached the Oxus River. They crossed the plain of Pamir and traveled across the incredible desolation of the Gobi desert into the ancient mercantile cities of Samarkand, Yarkand, and Kashgar, until they reached Tangut, in the extreme northwest of China. Finally, in the spring of 1275, the three Polos were made welcome at Shando, the summer capital of Kublai Khan, the Mongol emperor of China. Marco soon became a favorite at the Chinese court of the Great Kublai Khan. Polo studied the native languages and in 1277 became a commissioner in the Mongol government. The khan came

Marco Polo's famous account of his journeys, Il milione, *was the primary source for the European image of the Far East until the late nineteenth century.* (Archive Photos)

so to trust the young Venetian that he relied upon his advice in affairs of state and of commerce. Ser Marco's descriptions of the great emperor and of his mighty palace outside the capital fired the imaginations of generations of explorers and travelers, all of whom wished to view for themselves the eight square miles of enclosed barracks, parade grounds, vast arsenals, storerooms, living quarters, library, and especially the sumptuous treasury. As a trusted agent of Kublai Khan for seventeen years, Marco Polo had the unique opportunity, seldom offered later, to observe a developed and sophisticated way of life unknown to Western society. At one point, he served Kublai Khan as governor of Yang Chow. Fortunately, he was an enlightened observer who appreciated his responsibility to record this ancient civilization for all posterity.

In his long and loyal service to the great khan, Marco Polo visited nearly every part of both northern and southern China, employing the imperial horse and packet-boat system which was kept constantly in readiness for the comfort and convenience of government officials. Many are the provinces, the huge cities, the major commercial towns that he cataloged and described in lively and intriguing detail. Nothing escaped his notice; he was interested in commerce, the manufacturing arts, the character of the residents in each area, architecture, and even costumes. Ser Marco was especially impressed with the silk industry, the staple commerce between the Levant and the West; consequently the book contains our best early picture of silk culture, weaving, dyeing, and finishing.

To thirteenth century Europe the splendors of the Chinese cities must have seemed incredible. Polo's description of Hangchow, for example, included even the fabled "twelve thousand" bridges of the city, its many huge markets and bazaars, its cavernous warehouses for its trade with India, its state-owned pavilions for wedding feasts, and even its consumption of six tons of pepper daily.

On official business Marco Polo also visited India, and duly recorded its commercial life. In the same way he may also have visited the original homeland of the Moguls, the windswept steppes of Asia where the ancestors of the great khans had grazed their herds. There is even possible reference to Siberia, though it is doubtful that the adventurous and apparently indefatigable, Venetian ever traveled so far north. His account of his journey also indicates great interest in the islands to the south of China, including the Philippines.

In 1292, the Polos increasingly desired permission of the great khan to depart for their faraway home on the Adriatic. So favored were the Polos that Kublai Khan could not abide their leaving and it was with considerable reluctance he permitted the trio to depart, with an official commission to escort the Mogul prince's daughter to her wedding in Persia. The voyage homeward took the Polos three years. Traveling primarily by ship, Ser Marco records his impressions of Java or the "great island," Sumatra, Dragoian, Ceylon, Madagascar, Zanzibar, and many other exotic and exciting islands and landfalls. Crossing through the Red Sea, the adventurers finally reached Alexandria, and from there they were, by 1295, but a short distance from Venice, where they arrived unnoticed. An extraordinary mercantile odyssey of nearly twenty years' duration at last came to a satisfying end.

Shortly thereafter Polo was captured by the warring Genoese in a naval battle and imprisoned. In prison he dictated an account of his experiences to fellow-prisoner and writer, Rustichello of Pisa. *The Travels of Marco Polo* was received with awe and disbelief and it was not until other travelers to China verified portions of the tales that they came to be sanctioned. Polo's book is responsible for stimulating Occidental interest in Eastern commerce and influencing explorers such as Christopher Columbus.

—*Carl F. Rohne, updated by M. Casey Diana*

ADDITIONAL READING:

Bellonci, Maria, ed. and trans. *The Travels of Marco Polo*. Translated into English by Teresa Waugh. New York: Facts On File, 1985. This newer translation of Marco Polo's adventures contains many illustrations; some in color.

Hart, Henry. *Venetian Adventurer*. Stanford, Calif.: Stanford University Press, 1942. Approachable work detailing traveling life in the thirteenth century. Closely follows the first journey of Niccolò and Maffeo before describing life in Venice at the time of Marco's birth and his actual journey.

Polo, Marco. *The Travels of Marco Polo*. New York: Grosset & Dunlap, 1931. Standard translation of Marco Polo's adventures, including his arduous journey, his work for Kublai Khan, and his return to Venice.

Severin, Tim. *Tracking Marco Polo*. New York: Peter Bedrick Books, 1984. Entertaining account of late twentieth century motorcycling adventurer's determination to rediscover Polo's route. Concise history of Polo's journey with photographs and maps.

Wallen, David. "Stumbling in Marco Polo's Footsteps." *World Press Review* 42 (January, 1995): 46. Excerpted from an article published in the *South China Morning Post* of Hong Kong. In the article, Frances Wood asserts that Polo's route makes no geographical sense and alleges that he only reached Constantinople, never visited China, and obtained his information from a Persian guidebook.

SEE ALSO: 1150, Venetian Merchants Dominate Trade

with the East; 1415-1460, Prince Henry the Navigator Promotes Portuguese Exploration; 1492, Columbus Lands in America; 1583-1601, Matteo Ricci Travels to Peking as Jesuit Missionary; 1602, Dutch East India Company Is Founded.

1285
STATUTE OF WINCHESTER

The statute of Winchester defines the rights and obligations of kings and subjects in military affairs and establishes a national police force.

DATE: 1285

LOCALE: England

CATEGORY: Laws, acts, and legal history

KEY FIGURE:

Edward I (1239-1307), king of England, 1272-1307

SUMMARY OF EVENT. During his busy reign, Edward I, the so-called English Justinian, legislated a number of significant matters. The Statutes of Gloucester (1278), addressed land law. Westminster I (1275) changed a number of procedures, many of which were designed to relieve oppression of subjects. Westminster II (1285) and Westminster III (1290) reorganized feudalism in England, while the Statute of Mortmain (1279) attempted to limit the power of the Church to acquire land and deny feudal obligations to the king and nobles. Of great significance for future English fortunes was the Statute of Winchester (1285).

Apart from providing for various contingencies, such as the supervision of strangers, clearing highroads, and guarding city gates and walls, this law called for the maintenance of a national militia, the origins of which were in the ancient Anglo-Saxon concept of the universal military obligation of freemen. Certain modifications had been made in implementing this custom even before the Norman Conquest; the land unit for providing one fighting man had been increased from one hide to five or more as the equipment of the fighting knight became increasingly more expensive than that of the old Saxon *thegn* (or thane). Often, too, military service came to be commuted into a money payment called "scutage."

In 1181, Henry II took a step toward reorganization of local defense with his Assize of Arms that established a graded hierarchy of military obligations based on a single recruitment system extending down to the general military duty of all freemen. By assessing military service in terms of the economic resources of the individual, the Assize of Arms interpreted feudal custom. Further, by standardizing military obligations in monetary terms Henry set a precedent which similar reforms by Henry III in 1230 and 1242 were later to incorporate into the English constitution.

By Edward I's reign, subinfeudation—the process of creating subordinate tenancies out of one landholding—had damaged the system of military tenure. Under feudalism, a lord owed the king military service. When the lord subinfeudated his land, however, the military obligation was divided among his tenants. While in theory the process of subinfeudation should not damage the ability of the king to raise an army of knights, in reality, as landowners began to create long chains of tenure, it became increasingly difficult to determine exactly what each subtenant owed in terms of military service.

At least two considerations prompted the issuance of the Statute of Winchester. One was a general rise in prices during the eleventh, twelfth, and thirteenth centuries stemming from the commercial renaissance of the period. The royal revenues were increased but prices continued to rise ahead of income, especially the price of waging war which rose as the use of sophisticated weapons necessitated specialized training for the infantry and limited the effectiveness of the amateur militia levies. Crossbows and the use of professional soldiers required large cash outlays, and by reaffirming the military obligation of all freemen, Edward expected to increase his revenues through scutage.

Edward's second and total victory over the Welsh in 1284 was the second and immediate cause of the Statute of Winchester. The Welsh campaigns had required large formations of expensive mercenary foot soldiers to supplement the feudal host, and because he intended to conquer rather than merely punish, Edward needed additional men as carters, woodsmen, builders, diggers, carpenters, and masons to erect castles and field fortifications in order to keep the Welsh in check. The combined pressures of needing additional revenue and additional men led Edward, in 1285, to feel the urgent need to define the rights and obligations of the king and subjects in military affairs. The Statute of Winchester was a brilliant effort at definition.

Reflecting the old Anglo-Saxon *fyrd* and the Assize of Arms, the statute fixed everyone's military obligation on the price of scutage in lieu of each obligation. Every freeman between the ages of fifteen and sixty was required to have armor according to his wealth. The statute defined five classes, the highest of which were those whose lands were valued at fifteen pounds and forty marks in goods. These men had to be fully equipped cavalry men each with chain-mail coat, iron helmet, sword, knife, and horse. At the other extreme were those freemen of little property each of whom was obliged to have only a quilted coat, an iron helmet, a bow, and arrows. Two constables were appointed in each hundred to review this host twice every year, and they could use it to repel an invader or to maintain local law and order as a police force. Constables had their own hierarchy leading up from constables of townships, or "vills," through the hundreds and counties, to king's constable of the realm.

The Statute of Winchester also represented a major change in criminal law. It placed heavy demands on local government for the maintenance of law and order. Under the Statute of Winchester, for example, in a hundred in which a robbery was committed, the whole hundred was held responsible unless the robber was produced. The statute also standardized and consolidated earlier practices that required the vills to maintain night watchmen and provide necessary weapons for their constables. Furthermore, the statute specified that all people of a vill must answer the hue and cry armed with their weapons. The vill could be punished for failure to respond to the hue and cry raised in the discovery of a crime. The vill could also be fined for failure to capture the perpetrator. There seemed to be a great concern with the number of crimes that were going unreported, and the Statute of Winchester was designed to address this concern.

As with so many medieval decrees, the Statute of Winchester was administered differently in different parts of the realm. Strict enforcement would have provided too unwieldy a force besides depriving the land of its cultivators. There was also the question of the duration and extent of service. Rather than face this problem, Edward I and his successors chose to utilize the Commissions of Array. In this case, the king appointed certain prominent men to "elect" or conscript such forces from each area as were needed for royal service at a particular time. The area, hundred, or county, was responsible for supporting this force, but for strictly offensive operations the royal treasury often bore the expense, and the district provided its quota by hiring mercenaries. This arrangement paved the way for the "Bastard Feudalism" of the fourteenth and fifteenth centuries.

What did the Statute of Winchester accomplish? First, by reestablishing that all freemen owed the king military service or scutage in lieu of military service, it raised both the money and men needed by Edward I that the increasing cost of armament had depleted. Second, it strengthened the position of the king by creating a national force organized by counties and responsible to the monarch. Finally, the statute forced the financial burden of keeping the peace on local authorities and thus freed the king from increased outlays.

—Lynewood F. Martin,
updated by Diane Andrews Henningfeld

ADDITIONAL READING:

Baker, J. H. *An Introduction to English Legal History.* 3d ed. London: Butterworths, 1990. An accessible introduction to English law, including documents in Latin with accompanying English translations.

Lyon, Bryce. *A Constitutional and Legal History of Medieval England.* New York: Harper & Row, 1960. A study of the extent of centralization and consolidation in medieval England in comparison to France, which failed to establish a national militia as England did under the Statute of Winchester.

Maitland, F. W. *The Constitutional History of England.* Cambridge, England: Cambridge University Press, 1920. Maitland shows the connection between the old Anglo-Saxon national military force and the Statute of Winchester.

Plucknett, T. F. T. *Legislation of Edward I.* Oxford: Clarendon Press, 1949. An excellent study of Edward I's legislation dwelling on the significance of the Statutes of Westminster.

Prestwich, Michael. *Edward I.* Berkeley: University of California Press, 1988. A thorough biography, placing the importance of Edward I's legislation in a historical context.

SEE ALSO: 1154-1204, Establishment of the Angevin Empire; 1175, Common Law Tradition Emerges in England; 1215, Signing of the Magna Carta; 1258, The "Provisions of Oxford"; 1295, The Model Parliament.

1290-1306
JEWS ARE EXPELLED FROM ENGLAND, FRANCE, AND SOUTHERN ITALY

The Jews are expelled from England, France, and southern Italy, disrupting Jewish life, resulting in mass suffering, and impeding the economic development of these European countries.

DATE: 1290-1306

LOCALE: England, France, and southern Italy

CATEGORIES: Economics; Government and politics; Religion

KEY FIGURES:

Charles II (1227-1285), Angevin king of Sicily, 1266-1285

Edward I (1239-1307), king of England, 1274-1307

Frederick II (1194-1250), king of Germany and Sicily, 1220-1250

Philip IV (1268-1314), king of France, 1285-1314

SUMMARY OF EVENT. Between 1290 and 1306, Jewish communities in both England and France were expelled while in southern Italy many Jews were killed or forced to convert or to flee. In each case, the persecution followed religious oppression by the Catholic Church and economic frustration and jealousy both by the nobility and by

the local citizenry. The Jews eventually returned to England and France but the communities—both Jewish and non-Jewish—were changed in the process.

Although the particular details vary, the dynamics are generally parallel. Unlike the larger population, most Jews lived in towns rather than on farms. Their communal numbers were small, rarely exceeding one thousand, typically under three hundred. Their occupations were limited, in large part because of legal restrictions and social discrimination. Their communities were not well integrated with the larger Christian population, many of whom were raised on a deep-seated anti-Semitism promoted by the local clergy.

In opposition to the clerical antagonism stood the king—for economic reasons. The Jews were a source of income since they could be very heavily taxed. As the kings attempted to conquer territory, and especially during the Crusades, their economic needs increased substantially. In order to ensure that the Jews could provide money, they were sometimes released from obligatory Church taxes and they were granted certain economic rights.

The occasional special treatment of Jews by royalty infuriated both the Catholic clergy and those who hoped to compete economically with the Jews. Over time, these Christian interests triumphed. For example, in the Third Lateran Council (1179), church leaders forbade Jews to employ Christian servants or workers. A half century later in 1215, the Fourth Lateran Council limited economic interaction with Jews, denied them the right to hold any public office, and compelled them to wear a distinguishing badge on their outer garments. About twenty years later, the medieval Church Inquisition began to preoccupy itself with eradicating heresy, a process that led to the Spanish Inquisition of the fifteenth century and the complete destruction of Jewish life in Spain and Portugal.

In addition to the centralized religious pressure, powerful local clergy could often impose additional restrictions as could the local nobility, who were in an ongoing struggle with the monarchy. Combined with the greater royal tax burden, this increased pressure broke the back of many Jewish communities. Once their wealth was drained, they lost the special protection of the king.

The deteriorating financial conditions of the Jews led to additional restrictions. Across all three countries Jews were stripped of their wealth, pressured and sometimes forced to convert, and in a number of cases exiled from their local communities. Several precedents were set for the more widespread expulsion later, from 1290 to 1306 and afterward, too, in some communities.

Jews came to England very late, starting primarily after the Norman Conquest of 1066. Unlike in the other two nations, many English Jews were financiers who loaned money at interest, a vocation closed to Christians for religious reasons.

In 1130, the Jews of London were fined a very considerable sum based on a trumped-up murder charge against a Jewish physician. In 1144, coinciding with the Second Crusade, the Jews of Norwich were accused without evidence of the ritual murder of a Christian boy. The Jewish quarter was ransacked and the Jews forced to pay a fine. Thereafter, until 1255, about every fifteen years another major Jewish community faced the same charges, with the same general outcome. Not incidentally, these charges and attacks took place when the Royal Treasury needed replenishing.

The most terrible incident occurred in 1190 in York, where the entire Jewish community of about six hundred was killed—including those who asked to convert; their properties were destroyed or seized; and their receipts of debts owed them were burned.

The Oxford Council held in 1222 prohibited Jews from owning slaves and from building new synagogues and required that they wear a linen badge. Ten years later, Londoners petitioned against the completion of a magnificent synagogue, which was then seized and given to the Church.

The monarch's need for money pushed the tax on the communities' declining resources sufficiently to waste many of them. A series of regulations limited the ability of Jews to collect interest on money already loaned, thus drying up their businesses. Although it was omitted in later confirmations, the original Magna Carta contained a provision restricting the claims of Jewish creditors against the estates of deceased landowners.

Throughout the thirteenth century, oppression against the Jews increased, further limiting their economic opportunities. Starting in mid-century, Jews were expelled from several towns after refusing to convert. Eventually, with widespread poverty, they were of no use to the king. Finally, in order to placate the Church and lower nobility, on July 18, 1290, Edward I issued an edict of banishment for all the Jews in England—probably about six thousand. Most left for France, Germany, and Flanders.

In France, Jews had been present, in small numbers, since the first century A.D. Unlike in England, in addition to trade and finance, some Jews were involved with wine—more in production and trade than in grape cultivation. Until the ninth century, periodic attempts were made to force conversion on the Jews. In 624, King Dagobert expelled all Jewish residents—for about fifteen years. In spite of some anti-Jewish laws, from about 800 to 1096 the Jewish communities flourished and were relatively safe. That situation changed with the advent of the First Cru-

sade (1096-1099), after which the conditions under which the Jews lived worsened.

The first attacks on European Jews occurred in Rouen. In 1144, Louis VII issued a decree that banished converted Jewish Christians who returned to Judaism. The first of a series of blood libels occurred in 1171, when thirty-one innocent Jews were burned alive. In 1181, King Philip Augustus imprisoned all the wealthy Jews of Paris and freed them only upon receiving a large ransom. A year later, he expelled them and confiscated their real estate.

Attacks on Jewish communities continued through the thirteenth century. In 1242, both Church and king condemned and burned the Talmud, the collection of Jewish oral law. Although the order was not rigorously pursued, Jews were expelled from Poitou in 1249. In 1268, Thibaut V, count of the Champagne region, confiscated much of the Jewish wealth to pay for the Crusades. In 1283, Jews were forbidden by Philip III to live in small rural localities. In 1291, the Jews expelled from England were prohibited by Philip IV from settling in France. Finally, in July of 1306, most of the Jews of France were imprisoned, their possessions seized, and shortly thereafter they were expelled. A number of Jews were allowed to remain, mostly to collect debts which they then paid to the royal coffers. In 1311, these last remnants of the Jewish population were also expelled.

Jewish life in Italy differed from that in the rest of the continent. Jews were in Rome by the first century B.C., and their numbers may have swelled to fifty thousand with the Jews brought as captives following the Roman conquest of Israel in A.D. 70. Conditions improved until Constantine's acceptance of Christianity as the official religion in the fourth century, after which Jews were discriminated against. For example, new synagogues were not allowed to be built, and Jews were pressured to convert to Christianity.

Conditions for Jews improved with the fall of the Holy Roman Empire but they worsened after the conquest by the Byzantines in the sixth century, after which they improved in the south with the Arab conquest (827-1061). As a result, by the late Middle Ages, the bulk of the community was in the south. Despite the formal anti-Semitism of the Church, Jewish life developed under the rule of Emperor Frederick II, who provided protection and a monopoly in silk weaving and dyeing—in exchange for high taxes. Unlike in England and France, most Jews in Italy were craftsmen and merchants.

Frederick II's suspected liberalism brought a successful challenge by the papacy in 1265 to replace him with the French Charles I, after which Jewish life deteriorated significantly. A series of blood libels, physical attacks, and forced conversions decimated the communities.

In 1268, the Inquisition was introduced. Following the French example, in 1270 a Jewish apostate denounced classic rabbinic literature, leading to the hunt for and burning of religious books. In about 1290, a Dominican friar accused the Jews of Apulia of ritual murder of a Christian child, leading to a series of fatal attacks.

Although there was no formal widespread expulsion, by 1294 the overwhelming majority of the approximately thirteen thousand Jews in southern Italy were forced to convert, flee, or were killed. Southern Italy never reclaimed the important presence of its Jewish population.

—*Alan M. Fisher*

ADDITIONAL READING:

Chazan, Robert. *Medieval Jewry of Northern France.* Baltimore: The Johns Hopkins University, 1973. A detailed political history of Jewish life in medieval France.

Finestein, Israel. *A Short History of Anglo-Jewry.* London: Lincolns-Praeger, 1957. Short, but informative review of Jewish life.

Hyamson, Albert M. *A History of the Jews in England.* London: Methuen, 1928. An older study, but one that provides a detailed picture of Jewish life in England.

Roth, Cecil. *The History of the Jews of Italy.* Philadelphia: Jewish Publication Society, 1946. Comprehensive study of two thousand years of Jewish history in Italy.

Taitz, Emily. *The Jews of Medieval France.* Westport, Conn.: Greenwood Press, 1994. Focuses on Jewish family and domestic life.

SEE ALSO: 1095, Pope Urban II Calls the First Crusade; 1215, The Fourth Lateran Council; 1233, The Papal Inquisition; 1478, Establishment of the Spanish Inquisition; 1492, Expulsion of the Jews from Spain.

1291

FALL OF ACRE

The fall of Acre marks the end of crusader rule in Palestine and Syria and the resumption of Muslim control.

DATE: April, 1291

LOCALE: Acre, Palestine (also known as Akko or Akka)

CATEGORIES: Religion; Wars, uprisings, and civil unrest

KEY FIGURES:

Al-Ashraf Khalīl (1253-1293), Mamluk sultan of Egypt, 1290-1293

Amalric de Lusignan (died 1310), brother of Henry II, *bailie* (magistrate) of Jerusalem, 1289-1291, and regent of Cyprus, 1306-1310

Henry de Lusignan (1271-1324), ruled Cyprus as King Henry II, 1285-1324, and, concurrently ruled Jerusalem, 1286-1291, and as titular ruler, 1291-1324

Otto of Grandison (died 1320), knight errant at Acre

Qāla'ūn (Kalavun; died 1290), Mamluk sultan of Egypt, 1279-1290

William of Beaujeau (died 1291), Master of the Temple, 1273-1291

SUMMARY OF EVENT. A riot in late August, 1290, between Muslims and newly arrived Italian crusaders—undisciplined, drunken, and disorderly—in the streets of Acre ended with the killing of a number of Muslims. As a consequence, Sultan Qāla'ūn of Egypt was convinced that the massacre broke the existing truce between Egypt and the already greatly contracted kingdom of Jerusalem and began to gather his army to finally eliminate the Franks. Outraged by the incident, the barons and knights ruling Acre suppressed the rioters and rescued many Muslims. They also immediately apologized to the sultan, who sent an embassy demanding surrender of the leaders of the riot.

The *bailie*, Amalric, representative of the king of Jerusalem in Acre, convened a council to frame a response. The Master of the Temple, William of Beaujeau, proposed sending the criminals in the jails of Acre to Cairo as the guilty men, but the council refused. Instead of condemning Christians to die in Cairo, the council attempted to persuade the sultan's emissaries that Muslim merchants had precipitated the riot. After consulting his council, Qāla'ūn rejected this response, abandoned the truce, and began mobilizing his army. Templar agents at Cairo reported the sultan's intentions to William of Beaujeau, who earlier had sent his own envoy to Cairo. Qāla'ūn then offered a proposal to William; he would allow the residents to leave Acre safely for a ransom of one Venetian sequin per inhabitant. When William presented this proposal to the high court in Acre, it was rejected, and the court accused William of treason.

The sultan left Cairo with his army on November 4. The invasion, however, was halted when Qāla'ūn suddenly fell ill and died on November 10. The government and citizens of Acre then relaxed, concluding that their troubles were over in the light of the usual protracted disorders accompanying the succession of sultans. The Mamluk successional conflict, however, was settled quickly and, by March of 1291, Qāla'ūn's son, al-Ashraf Khalīl, was in control. The council at Acre then sent a final embassy seeking to flatter Khalīl and to seek terms of peace. Khalīl threw them in prison, where they died. He sent his army against Acre in March, 1291. On April 6, he invested Acre and the siege began.

The inhabitants of Acre had put the double walls of the city in good repair. In anticipation of an attack after the fall of Tripoli in 1289, the authorities in Acre had broadcast appeals for help. The military orders, Templars, Hospital-

After the fall of Acre in 1291, crusader forces were driven from other strongholds in Tyre, Sidon, and Beirut, leaving only ruined remains of their outposts. (Robin W. Diel)

ers, and Teutonic knights, called in all available members from Europe. No great crusade, however, came from Europe. The only reinforcements to arrive were Tuscan and Lombard crossbow troops, who provoked the riot in August, 1290, and scattered knights errant. A few English volunteers led by Otto of Grandison came at the expense of King Edward I of England. The Venetians and Pisans remained loyal, but the Genovese, whose business in Acre had been ruined by Venice, stood aside. King Henry II of Cyprus, immobilized by sickness in Cyprus, sent a Cypriot group, and his brother Amalric commanded the defense. Many noncombatants were ferried to Cyprus and supplies of food, water, and arms were in good order. In all, about a thousand mounted men and fifteen thousand foot soldiers manned the walls of Acre. The invaders reportedly brought sixty thousand mounted men, a hundred and sixty thousand infantry, and almost one hundred catapults and mangonels. Although these figures are probably exaggerated, the besiegers likely outnumbered defenders by ten to one.

During a month of battering, Italian catapults had knocked out some important Egyptian siege engines, and a ship fitted with a catapult did great damage behind the Mamluk lines until it was destroyed in a storm. A moonlight sally by the Templars on April 15 began well but ended in confusion. A second sally by the Hospitalers in the dark of the moon a few days later was ambushed. Thereafter, the defenders fought from within the walls in order to conserve men and armaments. On May 4, King Henry arrived from Cyprus with a hundred knights and two thousand foot soldiers. This was the last infusion of reinforcements.

Henry sent envoys to beg for peace. In reply, Khalīl demanded surrender of the city but offered to allow the defenders to leave alive. During the parley, a catapulted stone landed among the bystanders, and Khalīl had to be persuaded not to kill the ambassadors immediately. Khalīl's terms were refused and, on May 15, the Egyptians penetrated the outer wall, forcing the defenders back to the Gate of Saint Anthony and the inner wall. On May 18, they mounted a general assault, overrunning the inner wall and the Gate of Saint Anthony. By evening, the Christians were trying to organize an evacuation by sea. King Henry, Amalric, and many of the Cypriots left first. Otto of Grandison took command of the rear guard, filled the Venetian ships with wounded, and he himself was the last to embark. When the elderly Nicholas of Hannape was carried to a ship by his servants, he encouraged fugitives to crowd in with him. The overloaded boat then foundered, drowning all onboard. After the ships left, the docks still were crowded with refugees. The Templars retreated to their headquarters and resisted for a few more days. Finally, the Mamluks undermined the walls, collapsing the entire building and killing all of the defenders and many of their own men.

The Mamluks then sacked Acre, killing or enslaving all Christians. The sultan also deliberately destroyed Acre and all of the castles along the coast. Fearing Christian sea power, Khalīl then systematically wiped out the remaining Christian outposts in the Levant. On May 19, his army appeared before Tyre, the strongest city in the kingdom of Jerusalem. Although it might have endured a long siege, the Cypriot garrison sailed home without resisting. At Sidon, the Templars held out until July, when they left by sea. Beirut, although protected by a private truce, was taken by treachery in the same month. In August, the monasteries of Mount Carmel were sacked.

By the end of 1291, no Franks remained in Outremer. The Crusader states had lasted only 192 years from the capture of Jerusalem in 1099 to their final destruction in 1291. Throughout, Outremer was plagued by persistent shortcomings. Most important, the permanent Frankish population was never large enough to defend and expand the Crusader states. Indeed, continuous reinforcement from the West was a necessity. The many different and antagonistic European crusader contingents seldom acknowledged any "central" authority and frequently lapsed into civil conflict. Also, the crusaders were dependent upon commercially oriented, opportunistic, and unreliable Italian city-states for transportation and commercial activity. Crusader leadership generally was unable to impose stable policy and, in any event, dependence on feudal allegiances frequently frustrated effective organization of available resources.

Acre was eventually conquered by the Ottoman Turks in 1516, who ruled the area with minor interruptions until 1918, when the city was captured by the British. After 1922, it was governed under the British mandate of Palestine. Acre again was captured in 1948, by a Jewish terrorist group, and subsequently occupied by regular Israeli troops. In the process, most of the city's Arab population fled. —*Ralph L. Langenheim, Jr.*

ADDITIONAL READING:

Benvenisti, Meron. *The Crusaders in the Holy Land.* New York: Macmillan, 1970. Provides a historical geography of the Crusades.

Oldenbourg, Zoe. *The Crusades.* New York: Pantheon Books, 1966. A history of the Crusades through the conquest of Jerusalem by Saladin followed by a thorough discussion of the character of the Crusades and the Crusader states.

Payne, Robert. *The Dream and the Tomb: A History of the Crusades.* New York: Stein & Day, 1984. Good account of the end of Outremer drawn from Arab as well as European accounts.

Robinson, John. *Dungeon, Fire and Sword: The Knights Templar in the Crusade.* New York: M. Evans, 1991. Gives an account of the fall of Acre, including preceding and subsequent events.

Runciman, Steven. "The Crusaders States." In *The Later Crusades, 1189-1311*, edited by Robert Lee Wolff and Harry W. Hazard. Vol. 2 in *A History of the Crusades*, edited by Kenneth M. Setton. 2d ed. Madison: University of Wisconsin Press, 1969. Detailed scholarly account of the fall of Acre.

_____. *The Kingdom of Acre and the Later Crusades.* Vol. 3 in *A History of the Crusades.* Cambridge, England: Cambridge University Press, 1954. Comprehensive history of the crusaders from the Third Crusade through final dissolution of Outremer.

SEE ALSO: 1095, Pope Urban II Calls the First Crusade; 1120, Order of the Knights Templar Is Founded; 1147-1149, The Second Crusade; 1189-1192, The Third Crusade; 1204, Knights of the Fourth Crusade Capture Constantinople; 1217-1221, The Fifth Crusade; 1227-1230, Frederick II Leads the Sixth Crusade; 1228-1231, Teutonic Knights Bring Baltic Region Under Catholic Control; 1248-1254, Failure of the Seventh Crusade.

1295
THE MODEL PARLIAMENT

The Model Parliament establishes an important precedent by joining the shire knights and town burgesses with the spiritual and temporal lords, resulting in the widest representation to that point in English parliamentary history.

DATE: 1295

LOCALE: Westminster, London, England

CATEGORY: Government and politics

KEY FIGURES:

Edward I (1239-1307), king of England, 1272-1307

Philip IV (1268-1314), king of France, 1285-1314

SUMMARY OF EVENT. Political historians view the evolution of the English Parliament as one of the greatest legacies of the English Middle Ages to the theory and practice of representative democracy throughout the world. Parliament had its forerunners in both Anglo-Saxon and Norman traditions and practices. It was considered normal and necessary for feudal kings to rely on their barons for advice as well as for military aid. Usually kings turned to a small council of permanent advisers, a council comprising the chief barons of the realm and important ecclesiastics. There was a prevailing tension, however, between this small council of permanent advisers and the larger *magnum concilium regis*, or Great Council of peers of the realm, who felt more and more that they, too, had a right to be consulted on matters of policy that affected their own situation.

The English kings, particularly from the time of Henry II (1154-1189), found themselves increasingly involved in costly wars with France. To gain support for these wars, particularly financial support, the kings turned to the *magnum concilium regis* and also to lesser barons and burgesses who commanded sources of wealth. Not surprisingly, therefore, some historians have tended to interpret the evolution of Parliament largely, though not solely, in economic terms.

The immediate circumstances surrounding the Parliament of 1295 can be found in Edward I's foreign policy. The king had been involved in costly wars with the Welsh. A far grander enterprise, however, was on the horizon: a war against France. Edward claimed that war was necessary to prevent France from depriving England of Gascony, a French territory rich in wine production. Both the writs summoning the members to Parliament and accounts by medieval chroniclers attest that Edward used the threat of foreign war, which was probably real, as his chief reason for calling members of the realm together to give him support. The campaign that Edward envisioned was of such a scale that the unified support of all was imperative. After negotiations between France and England failed, the king issued writs in September and October through his Chancery that required those summoned to participate in a parliament beginning the second week of November, after the feast of Saint Martin.

In composition, the Parliament of 1295 was made up of the lords spiritual, or the great churchmen; the lords temporal, or the great barons; and representatives of what was eventually to become the House of Commons. These representatives of the "commoners" came from two groups: knights of the shire, or men who held considerable land but who were not barons of the first rank or direct vassals of the king, and burgesses, or representatives of incorporated towns. Edward summoned the two archbishops, all the bishops, the abbots of the larger monasteries, seven earls, and forty-one barons, besides knights and burgesses.

The composition of the 1295 Parliament thus involved the widest membership of any parliament up to that time. Edward I rarely summoned knights from the shire and burgesses from the cities and towns. In 1295, when they joined the temporal and spiritual lords in the assembly that came to be called the Model Parliament, they set an important precedent. Afterward, they began to meet in parliament with some regularity, although representation was proportional neither to geography or population. The famous principle cited in the summoning writs: "that what affects all, by all should be approved," is found in Justinian's *Code* and also in university statutes and in the Canon Law of the Roman Catholic Church. It expresses one of the most salient principles of democratic government and runs like a thread through medieval political history. The writ to the archbishop of Canterbury obligingly describes the common threat necessitating the Parliament: the king of France would "deprive us of our land of Gascony, by withholding it unjustly from us," and is conspiring "to destroy the English language altogether from the earth."

Like the lords spiritual, the great barons were also summoned by name. The summons is clearly a command, not an invitation, ordering the individual addressed to appear in person at Westminster on the Lord's day next after the feast of St. Martin in the approaching winter.

In the cases of the bishops and great barons, the summons to the Parliament was a personal one, and the work to be done by these members was in a real sense personal work, but such was not the case, however, with the knights of the shires and burgesses, as a writ to the sheriff of Northampton makes clear. The sheriff is told "to cause two knights from the aforesaid county, two citizens from each city in the same county, and two burgesses from each borough, to be elected without delay, and to cause them to come to us at the aforesaid time and place." The writ explains that the knights and burgesses are to be "discreet," "capable of laboring," and empowered to act for their constituencies so that the business at hand can be finished then and there, evidence of the principle of representative government. Furthermore, these representatives, according to the writ, must be registered. The sheriff is enjoined to have on record the names of all knights, citizens, and burgesses elected to the Parliament.

When the Parliament assembled in November, each group ended by giving the king only as much as it was compelled to give. The king had to settle for a tenth of the revenue of the archbishop of Canterbury instead of the third or fourth he requested. The barons and knights gave one eleventh of their income to the king, and the boroughs gave one seventh, an indication not only of the relative wealth of the various components of the realm but also of their bargaining power. As each group assented to aid, it was dismissed and went home.

In interpreting the Parliament of 1295, a number of important features should be considered. In this Parliament, all elements of the realm were represented, but they were not yet established in the two groups which eventually became a bicameral legislature, a future development when the burgesses and the knights of the shire joined together for common discussion apart from the lords spiritual and temporal. Clearly present in 1295 was the working principle of aid for redress of grievances. The members of the Parliament of 1295 still acted within the framework of feudal grant of aid to the king. Pragmatically, this aid was now given only after collective bargaining. Further, this Parliament took an important step forward in a gradually established custom of consulting the middle class in Parliament, not outside it.

The principle that "what affects all, should be approved by all" meant in effect that policies should have at least the passive support of those affected by them. This is the essential principle of broad participation in the political process and is perhaps the single most significant detail of the summons to the Model Parliament of 1295. Edward's parliaments were considered the most solemn of his councils, whose members were his representatives. With the Model Parliament it was not yet a full functioning legislative body, nor could it challenge the authority of the king; but it did establish the consultative function of parliament. The full implications of the Parliament of 1295 were only realized later, when law-making power was integrated with the consultative-judicial power of Parliament.

—*Mary Evelyn Jegen, updated by Xavier Baron*

ADDITIONAL READING:

Butt, Ronald. *A History of Parliament: The Middle Ages.* London: Constable, 1989. This valuable and authoritative study questions many of the assumptions about the actualities and later assessments of the Model Parliament by positioning it in the overall history of the most fundamental English political body. It is an impor-

tant study which combines original research that raises new questions.

Davies, R. G., and J. H. Denton, eds. *The English Parliament in the Middle Ages.* Philadelphia: University of Pennsylvania Press, 1981. The collected essays gathered here honor medieval parliamentary historian John Smith Roskell. They discuss parliament from its "prehistory" through 1509, with a good balance of constitutional and political historical analysis.

Harris, G. L. "The Formation of Parliament, 1272-1377." In *The English Parliament in the Middle Ages,* edited by R. G. Davies and J. H. Denton. Philadelphia: University of Pennsylvania Press, 1981. This essay is the best single overview of the political and historical context of the Model Parliament, focusing on the reigns of Edward I through Edward III.

Plucknett, Theodore F. T. *Taswell-Langmead's English Constitutional History.* 11th ed. London: Sweet and Maxwell, 1960. Plucknett points to precedents of representation before the Model Parliament and so establishes a broader context for interpretation of the importance of 1295 in the history of parliament.

Powicke, Sir Maurice. *The Thirteenth Century, 1216-1307.* 2d ed. Oxford: Clarendon Press, 1962. This volume of the Oxford History of England remains an indispensable account of the political history of the sequence of events around the Model Parliament.

Sayles, George O. *The King's Parliament of England.* London: Edward Arnold, 1974. This brief account by one of the most authoritative of British political historians is concise, accessible and based on a lifetime of research and study. It has an excellent bibliography.

SEE ALSO: 1175, Common Law Tradition Emerges in England; 1215, Signing of the Magna Carta; 1285, Statute of Winchester; 1485-1547, Tudor Monarchs Rule in England.

1302
BONIFACE VII ISSUES THE BULL UNAM SANCTAM

Boniface VII issues the bull Unam Sanctam *after much division between the church and state, stating that the pope held supreme power over the state.*

DATE: November 18, 1302
LOCALE: Rome
CATEGORIES: Laws, acts, and legal history; Religion
KEY FIGURES:
Boniface VIII (Benedict Gaetani; c. 1235-1303), Roman Catholic pope, 1294-1303

Celestine V (Pietro da Morrone; c. 1209-1296), Roman Catholic pope, July 5-December 13, 1294

Clement V (Bertrand de Got; c. 1260-1314), archbishop of Bordeaux, 1299-1305; Roman Catholic pope, 1305-1314

Guillaume de Nogaret (c. 1260-1313), French jurist and minister to Philip

Philip IV (1268-1314), king of France, 1285-1314

SUMMARY OF EVENT. After the death of Pope Nicholas IV in 1292, the papacy remained vacant for more than two years because of factionalism within the College of Cardinals. The Colonnas, a leading family in Roman politics, included two cardinals, James and Peter, who represented French interests, whereas their opponents, the Orsini, favored a Roman or Italian pontiff. The issue was resolved through the election of Peter of Murrone, an aged eighty-five-year-old hermit from the mountainous country of the Abruzzi. Calling himself Celestine V, the new pontiff's naïveté and inexperience made it possible for others to exploit the papal office to the extent that he affixed his signature to blank bulls, permitting the recipient to fill in whatever he chose. By the end of 1294, Peter, aware of his deficiencies, issued a bull declaring his right to resign, and he relinquished his office. Despite the fact that canonists affirmed the legality of Peter's decision, a papal resignation was without precedent, and it cast doubt upon the legitimacy of his successor. Within less than two weeks Benedict Gaetani was elected to succeed Celestine V, and he took the name Boniface VIII.

An aristocratic Roman who was also somewhat elderly, the new pope was reported to be of bad temper. A dispute arose between Pope Boniface and Philip IV, king of France, over the right of kings to tax the clergy in their realms. In 1296, France and England were at war, and each king taxed the Church in his lands to finance the project. The pope issued an edict or bull, *Clericis laicos*, in which he declared that any cleric who paid taxes to a secular lord, and any lord who levied or received taxes from the Church, automatically incurred excommunication. In effect the bull denied absolute authority to a sovereign within his own kingdom. Philip retaliated by forbidding the exportation of gold and silver, jewelry, and currency from France, thereby cutting off papal revenues, and French publicists began attacking the papal position. Early in 1297, pressured by bankers and a hostile group of cardinals who accused the pope of heresy, Boniface issued the bull *Romana mater* which largely suspended *Clericis laicos*. The pope not only agreed to the levying of taxes on the clergy, but in certain cases it was even permissible without the consent of Rome. A subsequent bull left to the king the decision as to whether there was a necessity for

such assessment. One explanation which has been proposed for the pope's abrupt change of opinion was his preoccupations with a crusade against the Colonnas in Italy. It was at the height of this quarrel that Boniface made peace with Philip. In 1299, the Colonna stronghold, Palestrina, was razed by papal troops, plowed under, and sown with salt.

In 1300, Boniface declared a Jubilee year during which thousands of pilgrims flocked to Rome to gain the special indulgences made available. Cynics view the Jubilee merely as an attempt to line the papal coffers, but the pope was undoubtedly also prompted by religious motives. The overwhelming success of the Jubilee may have given the pope a false idea of the support he commanded among the faithful in Europe. Buoyed up with misplaced confidence, he renewed the struggle with Philip.

In 1301, Bernard Saisset, bishop of Pamiers and Boniface's legate to Paris, was arrested by Philip's agents for treason, blasphemy, and heresy. He was tried in the king's court, declared guilty, and imprisoned. A basic principle of the Canon Law of the Church reserved the trial of churchmen for church courts, especially when the accusation involved heresy. Boniface was compelled either to acquiesce in Philip's complete control of the French Church or to offer vigorous opposition. He ordered Saisset to be set free, and he summoned all French bishops to Rome to discuss the state of the French Church. He declared that in the case of wicked rulers popes had the jurisdiction to take authority in temporal affairs. In a long personal letter to Philip, the pope sharply reproved him for his conduct toward the Church and went on to say, "Let no one persuade you that you have no superior or that you are not subject to the head of the ecclesiastical hierarchy, for he is a fool who so thinks. . . ."

Philip had the letter burned, and he forged another as having come from Boniface which made extreme claims for the papacy. The forgery was calculated to stir French indignation and prompt a feeling of national hostility toward the pope. In April, 1302, Philip held an assembly of clergy, nobles, and townsmen at the Cathedral of Notre Dame in Paris, an assembly which is considered the first meeting of the Estates General. The nobility and commons, supporting the king in his antipapal position, sent a letter to the cardinals in Rome, declaring their refusal to recognize Boniface as lawful pope. The French clergy composed a less radical reply. In November, 1302, the pope's council met with about half the French bishops in attendance. One of the bulls issuing from this council was *Unam Sanctam*, which was published on November 18.

In this bull, perhaps the most famous of all medieval bulls, no mention is made of the conflict with Philip.

Rather, it sets forth the theoretical justification for papal primacy in Christian society regardless of time and place. It opens with statements on the unity of the Church, outside which there is no salvation or remission of sins. Numerous analogies from Scripture are used to support this unity: Noah's ark, Christ's seamless garment, the body of Christ, and the Church as a flock. In the Church there are two swords, spiritual and temporal, "but the one is exercised for the church, the other by the church, the one by the hand of the priest, the other by the hand of kings and soldiers, though at the will and suffrance of the priest." When the earthly power errs, it can be judged by the spiritual; but when the spiritual power errs, it can be judged by God alone. The most frequently quoted assertion from the bull is its conclusion taken verbatim from a statement made by Thomas Aquinas: "Therefore we declare, state, define, and pronounce that it is altogether necessary to salvation for every human creature to be subject to the Roman pontiff."

Philip delayed a response to this challenge until the spring of 1303, when he had made plans to bring Boniface to France as a captive. In June, 1303, Philip held a council at the Louvre where charges were brought against the pope, including simony, fornication, demon possession, illegal deposition of Celestine V, and denying the Eucharist. At the same time, Philip received word that Boniface intended to excommunicate him and had written that all subjects should deny allegiance to France. Guillaume de Nogaret, in league with Sciarra Colonna, was dispatched to Anagni, outside Rome, where Boniface was staying. With three hundred horses and a thousand footmen, they stormed the papal residence and, according to an eyewitness of the "outrage of Anagni," physically abused the aged pontiff. While the conspirators were debating their course of action, the townspeople rose up and expelled the invaders. Although Boniface was spared the ignominy of capture, he died a month later in October, 1303.

His successor, Benedict XI, excommunicated Nogaret and attempted to negotiate with Philip, but he lived only a short time. Benedict was followed by Clement V, a Frenchman who succumbed to French pressure by removing the papal residence to Avignon and by lifting the excommunication from Nogaret in 1311. Clement also commended Philip for the piety and zeal he had displayed in his relations with Boniface. Both Clement and Philip died in 1314. The papal residency remained in France until 1377, during which seven popes were installed. This period became known as the Babylonian Captivity of the papacy.

—*Carl A. Volz,*
updated by Marilyn Elizabeth Perry

ADDITIONAL READING:

Barraclough, Geoffrey. *The Medieval Papacy.* New York: W. W. Norton, 1979. The pontificate of Boniface VIII was a disaster of the first magnitude for the Church; not Boniface but the system was at fault, according to this author.

Boase, Thomas Sherer. *Boniface VIII.* London: Constable and Company, 1933. In what is probably the best and most exhaustive work on Boniface available in English, Boase points out that the bull *Unam Sanctam* contains nothing new.

Eno, Robert B. *The Rise of the Papacy.* Wilmington, Del.: M. Glazier, 1990. The history and doctrines of the early and medieval Roman Catholic Church.

Flick, A. C. *The Decline of the Medieval Church.* New York: Burt Franklin, 1967. A thesis arguing that Boniface was challenged by forces which he did not understand: political forces undermining the papacy, nationalism, powerful monarchs, and Roman law.

Tierney, Brian. *The Crisis of Church and State, 1050-1300.* Medieval Academy Reprints for Teaching 21. Toronto: University of Toronto Press, 1988. A collection of documents with commentary viewing the dispute as one involving national sovereignty.

Wood, Charles T., ed. *Philip the Fair and Boniface VIII.* Huntington, N.Y.: R. E. Kreiger, 1976. The interpretations of fifteen historians, most of which are here translated for the first time into English, together with a useful annotated bibliography for further study.

SEE ALSO: 1356, The "Golden Bull"; 1414-1418, Council of Constance; 1440, Donation of Constantine Is Exposed as Fraudulent; 1545-1563, Council of Trent.

1310-1350
WILLIAM OF OCKHAM ATTACKS THOMIST IDEAS

William of Ockham attacks Thomist ideas in philosophical and theological writings that question the teachings of the Catholic Church, preparing the way for the Protestant Reformation.

DATE: 1310-c. 1350
LOCALE: England and continental Europe
CATEGORIES: Cultural and intellectual history; Religion
KEY FIGURES:
Saint Thomas Aquinas (Tommaso d'Aquino; 1225-1274), Dominican friar, scholar, and Christian theologian known for his masterwork, *Summa theologiae*
John XXII (Jacques Duèse; 1244-1334), Roman Catholic pope, 1316-1334

Louis of Bavaria (1287-1347), Holy Roman Emperor as
  Louis IV, 1328-1347

William of Ockham (1285-1349), English theologian,
  philosopher, and Franciscan scholar

SUMMARY OF EVENT. Although the philosophical and
theological system created by Saint Thomas Aquinas represents the highest point of medieval Scholastic thought
and has long been the official philosophy of the Catholic
Church, it was not without critics during its time, especially during the fourteenth century, when Thomism had
not yet completely established itself. One of the sharpest
and most influential of these critics was the English theologian and philosopher, William of Ockham, and his views
both reflected a differing vision of truth than that of Aquinas and helped prepare the way for the Protestant Reformation.

Aquinas' greatest and definitive work, the *Summa
theologiae* (c. 1265-1273; *Summa Theologica*), made use
of the thoughts and concepts of many of his philosophical
and theological forerunners, but its greatest debt is to the
Greek philosopher Aristotle. In a very real sense, Thomistic philosophy is Aristotelian philosophy Christianized,
and William of Ockham's criticisms of Aquinas were
inevitably linked to objections to Aristotle which stretched
back to classical Greece.

The basic quarrel between Saint Thomas Aquinas and
William of Ockham involved the issue of "realism" versus
"nominalism." Briefly stated, "realism" posits that universals, or the perfect form of earthly objects, exist in some
real yet abstract state. Plato had taught that these universals were in fact the only reality. Thus there is, in some
world beyond this one, the "perfect chair" of which all
earthly chairs are inferior copies. Aristotle believed that
universals could exist only in specific things, but those
specific things shared the essence of the universal. Aquinas, following Aristotle's lead, claimed that these universals existed in the mind of God prior to creation, but
thereafter were found only in specific objects, while still
retaining their universal character. A horse, for example,
shares with all other horses a certain *quidditas* (which
might be translated as "whatness," or even "horseness").
This *quidditas* is the essential quality which distinguishes
horses from all other creatures. Although we as human
beings can perceive *quidditas* only as it is resident in a
particular thing, it is a universal reality.

Aquinas used this relatively simple concept, linked
with Christian belief, as a key part in his work to produce
a broad and systematic philosophical and theological
scheme. William of Ockham objected to this system because he rejected its foundation. William's cardinal principle was that universals existed, not in reality, but only as

*In his theological writings, William of Ockham took issue with
many of the concepts set forth by Saint Thomas Aquinas, shown
here writing his* Summa theologiae. *(Archive Photos)*

constructs of the human mind. Everything outside of the
mind was individual. The philosophical term given to this
view is "nominalism," and William's view that a universal
is only a term to label a group of individuals has earned his
philosophy the name "Terminism." He taught that the
terms we use to group individuals may be useful but they
are not, in any ultimate sense, real. This led to sharp
divisions with Thomistic thought.

Aquinas had sought to unite faith and reason, and so
had defended the scientific character of theology. Indeed,
he claimed that theology was the noblest of all the sciences, since it gives us knowledge of the ultimate truths
regarding God and His creation. William, on the other
hand, denied that theology was a science at all, since it can
rest only on the faith of the individual and the divinely
granted authority of the church. For William, science is
knowledge gained from experience, principles, or conclusions drawn from the two; since the fundamental "facts"
of theology are outside human experience, theology cannot be a science.

Aquinas had taught that theology is universal and unlimited, able to use all philosophical and scientific truths

in order to fashion a higher and clearer vision of ultimate reality. In this way he could use what he would term universal truths to fashion various proofs for the existence of God from the natural world around him. William, who had a much more skeptical view of human reason, maintained that theology was basically a collection of mental habits, undoubtedly divinely inspired but limited by our human nature, which had the common purpose of leading human beings to salvation. He thus rejected Aquinas' belief that theology was a single characteristic of the human mind which was capable of unlimited development. Here, William anticipates a key tenet of later Protestant thought, which emphasizes the infinite gulf between God and human beings.

Saint Thomas Aquinas and William of Ockham diverge again on the question of ethics. For Aquinas, ethics and human goodness are questions which relate to the perfection which is possible through God's sharing of His own goodness and perfection. In essence, Aquinas seems to be arguing that God wants us to be good, perhaps even perfect, and will provide the means by which to attain this. In traditional Catholic belief, this is accomplished not solely by individual action but through the assistance of the Church, which includes both the earthly version of the institution and the saints in heaven.

Again, William takes a differing view. For him, ethics and morality are based on the obligation human beings have to follow the laws laid down by God. "Goodness," a universal, does not exist as a thing in itself; it is merely a term which signifies that something is as it ought to be according to God's commandments. Here, William makes a breath-taking step and claims that God's commandments are not set according to an abstract concept of "good," but are determined purely by God's pleasure. Since God is free to do as He chooses He can command as He pleases. We have been commanded to love God; therefore, to love Him is good. Had He chosen to command us to hate Him, however, "goodness" in human beings would consist of obeying that commandment, incomprehensible as that might seem. In a similar fashion, William explains, God has condemned and forbidden adultery, but God could change this and make adultery good and meritorious.

This view of God's universal authority, unmediated by the presence of the church and its traditions, has caused some to label William of Ockham "the first Protestant." Martin Luther was later to refer to William as one of his major influences, and traces of William's philosophy are clearly seen in Protestant theological thought. William's personal history adds some credence to this description. Accused, or at least suspected, of heresy by the papacy, he was for a time confined to the Franciscan house in Avi-

gnon, and later fled to the court of his protector, Louis of Bavaria, Holy Roman Emperor, where he lived until his death. As a dedicated Franciscan who rejected material goods and preached the virtues of poverty, William ran against the current of the established church of his time.

William's ideas on the importance of the individual in the religious scheme of things and his rejection of universals in favor of directly observed particulars were later taken up and developed by empirical philosophers such as his fellow Englishman, John Locke. His major importance for both philosophy and theology is in his systematic and comprehensive marshaling of logical arguments in favor of nominalism over realism and his emphasis on the individual and the particular over the universal and general. Both views would later become central elements in the thought of the Protestant Reformation.

—Michael Witkoski

ADDITIONAL READING:

Adams, Marilyn McCord. *William Ockham*. 2 vols. Notre Dame, Ind.: University of Notre Dame Press, 1987. A detailed and comprehensive review of William of Ockham's thought, which addresses in considerable detail his controversy with Thomist philosophy. While perhaps too advanced for the beginning student, it is an essential work in any thorough study of the subject.

Carre, Meyrick. *Realists and Nominalists*. Oxford: Oxford University Press, 1946. A relatively early yet still essential study of the real differences between Saint Thomas Aquinas and William of Ockham, within the setting of medieval Scholastic thought.

Dancy, Jonathan, and Ernest Sousa, eds. *A Companion to Epistemology*. London: Blackwell, 1992. Part of the "Blackwell Companions to Philosophy" series, this volume provides a brief but thorough introduction to William of Ockham's thought and helps place it within the context of general Scholastic philosophy.

Honderich, Ted, ed. *The Oxford Companion to Philosophy*. New York: Oxford University Press, 1995. The section on William of Ockham gives a basic introduction to his theories in an accessible fashion.

Maurer, Armand. *Medieval Philosophy*. New York: Random House, 1962. A volume in the History of Philosophy series with Etienne Gilson as general editor, this is an invaluable starting point for a study of Scholastic philosophy in general, as well as William of Ockham's individual contributions to the field.

SEE ALSO: 335-323 B.C., Aristotle Writes the *Politics*; 1265-1273, Thomas Aquinas Compiles the *Summa Theologiae*; 1517, Luther Posts His Ninety-five Theses; 1690, Locke Publishes *Two Treatises of Government*.

1314

BATTLE OF BANNOCKBURN

The Battle of Bannockburn marks the defeat of a superior English army by Scottish forces under Robert the Bruce, allowing him to secure his own reign and preserve Scotland's independence for another four centuries.

DATE: June 24, 1314

LOCALE: Stirling, Scotland

CATEGORY: Wars, uprisings, and civil unrest

KEY FIGURES:

Robert Bruce (c. 1276-1329), king of Scotland, 1306-1329

Edward I (1239-1307), king of England and Wales, 1272-1307, who lost to William Wallace at the Battle of Stirling Bridge in 1297

Edward II (1284-1327), king of England and Wales, 1307-1327, who lost to Bruce at the Battle of Bannockburn

Gilbert, earl of Gloucester (1291-1314), nephew of Edward II and commander of English army who was killed at the Battle of Bannockburn

William Wallace (c. 1272-1305), Scottish patriot who was the victor at the Battle of Stirling Bridge in 1297 and was later executed in 1305

SUMMARY OF EVENT. Margaret "the Maid of Norway," heir to the throne of Scotland, died in 1290 at the age of eight. Without a clear claimant to the crown, the Scottish clans permitted an eager King Edward I of England to choose between various aristocratic candidates. Edward chose John Balliol, whom he believed he could control, over a stronger Robert de Brus, a nobleman of Anglo-Norman descent. The choice proved unfortunate when Balliol made the famous "Auld Alliance" with Edward's enemy France; Edward invaded Scotland, forced Balliol to abdicate, carried away the sacred Stone of Scone to England, and left Scotland kingless.

Into the vacuum of power stepped William Wallace, a landowner but not noble, who would become a hero of Scottish nationalism. Wallace rallied the disparate and often feuding clans to attack English garrisons and won a decisive victory over superior English troops at the Battle of Stirling Bridge in 1297. Wallace was defeated in a subsequent battle at Falkirk and in 1305 was betrayed, captured, and convicted of "treason" against an English king to whom he had never declared allegiance. He was hanged, drawn, and quartered, and his arms and legs were sent to four cities as a lesson to rebels.

Inspired by the support Wallace had received from Scots, Robert the Bruce, grandson of Robert de Brus passed over for king fifteen years earlier, abandoned his earlier allegiance to England and took up Wallace's cause. He was about thirty years of age when Wallace died in 1305; and in 1306 he was crowned by the Scottish clans at Scone. He faced daunting odds. Scots rarely worked in unison. He was himself excommunicated from the Catholic Church for having murdered a rival, John (Red) Comyn, in a church. It was also certain that the English would once more invade Scotland to end the independence which a king represented.

Bruce got a brief breathing space when Edward I died in 1307 and his feckless son and heir Edward II showed little desire to pursue his father's ambitions in Scotland. Bruce took advantage of his reprieve to consolidate his power. He took several castles back from English control, including Edinburgh, and held a parliament of his clans at St. Andrews. He was even recognized as king of Scots by the French, although not by the pope.

It was not until early 1314 that Edward II came to Scotland and the struggle for independence was renewed. Edward mustered a seemingly invincible English army to end Bruce's reign and by the middle of summer was ready for attack. The two armies met just southeast of Stirling, only three miles from the spot where Wallace had defeated

SITE OF THE BATTLE OF BANNOCKBURN

the English seventeen years earlier.

Sometime during the day of Friday, June 21, 1314, Bruce and perhaps six thousand men arrived at a small stream (a "burn" in Scots) called Bannock, which flows south of Stirling Castle and meanders through bog lands between Stirling and Falkirk to the River Forth. Stirling Castle, visible from this spot, was still held by the English, and Bruce reasoned that Edward would try to use its security as a base of operation against him in the central lowlands. He carefully chose a place north of Bannockburn on a crest atop a slope. North of the stream were only two patches of solid turf, and to cross the stream to meet him Edward's army would have to narrow their ranks in order to avoid bogs. Strategy was particularly important because Bruce knew that he would be outnumbered almost three to one, his six thousand soldiers against between fourteen thousand and twenty thousand English. Patriotic enthusiasm alone would not be sufficient for victory.

On Saturday, June 22, scouts reported that Edward's army was proceeding along the old Roman road that connected Edinburgh to Stirling. Later reports confirmed the supposition that the English would camp for the night at Falkirk, only nine miles from Stirling.

On Sunday, June 23, the eve of St. John's Day, Bruce and the Scottish army proclaimed a vigil and spent the day both in preparation for battle and in prayer. Late in the day, after a tiring march from Falkirk, the English army approached Bannockburn; but because of the late hour—and perhaps also because it was Sunday—the English king gave orders for his army to make camp south of the stream, at some distance from the Scots. One of his commanders, the earl of Gloucester, either did not hear the command or chose not to heed it and sent his three thousand soldiers against the Scots. His charge was repulsed, demonstrating the determination of Bruce's army; but the English seemed not at all dismayed by this failure. As a matter of fact, their camp reverberated late into the night with sounds of revelry, while the Scots kept vigil with prayers to St. John. Later accounts credited Bruce with one of history's greatest speeches of inspiration.

Monday, June 24, proved the fateful day. The English attacked as Bruce had anticipated and hoped, crossing the stream (almost dry at this time of the year) in the narrow spaces between the bogs, then having to climb toward the Scots on higher ground. The Scottish army formed into *schiltrons*, small, compact rings of spearmen, each man with spear leveled, as observers testified "bristling like hedgehogs." The schiltrons counterattacked the English and broke through their ranks, forcing them into the bogs and persuing the English king. The earl of Gloucester was killed, and the English infantry fell into chaos. The En-

glish cavalry was crippled by the swampy turf; but the Scottish cavalry, choosing its path, disrupted the English archers. Estimates held that up to one-half of the English forces perished that day, most of their casualties coming in the bogs along Bannockburn.

His army disintegrated, Edward circled the battlefield and hurried to Stirling Castle; but its commander, knowing that he would have to surrender to Bruce, advised him to seek the safety of Dunbar. From there Edward made his way to the Lothian coast and eventually arrived back in London. He never returned to Scotland, and thirteen years later he was deposed and murdered in a most horrible way by his queen and her lover.

The victory at Bannockburn secured Robert Bruce's reign as certainly as it weakened that of Edward. Scots united behind him, and the European powers recognized him as king of Scots. In 1324, at the urging of Scots bishops, even Pope John XXII blessed his reign. In 1328, Edward III recognized his legitimacy and by implication the independence of Scotland. He reigned for twenty-three years, from his coronation in 1306 to his death from natural causes in 1329.

Scotland remained a kingdom of its own for another four centuries. Yet the gravitational pull toward the stronger England continued. Robert Bruce's son David (1329-1371) agreed to be Edward III's vassal; and the Stewart family that replaced the Bruces on the Scottish throne continually made concessions to the powerful neighbor to the south. In the fifteenth century James IV Stewart married Margaret Tudor, sister of Henry VIII, and his great-grandson James VI inherited the English throne as James I when the "virgin" Queen Elizabeth died. The two thrones, while occupied by the same person, remained separate until the official Act of Union in 1707, which created the United Kingdom.

Even though a Scottish king became king of England, many Scots still feel that union was a mistake accomplished by deceit, when the English bribed Scottish parliamentarians to vote for the United Kingdom. Many believe that Bruce's victory at Bannockburn only delayed the inevitable. Still, when Scots talk of heroes, they remember Robert the Bruce. When they desire renewal of their pride, they remember Bannockburn. —*James T. Baker*

ADDITIONAL READING:

Barrow, G. W. S. *Robert Bruce and the Community of the Realm of Scotland*. Berkeley: University of California Press, 1965. Barrow's is the most complete biography of Bruce. It places Bannockburn in the perspective of the king's whole career and corrects errors of earlier authors.

Fry, Plantagenet, and Fiona Somerset Fry. *The History*

of Scotland. London: Routledge & Kegan Paul, 1982. The Frys place Bannockburn in the larger context of Scottish history and thus demonstrate its symbolic significance for Scots.

Linklater, Eric. *The Survival of Scotland*. Garden City, N.Y.: Doubleday, 1968. In a book that portrays the history of Scotland as a struggle to survive against great odds, Bannockburn is described as an essentially Scottish victory against a superior opposing force.

Maxwell, Herbert. *Robert the Bruce and the Struggle for Scottish Independence*. London: G. P. Putnam's Sons, 1897. Although a hundred years old, this account of Bannockburn provides a balanced if romantic description of the battle. It contains a convenient fold-out map.

SEE ALSO: 1559-1561, Scottish Reformation; 1603, James I Becomes King of England and Scotland; 1706-1707, Act of Union Unites England and Scotland.

1315
SWISS VICTORY AT MORGARTEN

Swiss victory at Morgarten over Habsburg forces by the allied "forest cantons" of Schwyz, Uri, and Unterwalden lays the foundation for the modern Swiss Confederation.

DATE: November 15, 1315
LOCALE: Switzerland
CATEGORY: Wars, uprisings, and civil unrest
KEY FIGURES:
Duke Leopold I of Austria (c. 1293-1326), brother of Frederick the Fair of Habsburg
Rudolf Stauffacher (Stoupacher) of Schwyz,
Werner von Attinghausen, of Uri, and
Walter Furst, of Uri, leaders of the allied Swiss resistance against the Habsburgs
Wilhelm Tell, legendary leader of Swiss resistance whose historical authenticity is in doubt

SUMMARY OF EVENT. The Swiss Republic includes twenty-six districts or "cantons" not united by a common ethnic stock, language, religion, natural boundaries, or ancient roots. The Roman Empire never organized the Transalpine Celts into a political entity. The Germanic invaders became the majority of a population divided into four ethnic and lingual groups—Allemani, Franks, Italians, and Romansh. During the breakup of Charlemagne's empire, it would have been logical for these groups to be annexed by their German, French, and Italian neighbors, but this was forestalled by a thirteenth century central Alpine federative movement. Within the large and loose framework of the "Holy Roman Empire of the German Nation," three small mountain valley "forest cantons"—

Uri, Schwyz, and Unterwalden—bordering the shores of Lake Lucerne, formed the alliance of rebels who fought at Morgarten.

The origins of the battle and of Switzerland must be told in terms of the geography, local history, and legends of the "inner Alps." The thirteenth century brought significant changes to these forest cantons. Construction of the Devil's Bridge over the Schoellenen Gorge on the Reuss River opened a trade route through the central Alps. Travelers and pack animals could go from Milan via Lake Maggiore, the Saint Gotthard Pass and Lake Lucerne to the Basle road, the Rhine, and Flanders. The formerly poor and isolated forest cantons began to prosper. At the same time, an increasing power struggle in the Holy Roman Empire saw emperors, their rivals, and the greater princes ready to sell charters for lands, political and tax rights, or privileges to wealthy nobles, towns, and peasant communities. The forest cantons now had the money to join the bidding. As early as 1231, the freemen of Uri purchased rent freedom from their Habsburg lord, as confirmed by imperial charter. By the 1240 "Faenza Charter," the Schwyzois sought to escape dues or taxes to their Habsburg lord by payments to the emperor, a privilege not recognized by a later (Habsburg) emperor.

Ultimately, the Habsburgs were the threat against which the forest cantons would join in alliance. This family from the northwestern foothills of the Alps increased their feudal estates until by 1290 they held land, tax, or political rights in nine Swiss cantons, stretching from the Rhine through the Saint Gotthard Pass, in addition to sovereignty over Austria and Styria. Habsburg rents, taxes, tariffs, trade controls, and over-zealous bailiffs all seemed to threaten the local rights of the central Alpine burghers and peasants.

In August of 1291, Schwyz, Uri, and Unterwalden signed a written alliance. This alliance largely confirmed earlier agreements for settlement of disputes and mutual defense. No particular enemy was identified, and no formal declaration of sovereignty was made, but the demand for native and freeborn bailiffs and judges was clearly aimed at Habsburg lordship, and the alliance itself was inherently an act of independence. Schwyz and Uri supported an anti-Habsburg coalition which was crushed at Winterthur on April 12, 1292, and related disorders may have been the context for the legendary midnight oath of rebellion supposedly sworn at Rütli meadow in 1307. Oral tradition seems to have embellished the roles of actual leaders such as Rudolf Stauffacher (Stoupacher) of Schwyz, and Werner von Attinghausen and Walter Furst of Uri.

A greater complication is the legend of "Wilhelm Tell," supposedly an oath-taker at Rütli, resistance leader, and warrior at Morgarten. The story of the bailiff's hat, the apple shot from a son's head on the tyrant's command, the escape from the storm on Lake Lucerne, and the assassination of the bailiff sparking the war of rebellion, were recorded only in the late fifteenth century "White Book of Sarnen," polished a bit by Aegidius Tschudi in the sixteenth century, given historical context by Johannes von Muller in 1786, and popularized by Friedrich Schiller's 1804 play and Gioacchino Rossini's 1829 opera. Historians have pointed out that the apple story is a common northern tale, that the "Tell" version garbles actual history, that no fourteenth century chronicler mentions such a hero, and that "Tell" is really a Swiss equivalent to "Robin Hood" or "Paul Bunyan." Some Swiss, however, point to verifiable portions of the context and argue that "Tell" is a possible composite of several heroes as well as an embodiment of the Swiss spirit.

In the "Tell" legend, Swiss beginnings are explained as a revolt against Habsburg injuries and insults to the self-respect of Swiss men, women, and children. In actuality, Habsburg tariffs and trade controls may have been equally important, as well as cantonal opposition in imperial politics. Certainly the immediate cause of war was the Schwyzois raid in January of 1314 on disputed properties at Einsiedeln, an abbey under Habsburg protection. The Habsburg imperial contender, Frederick the Fair, ordered an expedition to destroy the revolutionary movement.

Frederick's brother, Duke Leopold of Austria, therefore prepared a comprehensive attack in November of 1315. One Habsburg army made a wide right-flank swing from Lucerne via the Entlebuch and Brunig Pass to attack Unterwalden, while ships from Lucerne crossed the lake to harass the western shores of Schwyz. Duke Leopold collected a main army of more than two thousand knights and perhaps seven thousand infantry at Zug, and on the moonlit night of November 14-15 set out for Schwyz. Perhaps the road through Arth was blocked, or perhaps Leopold sought a "back door" surprise, but in any case, on November 15, his army marched southward along the eastern shore of Lake Aegeri and then continued south with the Aegerisee swamp on their right, and Morgarten heights on their left. Apparently the aim was to cross the watershed to the Steiner valley and use the fairly level ground between Steinen and Schwyz for the battle which would defeat the rebels.

The knights headed a column stretching over more than half a mile of mediocre track, an obviously vulnerable situation, but an attack by untrained peasants was clearly not expected. About a mile south of Lake Aegeri, the knights were brought up short, either by a roadblock or rough footing. The spare narratives written later do not fit the present terrain with exact geographic perfection, but the main effect is clear. The defenders—thirteen hundred Schwyzois, two hundred from Uri, and others from Unterwalden—emerged from the forests along Morgarten heights, rolled boulders and tree trunks down the rocky slope of the Figlenfluh, and attacked on foot. In addition to using arrows, spears, clubs, and axes, the Swiss defenders used the halberd—a combination of spear, axe, and hook—in order to pull armored knights off their mounts. Surprised, the Austrian cavalry tried to deploy their undoubtedly panicked horses into a combat formation, but the narrow way gave no room for this. The battle was simply a running rout. In less than two hours, more than half the knights were killed, some drowning in the swamp or in Lake Aegeri, and the Habsburg army completely scattered. Duke Leopold survived only by flight, and, demoralized, also abandoned the unsuccessful flank attack on Unterwald.

For Europe, the defeat of mounted knights by infantry at Morgarten, like the similar case at Courtrai in 1302, threatened the military superiority which cavalry had claimed since the Battle of Adrianople in A.D. 378. That a small force of peasants only emerging from serfdom could outmaneuver and outfight a much larger army led by mounted knights threatened the very basis of European feudalism.

As for the forest cantons, Morgarten cemented their alliance and gained them *de facto* independence and credibility. Lucerne joined the alliance in 1332, Zürich in 1351, Zug and Glarus in 1352, and Bern in 1353, completing the "Eight Canton Federation" of the next century. In 1323, abolition of serfdom and canton government made "Switzerland" a republican exception among the feudal monarchies of Europe. The 1386 victory at Sembach followed by a treaty with Austria in 1394 effectually ended the Habsburg threat, although formal recognition by Austria came only with the 1648 Peace of Westphalia. Switzerland's expansive wars were checked, however, when a 1516 defeat by the French at Marignano and the divisive influence of the Protestant Reformation persuaded the Swiss to abandon great-power ambitions for what became a tradition of neutrality.

—K. Fred Gillum

ADDITIONAL READING:

Bonjour, E., H. S. Offler, and G. R. Potter. *A Short History of Switzerland*. Oxford: Clarendon Press, 1952. Scholarly overview of Swiss history that includes coverage of the battle at Morgarten.

Cooper, William Augustus Brevoort. "Switzerland: History." In *Encyclopedia Britannica*. 11th ed. Cambridge, England: Cambridge University Press, 1911. More comprehensive and clearer than many one-volume accounts.

McCrackan, William D. *The Rise of the Swiss Republic*. New York: Henry Holt, 1901. Deconstructs the legend of Wilhelm Tell.

Martin, William. *Switzerland*. New York: Praeger, 1971. Comprehensive Franco-Swiss scholarship, translated and updated.

Miller, Douglas, and G. A. Embleton. *The Swiss at War, 1300-1500*. London: Osprey, 1979. This pamphlet in the Men-at-Arms series incorporates some of the interpretation of Morgarten given in Hans Rudolf Kurz's *Schweizerschlachten*.

See also: 378, Battle of Adrianople; 1643-1648, Peace of Westphalia; 1848, Swiss Confederation Is Formed.

1323-1328
PEASANTS' REVOLT IN FLANDERS

A revolt in Flanders by a coalition of peasants and city dwellers against aristocratic rule succeeds until the rebels are defeated by the French five years later.

DATE: August 1, 1323-August 23, 1328
LOCALE: Flanders
CATEGORIES: Social reform; Wars, uprisings, and civil unrest
KEY FIGURES:
Charles IV (1294-1328), king of France, 1322-1328
Louis I (1304-1346), count of Flanders, 1322-1346
Philip VI (1293-1350), king of France, 1328-1350
SUMMARY OF EVENT. Flanders, a region of Europe bordering the North Sea and extending into areas that would later form parts of modern France, Belgium, and the Netherlands, was a separate nation during the Middle Ages. Conquered by France in a series of invasions from 1297 to 1300, Flanders won partial independence at the battle of Courtrai on July 11, 1302. A peace treaty negotiated at Athis-sur-Orge in June of 1305 restored political power to Robert of Bethune, count of Flanders, but required that the count remain loyal to the king of France and that Flanders pay large amounts of money to France. As a result of protests by the taxpayers of Flanders, delays by the count, and the inability of France to enforce the treaty, these debts went largely unpaid.

Upon the death of Robert of Bethune, his grandson, Louis II of Nevers, became Louis I, count of Flanders, on September 17, 1322. Raised in France and married to the daughter of the king of France, Louis I was far more loyal to France than the previous count. He promised to pay France all money owed and appointed pro-French aristocrats to positions of power.

CENTERS OF THE REVOLT IN FLANDERS

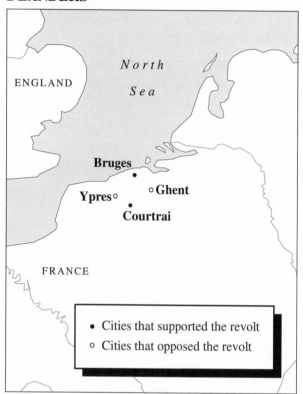

* Cities that supported the revolt
∘ Cities that opposed the revolt

On July 13, 1323, Louis I gave control of the Zwin waterway, which linked the city of Bruges to the North Sea, to his granduncle, John of Namur. The city leaders feared that John of Namur was planning to direct commerce away from Bruges to the town of Sluis, located at the mouth of the Zwin. A militia from Bruges attacked John of Namur's forces at Sluis on August 1, 1323. Sluis was burned and John of Namur was held prisoner until he escaped in late September.

Louis I left Flanders for France on October 15, 1323. Peasants began to rebel against the taxes that were being collected to make payments to France in late October. Officials in charge of collecting taxes were imprisoned or forced to flee. Despite the assistance of the militias of the three large cities of Bruges, Ghent, and Ypres, the government was able to do little against this well-organized, widespread rebellion.

Louis I returned to Flanders in early 1324. He arranged a truce with the rebels and set up commissions to investigate charges of corruption made against his officials. The commissions agreed to punish corrupt officials and offered amnesty to the rebels.

The effectiveness of these commissions varied from

region to region. In southwest Flanders, a commission led by Robert of Cassel, the uncle of Louis I, included representatives of city governments and listened to the testimony of the rebels. Because of this the rebels were inclined to agree with its decisions. In Bruges the settlement was made by Louis I and his advisers without the participation of city leaders or peasants. When Louis I later imposed heavy fines on Bruges and returned ousted officials to power, the region was ready to rebel again.

Louis I went back to France in July of 1324. Beginning in the late summer of 1324 peasants in the countryside north of Bruges attacked the strongholds of rural aristocrats, taking them prisoner or forcing them to flee. They also refused to pay tithes to monasteries. Local officials were driven out and replaced by representatives of the rebels.

Louis I returned to Flanders in December of 1324. Faced with a more serious rebellion than the tax protests of 1323, he gave permission for exiled aristocrats to attack the peasants with full force. He also allowed Robert of Cassel to use any means necessary to prevent the rebellion from spreading to southwest Flanders. The level of violence used on both sides quickly escalated into open warfare.

In February of 1325, peasant forces defeated the count's soldiers at the town of Gistel, southwest of Bruges. The city of Bruges joined the peasants in their rebellion at about the same time. Encouraged by their success and the support of Bruges, the rebels moved into southwest Flanders. The inhabitants of this region quickly joined the rebellion and forced Robert of Cassel to flee.

A truce was made with the rebels between March and June of 1325. A commission consisting of Robert of Cassel and representatives from the cities of Ghent and Ypres, which were still loyal to the count, was then set up. The rebels rejected the commission as too unsympathetic to their cause. Aristocrats led by John of Namur rejected it as too willing to compromise with the rebels. A meeting of the commission scheduled for June 11 failed to take place when Robert of Cassel learned that the aristocrats were conspiring to prevent him from reaching it. The other members of the commission were afraid to face the anger of the rebels waiting for them and knew that they could accomplish little without Robert of Cassel. The peace negotiations came to an end.

Louis I moved his soldiers to the town of Courtrai, between the cities of Ypres and Ghent, in an attempt to prevent the rebels from taking the town and driving a wedge between the two cities. An army of about five thousand rebels from Bruges began marching to Courtrai in mid-June of 1325. To block their approach, the count's forces set fire to the suburbs of Courtrai north of the Leie

River and destroyed the bridges crossing the river. A strong wind caused the fire to spread south of the river to Courtrai. The enraged citizens of Courtrai joined the rebellion and welcomed the approaching rebels. On June 20 and 21, the rebels inflicted heavy casualties on the count's forces and took Louis I prisoner. The peasant army then moved into Ypres, which joined the rebellion.

The leaders of Bruges forced Louis I to appoint Robert of Cassel as regent on June 30, 1325. In response, John of Namur produced a document, possibly forged, which had named him regent on June 12. The rebellion now evolved into a struggle between Robert of Cassel, allied with the rebels, and John of Namur, leading the aristocratic forces from Ghent. For several months the two armies fought many battles, losing and gaining territory, with neither side able to break the stalemate.

In November of 1325, King Charles IV of France became involved in the struggle. He recognized the regency of John of Namur, loaned money to Ghent, and prohibited trade between France and the rebel areas of Flanders. Hoping to prevent a French invasion, the rebels released Louis I on December 1, 1325, in exchange for a promise of amnesty. Despite his promise, Louis I went to Charles IV to request military aid.

Robert of Cassel abandoned his association with the rebels and obtained a pardon from the king on March 20, 1326. Reluctant to commit troops to Flanders at a time when he expected an invasion from England, Charles IV arranged for a peace treaty to be negotiated at the town of Arques on April 19, 1326. The treaty required payment of all fees owed to France and added additional fines. Although the rebel cities generally agreed to this treaty, the peasants mostly continued as before.

After Charles IV died in 1328, his successor, Philip VI, prepared to invade Flanders. On August 23, 1328, the French and rebel armies met near the town of Cassel. The French killed more than three thousand rebels, ending the uprising. Philip VI and Louis I punished the rebels severely and set up a strong centralized government which successfully resisted later attempts at rebellion.

—*Rose Secrest*

ADDITIONAL READING:

Fourquin, Guy. *The Anatomy of Popular Rebellion in the Middle Ages*. Translated by Anne Chesters. Amsterdam: North-Holland, 1978. An analysis of medieval uprisings which characterizes the Flanders revolt as a response to an agricultural and economic crisis.

Hilton, Rodney. *Bond Men Made Free: Medieval Peasant Movements and the English Rising of 1381*. New York: Viking, 1973. Deals with the Flanders revolt and other peasant rebellions of the Middle Ages and compares them to the later English revolt.

Nicholas, David. *Medieval Flanders*. New York: Longman, 1992. Provides background information on Flanders during the Middle Ages and discusses the revolt and its consequences.

_____. *Town and Countryside: Social, Economic, and Political Tensions in Fourteenth-Century Flanders*. Bruges, Belgium: De Tempel, 1971. Deals with the relationships between the cities of Bruges, Ghent, and Ypres and the rural areas of Flanders during the period of the revolt.

TeBrake, William H. *A Plague of Insurrection: Popular Politics and Peasant Revolt in Flanders, 1323-1328*. Philadelphia: University of Pennsylvania Press, 1993. A detailed account of the revolt and the complex political situation in which it took place.

SEE ALSO: 1214, Battle of Bouvines; 1346, Battle of Crécy; 1381, Wat Tyler Leads Peasants' Revolt; 1514, Hungarian Peasants Revolt; 1524-1526, German Peasants' War.

1330
BASARAB DEFEATS HUNGARIANS

Basarab defeats the Hungarians, establishing the resurgence of the indigenous Wallachian people, but ongoing strife between Hungary and the Danubian principalities ultimately weakens both, making them vulnerable to Turkish conquest.

DATE: November, 1330

LOCALE: Posada, north of Cimpulung, Wallachia

CATEGORIES: Expansion and land acquisition; Wars, uprisings, and civil unrest

KEY FIGURES:

Basarab I (c. 1310-1352), prince of Wallachia, c. 1330-1352

Charles Robert of Anjou (1288-1342), king of the Hungarians, 1308-1342

SUMMARY OF EVENT. Dacia, the area of southeastern Europe that was later to become part of modern Romania, was by the first century A.D. part of the Roman Empire, although later overrun by the Goths and other barbarian tribes that caused the Romans to abandon the Dacian colony in A.D. 271. The original inhabitants of this area north of the Danube, thought to be Romanized Dacians, were driven out of their original homeland by these invaders. Their territory was settled by Slavic tribes, Bulgars, Avars, and, at the end of the ninth century, by the Magyars (Hungarians) and other tribes from central Asia. The Daco-Romans (later Romanians) disappeared from his-

tory for nearly a millennium, then reappeared as Vlachs, although south of their original homeland, around the eleventh century. Although contemporary sources are scanty, it is thought that at least a sizable segment of the Daco-Roman native population retreated into the Carpathian Mountains of Transylvania, where they retained their language and culture, while the flatlands were settled by Slavs, Hungarians, Cumans, and Tatars. The extent to which this is true is still a matter of controversy between Romanians and Hungarians.

The geographical area now known as Romania formed a part of the Second Bulgarian (or Bulgaro-Vlach) Empire of the tenth and eleventh centuries, although whether Romanians made up the leadership of that empire is open to controversy. Although nominally Christianized, it was from their early contact with the Bulgarians that the Romanians were exposed to the Eastern Orthodox form of religion.

Around the end of the thirteenth century the people now known as Romanians reappeared in Wallachia, driven eastward and southward from the Carpathian Mountains of Transylvania because of religious persecution by the Catholic Hungarians and expropriation of their lands by Hungarian feudal lords. The fact that the Hungarians were still recovering from the terrible Mongol invasion of 1241, however, gave the Romanians some opportunity to rediscover their national identity. By the fourteenth century, the Wallachians and Moldavians, who were excluded from the cities founded by the Hungarian kings, were increasingly dissatisfied with the political and religious climate of their Magyar suzerains. They chose the Byzantine model for church and state in preference to that of the Catholic Hungarians, a model that was Eastern Orthodox, with an absolute monarch and dynastic succession. This autocratic power eventually became subject to abuse, since there were no rival estates which could limit the power of the ruler, who often rewarded his favorites at the expense of the peasant population.

The landowners of the territory south of the Carpathians chose Basarab, a prince of the district of Arges, to serve as grand voivode and prince. Basarab had gained recognition for his battles against the Mongol Tatars, although he was nominally a vassal of the Hungarian crown.

The Basarab dynasty, founded by Prince Basarab I of Wallachia, derived from the title of the prince as voivode, or military leader. His status was that of sole landowner, military leader, and chief ruler and lawmaker.

Basarab unified the area between the Carpathians and the Danube, and later the area north of the Danube as well, subsequently called Bessarabia after the Basarab dynasty. Basarab I's capital was at Cimpulung (Arges), which became his dynastic seat. His son and successor, Nicholas Alexander, continued to strengthen the dynasty and in 1359 was the founder of the Princely Church at Curtea de Arges, which under patriarchal approval became the Eastern Orthodox metropolitan church for Wallachia, thus confirming Wallachia's status as a principality.

Perhaps a further factor that provided the Romanians with a national goal was the development of the Danubian trade route that extended from the Black Sea north through Wallachia to Transylvania and the Adriatic Sea. This Danubian trade, and the taxes and tolls exacted from the mainly foreign merchant traders, enabled the Wallachian state and its rulers to become relatively wealthy by the middle of the fourteenth century.

In Hungary, after the extinction of the native Arpad dynasty in 1301 and a disputatious interregnum until 1310, the Angevin dynasty was established, with the election of Charles Robert of Anjou as King Charles I. As king, Charles Robert succeeded in ending the anarchy that had preceded his reign and in restoring the power of the Crown against the demands of the aristocracy. Charles founded his capital at Visegrad in 1323, a year which marked his resumption of full control over Hungary. As a ruler, Charles Robert was providential and careful, which contributed to the increasing power of Hungary during the Angevin reign.

At this time, Hungary included not only all the Danubian basin to the crests of the Carpathian Mountains, but also Wallachia, northern Serbia, Bosnia, and the coast of Dalmatia.

In November, 1330, Charles Robert invaded the domains of Basarab I in Wallachia in order to reestablish Hungarian supremacy over Wallachia, hoping to profit by Basarab's military reversals with his allies, the Bulgarians, who had recently been defeated by the Serbians at Velbuzhd. Although Basarab tried to buy off the Hungarian king with an indemnity of seven thousand silver marks, Charles refused. At Posada, a pass in the southern Carpathians, however, Charles was defeated by Basarab and barely escaped with his life. In spite of this victory, only a few years later Wallachia again became a dependency of Hungary, only achieving full independence from Hungary in 1380.

After the Battle of Posada, both nations continued to expand under the leadership of subsequent members of their respective dynasties. The Hungarians, under Charles's son, Louis I the Great, pursued an aggressive foreign policy against neighboring states, particularly the Venetian Republic and the Balkans, and yet the country enjoyed the benefits of domestic peace and stability. Prosperity was assured from the great mining wealth from the gold mines of Transylvania, which were mined largely by German Saxons invited by the Hungarian king. In contrast to the nobility, who held their estates as a hereditary elite, the lands newly conquered became the sole property of the king. These he used to establish a court aristocracy of his own supporters, as well as to build up a large treasury for the royal household. This social environment of wealth and privilege had a further effect of increasing the level of literacy and written documentation in Hungary at this time.

The principality of Wallachia, under the Basarab dynasty, together with the neighboring emerging principality of Moldavia, also continued to develop, although the advent of the Turks in the Balkans became an increasing threat, particularly after they defeated the Serbians and Bulgarians at the Battle of Marica in 1371. These Danubian principalities, with a large peasant population, a small boyar class under the authority of the voivode, and a disfranchised and landless class of Gypsy and Tatar slaves, continued to be coveted by the Hungarians. Nevertheless, after the Battle of Kosovo in Serbia in 1389, and the fall of Bulgaria in 1393, Wallachia also became an object of the Turkish sultan's interest. In 1394, the Turks invaded Wallachia, causing the voivode Mircea the Old to seek refuge with the Hungarians in Transylvania, and enabling a rival boyar to gain his throne. From 1395, the Wallachians began to pay a financial tribute to the Ottoman Turks. Although the Hungarians were not defeated by the Turks until 1526, the proximity of the Danubian principalities as Turkish vassals represented an enduring threat, and influenced the desire of the subsequent Hungarian rulers to wage crusades against the Ottoman Empire.   —*Gloria Fulton*

ADDITIONAL READING:

Castellan, Georges. *A History of the Romanians*. Boulder, Colo.: East European Monographs, 1989. A recent survey of Romanian history. Chapters 2 and 3 treat the origins and early development of the Romanians.

Chirot, Daniel. *Social Change in a Peripheral Society: The Creation of a Balkan Colony*. New York: Academic Press, 1976. A monograph describing the importance to the development of Wallachia of its location as a trading colony on the Danube.

Georgescu, Vlad. *The Romanians: A History*. Columbus: Ohio State University Press, 1991. A survey of Romanian history by a Romanian historian. Chapter 2 covers the Middle Ages.

Seton-Watson, R. W. *A History of the Roumanians: From Roman Times to the Completion of Unity*. Reprint. New York: Archon Books, 1963. Originally published in 1934, this work is a standard historical text on the formation of the Romanian nation-state.

Sugar, Peter F., ed. *A History of Hungary*. Bloom-ington: Indiana University Press, 1990. Chapter 5, written by Pal Angel, covers the age of the Angevins, 1301-1382.

SEE ALSO: 893, Beginning of Bulgaria's Golden Age; 896, Magyar Invasions of Italy, Saxony, and Bavaria; 955, Otto I Defeats the Magyars; 1389, Turkish Conquest of Serbia; 1442-1456, János Hunyadi Defends Hungary Against Ottoman Invaders.

1346
BATTLE OF CRÉCY

The Battle of Crécy not only establishes England as an important military power but also demonstrates that mounted knights and the age of chivalry are doomed.

DATE: August 26, 1346

LOCALE: Crécy, France

CATEGORIES: Science and technology; Wars, uprisings, and civil unrest

KEY FIGURES:

Edward III (1312-1377), king of England, 1327-1377

Philip VI (1293-1350), king of France, 1328-1350

SUMMARY OF EVENT. The Anglo-Norman kings of En-gland were so impressed with the powerful longbow they encountered in their military expeditions against Wales that they adopted it and ordered the inhabitants of every English village to practice its use on a regular basis. Thus the "Welsh" longbow had become the "English" longbow by 1346, when the Battle of Crécy occurred.

Longbows varied in length from slightly more than five and one-half feet to slightly less than six and one-half feet. The advantage of the longbow over its shorter cousins came from the increased leverage that resulted from draw-ing back its longer "arms." Knowledge of the principle involved was certainly no secret, but the longbow had significant disadvantages that limited its popularity. Its unwieldy length meant that the archer could carry few if any other weapons. He certainly could not put it over his back and use a sword in offensive operations. This limita-tion meant that it was unsuitable for any situations other than defensive battle. Perhaps more important, it was difficult to master without extensive practice, hence the royal order for regular training and practice.

Yew was the favored wood for longbow construction. Like the American aromatic cedar, the yew has an inner, red core of heartwood and an outer, white layer of sapwood. The former is strong under compression, while the latter has greater strength under tension. The bowyer took ad-vantage of these natural properties of the yew by splitting the bow staff from the log and shaping it in such a way that the red layer formed the "belly," which faced the archer in

use, and the white layer was on the "back" of the bow.

Arrows had to be straight to preserve their stability in flight and their accuracy. They were about thirty inches long with feathers, or "fletching," on one end to give stability in flight and a metal tip on the other. The favored tip shape was the "bodkin," which was a very elongated pyramid, square at the base and tapering to a point. On the fletched end was a notch, or "nock," made to receive the bowstring. To prevent repeated "nocking" from fraying the hemp bowstring, its central area had a thread wrap-ping. An archer might carry up to two dozen arrows, and an intelligent military commander would be careful to have plenty more in his baggage train.

Longbows had a "pull" of about eighty to one hundred pounds. They had an extreme range of more than one hundred yards and an effective range of about sixty yards. In other words, a good archer could expect to kill or disable an armored opponent out to sixty yards and could drop an arrow from a high trajectory on a general area as far as one hundred fifty yards away. It is difficult to be more precise, since much depended on the skill of the individual archer and weather conditions such as wind. A skilled man could shoot up to twelve arrows per minute, and this speed was the greatest advantage the longbow had over its major rival—the crossbow—at the Battle of Crécy.

The crossbow was even more powerful than the long-bow. Its power came from the sophisticated combination of materials in its much shorter bow. The bow was hardly more than two feet in length and was, essentially, a sand-wich of horn on the belly, wood in the middle, and animal sinew on the back. Just as with the longbow, this combina-tion provided materials strong under compression on the belly and strong under tension on the back but to a much greater degree. Most important, a crossbowman required little training. All of the crossbow's advantages over the longbow could not, however, compensate for one essential weakness: It was much slower to operate, and volume of fire is the most important battlefield feature of any missile weapon.

Many historians have claimed that the longbow caused a military revolution, beginning at the Battle of Crécy, by rendering the mounted knight obsolete. This is an exag-geration. The feudal system was already in decline be-cause of political, economic, and social developments before the Battle of Crécy. Even on the battlefield, the success of the longbow was a symptom more than a result. Although an individual on foot is almost helpless against an individual on horseback, formed infantrymen are prac-tically impervious to attack by cavalry as long as they maintain their formation. Newly forming centralized gov-ernments were acquiring the administrative and financial skills to field and maintain capable infantry.

The Battle of Crécy was the first important battle in the Hundred Years' War between England and France that began in 1337. King Edward III of England was actually closer by strict inheritance to the throne of France than King Philip VI, and Edward was eager to assert his rights through force of arms. A more substantial and deeper seated cause of the war was the attempt by King Philip to consolidate French territorial holdings and influence at the expense of England, which still had considerable land holdings and economic interests on the Continent. Hostile feelings and words led to open war by the late 1330's. The war proceeded in fits and starts with the French seeming to have the advantage until 1346, when Edward III mounted an invasion of Normandy. Philip came to defend his territory and the two forces met at Crécy on August 26, 1346.

The English had about seven thousand longbowmen, some two thousand men at arms (knights), and two or three thousand auxiliaries. Philip had at least twenty thousand men at arms—the flower of French chivalry, as is often said—and many other troops. Edward deployed his men on rising ground and awaited the French attack. He could hardly do otherwise, being so badly outnumbered and so dependent on the longbowmen who were useful only in defense. Fortunately for Edward, the French obliged by attacking and in a very inept way. As the men at arms rode onto the field in piecemeal fashion the sun was going down. Philip decided to wait until the next day to launch his attack after his men had rested and after they had all arrived, but he could not control the unwieldy mass, which continued to press forward despite his orders. He finally decided to make the best of a bad situation and ordered the attack.

Philip's Genoese crossbowmen led the assault. A brief rain shower fell on them, and this has led many historians to speculate that their wet bowstrings caused their poor performance. Whether or not this contributed, they could not withstand the more deadly shower of arrows that fell on them after the rain shower. The duke of Alençon, stationed behind the crossbowmen, decided they were acting in cowardly fashion when they hesitated and led the mounted men at arms in a charge over them. Neither side realized exactly what a toll the longbowmen were taking because of the dark, and the French continued to press on while the longbowmen continued to shoot into the confused mass at the foot of the rise. The horsemen charged fifteen times and the battle lasted until the "third quarter of the night." The next morning, the English discovered they had killed more than fifteen hundred French nobles and at least ten thousand others with a loss of less than one hundred on their side.

Although Crécy raised England's international reputation and led to considerable gains by Edward III, the war dragged on. In 1356, at the Battle of Poitiers, and again in 1415 at the Battle of Agincourt, the English were to win important victories with the aid of the longbow. By the end of the war, the proud mounted knights were no longer the dominant force on European battlefields. The age of chivalry was over, and the longbow had been a significant contributor to its demise. *—Philip Dwight Jones*

ADDITIONAL READING:

Burne, Alfred H. *The Crécy War: A Military History of the Hundred Years' War from 1337 to the Peace of Bretigny, 1360.* London: Eyre & Spottiswoode, 1955. A "drum and bugle" account of the battle and its aftermath in the first part of the Hundred Years' War.

Fuller, J. F. C. *The Decisive Battles of the Western World.* London: Eyre & Spottiswoode, 1954-1956. Contains a detailed account of the battle itself by one of the foremost military historians of the twentieth century.

McKisack, May. *The Fourteenth Century.* Oxford: Oxford University Press, 1959. Part of the Oxford History of England series, this large volume places the Hundred Years' War in context from an English perspective.

Myers, A. R. *A History of England in the Later Middle Ages.* London: Pelican, 1965. Also puts the war into a broader context but in the more concise form of a small paperback.

Seward, Desmond. *The Hundred Years' War: The English in France, 1337-1453.* New York: Atheneum, 1978. Probably the most readable account of the war.

SEE ALSO: 1429, Joan of Arc's Relief of Orléans; 1453, English Are Driven from France.

1347-1352
INVASION OF THE BLACK DEATH

The invasion of the Black Death creates physical and psychological devastation, bringing an end to the medieval period and Church domination and ushering in numerous social and economic reforms.

DATE: 1347-1352

LOCALE: Primarily western and central Europe

CATEGORIES: Environment; Health and medicine

KEY FIGURES:

Giovanni Boccaccio (1313-1375), Italian author of *The Decameron* (1349-1351), a series of graphic biographies explaining social dysfunction and class structure during the plague

Geoffrey Chaucer (c. 1343-1400), British author whose works *The Canterbury Tales* and *The Corbaccio*

describe various psychological and behavioral responses to the plague

Guy de Chauliac (1300-1368), French physician and author who stressed rational and professional courtesy, and who understood some of the demographics and social conditions that encouraged the spread of disease

Claudius Galen (129-c. 199), Greek physician and physiologist who expanded upon the Hippocratic four humors (blood, phlegm, and black and yellow bile)

Henry Knighton (died c. 1396), British chronicler who recorded economic and demographic results of the plague

William Langland (c. 1332-c. 1400), British poet whose *The Vision of William, Concerning Piers the Plowman* (c. 1395; known as *Piers Plowman*) describes rural sociocultural ramifications of population reduction

Jean de Venette (1308-1369), Carmelite friar who made many astute observations and descriptions of flagellism and widespread anti-Semitism

François Villon (1431-c. 1463), French criminal and brilliant poet who contended that cruelty and social dysfunction also prevailed with a general pursuit of happiness, a fascination with death, and festive funerals

SUMMARY OF EVENT. Apparently originating near Delhi in the 1330's, the plague spread to southern Asia by 1346, and to the cities of Kaffa and probably Constantinople by the end of the following year. Merchants traveling from Kaffa and probably from Constantinople effectively transmitted the plague to the ports of Genoa and Venice in northern Italy, to Messina in Sicily, and to Marseilles in southern France. The pandemic spread through Spain and France in 1348, arriving in England in the autumn of that year and eventually reaching Scandinavia and northern central Europe in 1349. Northern Russia first suffered its effects in 1352, after the plague had declined in western Europe. China experienced the disease between 1352 and 1369; Iceland and Cyprus were totally depopulated.

An increase in both maritime and overland trade facilitated the movement of the plague bacillus, and the southern European seaports were devastated first. Boats were loaded with two commodities: spices and disease-ridden rats. The "King of Terrors" ravaged populated areas so severely that at least one-fourth of Europe's inhabitants had died by 1350. Sometimes entire villages were depopulated by death, since sixty to eighty percent of those infected failed to survive. Half of Florence's ninety thousand people vanished; some two-thirds of the population of Siena and Hamburg died.

The spread of the black plague bacillus (*Yersinia pestis*) was facilitated when engorged, bacilli-infested fleas would leave their original animal hosts in search of new hosts, usually humans. The bite of the flea produced oval swellings called buboes. These chestnut-sized lumps commonly appeared near an area of lymph nodes, usually in the groin, the armpit, or the neck. The blackened color of these buboes gave the disease its common name—the Black Death. It appears that three types of plague existed. The first was the simple bubonic plague. The second and the most common type was pneumonic plague, which occurred when the bacillus invaded the lungs or was transmitted through exposure to a coughing plague victim. The third type was the always fatal septicemic plague, which occurred when the bacillus fully invaded the bloodstream and overwhelmed the nervous system before producing pustules.

Europe experienced great physical and mental anguish as whole families vanished. The plague created an even greater sense of demoralization, anomie, and relative deprivation, exacerbated by numerous viral epidemics, including measles, smallpox, influenza, dysentery, typhus, tuberculosis, and whooping cough. Medical treatment was

This medieval woodcut shows physicians studying the condition of a plague-stricken patient. During the initial outbreak of the Black Death, the infection was so virulent that most people died before they could seek medical care. (Archive Photos)

invariably irrational, even dangerous to the patient, as were numerous preventive procedures.

The practice of "sewage pharmacology" became widespread as people turned to unusual treatments in the hope of preventing the disease. Believing that strong odors could prevent transmission of the disease, some people would bathe daily in urine and even drank urine; others smeared human excrement on their clothing. Attempts were made to bottle flatulation; others allowed male goats to live in their houses, filling rooms with the malodorous smell of their urine. It was also the practice for people to hover over open latrines and inhale the stench. One witness reported "many were so courageous that they swallowed the pus from the mature boils in spoonfuls." Boils were incised, dried, and powdered for inhalation or administered orally in a drink.

Attempts at prevention assumed other procedures as when walls, furniture, and even a person's face and hands were washed in rose-water or vinegar. It was not an uncommon sight to see people with garlands, wearing nosegays, and even cloth masks with large noses stuffed with flowers, which were believed to act as a filter against miasma. Further evidence of this belief is revealed in the nursery rhyme "Ring Around the Rosey, Pocket Full of Posies," which signified the rose-colored swelling "ring" on the skin as an early stage of plague. Even the wearing of pointed shoes was avoided because such shoes were thought to resemble Satan's cloven hoof.

In keeping with Galenic medicine and the concept of humors, people were advised to avoid any excesses in eating, drinking, exercise, and even sexual relations. At the same time, many people felt doomed and frequently indulged in extreme forms of debauchery and antisocial behavior. Individuals and groups roamed streets robbing people or entering houses to rape and plunder. In Spain, the Tarrantella Dance (bite of the tarantula spider) was forbidden.

Mass hysteria became endemic to much of Europe. Various social movements became the focus of the people's frustration. In a display of piety, pilgrimages of the Brethren of the Cross or the Brotherhood of the Flagellants would go from village to village whipping themselves and others with metal-tipped leather thongs as penitence for presumed wrongs. This form of mortification of the flesh was actually based on an earlier concept of exorcism, one which the Church later came to despise. The Flagellants roamed throughout much of Europe, releasing criminals and patients from insane asylums.

A similar social movement was the so-called charisant mania, whereby hundreds, sometimes thousands, would dance and sing uncontrollably in village or city streets.

The sinister aspect of this mania was that some would dance themselves to death through exhaustion or trample others to death while performing awkward and erratic dances. Yet for some, the Dance of Death was not a psychological disorder but rather represented a later stage of plague, when the subcutaneous hemorrhaging created black blotches on the victim's skin. Eventually, the victim's central nervous system deteriorated, creating bizarre and painful neurological dysfunction and disorientation.

Unfortunately, another antisocial movement was the rise of anti-Semitism, particularly later in Germany and central Europe, although the first instances of widespread persecution were in Marseilles in 1348 when thousands of Jews were burned to death. The notion of anti-Semitism probably developed as early as the First Crusade (1096-1099), when the Catholic Church contended that Jews represented demons of Satan, poisoning the wells of plagued communities. By 1349, the number of persecutions had begun to decline, perhaps because the populace realized that Jews were also victims of the plague. With the decline of the Black Death in 1351, the persecution of the Jews waned.

The Black Death resulted in many lasting changes: better medical literature, programs of public sanitation, decline of feudalism and the manorial systems, end of the medieval period, and almost complete control of all ecclesiastical matters by the Catholic Church. For example, certain city governments imposed programs to prevent contagion and improved sanitation. Florence and Venice established commissions for public health in 1348; in the same year, the Italian city of Pistoia issued regulations on burial, clothing, and food to counter the spread of plague.

—John F. McGovern, updated by John Alan Ross

ADDITIONAL READING:

Campbell, Anna M. *The Black Death and Men of Learning*. New York: Columbia University Press, 1931. The author argues that education suffered a decline after the Black Death since the number as well as training of professors had deteriorated.

Coulton, George. *The Black Death*. New York: Robert M. McBride, n.d. In this work, published circa 1930, the author is convinced that the plague gave rise to the Protestant Reformation and was instrumental in major changes in land rights and sense of individualism.

Gasuet, Francis. *The Black Death of 1348 and 1349*. 2d ed. London: George Bell and Sons, 1908. A lucid treatment of the subject anticipating Coulton's thesis that the plague brought about a revolution in Church development.

Gottfried, Robert. *The Black Death: Natural and Human Disaster in Medieval Europe*. New York: Free Press,

1988. A thorough study of how the plague brought dramatic transformation to medieval Europe, particularly within the Church.

Shrewsbury, J. *A History of Bubonic Plague in the British Isles*. Cambridge, England: Cambridge University Press, 1970. Detailed descriptions of socioeconomic and demographic effects of the plague.

Twigg, Graham. *The Black Death: A Biological Reappraisal*. New York: Schocken Books, 1985. The author presents significant data to demonstrate that plague diseases produced clinical signs akin to anthrax, which was a major killer in medieval Europe.

Ziegler, Philip. *The Black Death*. London: Collins, 1969. A critical review of those major historians who argue the social and economic consequences of the plague.

SEE ALSO: 1350-1400, Petrarch and Boccaccio Recover Classical Texts; 1387, Chaucer Develops Vernacular Narrative in *The Canterbury Tales*; 1918-1919, Influenza Epidemic Strikes.

1347-1354
COLA DI RIENZO LEADS POPULAR UPRISING IN ROME

Cola di Rienzo leads a popular uprising in Rome against the aristocratic families of Rome, ruling the city as a dictator until he is murdered by the commoners who had supported him.

DATE: May 20, 1347-October 8, 1354

LOCALE: Rome

CATEGORIES: Social reform; Wars, uprisings, and civil unrest

KEY FIGURES:

Charles IV (1316-1378), king of Bohemia as Charles I, 1346-1378, and Holy Roman Emperor, 1355-1378

Clement VI (Pierre Roger; c. 1291-1352), Roman Catholic pope, 1342-1352

Innocent VI (Étienne Aubert; 1282-1362), Roman Catholic pope, 1352-1362

Cola di Rienzo (Niccolò di Lorenzo; 1313-1354), ruler of Rome, 1347 and 1354

SUMMARY OF EVENT. In 1309, Pope Clement V moved the headquarters of the papacy from Rome to Avignon, France, where it would remain until 1377. Although Rome was in the region of central Italy known as the Papal States and was therefore theoretically under the direct rule of the pope, the long absence of the papacy led to a struggle for power among Rome's aristocratic families.

Cola di Rienzo (a shortened version of his original name, Niccolò di Lorenzo) was an outspoken critic of the aristocrats. In 1343, he was a member of a delegation sent from Rome to Avignon to ask Pope Clement VI to return the papacy to Rome. Although Clement VI remained in Avignon, he appointed Cola di Rienzo to the post of notary of the civic treasury of Rome. He also declared 1350 to be a Holy Year, which would bring numerous pilgrims to Rome and help relieve the poverty of the Roman people.

On his return to Rome in 1344, Cola di Rienzo continued his public speeches denouncing the aristocrats. Although the common people were influenced by his oratory, the aristocrats failed to take him seriously. Some even amused themselves by inviting him to dinners, where they laughed at his verbal attacks. Secretly, Cola di Rienzo began planning a revolution with the commoners, financed by merchants who were eager to end the crime and bloodshed that filled Rome under the rule of the aristocrats.

On May 20, 1347, after attending a midnight mass at the church of Sant'Angelo in Peschiera, Cola di Rienzo led a group of his followers to the Capitoline Hill. Dressed in full armor with only his head bare, he made an impassioned speech against the aristocrats. A new constitution for Rome was read to the crowd, who accepted Cola di Rienzo as their leader. A few days later, he took the title of "tribune," from the title of an official of ancient Rome who served as a representative of the common people.

The aristocrats, intimidated by the number of Cola di Rienzo's supporters, some of whom bore weapons paid for by the merchants, were forced to swear loyalty to the new ruler of Rome. Cola di Rienzo proclaimed reforms of the financial, judicial, and political systems of Rome and enacted severe punishments for lawbreakers.

After these initial declarations, Cola di Rienzo announced his plan to unite Italy into a single nation. He sent representatives into all parts of Italy, inviting the rulers of its various regions to an assembly that would enact this goal. Many of these regional governments accepted the invitation, and the assembly began on August 1, 1347.

Following an elaborate ceremony in which he awarded himself a knighthood, Cola di Rienzo announced to the assembly that all the inhabitants of Italy were now Roman citizens and that Rome held jurisdiction over all other nations. He also declared that he and the pope held power over all other rulers. It seemed that Cola di Rienzo was attempting to transform Italy into a new Roman empire, with himself as emperor.

Many of Cola di Rienzo's followers withdrew their support because of his increasingly grandiose pronouncements. Meanwhile, the ousted aristocrats began gathering troops outside the city. On November 20, 1347, Cola di Rienzo's forces defeated the aristocrats' army, leaving eighty aristocrats dead.

Despite this victory, Cola di Rienzo continued to lose popular support. Although he had at first accepted Cola di Rienzo as the ruler of Rome, Pope Clement VI issued a decree declaring him a criminal and a heretic that the people of Rome should remove from power. Faced with his declining popularity as well as another uprising by the aristocrats, Cola di Rienzo resigned on December 15, 1347.

For two years, Cola di Rienzo lived as a hermit among monks in the mountains east of Rome. Meanwhile, the struggle between the aristocrats and the commoners continued. After the Holy Year, the aristocratic families seized all power in Rome, forcing the papal representative to flee. Encouraged by the pope, a group of Roman citizens appointed an elderly, respected Roman named Giovanni Gerroni as the ruler of Rome with the title of "rector" on December 26, 1351. He had not been in office long when he discovered a conspiracy plotting his downfall. Declaring himself unequal to the task of ruling Rome, he left the city.

The aristocrats took power again. Once again the commoners rose in rebellion, this time selecting Francesco Baroncelli as their leader. He proved to be no more effective against the aristocrats than the previous leader. Many Romans wished for the return of Cola di Rienzo. Despite his vanity and extravagant ambitions, he seemed to be the only popular leader capable of defeating the aristocrats.

In 1350, Cola di Rienzo traveled to the court of Charles IV, king of Bohemia (later to be the ruler of the Holy Roman Empire), in an attempt to win his aid in regaining power in Rome. Charles IV reported his visit to Pope Clement VI, who ordered him to be placed under the custody of the archbishop of Prague. Cola di Rienzo was again declared a heretic, given a death sentence, and held prisoner in Avignon beginning in August of 1352.

Clement VI died on December 6, 1352. The new pope, Innocent VI, was more sympathetic to Cola di Rienzo's cause and thought he might be useful in returning papal authority to Rome. Innocent VI lifted the charge of heresy and freed him from imprisonment. On August 1, 1354, Cola di Rienzo returned to Rome with the new title of "senator."

Cola di Rienzo's behavior during his second period as the ruler of Rome was even more dictatorial than before. Desperate for money to pay the soldiers who protected him from the aristocrats, he raised taxes to extremely high levels. He arrested wealthy merchants and forced their families to pay large ransoms for their release.

One of Cola di Rienzo's most notorious actions occurred when he arrested one of his supporters, Pandolfuccio di Guido dei Franchi, on suspicion of attempting to overthrow him. Without a trial, Cola di Rienzo had him beheaded. Many of the people of Rome had respected this man and were outraged by his execution. This act, along with heavy taxes and Cola di Rienzo's erratic behavior, turned many against him.

On October 8, 1354, a mob surrounded the palace in which Cola di Rienzo lived. He attempted to address the crowd from the balcony of the palace but could not be heard over their shouts. The mob began throwing stones at him and set fire to the wooden fortifications surrounding the palace. Cola di Rienzo attempted to escape by disguising himself to blend in with the crowd, but he was soon recognized and taken prisoner.

After confronting the crowd in silence for a time, Cola di Rienzo was stabbed with a sword by one of his former officials. The mob began to beat and tear at his body and his head was cut off. His corpse was left hanging by its feet for two days, then taken down and burned.

—*Rose Secrest*

ADDITIONAL READING:

Cheetham, Nicolas. "Avignon and the Great Schism (1305-1389)." In *Keepers of the Keys: A History of the Popes from Saint Peter to John Paul II*. New York: Charles Scribner's Sons, 1983. Describes the move of the papacy to Avignon and the career of Cola di Rienzo as seen by Clement VI.

Fleischer, Victor. *Rienzo: The Rise and Fall of a Dictator*. Port Washington, N.Y.: Kennikat Press, 1970. Reprint of a biography from 1948 which compares Cola di Rienzo to modern dictators.

Gregorovius, Ferdinand. *Rome and Medieval Culture*. Translated by Annie Hamilton. Edited by K. F. Morrison. Chicago: University of Chicago Press, 1971. An abridged version of the author's classic work *History of the City of Rome in the Middle Ages* (1871), including a detailed discussion of Cola di Rienzo.

Hibbert, Christopher. "Saints, Tyrants, and Anti-Popes." In *Rome: The Biography of a City*. New York: W. W. Norton, 1985. A colorful account of the life and times of Cola di Rienzo.

Wood, Diana. "Propriissima Sedes Beati Petri: The Problem of Old Rome." In *Clement VI: The Pontificate and Ideas of an Avignon Pope*. New York: Cambridge University Press, 1989. An account of the struggle between Clement VI and Cola di Rienzo.

SEE ALSO: 1302, Boniface VII Issues the Bull *Unam Sanctam*; 1347-1352, Invasion of the Black Death; 1831, Mazzini Founds Young Italy; 1848, Revolutions of 1848 in Italy; 1860, Garibaldi's Thousand "Redshirts" Land in Italy.

1350-1400
PETRARCH AND BOCCACCIO RECOVER CLASSICAL TEXTS

Petrarch and Boccaccio recover classical texts, bringing humanist ideals to the forefront of European education through the preservation and circulation of neglected manuscripts from the classical age.

DATE: c. 1350-1400

LOCALE: Florence and Naples, Italy; Avignon, France

CATEGORY: Cultural and intellectual history

KEY FIGURES:

Dante Alighieri (1265-1321), Italian poet and author of *The Divine Comedy*

Giovanni Boccaccio (1313-1375), Italian diplomat, poet, and storyteller, author of the *Decameron* (1350)

Geoffrey Chaucer (c. 1343-1400), English diplomat, poet, and author of *The Canterbury Tales*

Francesco Petrarch (or Petrarca; 1304-1374), Italian literary scholar, classicist, and author

Robert of Anjou (1278-1343), king of Naples, 1309-1343

SUMMARY OF EVENT. In 1350, Francesco Petrarch stopped over in Florence on his way to Rome for the mid-century Papal Jubilee. There, he met Giovanni Boccaccio who, like Petrarch, had already established himself as an innovative literary figure in Europe. Petrarch's reputation was reinforced by the *Canzoniere*—originally entitled *Rerum vulgarium fragmenta* and largely completed by 1335. This collection of 366 poems (317 sonnets, 29 canzoni, 9 sestine, 7 ballates, and 4 madrigals) represents a fusion of classical and Christian values. More important, it continued the enterprise, begun by Dante Alighieri, of writing in the vernacular—in this case, the refined Tuscan dialect of northern Italy.

Petrarch drew from numerous sources, chiefly the influential poets of Roman antiquity—Virgil, Horace, Catullus, Propertius, and especially Ovid. Augustine's moral precepts added a formidable coloring, as did Dante's *La vita nuova* (c. 1292; *The New Life*). The sprightly lyrical quality derives some of its vigor from the Provençal troubadours—notably Arnaut Daniel and Bernart de Ventadorn. In addition, courtly love resonances from Guido Cavalcanti's late thirteenth century poems are discernible. This extraordinary synthesis of biblical and classical themes inspired the humanist movement and contributed to Petrarch's celebrated moment of recognition on April 8, 1341, when he was crowned Poet Laureate of the Holy Roman Empire. This event was orchestrated by King Robert of Naples, perhaps the most dynamic patron of the arts during the formative years of Petrarch and Boccaccio.

Boccaccio's *Decameron* (1350) also relied upon classi-

Francesco Petrarch used his connections to the papal court at Avignon to travel in search of classical texts located in the libraries of European cathedrals and libraries. (Library of Congress)

cal sources and fourteenth century prose works. Among the latter, the *Gesta Romanorum*—a popular collection of tales and fables from antiquity that reached its final form during Boccaccio's lifetime—and the French *fabliaux* tradition represent noticeable influences. Boccaccio's Italian writings leading up to the *Decameron* reveal tendencies that clearly suggest the revival of classical literary modes. Early prose works from his Naples period of the 1330's, the *Filocolo* and the *Filostrato*, derive their energy from historical parallels. The *Ameto*, the *Fiammetta*, and the *Ninfale Fiesolano* from his Florentine period of the 1340's continue this pattern as Boccaccio added psychological and mythological elements to pastoral idylls.

The sensuality of these works can be traced to the Angevin court at Naples, where the chivalric codes of northern France were deeply embedded. Boccaccio's prose style, a mixture of classical decorum and robust local Italian color, became the model for Renaissance realists who admired the broad spectrum of his imagination, by which characters and social setting are vividly conveyed and at times viciously satirized.

Petrarch had a profound effect on Boccaccio's appreciation for classical writers. As Petrarch used his papal connections in Avignon to move around Europe visiting cathedrals and monasteries in search of ancient manuscripts, he developed a lively correspondence with Boccaccio. The two met regularly—in Milan (1359), Venice (1363 and 1367), and Padua (1368)—planning projects and trading books. Boccaccio translated into Italian the works of the Roman historian Titus Livius (Livy), studied the *Thebiad* of Statius, restored the reputation of Ovid, and wrote "eclogues" in imitation of Virgil. To Petrarch, he sent Dante's *The Divine Comedy*, Augustine's "Commentary on the Psalms of David," and excerpts from Cicero and Varro. Furthermore, Boccaccio popularized one of his favorite works, *The Metamorphoses* (better known as *The Golden Ass*) by Lucius Apuleius, and galvanized European interest in classical mythology in a series of Latin books written between 1350 and 1360.

Petrarch, on his part, elevated Seneca, Sappho, Cicero, Horace, and Quintilian to celebrated positions of esteem and contributed to new considerations of historical documentation by praising the accomplishments of Julius Caesar, Sallust, and Livy. Petrarch wrote a philological commentary on portions of Livy's *Decades* from a manuscript

In addition to inspiring Boccaccio's interest in vernacular writing, the Italian poet Dante Alighieri was the subject of a biography written by Boccaccio. (Library of Congress)

retrieved by Landolfo Coronna, one of his patrons. Many of the ideals of the humanist tradition concerning civic duty, eloquence, and moderation derive from Petrarch's study of lost manuscripts of Cicero's works—the *Pro Archia* and fragments of his letters—uncovered by Petrarch at Liège (1333) and at Verona (1345), respectively.

Petrarch and Boccaccio owned copies of Vitruvius' *De Architectura*, which they circulated. Developments in Renaissance architecture can be attributed to this effort. They also supervised the translations of Homer (the *Iliad* and the *Odyssey*) and Plato (the *Dialogues*) into Latin, along with annotations to the ecclesiastical chronicles of Eusebius. Petrarch continued to explore classical literature and history in several Latin books, notably *De viris illustribus*—an unfinished biography of famous Romans. Boccaccio concentrated on a *Life of Dante* (1355), which led to his appointment as a lecturer on Dante in Florence (1373). The scope and depth of the Latin writings of Petrarch and Boccaccio perhaps outweigh their contributions to the European vernacular traditions because they provided the essential materials for the blossoming of Humanism in the fifteenth century.

As Latinists and Italian lyric poets, Petrarch and Boccaccio paved the way for the secular spirit that imbues the work of Geoffrey Chaucer and a host of Renaissance vernacular writers. These authors attempted to capture, for the first time since classical antiquity, the complex world of human emotions seen freely from all sides, without class bias or religious restriction. They added a wealth of nuances and perspectives to the predetermined framework of Christian culture that houses their ideas. Chaucer's *The Canterbury Tales* (c. 1387), Boccaccio's *Decameron*, and, to a lesser extent, Petrarch's *Canzoniere* present a series of vignettes rooted in middle-class competitive practicality. Eroticism is equally as powerful as Christian morality, and the metaphysical dimensions of life are mirrors of worldliness.

The humanism articulated by Petrarch and Boccaccio introduced impulses at odds with scholastic thought, and thus it may be viewed as the mentality of a transitional phase, between the Medieval and the Modern. While discovering, editing, and restoring classical texts, Petrarch and Boccaccio also contributed to an imaginative understanding of ages past; this understanding gave classical literature a pedigree that it had not yet attained. Moreover, Petrarch and Boccaccio offered their contemporaries a new appreciation for the literary qualities of Greek, Roman, and early Christian authors, with a deeper sense of how they achieved their effects. As a result, humanist scholars were endowed with a finer vision of their own turbulent era.

—Robert J. Frail

ADDITIONAL READING:

Bergin, Thomas Goddard. *Petrarch.* New York: Twayne, 1970. This biographical portrait reinforces the wide influence that Petrarch generated in literary circles.

Bishop, Morris. *Petrarch and His World.* Bloomington: Indiana University Press, 1963. Examines Petrarch's inner circle of humanist scholars, their extravagant patrons, and their extensive contacts through the Avignon papacy. Includes selections from Petrarch's poems, essays, and correspondence.

Foster, Kenelm. *Petrarch: Poet and Humanist.* Edinburgh: Edinburgh University Press, 1987. A solid but academically predictable account of Petrarch's reputation.

Mazzotta, Giuseppe. *The World at Play in Boccaccio's "Decameron."* Princeton, N.J.: Princeton University Press, 1986. Connects the stories of the *Decameron* to commercial, legal, and political events in early fourteenth century culture.

Staples, Max. *The Ideology of the "Decameron."* Lewiston, N.Y.: Edwin Mellen Press, 1993. This wide-ranging study offers a fairly comprehensive account of Boccaccio's sources and demonstrates the classical depth established early in his writings.

Trinkhaus, Charles. *The Poet as Philosopher: Petrarch and the Formation of Renaissance Consciousness.* New Haven, Conn.: Yale University Press, 1979. These five essays examine the influence of Petrarch's Latin prose works on Renaissance humanism. Trinkaus presents a sociological inquiry into Petrarch's philosophic dualism.

Wilkins, Ernest Hat. *The Life of Petrarch.* Chicago: University of Chicago Press, 1961. This engaging profile by a renowned scholar includes references to Petrarch's abundant correspondence and studies the shifts in his thinking from the *Canzoniere* to the classical commentaries of his final years.

SEE ALSO: 1100-1300, Emergence of European Universities; 1150, Moors Transmit Classical Philosophy and Medicine to Europe; 1347-1352, Invasion of the Black Death; 1387, Chaucer Develops Vernacular Narrative in *The Canterbury Tales.*

1353
OTTOMAN EMPIRE ESTABLISHES FOOTHOLD IN RUMELIA

The Ottoman Empire establishes a foothold in Rumelia, pushing aside the Byzantines and heralding the beginning of the Ottoman advance into Europe.

DATE: 1353
LOCALE: Thrace

CATEGORIES: Expansion and land acquisition; Wars, uprisings, and civil unrest
KEY FIGURES:
Anne of Savoy, Byzantine empress and mother of John V Palaeologus
Orhan (Okhran) Gazi (c. 1288-c. 1360), second ruler of the Ottoman dynasty, 1324-1359
John V Palaeologus (1332-1391), Byzantine emperor, 1341-1391
John VI Cantacuzenus (1292-1383), co-emperor of the Byzantine Empire, 1341-1355
Stefan Dušan (1308-1355), king of Serbia, 1331-1346, and emperor of the Serbs and Greeks, 1346-1355
Süleyman Pasha (died 1357), son of Orhan

SUMMARY OF EVENT. Ottoman rule in Anatolia (modern Turkey) expanded more or less continuously at the expense of both the Byzantine Empire and other Anatolian Turkoman states during the thirteenth century. By 1330, the Ottomans had made the city of Brusa (Bursa), located about sixty miles south of Constantinople across the Sea of Marmora, their capitol. By 1345, they controlled the entire eastern shore of the Bosphorous, Sea of Marmora, and Dardanelles. Here, they were blocked, despite their complete domination of the Byzantine army, because there was no Ottoman navy.

The long Byzantine recession was characterized by repeated civil conflict, including military revolts. The empire also became more narrowly "Greek" in both religion and politics, thus undermining the loyalty of Slavs and others. Both the "legitimate" emperors and their challengers habitually employed mercenaries, including Ottomans and other Turkomans. In many cases, these mercenaries were "paid" by being allowed to sack segments of imperial territory. In other cases, they were accepted as vassals on imperial lands, or territory was ceded outright to them. Finally, the Venetians and Genoese gradually took over what had been Byzantine commerce.

When Andronicus III, the Byzantine emperor, died in June of 1341, he had not yet proclaimed or crowned his nine-year-old son John as co-emperor. This situation left the succession in doubt, but John Cantacuzenus, Andronicus' grand domestic (prime minister), claimed the regency and moved into the imperial palace in an attempt to organize a smooth transition of power. As grand domestic, Cantacuzenus had directed the empire's affairs for thirteen years and several times had declined Andronicus' invitations to become co-emperor. Cantacuzenus' claim to the regency, however, was contested by Patriarch Calecas and by Andronicus' widow, Anne of Savoy. As a result, the three jointly conducted the government. After a month, however, Cantacuzenus was called on to defend the empire against Serbian, Bulgarian, and Turkish incursions. After his success, he returned to Constantinople, where a delegation from the Morea waited on him, offering to return the principality of Acahaia to the empire. Following this opportunity, Cantacuzenus took his army into Thrace in September of 1341. During his absence, Empress Anne, Patriarch Calecas, and others raised a conspiracy against him. The patriarch assumed the regency, and the empress sent a dispatch relieving Cantacuzenus of command and disbanding his army. In addition, a mob destroyed his property and dispossessed his family. When the order for his dismissal reached him in the field, the army staged a revolt and proclaimed Cantacuzenus as emperor on October 26, 1341. In response, John V Paleologus was crowned in Hagia Sophia, Cantacuzenus was excommunicated, and civil war began.

Cantacuzenus first sought aid from an old ally, Umur Bey, the emir of Aydin (a Turkoman maritime principality near modern Smyrna or İzmir), who unfortunately was too far away to help in the immediate crisis. Thus, Cantacuzenus sought help from the Serbian leader Stefan Dušan, who immediately provided mercenaries. Later, in 1342-1343, Umur arrived and tipped the balance in favor of Cantacuzenus in Thessaly and Thrace. In return, Umur was allowed to ravage Macedonia, where he accumulated much booty. Umur Bey, however, died in 1344, and Aydin quickly disintegrated. Meanwhile, Stefan Dušan turned on Cantacuzenus and began advancing in Macedonia. Cantacuzenus then sought assistance from the Ottomans after Orhan captured Canicola (Çanakkale) on the south shore of the Hellespont opposite Gallipolli. Orhan then led approximately fifty-five thousand soldiers into Thrace and conquered the Black Sea north and west of Constantinople, defeating Empress Anne's armies. In return for Orhan's assistance, Cantacuzenus allowed men led by Orhan's son, Süleyman, to ravage Thrace and Gallipolli at will during 1345 and 1348. In response to Stefan Dušan's decision to crown himself emperor of the Serbs and Greeks on Easter, 1346, Cantacuzenus had himself crowned emperor with John V Paleologus as co-emperor. In 1346, Cantacuzenus also formalized his alliance with the Ottomans by giving his daughter Theodora to Orhan in marriage. On February 2, 1347, he forced his way into Constantinople, where he compelled the marriage of his second daughter, Helen, to John V Paleologus and was again crowned co-emperor with John in May of 1347.

In 1349, Stefan Dušan appeared at the gates of Salonica, and Cantacuzenus again sought Orhan's aid. Orhan sent his son, Süleyman Pasha, with an additional twenty thousand Ottoman cavalry, who relieved Salonica by dislodging Dušan's forces from the surrounding coastal cities

of Macedonia. These troops, with Orhan's approval, then withdrew with considerable loot. Orhan then aided the Genoese against their commercial rivals, the Venetians; in the process, he also fought against Cantacuzenus. When the Venetians and the Bulgarians then announced in favor of John V Paleologus, Cantacuzenus called for additional Ottoman reinforcements. Robbing the churches of Constantinople to pay Orhan, Cantacuzenus also promised Orhan a fortress in Thrace. With Orhan's assistance, Cantacuzenus attacked John V Paleologus, defeating a joint Bulgarian-Serbian army at Dimotica in 1352. In return, Orhan was given the fort of Çimpe (modern Tzympe), between Gallipolli and the Aegean Sea, and sent Süleyman across the Hellespont to occupy the fortress in 1353. Soon after, an earthquake destroyed part of the walls of Gallipolli, and Süleyman promptly captured that fortress as well.

In 1353, Süleyman advanced northward, capturing towns as far north as Tekirdağ (modern Rodosto), located some eighty miles west of Constantinople on the north shore of the Sea of Marmora, and established permanent Ottoman rule in the region. This was done with the aid of the Genoese who, seeking to displace the Venetians from their dominant commercial position within the Byzantine Empire, signed an alliance with Orhan in 1354. Cantacuzenus strongly objected, arguing that the Ottomans had only been given permission to ravage and that Çimpe had been given to them only as a temporary base. Orhan was willing to order his son to leave Çympe, but replied that Islamic law forbade surrendering lands conquered by the faithful. Thus, the fortress of Gallipolli became the base from which the initial Ottoman raids and conquests of Rumelia were mounted.

Süleyman made further raids throughout the western half of Thrace, reaching Corlu, Luleburgaz, Malkara, and Tekirdağ, making these locations serve as bases for more distant raids. Cantacuzenus called on the Serbians and Bulgarians for aid, but was forced from the throne in 1355 for his part in bringing the Ottomans into Thrace. John V Paleologus regained full control of the empire, but he was unable to dislodge the Ottomans from Europe. John was compelled to recognize Orhan's Thracian conquest in 1359 in return for promises to allow food and supplies to be brought into Constantinople. Orhan then began repopulating Thrace with Turkoman nomads imported from Anatolia, thus solidifying Ottoman occupation of parts of Thrace. Süleyman died in a hunting accident in 1357, and Orhan died two years later. Further Ottoman advances thus were led by Orhan's second son, Murad, who had succeeded Süleyman as rule of the Ottoman borderlands in Rumelia.

The Ottoman conquest of Rumelia and the remainder of the Balkans followed the pattern established in Thrace. A warrior caste known as the Ghazis ranged through the Ottoman borderlands, continually raiding into as yet unoccupied territory. States outside of the empire were supplied with mercenaries who were rewarded with rights to raid or were granted territory upon which to settle. States accepting Ottoman suzerainty generally were left in peace and protected from their neighbors. Peasants in conquered territory, for the most part, were left on their lands. Citizens of citadels or towns refusing to surrender were largely put to the sword or sold into slavery upon defeat.

The Ottoman conquest of Thrace also left Constantinople closely surrounded and in vassalage to the Ottoman sultan. With its commerce in the hands of the Genoese and Venetians, the city became more and more impoverished. Despite its impregnable walls, Constantinople had essentially placed itself at the mercy of the Ottomans.

—*Ralph L. Langenheim, Jr.*

ADDITIONAL READING:

Inalcïck, Halil. *The Ottoman Empire: The Classical Age, 1300-1600*. Translated by Norman Itzkowitz and Colin Imber. New Rochelle, N.Y.: Aristide D. Caratzas, 1973. Translated from Turkish, this source is heavily oriented toward the cultural and political history of the period.

_____. *The Ottoman Empire: Conquest, Organization, and Economy*. London: Variorum Reprints, 1978. Includes articles on Ottoman methods of conquest and the conquest of Edirne.

Kinross, Lord. *The Ottoman Centuries: The Rise and Fall of the Turkish Empire*. New York: William Morrow, 1977. A readable history of the Ottoman Empire that touches on its beginnings.

Norwich, John Julius. *Byzantium: The Decline and Fall*. New York: Alfred A. Knopf, 1996. A noted scholar, Norwich provides a comprehensive history of the Byzantine Empire up through the Ottoman capture of Constantinople in 1453.

Shaw, Stanford. *History of the Ottoman Empire and Modern Turkey*. Volume 1: *Empire of the Gazis: The Rise and Decline of the Ottoman Empire, 1280-1808*. Cambridge, England: Cambridge University Press, 1976. A short but detailed discussion of the initial Ottoman advance into Europe.

SEE ALSO: 1389, Turkish Conquest of Serbia; 1442-1456, János Hunyadi Defends Hungary Against Ottoman Invaders; 1536, Turkish Capitulations Begin; 1683, Ottoman Turks Are Defeated at Vienna.

1356
THE "GOLDEN BULL"

The "Golden Bull" reiterates the power of the electors of the Holy Roman Empire.

DATE: January 10, 1356, and December 25, 1356
LOCALE: Nuremberg, Germany, and Mete, France (then in the Holy Roman Empire)
CATEGORIES: Laws, acts, and legal history; Religion
KEY FIGURE:
Charles IV (1316-1378), king of Bohemia as Charles I, 1347-1378, and Holy Roman Emperor, 1355-1378

SUMMARY OF EVENT. Policies decreed in the Golden Bull of 1356 were intended to resolve constitutional problems remaining from the reign of Charles II's predecessor as Holy Roman Emperor, Louis of Bavaria. These problems concerned disputed claims to certain electorates of the Holy Roman Empire, the powers and functions of the electors, and papal prerogatives to decide the validity of elections and confer imperial authority on the elected candidate. Traditionally, the seven electors of the empire chose one of the German princes as king, who then usually went before the pope to be crowned emperor. After an Avignon pope refused to confirm claim to the *emperium*, the electors issued, in 1338, the Declaration of Rense and the ordinance *Licet Juris* proclaiming a prince's election as German king as tantamount to his election as emperor. Although the electors conceded the pope's right to crown the emperor, they rejected the assumption that the election required papal confirmation or that the emperor's authority stemmed from the pope.

During the medieval period, the Holy Roman Empire was beset by the intervention of France and the Avignon papacy. Behind a papacy seeking to meddle in imperial elections lurked a French monarch who hoped to secure territorial gains at the expense of the Holy Roman Empire in both the Rhoneland and the Rhineland. Thus Emperor Charles IV's German pacification problem was greatly facilitated by serious French losses at the hands of the English in the opening phases of the Hundred Years' War which broke out in 1238. The mutual desires of both the Avignon popes and the kings of France to benefit at the expense of imperial Germany thus were less threatening because the Avignon popes were henceforward supported by a weakened France.

Deterioration of Louis' popularity and support after 1338 finally enabled the papacy to depose him in favor of the Luxemburger, Charles of Bohemia, in 1346. Charles was elected emperor in July, 1346, but was not formally crowned in Rome by a papal legate until 1355, and only upon renouncing interference in Italian affairs.

One of Charles's basic intentions was to secure internal peace in Germany. He had already quelled one great disturbing element, the disgruntled Wittelsbach dynasty, by consolidating his own authority in Germany between 1346 and 1354. By strengthening the electoral process, perhaps future schisms might be contained.

Immediately after returning from Italy, Charles summoned a Reichstag, or diet, at Nuremberg. There, he presented proposals for a constitutional settlement clarifying membership in the electoral college and defining the territorial powers of princes governing territories officially designated as imperial electorates. Accepted by the Reichstag, these proposals were promulgated by Emperor Charles on January 10, 1356; together with a supplement approved by the Reichstag of Metz on December 25 of the same year. These acts comprise the "Golden Bull," so called after the golden seal affixed to important imperial documents.

To avoid long disrupting vacancies of the throne, the edict provided that the archbishop of Mains was to communicate with his fellow electors within one month after the emperor's death and summon them to appear within three months at Frankfort to choose a successor. Furthermore, subjects of the Holy Roman Empire were required to facilitate safe passage of the electors. To avoid misunderstandings and bickering, electors who failed to appear or send proxies forfeited their votes. To assure results, electors were required to remain in Frankfort until they named a successor. If they failed to reach a decision within thirty days, they were to be fed thereafter on bread and water. A majority vote constituted a valid election, which would be declared unanimous so as to preclude double elections.

The Golden Bull reaffirmed the right of the seven traditional electoral princes to choose the German king. The decree designated the seven electors by name and bestowed semiregal autonomy, immune from imperial jurisdiction, upon their principalities. All electoral territories were indivisible and retained their vote permanently. In the case of lay electorates, the law of primogeniture was invoked to exclude rival claimants for the same title and its attendant vote. The electors were granted full right to all metal and salt mines on their lands and to the taxes payable by Jews for protection. The electors also could coin their own money. No appeal would be recognized from an electoral court to any higher court of the empire. Finally, the bull forbade the formation of leagues of cities except under the emperor's patronage. The Golden Bull, seeking to eliminate papal interference in imperial elections and politics, stipulated that a simple majority of the seven votes conferred unqualified authority as emperor from the moment of an emperor's election. Designation of the count palatine of the Rhine and the duke of Saxony as regents during any

interregnum automatically excluded the pope's claim to act as vicar in such a period. These constitutional procedures of the Golden Bull thus ended the pope's authority in German affairs. They were Charles's response to his earlier exclusion by the papacy from Italy.

The Golden Bull of 1356 had several far-reaching effects on subsequent German history. In the first place, the Holy Roman Empire, by its prior withdrawal from Italy abandoned its universalism so that by the second half of the fifteenth century it became popular in the Germanies to speak of the "Holy Roman Empire of the German Nation." Charles IV designed the Golden Bull to strengthen his external position with respect to the pope. Also, recognition of the electors sovereignty created a conservative force contributing to maintaining peace among the German states. The edict did much to undermine the emperor's internal position, however, because it made the electoral princes the first estate of the empire. Almost immediately, the nonelectoral princes claimed the same sovereign rights, including the principles of indivisibility and primogeniture, enjoyed by the electors. Thus in 1359, Duke Rudolph IV of Habsburg Austria arbitrarily bestowed upon his house the so-called major privileges. Among other things, these privileges made the duchy of Austria an archduchy independent of the empire with the Habsburg lands indivisible. Other states, such Wurtemberg, Lippe, and Baden, soon did the same, adopting the principles of primogeniture and the indivisibility of principalities as well as privileges preventing recourse from electoral courts to the imperial *Hoffgerticht*. By 1500, most princes managed to consolidate their territorial authority at the expense of the emperor and the local aristocracy. Thus Charles, in his quest for peace, acknowledged the division within Germany and the futility of attempting to maintain a centralized monarchy. The electors of the Holy Roman Empire became upholders of the status quo, working with the emperor to preserve peace within the empire.

The Golden Bull, while containing some innovations, actually legally confirmed historical developments dating from the late eleventh century. Its effect was to accelerate further development of German particularism, thus blocking all attempts to unify Germany until well into the nineteenth century. It can be asserted that historical experiences following the Golden Bull were so firmly rooted in the German memory that they "constituted an iron framework, a mold so firm that it shaped subsequent German efforts to deal with contemporary problems as late as 1939. The Germany of the First Reich, the Holy Roman Empire, had a direct impact on the attitudes of the late Second and Third Reichs.

Not only did the provisions of the Golden Bull relate to international conditions impinging on Germany but its ultimate impact was international, since it encouraged a shift in the medieval theory of world government. Since 962, the emperor and pope had been, in theory, twin depositories of God's authority exercised through states. In breaking the imperial and papal interdependence, the ideal of Charlemagne and Otto was relinquished in favor of a secular justification for sovereignty, a move facilitating rationalization of the later system of the authority of states which emerged fully in the seventeenth century.

—Edward P. Keleher,
updated by Ralph L. Langenheim, Jr.

ADDITIONAL READING:

Barraclough, Geoffrey. *The Origins of Modern Germany*. 2d rev. ed. Oxford: Basil Blackwell, 1947. Probably the most useful account of German history in the English language.

De Booulay, F. R. H. *Germany in the Later Middle Ages*. London: Athlone Press, 1983. Includes a brief description of the Golden Bull, its purpose and result.

Ferguson, Wallace K. *Europe in Transition, 1300-1520*. Boston: Houghton Mifflin, 1962. This study of the Renaissance contains discussions of the background to the Golden Bull.

Kitchin, Martin. *The Cambridge Illustrated History of Germany*. New York: Cambridge University Press, 1996. Emphasizes cultural as well as political history, easy reading.

Waugh, W. T. "Germany: Charles IV." In *The Cambridge Medieval History*, Vol. 7 (chapter 5), edited by J. R. Tanner et al. Cambridge, England: Cambridge University Press, 1932. Discusses constitutional problems which Charles IV attempted to resolve in the Golden Bull.

SEE ALSO: 955, Otto I Defeats the Magyars; 1152, Frederick Barbarossa Is Elected King of Germany; 1156, Emergence of Austria; 1519, Charles V Is Elected Holy Roman Emperor; 1740, Accession of Frederick the Great.

1373-1410
JEAN FROISSART COMPILES HIS CHRONICLES

Jean Froissart compiles his Chronicles, *offering a vivid panorama of an age in transition that relies for its inspiration on waning codes of chivalry and a growing spirit of secular humanism.*

DATE: 1373-1410
LOCALE: England, France, Flanders, and Burgundy
CATEGORY: Cultural and intellectual history

KEY FIGURES:
Charles V (1337-1380), king of France, 1364-1380
Charles VI (1368-1422), king of France, 1388-1422
Edward III (1312-1377), king of England, 1327-1377
Edward, the Black Prince (1330-1376), Prince of Wales and eldest son of Edward III
Jean Froissart (c. 1337-c. 1404), Flemish poet, court historian, and secretary to Philippa of Hainaut, 1361-1366
John II (1319-1364), king of France, 1350-1364
John of Gaunt (1339-1399), duke of Lancaster and fourth son of Edward III
Philip the Bold (1342-1404), duke of Burgundy
Philippa of Hainaut (c. 1314-1369), queen of England, 1328-1369
Richard II (1366-1400), king of England, 1377-1399, and son of Edward, the Black Prince

SUMMARY OF EVENT. Jean Froissart entered the service of Margaret of Hainaut sometime between 1350 and her death in 1356. This was the first of many court appointments that enabled Froissart to establish a network of contacts in aristocratic circles. In 1362, he went to England to serve as secretary to Philippa of Hainaut, wife of Edward III. Froissart remained in Phillipa's entourage until her death in 1369. During these years of service, Froissart traveled to Scotland, France, Spain, and Italy. While in England, he present to the court a verse chronicle of the Battle of Poitiers (1356) and continued to write traditional poetry. Under the patronage of Wenceslas I of Luxembourg, duke of Brabant, Froissart received a position as rector of a small parish from 1373 to 1384. There, he began to formulate his principal literary and historical accomplishment: the four books entitled *Chroniques de France, d'Engleterre, d'Ëscoce, de Bretaigne, d'Espaigne, d'Italie, de Flandres et d'Alemaigne* (1373-1410; known simply as the *Chronicles*).

Froissart contributed to the formation of French historiography that began with the Crusades. In this tradition, the difference between chronicle and history depended upon the amount of information supplied. Chronicles, particularly those following the thirteenth century *annalist* method developed at the monastery of Saint-Denis, present a simplified narrative, whereas a historical approach demanded greater depth and detailed descriptions. Thus, Froissart relied not only upon original documents but also on eyewitness accounts and interviews. Once Froissart's reputation was established, members of the aristocracy sought to provide him with the financial resources and protection necessary to gather data. Even though he was a priest, Froissart was at ease in sophisticated society, and the *Chronicles* reflect the mannerisms, speech, dress, and value systems that characterize the period.

The *Chronicles* cover significant events in European history from 1326 until 1400. Book 1, completed in 1373, begins with the 1327 coronation of Edward III in England and the accession of Philip VI of Valois to the crown of France in 1328, thus setting the stage for the Hundred Years' War. This first volume was later revised to include events up to 1379 and serves as a valuable indicator of Froissart's methodic development as a historian. Book 2, written between 1385 and 1388, recapitulates the events of the last years of the preceding volume, with new information added, and concludes with the peace treaty of Tournai agreed upon in December, 1385.

Book 3, finished in 1392, recites events that had occurred since 1382, but gives a fuller account of them. This volume ends in 1389 with a three-year truce concluded between France and England. In his study of the political events in Portugal between 1383 and 1385 that led to the invasion launched by John of Gaunt, Froissart made considerable use of Portuguese narratives and anecdotal information provided by Gascon knights who served under Edmund Cambridge, duke of York.

The first fifty chapters of book 4 follow closely upon the material of book 3 as Froissart reexamined the political machinery of France under Charles VI. In 1392, a series of truces between England and France were announced, and Froissart took advantage of this opportunity to visit England for three months under the patronage of William, count of Ostrevant, a cousin of Richard II. Froissart was well received by Richard, but felt uncomfortable in what he sensed was a highly unstable environment. Thus, book 4 recounts the confusion in England leading to the deposition of Richard in 1399 and his death the following year.

The *Chronicles* do not constitute a formal history of the aristocracy, yet Froissart used a process of selection in order to demonstrate significant acts of gallantry, diplomacy, and heroism. Hence, he overlooked issues that attracted the attention of other chroniclers—administration of estates, enactment of laws, and collection of taxes. Nevertheless, Froissart commented openly on French policy during the reign of Charles V, on the relationship between the French monarchy and the vassals of Brittany and Flanders, and on the papal schism. These brief personal judgments reveal the techniques of composition and variations found in the different manuscripts of the *Chronicles*. The mobility evident in these texts is most likely the result of collaboration with other compilers who may have had a considerable part in the elaboration of certain episodes. Thus, the form of the *Chronicles* is derivative of the Arthurian romances, which usually included a fair number of overlapping accounts.

Froissart was an insightful observer of strategic warfare. One of his intentions was to give a faithful account of siege warfare and pitched battles. He commanded a wide military vocabulary, which he used to document changes in fourteenth century combat. He observed that warriors were motivated less by nationalism than by personal honor or monetary gain. One-to-one encounters on horseback no longer had the advantage over the use of well-disciplined archers. Froissart's saga of military exploits stresses individual action, yet his accounts make it clear that in large engagements, the victor was usually the side that managed some degree of coordinated tactics.

Froissart often repeated his contention that the purpose of the *Chronicles* was to illustrate "les grans merveilles et les beaux faits d'armes" (heroic exploits and military prowess). He accomplished this aim with astonishing regularity despite errors in topology and inconsistencies in dating. There is no attempt to outline historical patterns; instead, a strong emphasis on human factors, along with Froissart's objectivity, political acumen, variety, and poetic effects, gives the *Chronicles* a dramatic flair that is not always evident in historical works produced by his contemporaries. The scope and dynamism of Froissart's observations and his effort to create a social tableau of fourteenth century culture have contributed to his reputation as a narrative historian who compares favorably with Herodotus.

Froissart observed the decline of chivalry as the concept of courtesy often degenerated into greed and meaningless pageantry. His description of the tournament held at Smithfield in 1390 under the aegis of Richard II implies that courtesy had become a code of etiquette observed by members of the upper class in dealing with one another; it was rarely associated with the protection of the weak by the strong. Froissart did not openly take sides in the conflicts of knights, although in the evolution of the *Chronicles* there are shifts in partisanship from the English to the French, and, in book 4, to the Burgundian side. He consistently chose to accentuate moderation as an ideal, exemplified by the conduct of Philip the Bold. Although the Black Prince was the hero of the Battle of Poitiers, Froissart criticized the massacre of civilians at Limoge (1370), just as he condemned the brutality of Edward III's treatment of the burghers of Calais in 1347. In general, Froissart was concerned with deeds and actions, not with biography. Because of his accomplished literary talent, the portraits of the protagonists of the *Chronicles* are imbued with a legendary quality.

Froissart often invoked divine Providence to justify the outcome of events. His philosophical observations reveal a trust in social order controlled by a just prince who watches over the commonweal. His accounts of the *Jacquerie* movement in France (1358) and the English Peasants' Revolt of 1381 clearly indicate that urban disintegration was a threat to national stability. Nevertheless, his portrayal of John Ball, the vagrant priest who incited the English revolt, conveys a well-intentioned sympathy for lower-class misery. Froissart's ability to synthesize epic conflicts, like the struggle for dominance in Europe between the Plantagenet and Valois dynasties, gives the *Chronicles* their distinctive pedigree. The comparison of the Last Crusade, which ended in the defeat of the French at Nicopolis, to the French epic *La Chanson de Roland* implied that the history of Europe was irrevocably changed.

The *Chronicles* benefited greatly from the advent of the printing press, and in the hundred years after Froissart's death at least ten editions appeared, including a Latin abridgment—which was, in turn, translated into English, French, and Dutch. This transmission made the work available to humanist scholars and aristocratic readers across Europe who considered it a sign of prestige to own a copy. By the mid-sixteenth century, the *Chronicles* emerged as the most widely read account of the first half of the Hundred Years' War.   —*Robert J. Frail*

ADDITIONAL READING:

Ainsworth, Peter F. *Jean Froissart and the Fabric of History: Truth, Myth, and Fiction in the "Chroniques."* New York: Oxford University Press, 1991. An impressive, comprehensive account of Froissart's ability to weave an intricate narrative out of such diverse strands of information.

Archambault, Paul. *Seven French Chroniclers: Witnesses to History.* Syracuse, N.Y.: Syracuse University Press, 1974. Contains an informative essay on Froissart that places him within the context of the French *annalist* tradition.

Damus, Joseph. *Seven Medieval Historians.* Chicago: Nelson-Hall, 1982. Damus' thirty-five-page chapter on Froissart emphasizes a conception of history as a conflict of interest among individuals of rank and privilege.

Palmer, J. J. N., ed. *Froissart: Historian.* Totowa, N.J.: Boydell Press, 1981. This work, with ten chapters—two written in French—represents an appraisal of Froissart's technique in light of modern historical scholarship.

Tuchman, Barbara. *A Distant Mirror: The Calamitous Fourteenth Century.* New York: Alfred A. Knopf, 1978. A spirited and kaleidoscopic re-creation of European culture during the Hundred Years' War.

SEE ALSO: 1346, Battle of Crécy; 1381, Wat Tyler Leads Peasants' Revolt.

1377-1378
JOHN WYCLIFFE IS CONDEMNED FOR ATTACKING CHURCH AUTHORITY

John Wycliffe is condemned for attacking Church authority and advocating a separation of church and state, but a number of theological reforms which he propounds are later adopted by the Protestant Reformers of the sixteenth century.

DATE: 1377-1378

LOCALE: Oxford and London, England

CATEGORIES: Government and politics; Religion

KEY FIGURES:

John of Gaunt (1340-1399), the fourth son of King Edward III and an early and staunch supporter of Wycliffe

Marsiglio of Padua (c. 1275-1342), political theoretician who influenced markedly the young Wycliffe's conceptions of state and sovereignty

Simon of Sudbury (died 1381), archbishop of Canterbury who summoned Wycliffe to answer charges at Lambeth Palace in 1378

William of Ockham (c. 1285-1349), Oxford philosopher and political thinker whose work strongly influenced Wycliffe

John Wycliffe (c. 1320-1384), Oxford professor and English ecclesiastical reformer

SUMMARY OF EVENT. John Wycliffe (also spelled Wyclif), born in the early 1320's, was an English ecclesiastic and statesman of the first order. His early life, partly spent preparing himself at Oxford for an ecclesiastical career, saw England in the throes of great changes. Everywhere an air of restlessness prevailed as a result of the long and costly Hundred Years' War with France, to which the Black Death (bubonic plague) added social, physical, and psychological horrors. A rising middle class caused dislocations of society, and the increasingly heavy taxation levied upon England by an unsympathetic papal court at Avignon aroused national resentments. Wycliffe, quick in mind, tenacious of memory, and profound in religious sympathies, hungered for security in a cleansed Church. He carried out his campaign for a reformed Church both as an academic and as a popular preacher. He was ordained a priest in 1355 and established himself as a popular preacher. In 1374, the Crown presented him with the rectory of Lutterworth in Leicestershire which would serve as the base of his reform movement until his death. Additionally, however, he continued his academic training and accepted a position a Oxford where he lectured with few interruptions from 1360 to 1381. He served as a member of the famous Good Parliament, and early advo-

JOHN WYCLIFFE IS CONDEMNED FOR ATTACKING CHURCH AUTHORITY

cated English national resistance to unjust financial claims made by the papacy. His work, *De Civili Dominio* (on civil lordship), presented the arguments that were used by the Good Parliament to resist papal claims.

While it is extremely difficult to trace the precise course of Wycliffe's intellectual maturation and the development of his controversial views, his impact upon his contemporaries was so great that he became an intellectual institution among European liberals and reformers by the time of his death in 1384. His initial attacks on the Church focused on the abuse of Church power. Skeptical of the famous Donation of Constantine, Wycliffe was firmly against the Roman clergy possessing either secular property or office. As a close corollary, Wycliffe later held that the Church ought not to interfere in the secular affairs of Christians, least of all in the affairs of Christian princes who were themselves ordained by God to their high offices. Finally, Wycliffe argued that secular rulers had a moral obligation to restrain the excesses of clergymen who trafficked in secular matters, and supported the right of civil authorities to confiscate the properties of clerics that were improperly attained or legally misused. He was supported in these attacks and received political protection from John of Gaunt who shared his anticlerical views.

Wycliffe's criticisms escalated following the Great Schism. The French, angered by the appointment of Urban VI as pope, appointed their own pope, Clement VII, leading to a conflict in Church authority. Angered by the obvious political intrigue in Church politics, Wycliffe gradually evolved a series of doctrines which served effectively to undermine the whole structure of the organized Church. In pamphlets and lectures he began to attack historical papal claims and prerogatives in both the religious and the secular spheres. He questioned the time-honored concept of Petrine supremacy and the power of the pope to excommunicate and went so far as to call the pope the Antichrist, a claim later to be reiterated by Martin Luther. The sale of indulgences he viewed as fraudulent, and he declared that there could be no justification for the hierarchy within the Church itself, much less for a differentiation between priest and layman. He also attacked such standard medieval practices as the veneration of relics, communion in one kind for the laity, pilgrimages, confession, penance, and absolution, asserting that each Christian had ultimately to be responsible for his own conduct.

Wycliffe sharpened his attack upon Church authority by offering sweeping doctrinal claims that stood in opposition to orthodox beliefs. He proclaimed that Scripture alone is the final authority in matters of faith. He likewise declared that each individual stands alone before God and has no need for a priest or Church to act as mediator. One of the most radical views was his denial of Transubstantiation, the belief that the bread and wine are transformed into the body and blood of Christ during the celebration of the Eucharist. In order to popularize his views, he made his most outstanding contribution to popular religion by supporting the translation of the Bible into the developing English vernacular. In 1378, he also supported the commissioning of lay preachers, the Lollards, to preach his doctrines in a simple style to the masses.

That Wycliffe was allowed to preach such doctrines at Oxford is a revealing commentary upon the dissatisfaction then current in England. Only twice was Wycliffe required to testify about his views; and on neither occasion was he permanently silenced. It was obvious that the authorities of Oxford were not willing to interfere with his brilliant lecturing, and the Church was also apparently hesitant to make a formal issue of his views. In 1377, however, Archbishop Sudbury commanded Wycliffe to appear before a special convocation at St. Paul's, London. Wycliffe's supporters of all classes came out in force, and a large crowd of Londoners invaded the hall of convocation to defend him. A near riot resulted and the proceedings were canceled.

Eventually, the pope took note of his heretical views and formally requested an inquiry into his work. In 1377, Gregory XI addressed letters to the archbishop of Canterbury and other dignitaries, declaring a number of points in Wycliffe's writings heretical and demanding that he be silenced. Wycliffe was to be arrested and taken before the archbishop of Canterbury and the bishop of London, who were to conduct the inquiry into his revolutionary views. Part of the basis for the attack on Wycliffe was his heavy reliance on the work of both William of Ockham, a Realist whose views challenged some Church doctrines, and Marsiglio of Padua who had seriously attacked the right of the Church to be involved in the affairs of the secular state. For several reasons the two prelates did not take action against the heretical Oxford don for many months. Perhaps they resented orders from a "schismatic" pope, who was suspected of being a tool of French foreign policy. Perhaps the nation was too preoccupied with the death of Edward III and preparations for the coronation of the new king. It is also possible the Wycliffe's support among many of the British intelligentsia of the period made circumspection necessary. In 1378, Wycliffe was again summoned by the archbishop to London, but this time to the relative privacy of Lambeth Palace. Word again reached Wycliffe's supporters, however, and a noisy crowd quickly gathered outside the gates. The clergy present, wishing to avoid a debacle like the one they had witnessed the year before, merely recommended that Wycliffe cease discussing such controversial matters in public.

The year 1381, however, marked the outbreak of the short-lived Peasants' Revolt and a change in Wycliffe's fortunes. While Wycliffe had no direct role in the revolt, many of those involved had been influenced by Wycliffe's attack on Church authority. In response to the revolt, political and religious conservatives banded together and Wycliffe lost much of his royal political support. Wycliffe was again summoned by the archbishop to London to the Blackfriar's convent for a hearing. The new archbishop was William of Courtenay, a long time opponent of Wycliffe. Despite continued support from the Oxford faculty for Wycliffe as a person, the faculty found it necessary to bow to Church pressure. While Wycliffe was not arrested, he was required to withdraw from Oxford and from public preaching. He retired to Lutterworth where he engaged in an intense period of pamphlet and treatise writing and from which he continued to direct the Lollard movement. After the Council of Constance condemned 251 articles of his writings in 1415, Wycliffe's body was disinterred, burned and scattered on unconsecrated ground. His movement was nothing short of a revolution in the medieval Church; he greatly influenced Jan Hus in Bohemia, and his views merely went underground for a time to reappear later in the Reformation.

—*Carl F. Rohne, updated by Charles L. Kammer III*

ADDITIONAL READING:

Hall, Louis Brewer. *The Perilous Vision of John Wyclif.* Chicago: Nelson-Hall, 1983. A comprehensive biography of Wycliffe that is grounded solidly in the political and social unrest of the time.

Hudson, Anne, *The Premature Reformation: Wycliffe Texts and Lollard History.* Oxford: Clarendon Press, 1988. A comprehensive account of the political and theological views of Wycliffe and the Lollards with a discussion of their influence on the later Reformation.

Hudson, Anne, and Michael Wilks, eds. *From Ockham to Wyclif.* Oxford: Blackwell, 1987. Includes essays on Wycliffe and locates his work in the context of early Church reformers.

Lechler, Gotthard. *John Wycliffe and His English Precursors.* London: Religious Tract Society, 1878. This work remains a standard for all research done on Wycliffe.

Stacey, John. *John Wyclif and Reform.* Philadelphia: Westminster Press, 1964. A good study of Wycliffe's influence on Church reform in England and on the later Reformation.

SEE ALSO: 1381, Wat Tyler Leads Peasants' Revolt; 1414-1418, Council of Constance; 1415, Martyrdom of Jan Hus.

1380
BATTLE OF KULIKOVO

The Battle of Kulikovo marks the decisive defeat of the Mongols by Grand Duke Dmitry Ivanovich of Moscow, dispelling the myth of Mongol invincibility and elevating Dmitry as a legendary hero in Russia.

DATE: September 8, 1380
LOCALE: Tula region of Russia, south of Moscow
CATEGORY: Wars, uprisings, and civil unrest
KEY FIGURES:

Dmitry Ivanovich (Dmitry Donskoi; 1350-1389), grand duke of Moscow, 1359-1389

Jogaila (c. 1351-1434), grand prince of Lithuania, later ruled Poland as Władysław II Jagiełło, 1386-1434

Mamai (died 1380), Mongol general and leader of western part of the Golden Horde

Oleg (1350-1402), grand prince of Riazan principality

SUMMARY OF EVENT. For much of the thirteenth and fourteenth centuries, Russia was under domination by the Mongols, or "Tatars" as they were known in Russian. The Mongols had invaded southern Russia in 1237, and by 1241 had succeeded in conquering Kiev. Thus began a long period known as the "Tatar yoke," whereby the Mongols maintained exploitive control over the Russian lands. Although the Mongol conquest was savage, the "Golden Horde" allowed Russian princes to rule the day-to-day affairs of their regions. The Mongol yoke largely took the form of periodic demands for tribute and, less frequently, plunderous raids.

During this time, Muscovy (Moscow) was surpassing Kiev and Novgorod as the preeminent Russian principality. First emerging as a significant principality in the late thirteenth century, Muscovy grew partly as a result of the sycophancy of its princes toward the Golden Horde. In 1327, Muscovy became the residence of the metropolitan (chief religious leader) of the Russian Orthodox Church, which not only elevated the city's status as a religious capital but also laid the groundwork for the claim of Moscow to be the "Third Rome." During the middle of this important period in Muscovy's (and Russia's) development came the reign of Grand Duke Dmitry Ivanovich in the late fourteenth century, setting the stage for an eventual escape from Mongol domination and the consolidation of a Muscovite state.

The Golden Horde was experiencing internecine struggles among its rival khans when Dmitry came to power in Muscovy. One especially powerful khan named Mamai sought to recentralize Mongol authority. At the same time, Mamai was concerned about the growing independence of the Russian princes and particularly about the growing strength of Muscovy. In 1378, Mamai sent a Mongol force under the command of one of his generals, Begich, to Riazan, a principality at the southeastern border of Muscovy. Dmitry interpreted this as a threat to his own domain, and responded by personally leading his troops to head off Begich's advance. A battle ensued between the two forces at the Vozha River on August 11, with Dmitry's troops emerging victorious.

The Mongol defeat in that small battle only served to enrage Mamai, who already had resolved to reimpose upon the Russians stricter discipline and extract from them greater tribute. In the months following Begich's defeat, Mamai prepared for a major assault on Muscovy. His decision to personally lead his army into battle ensured that the resulting clash would have epic-heroic aspects. Mamai also secured promises of assistance from the princes of Riazan and Lithuania. Oleg of Riazan felt compelled to acquiesce to Mamai's demand for assistance in order to save his region from yet another assault. Oleg did, however, alert Dmitry to Mamai's planned attack, and delayed the deployment of his troops for so long that they failed to meet up with Mamai's army.

Having been alerted to Mamai's plan by Oleg in the summer of 1380, Dmitry prepared for the Mongol attack. Legend has it that Dmitry was blessed by Abbot (later Saint) Sergius of Zagorsk, who also foretold the Mongols' defeat at Dmitry's hand. Dmitry assembled a large force of men from Muscovy, but received little assistance from the other major Russian cities and principalities. He did secure men from other lands, including Lithuanians, Belorussians, and Ukrainians. As these forces were being assembled, Mamai's emissaries approached Dmitry with a demand for tribute backed by a threat of attack. Dmitry stalled for a time in diplomatic negotiations through his own envoy, but shortly began moving his troops toward the Don River without the knowledge of Mamai. On September 7, they crossed the Don near the point where it was met by the Nepriadva River, and set up positions in Kulikovo Pole ("Snipes' Field").

Mamai had planned for his army to be joined by Jogaila's Lithuanian forces on September 1. Jogaila's forces were late, however, and Mamai went on toward Moscow without those reinforcements. In the early morning of September 8, Mamai's army entered the Kulikovo Pole from the opposite end as Dmitry's forces, as Dmitry had anticipated. As a thick fog obscured the vision of the two armies, however, both sides waited in relative silence for several hours. When the fog lifted, both armies immediately sprang into preparations for battle. True to his somewhat self-styled heroic character, Dmitry chose to ride with his central mounted units as a soldier under the grand prince's banner. Mamai directed his troops' attack from behind the front lines.

The first hours of the battle were favorable for the Mongols, who began compressing the Russian troops against the Don. Yet Dmitry had earlier hidden an elite group of cavalrymen behind his left flank. This "ambush force" now came into play, taking the Mongols entirely by surprise. The Mongol cavalry panicked and fled the battlefield, driving off and trampling their own infantry. As they had at Vozha two years earlier, Dmitry's forces pursued the fleeing Mongols to seize spoils. Mamai himself managed to escape even before the battle had subsided. Dmitry had fallen unconscious on the battlefield, but survived.

The Russian victory did not owe entirely to Dmitry's tactics and his forces' fighting ability. Certainly the absence of Jogaila's forces contributed to Mamai's defeat. Still a day's ride away when Mamai fled the battlefield, Jogaila chose to turn back rather than face Dmitry's army alone. Dmitry's victory was further diminished by the heavy losses sustained by Russian troops. Nevertheless, Dmitry was credited with standing up to the Mongols, halting Mamai's raid, and weakening the Golden Horde. Out of respect for these accomplishments Dmitry became known as Dmitry Donskoi, or Dmitry "of the Don." Russians in Muscovy and far beyond looked to Dmitry as a leader of the Russian people against the "Tatars," thus marking a step toward an eventual consolidation of the Russian principalities into a national Russian state.

Despite the symbolic power of Dmitry's success at Kulikovo in destroying the myth of Mongol invincibility, Russia would suffer under the Mongol yoke for another century. It was not until 1480 that Ivan III ("the Great") of Moscow successfully renounced Russian subordination to the khan. During that century, Kulikovo would remain a source of pride and hope for the Russians, and Dmitry Donskoi became a symbol of Russian strength and resistance to invaders throughout Russian and later Soviet history.

—Steve D. Boilard

ADDITIONAL READING:

Crummey, Robert O. "Moscow and Its Rivals, 1304-1380." In *The Formation of Muscovy, 1304-1613*. London: Longman, 1987. A discussion of Moscow's conflicts and rivalries in the fourteenth century, culminating in the Battle of Kulikovo.

Halperin, Charles J. *Russia and the Golden Horde.* Bloomington: Indiana University Press, 1985. An analysis of Russia under the Tatar yoke. The Battle of Kulikovo is noted in various parts of the narrative.

"Moscow's First Successful Challenge of the Mongols, 1380." In *Medieval Russia: A Source Book, 850-1700,* edited by Basil Dmytryshyn. 3d ed. Fort Worth, Tex.: Holt, Rinehart and Winston, 1991. A translated excerpt from a nineteenth century Russian source. This account is heavily biased, with reference, for example, to the "godless Tatars."

Neville, Peter. "The Rise of Muscovy." In *A Traveler's History of Russia and the USSR*. Brooklyn, N.Y.: Interlink, 1990. A brief description of Muscovy's rise to prominence in the thirteenth and fourteenth centuries, focusing on the Russians' efforts to escape the Mongol yoke.

"Orison on the Life and Death of Grand Prince Dmitry Ivanovich." In *Medieval Russia's Epics, Chronicles, and Tales*, edited by Serge A. Zenkovsky. New York: E. P. Dutton, 1974. A highly symbolic and reverent tribute to Dmitry written shortly after his death, with particular focus on his defeat of Mamai. This work conveys the idolization felt by Russians toward Dmitry, and their epic-heroic interpretation of Kulikovo.

SEE ALSO: 1240, Mongols Take Kiev; 1391-1395, Timur Devastates Southern Russia; 1480-1502, Destruction of the Golden Horde.

1381
WAT TYLER LEADS PEASANTS' REVOLT

Wat Tyler leads a peasants' revolt, consolidating agrarian discontent in this major popular protest against an oppressive tax that eventually brings about the demise of villeinage in England.

DATE: May-June, 1381
LOCALE: Southeastern England
CATEGORIES: Social reform; Wars, uprisings, and civil unrest
KEY FIGURES:
John Ball, priest from Blackheath, Kent, with radical (reportedly Lollard) ideas
Robert Cave, rebel leader from Dartford, Kent
Robert Hales, treasurer of England
Abel Ker, rebel leader from Erith, Essex
Richard II (1367-1400), king of England, 1377-1399
Simon of Sudbury (died 1381), archbishop and chancellor of England
Wat Tyler (or Walter; died 1381), chief rebel leader from Maidstone, Kent

SUMMARY OF EVENT. Wat Tyler was the leader of the Peasants' Revolt, which lasted from late May to the end of June, 1381. It was an outcome of the growing conflict between landlords and tenants since the Black Death (bubonic plague) of the mid-century, declining population,

and the consequent shortage of laborers. Landowners before the epidemic used to charge high rents for leasing their lands, and pay low wages to men eager for a livelihood. After the plague, the scarcity of labor threatening a rise in wages led to the Ordinance of Laborers of 1349 and the Statute of 1351, which limited mobility of labor and pegged wage rates at the 1346 level. These measures provoked agricultural unrest. From 1372, basic food prices fell as a result of improved harvests as well as a declining population in the wake of later outbreaks of plague, but wages did not drop, thus threatening the profit margins of the manorial landlords. Consequently, there were attempts to control wages by law, and these efforts contributed to the outbreak of the Peasants' Revolt in 1381.

Another contributing factor to the revolt was a crisis of confidence in government, generated partly by England's failures in the so-called Hundred Years' War. From the later part of the 1360's through the 1370's, the French commanded greater advantage over the English. English leadership suffered as Edward III was aging with no adult male to succeed him, his two eligible sons having predeceased him. The surviving third son, John of Gaunt, was inexperienced and unpopular. When Edward III died, no regent was appointed for Richard II, the Black Prince's son, who succeeded to the throne in 1377 at the age of ten.

Since 1371, parliament had been disenchanted with clerical incompetence. The clergy was also accused of avoiding taxes. In the Good Parliament of 1376, the Commons meeting at Westminster indicted a number of royal servants for corruption and the accused were tried before the Lords. Although the leader of the Commons, Sir Peter de la Mare, was arrested in the spring parliament of 1377, he was back again as the speaker in autumn, demanding a list of the members of the king's council.

In spite of these signs of uneasiness Parliament throughout 1377-1381 was generous with money grants, though demanding accountability from the government. It granted a poll tax of four shillings per head on all males between the ages of twelve and sixty in the spring of 1377, a double subsidy in autumn, and another poll tax in the spring of 1379. In 1380, a subsidy was granted on condition that the king's continual council be dismissed. The parliament meeting at Northampton in autumn approved a poll tax at the rate of a shilling a head for all males above the age of fifteen. This tax was to be collected in two installments in January and June of 1381. The attempt to collect it led to the Peasants' Revolt of 1381.

The earliest decisive event occurred in Essex on May 30, when about one hundred peasants and fishermen of Fobbing, Corringham, and Stanford refused to pay and stoned the party of collectors headed by the commis-

As captured in this engraving, Wat Tyler and his supporters were not afraid to target tax collectors and other unpopular royal officials as responsible for their financial woes. (Archive Photos)

sioner John Bampton out of Brentwood. On June 2, the chief justice of the common pleas, Robert Belknap, who came with a commission of trailbaston (special judicial power to put down hoodlums), was manhandled and forced to swear never to hold such a session. Although Belknap's life was spared, six of his local aides were killed. The Brentwood murders were followed by a general outbreak of violence throughout the county during the first week of June.

In Kent, rebel gangs under the leadership of Abel Ker of Erith invaded the monastery of Lesnes and incited the men of Dartford, where a baker named Robert Cave led men from the neighboring villages to Rochester. On June 7, at Maidstone, Wat Tyler (also spelled Tegheler and Heller) emerged as the leader of the rebels. An artisan from Dartford, Tyler reportedly was a discharged soldier from the French wars who had become a felon. His military background perhaps helped him command the insurgents many of whom were probably war veterans. His success in rallying the rebels was no doubt owed also to

the fiery sermons of John Ball, a vagrant priest from Blackheath, held at the archbishop's prison, whom he freed.

On June 8-9, the rebellion spread in all directions and fresh recruits from every village between Weald and the Thames estuary joined the horde targeting royal officials, lawyers and unpopular landlords. They seized as hostages four prominent country gentlemen and made them swear an oath of fealty to "King Richard and the Commons of England." They also broke open all the gaols, releasing the inmates. On June 10, Tyler turned toward Canterbury, sacked the palace of the archbishop and chancellor Simon Sudbury, and forcibly entered the cathedral to terrorize the monks. Thereafter, the rebels made the Kentish sheriff William Septvans surrender all judicial records and financial rolls which were destroyed.

On the same day a band of rebels from southwest Essex destroyed the properties connected with the treasurer, Sir Robert Hales, and with the sheriff, John Sewell. On June 13, the rebels from Essex and Kent entered London and destroyed numerous properties, including John of Gaunt's manor of the Savoy. The royal court, besieged in the Tower of London, was forced to negotiate with the rebels. On June 14, at the meeting at Mile End in east London, Richard agreed to abolish villeinage and declared that the rebels could seize those they regarded as traitors and bring them to the king's justice. Consequently, Tyler and his men entered the Tower and beheaded chancellor Sudbury and treasurer Hales. These murders were followed by a massacre of alien workers of the city.

These acts of violence resulted in a decline of the rebel force as many of the insurgents joined in a drinking spree to celebrate their success. Meanwhile mayor William Walworth had organized the city's defence and advised Richard to meet the rebels at Smithfield. Here, on June 15, came mostly Kentish men, their Essex cohorts having departed after the Mile End meeting. Desperate and defensive, Tyler behaved rudely, addressing the king as "brother" and shaking the boy's hands "forcefully and roughly." He demanded that there be only one bishop and one prelate for the whole of England; and that the properties of the rest of the clergy be distributed among the people; and that "there should be no . . . serfdom nor villeinage . . . but that all men should be free." He further demanded that "there should be no law except for the Law of Winchester [probably the Statute of Winchester of 1285, which provided for mutilation instead of death of felons] . . . and that no lord should have lordship in future . . . except for the king's own lordship."

Showing remarkable tact and courage, the king promised everything and urged Tyler to go home. The latter, feeling thirsty as a result of the heat, called for beer, drank a great draught in the king's presence, and mounted his horse. At that point, he was recognized by one of the royal valets, Sir John Newentone, to be "the greatest thief and robber in all Kent." As Tyler proceeded to kill his accuser, he was intercepted and wounded by Walworth. Thereupon another king's man, Ralph Standish, delivered the coup de grâce. Yet Wat did not succumb but spurred his horse though only to ride some thirty yards before collapsing from his charge half dead. His followers carried him into the adjoining hospital of St. Bartholomew from where he was dragged out later by Walworth and beheaded. Tyler's death brought the rebellion to its end, but its memories lingered on to wipe out villeinage from English society in the course of a century.   —*Narasingha P. Sil*

ADDITIONAL READING:

Dobson, R. B. *The Peasants' Revolt of 1381*. London: Macmillan, 1970. A useful collection and translation of all the important contemporary chronicles of the revolt together with a masterful introduction.

Fryde, E. B. *The Great Revolt of 1381*. London: Historical Association, 1981. The most succinct and up-to-date account by a specialist.

Galbraith, V. H. "Thoughts About the Peasants' Revolt." In *The Reign of Richard II*, edited by F. R. H. Du Boulay and Caroline M. Barron. London: Athlone Press, 1971. A valuable study claiming William Parkington, keeper of the king's wardrobe, as the author of the *Anonimalle Chronicle, 1333-1381*, a major eyewitness account of the revolt in London.

Hilton, R. H. *Bond Men Made Free: Medieval Peasant Movements and the English Rising of 1381*. New York: Viking Press, 1973. The second part of this two-part book contains a persuasive analysis of the nature and origins of this uprising.

Hilton, R. H., and T. H. Aston, eds. *The English Rising of 1381*. New York: Cambridge University Press, 1984. A collection of eight specialized articles on the revolt.

Oman, C. *The Great Revolt of 1381*. Introduction by E. B. Fryde. 1906. Rev. ed. Oxford: Clarendon Press, 1969. A pioneering study of the revolt by using A. Réville, *Le Soulèvement des travailleurs d'Angleterre en 1381* (1898) and the *Anonimalle Chronicle*.

Stephen, L., and S. Lee, eds. *The Dictionary of National Biography*. 30 vols. London: Oxford University Press, 1917-1986. Volume 19 contains one of the few biographical accounts of Tyler.

SEE ALSO: 1285, Statute of Winchester; 1347-1352, Invasion of the Black Death; 1377-1378, John Wycliffe Is Condemned for Attacking Church Authority.

1387
CHAUCER DEVELOPS VERNACULAR NARRATIVE IN THE CANTERBURY TALES

Chaucer develops vernacular narrative in The Canterbury Tales, *creating a unique English literary language and bringing to life a distinctly English scene.*

DATE: c. 1387
LOCALE: England
CATEGORIES: Communications; Cultural and intellectual history
KEY FIGURE:
Geoffrey Chaucer (c. 1343-1400), English author and diplomat

SUMMARY OF EVENT. Geoffrey Chaucer's decision to write poetry in English was a watershed event in the English linguistic and literary traditions. His use of English helped to bring prestige to that language, and it demonstrated the fluency and stylistic variety of which the language was capable. In *The Canterbury Tales* in particular, Chaucer contributes important stylistic innovations as well as humanistic values to the development of English literature.

Chaucer was born around 1340 in London. His father was a well-to-do vintner (wine importer), whose connections to the court of King Edward III undoubtedly enabled him to place his son, Geoffrey, in a royal household as a page. In such a position, Chaucer would have imbibed the values of the aristocracy and would have made valuable connections with powerful people. Those connections, along with his native intelligence and talents, led to a long career as a public servant, which included stints as a soldier, diplomat, controller of wool customs for the port of London, justice of the peace, member of Parliament, and clerk of the king's works. It was while on diplomatic missions to Italy that Chaucer came in contact with and was deeply influenced by the literary works of Dante Alighieri, Francesco Petrarch, and Giovanni Boccaccio. In 1399, Chaucer leased a house near Westminster Abbey; when he died the following year, he was buried in the Abbey in a location that would later become known as Poets' Corner.

Although as an active public servant, Chaucer's life is relatively well documented, the official records never mention his poetry. Clearly, however, he seems to have written a variety of literature throughout his adult life. The once-traditional division of his literary career into three successive periods is considered overly simplistic by modern scholars. If these divisions are not rigidly imposed, however, they do help readers grasp a general movement in the poet's reading interests, which are reflected in his own writing: the French period, when he was influenced by French courtly poetry; the Italian period, when he later discovered and was influenced by Italian literature; and finally, the English period, in which he synthesized the earlier influences and produced his own unique poetry, specifically representing the English scene in *The Canterbury Tales*.

Chaucer's decision to write poetry in English (later known as Middle English) was by no means inevitable in fourteenth century England. From the time of the Norman Conquest in 1066 right up until Chaucer's lifetime, the prestige language in England was French, the spoken language of royalty and the aristocratic ruling class. Meanwhile, the written language of learning (in the universities), of the church, and of government was Latin. By contrast, English was the unassuming language of the common people. By Chaucer's time, however, the common spoken language, or vernacular, had reasserted itself, to the point that, in 1362, Parliament decreed that legal proceedings should be conducted in English instead of French. Thus, Chaucer lived in a period of linguistic transition. He prob-

ably would have heard English spoken in his home but would have studied Latin and French at school.

Chaucer's decision to write in English should also be seen in the context of the emerging vernacular literatures in western Europe. Well before Chaucer's time, sophisticated literature began to be written in the vernacular in France, Italy, and Spain. As noted earlier, Chaucer was especially influenced by artful and complex literary works written in French (for example, *Roman de la Rose*) and Italian. Although there were certainly literary works written in English before Chaucer's time, including lyrics and romances, these did not provide him with major literary models, as did continental and Latin writing. One of Chaucer's main contributions is to fashion a literature in English that is capable of the complexities and sophistication of some of his continental and Latin models.

Given the prestige of French language and literature during Chaucer's formative years, it is not unlikely that some of his earliest writing would have been poetry in French imitating French literary styles. In any event, it is clear that Chaucer from early in his writing career successfully adapted into English the styles and subject matters of

This illustration represents an artist's conception of the real-life Tabard Inn. Geoffrey Chaucer was familiar with the inn, which served as a logical starting point for the pilgrims who appear in his famous narrative, The Canterbury Tales. *(Archive Photos)*

the French courtly tradition. For Chaucer, it is important to note, such adaptations were not servile renderings of the originals. For example, the French courtly or chivalric love (the idealistic code of romantic love in which the male is a humble supplicant and the lady an impossibly high ideal) is treated by Chaucer in a lighter, often ironic way, that undercuts the courtly sentiment.

In his adaptations from the French, and from Italian and Latin as well, Chaucer also enriched English literature by integrating into his writing a range of classical allusions, references to philosophical and theological topics, and to a host of other subject matters—dream-lore, astrology, literary genres. In this way, Chaucer pioneers (creates, really) English literature capable of sophistication and intellectual complexity equal to that of his continental models. Again, however, Chaucer does not in this enterprise simply translate literally from one culture to another. He must create an English idiom to express these complexities, and in so doing he succeeded in creating a unique English literary language.

Chaucer also adapted, primarily from the French literary tradition, metrical patterns that have been hugely influential in English literature since his day. In place of the native alliterative verse form (for example, in William Langland's *Piers Plowman*, 1362, 1377, and 1393), Chaucer characteristically looked to and adapted the metrical verse form employed by French poets. Metrical verse provided a set number of syllables and a regular pattern of alternating stressed and unstressed syllables. Some Middle English poetry had been written in metrical verse before Chaucer's time, but it had followed the French model of employing eight syllables per line (octosyllabic). Chaucer adapted the greater flexibility of the ten-syllable line (decasyllabic) for English poetry. This resulted in Chaucer's characteristic iambic pentameter line, in which there is an unstressed syllable followed by a stressed syllable (an iambic foot) in a regular pattern in a ten-syllable line: "A Knyght ther was, and that a worthy man." Chaucer's additional important innovation was to employ these iambic pentameter lines in rhyming couplets, the form seen in the general prologue to *The Canterbury Tales* and other well-known tales from that work. In Chaucer's hands, the pentameter couplets became a remarkably supple form, capable of narrative momentum as well as conversational tone and exchange. The pentameter line became a staple verse form in the English literary tradition, making possible the blank verse later used by William Shakespeare and John Milton, among others.

Another important contribution of Chaucer to English literature is the reflection in his writing of lifelike experience, of credible characters in ordinary circumstances, if not actions. Again, Chaucer in this development of verisimilitude is heir to many continental influences, notably the comic realism of the bawdy French fabliaux, which he exploited fully in "The Miller's Tale." Yet when, in the general prologue to *The Canterbury Tales*, he gathers an assorted company of "nine and twenty" pilgrims, representing a wide cross-section of fourteenth century English society, in Southwark at the Tabard Inn (which actually existed and would have been a natural starting point for pilgrimages to Canterbury), he succeeds in bringing this distinctly English scene to life using the subtle illusions of his art. Furthermore, in describing the pilgrims, Chaucer makes them both representatives of their vocation or "estate" and individuals, who are possessed of unique characteristics and intentions. Through an apparently haphazard description of details about each pilgrim, Chaucer's narrator allows readers to glimpse the character's internal world of values, although the Chaucerian narrator himself is remarkably free from value judgments about the pilgrims, except for comments of general approval about everyone, including the obvious scoundrels. The result is a complexity of "characterization" and motivation that is central to the English literary tradition.

Finally, Chaucer's arguably most important contribution to the development of vernacular narrative is the way he matches the unique personalities of his pilgrims to the tales they tell on the way to Canterbury. Thus, the knight tells a courtly romance, the miller a bawdy fabliau, and prioress a miracle of the virgin, and so forth. This stylistic enhancement has long been recognized as one of Chaucer's greatest innovations in the vastly influential *Canterbury Tales.*   —*James Flynn*

ADDITIONAL READING:

Cooper, Helen. *Oxford Guides to Chaucer: The Canterbury Tales*. New York: Oxford University Press, 1989. Provides detailed introductions to each of the tales. Comprehensive, reliable, and extremely useful as a reference tool.

Donaldson, E. Talbot. *Speaking of Chaucer*. New York: W. W. Norton, 1970. A collection of essays, notable for their learning and wit; many are classics concerning *The Canterbury Tales.*

Fisher, John H. *The Importance of Chaucer*. Carbondale: Southern Illinois University Press, 1992. A judicious overview of Chaucer's accomplishments and innovations, especially with respect to linguistic matters.

Muscatine, Charles. *Chaucer and the French Tradition*. Berkeley: University of California Press, 1957. A landmark critical work that remains useful for its scholarly insights.

Pearsall, Derek. *The Canterbury Tales*. London: Allen & Unwin, 1985. Insightful critical account of the work, along with some helpful reviews of scholarship.

SEE ALSO: 1170, Murder of Thomas à Becket; 1347-1352, Invasion of the Black Death; 1350-1400, Petrarch and Boccaccio Recover Classical Texts; 1589-1613, Shakespeare Writes His Dramas; 1667, John Milton Publishes *Paradise Lost*.

1389
TURKISH CONQUEST OF SERBIA

The Turkish conquest of Serbia heralds the end of Serbia's "Golden Age" as a major power in the Balkan Peninsula and the beginning of more than four hundred years of Ottoman occupation and domination of southeast Europe.

DATE: June 28, 1389

LOCALE: Kosovo Plain, Serbia

CATEGORIES: Expansion and land acquisition; Wars, uprisings, and civil unrest

KEY FIGURES:

Bayezid I (1354-1403), Ottoman sultan, 1389-1402

George Brankovich (c. 1374-1456), Serbian despot, 1426-1456

Lazar I Hrebeljanovich (c. 1329-1389), prince of Serbia, 1371-1389

Mehmed II (1432-1481), Ottoman sultan, 1444-1446 and 1451-1481, and conqueror of Constantinople

Milica, princess of Serbia and wife of Lazar I

Murad I (c. 1326-1389), Ottoman sultan, 1360-1389

Stefan Dušan, (1308-1355), king of Serbia, 1331-1346, and emperor of the Serbs and Greeks, 1346-1355

Stefan Lazarevich, prince of Serbia, 1389-1427

Tvrtko I (c. 1338-1391), king of Bosnia, 1353-1391, and ally of Lazar I

SUMMARY OF EVENT. The Ottoman Turks conquered Serbia between 1389 and 1459. The conquest began less than a century after the Ottoman Turks first appeared in Europe from their homeland in Asia Minor where they had emerged around 1290 under the leadership of Osman, or Othman. In 1345, John Cantacuzenus, one of the claimants to the throne of the shrinking Byzantine Empire, had called upon the Turks for military support as mercenaries, but they had seized upon the opportunity to extend their domains into southeastern Europe. They captured the city of Gallipoli and under Murad I occupied Byzantine Thrace, clashing for the first time with Slavic kingdoms in the central Balkans.

The condition of these kingdoms made them ripe for conquest by Murad. Serbia, Bosnia, and Bulgaria were racked by the internal strife of rival pretenders, rival religions, rebellious nobles, and oppressed peasants. Under the strong Serbian dynasty of the Nemanyids, particularly the Serbian "Czar of the Serbs and Greeks" Stefan Dušan, the Serbs had extended their state to include Albania, Epirus, Thessaly, Macedonia, and most of the Adriatic and Ionian coasts. The Serbian Orthodox Church, under its patriarchate at Pech, was autocephalous and a center of cultural life. Serbia had a strong economy, with considerable activity in mining, trade, and agriculture. Ostensibly the strongest state in the Balkans at the time of the Turkish arrival in Europe, Serbia had in reality overextended itself; to some of the peoples languishing under Serbian oppression, the Turks appeared as liberators.

In 1365, Murad captured Adrianople and made it the Ottoman capital, a status it retained until the Turkish conquest of Constantinople in the fifteenth century. Having smashed a Christian crusading army of Hungarians, Serbs, Bosnians, and Wallachians which had set out to recapture the city, Murad overran western Bulgaria in 1366, forcing its leaders to become his vassals. After disastrously defeating the Serbs in 1371 at the Battle of Marica near Adrianople, the strong Nemanyid dynasty of the Serbs was at an end and the throne of Serbia passed to weaker incumbents.

The Ottomans turned their attentions to Anatolia and the dynastic troubles of the Byzantine Empire after 1371. Then they again entered the Balkans, conquering Sofija in Bulgaria and the Byzantine city Salonika (Thessaloniki). Finally, the sultan invaded Serbian Macedonia and the Serbian homeland itself. Murad had left most of Serbia under the rule of its prince, Lazar I, as a vassal. Unwilling to accept Turkish suzerainty, Lazar formed an alliance with the king of Bosnia, Tvrtko I, and John Stratsimir of Vidin Bulgaria. While Murad was quieting disorders in Asia Minor, the two Slavic rulers organized a military coalition of Bosnians, Serbs, Croats, Bulgarians, Wallachians, and Albanians. In 1388, the coalition won three successive victories over the Turks. Murad, in response to this challenge, hurried back to Europe and on June 28, 1389, inflicted an overwhelming defeat upon the South Slavic and other Balkan forces at Kosovo, although he was assassinated in the course of the battle.

The Battle of Kosovo, because of its dramatic consequences for the entire Balkan Peninsula, and especially for the Serbs, has been the subject of myth and legend since shortly after its occurrence. It is the subject of an oral epic cycle, Prince Lazar and other combatants have been given semilegendary status, and the region of Kosovo, the site of the battle as well as the location of a number of ancient Serbian monasteries and other monuments, has achieved an importance to the Serbs that goes beyond the merely geographical.

After the decisive Battle of the Kosovo Plain, or the Field of Blackbirds, Bayezid, the new sultan, avenged his father Murad's death by ordering the execution of the captive Lazar. Princess Milica, Lazar's wife, ruled Serbia until her infant son, Stefan Lazarevich, was of age. She founded several monasteries, became a nun, and assembled around her the widows of men who died at Kosovo.

When Lazar's son and successor, Stefan Lazarevich, was made a tributary vassal of the Ottoman Turks, Serbia's real independence ended, though the ruling dynasty and some measure of limited autonomy were retained. Stefan Lazarevich even took part in later battles on the side of the Turks, although he visited the Byzantine Emperor on his return from Bayezid's battle at Ankara in 1402.

In the wake of the Battle of Kosovo, Bayezid managed by 1395 to incorporate eastern Bulgaria, to extend his influence over Wallachia, and to begin the first Turkish siege of Constantinople.

The Ottoman Turks continued to strengthen their hold over the Balkans during the fifteenth century. In 1402, Bayezid's devastating defeat at Ankara at the hands of the great Mongol conqueror Tamerlane marked a temporary setback for Ottoman fortunes in Asia Minor, but in Europe, the Turks remained strong, waging war intermittently with the Venetian Republic, Hungary, Serbia, and the Byzantine Empire. When Stefan Lazarevich died without heirs his nephew George Brankovich became ruler of Serbia, which by this time had the status of a despotate, a title conferred on Stefan Lazarevich by the Byzantine emperor. Brankovich built a new fortified city at Smederovo, on the Danube, in 1430, whence he, with the help of his Hungarian ally János Hunyadi, was able to throw off the Turkish yoke in 1444. Yet the Turks more than recovered their losses within a few years, and at a second battle at Kosovo, in 1448, defeated the forces of the Hungarian leader Hunyadi. In the meantime Murad II had died, and the new sultan, Mehmed II, set about capturing the silver mining town of Novo Brdo, the source of George Brankovich's wealth. In 1456, the Serbian despot George Brankovich died at Smederovo. Three years later, Mehmed led his troops to the fortress and captured it. This signaled the final defeat of Serbia, which was not to revive as a nation until the nineteenth century. In Europe, the fall of the fortress at Smederovo was considered a disaster equal to the fall of Constantinople, because it signaled the fact that the Turkish menace had the potential of overrunning the entire continent. Under Sultan Mehmed II, the Ottoman Turks finally captured Constantinople in May, 1453, thus terminating the thousand-year-old Byzantine state.

The definitive Turkish conquest of Serbia in 1459 had several important consequences. It gave the Ottoman Empire control over the entire southern bank of the lower Danube River. Fearing Hungarian attacks, the Turks extended their complete sway over Wallachia in 1462, to gain control over most of the northern bank of the lower Danube. The Turkish occupation of Serbia facilitated Mehmed's conquest of Bosnia in 1463 and neighboring Herzegovina by his successor some twenty years later. These Turkish acquisitions had the net effect of transforming Hungary, as Byzantium of old, into an outpost of Christian civilization against the infidels. In its subsequent defeat by the Turks in 1526, Hungary abdicated this mission to neighboring Habsburg Austria. Against the impenetrable walls of Vienna, the Turkish advance was finally shattered toward the end of the seventeenth century, and Turkish power thereafter declined at the hands of Austria, Russia, and the reemerging Balkan states.

—Edward P. Keleher, updated by Gloria Fulton

ADDITIONAL READING:

Edwards, Lovett. *Yugoslavia*. New York: Hastings House, 1971. Chapters 3 and 4 contain an account of the aftermath of the Kosovo battle, as well as cultural history of the region.

Fine, John V. A. *The Late Medieval Balkans: A Critical Survey from the Late Twelfth Century to the Ottoman Conquest*. Ann Arbor: University of Michigan Press, 1987. Scholarly work covering the rise of the Serbian state and the Ottoman invasion.

Singleton, Fred. *A Short History of the Yugoslav Peoples*. New York: Cambridge University Press, 1985. Chapters 3 and 4 cover the Ottoman invasion and occupation of the Yugoslav lands.

Sugar, Peter F. *Southeastern Europe Under Ottoman Rule, 1354-1804*. Seattle: University of Washington Press, 1977. A detailed scholarly treatment of the changes wrought in the Balkans by the introduction of Ottoman rule.

Temperley, Harold W. V. *History of Serbia*. Reprint. New York: AMS Press, 1970. First published in 1917, Temperley includes a detailed discussion of the battle at Kosovo and its importance for the Serbs in chapter 6.

West, Rebecca. *Black Lamb and Grey Falcon: A Journey Through Yugoslavia*. New York: Viking Press, 1943. Discussion of the Kosovo myth and its importance for the Serbs.

SEE ALSO: 1168, Nemanyid Dynasty Is Founded in Serbia; 1353, Ottoman Empire Establishes Foothold in Rumelia; 1442-1456, János Hunyadi Defends Hungary Against Ottoman Invaders; 1453, Fall of Constantinople; 1457-1504, Reign of Stephen the Great; 1526, Battle of Mohács.

1391-1395
Timur Devastates Southern Russia

Timur devastates southern Russia in fierce fighting against the Golden Horde, weakening the latter to the point that the grand duchy of Moscow increases in importance and independence.

Date: 1391-1395

Locale: The steppes of southern Russia

Categories: Expansion and land acquisition; Wars, uprisings, and civil unrest

Key figures:

Dmitry Ivanovich (Dmitry Donskoi; 1350-1389), prince of Moscow, 1359-1389, and grand duke of Vladimir, 1368-1389

Edigei, emir of the Golden Horde, 1396-1411, who ruled via puppet khans

Mamai (died 1380), emir of the Golden Horde, 1361-1380, who ruled via puppet khans

Timur (Tamerlane), great lord of the Mongol empire, 1370-1405

Tokhtamysh, khan of the Golden Horde, 1381-1395

Vasily I (1371-1425), grand duke of Moscow, 1389-1425

Vytautas (Vitovt or Witold; 1350-1430), grand duke of Lithuania, 1392-1430

Summary of event. Born in 1336 near Samarkand, Timur was the son of a petty Mongol lord and entered a many-sided struggle for power in the collapsing Chagatai realm of the former empire of Genghis (Chingis) Khan. He emerged from the civil wars as victor and took the title of emir of Transoxiana in 1370, the formal beginning of his empire. Unable to assume the title of khan, which was reserved for blood relatives of Genghis, Timur was granted the title of great lord. He extended his authority into southern Khorezm and eastward into eastern Turkestan. From 1380 to 1393, Timur conquered all of Persia, including Mesopotamia and Azerbaijan, and the Caucasus.

In 1375, Timur had helped to make Tokhtamysh, a Chingisid, khan of the Blue Horde in Kazakhstan, and a few years later supported his effort to displace Emir Mamai as ruler of the Golden Horde, which included most of the Russian principalities. Mamai, ruling via puppet Chingisid khans, was powerful enough to retain control of the western half of the Horde. Then in 1380, after Grand Duke Dmitry of Moscow defeated the Tatars of the Horde in a battle at Kulikovo Field in a premature bid for independence, Tokhtamysh seized the opportunity to overthrow Mamai and defeated him in battle at the Kalka River. The other Mongol princes deserted Mamai, and Tokhtamysh, who called himself a vassal of Timur, took

the throne of the Golden Horde for himself. Mamai fled with his jewels to Kaffa, where Genoese merchants robbed and killed him.

In 1382, after securing an alliance with Lithuania and compelling Russian princes of Riazan, Suzdal, and Nizhny Novgorod to join him, the new khan took his Tatar-Mongol armies northward to Moscow. Dmitry hoped the walls of the city would prevent a sack, but Tokhtamysh was able to seize the Moscow kremlin anyway, plundering and killing many Muscovites in retribution for the Kulikovo encounter. Tokhtamysh saw to it that the Russian principalities renewed their tribute to his court at Sarai on the Volga. Meanwhile, Dmitry returned to his capital to preside over the burial of some twenty-four thousand bodies, pledging allegiance to the Mongol court in 1383.

Events were to turn in Moscow's favor, however, owing to the arrival of Timur. Tokhtamysh wished to prove that he was no puppet of Timur and broke relations with his former patron in 1386 by sacking the city of Tabriz, then in Timur's domain. He regarded Timur as beneath him because Timur lacked kinship with the founder of the Mongol destinies. Furthermore, Tokhtamysh's head was turned by the many accolades he received after subduing the Muscovites so soon after the humiliation at Kulikovo.

Two years later, while Timur was busy restoring his imperial command in southern Persia, Azerbaijan, Georgia, and Daghestan, Tokhtamysh took his warriors into central Asia and raided the lands of Transoxiana, reaching as far as Bokhara in 1388 before turning back to the Volga region. The next year, he launched a similar venture, this time armed with a larger force including Russian conscripts. Timur, against the advice of his generals, decided to march on Tokhtamysh in January of 1389, when the snow was deep. This so surprised the Horde that many of them were massacred by Timur's troops. Nevertheless, the khan returned to pillage Timur's possessions north of the Syr Darya.

Timur was unable to retaliate against Tokhtamysh until 1391. He gathered a 200,000-man force and mounted a campaign against the Golden Horde from the East, defeating Tokhtamysh in the steppes using new tactics, including the use of trenches and shields, and dividing his troops into seven corps, two in reserve. Tokhtamysh kept retreating but could not avoid battle forever and made his stand at the Kondurch River on June 18, 1391. Although the outcome was not immediately apparent, the armies of Tokhtamysh were defeated and he was deposed as khan of the Golden Horde. The losses of the Horde reached one hundred thousand men, owing mainly to the defection of two military commanders of the khan in the heat of battle.

After Timur departed, Tokhtamysh regained the west-

TIMUR'S EMPIRE CIRCA 1400

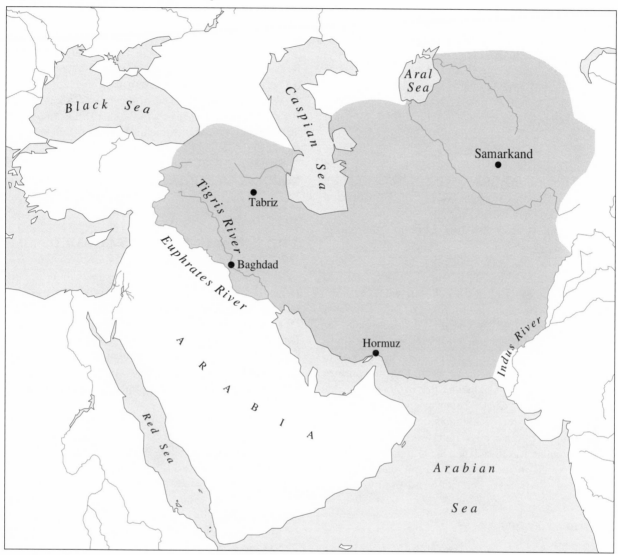

ern half of the Golden Horde. In need of support, how-ever, Tokhtamysh granted Moscow control of Nizhny Novgorod in return for acknowledging his suzerainty. He also secured an alliance with Grand Duke Vytautas of Lithuania and with the Mamelukes in Egypt. With new confidence, Tokhtamysh attacked Timur's empire in the Caucasus, setting the stage for the final clash between these two titans. This time, Timur led an expedition north-ward from his base in the Caucasus and inflicted a crush-ing defeat on the Golden Horde near the Terek River in February, 1395. Timur followed up this victory by de-stroying the capital of the Horde at Sarai, including its imperial archives, then devastated the Tatar commercial centers at Kaffa, Azov, and Astrakhan. He went north to

crush the Bulgar kingdom, a dependency of the Horde. Timur turned his depredations into Russian territories, most notably at Elets, but, contrary to some reports, he did not advance as far as Moscow.

Meanwhile, Dmitry had died in Moscow and was re-placed by his son Vasily, once a hostage at the court of the Golden Horde. The new Muscovite grand duke married a daughter of the Lithuanian prince, linking the fortunes of both states. Vasily had set up defenses along the Oka River and ordered the great icon of Our Lady of Vladimir moved to Moscow to raise the spirits of the people. Hesitant to lose many men far from home, Timur ordered the end of the Russian campaigns. While en route south, however, he devastated the Circassian lands in the northern Caucasus and burned Sarai and Astrakhan on the lower Volga. Once home, Timur prepared his invasion of India the following year.

The results of Timur's onslaughts into Tatar and Russian lands left the Golden Horde weakened beyond recovery. Although Timur chose not to add the Russian steppes to his dominions, trading centers were destroyed and the China-India trade was now rerouted from the North Caspian Sea region to Persia and Syria. Urban crafts and industries of the Golden Horde were devastated as well. Such destruction, coming after the losses from the bubonic plague earlier in the century, left the Horde in a weakened position. Consequently, there was little money with which to purchase firearms from the West, and the peripheral states, Crimea and Kazan, became more independent. Lithuania and Moscow also grew more powerful during the next century as well.

There was one odd postscript to this episode. Tokhtamysh, who had escaped Timur's troops, launched yet another comeback after 1396. Within two years, however, Mongol rebels ousted him from the throne in favor of Edigei, who defeated the Polish, Lithuanian, and West Russian allies of Tokhtamysh in 1399. Again, Tokhtamysh survived and fled to eastern Siberia, where he intended to raise new armies to recover his throne. In 1405, he appealed to his old adversary Timur, then resting in Otrar before his planned invasion of China. Timur received the embassy from his former foe, Tokhtamysh, who now wanted Timur's support. Apparently Timur was not hostile to the invitation but he was ill and died in Otrar on February 18. He was buried in the famed Gur-Emir mausoleum in Samarkand. Tokhtamysh was not heard from again and presumably died soon after.   —*John D. Windhausen*

ADDITIONAL READING:

Adshead, S. A. M. *Central Asia in World History*. New York: St. Martin's Press, 1993. In a provocative work on the nature of world history, the author suggests that the reorientation of Lithuania westward after the death of Vytautas may have had more to do with the rise of Moscow than the destruction of the Horde by Timur.

Crummey, Robert O. *The Formation of Muscovy, 1304-1613*. London: Longman, 1987. Crummey argues that Vytautas hoped to capitalize upon Timur's depredations to enhance his own power over the Horde and Muscovy.

Halperin, Charles J. *Russia and the Golden Horde: The Mongol Impact on Medieval Russian History*. Bloomington: Indiana University Press, 1985. The most recent scholarly study of this subject, describing well the symbiosis of the Tatar bureaucracy and the nomad world.

Manz, Beatrice Forbes. *The Rise and Rule of Tamer-

lane. New York: Cambridge University Press, 1989 (reprinted 1993). The best single study of this ruler, although the author does relate the apocryphal story that Timur marched his forces to Moscow.

Sokol, Edward D. *Tamerlane*. Lawrence: University of Kansas Press, 1977. This biography contains useful detail, but suffers from the absence of maps.

Vernadsky, George. *The Mongols and Russia*. New Haven, Conn.: Yale University Press, 1953. Contains the most comprehensive treatment of Timur's invasions and the intrigues among the Tatar leaders.

SEE ALSO: 1240, Mongols Take Kiev; 1380, Battle of Kulikovo; 1480-1502, Destruction of the Golden Horde.

1397
THE KALMAR UNION IS FORMED
The Kalmar Union is formed through the diplomatic skills of Margaret I, bringing Sweden, Norway, and Denmark under the rule of a single sovereign in a union that lasts more than a century.

DATE: June 17, 1397
LOCALE: Sweden, Norway, and Denmark
CATEGORY: Government and politics
KEY FIGURES:
Albert (Albert III of Mecklenburg; 1340-1412), king of Sweden, 1363-1389
Christian II (1481-1559), king of Denmark and Norway, 1513-1523, and king of Sweden, 1520-1523
Erik of Pomerania (1382-1459), king of Denmark, Norway, and Sweden, 1397-1439
Gustav I Vasa (Gustav Eriksson; c. 1496-1560), king of Sweden, 1523-1560
Margaret I (1353-1412), regent of Denmark, 1375-1401, regent of Norway, 1380-1401, and regent of Sweden, 1389-1401

SUMMARY OF EVENT. During the fourteenth century, the three Scandinavian nations of Denmark, Norway, and Sweden were involved in numerous complex struggles for political power. In addition to wars among the three nations and conflicts between the nations of Scandinavia and the Hanseatic League (a powerful federation of German trading towns), there were internal struggles as well.

During one of these struggles, the nobles of Sweden, in alliance with the Hanseatic League, invited Albert of Mecklenburg, a German prince, to drive out the current king of Sweden, Magnus II, who was his uncle. Albert of Mecklenburg invaded in 1364, taking the title of king. He defeated the forces of Magnus II in 1365 and took him prisoner. Magnus II was released in 1371 in exchange for recognizing Albert of Mecklenburg as king.

The reign of Albert of Mecklenburg was a constant struggle with the Swedish nobles, who held most of the real power. The most powerful of these nobles was Bo Jonsson Grip, who owned large amounts of land in Sweden, including all of Finland (which was at the time a part of Sweden). When Grip died in 1386, Albert of Mecklenburg attempted to seize his estates, and this act caused the nobles to unite against him.

Meanwhile, the future ruler of all three nations was consolidating her own power. The daughter of King Valdemar IV of Denmark, Margaret I married King Haakon VI of Norway, the son of Magnus II, in 1363, when she was ten years old. During the reign of Albert of Mecklenburg, Haakon VI lost his claim to the throne of Sweden but retained Norway.

In 1370, Margaret gave birth to a son, Olaf. When Valdemar IV died in 1375, she was able to convince the nobles of Denmark to elect Olaf as king. Since he was still a child, Margaret ruled Denmark as regent in his place.

In 1380, Haakon VI died and Olaf inherited the throne of Norway. Margaret was now the regent of both Denmark and Norway. When the Swedish nobles turned against Albert of Mecklenburg in 1386, Margaret was ready to offer military aid to them in exchange for making Olaf king of Sweden as well. Her plans were destroyed when Olaf died suddenly on August 3, 1387, possibly from poison.

During this crisis, Margaret proved to have great skill at diplomacy. She had no claim to the throne of any of the three nations, and Scandinavian law and tradition prevented a woman from reigning as a monarch. Despite this restriction, she managed to persuade the nobles of both Denmark and Norway to allow her to continue to rule as regent, with the right to name her heir. The heir she chose was her grandnephew, Erik of Pomerania, who was a young child at the time.

In March of 1388, the Swedish nobles accepted Margaret as regent of Sweden also, beginning a war for control of Sweden between Margaret and Albert of Mecklenburg. On February 24, 1389, a decisive battle was fought near the Swedish town of Falköping. The forces of Margaret defeated the forces of Albert of Mecklenburg and he was taken prisoner. Margaret was now the ruler of all three Scandinavian nations.

The Swedish city of Stockholm continued to be controlled by the supporters of Albert of Mecklenburg. These supporters allied themselves with pirates who were disrupting trade on the Baltic Sea. The Hanseatic League, which depended on the Baltic trade routes, formed an alliance with Margaret against the pirates. In 1395, Margaret made an agreement with the supporters of Albert of

Mecklenburg to release him from imprisonment in exchange for a large ransom. If the ransom was not paid, Stockholm would be turned over to the Hanseatic League for three years, after which it would be given to Margaret. Albert of Mecklenburg was unable to raise enough money for the ransom, so the Hanseatic League took over the city and spent the next three years destroying the pirates.

Erik of Pomerania was accepted as king of Norway in 1389, and was elected king of Denmark and Sweden in 1396. On June 17, 1397, representatives of all three nations, nobles and clergymen, gathered at Kalmar, Sweden, to witness the coronation of Erik of Pomerania. This ceremony was the birth of what would later be known as the Kalmar Union.

Little is known of the negotiations which took place between Margaret and the nobles at Kalmar at this time, but they seem to have taken about a month to complete. The two documents which were produced by these negotiations were both dated July 13, 1397. The first document, known as the Coronation Letter, was written on parchment and announced the coronation of Erik of Pomerania in a way which implied a centralized, hereditary monarchy.

The second document, known as the Union Letter, has been closely studied by historians because it poses several questions. Although the text of this document states that it is written on parchment and that it is hung with seventeen seals, it is actually written on vellum and contains only ten seals, which are stamped into it rather than hanging from it. These discrepancies, along with the fact that the Union Letter contains written corrections, leads scholars to believe that it is an unapproved draft of an agreement which was never completed.

Apparently Margaret wanted a closer union of the three nations than the nobles, who wanted to ensure that each nation would retain its own laws and customs. Unable to come to a formal agreement with the nobles about the exact details of the union, Margaret continued to rule as before, relying on her diplomatic skill to avoid conflicts.

Although Erik of Pomerania reached the age at which he no longer needed a regent in 1401, Margaret remained the unofficial power behind the throne until her death on October 28, 1412. She spent the last years of her life strengthening the union and increasing the power of the sovereign by appointing loyal and efficient officials to administer her government.

Erik of Pomerania proved to be a less effective ruler than Margaret. His attempt to build an empire on the Baltic coast led to an expensive war with the Hanseatic League. A blockade of Swedish exports of iron and copper by the Hanseatic League in 1434 led to a rebellion by Swedish miners. Eventually Erik of Pomerania was deposed from the thrones of Denmark and Sweden in 1439 and Norway in 1442.

Erik of Pomerania was replaced by Christopher III, who died in 1448 with no heir. Danish nobles selected Christian I as his successor while Swedish nobles selected Karl Knutsson. The conflict between Denmark and Sweden continued for the next several decades, as one side or the other gained control over the throne of Sweden.

On January 19, 1520, Christian II, the king of Denmark and Norway, defeated the forces of Sten Sture the Younger, the regent of Sweden. After months of attempting to take the city of Stockholm by force, Christian II convinced it to surrender by promising amnesty to his opponents. He was crowned king of Sweden on November 4, 1520. Four days later, despite his promise of amnesty, he executed eighty-two supporters of Sten Sture the Younger in an event later known as the Stockholm Bloodbath.

The Swedish nobleman Gustav Vasa led a war of independence against Christian II, defeating him with the financial help of the rich German trading city of Lübeck. He was crowned king of Sweden on June 6, 1523, ending the Kalmar Union.   —*Rose Secrest*

ADDITIONAL READING:

Butler, Ewan. "Royal Union, Peasant Separatism." In *The Horizon Concise History of Scandinavia*. New York: American Heritage, 1973. Focuses on the wars and rebellions that threatened the Kalmar Union throughout its history.

Derry, T. K. "The Union of Three Crowns." In *A History of Scandinavia*. Minneapolis: University of Minnesota Press, 1979. A detailed account of the rise and fall of the Kalmar Union.

Larsen, Karen. "Scandinavian Union." In *A History of Norway*. Princeton, N.J.: Princeton University Press, 1948. An account of the Kalmar Union from the viewpoint of Norway.

Scott, Franklin D. "Margareta and the Union of Kalmar." In *Sweden: The Nation's History*. Carbondale: Southern Illinois University Press, 1988. Discusses Margaret I and the Kalmar Union as seen by Sweden.

Singleton, Fred. "Finland and Sweden." In *A Short History of Finland*. New York: Cambridge University Press, 1989. Describes the effect of the Kalmar Union on Finland.

SEE ALSO: 1150-1200, Rise of the Hansa; 1240, Alexander Nevsky Defends Novgorod from Swedish Invaders; 1700, Battle of Narva.

1410-1440
FLORENTINE SCHOOL OF ART EMERGES

The Florentine School of Art emerges, establishing the principal characteristics of Italian Renaissance art through the works of Donatello, Masaccio, and Filippo Brunelleschi.

DATE: 1410-1440

LOCALE: Florence, Italy

CATEGORY: Cultural and intellectual history

KEY FIGURES:

Filippo Brunelleschi (1377-1446), a Florentine artist and master goldsmith who turned his attention to architectural engineering and design and became the first architect of the new Renaissance style

Donatello (Donato di Niccolò di Betto Bardi; 1386-1446), a Florentine artist who trained as a goldsmith, engraver, and carver before becoming a sculptor

Lorenzo Ghiberti (1378-1455), a Florentine artisan and master of perspective under whom Donatello worked

Masaccio (Tommaso di Giovanni di Simone Guidi; 1401-c. 1428), a Florentine painter whose altarpieces and frescoes were influenced by Giotto, Brunelleschi, and Donatello

SUMMARY OF EVENT. Although they built on foundations and developments in early Italian Renaissance art during the fourteenth century, the work of three artists, Brunelleschi, Donatello, and Masaccio, converged in the early fifteenth century to define the character of Italian Renaissance art and establish Florence as a leading artistic center. Because their work represented the major art forms—architecture for Brunelleschi, sculpture for Donatello, and painting for Masaccio—collectively they articulated the principal ideals of Italian Renaissance art.

A famous competition of 1401 for the design of a pair of bronze doors for the Baptistery of Florence was important for the emergence of Florentine art. The winner, Lorenzo Ghiberti, narrowly beat out Filippo Brunelleschi, who then turned to architecture. Ghiberti's assistant while working on the doors was Donatello. Thus, while Ghiberti's doors were significant artistic achievements in their own right, they can also be said to have influenced the careers of Brunelleschi and Donatello.

When Brunelleschi lost the competition, he went to Rome to study the ancient architectural monuments. The subsequent architectural projects which Brunelleschi designed in Florence are marked by a consistent application of harmonious geometrical proportions and the use of classically inspired architectural members and ornament.

The most famous of Brunelleschi's architectural works

is the dome of Florence cathedral which was begun in 1420 and completed around 1436. As the largest dome since Roman times, its octagonal structure was composed of an inner and outer shell. The structural ingenuity combined with the simple, basic shapes point to the ideals that Brunelleschi's architecture conveyed.

Because it was added to an earlier essentially Gothic structure, Brunelleschi's dome did not reveal the full extent of his architectural innovations. Several buildings that he designed between 1420 and his death in 1446, however, demonstrate the classicism of his approach to architecture. In the Ospedale degli Innocenti (Hospital of the Innocents), an orphanage begun in 1419, the plan and elevation rely on modular proportions based on the geometrical system of the ancient Greek mathematician, Pythagoras, as revealed in the exterior arcade with its rhythmical row of arches supported on slender Corinthian columns. A similar use of proportion as well as nave arcades with rounded arches and Corinthian columns characterize two Florentine churches: San Lorenzo, which was begun sometime around 1425 and completed 1470, and Santo Spirito, which was designed in 1434-1436. In many ways, the most perfect structure that Brunelleschi designed was the Pazzi Chapel, the chapter house of the church of Santa Croce in Florence, begun in 1433. The plan focuses on a central square with the space of half a square to either side covered by a dome. The consistency of the proportional module and the centralized space give this structure a feeling of perfect balance and harmony that became a hallmark of Renaissance culture.

Donatello assisted Ghiberti but soon established himself as a sculptor. Whereas Ghiberti's reliefs were still marked by active diagonals in the compositional lines and sharp drapery folds that had a decorative quality reminiscent of the late Gothic style, Donatello's early works such as the Saint George for one of the exterior niches of the Florentine guildhall of Orsanmichele portrayed a fully three-dimensional body whose taut form protrudes into the viewer's space. A low relief of Saint George slaying the dragon just beneath this statue uses architectural forms with the kind of perspective that Brunelleschi constructed with his architecture.

Throughout a long career, Donatello combined several important features that characterized Renaissance art. First, he brought a three-dimensional corporeality to depictions of the human body. Second, his sculptures emanated a powerful psychological persona appropriate to the subject. Third, he revived several classical sculptural types such as the nude body and the equestrian statue. Finally, his technique of low relief utilized perspective to create a believable spatial context.

The three-dimensional reality of the human body combined with the idealistic beauty of the nude figure to produce a bronze sculpture of *David* (c. 1450) for Cosimo de' Medici. The unusual depiction of a nude David posed in classical *contrapposto* is the first freestanding nude sculpture since antiquity. In Padua, Donatello executed an equestrian statue of a *condottiere*, or soldier, nicknamed *Gattamelata* (c. 1445), which revives the Roman equestrian monument. Done in bronze, both horse and rider have a powerful physical presence. The individual personality that emerges from the portrait-quality of the soldier's face also draws inspiration from Roman portrait sculpture.

Part of Donatello's genius was the ability to infuse many of his subjects with psychological insight. His prophets for Florence Cathedral emanate a striking sense of their calling. The large bald head and penetrating eyes of *Habbakuk* (c. 1430), give this prophet an intense inner character. Most startling is his wooden statue of Mary Magdalene carved in the last decade of his life whose gaunt face and body graphically portray spiritual strength through physical mortification.

Donatello continued to perfect the depiction of space using low relief that he pioneered in the early scene of Saint George and the dragon. He created the effects of aerial perspective with landscape elements as in a relief of the *Ascension of Christ and the Giving of the Keys to St. Peter* (c. 1425-1430). He used architectural perspective not only to convey three-dimensional space but also to unify several narrative scenes, for example in the gilt bronze relief of the *Feast of Herod* done around 1425 for the font in the Baptistery of Siena. Thus, in many forms, Donatello's work epitomized the new directions in Renaissance art that focused on human qualities within a believable spatial setting.

Of the three artists whose work revolutionized not only Florentine but also Italian Renaissance art in general, Masaccio, the painter, was the youngest. He was born in a small town near Florence in 1401, the year that the competition for the bronze doors of the Florentine Baptistery took place. Thus, Masaccio benefited from some of the visual ideas about architectural perspective and the monumentality of the human figure articulated by Brunelleschi and Donatello.

Masaccio's life was quite brief; he died before he was thirty years old. In this short time, however, he painted several works that summarized the innovations in form and space with his own artistic creativity and vision. His most famous works are the frescoes of the *Lives of Saints Peter and Paul* in the Brancacci Chapel of Santa Maria del Carmine in Florence (c. 1425-1428) and a fresco of the Trinity in the Florentine church of Santa Maria Novella

(c. 1427-1428). These paintings share several characteristics. The figures have a sculptural monumentality achieved by modeling with a consistent light source. They also display an inner awareness of the psychological import and drama of a scene. The *Expulsion of Adam and Eve* in the Brancacci Chapel illustrates these characteristics. The weightiness and corporeal quality of the nude bodies of Adam and Eve accentuate their expression of shame at the realization of their human fallibility.

To create a spatial context, Masaccio combined the unifying force of a single light source with the device of one-point perspective. The spatial recession in *The Tribute Money*, a fresco from the Brancacci Chapel, gives a convincing pictorial illusion of the depth of the landscape setting while simultaneously unifying several different scenes into a continuous narrative. In the fresco of the Trinity in Santa Maria Novella, a single-point perspective is used to create spatial unity that connects the spectator's viewpoint with the illusion of architectural space in the painting.

The work of these artists shared common aesthetic ideas. While they did not work as a group, they knew each other. Brunelleschi and Donatello studied ancient monuments in Rome together. Masaccio included a portrait of Donatello in one his frescoes which is now lost. Beyond these personal ties are the visual interrelationships that their work displays. Revival of the aesthetic principles of classical architecture and sculpture led to the use of proportion and perspective to articulate space in all media. It also helped to develop portrayal of human figures as substantial, three-dimensional bodies. For Donatello and Masaccio, the expression of inner emotion and character was an integral part of the human condition that they depicted in the sculpture and painting. The convergence of these three great artists in Florence during the first half of the fifteenth century set the direction of Renaissance art that accorded with the new spirit of the age.

—*Karen Gould*

ADDITIONAL READING:

Andres, Glenn, John M. Hunisak, and A. Richard Turner. *The Art of Florence, Volume 1*. New York: Abbeville Press, 1988. A comprehensive study of Florentine art with lavish plates that sets the work of Brunelleschi, Donatello, and Masaccio in context.

Avery, Charles. *Donatello: An Introduction*. London: John Murray, 1994. A concise overview of Donatello's life and work with a chronology and location list of Donatello's sculptures.

Cole, Bruce. *Masaccio and the Art of Early Renaissance Florence*. Bloomington: Indiana University Press,

1980. A study of Masaccio's painting that places him in the context of Florentine art and society.

Hartt, Frederick. *History of Italian Renaissance Art*. 4th ed. Revised by David G. Wilkins. New York: Harry N. Abrams, 1994. A comprehensive history of Italian Renaissance art with discussions of Brunelleschi, Donatello, and Masaccio and their influence on the development of Renaissance art.

Saalman, Howard. *Filippo Brunelleschi: The Buildings*. London: A. Zwemmer, 1993. A study of the major buildings designed by Brunelleschi including documentation, patronage, and architectural structure.

SEE ALSO: 1150-1200, Development of Gothic Architecture; 1500, Botticelli Leads the Renaissance Revival of Classical Themes in Painting.

1410
BATTLE OF TANNENBERG

The Battle of Tannenberg marks the declining dominance of the Teutonic Knights along the Baltic coast, the consequent rise of Poland as the most powerful state in east central Europe, and the preeminence of Lithuania in eastern Europe.

DATE: July 15, 1410

LOCALE: Between the village of Tannenberg and the forest of Grunwald in southern East Prussia

CATEGORY: Wars, uprisings, and civil unrest

KEY FIGURES:

Ulrich von Jungingen, grandmaster of the Teutonic Knights since 1407 and ruler of Prussia

Vytautas (Vitovt or Witold; 1350-1430), grand prince of Lithuania, 1392-1430, and cousin of Jagiełło

Władysław II Jagiełło (Jogaila; c. 1351-1434), king of Poland, 1386-1434, who converted to Christianity in 1386

SUMMARY OF EVENT. Since the thirteenth century, the Teutonic Order had led crusades against the pagans in Lithuania and "schismatics" (Orthodox Christians) in Russia. During much of this time, the Germans of the Teutonic Order had been allied with the Polish kings, who were advancing eastward to the south against the same combination of enemies. It had seemed that the Peace of Kalish (1343) had brought an end to the conflicts over possession of Pomerellia (West Prussia). The conversion of the Lithuanian grand duke, Jogaila, and his 1386 marriage to the Polish heiress, Jadwiga, ended the Polish need for an alliance with the Germans. Jadwiga's death in 1399 removed the last voice for peace.

Nevertheless, war was not inevitable. The Teutonic Knights had once been allied with Jogaila (Jagiełło)

against Vytautas' father, and Vytautas had held him partly culpable for his murder. Twice Vytautas had been allied with the Teutonic Knights against Jagiełło. Each time Vytautas had rebelled, cleverly disguising his intent until he could do maximum damage to the Teutonic Order's position in Samogitia. Afterward, when Vytautas realized that he could seize Russia from the weakening hands of the Tatars, he made peace with the Teutonic Order, surrendering Samogitia at the Treaty of Sallinwerder (1398) in return for military aid. Having similarly reconciled himself with Jagiełło, he could count on having Polish knights support his campaigns against Tatars, the grand duke of Moscow, and Novgorod the Great.

Samogitia was important to the Teutonic Knights as the land bridge to their possessions in Livonia. It was also home to the last pagans in Europe, doughty warriors who had refused to convert when the rest of the Lithuanians obeyed Jagiełło's instructions to consider themselves henceforth Roman Catholics. Samogitia was also the homeland of Vytautas' mother, and most of Vytautas' boyars were unhappy that it was in foreign hands. In 1409, after an unusually cold winter and a very dry summer, the crops failed. Several thousand Samogitians fled to Vytautas. Grandmaster Ulrich asked Vytautas to return the "serfs" according to treaty promises. Vytautas responded that they were not serfs and, therefore, he was allowing them to stay. Ulrich then ordered vessels carrying Polish grain to Lithuania searched, and when weapons were allegedly found, supposedly destined for Samogitian rebels, he confiscated the cargos. Vytautas was furious. Soon thereafter a rebellion began in Samogitia, and Vytautas appeared with an army, supposedly in support of the crusader order, but in actuality aiding the rebels. Grandmaster Ulrich then attacked Jagiełło, hoping to intimidate him into abandoning his support of Vytautas.

The grandmaster had good reason for confidence in his ability to challenge two great powers at once: Most of the border wilderness between Prussia and Poland's northeast province, Masovia, was impassible for large armies. In addition, the Masovian dukes were not eager to become involved in the war. The Polish forces were on the west bank of the Vistula River and could not easily cross to join the Lithuanians. At the time, the armies of the Teutonic Order were considered invincible, and their border fortifications were the best in east central Europe. Finally, Sigismund of Hungary and Holy Roman Emperor Wenceslas of Bohemia were expected to attack Poland's southern and western frontiers, while the Livonian forces would ravage Lithuania.

Sigismund and Wenceslas had other problems to deal with, however, and the Livonians had signed a truce with Vytautas. The grandmaster prepared for war, anticipating an invasion of West Prussia. To Ulrich von Jungingen's surprise, Vytautas marched into Masovia in June with eleven thousand men, while Jagiełło's engineers built a pontoon bridge and transported his eighteen to twenty-one thousand men across the Vistula. The grandmaster had to hurry to take his own twenty thousand men into East Prussia and cut off the invaders at the Dzewa (Drwęca) River. Jagiełło then feigned a retreat and marched around the eastern flank of the crusader forces through the Grunwald forest. Von Jungingen again cut off the invaders' line of march, passing through Tannenberg before dawn on July 15 to confront the Poles and Lithuanians on a broad field at the edge of the forest.

Von Jungingen did not exploit the advantage of surprise. He apparently wanted to fight a defensive battle, holding his heavy cavalry in reserve for the moment that his light cavalry and infantry drove their opponents back, then charging into the rear of the retreating forces. Yet Jagiełło delayed deploying his forces. He remained in his tent, hearing mass after mass. After a while, the grandmaster pulled his forces back somewhat so that his enemies would have space to line up their forces. This strategy had the disadvantage of placing the order's excellent artillery in a poor location and abandoning the obstacles the infantry had erected to protect their position. Meanwhile, his troops had nothing to eat or drink. As the morning wore on, the grandmaster sent two swords to the king, challenging him to come out and fight. At that Jagiełło ordered the attack.

Vytautas' Lithuanians, Russians, and Tatars swept down on the crusader lines; the Poles advanced singing their anthem. After a desperate struggle, most of Vytautas' cavalry fled the field, pursued by elated, undisciplined crusaders from Germany. Vytautas, however, remained on the field, exhausting horse after horse in directing the fighting. Polish units, meanwhile, noticed the gap the crusaders had left in their lines. Charging into that gap, the Poles began to roll up the German position. Grandmaster Ulrich, instead of ordering a retreat (perhaps because he did not think he could extract his forces successfully), collected every knight he could into a column and charged directly toward Jagiełło's great banner. The attack had a good chance of success, and one knight almost struck down the king before he himself was unhorsed. When Ulrich's banner went down, however, the advance stalled. The order to retreat could not be obeyed. Ulrich, most of his officers, and most of his knights were surrounded and killed; a few were taken prisoner.

Panic set in among the German forces, a panic which became worse when they realized that even abandoning weapons and armor could not speed their flight through the forest significantly. The pursuers cut down the slowest, stopping only to loot the dead, steal the belongings of the prisoners before murdering them, and protect those they considered sufficiently wealthy to ransom.

About eight thousand soldiers had fallen in each army. Jagiełło ordered a search for the grandmaster's body, the collection of weapons, the burial of the dead in mass graves, and care for the wounded. His army, though victorious, was too exhausted to move for three days. Vytautas, more active and a better leader, sent his Tatars to burn and loot throughout East Prussia.

When Jagiełło did move north, he was met by delegations of clerics, towns, secular knights, all eager to obtain favorable terms of surrender. He expected that the entire country would come under his sway. He did not reckon on the unusual initiative of a minor officer of the Teutonic Order, Heinrich von Plauen, who took his small force directly to Marienburg, the greatest fortress in Prussia, where grandmasters had entertained the thousands of crusaders who used to come annually to earn knighthood, to witness the elaborate chivalric spectacles and, if sufficiently prominent, to sit at the Table Round. In three days, he made Marienburg defensible, so that all Jagiełło could do was sit outside the walls, without siege guns or a sufficient supply of food. When disease began to break out among Vytautas' troops, Jagiełło ordered a retreat. Heinrich von Plauen followed, recapturing the towns and castles one by one easily because the king could not leave behind a large occupation force. Such was the disadvantage of the king having to rely on a feudal levy and foreign allies.

Although Jagiełło did not occupy Prussia, he had struck a deadly blow at the order, destroying the flower of its fighting machine, its most experienced leaders, and its reputation for invincibility. The Treaty of Thorn (1411) imposed a crushing indemnity on the Teutonic Order that ultimately drained its resources beyond recovery. Poland was henceforth the dominant power in the region.

—*William L. Urban*

ADDITIONAL READING::

Christiansen, Eric. *The Northern Crusades* and *The Baltic and the Catholic Frontier, 1100-1525*. Minneapolis: University of Minnesota Press, 1980. The best of the general surveys which set the battle in context.

Davies, Norman. *God's Playground: A History of Poland in Two Volumes*. Vol. 1. New York: Columbia University Press, 1982. A lively account with no controversial opinions repressed.

Evans, Geoffrey. *Tannenberg 1410:1914*. London: Hamish Hamilton, 1970. Succinct standard interpretation of two major battles at this site by a military historian.

Jasienica, Pawel. *Jagiellonian Poland*. Miami, Fla.: American Institute of Polish Culture, 1978. Polish interpretation of the battle that gives credit for victory to King Jagiełło.

Koncius, Joseph. *Vytautas the Great, Grand Duke of Lithuania*. Miami, Fla.: Franklin Press, 1964. Lithuanian interpretation of the battle that gives credit to Grand Prince Vytautas.

SEE ALSO: 1228-1231, Teutonic Knights Bring Baltic Region Under Catholic Control; 1380, Battle of Kulikovo; 1450-1466, Second Peace of Thorn.

1414-1418
COUNCIL OF CONSTANCE

The Council of Constance ends the Great Schism within the Catholic Church, but fails to institute basic reforms, especially the sharing of papal powers with regular assemblies of churchmen, and sparks Hussite revolt in Bohemia.

DATE: 1414-1418
LOCALE: Constance, in modern-day Switzerland
CATEGORY: Religion
KEY FIGURES:
Benedict XIII (Pedro de Luna; c. 1328-1423), Catholic pope in Avignon, 1394-1423
Gregory XII (Angelo Correr; c. 1325-1417), Catholic pope in Rome, 1406-1415
Jan Hus (c. 1372-1415), Bohemian reformer accused of heresy
John XXIII (Baldassare Cossa; died 1419), a former mercenary general who was elected pope by the Council of Pisa in 1410
Sigismund of Luxembourg (1368-1437), king of Hungary, 1387-1437, and Holy Roman Emperor, 1433-1437

SUMMARY OF EVENT. In the early fourteenth century European public life seemed to be unraveling. There had been divisions in the Roman Church before, but the Great Schism that began in 1378 was worse than any previous contest of pope and antipope. After the Council of Pisa met in 1408 in an effort to remove both the Roman and Avignon popes, they achieved little more than declaring a third pope, who was soon succeeded by a former mercenary soldier, John XXIII, whose personal life and politics were more distasteful than those of either of his rivals.

Similarly, the Holy Roman Empire was being contested by three claimants: Wenceslas of Bohemia, who had refused to accept his deposition by the electors on the grounds of incompetence and alcoholism; Ruprecht of the Rhine, a minor prince; and Wenceslas' half brother, Sigismund of Hungary, whose qualifications were geniality, a gift for foreign languages, and the expectation that he would be Wenceslas' heir. France was ruled by an insane king, with the regency contested between Burgundian and Orléanist factions. England, having finally resolved its internal problems, saw an opportunity to resume the Hundred Years' War. Bulgaria and Serbia had fallen to the Ottoman Turks, Constantinople was surrounded, and the French and Hungarian crusaders of 1396 had suffered a humiliating defeat at Nicopolis on the Danube.

In the end, everyone turned to Sigismund for leadership. Ruprecht had died, Wenceslas was unable even to maintain peace in his own kingdom, and John XXIII had been driven out of Rome by King Ladislas of Naples. In 1413, the electors of the Holy Roman Empire proclaimed Sigismund as the German king and saw to his coronation in Aachen; then they contributed a small number of knights to accompany him to Italy. There, Sigismund won general agreement to participating in General Council, which would attempt to resolve some of Christendom's most pressing crises.

The site was to be Constance, a beautiful city on a lake that everyone could reach easily via the Rhine and the Alpine passes, which had sufficient lodgings and food, enjoyed a mild climate, and was relatively neutral in politics. For convenience, the delegates would be divided into four "nations" according to the practice common in universities, allocating the delegations to the largest nation according to the cardinal points: the German, the Italian, the French, and the Spanish. Since the Spanish refused to attend, however, their place was awarded to the English.

Because it was not easy to get all the representatives to Constance on time, the council took up important business slowly even after John XXIII formally opened its sessions in late 1414. Sigismund did not appear until Christmas Eve. This time, however, was not wasted. The adherents of the three popes conducted informal discussions which led them to the conclusion that the present claimants had to go. As it dawned on John XXIII that he would not have an honorable retirement, he slipped out of Constance on March 20, a day when the entire populace and most of the council members were watching a tournament, leaving behind a proclamation that the council was dissolved.

Sigismund responded promptly by ordering the councilmen to stay in session, setting pursuers on the fugitive's trail, and raising an army to attack John's protector, Friedrich of Austria. In late April, John XXIII was captured and brought to Constance. In early May, he was put on trial for heresy, simony, and a long catalog of crimes mortal and venal. By the end of the month, John XXIII had been convicted and deposed.

Meanwhile, another trial was in process, that of Jan Hus of Bohemia. Hus was the leader of the Czech reformers, a brilliant orator, a man of highest personal integrity, but hated by the German churchmen in Prague who were the target of his unrelenting attacks. Because Hus's philosophy was strikingly similar to that of John Wycliffe, he was repeatedly accused of heretical beliefs and practices. The council was an opportunity for Hus to defend himself against his enemies' charges and to persuade others to make the kind of basic reforms that would transform the Church into a servant of the people rather than the great landed families. Sigismund had given Hus safe conduct to Constance, then rather shamefacedly arrested him when churchmen threatened to break up the council and go home unless the excommunicated scholar was put on trial for heresy. The trial was a travesty. Hus was condemned and burned at the stake in July. His follower, Jerome of Prague, came to Constance to defend Hus's teachings. He was burned in May of 1416, shouting his defiance to his last breath.

Immediately, the smoldering unrest in Bohemia burst into flame. Czech nationalism joined religious and class motives to create several Hussite parties. Soon, moderate Hussites were celebrating communion "in both kinds," with the communicants drinking from the chalice as well as the priest; radicals were advocating social revolution.

Sigismund's personal diplomacy persuaded the remaining popes to resign, which required the creation of a fifth nation in order to seat the Spanish delegates. Sigismund visited France and England, hoping to bring an end to the Hundred Years' War (Henry V had landed in Normandy in August and fought the battle of Agincourt). The repercussions of this conflict were felt in Constance, where it was widely believed that the French nation wanted to break up the council.

There were two trials which touched on the question of tyrannicide. The first was that of John Petit, who had defended the assassination of Louis of Orléans. The second concerned the Dominican Johannes Falkenberg, who had called for the murder of King Władysław II Jagiełło of Poland, whom he accused of being an idolater and a secret pagan. In the end, it was decreed that Catholics cannot commit murder, even for a good cause.

With the French not cooperating, with the cardinals angry at having lost influence, with national issues intruding on the deliberations at every level, and with Sigismund absent on diplomatic missions, management of the council fell to the archbishops of Milan, Antioch, Riga, and Salisbury. Only in October of 1417 were they able to bring the nations together to pass several important decrees: *Frequens* established the principle of holding regular General

Council, the next in five years, the following in seven years, and thereafter every ten years; another established a procedure for dealing with future schisms; and a commission was established to determine a method of electing a pope.

In November, the electoral conclave met. Consisting of all the cardinals and delegates from each of the nations, this conclave came to agreement within three days on Cardinal Odo Colonna, who took the name Martin V. The enthusiasm of the moment hardly lasted past the naming of a reform commission; in January of 1418, the pope listed matters which the commission should study, but he insisted on an impossible unanimity before any changes could be adopted. Papal authority was safe.

Martin V was not eager to call another council, nor was his successor, Eugenius IV. They, the cardinals, and the papal bureaucrats recognized the danger presented by an effort to create a representative government for the Church. Who could resolve matters quickly and effectively, who could call for a crusade, who could decide whether a Holy Roman Emperor had been properly elected, if not the pope? Reforms would win public respect at the cost of bankrupting the papacy and tying the pope's hands.

The Council of Constance had been a magnificent effort. The councilmen had restored the unity of the Roman Catholic Church, but they left some important disputes to be resolved by Martin Luther, others by the Council of Trent, and the rest by time.   —*Roger Smith*

ADDITIONAL READING:

Hughes, Philip. *The Church in Crisis: A History of the General Councils, 325-1870.* Garden City, N.Y.: Doubleday, 1964. Narrative account for a general audience by a prominent Roman Catholic scholar.

Oberman, Heiko. *Forerunners of the Reformation: The Shape of Late Medieval Thought Illustrated by Key Documents.* New York: Holt, Rinehart and Winston, 1966. A chapter on the nature of the Church, with emphasis on Hus's views, by a prominent theologian.

Pelikan, Jaroslav. *Reformation of Church and Dogma, 1300-1700.* Vol. 4 in *The Christian Tradition: A History of Development of Doctrine.* Chicago: University of Chicago Press, 1984. Citation-filled scholarly work for theological students and scholars.

Spinka, Matthew. *John Hus at the Council of Constance.* New York: Columbia University Press, 1965. Contains the lengthy account of Petr z Mladenovic of Hus's trial and execution.

Waugh, W. T. "The Councils of Constance and Basle." In *The Cambridge Medieval History.* Cambridge, England: Cambridge University Press, 1964. Straightfor-ward account of the council for well-informed scholars.

SEE ALSO: 1054, Beginning of the Rome-Constantinople Schism; 1215, The Fourth Lateran Council; 1415, Martyrdom of Jan Hus; 1521, Martin Luther Appears Before the Diet of Worms; 1545-1563, Council of Trent.

1415-1460
PRINCE HENRY THE NAVIGATOR PROMOTES PORTUGUESE EXPLORATION

Prince Henry the Navigator sends out exploratory expeditions under the aegis of his center for the study of navigation, science, and geography, removing the imagined terrors of the deep, and establishing the first exploring and commercial companies of modern times.

DATE: 1415-1460

LOCALE: Sagres, Largos, and Lisbon, Portugal

CATEGORIES: Education; Exploration and discovery; Science and technology

KEY FIGURES:

Prince Edward (1391-1438), John I's eldest son who succeeded his father as king in 1433 and supported Henry's work

Diogo Gomes (fl. 1440-1484), explorer of Cape Verde Islands between 1458 and 1460

Anton Gonsaluez and *Nuno Tristam*, originators of Portuguese slave interests in 1441

John Gonsaluez, explorer who rediscovered the Canary Islands and Madeira in 1418

Prince Henry the Navigator (1394-1460), fourth son of King John of Portugal

John I (1357-1433), king of Portugal, 1385-1433, who established a strong, centralized monarchy

Prince Peter, John I's second son who later became regent

Queen Philippa of Portugal (1359-1415), daughter of John of Gaunt and wife of John I in 1387

SUMMARY OF EVENT. The court of Prince Henry the Navigator at Sagres became famous as a center which attracted mathematicians, geographers, and, in general, any scientific-minded person from East or West interested in exploration, discovery, and the expansion of maritime knowledge. The center of Henry's maritime activity was not his court at Sagres, but at Lagos, where nearly all the early expeditions were equipped. Although Henry financed and directed many expeditions along the coast of Africa, he did not accompany them. His aim was not personal adventure, but rather the expansion of scientific knowledge and the extension of Portugal's wealth. Inspired by the crusading zeal of his mother, he claimed that his primary goal was the propagation of Christianity even beyond Moorish lands. While he also sought to draw commercial profit from the new-found lands to underwrite the vast expense of the voyages, the sincerity of his religious and scientific motives is not easily discredited. Determined to wipe out medieval fears of the sea and unknown lands, he was passionately involved in supervising the compilation and dissemination of the knowledge gained from new voyages. The influence of the ancient Greek astronomer Ptolemy was still great: His view that the world was flat attracted supporters, and many believed that while the known portion of the earth was neatly divided into ordered segments, the unknown area was full of sea monsters and boiling waters. Henry not only studied the ancient geographers and medieval maps, but engaged an expert map and instrument maker, James of Majorca, so that his explorers might have the best nautical information.

Henry's enthusiasm was fed not only by the experiences of the traders of his own day, but also by his knowledge of past expeditions of crusaders and explorers such as Marco Polo and John de Plano Caprini. Little was known of the Viking adventures in crossing the Atlantic to Greenland and America or their penetration of Russia, but Henry became interested in studying their sea ventures and was strongly influenced by them. Between 1250 and 1410, many new geographical vistas had opened up. In 1270, the Italian Lancelot Malocello found the Canary Islands, and in 1281 and 1291, the Italians Tedisio Doria and Vivaldi discovered Cape Horn while trying to reach India by sea. Around 1350, the Catalonians found Guinea. The Englishman Robert Machin reached Madeira, only to die there; however, his servant managed to escape from the island and eventually reported the discovery to Henry.

Henry's captains used all the reliable knowledge of the sea available to them from such explorations, and used the compass and other instruments to navigate in the open sea. Henry's first venture in expansion, however, was the Portuguese conquest in 1415 of Ceuta, the Moorish port opposite Gibraltar. Fulfilling the mission of the Military Order of Christ, of which he was grandmaster, his ships carried on a constant war against the Muslims. He envisioned the conquest of Ceuta as part of the crusade against Islam. The permanent occupation of Ceuta marks the beginning of imperialism by nation-states three generations in advance of the general movement. Again in 1418, when John Gonsaluez rediscovered the Canaries and Madeira, colonization followed. It was after the fall of Ceuta that Henry entered his career of discovery, and his immediate objects were to know the country beyond Cape Bojador, the farthest limit of the known world on the west

AFRICAN EXPLORATION SPONSORED BY HENRY THE NAVIGATOR

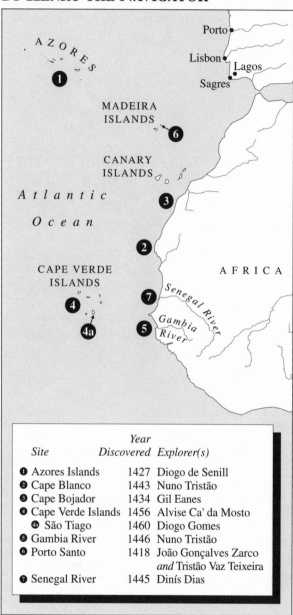

Site	Year Discovered	Explorer(s)
❶ Azores Islands	1427	Diogo de Senill
❷ Cape Blanco	1443	Nuno Tristão
❸ Cape Bojador	1434	Gil Eanes
❹ Cape Verde Islands	1456	Alvise Ca' da Mosto
❹ᵇ São Tiago	1460	Diogo Gomes
❺ Gambia River	1446	Nuno Tristão
❻ Porto Santo	1418	João Gonçalves Zarco *and* Tristão Vaz Teixeira
❼ Senegal River	1445	Dinís Dias

side of Africa, to open up trade relations and to spread the Christian faith. After twelve years of voyages down the African coast, one of his seamen, Gil Eannes, finally rounded Cape Bojador off the coast of modern Rio de Oro in 1435. He found habitable land and not sea monsters. From that date events moved quickly. An unsuccessful attempt to take Tangier occupied Henry's attention between 1437 and 1445. Nevertheless, Anton Gonsaluez landed on the coast of Africa in 1441 and brought back the first captives. Nuno Tristam penetrated as far as Cape Branco, and a few years later to Arguim Bay, and also returned with captured natives, thus inaugurating the slave trade of Guinea. Although Henry's school has been reproached with encouraging slavery, it was an age that saw no harm in the traffic, and he would claim that the Africans brought to Portugal were employed in domestic offices and fairly treated, and that nearly all of them became Christians. There is little doubt, however, about his interest in the discovery of gold around Guinea. In 1445, a number of caravels sailed to Cape Verde. Ten years later Cadamostro (whose narrative proved a most significant contribution to the knowledge of Africa and its adjoining waters) sailed five hundred miles farther to Cape Palmar. The discovery of the Azores to the west of Spain by Gonzalo Cibial in 1436, and the further discovery of two more groups of islands before 1450, led to the colonization of the whole archipelago before Henry's death in 1460.

From 1458 to 1460, Diogo Gomes explored the Senegal and the Gambia, and sailed down the coast as far as Sierra Leone, marking the final exploring effort during Henry's lifetime. Henry's last labor was the commissioning and supervision of the beautiful Camaldalese Chart of Fra Mauro, which carefully illustrated the systematic and scientific discoveries of Henry's "school." He died in November, 1460, deeply in debt as the price of his lifelong service to the cause of Christianity and science and to the pursuance of his motto, *Talent de bien faire* ("The desire to do well").

The more remote achievements resulting from the pioneering efforts of Henry and his court include the voyage of Bartholomeu Dias around Cape Horn in 1486, the voyage to India round Africa by Vasco da Gama from 1497 to 1499, and the establishment of the first outpost of empire by Albuquerque between 1506 and 1515. All of these men were trained in the techniques of Prince Henry's techniques, and their voyages were inspired or encouraged by his school. Ultimately, the discovery of America by Columbus and the circumnavigation of the globe by Magellan's crew were inspired by the achievements of Henry's captains and their successors. Thus, Henry's thirst for inquiry, empire, and crusading led to the opening of a new age and a new world.

—*Carl F. Rohne, updated by Marian T. Horvat*

ADDITIONAL READING:

Beazley, C. Raymond. *Prince Henry, the Navigator.* New York: Knickerbocker Press, 1903. Considered a basic biography of Prince Henry that closely follows primary sources and presents a sympathetic picture of Prince Henry.

Bradford, Ernle D. S. *A Wind from the North: The Life*

of Henry the Navigator. New York: Harcourt, Brace, 1960. A favorable assessment of the character and outlook of Prince Henry based on source documents.

Oliveira Martins, J. P. *The Golden Age of Prince Henry, the Navigator.* Translated by James Johnston Abraham and W. Edward Reynolds. London: Chapman and Hall, 1914. Classic Portuguese work by noted scholar in the field with a primary emphasis on politics and the personalities of the court. Oliveira Martins makes a critical portrayal of the prince and pays little attention to his scientific school.

Sanceau, Elaine. *Henry the Navigator: The Story of a Great Prince and His Times.* New York: W. W. Norton, 1947. A factual and easy-reading narrative by a noted English scholar of Portuguese history.

Ure, John. *Prince Henry the Navigator.* London: Constable, 1977. Ure portrays Henry as a more complex figure, a man torn between the conflicting influences of his medieval background and a pragmatic, forward-looking personality. Presents new perspectives.

SEE ALSO: 1487-1488, Dias Rounds the Cape of Good Hope; 1494, Treaty of Tordesillas; 1500-1530's, Portugal Begins to Colonize Brazil; 1505-1515, Portuguese Viceroys Establish Overseas Trade Empire; 1519-1522, Magellan Expedition Circumnavigates the Globe.

1415
MARTYRDOM OF JAN HUS

The martyrdom of Jan Hus at the Council of Constance makes him a Bohemian national hero and leads to a Hussite revolt against the Holy Roman Emperor and a new schism within the Catholic Church.

DATE: July 6, 1415

LOCALE: Constance, South Germany, and Bohemia

CATEGORIES: Government and politics; Religion

KEY FIGURES:

Jan Hus (c. 1372-1415), Bohemian theologian and martyr

Jerome of Prague (1380-1416), fellow martyr, who brought John Wycliffe's writings to Bohemia

John XXIII (Baldassare Cossa; died 1419), Pisan pope, 1410-1415, during a schism in the papacy

Sigismund (1368-1437), king of Hungary, 1387-1437, king of Bohemia, 1419-1437, and Holy Roman Emperor, 1433-1437

Wenceslas IV (1361-1419), king of Bohemia, 1378-1419, and a supporter of Hus

Zajic Zbyněk, archbishop of Prague, 1403-1411, who condemned Wycliffe's teachings and tried to thwart Hus

SUMMARY OF EVENT. About 1380, a Bohemian princess became queen of England's Richard II (1377-1399), and through that connection Czech students went to Oxford University and came under the influence of John Wycliffe's teaching. Although the Catholic Church had condemned Wycliffe for holding heretical beliefs, the legacy of his teaching at Oxford remained after he had to leave the faculty. Jerome of Prague became acquainted with the writings of the English theologian and took them to Bohemia where he presented them to Jan Hus, who already had been assailing abuses and corruptions in the late medieval church.

Hus, a Master of Arts at the University of Prague, joined its faculty in 1398 and was dean in 1401-1402. He was a popular preacher at Bethlehem Chapel, where he expounded Scripture in the Czech language and called for reforms in the church in a manner similar to that of Wycliffe.

As in Wycliffe's England, the religious issues in Bohemia were connected with national resentment against foreign interference. Until the fourteenth century, Bohemia inclined more toward Constantinople than toward Rome for leadership in religion, because the country had received Christianity originally from the Eastern Church. The University of Prague had Czech and German faculties that opposed each other over various teachings of Wycliffe. The Czechs distrusted the Germans and Rome, and antipapal sects such as the Waldenses had gained a following in Bohemia.

At first Archbishop Zbyněk Zajic supported Hus's efforts to cleanse the church, but his vehement attacks upon clergymen involved in corruptions led Zybněk to oppose Hus and other reformers. The papacy at that time was divided between rivals at Rome and Avignon, and both would-be pontiffs urged the archbishop to suppress the dissidents on the grounds that they promoted Wycliffe's heresies.

Hus, like Wycliffe, espoused the Augustinian understanding of the true church as the body of people God predestined for salvation. While the Bohemian reformer acknowledged the authority of the visible Catholic Church, he refused to equate it with the true church because so many of its members led evil lives and some of its practices were corrupt. In a book entitled *Concerning the Church*, Hus published his doctrine, which ecclesiastical leaders deemed subversive. When Pisan Pope Alexander V ordered the burning of Wycliffe's books, Hus defended some, but not all, of the English reformer's doctrines. King Wenceslas IV of Bohemia protected Hus, so Archbishop Zbyněk and Alexander V denounced him. Zybněk ordered the execution of several Hussite students.

The Catholic Church at that time was seething with dissension over the divided papacy, as rival claimants sat in Rome, Avignon, and Pisa, and a general council of bishops convened at Constance in an effort to heal the schism. Any unconventional teaching about the character of the true church was therefore unwelcome.

The archbishop of Prague tried to silence Hus, but he preached anyway. Zybněk accused him of heresy. When the pope at Pisa, John XXIII, announced a sale of indulgences, Hus cited that as evidence of financial abuses in the highest church office. King Wenceslas broke with Hus over this issue, so the reformer lost his protector. In 1414, Sigismund, king of Hungary and of Bohemia, who was to become Holy Roman Emperor, requested that Hus and Jerome appear before the Council of Constance to answer charges of heresy. He promised them safe conduct to and from the council, but a trial led to condemnation and death by burning for both of the accused.

Perhaps Sigismund thought the executions at Constance would intimidate Bohemian dissidents, but they provoked a violent revolt instead. It began in Prague in 1419, under the leadership of Hussite noblemen, and so several Bohemian cites adhered to the defense against the Catholic forces. Sigismund's efforts to suppress the Hussites by force failed, but the rebels weakened their own cause by dividing among themselves. The conservative faction sought church reforms in accord with Hus's teachings, but the radicals wanted sweeping social and political changes as well. The Taborites, as the radicals were known, decried the traditional feudal society and enlisted common people and lowly knights and clergymen, as they fought tenaciously until 1434, when imperial forces defeated them with aid from conservative Hussites.

Defeat in battle did not destroy the Hussites. Emperor Sigismund and the Catholic hierarchy agreed to a compromise in 1436 that allowed the Hussites to practice their religion and to enjoy the same political rights as Catholics. Many Hussite nobles kept Catholic properties they had seized during the revolt. The papacy, reunited at the Council of Constance, did not accept the compromise, but it lacked the means to thwart it. The Hussites had won politically as well as religiously, perhaps because of the defeat of the Taborite radicals. Large numbers of Bohemians and some Moravians aligned with the Hussite movement in opposition to the Roman Catholic Church. Bohemian nobles continued to elect their kings and to exert decisive influence in the national diet and thereby to maintain protection of the Hussites until the forces of the Habsburg Empire conquered Bohemia in the Thirty Years' War (1618-1648). The remaining Taborites who resisted absorption into the major Hussite Church became known as United Brethren, which maintained a separate existence and refused all agreements with the Catholics and did not enjoy legal recognition. The Brethren were very receptive toward Lutheranism and Calvinism, when those beliefs entered Bohemia in the sixteenth century. Hussites of both connections suffered horribly during recurrent persecutions by Catholic authorities well into the eighteenth century.

Although the Hussites eventually became Protestants, Hus himself was almost completely orthodox when judged by the standards of medieval Catholicism. The account of his trial at the Council of Constance shows clearly that he accepted all seven sacraments and that he believed in transubstantiation, the teaching that the bread and wine of the Eucharist become the actual body and blood of Christ when a priest consecrates them. Hus believed in Purgatory and in prayers for the dead who were confined there, and he thought that living believers could perform good works to benefit the deceased in Purgatory. He believed the Virgin Mary had been raised from the dead and exalted to Heaven above the angels, where she intercedes for Chris-

tians on Earth and in Purgatory. While he awaited execution, Hus confessed his sins to another priest, and he implored Saint John the Baptist to intercede for him with God. It appears that his rejection of papal supremacy was Hus's only actual heresy. He upheld the authority of the Bible but as interpreted by the early ecumenical councils and the church fathers. He would not affirm the right of the pope to issue the infallible interpretations of either the Scriptures or the fathers. Hus preached and wrote in an era when the matter of supreme ecclesiastical authority was hotly contested, so his views appeared dangerous both to the papacy and to advocates of the conciliar theory of church government.   —*James Edward McGoldrick*

ADDITIONAL READING:

Budgen, Victor. *On Fire for God*. Welwyn, England: Evangelical Press, 1983. A readable biography that extols Hus as an example of heroic faith.

Hus, John. *The Church*. Translated by David Schaff. Reprint. Westport, Conn.: Greenwood Press, 1974. A reprint of an edition of Hus's most controversial writing

Excommunicated because of his support for church reform, Jan Hus was tried for heresy at the Council of Constance and was sentenced to burn at the stake. (Archive Photos)

published in translation in 1915. Essential reading for an understanding of his beliefs.

_____. "Hus on Simony." In *Advocates of Reform*, edited by Matthew Spinka. Vol. 14 of Library of Christian Classics. Philadelphia: Westminster Press, 1953. An important tract that shows Hus's exposé of ecclesiastical corruption.

Kaminsky, Howard. *A History of the Hussite Revolution*. Berkeley: University of California Press, 1967. A thorough study of Hussite ideas and their revolutionary consequences.

Roubiczek, Paul, and Joseph Kalmer. *Warrior of God*. London: Nicholson and Watson, 1947. A valuable biography by enthusiasts who portray Hus as a saint.

Schaff, David. *John Hus After Five Hundred Years*. New York: Charles Scribner's Sons, 1915. A scholarly biography that assesses Hus's influence upon Luther and other Protestant reformers.

Spinka, Matthew. *John Hus*. Princeton, N.J.: Princeton University Press, 1968. The best biography of Hus published in English. Scholarly, readable, and fair.

_____. *John Hus and the Czech Reform*. Chicago: University of Chicago Press, 1941. An important study of Hus's concept of reform and the extent of his debt to Wycliffe.

_____, ed. and trans. *John Hus at the Council of Constance*. New York: Columbia University Press, 1965. The records of Hus's trial and execution; shows clearly that he was not a proto-Protestant.

SEE ALSO: 1414-1418, Council of Constance; 1517, Luther Posts His Ninety-five Theses; 1521, Martin Luther Appears Before the Diet of Worms; 1618, Defenestration of Prague; 1635, Peace of Prague; 1643-1648, Peace of Westphalia.

1429

JOAN OF ARC'S RELIEF OF ORLÉANS

Joan of Arc's relief of Orléans begins a series of French victories that shatter the myth of English invincibility and turn the tide in the Hundred Years' War.

DATE: May 4-8, 1429

LOCALE: France

CATEGORIES: Government and politics; Religion; Wars, uprisings, and civil unrest

KEY FIGURES:

Charles VII (1403-1461), Valois claimant to the French throne

Jean Dunois (1403-1468), bastard of the duke of Orléans, later comte de Dunois, French commander at Orléans

Joan of Arc (c. 1412-1431), French heroine known as the Maid of Orléans

John of Lancaster, duke of Bedford (1389-1435), regent in France for Henry VI

John Talbot, earl of Shrewsbury (c. 1384-1453), English troop commander at Orléans

SUMMARY OF EVENT. During the Anglo-French Hundred Years' War (1337-1453), the English invaders repeatedly defeated France's feudal armies in battles such as Crécy (1337) and Poitiers (1356). With Henry V's victory at Agincourt in 1415, English mastery of all France seemed possible. Defeated and demented, King Charles VI of France, by the 1420 Treaty of Trois, gave Henry his daughter Catherine in marriage and regency powers and inheritance rights, in effect disinheriting his own son, the dauphin Charles. Henry V and Charles VI died in 1422, leaving an infant Henry VI as sovereign of both kingdoms. Henry's regent for France, John, duke of Bedford, held Paris and northern France with the alliance of Burgundy and the acquiescence of Brittany. The former dauphin, claiming the throne as Charles VII, was an uncrowned and generally unsuccessful challenger. His "capital" at Bourges and a residence at Chinon were threatened as Bedford's commanders advanced. On October 12, 1428, the English attacked the key city of Orléans on the north bank of the Loire.

The invaders had scattered so many troops in Loire valley garrisons that less than five thousand were at hand to take the walled city, and even these forces were dispersed—some in connected forts northwest of Orléans, others in isolated forts upstream or downstream or at the south end of the nine-span Loire bridge. Despite this, river traffic continued, there was an upstream ford, and the city's eastern gate admitted supplies. Orléans' seventy-one heavy cannon and numerous field pieces outgunned the besiegers. John Talbot, the effective English siege commander, was essentially waiting for the city of perhaps forty thousand, including refugees, to starve. On the other hand, the capable French commander, Jean Dunois, felt that with only two thousand troops and two thousand militia, he could not attack, and so waited for reinforcements. The bishop and several leading citizens left, and, by early 1429, the people of Orléans began to feel abandoned. At Chinon in March, while King Charles was trying to organize a relief force, a seventeen-year-old peasant girl arrived and volunteered to lead the expedition.

Joan the Maid, or Jehanne la Pucelle, as she described herself, was one of five children born to Jacques "Darc" and Isabelle in the Lorraine village of Domremy. Her childhood was "like the others" until about 1425, when she began to sense voices and visions of saints telling her

Despite her lack of fighting experience, Joan of Arc rallied French troops to capture English garrisons along the Loire River and break the lengthy siege of Orléans. (Archive Photos)

that God wished Joan to drive the English from France. By 1428, she was petitioning local officials for support, and in February of 1429, Joan was given an escort for the 240-mile journey to Chinon. There the court awaited her with a mixture of curiosity, skepticism, and faint hope. Joan presented to Charles a still secret "personal message" as well as her service toward raising the siege of Orléans and leading the troops to Rheims, where Charles could be anointed with the sacred oil kept there for traditional French coronations. Charles was impressed by Joan's confidence, but cautiously had her examined by clerics and matrons, to make sure the virgin claiming divine inspiration was not a witch deceived and seduced by the devil. Once cleared of Satanic associations, Joan was equipped with white armor, a sword, a small battle ax, a white religious standard of her own design, a large black charger which she rode with admirable skill, and a vague status as a "commander" (but not a knight or "chevalier") in the

four-thousand-man relief force that set out from Blois for Orléans on April 27. The march seemed an uncertain combination of supplies, military force, religious devotion, and showmanship.

The French relief army, keeping south of the Loire, arrived upstream from Orléans on the afternoon of April 29, and were met by Dunois. He was impressed by Joan's forcefulness and anxious to show this much-expected arrival to the people of Orléans. Accordingly, at 8:00 P.M. Joan rode through the eastern gate, escorted by Dunois and other captains. Torches dramatized the procession and crowds pressed forward to touch the garments or at least the horse of this girl they hoped would save them. For several days, while the French commanders debated plans of attack, Joan mingled with the garrison and citizens of Orléans, while also sending surrender demands to the English commanders. The English troops hailed her with earthy insults, but the French soldiers increasingly accepted her as a leader.

On May 4, French troops attacked St. Loup, an English fort east of Orléans. Joan hastened to the fight, which Dunois was ready to discontinue, and rallied the French to capture the position. Thereafter, Joan was one of the military council, and she also played a leading part in taking Les Augustins near the south end of the bridge. On May 7, while attacking Les Tourelles guarding the bridge itself, Joan was seriously wounded by an arrow, but still took charge of the attack which captured the towers. By nightfall of May 7, the Loire bridge was in French hands, and Orléans was no longer isolated. The following day, after challenging the French to battle (declined) the English army marched north. On the evening of May 8, the long-besieged citizens celebrated their rescue by the Maid of Orléans.

The relief of Orléans was accomplished without a major battle of main forces—only a few hundred lives were lost on each side, and the odds clearly favored the French after April 29. Nevertheless, the prolonged September to May "siege" was lifted unexpectedly only nine days after Joan's arrival, enough of a "miracle" to encourage the French and disquiet the English, as Bedford reported to London. Joan, Dunois, and other French commanders captured English garrisons along the Loire at Jargeau, Meury, and Beaugency. On June 18, the English and French main armies, each numbering about five thousand, encountered each other near Patay. While Talbot and Sir John Fastolf began to deploy in the usual English "hedgehog" defense line of stakes and archers, Joan's insistence on immediate attack took them by surprise. In a paralyzing defeat, the English lost thousands, Talbot was captured, Fastolf fled, and the English, decisively beaten in the field, fell back on Paris. Patay ranked with Orléans as a decisive French victory and a blow to English morale.

French debates over strategic direction continued until Charles reluctantly tried Joan's plan to advance through Champagne for a coronation at Rheims. The march became a triumph—popular enthusiasm (and a few bribes) disarmed opposition and avoided any divisive battle between Frenchmen. The idolized girl on horseback achieved her greatest political success with the Rheims coronation, which dramatized Charles as the crowned, anointed, and rightful king of France.

In 1430, however, Joan failed to take Paris, was captured near Compiègne by Burgundian forces, sold to the English-controlled Paris authorities, and tried by a church court at Rouen from January through May, 1431. The judges and Joan disagreed somewhat dogmatically concerning God's will, and the court predictably insisted that Joan's anti-English voices must be either imaginary or proof of Satanic possession. After a brief "recantation" of the voices, Joan "relapsed" and as a convicted heretic and tool of the devil, was turned over to the civil authorities and burned at the stake in Rouen on May 30, 1431.

The popular nationalism which Joan had harnessed so dramatically in 1429 did not by itself drive the English from France. Those who could pay for such a war wanted to be able to profit from the outcome. King Charles (who made no attempt to ransom Joan in 1430) methodically pursued governmental, fiscal, and military reforms and in 1435 also won the support of Burgundy for expelling the English. Only in 1450, with success assured, did Charles order the inquiry which cleared Joan (and the king) of any taint of witchcraft or heresy. Papal authorities declared Joan rehabilitated in 1456, and in a later and different context, the Church declared her "venerable" in 1904, "blessed" in 1909, and canonized in 1920 as "Saint Joan."

Joan's role at Orléans was to add the spark of moral and combat leadership needed to give the French a season of military and political success, and the confidence and credibility for ultimate victory. Yet in the long run, Joan's life was seen as a human drama even more compelling than the war itself. A "guided" national savior, victim, and martyr, all by the age of nineteen—a sort of fairy tale, but with a brutal ending.   —*K. Fred Gillum*

ADDITIONAL READING:

Belloc, Hilaire. *Joan of Arc*. London: Cassell, 1929. A popular biography by an inimitable French stylist.

Burne, Alfred. *The Agincourt War*. London: Eyre & Spottiswode, 1956. An English military analysis of the Battle of Agincourt.

Gies, Frances. *Joan of Arc: The Legend and the Reality*. New York: Harper & Row, 1981. Scholarly, but omits some "legends."

Raknen, Ingvald. *Joan of Arc in History, Legend, and Literature*. Oslo, Norway: Universitets vorlaget, 1971. A brief survey and useful bibliography.

Sackville-West, Vita. *Saint Joan of Arc*. New York: Doubleday Doran, 1936. Comprehensive and well-balanced biography of Joan written by the noted British author.

Scott, W. S. *Jeanne d'Arc*. London: George G. Harrap, 1974. Scott's biography of Joan includes an invaluable annotated bibliography.

SEE ALSO: 1346, Battle of Crécy; 1453, English Are Driven from France.

1440

DONATION OF CONSTANTINE IS EXPOSED AS FRAUDULENT

The Donation of Constantine is exposed as fraudulent, casting doubts on the legitimacy of papal authority.

DATE: 1440

LOCALE: The kingdom of Naples

CATEGORIES: Cultural and intellectual history; Religion

KEY FIGURES:

Alfonso V (1396-1458), king of Aragon, 1416-1458, and king of Naples, 1442-1458

Eugenius IV (Gabriele Condulmer; 1383-1447), Roman Catholic pope, 1431-1447

Nicholas of Cusa (1401-1464), philosopher and theologian

Lorenzo Valla (1407-1457), philosopher

SUMMARY OF EVENT. The Donation of Constantine (known in Latin as the *Constitutum Constantini*) is a document supposedly written by Constantine I, the first Christian emperor of Rome, to Pope Sylvester I in the early fourth century. The document consists of about three hundred lines of Latin text and is divided into two parts. The first half is known as the *Confessio* and the second half is known as the *Donatio*.

The *Confessio* describes how Constantine I rejected the advice of pagan priests to bathe in the blood of children to cure his leprosy. He then had a dream in which Saint Peter and Saint Paul appeared to him and told him he would be cured if he visited Pope Sylvester I and became baptized as a Christian by him. Constantine I followed this advice and was miraculously cured.

The *Donatio* relates how Constantine I, in gratitude for his cure, declared that Pope Sylvester I and his successors would have rule over all Christian churches in the world. He also granted them the use of his Lateran Palace and the use of numerous imperial insignias. Most important, he gave them political power over all of the western part of the Roman Empire and stated that he would move his own court to a new capital (Constantinople) in the eastern part.

Throughout the Middle Ages, the Donation of Constantine was used to defend the authority of the pope over all other Christian clergy and over the secular rulers of western Europe. Although some questioned the validity of the Donation of Constantine on the grounds that the emperor could not legally donate his authority over the empire, the authenticity of the document itself was rarely challenged. The only known accusation of forgery before the fifteenth century came from Otto III, ruler of the Western Roman Empire, in 1001.

The first important attempt to prove that the Donation of Constantine was a forgery came from the German priest, philosopher, theologian, and mathematician Nicholas of Cusa. In his book *De concordantia catholica* (1433, on unity), he noted that the Donation of Constantine was not mentioned in any of the numerous church histories of its time. He also used historical records to show that the pope acknowledged the authority of the emperor in western Europe until the eighth century.

The most critical attack on the authenticity of the Donation of Constantine came seven years later when the Italian philosopher Lorenzo Valla wrote *De Falso Credita et Ementita Constantini Donatione* ("On the Falsely Believed and Forged Donation of Constantine," written in 1440, published in 1517). In this work, Valla used both historical evidence and linguistic analysis to demonstrate that the Donation of Constantine could not have been written during the time of Constantine I.

Like Nicholas of Cusa, Valla noted the lack of historical records mentioning the document. He also noted that the Donation of Constantine made reference to the controversy over the use of images in worship services, an issue which did not come up until the eighth century. The document also mentioned satraps, a type of official which did not exist in the government of Constantine I.

Valla also studied the style of Latin used in the Donation of Constantine to prove that it could not have been written in the fourth century. By carefully examining the grammar and vocabulary used in the document, he was able to demonstrate that the Latin of the Donation of Constantine was not the Latin used during the time of Constantine I but the Latin used hundreds of years later.

Valla had many political, theological, and philosophical reasons for his attack on the authenticity of the Donation of Constantine. Besides a concern for exposing the truth, he also hoped to demonstrate that it would be evil for the pope to accept secular power from Constantine I because his Roman Empire was tyrannic. In a similar way, he advocated the spiritual freedom of the individual over the absolute spiritual authority of the pope. Philosophi-

cally, he defended the use of objective evidence over reliance on accepted authority.

Valla also had a more practical reason for denying the authenticity of the Donation of Constantine. He was employed as a secretary and historian to Alfonso V, king of Aragon, who was at war with Pope Eugenius IV over control of the kingdom of Naples. By exposing the Donation of Constantine as a forgery, Valla denied the authority of the pope to determine who would rule the kingdoms of western Europe.

Valla's book was not published until sixty years after his death, at the beginning of the Reformation. The leaders of the Protestant movement used it to demonstrate that the power of the pope was based on falsehoods. In defense of the Catholic Church, the Italian philosopher Agostino Steuco pointed out that Valla's work was seriously flawed by being based on an abridged and distorted version of the Donation of Constantine rather than on the best text available.

Despite this attack on Valla's methods, modern scholars agree that the Donation of Constantine is a forgery. The evidence suggests that it was composed shortly after the year 750, probably by a cleric at the Church of the Savior, which was built within the Lateran Palace mentioned in the document.

Several theories have been advanced to explain the motive behind the forgery of the Donation of Constantine. In the 1960's, it was suggested that it was used to defend the authority of the pope during diplomatic negotiations with the Franks in the eighth and ninth centuries. More recently it has been suggested that the Donation of Constantine was composed to associate the Church of the Savior with the glory of the first Christian emperor and that it was more an embellished version of what was believed to be the truth rather than a deliberate fraud.

The author of the Donation of Constantine apparently based the *Confessio* section of the document on well-known fifth century legends about Pope Sylvester I. The *Donatio* section is more original, although such a donation was vaguely mentioned in the same legends. The final part of this section, in which the pope was given power over all other rulers in western Europe, was of great political and theological importance from the eleventh century to the fifteenth century.

Despite its later significance, this section may have been an afterthought added by the author after the importance of the Church of the Savior had been established earlier in the document. The claims of papal power made at the end of the Donation of Constantine were either well-established by the middle of the eighth century or were so broadly expressed as to be virtually without any specific meaning.

The critiques of the authenticity of the Donation of Constantine by Nicholas of Cusa and Lorenzo Valla in the middle of the fifteenth century were important precedents in the development of textual criticism in the early Renaissance. Later philosophers would use their methods to question the validity of other old documents. This movement away from accepting the writings of ancient authorities to making use of scientific evidence was one of the important factors in the philosophical transition from medieval Scholasticism to Renaissance Humanism.

—*Rose Secrest*

ADDITIONAL READING:

Bainton, Roland H. "The Search for Order" and "Decline of the Papacy." In *The Horizon History of Christianity*. New York: American Heritage Publishing Company, 1964. Describes the origin of the Donation of Constantine and the methods Lorenzo Valla used to prove that it was a forgery.

Bettenson, Henry, ed. "The Empire and the Papacy." In *Documents of the Christian Church*. 2d ed. London: Oxford University Press, 1963. Includes an English translation of the Donation of Constantine.

Camporeale, Salvatore I. "Lorenzo Valla's Oratio on the Pseudo-Donation of Constantine: Dissent and Innovation in Early Renaissance Humanism." *Journal of the History of Ideas* 57 (January, 1996): 9-26. Discusses the political and theological implications of Lorenzo Valla's attack on the authenticity of the Donation of Constantine.

Delph, Ronald K. "Valla Grammaticus, Agostino Steuco, and the Donation of Constantine." *Journal of the History of Ideas* 57 (January, 1996): 55-77. Describes Agostino Steuco's criticism of the methods used by Lorenzo Valla to expose the Donation of Constantine as a forgery.

Fubini, Riccardo. "Humanism and Truth: Valla Writes Against the Donation of Constantine." *Journal of the History of Ideas* 57 (January, 1996): 79-86. An analysis of the philosophical motivations behind Lorenzo Valla's critique of the Donation of Constantine.

SEE ALSO: 312, Conversion of Constantine; 326-330, Constantinople Is Founded; 1377-1378, John Wycliffe Is Condemned for Attacking Church Authority; 1517, Luther Posts His Ninety-five Theses.

1442-1456
JÁNOS HUNYADI DEFENDS HUNGARY AGAINST OTTOMAN INVADERS

János Hunyadi defends Hungary against Ottoman invaders, delaying the Ottoman conquest and contributing to development of a Hungarian national identity.

DATE: 1442-1456
LOCALE: Hungary and the Balkan Peninsula
CATEGORY: Wars, uprisings, and civil unrest
KEY FIGURES:

Giovanni di Capestrano (János Kapisztrán; 1386-1456), sent to Hungary by the pope to raise a crusade against the Turks; co-leader with Hunyadi in defending Belgrade in 1456, and later canonized by the Catholic Church

János Hunyadi (John Huniades; c. 1407-1456), Hungarian national hero; effectively preserved Hungary from Ottoman conquest during his lifetime and for seventy years thereafter

Ladislas V Posthumous (1440-1457), succeeded father Albrecht of Habsburg as king of Hungary, 1444-1457, later king of Bohemia, 1453-1457; ward of Frederick III of Austria until 1453

Murad II (1404-1451), Ottoman sultan, 1421-1444 and 1446-1451, who campaigned against Hunyadi in 1443, 1445, and 1448

Mehmed II (1432-1481), Ottoman sultan, 1444-1446 and 1451-1481), who captured Constantinople in 1453, but was defeated by Hunyadi and Capestrano at Belgrade in 1456

Władysław III (1424-1444), king of Poland, 1434-1444, and king of Hungary (as Ulászló I), 1440-1444; elected king of Hungary by opponents of Ladislas Posthumous, who also was crowned

SUMMARY OF EVENT. In 1437, Hungary fell into chaos when King Sigismund died without leaving a male heir. Sigismund's daughter, Elizabeth, however, was married to Albrecht, king of Austria, whom Sigismund had designated his successor. Albrecht, however, died after two years without an heir but leaving Elizabeth pregnant. Some Hungarians then supported Elizabeth as regent but others, demanding a male king, elected Władisław III, then king of Poland, as King Ulászló I of Hungary. This action precipitated a civil war.

Sultan Murad II, taking advantage of the confusion, expanded into Wallachia (part of modern Romania) and resumed raids into Hungary across the Danube River. In response, Władisław III appointed János Hunyadi (nicknamed Yanko by the Turks) as captain general of Belgrade and voivade of Transylvania and charged him with defending Hungary's southern border. Hunyadi, son of a minor Vlalch (Romanian) nobleman, Vajk Oláh, and reputed to be an illegitimate son of King Sigismund, was an effective leader. Previously, Hunyadi had been appointed to high command by Sigismund and had been made ban of Szörény by Albrecht. As the "White Knight" of the Serbs and Hungarians, Hunyadi led cavalry charges wearing shining silver armor, quickly winning victories over Władisław's domestic opponents and over the Ottomans along the two-hundred-mile-long southern Hungarian border. His decisive victory at Bataszek in 1441 against Elizabeth's supporters was his first victory of national significance. He defeated a Turkish army under Mezit Beg at Nagyszeben in Transylvania and routed another Turkish army of an estimated eighty thousand men near the Iron Gates on the Danube in 1442. Soon after, Sultan Murad II offered to sign a treaty of peace, but Hunyadi persuaded Władisław to take the offensive against the Turks in 1443. Following Sigismund's prior effort, Hunyadi attempted to generate enthusiasm for a new crusade to drive the Turks out of Europe. Support from western Europe was minimal; only Pope Julian accompanied the crusade. Thus, the crusaders were primarily Poles and Hungarians and, later, Wallachians, along with a few Serbs, Bulgarians, Bosnians, and Albanians. The crusade crossed the Danube in July of 1443, and captured Nish in what is now western Serbia with great losses to the Ottomans. Next, they occupied Sofia (capital of modern Bulgaria), and attempted crossing the Balkan Range in mid-winter. After winning a victory on Christmas Eve near Phillipolis, they found the weather, supply problems, and increased Turkish pressure insurmountable, so Hunyadi ordered a return to Buda. Arriving in February, 1444, his chilled and gaunt army, led by King Władisław on foot, triumphantly entered the city singing hymns and flaunting Ottoman banners. Murad II, essentially a man of peace, did not pursue the crusaders across the Danube but negotiated a ten-year truce on July, 1444, at Szeged, in which Serbia and Wallachia were freed from Ottoman rule and the Hungarians agreed to not cross the Danube or press claims on Bulgaria.

Julian Cesarini, the papal cardinal legate, however, persuaded Władisław that word given to an "infidel" need not be honored, so Hunyadi and Władisław again invaded the Balkans in 1444, leading an army of about twenty thousand Hungarians and Wallachians. Murad, however, succeeded in returning from a campaign in Asia Minor and confronted the Hungarians with one hundred thousand men at Varna on November 10, 1444. Hunyadi and Władisław were decisively defeated. Władisław was unhorsed and decapitated, and his head was mounted on a lance, as was a copy of the broken treaty. These "symbols" were returned to Bursa, then the Ottoman capital, for public display as a warning to the perfidious. Cardinal Julian fled and was never seen again, dead or alive, reportedly having been executed by his own defeated troops. Most of the army was killed in battle or beheaded on the field.

Hunyadi, however, escaped and returned to Hungary, where he successfully mediated the dynastic conflict.

Elizabeth had died, leaving her very young son, King Ladislas V Posthumous, under the protection of his uncle, Emperor Frederick. The Hungarian diet of 1445, an assemblage of nobles, sent negotiators to Frederick requesting return of Ladislas as king, but in the interim the Diet appointed a council of regency to restore internal peace. Failing to retrieve Ladislas, the 1447 Diet elected Hunyadi governor with limited sovereign rights. Hunyadi succeeded in restoring peace in most of the country, although he was defeated by a Czech leader Giskra, who retained control of Northwestern Hungary. In 1448, allied with Albania's leader, Skanderbeg, he again invaded the Balkans. They were again defeated by Murad II in the second battle of Kossovo Polje (Rígomezö in Hungarian). As a result, Serbia lost its independence, Bosnia became an Ottoman vassal state, and Hungarian military power was crippled. Skanderbeg retreated to Croia in Albania, where he remained independent for two decades. Hunyadi, however, still succeeded in holding back Ottoman advance into Hungary.

In 1450, Hunyadi abandoned his supporters in the Diet and allied himself with the Habsburg party. In this way he acquired new Moravian territories and became the legitimate regent for the child king. In 1452, the Austrian and Bohemian Estates forced Emperor Frederick to release Ladislas from tutelage. Ladislas was then instated as king of Hungary, but allowed Hunyadi to remain de facto regent.

After capturing Constantinople in 1453, Mehmed II, the son of Murad II, conquered most of Serbia during 1454 and 1455. In 1456, he besieged about seven thousand men in the fortress of Nándofehérvár (Belgrade) with an army of about one hundred thousand. Hunyadi and the monk, Giovanni di Capestrano, broke through the Ottoman fleet blockading the Danube and entered the citadel of Nándofehérvár. After severe bombardment breached the fortress walls, the Turks penetrated the citadel. Here, Hunyadi ordered his men to hide, while the Janissaries scattered to plunder the town. At a prearranged signal the Hungarians fell upon the disorganized Turks, killed many, and drove the remainder out of the city where many more were trapped in the moats and burned to death. The Hungarians and Capestrano's crusaders then charged the remaining Turks, wounded the sultan, and broke the Ottoman army on July 22. The Ottomans thereafter retreated, leaving their siege guns behind and did not again invade Hungary for seventy years. Hunyadi died of the plague two weeks after the battle, and Capestrano also died a few months afterward. Hungarian affairs again lapsed into internal conflict.

Hunyadi was immediately and uncritically hailed as the man who saved Hungary and Europe from the Ottomans.

He thus became the national hero around whom Hungarian national identity has centered. Critical analysis, however, shows that Hunyadi was far from an invincible military leader, having commanded at two major military disasters. He also failed to end the Ottoman threat, since his actions only delayed the advent of Ottoman control. His effect on Hungarian political evolution lies mostly in having prepared the way for Hungary's first centralized royal government. This government, however, did not survive Ottoman conquest seventy years after Hunyadi's death.
                                            —*Ralph L. Langenheim, Jr.*

ADDITIONAL READING:

Bak, János M., and Béla K. Király, eds. *From Hunyadi to Rákóczi: War and Society in Medieval and Early Modern Hungary.* New York: Columbia University Press, 1982. Includes a critical essay, "János Hunyadi, the Decisive Years of His Career, 1440-1444," written by Pál Engel. Also contains useful background material on fifteenth century Hungary.

Held, Joseph. *Hunyadi: Legend and Reality.* Boulder, Colo.: Westview Press, 1985. Critical evaluation of Hunyadi's career and an extensive description of the social and political environment of the times.

Kinross, Lord. *The Ottoman Centuries: The Rise and Fall of the Turkish Empire.* New York: William Morrow, 1977. Analyzes Hunyadi's battles with the Turks from the Turkish point of view.

Pamlényi, Erving, ed. *A History of Hungary.* London: Collets, 1975. A detailed history of Hungary.

Sugar, P. F., ed. *A History of Hungary.* Bloomington: Indiana University Press, 1990. Includes an essay by János M. Bak entitled "The Late Medieval Period," which outlines the political and cultural history of Hunyadi's regime.

SEE ALSO: 1353, Ottoman Empire Establishes Foothold in Rumelia; 1457-1504, Reign of Stephen the Great; 1458-1490, Hungarian Renaissance Under Mátyás Hunyadi.

1444-1446
ALBANIAN CHIEFTAINS ARE UNITED UNDER SKANDERBEG

Albanian chieftains are united under Skanderbeg as part of the League of Lezha, preserving Albanian freedom for nearly forty years and establishing Albanian national identity.

DATE: 1444-1446
LOCALE: Albania
CATEGORIES: Government and politics; Wars, uprisings, and civil unrest

KEY FIGURES:
Moïse Golem (fl. 1443-1456), a principal commander under Skanderbeg
John Kastriote (fl. 1410), prince of Emathia and father of Skanderbeg
Mehmed II (1432-1481), Ottoman sultan, 1451-1481
Murad II (1404-1451), Ottoman sultan, 1421-1451
Skanderbeg (George Kastriote; 1405-1468), prince of Emathia

SUMMARY OF EVENT. Born George Kastriote, Skanderbeg was the youngest son of John Kastriote, prince of Emathia. Although John Kastriote was a vassal of the Ottoman Turks, he participated in a series of unsuccessful revolts against them during the 1430's. His youngest son, George, was sent to the sultan as a hostage in 1414, and probably was sent again in 1423. Here, George was given the name Skander (Alexander) and was enrolled as a Janissary, a corps of troops recruited by taking non-Muslim children as slaves of the sultan. Here, Skander attended the military school for pages. In 1426 or 1427, he became a *Siphai*, a landed vassal required to supply mounted troops to the sultan. In 1438, Skander was made a "Beg" (or *bey*, a title of nobility) and was appointed governor (*vali*) of three small communities in the *Vilayet*, or province, of Kruja. Later, in 1440, he apparently moved to the large province of Dibra.

In 1443, the Hungarian leader János Hunyadi organized a campaign against the Ottomans and called the Balkan princes to join him as his Hungarians marched south. The sultan rallied his vassals, and Skanderbeg marched to join him. On November 3, the Hungarians attacked at Niš and forced an Ottoman retreat. At this point, Skanderbeg deserted the Ottomans and returned to Dibra with three hundred Albanian horsemen. Finding Dibra ready for revolt, Skanderbeg proceeded to Kruja, where he presented a false *firman* (order from the sultan) giving him command of the town and citadel. That night, Skanderbeg attacked and annihilated the Ottoman garrison. He then spread the rebellion, evicting Ottoman landed vassals from the region. After triumphantly returning to Kruja, he proclaimed Albanian freedom on November 28, 1443, and raised the Kastriote banner over the citadel. Skanderbeg then organized volunteers to capture several citadels in central Albania during December. He also called a conclave of Albanian lords in Venetian territory at Lezha.

At this conclave, he organized an alliance or confederation known as the League of Lezha. This league was an important innovation, since it marked the first embryonic centralized state in the region. A league army supported by a common fund was organized to counter the much larger

Ottoman forces. Skanderbeg was appointed commander in chief and head of the league. Loyal garrisons were installed in fortresses, some lords were deposed, and outstanding soldiers were rewarded with domains of their own. The league, however, was a confederation in which individual nobles retained local authority and the right to withdraw. Encroachments on feudal authority and opportunism made defections a recurring problem and ultimately destroyed the league.

During the spring of 1444, Skanderbeg enrolled an army of some eight thousand to ten thousand regular troops with approximately ten thousand reserves. He also reinforced fortresses and organized a look-out system to warn of attack. About three thousand troops, mostly mounted cavalry, were under his direct command with another three thousand under Moïse Golem guarding the eastern frontier. The remaining troops were under the command of individual nobles.

In June, 1444, twenty-five thousand Ottomans under the command of Ali Pasha invaded Albania through Ochrid. After they were routed by Skanderbeg, the Ottomans withdrew to combat a Hungarian-Polish invasion. After annihilating the Hungarians and Poles at Varna in November of 1444, the Ottomans again invaded Albania. Skanderbeg and his troops defeated the Ottomans at Modr in October, 1445, and at Dibra in September, 1446. The Ottomans did not attempt another invasion in 1447, but war did break out between the league and the Venetian Republic over Danja and Lezha. Lacking artillery, the Albanians were unable to take these citadels.

In 1448, Murad II laid siege to Sfetigrad (Kodjadjik) on Albania's eastern border. Failing to arrange a peace, Skanderbeg quickly defeated the Venetians near Drin in July, 1448, and immediately set off to relieve Sfetigrad. The city capitulated in August, however, so Skanderbeg compromised with the Venetians, giving up Danja for a payment of fourteen thousand ducats per year. The Venetians also agreed to subsidize a Hungarian-Albanian alliance under which Skanderbeg joined János Hunyadi's new offensive against the Turks. The Hungarians, however, were defeated in the second Battle of Kossovo on October 12, 1448, and the alliance ended.

In early May of 1450, Murad again invaded Albania with about one hundred thousand men. Skanderbeg's call to arms raised nearly eighteen thousand men. Besieged by Murad's army, Kruja was garrisoned with fifteen hundred men, but Skanderbeg held eight thousand men on nearby Mount Tumenisht, from which he repeatedly attacked Murad's troops. The remaining Albanian units ambushed Ottoman reinforcements and supply caravans. After a siege of four and a half months, Murad purportedly lost twenty thousand men and was forced to retreat to Adrianople (modern Edirne).

The Treaty of Gaeta between Skanderbeg and Alfonso V of Aragon on March 26, 1451, brought minor support against Ottoman offensives in 1452-1453. In 1453, Skanderbeg personally traveled to Naples and persuaded Alfonso to send troops and artillery to Albania. He also persuaded Ragusa to organize a coalition of troops from Albania, Hungary, and Serbia to fight against the Ottomans. With this support, Skanderbeg laid siege to Berat. Just as the citadel was at the point of surrendering, however, he was assaulted from the rear by forty thousand Ottoman troops who had crossed the frontier through the connivance of Moïse Golem, who had defected. Skanderbeg's defeat renewed Venetian opposition, and Alfonso withdrew his support. In 1456, Golem led fifteen thousand Ottoman cavalry into Albania, but was defeated by Skanderbeg at Oranik. Skanderbeg's nephew, George Stres Balsa, became the next to defect and gave up the frontier citadel of Modrica to the Ottomans. Skanderbeg's other nephew, Hamza Kastriote, also joined the Ottomans.

In 1457, some eighty thousand Ottomans under the command of Isaac Bey Evernos entered Albania accompanied by Hamza Kastriote, who had been named governor of Kruja by the sultan. Skanderbeg avoided direct combat with the invaders until September 7, when he surprised the Ottomans near Kruja and captured thousands of prisoners, including Hamza Kastriote. Skanderbeg then signed a three-year truce; during this period, he took his army to Italy to support Ferdinand of Naples in 1461. In Italy, Skanderbeg won battles at Barletta and Trani. Returning to Albania in 1462, he defeated three separate invasions at Mokra, Pollog, and Livad. After these victories, Skanderbeg persuaded Mehmed II to sign a ten-year peace treaty in April, 1463. Shortly thereafter, Venice declared war on the Ottomans and promised aid to the Albanians. Pope Pius II announced a crusade, and Skanderbeg renewed hostilities. Unfortunately, the crusade collapsed after Pius II's death in 1464, leaving the Albanians unsupported.

Mehmed sent an army of fourteen thousand into Albania from Ochrid, but was promptly crushed in August, 1464. In June, 1466, he proclaimed a holy war of extermination and besieged Kruja with the entire Ottoman army of 150,000 men. In July, Mehmed left with part of the army, leaving Ballaban Pasha to continue the siege. During the winter of 1466-1467, Skanderbeg went to Rome and Naples seeking aid, but accomplished little. In April, 1467, the Albanians defeated reinforcements who were advancing to strengthen Ballaban Pasha; a few days later, they broke the siege and killed Ballaban. Mehmed countered by again invading Albania with his entire imperial army. Winning a bloody battle at Buzurshek (near modern Elbasan), he again laid siege to Kruja. After three weeks, however, Mehmed left the field of battle and Skanderbeg again freed his capital.

In the face of continuing hostilities, depleted forces, and low finances, Skanderbeg planned an assembly of nobles at Lezha to be held in 1468. In midwinter, however, Skanderbeg contracted fever and died on January 17, 1468. His son, John, fled with his mother to Naples. Resistance continued, but depended heavily upon Venetian support. Venice quit the war in 1479, and the Ottomans quickly captured the Albanian citadels. At this point, Skanderbeg's son returned but was unable to stem the tide. After he fled the country in 1482, Albanian independence was lost.

Skanderbeg's League of Lezha began the process of creating a nation-state in Albania. It successfully maintained an independent Albania for some twenty-five years, thus delaying and partially checking the Ottoman advance into Europe. Skanderbeg's successors, however, were unable to keep the league together, and most of Skanderbeg's accomplishments were undone. As a result of his efforts to establish Albanian independence, Skanderbeg has been honored as the national hero of modern Albania.

—*Ralph L. Langenheim, Jr.*

ADDITIONAL READING:

Chekrezi, Constantine A. *Albania Past and Present.* New York: Macmillan, 1919. Reprint. New York: Arno Press, 1971. Within this work, a section on Skanderbeg covers the highlights of his career.

Jacques, Edwin C. *The Albanians: An Ethnic History from Prehistoric Times to the Present.* Jefferson, N.C.: McFarland, 1995. Written by an American who was a former Protestant missionary teacher, this work presents a history of Albania through the early 1990's.

Marmullaku, Ramadan. *Albania and the Albanians.* Translated from the Serbo-Croatian by Margot and Boško Milosavljevic. Hamden, Conn.: Archon Books, 1975. Includes a brief account of Skanderbeg's career, placing him within the context of his times.

Pollo, Stefanaq, and Arben Puto. *The History of Albania from Its Origins to the Present Day.* London: Routledge & Kegan Paul, 1981. Contains a fairly detailed discussion of Skanderbeg from the perspective of communist historians.

Swire, J. *Albania: The Rise of a Kingdom.* London: William & Northgate, 1929. Reprint. New York: Arno Press, 1971. This work includes a readable short account of the military and political accomplishments of Skanderbeg.

SEE ALSO: 1442-1456, János Hunyadi Defends Hungary Against Ottoman Invaders; 1990, Albania Opens Doors to Foreign Nationals.

1450
GUTENBERG PIONEERS THE PRINTING PRESS

Gutenberg pioneers the printing press, developing the technology of printing with movable metal type and ushering in a revolution in communications by making written materials more widely available at a lower cost.

DATE: c. 1450

LOCALE: Germany

CATEGORIES: Communications; Cultural and intellectual history; Science and technology

KEY FIGURES:

William Caxton (c. 1422-1491), English translator and first printer in England

Laurens Janszoon Coster (fl. 1440), Harlem sexton

Johann Fust (c. 1400-1466), Mainz businessman who backed Gutenberg before establishing a printing firm with Peter Schöffer

Johann Gutenberg (Johannes Gensfleisch zur Laden; c. 1399-1468), probable inventor of movable type

Anthony Koberger, published the illustrated *Nuremberg Chronicle* of 1493

Aldus Manutius (Aldo Mannucci; 1449-1515), Venetian printer of classical texts

Peter Schöffer (c. 1425-1502), an early Mainz printer

Konrad Sweinheim and *Arnold Pannartz*, German clerics who set up presses in Italy, 1464-1473

SUMMARY OF EVENT. A concise, factual account of the invention of printing with movable type is not possible because surmises far outnumber facts. The few early printed works bearing dates and names are of little help in identifying early experimenters.

Wang Chieh used the first block print in China in 868; in the eleventh century his fellow countryman Pi Sheng arranged molded and baked clay characters on a frame for printing. Except in Arabic Spain, the West did not make paper until 1270, in Fabriano, Italy; Germany did not begin the process until the fourteenth century.

Between the painstaking copying of manuscripts by hand and the earliest printing with movable type which imitated their calligraphy, an intermediate process of "block books" or *xylographica* appeared. As early as 1418, pictures were carved in wood and printed in thin brownish ink on one side of a leaf. Later, descriptive text accompanied the picture, and printing was done on both sides of the paper in improved ink made of pine shavings and soot. Examples of block books are the *Biblia pauperum* (poor man's Bible), the *Apocalypse*, and the *Ars moriendi* (the art of dying).

Between the middle and end of the fifteenth century about thirty thousand editions of "cradle books," or *incunabula*, appeared in Europe. Unlikely credit has been given to Laurens Janszoon Coster, a Harlem sexton, for the invention of movable type in 1423; however, contemporary documents fail to mention him. Only about 1570 did Adrian Young's book *Batavia* give Coster credit, and most modern scholars ignore this shadowy claim. Although no extant book bears his name, a more plausible inventor of printing with movable type is Johann Gutenberg, from Mainz, Germany. During a time when he was working in Strasbourg between 1430 and 1440, he seems to have been adapting the *prelum*, or winepress, for printing. Although he produced fewer than thirty works, he devoted years to mechanical perfection of the new process of printing. Among his alleged works are a thirty-one-line

Johann Gutenberg is believed to have developed the technology of printing with movable metal type while working in the German city of Strasbourg in the 1430's and 1440's. (Library of Congress)

Indulgence (1454); *Indulgence* (1455); a thirty-six-line Bible; a forty-two-line Bible (the Mainz or Gutenberg Bible); *Catholicon*, a theological grammar of Johannes Balbus; and some calendars, including one for the year 1448. Supporting Gutenberg as the inventor of printing are court records and documents of Mainz, which show his need for funds and detail his lawsuits regarding the press. In 1448, a loan made by Johann Fust facilitated the printing with movable type of the forty-two-line or Gutenberg Bible between 1452 and 1455, antedating the thirty-six-line Bible of 1459-1460. That Gutenberg's press produced the early calendars of 1447 or 1448, and the 1454 and 1455 indulgence slips seems plausible because of the similarity of type. The appearance of printed indulgence slips has tempted some to suggest that the papacy was planning a great retaliatory campaign against the Turks after the fall of Constantinople in 1453. The papal legate in Mainz supposedly ordered both Gutenberg and Johann Fust to print indulgences to help defray the expenses of the campaign.

A lawsuit of 1455 indicates that Johann Fust sued to recover his expenses incurred in the loans he made to Gutenberg. Around this time, Fust and Gutenberg's former chief workman, Peter Schöffer, formed a new printing firm. Before this setback, however, Gutenberg's press yielded 210 copies of the forty-two-line Bible using 290 different typefaces. From 1455 to 1460, Gutenberg used equipment supplied by his new patron, Dr. Humery of Mainz. The 1460 *Catholicon* marks the end of Gutenberg's supposed work. In that year, he accepted a court position offered by the archbishop of Mainz, leaving Fust and Schöffer dominant in the new art in that city.

The chief credit given to Fust and Schöffer derives from their 1457 *Psalter*, the first book whose colophon dates and names its printer. Some scholars claim its U and V capitals link it to the 1454 and 1455 indulgence slips. The *Psalter* contains black and red print and blue initials, an innovation since earlier rubrication had been done by hand. In addition, the woodcuts in the *Psalter* are delicate and profuse. Fust and Schöffer followed this work in 1462 by a forty-eight-line Bible. From 1466 until his death, Schöffer worked alone. He was known for his use of marginal notes, Greek printed characters, and spacing between lines. A poster of his—the first of its kind—that advertised printed books shows that he had become a large-scale businessman.

In Cologne in 1466, Ulrich Zell produced perhaps the first printed Latin classic, Cicero's *De officiis*. Elsewhere in Germany, Anthony Koberger published the *Nuremberg Chronicle* in 1493, using much illustration and both Gothic and Roman typefaces. In Augsburg, Erhard Ratdolt

After returning to his birthplace in Mainz, Gutenberg became responsible for printing the two-volume Gutenberg Bible, which was bound and decorated in August of 1456. (AP/Wide World Photos)

printed missals and ecclesiastical books with border designs and engraved initials, such as his *Obsequiale Augustense* (1487).

In Italy, two German clerics, Konrad Sweinheim and Arnold Pannartz, established presses in a Subiaco monastery (1461) and in Rome (1467). These originators foreshadowed the Humanist Aldus Manutius, most famous of all Italian printers. In Venice from 1485 until about 1505, he printed Greek and Latin editions of works by Aristotle, Aristophanes, Bion, Moschus, and others. His small pocket-size books of cheap quality and legible italic typeface helped to disseminate learning to the less wealthy classes.

A Frenchman, Nicolaus Jenson, studied in Mainz and worked in Venice in the 1460's. Printing in France itself produced the early names of Jean Heynlin and Guillaume Fichet of the Sorbonne, and of others such as Ulrich Gering, Martin Krantz, and Michael Freiburger. In 1470, a volume of the letters of Gasparino Barzizi of Bergamo

appeared followed by the first Bible printed in France, in 1476.

Printing in Spain started in 1468, when a Barcelona press produced a grammar book. Later, Lambert Palmart of Valencia published its city laws during 1477-1490 in fifteen volumes. Spain produced mostly ecclesiastical works, with some poetry and romances.

In the Low Countries, the Brothers of the Common Life set up a press at Marienthal in 1468; by 1490, more than sixty establishments acknowledged their supervision. In Bruges, Colard Mansion taught William Caxton, an Englishman who translated and printed Le Fever's *Recuyell of the Historyes of Troye* in 1475. By 1477, Caxton returned to England to print the country's first book, significantly in the vernacular. Thus within fifty years, printing by movable type spread over Europe to become—as a vehicle for the mass dissemination of information—one of the most significant events in the history of Western culture.   —*John J. Healy, updated by Karen Gould*

ADDITIONAL READING:

Chappell, Warren. *A Short History of the Printed Word*. Reprint. Boston: Nonpareil Books, 1980. Contains a good introduction to the basics of printing technology along with a survey of the history that puts the invention of printing and the incunable era in context.

Davies, Martin. *Aldus Manutius: Printer and Publisher of Renaissance Venice*. London: The British Library, 1995. A concise introduction to the works of Aldus and his contributions to the development of printing.

Febvre, Lucien, and Henri-Jean Martin. *The Coming of the Book: The Impact of Printing, 1450-1800*. Translated by David Gerard. London: NLB, 1976. A study of the transformations that printing brought to book production and the book trade.

Ing, Janet. *Johann Gutenberg and His Bible*. 2d ed. New York: The Typophiles, 1990. A concise, readable account of the evidence about Gutenberg and his role in the invention of printing and the production of the Gutenberg Bible.

Lehmann-Haupt, Hellmut. *Peter Schoeffer of Gernsheim and Mainz*. Rochester, N.Y.: L. Hart, 1950. A short biography of this pioneer in the development of printing.

Painter, George D. *William Caxton: A Quincentenary Biography*. New York: G. P. Putnam's Sons, 1977. A complete biography of England's first printer from his first career as a merchant-trader to his later years when he set up a printing establishment in England.

Scholderer, Victor. *Johann Gutenberg: The Inventor of Printing*. 2d ed. London: British Museum, 1970. An overview of Gutenberg's life and his accomplishments in developing printing with movable type.

SEE ALSO: 1517, Luther Posts His Ninety-five Theses; 1611, The King James Bible Is Published.

1450-1466
SECOND PEACE OF THORN

The Second Peace of Thorn brings an end to the Thirteen Years' War between Poland and the Teutonic Knights of Prussia, expanding the territory of Poland to reach the Baltic coast.

DATE: 1450-1466

LOCALE: Prussia

CATEGORIES: Diplomacy and international relations; Expansion and land acquisition

KEY FIGURES:

Casimir IV (1427-1492), king of Poland, 1447-1492

Conrad von Erlichshausen (1441-1449), grandmaster of the Teutonic Knights

Louis von Erlichshausen (1450-1467), grandmaster of the Teutonic Knights

Aeneas Silvius Piccolomini (1405-1464), papal legate and later Roman Catholic pope as Pius II, 1458-1464

SUMMARY OF EVENT. Continual tension, broken occasionally by war, had characterized the relationship of the Teutonic Order with the neighboring Polish princes from the late thirteenth century to the Peace of Kalisch (1343), when King Casimir the Great agreed that West Prussia and Culm were indeed rightful possessions of the Teutonic Order. Peace was then predominant until the crises that led to the famous Battle of Tannenburg (Grunwald) in 1410, where the combined forces of Poland and Lithuania, led by cousins King Władysław II Jagiełło and Grand Duke Vytautas, crushed the hitherto invincible army of the Teutonic Order.

The surviving members of the Teutonic Order were at first consumed with the desire to restore the order's pride and political power to the position it had once enjoyed, but their resources were drained every year a little more by the need to maintain a high state of readiness in case King Jagiełło invaded again; also, the grandmaster was attempting to win imperial favor (and perhaps an alliance against Poland) by assisting the Holy Roman Emperor in his crusade against religious rebels in Bohemia, the Hussites. The Polish king, for his part, knew how expensive and risky it would be to besiege the massive castles of the Teutonic Knights, and he understood well that his knights and prelates were not willing to authorize or take part in another campaign into Prussia. Therefore, Jagiełło contented himself with diplomatic efforts at the papal court, at the Council of Constance, and elsewhere, meanwhile allowing the grandmasters to imagine that an invasion was imminent. Moreover, when the Hussites wanted to strike at the principal supporters of the Holy Roman Emperor, the Polish king allowed them passage through his lands to invade Prussia.

The famed discipline of the Teutonic Order broke down. The knights removed one grandmaster, the convents in Germany refused to recognize his successor, and military defeat dogged every effort in Prussia, Livonia, and Bohemia.

Conrad von Erlichshausen became grandmaster of the Teutonic Order in 1441 with a mandate to bring order into the chaotic situation. His solution was to centralize power in his own hands, raise new taxes, and see that even the traditionally autonomous cities contributed more to the order's political and military ambitions. Conrad was essentially successful in dealing with the order's knights, partly because there were fewer of them than ever before and partly because current military theory stressed the wisdom of hiring mercenaries when war threatened rather than housing and feeding knights in both war and peace. Conrad's threats, however, provoked only resistance from the secular knights and burghers, especially those of Danzig. By the time Conrad died in 1449, his enemies had expanded an existing forum for discussion of mutual concerns, the Prussian League, into a military alliance.

The new grandmaster, Louis von Erlichshausen, took the matter to Pope Nicholas V and the Holy Roman Emperor and obtained rulings that the Prussian League was an illegal organization. In 1454, when the Prussian League realized that further negotiations were hopeless, it struck before the grandmaster could raise a mercenary army. The league quickly captured all but a few castles in West Prussia.

Grandmaster Louis was taken completely by surprise; little had he realized that the long-standing fear of King Jagiełło had died away in the two decades since that monarch's demise. While the army of the Prussian League besieged the grandmaster's seemingly invincible residence at Marienburg, the league's diplomats were at the court of King Casimir, offering to become his subjects.

Casimir could not send much help. His activities were restricted by a small number of nobles and prelates who mistrusted every royal action which might make the king powerful. He nevertheless made an armed entry into West Prussia which had all the appearance of a triumphal parade until he reached the fortress of Könitz. There, surprised by the simultaneous arrival of mercenaries from Germany and a sally by the garrison, Casimir's army was cut to pieces. The king fled back to Poland, the grandmaster recovered his confidence, and the Prussian League prepared for a long struggle—the Thirteen Years' War had begun.

At length, Pope Calixtus III decided that the conflict had lasted long enough. The pope's legates would never be able to organize a crusade against the Turks to recover Constantinople until there was peace in Poland. Awkwardly, the pope had an obligation to protect the Teutonic Order, he had to respect the wishes of the Holy Roman Emperor (who was, like the pope, also the Teutonic Knights' overlord), and he had a moral obligation to uphold the established order and the rule of law. On the other hand, Poland was a powerful land, the Prussian League had valid complaints, and no one was going to quit fighting just because the pope said to stop. All that Pope Calixtus could do was to tell Aeneas Silvius Piccolomini to look into the matter. Piccolomini was the most prominent humanist in the Church's service and a master of persuasion.

Piccolomini's efforts proved largely in vain. When he realized that the war would not cease until either one side won a clear-cut military victory or until everyone became exhausted, he adopted a policy of patient waiting. When his elevation to the papacy allowed him to offer inducements to various participants for cooperation, he sent legates to move the negotiations along. This proved ineffective, too.

When the grandmaster's mercenaries, unhappy with not being paid, turned over Marienburg to the league in 1457, it appeared that the war was at its end. Yet Louis managed to escape to Königsberg, the Prussian League ran out of money to pay its mercenaries, and the war resumed. At length, in 1462, Casimir sent some troops and a competent general, but it was the league's naval strength that proved the difference; in the fall of 1463, the coalition led by Danzig destroyed the grandmaster's fleet.

The Second Peace of Thorn was mediated by a second papal emissary, Rudolf von Rudesheim. West Prussia and Culm (in the southern elbow of the Vistula River) were returned to the king of Poland, the bishopric of Ermland in the center of East Prussia became independent, and the East Prussian districts of Marienburg, Elbing, and Christburg became Polish.

The long-term results of the war were significant. Most important, Poland reached the sea. It was insignificant that its subjects were largely German-speaking: The Commonwealth was multilingual and multiconfessional; it was bound together by ties of trade and culture, toleration for diversity, and a high degree of local self-government. "German" nobles adopted Polish customs and spoke Polish; German burghers went about their business, trading with German-speaking merchants clear to the other ends of the Lithuanian grand duchy and the Polish kingdom; all prized their right to govern themselves with minimum interference from the king and his council.

The grandmaster regrouped his resources, trying to make something out of his shrunken state in East Prussia, periodically assisting the Polish king in his wars against the Turks. A new noble class was establishing itself in both East and West Prussia, a class composed of former mercenaries who had accepted fiefs in lieu of payment for their services; this class eventually developed into the famous Junker nobility of Prussia.

The peasantry never recovered completely from the ravages of war. The native Prussian freeholders and knights who had thrived in the service of the order's armies were now refugees. Dispersed around the countryside, taking refuge in German-speaking towns and villages, within decades they ceased to pass their native language to their descendants. Some, like many dispossessed German farmers, became serfs.

The Thirteen Years' War, fought to avoid tyranny, taxation, and war with Poland, did at least avoid tyranny for some. The burghers of Danzig and the other large towns profited from the enhanced opportunities for trade and the greater protection that the king could provide against competitors; the nobles enhanced their rights and privileges at the expense of the peasants. Royal prestige was enhanced; in fact, if royal authority had benefited equally, King Casimir would have been powerful indeed. As was the case so often in this era, Casimir's authority in his new lands was dependent upon his new subjects' willingness to allow him to exercise it.

—*William L. Urban*

ADDITIONAL READING:

Burleigh, Michael. *Prussian Society and the German Order: An Aristocratic Corporation in Crisis, c. 1410-1466.* New York: Cambridge University Press, 1984. Somewhat dour, but solid.

Christiansen, Eric. *The Northern Crusades: The Baltic and the Catholic Frontier, 1100-1525.* Minneapolis: University of Minnesota Press, 1980. Contains a first-class summary.

Davies, Norman. *God's Playground: A History of Poland in Two Volumes.* New York: Columbia University Press, 1982. Solid on Poland, though holding strong opinions; weak on the Teutonic Order.

Jasienica, Pawel. *Jagiellonian Poland.* Translated by Alexander Jordan. Miami, Fla.: American Institute of Polish Culture, 1978. Good on internal Polish politics.

Urban, William. "Renaissance Humanism in Prussia." *Journal of Baltic Studies* 22 (Spring, 1991): 5-72; 22 (Summer, 1991): 95-122; 22 (Fall, 1991): 195-232. A useful series of articles on the cultural consequences of the Thirteen Years' War.

SEE ALSO: 1228-1231, Teutonic Knights Bring Baltic Region Under Catholic Control; 1410, Battle of Tannenburg; 1414-1418, Council of Constance; 1457-1504, Reign of Stephen the Great.

1453

ENGLISH ARE DRIVEN FROM FRANCE

The English are driven from France through French numerical superiority, nationalism, Burgundian support, and the creation of the national army that later gives France the leadership of early modern Europe.

DATE: 1453

LOCALE: France

CATEGORIES: Government and politics; Wars, uprisings, and civil unrest

KEY FIGURES:

Charles VII (1403-1461), king of France, 1422-1461

Joan of Arc (c. 1412-1431), patriotic heroine of France (canonized 1920)

John of Lancaster, duke of Bedford (1389-1435), English regent in France, 1422-1435

Philip the Good (1396-1467), duke of Burgundy, 1419-1467

John Talbot, earl of Shrewsbury (c. 1384-1453), English commander in defeat

SUMMARY OF EVENT. After 1066, when Duke William of Normandy conquered England and became its king, English monarchs also ruled provinces in France. These holdings, extensive under Henry II (1154-1189), were lost by his son John (1199-1216) to the French ruler Philip II (1180-1223) except for the wine-producing Guienne of southwestern France. From 1337 to 1453, English monarchs repeatedly invaded France hoping to regain lost provinces and claiming that their descent from Philip IV (1285-1314) through his daughter Isabella gave them title to the French throne itself. English victories at Crécy (1346) and Poitiers (1356), thanks to their longbows, brought territorial gains under the 1360 Treaty of Bretigny, although French guerrilla tactics regained most of these by 1396.

The war was renewed in 1415, however, when Henry V soundly defeated the French army at Agincourt and then launched a major English effort to gain control of all France. This was an ambitious project. There were about six Frenchmen for every Englishman, and the recruitment, equipment, transport, conquest, and occupation costs would require special taxes voted by Parliament.

Meanwhile, the French people were becoming increasingly hostile to the English invaders, and the French feudal levies (conscripts) were learning to avoid futile frontal assaults. Henry's second invasion of Normandy in 1417,

however, met little opposition from France's Valois king, the intermittently insane Charles VI. His teenage son, the dauphin Charles, trying to organize a patriotic front, blundered with a treacherous assassination of Duke John the Fearless of Burgundy in 1419. This threw John's son, Philip the Good, into the English camp, and King Charles capitulated. By the Treaty of Troyes, signed on June 14, 1420, Charles VI accepted Henry as his regent and heir, disinherited the dauphin as a dishonorable murderer, and gave his daughter Catherine in marriage to Henry. Their anticipated son (the future Henry VI, born in 1421), was to rule France as well as England. Paris opened its gates, and Henry's conquest of France seemed well under way.

Unfortunately, both Henry V and Charles VI died in 1422, leaving Henry VI as an infant sovereign for France and England. While his regent in France, John, duke of Bedford, was capable, the regent in England, Humphrey, duke of Gloucester, failed to provide money or control policy.

One result was London's insistence on an advance to Orléans on the Loire without providing enough men, supplies, and artillery to take this fortified city. Consequently, the scene was set for an English reverse when Charles reinforced the capable leaders at Orléans with five thousand troops plus Joan of Arc, a teenage country girl claiming a divine mission. She took center stage with remarkable effect. Her infectious confidence was a factor in breaking the siege of Orléans, and her participation and influence increased with the victories at Jargeau and Patay, culminating in the march through Champagne to a ceremonious coronation of Charles at Rheims on July 17, 1429.

These spectacular victories, however, did not dislodge the English from northwestern France and the Guienne. After Joan's capture in 1430 and execution in 1431, the war languished. While English war policy in the 1430's was hampered by financial shortages and the death in 1435 of Bedford, Charles methodically prepared. An essential reconciliation with Burgundy by the 1435 Treaty of Arras meant the recovery of Paris on April 13, 1436. Expelling the capable English army commanders from northwestern France required war, which in turn required money and an improved army. Indirect taxes and a hearth tax became permanent (if unpopular) annual revenues for the central government. The feudal levies of local lords were replaced by a national army under royal control while on the technical side, Jean and Gaspard Bureau developed more effective artillery. With "corned" gunpowder firing cast iron or lead shot, the new French army gained missile superiority over the English.

Finally, in 1441, Charles launched a well-prepared attack. Pontoise fell to French artillery, weakening the English position in the lower Seine valley, and in 1442 sieges reduced the English outer fortresses in Guienne. A 1443 English expedition proved fruitless; in 1444, Henry VI and the English "peace party" tried the path of negotiation. The Truce of Tours provided for the 1445 marriage of Henry with Margaret of Anjou, a niece to Charles VII, with a secret clause calling for the cession of Maine, including its line of strong fortresses, to France. These surrenders dragged on through 1448, but when English aggression against Brittany broke the truce, Charles invaded Normandy in 1449. The new French armies swiftly took many fortified towns and held the countryside, gaining a major success for "Charles the Well-Served."

Early in 1450, the English made a belated effort to save Normandy. An army under Sir Thomas Kyriell landed at Cherbourg, recovered Valognes, and moved east through Carentan to reinforce the Bayeux garrison. Kyriell's force of perhaps five to six thousand spent the night of April 14 at the village of Formigny and early on April 15 found the road back to Carentan blocked by a French army of three thousand under the Count de Clermont. The English deployed west of Formigny and for some hours the opposing forces sought to provoke the other to attack, each hoping for a defensive victory. A melee eventually developed over two French culverins (light cannon) but the decisive factor was the arrival from St. Lo of about twelve hundred

French troops under the Constable de Richemont, on the English left flank. Simultaneous French attacks broke the disjointed English defenses. The French claimed 3,774 English dead on the field, plus "more than a thousand whom shameful flight . . . did not save," as well as fifteen hundred prisoners, including Kyriell. The reported French loss of only six, eight, or twelve is not credible, but the significant result of this decisive battle was that Kyriell's army no longer existed. English garrisons at Bayeux, Avranches, Caen, Falaise, and elsewhere fell quickly. Cherbourg surrendered on August 12, 1450, after "such a heavy battering from cannons and bombards that the like had never been seen before," and no part of France remained under English rule except Guienne, Calais, and the Channel Islands.

Following the defeat at Formigny, the English government was shaken by disorders at home leading to Cade's Rebellion of 1450, and Charles VI seized the opportunity to attack in the Guienne. Again the French employed a broad-front invasion, brief sieges, threats, and bribery to converge on the English positions. The Bordeaux garrison surrendered on June 30, and Bayonne on August 20, 1451. The expulsion of the English from southwestern France was complete, although only for a year's space. King Charles's administrators and tax collectors became so immediately unpopular that influential Guiennese leaders

Joan of Arc inspired confidence in the French troops at Orléans, but her execution in 1431 discouraged French efforts in the Hundred Years' War. (Archive Photos)

MAJOR SITES IN THE HUNDRED YEARS' WAR, 1337-1453

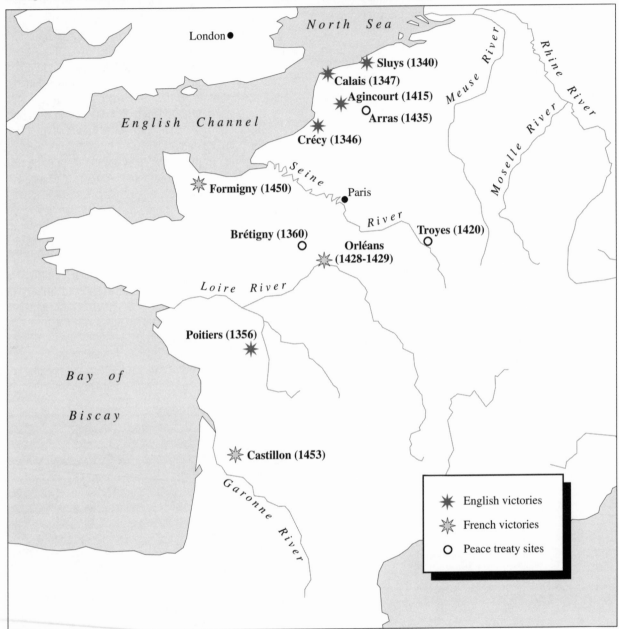

promised in 1452 to support whatever expedition London could send to restore English rule. Accordingly, in October of 1452, the English sent an army of three thousand commanded by John Talbot, earl of Shrewsbury, a veteran of close to fifty years of campaigning, to liberate Guienne. Bordeaux indeed rose against its French garrison, and all western Guienne rallied to Talbot, soon strengthened by a reinforcement of three thousand more troops from England. In July of 1453, however, French armies advanced into Guienne, and a force of seven thousand under the direction of artillery master Jean Bureau besieged Castillon in the Dordogne valley. Talbot marched from Bordeaux to relieve Castillon with an Anglo-Guiennese army of about the same number, but these forces were evidently scattered by the time he arrived before Castillon on July 17. Exactly why Talbot chose to make a dismounted frontal assault on the French lines with his straggling force is unclear. The attack was riddled by enfiladed artillery fire and the right flank crumpled by Franco-Breton reinforcements. In the rout, Talbot was killed and the Anglo-Guiennese army destroyed. Bordeaux surrendered to France on October 19. Only Calais remained, until 1558, as part of continental France under the English flag. The war was over, and the French king emerged as "Charles the Very Victorious" while English frustration in defeat helped cause their own divisive "War of the Roses."

Throughout the Hundred Years' War, England's apparent initiative depended on battles won by superior archery. Their invasions, however, antagonized the French population, gradually creating the nationalism dramatically embodied by Joan of Arc. Equally important were the systematic administrative reforms of Charles VII in giving France an army decisively superior in equipment and method to the English forces. —*K. Fred Gillum*

ADDITIONAL READING:

Allmand, C. T., ed. *War, Literature and Politics in the Late Medieval Ages.* New York: Barnes & Noble, 1976. Several informative articles, including espionage and artillery.

Burne, Alfred H. *The Agincourt War.* London: Eyre & Spottiswoode, 1956. A military analysis of the war from 1369 to 1453.

Contamine, Philippe. *War in the Middle Ages.* Translated by Michael Jones. Oxford: Basil Blackwell, 1984. Rich in details, surpassing even Sir Charles Oman's earlier work, *A History of the Art of War in the Middle Ages* (1924).

Gies, Frances. *Joan of Arc: The Legend and the Reality.* New York: Harper & Row, 1981. Scholarly and nonmiraculous account.

Perroy, Edouard. *The Hundred Years' War.* London: Eyre & Spottiswoode, 1951. Gives a broad view of French politics and society.

Vale, M. G. A. *Charles VII.* Berkeley: University of California Press, 1974. Scholarly analysis of war policies.

SEE ALSO: 1346, Battle of Crécy; 1429, Joan of Arc's Relief of Orléans.

1453
FALL OF CONSTANTINOPLE

The fall of Constantinople signifies the collapse of the Byzantine Empire and the rise of the Ottoman Empire, considered by some to mark the close of the Middle Ages.

DATE: May 29, 1453
LOCALE: Constantinople
CATEGORIES: Government and politics; Wars, uprisings, and civil unrest

KEY FIGURES:
Constantine XI Palaeologus (1404-1453), Byzantine emperor, 1448-1453
Giovanni Giustiniani (died 1453), Genoese soldier who assisted the Greeks during the siege
Mehmed II (1432-1481), Ottoman sultan, 1451-1481
Zagan Pasha, Turkish commander and zealot

SUMMARY OF EVENT. By 1453, relations between the Greek East and the Latin West were near the breaking point. The mass of the Greeks remembered with bitterness the capture of Constantinople in 1204 at the hands of Western crusaders. This led to a struggle between the Greeks and Latins to control Constantinople after 1261, with control eventually going to the Greeks. By the fifteenth century, the failure of the Orthodox Church and the Catholic Church to reconcile their differences and present a united front against the encroaching Turks left Constantinople and the Byzantine Empire vulnerable to invasion. The young sultan of the Turks, Mehmed II, saw in this division within Christendom the chance to crush the might of the Byzantine Empire. He had decided early in his reign that one of his principal objectives would be the seizure of the "God-protected city," and by the spring of 1453 he had determined his plan of attack. When the Greeks awoke on the morning of April 5, 1453, they were amazed at the sight of more than one hundred thousand Turkish troops outside the high walls of Constantinople, stretching in a formidable line from the Sea of Marmora to the Golden Horn. The city had withstood sieges from all the migratory barbarians of the East, yet never had it faced such peril as it did on that April morning.

The hosts of the Turkish sultan seemed numberless. Cattle, supply wagons, tents, heavily armed soldiers, and cursing officers intermingled in a terrifying scene of purposeful confusion. By the middle of the morning, the defenders on top of the stout walls could see the hugh Turkish cannon being maneuvered into place by thousands of sweating laborers.

While the Turkish land army had been making its preparations, the sultan's navy had not been idle; soon the harried defenders saw 493 Turkish ships sail quickly into the Bosphorus, fully armed and ready to match the Greek fleet.

The opposing forces were unevenly matched. The sultan, having mustered more than one hundred thousand men including the elite Janissaries and five hundred ships, could surely overwhelm the legions of beleaguered Byzantium, which numbered some seven to eight thousand supported by fifteen ships. Mehmed II had built forts to control the naval approaches to Constantinople, forestalling any naval reinforcements coming to the aid of the emperor. It was impossible to doubt the outcome of such odds; yet the defense of Constantinople was maintained brilliantly and bravely for nearly two months.

The Byzantines, it is to be noted, had more than high walls on their side. The leader of their forces, the Genoese Giovanni Giustiniani, was a man of outstanding military ability, as he proved time and time again in repelling successive attacks of the Turks. Giustiniani was part of the force sent from Venice and Genoa, whose traders and merchants had realized that Constantinople was the central crossroads to trade with the East. The Greeks also had their famous chain boom with which they could block off their harbor, and they had courage and belief in the protection of the Christian God.

On April 12, the siege began in earnest. The Royal One, the biggest siege gun the Turks possessed, was moved ponderously into position. The barrel of this gargantuan weapon was three feet in diameter and fired stone projectiles weighing nearly a ton. From its first shot the huge gun posed a dramatic threat to the garrison on the walls. Week after week, it hammered slowly and inexorably at the crumbling defenses. Citizens were roused at any hour of the day to repair the holes in the battlements. The strain told. Nerves stretched tighter, and fatigue began to take its enervating toll. In actual fighting, however, the vastly outnumbered Greeks decisively won the first two major engagements of the siege. On April 18, Giustiniani and his armored Genoese followers beat back wave after wave of Turks who attempted to scale the walls, while the very next day the Greek naval forces successfully repelled a frenzied attack by almost three hundred of the smaller Turkish men-of-war. In a crescendo of death, even more attacks by the Turks took place throughout the following weeks. Slowly and grimly, they set out to wear down the defenders. Day after hot day, the siege continued. The Greeks stayed at the walls, their numbers so low that they had their food and ammunition brought to them on the parapets.

Even the redoubtable Mehmed II began to doubt the wisdom of the siege when it had become obvious that the Greeks would fight to the bitter end. His own troops were becoming restive, and he suspected that help for the Greeks might soon arrive. By the evening of May 27, 1453, Mehmed II was in favor of negotiating with the stubborn defenders. At a council meeting that evening, however, the zealous warrior Zagan Pasha rose to his feet and passionately exhorted his colleagues to finish the task they had begun nearly two month before. The Turks broke up their conference determined once more to take the city.

On the morning of May 28, the final attack upon the city of Constantinople began. Assault after assault was beaten back by the exhausted Greeks. On the night of the last day of the Empire, the citizens of Constantinople, Greek and Latin, gathered together for Mass at the hallowed shrine of Byzantine Christendom, Santa Sophia, known as Hagia Sophia. Old differences between Latins and Greeks were forgotten in these final moments as haggard soldiers of the East and the West worshiped together in the sacred basilica. The ancient lights, the gold decorations, the priceless icons, must have moved those tired warriors.

On May 29, 1453, the Turkish forces at last forced their way into the city. Finally, even Emperor Constantine XI, the last of the Caesars, descended from his horse. With an air of fatality he removed his imperial vestments and, clad only in his simple tunic and the red leather imperial boots, took up his sword to fight to the death at the side of his last troops. The last link with ancient Rome was broken. The empire of a thousand years had ended.

The consequences of the fall of Constantinople are vast. Besides the cultural impact on the West from refugee Greeks, the East slowly sank into poverty and an intellectual decline. The foothold of the Turks into southern Europe consolidated their base for further invasion of central and southern Europe, eventually resulting in the complete conquest of the Balkans.

The Ottoman Empire, whose attachment to Constantinople was as strong as the Greeks and Latins, made Constantinople their capital and principal city. Mehmed II himself destroyed the altar at Hagia Sophia and turned the church into a Muslim mosque. It later became a museum. Constantinople is still the seat of the patriarch of the Orthodox Church, and one of the most important cities for the Turkish Muslims. Constantinople, whose name was changed to Istanbul in the early 1900's, is truly a cosmopolitan city.

—Carl F. Rohne, updated by Elizabeth L. Scully

ADDITIONAL READING:

Diehl, Charles. *Byzantium: Greatness and Decline*. Translated from the French by Naomi Alford, with an introduction and bibliography by Peter Charanis. New Brunswick, N.J.: Rutgers University Press, 1957. An interpretive account of the factors in Byzantine life which contributed both to the maintenance of the empire and its gradual decline.

Nicol, Donald M. *The Last Centuries of Byzantium 1261-1453*. 2d ed. New York: Cambridge University Press, 1993. Updated political and social history of the Byzantium Empire from the Greek restoration in 1261 until the fall of Constantinople in 1453.

Palmer, Alan. *The Decline and Fall of the Ottoman Empire*. New York: Barnes & Noble, 1994. Although only the introduction deals with the actual fall of Constantinople, the book explores the consequences of the fall until World War I.

Pears, Edwin. *The Destruction of the Greek Empire and the Story of the Capture of Constantinople by the Turks.* London: Longmans, Green, 1903. While somewhat outdated because of new research, one of the best balanced accounts regarding the political, social and religious aspects of the fall.

Runciman, Steven. *The Fall of Constantinople, 1453.* Cambridge, England: Cambridge University Press, 1965. A complete full-length narrative account of the siege of Constantinople, with a brief synopsis of primary sources from both sides.

SEE ALSO: 476, "Fall" of Rome; 1204, Knights of the Fourth Crusade Capture Constantinople; 1353, Ottoman Empire Establishes Foothold in Rumelia; 1389, Turkish Conquest of Serbia; 1442-1456, János Hunyadi Defends Hungary Against Ottoman Invaders; 1536, Turkish Capitulations Begin; 1683, Ottoman Turks Are Defeated at Vienna.

1454
PEACE OF LODI

The Peace of Lodi ends the war between Venice and Milan and establishes a renewable mutual defense pact that is later expanded to include Florence, Naples, and the papacy, bringing peace and modern diplomatic practices to Italy and the world.

DATE: April 9, 1454
LOCALE: Lodi, Italy
CATEGORY: Diplomacy and international relations
KEY FIGURES:

Alfonso V of Aragon (1396-1458), king of Aragon, 1416-1458, and king of Naples, 1435-1458
Simonetto da Camerino, Augustinian friar and secret mediator between Milan and Venice
Francesco Foscari (c. 1373-1457), doge of Venice, 1423-1457
Cosimo de' Medici (1389-1464), ruler of Florence, 1434-1464
Mehmed II (1432-1481), Ottoman sultan and founder of the Ottoman Empire, 1444-1446 and 1451-1481
Nicholas V (Tommaso Parentucelli; 1397-1455), Roman Catholic pope, 1447-1455
Francesco Sforza (1401-1466), duke of Milan, 1450-1456

SUMMARY OF EVENT. The fall of Constantinople to the Ottoman Turks on May 29, 1453, had a profound effect on Italy's internal politics and helped solidify the foundation

for increased diplomatic cooperation between the peninsula's five principal states. Mehmed II's victory exposed the Balkans and threatened the Venetian commercial empire in the eastern Mediterranean. Italians everywhere feared the imminent advance of Ottoman power toward the Adriatic and their homeland. Compounding the pressures against Venice, the state closest to Turkish expansion, stood a dangerous alliance along its western frontier. France had recently joined Milan and Florence in a war against the republic over Francesco Sforza's succession to Milan. Before the French entered the conflict, the combatants had been fairly equal in strength and Venice actually entertained hopes of annexing Milan. While French presence certainly tipped the balance in favor of Milan, it also encouraged Venice and Milan to search for peace as neither side welcomed a powerful foreign presence in Italy. Pope Nicholas invited the combatants and the lesser Italian states to assemble in Rome to settle their disputes and prepare for the anticipated confrontation with Mehmed's armies. Despite common fears of impending disaster, the pope offered little constructive leadership during the extended debates. As a result, the sessions were inconclusive and the congress disbanded in failure by March, 1454.

Both Sforza and the Venetians understood the advantages of peace, however, and, with the assistance of a secret intermediary, the Augustinian friar Simonetto da Camerino, settled their differences and signed the Peace of Lodi on April 9, 1454. Under the terms of this agreement, Francesco Sforza was acknowledged as the rightful ruler of Milan, Venice held on to her territorial gains in northern Italy, and all began to prepare for war against the Turks. Simonetto reported to Francesco Sforza later in the same month that the Venetians were vigorously arming galleys and urged the Milanese to ready themselves as well.

Although the immediate cessation of hostilities was significant and restrained French influence in Italy for many years, other aspects of the treaty were probably more important. In particular, one clause called for a new defensive military alliance for twenty-five years between Venice and Milan. Through the extension and application of this clause, the Peace of Lodi achieved its lasting historical value. Cosimo de' Medici brought Florence into the new alliance on August 30, Naples agreed the following January, and Nicholas V sanctioned the treaty a month later. In an official announcement from Rome on March 2, 1455, the five principal Italian powers bound themselves in a defensive league for a quarter of a century. Smaller states soon agreed to follow suit until all but Genoa and Rimini were members.

Venice, Milan, Florence, the papacy, and Naples then established an Italian League through which they pledged

TERRITORIAL BOUNDARIES OF VENICE AND MILAN AFTER THE PEACE OF LODI, 1454

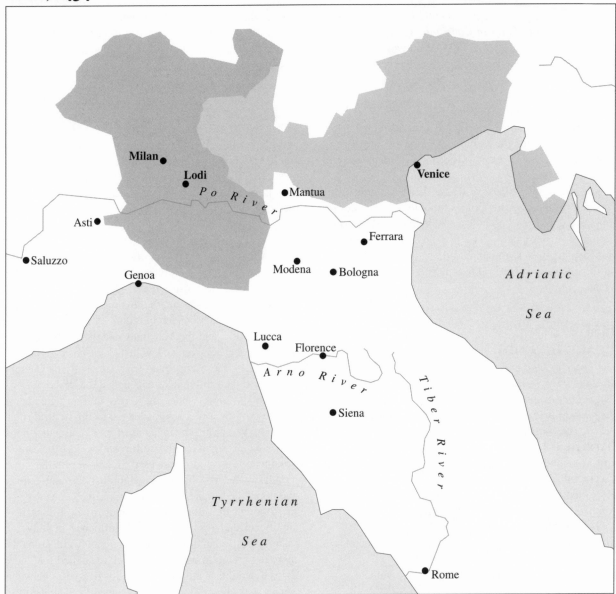

to defend one another in the event of attack from powers outside Italy, especially the awaited invasion from the East. Venice committed six thousand cavalry and two thousand infantry to assist against foreign aggression and the others pledged like forces. All signatories accepted existing territorial boundaries, and each vowed to consult the other before altering individual military or diplomatic arrangements which might upset the common peace. Though uneasy at times and not always successful in preventing minor wars between individual Italian states,

the overall peace endured for almost forty years until the French invasion of 1494.

Another critical dimension of the treaty was the establishment of a balance among the several powers of Italy. In the north, Venice, though the strongest individual state in the peninsula, was balanced by a union between Milan and Florence. In a like manner, the papacy checked Naples in the south. Though each state continued to place its own interests first and the balance was not always a comfortable one, it served to constrain the aspirations of individual states at the expense of their neighbors and to stabilize Italian affairs for nearly half a century.

Perhaps the most enduring legacy of the Peace of Lodi and its collateral agreements occurred in the area of diplomacy. By 1460, resident ambassadors had become a permanent feature among the principal secular powers of Italy. Such exchanges were bilateral from the outset, except for the papacy which only received ambassadors but did not send them. Naples was the last secular state to set up resident ambassadors, sending one to Venice in 1457 and another to Milan the next year. Smaller states and principalities were considerably slower and less consistent in establishing their own. Except during times of war when ambassadors were recalled by the home state, the custom of exchanging permanent ambassadors was now firmly in place, replacing the earlier system of sending an ambassador or envoy to another state for a specific purpose and a clearly defined time. The practice was quickly imitated across Europe and later became the cornerstone for the global system of diplomacy. Even the Italian word *ambasciator* came to be universally adopted.

The need for member states to consult about common threats on a regular basis necessitated resident ambassadors after 1454. The various states entrusted these ambassadors with special authority to negotiate on their behalf and over time created the structures of permanent embassies. During the fifteenth century, the standard house and personal staff for an embassy came to include ten to twelve men with a complement of six to eight horses. The staff was paid for by the ambassador and responsible to him. In the same period, states began to provide their resident ambassadors with secretaries. The first to adopt this custom were the Venetians and Florentines. These secretaries were separately appointed and separately paid. As time passed, they came to be the permanent diplomatic bridge between ambassadorial appointments, remaining at their posts when an ambassador resigned, retired, or was recalled, and thereby represented continuity and informed instruction for the successor.

These new, resident embassies served, according to the Renaissance historian, Francesco Guicciardini, as the "eyes and ears" of their governments, gathering daily information, preparing detailed reports, and sending them to their home governments through diplomatic couriers on a steady basis. The Venetians, in particular, excelled in collecting thorough intelligence about all political figures, customs, practices, and physical characteristics of those countries where embassies were received and their *relazioni* became the standard against which all other reports were measured. Rome remained the center of the Italian diplomatic community, receiving ambassadors but not

sending any. The city functioned throughout the Renaissance as a place to train future diplomats because each state was careful to send only its most experienced there to serve. Thus, would be ambassadors had an opportunity to learn from the very best diplomats of their time. The Peace of Lodi generally preserved the peace in Italy for nearly forty years. It maintained a balance of power and discouraged any state from appealing to outside force to augment its authority at the expense of a neighboring state. It encouraged military and diplomatic cooperation among the signatories. Finally, it established a lasting system of permanent embassies.   —*Michael J. Galgano*

ADDITIONAL READING:

Hale, John. *The Civilization of Europe in the Renaissance*. New York: Atheneum, 1994. A scholarly, readable, though traditional survey of the period by a leading English scholar.

Mallett, M. E., and J. R. Hale. *The Military Organization of a Renaissance State: Venice c. 1400 to 1617*. New York: Cambridge University Press, 1984. Examines relationship between the Venetian government and its mercenary armies; illustrates development of standing army.

Mattingly, Garrett. *Renaissance Diplomacy*. Reprint. New York: Dover, 1988. Originally published in 1955, this work is a classic study of diplomacy and the development of diplomatic institutions in Renaissance Italy and Europe.

Nicol, Donald M. *Byzantium and Venice: A Study in Diplomatic and Cultural Relations*. Cambridge and New York: Cambridge University Press, 1988. Surveys relations between the two culminating in the fall of Constantinople.

Setton, Kenneth M. *The Papacy and the Levant, 1204-1571*. 4 vols. Philadelphia: American Philosophical Society, 1976-1984 (Memoirs of the American Philosophical Society, 114, 127, 161, 162). Describes military, political, and diplomatic history of Christian Europe and the Ottoman Empire leading to the battle of Lepanto. Rich in detail.

SEE ALSO: 1150, Venetian Merchants Dominate Trade with the East; 1453, Fall of Constantinople; 1494-1495, Charles VIII of France Invades Italy; 1513, Machiavelli Writes *The Prince*.

1457-1504
REIGN OF STEPHEN THE GREAT

The reign of Stephen the Great establishes Moldavian independence, blocks Ottoman expansion in the region, and ensures the necessary prosperity for cultural accomplishments.

DATE: April 14, 1457-July 2, 1504
LOCALE: Moldavia
CATEGORY: Government and politics
KEY FIGURES:
Bayezid II (c. 1447-1512), Ottoman sultan, 1481-1512
Casimir IV (1447-1492), king of Poland, 1447-1492
Mátyás Hunyadi (1443-1490), king of Hungary as
  Matthias Corvinus, 1458-1490
John I Albert Jagiełło (1459-1501), king of Poland,
  1492-1501
Maria de Mangop, wife of Stephen the Great
Mehmed II (1432-1481), Ottoman sultan, 1444-1446
  and 1451-1481
Stephen IV the Great (1435-1504), prince of Moldavia,
  1457-1504
Süleyman I ("the Magnificent"; c. 1494-1566), Ottoman
  sultan, 1520-1566
Vlad III the Impaler (Vlad Tepes; died 1476), prince of
  Wallachia, 1448, 1456-1462, and 1476

SUMMARY OF EVENT. In 1457, Stephen Musat was proclaimed prince of Moldavia, ending the dynastic strife
that had weakened Moldavia since the death of his grandfather in 1432. Having consolidated power by eliminating rivals and nobles of doubtful loyalty, he strengthened the defenses of Suceava, his capital, reenforcing the
walls with stone able to withstand the increasing use
of explosives and artillery. Eventually he constructed or
improved a series of frontier fortifications, including those
on vital trade routes through Cetatea-Alba at the mouth
of the Dniester River and Chilia near the delta of the
Danube.

Recurring invasions and ceaseless diplomacy characterized Stephen's reign. The principle powers allied or at
war with Moldavia included Hungary and Poland, both of
which wanted Moldavia as a vassal principality, and the
Ottoman Empire, which was consolidating its hold on the
Balkans and ensuring its flanks before advancing up the
Danube. Additionally, there were the Crimean Tatars, intermittently allied with the Ottomans and threatening
Moldavia from the northeast, and Wallachia, a buffer principality where both Moldavia and the Ottoman Empire
jostled for influence. In this, the Ottomans were the more
successful, especially after Vlad IV the Impaler was de-
throned in 1462; thereafter, Moldavians frequently fought
the sultan's Wallachian allies, despite their common language, culture, and religion.

The challenges threatening Stephen divide into three
periods. The first began November, 1467, when King
Matthias Corvinus of Hungary invaded Moldavia to punish Stephen for aiding some disloyal Hungarian nobles the
previous summer and to regain the Chilia fortress that had

been captured by Stephen in 1465. The Hungarian army
moved eastward, plundering towns and capturing Baia on
December 14. Stephen's forces set the town afire. In the
confusion, the Hungarians sustained heavy losses and
Matthias Corvinus himself was wounded, thus ending
Hungary's last attempt to gain Moldavia as a vassal.

Stephen faced an Ottoman challenge in the second
period, dating from 1471, when he refused to pay the
annual tribute. In November, 1473, he replaced the sultan's appointee as prince of Wallachia, Radu III the Handsome, with his own man, Basarab Laiota. Thus provoked,
Sultan Mehmed II ordered his forces, aided by the traitor-
ous Basarab Laiota, into Moldavia. On January 10, 1475,
at Podul Inalt, located south of Vaslui in a foggy marsh
surrounded by forests, the Moldavians attacked. Stephen
had carefully selected the site to nullify the enemy's numerical superiority and to ensure the overwhelming
Moldavian victory that followed. On January 25, Stephen
addressed a circular letter to the rulers of Europe, inviting
their participation in an anti-Ottoman crusade. This invitation was not accepted, but Pope Sixtus IV increased
Stephen's growing fame by calling him "the athlete of
Christ."

Mehmed II took revenge in 1476, ordering the Crimean
Tatars to cross the Dniester River and attack Suceava.
Elements of the Moldavian army rushed north to meet the
threat and thus were unavailable when Ottoman forces
entered Moldavia that July. At Razboieni in the Valea
Alba, the Turks, commanded by Mehmed II himself, defeated the Moldavians on July 26. The sultan continued his
advance and laid siege to Suceava. Thereafter, the detachments sent to confront the Tartars rejoined Stephen, Ottoman supplies ran short, cholera broke out in the Ottoman
camp, and the Hungarians advanced eastward, threatening
the Turkish lines of supply and retreat. As a result,
Mehmed II ordered withdrawal on August 10.

In 1477, Stephen again set about building an anti-
Ottoman coalition. When Venice signed a peace treaty
with the Turks in January of 1479, Stephen also realized
he must negotiate. That year, he resumed tribute payments
to the sultan. Nevertheless, in July of 1484, Sultan
Bayezid II captured Chilia and Cetatea Alba. Seeking
Polish support, Stephen reconfirmed the old Moldavian-
Polish treaty and swore fealty to King Casimir IV on
September 15, 1485. Taking advantage of Stephen's absence in Poland, the Ottoman army invaded Moldavia and
burned down Suceava on September 19, 1485. A combined Polish-Moldavian army forced the Turks to retreat,
but hope of reconquering the two fortresses disappeared in
1489, when Poland also concluded a treaty with the sultan.
Stephen was forced to do the same and resume the tribute,

thus bringing to an end his anti-Ottoman efforts.

The third period of Stephen's reign dates from the death of Matthias Corvinus in 1490. John Albert Jagiełło, the Polish heir apparent, advanced claims to the Hungarian throne. To forestall a Polish-Hungarian union, Stephen invaded Poland, annexing the territory of Pocutia. Complicated diplomatic activity followed for several years between the countries of the area. Finally, John Albert invaded Moldavia in August of 1497, and laid siege to Suceava. Successful negotiations lifted the siege, but the Poles failed to follow the stipulated withdrawal route. Stephen attacked and defeated them at Codii Cosminului on October 26, 1497. Pressing his advantage, Stephen invaded Poland the following year. Hungarian mediation restored peace on July 12, 1499, and John Albert abandoned hope of making Moldavia a vassal. The years immediately before Stephen's death on July 2, 1504, were peaceful. The years thereafter, however, were marked by a succession crisis, revolts by Moldavian nobles, and further conflicts with Wallachia and Poland. Weakened and unable to resist the Ottomans, led by Süleyman the Magnificent, Moldavia became a Turkish vassal in 1538 and so remained until the nineteenth century.

The rapid decline after Stephen's death only underlines his skill in maintaining Moldavian independence for forty-seven years. Because his wars were usually fought in Moldavia, he almost invariably enjoyed better intelligence, superior knowledge of the terrain, and shorter supply lines than his enemies. These advantages were coupled with Stephen's uncanny ability to coax his enemies into pursuit as he retreated behind scorched earth until they were positioned where superior numbers were no advantage and their baggage and artillery a distinct disadvantage. Although his army fought as infantry, it maneuvered on horseback for speed and surprise.

Stephen was equally a skilled diplomat, making and discarding treaties with a sure sense of Moldavia's shifting needs. Although the grand anti-Ottoman coalition of which he dreamed eluded him, he was a master at dividing his enemies and setting them against each other.

Beyond his military and diplomatic successes, however, in Romanian history Stephen is known as "the Great" because he presided over and generously patronized one of the richest periods of Romanian culture. The Moldavian ecclesiastical architectural style, combining Byzantine and Gothic with traditional Moldavian elements, was perfected during his reign. The resulting structures reveal balance, proportion, and unexpected unity of design. Best known are the painted monasteries at Voronet and Neamt, whose exterior frescoes were added after his death. Many churches he endowed were built during the peaceful, prosperous period after the Ottoman invasions. Putna monastery, however, was finished in 1466, and Stephen was buried there with his wife, Maria de Mangop, whose tomb covering is considered a masterpiece of medieval embroidery.

Stephen was a generous patron of many arts. The illuminated manuscripts, icons, frescoes, richly embroidered vestments, gold and silver liturgical vessels, and book bindings which he donated to churches throughout the Romanian area preserved the memory of his glorious reign long after his death, as he doubtless hoped would be the case. Also helpful in preserving his memory was *The Chronicle from the Origins of the Moldavian Land*, which he commissioned and to which he himself contributed some passages concerning his accomplishments.

For his piety, generosity, and determined defense of Christendom, Stephen the Great was canonized by the Romanian Orthodox Church on June 20, 1992.

—*Ernest H. Latham, Jr.*

ADDITIONAL READING:

Papacostea, Serban. *Stephen the Great, Prince of Moldavia: 1457-1504.* 2d ed. Bucharest: Editura stiintifica si enciclopedica, 1981. Biographical monograph by a noted Romanian historian with useful bibliography.

Rosetti, R. "Stephen the Great of Moldavia and the Turkish Invasion." *The Slavonic Review* VI, no. 16 (June, 1927): 87-103. Romanian military historian's examination of Stephen's army, its organization, tactics, and strategy in the Ottoman wars.

Sadoveanu, Mihail. *The Life of Stephen the Great.* Vol. 3 in *Classics of Romanian Literature*. New York: East European Monographs, distributed by Columbia University Press, 1991. Romantic narrative by a famous Romanian novelist, underlining the rich legends surrounding Stephen.

Sedlar, Jean W. *East Central Europe in the Middle Ages, 1000-1500.* Vol. 3 in *A History of East Central Europe*. Seattle: University of Washington Press, 1994. A series of essays by a noted medievalist on social, economic, intellectual, and political topics.

Sugar, Peter F. *Southeastern Europe Under Ottoman Rule, 1354-1804.* Vol. 5 in *A History of East Central Europe*. Seattle: University of Washington Press, 1977. Authoritative study of Ottoman penetration and rule in the Balkans with separate chapters on such vassal states as Moldavia.

Sweeney, James Ross. "Walachia/Moldavia." In *Dictionary of the Middle Ages*, vol. 12. New York: Charles Scribner's Sons, 1989. Introduction to the political, social, economic, and military situations of the Romanian principalities before the Ottomans.

Treptow, Kurt W. "Stefan cel Mare—Images of a Medieval Hero." *Romanian Civilization* 1, no. 2 (Fall, 1992): 35-41. Contrasts Stephen's image as heroic symbol of Romanian national unity with historical reality.

See also: 1410, Battle of Tannenburg; 1442-1456, János Hunyadi Defends Hungary Against Ottoman Invaders; 1453, Fall of Constantinople; 1458-1490, Hungarian Renaissance Under Mátyás Hunyadi.

1458-1490
Hungarian Renaissance Under Mátyás Hunyadi

The Hungarian renaissance under Mátyás Hunyadi expands the boundaries of Hungary, establishes an advanced legal code and court system, ushers in enlightened social and judicial policies, and inspires lasting cultural achievements in Hungary.

Date: 1458-1490

Locale: Hungary

Categories: Cultural and intellectual history; Government and politics

Key figures:

Mátyás Hunyadi (1443-1490), king of Hungary as Matthias Corvinus, 1458-1490, and son of János Hunyadi

Ladislas V Posthumous (1440-1458), king of Hungary, 1453-1457

János Pannonius (John Cszemecei; 1434-1472), poet and bishop of Pécs, 1457-1472

Mihály Szilágyi (died 1461), uncle of Mátyás Hunyadi and sometime regent of Hungary

János Vitez (1408-1472), bishop of Nagyvárad until 1465, and archbishop of Esztergom, 1465-1472

Summary of event. When Ladislas V Posthumous, king of Hungary, died in Prague without an heir, Mátyás Hunyadi, the eighteen-year-old second son of the Hungarian national hero, János Hunyadi, became a leading candidate for the crown. Mihály Szilágyi, the young Hunyadi's uncle, organized the small nobles in his favor and, on January 24, 1458, a Diet in Buda elected him king. Claims of Casimir of Poland and Holy Roman Emperor Frederick II, respectively the brother-in-law and uncle of Ladislas, were rejected. Szilágyi and János Vitez, Hunyadi's tutor and mentor, then negotiated the release of the young king from Prague. George Podiebrad, king of Bohemia, extracted a substantial ransom, but he also betrothed his daughter, Catherine, to Hunyadi. The Diet enacted a law forbidding the new king to impose taxes without their

consent; to which Hunyadi pledged in his coronation oath. Nobles also were prohibited from bringing armed retainers to Diet meetings, thus bringing peace and calm to such meetings and allowing the king to rule effectively. With the aid of Vitez, Mátyás Hunyadi quickly repaid his uncle for the ransom payment to Podiebrad. Hunyadi also negotiated a settlement with Emperor Frederick II and ransomed the sacred crown of Saint Stephen. Thereafter, Hunyadi was crowned King Matthias Corvinus in 1464.

Appointed regent, Szilágyi sought to dominate his nephew but was quickly outmaneuvered with Vitez's assistance. Matthias took full control and established a strong centralized government, conducting state affairs through his own chancellery and royal council. These bodies were largely composed of younger men selected by Matthias for their capabilities rather than familial connections or wealth. In this way, he minimized the influence of the Diet and reduced the political power of the magnates.

To pursue an effective foreign policy and maintain his position as king, Matthias reinforced the militia in 1458 by ordering every twenty *jobbagy* (households on the lands of great lords) to supply one mounted soldier. This quota was increased to one soldier per ten households in 1465. More important, beginning in 1462, he organized the "Black Army," a hired standing army of twenty thousand cavalry and ten thousand foot soldiers. This force, an innovation for the time, gave Matthias a reliable standing army independent of the nobles.

To support his army, Matthias reorganized finances under royal administration and greatly increased taxation. He canceled existing tax exemptions granted by his predecessors for many properties, communes, and districts. A new treasury tax of one-fifth of a gold florin for every town house or peasant homestead was introduced in 1467 and was quintupled in 1468. In addition, Matthias regularly levied special taxes. The actual taxes fell on the *jobbagys*, except for the poorest nobles. Nobles having no *jobbagys* were required to pay the taxes personally. In this way, Matthias more than doubled royal revenues to almost two million gold florins. This increased wealth proved a burden, however, that provoked unsuccessful conspiracies against him in 1467 and 1471.

Matthias' legal code, the *Decretum Majus*, proclaimed in 1486, protected and defined individual rights. His reformed legal administration speeded legal procedures, which formerly were a function of the periodic meetings of the Diet, and largely prevented bribery. It also curbed the influence of the magnates. Lower courts were organized in each *megye* (county) and met at regular intervals. Courts consisted of a *föispán*, the king's administrative representative in the *megye*, four elected judges from the *megye*, and ten *homini regius*. Appeals were first submitted to the *tabula regia judicaria*, presided over by a professional judge known as the *protonotarius*. Above this, the supreme court consisted of the king and assisting members of the royal council.

Matthias also encouraged Hungarian cultural development. János Vitez, who was one of his principal agents and became archbishop of Esztergom in 1465, had begun his humanistic career under King Sigismund, but served the Hunyadis for more than thirty years. Vitez made his bishopric a center of culture and began accumulating the library that became the Corvina. He employed talented copyists whose works were distributed among distinguished humanists. His interest in astrology led him to commission a treatise for calculating solar and lunar eclipses. Vitez also founded the short-lived University at Pozsony. Another outstanding Hungarian humanist of the time, John Cszemecei, known as János Pannonius, served as bishop of Pécs and was Vitez's nephew. Pannonius was a prolific and influential poet, but much of his work was written in Italy and is unrelated to Hungarian life. While he served as bishop of Pécs, however, his poetry became more serious and more Hungarian in character.

Matthias' most significant achievement was his magnificent library. Starting in the early 1460's, the Corvina grew rapidly under the management of Tadeo Ugoleto. Buyers, copyists, and illustrators were engaged in Vienna and many Italian towns. A library workshop at Buda employed some thirty men in copying and illustrating. Some early printed works also were acquired and a short-lived press was established at Buda in 1478. The first map of Hungary was also produced in Matthias' court. After Matthias' death, many books were lost as scholars failed to return volumes borrowed from the Corvina. Finally, the Ottoman Turks captured the library and added its contents to the sultan's library in Istanbul after the fall of Buda in 1541. About 170 of approximately two thousand volumes contained in the Corvina survived to the late twentieth century, and titles of an additional three hundred books are known. A significant number of early editions of the classics are based on volumes from the Corvina.

Matthias effectively protected his royal position, but in hindsight appears misguided for not having opposed the Ottomans more vigorously. When Matthias returned to Hungary from Prague as king, he was engaged to the Czech king's daughter and, under pressure from the Hungarian magnates, loyally refused to break the alliance. In 1464, after the death of his first wife, Matthias severed connections with King George of Bohemia, a Hussite, and, in pursuit of his ambition to be elected Holy Roman Emperor, volunteered to lead a crusade against "heretical"

Bohemia. Matthias attacked Moravia, occupied Brno and Olomouc, and with the aide of Catholic lords, was crowned king of Bohemia in 1468. Seeking support, Podiebrad, king of Bohemia, immediately made Ladislas, son of the Polish king, his heir. Upon Podiebrad's death, Emperor Frederick recognized Ladislas as king of Bohemia, leaving Matthias to face both the Poles and Bohemians. The war's expense forced Matthias to request a tax increase at the Diet of 1470. Refused, he collected the taxes without consent, thus igniting a conspiracy, involving a his longtime allies, János Vitez and János Pannonius, to replace him as king by Casimir, the younger son of the king of Poland. Casimir invaded with seventeen thousand men, but quickly withdrew when Matthias successfully reenlisted the sympathy of many magnates and proposed remedies for many of the conspirator's complaints at the Diet of 1471. Vitez reconciled with Matthias, but soon died. Pannonius died while fleeing the country, and the Diet adjourned itself for two years. The war in Bohemia, however, continued until 1478, when the Treaty of Olomouc affirmed Matthias' possession of Moravia, Silesia, and Lausitz and allowed both Matthias and Ladislas the title "king of Bohemia." Meanwhile, the Ottoman Turks successfully invaded southern Hungary and constructed a fortress, Sabach, on Hungarian territory. Matthias mounted a campaign against the Ottomans and besieged Sabach, which surrendered in 1476.

Throughout his reign, Matthias was forced to contend with Emperor Frederick's unrelinquished claim to the Hungarian throne. After his Polish-Bohemian war, Matthias fought three campaigns against Frederick between 1477 and 1490 in order to end Frederick's influence. The first two wars ended on Matthias' terms and gave him all of Bohemia. Frederick did not comply with all of the terms, however, and hostilities were resumed. In the third war, Matthias captured Vienna in 1485. Here, Matthias died on December 6, 1490.

Matthias' conquests were soon lost after his death, and Hungary was left alone to face the Ottomans. Matthias' code and courts were more advanced and more humane than most contemporary systems and have been memorialized by the saying, "Matthias is dead—justice is lost." His enlightened social and judicial policies also did not long survive following his reign. The cultural achievements of his regime, however, had a more lasting effect, resulting in his reign being designated as the "Hungarian Renaissance."   —*Ralph L. Langenheim, Jr.*

ADDITIONAL READING:

Bak, János. "The Late Medieval Period." In *A History of Hungary*, edited by Peter F. Sugar, Peter Hanak, and

Frank Tibor. London: I. B. Tauris, 1990. Comprehensive short account of Matthias' life and times.

Erdei, Ferenc. *Information Hungary*. Vol. 2 in *Countries of the World*, edited by Robert Maxwell. Oxford: Pergamon Press, 1968. A Marxist account of Matthias' reign.

Macartney, C. A. *Hungary: A Short History*. Chicago: Aldine, 1961. Includes a brief account of Matthias' reign.

Pamlenyi, Erving, ed. *A History of Hungary*. London: Collets, 1975. A detailed history of Hungary that includes discussion of Matthias and his accomplishments.

Sinor, Denis. *History of Hungary*. New York: Frederick A. Praeger, 1959. Includes a chapter on Matthias Corvinus.

SEE ALSO: 1442-1456, János Hunyadi Defends Hungary Against Ottoman Invaders; 1514, Hungarian Peasants Revolt; 1703-1711, Hungarian Revolt Against Habsburg Rule.

1469
MARRIAGE OF FERDINAND AND ISABELLA

The marriage of Ferdinand and Isabella combines the power and prestige of Aragon and Castile, the two largest kingdoms on the Iberian Peninsula, thus defining the future Spanish nation.

DATE: October 19, 1469

LOCALE: Valladolid, Castile, Spain

CATEGORIES: Government and politics; Religion

KEY FIGURES:

Alfonso Carrillo (c. 1422-1482), archbishop of Toledo

Ferdinand V (1452-1516), king of Castile, 1474-1504, and later king of Aragon, 1479-1516

Pedro González de Mendoza (1428-1495), cardinal of Spain

Henry IV (1425-1474), king of Castile, 1454-1474

Isabella I (1451-1504), half sister of Henry and queen of Castile, 1474-1504

John II (1397-1479), king of Aragon, 1458-1479

SUMMARY OF EVENT. When Ferdinand, crown prince of Aragon, married his cousin, Isabella, disputed heiress of Castile, they seemed pawns of their elders, notably his father. John II had made Ferdinand king of Sicily to strengthen his position in marriage negotiations. Castile dominated the Iberian Peninsula with about half of its land and three-fifths of its population. Internal rebellion under weak Henry IV, "the Impotent," had brought intervention by rulers of Iberia's other kingdoms (Aragon, Portugal, Granada, and Navarre). Henry IV preferred that his sister,

Isabella, marry a Castilian lord to strengthen his own position or a foreign ally to secure the succession rights of his own daughter, Princess Juana. Also opposed to this marriage, but ready to play a double game, was Juan Pacheco, master of the military Order of Santiago and Henry IV's favorite. Most nobles adopted a wait-and-see attitude. Supporting Isabella's marriage to Aragon's heir were the Enríquez family (Ferdinand's maternal kinspeople) and Alfonso Carrillo, archbishop of Toledo, who became Isabella's chief protector. Their marriage required considerable derring-do by the principals (who had never seen each other). Ferdinand traveled from Aragon disguised, with a few retainers. Isabella defied her brother and fled to Carrillo's protection. In their haste to present Henry IV with a fait accompli, they married without requisite papal dispensation, which was needed because of their close kinship.

During the first years of their marriage, the young couple asserted their independence against their elders and built their own power base, including an uneasy reconciliation with Henry IV and an alliance with the Mendoza family. In 1472, support came from papal legate Rodrigo Borgia (later Pope Alexander VI), facilitated by Pedro González de Mendoza, who thereby gained a cardinal's hat. A vassal of John II, Borgia provided the needed dispensation in part because of a barrage of slander against Princess Juana. Queen Juana, wife of Henry IV, had recently borne an illegitimate son, and rumors circulated that her (older) daughter was also illegitimate. Princess Juana appears in history as "Juana la Beltraneja"; her supposed father, Beltrán de la Cueva, was another royal favorite and a Mendoza in-law. Despite such rumors, many modern historians accept Juana's legitimacy.

The death of Henry IV, about the same time as those of Juan Pacheco and Queen Juana, brought civil war to the peninsula. Aragon backed Isabella; King Alfonso V of Portugal, affianced to his niece, Princess Juana, invaded Castile in her interest. Surviving members of the Pacheco family also supported Juana, as did Carrillo, who was upset over the independence of Ferdinand and Isabella and blamed them for his failure to secure a cardinalate. After the couple's five years of marriage, Castilians identified Ferdinand with his wife's cause more than with Aragon; Portugal's king seemed a foreign invader. Isabella played an active political role, whereas the juvenile Juana could not. Thus, Ferdinand and Isabella gained adherence from most of Castile's nobles and cities. John II supported them unconditionally, although he was harassed by Louis XI of France, who pursued his own interests in Navarre and Aragon, promising much and delivering nothing to Alfonso V. Historians usually consider the Battle of Toro (or

Peleagonzalo), fought on March 1, 1476, to have been decisive. Nevertheless, Ferdinand and Isabella did not control Castile until 1479, with the signing of the Treaty of Alcaçovas; by then, John II had died, and the couple also ruled Aragon.

In building control during the civil war, Ferdinand and Isabella shaped the Spanish nation. The Holy Brotherhood, a league of municipalities, had provided mutual assistance and protection to members. In 1476, the monarchs took control and used Brotherhood armies against Juana's supporters. In the period from 1488 to 1495, Ferdinand tried to develop a brotherhood in Aragon. Isabella forced her husband's election as master of the military orders of Santiago in 1477, Calatrave in 1487, and Alcantará in 1494, all of which provided sources of money and military power.

Between 1476 and 1480, the monarchs enacted major reforms through the Cortes (parliament). Afterward, having received its mandate, Ferdinand and Isabella used the Cortes infrequently and governed through the bureau-

Although shown taking part in a regal state wedding in this artist's rendition, Ferdinand and Isabella married in haste without the papal dispensation that would allow them to marry despite their close blood ties as cousins. (Archive Photos)

cratic royal council, the Brotherhood (for military expenses), and special agents, such as *corregidores*, to handle local problems. The Council of Aragon, established in 1494 and composed of Aragonese personnel, was quite separate, but, meeting in Castile, it demonstrated an osmotic process of national unification. On the other hand, having established royal authority, the monarchs allowed great nobles considerable local autonomy. Similarly, fiscal dependence on the wool trade encouraged Ferdinand and Isabella to allow its guild, the *Mesta*, great independence. In 1498, no longer needing the Brotherhood, the monarchs allowed it to revert to local control.

In 1478, the pope authorized establishment of Spain's Inquisition, and, from 1483, the same inquisitor general served in both Aragon and Castile. In 1486, the pope granted Ferdinand and Isabella control of church appointments and finances in the Canary Islands and territory conquered from the Muslim kingdom of Granada. This royal patronage extended to the Americas in 1501-1508 and eventually pertained to all of Spain. The Synod of Seville in 1478 witnessed genuine royal concern for church reform. In 1495, Francisco Jiménez de Cisneros, an ascetic Franciscan friar, succeeded mighty Pedro González de Mendoza as archbishop of Toledo. Royal piety and political acumen combined in rallying Spaniards in the crusade that conquered Granada for Castile (1481-1492). Pope Alexander VI recognized this triumph with the title "Catholic Monarchs," also held by subsequent Spanish kings. Decrees in 1492 and 1502 obliged Jews and Muslims to convert to Christianity or leave Spain. Thus, the nation became Europe's most formidable Catholic power.

Control within Spain made possible ambitious projects abroad. After Christopher Columbus returned from America, Castile became a world power; with American treasure, Spain dominated Europe. From 1495, Ferdinand pursued Aragon's rivalry against France in Italian wars in which Castilian Gonzalo Fernández de Córdoba emerged as Europe's greatest commander. Archbishop Jiménez led an army into North Africa serving Aragonese interests. Capping his career, Ferdinand annexed Navarre to Castile in 1512. Ferdinand and Isabella carefully educated their children and made strategic marriages for them with two aims: union with Portugal and encirclement of France. Princess Isabella and (after her death in childbirth) her sister Maria were married to Manuel I of Portugal. Their siblings Juan and Juana married Habsburgs of Germany and the Netherlands (Austria and Burgundy), and Princess Catherine married King Henry VIII of England. Thus, despite the stipulations in the marriage treaty of Ferdinand and Isabella that Aragon and Castile must remain separate

kingdoms, the two kingdoms functioned together in their common interest in foreign and domestic affairs.

Circumstances, however, determined the separation of the two kingdoms. When Queen Isabella died in 1504, the throne of Castile passed to Juana and her husband, Philip I, ending the Trastámara dynasty there. Aragon was ruled separately under Ferdinand. The death of Philip I in 1506 and the mental instability of Juana (who became known as "la Loca") enabled a restoration of unity under Ferdinand's regency. By then, Ferdinand had married his great-great niece, Germaine de Foix of Navarre, to strengthen his position in that kingdom. Germaine's baby, who might have continued Aragonese separation, died. After Ferdinand's death in 1516, Archbishop Jiménez served as regent for Charles I (also known as Charles V of the Holy Roman Empire), son of Philip I and Juana, who ruled a united Spain. As the heir of Charles and his wife, Isabella of Portugal, Philip II conquered Portugal in 1580. The political union of Spain and Portugal continued until it was dissolved in a war for Portuguese independence (1640-1685).

—*Paul Stewart*

ADDITIONAL READING:

Fernández-Armesto, Felipe. *Ferdinand and Isabella*. New York: Taplinger, 1975. Reliable and filled with humanizing details, this book provides an admirably balanced portrait, giving proper recognition to both husband and wife.

Hillgarth, J. N. *The Spanish Kingdoms, 1250-1516*. Vol. 2. Oxford: Clarendon Press, 1978. More detailed than the work of Kamen (cited below), this book surpasses earlier standard works on the period.

Kamen, Henry. *Spain, 1469-1714: A Society of Conflict*. 2d ed. New York: Longman, 1991. A revisionist study that parallels coverage of the period provided in John H. Elliott's *Imperial Spain, 1469-1714* (1963), which tends more to facts and figures.

Liss, Peggy K. *Isabel the Queen*. New York: Oxford University Press, 1992. Notable for its superior scholarship, Liss's biography provides an in-depth study of Isabella and the full range of her accomplishments.

Rubin, Nancy. *Isabella of Castile: The First Renaissance Queen*. New York: St. Martin's Press, 1992. Issued the same year as the work of Liss (cited above), Rubin's biography takes a more popular approach that renders it more accessible for general readers.

SEE ALSO: 1230, Kingdoms of Castile and Léon Are Unified; 1478, Establishment of the Spanish Inquisition; 1492, Expulsion of the Jews from Spain; 1492, Fall of Granada; 1492, Columbus Lands in America.

KEY WORD INDEX

CATEGORY LIST

NOTE: The entries in this publication are listed below under all categories that apply. The chronological order under each category corresponds to the chronological order of the entries in these volumes.

EDUCATION

ENVIRONMENT

EXPANSION AND LAND ACQUISITION

1933	The Reichstag Fire
1934	Stalin Begins the Purge Trials
1934	Stavisky Riots
1934	The Great Blood Purge
1935	Italy Conquers Ethiopia
1936	Spanish Civil War Begins
1936	Edward VIII Abdicates the British Throne
1938	The *Anschluss*
1939	Gypsies Are Exterminated in Nazi Death Camps
1939	Nazi Extermination of the Jews
1939	Germany Invades Poland
1939	Russo-Finnish War
1940	German Invasion of Norway
1941	Atlantic Charter Is Signed
1943	The Casablanca Conference
1945	The Yalta Conference
1945	The Potsdam Conference
1945	Labour Party Forms Majority Government
1945	Nuremberg Trials
1946	Churchill's "Iron Curtain" Speech
1949	Creation of Two German Republics
1950	Italy's Postwar Economic Boom
1953	Death of Stalin
1956	Hungarian Revolution
1957	Common Market Is Formed
1958	Race Riots Erupt in London
1961	Building of the Berlin Wall
1961	Organization for Economic Cooperation and Development Forms
1963	Soviet Jews Demand Cultural and Religious Rights
1963	Greek and Turkish Cypriots Clash over Political Rights
1964	Khrushchev Falls from Power
1966	Soviet Intellectuals Express Disagreement with Party Policy
1967	Greek Coup Leads to a Military Dictatorship
1968	French Workers Engage in a National Strike
1968	Soviet Union Invades Czechoslovakia
1968	Caetano Becomes Premier of Portugal
1969	De Gaulle Steps Down
1969	Pesticide Poisons the Rhine River
1970	Parliament Passes the Equal Pay Act of 1970
1972	"Bloody Sunday" in Northern Ireland
1972	United Nations Environmental Conference
1972	Munich Olympic Massacre
1973	European Space Agency Is Formed
1973	West Germany Restricts Immigration of Foreign Workers
1974	Portugal Grants Independence to Its African Colonies
1974	Solzhenitsyn Is Expelled from the Soviet Union
1974	IRA Terrorists Bomb Parliament Building
1975	Death of Franco
1976	IRA Hunger Striker Dies in an English Prison
1978	Aldo Moro Is Kidnapped and Murdered by Italian Terrorists

1979	Margaret Thatcher Becomes Britain's First Woman Prime Minister
1979	Soviet Union Invades Afghanistan
1980	Death of Tito
1980	Solidarity Is Founded in Poland
1981	Mitterrand Is Elected to the French Presidency
1981	Greek Socialists Win Parliamentary Majority
1981	Construction of Siberian Gas Pipeline Begins
1982	Great Britain Recovers the Falkland Islands
1983	Klaus Barbie Faces Nazi War Crimes Charges
1983	Green Party Wins Seats in West German Parliament
1983	Martial Law in Poland Ends
1985	Gorbachev Is Elected General Secretary of the Communist Party
1985	Sinking of the *Rainbow Warrior*
1986	Olof Palme Is Assassinated
1986	Chernobyl Nuclear Disaster
1986	Election of Kurt Waldheim as President of Austria Stirs Controversy
1986	Riots in Kazakhstan
1987	European Community Adopts the Single Europe Act
1988	Ethnic Riots Erupt in Armenia
1989	Hungary Adopts a Multiparty System
1989	The Berlin Wall Falls
1989	Velvet Revolution in Czechoslovakia
1989	Ceausescu Is Overthrown in Romania
1990	German Reunification
1991	Soviet Attack on Baltic Separatists
1991	Coalition Defeats Iraq in Gulf War
1991	Civil War Rages in Yugoslavia
1991	Soviet Union Dissolves into Loosely Allied Republics
1992	Protests and Violence Against Immigrants in Germany
1993	Czechoslovakia Splits into Two Republics
1993	Maastricht Treaty Is Ratified
1994	Channel Tunnel Is Officially Opened
1994	Russian Troops Invade Chechnya
1995	Chirac Takes Office as President of France
1997	Labour Party Wins Majority in British National Elections

HEALTH AND MEDICINE

500 B.C.	Greek Physicians Develop Scientific Practice of Medicine
A.D. 157	Galen Synthesizes Ancient Medical Knowledge
1010	Avicenna Writes His *Canon of Medicine*
1150	Moors Transmit Classical Philosophy and Medicine to Europe
1347	Invasion of the Black Death
1865	Lister Promotes Antiseptic Surgery
1882	First Birth Control Clinic Is Established in Amsterdam
1882	Koch Isolates Microorganisms That Cause Tuberculosis and Cholera

1983	Klaus Barbie Faces Nazi War Crimes Charges
1986	Election of Kurt Waldheim as President of Austria Stirs Controversy
1991	Soviet Attack on Baltic Separatists
1991	Coalition Defeats Iraq in Gulf War
1991	Civil War Rages in Yugoslavia
1992	Protests and Violence Against Immigrants in Germany
1994	Russian Troops Invade Chechnya

WOMEN'S ISSUES

1792	Mary Wollstonecraft Publishes *A Vindication of the Rights of Woman*
1882	First Birth Control Clinic Is Established in Amsterdam
1915	International Congress of Women
1918	British Women Gain the Vote
1967	United Nations Issues a Declaration on Equality for Women
1970	Parliament Passes the Equal Pay Act of 1970